Handbook of Depression in Adolescents

Handbook of Depression in Adolescents

Edited by
Susan Nolen-Hoeksema • Lori M. Hilt

Routledge
Taylor & Francis Group
New York London

Routledge
Taylor & Francis Group
711 Third Avenue,
New York, NY 10017

Routledge
Taylor & Francis Group
2 Park Square
Milton Park, Abingdon
Oxon OX14 4RN

Routledge is an imprint of Taylor & Francis Group, an Informa business

First issued in paperback 2012

Library of Congress Cataloging-in-Publication Data

Handbook of depression in adolescents / [edited by] Susan Nolen-Hoeksema and Lori M. Hilt.
p. ; cm.
Includes bibliographical references and index.
ISBN 978-0-8058-6235-5 (hardbound : alk. paper)
1. Depression in adolescence--Handbooks, manuals, etc. I. Nolen-Hoeksema, Susan, 1959- II. Hilt, Lori M.
[DNLM: 1. Depression. 2. Depressive Disorder. 3. Adolescent. WM 171 H2108 2008]

RJ506.D4H357 2008
616.85'2700835--dc22 2008016556

Visit the Taylor & Francis Web site at
http://www.taylorandfrancis.com

and the Routledge Web site at
http://www.routledge.com

ISBN13: 978-0-805-86235-5 (hbk)
ISBN13: 978-0-415-64820-2 (pbk)

Contents

Preface

Depressive disorders are among the most common types of psychopathology in the United States (Kessler et al., 2003). These disorders are associated with significant psychosocial impairment across multiple domains of functioning, including work, family, and social functioning (Kessler et al., 2003; Stein, Torgrud, & Walker, 2000). Depression is estimated to cost the United States about $43 billion per year, was named as the second leading cause of disability in the United States in 1990, and is estimated to be the leading cause of disability by 2020 (Hirschfield et al., 1997; Murray & Lopez, 1996).

One reason these disorders are so costly to individuals and to society is that they are often chronic and recurrent conditions (Judd, 1997). When these conditions strike early in adolescence, they are even more likely to be associated with chronicity and relapse over the life span (Fombonne, Wostear, Cooper, Harrington, & Rutter, 2001; Lewinsohn, Rohde, Klein, & Seeley, 1999; Pine, Cohen, Gurley, Brook, & Ma, 1998). Adolescents who have experienced a major depressive episode, experience a high risk for relapse in adulthood, and the majority of adults who develop major depression, experienced problems with anxiety and depressive disorders in adolescence (Pine et al., 1998). As such, adolescent-onset depressive disorders represent particularly insidious conditions because of their strong association with chronic and recurrent emotional problems in adulthood.

Scientific interest in the nature, causes, and treatments of depression in adolescents has grown dramatically in the last decade. A search of the PsychInfo database using the keywords "adolescent and depression" yielded 6,085 references, 3,400 of which were published since the year 2000. Most importantly, the literature on adolescent depression that has emerged in the last decade has been largely empirically based. We now have many studies of the nature and assessment of adolescent depression, biological and psychosocial contributors to adolescent depression, and the efficacy of treatments for adolescent depression. Thus, there is much new information to review. There are many remaining questions and controversies in the field, however. For example, the safety of antidepressant medications for adolescents has been a heated topic in both the academic and popular press. The chapters in *Handbook of Depression in Adolescents* provide both comprehensive review of state-of-the-art knowledge about adolescent depression and roadmaps for future research.

GOALS FOR THE BOOK

Our first goal for this volume was to shine a light *specifically on adolescents* who suffer depression. Depressions that occur during adolescence have different characteristics, and possibly different causes and consequences, compared to depressions that occur in childhood or adulthood. It is no longer necessary or appropriate to make inferences about adolescent depression that are based on studies of depressed children or adults. The chapters of *Handbook of Depression in Adolescents* center specifically on the period of adolescence, and on the transitions from childhood to adolescence and from adolescence to adulthood.

Our second goal was to take a *developmental psychopathology* perspective on adolescent depression, and thus our first chapter, by Cicchetti and Toth, is "A Developmental Psychopathology Perspective on Adolescent Depression." Adolescence is a period of tremendous physiological, cognitive, and social change and growth, and there is now a large literature on typical development in adolescence. We can use this literature to understand how development can go awry in adolescents who suffer depression.

Our third goal was to maintain a consistent focus on *empirical research* in the chapters of this book. Even just a decade ago, much of what was written about adolescent depression was highly theoretical and not based on empirical studies. The authors of chapters in this volume are researchers who have produced the best evidence concerning the nature, causes, and treatments of adolescent depression. Although theories are obviously used to organize and interpret research results, the authors focus on theories that have been empirically supported.

STRUCTURE OF THE HANDBOOK

The first section of *Handbook of Depression in Adolescents* focuses on the assessment, diagnosis, and epidemiology of adolescent depression. After the opening chapter by Dante Cichetti and Sheree Toth on developmental psychopathology, Cecilia Essau and Thomas Ollendick address how depression is assessed and diagnosed in adolescents, including the pros and cons of different self-report questionnaires and diagnostic interviews. In the third chapter, Kathleen Merikangas and Erin Knight describe the results of community-based studies of the epidemiology of adolescent depression, which point to an alarmingly high prevalence of the disorder. LaRue Allen and Jennifer Astuto address what we know about the influence of culture, ethnicity, and socioeconomic status on vulnerability to, and expression of, depression in Chapter 4. Chapter 5, by Lori Hilt and Susan Nolen-Hoeksema, focuses on the fact that the gender difference in depression (girls showing more depression than boys) emerges in early adolescence.

The second section of *Handbook of Depression in Adolescents* focuses on conditions that are often comorbid with or related to depression in adolescence. In Chapter 6, Paul Rohde reviews evidence that many other disorders tend to co-occur with depression in adolescence, including anxiety disorders, eating disorders, and substance use disorders, increasing disability in afflicted adolescents. Dawn Taylor and David Miklowitz address, in Chapter 7, the growing literature on bipolar disorder in adolescence, including how it is distinguished from unipolar depression, and controversies about its diagnosis and treatment. In Chapter 8, Colleen Jacobson and Madelyn Gould describe the epidemiology and risk factors for self-injurious behavior that may be related to adolescent depression by focusing on suicide and non-suicidal self-injury in adolescence.

Section III of *Handbook of Depression in Adolescents* focuses specifically on biological factors implicated in adolescent depression. We have chosen to have separate sections on biological and psychosocial variables because there are a large number of specific topics to be addressed within each section. In Chapter 9, Ian Goodyer provides an overview of the literature on neurotransmitters and depression, highlighting those studies that have used adolescent samples. In Chapter 10, Jennifer Lau and Thalia Eley address the genetics of depression in general, and what we know about genetic contributors to adolescent depression specifically. Finally, Amy Wolfson and Roseanne Armitage, in Chapter 11, review the growing literature on the importance of sleep physiology in adolescence in general and adolescent depression specifically.

Psychosocial factors are the focus of Section IV of *Handbook of Depression in Adolescents*. Chapter 12, by Constance Hammen, addresses the dual hypothesis that stressful events both lead to, and are the result of, depression, with an emphasis on studies that have been done with depressed adolescents. Chapter 13, by John Abela and Benjamin Hankin, and Chapter 14, by Karen Rudolph, review the large literatures on cognitive and interpersonal factors implicated in adolescent depression. Bruce Compas, Sarah Jaser, and Molly Benson bring together the work on coping with stress and the emerging field of emotion regulation in a discussion of their development over adolescence and their relationship to depression, in Chapter 15. The impact of parental depression on risk for depression in adolescence is discussed by Jutta Joormann, Fanny Eugène, and Ian Gotlib in Chapter 16.

Section V highlights several recent studies on treatment of adolescent depression. Many of these studies have employed cognitive-behavioral treatments, and these are the focus of Chapter 17 by Kevin Stark, Lauren Krumholz, Kristen Ridley, and Amy Hamilton. Meredith Gunlicks and Laura Mufson describe the application of interpersonal therapy to adolescent depression in Chapter 18. Nadine Kaslow, Michelle Broth, Natalie Arnette, and Marietta Collins discuss the family-based treatments for depression in adolescents in Chapter 19. The various medications used to treat depressed adolescents, and the recent controversies over the effectiveness and safety of these medications are the subject of Chapter 20 by Gil Zalsman, Gil Shoval, and Liad Rotstein. Finally, Robin Weersing and Araceli Gonzalez present the results from a recent meta-analyses of studies of treatments for depression in children and adolescents in Chapter 21.

Because adolescent depression tends to be chronic and recurrent, and has such a devastating impact on adolescents' lives, a critical goal is to prevent first onsets or recurrences. In the final section of *Handbook of Depression in Adolescents*, Judy Garber, Christian Webb, and Jason Horowitz discuss prevention programs directed at high-risk youth in Chapter 22, then Katie McLaughlin discusses universal programs designed to prevent first onsets in general communities of adolescents in Chapter 23. The handbook concludes with an integrative chapter written by the editors on the interplay of biological, psychological, and social factors in adolescent depression.

The chapters of *Handbook of Depression in Adolescents* are authoritative reviews of research on the nature, causes, and treatments for depression in adolescents. These chapters also raise critical questions and gaps in our understanding. We believe they will serve to inform and inspire research on adolescent depression for years to come.

Susan Nolen-Hoeksema and Lori M. Hilt

REFERENCES

Fombonne, E., Wostear, G., Cooper, V., Harrington, R., & Rutter, M. (2001). The Maudsley long-term follow-up of child and adolescent depression. *British Journal of Psychiatry, 179,* 210–217.

Hirschfield, R. M. A., Keller, M. B., Panico, S., Arons, B. S., Barlow, D., Davidoff, F., et al. (1997). The National Depressive and Manic-Depressive Association consensus statement on the undertreatment of depression. *Journal of the American Medical Association, 277,* 333–340.

Judd, L. L. (1997). The clinical course of unipolar major depressive disorders. *Archives of General Psychiatry, 54,* 989–991.

Kessler, R. C., Berglund, P., Demler, O., Jin, R., Koretz, D., Merikangas, K. R., et al. (2003). The epidemiology of major depressive disorder: Results from the National Comorbidity Survey Replication (NCS-R). *Journal of the American Medical Association, 289,* 3095–3105.

Lewinsohn, P. M., Rohde, P., Klein, D. N., & Seeley, J. R. (1999). Natural course of adolescent major depressive disorder: I. Continuity into young adulthood. *Journal of the American Academy of Child & Adolescent Psychiatry, 38,* 56–63.

Murray, C., & Lopez, A. (Eds.). (1996). *The global burden of disease, injuries, and risk factors in 1990 and projected to 2020.* Cambridge, MA: Harvard University Press.

Pine, D. S., Cohen, P., Gurley, D., Brook, J., & Ma, Y. (1998). The risk for early-adulthood anxiety and depressive disorders in adolescents with anxiety and depressive disorders. *Archives of General Psychiatry, 55,* 56–64.

Stein, M. B., Torgrud, L. J., & Walker, J. R. (2000). Social phobia symptoms, subtypes, and severity: Findings from a community survey. *Archives of General Psychiatry, 57,* 1046–1052.

About the Editors

Susan Nolen-Hoeksema, PhD, is professor of psychology at Yale University. She received her BA from Yale University and her PhD from the University of Pennsylvania, and has previously held faculty positions at Stanford University and University of Michigan. Dr. Nolen-Hoeksema has received numerous awards for her research on depression, mood regulation, and gender, including the David Shakow Early Career Award from the American Psychological Association, and the Leadership Award from the Committee on Women of the American Psychological Association. Her research has been funded by grants from private foundations and the National Institute on Mental Health.

Lori M. Hilt, PhD, is currently completing a clinical internship at the University of Wisconsin, Department of Psychiatry. She received her BA from Lawrence University, her MA in Education from Viterbo University, and her MS, MPhil, and PhD (2009) from Yale University. Her research focuses on the development of psychopathology in early adolescence, and she has published studies on cognitive, interpersonal, and biological processes involved in depression and self-injurious behavior. A former high school teacher, she is also the recipient of two teaching awards and served as co-ordinator of the Yale Graduate Teaching Center for three years.

Contributors

John R. Z. Abela, PhD
Department of Psychology and Psychiatry
McGill University
Montreal, Quebec, Canada

LaRue Allen, PhD
Department of Applied Psychology
New York University
New York, New York

Roseanne Armitage, PhD
Department of Psychiatry
Department of Psychology
Sleep and Chronophysiology Laboratory
University of Michigan
Ann Arbor, Michigan

Natalie Cowles Arnette, PhD
Virtually Better Inc
Decatur, Georgia

Jennifer Astuto, PhD
School of Education
Long Island University
New York, New York

Molly A. Benson, PhD
Department of Psychiatry
Children's Hospital
Boston, Massachusetts
and
Harvard University
Cambridge, Massachusetts

Michelle Robbins Broth, PhD
Emory University School of Medicine
Atlanta, Georgia

Dante Cicchetti, PhD
Institute of Child Development and Department of Psychiatry
University of Minnesota
Minneapolis, Minnesota

Marietta H. Collins, PhD
Emory University School of Medicine
Atlanta, Georgia

Bruce E. Compas, PhD
Department of Psychology and Human Development
Vanderbilt University
Nashville, Tennessee

Thalia C. Eley, PhD
Social, Genetic and Developmental Psychiatry Centre
Institute of Psychiatry
King's College London
London, U.K.

Cecilia A. Essau, PhD
Developmental Psychopathology
School of Human and Life Sciences
Roehampton University
Whitelands College
London, U.K.

Fanny Eugène, PhD
Department of Psychology
Concordia University
Montreal, Quebec, Canada

Judy Garber, PhD
Department of Psychology and Human Development
Vanderbilt University
Nashville, Tennessee

Araceli Gonzalez, MA
SDSU/UCSD Joint Doctoral Program in Clinical Psychology
San Diego, California

Ian M. Goodyer, MA, MD, FRCPsych, FmedSci
Department of Psychiatry
University of Cambridge
Cambridge, U.K.

Ian H. Gotlib, PhD
Department of Psychology
Stanford University
Stanford, California

Madelyn Gould, PhD, MPH
Columbia University
Division of Child and Adolescent Psychiatry
Department of Epidemiology
New York State Psychiatric Institute
New York, New York

Meredith L. Gunlicks, PhD
Columbia University College of Physicians and Surgeons
New York, New York

Amy Hamilton, MS
Department of Educational Psychology
University of Texas
Austin, Texas

Constance Hammen, PhD
Department of Psychology
University of California
Los Angeles, California

Benjamin L. Hankin, PhD
Department of Psychology
University of Denver
Denver, Colorado

Lori M. Hilt, MA, MPhil
Department of Psychology
Yale University
New Haven, Connecticut

Jason L. Horowitz, PhD
Department of Psychiatry
University of Wisconsin
Madison, Wisconsin

Colleen M. Jacobson, PhD
Department of Child and Adolescent Psychiatry
Columbia University
New York Psychiatric Institute
New York, New York

Sarah S. Jaser, MA
Department of Psychology and Human Development
Vanderbilt University
Nashville, Tennessee

Jutta Joormann, PhD
Department of Psychology
University of Miami
Coral Gables, Florida

Nadine J. Kaslow, PhD
Emory University School of Medicine
Atlanta, Georgia

Erin Knight, BA
National Institute of Mental Health
Bethesda, Maryland

Lauren S. Krumholz, MS
Department of Educational Psychology
University of Texas
Austin, Texas

Jennifer Y. F. Lau, PhD
Department of Experimental Psychology
University of Oxford
Oxford, U.K.

Katie A. McLaughlin, PhD
School of Public Health
Harvard University
Boston, Massachusetts

Kathleen Ries Merikangas, MD
National Institute of Mental Health
Bethesda, Maryland

David J. Miklowitz, PhD
Department of Psychology
University of Colorado
Boulder, Colorado

Laura Mufson, PhD
Columbia University College of Physicians and Surgeons
Department of Clinical Psychology
New York State Psychiatric Institute
New York, New York

Susan Nolen-Hoeksema, PhD
Department of Psychology
Yale University
New Haven, Connecticut

Thomas H. Ollendick, PhD
Department of Psychology
Virginia Tech University
Blacksburg, Virginia

Kristen P. Ridley, MS
Department of Educational Psychology
University of Texas
Austin, Texas

Paul Rohde, PhD
Oregon Research Institute
Eugene, Oregon

Liad Rotstein, MD
Geha Mental Health Center
Tel Aviv University
Petach Tiqwa, Israel

Karen D. Rudolph, PhD
Department of Psychology
University of Illinois
Urbana-Champaign, Champaign, Illinois

Gal Shoval, MD
Geha Mental Health Center
Tel Aviv University
Petach Tiqwa, Israel

Kevin D. Stark, PhD
Department of Educational Psychology
University of Texas
Austin, Texas

Dawn O. Taylor, PhD
Department of Psychology
University of Colorado
Boulder, Colorado

Sheree L. Toth, PhD
Clinical and Social Sciences in Psychology
University of Rochester
Rochester, New York

Christian A. Webb, MA
Department of Psychology
University of Pennsylvania
Philadelphia, Pennsylvania

V. Robin Weersing, PhD
SDSU/UCSD Joint Doctoral Program in Clinical Psychology
San Diego, California

Amy R. Wolfson, PhD
Department of Psychology
College of the Holy Cross
Worcester, Massachusetts

Gil Zalsman, MD
Child and Adolescent Department
Geha Mental Health Center
Psychiatry Department
Tel Aviv University, Israel
and
Neuroscience Division, Psychiatry Department
Columbia University
New York, New York

Section I

ASSESSMENT, DIAGNOSIS, AND EPIDEMIOLOGY

Chapter One

A Developmental Psychopathology Perspective on Adolescent Depression

DANTE CICCHETTI AND SHEREE L. TOTH

CONTENTS

A developmental psychopathology perspective can help to elucidate the understanding of depression in adolescence. Such an approach espouses the viewpoint that in order to comprehend the genesis and epigenesis of adaptation and maladaptation, it is essential to understand the integration of diverse biological and psychological systems at multiple levels of complexity within individuals over the course of development. The developmental psychopathology position challenges researchers investigating adolescent mood disorders to move beyond identifying isolated cognitive, social-cognitive, affective, interpersonal, and biological aberrations in depressive presentations in adolescence, to understanding the processes by which these components have evolved and are integrated within and across the biological and psychological systems of the depressed adolescent embedded within a multilevel and dynamic social ecology (Cicchetti & Toth, 1995, 1998; Masten, 2006).

In this chapter, we begin by explicating why a developmental psychopathology perspective can be usefully applied toward enhancing our understanding of adolescent depression. Next, we discuss the parameters of developmental psychopathology, including the core principles of the discipline. Throughout this presentation, we highlight aspects of a developmental psychopathology approach that are particularly relevant to the study and treatment of adolescent depression. We conclude by providing an integrative summary and addressing social policy and treatment implications that emanate from a developmental psychopathology framework.

Adolescence is a particularly compelling period of development and one that lends itself well to investigations guided by a developmental psychopathology perspective. Neurobiological, hormonal, psychological, and social systems undergo marked developmental changes during adolescence (Cameron, 2004; Cicchetti & Toth, 1996; Dahl, 2004; Feldman & Elliott, 1990; Giedd, 2004; Masten, 2004; Nelson, Leibenluft, McClure, & Pine, 2005; Romer & Walker, 2006; Spear, 2000; Steinberg & Morris, 2001; Steinberg et al., 2006).

Adolescence is characterized by a rather lengthy transition phase in which the individual is neither a child nor an adult. Although the adolescent strives to move toward acquiring independence and the attainment of the perceived rewards of adulthood, parents and social institutions, recognizing the adolescent's relative lack of preparedness for the assumption of full adult responsibilities, struggle with relinquishing their perception of the adolescent as a child. Consequently, the flux and renegotiation inherent in this developmental period increase the potential for both internal and external conflict. Concomitantly, however, opportunities for growth and the realization of new possibilities occur (Cicchetti & Toth, 1996).

In an influential article, Arnett (1999) identified three central features of the stress and turmoil that is experienced by some, but not all, adolescents: mood disruptions, engaging in risky behaviors, and conflict with parents. Although adolescents exhibit wide variability in these areas, the fact that mood disruptions and increased risk taking are not atypical during this period of development suggests that behaviors commonly associated with internalizing and externalizing forms of psychopathology are in ascendance. Thus, the boundaries between normal and abnormal, as well as between normative struggles and psychopathology, become less clear.

When are irritability, dysphoria, and emotional lability part of normative adolescent self-searching versus symptoms of mood disorder? When does experimentation with alcohol and drugs lapse into substance abuse? Which adolescents are most vulnerable to moving into the psychopathological extremes? Why do many adolescents adapt successfully, and what protects adolescents from developing significant disturbance? What current and historical developmental factors influence the trajectories engaged that involve normative struggles versus emerging disorder? What are the future ramifications of adolescent psychopathology? These are some questions relevant to adolescence that can be better understood by invoking a developmental psychopathology perspective.

Adolescent depression constitutes a particularly important area of study for developmental psychopathologists because of the diverse biological, psychological, and social systems that are influenced by the disorder (Cicchetti & Toth, 1995, 1998; Goodman, 2003; Goodman & Gottlib, 1999). Aberrations in the broad domains of cognition, affect, interpersonal relations, genetics, and neurobiology are present to varying degrees among individuals with adolescent depression. Notably, these varied systems do not exist in isolation; rather, they are complexly interrelated and mutually interdependent (Cicchetti & Toth, 1998; Goodman & Gottlib, 1999). Thus, understanding the interrelations among these biological, psychological, and social systems is critical for delineating the nature of the disorder, as well as for elucidating how the organization of these systems also promotes adaptive functioning.

Given the multiplicity of systems affected by depressive disorder, the developmental psychopathology approach also directs attention to an examination of early developmental attainments (i.e., prior development) that may be theoretically related to later appearing patterns of depression in adolescence (Cicchetti & Aber, 1986; Cicchetti & Schneider-Rosen, 1986; Cicchetti & Toth, 1995; Goodman, 2003; Goodman & Gottlib, 1999). For example, obtaining an understanding of the deviations in affect regulation, close interpersonal relationships, or the core negative attributions about the self observed in depressed adolescents may begin by examining the early development of these features (e.g., Cicchetti, Rogosch, & Toth, 1998; Cicchetti, Rogosch, Toth, & Spagnola, 1997; Maughan, Cicchetti, Toth, & Rogosch, 2007; Toth, Cicchetti, Rogosch, & Sturge-Apple, in press; Toth, Rogosch, Manly, & Cicchetti, 2006), their developmental course, and their interrelations with other psychological and biological systems of the individual (Alloy & Abramson, 2006; Cicchetti & Toth, 1995; Cummings & Davies, 1994; Goodman & Gottlib, 1999).

A number of issues that have been examined by investigators of normative adolescent development mirror areas of interest to a developmental psychopathology approach to depression. These include: (1) the use of interdisciplinary models of development; (2) the examination of the continuity or discontinuity of development from childhood to adolescence and, more recently, from adolescence to adulthood (see Schulenberg, Sameroff, & Cicchetti, 2004); (3) the boundary and linkages between normal and maladaptive or psychopathological functioning; (4) the transactions that occur between environmental and more person-specific characteristics; (5) processes associated with risk and resilience; and (6) the translation of basic research into the design and provision of prevention and intervention strategies. Building on the normative advances accompanying adolescence, research investigations conducted within a developmental psychopathology framework not only can inform knowledge of adolescent depression, but also can contribute to an enhanced understanding of developmental processes and mechanisms more generally (Cicchetti, 1984, 1990, 2006; Cicchetti & Toth, 2006; Sroufe, 1990).

Adolescent affective disturbances may be conceived of as forming a spectrum of severity, from transient dysphoria universally experienced, to elevated levels of depressive symptoms that meet the diagnostic criteria for disorder, to extended periods of dysthymia and episodes of major depressive disorder (MDD). Because of the continuities and divergences from normal functioning manifested in depressive disorders across the life course, empirical research on the pathways to depression, as well as longitudinal studies of its developmental course and sequelae, hold promise for enhancing the understanding of the relation between normality and psychopathology. Given the increased prevalence of depressive disorders that takes place during adolescence (Costello & Angold, 2006; Merikangas & Knight, this volume), as well as the various risk factors associated with adolescent depression and its comorbid forms of psychopathology, it is essential for researchers and clinicians to acquire a firm grasp of the multilevel biological and psychological processes and mechanisms that contribute to the emergence, maintenance, and recurrence of depressive disorders.

WHAT IS DEVELOPMENTAL PSYCHOPATHOLOGY?

Although developmental psychopathology has frequently been equated with the study of mental disorders among children and youth, this perspective encompasses a much broader approach to studying development, normal and abnormal, across the life span (Cicchetti, 1993; Cicchetti & Toth, 1991). A developmental psychopathology analysis is necessary for tracing the roots, etiology, and nature of maladaptation in depressed adolescents, so that treatment interventions may be appropriately timed and guided, as well as developmentally appropriate.

In contrast to the field of classic developmental psychology, which strives to comprehend central tendencies and uniformities in normative processes of growth and development, the discipline of developmental psychopathology is concerned with expanding the knowledge base of developmental psychology by focusing on the extremes of adaptation and nonnormative processes of development. Thus, developmental psychopathology emphasizes and highlights the dialectic between normal and abnormal development (Cicchetti, 1984, 1990, 1993; Rutter & Sroufe, 2000; Sroufe, 1990; Sroufe & Rutter, 1984). Through comparing and contrasting abnormal development with typical, normative developmental patterns, and through investigating the similarities as well as differences between normality and psychopathology, the strengths and aberrations associated with atypical development are underscored (Cicchetti, 1993; Karmiloff-Smith, 2007). Just as importantly for developmental psychopathologists is the comparison of normal and pathological for illuminating the understanding of normative developmental processes (Cicchetti, 1984, 1993; Cicchetti & Toth, 1991; Sroufe, 1990). The unique delays, deficits, and atypicalities of psychopathological conditions can provide insights into essential aspects of normal development that might not otherwise be apparent.

It is important to note that developmental psychopathology is not limited to the study of mental disorders. Rather, developmental psychopathologists are interested in the full range of developmental processes and functioning. In addition to the disordered extremes, the subclinical range of functioning is also important. Individuals at this range of adaptation may be vulnerable to the subsequent emergence of psychopathology on the basis of the developmental organization of their biological, psychological, and social systems, and the investigation of processes that contribute to the later emergence of a disorder, such as adolescent depression, as well as processes that mitigate against disordered outcomes, provides further insight into the full range of developmental phenomena.

The developmental approach seeks to examine the specific evolving characteristics of individuals at varying developmental periods across the life span. Accordingly, in order to understand a complex phenomenon such as adolescent depression, researchers must consider variations in cognitive, social-cognitive, and socioemotional capacities, in addition to other psychological and biological domains of functioning, in order to discover how particular outcomes are manifested during different developmental epochs. Moreover, a developmental analysis seeks to examine the prior sequence of adaptation in development contributing to an outcome in a particular developmental period. With respect to adolescent depression, this would require that the current status of an individual's functioning be examined in the context of how that status was attained across the course of development. Thus, the life span perspective strives to move beyond the proximal causes of current outcomes to an examination of the developmental progression of distal sources of influences that eventuated in the current outcomes. Prospective longitudinal designs are particularly critical for tracing the pathways, sequelae, and course of adolescent depression.

The discipline of developmental psychopathology has its roots embedded in multiple areas, including genetics, embryology, the neuro sciences, psychiatry, psychology, and sociology (Cicchetti, 1990). Developmental psychopathology has evolved into an interdisciplinary field that seeks to unify these multiple fields of inquiry in order to understand diverse forms of adaptation and maladaptation, the interrelations and integrations of these varied systems across the life course, the spectrum of potential developmental pathways that evolve, and the causal processes contributing to these varied trajectories (Cicchetti, 1993; Cicchetti & Sroufe, 2000). Thus, a developmental psychopathology perspective holds considerable potential for fostering cross-disciplinary efforts directed toward understanding variations in adolescent affective functioning.

PRINCIPLES OF DEVELOPMENTAL PSYCHOPATHOLOGY

In this section, we discuss the major developmental principles that are central to elucidating the understanding of both normal and atypical patterns of development, and highlight their relevance to adolescence. We believe that the incorporation of these principles into the design and implementation of longitudinal investigations from their inception will provide a powerful framework for guiding and informing the future research agenda on the causes, sequelae, course, and treatment of adolescent depression.

The Interplay Between Normal and Abnormal Development

One of the central foci of developmental psychopathology concerns the boundary between normality and psychopathology. This principle emphasizes not only how knowledge from the study of normal development can inform the study of high-risk conditions and mental disorders, but also how the study of risk and disorder can contribute to an understanding of normal development (Cicchetti, 1993; Sroufe, 1990). Accordingly, the study of abnormal and normal processes is intimately intertwined, and it is through that dialectic that enhanced understanding in both domains can be attained. Thus, the application of knowledge concerning normal biological, cognitive, social-cognitive, and affective development to depression in adolescence results in a clarification of how the organization of components of individual functioning in depressed adolescents contributes to their symptomatic presentation.

Conversely, the investigation of atypicalities in functioning within adolescents with depression may assist in providing a more complete understanding of how these same processes function in the normal course of development. Despite the fact that developmental psychopathologists emphasize the mutual interplay between normal and abnormal development, most contemporary theory and research have focused on the contributions that normal development can make to advancing our knowledge of psychopathological processes.

Understanding how psychopathological conditions evolve, and how aberrations of component developmental systems that exist among disordered individuals eventuate, may be informative for elucidating critical components that are not typically evident (Chomsky, 1968; Cicchetti, 1990; Lenneberg, 1967; O'Connor, 2003). Often, the examination of a system in its smoothly operating normal or healthy state does not afford us the opportunity to comprehend the interrelations among its component subsystems. In usual circumstances, the integration of component developmental systems may be so well established that it is difficult to determine how normal functioning is dependent on this confluence. When there are clear aberrations in component systems, as is the case for adolescents with mood disorder, examination of how that atypicality relates to the organization of other component systems can reveal information regarding the interdependence of components not readily apparent under normal conditions.

The Role of Prior Development in Current and Future Adaptive or Maladaptive Processes

A developmental analysis also requires that the current functioning of the adolescent be considered within the context of how that level of functioning evolved over the course of development. Distal influences and their dynamic relation to proximal causes need to be delineated (Cicchetti & Toth, 1998; Sroufe, Egeland, & Kreutzer, 1990). A developmental analysis also benefits not only from knowing the progression of experiences prior to adolescence, but also from attending to the subsequent trajectories of individuals into adulthood (Schulenberg et al., 2004). For example, seemingly comparable groups of depressed individuals may appear indistinguishable in adolescence, but may manifest very different patterns of adaptation in adulthood. Accordingly, the life span orientation is central to how questions are framed, and how psychopathology is to be understood more broadly. Investigation of psychopathological functioning during adolescence not only provides information about parameters and origins of a disorder during this particular developmental period, but also, by means of comparison and contrast across the life course, offers insight into potential variation in causal processes that may operate according to when a disorder emerges.

For example, there is evidence that depressive disorders that occur in childhood and those that occur during adolescence may be differentially influenced by genetic and psychosocial factors. Both childhood and adolescent depressive disorders increase the risk for subsequent depression in adulthood. However, the linkage to adult depressive disorder is much stronger for adolescent onset depression than it is for childhood onset depression (Harrington, Fudge, Rutter, Pickles, & Hill, 1990). Furthermore, for both childhood and adolescent onset depressive disorders, there is a higher familial loading for adult depression in first- and second-degree relatives. For children with depressive disorder, higher rates of criminality, alcohol abuse, and family discord are found in their families compared with the adolescent cases, and among relatives of children with depression, there also is higher comorbidity with criminality (Harrington et al., 1997). These findings suggest that psychosocial stressors may play a more prominent role in childhood onset depression compared with adolescent onset depression, underscoring the need for attention to the differential matrix of processes that may contribute to psychopathology during different periods of development. Because children are largely reliant on their family contexts for support, it is not surprising that stressors embedded in this proximal ecology increase the likelihood of childhood depression occurring. Conversely, because adolescence encompasses a period of increased autonomy, factors less directly linked with the family milieu become more ascendant and are likely to be relevant to the emergence of depression.

The Importance of a Life Span Perspective

Development extends throughout the entire course of life, and adaptive and maladaptive processes emerge over the life span. From infancy through senescence, each period of life has its own developmental agenda and contributes in a unique fashion to the past, present, and future organization of individual development. Thus, individuals with a mental disorder, such as adolescent depression, may move between pathological and nonpathological forms of functioning. Moreover, even in the midst of a disordered period, individuals may display adaptive as well as maladaptive processes so that it becomes possible to delimit the presence, nature, and boundaries of the underlying psychopathology.

With respect to the emergence of psychopathology, all periods of life are consequential in that the developmental process may undergo a pernicious turn toward mental disorder at any phase. Many mental disorders have several distinct phases (Rutter & Sroufe, 2000). The factors that are associated with the onset of a disorder may be very different from those that are associated with the cessation of a disorder or with its repeated occurrence. In contrast to the often dichotomous world of mental disorder/nondisorder depicted in psychiatry, a developmental psychopathology perspective recognizes that normality often fades into abnormality, that adaptive and maladaptive may assume differing definitions depending on whether one's time referent is immediate circumstances or long-term development, and that processes within the individual can be characterized as having shades or degrees of psychopathology. With respect to adolescence, such a life span perspective suggests that even when depression has occurred, future remission and more adaptive functioning are possible.

Developmental Pathways: Diversity in Process and Outcome

Since its inception as an interdisciplinary science, diversity in process and outcome has been conceived as among the hallmarks of the developmental psychopathology perspective. As Sroufe (1990, p. 335) has asserted, "One of the principal tasks of developmental psychopathology is to define families of developmental pathways, some of which are associated with psychopathology with high probability, others with low probability." Even before a mental disorder emerges, certain pathways signify adaptational failures that probabilistically forebode subsequent psychopathology (Sroufe, 1990). Thus, developmental psychopathologists have articulated the expectation that there are multiple contributors to adaptive and maladaptive outcomes in any individual, that these factors and their relative contributions vary among individuals, and that there are myriad pathways to any particular manifestation of adaptive and disordered behavior (Cicchetti, 1993; Robins, 1966; Sroufe & Jacobvitz, 1989). In addition, it is believed that there is heterogeneity among individuals who develop a specific disorder with respect to the features of their disturbance, as well as among individuals who evidence maladaptation but do not develop a disorder. In accord with this view, the principles of equifinality and multifinality, derived from general systems theory (von Bertalanffy, 1968) are germane.

Equifinality refers to the observation that in any open system (cf. Mayr, 1964, 1988), a diversity of pathways, including chance events or what biologists refer to as nonlinear epigenesis, may lead to the same outcome. Stated differently, in an open system (i.e., one where there is maintenance in change, dynamic order in processes, organization, and self-regulation), the same end state may be reached from a variety of different initial conditions and through different processes. This is referred to as equifinality, an organismic process that possesses significant implications for biological and psychological regulatory systems and for behavioral and biological plasticity (Cicchetti & Tucker, 1994; Curtis & Cicchetti, 2003). In contrast, in a closed system, the end state is inextricably linked to and determined by the initial conditions. If either of the conditions changes or if the processes are modified, then the end state also will be modified (von Bertalanffy, 1968).

Initial descriptions of equifinality emanated from work in embryology. For example, the development of a normal organism was shown to occur from a whole ovum, a divided ovum, or two fused ova. Further, it was demonstrated that different initial sizes and different courses of growth can eventuate in the same ultimate size of an organism (von Bertalanffy, 1968; Waddington, 1957). Within the discipline of developmental psychopathology, equifinality has been invoked to explain why a variety of developmental pathways may eventuate in a given outcome, rather than expecting a singular primary pathway to the adaptive or maladaptive outcome.

For example, some individuals who develop a depressive disorder in adolescence may have a genetic predisposition to develop the disorder (Lau & Eley, this volume), others may have grown up in a home with substance abusing parents or experienced child maltreatment (Cicchetti, Rogosch, & Sturge-Apple, 2007; Kaufman et al., 2006; Toth, Manly, & Cicchetti, 1992). Still other adolescents may have more benign early experiences, but may have struggled with the physical changes of puberty occurring as they entered junior high school. Thus, the common outcome of depression in adolescence is likely to result from diverse processes across different individuals rather than from all adolescents following the same progression to depression. Understanding these divergent pathways holds implications for approaches to treatment.

Gjerde and Block (1996) have proposed different gender-based pathways to depression by early adulthood. In terms of expression of dysphoria, girls tend to be more autocentric, or inner-oriented, resulting in heightened attention to their own thoughts and feelings of distress, low self-esteem, and preoccupations with adequacy of the self. In contrast, allocentric, or outer-directed, modes of symptom expression are more common in boys, resulting in them enacting their frustrations on the world with impulsiveness, anger, and antagonism. For adolescents, both forms of symptom expression are likely to interfere with the successful resolution of adolescent adaptational tasks. The two different forms of expression result in girls ruminating and having a negative self-focus when experiencing sadness and anger, and boys being more likely to be aggressive and antagonistic and to exhibit poor impulse control. Gjerde and Block found that the different sets of characteristics for girls and boys at age 14 predicted depressive feelings at age 18. However, in early adulthood at age 23, the manifestations of depression tended to converge for men and women, with men beginning to evidence more internal distress and women exhibiting more antagonism. It is important to note that the predictors of depression in boys were evident as early as nursery school, in terms of undersocialization of impulse and antagonism (Block, Gjerde, & Block, 1991). Observable predictors for girls did not appear until adolescence, reflecting girls' tendency to suppress outward expression of distress. Thus, females and males appeared to follow different developmental trajectories to depression through adolescence into early adulthood (see also Hilt & Nolen-Hoeksema, this volume).

Relatedly, Duggal, Carlson, Sroufe, and Egeland (2001) reported that there appear to be different predictors of childhood onset compared with adolescent onset depression, suggesting variation in processes promoting depression in different developmental periods. Maternal depression during childhood was related to both childhood and adolescent onset of depression. In contrast, childhood onset depression also was strongly influenced by additional factors related to pervasive deficits in the overall family context, including poor early supportive care of the child, abuse, and early maternal stress. Among adolescents, gender differences emerged for the predictors of depression. For girls, maternal depression during childhood was strongly associated with high depressive symptomatology during adolescence, whereas for boys, high depressive symptomatology was linked to deficits in the early supportive care they received. Thus, different processes appear to be prominent in promoting a common depressive outcome for boys versus girls during adolescence.

The principle of multifinality (Wilden, 1980) suggests that any one component may function differently depending on the organization of the system in which it operates. Multifinality states that the effect on functioning of any one component's value may vary in different systems. Actual effects will depend on the conditions set by the values of additional components with which it is structurally linked. Consequently, the pathology or health of the system must be identified in terms of how adequately its essential functions are maintained. Stated differently, a particular adverse event should not necessarily be seen as leading to the same psychopathological or nonpsychopathological outcome in every individual. Likewise, individuals may begin on the same major pathway and, as a function of their subsequent "choices," exhibit very different patterns of adaptation or maladaptation (Cicchetti & Tucker, 1994; Sroufe, 1989; Sroufe et al., 1990).

The principles of equifinality and multifinality suggest that investigations examining adolescent depression should occur within a broad framework. A specific form of psychopathology may develop in different individuals through alternative developmental processes, and different outcomes, adaptive and maladaptive, should be considered potential results of a common risk condition (Cicchetti & Rogosch, 1996; Masten, 2004).

A pathway approach builds on knowledge gained from variable-oriented studies; however, attention is shifted to exploring the common and the uncommon outcomes, as well as alternative routes by which outcomes are achieved by different individuals (cf. Cicchetti & Schneider-Rosen, 1986).

Thus, what might be considered error variance at the group level must be critically examined for understanding diversity in process and outcome. The emphasis on person-centered observation highlights the transition from a focus on variables to a focus on individuals, and this transition is essential for demonstrating equifinality and multifinality in the developmental course.

The examination of patterns of commonality within relatively homogeneous subgroups of individuals and concomitant similarity in profiles of contributory processes becomes an important data analytic strategy. Moreover, the need to examine the totality of attributes, psychopathological conditions, and risk and protective processes in the context of each other rather than in isolation is seen as crucial for understanding the course of development taken by individuals. For example, the presence of a childhood depressive disorder has different developmental implications depending on whether it occurs alone or in conjunction with conduct disorder. The meaning of any one attribute, process, or psychopathological condition needs to be considered in light of the complex matrix of individual characteristics, experiences, and social-contextual influences involved, the timing of events and experiences, and the developmental history of the individual.

This attention to diversity in origins, processes, and outcomes in understanding developmental pathways does not suggest that prediction is futile as a result of the many potential individual patterns of adaptation (Sroufe, 1989). There are constraints on how much diversity is possible and not all outcomes are equally likely (Cicchetti & Tucker, 1994; Sroufe et al., 1990). Nonetheless, the appreciation of equifinality and multifinality in development encourages theorists and researchers to entertain more complex and varied approaches to how they conceptualize and investigate development and psychopathology. Researchers should increasingly strive to demonstrate the multiplicity of processes and outcomes that may be articulated at the individual, person-oriented level within existing longitudinal data sets. Ultimately, future endeavors must conceptualize and design research at the outset with these differential pathways concepts as a foundation (Richters, 1997). In so doing, progress toward achieving the unique goals of developmental psychopathology to explain the development of individual patterns of adaptation and maladaptation will be realized (cf. Sroufe & Rutter, 1984).

Contextual Influences

Developmental psychopathologists also stress the importance of contextual influences in defining what constitutes abnormality. Clearly, no behavior or pattern of adaptation can be viewed as psychopathological except in particular contexts (Richters & Cicchetti, 1993; Werner & Kaplan, 1963). Furthermore, chronological age and developmental stage or level of biological and psychological organization are important defining features of context for clinicians and researchers interested in chronicling the development and treatment of adolescent depression and other forms of psychopathology.

Despite the growing awareness that contextual factors play an important role in defining phenomena as psychopathological, there are vast differences in how the contexts for human development can be conceptualized (Jensen & Hoagwood, 1997; Wakefield, 1992). Bronfenbrenner's (1979) articulation of nested levels in the ecology of human development marked a great stride forward in the conceptualization of contexts (see also Belsky, 1993; Cicchetti

& Aber, 1998; Cicchetti & Lynch, 1993). The macro-, exo-, meso-, and microsystems delineated by Bronfenbrenner, clearly and compellingly alert the developmental psychopathologist studying depression or other forms of psychopathology in adolescence to important and vastly different sources of contextual influence on individual development.

Situational and interpersonal influences operate at the microsystem level in Bronfenbrenner's (1979) schema and have been the traditional focus of psychological study. However, it has thus far proven to be far more difficult to conceptualize specific macro-, exo-, and mesosystem influences on development. Part of the difficulty in pinpointing the effects of these more distal contexts is that documenting their impact on individual development requires cross-fertilization with the disciplines that study these macrophenomena: anthropology, demography, sociology, economics, and epidemiology. Parental workplace, school transitions, violent communities, persistent poverty, and unsupportive stress-laden ecologies are all examples of contexts that exert influence on the development of psychopathology in children, adolescents, and adults. Consequently, societal-, community-, and institutional-level influences on individual development are now being examined in systemic, rigorous, fashion (Cicchetti & Aber, 1998; Raver, Gershoff, & Aber, 2007). Researchers investigating adolescent depression should incorporate the examination of the effects that these various ecological systems exert on the adaptive process—be they exacerbators of risk or promoters of protection.

Another important aspect to consider with respect to contextual influences on development pertains to culture. Cultural considerations are relevant to understanding psychopathology on two interrelated dimensions (Serafica & Vargas, 2006). First, the role of culture in human development must be considered, whether development is normal or abnormal. Second, the role of culture in informing societal perspectives on psychopathology, including its etiology, course, assessment, prevention, and treatment, is critical. Because of the importance of culture, some theorists have urged that developmental psychopathology must avoid becoming a monocultural science (Cicchetti & Toth, 1998; Spencer & Dupree, 1996). Historically, mainstream developmental psychology has revealed a dearth of research on cultural influences on adaptation (Garcia-Coll, Akerman, & Cicchetti, 2000). Since our knowledge of atypical development usually lags behind that of normative development, and because developmental psychopathology is based on the interplay between normality and atypicality, it is not surprising that our understanding of the etiology, course, and treatment of disorders in children and adolescents from diverse ethnic and racial backgrounds is less developed. Unfortunately, the extant research literature on culture and psychopathology during infancy, childhood, and adolescence remains sparse (Serafica & Vargas, 2006). Although the number of ethnic and cultural investigations addressing adult psychopathology has burgeoned, studies that examine culture and psychopathology among children and adolescents are more recent (Allen & Astuto, this volume). With respect to depressive disorders, few investigations have sought to examine ethnic differences among minority youth. In general, some ethnic differences in the prevalence rates and symptomatology associated with mood disorders have been identified. However, the overall paucity of investigations examining adolescent depression and ethnicity and possible confounds with socioeconomic status suggest that firm conclusions regarding adolescent depression and ethnic influences cannot yet be drawn. It is therefore incumbent upon investigators to incorporate ethnocultural considerations into their examinations of adolescent depression.

Resilience

Developmental psychopathologists are as interested in individuals at high risk for the development of psychopathology who do not manifest disorder over time, as they are in individuals who develop an actual mental disorder (Luthar, Cicchetti, & Becker, 2000). Moreover, developmental psychopathologists strive to discover the pathways to competent adaptation despite exposure to conditions of adversity (Luthar, 2006; Masten, 2001). Thus, it is as critical for researchers to understand the mechanisms that promote resilient functioning among adolescents at risk for maladaptive developmental organizations and depression, as it is to investigate developmental trajectories toward psychopathology.

In order for resilience research to elucidate the mechanisms through which individuals are able to initiate or maintain their self-righting tendencies when confronted with adversity, it is important that the construct of resilience be conceptualized as a dynamic process, not a static or trait-like condition (Egeland, Carlson, & Sroufe, 1993; Luthar et al., 2000). Understanding resilience will contribute to our understanding of how the organization of an individual's biological, psychological, and social-contextual systems play critical roles in determining whether adaptation or maladaptation will become manifest at each stage of development (Cicchetti & Toth, 1995; Cicchetti & Tucker, 1994).

To date, research on the determinants of resilience has predominantly focused on psychosocial processes. For example, Garber and Little (1999), in a prospective longitudinal investigation, followed up a large cohort of children of mothers with MDD. In the sixth grade, 51 of the 185 offspring of depressed mothers were identified as being in the high-competence group (i.e., high functioning and without psychopathology). Two years later, 18 of the high-competence children developed problems by early adolescence. In comparison with the children who manifested a decrease in competence during the transition to adolescence, the 33 continuously competent children demonstrated more positive coping, an enhanced commitment to school achievement, greater social support, and better family relationships. Additionally, Garber and Little (1999) discovered that the group manifesting decreased competence experienced a greater number of hassles during junior high school. It is interesting to note that among the adolescents experiencing higher levels of hassles during junior high school, high commitment to achievement and a positive family environment each moderated the relation between school hassles and competence.

Furthermore, Luthar and colleagues (Luthar, 1991; Luthar, Doernberger, & Zigler, 1993) found that disadvantaged adolescents who manifested resilient functioning in some domains often were at risk for difficulties in other realms of functioning, including the development of high levels of depressive symptomatology. These findings suggest that resilient adolescents may need support to deal with the emotional difficulties and distress that are often associated with coping with the emotional difficulties they have had to address and surmount.

Multiple Levels of Analysis

Developmental psychopathologists strive to engage in a comprehensive evaluation of biological, psychological, and social-contextual processes, and to ascertain how the interaction among these multiple-levels-of-analysis may influence individual differences, the continuity or discontinuity of adaptive or maladaptive behavioral patterns, and the pathways by which normal and pathological developmental outcomes may be achieved (Cicchetti & Dawson, 2002; Cicchetti & Sroufe, 2000). To date, much of what is known about the causes, pathways, and sequelae of mental disorders, including adolescent depression, has been gleaned from investigations that focused on relatively narrow domains of variables. To fully comprehend the complexity of mental disorders, it is essential that a multiple-levels-of-analysis approach and an interdisciplinary perspective be incorporated into the research methods of developmental psychopathologists. The sophisticated and comprehensive portrayals of adaptation and maladaptation that ensue will serve not only to advance scientific understanding, but also to inform efforts to prevent and ameliorate psychopathology, including adolescent depression (Ialongo et al., 2006).

An example of how a multiple-levels-of-analysis approach can augment our understanding of the developmental pathways to depression can be seen in the upsurge of interest in molecular genetics and gene–environment interaction (G×E) within the social- and neurosciences. Developmental psychopathologists have begun to examine behavioral effects that are the outcomes of the interdependence between a specific identified variation in the DNA sequence and a specific, well-defined environmental pathogen—known as G×E. In G×E, environmental experiences moderate genetic effects (or vice versa) on normal, psychopathological, and resilient outcomes. For example, genetic effects on functioning outcomes may be observed only under certain environmental contexts, or in conjunction with different histories of experience, or conversely, experience may only relate to outcomes among individuals with specific genetic characteristics. One of the most compelling reasons for encouraging increased research on G×E interactions in the field of developmental psychopathology is gleaned from the animal and human literatures on behavioral responses to environmental challenges. Consistent with a developmental psychopathology perspective, multifinality is characteristic of the response to even the most pernicious and hazardous traumas, including the array of environmental risk factors for mental disorder, including adolescent depression (Moffitt, Caspi, & Rutter, 2006). It has been empirically demonstrated that individual differences in response to environmental risks are associated with pre-existing individual variations that are under genetic influence (Moffitt et al., 2006; Rutter, 2006). Accordingly, in instances where there is individual variation among the psychological responses of humans to environmental risk factors for psychopathology, it is highly probable that G×E may be operating in some fashion.

Children who have been abused and/or neglected have been shown to be at high risk for the development of depressive disorder and high levels of depressive symptomatology (Kaufman, 1991; Manly, Kim, Rogosch, & Cicchetti, 2001; Toth et al., 1992; Widom, DuMont, & Czaja, 2007). A variety of factors have been theorized to mediate or moderate the impact of maltreatment on depression (Gibb, Wheeler, Alloy, & Abramson, 2001; Kaufman, 1991; Toth & Cicchetti, 1996a, 1996b).

Dysregulation of the neurotransmitter serotonin has been implicated in the development of depressive disorder (Cicchetti & Toth, 1995; Goodyer, this volume; Spoont, 1992). The serotonin transporter gene (5-HTT), one of the major genes involved with serotonergic transmission, has a functional insertion/deletion polymorphic region labeled the serotonin transporter linkage promoter region (5-HTTLPR), that has two allelic forms—the long ("l") and the short ("s") variants. Investigations with nonhuman primates and clinical studies of humans have demonstrated that individuals who possess the s/s and s/l genotypes have lower levels of serotonergic activity than individuals with the l/l genotype (Lesch & Hiels, 2000; Williams et al., 2001). The diversity in behavioral outcomes associated with 5-HTTLPR suggests the likely plausibility of its genetic influences being moderated by environmental pathogens.

Several studies have investigated the interaction of social adversity (e.g., child maltreatment) or stressful life events and the serotonin transporter polymorphism on the development of depression. A number of investigations of 5-HTT and child maltreatment have revealed G×E interactions for the presence of the s/s or s/l genotype and severe child maltreatment on depression in adults (Caspi et al., 2003), adolescents (Cicchetti et al., 2007; Eley et al., 2004), and children (Kaufman et al., 2004, 2006).

Future G×E investigations examining the development of depression should increasingly seek to discover endophenotypes that may be intermediate between genes, environments, and behavioral outcomes (Gottesman & Gould, 2003). Such endophenotypes are heritable constituents of mental disorders and may be, among other possibilities, neurophysiological, neurochemical, endocrinological, neuropsychological, or cognitive (Gottesman & Hanson, 2005; Moffitt et al., 2006). The inclusion of measures that can reveal the presence of endophenotypes in future G×E studies should further enhance our understanding of the development of depression within a multiple-levels-of-analysis perspective.

In recent years, a number of developmental scientists have urged researchers studying resilience to incorporate neurobiological and molecular genetic measures into their investigations of the pathways to resilient functioning (Charney, 2004; Cicchetti & Curtis, 2006; Curtis & Cicchetti, 2003). We believe that the concurrent examination of biological, psychological, and social-contextual processes, and their interplay at varying developmental periods will provide a more integrative conceptualization of resilience.

G×E research has not only been important in elucidating pathways to psychopathology, but also it has shown that specific genetic polymorphisms can moderate the impact of various environmental pathogens on the development of psychopathology. For example, in G×E research on depression, the presence of the l/l genotype has been shown to moderate the effects of child maltreatment or stressful life events on depression and depressive symptomatology (Caspi et al., 2003; Cicchetti et al., 2007; Eley et al., 2004; Kaufman et al., 2004, 2006). Furthermore, the presence of positive social supports (Kaufman et al., 2004) and self-coping processes (Cicchetti et al., 2007) also have been shown to moderate the impact of child maltreatment and the s/s or s/l genotype on depressive symptomatology. Thus, the negative effects commonly associated with child maltreatment are not inevitable. Knowledge of genetic variation may help to identify which individuals are most vulnerable to adverse experiences. Through studying G×E, protective functions of genes also can be discovered.

In another multilevel investigation, Cicchetti and Rogosch (2007) examined resilient functioning in maltreated and nonmaltreated low income children. The regulation of two stress-responsive adrenal steroid hormones, cortisol and dehydroepiandosterone (DHEA), and the personality constructs of ego-resiliency and ego-control served as predictors of resilient adaptation, assessed through a multidomain, multi-informant composite of adaptive functioning that also included assessments of depression.

Maltreatment status was not related to differences in average levels of morning or afternoon cortisol or DHEA; however, lower morning cortisol was related to higher resilient functioning, but only in nonmaltreated children. In contrast, among physically abused children, high morning cortisol was related to resilient functioning. Typically, physically abused children have been found to exhibit low levels of cortisol; the subgroup of physically abused youth who elevated their cortisol levels to adapt to stressors in their lives may have been demonstrating greater resilient self-strivings for competent adaptation (cf. Cicchetti, Rogosch, Lynch, & Holt, 1993).

Although diurnal change in cortisol was not related to resilience, for DHEA, maltreated children with high levels of resilience showed an atypical rise in DHEA from morning to afternoon. Morning and afternoon cortisol/DHEA ratios were positively related to resilient functioning, but did not interact with maltreatment status. Ego-resiliency and ego-control strongly differentiated maltreated and nonmaltreated children, and the personality variables were substantially predictive of resilience. When considered together, the demonstrated multilevel effects of personality, cortisol, and DHEA maintained independent contributions in predicting resilience among these high-risk youth.

In another illustration of a multilevel approach to resilience, Curtis and Cicchetti (2007) examined the contribution of emotion regulation and hemispheric electroencephalogram (EEG) asymmetry to competent adaptation in a sample of maltreated and nonmaltreated children. The left hemisphere participates more heavily in positive affect (i.e., approach), whereas the right hemisphere mediates negative emotion (i.e., withdrawal; depression) (Davidson, 2000).

Findings indicated that EEG asymmetry across central cortical regions distinguished between resilient and nonresilient children, with greater left hemisphere activity characterizing those who were resilient. In addition, nonmaltreated children showed greater left hemisphere EEG activity across parietal cortical regions. There also was a significant interaction between resilience, maltreatment status, and gender for asymmetry at anterior frontal electrodes, where nonmaltreated resilient females had greater relative left frontal activity compared to more right frontal activity exhibited by resilient maltreated females. An observational measure of emotion regulation significantly contributed to the prediction of resilience in the maltreated and nonmaltreated children; however, EEG asymmetry in central cortical regions independently predicted resilience only in the maltreated group.

The investigation of a neural-level phenomenon, such as hemispheric EEG asymmetry, in the context of resilience provides further evidence that resilience cannot be reduced to or defined by one or more biological/individual characteristics. Viewed across development, the relative importance of various biological systems for promoting resilience may vary with an individual, and the relative importance of biological and psychological processes, although invariably interrelated, may also vary across development.

Biological, psychological, and social-contextual domains are each essential to include in basic research on resilience. The application of such a multiple-levels-of-analysis perspective to adolescents at risk for depression will enable scientists to grasp resilience in its full complexity. The incorporation of such an approach into the study of resilience will also be useful for informing efforts to translate research on positive adaptation in the face of adversity into the development of interventions to promote resilient functioning in adolescents.

Translational Research

In a report of the National Advisory Mental Health Council on Behavioral Sciences (2000) entitled *Translating Behavioral Science into Action*, strategies for enhancing the contributions of behavioral science to society more broadly were proposed. In this report, translational research is defined as "research designed to address how basic behavioral processes inform the diagnosis, prevention, treatment, and delivery of services for mental illness, and, conversely, how knowledge of mental illness increases our understanding of basic behavioral processes" (p. iii). This formulation of translational research is in direct accord with two of the key tenets of a developmental psychopathology perspective we described earlier—namely, the reciprocal interplay between basic and applied research and between normal and atypical development.

In order to improve the health and well-being of all members of society, it is clear that scientific discoveries must be translated into practical applications (Insel & Fernald, 2004; Moses, Dorsey, Matheson, & Their, 2005). The parameters of developmental psychopathology lend themselves to fostering translational research that has implications for society, policymakers, and individuals with mental disorders and their families. The very subject matter of the field, which encompasses risk and resilience, prevention and intervention, the elucidation of precipitants of mental illness, the mediating and moderating processes that contribute to or mitigate against the emergence and maintenance of psychopathology, a multiple-levels-of-analysis approach, and the incorporation of principles of normal development into the conduct of empirical investigations, necessitates thinking clearly about the implications of the work and devising strategies that can be directed toward the remediation of the problems being studied.

In one interesting explication of how social-cognitive processes that become prominent during adolescence may account for the increased risk for depression among adolescent girls, Papadakis, Prince, Jones, and Strauman (2006) found that adolescent girls who manifested both high levels of actual versus ideal discrepancy and a tendency to ruminate in response to stress and failure were at particularly high risk for reporting depressive symptoms. The work conducted by these investigators built upon theory and basic research derived from social psychology, thereby illustrating the value that such a translational approach can impart to understanding adolescent depression.

In order to truly facilitate the translation of research to the real-world problems associated with adolescent depression, increased interdisciplinary efforts will be necessary (Pellmar & Eisenberg, 2000). Such interdisciplinary efforts have repeatedly been advocated by developmental psychopathologists (Cicchetti & Toth, 2006), and they hold considerable value for advancing our understanding of adolescent depression.

PREVENTION AND INTERVENTION

Now that we have examined some illustrative principles of the developmental psychopathology framework and their relevance to investigating the development of adaptation and psychopathology in adolescents with depressive disorder, we next discuss how the developmental psychopathology perspective can similarly assist in the development and provision of prevention and intervention to adolescents who are at heightened risk for, or who have developed, a depressive disorder.

Theory and research on basic developmental processes and on the causes and consequences of adolescent depression can, and should, inform prevention and intervention efforts. Clinical research on treatment and preventive strategies can provide unprecedented and essential insights translatable to the making of further theoretical and empirical advances (Cicchetti & Hinshaw, 2002; Cicchetti & Toth, 2006; Garber, Webb, & Horowitz, this volume; Kellam & Rebok, 1992; McLaughlin, this volume; Toth & Cicchetti, 1999; Toth et al., 2006).

For example, if the developmental course is altered as a result of the implementation of a randomized preventive intervention trial and the risk for negative outcomes is reduced, then prevention research has contributed to specifying the processes that are involved in the emergence of maladaptive developmental outcomes and psychopathology. Accordingly, preventive intervention research can be conceptualized as true experiments in modifying the course of development, thereby providing insights into the etiology and pathogenesis of disordered outcomes.

Prevention research is based on theoretical models of how risk conditions are related to adverse outcomes. As such, it posits processes that link the risk condition to the negative outcome (Institute of Medicine, 1994). Intervention efficacy may be enhanced by knowledge of developmental norms, appreciation of how a developmental level may vary within the same age group, sensitivity to the changing meaning that problems and disorders have at different developmental levels, attention to the effects of developmental transitions and reorganizations, and an understanding of the factors that are essential to incorporate into the design and implementation of preventive interventions (Cicchetti & Toth, 1999; Institute of Medicine, 1994; Reiss & Price, 1996; Toth & Cicchetti, 1999).

As stated earlier, a central principle of developmental psychopathology is that the understanding of atypical development can inform the understanding of normal development, and vice versa. We extend this assertion through our contention that methodologically rigorous prevention and intervention science can provide a unique lens through which to discern the processes responsible for the development, maintenance, and alteration of both typical and atypical developmental patterns (Cicchetti & Toth, 1992; Hinshaw, 2002; Kellam & Rebok, 1992). The experimental nature of randomized prevention and intervention trials provides an unprecedented opportunity to make causal inferences (Hinshaw, 2002; Kraemer, Wilson, Fairburn, & Agras, 2002).

In recent years, there has been an increased call to develop and provide empirically supported treatments and to disseminate them to real-world settings. Even when treatments have been supported by empirical evidence and exported to broader clinical contexts, the developmental appropriateness of the modality must be considered if the treatment is to be optimally effective.

Although a seeming oxymoron, most treatments for children and adolescents are not developmentally informed (Holmbeck, Greenley, & Franks, 2003; Toth & Cicchetti, 1999). It is critical that developmental change and level be considered when providing interventions. A behavior that is normative at one period of development may become abnormal at a subsequent period. Moreover, the same psychopathology may be expressed differently at different stages of development, and similar psychopathologies may eventuate via very different developmental pathways (Cicchetti & Rogosch, 1996). Therefore, an understanding of diversity in developmental processes is critical to the development and delivery of efficacious services to depressed adolescents.

Unfortunately, results are not encouraging with respect to the developmental sensitivity of treatments for adolescents. In a review of treatment outcome studies that utilized cognitive-behavioral therapy (CBT) with adolescents, only 26% of studies reviewed considered developmental issues when discussing the design or evaluation of treatments (Holmbeck et al., 2000). In another review of treatments for adolescents, Weisz and Hawley (2002) reported that 14 of the 25 therapies that they examined were effective with adolescents. However, of those 14, seven involved downward modifications of treatments utilized with adults, and six involved upward extensions of treatments designed for children (Henggeler, Schoenwald, Borduin, Rowland, & Cunningham, 1998). Thus, only one of the efficacious treatments was designed specifically for adolescents, a fact that underscores the paucity of attention to developmental considerations.

With respect to depression, Weisz and Hawley (2002) reported that only 9% of published outcome research studies with adolescents involved treatments for depression. In general, the intervention evaluation literature for depressed youth has not been extensive and has been based largely on case studies and small samples (Mufson, Dorta, Moreau, & Weissman, 2004). More recently, randomized clinical trials of efficacy studies of CBT and interpersonal psychotherapy for adolescents (IPT-A) have been initiated, with promising results (Gunlicks & Mufson, this volume; Mufson et al., 2004). To date, however, CBT has the most extensive base of empirical support with respect to the treatment of depression in adolescents (Stark, Krumholz, Ridley, & Hamilton, this volume; Weisz, 2004).

When evaluating the efficacy of treatments for adolescent depression, considerations specific to that developmental period must be considered. In their presentation of IPT-A, Mufson and colleagues (2004) discuss a number of patient, family, and depression-specific influences to address when treating adolescents (see Gunlicks & Mufson, this volume). In addition to issues that may derive from these domains, we believe that the role of adolescent development also needs to be highlighted. For example, in the prefrontal cortex, peak overproduction of synapses occurs at approximately 1 year of age, but it is not until middle to late adolescence that synapses consistent with adult numbers are obtained (Spear, 2000). Moreover, key structures of the brain are not completely myelinated or fully developed during adolescence (Giedd, 2004; Spear, 2000). Therefore, brain physiology warns against assuming that adolescents are capable of consistently utilizing higher-level thought processes that may govern judgment and decision making, and that are requisite for the effective utilization of many treatment modalities (Dahl, 2004; Dahl & Spear, 2004; Steinberg et al., 2006).

In a review of research on the determinants of resilience, Luthar and Cicchetti (2000) stated that interventions aimed at promoting competent adaptation in diverse high-risk populations that have experienced significant adversity "should target protective and vulnerability forces at multiple levels of influence" (p. 878). The time has now come to design and implement randomized clinical trials aimed at ameliorating psychopathology, preventing its occurrence and relapse, and promoting resilience that not only assess behavioral changes, but also ascertain whether abnormal neurobiological structures, functions, and organizations are modifiable or are refractory to intervention (Cicchetti & Curtis, 2006; Curtis & Cicchetti, 2003). There is growing evidence that successful intervention modifies not only maladaptive behavior, but also the cellular and physiological correlates of behavior (Kandel, 1998, 1999). Efficacious interventions should change both behavior and physiology through producing alterations in gene expression (transcription) that produce new structural changes in the brain (Cicchetti & Curtis, 2006; Kandel, 1999).

In addition to more typical approaches to the treatment of depression in adolescents, a developmental psychopathology approach also suggests the importance of utilizing preventive strategies. According to prevention science, its overarching goal is to intervene in the course of development in order to reduce or eliminate the emergence of maladaptation and psychopathology (Ialongo et al., 2006). Such an approach requires an understanding of the course of normal development. Because a primary objective of a developmental psychopathology perspective involves understanding the boundary between normal and abnormal development, it is uniquely poised to provide a foundational base on which to build strategies to prevent the emergence of adolescent depression. For example, Cicchetti and Toth (1998) describe how aberrations in psychological and biological developmental domains during the early years of life may portend the emergence of future depressive disorder. Identifying the roots of such a depressotypic organization can lend itself to preventing the origins of such atypicality from eventuating in actual disorder.

One example of such a preventive strategy involved a randomized clinical trial of a preventive intervention conducted at Mt. Hope Family Center that was directed toward the offspring of mothers with MDD. The development of insecure attachment relationships in the offspring of mothers with MDD may initiate a negative trajectory that leads to future psychopathology (Cicchetti & Toth, 1995, 1998). Therefore, the provision of theoretically guided interventions designed to promote secure attachment is of paramount importance, and may ultimately prevent the emergence of future depression. In an intervention designed to prevent insecure attachment relationships in toddlers of mothers with MDD, dyads were randomized to toddler-parent psychotherapy (DI), or to a treatment-as-usual control group (DC). At baseline, higher rates of insecure attachment were present in both the DI and DC groups than in a normal comparison group (NC) of toddlers whose parents had no history of present or past Axis I mental disorder.

At postintervention at age 36 months, insecure attachment continued to predominate in the DC group. In contrast, the rate of secure attachment had increased substantially in the DI group, and was significantly higher than that for the DC group. There were no differences between the DI and the NC groups in attachment security at the conclusion of the intervention (Toth et al., 2006). These results demonstrate the efficacy of toddler-parent psychotherapy in fostering secure attachment relationships in offspring of depressed mothers, and highlight how preventive strategies that are implemented in at-risk groups of children during the early years of life may ultimately prevent the emergence of depression during later childhood or adolescence.

CONCLUSION AND IMPLICATIONS

The developmental psychopathology perspective described herein proffers important insights regarding the formulation of a research agenda for examining affective disturbances of adolescence. In addition, developmental considerations can contribute to the design, implementation, and evaluation of preventive and intervention strategies. By understanding the normative organization of psychological and biological developmental domains, the meaning of symptom expression and the capacity of depressed adolescents to benefit from varied treatment approaches can be elucidated. Moreover, information from intervention outcome studies can be used to challenge and extend normative theories of development.

Despite the fact that depression is a preventable and treatable illness, social stigma continues to be associated with seeking treatment for depressive disorders, and far too many individuals suffer needlessly due to an avoidance of help-seeking (Cicchetti & Toth, 1998; Hinshaw & Cicchetti, 2000). The failure to obtain treatment is particularly problematic for adolescents, as the prevalence of depressive symptoms and disorders increases sharply during this period of development, with rates rising from 2 to 6% (Angold, Costello, & Erkanli, 1999; Avenevoli & Steinberg, 2001; Weisz & Hawley, 2002). As knowledge that is guided by a developmental psychopathology perspective on the etiology and course of adolescent depression increases, and as more developmentally informed treatments are developed, evaluated, and disseminated, it is critical that commensurate increases in the willingness of adolescents and their families to seek treatment will occur.

In order to facilitate access to empirically validated and developmentally appropriate strategies for preventing and treating adolescent depression, social policy impediments also must be addressed. Although Congress passed the Domenici-Wellstone Mental Illness Parity Provision over a decade ago, this provision does not require that employers provide coverage for mental disorders; rather they must meet parity requirements with physical illness only if they offer some form of mental health coverage. Obviously, this approach can result in inadequate coverage for many children and families. Moreover, emerging policies suggest that it is mental illnesses that are consistent with underlying "brain" dysfunction that are most likely to be covered under mental health parity laws (Shirk, Talmi, & Olds, 2006). Such a medical model approach, wherein parity is based on the conceptualization of mental disorders as commensurate with physical illnesses, is antithetical to a developmental psychopathology perspective on risk and disorder. In addition, the ability to intervene early in the course of development, before an actual disorder may emerge, is precluded by policies such as these. Because the mental health system, since its inception, has operated in a "repair" mode (Cowen & Durlak, 2006), opportunities to promote positive functioning and to prevent mental illness have been rare. In fact, currently preventive strategies are more likely to be found in the child welfare than in the mental health arenas (Toth, Manly, & Nilsen, in press). The inability to obtain preventive services also may contribute to the stigmatization of access to mental health services, as it is only in the most severe "diagnosable" cases where mental health systems are sought.

As developmental psychopathologists, it is imperative that we work to ensure that the principles and values of a developmental approach to risk and disorder be incorporated into both clinical and social policy arenas. Such a perspective has much to offer to children, adolescents, and their families, and the failure to export the breadth of knowledge offered by this approach with respect to adolescent depression will impede advances in understanding and treating this devastating disorder.

REFERENCES

Alloy, L. B., & Abramson, L. Y. (2006). The adolescent surge in depression and emergence of gender differences: A biocognitive vulnerability-stress model in developmental context. In D. Romer & E. F. Walker (Eds.), *Adolescent psychopathology and the developing brain: Integrating brain and prevention science* (pp. 284–312). New York: Oxford University Press.

Angold, A., Costello, E. J., & Erkanli, A. (1999). Comorbidity. *Journal of Child Psychology and Psychiatry, 40*, 57–87.

Arnett, J. J. (1999). Adolescent storm and stress, reconsidered. *American Psychologist, 54*, 317–326.

Avenevoli, S., & Steinberg, L. (2001). The continuity of depression across the adolescent transition. In H. Reese & R. Kail (Eds.), *Advances in child development and behavior* (Vol. 28, pp. 139–173). New York: Academic Press.

Belsky, J. (1993). Etiology of child maltreatment: A developmental-ecological analysis. *Psychological Bulletin, 114*, 413–434.

Block, J. H., Gjerde, P. F., & Block, J. H. (1991). Personality antecedents of depressive tendencies in 18-year-olds: A prospective study. *Journal of Personality and Social Psychology, 60*, 726–738.

Bronfenbrenner, U. (1979). *The ecology of human development: Experiments by nature and design*. Cambridge, MA: Harvard University Press.

Cameron, J. L. (2004). Interrelationships between hormones, behavior, and affect during adolescence: Understanding hormonal, physical, and brain changes occurring in association with pubertal activation of the reproductive axis. *Annals of the New York Academy of Science, 1021*, 110–123.

Caspi, A., Sugden, K., Moffitt, T. E., Taylor, A., Craig, I. W., Harrington, H. L., et al. (2003). Influence of life stress on depression: Moderation by a polymorphism in the 5-HTT gene. *Science, 301*, 386–389.

Charney, D. (2004). Psychobiological mechanisms of resilience and vulnerability: Implications for successful adaptation to extreme stress. *American Journal of Psychiatry, 161*, 195–216.

Chomsky, N. (1968). *Language and mind*. New York: Harcourt Brace Jovanovich.

Cicchetti, D. (1984). The emergence of developmental psychopathology. *Child Development, 55*, 1–7.

Cicchetti, D. (1990). A historical perspective on the discipline of developmental psychopathology. In J. Rolf, A. Masten, D. Cicchetti, K. Nuechterlein & S. Weintraub (Eds.), *Risk and protective factors in the development of psychopathology* (pp. 2–28). New York: Cambridge University Press.

Cicchetti, D. (1993). Developmental psychopathology: Reactions, reflections, projections. *Developmental Review, 13*, 471–502.
Cicchetti, D. (2006). Development and psychopathology. In D. Cicchetti & D. J. Cohen (Eds.), *Developmental psychopathology, Vol. 1: Theory and method* (2nd ed., pp. 1–23). New York: Wiley.
Cicchetti, D., & Aber, J. L. (1986). Early precursors to later depression: An organizational perspective. In L. Lipsitt & C. Rovee-Collier (Eds.), *Advances in infancy* (Vol. 4, pp. 87–137). Norwood, NJ: Ablex.
Cicchetti, D., & Aber, J. L. (Eds.). (1998). Contextualism and developmental psychopathology [Special Issue]. *Development and Psychopathology, 10*(2), 137–426.
Cicchetti, D., & Cohen, D. J. (Eds.). (2006). *Developmental psychopathology* (2nd ed.). New York: Wiley.
Cicchetti, D., & Curtis, W. J. (2006). The developing brain and neural plasticity: Implications for normality, psychopathology, and resilience. In D. Cicchetti & D. Cohen (Eds.), *Developmental psychopathology, Vol. 2: Developmental neuroscience* (2nd ed., pp. 1–64). New York: Wiley.
Cicchetti, D., & Dawson, G. (Eds.). (2002). Multiple levels of analysis [Special Issue]. *Development and Psychopathology, 14*(3), 417–666.
Cicchetti, D., & Hinshaw, S. P. (2002). Prevention and intervention science: Contributions to developmental theory. *Development and Psychopathology, 14*, 667–671.
Cicchetti, D., & Lynch, M. (1993). Toward an ecological/transactional model of community violence and child maltreatment: Consequences for children's development. *Psychiatry, 56*, 96–118.
Cicchetti, D., & Rogosch, F. A. (1996). Equifinality and multifinality in developmental psychopathology. *Development and Psychopathology, 8*, 597–600.
Cicchetti, D., & Rogosch, F. R. (2007). Personality, adrenal steroid hormones, and resilience in maltreated children: A multi-level perspective. *Development and Psychopathology, 19*(3), 787–809.
Cicchetti, D., Rogosch, F. A., Lynch, M., & Holt, K. (1993). Resilience in maltreated children: Processes leading to adaptive outcome. *Development and Psychopathology, 5*, 629–647.
Cicchetti, D., Rogosch, F. R., & Sturge-Apple, M. L. (2007). Interactions of child maltreatment and 5-HTT and MAOA polymorphisms: Depressive symptomatology among adolescents from low-socioeconomic status backgrounds. *Development and Psychopathology, 19*(4), 1180–1161.
Cicchetti, D., Rogosch, F. A., & Toth, S. L. (1998). Maternal depressive disorder and contextual risk: Contributions to the development of attachment insecurity and behavior problems in toddlerhood. *Development and Psychopathology, 10*, 283–300.
Cicchetti, D., Rogosch, F. A., Toth, S. L., & Spagnola, M. (1997). Affect, cognition, and the emergence of self-knowledge in the toddler offspring of depressed mothers. *Journal of Experimental Child Psychology, 67*, 338–362.
Cicchetti, D., & Schneider-Rosen, K. (1986). An organizational approach to childhood depression. In M. Rutter, C. Izard & P. Read (Eds.), *Depression in young people, clinical and developmental perspectives* (pp. 71–134). New York: Guilford Press.

Cicchetti, D., & Sroufe, L. A. (2000). Editorial: The past as prologue to the future: The times, they've been a changin'. *Development and Psychopathology, 12,* 255–264.
Cicchetti, D., & Toth, S. L. (1991). The making of a developmental psychopathologist. In J. Cantor, C. Spiker & L. Lipsitt (Eds.), *Child behavior and development: Training for diversity* (pp. 34–72). Norwood, NJ: Ablex.
Cicchetti, D., & Toth, S. L. (1992). The role of developmental theory in prevention and intervention. *Development and Psychopathology, 4,* 489–493.
Cicchetti, D., & Toth, S. L. (1995). Developmental psychopathology and disorders of affect. In D. Cicchetti & D. J. Cohen (Eds.), *Developmental psychopathology, Vol. 2: Risk, disorder, and adaptation* (pp. 369–420). New York: Wiley.
Cicchetti, D., & Toth, S. L. (Eds.). (1996). *Rochester Symposium on Developmental Psychopathology: Adolescence: Opportunities and challenges* (Vol. 7). Rochester, NY: University of Rochester Press.
Cicchetti, D., & Toth, S. L. (1998). The development of depression in children and adolescents. *American Psychologist, 53,* 221–241.
Cicchetti, D., & Toth, S. L. (Eds.). (1999). *Rochester Symposium on Developmental Psychopathology: Developmental approaches to prevention and intervention* (Vol. 9). Rochester, NY: University of Rochester Press.
Cicchetti, D., & Toth, S. L. (Eds.). (2006). Translational research in developmental psychopathology. [Special Issue]. *Development and Psychopathology, 18*(3), 619–933.
Cicchetti, D., & Tucker, D. (1994). Development and self-regulatory structures of the mind. *Development and Psychopathology, 6,* 533–549.
Coie, J. D., Watt, N. F., West, S. G., Hawkins, J. D., Asarnow, J. R., & Markman, H. J. (1993). The science of prevention: A conceptual framework and some directions for a National Research Program. *American Psychologist, 48,* 1013–1022.
Costello, E. J., & Angold, A. (2006). Developmental epidemiology. In D. Cicchetti & D. J. Cohen (Eds.), *Developmental psychopathology, Vol. 1: Theory and method* (2nd ed., pp. 41–75). New York: Wiley.
Cowen, E. L., & Durlak, J. A. (2006). Social policy and prevention in mental health. *Development and Psychopathology, 12,* 815–834.
Cummings, E. M., & Davies, P. T. (1994). Maternal depression and child development. *Journal of Child Psychology and Psychiatry, 35,* 73–112.
Curtis, W. J., & Cicchetti, D. (2003). Moving research on resilience into the 21st century: Theoretical and methodological considerations in examining the biological contributors to resilience. *Development and Psychopathology, 15,* 773–810. Re-printed in *Dziecko Autystyczne* (2003); reprinted in *Audiofonologia* (2004).
Curtis, W. J., & Cicchetti, D. (2007). Emotion and resilience: A multi-level investigation of hemispheric electroencephalogram asymmetry and emotion regulation in maltreated and non-maltreated children. *Development and Psychopathology, 19,* 811–840.
Dahl, R. E. (2004). Adolescent brain development: A period of vulnerabilities and opportunities. *Annals of the New York Academy of Sciences, 1021,* 1–22.
Dahl, R. E., & Spear, L. P. (Eds.). (2004). *Adolescent brain development: Vulnerabilities and opportunities.* New York: New York Academy of Sciences.

Davidson, R. J. (2000). Affective style, psychopathology, and resilience: Brain mechanisms and plasticity. *American Psychologist, 55*, 1196–1214.

Duggal, S., Carlson, E .A., Sroufe, L. A., & Egeland, B. (2001). Depressive symptomatology in childhood and adolescence. *Development and Psychopathology, 13*, 143–164.

Egeland, B., Carlson, E. A., & Sroufe, L. A. (1993). Resilience as process. *Development and Psychopathology, 5*, 517–528.

Eley, T. C., Sugden, K., Corsico, A., Gregory, A. M., Sham, P., McGuffin, P., et al. (2004). Gene–environment interaction analysis of serotonin system markers with adolescent depression. *Molecular Psychiatry, 9*, 908–915.

Feldman, S. S., & Elliot, G. R. (Eds.). (1990). *At the threshold: The developing adolescent*. Cambridge, MA: Harvard University Press.

Garber, J., & Little, S. (1999). Predictors of competence among offspring of depressed mothers. *Journal of Adolescent Research, 14*, 44–71.

Garcia-Coll, C., Akerman, A., & Cicchetti, D. (2000). Cultural influences on developmental processes and outcomes: Implications for the study of development and psychopathology. *Development and Psychopathology, 12*, 333–356.

Giedd, J. N. (2004). Structural magnetic resonance imaging of the adolescent brain. *Annals of the New York Academy of Science, 1021*, 77–85.

Gjerde, P., & Block, J. (1996). A developmental perspective on depressive symptoms in adolescence: Gender differences in autocentric-allocentric modes of impulse regulation. In D. Cicchetti & S. L. Toth (Eds.), *Rochester Symposium on Developmental Psychopathology: Adolescence: Opportunities and challenges* (Vol. 7, pp. 167–196). Rochester, NY: University of Rochester Press.

Goodman, S. H. (2003). Genesis and epigenesis of psychopathology in children with depressed mothers: Toward an integrative biopsychosocial perspective. In D. Cicchetti & E. F. Walker (Eds.), *Neurodevelopmental mechanisms in psychopathology* (pp. 428–460). New York: Cambridge University Press.

Goodman, S. H., & Gottlib, I. H. (1999). Risk for psychopathology in the children of depressed mothers: A developmental model for understanding mechanisms of transmission. *Psychological Review, 106*, 458–490.

Gottesman, I. I., & Gould, T. D. (2003). The endophenotype concept in psychiatry: Etymology and strategic intentions. *American Journal of Psychiatry, 160*, 636–645.

Gottesman, I. I., & Hanson, D. R. (2005). Human development: Biological and genetic processes. *Annual Review of Psychology, 56*, 263–286.

Harrington, R., Fudge, H., Rutter, M., Pickles, A., & Hill, J. (1990). Adult outcomes of childhood and adolescent depression: I. Psychiatric status. *Archives of General Psychiatry, 47*, 465–473.

Harrington, R., Rutter, M., Weissman, M., Fudge, H., Groothues, C., Bredenkamp, D., et al. (1997). Psychiatric disorders in the relatives of depressed probands, I: Comparison of prepubertal, adolescent and early adult onset cases. *Journal of Affective Disorders, 42*, 9–22.

Henggeler, S. W., Schoenwald, S. K., Borduin, C. M., Rowland, M. D., & Cunningham, P. B. (1998). *Multisystemic treatment of antisocial behavior in children and adolescents.* New York: Guilford Press.

Hinshaw, S. P. (2002). Intervention research, theoretical mechanisms, and causal processes related to externalizing behavior problems. *Development and Psychopathology, 14*(4), 789–818.

Hinshaw, S. P., & Cicchetti, D. (2000). Stigma and mental disorder: Conceptions of illness, public attitudes, personal disclosure, and social policy. *Development and Psychopathology, 12*, 555–598.

Holmbeck, G. N., Colder, C., Shapera, W., Westhoven, V., Kenealy, L., & Updegrove, A. L. (2000). Working with adolescents: Guides from developmental psychology. In P. C. Kendall (Ed.), *Child & adolescent therapy: Cognitive-behavioral procedures* (2nd ed., pp. 334–385). New York: Guilford Press.

Holmbeck, G. N., Greenley, R. N., & Franks, E. A. (2003). Developmental issues in evidence-based practice. In P. Barrett & T. H. Ollendick (Eds.), *Handbook of interventions that work with children and adolescents: Prevention and treatment* (pp. 27–48). London: Oxford.

Ialongo, N., Rogosch, F. A., Cicchetti, D., Toth, S. L., Buckley, J., Petras, H., et al. (2006). A developmental psychopathology approach to the prevention of mental health disorders. In D. Cicchetti & D. Cohen (Eds.), *Developmental psychopathology, Vol. 1: Theory and method* (2nd ed., pp. 968–1018). New York: Wiley.

Insel, T. R., & Fernald, R. D. (2004). How the brain processes social information: Searching for the social brain. *Annual Review of Neuroscience, 27*, 697–722.

Institute of Medicine. (1994). *Reducing risks for mental disorders: Frontiers for preventive intervention research.* Washington, DC: National Academy Press.

Jensen, P. S., & Hoagwood, K. (1997). The book of names: DSM-IV in context. *Development and Psychopathology, 2*, 231–249.

Kandel, E. R. (1998). A new intellectual framework for psychiatry. *American Journal of Psychiatry, 155*, 475–469.

Kandel, E. R. (1999). Biology and the future of psychoanalysis: A new intellectual framework for psychiatry revisited. *American Journal of Psychiatry, 156*, 505–524.

Karmiloff-Smith, A. (2007). Atypical epigenesis. *Developmental Science, 10*, 84–88.

Kaufman, J. (1991). Depressive disorders in maltreated children. *Journal of the American Academy of Child & Adolescent Psychiatry, 30*, 257–265.

Kaufman, J., Yang, B., Douglas-Palumberi, H., Grasso, D., Lipschitz, D., Houshyar, S., et al. (2006). Brain-derived neurotrophic factor: 5-HTTLPR gene interactions and environmental modifiers of depression in children. *Biological Psychiatry, 59*, 673–680.

Kaufman, J., Yang, B., Douglas-Palumberi, H., Houshyar, S., Lipschitz, D., Krystal, J., et al. (2004). Social supports and serotonin transporter gene moderate depression in maltreated children. *Proceedings of the National Academy of Sciences of the United States of America, 101*(49), 17316–17321.

Kellam, S. G., & Rebok, G. W. (1992). Building developmental and etiological theory through epidemiologically based preventive intervention trials. In J. McCord & R. E. Tremblay (Eds.), *Preventing antisocial behavior: Interventions from birth through adolescence* (pp. 162–195). New York: Guilford Press.

Kraemer, H. C., Wilson, G. T., Fairburn, C. G., & Agras, W. S. (2002). Mediators and moderators of treatment effects in randomized clinical trials. *Archives of General Psychiatry, 59*, 877–884.

Lenneberg, E. (1967). *Biological foundations of language.* New York: Wiley.

Lesch, K. P., & Hiels, A. (2000). Serotonergic gene transcription control regions: Targets for antidepressant drug development. *International Journal of Neuropsychopharmacology, 3*, 67–79.

Luthar, S. S. (1991). Vulnerability and resilience: A study of high-risk adolescents. *Child Development, 62*, 600–616.

Luthar, S. S. (2006). Resilience in development: A synthesis of research across five decades. In D. Cicchetti & D. Cohen (Eds.), *Developmental psychopathology, Vol. 3: Risk, disorder, and adaptation* (2nd ed., pp. 739–795). New York: Wiley.

Luthar, S. S., & Cicchetti, D. (2000). The construct of resilience: Implications for intervention and social policy. *Development and Psychopathology, 12*, 857–885.

Luthar, S. S., Cicchetti, D., & Becker, B. (2000). The construct of resilience: A critical evaluation and guidelines for future work. *Child Development, 71*, 543–562.

Luthar, S. S., Doernberger, C. H., & Zigler, E. (1993). Resilience is not a unidimensional construct: Insights from a prospective study on inner-city adolescents. *Development and Psychopathology, 5*, 703–717.

Manly, J. T., Kim, J. E., Rogosch, F. A., & Cicchetti, D. (2001). Dimensions of child maltreatment and children's adjustment: Contributions of developmental timing and subtype. *Development and Psychopathology, 13*, 759–782.

Masten, A. S. (2001). Ordinary magic: Resilience processes in development. *American Psychologist, 56*, 227–238. Reprinted in M. E., Hertzig & E. A. Farber (Eds.). (2005). *Annual progress in child psychiatry and child development: 2002*. New York: Routledge.

Masten, A. S. (2004). Regulatory processes, risk and resilience in adolescent development. In R. E. Dahl & L. P. Spear (Eds.), *Adolescent brain development: Vulnerabilities and opportunities* (Vol. 1021). New York: New York Academy of Sciences.

Masten, A. S. (2006). Developmental psychopathology: Pathways to the future. *International Journal of Behavioral Development, 31*, 47–54.

Maughan, A., Cicchetti, D., Toth, S. L., & Rogosch, F. A. (2007). Early-occurring maternal depression and maternal sensitivity in predicting young children's emotional regulation and socioemotional difficulties. *Journal of Abnormal Child Psychology, 35*, 685–703.

Mayr, E. (1964). The evolution of living systems. *Proceedings of the National Academy of Sciences, 51*, 934–941.

Mayr, E. (1988). *Toward a new philosophy of biology.* Cambridge, MA: Harvard University Press.

Moffitt, T., Caspi, A., & Rutter, M. (2006). Measured gene–environment interactions in psychopathology: Concepts, research strategies, and implications for research, intervention, and public understanding of genetics. *Perspectives on Psychological. Science, 1*, 5–27.

Moses, H., 3rd., Dorsey, E. R., Matheson, D. H., & Their, S. O. (2005). Financial anatomy of biomedical research. *Journal of the American Medical Association, 294*, 1333–1342.

Mufson, L., Dorta, K. P., Moreau, D., & Weissman, M. M. (2004). *Interpersonal psychotherapy for depressed adolescents* (2nd ed.). New York: Guildford Press.

National Advisory Mental Health Council on Behavioral Sciences (2000). *Translating behavioral science into action*. NIH Publication 00-4699. Bethesda, MD: National Institute of Mental Health.

Nelson, E. E., Leibenluft, E., McClure, E. B., & Pine, D. S. (2005). The social reorientation of adolescence: A neuroscience perspective on the process and its relation to psychopathology. *Psychological Medicine, 35*, 163–174.

Noam, G. (1992). Development as the aim of clinical intervention. *Development and Psychopathology, 4*, 679–696.

O'Connor, T. G. (2003). Natural experiments to study the effects of early experience: Progress and limitations. *Development and Psychopathology, 15*, 837–852.

Papadakis, A. A., Prince, R. P., Jones, N. P., & Strauman, T. J. (2006). Self-regulation, rumination, and vulnerability to depression in adolescent girls. *Development and Psychopathology, 18*, 815–829.

Pellmar, R., & Eisenberg, L. (Eds.). (2000). *Bridging disciplines in the brain, behavioral, and clinical sciences*. Washington, DC: National Academies Press.

Raver, C. C., Gershoff, E. T., & Aber, J. L. (2007). Testing equivalence of mediating models of income, parenting, and school readiness for White, Black, and Hispanic children in a national sample. *Child Development, 78*, 96–115.

Reiss, D., & Price, R. H. (1996). National Research Agenda for Prevention Research: The National Institute of Mental Health Report. *American Psychologist, 51*, 1109–1115.

Richters, J. E. (1997). The Hubble hypothesis and the developmentalist's dilemma. *Development and Psychopathology, 9*, 193–229.

Richters, J. E., & Cicchetti, D. (1993). Mark Twain meets DSM-III-R: Conduct disorder, development, and the concept of harmful dysfunction. *Development and Psychopathology, 5*, 5–29.

Robins, L. (1966). *Deviant children grow up*. Baltimore, MD: Williams & Wilkins.

Romer, D., & Walker, E. F. (Eds.). (2006). *Adolescent psychopathology and the developing brain: Integrating brain and prevention science*. New York: Oxford University Press.

Rutter, M. (2006). *Genes and behavior: Nature-nurture interplay explained*. Oxford, UK: Blackwell.

Rutter, M., & Sroufe, L. A. (2000). Developmental psychopathology: Concepts and challenges. *Development and Psychopathology, 12*, 265–296.

Schulenberg, J. E., Sameroff, A. J., & Cicchetti, D. (Eds.). (2004). Transition from adolescence to adulthood [Special Issue]. *Development and Psychopathology, 16*, 799–1171.

Serafica, F. C., & Vargas, L. A. (2006). Cultural diversity in the development of child psychopathology. In D. Cicchetti & D. Cohen (Eds.), *Developmental psychopathology, Vol. 1: Theory and method* (2nd ed., pp. 588–626). New York: Wiley.

Shirk, S. R., Talmi, A., & Olds, D. (2000). A developmental psychopathology perspective on child and adolescent treatment policy. *Development and Psychopathology, 12*, 835–855.

Spear, L. P. (2000). The adolescent brain and age-related behavioral manifestations. *Neuroscience and Behavioral Reviews, 24*, 417–463.

Spencer, M. B., & DuPree, D. (1996). African-American youths' ecocultural challenges and psychosocial opportunities: An alternative analysis of problem behavior outcomes. In D. Cicchetti & S. L. Toth (Eds.), Rochester Symposium on Developmental Psychopathology: Adolescence: Opportunities and challenges (Vol. 7, pp. 259–282). Rochester, NY: University of Rochester Press.

Spoont, M. (1992). Modulatory role of serotonin in neural information processing: Implications for human psychopathology. *Psychological Bulletin, 112*, 330–350.

Sroufe, L. A. (1989). Pathways to adaptation and maladaptation: Psychopathology as developmental deviation. In D. Cicchetti (Ed.), *Rochester Symposium on Developmental Psychopathology: The emergence of a discipline* (Vol. 1, pp. 13–40). Hillsdale, NJ: Lawrence Erlbaum Associates.

Sroufe, L. A. (1990). Considering normal and abnormal together: The essence of developmental psychopathology. *Development and Psychopathology, 2*, 335–347.

Sroufe, L. A., Egeland, B., & Kreutzer, T. (1990). The fate of early experience following developmental change: Longitudinal approaches to individual adaptation in childhood. *Child Development, 61*, 1363–1373.

Sroufe, L. A., & Jacobvitz, D. (1989). Diverging pathways, developmental transformations, multiple etiologies, and the problem of continuity in development. *Human Development, 32*, 196–203.

Sroufe, L. A., & Rutter, M. (1984). The domain of developmental psychopathology. *Child Development, 55*, 17–29.

Steinberg, L., Dahl, R., Keating, D., Kupfer, D., Masten, A. S., & Pine, D. S. (2006). The study of developmental psychopathology in adolescence: Integrating affective neuroscience with the study of context. In D. Cicchetti & D. Cohen (Eds.), *Developmental psychopathology, Vol. 2: Developmental neuroscience* (2nd ed., pp. 710–741). New York: Wiley.

Steinberg, L., & Morris, A. S. (2001). Adolescent development. *Annual Review of Psychology, 52*, 83–110.

Toth, S. L., & Cicchetti, D. (1996a). The impact of relatedness with mother on school functioning in maltreated youngsters. *Journal of School Psychology, 3*, 247–266.

Toth, S. L., & Cicchetti, D. (1996b). Patterns of relatedness and depressive symptomatology in maltreated children. *Journal of Consulting and Clinical Psychology, 64*, 32–41.

Toth, S. L., & Cicchetti, D. (1999). Developmental psychopathology and child psychotherapy. In S. Russ & T. Ollendick (Eds.), *Handbook of psychotherapies with children and families* (pp. 15–44). New York: Plenum Press.

Toth, S. L., Cicchetti, D., Rogosch, F. A., & Sturge-Apple, M. (in press). Attachment security and representational development in offspring of depressed mothers: An organizational perspective. *Child Development.*

Toth, S. L., Manly, J. T., & Cicchetti, D. (1992). Child maltreatment and vulnerability to depression. *Development and Psychopathology, 4*, 97–112.

Toth, S. L., Manly, J. T., & Nilsen, W. (in press). From research to practice: Lessons learned. *Journal of Applied Developmental Psychology.*

Toth, S. L., Rogosch, F. A., Manly, J. T., & Cicchetti, D. (2006). The efficacy of toddler-parent psychotherapy to reorganize attachment in the young offspring of mothers with major depressive disorder. *Journal of Consulting & Clinical Psychology, 74*(6), 1086–1097.
von Bertalanffy, L. (1968). *General system theory.* New York: Braziller.
Waddington, C. H. (1957). *The strategy of genes.* London: Allen & Unwin.
Wakefield, J. C. (1992). Disorder as harmful dysfunction: A conceptual critique of DSM-III-R's definition of mental disorder. *Psychological Review, 99*, 232–247.
Weisz, J. R. (2004). *Psychotherapy for children and adolescents: Evidence-based treatments and case examples.* New York: Cambridge University Press.
Weisz, J. R., & Hawley, K. M. (2002). Developmental factors in the treatment of adolescents. *Journal of Consulting and Clinical Psychology, 70*, 21–43.
Werner, H., & Kaplan, B. (1963). *Symbol formation.* New York: Wiley.
Widom, C. S., DuMont, K., & Czaja, S. J. (2007). A prospective investigation of major depressive disorder and comorbidity in abused and neglected children grown up. *Archives of General Psychiatry, 64*, 49–56.
Wilden, A. (1980). *System and structure.* London: Tavistock.
Williams, R. B., Marchuk, D. A., Gadde, K. M., Barefoot, J. C., Grichnik, K., Helms, M. J., et al. (2001). Central nervous system serotonin function and cardiovascular responses to stress. *Psychosomatic Medicine, 63*, 300–305.

Chapter Two

Diagnosis and Assessment of Adolescent Depression

CECILIA A. ESSAU AND THOMAS H. OLLENDICK

CONTENTS

The existence of a sound classification system is a prerequisite for enhanced understanding of the etiology, assessment, treatment, and prevention of depressive disorders. With regard to adolescent psychopathology in general, and to adolescent depression in particular, a robust classification system must meet at least four standards: (1) it must be based on clearly defined rules and criteria, (2) it must be reliable and valid across diverse populations and settings, (3) it must be able to differentiate adolescents with depression from those without, and (4) it must contain clinically useful information for treatment planning and treatment evaluation. Classification systems that meet these requirements should provide researchers with a common framework for theory building on depressive and other psychiatric disorders, clinicians with a nomenclature for effective communication, and administrators with a rationale for planning and resource allocation (Remschmidt, 1995).

This chapter will focus on the comparison between DSM-IV and ICD-10, the distinction between categorical and dimensional approaches, and a review of methods for assessing depressive symptoms and structured diagnostic interviews commonly used in making a diagnosis of depressive and other psychiatric disorders.

CLASSIFICATION OF ADOLESCENT DEPRESSION

Categorical Systems (DSM/ICD)

Categorical systems view depression as a psychiatric disorder based on the number, severity, persistence, and impairment of symptoms (Kazdin, 1995). The most commonly used categorical systems for depressive disorder are the Diagnostic and Statistical Manual currently in its fourth edition (DSM-IV; APA, 1994), and the International Classification of Diseases currently in its 10th revision (ICD; WHO, 1993). The DSM-IV criteria were established by empirical studies via systematic field trials, and then balanced by expert opinion (Frances et al., 1994). The diagnostic criteria in the ICD-10 are based primarily on expert consensus that was later tested with field trials in various countries. Although the most recent versions of these systems have increasingly resulted in greater convergence between them, some differences remain (Table 2.1; Essau, Feehan, & Üstun, 1997).

Major depressive disorder (MDD) denotes a severe and an acute form of a depressive disorder (APA, 1994). In DSM-IV, MDD is diagnosed when the adolescent has either depressed mood or anhedonia together with the presence of at least four other symptoms that involve vegetative, psychomotor, and cognitive domains. In adolescents, depressed mood may be replaced by irritable mood; failure to make expected weight gains may be observed in lieu of significant weight loss or weight gain, or decrease or increase in appetite. In ICD-10, the criteria of a depressive episode is met when at least two of the three core symptoms (i.e., depressed mood, loss of interest and enjoyment, and reduced energy leading to increased fatigability and diminished activity) are present for most of the day, nearly everyday for a minimum of 2 weeks.

Dysthymic disorder represents a chronic, but less severe form of a depressive disorder (APA, 1994). In DSM-IV, the adolescents must have depressed or irritable mood for most days for at least a year together with at least two depressive symptoms; the 1-year duration for adolescents is in contrast to the 2-year duration required for adults. In ICD-10, the diagnosis of dysthymia is met when there is a constant recurring depressed mood for at least 2 years, during which no or few depressive episodes are severe or long-lasting enough to meet the criteria for recurrent depressive disorder.

Criticism of Categorical Systems

Despite the widespread application of the categorical approach in studying adolescent depression, questions have been raised as to whether criteria created for adults are appropriate for children and adolescents. In DSM-IV, two adjustments made for children and adolescents were related to "depressed mood" and "significant weight loss or weight gain," which can be substituted with "irritable mood," and with "a failure to make expected weight gains," respectively. Empirical basis for the differences and similarities in the manifestation of depressive symptoms at different ages are however lacking (Angold & Worthman, 1993; Ollendick, Shortt, & Sander, 2005). Furthermore, a study by Luby and colleagues (2002) indicated that DSM-IV criteria failed to capture 76% of preschoolers who

Table 2.1 Classification of depressive disorders according to ICD-10 and DSM-IV

	DSM-IV	ICD-10
Depressive symptoms	At least five of the following symptoms, one of which should be either depressed mood or loss of interest: (1) Depressed mood (2) Loss of interest (3) Significant weight loss when not dieting or weight gain, or increase in appetite (4) Insomnia or hypersomnia (5) Psychomotor agitation or retardation (6) Fatigue or loss of energy (7) Feelings of worthlessness or excessive or inappropriate guilt (8) Diminished ability to think or concentrate or indecisiveness (9) Recurrent thoughts of death, recurrent suicidal ideation without a specific plan, or a suicide attempt or a specific plan	Depressed mood, loss of interest or enjoyment, and decreased energy or increased fatigability. Other common symptoms include: loss of confidence or self-esteem; unreasonable feelings of self-reproach or excessive and inappropriate guilt; recurrent thoughts of death or suicide, or any suicidal behavior; diminished ability to think or concentrate; change of psychomotor activity, with agitation or retardation; sleep disturbance; and change in appetite with corresponding weight change. Some depressive symptoms have a clinical significance and are referred to as "somatic." To meet the criteria for the somatic syndrome, four of the following symptoms should be present: marked loss of interest or pleasure in activities that are normally pleasurable; lack of emotional reactions to events or activities that normally produce an emotional response; waking up 2 hours or earlier before the usual time in the morning; depression being worse in the morning; objective evidence of marked psychomotor retardation or agitation; marked loss of appetite; weight loss; and marked loss of libido.
Duration of symptoms	Nearly every day for at least 2 weeks at a level that represents a change from previous functioning.	Last for a minimum of 2 weeks.
Clinical significance	Symptoms cause clinically significant stress or impairment in social, occupational or other important areas of functioning.	Major depressive episode can be categorized as mild (i.e., distressed by the symptoms, but will not cease to function completely), moderate (i.e., have considerable difficulty in continuing with social, work, or domestic activities), and severe (i.e., considerable distress or agitation; social, work or domestic activities are likely to be discontinued, except to a very limited extent).
Exclusion criteria	Symptoms meet criteria for a mixed episode (i.e., symptoms of a manic and major depressive episode) that occur almost daily for a period of at least 1 week; symptoms are a result of direct physiological effects of a substance or a general medical condition; symptoms are accounted for by a normal reaction to the loss of a loved one (bereavement).	Hypomanic or manic symptoms enough to meet the criteria for hypomanic or manic episode; depressive episode is caused by psychoactive substance use or by an organic mental disorder.

met MDD when criteria were age-appropriately modified. Weiss and Garber (2003) reported developmental differences in depressive symptoms among adolescents. Specifically, guilt tended to be more related to depression in children than in adolescents, whereas affective symptoms (e.g., sadness) and concerns about the future were more strongly related to depression in adolescents than in children (Weiss et al., 1991). This study suggested the inadequacy of a global set of criteria for the under 18-year-olds.

Some concerns have also been raised about the validity of the current taxonomy in general. First, our classification systems have been developed largely from data derived from adults; thus, limitations of these nomenclatures observed in adults also apply to adolescents. For example, in the DSM-IV, once one core symptom is present (i.e., depressed mood, or loss of interest or pleasure) all subsequent symptoms are given equal weight in making a diagnosis of MDD. This notion of symptom equivalency defies common sense. For example, why should "suicide attempt" and "fatigue" be given the same weight?

Second, the use of categorical approach could lead to a loss of useful information about the nature of the disorders because individuals with scores just below the diagnostic threshold are regarded as noncases. As reported by Lewinsohn, Solomon, Seeley, and Zeiss (2000), adolescents with subthreshold depression were not only psychosocially impaired similarly to those who meet full diagnostic criteria, but they were also at increased risk for future psychiatric diagnoses. Third, comorbidity seems to be a rule rather than an exception among adolescents with depressive disorders, with about 40–70% of the adolescents who meet the diagnosis of MDD, meeting criteria for at least one other psychiatric disorder (Angold, Costello, & Erkanli, 1999a; Essau, 2007; Ford, Goodman, & Meltzer, 2003). The high comorbidity rate has raised questions about the meaningfulness of the system; it suggests that disorders may not be distinct or, at the least, have not been defined adequately (Caron & Rutter, 1991; Seligman & Ollendick, 1998).

Despite these limitations, categorical systems such as the DSM and ICD are important for guiding research, education/training, and clinical practice. Moreover, in clinical settings, the two systems are often associated with reimbursement for treatment services.

Dimensional System

In the dimensional system, depression is defined as a set of emotions and behaviors that occur together in a specific pattern. The general assumption of this approach is that the entities are quantitative, continuous, and linear; differences among individuals are considered in terms of deviations in the quantitative levels of symptoms. The dimensional approach is relatively atheoretical, although it is not theory free because the type of behavior to be assessed and to be entered into the statistical analyses has to be decided upon.

One of the most widely used standardized dimensional tests is the Child Behavior Checklist (CBCL; Achenbach, 1991a) and its companion measures, the Youth Self-Report (YSR; Achenbach, 1991b) which is completed by the adolescents themselves, and the Teacher's Report Form (TRF; Achenbach, 1991c) which is completed by a teacher who is familiar with the child. In the CBCL, YSR, and TRF, the syndrome labeled anxious/depressed comprises symptoms of anxiety and depression. Large-scale studies (e.g., Lambert, Essau, Schmitt, & Samms-Vaughan, 2007) conducted in many countries have successfully replicated the anxious/depressed syndrome.

The main advantage of the dimensional approach to classification is that constellations of behavior and emotions are obtained through empirical data. By conceptualizing the adolescent's problem on a specific dimension, the adolescent's behavior can also be compared to normative standards. That is, developmental variables are accounted for and clinical profiles for specific populations can be based on separate age (4–5, 6–11, and 12- to 16-year-olds) and gender groupings. In clinical and research settings, they can also be used to compare any significant changes due to treatment. A major problem with the dimensional approach, however, is that it does not allow the formulation of a clinical diagnosis of depression, and that the cut-off used to indicate depressive "caseness" can be arbitrary. Furthermore, the results obtained may depend on the type of statistical procedures, the number and content of items, and the number of adolescents used in the analyses.

ASSESSMENT

Goals of Assessment

Assessment represents a fundamental step in understanding depressive disorders in adolescents. Goals of assessment include diagnosis and prognosis, treatment planning, and treatment monitoring and evaluation. In clinical practice, assessment precedes treatment, but is also an ongoing, fluid, and dynamic process. The success of the intervention often depends on the information obtained during the initial assessment process, and the dynamic interplay between ongoing assessments throughout treatment.

Due to the complexity and the multiple facets of dysfunction associated with adolescent depression, assessment should not be limited to the characteristics of the adolescents, but also include external contexts (e.g., characteristics of the parents, peer groups, social context; Kazdin & Kagan, 1994), and related constructs (cognitive function, social competence, and psychosocial impairment). The assessment of adolescent depression should ideally use multiple methods (interview, questionnaire) and multiple informants (adolescent, parent). Multiple-method assessment enables capturing different manifestations of behavior or of responses in given situations (Ollendick & Hersen, 1984, 1993).

Sources of Information

Although the diagnostic criteria for depression are similar in adults, adolescents, and children, the process of determining the diagnosis differs. In adults, the major method is through the use of individual interviews, whereas in children and adolescents multiple informants are needed. The multi-informant recommendation is based on the notion that different informants have unique and valid perspectives on the adolescent given their access to different samples of behavior in different settings (Achenbach, 1995). Achenbach (1995) has argued that in order to help decrease bias that may result from any one informant, information should be obtained from parent reports (e.g., child's developmental history, parent interview), teacher reports (e.g., child's school reports, teacher interview), cognitive assessment (e.g., ability tests, achievement tests, perceptual-motor tests), physical assessment (e.g., medical and neurological examination), and self-report assessment (e.g., clinical interview, standardized self-ratings by the child/adolescent) of the child or adolescent.

Unfortunately, the agreement among informants on the frequency and severity of childhood and adolescent depression has been relatively low (Angold et al., 1987). For example, on the Oregon Adolescent Depression Project (OADP), parent–adolescent agreement for major depression ($K=0.31$) and dysthymia ($K=0.23$) has been low (Cantwell, Lewinsohn, Rohde, & Seeley, 1997). Parent-reported rate of dysthymic disorder (4.6%) was slightly higher than the adolescent-reported rate (3.6%). By contrast, adolescents (19.2%) reported significantly higher rates of major depression than their parents (9.3%).

The reasons for the low agreement reported in some studies are unclear; however, some hypotheses may be put forward. First, adolescents have the cognitive maturity and insight to answer questionnaires assessing their thoughts and feelings, but they may be reluctant to provide certain information (e.g., about suicidal thoughts) due to embarrassment or social desirability (Reynolds, 1994). In addition, among preadolescents, a lack of developmentally relevant methods for the assessment of depression may result in them failing to understand the questions. Second, parents and adolescents may have a different threshold as to what constitutes a "depressed symptom." Third, it could be that parents do not have an accurate understanding of the adolescent's difficulty, and that they may not be aware of all the adolescent's internal feelings. Regardless of the reasons for the low agreement between informants, a major challenge is to decide which information to use when a significant discrepancy exists between the child and the parent's report. Authors differ in their view as to which information should be used. Angold et al. (1987), for example, recommended that the children's report be used to judge the accuracy of the adult's report, whereas others have recommended the use of parents' report as the primary criterion (Rapee, Barrett, Dadds, & Evans, 1994). However, because each case may differ, it is important to know the interpersonal dynamics between the child and the parents before determining which informant to rely upon (Dadds, James, Barrett, & Verhulst, 2003). Still, others have recommended the value of both informants, even though they might disagree with one another (Silverman & Ollendick, 2005). Each provides valuable information.

ASSESSMENT METHODS

The assessment of depression in adolescents has generally used self-report instruments, behavior rating scales, and diagnostic interviews (Table 2.2). When choosing an assessment approach for measuring depressive disorder, an important consideration is the reliability and validity of the instruments (Table 2.3). Decisions as to which instruments to use also rely on the research and clinical questions to be addressed, as well as the study design. Achenbach (1995) recommended that the instruments used should be standardized, contain multiple items to assess different level of functioning, and have normed scores to compare the individual with relevant reference groups. Kazdin (1990) similarly stated that an assessment battery should have different sources of information (e.g., the child and a significant other), assess performance at home and at school, examine multiple domains of depressive symptoms (e.g., affect, cognitions, and behavior), and measure overall adjustment (e.g., adjustment or psychopathology). Also, in assessing children and adolescents, there is a need to consider measures appropriate to their age and level of development.

Table 2.2 Advantages and limitations of different assessment methods

Assessment Method	Advantages/Unique Contribution	Limitations
Unstructured interview	Rapport building; flexible; personally-tailored to the adolescent's problems; direct observation of behavior.	Unsystematic; unreliable.
Structured interview	Reliable and comprehensive coverage of DSM and ICD disorders; allows documentation of information on age of onset, duration, and impairment of depressive disorders; reduce observer, information, and criterion variance in obtaining information; direct observation of behavior.	Time consuming to administer; in some interviews, the items are "gated" which lead to loss of information; lack normative data. Semistructured interview needs to be conducted by clinicians, which can be expensive for large sample size.
General omnibus measures and single-domain questionnaires	Inexpensive and easy to administer; mostly psychometrically sound; available normative data which enable the determination of severity; enable multi-informant comparisons.	Low level of agreement among informants; lack of information related to the onset and duration of depression; information is limited to the informant's perspective.

Source: Modified from Essau and Barrett (2001).

Table 2.3 Guidelines in selecting assessment instruments for depressive disorders

Areas of Consideration	Alternatives/Comments
Depressive phenomena	Frequency of depressive disorders and comorbid disorders • Highly structured interview • Semistructured interview Frequency and severity of depressive symptoms • Questionnaire/rating scales • Some structured interviews Effect of treatment • Structured interviews • Questionnaire/rating scales • Measures of psychosocial impairment or quality of life
Age of the sample	Consider the developmental aspects of self-reports and interviews • Characteristics of self-report questionnaires – consider the adolescent's language, reading, writing skills • Characteristics of the interviews – establish rapport and co-operation using age-appropriate communication
Informants	Adolescent; parent; teacher; peer
Psychometric properties	Reliability; validity; sensitivity; specificity
Content of the instrument	Types and number of depressive symptoms
Coverage of other psychopathology	Use interview schedules that include a broad range of disorders due to high comorbidity rates in depressive disorders
Comparability with other studies	Use existing instruments in order to compare findings across studies
Resources	Personnel availability: clinicians, lay interviewers, nonprofessional staff

Source: Modified from Essau and Barrett (2001).

Self-Report Questionnaires

The fact that many depressive symptoms reflect subjective feelings and self-perceptions lends credence to the use of self-report questionnaires. In self-report questionnaires, adolescents respond to the questions or statements by marking one of the given sets of responses. The information elicited by these questionnaires can be used to assess the presence, frequency, and severity of depressive symptoms (Reynolds, 1994). Some examples of self-report questionnaires for the assessment of adolescent depression include: the Depression Self-Rating Scale (Birleson, 1981), the Center for Epidemiological Studies-Depression Scale (Radloff, 1991), the Beck Depression Inventory (BDI; Beck, Steer, Ball, & Ranieri, 1996), the Reynolds Adolescent Depression Scale (Reynolds, 1987), the Children's Depression Inventory (CDI; Kovacs, 1992), and the Children's Depression Scale (CDS; Tisher, Lang-Takac, & Lang, 1992). One common feature of these self-report questionnaires is that they contain emotions and symptoms of core characteristics of depressive disorders. In most of these questionnaires, symptoms are based on DSM criteria or are downward version of the measure of adult depression (e.g., BDI; Beck et al., 1996). Because detailed description and a summary of the psychometric properties of these instruments have been presented by several authors (e.g., Essau, Hakim-Larson, Crocker, & Petermann, 1999; Myers & Winters, 2002; Nezu, Nezu, McClure, & Zwick, 2002; Reynolds, 1994), we will not discuss them in this chapter.

There are several advantages of using questionnaires for assessing depressive symptoms (Table 2.2). First, because the adolescents themselves are much closer to the issues in question than other individuals, the information they give in a self-report questionnaire tends to be more accurate. Others are limited to reporting only the obvious side of adolescent's experience through their behavior and verbal responses. As reported in several studies, adolescents are better informants in assessing covert symptoms of depression (e.g., self-worth and suicidal ideation; Crocker & Hakim-Larson, 1997), whereas significant others are better informants for vegetative and externally observable problems associated with depressed affect (Robinson, Garber, & Hilsman, 1995). Second, because the questionnaires are completed by the adolescents, they can be administered and assessed by personnel with limited clinical experience. Furthermore, they can be administered relatively quickly to large groups of adolescents without much financial cost. For this reason, self-reported questionnaires are often used as screening instruments in the first stage of a two-stage process to determine those who have an elevated probability of being or becoming depressed, or those in need of professional help (e.g., Clarke et al., 1996). Third, in clinical practice, self-report instruments are typically administered as part of a comprehensive assessment. The responses can be used to assist a clinician in the initial evaluation by providing a guide about a particular problem, and as a tool for quantifying the adolescent's presenting symptoms.

Although important for assessing the depressed experience from the perspective of the adolescents, self-report questionnaires are insufficient to determine the diagnosis of depressive disorders. Furthermore, response bias (e.g., social desirability) may distort an adolescent's self-evaluation. Further work is needed to overcome limitations of existing measures by designing developmentally appropriate, depression-specific, self-report instruments, and to design self-report measures that can be used to adequately identify adolescents who require treatment, and appropriate for use in the assessment of treatment outcome. The former point is of importance given the fact that certain depressive symptoms may be affected by one's cognitive development (Cicchetti & Toth, 1998).

Diagnostic Interview Schedules

In both clinical practice and research, the clinical interview remains the main source of information about an adolescent's presenting symptomatology. Interviews can be classified as structured and unstructured. Unstructured interviews make few attempts to standardize the gathering of information across respondents and are commonly used in clinical settings. When the goal of the interview is to establish a reliable diagnosis of depressive disorders by accurately identifying key DSM-IV symptoms, structured diagnostic interviews are the method of choice (Klein, Dougherty, & Olino, 2005; March & Albano, 1998).

Efforts in the development of more structured diagnostic interviews for adolescents have been spurred by the development of structured interview schedules for adults (Robins, Helzer, Croughan, & Ratcliff, 1981). The development of more differentiated taxonomies of psychiatric disorders and more explicit diagnostic criteria has also required, and consequently led to, a more standardized approach for the assessment of psychiatric symptoms (Essau et al., 1997). Diagnostic interviews are based on strict formalizations of the diagnostic process by using specific symptoms and probe questions, detailed coding rules, and diagnostic algorithms. The questions in each diagnostic category are formulated to evaluate the symptoms of the disorder, their duration, and potential exclusion. The availability of clear diagnostic criteria has the advantage of reducing observer, information, and criterion variance.

All structured interviews contain lists of target behaviors, symptoms, and guidelines for conducting the interview and recording responses, and allow a derivation of diagnoses (Essau et al., 1997). However, the nature of the target behaviors or diagnostic coverage that are to be assessed, the time frames (i.e., lifetime, past 6 or 12 months), the answer format (i.e., yes–no responses, or graded responses as indicators of symptoms severity), and the degree of structure (highly structured versus semistructured) imposed on the interview can differ across interviews. Interviews also differ in the systems (DSM-IV versus ICD-10) they serve, and the expertise (clinician versus lay interviewer) needed to administer them (Table 2.3).

Since diagnostic interview schedules allow assessment of a broad range of psychiatric disorders in addition to depression, they tend to be time consuming to administer. As shown by Piacentini, Shaffer, & Fischer (1993), an average administration time for the Diagnostic Interview Schedule for Children (DISC) was 90 minutes. Furthermore, adolescents' ability to recall the date on which the symptom first manifests is questionable. In the study by Angold, Erkanli, and Rutter (1996), adolescents were unreliable in dating the onset of a symptom for recall period longer than 3 months. About 31% of the individuals reported depressed mood that lasted longer than 1 year during one interview, and in another interview less than 1 year. The rest (69%) reported the length of depressed mood either less than 1 year or more than 1 year at both interviews. Such low reliability could mean that the depressed mood counted towards a diagnosis of MDD in one interview, but not in the other. Many interview schedules (e.g., K-SADS-E and DICA-R) have "skipouts." Thus, if the question is answered negatively, none of the subsequent symptoms are asked and the interviewer moves on to the next diagnostic category. This may lead to some loss of information.

Structured interviews can be further divided into highly structured and semistructured. Highly structured interviews contain exact wording and sequence of questions, well-defined rules for recording, and rating of the respondents' answers. Due to their highly structured forms, little or no clinical judgment is needed, and they can be administered by lay interviewers with minimal training in using the instruments. As such, highly structured interviews are commonly used in large epidemiologic studies in which a large number of respondents are interviewed. The items of most structured interviews are often "gated," which may lead to loss of information. That is, if the essential "symptoms" are answered negatively, none of the subsequent symptoms will be asked and the interviewer will then skip to the next diagnostic category. Some examples of structured interview schedules are the Diagnostic Interview Schedule for Children version IV (DISC-IV; Shaffer, Fisher, Lucas, Dulcan, & Schwab-Stone, 2000) and the Child and Adolescent Psychiatric Assessment (CAPA; Angold & Costello, 2000).

Semistructured interviews contain flexible guidelines for conducting the interview to ensure consistent coverage of topics and recording of information. As such, they are primarily designed for use by more highly trained clinicians, usually in a clinical setting. Because the interview may be conducted in a slightly different way by each clinician, close attention needs to be paid to reliability. Some examples of semistructured interviews are the Kiddie-Schedule for Affective Disorders and Schizophrenia for School-Age Children (K-SADS; Ambrosini, 2000), and the Diagnostic Interview for Children and Adolescents (DICA; Reich, 2000). The following discussion will focus on a brief description of the DISC-IV (Shaffer et al., 2000), the CAPA (Angold & Costello, 2000), the K-SADS (Ambrosini, 2000), and the DICA (Reich, 2000) as examples of structured diagnostic interviews.

The DISC-IV (Shaffer et al., 2000) is a highly structured diagnostic interview, designed for 9- to 17-year-olds to assess the presence of affective disorder and other psychiatric disorders, including attention-deficit disorder, conduct disorder, anorexia nervosa, bulimia, functional enuresis and encopresis, alcohol abuse/dependence, cannabis abuse/dependence, tobacco dependence, schizophrenia, cyclothymic disorder, and substance abuse, and anxiety disorders. The DISC-IV questions can be grouped into two categories: (a) "stem" questions that ask about the presence of behaviors. A "no" response to the "stem question" means that the interviewer has to move forward past more specific prompts of that general question; (b) "contingent" questions are asked only if a stem question is answered positively to determine whether the elicited behavior meets a diagnostic criterion. Finally, when a certain number of symptoms have been positively answered, the adolescents are asked about the age at which the first "episode" appeared, impairment associated with the current episode, the context in which the current symptoms may have arisen or been exacerbated, and the need for or receipt of any treatment intervention for the specific conditions.

CAPA contains diagnostic algorithms that provide diagnoses according to DSM-III-R, DSM-IV, and ICD-10 systems for depressive disorders, anxiety disorders, somatization disorders, food-related disorders, sleep problems, and elimination disorders. The interview comprises three phrases: (i) the introduction, which is usually used to establish a rapport with the child; (ii) the symptom review; and (iii) the incapacity rating for measuring the effects of symptoms on various life areas. When questioning about the symptom, the context in which it has occurred and its consequences are asked. The information obtained is then matched with the operational definitions and levels of severity given in the glossary.

DICA (Reich, 2000) is a semistructured interview designed to assess depressive and other major psychiatric disorders (i.e., anxiety disorders, attention-deficit disorder, oppositional disorder, conduct disorder, alcohol use, cigarette smoking, drug use, anorexia nervosa, bulimia, somatization disorder, enuresis, encopresis, and gender identity disorder), together with onset, duration, severity, and associated impairments of the symptoms. This interview schedule is available in three versions, one for children (ages 6–12), one for adolescents (ages 13–17), and another for parents. Questions are also available for the interviewer to evaluate the adolescent's general appearance, affect, motor behavior, speech, attention, flow of thought, general responses to the interview, and subjective clinical impressions of the interview.

K-SADS (Ambrosini, 2000) is a semistructured diagnostic interview designed to measure the presence of disorders, according to DSM and research diagnostic criteria. The interview begins with an unstructured interview to establish rapport, to gain information about the child's social environment and social functioning (e.g., family relations, peer relations), and to obtain a history of the present illness, as well as to determine current symptoms, their severity, and chronicity. The structured section of the K-SADS focuses on specific symptoms. The six-point severity ratings are scaled from "no information" to "extreme." The "essential symptoms" (i.e., screening or gating question) of a disorder are first asked to evaluate the presence of an episode of illness before evaluating additional "qualifying symptoms." If the response to the screening question is negative, the clinician then skips to the next diagnostic category.

Diagnostic interview schedules designed for adults have also been used to assess the presence of depressive disorders in adolescents, including the Diagnostic Interview Schedule-IV (DIS-IV; Robins, Cottler, Bucholz, & Compton, 1996), the Composite International Diagnostic Interview (CIDI; Essau & Wittchen, 1993), and the Structured Clinical Interview for DSM-IV Axis I Disorder (SCID-IV) (First, Spitzer, Gibson, & Williams, 1997). For example, the CIDI has been used in two large studies on the epidemiology of depressive and other psychiatric disorders among adolescents (e.g., Essau, 2007; Wittchen, Nelson, & Lachner, 1998).

While the use of highly structured and semistructured interviews has increased the reliability of DSM diagnoses, the problems of clinician error and disagreement (Silverman & Serafini, 1998) and cross-informant inconsistencies (Seligman & Ollendick, 2005) remain. Interviews rely on the accurate reporting of the adolescent's presenting symptoms which may be affected by the motivation of their parents to have their child accepted into treatment ("faking bad") and by the adolescent's social desirability ("faking good") (Kendall & Flannery-Shroeder, 1998).

General Omnibus Measures

The YSR (Achenbach, 1991b) is a self-report questionnaire designed for measuring behavioral and emotional problems in the previous 6 months among 11- to 18-year olds. The YSR contains 113 items which are to be rated on a three-point score (0=not true, 1=somewhat or sometimes true, 2=very or often true). The scores are computed for both clinical scales and social and academic competence. The child also receives scores for internalizing and externalizing behavior as well as for total problem behaviors. The three scales likely to be clinically elevated in children and adolescents with depressive disorders are the scales for withdrawn, anxious/depressed, and social problems (Kronenberger & Meyer, 1996). Although the reliability and validity of the YSR (Achenbach, 1991a, 1991b, 1991c) have been reported in several studies, symptoms of anxiety and depressive disorders are not teased out in these scales, and DSM-IV criteria for diagnosing depressive disorders per se were not specifically used in developing the YSR (Kronenberger & Meyer, 1996). Furthermore, the correspondence between the YSR scale anxious/depressed and DSM-IV anxiety and depression is low (Kasius, Ferdinand, van den Berg, & Verhulst, 1997). This problem has led to the development of DSM-IV scales for YSR/CBCL problem behavior (Achenbach, Dumenci, & Rescorla, 2003). The DSM-IV scale affective problems contains 13 symptoms of DSM-IV MDD and dysthmia; 11 of these items were from the YSR subscales (anxious/depressed, withdrawn, somatic complaints, and thought problems), and two items which did not belong to any syndrome scale. Recent studies have shown moderate to good correspondence with DSM-IV affective disorder (e.g., Van Lang, Ferdinand, Oldehinkel, Ormel, & Verhulst, 2005).

Other examples of the general omnibus measures include the Symptom Checklist-90-Revised (SCL-90-R; Derogatis, 1983) and the Revised Ontario Child Health Study Scales (Boyle et al., 1993). The SCL-90-R can be used measure depressive symptoms and eight other symptom dimensions (i.e., somatization, obsessive-compulsive behavior, interpersonal sensitivity, anxiety, hostility, phobic anxiety, paranoid ideation, and psychoticism) and three global indices of distress. The depressed factor of the SCL-90 contains 13 items, with each individual items focus on mood and loss of interest, with two items related to somatic symptoms, and one each about self-blame, suicidal thoughts, hopelessness, and worthlessness.

The Revised Ontario Child Health Study Scales (Boyle et al., 1993) contain items to measure depressive symptoms and symptoms of major childhood and adolescent disorders based on DSM-III-R criteria. Some symptoms are operationalized using two or more items. For example, "depressed mood" is operationalized in two items: "unhappy, sad or depressed" and "cranky." A value of 0, 1, or 2 is assigned to this symptom, with this value corresponding to the highest value to be obtained between the two items.

MEASURES OF RELATED CONSTRUCTS

In order to have a complete understanding of the cause of adolescent depression, it is important to assess depression-related constructs in addition to the assessment of depressive symptoms and disorders. The inclusion of the depression-related constructs may give hints about the precipitating factors of depression, or to factors which contribute to the course and outcome of depression (Gotlib & Hammen, 1992). The number of related constructs is however vast, and is therefore beyond the scope of this chapter to review all of these constructs. We will focus on social-cognitive factors (e.g., cognitive dysfunction, self-schemas) and their assessments.

Based on Beck's cognitive model of depression in adults, several questionnaires have been developed to measure cognitive dysfunction. Most of these questionnaires (e.g., the Automatic Thoughts Questionnaire for Children [Stark, Best, & Adam, 1990], the Cognitive Triad Inventory for Children [Kaslow, Stark, Printz, Livingston, & Tsai, 1992]) are downward extensions of adult instruments, and have therefore been criticized in light of evidence that children' and adolescents' understanding of items may differ to that of adults (Campbell, Rapee, & Spence, 2001). Recently, the Children's Automatic Thoughts Scale (CATS; Schniering & Rapee, 2004) was developed to assess negative self-statements in children and adolescents. Both the reliability and validity of the subscales of the CATS (physical threat, social threat, personal failure, and hostility) have been established; the subscale, personal failure, significantly differentiated depressed from nonclinical groups.

Another major component of the cognitive models of depression is a negative view of the self. The Self-perception Profile for Adolescents (Harter, 1988) is the most widely used instrument to measure the adolescent's self-perception in specific domains, including scholastic competence, social acceptance, athletic competence, physical appearance, job competence, romantic appeal, behavioral conduct, close friendship, and global self-worth. In each item, adolescents were given two contrasting descriptions and asked which was more true of them. Although the Self-perception Profile for Adolescents has been shown to be related to depressive symptoms (Harter, 1988), it failed to predict the chronicity of depressive disorders in adolescents (Essau, 2007).

PSYCHOSOCIAL IMPAIRMENT

The lack of acceptable "gold standards" in validating "depressive caseness" accentuates the importance of including psychosocial impairment as an external validator. This is especially important for adolescents whose scores lie slightly above the diagnostic threshold for depressive disorders (i.e., subthreshold level), and when individuals who meet diagnostic criteria for these disorders are not seeking treatment (Bird & Gould, 1995). Studies differ in the instruments used to assess psychosocial impairment, and in the areas of functioning measured. The most common areas addressed are interpersonal relations, academic functioning, and leisure time activities. Because depressed adolescents are often impaired in various life domains, a summary of the adolescent's level of disturbance is of importance to clinicians.

Some examples of instruments to measure the severity of disturbance and adequacy of social functioning (i.e., psychosocial impairment) among adolescents with depressive and other psychiatric disorders include: the Children's Global Assessment Scale (CGAS; Shaffer et al., 1983), the Social Adjustment Inventory for Children and Adolescents (SAICA; John, Gammon, Prusoff, & Warner, 1987), and the Columbia Impairment Scale (CIS; Bird, Gould, & Staghezza, 1993). A recent scale by Essau (2007), for example, has shown adolescents with depressive disorders (chronic and new depressed cases) to be significantly more impaired in the total scores of the CIS and in CIS subscales (i.e., interpersonal relationship and general psychopathology) when compared to adolescents without any psychiatric disorders.

QUALITY OF LIFE

"Quality of life" is an under-researched area in the field of mental health. Historically, the concept evolved from the field of medicine. In the mid-1900s, advances in medical technologies and therapies resulted in increased preservation and extension of life, but oftentimes neglected patients' basic needs, autonomy, and well-being (Katschnig, 1997). As a result, "health" was viewed as "a state of complete physical, mental, and social well-being and not merely the absence of disease or infirmity" (WHO, 1948). Over time, this broader conceptualization of health was extended to the fields of clinical psychiatry and psychology as well. As such, quality of life typically is used to refer to those "aspects of life that make life particularly fulfilling and worthwhile" (Quilty, Van Ameringen, Mancini, Oakman, & Farvolden, 2003, p. 406).

In addition to psychoses and other psychiatric disorders, researchers have examined the quality of life associated with depression, particularly in adults. Initial results support pervasive and debilitating effects resulting from depression. In one of the earliest studies, Wells and colleagues (1989) reported on over 11,000 patients with depression in the Medical Outcomes Study. Their results indicated that patients with depression had worse physical functioning, social functioning, role functioning, perceived current health, and bodily pain than patients without clinical depression. In addition, they demonstrated that individuals with depression functioned worse than patients with chronic medical conditions, such as hypertension, diabetes, and arthritis. In another study, Gaynes, Burns, Tweed, and Erickson (2002) affirmed the findings of Wells et al. (1989), and further established that depression interacted with these same chronic medical conditions to amplify the effects of those illnesses. Studies examining depression, such as these, are relatively common in the quality of life literature (Mendlowicz & Stein, 2000).

Unfortunately, quality of life has not yet been examined systematically in children and adolescents with depressive disorders. To address this matter, we (Ollendick & Davis, 2002) recently designed a measure for use with children, and are presently field testing it in our clinic. Basically, children are asked to indicate the importance of 10 areas in their life, and then to indicate their happiness associated with each of those areas. Directions to the measure are as follows: the following 10 questions ask how you feel about different parts of your life such as your friends and your health. For each question you will first be asked how important that thing is in your life; then you will be asked how happy you are with that part of your life. You can say how important something is to you by circling one of three answers: "Not important," "Important," or "Very Important." You can say how happy you are by picking one of six answers ranging from "Very Unhappy" to "Very Happy." Although the scale is still in the early stages of development, we have found that our depressed children and adolescents report similar levels of importance of these events in their lives as those with other disorders (e.g., anxiety disorders, disruptive behavioral disorders), but to report lower levels of happiness. The scale appears promising, but obviously much important work remains to be accomplished.

CONCLUDING REMARKS

Our review has shown two major approaches to classifying depressive disorders, and a wide range of methods for assessing depressive symptoms and psychiatric disorders, including depression in adolescents. The most important implication of this review has made us aware of numerous problems with our current classification systems and with regards to assessment of depression in adolescents, which warrant consideration in future studies:

- Both the DSM-IV and ICD-10 systems make little attempt to adequately address developmental perspectives in the depressive disorders, which is surprising given substantial age differences in the occurrence and manifestation of depression.
- The validity of using DSM-IV and ICD-10 diagnostic criteria, which have been designed for adults, to diagnose depression in adolescents is yet to be determined.
- The lack of clear or consistent cut-off criteria in studies based on self-report questionnaires to define which adolescents experience clinical levels of depression limits our ability to describe "depressed cases," and to compare findings across studies.
- Due to differences in the clinical phenomenology of depressive symptoms across age groups, certain instruments may be appropriate for certain ages and not others.
- There is a need to integrate data from multiple informants (e.g., child, parent, and teacher) given the low level of agreement among the different informants. There are real limitations to what the different informants can know about adolescents' experiences of depression.
- Measurement of depression should include numerous methods of assessment (e.g., interview, rating scales, self reports) and psychosocial impairment, since depression involves multiple dysfunctions in various domains (e.g., cognitive, affective, behavioral). As argued by Gotlib and Hammen (1992), there is a real need to go beyond symptom measures, and to develop adequate instruments that measure what depressed adolescents do which may prolong, intensify, or maintain their depression.

REFERENCES

Achenbach, T. M. (1991a). *Manual for the youth self-report and 1991 profile.* Burlington, VT: University of Vermont Department of Psychiatry.

Achenbach, T. M. (1991b). *Manual for the child behavior checklist/4-18 and 1991 profile.* Burlington, VT: University of Vermont Department of Psychiatry.

Achenbach, T. M. (1991c). *Manual for the teacher's report form and 1991 profile.* Burlington, VT: University of Vermont Department of Psychiatry.

Achenbach, T. M. (1995). Epidemiological applications of multiaxial empirically based assessment and taxonomy. In F. C. Verhulst & H. M. Koot (Eds.), *The epidemiology of child and adolescent psychopathology* (pp. 22–41). Oxford: Oxford University Press.

Achenbach, T. M., Dumenci, L., & Rescorla, L. A. (2003). DSM-oriented and empirically based approaches to constructing scales from the same item pools. *Journal of Clinical Child and Adolescent Psychology, 32,* 328–340.

Ambrosini, P. J. (2000). Historical development and present status of the Schedule for Affective Disorders and Schizophrenia for School-Age Children (K-SADS). *Journal of the American Academy of Child & Adolescent Psychiatry, 39*, 49–58.

Angold, A., & Costello, E. J. (2000). The child and adolescent psychiatric assessment (CAPA). *Journal of the American Academy of Child & Adolescent Psychiatry, 39*, 39–48.

Angold, A., Costello, E. J., & Erkanli, A. (1999). Comorbidity. *Journal of Child Psychology and Psychiatry and Allied Disciplines, 40*, 57–87.

Angold, A., Erkanli, A., & Rutter, M. (1996). Precision, reliability and accuracy in the dating of symptom onsets in child and adolescent psychopathology. *Journal of Child Psychology and Psychiatry, 37*, 657–664.

Angold, A., Weissman, M. M., John, K., Merikangas, K. R., Prusoff, P., Wickramaratne, G., et al. (1987). Parent and child reports of depressive symptoms in children at low and high risk of depression. *Journal of Child Psychology and Psychiatry, 28*, 901–915.

Angold, A., & Worthman, C. W. (1993). Puberty onset of gender differences in rates of depression: A developmental, epidemiologic and neuroendocrine perspective. *Journal of Affective Disorders, 29*, 145–158.

American Psychiatric Association (1994). *Diagnostic and statistical manual of mental disorders* (4th ed.). Washington, DC: Author.

Beck, A. T., Steer, R. A., Ball, R., & Ranieri, W. F. (1996). Comparison of Beck Depression Inventories-IA and -II in psychiatric outpatients. *Journal of Personality Assessment, 67*, 588–597.

Bird, H. R., & Gould, M. S. (1995). The use of diagnostic instruments and global measures of functioning in child psychiatry epidemiological studies. In F. C. Verhulst & H. M. Koot (Eds.), *The epidemiology of child and adolescent psychopathology*. Oxford: Oxford University Press.

Bird, H. R., Gould, M. S., & Staghezza, B. M. (1993). Patterns of diagnostic comorbidity in a community sample of children aged 9 through 16 years. *Journal of the American Academy of Child & Adolescent Psychiatry, 32*, 361–368.

Birleson, P. (1981). The validity of depressive disorders in childhood and the development of a self-rating scale: A research report. *Journal of Child Psychology and Psychiatry, 22*, 73–88.

Boyle, M. H., Offord, D. R., Racine, Y., Fleming, J. E., Szatmari, P., & Sanford, M. (1993). Evaluation of the revised Ontario Child Health Study scales. *Journal of Child Psychology and Psychiatry, 34*, 189–213.

Cantwell, D. P., Lewinsohn, P. M., Rohde, P., & Seeley, J. R. (1997). Correspondence between adolescent report and parent report of psychiatric diagnostic data. *Journal of the American Academy of Child & Adolescent Psychiatry, 36*, 610–619.

Caron, C., & Rutter, M. (1991). Comorbidity in child psychopathology: Concepts, issues, and research strategies. *Journal of Child Psychology and Psychiatry, 32*, 1063–1080.

Cicchetti, D., & Toth, S. L. (1998). A development of depression in children and adolescents. *American Psychologist, 53*, 221–241.

Clarke, G. N., Hawkins, W., Murphy, M., Sheeber, L., Lewinsohn, P. M., & Seeley, J. R. (1995). Targeted prevention of unipolar depressive disorder in an at-risk sample of high school adolescents: A randomized trial of a group cognitive intervention. *Journal of the American Academy of Child & Adolescent Psychiatry, 34*, 312–321.

Crocker, A. D., & Hakim-Larson, J. (1997). Predictors of pre-adolescent depression and suicidal ideation. *Canadian Journal of Behavioural Science, 29,* 76–82.

Dadds, M. R., James, R. C., Barrett, P. M., & Verhulst, F. C. (2003). Diagnostic issues. In T. H. Ollendick & J. S. March (Eds.), *Phobic and anxiety disorders in children and adolescents* (pp. 3–33). New York: Oxford University Press.

Derogatis, L. R. (1983). *SCL-90-R administration, scoring, and procedures manual-II.* Towson, MD: Clinical Psychometric Research.

Essau, C. A. (2007). Course of depressive disorders in adolescents. *Journal of Affective Disorders, 99,* 191–201.

Essau, C. A., & Barrett, P. (2001). Developmental issues in the assessment of anxiety. In C. A. Essau & F. Petermann (Eds.), *Anxiety disorders in children and adolescents: Epidemiology, risk factors, and treatment* (pp. 75–110). London: Brunner-Routledge.

Essau, C. A., Feehan, M., & Üstun, B. (1997). Classification and assessment strategies. In C. A. Essau & F. Petermann (Eds.), *Developmental psychopathology: Epidemiology, diagnostics, and treatment* (pp. 19–62). London: Harwood Academic.

Essau, C. A., Hakim-Larson, J., Crocker, A., & Petermann, F. (1999). Assessment of depressive disorders in children and adolescents. In C. A. Essau & F. Petermann (Eds.), *Depressive disorders in children and adolescents: Epidemiology, risk factors, and treatment* (pp. 27–67). Northvale, NJ: Jason Aronson.

First, M. B., Spitzer, R. L., Gibson, M., & Williams, J. B. (1997). *User's guide for the structured clinical interview for DSM-IV Axis I disorders.* Washington, DC: American Psychiatric Press.

Ford, T., Goodman, R., & Meltzer, H. (2003). The British Child and Adolescent Mental Health Survey 1999: The prevalence of DSM-IV disorders. *Journal of the American Academy of Child & Adolescent Psychiatry, 42,* 1203–1211.

Frances, A., Pincus, H., Widiger, T., First, M., Davis, W., Hall, W., et al. (1994). DSM-IV and international communication in psychiatric diagnosis. In J. E. Mezzich, Y. Honda & M. C. Kastrup (Eds.), *Psychiatric diagnosis: A world perspective* (pp. 11–22). New York: Springer-Verlag.

Gaynes, B. N., Burns, B. J., Tweed, D. L., & Erickson, P. (2002). Depression and health-related quality of life. *Journal of Nervous & Mental Disease, 190,* 799–806.

Gotlib, I. H., & Hammen, C. L. (1992). *Psychological aspects of depression: Toward a cognitive-interpersonal integration.* Chichester: Wiley.

Harter, S. (1988). *Manual: Self-perception profile for adolescents.* Denver, CO: University of Denver.

John, K., Gammon, G. D., Prusoff, B. A., & Warner, V. (1987). The social adjustment inventory for children and adolescents (SAICA): Testing of a new semistructured interview. *Journal of the American Academy of Child & Adolescent Psychiatry, 26,* 898–911.

Kasius, M. C., Ferdinand, R. F., van den Berg, H., & Verhulst, F. C. (1997). Associations between different diagnostic approaches for child and adolescent psychopathology. *Journal of Child Psychology and Psychiatry, 38,* 625–632.

Katschnig, H. (1997). How useful is the concept of quality of life in psychiatry? *Current Opinion in Psychiatry, 10,* 337–345.

Kazdin, A. E. (1990). Assessment of childhood depression. In A. M. LaGreca (Ed.), *Through the eyes of the child: Obtaining self-reports from children and adolescents* (pp. 189–233). Boston, MA: Allyn & Bacon.

Kazdin, A. E. (1995). *Conduct disorders in childhood and adolescence* (2nd ed.). Thousand Oaks, CA: Sage.

Kazdin, A. E., & Kagan, J. (1994). Models of dysfunction in developmental psychopathology. *Clinical Psychological: Science and Practice, 1* (summer), 35–52.

Kendall, P. C., & Flannery-Shroeder, E. C. (1998). Methodological issues in treatment research for anxiety disorders in youth. *Journal of Abnormal Child Psychology, 26*, 27–38.

Klein, D. N., Dougherty, L. R., & Olino, T. M. (2005). Toward guidelines for evidence-based assessment of depression in children and adolescents. *Journal of Clinical Child and Adolescent Psychology, 34*, 412–432.

Kovacs, M. (1992). *Children's depression inventory.* Toronto: Multi-Health Systems.

Kronenberger, W. G., & Meyer, R. G. (1996). *The child clinician's handbook.* Boston, MA: Allyn & Bacon.

Lambert, M. C., Essau, C. A., Schmitt, N., & Samms-Vaughan, M. E. (2007). Dimensionality and psychometric invariance of the youth self-report form of the child behavior checklist in cross-national settings. *Assessment, 14*, 231–245.

Lewinsohn, P. M., Solomon, A., Seeley, J. R., & Zeiss, A. (2000). Clinical implications of "subthreshold" depressive symptoms. *Journal of Abnormal Psychology, 109*, 345–351.

Luby, J. L., Heffelfinger, A. K., Mrakotsky, C., Brown, K. M., Hessler, M. J., Wallis, J. A., et al. (2002). The clinical picture of depression in preschool children. *Journal of the American Academy of Child & Adolescent Psychiatry, 42*, 340–348.

March, J. S., & Albano, A. M. (1998). New developments in assessing pediatric anxiety disorders. *Advances in Clinical Child Psychology, 20*, 213–241.

Mendlowicz, M. V., & Stein, M. B. (2000). Quality of life in individuals with anxiety disorders. *American Journal of Psychiatry, 157*, 669–682.

Myers, K., & Winters, N. C. (2002). Ten-year review of rating scales. II: Scales for internalizing disorders. Research update review. *Journal of the American Academy of Child & Adolescent Psychiatry, 41*, 634–659.

Nezu, A. M., Nezu, C. M., McClure, K. S., & Zwick, M. L. (2002). Assessment of depression. In I. Gotlib & C. Hammen (Eds.), *Handbook of depression* (pp. 61–85). New York: Guilford Press.

Ollendick, T. H., & Hersen, M. (Eds.). (1984). *Child behavioral assessment: Principles and procedures.* New York: Pergamon Press.

Ollendick, T. H., & Hersen, M. (Eds.). (1993). *Handbook of child and adolescent assessment.* Boston, MA: Allyn & Bacon.

Ollendick, T. H., Shortt, A., & Sander, J. B. (2005). Internalizing disorders in children and adolescents. In J. E. Maddux & B. A. Winstead (Eds.), *Psychopathology: Foundations for a contemporary understanding* (pp. 353–376). Mahwah, NJ: Lawrence Erlbaum Associates.

Piacentini, J., Shaffer, D., & Fischer, P. W. (1993). The diagnostic interview schedule for children—revised version (DISC-R): II. Concurrent criterion validity. *Journal of the American Academy of Child & Adolescent Psychiatry, 32*, 658–665.

Quilty L. C., Van Ameringen, M., Mancini, C., Oakman J., & Farvolden, P. (2003). Quality of life and the anxiety disorders. *Journal of Anxiety Disorders, 17*, 405–426.

Radloff, L. S. (1991). The use of the Center for Epidemiologic Studies Depression scale in adolescents and young adults. *Journal of Youth and Adolescence, 20*, 149–166.

Rapee, R. M., Barrett, P. M., Dadds, M. R., & Evans, L. (1994). Reliability of the DSM-III-R childhood anxiety disorders using structured interview: Interrater and parent-child agreement. *Journal of the American Academy of Child & Adolescent Psychiatry, 33*, 984–992.

Reich, W. (2000). Diagnostic interview for children and adolescents (DICA). *Journal of the American Academy of Child & Adolescent Psychiatry, 39*, 59–66.

Remschmidt, H. (1995). Grundlagen psychiatrischer Klassifikation und Psychodiagnostik. In F. Petermann (Ed.), *Lehrbuch der Klinischen Kinderpsychologie* (pp. 3–52). Göttingen: Hogrefe.

Reynolds, W. M. (1987). *Assessment of depression in adolescents: Manual for the Reynolds Adolescent Depression Scale (RADS).* Odessa, FL: Psychological Assessment Resources.

Reynolds, W. M. (1994). Assessment of depression in children and adolescents by self-report questionnaires. In W. M. Reynolds & H. F. Johnston (Eds.), *Handbook of depression in children and adolescents* (pp. 209–234). New York: Plenum Press.

Robins, L. N., Cottler, L., Bucholz, K., & Compton, W. (1996). *The diagnostic interview schedule, version IV.* St. Louis, MO: Washington University.

Robins, L. N., Helzer, J. E., Croughan, J., & Ratcliff, K. F. (1981). National Institute of Mental Health diagnostic interview schedule: Its history, characteristics and validity. *Archives of General Psychiatry, 38*, 381–389.

Robinson, N. S., Garber, J., & Hilsman, R. (1995). Cognitions and stress: Direct and moderating effects on depressive versus externalizing symptoms during junior high school transition. *Journal of Abnormal Psychology, 104*, 453–463.

Sattler, J. M. (2002). *Assessment of children: Behavioral and clinical applications* (4th ed.). La Mesa, CA: Jerome M. Sattler.

Schiering, C. A., & Rapee, R. M. (2004). The structure of negative self-statements among children and adolescents: A confirmatory factor-analytic approach. *Journal of Abnormal Child Psychology, 32*, 95–109.

Seligman, L. D., & Ollendick, T. H. (1998). Comorbidity of anxiety and depression in children and adolescents: An integrative review. *Clinical Child and Family Psychology Review, 1*, 125–144.

Shaffer, D., Fisher, P., Lucas, C. P., Dulcan, M. K., & Schwab-Stone, M. E. (2000). NIMH diagnostic interview schedule for children version IV (NIMH DISC-IV): Description, differences from previous versions, and reliability of some common diagnoses. *Journal of the American Academy of Child & Adolescent Psychiatry, 39*, 28–38.

Shaffer, D., Gould, M. S., Brasic, J., Ambrosini, P., Fisher, P., Bird, H., et al. (1983). A children's global assessment scale (CGAS). *Archives of General Psychiatry, 40*, 1228–1231.

Silverman, W. K., & Ollendick, T. H. (2005). Evidence-based assessment of anxiety and its disorders in children and adolescents. *Journal of Clinical Child and Adolescent Psychology, 34*, 380–411.

Silverman, W. K., & Serafini, L. T. (1998). Assessment of child behavior problems: Internalizing disorders. In A. S. Bellack & M. Hersen (Eds.), *Behavioral assessment: A practical handbook* (4th ed., pp. 342–360). Boston, MA: Allyn & Bacon.

Tisher, M., Lang-Takac, E., & Lang, M. (1992). The children's depression scale: Review of Australian and overseas experience. *Australian Journal of Psychology, 44*, 27–35.

Van Lang, N. D. J., Ferdinand, R. F., Oldehinkel, A. J., Ormel, J., & Verhulst, F. C. (2005). Validity of the DSMIV scales affective problems and anxiety problems of the youth self-report. *Behavior Research and Therapy, 43*, 1485–1494.

Weiss, B., & Garber, J. (2003). Developmental differences in the phenomenology of depression. *Development and Psychopathology, 15*, 403–430.

Weiss, B., Weisz, J. R., Politano, M., Carey, M., Nelson, W. M., & Finch, A. J. (1991). Developmental differences in the factor structure of the children's depression inventory. *Psychological Assessment: A Journal of Consulting and Clinical Psychology, 3*, 38–45.

Wells, K. B., Stewart, A. L., Hays, R. D., Burnam, A., Rogers, W., Daniels, M., et al. (1989). The functioning and well-being of depressed patients: Results from the Medical Outcomes Study. *Journal of the American Medical Association, 262*, 914–919.

Wittchen, H.-U., Nelson, C. B., & Lachner, G. (1998). Prevalence of mental disorders and psychosocial impairments in adolescents and young adults. *Psychological Medicine, 28*, 109–126.

Wittchen, H.-U., Robins, L. N., Cottler, L., Sartorious, N., Burke, J., Regier, D., & participants of the field trials (1991). Cross-cultural feasibility, reliability, and sources of variance of the composite international diagnostic interview (CIDI) – results of the multicenter WHO/ADAMHA field trials (Wave I). British Journal of Psychiatry, 159, 645–653.

World Health Organization (1948). *Manual of the international statistical classification of diseases, injuries, and causes of death: Sixth revision of the International lists of diseases and causes of death.* Geneva: World Health Organization.

World Health Organization (1993). *The ICD-10 classification of mental and behavioural disorders.* Geneva: World Health Organization.

Chapter Three

The Epidemiology of Depression in Adolescents

KATHLEEN RIES MERIKANGAS AND ERIN KNIGHT

CONTENTS

INTRODUCTION

There has been a substantial increase in public awareness of the high prevalence and serious consequences of depression in youth, particularly suicide. Black box warnings, direct consumer marketing of antidepressant medications, reports that depression in youth has reached epidemic proportion, and a fortyfold increase in the diagnosis of bipolar disorder in children have led to widespread debate about appropriate definitions and treatments of depression in children and adolescents. These controversies have highlighted the lack of information from population-based samples of youth that could address some of these issues. This chapter provides (1) background on the definition, methods, and goals of epidemiology; (2) a comprehensive review of population-based studies of the prevalence of depression in adolescents; (3) the population impact of depression in youth; and (4) a summary of service patterns for adolescent depression in the community.

OVERVIEW OF THE DISCIPLINE OF EPIDEMIOLOGY

Definition and Goals

The field of epidemiology is defined as the study of the distribution and determinants of diseases in human populations. Epidemiologic studies are concerned with the extent and types of illnesses in groups of people, and with the factors that influence their distribution (Gordis, 2000). Epidemiologists investigate the interactions that may occur among the host, agent, and environment (the classic epidemiologic triangle) to produce a disease state. The important goal of epidemiologic studies is to identify the *etiology* of a disease in order to prevent or intervene in the progression of the disorder. To achieve this goal, epidemiologic studies generally proceed from studies that specify the prevalence and distribution of a disease within a population by person, place, and time (that is, *descriptive* epidemiology), to more focused studies of the determinants of disease in specific groups (that is, *analytic* epidemiology) (Gordis, 2000).

Descriptive epidemiologic studies are important in specifying the rates and distribution of disorders in the general population. These data can be applied to identify biases that may exist in treated populations, and to construct case registries from which persons may serve as probands for analytic epidemiologic studies. Such attention to sampling issues is a major contribution of the epidemiologic approach, as individuals identified in clinical settings often constitute the biased tip of the iceberg of the disease and may not be representative of the general population of similarly affected individuals with respect to demographic, social, or clinical characteristics. Associations, which are identified at the descriptive level, may then be tested systematically with case-control designs that compare the relationship between a particular risk factor or disease correlate and the presence or absence of a given disease, after controlling for relevant confounding variables. Case-control studies involve a retrospective design to investigate these particular associations. Researchers then proceed to prospective cohort studies, which can formally test the temporal direction of such associations.

The identification of risk factors for a disease is an intermediate step in the process of identifying a discrete and valid disorder in the general population, which then culminates in analytic studies that attempt to identify etiologic factors. There are several criteria for assessing the extent to which a risk factor is causally involved in a trait or disease. These include the strength of the association, a dose-response effect, and a lack of temporal ambiguity. Broader criteria that can be applied to a set of studies on a putative etiologic risk factor include: consistency of the findings, biologic plausibility of the hypothesis, and a specificity of association (Hill, 1953; Kleinbaum & Shamoon, 1982). Each of these analytic approaches is germane to epidemiologic research and can be applied to the field of psychiatry to identify risk factors for mental disorders and potential mechanisms of etiology.

Whether descriptive or analytic, the ultimate goal of epidemiologic investigations is prevention. The traditional epidemiologic concept of prevention is comprised of three levels: (1) primary prevention to reduce the incidence of a disease, (2) secondary prevention to reduce the risk of disease among susceptible individuals, and (3) tertiary prevention to reduce the impact or consequences of a disease.

Application of Epidemiology to Psychiatry

The traditional contributions of the application of the tools of epidemiology to psychiatry were comprised of methodological developments including the introduction of structured and semistructured diagnostic interviews, statistical methods for estimating prevalence and correlates of mental disorders, and the focus on population-based samples to obtain estimates of the magnitude and correlates of mental disorders unbiased by treatment seeking. The results of recent epidemiological studies have illustrated the need for further development of the psychiatric diagnostic system (First et al., 2004; Kessler et al., 2006; Kessler et al., 2003; Kessler et al., 1994; Merikangas et al., 2007; Regier, 1990). As demonstrated by growing research on the dimensional classification of disorders, inclusion of subthreshold diagnostic categories and diagnostic spectra, and pervasive comorbidity between purportedly distinct diagnostic entities, there is widespread agreement that the categorical classification system in psychiatry lacks validity (Angst, 2007; Lenox, Gould, & Manji, 2002; Tsuang, 2001).

Recent studies have begun to expand the diagnostic criteria for mental disorders to collect information on the spectra of expression of particular conditions. Several studies have begun to deconstruct psychiatric phenotypes by their component features or subtypes including bipolar disorder (Angst, 2007), general anxiety disorder (Angst et al., 2006), obsessive compulsive disorder (Eapen, Pauls, & Robertson, 2006), schizophrenia (Braff & Light, 2005), and panic disorder (Smoller & Tsuang, 1998). For example, recent findings from the National Comorbidity Survey-Replication (NCS-R) demonstrated the validity of the spectrum concept of bipolar disorder (Merikangas et al., 2007) that had been proposed by clinicians for more than a decade (Akiskal & Benazzi, 2006; Angst, 2007).

EPIDEMIOLOGY OF MOOD DISORDERS IN ADULTS

During the last two decades, the results of several surveys of mental disorders of adults in the US population using contemporary diagnostic criteria have become available. The Epidemiologic Catchment Area (ECA) program sampled community and institutionalized residents from numerous sites across the United States (Freedman, 1984). This was followed by the National Comorbidity Survey (NCS) in 1990, and the NCS-R conducted a decade later. The NCS studies have provided the first estimates of mental disorders in a probability sample of the general population of the United States. More recently, another large study of a probability sample of the United States that focused on the epidemiology of alcoholism has also provided information on base rates of mental disorders and their association with substance use disorders (Hasin, Goodwin, Stinson, & Grant, 2005). Perhaps the most important finding from these diverse investigations is the high prevalence of mood disorders in community residents, with as many as one-quarter of all adults having experienced a major depressive episode during their lifetime. Despite the high magnitude of these conditions, few people receive adequate services, particularly in the mental health sector.

MAGNITUDE OF DEPRESSION IN ADOLESCENTS

Several years ago, the landmark US Surgeon General's report on Mental Health (Substance Abuse and Mental Health Services Administration, 1999) cited the urgent need for information tracking knowledge on the prevalence and distribution of mental disorders and patterns of service utilization in the United States. Although there has been substantial research on the epidemiology of mental disorders in children and adolescents in specific regions of the United States, there is still a striking lack of information on the national estimates of the prevalence and distribution of mental disorders in children in the US population. Aggregation of the findings of several of these local community surveys of children and adolescents in Connecticut (Schwab-Stone et al., 1995), Illinois (Buka et al., 2001), Massachusetts (Reinherz, Giaconia, Lefkowitz, Pakiz, & Frost, 1993a), Missouri (Kashani et al., 1987), New York State (Cohen et al., 1993; Shaffer et al., 1996), North Carolina (Costello et al., 1996b), and Oregon (Lewinsohn, Rohde, Seeley, & Hops, 1991) have provided a range of estimates of the magnitude and socioeconomic correlates of mental disorders in youth. A recent summary by Costello, Egger, and Angold (2005) yielded the following estimates of the median and range of the prevalence of disorders in youth: any disorder—26% (8–42%); any anxiety—8% (2–24%); attention deficit disorder—3% (0.3–11%); disruptive behavior disorders—6% (5–14%); alcohol or drug abuse/dependence—5% (1–24%); and mood disorders—4% (0.2–17%). The most important finding was that in any given year approximately 12% of children in the United States suffers from a serious emotional disturbance that leads to functional impairment. This implies that one out of every eight children in the United States is in need of mental health treatment.

Unfortunately, the results of these epidemiologic surveys also reveal that the vast majority of children with serious emotional disturbances do not receive treatment for their condition. Of particular concern is the finding that service use is particularly low among ethnic minority youth (Costello et al., 2005).

Prevalence Estimates of Depressive Disorders

An updated summary of the prevalence rates of depressive disorders is presented in Table 3.1. There is remarkable variability in the prevalence estimates of major depression, dysthymia, and other depressive disorders across national and international population-based studies. This can be attributed to both methodological and true differences across samples in different geographic regions.

As demonstrated in Table 3.1, point prevalence estimates for major depression among adolescents range from about 0.7% (Fergusson, Horwood, & Lynskey, 1993) to 3.4% (Feehan, McGee, Raja, & Williams, 1994). As expected, 6- and 12-month prevalence estimates for major depression in adolescents were somewhat higher, with ranges from 2.5% (Velez, Johnson, & Cohen, 1989) to 13.3% (Feehan et al., 1994). In the two studies that assessed young adults, 12-month prevalence estimates were 8.2% (Pine, Cohen, Gurley, Brook, & Ma, 1998) and 16.8% (Newman et al., 1996).

Several studies reported lifetime prevalence in adolescents, with estimates ranging from 9.3% (Wittchen, Nelson, & Lachner, 1998) to 24.0% (Lewinsohn, Hops, Roberts, Seeley, & Andrews, 1993). Estimates for young adults were at the upper end of the adolescent range, 23.2% according to Reinherz, Paradis, Giaconia, Stashwick, and Fitzmaurice (2003). The only study based on a national probability sample of adolescents and young adults reported a 15% lifetime prevalence of major depression (Kessler & Walters, 1998).

Table 3.1 Prevalence estimates of depressive disorders in community samples of children and adolescents using DSM-IIIR and DSM-IV criteria

Author/Date	Location	Wave	n	Age	DX Criteria	DX Intvw[a,b]	Period[c]	MDE/D[d,e]	Other Depression[f]
United States									
Angold et al. (2002)	North Carolina		920	9–17	DSM-IV	CAPA	3M	1.0%	0.3% (DY) 1.7% (mDep)
Canino et al. (2004)	Puerto Rico		1,886	4–17	DSM-IV	Spanish DISC	12M	3.6%, 3.0 (I)	0.6% (DY) 0.5% (DY; I)
Gonzalez-Tejera et al. (2005)			891	11–17				4.4%	5.3% (mDep)
Costello et al. (1996a)	North Carolina	1	1,015	9, 11, 13	DSM-III-R	CAPA	3M	0.03%	0.1% (DY), 1.5% (NOS)
Costello et al. (2003)		FU to 16		9–16	DSM-IV			0.4%	0.3% (DY), 1.5% (NOS) 2.2% (Any)
Kessler and Walters (1998)	United States		1,769	15–24	DSM-III-R	CIDI	30D, 12M, LT	5.8% (30D) 12.4% (12M) 15.3% (LT)	2.1% (mDep, 30D) 7.1% (mDep, 12M) 9.9% (mDep, LT)
Kilpatrick et al. (2003)	U.S. probability		4,023	12–17	DSM-IV	NWS	6M	M: 7.4%, F:13.9%	
Lewinsohn et al. (1991), Lewinsohn et al. (2004)	Oregon	1	1,709	14–18	DSM-III-R	K-SADS-E	PT, LT	2.9% (PT) 20.4% (LT)	3.2% (DY, LT) 25.9% (sMDD, LT)
Lewinsohn et al. (1993)		2	1,507	15–19		LIFE	PT, LT	3.1% (PT) 24.0% (LT)	0.1% (DY, PT) 3.0% (DY, LT)
Lewinsohn et al. (2006)		3	941	24	DSM-IV		PT	2.4%	0.5% (DY)
		4	816				PT	4.1%	0.8% (DY)
Giaconia et al. (1994), Reinherz et al. (1993)	Northeastern, USA	1	386	18	DSM-III-R	DIS	1M, 6M, LT	2.9% (1M) 6.0% (6M) 9.4% (LT)	
Reinherz et al. (1999)		2	375	21			LT	10%	

(Continued)

Table 3.1 (Continued)

Author/Date	Location	Wave	*n*	Age	DX Criteria	DX Intvw[a,b]	Period[c]	MDE/D[d,e]	Other Depression[f]
Reinherz et al. (2003)		3	354	18–26	DSM-IV		LT	23.2%	
Shaffer et al. (1996)	Atlanta, New Haven, New York, Puerto Rico		1,285	9–17	DSM-III-R	DISC	6M	5.6% (I) 7.1% (noI)	7.2% (Any, I), 8.8% (Any, noI)
Simonoff et al. (1997)	Virginia		2,762 twins	8–16	DSM-III-R	CAPA	3M	1.2% (I) 1.3% (noI)	
Velez et al. (1989)	New York State	1	776	1–10		No assessment			
		2 3	760 716	9–12 13–18 11–14 15–20	DSM-III-R	DISC	12M	2.5% 3.7% 2.5% 3.1%	
Pine et al. (1998)		4	716	17–26				M: 5.0%, F: 11.5%	
International									
Feehan et al. (1994)		4	930	18	DSM-III-R	DIS	PT, 12M	3.4% (PT) 13.3% (12M)	3.2% (DY, 12M)
Newman et al. (1996)		5	961	21			12M	16.8%	3.0% (DY)
Kim-Cohen et al. (2003)		6	976	26	DSM-IV		12M	16.5%	0.8% (DY)
Canals et al. (1995)	Spain	1	500	10–11	DSM-III-R	No assessment			
Canals et al. (1997)		2	290	18 (FU)	DSM-III-R	SCAN	PT	2.4%	5.8% (DY) 0.7% (mDep)
Fergusson et al. (1993)	Christchurch, New Zealand	1	1,265	15	DSM-III-R	DISC	PT, 12M	0.7% (PT) 4.2% (12M)	0.4% (DY, PT)
Fergusson and Woodward (2002)		2–4	1,006	16–21	DSM-IV	CIDI	Interval	33.5% (cumulative)	

Gau et al. (2005)	Taiwan	3 year	1,070	7th	DSM-IV	Chinese	Unk	0.5%	0.2% (DY)
		Panel		8th		KSADS-E		2.5%	0.2% (DY)
				9th				4.4%	0.6% (DY)
Goodyer and Cooper (1993)	Cambridgeshire, England		1,068 girls	11–16	DSM-III-R	DISC	PT, 12M	3.6% (PT) 6.0% (12M)	
Rutter et al. (1970)	Isle of Wight		2,303	14–15	–	Clinical intvw	PT	1.5%	
Verhulst et al. (1997)	Netherlands		780	13–18	DSM-III-R	DISC	6M	3.6%	2.3% (DY)
Wittchen et al. (1998)	Munich, Germany		3,021	14–24	DSM-IV	CIDI	12M LT	3.6% (12M) 9.3% (LT)	2.9% (DY, 12M) 3.0% (DY, LT)
Pezawas et al. (2003)			2,548	14–22			LT		2.6% (RBD/sRBD)
Yang et al. (2004)	Taipei		178	12–16	DSM-IV	K-SADS	PT	3.7 (no I) 2.4 (I)	2.7 (DY, no I) 0.3 (DY, I)

[a] Diagnostic interview.

[b] Abbreviations of diagnostic interviews: CAS = Child Assessment Schedule; CAPA = Child and Adolescent Psychiatric Assessment; CIDI = Composite International Diagnostic Interview; DICA = Diagnostic Interview for Children and Adolescents; DIS = Diagnostic Interview Schedule; DISC = Diagnostic Interview Schedule for Children; K-SADS = Schedule for Affective Disorders and Schizophrenia for School-Aged Children; NWS = National Women's Study, major depression module; SCAN = Schedules for Clinical Assessment in Neuropsychiatry; SDI = Survey Diagnostic Instrument (Boyle, Offord, & Hoffman, 1987).

[c] Time period abbreviations: PT = point, 30D = 30 days, 1M = 1 month, 6M = 6 months, 12M = 12 months, LT = lifetime.

[d] Major depressive episode or disorder.

[e] Abbreviations: I = with impairment, noI = without impairment, M = males, F = females.

[f] Other depressive disorders abbreviations: Any = any depressive disorder, DY = dysthymia, mDep = minor depression, NOS = not otherwise specified, RBD = recurrent brief depression, sMDD = subthreshold major depression, sRBD = subthreshold recurrent brief depression.

Note: Unk = unknown.

Estimates of prevalence for dysthymic disorder follow the same general pattern as for major depression, with prevalence estimates higher in adolescents than in children.

Prevalence estimates of dysthymia among adolescents and young adults are typically lower than those of major depression (Feehan et al., 1994; Kim-Cohen et al., 2003; Lewinsohn et al., 1993; Newman et al., 1996; Verhulst, van der Ende, Ferdinand, & Kasius, 1997; Wittchen et al., 1998). In contrast, prevalence estimates of subthreshold depressive disorders and syndromes, including minor depression and depression not otherwise specified, are generally higher than those of major depression across all age groups (Angold et al., 2002; Costello, Mustillo, Erkanli, Keeler, & Angold, 2003; Gonzalez-Tejera et al., 2005; Lewinsohn, Shankman, Gau, & Klein, 2004). Although some studies have shown increased rates of depression in children and adolescents, a recent meta-analysis by Costello, Erkanli, and Angold (2006) found no increase in child or adolescent depression over the past 30 years.

Age and Sex Patterns of Prevalence

Retrospective studies of adults with depression suggest that first onset is most likely to occur between mid-adolescence and young adulthood (Burke, Burke, Regier, & Rae, 1990; Kessler, McGonagle, Swartz, Blazer, & Nelson, 1993; Lewinsohn, Duncan, Stanton, & Hautzinger, 1986). In the only nationally representative general population sample to examine age of onset, approximately 25% of adults with major depression or dysthymia reported onset prior to young adulthood, and almost 50% reported onset by age 30 (see Table 3.1). Longitudinal studies of treatment and community samples of children and adolescents suggest an earlier average age of onset: between 11 and 14 years for major depression and dysthymia (Kovacs, Feinberg, Crouse-Novak, Paulauskas, & Finkelstein, 1984; Lewinsohn et al., 1993). Additionally, prospective studies that follow the same children over time reveal a dramatic increase in the prevalence of major depressive episodes after age 11 and again after age 15, with a flattening of rates in young adulthood (ages 21–26) (Kim-Cohen et al., 2003; McGee, Feehan, Williams, & Anderson, 1992; Newman et al., 1996).

National epidemiological studies have clearly documented that the prevalence of depression is nearly twice as high among adult females as adult males in developing countries (Kessler et al., 1993). Among preadolescents, community studies report either no sex differences in depression (Fleming, Offord, & Boyle, 1989; Kashani et al., 1987; Velez et al., 1989), or somewhat higher prevalence among preadolescent boys than girls (Anderson, Williams, McGee, & Silva, 1987; Angold, Costello, & Worthman, 1998; Costello et al., 1988). During adolescence and young adulthood, however, depression becomes more common among females than males (Cohen et al., 1993; Costello et al., 2003; Kessler & Walters, 1998; Reinherz et al., 1993a; Whitaker et al., 1990; Wittchen et al., 1998). While sex differences in depression are evident for both major depression and dysthymia, findings on sex differences in minor depression (Gonzalez-Tejera et al., 2005; Kessler & Walters, 1998), recurrent brief depression (Pezawas et al., 2003), and depressive symptoms (Petersen, 1991) are mixed across studies.

The female preponderance of depression begins to emerge around the age of 13 (McGee et al., 1992; Nolen-Hoeksema & Girgus, 1994). In a longitudinal follow-up of a large birth cohort, the change in the sex ratio was attributable to an increase in the incidence of depression among females after age 11 and again between ages 15 and 18 (Hankin et al., 1998). Although depression increases among both males and females during the middle adolescent years, incidence among females is far greater than among males (Hankin et al., 1998; Lewinsohn et al., 1993).

Social Class, Race, Ethnicity, Culture

Although studies of adults suggest that depression is associated with lower social class (Kessler et al., 2003), studies of children and adolescents are less consistent. Whereas some studies report a lack of association between depressive disorders and social class (Costello et al., 1988; Costello et al., 2003; Whitaker et al., 1990), others report a significant association, at least for the most impoverished groups (Bird et al., 1988; Costello et al., 1996b; Gilman, Kawachi, Fitzmaurice, & Buka, 2003; Reinherz et al., 1993b). A large meta-analysis of 310 samples of children who completed the Children's Depression Inventory (CDI) found no association between depressive symptoms and social class (Twenge & Nolen-Hoeksema, 2002).

Because of differing measures, samples, and reporting techniques, difficulties arise in attempting to compare depressive symptoms across studies of racial and ethnic groups (see Table 3.2). The small sample size of ethnic minority youth in most community studies of children and adolescents diminishes the statistical power to test differences in prevalence of disorders between specific ethnic subgroups. The few studies that have compared racial or ethnic groups yielded no differences in prevalence of depressive disorders between Caucasian and African American (Angold et al., 2002; Costello et al., 1988) or American Indian youth (Costello, Farmer, Angold, Burns, & Erkanli, 1997). There is some evidence for differences in depressive symptoms among racial and ethnic groups, however this evidence is inconclusive. Studies show some support for increased depressive symptoms among Hispanic youth compared to their white and African American counterparts (Guiao & Thompson, 2004; Twenge & Nolen-Hoeksema, 2002). Two studies showed increased depressive symptoms in African American as opposed to white males (Kistner, David, & White, 2003; Schoenbach, Kaplan, Grimson, & Wagner, 1982).

IMPACT OF MENTAL DISORDERS

One of the major advances in epidemiology during the past decade has been the increasing focus on the impact and burden of mental disorders. The importance of role disability has become increasingly recognized as a major source of indirect costs of illness because of its high economic impact on ill workers, their employers, and society (Angst, Merikangas, & Preisig, 1997; First et al., 2004; Judd et al., 1998).

The introduction of the concept of Disability Adjusted Life Years, which estimates the disease-specific reduction in life expectancy attributable to disability and increased mortality, has highlighted the dramatic public health impact of mental disorders (Murray & Lopez, 1996). By the year 2020, it is estimated that psychiatric and neurologic disorders will account for 15% of the total burden of all diseases. Major depression is the leading cause of disability among those age five and over, and the second leading source of disease burden surpassing cardiovascular diseases, dementia, lung cancer, and diabetes.

Table 3.2 Racial/ethnic differences in depressive symptoms in adolescents

Author/Date	Age	*n*	Race	Sex	Depressive Symptoms	Diagnostic Instrument
Schoenbach et al. (1982)	Junior High School	384			RDC-like depressive syndrome	RDC-like classification algorithm from The Center for Epidemiologic Studies Depression Scale (CES-D) scale symptom responses
		253	White	Males	0.90%	
				Females	2.90%	
		131	Black	Males	8.5%[a]	
				Females	1.40%	
Garrison et al. (1989)	11–17	677			Mean CES-D scores	The Center for Epidemiologic Studies Depression Scale (CES-D)
		253	White	Boys	15.21	
		292		Girls	16.54	
		60	Black	Boys	15.73	
		72		Girls	20.02	
Angold et al. (2002)	9–17	920			Three-month prevalence—any depressive disorder	Child and Adolescent Psychiatric Assessment (DSM-IV)
		379	White		4.6%[b]	
		541	Black		1.40%	
Twenge and Nolen-Hoeksema (2002)	8–16	61,424			CDI score	Children's Depression Inventory (CDI)
			Hispanic		10.34[c]	
			White		8.84	
			Black		8.67	

Kistner et al. (2003)	8–14	272	African American		CDI score	Children's Depression Inventory (CDI)
				Boys	12.62[d]	
				Girls	10.1	
		630	Euro-American			
				Boys	8.82	
				Girls	10.1[e]	
Kubik et al. (2003)	12–13	3,621			Percentage with elevated depressive symptoms	The Center for Epidemiologic Studies Depression Scale (CES-D)
		64	Native American		52%	
		248	Asian		47%	
		155	Other		45%	
		350	African American		44%	
		219	Multiethnic		42%	
		97	Hispanic		40%	
		2458	White		30%	
Guiao and Thompson (2004)	12–19	3,310			CES-D scores	The Center for Epidemiologic Studies Depression Scale (CES-D)
		385	Latinas		14.19[f]	
		1,911	Euro-American	Girls	10.97	

(Continued)

Table 3.2 (Continued)

Author/Date	Age	*n*	Race	Sex	Depressive Symptoms	Diagnostic Instrument
Saluja et al. (2004)	11–15	9,863			Percent with elevated depressive symptoms	U.S. Health Behavior in School Children Study School-Based Survey
		4,434	Non-Hispanic White			
				Boys	10.3%	
				Girls	25.7%	
		1,252	Non-Hispanic African American			
				Boys	8.7%	
				Girls	19.5%	
		803	Non-Hispanic Asian American			
				Boys	11.5%	
				Girls	20.0%	
		2,603	Hispanic			
				Boys	11.5%	
				Girls	32.2%	
		141	Non-Hispanic American Indian/Alaskan Native			
				Boys	16.1%	
				Girls	42.8%	

Wight et al. (2005)	Grades 7–12	18,473		CES-D scores	The Center for Epidemiologic Studies Depression Scale (CES-D)
		3,927	African American	10.51[g]	
		1,305	Asian or Pacific Islander	10.44	
		3,151	Hispanic	10.85	
		9,741	White—not Hispanic	8.94	
		349	Other	9.85	

[a] Black males had a statistically significant higher prevalence of symptoms than white males.
[b] African American children had statistically significant lower rates of any depressive disorder than white children.
[c] Hispanic children had statistically significant higher rates of symptoms than black or white children.
[d] African American boys had statistically significant higher rates of symptoms than Euro-American boys.
[e] Euro-American girls had statistically significant higher rates of symptoms than Euro-American boys.
[f] Latinas had statistically significant higher rates of symptoms than Euro-American girls.
[g] Non-Hispanic White children had statistically significant lower CES-D scores than African American and Hispanic children.

The dramatic impact of mood disorders on lifetime disability highlights the importance of epidemiology in surveillance, understanding, and control of the major mental disorders.

Comparative studies of role disability reveal that the effects of mental conditions are as large as those of most chronic physical conditions (Buka et al., 2001; Costello et al., 1996a; Freedman, 1984; Kendell, 1989). The global burden of mental disorders in children and adolescents up to 24 years of age has also been examined. Similar to studies within the United States, there is a broad range of estimates of the rates of mental disorders. A recent review reported estimates that ranged from 8% (in the Netherlands) to 57% (for young people receiving services in five sectors of care in San Diego, CA, USA) (Patel, Flisher, Hetrick, & McGorry, 2007). Results from The Australian National Survey of Mental Health and Well Being showed that at least 14% of adolescents younger than 18 years had a diagnosable mental or substance use disorder within the previous 12 months, and this figure rose to 27% in the 18–24 year age-group (Sawyer et al., 2000). Meta-analysis of the childhood and adolescent data by Patel and colleagues (Patel et al., 2007) showed that at least one out of every four to five young people in the general population will suffer from at least one mental disorder in any given year. However, there is much less information on the burden of mental disorders in developing countries and substantial cross-cultural variations are likely.

HELP SEEKING AND TREATMENT

Despite the magnitude and serious consequences of depression in youth, only about one-quarter to less than half of those with mental disorders receive mental health services (Angold et al., 2002; Canino et al., 2004; Costello et al., 1988; Kessler & Walters, 1998; Wu et al., 1999). Factors associated with service utilization include ethnicity, high global impairment, comorbidity, prior history of depression, suicide attempt, and impact of the child's problem on the family (Angold et al., 2002; Canino et al., 2004; Fergusson & Horwood, 2001; Lewinsohn, Rohde, & Seeley, 1998; Wittchen et al., 1998). School services are the most common point of entry for children seeking services, although those who enter through the education sector are least likely to transition to specialty mental health services (Farmer, Burns, Phillips, Angold, & Costello, 2003). The actual diagnostic process and services provided differ dramatically according to the context of entry to service (Hoagwood, Burns, Kiser, Ringeisen, & Schoenwald, 2001).

There has been accumulating controlled research on the effects of antidepressants in youth (Hetrick, Merry, McKenzie, Sindahl, & Proctor, 2007), but few studies of either the comparative efficacy of various agents that are commonly used in clinical practice or of individual and family therapies either in conjunction with or independent from drug treatments. One study that demonstrated the efficacy of combined pharmacologic and psychotherapeutic treatment has provided a model for future studies that can guide policy in health services for adolescents (March et al., 2004; Pathak et al., 2005). Recent controversy about the potential dangers versus the benefits of the serotonin-reuptake inhibitors in adolescents (Gibbons et al., 2007; Hetrick et al., 2007) highlights the urgent need for population-based studies of services in youth in the United States.

SUMMARY AND FUTURE RESEARCH

Although there has been substantial research on the epidemiology of mental disorders in children and adolescents in specific regions of the United States (Buka et al., 2001; Cohen et al., 1993; Costello et al., 1996b; Kashani et al., 1987; Lewinsohn et al., 1991; Shaffer et al., 1996; Whitaker et al., 1990), there is a striking lack of information on the prevalence and distribution of mental disorders in children in the US population. The information that does exist for prevalence (see Table 3.1), racial differences (see Table 3.2), and socioeconomic status (Bird et al., 1988; Costello et al., 1996b; Costello et al., 1988; Costello et al., 2003; Gilman et al., 2003; Reinherz et al., 1993a; Twenge & Nolen-Hoeksema, 2002; Whitaker et al., 1990) is inconsistent and varies greatly across studies. There is more agreement in the literature for sex differences (Burke et al., 1990; Kessler et al., 1993; Lewinsohn et al., 1986) and age of onset of major depression (Cohen et al., 1993; Costello et al., 2003; Kessler & Walters, 1998; Lewinsohn et al., 1993; McGee et al., 1990; Reinherz et al., 1993a; Whitaker et al., 1990; Wittchen et al., 1998), but not for minor depression (Gonzalez-Tejera et al., 2005; Kessler & Walters, 1998), recurrent brief depression (Pezawas et al., 2003), and depressive symptoms (Petersen, 1991). The landmark U.S. Surgeon General's report on Mental Health (Substance Abuse and Mental Health Services Administration, 1999) and a National Institute of Mental Health National Advisory Mental Health Council Workgroup on Child and Adolescent Mental Health Intervention Development and Deployment (National Institute of Mental Health, 2001) cited the urgent need for information tracking knowledge on the prevalence and distribution of mental disorders and patterns of service utilization in the United States. Two forthcoming results of national surveys of adolescent mental health in the United States, the NCS-Adolescent Extension (http://www.hcp.med.harvard.edu/ncs/) and the National Health and Nutrition Examination Survey (NHANES) (http://www.cdc.gov/nchs/nhanes.htm) should begin to address the gap in knowledge regarding the epidemiology of adolescent mood disorders in the United States.

REFERENCES

Akiskal, H. S., & Benazzi, F. (2006). The DSM-IV and ICD-10 categories of recurrent [major] depressive and bipolar II disorders: Evidence that they lie on a dimensional spectrum. *Journal of Affective Disorders, 92*(1), 45–54.

Anderson, J. C., Williams, S., McGee, R., & Silva, P. A. (1987). DSM-III disorders in preadolescent children. Prevalence in a large sample from the general population. *Archives of General Psychiatry, 44*(1), 69–76.

Angold, A., Costello, E. J., & Worthman, C. M. (1998). Puberty and depression: The roles of age, pubertal status and pubertal timing. *Psychological Medicine, 28*(1), 51–61.

Angold, A., Erkanli, A., Farmer, E. M., Fairbank, J. A., Burns, B. J., Keeler, G., et al. (2002). Psychiatric disorder, impairment, and service use in rural African American and white youth. *Archives of General Psychiatry, 59*(10), 893–901.

Angst, J. (2007). The bipolar spectrum. *British Journal of Psychiatry, 190*, 189–191.

Angst, J., Gamma, A., Joseph Bienvenu, O., Eaton, W. W., Ajdacic, V., Eich, D., et al. (2006). Varying temporal criteria for generalized anxiety disorder: Prevalence and clinical characteristics in a young age cohort. *Psychological Medicine, 36*(9), 1283–1292.

Angst, J., Merikangas, K. R., & Preisig, M. (1997). Subthreshold syndromes of depression and anxiety in the community. *The Journal of Clinical Psychiatry, 58*(Suppl 8), 6–10.

Bird, H. R., Canino, G., Rubio-Stipec, M., Gould, M. S., Ribera, J., Sesman, M., et al. (1988). Estimates of the prevalence of childhood maladjustment in a community survey in Puerto Rico. The use of combined measures. *Archives of General Psychiatry, 45*(12), 1120–1126.

Braff, D. L., & Light, G. A. (2005). The use of neurophysiological endophenotypes to understand the genetic basis of schizophrenia. *Dialogues in Clinical Neuroscience, 7*(2), 125–135.

Buka, S. L., Tsuang, M. T., Torrey, E. F., Klebanoff, M. A., Bernstein, D., & Yolken, R. H. (2001). Maternal infections and subsequent psychosis among offspring. *Archives of General Psychiatry, 58*(11), 1032–1037.

Burke, K. C., Burke, J. D., Jr., Regier, D. A., & Rae, D. S. (1990). Age at onset of selected mental disorders in five community populations. *Archives of General Psychiatry, 47*(6), 511–518.

Canals, J., Domenech, E., Carbajo, G., & Blade, J. (1997). Prevalence of DSM-III-R and ICD-10 psychiatric disorders in a Spanish population of 18-year-olds. *Acta Psychiatrica Scandinavica, 96*(4), 287–294.

Canals, J., Marti-Henneberg, C., Fernandez-Ballart, J., & Domenech, E. (1995). A longitudinal study of depression in an urban Spanish pubertal population. *European Child and Adolescent Psychiatry, 4*(2), 102–111.

Canino, G., Shrout, P. E., Rubio-Stipec, M., Bird, H. R., Bravo, M., Ramirez, R., et al. (2004). The DSM-IV rates of child and adolescent disorders in Puerto Rico: Prevalence, correlates, service use, and the effects of impairment. *Archives of General Psychiatry, 61*(1), 85–93.

Cohen, P., Cohen, J., Kasen, S., Velez, C. N., Hartmark, C., Johnson, J., et al. (1993). An epidemiological study of disorders in late childhood and adolescence—I. Age- and gender-specific prevalence. *Journal of Child Psychology and Psychiatry, 34*(6), 851–867.

Costello, E. J., Erkanli, A., & Angold, A. (2006). Is there an epidemic of child or adolescent depression? *Journal of Child Psychology and Psychiatry, 47*(12), 1263–1271.

Costello, E. J., Angold, A., Burns, B. J., Erkanli, A., Stangl, D. K., & Tweed, D. L. (1996a). The Great Smoky Mountains Study of Youth. Functional impairment and serious emotional disturbance. *Archives of General Psychiatry, 53*(12), 1137–1143.

Costello, E. J., Angold, A., Burns, B. J., Stangl, D. K., Tweed, D. L., Erkanli, A., et al. (1996b). The Great Smoky Mountains Study of Youth. Goals, design, methods, and the prevalence of DSM-III-R disorders. *Archives of General Psychiatry, 53*(12), 1129–1136.

Costello, E. J., Costello, A. J., Edelbrock, C., Burns, B. J., Dulcan, M. K., Brent, D., et al. (1988). Psychiatric disorders in pediatric primary care. Prevalence and risk factors. *Archives of General Psychiatry, 45*(12), 1107–1116.

Costello, E. J., Egger, H., & Angold, A. (2005). 10-year research update review: The epidemiology of child and adolescent psychiatric disorders: I. Methods and public health burden. *Journal of the American Academy of Child & Adolescent Psychiatry, 44*(10), 972–986.

Costello, E. J., Farmer, E. M., Angold, A., Burns, B. J., & Erkanli, A. (1997). Psychiatric disorders among American Indian and white youth in Appalachia: The Great Smoky Mountains Study. *American Journal of Public Health, 87*(5), 827–832.

Costello, E. J., Mustillo, S., Erkanli, A., Keeler, G., & Angold, A. (2003). Prevalence and development of psychiatric disorders in childhood and adolescence. *Archives of General Psychiatry, 60*(8), 837–844.

Eapen, V., Pauls, D. L., & Robertson, M. M. (2006). The role of clinical phenotypes in understanding the genetics of obsessive-compulsive disorder. *Journal of Psychosomatic Research, 61*(3), 359–364.

Farmer, E. M., Burns, B. J., Phillips, S. D., Angold, A., & Costello, E. J. (2003). Pathways into and through mental health services for children and adolescents. *Psychiatric Services, 54*(1), 60–66.

Feehan, M., McGee, R., Raja, S. N., & Williams, S. M. (1994). DSM-III-R disorders in New Zealand 18-year-olds. *Australian and New Zealand Journal of Psychiatry, 28*(1), 87–99.

Fergusson, D. M., & Horwood, L. J. (2001). The Christchurch Health and Development Study: Review of findings on child and adolescent mental health. *Australian and New Zealand Journal of Psychiatry, 35*(3), 287–296.

Fergusson, D. M., Horwood, L. J., & Lynskey, M. T. (1993). Prevalence and comorbidity of DSM-III-R diagnoses in a birth cohort of 15 year olds. *Journal of the American Academy of Child & Adolescent Psychiatry, 32*(6), 1127–1134.

First, M. B., Pincus, H. A., Levine, J. B., Williams, J. B., Ustun, B., & Peele, R. (2004). Clinical utility as a criterion for revising psychiatric diagnoses. *American Journal of Psychiatry, 161*(6), 946–954.

Fleming, J. E., Offord, D. R., & Boyle, M. H. (1989). Prevalence of childhood and adolescent depression in the community. Ontario Child Health Study. *British Journal of Psychiatry, 155*, 647–654.

Freedman, D. X. (1984). Psychiatric epidemiology counts. *Archives of General Psychiatry, 41*(10), 931–933.

Gibbons, R. D., Brown, C. H., Hur, K., Marcus, S. M., Bhaumik, D. K., Erkens, J. A., et al. (2007). Early evidence on the effects of regulators' suicidality warnings on SSRI prescriptions and suicide in children and adolescents. *American Journal of Psychiatry, 164*(9), 1356–1363.

Gilman, S. E., Kawachi, I., Fitzmaurice, G. M., & Buka, L. (2003). Socio-economic status, family disruption and residential stability in childhood: Relation to onset, recurrence and remission of major depression. *Psychological Medicine, 33*(8), 1341–1355.

Gonzalez-Tejera, G., Canino, G., Ramirez, R., Chavez, L., Shrout, P., Bird, H., et al. (2005). Examining minor and major depression in adolescents. *Journal of Child Psychology and Psychiatry, 46*(8), 888–899.

Gordis, E. (2000). Contributions of behavioral science to alcohol research: Understanding who is at risk and why. *Experimental and Clinical Psychopharmacology, 8*(3), 264–270.

Guiao, I. Z., & Thompson, E. A. (2004). Ethnicity and problem behaviors among adolescent females in the United States. *Health Care for Women International, 25*(4), 296–310.

Hankin, B. L., Abramson, L. Y., Moffitt, T. E., Silva, P. A., McGee, R., & Angell, K. E. (1998). Development of depression from preadolescence to young adulthood: Emerging gender differences in a 10-year longitudinal study. *Journal of Abnormal Psychology, 107*(1), 128–140.

Hasin, D. S., Goodwin, R. D., Stinson, F. S., & Grant, B. F. (2005). Epidemiology of major depressive disorder: results from the National Epidemiologic Survey on Alcoholism and Related Conditions. *Archives of General Psychiatry, 62*, 1097–1106.

Hetrick, S., Merry, S., McKenzie, J., Sindahl, P., & Proctor, M. (2007). Selective serotonin reuptake inhibitors (SSRIs) for depressive disorders in children and adolescents. *Cochrane Database of Systematic Reviews* (3), CD004851.

Hill, A. (1953). Observation and experiment. *New England Journal of Medicine, 248*, 995–1001.

Hoagwood, K., Burns, B. J., Kiser, L., Ringeisen, H., & Schoenwald, S. K. (2001). Evidence-based practice in child and adolescent mental health services. *Psychiatric Services, 52*(9), 1179–1189.

Judd, L. L., Akiskal, H. S., Maser, J. D., Zeller, P. J., Endicott, J., Coryell, W., et al. (1998). A prospective 12-year study of subsyndromal and syndromal depressive symptoms in unipolar major depressive disorders. *Archives of General Psychiatry, 55*(8), 694–700.

Kashani, J. H., Beck, N. C., Hoeper, E. W., Fallahi, C., Corcoran, C. M., McAllister, J. A., et al. (1987). Psychiatric disorders in a community sample of adolescents. *American Journal of Psychiatry, 144*(5), 584–589.

Kendell, R. E. (1989). Clinical validity. *Psychological Medicine, 19*(1), 45–55.

Kessler, R. C., Akiskal, H. S., Angst, J., Guyer, M., Hirschfeld, R. M., Merikangas, K. R., et al. (2006). Validity of the assessment of bipolar spectrum disorders in the WHO CIDI 3.0. *Journal of Affective Disorders, 96*(3), 259–269.

Kessler, R. C., Berglund, P., Demler, O., Jin, R., Koretz, D., Merikangas, K. R., et al. (2003). The epidemiology of major depressive disorder: Results from the National Comorbidity Survey Replication (NCS-R). *Journal of the American Medical Association, 289*(23), 3095–3105.

Kessler, R. C., McGonagle, K. A., Swartz, M., Blazer, D. G., & Nelson, C. B. (1993). Sex and depression in the National Comorbidity Survey. I: Lifetime prevalence, chronicity and recurrence. *Journal of Affective Disorders, 29*(2–3), 85–96.

Kessler, R. C., McGonagle, K. A., Zhao, S., Nelson, C. B., Hughes, M., Eshleman, S., et al. (1994). Lifetime and 12-month prevalence of DSM-III-R psychiatric disorders in the United States. Results from the National Comorbidity Survey. *Archives of General Psychiatry, 51*(1), 8–19.

Kessler, R. C., & Walters, E. E. (1998). Epidemiology of DSM-III-R major depression and minor depression among adolescents and young adults in the National Comorbidity Survey. *Depression and Anxiety, 7*(1), 3–14.

Kim-Cohen, J., Caspi, A., Moffitt, T. E., Harrington, H., Milne, B. J., & Poulton, R. (2003). Prior juvenile diagnoses in adults with mental disorder: Developmental follow-back of a prospective-longitudinal cohort. *Archives of General Psychiatry, 60*(7), 709–717.

Kistner, J. A., David, C. F., & White, B. A. (2003). Ethnic and sex differences in children's depressive symptoms: Mediating effects of perceived and actual competence. *Journal of Clinical Child and Adolescent Psychology, 32*(3), 341–350.

Kleinbaum, J., & Shamoon, H. (1982). Selective counterregulatory hormone responses after oral glucose in man. *Journal of Clinical Endocrinology Metabolism, 55*(4), 787–790.

Kovacs, M., Feinberg, T. L., Crouse-Novak, M. A., Paulauskas, S. L., & Finkelstein, R. (1984). Depressive disorders in childhood. I. A longitudinal prospective study of characteristics and recovery. *Archives of General Psychiatry, 41*(3), 229–237.

Lenox, R. H., Gould, T. D., & Manji, H. K. (2002). Endophenotypes in bipolar disorder. *American Journal of Medical Genetics, 114*(4), 391–406.

Lewinsohn, P. M., Duncan, E. M., Stanton, A. K., & Hautzinger, M. (1986). Age at first onset for nonbipolar depression. *Journal of Abnormal Psychology, 95*(4), 378–383.

Lewinsohn, P. M., Hops, H., Roberts, R. E., Seeley, J. R., & Andrews, J. A. (1993). Adolescent psychopathology: I. Prevalence and incidence of depression and other DSM-III-R disorders in high school students. *Journal of Abnormal Psychology, 102*(1), 133–144.

Lewinsohn, P. M., Rohde, P., & Seeley, J. R. (1998). Major depressive disorder in older adolescents: Prevalence, risk factors, and clinical implications. *Clinical Psychology Review, 18*(7), 765–794.

Lewinsohn, P. M., Rohde, P., Seeley, J. R., & Hops, H. (1991). Comorbidity of unipolar depression: I. Major depression with dysthymia. *Journal of Abnormal Psychology, 100*(2), 205–213.

Lewinsohn, P. M., Shankman, S. A., Gau, J. M., & Klein, D. N. (2004). The prevalence and co-morbidity of subthreshold psychiatric conditions. *Psychological Medicine, 34*(4), 613–622.

March, J., Silva, S., Petrycki, S., Curry, J., Wells, K., Fairbank, J., et al. (2004). Fluoxetine, cognitive-behavioral therapy, and their combination for adolescents with depression: Treatment for Adolescents with Depression Study (TADS) randomized controlled trial. *Journal of the American Medical Association, 292*(7), 807–820.

McGee, R., Feehan, M., Williams, S., & Anderson, J. (1992). DSM-III disorders from age 11 to age 15 years. *Journal of the American Academy of Child & Adolescent Psychiatry, 31*(1), 50–59.

McGee, R., Feehan, M., Williams, S., Partridge, F., Silva, P. A., & Kelly, J. (1990). DSM-III disorders in a large sample of adolescents. *Journal of the American Academy of Child & Adolescent Psychiatry, 29*(4), 611–619.

Merikangas, K. R., Akiskal, H. S., Angst, J., Greenberg, P. E., Hirschfeld, R. M., Petukhova, M., et al. (2007). Lifetime and 12-month prevalence of bipolar spectrum disorder in the National Comorbidity Survey Replication. *Archives of General Psychiatry, 64*(5), 543–552.

Murray, C. J., & Lopez, A. D. (1996). The incremental effect of age-weighting on YLLs, YLDs, and DALYs: A response. *Bulletin of the World Health Organization, 74*(4), 445–446.

National Institute of Mental Health. (2001). Report of the National Advisory Mental Health Council's workgroup on child and adolescent mental health intervention development and deployment. Paper presented at the Blueprint for Change: Research on Child and Adolescent Mental Health.

Newman, D. L., Moffitt, T. E., Caspi, A., Magdol, L., Silva, P. A., & Stanton, W. R. (1996). Psychiatric disorder in a birth cohort of young adults: Prevalence, comorbidity, clinical significance, and new case incidence from ages 11 to 21. *Journal of Consulting and Clinical Psychology, 64*(3), 552–562.

Nolen-Hoeksema, S., & Girgus, J. S. (1994). The emergence of gender differences in depression during adolescence. *Psychological Bulletin, 115*(3), 424–443.

Patel, V., Flisher, A. J., Hetrick, S., & McGorry, P. (2007). Mental health of young people: A global public-health challenge. *Lancet, 369*(9569), 1302–1313.

Pathak, S., Kratochvil, C. J., Rogers, G. M., Silva, S., Vitiello, B., Weller, E. B., et al. (2005). Comparative efficacy of cognitive behavioral therapy, fluoxetine, and their combination in depressed adolescents: Initial lessons from the treatment for adolescents with depression study. *Current Psychiatry Reports, 7*(6), 429–434.

Petersen, A. C., Sarigiani, P. A., & Kennedy, R. E. (1991). Adolescent depression: Why more girls? *Journal of Youth and Adolescence, 20*, 247–271.

Pezawas, L., Wittchen, H. U., Pfister, H., Angst, J., Lieb, R., & Kasper, S. (2003). Recurrent brief depressive disorder reinvestigated: A community sample of adolescents and young adults. *Psychological Medicine, 33*(3), 407–418.

Pine, D. S., Cohen, P., Gurley, D., Brook, J., & Ma, Y. (1998). The risk for early-adulthood anxiety and depressive disorders in adolescents with anxiety and depressive disorders. *Archives of General Psychiatry, 55*(1), 56–64.

Regier, D., Burke, J. D., and Bruke, K. C. (1990). *Comorbidity of affective and anxiety disorders in the NIMH epidemiologic catchment area (ECA) program*. Washington, DC: American Psychiatric Press.

Reinherz, H. Z., Giaconia, R. M., Lefkowitz, E. S., Pakiz, B., & Frost, A. K. (1993). Prevalence of psychiatric disorders in a community population of older adolescents. *Journal of the American Academy of Child & Adolescent Psychiatry, 32*(2), 369–377.

Reinherz, H. Z., Giaconia, R. M., Pakiz, B., Silverman, A. B., Frost, A. K., & Lefkowitz, E. S. (1993). Psychosocial risks for major depression in late adolescence: A longitudinal community study. *Journal of the American Academy of Child & Adolescent Psychiatry, 32*(6), 1155–1163.

Reinherz, H. Z., Paradis, A. D., Giaconia, R. M., Stashwick, C. K., & Fitzmaurice, G. (2003). Childhood and adolescent predictors of major depression in the transition to adulthood. *American Journal of Psychiatry, 160*(12), 2141–2147.

Sawyer, M. G., Arney, F. M., Baghurst, P. A., Clark, J. J., Graetz, B. W., Kosky, R. J., et al. (2000). *The Mental Health of Young People in Australia*. Canberra Mental Health and Special Programs Branch, Commonwealth Department of Health and Aged Care.

Schoenbach, V. J., Kaplan, B. H., Grimson, R. C., & Wagner, E. H. (1982). Use of a symptom scale to study the prevalence of a depressive syndrome in young adolescents. *American Journal of Epidemiology, 116*(5), 791–800.

Schwab-Stone, M. E., Ayers, T. S., Kasprow, W., Voyce, C., Barone, C., Shriver, T., et al. (1995). No safe haven: A study of violence exposure in an urban community. *Journal of the American Academy of Child & Adolescent Psychiatry, 34*(10), 1343–1352.

Substance Abuse and Mental Health Services Administration (1999). Mental Health: A Report of the Surgeon General—Executive Summary. Rockville, MD: National Institute of Health.

Shaffer, D., Fisher, P., Dulcan, M. K., Davies, M., Piacentini, J., Schwab-Stone, M. E., et al. (1996). The NIMH Diagnostic Interview Schedule for Children Version 2.3 (DISC-2.3): Description, acceptability, prevalence rates, and performance in the MECA study. Methods for the Epidemiology of Child and Adolescent Mental Disorders Study. *Journal of the American Academy of Child & Adolescent Psychiatry, 35*(7), 865–877.

Smoller, J. W., & Tsuang, M. T. (1998). Panic and phobic anxiety: Defining phenotypes for genetic studies. *American Journal of Psychiatry, 155*(9), 1152–1162.

Tsuang, M. T. (2001). Defining alternative phenotypes for genetic studies: What can we learn from studies of schizophrenia? *American Journal of Medical Genetics, 105*(1), 8–10.

Twenge, J. M., & Nolen-Hoeksema, S. (2002). Age, gender, race, socioeconomic status, and birth cohort differences on the Children's Depression Inventory: A meta-analysis. *Journal of Abnormal Psychology, 111*(4), 578–588.

Velez, C. N., Johnson, J., & Cohen, P. (1989). A longitudinal analysis of selected risk factors for childhood psychopathology. *Journal of the American Academy of Child & Adolescent Psychiatry, 28*(6), 861–864.

Verhulst, F. C., van der Ende, J., Ferdinand, R. F., & Kasius, M. C. (1997). The prevalence of DSM-III-R diagnoses in a national sample of Dutch adolescents. *Archives of General Psychiatry, 54*(4), 329–336.

Whitaker, A., Johnson, J., Shaffer, D., Rapoport, J. L., Kalikow, K., Walsh, B. T., et al. (1990). Uncommon troubles in young people: Prevalence estimates of selected psychiatric disorders in a nonreferred adolescent population. *Archives of General Psychiatry, 47*(5), 487–496.

Wittchen, H. U., Nelson, C. B., & Lachner, G. (1998). Prevalence of mental disorders and psychosocial impairments in adolescents and young adults. *Psychological Medicine, 28*(1), 109–126.

Wu, P., Hoven, C. W., Bird, H. R., Moore, R. E., Cohen, P., Alegria, M., et al. (1999). Depressive and disruptive disorders and mental health service utilization in children and adolescents. *Journal of the American Academy of Child & Adolescent Psychiatry, 38*(9), 1081–1090.

Chapter Four

Depression Among Racially, Ethnically, and Culturally Diverse Adolescents

LARUE ALLEN AND JENNIFER ASTUTO

CONTENTS

CULTURE, RACE/ETHNICITY AND SOCIOECONOMIC STATUS

Symptoms of depression represent a significant health problem for adolescents (Peterson et al., 1993). Increasingly, evidence points to greater risk for depression among adolescents from racial and ethnic minority groups (Angold & Costello, 2001). Given that this evidence comes from studies that focus on different populations, of different ages, and use different measures, it is a major challenge to draw any firm conclusions about how great this differential risk actually is, or how this risk might vary for different sociodemographic groups (Roberts, Roberts, & Chen, 1997). The need to meet this challenge is urgent, given that high rates of depressive symptoms in adolescence create a considerable risk for depression in later life (Reinherz et al., 2006). The population of minority youth, currently at 46% of the young people (U.S. Census Bureau, 2000), is expected to increase even further over the next several years. Current immigration trends will further contribute to their number, and their racial, ethnic and cultural diversity (Holmes, 2001). Their increasing numbers, combined with the debilitating impact of depressive symptoms, and the wide disparities in access to competent diagnosis and treatment (U.S. Department of Health and Human Services [HHS], 2001) all suggest that it is indeed time for a review of the current state of knowledge.

We begin with a brief overview of data on prevalence of depressive symptoms, and then review empirical studies that attend to racial/ethnic group differences in the United States, some of which consider the role of socioeconomic status (SES) as well. In our focus on cultural explanations for differences found, we also incorporate information from the international empirical literature that touches on the question of minority/majority differences in prevalence and expression of disorders. Next, we examine how risk and protective factors influence depression trajectories, focusing on personal group identity, social support, stress and negative life events, and biological and body image problems. Finally, we address problems in measurement that compromise our ability to generate clear and consistent information on depression in youth.

The answers to our questions about racial/ethnic, cultural and SES influences on the prevalence and expression of depression can only come from nonclinical studies, given the disparities in access to clinical care across sociodemographic groups. From diagnosis, to access to treatment, to type and quality of treatment offered, racial/ethnic and social class differences are evident (HHS, 2001). Given this, the chances of drawing representative samples of minority groups from clinic populations are quite low. Additionally, given the racial/ethnic differences in the tendency to seek help (e.g., Sen, 2004), we expect that including clinical samples would compound the existing problems of getting representative samples of racial and ethnic minority group members into research studies (Cauce, Ryan, & Grove, 1998). Thus, our focus is on depressive symptoms measured using scales and checklists rather than on the truly rare study that looks at clinically diagnosed major depressive disorders in non-White youth. Finally, we offer our conclusions and our recommendations for further research aimed at increasing the chances that theories and interventions will address the needs of sociodemographically diverse youth in culturally sensitive ways.

RACIAL AND ETHNIC VARIATIONS IN ADOLESCENT DEPRESSION

Though many think of race as a biological category, there is, in fact, more genetic variation within race groups than between them (Lewontin, 1972). Race has powerful meaning as a social category given its frequent association with discrimination, which ranges from blatant to subtle, and is a source of stress for its victims (Clark, Anderson, Clark, & Williams, 1999; HHS, 2001). Ethnicity, an even more complex concept (Rutter & Tienda, 2005), implies a set of characteristics—which could include cultural values, language, race, traditions, and behaviors—shared by a geographically contiguous group of people. These characteristics are transmitted through socialization as well as heredity (Ocampo, Bernal, & Knight, 1993). The term ethnicity has come to be used in research involving a variety of groups, including Latinos, Blacks, Asian-Americans, and non-Latino Whites (NLW) (Aboud, 1987; Rice, Ruiz, & Padilla, 1974, Smith & Brookins, 1997; Waters, 1990).

Both constructs are measured through self-identification, though respondents are usually limited to a fixed set of options that may or may not allow them to name the groups that they identify with most closely. We know, though, that people respond inconsistently over time (Peterson, 1987), an issue that is particularly relevant for adolescents, whose social identities are emerging and fluid (Allen, Bat-Chava, Aber, & Seidman, 2005). For researchers looking to open the "black box" that connects race and ethnicity to various developmental outcomes such as depression, clearly a dimensional approach to these identities is preferred over categorical assessment. The preference for parsimony over dimensionality conflicts with the goal, supported by individuals of multidimensional racial/ethnic background themselves, that data collection efforts as large as the US Census allow individuals to choose as many self-descriptors as they care to (Howell, 2001).

Being a member of a low-status racial group (e.g., a group frequently subjected to racial discrimination) is thought to be a risk factor for compromised development with risk increasing as skin color deepens (Russell, Wilson, & Hall, 1992). Given the differences in experience that groups encounter, race does not have the same meaning for US NLW and African-Americans that it does for Asian-Americans, Latinos and even immigrant Blacks. For example, Caribbean Blacks move from nations in which race is not a salient dimension of their social identity (Akbar, Chambers, & Thompson, 2001) to the United States where skin color is a prominent factor in how people perceive one another. This mixture of peoples of African descent creates ethnic differences within the Black race (e.g., African-American versus Jamaican-American) that we find within all racial groups (e.g., Italian-American versus Greek-American). In this chapter, we use the hybrid term race/ethnicity to describe the overarching category that contains the Asian-American, American Indian, Black, Latino and NLW youth who are the focus of this chapter. While we recognize that this is a complex term, we advocate its use when neither term alone adequately describes the groups being compared.

Estimates of Prevalence of Symptoms of Depression

Large sample research on racial/ethnic minority youth and depression has increased since Fleming and Offord's review (1990) found only five studies, and those compared small numbers of Black and White children. A decade later, Angold and Costello (2001) concluded that there was some evidence that ethnic differences in rates of depression may exist, and that these rates may be higher for Latinos. Still today, given the variation in measures used, in the ages sampled, uncertainty about reliability and validity of our constructs over the adolescent age range, and variation, in which relevant control variables are considered (e.g., SES), research on depression among racial and ethnic minority adolescents continues to reflect confusion and underdevelopment.

In this section, we summarize the point prevalence of depression using studies that provided specific information on rates from racial and ethnic samples in the United States. We use only large (at least 500 participants), community- and school-based samples from epidemiological studies that provide prevalence estimates for each group studied and included at least two groups. The two exceptions (see Table 4.1) are Manson, Ackerson, Dick, Baron, and Fleming (1990), the only recent major study of American Indians. The second exception is Rushton, Forcier, and Schectman's research (2002), included because they analyze data from the large, diverse National Longitudinal Study of Adolescent Health (Add Health), though prevalence estimates are provided only for White and "Other."

In Table 4.1, we see that rates for depressive symptoms among NLW range from 18 to 36%, for African-Americans from 15 to 44%, for Latinos from 13 to 48%, for Asian-Americans from 17 to 47%, and American Indians a stunning 58%. Prevalence estimates for moderate depression for NLW range from 9 to 20%, African-Americans, 9 to 17%, and Latinos, 8 to 29%. Estimates for major depression range from 6 to 12% for NLW, 9 to 13% for African-Americans, and 3 to 18% for Latinos. Based on these data, and remembering that there are measurement and methodological issues that may well influence the "consistency" of these figures across studies and across groups, which we will discuss later in this chapter, prevalence trends suggest that American Indians and Latinos may have the highest rates of prevalence as well as the greatest range in estimates of all five groups. Overall, these studies find that African-Americans prevalence rates are higher than NLW, although NLW estimates are slightly higher than African-Americans in the moderate and major depression categories.

Comparing Rates of Depression

Research evidence on rates of depression across racial and ethnic groups is scarce but growing in the last decade, helped considerably by large projects such as the National Longitudinal Study on Adolescent Health (Add Health), "a nationally representative study that explores the causes of health-related behaviors of adolescents in grades 7 through 12 and their outcomes in young adulthood" (http://www.cpc.unc.edu/addhealth). This recent research, based on both large school-based samples and an increasing number of nationally representative samples (such as Add Health), points toward Blacks, and even more so Latinos, as the most frequent targets of discrimination, and at greatest risk for high scores on depression symptom checklists. The little information that we have on American Indians strongly suggests that they, victims of discrimination since before the United States became a country, are also at the high-risk end of the continuum. We provide details on these findings, as well as some exceptions, in the following sections.

Table 4.1 Prevalence rates of depression across different groups

Study	Sample Characteristics	Group Size	Depression Measure	Point Prevalence		
Roberts et al. (1997)	School-based; grades 6–8	n=5,423 NLW –17% AfAm – 26% L – 16%	DSM Scale for Depression (DSD) (major depression)	Full sample – 8.4% NLW – 6.3% AfAm – 9.0% L – 12.0%		
Doi et al. (2001)	School-based; ages 12–15	n=2,046 NLW – 26% AfAm – 31% L – 20% As – 23%	DSD (major depression)	NLW – 9.6% AfAm – 13.4% L – 16.9% As/PI – 5.6%		
Franko et al. (2005)	Community-based; girls ages 16–22	n=2,221 NLW – 48% AfAm – 52%	Center for Epidemiological Studies of Depression Scale (CES-D)	Age	NLW >24	AfAm >24
				16	20.8%	13.7%
				17	20.3%	13.2%
				18	10.8%	9.2%
				19	13.1%	12.9%
				20	12.3%	13.0%
				21	14.5%	16.6%
				22	13.7%	14.9%
Mason et al. (1990)	School-based; grades 9–12	n=188 AI – 100%	CES-D ($\geq$16)	AI – 58.1%		
Rushton et al. (2002)	Community-based; ages 12–17 (Add Health)	n=13,568 NLW – 68% AfAm – 15% L – 12.3% As – 3.4%	CES-D	NLW – 8.5% Other – 10.2%		

(Continued)

Table 4.1 (Continued)

Study	Sample Characteristics	Group Size	Depression Measure	Point Prevalence				
Roberts and Sobhan (1992)	Community-based; ages 12–17	n=2,250 NLW – 41.5% AfAm – 26% L – 5% Mexican – 9%	Twelve-item version of the CES-D (for prevalence, scores x 1.667 to reflect CES-D20)			Mild (≥16)	Mod (>20)	MDD (>30)
					Female			
					NLW	20.5%	9.0%	.8%
					AfAm	19.9%	8.9%	1.1%
					L	17.1%	7.7%	N/A
					Mexican	26.9%	15.8%	3.1%
					Males			
					NLW	26.6%	14.0%	2.6%
					AfAm	32.3%	17.2%	2.5%
					L	24.8%	12.8%	1.8%
					Mexican	37.1%	19.8%	3.6%
Roberts and Chen (1995)	School-based; grades 6–8	n=2,614 NLW – 35.3% L – 51.7%	CES-D (20)			Mild (>16)	Mod (>24)	MDD(>30)
					NLW	35.7%	19.9%	12.3%
					L	47.5%	29.8%	18.0%
Saluja et al. (2004)	School-based; grades 6, 8, 10	n=9,863 NLW – 48% AfAm – 13.6% L – 28.2% As – 8.6%	Twelve items selected from the DSM-IV interview	NLW – 18.4% AfAm – 14.6% L – 21.7% As – 16.6%				
Kubik et al. (2003)	School-based; grade 7	n=3,621 NLW – 68% AfAm – 10% L – 3% As – 7% AI – 2%	CES-D	Elevated symptoms (16+) NLW – 30% AfAm – 44% L – 40% As – 47% AI – 52%				

Note: NLW = Non-Latino White; AfAm = African-American; L = Latino; As = Asian; AI = American Indian; CES-D = Center for Epidemiological Studies of Depression Scale; DSD = DSM Scale for Depression

Early-to-Middle Adolescence

Three papers comparing a minority group to White youth find either no group differences, or that racial/ethnic minority youth are disadvantaged. First, in a convenience sample of junior high school students ($n = 735$), Blacks had higher scores than NLW, even after introducing parent's education as a control for SES (Garrison, Schluchter, Schoenbach, & Kaplan, 1989). In both racial groups, females scored higher than males, a common gender finding in research on depression beyond the childhood years.

Comparing young Mexican-Americans and Whites, Roberts and Chen (1995) found that youth of Mexican origin reported about 50% more depression than NLW in their school-based survey of 2,614 middle school students. Youth who spoke English more had lower rates of depression, suggesting that perhaps acculturation (for which English use is a proxy) in some cases protects from depression.

In the third study, Chinese-Americans, one of the first Asian groups to arrive in the United States, were compared to White middle school students in the Teen Life Changes study (Chen, Roberts, & Aday, 1998). Responses from 952 students revealed that total scores did not differ significantly for the two groups.

Two studies that compare more than two groups also find that minority status is a risk factor for adolescent depression. Data from the Teen Life Changes Survey (Doi, Roberts, Takeuchi, & Suzuki, 2001) provides comparative information on more serious depression for three major groups. The researchers analyzed data from 5,496 children in grades 6 to 8 in Texas and found that of the "cases" identified with the DSM Scale for Depression (DSD) (Roberts et al., 1997), Whites had the lowest rates, Mexican-Americans had the highest rates, and African-Americans were in between. However, there were no racial/ethnic differences once fathers' education and the family financial status were controlled.

In one of the first studies to focus on younger adolescents from all five of the major racial/ethnic categories commonly used in the United States, Kubik, Lytle, Birnbaum, Murray, and Perry (2003) studied a large ($n = 3{,}621$) school-based sample of seventh graders in the Minneapolis/St. Paul metropolitan area. The researchers emphasized that even for 12- and 13-year-olds, depression was a significant problem, with American-Indians scoring highest, and NLW the lowest, and Asian/Pacific Islanders, African-Americans, and Latinos in between. In addition to race/ethnicity as a predictor, substance use and low SES were also significantly related to depression's prevalence. Both of these studies anticipate our later discussion of the role of SES in research on adolescent depression.

Thus, studies with samples of youth during early and mid-adolescence suggest that minority group adolescents are at greater risk than NLW, and that even for 12-year-olds, depressive symptoms may be a real problem. Next, we will review a set of studies that focus on later adolescence, then we will turn to a group of studies that cover the full adolescent range.

Late Adolescence

Two high school studies found greater risk for Whites. The Massachusetts Adolescent Health Survey (Brooks, Harris, Thrall, & Woods, 2002) is a study of 2,224 Black, White, and Latino students from all four high school grades in a convenience sample of 32 schools. The investigators found no mean differences across groups on their dichotomized variable created from responses to the question "In the last 30 days, how many days did you feel depressed/stressed? However, when demographics and statistically relevant risk factors were controlled, they found that both Blacks and Latinos had *reduced* odds of feeling depressed/stressed. Similarly, Dornbusch, Mont-Reynaud, Ritter, Chen, and Steinberg (1991) reported, using data from 10,041 high schools students from the San Francisco Bay Area and Wisconsin, that Asian-Americans, Blacks and Latinos all reported fewer depressive symptoms than did Whites.

In contrast, Emslie, Weinberg, Rush, Adams, and Rintelmann (1990), focusing on 3,294 tenth grade students from largely low SES schools, found just the reverse—that both more Blacks and Latinos fell into the moderate to severe range of symptoms than Whites. Further analyses found group similarities in endorsement of items related to, for example, school difficulties, sadness, and feelings of failure. But there were also significant differences in patterns of endorsement that were summarized as follows: Whites internalized, endorsing self-punitive items (e.g., I cause trouble for everybody); Blacks externalized with a negative view of their immediate contexts (e.g., School makes me nervous); and Latinos showed a mixture of negative views about themselves and their contexts, but leaning toward internalizing.

Across the Full Adolescent Range

Studies of the full adolescent range often point to the increased vulnerability of racial/ethnic minority youth. Maag and Irvin (2005), with their sample of 524 seventh through twelfth grade adolescents from the Midwest, found that, though there were no mean differences on depression scores between their Black and White groups, Whites had a significantly *higher* probability of being in the severe depressive symptoms group. However, there were no mean differences in depression scores. In contrast, Sen (2004), using a representative sample of 9,000 youth from grades 6 to 10, found that Whites were significantly *less* at risk of reporting depressed mood compared to all other groups (i.e., Black, Latinos, and Asians).

The Commonwealth Fund's 1997 Adolescent Health Survey is a large, nationally representative sample of 6,943 students from grade 5 through 12 from private and parochial schools in addition to the usual public school sampling (Schraedley, Gotlib, & Hayward, 1999). Whites were among the lowest risk, as might be expected, but the surprise here is that African-Americans joined them as the students with lowest scores. Asian-Americans joined Latinos among those at greatest risk. The authors note the inconsistency with other research. One avenue of clarification is to address the possible confound between racial/ethnic group membership and SES. The use of private and parochial schools, along with public schools, is a welcome addition to research on understanding depression across all racial and ethnic groups, but may have introduced unobserved sources of variation that warrant further investigation.

Twenge and Nolen-Hoeksema (2002), in their meta-analysis of 134 samples of youth ages 8 to 16, concurred that Latinos (from diverse national backgrounds) were at greatest risk, with significantly higher scores than both Blacks and Whites in the largest effect size of all of the individual differences they analyzed.

Siegel, Aneshensel, Taub, Cantwell, and Driscoll (1998), with their area probability sample of 877 African-Americans, Euro-Americans, Asian-Americans, and Latinos from Los Angeles County, aged 12 to 17 years, came to the same conclusion that Latinos are at greatest risk. Notable here is the over sampling of African- and Asian-Americans to assure adequate power to test for group differences. Latinos had the highest scores with no differences across the other three groups (White, Asian-, African-American), even when SES (parent report of income and education) was controlled. Focusing on Latinos, this team found, as did Roberts and Chen (1995) with their middle school sample, that acculturation tended to serve a protective role. Here, lower scores occurred among those who chose to be interviewed in English. But the relations across groups held even when Spanish-preference Latinos were removed from the analyses.

Greater Latino risk was again confirmed in Guiao and Thompson's (2004) look at depression and suicidal behaviors across the five major racial/ethnic groups. Their Add Health sample of 23,310 females ranged from 12- to 19-years-old. Though there were no significant differences in suicidal behavior, once again, NLW reported significantly less depression than Latinas who had the highest scores.

Giving nuance to the increasingly clear view that Latinos are at greatest risk is Roberts and Sobhan's (1992) study, using data from a national in-home survey of 2,250 adolescents aged 12 to 17. They analyzed depression scores across NLW, Blacks, Mexican-Americans, and other Latinos and found that youth of Mexican origin had the highest scores, and that Blacks scored higher than Whites. A mixed group of "other Hispanics" had the lowest scores, underlining the pressing need to attend to differences within racial and ethnic groups and not just focus on between-group studies.

In one of the rare opportunities to gain insight into depressive symptoms among American Indian youth, Saluja et al. (2004) examined a large nationally representative sample of sixth, eighth, and tenth graders from all five major racial/ethnic groups. Here, it was American Indians who were most likely to report being depressed. African-Americans, unexpectedly, were the lowest of all five groups. Whites were higher than African-Americans; Latinos and Asians were equal in percentage depressed, and between Whites and American Indians. These percentages were based on responses to a list of 10 statements based on DSM-III-R criteria that were then dichotomized into reporting or not reporting depressive symptoms, rather then being based on responses to one of the commonly used symptom checklists. High rates for American Indians compared to non-Indians were reported in earlier research (Beiser & Attneave, 1982; Kleinfeld & Bloom, 1977). Clearly, much more information is needed both comparing the nature of depression for American Indians compared to the other major racial/ethnic groups as well as work examining within-American Indian ethnic/tribal differences.

Looking Within Racial/Ethnic Groups

Within-group diversity can only be examined when samples are large enough to power the desired analyses. The findings available do point to the need to be wary when research samples only permit analysis of heterogeneous groups, for example studying Latinos without regard to national origin. Within the Latino group (Malgady, Rogier, & Constantino, 1990), Puerto Ricans have sometimes evidenced more depressive symptoms than Mexican-Americans or Cubans. More often though, it is Mexican-Americans who score the highest, as with Roberts and Sobhan's (1992) national sample showing Mexican-Americans with scores higher than those of NLW and Black adolescents, and "other Hispanics" having scores that were lower still. As already seen, even within a single national group, unmeasured variables such as acculturation/English use (e.g., Roberts & Chen, 1995) or type of community (e.g., urban vs. rural) may introduce noise and confusion into our findings.

An unusual sample of youth who had the option of identifying themselves to be of mixed racial/ethnic heritage provided Ramos, Jaccard, and Guilamo-Ramos (2003) the opportunity to test their competing hypotheses that declaring oneself a member of two cultural communities—here, Afro-Latino—confers a double advantage, or alternatively, places one in double jeopardy. The authors used the Add Health dataset to create a sample of 17,839 White, African-American, Latino and Afro-Latino students from grades 7 to 12. They found it necessary to use a subset of the Center for Epidemiologic Studies Depression Scale (CES-D) items in order to create four subscales that were appropriate for all four racial/ethnic groups. Across the four subscales—negative affect, positive affect, negative interpersonal feelings, and somatic symptomatology—Whites showed the lowest risk levels and Afro-Latinos the highest, with Latinos and African Americans in between. The authors suggest that rather than being protected by a broader repertoire of social and cultural traditions than African-Americans or Latinos, the mixed cultural group may be subject to conflicting ethnic loyalties and additive burdens of being a double minority. We also note that any of the multiethnic group studies cited earlier may well have introduced unmeasured variance into their analyses by failing to address the degree to which youth feel they belong to one or more than one culture.

Twenge and Nolen-Hoeksema (2002) indicated in their meta-analysis of 310 samples of youth ages 8 to 16 that we still do not have enough data on depression in various racial and ethnic groups to explain why Latinos have significantly higher scores than both Blacks and Whites. We would add, from several of the studies we have reviewed here, that Latinos are at greatest risk, Whites are at lowest risk, and American Indians may be at even higher risk than Latinos. Why? The high rates for Latinos point to cultural factors, since Latinos can be of any race (Twenge & Nolen-Hoeksema, 2002). But the addition of the findings regarding the double jeopardy that Afro-Latinos face (Ramos et al., 2003), suggest that we should look at practices and experiences that are related to both racial (e.g., discrimination) and cultural (e.g., patterns of immigration) group memberships.

CONTINUITY OF DEPRESSION OVER TIME

The question of continuity or discontinuity in the manifestation of depression among racial and ethnic minority youth is an important one that is largely unaddressed. Although some cross-sectional analyses that specifically test age effects find none (e.g., Roberts & Chen, 1995), there are as many that find at least small significant trends for depression symptoms to increase with age (Rushton, Forcier, & Schetman, 2002; Saluja et al., 2004; Schraedley, Gotlib, & Hayward, 1999). Guiao and Thompsons's analyses (2004) of Wave I Add Health data focused on females from five racial/ethnic groups and in three age cohorts, early (ages 12–14), middle (15–16) and late (17–19). Risk of depression increased significantly from early to late adolescence for three groups, African-American, NLW, and Asian-Americans. Native Americans also showed this pattern, but the sample was too small to detect significance. Only Latinas showed no significant differences across the age cohorts.

Longitudinal data are even rarer for racially and ethnically diverse adolescent samples. Research using data from the Adolescent Pathways Project (APP), a longitudinal study of development among urban adolescents from low-income communities (Seidman, 1991), examined depressive symptoms for 528 Black, Latino, and White adolescents (Clements, 2003). After adjusting for neighborhood-level poverty, there was both a main effect for time, and a significant race/ethnic group by time interaction. Black and Latino participants reported significant declines in depressive symptoms over the 3 years of the study, while levels for White adolescents remained relatively stable across the three waves. The APP group recently examined four waves of data ($n=768$) and utilized latent growth modeling (LGM) to identify individual change trajectories of depressive symptoms for each race/ethnic group. Analyses comparing the fit of the curvilinear (compared to a poorer fitting linear) model for Black, Latino, and White adolescents indicated that while a curvilinear model provided the best fit for all three groups, the initial level of depressive symptoms as well as the rate of change varied significantly for the three groups. For most adolescents, depressive symptoms declined throughout early adolescence (specifically, the last year of elementary school through middle school), but then increased by the time they were midway through high school. However, Latino early adolescents' depressive symptoms were both initially higher than those of either Black or White adolescents, and demonstrate a more dramatic decrease and subsequent increase. Black adolescents' initial level of depressive symptoms fell between that of White and Latino adolescents, but the rate of change was similar to that of the Latino adolescents. White adolescents reported the lowest levels of depressive symptoms and manifested the least amount of change over the period of study (Allen et al., in preparation).

Latent growth curve analyses of longitudinal data from the Children of the National Longitudinal Surveys of Youth data set (McLeod & Owens, 2004), showed different patterns for the Black, White, and Latino children followed across the same ages as the APP study just discussed. Here, Black and Latinos reported *lower* scores at age 10–11 along with more pronounced declines in scores than Whites over time. Franko et al. (2005), with their sample of 2,221 girls, found that it was African-American girls who were consistent and White girls whose scores decreased across the transition from adolescence to emerging adulthood. This difference may be due to the older age of these participants, a hypothesis that can only be confirmed by appropriately designed longitudinal studies.

These few investigations of the developmental course of depression for young people of different racial and ethnic backgrounds point to the role of cultural as well as developmental factors in influencing patterns of depressive symptoms (Guiao & Thompson, 2004). How do age, gender, racial and ethnic membership experiences, cultural values and behaviors interact to protect or increase the vulnerability of adolescents passing into, through, and beyond this developmental stage? This set of questions should guide future research to lead us to theories and interventions that fit the experience of these diverse groups. Research must also attend to the frequent confound between race/ethnicity and SES if we are to understand their separate and combined effects. We turn to a consideration of SES next.

SOCIOECONOMIC STATUS

Research on SES and human development has a long history based largely on the belief that high SES affords children and youth access to resources that benefit development in ways that could advance theory and intervention if these mechanisms were better understood (Bradley & Corwyn, 2002). How to define social class or social status triggers debate in sociology, psychology, and beyond. Adopting the current idea that SES conveys human, economic, and social capital (Coleman, 1988) is a reasonable way of capturing how developmental psychology currently uses SES. Many have argued that SES can only be captured well with some combination of measures of income, occupational prestige, and education (e.g., Bradley & Corwyn, 2002). In practice, however, researchers often adopt a single measure in efforts to "control" its effects. We argue that the effects of this complex construct will only be understood when we have explored both the main and interactive effects of SES.

An additional obstacle is that the meaning and impact of measures of education and wealth may vary across racial and ethnic groups when, at any given level of income, the proportion of each group at that level varies considerably (Braveman et al., 2005). The Braverman et al. analysis of National Health Interview Survey data showed that, at every level of education, African- and Mexican-Americans had lower incomes than Whites, underlining the danger of using education alone as one's proxy for SES to compare racial/ethnic groups. Measuring even these single factors in research on adolescent depression is further complicated by the fact that young people are often unaware of their family's income, education, or occupation. A teen may say that his mother works in a bank, but is this as the bank vice president or as a bank clerk?

Research that carefully attends to SES in research with diverse adolescent populations is critical to our understanding of both race/ethnicity and social class as correlates and predictors of depressive symptoms given the degree to which these two factors are often confounded (Wight, Aneshensel, Botticello, & Sepulveda, 2005). One of the main hypotheses to explain ethnic differences in rates of depression suggests that the two are totally confounded, and that ethnic differences are actually class differences. The main competing hypothesis asserts that social class has an effect on depression over and above the contribution of race or ethnicity (Roberts et al., 1997). But pursuit of these hypotheses is hampered in several ways: empirical evidence on the relationship of SES and adolescent depression is not well-developed, and is characterized by inconsistent and weak measurement; race/ethnicity and social class are not often enough conceptualized and operationalized separately (see Steward & Napoles-Springer, 2003 for further discussion); and until recently, samples were insufficient in power for real tests of the impact of this factor.

The findings of "no relationship" are numerous and are often hypothesized when researchers believe that "controlling" for SES will eliminate its impact on racial/ethnic differences. In a convenience sample of 681 African-Americans ages 14 to 17, depressive symptoms were not related to parent occupation, perhaps because of the narrow range of SES in the sample (Repetto, Caldwell, & Zimmerman, 2004). Waschbusch, Sellers, LeBlanc, and Kelley (2003) looked at income and education combined in the Hollingshead Four-Factor Index (Hollingshead, 1975) and found no relationship between SES and depression in a sample of 425 African-American and NLW adolescents (mean age=15 years).

Large samples with more complex measures of SES generally find the reverse. For example, Rushton et al. (2002) did see differences in scores with a sample of over 13,000 adolescents (mean age=15.6 years) from the Add Health data. They used three indices of SES—receipt of public assistance, single-parent versus two-parent household, and maternal education. Goodman, Slap, and Huang (2003) used the Add Health sample to examine this question at the population rather than the individual level. After calculating something that they call the "population attributable risk" (a measure of the population-level impact) of exposure to low SES on depression, they determined that fully one-third of the depression in the sample was associated with lower household income and parental education. Goodman's analyses of the same data focused on the search for an SES gradient (inverse linear relationship) in contrast to a threshold (level of income below which outcomes are compromised) relationship between SES and depression symptom scores. She did indeed find this linear relationship, and further, found that it persisted even after race/ethnicity was controlled (Goodman, 1999). Schraedley et al.'s, (1999) nationally representative sample of young people from a wider age range—grades 5 through 12—also confirmed this inverse relationship.

Additional studies support the existence of SES differences in depression even when focusing on the youngest adolescents. Roberts et al. (1997) studied over 6,000 middle school students from more than 20 racial/ethnic categories (e.g., Cuban, Indian American), but largely African-American, White, Latino and Asian. Depression rates were higher among students who said that they were somewhat or much worse off economically than others. Further, this relationship was not moderated by racial/ethnic group membership. This relationship was also found by Kubik et al. (2003), using an SES index composed of four variables—reduced/free lunch, parents' education, number of parents in the home, and number of parents working full time. High depression was related to low SES in this sample of 3,621 middle school students (seventh graders) from all five major racial/ethnic groups. Finally, Garrison, Addy, Jackson, McKeown, and Waller (1991), with their diverse public middle school sample (seventh, eighth, and ninth graders), were surprised to find that after controlling for education of head of household, scores for Blacks were still higher than scores for Whites.

Complementing (and complicating) these studies that focus on risk at the low end of the SES scale, we have work by Luthar and D'Avanzo (1999) that focuses on the other end of the socioeconomic continuum. They find that affluent suburban teens evidenced higher depressive symptoms than an inner-city, much less affluent comparison group. Taken together, these studies suggest that exploration of the full range of SES is required if we are to fully understand how such resources are related to depressive symptoms. Studies that include affluent racial and ethnic minority families, for example, would help us to test the hypotheses that have race/ethnicity equaling social class, versus the approach that says that social class is a contributor to adolescent depression over and above race/ethnic category.

To untangle these variables, we also need studies that consider how individuals, nested within a given SES context, vary in depressive symptoms. Wight et al. (2005) used hierarchical linear modeling to look at the simultaneous effects of variables capturing race/ethnicity and SES at both the individual and the community levels. Their more than 18,000 youth (ages 11–17) from the Add Health study were nested in geographic "sampling areas" for which they defined two indicators of SES: median household income and proportion of NLW households. When African-Americans were compared to NLW, African-Americans in neighborhoods with a high proportion of NLW reported higher scores more often than NLW youth living in similar areas. But, when African-American and White youth lived in neighborhoods with a low proportion of NLW, the frequency of symptoms was more similar.

What is it about such a setting that makes for these relations? Is it the low education of the residents? The absence of good health, education, and social resources? The high rates of unemployment? Research will advance when we develop good ideas about what makes SES "work," then operationalize those ideas with measures of SES consistent with our hypotheses. Brindis, Park, Paul, and Burg (2002), in their article on disparities in health status by race/ethnicity, conclude that data on SES across adolescent health problems is lacking, and that this variable, SES, "may prove to be one of the most important elements in understanding which young people are at most risk and will also likely explain many of the ethnic and racial differences ..." (p. 27)

Researchers from the Center on Social Disparities in Health at UCSF warn that racial and ethnic differences are likely to reflect unmeasured SES effects (Braveman et al., 1999) and only careful measurement derived from consideration of possible explanatory pathways between aspects of SES and depression will ever allow us to eliminate the persistent confound between race/ethnicity and SES in social science research. Our hope is that this summary of the main issues in research that has looked at SES and racial/ethnic minority youth depression will encourage researchers to more carefully select measures of SES that will capture variations in resources across racial/ethnic groups, and will capture a wide range of SES groups. We also hope that researchers, using more complex measures of SES, will increase our understanding of the active ingredients that lead to poor outcomes for youth. Is it low income, or is it the family dynamics set into motion by the stress of economic disadvantage? How do we fit the high-income youth into a comprehensive theory? Is it parents' education or their parenting style? Increased understanding also demands that we go to the expense of collecting SES data from sources other than youth, whether from parents or from communities in multilevel designs. Culturally sensitive depression theory and intervention depend on a commitment to take these steps to improve research on these questions.

CULTURE AND DEPRESSION

The unique role culture plays in understanding mental health issues is widely recognized (U.S. Department of Health and Human Services [DHHS], 2001). Although symptoms, presentation, and meaning of mental health outcomes are understood as universal processes, the identification of "culture-bound syndromes"—sets of symptoms which are distinct to specific social-cultural groups—indicates an effort to understand the complexity of preventing, assessing, and treating ethnically diverse populations (DSM-IV; American Psychiatric Association, 1994). Research with ethnically diverse and immigrant populations gives us insight into how depressive symptomatology varies among groups, and how acculturative processes create a unique context for the development of adolescent depression for those from immigrant families and the role that familial factors play in the development of depression for youth. We turn now to acculturation because it is most often looked to as a significant explanatory variable in the study of psychological issues, such as depression, in ethnically diverse groups (Zane & Mak, 2002).

Acculturation

Mental health outcomes are influenced by immigration and acculturation processes (Organista, Organista, & Kurasaki, 2002). Acculturation has been broadly defined as the process individuals experience as a result of being in contact with a different culture (Berry, Poortinga, Segall, & Dasen, 1992). Modes of acculturation have been used to describe the ways individuals reject the old and embrace a new culture which include, separation (preserve the old and reject the new), assimilation (preserve the old and accept the new), biculturality/integration (accept both cultures) and marginality (reject both cultures) (Berry, 1997). How one "acculturates" relates to how individuals go about their daily lives. The language one chooses to speak (and when and how often they choose to speak it), the values they use to guide decisions, and the behaviors (or shedding of) one engages in are some examples. When an individual or group has contact with a "new" culture, they are engaged in a process of acculturation. Although there are a number of acculturating groups in the United States, such as, American Indians, African Americans, Asian Americans and Latinos (Organista, Organista, & Kurasaki, 2002), recent demographic trends and projections have encouraged empirical focus on Latino (particularly from Mexican decent) and Asian-American subgroups in examining the role acculturation processes play in understanding depression in adolescents. In our review of this literature, we have included only studies that focused on adolescents, and used comprehensive, multidimensional measures of acculturation, rather than proxies such as language use or parental immigrant status.

How does acculturation explain differences in depressive symptoms in diverse youth? As we saw earlier, Latinos, and especially Mexican-Americans who prefer to be interviewed in Spanish, show highest depression scores when compared to other Latino groups or Whites (Roberts & Sobhan, 1992), and to Blacks and Asians as well (Siegel et al., 1998). Authors suggest that acculturation stress, language factors, and having immigrant parents (who tend to be depressed and/or unemployed) (Roberts et al., 1992) contribute to greater exposure to stressors associated with being Latino (Siegel et al., 1998), and are factors that may explain these high rates of depressive symptoms. Roberts et al. (1997), discussed above, suggested that culturally anchored factors, such as a fatalistic orientation, external locus of control, and acculturative stress may contribute to high rates of depressive symptomatology for Mexican-Americans. It is important to note that acculturative stress was not a significant predictor of depression with a sample of rural Latino adolescents, although other stressors that are associated with the process of acculturation were (e.g., not understanding teacher; parents not making enough money; not making new friends at school) (Chandrika, Katragadda, & Tidwell, 1998). The authors suggest that this result reflects the complex relationship between depression and acculturation processes.

In a study with 144 high school students, Wong (2001) examined the effects of cultural orientation and interpersonal relationships on depression among inner-city Asian Americans. This contextual setting is important to note because research with Asian-American populations rarely samples from urban areas (or low income samples), which expose inhabitants to distinct stressors that may contribute to depressive symptoms (Wong, 2001). Individuals who were separated (high orientation towards ethnic culture and low orientation towards mainstream) were more depressed than those who were assimilated (high orientation toward American culture and low toward ethnic culture). Late immigrants (those who immigrated after age 12) were more depressed than American-born adolescents. When compared to non-Hawaiian youth, indigenous Hawaiian youth in a community-based sample showed rates of depression that resembled patterns for other high-risk groups, such as Native Americans (Andrade et al., 2006). A reasonable conjecture is that it is acculturation stress that makes being a part of the nondominant group a risk factor for higher rates of depression.

Empirical evidence of the role of acculturation leads us to the consideration of acculturation's most important contexts—the family. Gonzales et al. (2006) provide evidence that more acculturated Mexican-American adolescents are at increased risk for depressive symptoms due to increases in family conflict not found in less acculturated families. And while family pressure has been found to exacerbate risk for depression among, for example, Filipino immigrant adolescents (Guerrero, Hishinuma, Andrade, Nishimura, & Cunanan, 2006), there are also situations in which family support seems to protect youth from low status racial/ethnic groups from the stressors often related to depression (e.g., Carlton et al., 2006; Guerrero et al., 2006).

International Studies

Studies exploring depression in non-American non-White samples of adolescents provide further evidence of how cultural context relates to development. In a community sample of Hong Kong adolescents (Stewart et al., 2003), cultural differences in orientation (e.g., personal self-efficacy versus interpersonal evaluations) predicted variation in depressive mood. Consistent with collectivist ideology that characterizes Chinese cultures, interpersonal relationship harmony was more strongly associated with mood than was personal self-efficacy. A sense of mastery, an orientation with high predictive validity in Western samples, is not as relevant when predicting depression with adolescents from collectivist cultures. Working with a sample of approximately 1,100 adolescents from Hong Kong, Stewart et al. (2002) also reports that interpersonal relationship harmony is a significant predictor of depressive mood.

Cross-cultural studies examining depressive patterns across the United States and international samples add to the complexity of how cultural factors explain depression trajectories in non-White and/or acculturating youth. Some studies point to the role of traditional culture in determining cultural group differences. For example, in a cross-cultural comparison of American and Hong Kong youth, general patterns (e.g., hopelessness, negative cognitive errors) existed for both samples. However, general cognitive tendencies tended to be weaker predictors of depression among Hong Kong youth who also reported higher levels of symptomatology than the American sample (Stewart et al., 2004). These data suggest that although cognitive mechanisms such as self-efficacy may serve to protect youth in Western cultures against depressed mood, this may not be the case for youth who value interpersonal interdependence more than autonomy and personal agency. Similarly, peer networks may or may not serve as a protective mechanism for youth depending on the collectivist-individualistic nature of their culture of origin (Oppedal & Roysamb, 2004). Chen, Chan, Bond, and Stewart (2006) compared the effects of self-efficacy and relationship harmony on depression among adolescents in the United States and Hong Kong. The pathway from self-efficacy to depressive symptomatology was stronger for US youth, while harmonious relationships were equally significant predictors of depression for both groups. The authors suggest theories of collectivism and individualism are indeed a factor in understanding pathways to depression for youth.

There is also recent data suggesting that globalization may be reaching into non-Western cultures and influencing even the expression of mental distress. Dmitrieva, Chen, Greenberger, and Gil-Rivas (2004) examined the role of parent–adolescent relationships as a mediator between negative life events and depressive symptoms, with youth from China, Korea, United States, and Czech Republic. Although depressed mood varied significantly across cultural groups, with Korean and Czech youth reporting significantly higher levels of depressed mood than youth from the United States or China, cross-cultural similarities in patterns of associations among family variables and depressive symptomatology were evident. This work supports culture-general developmental processes (although there are differences in the magnitude of association between variables that may be explained by culture), suggesting that globalization trends are changing the norms of expression in Asian contexts. Another study suggesting the increasing influence of Western culture explored patterns of symptoms among adolescents in Hong Kong and the United States. Using a community sample of youth, the investigators suggested that somatic symptoms as well as affective/cognitive symptoms of depression were equally relevant for Asian youth growing up in a modernized, Westernized city (Stewart et al., 2003). This work suggests that as context changes (e.g., becomes more Western) the expression of depression in non-Western cultures may also be changing.

Efforts to identify universal processes in depression symptomatology must be balanced with the pursuit of the possible cultural particularities of their expression, or we may unintentionally cloud our understanding of culture and depressive symptomatology for youth. Ruchkin, Sukhodolsky, Vermeiren, Koposov, and Schwab-Stone (2006) systematically compared patterns of associations in depressive symptoms and internalizing and externalizing behaviors in large community samples of youth from three nations; the United States, Belgium and Russia. Although the US and Belgium samples included a substantial proportion of ethnic minorities, ethnicity/race was not included as a variable in the analyses possibly occluding within and across culture differences in depressive symptomatology. We will address the issue of cultural-symptom variability in greater depth in the upcoming discussion of measurement.

What then, does cultural mean when we are trying to understand adolescent depression? This inquiry, posed by Kleinman and Good (1985) over two decades ago continues to be a critical question for increasing our understanding of adolescent depression. There are two dominant positions that drive our understanding of the way culture influences depression. The etic position assumes universality regarding the expression, manifestation, and ways of diagnosing depression. The assumption is that universal developmental patterns of depression are identifiable within and across populations despite differences in ethnicity, race, culture, and social class. In contrast, the emic position suggests that individuals cannot be compared cross-culturally on measures of depression that do not capture the variability in expression which emerges from non-Western or nonhegemonic social practices and norms regarding behavior. Clearly, neither extreme will allow us to understand variations in depression at the same time that we build theory and models of intervention that, at the policy level, can address the health disparities between majority and minority populations in this country (HHS, 2001).

One way to reconcile the polarizing etic–emic framework is to consider a "multicultural position," which argues that in pluralistic societies where many different cultures coexist, the emergence of adaptive or maladaptive mechanisms will occur, reflecting the individuals' sociocultural experiences (Tanaka-Matsumi & Draguns, 1997). Across these conceptual frameworks exists another layer of influence that has been demonstrated to have a great impact on the language and culture of depression—the individualistic and collectivistic dimensions of a culture and/or a society (e.g., Stewart et al., 2003). Global values, such as interdependence and communality, most common in collectivistic cultures will effect individual-level depressogenic processes (e.g., awareness and recognition of depression), which are in effect moderated by the synergy of culture, social class, race, and ethnicity.

Since the development and expression of depressive symptomatology is embedded within this complex sociocultural framework, it is necessary to evaluate the "in-between" space of an individuals' value system (which is clearly shaped by cultural, socioeconomic, and ethnic norms) and the global system within which the individual develops. By examining this space we will identify the fractures between mainstream conceptualizations and expectations of depressiveness in youth, and the less obvious, varied ways depressions occurs and is expressed by individuals who share common sociocultural norms and experiences—leading to more cost effective, culturally competent services and programs. We will also increase our understanding of when and how cultural variables expose one to greater risk or indeed protect one from the onset of depressive symptoms. We turn now to a look at empirical clues to what other factors may serve as risks or protectors for depression among diverse youth.

RISK AND PROTECTIVE FACTORS

Developmental psychopathology has taken great interest in environmental and personal factors that protect youth from challenging circumstances (Luthar & Zigler, 1991; Masten, Best, & Garmezy, 1990). For youth, such factors warrant greater attention given the probability that they will help to explain the contradictory findings in research on depression across racial/ethnic groups. Indeed, racial and ethnic labels and group membership themselves deserves attention as potential risk and protective factors, given that the opportunities and burdens of group membership vary considerably, from Blacks who are often the victims of blatant discrimination, to Asian-Americans who suffer the mixed blessing of being called a "model minority" (HHS, 2001). We might hypothesize in fact that race is more likely to be a risk factor, at least for some lower status groups, while ethnicity is protective for those who proactively include themselves in the group and seek to derive the benefits of belonging (Ashmore, Deaux, & McLaughlin-Volpe, 2004).

Personal Group Identity

One dimension of individual identity that shows promise for helping us to understand what mediates or moderates the relationship between racial/ethnic group membership and risk of depression is the attachment one feels to that identity (Rutter & Tienda, 2005). Racial, ethnic, or cultural identity are all multidimensional constructs that reflect attachment to, importance of, and feelings about one's group memberships (Allen et al., 2005). These identities are thought to be risk factors when they are weak, and may be the mechanisms that explain inconsistencies in group differences in manifestations of adolescent depression. Support for this conjecture comes from Williams et al.'s (2005) examination of Japanese cultural identity scores from a small sample ($n=140$) of Japanese American and Part-Japanese American high school seniors in Hawaii. Japanese American adolescents' lower scores were related to their stronger Japanese cultural identity. Roberts and Chen (1995) found that English language use, a simplistic measure of acculturation and presumably related to one's personal identity, was also related to a decreased Mexican-American's risk of depression. Here, however, though we are assuming that acculturation is positively correlated with a sense of group belonging, empirical evidence is needed before we can assume that these two measures can substitute for each other in studies of adolescent depression. Yasui, Dorham, and Dishion (2004) studied a small cross-sectional sample ($n=159$) including both successful and high-risk Black and White middle school students using Phinney's (1992) Multigroup Ethnic Identity Measure. In predicting depression, two interactions were related to depressive symptoms across all groups: the interaction between race/ethnicity and ethnic affirmation, along with the interaction between race/ethnicity and ethnic belonging. However, for ethnic identity achievement, its interaction with race/ethnicity predicted symptoms only for African-American youth, despite the fact that levels of ethnic identity were comparable across the White and African-American groups. Though confirming their initial hypothesis that ethnic identity would have a stronger association to depression for African-Americans, the authors point out that with cross-sectional data, it is impossible to determine whether depression achievement protects from depression or whether depression suppresses this achievement. Nonetheless, the results bolster the view that research on racial/ethnic identity may well lead to increased understanding of racial/ethnic differences in depressive symptoms.

The influence of ethnic identity may depend not just on its relative strength or weakness, but also on one's immediate context. Data from the APP showed complex interactions among context, identity, and depression, such that racial group esteem protected youth from the stress of being in a neighborhood that was not congruent with the youths' racial group membership, but only for Black youth. But when looking at congruence with the racial/ethnic makeup of the school context, it was White students who, when in the minority in their setting, showed that those with low levels of ethnic group esteem were more vulnerable to symptoms of depression (Allen et al., 2005). Additional evidence of the importance of context, over and above the impact of any individual factors, comes from a multilevel analysis of data from the Add Health study (Wight et al., 2005). The researchers found that the impact of individual level ethnicity on depressive symptoms changed depending on the individual and community level SES of the larger context. Consistent with the findings from the Allen et al. study (2005),

African-American adolescents were especially at risk if they lived in areas that were largely White. Wight and coauthors (2005) add that their analyses could have been even more revealing had they had sufficient sample sizes to address the heterogeneity within their large racial/ethnic groups given the strong possibility that risk factors at both the individual and community level may affect Chinese differently from Koreans, and Mexicans differently from Cubans.

Social Support

Among potentially protective factors often explored is social support from a variety of sources including friends, family, and others (e.g., Demaray & Malecki, 2002). Perceived social support has been shown to protect against depressive symptoms, but it seems clear that the source of support can make a crucial difference in its impact. Results from a school-based sample of Asian/Pacific Islander adolescents (mean=tenth grade) (Hishinuma et al., 2004) evinced protective roles for social support from family and friends, noting much stronger effects for family support. This difference varied little across the Hawaiian, Japanese, Filipino, mixed/non-Hawaiian, and Caucasian groups.

Focusing on supportive and nonsupportive aspects of friendship and peer relationships, La Greca and Harrison (2005) found that being part of a high status peer group offered protection against depression in their 67% Latino sample. Beck Depression Inventory scores were higher when adolescents reported being victimized by peers, and when they perceived negative aspects of their best friend and romantic relationships. The main effects were moderated by racial/ethnic group membership in two ways. First, the overt victimization effect was present for White but not for Latino adolescents. Second, negative interactions with romantic partners predicted depression for both Whites and Latinos, but the relation was stronger for Whites. Since little is known about peer victimization or the development and conduct of romantic relationships among minority youth, both of these areas of socioemotional development offer opportunities for important discoveries.

Stress and Negative Life Events

Negative life events have been related to depression in adults (e.g., Kendler, Karkowski, & Prescott, 1999) and adolescents (e.g., Compas, Howell, Phares, Williams, & Giunta, 1989), but rarely have racial/ethnic differences been examined. Debra Franko and her team are among the few who have examined such differences longitudinally (Franko et al., 2004). They measured five domains of life events among Black and White females age 16, and measured depressive symptoms at ages 18 and 21. Negative life events increased the likelihood of depression for both racial groups. This relationship is important to pursue further given the higher negative life events reported for Black females in this sample despite the fact that the vast majority came from families in which parents had at least some college education. Lower SES samples would likely show even higher levels of negative life events, and therefore even greater risk of depressive symptoms.

Dornbusch et al. (1991), with their sample of over 10,000 adolescents from California and Wisconsin, found that those who reported more stressful life events, reported more symptoms of depression whether Asian- and African-American, Latino or White, though the relationship is weakest among African-Americans. Stressful events were the second greatest influence in predicting depression, after gender. In examination of interaction effects, Asian and Black youth showed fewer symptoms of depressive symptoms, compared to Whites. The addition of measures of coping might help to clarify this kind of relationship. Such examination would need to take a lifetime perspective, since we hypothesize that a lifetime of coping with discrimination and other stressors related to being Black in the United States may enhance resilience. Alternatively, the usual list of stressful life events may fail to include stressors that are particular to the lives of African-American youth.

Gerard and Buehler (2004) examined cumulative risk and maladjustment using a longitudinal Add Health sample of over 5,000 Black, White, and Latino youth ages 11 to 18. Depression was measured using the CES-D, and risk was assessed across five different contexts: family sociodemographic risk; family process risk (e.g., family detachment); peer support and rejection; school detachment and prejudice; and neighborhood quality. Youth attributes or protective factors tested were scholastic achievement, problem-solving ability, and self-esteem.

Results confirmed the team's hypothesis that cumulative risk would be associated with a linear increase in depressive symptoms, a relationship that was moderated by racial/ethnic group membership. Specifically, the relationship was stronger for White youth when compared to both Blacks and Latinos. Of the hypothesized protective factors, self-esteem buffered the impact of risk on depression for Whites and Latinos, but not for African-American youth. Problem solving, hypothesized as a protective factor, was actually a risk factor, but only for African-American youth. Further, the higher the levels of risk for African-American youth, the more high levels of problem-solving skill heightened the risk of depression. The problem solving findings deserve particular attention from those who design preventive and other interventions for dealing with adolescent depression. Consistent with research on "stereotype threat," the authors suggest that for Black students, in contrast to both the Latinos and Whites, problem-solving skills are in conflict with their environments in that they are behaving counter to peer culture stereotypes and expectation (Steele & Aronson, 1995) and are, paradoxically, placed at greater risk the greater their ability to analyze and understand their place in their context. So, it may be that White students are harmed more by cumulative risk, but then known protective factors seem to protect them effectively. The search for protective factors that are unique or common across groups, and using data that follow the longitudinal course of depressive symptoms longer that the two waves in this study, is the next important step toward complete theories of risk and protective that take full advantage of what we can learn about the roles of racial and ethnic cultural factors.

Another important source of stress for low-income youth can come from their neighborhoods. We discussed neighborhood effects earlier as we focused on neighborhood SES as a contextual risk factor for depression (Allen et al., 2005). Aneshensel and Sucoff (1996) sought to "unpack" the effects of low SES neighborhoods to better understand what about them constitutes a risk factor. While social cohesion did not explain group differences in depression, ambient hazards (e.g., graffiti, drug dealing) did indeed offer some insights. Depression was lowest when neighborhoods were perceived as less threatening. African-Americans rated their neighborhoods as more threatening than other groups, net of the effects of both racial/ethnic composition of the neighborhood and its

SES status. Though these effects were modest in size, they point to the value of operationalizing specific theories about the "active ingredients" in neighborhoods that have an impact on adolescent mental health.

Puberty and Self-Perception

Pubertal stage (e.g., menarche) and pubertal timing (e.g., early compared to peers) have both been related to the consistent finding that after adolescence, females show more depressive symptoms than males (Hayward & Sanborn, 2002). Nolen-Hoeksema and Girgus (1994), examining models to explain this persistent result, found the strongest empirical support for the idea that risk factors for depression are more common in girls than boys, and that the challenges of adolescence, whether personality, biological, or social challenges, or some combination of these, are more common for females, leading to the gender difference often observed. Puberty, with its biological and social challenges, is an example of a challenge that seems to affect girls more than boys. But whether this relationship between puberty and depressive symptoms exists among racial/ethnic minority youth is an open question and one that speaks directly to the generalizability of theories of adolescent depressive symptoms.

Hayward and Sanborn (2002) evaluated this question with a large, nationally representative sample and found that the relationship held for White girls in grades 5 to 8, but not for African-American girls. However, in the diverse sample ages 12 to 17 from the Los Angeles County probability sample discussed earlier (Siegel et al., 1998), though African Americans had more positive body images than all other groups, they were more affected by changes in body image than others (Siegel, 2002). The presumed lack of a relationship, for African-American females, between depression and puberty and its concomitant body changes might have led one to believe that change in body image would affect them least. But in fact, girls whose body image remained unchanged or became more negative 13 months later showed relatively more negative depression scores.

Analyses of pubertal timing using the same data set (Siegel et al., 1998) showed that all teens who were in the early stages of puberty reported fewer symptoms of depression. But, if one were in this early stage longer than one's peers (late pubertal timing), or left the stage well ahead of one's peers (early pubertal timing) mattered too, but only for Latinos. Those who did not conform to peer pubertal norms had higher levels of depression relative to those who reached puberty on time. Clearly, there is not enough data to draw real conclusion about how puberty and body image relate to the onset of depression in racial/ethnic minority groups. However, there is enough to suggest that further research might be fruitful in testing the limits of theories of depression in which biological change and body image play an important role.

These findings, from studies of personal group identity, of support from family, friends, and others, of negative life events, and from examination of the risk of the biological change and self-perception changes that accompany puberty in girls all point to one conclusion—that research on risk and protective factors can lead to levers for intervention, and that these levers will surely not be a one-size-fits-all solution. Yet, we caution that the findings we review can be no better than the measurement tools used to define the depression phenomena under consideration. We turn now to a fuller discussion of the problems in measurement that characterizes this area of research.

MEASUREMENT OF ADOLESCENT DEPRESSION

In this section, we review the most commonly used measures of depression and illustrate how issues of measurement and cultural equivalence complicate our ability to rely on a one-size-fits-all approach to assessing youth depression. It is important to note, however, that we are not taking the position described in cross-cultural psychology as "relativist," in which it would be impossible for any cross-group analysis of depression to occur because depression in each group would be understood only from the perspective of that group. Rather, our "universalist" position, which assumes our belief that there are indeed psychological processes that exist across human groups, is core to our understanding of depression in racial and ethnic minority youth. Added to this, however, is the belief that cultural factors influence both the development and the display of these processes (Berry, Poortinga, Segall, & Dasen, 2002). Thus, the goal is to find expressions of depression that are common across groups, as well as to acknowledge, identify, and measure symptoms that occur in some groups but not others, leading to culturally meaningful versions of measures of depressive symptoms. The common indicators permit meaningful epidemiological comparisons as well as the formulation and evaluation of health policy, while the unique factors will lead us more quickly to culturally sensitive prevention and treatment interventions (APA, 2003). We begin with a brief description of each measure, and then discuss further how to understand and deal with the influence of culture in research and intervention with adolescents showing symptoms of depression.

MEASURES OF YOUTH DEPRESSION

There are four measures of depression commonly used to assess depression in American youth. The CES-D, designed to measure depressive symptoms, is a 20-item self-report scale, which was originally developed by Radloff (1977) for use in the general adult population. The Youth Self-Report (YSR) developed by Achenbach (1991) includes eight symptom subscales loading onto two factors; internalizing and externalizing behaviors. The anxious/depressed subscale is utilized to assess symptoms of depression with youth (e.g., Grant et al., 2004). The Children's Depression Inventory (CDI) is a downward extension of the Beck Depression Inventory (Beck et al. 1961) by Kovacs (Kovacs, 1985), and measures the level of depressive symptoms in ages 7–17. Lastly, the DSD is designed to measure depressive symptoms in adolescents ages 10–17 (e.g., Roberts et al., 1997). Its 31 items are rephrasings of questions on the Diagnostic Interview Schedule for Children (DISC) that are related to major depression.

Achieving "Equivalence" Across Groups

Comparing depression symptoms across groups requires measures that are equivalent across groups in several ways. Measures should have factorial equivalence such that items relate to dimensions or subscales of the measure in the same general order and to the same degree (Hales et al., 2006). Cultural equivalence means that the items have the same value, weight, importance, and meaning across groups, and tap the same construct. "I have a stomachache," for a group that is prone to somatic expression of pain could have different meaning for a group more used to admitting that "I am sad." But, as Crockett,

Randall, Shen, Russell, and Driscoll (2005) indicate, even if the construct is exactly the same, a measure might not measure it equally across groups. Crockett et al. also point out that a measure whose constructs are equivalent across all groups studied might still not measure depression in the same way if the groups react to the response scale differently. Bachman and O'Malley (1984) found, for example, that African-American youth were more likely to use extreme response options than were White respondents. In all of these cases, real depressive symptoms might be misreported, a risk not just between major racial/ethnic groups, but extending, as we have indicated, to cultural differences within major groups (e.g., Cuban- compared to Mexican-Americans).

Given that most scales and checklists were based on diagnostic practices of the dominant culture and tested largely with White samples, as is still surprisingly common in research with adolescent populations in the United States (Doucette-Gates, Brooks-Gunn, & Chase-Lansdale, 1998), we assume that the burden is on the measure to prove that it is indeed useful for racial/ethnic and language minority groups. With these equally important issues in mind—measurement and cultural equivalence—we turn next to a review of empirical literature in this area.

The CES-D

One of the most commonly used measurements of depression for youth is the CES-D. Evidence for its equivalence across groups comes from several studies. Prescott et al. (1998) concluded that the CES-D's ability to predict major depression did not differ by ethnicity (Hawaiian compared to a mixed group of non-Hawaiians) after group differences in gender and grade level were controlled. Similarly, Hales et al. (2006) reported that the measure had a similar factor structure for African-American (n=610) and White (n=452) twelfth grade girls. Wight et al. (2005), too, show strong internal consistency in African Americans (α=.82), Asian/Pacific Islanders (α=.84), and Hispanics (α=.85) using a shortened version (16 of 20 items) of the CES-D, as have others (e.g., Garrison et al., 1989).

However, Perreira, Deeb-Sossa, Harris, and Bollen (2005) pointed out that the CES-D violates one of the basic assumptions of the alpha statistic as a measure of internal consistency because it contains both cause and effect items. "I feel depressed" and "I felt sad" are clearly effect or indicator items, but "I felt lonely" could easily be a cause of depression rather than an indicator of the latent construct. This confusion creates the need for caution when interpreting studies primarily using internal reliability statistics to establish measurement or cultural robustness. These authors further investigated the psychometric properties of the measure across 12 distinct cultural groupings of adolescent youth by immigration status (four racial/ethnic groups x across 1st/2nd/3rd generations), and the equivalence story is indeed challenged. Based on multigroup comparative factor structure analysis, the authors argued that a four-factor solution model does not fit the non-White groups in the sample because the CES-D mixes items measuring causes with outcomes of depression. They were able to develop an abbreviated CES-D with five items, all indicating effects, and established that all parameter estimates were equivalent across ethno-cultural groups.

Within Latinos there is also mixed support for measurement equivalence of the original scale (Crockett et al., 2005). In a study of NLW, Mexican-American, Cuban-American and Puerto-Rican youth, a four-factor structure was supported for Mexican-American and NLW, although full metric invariance was not—suggesting some items may be more significant indicators of depression for Mexican-American youths than their White counterparts. In contrast, the four-factor structure did not hold for the Puerto Rican or Cuban youth. The different factor structures observed for these groups suggest that the symptomatic experience of depression may differ within major groups, such as Latinos, as well as between minority and majority group youth.

Finally, Manson, Ackerson, Dick, Baron, and Fleming (1990) found that the measure showed good internal consistency ($\alpha = .82$) with a sample of American Indian boarding school students ($n = 188$; grades 9–12). But comparison of the recommended cutoff score of 16 with cross-classifications based on DSM-III diagnoses for depression showed that the CES-D, showing as many as 58.1% of the students as depressed, gave a high rate of false-positives. Knight and Hill (1998) remind us that even if we have good internal consistency, if the scale does not represent the same degree of "depressed-ness" for all groups, then using a common cutoff score will naturally introduce systematic bias. Qualitative exploration of the meaning of items is strongly recommended to uncover such group differences.

The YSR

Original normative data from the YSR showed an internal consistency on the anxious/depressed subscale of .86 for males and .90 for females. Grant et al. (2004b) reported an internal consistency of .83 in a sample of 622 low income African Americans (mean age=12.73). Using a sample of 1,520 low income early adolescents (64% Black, 13% Latino, 9% Asian, and 5% White), Grant et al. (2004a) reported $\alpha = .86$ on the internalizing behavior scale as a whole. However, we find no research on the factorial invariance across diverse populations, though a number of studies have shown this widely translated scale to result in similar scores (though with differences in specific items) in Australian (Achenbach, Hensley, Phares, & Grayson, 1990), Puerto Rican (Achenbach et al., 1990) and European community samples (de Groot, Koot, & Velhulst 1996; Walter, Remschmidt, & Deimel, 1994) among others.

The CDI

Research on the appropriateness of the CDI for diverse community populations is also limited. Steele and colleagues (2006) explored its construct validity and found an adequate fit to the original five-factor structure in both African Americans ($n = 523$, mean age = 12.76) and Whites ($n = 564$, mean age = 12.43). But upon closer examination, using factors based on the original five identified by Kovacs (1985), Steele et al. (2006) found that only the "social" factor was differentiated in the White sample, while both the "social" and "in-effectual" factors were differentiated as separate elements of depression in the Black sample. Fit to the original factor structure has also varied using samples that do not focus on ethnic/racial diversity, with analysis yielding as many as six (Craighead Smucker, Craighead, & Ilardi, 1998) and as few as three factors (Cole, Hoffman, Tram, & Maxwell, 2000) using both confirmatory and exploratory factor analysis. Finally, internal consistency for the CDI has not been reported for individual ethnic/racial minority groups, despite its having been used in a few community samples that include substantial proportions of racial/ethnic minorities (e.g., Cole & Jordan, 1995; Cole et al., 2004).

The DSD

Construct validity of the DSD has been demonstrated in racially and ethnically diverse populations by providing statistically significant negative correlations with existing measures of self-esteem, social support, active coping, happiness, and optimism (Chen et al., 1998). We find additional cultural group information from two single group studies only. Excellent internal consistency was demonstrated by Chen et al. (1998) in a sample of Chinese Americans ($\alpha = .91$, $n = 177$), and by Choi et al. (2002) in a sample of Korean Americans ($\alpha = .92$, $n = 104$). Finally, Chen et al.'s (1998) analysis of the DSD revealed no mean difference for Chinese-Americans and Whites, challenging their hypothesis that Chinese-Americans would score lower because the measure did not address culture-specific notions of depression. In fact, only 5 of 26 items functioned differently between the two groups. For instance, Chinese- and Anglo-Americans who were equally depressed responded differently to items including "trouble with sleep" and "trouble taking care of self." Further, depression prevalence rates were unchanged when these items were deleted from the total score. The authors concluded that the measure was an accurate measure of depression for Chinese Americans. At the same time, the five items that functioned differently between the groups found the Chinese higher on somatic symptoms and lower on symptoms of guilt.

In summary, though response patterns of non-White youth can sometimes be matched to the structure of measures developed for the dominant culture, the need for culturally sensitive identification of depressive symptoms, that can then be linked to culturally appropriate treatment (HHS, 2001), suggests that the accumulating evidence that racial and ethnic groups show variations in the expression of depression warrant continued investigation. Epidemiological studies require measures that can be administered to entire populations. The work by Perreira and colleagues (2005) shows that subsets of questions from existing measures can be developed that will serve these group comparison purposes. In concert with this "etic" approach, and consistent with our "universalistic" view that common psychological processes across groups may not show identical manifestations, the search for additional items particularly salient for certain groups may increase diagnostic precision and suggest fruitful avenues for culturally sensitive prevention and treatment efforts. In addition to the exploration of widely used measures, attempts have been made to develop and validate measures for specific groups. These may be useful when in-depth study of symptoms in a certain community, rather than cross-group comparison, is the goal. An example, developed in Singapore, is the Asian Adolescent Depression Scale (AADS) (Woo et al., 2004). Grounded in an "emic" perspective, this work underscores the importance of identifying "culture-specific" symptoms of Asian collectivist cultures as well as core symptoms of depression. Notably, the authors used a combination of qualitative and quantitative methods, a highly effective approach to construct development with culturally diverse communities (Knight & Hill, 1998).

CONCLUSION

Research cited in this chapter challenges researchers to question the validity of current ways of measuring the construct of depression for non-Western cultures as it has been defined for the dominant United States culture. Burgeoning evidence from research with immigrant, non-Western, and from ethnically and racially diverse samples illustrate the variability in symptomatology expression, meaning and coherence (e.g., Chen, Roberts, & Aday, 1998; Kleinman & Good, 1985; Tseng, 2001). In response to these critiques, an effort to establish measurement validity for non-Western samples is slowly emerging. Researchers must continue to find ways to identify the measurement universality of depression while maintaining enough conceptual flexibility to account for the apparent differences in expressions of depression that are culturally determined. In the meantime, measures such as Perreira et al.'s (2005) five-item CES-D, shown to be equivalent across several cultural groups, encourages our belief that depression involves a universal underlying process with cultural variations is what we are dealing with. This measure and others like it to be constructed should be used when group comparisons are intended. Additionally, the convergence of such measures, proven to be effective across groups, can also be a valuable tool in efforts to determine the validity of other measures of depression symptoms.

Our review has highlighted several emerging developments in this area of research that must be encouraged and fostered. Along with the pursuit of sound measures, we then need to be thoughtful about to whom we administer them. Youth should be offered the chance to define themselves with regard to both race and ethnicity. We encourage researchers to include measures of racial and ethnic identity when they study youth from diverse backgrounds, so that they learn not only what group(s) youth belong to, but how they feel about being members of those groups as well. Mounting large well-defined samples with the statistical power to explore group differences is, of course, of paramount importance. We want to also emphasize that findings from small, culturally well-defined samples explored with both qualitative and quantitative methods can also be very revealing.

The same deliberateness needs to be applied to measuring SES, which must be further explored as a means for clarifying differences in rates of depression within and between racial and ethnic groups. Given the extent to which indices of status vary across racial groups, it is unlikely that statistical controls lead to groups truly equal in human, social, and economic resources. Thus "controlling" for SES is of as limited utility as is "controlling" for race and ethnicity. Further, we must be thoughtful about what aspects of status we believe are relevant to our research hypotheses (e.g., what about parental education level do we believe will differentiate status groups), and then measure those aspects as carefully as we can. Ideally, this will include collecting SES data from sources in addition to youth themselves. Multilevel designs are also important here to distinguish individual and familial variables from larger contextual factors (e.g., Wight et al., 2005), distinctions important to define and understand for the design of appropriate interventions. The one clear conclusion in this area is that ignoring SES is not an option, given its omnipresence in defining the lives of different racial and ethnic groups.

The search for risk and protective factors is another area where sound cultural knowledge will be valuable. Much more research is needed on what dimensions of competence should be promoted to increase the resilience of given groups and which risk factors are most important to target for each group. A one-size-fits-all approach will serve us only if we dilute our efforts to the lowest common denominator. Programs with core, universal elements and culturally specific add-ons are likely to meet diverse group needs more meaningfully.

Improving research on depression among sociodemographically diverse youth requires careful thought about every stage of the research process, from capturing how youth define themselves, to interpreting and understanding the implications of differences that might be found. Paramount to success with this work is the willingness and ability to question every assumption we make when choosing, administering, and analyzing responses to measures, and the willingness to confirm the validity and reliability of measures' results through use of current more sophisticated methods, such as Item-Response Theory and Confirmatory Factor Analysis (Meade & Lautenschlager, 2004). These must be combined with a willingness to become deeply knowledgeable about any cultural group one decides to work with, through continued professional development as well as through collaboration with knowledgeable colleagues and the communities we work in. Closing the pronounced disparities in rates of mental health problems and access to necessary care requires (HHS, 2001) nothing less.

REFERENCES

Aboud, F. (1987). The development of ethnic self-identification and attitudes. In J. S. Phinney & M. J. Rotheram (Eds.), *Children's ethnic socialization – pluralism and development* (pp. 32–55). Newbury Park, CA: Sage.

Achenbach, T. (1991). *Manual for the youth self-report and 1991 profile.* Burlington, VT: University of Vermont.

Achenbach, T., Bird, H. R., Canino, G., Phares, V. Gould, M. S., & Rubio-Stipec, M. (1990). Epidemiological comparisons of Puerto Rican and U.S. mainland children: Parent, teacher, and self-reports. *Journal of the American Academy of Child & Adolescent Psychiatry, 29*(1), 84–93.

Achenbach, T., Hensley, V. R., Phares, V. G., & Grayson, D. (1990). Problems and competencies reported by parents of Australian and American children. *Journal of Child Psychology and Psychiatry, 31*(2), 265–286.

Akbar, M., Chambers, J. W., & Thompson, V. L. S. (2001). Racial identity, Africentric values, and self-esteem in Jamaican children. *Journal of Black Psychology, 27*(3), 341–358.

Allen, L., Astuto, J., & Aber, L. (in preparation). Developmental trajectory of depressive symptoms in urban youth.

Allen, L., Bat-Chava, Y., Aber, J. L., & Seidman, E. (2005). Adolescent racial and ethnic identity in context. In G. Downey, J. Eccles & C. Chatman (Eds.), *Navigating the future: Social identity, coping, and life tasks* (pp. 143–166). New York: Russell Sage Foundation.

American Psychological Association. (2003). Guidelines on multicultural education, training, research, practice, and organizational change for psychologists. *American Psychologist, 58*(5), 377–402.

Andrade, N. N., Hishinuma, E. S., McDermott, J. F., Johnson, R. C., Goebert, D. A., Makini, G. K., et al. (2006). The national center on indigenous Hawaiian behavioral health study of prevalence of psychiatric disorders in Native Hawaiian adolescents. *Journal of the American Academy of Child & Adolescent Psychiatry, 45*(1), 26–36.

Aneshensel, C. S., & Sucoff, C. A. (1996). The neighborhood context of adolescent mental health. *Journal of Health and Social Behavior, 37*(4), 293–310.

Angold, A., & Costello, E. J. (2001). The epidemiology of depression in children and adolescents. In I. M. Goodyer (Ed.), *The depressed child and adolescent* (pp. 143–178). UK: Cambridge University Press.

Ashmore, R. D., Deaux, K., & McLaughlin-Volpe, T. (2004). An organizing framework for collective identity: Articulation and significance of multidimensionality. *Psychological Bulletin, 130*(1), 80–114.

Beardslee, W. R., Versage, E. M., & Gladstone, T. R. G. (1998). Children of affectively ill parents: A review of the past 10 years. *Journal of the American Academy of Child & Adolescent Psychiatry, 37*(11), 1134–1141.

Beck, A. T., Ward, C. H., Mendelson, M., Mock, J., & Erbaugh, J. (1961). An inventory for measuring depression. *Archives of General Psychiatry, 4*, 561–571.

Beiser, M., & Attneave, C. M. (1982). Mental disorders among Native American children: Rate and risk periods for entering treatment. *American Journal of Psychiatry, 139*, 193–198.

Berry, J. W. (1997). Immigration, acculturation, and adaptation. *Applied Psychology: An International Review, 46*(1), 5–34.

Berry, J. W., Poortinga, Y. H., Segall, M. H., & Dasen, P. R. (1992). *Cross-cultural psychology: Research and applications* (2nd ed.). New York: Cambridge University Press.

Bradley, R. H., & Corwyn, R. F. (2002). Socioeconomic status and child development. *Annual Review of Psychology, 53*(1), 371–399.

Braveman, P. A., Cubbin, C., Egerter, S., Chideya, S., Marchi, K. S., Metzler, M., et al. (2005). Socioeconomic status in health research: One size does not fit all. *Journal of the American Medical Association, 294*(22), 2879–2888.

Brindis, C., Park, M. J., Paul, T., & Burg, S. (2002). A profile of adolescent health: The role of race, ethnicity and gender. *Journal of Ethnic and Cultural Diversity in Social Work, 11*(1–2), 1–32.

Brooks, T. L., Harris, S. K., Thrall, J. S., & Woods, E. R. (2002). Association of adolescent risk behaviors with mental health symptoms in high school students. *Journal of Adolescent Health, 31*(3), 240–246.

Carlton, B. S., Goebert, D. A., Miyamoto, R. H., Andrade, N. N., Hishinuma, E. S., Makini, G. K., et al. (2006). Resilience, family adversity and well-being among Hawaiian and non-Hawaiian adolescents. *International Journal of Social Psychiatry, 52*(4), 291–308.

Casey-Cannon, S., Pasch, L. A., Tschann, J. M., & Flores, E. (2006). Non-parent adult social support and depressive symptoms among Mexican American and European American adolescents. *The Journal of Early Adolescence, 26*(3), 318–343.

Cauce, A. M., Ryan, K. D., & Grove, K. (1998). Children and adolescents of color, where are you? Participation, selection, recruitment, and retention in developmental research. In V. C. McLoyd & L. Steinberg (Eds.), *Studying minority adolescents* (pp. 147–156). Mahwah, NJ: Lawrence Erlbaum Associates.

Chen, I. G., Roberts, R. E., & Aday, L. A. (1998). Ethnicity and adolescent depression: The case of Chinese Americans. *Journal of Nervous and Mental Disease, 186*(10), 623–630.

Chen, S. X., Chan, W., Bond, M. H., & Stewart, S. M. (2006). The effects of self-efficacy and relationship harmony on depression across cultures: Applying level-oriented and structure-oriented analyses. *Journal of Cross-Cultural Psychology, 37*(6), 643–658.

Choi, H., Stafford, L., Meininger, J. C., Roberts, R. E., & Smith, D. P. (2002). Psychometric properties of the DSM scale for depression (DSD) with Korean-American youths. *Issues in Mental Health Nursing, 23*(8), 735–756.

Clark, R., Anderson, N. B., Clark, V. R., & Williams, D. R. (1999). Racism as a stressor for African Americans. *American Psychologist, 54*(10), 805–816.

Clements, M. (2004). Negative life events, daily hassles, and the development of depressive symptoms: A longitudinal study of urban adolescents (Doctoral dissertation, New York University). *Dissertation Abstracts International: Section B: The Sciences and Engineering, 64*(9-B), 4651.

Cole, D. A., Hoffman, K., Tram, J. M., & Maxwell, S. E. (2000). Structural differences in parent and reports of children's symptoms of depression and anxiety. *Psychological Assessment, 12*(2), 174–185.

Cole, J. C., Motivala, S. J., Dang, J., Lucko, A., Lang, N., Levin, M. J., et al. (2004). Structural validation of the Hamilton depression rating scale. *Journal of Psychopathology and Behavioral Assessment, 26*(4), 241–254.

Coleman, J. S. (1988). Social capital in the creation of human capital. *The American Journal of Sociology, 94*, 95–120.

Compas, B. E., Howell, D. C., Phares, V., Williams, R. A., & Giunta, C. T. (1989). Parent and child stress and symptoms: An integrative analysis. *Developmental Psychology, 25*(4), 550–559.

Craighead, W. E., Smucker, M. R., Craighead, L. W., & Ilardi, S. S. (1998). Factor analysis of the Children's Depression Inventory in a community sample. *Psychological Assessment, 10*(2), 156–165.

Crockett, L. J., Randall, B. A., Shen, Y.-L., Russell, S. T., & Driscoll, A. K. (2005). Measurement equivalence of the center for epidemiological studies depression scale for Latino and Anglo adolescents: A national study. *Journal of Consulting and Clinical Psychology, 73*(1), 47–58.

de Groot, A., Koot, H. M., & Velhulst, F. C. (1996). Cross-cultural generalizability of the Youth Self-Report and Teacher's Report Form cross-informant syndromes. *Journal of Abnormal Psychology, 24*(5), 651–664.

del Barrio, V., Frías, D., & Mestre, V. (1994). Autoestima y depresión en niños [Self-esteem and depression in children]. *Revista de Psicología General y Aplicada, 47*(4), 471–476.

Demaray, M. K., & Malecki, C. K. (2002). Critical levels of perceived social support associated with student adjustment. *School Psychology Quarterly, 17*(3), 213–241.

Dmitrieva, J., Chen, C., Greenberger, E., & Gil-Rivas, V. (2004). Family relationships and adolescent psychosocial outcomes: Converging findings from Eastern and Western cultures. *Journal of Research on Adolescence, 14*(4), 425–447.

Doi, Y., Roberts, R. E., Takeuchi, K., & Suzuki, S. (2001). Multiethnic comparison of adolescent major depression based on the DSM-IV criteria in a U.S.–Japan study. *Journal of the American Academy of Child & Adolescent Psychiatry, 40*(11), 1308–1315.

Dornbusch, S. M., Mont-Reynaud, R., Ritter, P. L., Chen, Z., & Steinberg, L. (1991). Stressful events and their correlates among adolescents of diverse backgrounds. In M. E. Colton & S. Gore (Eds.), *Adolescent stress: Causes and consequences* (pp. 111–130). Hawthorne, NY: Aldine de Gruyter.

Doucette-Gates, A., Brooks-Gunn, J., & Chase-Lansdale, L. P. (1998). The role of bias and equivalence in the study of race, class, and ethnicity. In V. C. McLoyd & L. Steinberg (Eds.), *Studying minority adolescents: Conceptual, methodological, and theoretical issues* (pp. 211–236). Mahwah, NJ: Lawrence Erlbaum Associates.

DSM-IV (1994). *Diagnostic and statistical manual of mental disorders* (4th ed.). Washington, DC: American Psychiatric Association.

Emslie, G. J., Weinberg, W. A., Rush, A. J., Adams, R. M., & Rintelmann, J. W. (1990). Depressive symptoms by self-report in adolescence: Phase I of the development of a questionnaire for depression by self-report. *Journal of Child Neurology, 5*(2), 114–121.

Fleming, J. E., & Offord, D. R. (1990). Epidemiology of childhood depressive disorders: A critical review. *Journal of the American Academy of Child & Adolescent Psychiatry, 29*(4), 571–580.

Franko, D. L., Striegel-Moore, R. H., Bean, J., Barton, B. A., Biro, F., Kraemer, H. C., et al. (2005). Self-reported symptoms of depression in late adolescence to early adulthood: A comparison of African-American and Caucasian females. *Journal of Adolescent Health, 37*(6), 526–529.

Franko, D. L., Striegel-Moore, R. H., Brown, K. M., Barton, B. A., McMahon, R. P., Schreiber, G. B., et al. (2004). Expanding our understanding of the relationship between negative life events and depressive symptoms in black and white adolescent girls. *Psychological Medicine, 34*(7), 1319–1330.

Garrison, C. Z., Addy, C. L., Jackson, K. L., McKeown, R. E., & Waller, J. L. (1992). Major depressive disorder and dysthymia in young adolescents. *American Journal of Epidemiology, 135*(7), 792–802.

Garrison, C. Z., Schluchter, M. D., Schoenbach, V. J., & Kaplan, B. K. (1989). Epidemiology of depressive symptoms in young adolescents. *Journal of the American Academy of Child & Adolescent Psychiatry, 28*(3), 343–351.

Gerard, J. M., & Buehler, C. (2004). Cumulative environmental risk and youth maladjustment: The role of youth attributes. *Child Development, 75*(6), 1832–1849.

Gonzales, N. A., Deardorff, J., Formoso, D., Barr, A., & Barrera, M. (2006). Family mediators of the relation between acculturation and adolescent mental health. *Family Relations, 55*(3), 318–330.

Goodman, E. (1999). The role of socioeconomic status gradients in explaining differences in US adolescents' health. *American Journal of Public Health, 89*(10), 1522–1528.

Goodman, E., Slap, G. B., & Huang, B. (2003). The public health impact of socioeconomic status on adolescent depression and obesity. *American Journal of Public Health, 93*(11), 1844–1850.

Grant, K. E., Katz, B. N., Thomas, K. J., O'Koon, J. H., Meza, C. M., & DiPasquale, A., et al. (2004a). Psychological symptoms affecting low-income urban youth. *Journal of Adolescent Research, 19*(6), 613–634.

Grant, K. E., Lyons, A. L., Finkelstein, J. S., Conway, K. M., Reynolds, L. K., O'Koon, J. H., et al. (2004b). Gender differences in rates of depressive symptoms among low-income, urban, African American youth: A test of two mediational hypotheses. *Journal of Youth and Adolescence, 33*(6), 523–533.

Gray-Little, B., & Hafdahl, A. R. (2000). Factors influencing racial comparisons of self-esteem: A quantitative review. *Psychological Bulletin, 126*(1), 26–54.

Guerrero, A. P. S., Hishinuma, E. S., Andrade, N. N., Nishimura, S. T., & Cunanan, V. L. (2006). Correlations among socioeconomic and family factors and academic, behavioral, and emotional difficulties in Filipino adolescents in Hawaii. *International Journal of Social Psychiatry, 52*(4), 343–359.

Guiao, I., & Thompson, E. A. (2004). Ethnicity and problem behaviors among adolescent females in the United States. *Health Care for Women International, 25*(4), 296–310.

Hales, D. P., Dishman, R. K., Motl, R. W., Addy, C. L., Pfeiffer, K. A., & Pate, R. R. (2006). Factorial validity and invariance of the Center for Epidemiologic Studies Depression (CES-D) scale in a sample of black and white adolescent girls. *Ethnicity & Disease, 16*(1), 1–8.

Hayward, C., & Sanborn, K. (2002). Puberty and the emergence of gender differences in psychopathology. *Journal of Adolescent Health, 30*(4), 49–58.

Hishinuma, E. S., Johnson, R. C., Carlton, B. S., Andrade, N. N., Nishimura, S. T., Goebert, D. A., et al. (2004). Demographic and social variables associated with psychiatric and school-related indicators for Asian/Pacific-Islander adolescents. *International Journal of Social Psychiatry, 50*(4), 301–318.

Hollingshead, A. B. (1975). *Four factor index of social status.* New Haven, CN: Yale University.

Holmes, S. (2001, June 3). The nation: True colors; the confusion over who we are. *The New York Times,* Weekend Review.

Katragadda, C. P., & Tidwell, R. (1998). Rural Hispanic adolescents at risk for depressive symptoms. *Journal of Applied Social Psychology, 28*(20), 1916–1930.

Kendler, K. S., Karkowski, L. M., & Prescott, C. A. (1999). Causal relationship between stressful life events and the onset of major depression. *American Journal of Psychiatry, 156*(6), 837–848.

Kleinfeld, J., & Bloom, L. D. (1977). Boarding schools: Effects on the mental health of Eskimo adolescents. *American Journal of Psychiatry, 134*, 411–417.

Kleinman, A., & Good, B. J. (1985). *Culture and anxiety: Cross-cultural evidence for the patterning of anxiety disorder.* Hillsdale, NJ: Lawrence Erlbaum Associates.

Knight, G. P., & Hill, N. E. (1998). Measurement equivalence in research involving minority adolescents. In V. C. McLoyd & L. Steinberg (Eds.), *Studying minority adolescence* (pp. 183–210). Mahwah, HJ: Lawrence Erlbaum Associates.

Kovacs, M. (1985). The children's depression inventory. *Psychopharmacology Bulletin, 21*, 995–998.

Kubik, M. Y., Lytle, L. A., Birnbaum, A. S., Murray, D. M., & Perry, C. L. (2003). Prevalence and correlates of depressive symptoms in young adolescents. *American Journal of Health Behavior, 27*(5), 546–553.

La Greca, A. M., & Harrison, H. M. (2005). Adolescent peer relations, friendships, and romantic relationships: Do they predict social anxiety and depression? *Journal of Clinical Child and Adolescent Psychology, 34*(1), 49–61.

Lewontin, R. C. (1972). The apportionment of human diversity. *Evolutionary Biology, 6*, 381–398.
Luthar, S. S., & D'Avanzo, K. (1999). Contextual factors in substance use: A study of suburban and inner-city adolescents. *Development and Psychopathology. Special Issue: Developmental Approaches to Substance Use and Abuse, 11*(4), 845–867.
Luthar, S. S., & Zigler, E. (1991). Vulnerability and competence: A review of research on resilience in childhood. *American Journal of Orthopsychiatry, 61*(1), 6–22.
Maag, J. W., & Irvin, D. M. (2005). Alcohol use and depression among African-American and Caucasian adolescents. *Adolescence, 40*(157), 87–101.
Malgady, R. G., Rogler, L. H., & Constantino, G. (1990). Culturally sensitive psychotherapy for Puerto Rican children and adolescents: A program of treatment outcome research. *Journal of Consulting and Clinical Psychology, 58*(6), 704–712.
Manson, S. M., Ackerson, L. M., Dick, R. W., Baron, A. E., & Fleming, C. M. (1990). Depressive symptoms among American Indian adolescents: Psychometric characteristics of the Center of Epidemiologic Studies Depression Scale (CES-D). *Psychological Assessment, 2*, 231–237.
Masten, A. S., Best, K. M., & Garmezy, N. (1990). Resilience and development: Contributions from the study of children who overcome adversity. *Development and Psychopathology, 2*(4), 425–444.
Mcleod, J. D., & Owens, T. J. (2004). Psychological well-being in the early life course: Variations by socioeconomic status, gender, and race/ethnicity. *Social Psychology Quarterly, 67*(3), 257–278.
Meade, A. W., & Lautenschlager, G. J. (2004). A comparison of item response theory and confirmatory factor analytic methodologies for establishing measurement equivalence/invariance. *Organizational Research Methods, 7*(4), 361–388.
Nettles, S. M., & Pleck, J. H. (1994). Stress, risk, resilience, and development: The multiple ecologies of black adolescents in the United States. In L. R. Haggerty, N. Sherrod, N. Garmezy & M. Rutter. (Eds.), *Risk and resilience in children and adolescents: Processes, mechanisms, and interventions* (pp. 147–181). New York: Cambridge University Press.
Nolen-Hoeksema, S., & Girgus, J. S. (1994). The emergence of gender differences in depression during adolescence. *Psychological Bulletin, 115*(3), 424–443.
Ocampo, K. A., Bernal, M. E., & Knight, G. P. (1993). Gender, race, and ethnicity: The sequencing of social constancies. In M. Bernal & G. P. Knight (Eds.), *Ethnic identity: Formation and transmission among Hispanics and other minorities* (pp. 11–30). Albany, NY: State University of New York Press.
Oppedal, B., & Roysamb, E. (2004). Mental health, life stress and social support among young Norwegian adolescents with immigrant and host national background. *Scandinavian Journal of Psychology, 45*(2), 131–144.
Organista, P. B., Organista, K. C., & Kurasaki, K. (2002). The relationship between acculturation and ethnic minority mental health. In K. M. Chun, P. B. Organista & G. Marin (Eds.), *Acculturation: Advances in theory, measurement, and applied research* (pp. 139–162). Washington, DC: American Psychological Association.

Perreira, K. M., Deeb-Sossa, N., Harris, K. M., & Bollen, K. (2005). What are we measuring? An evaluation of the CES-D across race/ethnicity and immigrant generation. *Social Forces, 83*(4), 1567–1602.
Petersen, A. C., Compas, B. E., Brooks-Gunn, J., Stemmler, M., Ey, S., & Grant, K. E. (1993). Depression in adolescence. *American Psychologist, 48*(2), 155–168.
Peterson, W. (1987). Politics and the measurement of ethnicity. In W. Alonso & P. Starr (Eds.), *The politics of numbers* (pp. 187–233). New York: Russell Sage Foundations.
Phinney, J. S. (1992). The multigroup ethnic identity measure: A new scale for use with diverse groups. *Journal of Adolescent Research, 7*(2), 156–176.
Prescott, C. A., McArdle, J. J., Hishinuma, E. S., Johnson, R. C., Miyamoto, R. H., Andrade, N. N., et al. (1998). Prediction of major depression and dysthmia from CES-D scores among ethnic minority adolescents. *Journal of the American Academy of Child & Adolescent Psychiatry, 37*(5), 495–503.
Radloff, L. S. (1977). A self-report depression scale for research in the general population. *Applied Psychological Measurements, 1*(3), 385–401.
Ramos, B., Jaccard, J., & Guilamo-Ramos, V. (2003). Dual ethnicity and depressive symptoms: Implications of being Black and Latino in the United States. *Hispanic Journal of Behavioral Sciences, 25*(2), 147–173.
Reinherz, H. Z., Tanner, J. L., Paradis, A. D., Beardslee, W. R., Szigethy, E. M., & Bond, A. E. (2006). Child and adolescent psychopathology: Theoretical and clinical implications. In C. A. Essau (Ed.), *Depressive disorders* (pp. 113–139). New York: Routledge/Taylor & Francis Group.
Repetto, P. B., Caldwell, C. H., & Zimmerman, M. A. (2004). Trajectories of depressive symptoms among high risk African-American adolescents. *Journal of Adolescent Health, 35*(6), 468–477.
Reynolds, W. M., Anderson, G., & Bartell, N. (1985). Measuring depression in children: A multimethod assessment investigation. *Journal of Abnormal Child Psychology, 13*(4), 513–526.
Rice, A., Ruiz, R., & Padilla, A. (1974). Person, perception, self-identity, and ethnic group preference in Anglo, black, and Chicano pre-school and third grade children. *Journal of Cross-Cultural Psychology, 5*, 100–108.
Roberts, R. E., & Chen, Y. (1995). Depressive symptoms and suicidal ideation among Mexican-origin and Anglo adolescents. *Journal of the American Academy of Child & Adolescent Psychiatry, 34*(1), 81–90.
Roberts, R. E., Roberts, C. R., & Chen, Y. R. (1997). Ethnocultural differences in prevalence of adolescent depression. *American Journal of Community Psychology, 25*(1), 95–110.
Roberts, R. E., & Sobhan, M. (1992). Symptoms of depression in adolescence: A comparison of Anglo, African, and Hispanic Americans. *Journal of Youth and Adolescence, 21*(6), 639–651.
Ruchkin, V., Sukhodolsky, D. G., Vermeiren, R., Koposov, R. A., & Schwab-Stone, M. (2006). Depressive symptoms and associated psychopathology in urban adolescents: A cross-cultural study of three countries. *Journal of Nervous and Mental Disease, 194*(2), 106–113.
Rushton, J. L., Forcier, M., & Schectman, R. M. (2002). Epidemiology of depressive symptoms in the National Longitudinal Study of Adolescent Health. *Journal of the American Academy of Child & Adolescent Psychiatry, 41*(2), 199–205.

Russell, K. Y., Wilson, M., & Hall, R. E. (1992). *The color complex: The politics of skin color among African Americans.* San Diego, CA: Harcourt Brace Jovanovich.
Rutter, M., & Tienda, M. (2005). *Ethnicity and causal mechanisms.* Cambridge: Cambridge University Press.
Saluja, G., Iachan, R., Scheidt, P. C., Overpeck, M. D., Sun, W., & Giedd, J. N. (2004). Prevalence of and risk factors for depressive symptoms among young adolescents. *Archives of Pediatrics and Adolescent Medicine, 158*(8), 760–765.
Sam, D. L. (1994). The psychological adjustment of young immigrants in Norway. *Scandinavian Journal of Psychology, 35*(3), 240–253.
Schraedley, P. K., Gotlib, I. H., & Hayward, C. (1999). Gender differences in correlates of depressive symptoms in adolescents. *Journal of Adolescent Health, 25*(2), 98–108.
Seidman, E. (1991). Growing up the hard way: Pathways of urban adolescents. *American Journal of Community Psychology, 19*(2), 173–205.
Sen, B. (2004). Adolescent propensity for depressed mood and help seeking: Race and gender differences. *Journal of Mental Health Policy and Economics, 7*(3), 133–145.
Siegel, J. M. (2002). Body image change and adolescent depressive symptoms. *Journal of Adolescent Research, 17*(1), 27–41.
Siegel, J. M., Aneshensel, C. S., Taub, B., Cantwell, D. P., & Driscoll, A. K. (1998). Adolescent depressed mood in a multiethnic sample. *Journal of Youth and Adolescence, 27*(4), 413–427.
Smith, E. P., & Brookins, C. C. (1997). Towards the development of an ethnic identity measure for African American youth. *Journal of Black Psychology, 23*(4), 358–377.
Steele, C. M., & Aronson, J. (1995). Stereotype threat and the intellectual test performance of African Americans. *Journal of Personality and Social Psychology, 69*(5), 797–811.
Steele, R. G., Little, T. D., Ilardi, S. S., Forehand, R., Brody, G. H., & Hunter, H. L. (2006). A confirmatory comparison of factor structure of the Children's Depression Inventory between European American and African American youth. *Journal of Child and Family Studies, 15*, 773–788.
Stewart, S. M., Byrne, B. M., Lee, P. W. H., Ho, L. M., Kennard, B. D., Hughes, C. W., et al. (2003). Personal versus interpersonal contributions to depressive symptoms among Hong Kong adolescents. *International Journal of Psychology, 38*(3), 160–169.
Stewart, S. M., Lewinsohn, P. M., Lee, P. W. H., Ho, L. M., Kennard, B. D., Hughes, C. W., et al. (2002). Symptom patterns in depression and "subthreshold" depression among adolescents in Hong Kong and the United States. *Journal of Cross-Cultural Psychology, 33*(6), 559–576.
Tanaka-Matsumi, J., & Draguns, J. G. (1997). *Culture and psychopathology – Handbook of cross-cultural psychology.* Boston, MA: Allyn and Bacon.
Tseng, W. (2001). *Handbook of cultural psychiatry.* San Diego, CA: Academic Press.
Twenge, J. M., & Nolen-Hoeksema, S. (2002). Age, gender, race, socioeconomic status, and birth cohort differences on the Children's Depression Inventory: A meta-analysis. *Journal of Abnormal Psychology, 111*(4), 578–588.

U.S. Census Beureau. (2000). *American FactFinder.* Retrieved May 31, 2007, from the World Wide Web: http://factfinder.census.gov.

U.S. Department of Commerce, Economics and Statistics Administration & Bureau of the Census. (1996). *Current population reports: Population projections of the United States by age, sex, race, and Hispanic origin: 1995–2050.* Washington, DC: U.S. Government Printing Office.

U.S. Department of Health and Human Services. (2001). *Mental health: Culture, race, and ethnicity: A supplement to mental health: A report of the Surgeon General.* Rockville, MD: U.S. Public Health Service.

Walter, R., Remschmidt, H., & Deimel, W. (1994). Gütekriterien und Normierung einer deutschen Version des Youth Self-Report [Reliability and validity of a German version of the Youth Self-Report]. *Zeitschrift für Kinder– und Jugendpsychiatrie, 22*(1), 23–38.

Waters, M. C. (1990). *Ethnic options: Choosing identities in America.* Berkeley, CA: University of California Press.

Weinberg, W. A., & Emslie, G. J. (1998). Weinberg Screening Affective Scales (WSAS and WSAS-SF). *Journal of Child Neurology, 3*(4), 294–296.

Wight, R. G., Aneshensel, C. S., Botticello, A. L., & Sepúlveda, J. E. (2005). A multilevel analysis of ethnic variation in depressive symptoms among adolescents in the United States. *Social Science and Medicine, 60*(9), 2073–2084.

Williams, J. K. Y., Else, I. R. N., Hishinuma, E. S., Goebert, D. A., Chang, J. Y., Andrade, N. N., et al. (2005). A confirmatory model for depression among Japanese American and part-Japanese American adolescents. *Cultural Diversity and Ethnic Minority Psychology, 11*(1), 41–56.

Wong, S. L. (2001). Depression level in inner-city Asian American adolescents: The contributions of cultural orientation and interpersonal relationships. *Journal of Human Behavior in the Social Environment, 3*(3–4), 49–64.

Woo, B. S. C., Chang, W. C., Fung, D. S. S., Koh, J. B. K., Leong, J. S. F., Kee, C. H. Y., et al. (2004). Development and validation of a depression scale for Asian adolescents. *Journal of Adolescence, 27*(6), 677–689.

Yasui, M., Dorham, C. L., & Dishion, T. J. (2004). Ethnic identity and psychological adjustment: A validity analysis for European American and African American adolescents. *Journal of Adolescent Research, 19*(6), 807–825.

Yeung, A., Chan, R., Mischoulon, D., Sonawalla, S., Wong, E., Nierenberg, A. A., et al. (2004). Prevalence of major depressive disorder among Chinese-Americans in primary care. *General Hospital Psychiatry, 26*(1), 24–30.

Zane, N., & Mak, W. (2002). Major approaches to the measurements of acculturation among ethnic minority populations: A content analysis and an alternative empirical strategy. In K. M. Chun, P. B. Organista & G. Marin (Eds.), *Acculturation: Advances in theory, measurement, and applied research* (pp. 39–60). Washington, DC: American Psychological Association.

Chapter Five

The Emergence of Gender Differences in Depression in Adolescence

LORI M. HILT AND SUSAN NOLEN-HOEKSEMA

CONTENTS

During adolescence, there is a remarkable shift in the relative risk of depression in girls and boys. Prior to about the age of 13, girls and boys have fairly equal levels of depressive symptoms and rates of depressive disorders. Between ages 13 and 15, girls' rates of symptoms and disorders rise precipitously, while boys' rates remain relatively stable (Galambos, Leadbeater, & Barker, 2004; Twenge & Nolen-Hoeksema, 2002). By early adulthood, women are twice as likely as men to suffer depression. Several biological and psychosocial factors have been identified that may help to explain this gender difference.

We propose an integrated bio-psycho-social model to account for the greater prevalence of depression among girls beginning in adolescence (see Figure 5.1). According to this model, adolescents most at risk for developing depression in

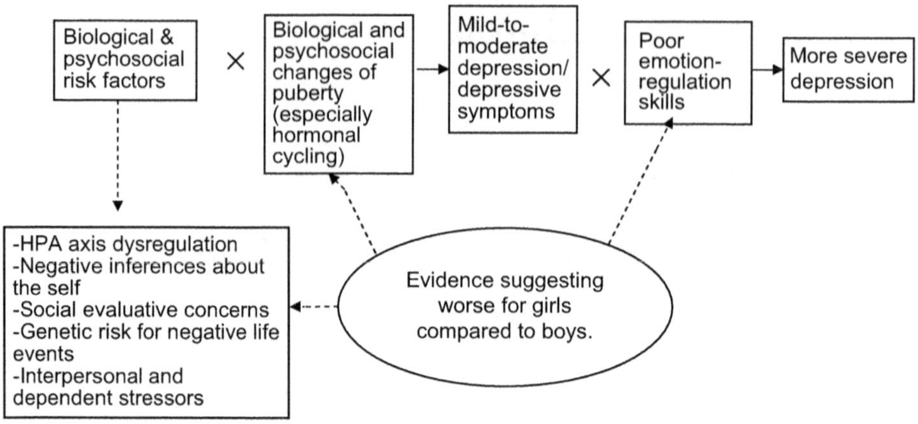

Figure 5.1 Bio-psycho-social model of the development of depression in adolescents.

early adolescence carry genetic risk factors for the disorder, including certain alleles for the brain-derived neurotrophic factor (BDNF) and serotonin transporter genes. In addition, they carry certain other neurobiological risk factors including hypothalamic-pituitary axis dysregulation. They also carry certain psychosocial risk factors, including negative cognitive styles and difficulty in social relationships. Although boys and girls have many similar risk factors, some are more common among girls. Additionally, these biological and psychosocial risk factors interact with the neurobiological and psychosocial changes associated with puberty to trigger increases in depressive symptoms. Girls become more distressed from these changes, which contributes to higher symptoms in adolescent girls compared to boys. These depressive symptoms, which may be mild-to-moderate initially, are amplified and prolonged in adolescents with poor emotion-regulation skills. Further, girls are more likely to engage in maladaptive emotion-regulation strategies that may result in depression. As a result, these initially mild depressive symptoms grow into more severe symptoms and depressive disorders.

In this chapter, we first review the research on gender differences in adolescent depressive symptoms and disorders. Next, we describe some of the biological and psychoscocial changes of puberty that serve as a backdrop or trigger for potential risk factors and highlight how these changes may be more difficult for girls. In the next section, we discuss putative biological and psychosocial risk factors that may be triggered in puberty resulting in depressive symptoms, and review which factors are more common among girls and boys. In the final section, we describe how emotion-regulation skills may exacerbate existing symptoms, resulting in more severe depression. We end by suggesting which parts of this model are in need of empirical support and how intervention programs may be informed by testing of this model.

EPIDEMIOLOGICAL DIFFERENCES

Diagnostic Differences

There is ample evidence for gender differences in depressive disorders in adolescence. A recent longitudinal study of 12- to 19-year-olds found that girls experienced more major depressive episodes (MDEs) than boys at each wave of the study, with a median ratio of 2:1; furthermore, one in five girls and one in ten boys experienced a probable MDE during the study (Galambos et al., 2004). A recent meta-analysis also found a higher prevalence of depression among 13- to 18-year-old adolescent girls (5.9%) compared to boys (4.6%) (Costello, Erkanli, & Angold, 2006). Additionally, a longitudinal birth-cohort study found a gender difference in MDEs with girls having higher rates beginning at age 13 and the difference becoming more pronounced by age 15 (Hankin et al., 1998). Therefore, it appears that the gender difference in depression diagnosis emerges between ages 12 and 15.

Some studies have examined whether the gender difference in depression diagnosis is due to girls experiencing more first onsets or more recurrence of depression. One longitudinal study of high school students found that girls with major depressive disorder (MDD) were more likely than boys to experience recurrence in childhood or adolescence (Lewinsohn, Pettit, Joiner, & Seeley, 2003). However, another longitudinal study failed to find a gender difference in recurrence of depression, and instead found that girls experienced significantly more first onsets of depression than boys during adolescence (Hankin et al., 1998). Similarly, a study of 11- to 17-year-olds with MDD did not find a gender difference in risk of recurrent episodes (Kovacs, 2001). This pattern fits patterns found in studies of adult gender differences in depression. Data from three large epidemiological studies conducted in the United States suggest that the adult gender difference is primarily due to a greater number of first onsets of depression in women than men, and not to gender differences in the duration or recurrence of depression (Eaton et al., 1997; Keller & Shapiro, 1981; Kessler, McGonagle, Swartz, Blazer, & Nelson, 1993).

Levels and Types of Symptoms

Multiple studies have found higher symptom levels of depression among girls compared to boys during adolescence, although the age at which this gender difference first emerges has varied by study. In their meta-analysis of studies using the Children's Depression Inventory (CDI; Kovacs, 1980/1981, 1992), Twenge and Nolen-Hoeksema (2002) found that boys' depression scores were slightly higher than girls' in childhood, but beginning at age 13, girls scored higher while boys stayed relatively the same. In a recent study of 12- to 19-year-olds, girls had higher depressive symptoms across all time points, suggesting that the gender difference was already present at baseline, i.e., age 12 (Galambos et al., 2004). A longitudinal study of 9- to 17-year-olds found that the gender difference emerged after age 13 (Ge, Lorenz, Conger, Elder, & Simons, 1994). Finally, a longitudinal birth-cohort study examining the number of depressive symptoms endorsed during a clinical interview by participants ages 11–21 found trend level differences in the number of symptoms at age 15 only (Hankin et al., 1998). It appears that the gender difference in symptom level emerges sometime between 12 and 15.

In addition to gender differences in overall symptom level during adolescence, some studies have investigated potential differences in symptom severity among those diagnosed with MDD. For example, a study of high school students with MDD found that adolescent girls had slightly more depressive symptoms than adolescent boys during a first depressive episode (7.0 vs. 6.7; Lewinsohn et al., 2003). Another recent study of 11- to 20-year-olds with MDD also found that girls had higher symptom severity compared to boys using two different measures of depressive symptoms (Bennett, Ambrosini, Kudes, Metz, & Rabinovich, 2005). However, at least two studies of adolescents with MDD did not find evidence for gender differences in symptom severity based on number of symptoms endorsed during a clinical interview (Hankin et al., 1998; Kovacs, 2001).

A few studies have also examined whether there are gender differences in the specific symptoms experienced by adolescents with depression. Lewinsohn et al. (2003) found that adolescent girls had more weight and appetite symptoms (i.e., weight loss and gain and increased appetite) compared to adolescent boys. In another study of adolescents with MDD, girls were found to have the symptoms of excessive guilt and concentration problems more often than boys who were found to have more morning fatigue and psychomotor retardation than girls (Bennett et al., 2005). Both of these studies found very few differences in symptom presentation between adolescent boys and girls with MDD, suggesting that they are more similar than different in this domain. Another study found no gender differences in symptom profiles among a sample of 8- to 13-year-olds (Sorensen, Nissen, Mors, & Thomsen, 2005).

In sum, there is a reliable gender difference in symptom and diagnosis rates, with more adolescent girls experiencing depression compared to boys. The age at which this gender difference first emerges seems to be between ages 12 and 15. Evidence regarding whether or not adolescent girls with MDD experience greater severity of symptoms or more recurrence compared to adolescent boys is mixed. Finally, among those adolescents diagnosed with MDD, there appear to be more similarities in symptom profile than differences.

PUBERTAL CHANGES: TRIGGERS FOR RISK FACTORS

There are many neurobiological and morphological changes that accompany puberty (for an extended discussion, see Steinberg et al., 2006). Additionally, more advanced pubertal development is associated with more stress, at least for girls (Simon, Wardle, Jarvis, Steggles, & Cartwright, 2003). Because the gender difference in depression first emerges around age 12 or 13, we will first consider some of the biological and psychosocial changes that accompany puberty as factors that may interact with putative pre-existing risk factors. Following this section, we will detail the risk factors that may then interact with these pubertal changes to result in depressive symptomology.

Reproductive Hormones and Morphological Change

In a report on 1,073 US children 9 to 13 years of age, depression levels were significantly higher in girls at midpuberty, whereas boys' depression levels were not associated with pubertal stage (Angold, Costello, & Worthman, 1998). This study also found that pubertal status was a better predictor of the gender difference in diagnosis of depression than age (Angold et al., 1998), perhaps suggesting that morphological changes trigger depression for girls.

The morphological changes of puberty only grossly reflect the underlying endocrine changes (Buchanan, Eccles, & Becker, 1992; Nottelmann et al., 1987). There is some evidence of direct relationships between reproductive hormone levels and depressive symptoms in early adolescent girls (for reviews, see Angold & Worthman, 1993; Buchanan et al., 1992; Steiner, Dunn, & Born, 2003). The largest study of hormones and depressive symptoms to date has been the study by Angold and colleagues (Angold, Costello, Erkanli, & Worthman, 1999). In analyses of hormonal data from the 339 girls in this study, testosterone and estradiol levels (the main sex hormones, respectively) better accounted for increases in depressive symptoms in the girls than did pubertal stage or age (Angold et al., 1999).

Several other studies have found no relationship between pubertal stage, or hormonal levels, and mood in adolescent girls or boys (see Buchanan et al., 1992). For example, in a study of 103 girls, 10 to 14 years of age, Brooks-Gunn and Warren (1989) found no relationship between depressive symptom levels and any of five different reproductive hormones. In an analysis of follow-up data on 72 of these girls, Paikoff and colleagues found a positive linear relationship between levels of estradiol and one self-report measure of depressive symptoms, but estradiol levels were not significantly correlated with maternal reports of the girls' depressive symptom levels or with a second self-report measure of depressive symptoms (Paikoff, Brooks-Gunn, & Warren, 1991). Susman, Dorn, and Chrousos (1991) and Susman and colleagues (1987) found no significant relationship between hormone levels (including estradiol) and depressive symptoms in either early adolescent girls or boys. In a recent study of 100, 10 to 14-year-old girls, we did not find a significant correlation between estradiol serum levels and depressive symptoms from a clinical interview.

It may not be fruitful to examine simple correlations between hormone levels and depressive symptoms among adolescents. For example, estradiol levels fluctuate dramatically during different menstrual cycle phases (i.e., they are typically low during menstruation and begin to rise and peak during the follicular phase and then level off and drop through the luteal phase). Because adolescents often do not have regular cycles (ACOG; Committee on Adolescent Health Care, 2006) and because they may not be accurate reporters of when they last menstruated, data on estradiol levels may simply reflect the menstrual cycle phase a girl is in. If one wanted to examine whether estradiol levels predicted depressive symptoms, it would be important to standardize hormone data collection. For example, blood could be drawn from all participants 3 days after their last menses in order to have all girls in the same phase. For girls who have not started menstruating, this would not be possible; therefore, estradiol levels in premenstruating girls may simply reflect more advanced pubertal development. Rather than examine correlations, we suggest that estradiol should be examined with respect to functioning of neurotransmitter systems and the hypothalamic-pituitary-adrenal (HPA) axis. It is the changes in these systems (which may be triggered by surges and cycling of hormones) that ultimately tip the scale to result in depressive symptoms in adolescent girls.

Psychosocial Aspects of Pubertal Changes

Some studies have focused on the relative timing of pubertal change and found that girls who mature earlier than their peers have more negative affective symptoms, including depression (e.g., Graber, Lewinsohn, Seeley, & Brooks-Gunn, 1997; Kaltiala-Heino, Kosunen, & Rimpela, 2003; Petersen, Sarigiani, & Kennedy, 1991; Rierdan & Koff, 1991; Siegel, Yancey, Aneshensel, & Schuler, 1999; Stattin & Magnusson, 1990; Stice, Presnell, & Bearman, 2001), although other studies have found no effects of early maturation for girls (e.g., Angold et al., 1998; Paikoff et al., 1991). For boys, it may be that late maturation is a risk factor for increases in depressive symptoms (e.g., Siegel et al., 1999), although two other studies found that both early and late perceived timing predicted higher depressive symptoms for boys (Graber et al., 1997; Kaltiala-Heino et al., 2003). The mixed findings regarding the effects of pubertal timing may be due to differences in measurement method (e.g., informant, retrospective recall, perceived vs. actual timing; see Dorn, Dahl, Woodward, & Biro, 2006). It may also be due to individual differences in self-perceptions and feelings about the attention received from others due to differences in timing. For example, some young adolescent girls may enjoy the extra attention received from early pubertal timing, especially if they are confident with their appearance, while others may feel extremely uncomfortable with unwanted attention due to anxiety and/or negative self-perception regarding appearance. Similarly, some young adolescent boys may not care as much about fitting in with his peers regarding appearance, while other boys may feel distressed by lagging behind their peers in appearance, especially if appearance is salient.

In addition to timing, there may be individual differences in the effects of pubertal change among adolescents regardless of timing. As Angold and Worthman (1993) note, the onset of puberty is likely to have very different personal and social meanings to a 12-year-old girl who gains considerable body fat and is teased for it versus an athletic 12-year-old girl who gains useful muscle mass as a result of puberty. Similarly, cultures view pubertal changes differently, so the meaning of these changes to Caucasian, Latina, and African-American adolescents may be different (Smolak & Striegel-Moore, 2001). In fact, one study found that pubertal status was a better predictor of depressive symptoms than age among Caucasian adolescents, but not among Hispanic or African-American adolescents (Hayward, Gotlib, Schraedley, & Litt, 1999). Finally, some theorists have argued that the normal reproductive hormonal changes of puberty may only trigger depression in girls with a genetic or other biological vulnerability to the disorder (Steiner et al., 2003; Young & Korszun, 1999).

In sum, puberty brings a myriad of biological changes that may result in stress for some adolescents. We suggest that hormonal cycling and other pubertal changes may interact with several potential risk factors that may be present before puberty, resulting in increases in depression among adolescents, especially girls.

RISK FACTORS

In this section, we examine some of the putative biological and psychosocial risk factors for depression that may interact with the changes of puberty to result in increases in depression for adolescents. We first review biological factors followed by psychosocial factors.

Biological Risk Factors

Several biological factors have been associated with depression among adults, and more recently among adolescents. These include dysregulation of the HPA axis, genetic factors, and dysregulation of neurotransmitter systems that regulate mood. We suggest that these biological factors interact with the changes of puberty, particularly the changes in hormonal cycling, and may contribute to increases in depressive symptoms.

HPA Axis

The HPA axis is an intricate neuroendocrine system that is largely controlled by the hippocampus. Its main function is to maintain homeostasis of various bodily processes, and it is especially important in regulation of stress. One of the main hormones released via the HPA axis is cortisol, which functions to help the individual adapt to stress. While cortisol and the resulting "fight-or-flight" response is adaptive for responding to acute stressors, chronically high levels of cortisol result in many deleterious physical and psychological effects (see Bale, 2006 for a review). Dysregulation of the HPA axis has been found in depressed adults: approximately 50% of depressed adults tend to have chronic hyperactivity in the HPA axis and a slowing of the HPA axis to return to normal functioning following a stressor (Southwick, Vythilingam, & Charney, 2005; Young & Korszun, 1999). In turn, the excess hormones produced by heightened HPA activity seem to have an inhibiting effect on receptors for the monoamines, including serotonin. One model for the development of depression is that people exposed to chronic stress may develop poorly regulated neuroendocrine systems. Then, when they are exposed even to minor stressors later in life, the HPA axis over-reacts and does not easily return to homeostasis. This creates change in the functioning of the monoamine neurotransmitters in the brain, and symptoms of depression and anxiety are likely to ensue (Southwick et al., 2005).

The ovarian hormones estradiol and progesterone have been shown modulate the regulation of the HPA axis, with some studies showing the hormones heighten HPA activity and others showing they diminish HPA activity (Kudielka & Kirschbaum, 2005; Steiner et al., 2003). The radically changing hormonal milieu during the pubertal transition could affect the functioning of the HPA axis, influencing adolescents' physiological and psychological reactions to stressors (Young & Korszun, 1999). For example, some studies of pubertal girls have shown that it is the interaction of major stressors and peak hormonal change that predict increases in distress, rather than either factor alone (Brooks-Gunn & Warren, 1989; Steiner, Born, & Marton, 2000).

Relationships between indicators of HPA functioning, such as cortisol levels, and depression tend to be less consistently found in depressed youth than in depressed adults (Feder et al., 2004; Kaufman, Martin, King, & Charney, 2001; Ryan, 1998), but hypercortisolemia has been observed in depressed adolescents (Dahl et al., 1991; Forbes et al., 2006c; Goodyer, Tamplin, Herbert, & Altham, 2000; Susman et al., 1987). In one intriguing study, Forbes and colleagues (2006c) found no differences between depressed and nondepressed children in cortisol levels, but differences approaching significance ($p<0.08$) between depressed and nondepressed adolescents. Interestingly, Forbes et al. (2006) did find significant differences between children with anxiety disorders and children with no disorders in cortisol levels (but no differences between anxious and nonanxious adolescents). This pattern raises the interesting possibility that HPA dysregulation in childhood is a risk factor for anxiety, but becomes a risk factor for depression over the pubertal change. Forbes and colleagues note that there was significant heterogeneity in cortisol levels among both the anxious children and depressed adolescents, and none of their measured variables accounted for this variability. They suggest it will be valuable in future studies to assess reproductive hormone levels, psychosocial stressors, and emotion-regulation styles as possible predictors of HPA functioning in youth as they go through pubertal development.

In sum, people exposed to chronic stress may develop poorly regulated neuroendocrine systems resulting in an overactive HPA axis and changes in the functioning of the monoamine neurotransmitters which may lead to depression (Southwick et al., 2005). Such stress sensitization is thought to be analogous to electrical kindling in animal studies where structural changes, including the induction of gene transcription factors, results from electrical stimulation of limbic areas (Post, 1992). It may be the case that early biological changes resulting from HPA dysregulation cause other brain changes, such as allowing the prefrontal cortex to go "offline" more easily, resulting in increased limbic system activity when encountering mild stress and subsequent increases in depressive symptoms (Arnsten, 1999). Adolescence is an important time for prefrontal cortical remodeling (Yurgelun-Todd, 2007), so HPA dysregulation during this time may have important consequences later in life. Because ovarian hormones modulate the regulation of the HPA axis (Steiner et al., 2003), adolescent girls may be particularly vulnerable to depression from HPA axis dysregulation.

Genetic Factors

Behavioral genetics research has indicated that depression, including adolescent-onset, is caused in part by genetic factors that interact with various aspects of the environment (see Chapter 10 by Lau and Eley in this volume). In addition, some specific genes have been identified that are associated with adolescent depression. Genetic factors seem to account for more variance in depressive symptoms in older adolescents compared to younger children (e.g., Rice, Harold, & Thapar, 2002; Silberg et al., 1999). This suggests that the hormonal cycling and other changes of puberty may "turn on" some of the genes that influence depression. A recent genetic epidemiology study of female adolescent twins reported that 40% of the variance in depression was accounted for by genetic factors and the remaining variance was accounted for by nonshared environmental factors (Glowinski, Madden, Bucholz, Lynskey, & Heath, 2003). Other research has found that shared environmental factors account for much of the variance in depressive symptoms, especially for adolescent girls (Eley & Stevenson, 1999).

Findings regarding gender differences in genetic factors are somewhat mixed, as the few twin studies that have examined genetic factors in adolescent depression have found quite different patterns. Silberg et al. (1999) reported a greater genetic influence on depressive symptoms for adolescent girls compared to boys. They also found that latent genetic factors (e.g., the genetic influence on experiencing negative life events) explained the higher rates of depression in adolescent girls. In contrast, Rice et al. (2002) found that genetic factors are stronger for adolescent boys' depressive symptoms compared to girls'. Similarly, Eley and Stevenson (1999) found stronger heritability for depression among adolescent boys, and stronger influence of shared environment for adolescent girls. Until more research is done, the influence of genetic factors in explaining the gender difference in adolescent depression remains inconclusive. One reliable finding is that genetic factors become important in explaining depression beginning in adolescence, and there are likely to be multiple mechanisms to account for this (e.g., gene–environment correlations and gene × environment interactions; see Chapter 10 by Lau and Eley in this volume for further discussion).

Research in molecular genetics has revealed several candidate genes that influence the likelihood of developing depression. One of the most reliable findings involves a polymorphism on the serotonin transporter gene (5-HTTLPR). Multiple studies, including one with adolescents (Eley et al., 2004), have found that individuals with the short allele are at increased risk for depression in the presence of negative life events (e.g., Caspi et al., 2003). In our recent study of 100 young adolescent girls, we found that those with two copies of the short allele on the serotonin transporter gene had higher levels of clinical symptoms, including depression, compared to girls with one or two long alleles.

Another body of research has pointed to a polymorphism on the BDNF gene (val66met). This polymorphism has been found to confer an increased risk of depression, especially childhood-onset (e.g., Strauss et al., 2005; Strauss et al., 2004), with the val allele being associated with depression early in life. We also found that the val allele was associated with depressive symptoms in our study with adolescent girls (Hilt, Sander, Nolen-Hoeksema, & Simen, 2007). Although we know of no gender differences in the presence of these "risky" alleles, girls may be more at risk for developing depression from gene interactions with increased stress beginning during the pubertal transition.

Neurotransmitter Dysregulation

One of the ways in which genetic factors may affect mood is through neurotransmitter regulation. For example, the serotonin transporter gene is important for the regulation of serotonin, which has many functions in the brain including mood regulation (Lesch et al., 1996), while the BDNF gene is important for regulating BDNF in the brain, which also functions to regulate mood and has important cognitive functions (Egan et al., 2003). Additionally, there are multiple, complex relationships between gonadal hormones and the neurotransmitters that regulate mood. In genetically vulnerable girls, normal hormonal cycling, which begins in puberty, may trigger dysregulation of neurotransmitter systems, leading to increases in depressive symptoms. For example, gonadal hormones influence the production of serotonin receptors, which could influence vulnerability to mood disorders in girls with a genetic risk for dysregulation of serotonergic systems (Amin, Canli, & Epperson, 2005; Steiner et al., 2003). Additionally, there is preclinical evidence that estrogen levels are associated with levels of BDNF, particularly in certain areas of the hippocampus (e.g., Franklin & Perrot-Sinal, 2006; Sun & Akon, 2006). In studies with adult humans, low levels of BDNF have been reliably associated with elevated depressive symptoms (e.g., Aydemir et al., 2006; Shimizu et al., 2003). One recent study of pregnant women found lower BDNF and serotonin serum levels just before and just after childbirth, adding evidence that changing hormone levels in women may be a risk factor for depression (Lommatzsch et al., 2006). The hormonal cycling of puberty may put adolescent girls at greater risk of experiencing dysregulation of BDNF and other neuroregulatory systems, setting off a cascade of events in the brain that are associated with depression. In our recent study of young adolescent girls, we found significantly lower BDNF serum levels (measured as picograms per milliliter) in girls of mothers with a history of depression (M=2.53, n=31) compared to girls of mothers with no history of psychopathology ($M=2.73$, $n=27$), $t(56)=-2.04$, $p<0.05$. Although we did not find a significant negative correlation between BDNF level and depressive symptoms among the adolescent girls, the lower BDNF level in the high-risk girls may be a biomarker for future depression. Furthermore, we found a marginally significant relationship between estradiol and BDNF level ($r=-0.22$, $p=0.07$), suggesting that multiple biological systems may be involved in the development of mood symptoms.

Psychosocial Factors

There are also several psychosocial risk factors that may be present before puberty but interact with stresses caused by the pubertal transition to cause increases in depressive symptoms, especially for adolescent girls. We review some of the literature on negative cognitive style, interpersonal orientation, and negative life stress, and discuss how these risk factors may interact with the changes of puberty to put girls at increased risk for developing depression. For more extensive reviews of the literatures on cognitive styles, interpersonal orientation, and negative life stress, see Chapters 12, 13, and 14 in this volume.

Negative Cognitive Style

Certain maladaptive patterns of thinking that develop beginning in childhood predict increases in depression in adolescents and adults. One example is a negative attributional style, or the tendency to attribute negative events to internal, stable, and global causes (e.g., *I did poorly on the test because I'm not smart).* Numerous studies have found that a negative attributional style interacts with negative life events (i.e., diathesis-stress model) to predict increases in depression over time, especially hopelessness depression, by midadolescence (see reviews by Garber & Horowitz, 2002; Hankin & Abramson, 2001). Few gender differences in negative attributional style have been reported; however, Hankin and Abramson (2002) found that high school girls had a more negative attributional style than boys, and this cognitive vulnerability mediated the gender difference in depression. The mixed gender findings regarding attributional style may reflect the different measures of attributional style used which vary widely in their reliability (see Conley, Haines, Hilt & Metalsky, 2001; Hankin & Abramson, 2001).

There are other maladaptive cognitive styles that have been associated with depression, including dysfunctional attitudes (Beck, Rush, Shaw, & Emery, 1979) and negative inferences about the self and consequences of negative events (Abramson, Metalsky, & Alloy, 1989). Although there do not appear to be gender differences in dysfunctional attitudes, some research has suggested that the tendency to make negative inferences about the self is a vulnerability factor for the development of depression in adolescent girls, but not boys (Abela, 2001). Additionally, Hankin and Abramson (2002) found that high school girls reported a more negative inferential style about the self, and this mediated the gender difference in depression. Adolescent girls may make more negative inferences about the self because of the importance they place on peer evaluation (Rudolph & Conley, 2005) and the high rates of body dissatisfaction among this group (e.g., Stice, Hayward, Cameron, Killen, & Taylor, 2000). In fact, one study found that body image and self-esteem were more important than other variables (such as life events, gender-related attributes, etc.) in explaining the higher rate of depression among adolescent girls in a sample of high school students (Allgood-Merten, Lewinsohn, & Hops, 1990).

In sum, although negative cognitive styles do appear to be a risk factor for depression in adolescence, there is mixed evidence as to whether girls have more negative cognitive styles than boys, or these styles are a greater risk factor for girls than for boys. We propose that negative cognitive styles interact with the biological and psychosocial changes of puberty that may affect girls more than boys to contribute to depression among adolescent girls.

Interpersonal Orientation and Social Support

Many of the stressful transitions of early adolescence concern interpersonal relationships: changes in friendship patterns as students move from one school to the next or change interests, new romantic relationships, and changes in adolescents' relationships with their parents (Cyranowski, Frank, Young, & Shear, 2000). Girls tend to show a more interpersonal orientation compared to boys, and their strong emotional relationships with others are important sources of support for girls during early adolescence (Rose & Rudolph, 2006). Some girls cross a line, however, from emotional closeness to emotional dependency on their relationships with others (Cyranowski et al., 2000; Rose & Rudolph, 2006). When these relationships are going well, these girls feel good about themselves, but when the relationships falter, as they often do, these girls sometimes sacrifice their own needs to please others (LaGreca & Lopez, 1998; Leadbeater, Blatt, & Quinlan, 1995; Rudolph & Conley, 2005). They may engage in excessive reassurance seeking, a pattern of desperate attempts to seek reassurance of others' love that can annoy and alienate others (Joiner & Metalsky, 2001). Recent students of children and adolescents find that girls who have greater need for social approval, engage in more reassurance seeking, and have greater social-evaluative concerns are more prone to develop symptoms of depression (Little & Garber, 2005; Prinstein, Borelli, Cheah, Simon, & Aikins, 2005; Rudolph, Caldwell, & Conley, 2005; Rudolph & Conley, 2005). For example, Rudoph and Conley (2005) found that social evaluative concerns fully mediated the gender difference in depression among a group of adolescents.

Additionally, a strong interpersonal orientation may put children at risk if their relationships are characterized by negative communication. Rose (2002) found that children and adolescents who engage in co-rumination (i.e., discussing negative feelings and focusing on problems in discussions with close friends) report having high-quality friendships but also more depressive symptoms. Furthermore, girls reported engaging in more co-rumination compared to boys and this partially explained the gender difference in depression.

One *beneficial* consequence of a strong interpersonal orientation is greater levels of social support. In fact, high quality social support in the face of significant stress has been shown to reduce children's vulnerability to depression and related problems (Prinstein, Boergers, & Vernberg, 2001; Storch & Masia-Warner, 2004). Conversely, social isolation has been associated with depression, especially for adolescent boys (Larson, Richards, Raffaelli, Ham, & Jewell, 1990). Social support can protect against mental health problems through a number of mechanisms, including by fostering positive self-appraisals and self-efficacy and encouraging positive emotion-regulation strategies (Holahan,

Moos, Holahan, & Brennan, 1996). Steinberg and colleagues (2006) suggest that social support, especially from parents, is especially crucial in early adolescence when the individual is confronted with rapidly changing emotions and social situations but does not yet have mature emotion-regulation strategies, particularly cognitive strategies, for coping with the arousal created by emotional and social change.

Several studies have found that social support buffers the otherwise deleterious effects of certain risk factors for depression. For example, Prinstein and colleagues (2001) found that social support from close friends served as a buffer against developing depressive symptoms when experiencing peer victimization. Additionally, Kaufman and colleagues (2004, 2006) found evidence for an interaction between the presence of a genetic vulnerability to depression (indexed by polymorphisms on 5-HTTLPR and BDNF) and social support to predict which children were most at risk for depression. Specifically, among maltreated children, social support moderated the impact of the val66met variant of BDNF and/or the s/s combination of 5-HTTLPR on risk for depression.

Adolescent girls' strong interpersonal orientation seems to play a complex role in risk for depression. If relationships are going well and provide good social support, adolescents with other risk factors may be protected from developing serious depression. However, a strong investment in interpersonal relationships can contribute to depression when relationships are not going well as often happens in adolescence, especially among girls.

Negative Life Events

The presence of negative life events is a reliable risk factor for depression in adolescent boys and girls (e.g., Ge et al., 1994). In addition to the stressors associated with pubertal changes, girls appear to be at greater risk for depression in adolescence because they have a greater genetic risk for negative life events, experience more negative life events (especially in interpersonal domains), and are more distressed by negative life events.

As discussed earlier, Silberg et al. (1999) found that girls had a greater genetic risk for experiencing negative life events after puberty and this helped to explain the higher rate of depression in adolescent girls. Both boys and girls report increases in negative life events in adolescence compared to childhood; however, the increase in exposure to negative life events is especially pronounced for adolescent girls (e.g., Ge et al., 1994; Larson & Ham, 1993). Additionally, girls report more interpersonal stressors compared to boys who report more academic stressors (Larson & Ham, 1993; Rudolph & Hammen, 1999; Shih, Eberhart, Hammen, & Brennan, 2006). One study found that girls' higher rate of interpersonal stressors partially accounted for the gender difference in subjective distress (Liu & Kaplan, 1999), and another study found that the higher levels of stress experienced by girls was largely due to girls' higher levels of interpersonal stressors (Shih et al., 2006).

In addition to experiencing more interpersonal stressors, girls are more often the victims of child abuse (physical and especially sexual) compared to boys (see Gorey & Leslie, 1997 for a review). In turn, being the victim of child abuse has been shown to be a risk factor for the development of depression (see Weiss, Longhurst, & Mazure, 1999), possibly through heightened HPA axis activity, which can lead to the development of depression (see Tarullo & Gunnar, 2006). Although most of the studies in this area are retrospective, one recent prospective study of several hundred children and matched controls followed through early adulthood found that child abuse predicted current and lifetime MDD (Widom, DuMont, & Czaja, 2007). Furthermore, this study found that abused children had earlier onset of MDD compared to controls (Spatz Widom et al., 2007). It may be that the higher rate of child sexual abuse places adolescent girls at increased risk for depression. In fact, one review estimated that 35% of the gender difference in adult depression could be attributed to the higher rate of childhood sexual assault experienced by girls (Cutler & Nolen-Hoeksema, 1991).

A potential mechanism for this involves a genetic predisposition that may be triggered by child abuse or neglect leading to depression. One recent study found a gene × gene interaction among maltreated children that predicted higher depression scores; specifically, having the met allele for BDNF and two short serotonin transporter alleles predicted higher depression scores in maltreated (but not nonmaltreated) children (Kaufman et al., 2006). Even though we know of no gender difference in genotypes, girls' higher likelihood of being abused places them at greater risk for triggering a genetic vulnerability.

In addition to experiencing more interpersonal stressors and more often being the victims of abuse, girls may also engage in more stress generation. Hammen's (1991) model of stress generation conceptualizes certain stressors as dependent (i.e., contributed to, in part or in whole, by the individual), and she finds that women are more likely than men to experience dependent stressors. Studies with adolescents have also found that adolescent girls are more likely to report dependent stressors (especially within the interpersonal domain such as peer conflict) compared to adolescent boys (Rudolph & Hammen, 1999; Shih et al., 2006). Furthermore, Shih et al. (2006) found that dependent interpersonal stress mediated the gender difference in adolescent depression. There was also evidence of higher stress reactivity among the adolescent girls in this study as they were more likely than adolescent boys to become depressed when experiencing stressful life events.

In sum, research in the domain of negative life events suggests that adolescent girls may be at higher risk for depression for a variety of reasons. Girls are exposed to more stressors, especially in the interpersonal domain, and this may be due to social factors (see Nolen-Hoeksema & Girgus, 1994) and/or a greater genetic propensity to experience negative life events. Additionally, adolescent girls seem to generate more dependent stressors that also contribute to their depression. Finally, adolescent girls appear to be more reactive to stress than adolescent boys, as they are more likely to develop depression in the presence of stress. We propose that the stress associated with the biological changes of puberty, along with stress in the interpersonal domain regarding peers, which becomes more important for girls in adolescence, may be overwhelming for girls. It taxes them cognitively and also biologically via HPA axis activity. Unless they have adequate skills to cope with these stressors, adolescent girls are susceptible to developing depressive symptoms.

POOR EMOTION-REGULATION SKILLS: FURTHER EXACERBATION OF DEPRESSIVE SYMPTOMS

Stressful events and transitions create difficult emotions and moods for adolescents to respond to (Steinberg et al., 2006). The new and challenging demands of middle school or high school can create anxiety about being able to perform, sadness when one cannot meet standards, and a general sense of negative arousal. Similarly, losses of friendships, teasing by others, and rejections by early romantic interests can create negative moods. The physical changes of puberty can also bring negative moods, particularly in girls, because some girls do not like the ways their bodies are changing. All of these emotions may be regulated through effective coping, but when adolescents have not developed such skills, depressive symptoms will be exacerbated.

A growing body of research shows that youth differ in their skills at regulating initial symptoms of distress, and these emotion-regulation skills are important predictors of the development of more severe symptoms of depression and other psychopathology (e.g., Cicchetti, Ackerman, & Izard, 1995; Eisenberg et al., 2001; Southam-Gerow & Kendall, 2000; Zeman, Shipman, & Suveg, 2002). Indeed, some theorists have argued that a central psychological task of adolescence is to learn to regulate affect and behavior in adaptive ways, increasingly without the aid of the adults who provide guidance in childhood (Steinberg & Avenevoli, 2000; Steinberg et al., 2006). For girls, this task is made more difficult by the historical changes toward earlier onset of puberty and its neurobiological and morphological changes. For some girls, these biological changes, which bring changes in emotional and motivational systems, and reactions of the social environment to the girls, come well before they have experienced cognitive maturation that would facilitate good emotion regulation. Steinberg and colleagues (2006) suggest the disjunction between pubertal change and cognitive emotion-regulation skills is a major risk factor for the development of depression in adolescence.

One particularly maladaptive emotion-regulation strategy that we have studied extensively is rumination, the tendency to repetitively and passively dwell on one's negative emotions without engaging in active problem solving (Nolen-Hoeksema, 2000). Studies have shown that adults prone to rumination are more vulnerable to depressive and anxiety symptoms and to MDD (Nolen-Hoeksema, 2000; Nolen-Hoeksema, Larson, & Grayson, 1999), and the greater tendency for women to engage in rumination partially explains the gender difference in depression among adults (e.g., Nolen-Hoeksema et al., 1999).

A few studies have examined gender differences in rumination among children and adolescents, and the findings are not as clear. Grant et al. (2004) found the expected gender difference in rumination among a sample of African-American fourth and sixth graders, and also found that rumination accounted for the gender difference in depression, replicating work with adults. Additionally, we found that girls reported higher rumination compared to boys and that this accounted for the gender difference in depression in our study of a large group of ethnically diverse middle school students (Hilt, McLaughlin, & Nolen-Hoeksema, 2008). Two other studies found the expected gender difference in rumination (Hampel & Petermann, 2005; Schwartz & Koenig, 1996). Schwartz and Koenig (1996) did not, however, find that rumination accounted for the gender difference in depression, and Hampel and Petermann (2005) did not examine depression. Two additional studies of 8- to 13-year-olds did not find a gender difference in rumination (Abela, Brozina, & Haigh, 2002; Broderick & Korteland, 2004). One explanation for these varied findings may have to do with sample size. The effect size for the gender difference in rumination may be small in adolescence (e.g., ES=0.30 in Hilt et al., 2008), so a large sample size may be needed to detect a difference. The two studies of youth that did not find a gender difference in rumination had relatively small sample sizes compared to the studies that did find a difference. We propose that although the tendency to ruminate predicts depression among boys and girls, girls' greater likelihood to ruminate will further exacerbate their depressive symptoms in adolescence, leading to onset of MDEs over time.

In our work with young adolescent girls, we found evidence that rumination may be an endophenotype (mediating factor) in the path between the BDNF gene and depression (Hilt et al., 2007). We found that the val allele for BDNF was associated with rumination, and rumination mediated the relationship between val66met and depressive symptoms. This suggests that rumination may serve as an endophenotype (mediating factor) in the link between genotype and phenotype.

Some potentially positive alternatives to rumination are problem solving, distraction, and reappraisal (Folkman, 1984; Gross, 1998; Nolen-Hoeksema, 1991). Studies of adults generally show that these coping strategies are associated with lower levels of depression in the face of stress (see Holahan et al., 1996; Lazarus & Folkman, 1984). A meta-analysis of the relationship between coping and mental health symptoms in children and adolescents (Compas, Connor-Smith, Saltzman, Thomsen, & Wadsworth, 2001) found that problem-focused coping and reappraisal were associated with fewer internalizing symptoms in some studies; the number of studies specifically measuring these coping strategies was small, however. One study found that young adolescent girls were less likely than young adolescent boys to report employing adaptive coping strategies (e.g., distraction) when encountering common stressors; however, the researchers did not examine depression in this study (Hampel & Petermann, 2005). In the few studies that have examined self-reported problem solving and distraction and depression, these coping strategies were not associated with decreases in depression (Abela et al., 2002; Schwartz & Koenig, 1996).

Research on adolescent brain development helps to explain why emotion regulation may be difficult, especially for young adolescents. The typical adolescent brain is characterized by a strong reward system (nucleus acumbens), a weak avoidant system (amygdala), and an underdeveloped prefrontal cortex (which is important for tempering limbic system/impulsive responses) (see Ernst, Pine, & Hardin, 2005). One of the most significant physical changes for adolescents is reorganization of the prefrontal cortex that eventually allows for greater executive functioning and emotion regulation (see Yurgelun-Todd, 2007 for a review). Furthermore, there is evidence that the neuroendocrine changes associated with puberty may impact brain organization during adolescence. At least one imaging study found a gender difference in prefrontal cortex activation during an emotional processing task (Yurgelun-Todd & Killgore, 2006). In this study, adolescents ages 8 to 15 viewed fearful faces while in the scanner. For girls, there was a significant correlation between age and prefrontal cortex activity in both hemispheres, and for boys this correlation only held for right prefrontal activity. This difference may reflect differences in emotional processing and be associated with behavioral outcomes, such as the greater tendency for girls to internalize and boys to externalize.

Prefrontal re-organization allows for more reliance on the prefrontal cortex and less reliance on the subcortical structures for cognitive processing. There is some evidence that adolescents with depression have abnormal functioning in these subcortical structures. For example, research on adolescents with depression suggests poor functioning (i.e., lowered response compared to controls) in the brain's reward system (e.g., Forbes et al., 2006b) and stronger avoidant responses (e.g., Thomas et al., 2001). To our knowledge, no gender differences have emerged in these studies.

The differences in emotion regulation may be apparent before symptoms of depression and anxiety appear. For example, children of depressed parents have been shown to have different patterns of prefrontal cortex response to frustrating situations (e.g., receiving a disappointing toy) (Forbes, Fox, Cohn, Galles, & Kovacs, 2006a). However, we believe that poor emotion regulation will also exacerbate depressive symptoms, especially during times of increased stress during the pubertal transition, which may explain why girls have a more difficult time than boys. Most of the research to date has focused on neural correlates of depressive symptoms, without teasing apart gender differences and/or temporal associations between brain activity and symptom onset. It will be important for future work in this area to focus on these areas.

SUMMARY

In sum, we propose that some children carry genetic, neurobiological, and psychosocial risk factors for depression prior to adolescence. The specific genetic risk factors include certain polymorphisms of the serotonin transporter and BDNF genes. The neurobiological risk factors include HPA hyperactivity which results in increased cortisol and dysregulation of neurotransmitter systems. The psychosocial risk factors include negative cognitive styles, excessive concern about social relationships, and lower social support. It is unclear whether girls are more likely than boys to carry the genetic and neurobiological risk factors, or to have more negative cognitive styles. Girls do tend to have greater concern about social relationships and because of their relatively stronger investment in interpersonal relationships, may be more vulnerable to disruptions in their relationships compared to boys.

These risk factors for depression then interact with the numerous stressful changes of early adolescence, many of which occur more in girls than in boys, to trigger depressive symptoms. Pubertal changes that may be associated with depressive symptoms include gains in body fat and changes and variability in hormone levels. In addition, girls report more stressors in early adolescence than boys, particularly interpersonal stressors and dependent stressors, and may also have higher stress reactivity.

Girls are more likely than boys to engage in certain maladaptive emotion-regulation strategies, particularly rumination. These maladaptive emotion-regulation strategies then exacerbate the depressive symptoms triggered by early adolescent stressors and their interactions with pre-existing risk factors.

The result is an escalation of depressive symptoms in girls that may develop into diagnosable depressive disorders.

Many elements of our proposed bio-psycho-social model have received empirical support, but there is much more research to be done. In particular, one aspect of our model involves the interaction of hormonal cycling with other biological and psychosocial changes of puberty. Most research to date with hormones has involved examining linear relationships between hormone level and depressive symptoms. More sophisticated models that examine changes in hormone levels and their interaction with other factors, such as neurotransmitter expression and HPA axis functioning, is needed to test this aspect of our model. There is also a need for research regarding the relationships among hormones and neurotransmitter systems in predicting depression and how these relationships change over time, especially during adolescence. Additionally, there is some evidence that individual differences in personality and biology interact with pubertal timing to predict which individuals become depressed during adolescence, but more research is needed to better understand these differences. In general, there is a trend toward integrating biological and psychosocial factors in research, and we believe this kind of research is especially important in the case of depression that rises significantly among girls beginning in adolescence. One exciting area of research involves brain imaging studies that begin to show some of the structural and functional mechanisms that are important for emotional processing and cognitive control of emotion, and an important direction for this research is to examine potential gender differences. Understanding why depression increases for girls beginning in adolescence is complex, and while studies are needed to tease apart various aspects of the model, the field also needs integrated, longitudinal studies that can examine how these processes unfold and interact among a sample over time.

Understanding the causes of the increases in depressive symptoms and disorders in girls during adolescence is critical to the development of prevention and intervention programs. In particular, if emotion-regulation styles play an important role in the emergence of gender differences in depression, then interventions designed to improve emotion-regulation strategies may help to reduce girls' vulnerability to depression, not only in adolescence, but into adulthood. Such interventions should involve helping younger adolescent girls better cope with the biological and psychosocial changes of puberty. This may involve psychoeducation along with the development of coping strategies as reappraisal and problem-solving skills. In addition, interventions can help girls develop positive interpersonal relationships, which have been shown to be protective against the development of depression. Interventions for older adolescent girls should focus even more on effective emotion-regulation strategies as their brains are changing and better able to handle more cognitive control tasks.

REFERENCES

Abela, J. R. Z. (2001). The hopelessness theory of depression: A test of the diathesis-stress and causal mediation components in third and seventh grade children. *Journal of Abnormal Child Psychology, 29*, 241–254.

Abela, J. R. Z., Brozina, K., & Haigh, E. P. (2002). An examination of the response-styles theory depression in third- and seventh-grade children: A short-term longitudinal study. *Journal of Abnormal Child Psychology, 30*, 515–527.

Abramson, L. Y., Metalsky, G. I., & Alloy, L. B. (1989). Hopelessness depression: A theory-based subtype of depression. *Psychological Review, 96*, 358–372.

ACOG Committee on Adolescent Health Care. (2006). ACOG Committee Opinion No. 349, November 2006: Menstruation in girls and adolescents: Using the menstrual cycle as a vital sign. *Obstetrics & Gynecology, 108*, 1323–1328.

Allgood-Merten, B., Lewinsohn, P. M., & Hops, H. (1990). Sex differences and adolescent depression. *Journal of Abnormal Psychology, 99*, 55–63.

Amin, Z., Canli, T., & Epperson, C. N. (2005). Effective of estrogen-serotonin interactions on mood and cognition. *Behavioral and Cognitive Neuroscience Reviews, 4*, 43–58.

Angold, A., Costello, E. J., Erkanli, A., & Worthman, C. M. (1999). Pubertal changes in hormone levels and depression in girls. *Psychological Medicine, 29*, 1043–1053.

Angold, A., Costello, E. J., & Worthman, C. M. (1998). Puberty and depression: The roles of age, pubertal status and pubertal timing. *Psychological Medicine, 28*, 51–61.

Angold, A., & Worthman, C. W. (1993). Puberty onset of gender differences in rates of depression: A developmental, epidemiological, and neuroendocrine perspective. *Journal of Affective Disorders, 29*, 145–158.

Arnsten, A. F. (1999). Development of the cerebral cortex: XIV. Stress impairs prefrontal cortical function. *Journal of the American Academy of Child & Adolescent Psychiatry, 38*, 220–222.

Aydemir, C., Yalcin, E. S., Aksaray, S., Kisa, C., Yildirim, S. G., Uzbay, T., et al. (2006). Brain-derived neurotrophic factor (BDNF) changes in the serum of depressed women. *Progress in Neuro-Psychopharmacology & Biological Psychiatry, 30*, 1256–1260.

Bale, T. L. (2006). Stress sensitivity and the development of affective disorders. *Hormones & Behavior, 50*, 529–533.

Beck, A. T., Rush, A. J., Shaw, B. F., & Emery, G. (1979). *Cognitive therapy of depression.* New York: Guilford Press.

Bennett, D. S., Ambrosini, P. J., Kudes, D., Metz, C., & Rabinovich, H. (2005). Gender differences in adolescent depression: Do symptoms differ for boys and girls? *Journal of Affective Disorders, 89*, 35–44.

Broderick, P. C., & Korteland, C. (2004). A prospective study of rumination and depression in early adolescence. *Clinical Child Psychology and Psychiatry, 9*, 383–394.

Brooks-Gunn, J., & Warren, M. P. (1989). Biological and social contributions to negative affect in young adolescent girls. *Child Development, 60*, 40–55.

Buchanan, C. M., Eccles, J. S., & Becker, J. B. (1992). Are adolescents the victims of raging hormones? Evidence for activational effects of hormones on moods and behavior at adolescence. *Psychological Bulletin, 111*, 62–107.

Caspi, A., Sugden, K., Moffitt, T. E., Taylor, A., Craig, I. W., Harrington, H. L., et al. (2003). Influence of life stress on depression: Moderation by a polymorphism on the 5-HTT gene. *Science, 301*, 386–389.

Cicchetti, D., Ackerman, B. P., & Izard, C. E. (1995). Emotions and emotion regulation in developmental psychopathology. *Development and Psychopathology, 7*, 1–10.

Compas, B. E., Connor-Smith, J. K., Saltzman, H., Thomsen, A. H., & Wadsworth, M. E. (2001). Coping with stress during childhood and adolescence: Problems, progress, and potential in theory and research. *Psychological Bulletin, 127,* 87–127.

Conley, C. S., Haines, B. A., Hilt, L. M., & Metalsky, G. I. (2001). The children's attributional style interview: Developmental tests of cognitive diathesis-stress theories of depression. *Journal of Abnormal Child Psychology, 29,* 445–463.

Costello, E. J., Erkanli, A., & Angold, A. (2006). Is there an epidemic of child or adolescent depression? *Journal of Child Psychology and Psychiatry and Allied Disciplines, 47,* 1263–1271.

Cutler, S. E., & Nolen-Hoeksema, S. (1991). Accounting for sex differences in depression through female victimization: Childhood sexual abuse. *Sex Roles, 24,* 425–438.

Cyranowski, J. M., Frank, E., Young, E., & Shear, K. (2000). Adolescent onset of the gender difference in lifetime rates of major depression. *Archives of General Psychiatry, 57,* 21–27.

Dahl, R. E., Ryan, N. D., Puig-Antich, J., Nguyen, N. A., Al-Shabbout, M., Meyer, V. A., et al. (1991). 24-hour cortisol measures in adolescents with major depression: A controlled study. *Biological Psychiatry, 30,* 25–36.

Dorn, L. D., Dahl, R. E., Woodward, H. R., & Biro, F. (2006). Defining the boundaries of early adolescence: A user's guide to assessing pubertal status and pubertal timing in research with adolescents. *Applied Developmental Science, 10,* 30–56.

Eaton, W., Anthony, J., Gallo, J., Cai, G., Tien, A., Romanoski, A., et al. (1997). Natural history of diagnostic interview schedule/DSM-IV major depression. *Archives of General Psychiatry, 54,* 993–999.

Egan, M. F., Kojima, M., Callicott, J. H., Goldberg, T. E., Kolachana, B. S., Bertolino, A., et al. (2003). The BDNF val66met polymorphism affects activity-dependent secretion of BDNF and human memory and hippocampal function. *Cell, 112,* 257–269.

Eisenberg, N., Cumberland, A., Spinrad, T. L., Fabes, R. A., Shepard, S. A., Reiser, M., et al. (2001). The relations of regulation and emotionality to children's externalizing and internalizing problem behavior. *Child Development, 72,* 1112–1134.

Eley, T. C., & Stevenson, J. (1999). Exploring the covariation between anxiety and depression symptoms: A genetic analysis of the effects of age and sex. *Journal of Child Psychology and Psychiatry, 40,* 1273–1284.

Eley, T. C., Sugden, K., Corsico, A., Gregory, A. M., Sham, P., McGuffin, P., et al. (2004). Gene-environment interaction analysis of serotonin system markers with adolescent depression. *Molecular Psychiatry, 9,* 908–915.

Ernst, M., Pine, D. S., & Hardin, M. (2005). Triadic model of the neurobiology of motivated behavior in adolescence. *Psychological Medicine, 35,* 1–14.

Feder, A., Coplan, J. D., Goetz, R. R., Mathew, S. J., Pine, D. S., Dahl, R. E., et al. (2004). Twenty-four-hour cortisol secretion patterns in prepubertal children with anxiety or depressive disorders. *Biological Psychiatry, 56,* 198–204.

Folkman, S. (1984). Personal control and stress and coping processes: A theoretical analysis. *Journal of Personality and Social Psychology, 46,* 839–852.

Forbes, E. E., Fox, N. A., Cohn, J. F., Galles, S. F., & Kovacs, M. (2006a). Children's affect regulation during a disappointment: Psychophysiological responses and relation to parent history of depression. *Biological Psychology, 71*, 264–277.

Forbes, E. E., May, J. C., Siegle, G. J., Ladouceur, C. D., Ryan, N. D., Carter, C. S., et al. (2006b). Reward-related decision-making in pediatric major depressive disorder: An fMRI study. *Journal of Child Psychology and Psychiatry, 47*, 1031–1040.

Forbes, E. E., Williamson, D. E., Ryan, N. D., Biraher, B., Axelson, D. A., & Dahl, R. E. (2006c). Peri-sleep-onset cortisol levels in children and adolescents with affective disorders. *Biological Psychiatry, 59*, 24–30.

Franklin, T. B., & Perrot-Sinal, T. S. (2006). Sex and ovarian steroids modulate brain-derived neurotrophic factor (BDNF) protein levels in rat hippocampus under stressful and non-stressful conditions. *Psychoneuroendocrinology, 31*, 38–48.

Galambos, N. L., Leadbeater, B. J., & Barker, E. T. (2004). Gender differences in and risk factors for depression in adolescent: A 4-year longitudinal study. *International Journal of Behavior Development, 28*, 16–25.

Garber, J., & Horowitz, J. L. (2002). Depression in children. In I. H. Gotlib & C. L. Hammen (Eds.), *Handbook of depression* (pp. 510–540). New York: Guilford Press.

Ge, X., Lorenz, F. O., Conger, R. D., Elder, G. H., & Simons, R. L. (1994). Trajectories of stressful life events and depressive symptoms during adolescence. *Developmental Psychology, 30*, 467–483.

Glowinski, A. L., Madden, P. A. F., Bucholz, K. K., Lynskey, M. T., & Heath, A. C. (2003). Genetic epidemiology of self-reported lifetime DSM-IV major depressive disorder in a population-based twin sample of female adolescents. *Journal of Child Psychology and Psychiatry, 44*, 988–996.

Goodyer, I. M., Tamplin, A., Herbert, J., & Altham, P. M. (2000). Recent life events, cortisol, dehydroeplandrosterone and the onset of major depression in high-risk adolescents. *British Journal of Psychiatry, 177*, 499–504.

Gorey, K. M., & Leslie, D. R. (1997). The prevalence of child sexual abuse: Integrative review adjustment for potential response and measurement biases. *Child Abuse & Neglect, 21*, 391–398.

Graber, J. A., Lewinsohn, P. M., Seeley, J. R., & Brooks-Gunn, J. (1997). Is psychopathology associated with the timing of pubertal development? *Journal of the American Academy of Child & Adolescent Psychiatry, 36*, 1768–1776.

Grant, K. E., Lyons, A. L., Finkelstein, J. S., Conway, K. M., Reynolds, L. K., Koon, J. H., et al. (2004). Gender differences in rates of depressive symptoms among low-income, urban, African American youth: A test of two mediational hypotheses. *Journal of Youth and Adolescence, 33*, 523–533.

Gross, J. J. (1998). Antecedent- and response-focused emotion regulation: Divergent consequences for experience, expression, and physiology. *Journal of Personality and Social Psychology, 74*, 224–237.

Hammen, C. (1991). *Depression runs in families: The social context of risk and resilience in children of depressed mothers.* New York: Springer-Verlag.

Hampel, P., & Petermann, F. (2005). Age and gender effects on coping in children and adolescents. *Journal of Youth and Adolescence, 34*, 73–83.

Hankin, B. L., & Abramson, L. Y. (2001). Development of gender differences in depression: An elaborated cognitive vulnerability-transactional stress theory. *Psychological Bulletin, 127,* 773–796.

Hankin, B. L., & Abramson, L. Y. (2002). Measuring cognitive vulnerability to depression in adolescence: Reliability, validity, and gender differences. *Journal of Clinical Child and Adolescent Psychology, 31,* 491–504.

Hankin, B. L., Abramson, L. Y., Moffitt, T. E., McGee, R., Silva, P., & Angell, K. E. (1998). Development of depression from preadolescence to young adulthood: Emerging gender differences in a 10-year longitudinal study. *Journal of Abnormal Psychology, 107,* 128–140.

Hayward, C., Gotlib, I. H., Schraedley, P. K., & Litt, I. F. (1999). Ethnic differences in the association between pubertal status and symptoms of depression in adolescent girls. *Journal of Adolescent Health, 25,* 143–149.

Hilt, L. M., McLaughlin, K., & Nolen-Hoeksema, S. (2006). *Gender and ethnic group differences in response styles among adolescents.* Paper presented at the Association for Psychological Science Annual Convention, New York.

Hilt, L. M., Sander, L. C., Nolen-Hoeksema, S., & Simen, A. A. (2007). The BDNF Val66Met polymorphism predicts rumination and depression differently in young adolescent girls and their mothers. *Neuroscience Letters, 429,* 12–16.

Holahan, C. J., Moos, R. H., Holahan, C. K., & Brennan, P. L. (1996). Social support, coping strategies, and psychosocial adjustment to cardiac illness: Implications for assessment and prevention. *Journal of Prevention & Intervention in the Community, 13,* 33–52.

Joiner, T. E., Jr., & Metalsky, G. I. (2001). Excessive reassurance seeking: Delineating a risk factor involved in the development of depressive symptoms. *Psychological Science, 12,* 371–378.

Kaltiala-Heino, R., Kosunen, E., & Rimpela, M. (2003). Pubertal timing, sexual behaviour and self-reported depression in middle adolescence. *Journal of Adolescence, 26,* 531–545.

Kaufman, J., Martin, A., King, R. A., & Charney, D. (2001). Are child-, adolescent-, and adult-onset depression one and the same disorder? *Biological Psychiatry, 49,* 980–1001.

Kaufman, J., Yang, B.-Z., Douglas-Palumberi, H., Grasso, D., Lipschitz, D., Houshyar, S., et al. (2004). Social supports and serotonin transporter gene moderate depression in maltreated children. *Proceedings of the National Academy of Science of the United States of America, 101,* 17316–17321.

Kaufman, J., Yang, B.-Z., Douglas-Palumberi, H., Grasso, D., Lipschitz, D., Houshyar, S., et al. (2006). Brain-derived neurotrophic factor-5-HHTLPR gene interactions and environmental modifiers of depression in children. *Biological Psychiatry, 59,* 673–680.

Keller, M., & Shapiro, R. (1981). Major depressive disorder: Initial results from a one-year prospective naturalistic follow-up study. *Journal of Nervous Mental Disorders, 169,* 761–768.

Kessler, R. C., McGonagle, K. A., Swartz, M., Blazer, D. G., & Nelson, C. B. (1993). Sex and depression in the National Comorbidity Survey: I. Lifetime prevalence, chronicity and recurrence. *Journal of Affective Disorders, 29,* 85–96.

Kovacs, M. (1980/1981). Rating scales to assess depression in school-aged children. *Acta Paedopsychiatry, 46,* 305–315.

Kovacs, M. (1992). *Children's Depression Inventory manual.* North Tonawanda, NY: Multi-Health Systems.

Kovacs, M. (2001). Gender and the course of major depressive disorder through adolescence in clinically referred youngsters. *Journal of the American Academy of Child & Adolescent Psychiatry, 40,* 1079–1085.

Kudielka, B. M., & Kirschbaum, C. (2005). Sex differences in HPA axis responses to stress: A review. *Biological Psychology, 69,* 113–132.

LaGreca, A. M., & Lopez, N. (1998). Social anxiety among adolescents: Linkages with peer relations and friendships. *Journal of Abnormal Child Psychology, 26,* 83–94.

Larson, R., & Ham, M. (1993). Stress and "storm and stress" in early adolescence: The relationship of negative events with dysphoric affect. *Developmental Psychology, 29,* 130–140.

Larson, R. W., Richards, M. H., Raffaelli, M., Ham, M., & Jewell, L. (1990). Ecology of depression in late childhood and early adolescence: A profile of daily states and activities. *Journal of Abnormal Psychology, 99,* 92–102.

Lazarus, R. S., & Folkman, S. (1984). *Stress, appraisal, and coping.* New York: Springer.

Leadbeater, B. J., Blatt, S. J., & Quinlan, D. M. (1995). Gender-linked vulnerabilities to depressive symptoms, stress, and problem behaviors in adolescents. *Journal of Research on Adolescence, 5,* 1–29.

Lesch, P. K., Dietmar, B., Heils, A., Sabol, S. Z., Greenberg, B. D., Petri, S., et al. (1996). Association of anxiety-related traits with a polymorphism in the serotonin transporter gene regulatory region. *Science, 274,* 1527–1531.

Lewinsohn, P. M., Pettit, J. W., Joiner, T. E., Jr., & Seeley, J. R. (2003). The symptomatic expression of major depressive disorder in adolescents and young adults. *Journal of Abnormal Psychology, 112,* 244–252.

Little, S. A., & Garber, J. (2005). The role of social stressors and interpersonal orientation in explaining the longitudinal relation between externalizing and depressive symptoms. *Journal of Abnormal Psychology, 114,* 432–443.

Liu, X., & Kaplan, H. B. (1999). Explaining gender differences in symptoms of subjective distress in young adolescents. *Stress Medicine, 15,* 41–51.

Lommatzsch, M., Hornych, K., Zingler, C., Schuff-Werner, P., Hoppner, J., Virchow, J. C. (2006). Maternal serum concentrations of BDNF and depression in the perinatal period. *Psychoneuroendocrinology, 31,* 388–394.

Nolen-Hoeksema, S. (1991). Responses to depression and their effects on the duration of depressive episodes. *Journal of Abnormal Psychology, 100,* 569–582.

Nolen-Hoeksema, S. (2000). The role of rumination in depressive disorders and mixed anxiety/depressive symptoms. *Journal of Abnormal Psychology, 109,* 504–511.

Nolen-Hoeksema, S., & Girgus, J. S. (1994). The emergence of gender differences in depression in adolescence. *Psychological Bulletin, 115,* 424–443.

Nolen-Hoeksema, S., Larson, J., & Grayson, C. (1999). Explaining the gender difference in depressive symptoms. *Journal of Personality and Social Psychology, 77,* 1061–1072.

Nottelmann, E. D., Susman, E. J., Blue, J. H., Inoff-Germain, G., Dorn, L. D., Loriaux, D. L., et al. (1987). Gonadal and adrenal hormone correlates of adjustment in early adolescence. In R. M. Lerner & T. T. Foch (Eds.), *Biological-psychosocial interactions in early adolescence* (pp. 303–323). Hillsdale, NJ: Lawrence Erlbaum Associates.

Paikoff, R. L., Brooks-Gunn, J., & Warren, M. P. (1991). Effects of girls' hormonal status on depressive and aggressive symptoms over the course of one year. *Journal of Youth and Adolescence, 20*, 191–215.

Petersen, A. C., Sarigiani, P. A., & Kennedy, R. E. (1991). Adolescent depression: Why more girls? *Journal of Youth and Adolescence, 20*, 247–271.

Post, R. M. (1992). Transduction of psychosocial stress into the neurobiology of recurrent affective disorder. *American Journal of Psychiatry, 149*, 999–1010.

Prinstein, M. J., Boergers, J., & Vernberg, E. M. (2001). Overt and relational aggression in adolescents: Social-psychological adjustment of aggressors and victims. *Journal of Clinical Child Psychology, 30*, 479–491.

Prinstein, M. J., Borelli, J. L., Cheah, C. S. L., Simon, V. A., & Aikins, J. W. (2005). Adolescent girls' interpersonal vulnerability to depressive symptoms: A longitudinal examination of reassurance-seeking and peer relationships. *Journal of Abnormal Psychology, 114*, 676–688.

Rice, F., Harold, G., & Thapar, A. (2002). The genetic aetiology of childhood depression: A review. *Journal of Child Psychology and Psychiatry, 43*, 65–79.

Rierdan, J., & Koff, E. (1991). Depressive symptomatology among very early maturing girls. *Journal of Youth and Adolescence, 20*, 415–425.

Rose, A. J. (2002). Co-rumination in the friendships of girls and boys. *Child Development, 73*, 1830–1843.

Rose, A. J., & Rudolph, K. D. (2006). A review of sex differences in peer relationship processes: Potential trade-offs for the emotional and behavioral development of girls and boys. *Psychological Bulletin, 132*, 98–131.

Rudolph, K. D., Caldwell, M. S., & Conley, C. S. (2005). Need for approval and children's well-being. *Child Development, 76*, 309–323.

Rudolph, K. D., & Conley, C. S. (2005). The socioemotional costs and benefits of social-evaluative concerns: Do girls care too much? *Journal of Personality, 73*, 115–137.

Rudolph, K. D., & Hammen, C. (1999). Age and gender as determinants of stress exposure, generation, and reactions in youngsters: A transactional perspective. *Child Development, 70*, 660–677.

Ryan, N. D. (1998). Psychoneuroendocrinology of children and adolescents. *Psychiatric Clinics of North America, 21*, 435–441

Schwartz, J. A. J., & Koenig, L. J. (1996). Response styles & negative affect among adolescents. *Cognitive Therapy and Research, 20*, 13–36.

Shih, J. H., Eberhart, N. K., Hammen, C. L., & Brennan, P. A. (2006). Differential exposure and reactivity to interpersonal stress predict sex differences in adolescent depression. *Journal of Clinical Child & Adolescent Psychology, 35*, 103–115.

Shimizu, E., Hashimoto, K., Okamura, N., Koike, K., Komatsu, N., Kumakiri, C., et al. (2003). Alterations of serum levels of brain-derived neurotrophic factor (BDNF) in depressed patients with or without antidepressants. *Biological Psychiatry, 54*, 70–75.

Siegel, J. M., Yancey, A. K., Aneshensel, C. S., & Schuler, R. (1999). Body image, perceived pubertal timing, and adolescent mental health. *Journal of Adolescent Health, 25*, 155–165.

Silberg, J. L., Pickels, A., Rutter, M., Hewitt, J., Simonoff, E., Maes, H., et al. (1999). The influence of genetic factors and life stress on depression among adolescent girls. *Archives of General Psychiatry, 56*, 225–232.

Simon, A. E., Wardle, J., Jarvis, M. J., Steggles, N., & Cartwright, M. (2003). Examining the relationship between pubertal stage, adolescent health behaviours and stress. *Psychological Medicine, 33,* 1369–1379.

Smolak, L., & Striegel-Moore, R. H. (2001). Challenging the myth of the golden girl: Ethnicity and eating disorders. In R. H. Striegel-Moore & L. Smolak (Eds.), *Eating disorders: Innovative directions in research and practice* (pp. 111–132). Washington, DC: American Psychological Association.

Sorensen, M. J., Nissen, J. B., Mors, O., & Thomsen, P. H. (2005). Age and gender differences in depressive symptomatology and comorbidity: An incident sample of psychiatrically admitted children. *Journal of Affective Disorders, 84,* 85–91.

Southam-Gerow, M. A., & Kendall, P. C. (2000). A preliminary study of the emotional understanding of youth referred for treatment of anxiety disorders. *Journal of Clinical Child Psychology, 29,* 319–327.

Southwick, S. M., Vythilingam, M., & Charney, D. S. (2005). The psychobiology of depression and resilience to stress: Implications for prevention and treatment. *Annual Review of Clinical Psychology, 1,* 255–292.

Spatz Widom, C., DuMont, K., & Czaja, S. J. (2007). A prospective investigation of major depressive disorder and comorbidity in abused and neglected children grown up. *Archives of General Psychiatry,* 64, 49–56.

Stattin, H., & Magnusson, D. (1990). *Pubertal maturation in female development.* Hillsdale, NJ: Lawrence Erlbaum Associates.

Steinberg, L., & Avenevoli, S. (2000). The role of context in the development of psychopathology: A conceptual framework and some speculative propositions. *Child Development, 71,* 66–74.

Steinberg, L., Dahl, R., Keating, D., Kupfer, D. J., Masten, A. S., & Pine, D. (2006). The study of developmental psychopathology in adolescence: Integrating affective neuroscience with the study of context. In D. Cicchetti & D. Cohen (Eds.), *Developmental psychopathology, Vol. 2: Developmental neuroscience* (pp. 710–741). New York: Wiley.

Steiner, M., Born, L., & Martin, P. (2000). Menarche and mood disorders in adolescence. In M. Steiner, K. A. Yonkers, & E. Erikkson (Eds.), *Mood disorders in women* (pp. 247–268). London: Martin Dunitz.

Steiner, M., Dunn, E., & Born, L. (2003). Hormones and mood: From menarche to menopause and beyond. *Journal of Affective Disorders, 74,* 67–83.

Stice, E., Hayward, C., Cameron, R. P., Killen, J. D., & Taylor, C. B. (2000). Body-image and eating disturbances predict onset of depression among female adolescents: A longitudinal study. *Journal of Abnormal Psychology, 109,* 438–444.

Stice, E., Presnell, K., & Bearman, S. K. (2001). Relation of early menarche to depression, eating disorders, substance abuse, and comorbid psychopathology among adolescent girls. *Developmental Psychology, 37,* 608–619.

Storch, E. A., & Masia-Warner, C. (2004). The relationship of peer victimization to social anxiety and loneliness in adolescent females. *Journal of Adolescence, 27,* 351–362.

Strauss, J., Barr, C. L., George, C. J., Devlin, B., Vetro, A., Kiss, E., et al. (2005). Brain-derived neurotrophic factor variants are associated with childhood-onset mood disorder: Confirmation in a Hungarian sample. *Molecular Psychiatry, 10,* 861–867.

Strauss J., Barr, C. L., George, C. J., King, N., Shaikh, S., Devlin, B., et al. (2004). Association study of brain-derived neurotrophic factor in adults with a history of childhood-onset mood disorder. *American Journal of Medical Genetics (Neuropsychiatry Genetic), 131B*, 16–19.

Sun, M., & Akon, D. L. (2006). Differential gender-related vulnerability to depression induction and converging antidepressant responses in rats. *Journal of Pharmacology and Experimental Therapeutics, 316*, 926–932.

Susman, E. J., Dorn, L. D., & Chrousos, G. P. (1991). Negative affect and hormone levels in young adolescents: Concurrent and predictive perspectives. *Journal of Youth and Adolescence, 20*, 167–190.

Susman, E. J., Inoff-Germain, G., Nottelmann, E. D., Loriaux, D. L., Cutler, G. B., Jr., & Chrousos, G. P. (1987). Hormones, emotional dispositions, and aggressive attributes in young adolescents. *Child Development, 58*, 1114–1134.

Tarullo, A. R., & Gunnar, M. R. (2006). Child maltreatment and the developing HPA axis. *Hormones & Behavior, 50*, 632–639.

Thomas, K. M., Drevets, W. C., Dahl, R. E., Ryan, N. D., Birmahe, B., Eccard, C. H., et al. (2001). Amygdala response to fearful faces in anxious and depressed children. *Archives of General Psychiatry, 58*, 1057–1063.

Twenge, J. M., & Nolen-Hoeksema, S. (2002). Age, gender, race, socioeconomic status, and birth cohort differences on the Children's Depression Inventory: A meta-analysis. *Journal of Abnormal Psychology, 111*, 578–588.

Weiss, E. L., Longhurst, J. G., & Mazure, C. M. (1999). Childhood sexual abuse as a risk factor for depression in women: Psychosocial and neurobiological correlates. *American Journal of Psychiatry, 156*, 816–828.

Widom, C. S., DuMont, K., & Czaja, S. J. (2007). A prospective investigation of major depressive disorder and comorbidity in abused and neglected children grown up. *Archives of General Psychiatry, 64*, 49–56.

Young, E., & Korszun, A. (1999). Women, stress, and depression: Sex differences in hypothalamic-pituitary-adrenal axis regulation. In E. Leibenluft (Ed.), *Gender differences in mood and anxiety disorders: From bench to bedside* (pp. 31–52). Washington, DC: American Psychiatric Press.

Yurgelun-Todd, D. A. (2007). Emotional and cognitive changes during adolescence. *Current Opinions in Neurobiology, 17*, 251–257.

Yurgelun-Todd, D. A., & Killgore, W. D. (2006). Fear-related activity in the prefrontal cortex increases with age during adolescence: A preliminary fMRI study. *Neuroscience Letters, 406*, 194–199.

Zeman, J., Shipman, K., & Suveg, C. (2002). Anger and sadness regulation: Predictions to internalizing an externalizing symptoms in children. *Journal of Clinical Child & Adolescent Psychology, 31*, 393–398.

Section II

RELATED CONDITIONS

Chapter Six

Comorbidities with Adolescent Depression

PAUL ROHDE

CONTENTS

Psychiatric comorbidity can be defined as the co-occurrence of two or more disorders within a diagnostic system at rates that are higher than expected by chance. Comorbidity generally refers to either the *lifetime* (but not necessarily simultaneous) or *concurrent* co-occurrence of disorders. The issue of psychiatric comorbidity received a great deal of attention in the 1990s (e.g., Angold & Costello, 1993; Lewinsohn, Rohde, & Seeley, 1995; Nottelmann & Jensen, 1999; Rohde, Lewinsohn, & Seeley, 1991), and it is now generally recognized that comorbidity represents an important factor to consider in research and clinical decisions, although the empirical basis for understanding how to actually intervene effectively with comorbid depressed adolescents remains surprisingly limited.

The purpose of this chapter is to review the research on comorbidity with major depressive disorder (MDD) in adolescents. The most common categories of comorbid disorders will be examined, including dysthymia, anxiety disorders, disruptive behavior/attention-deficit/hyperactivity disorder (ADHD), substance use disorders (i.e., abuse and dependence), and eating disorders. Psychiatric conditions with lower base rates (e.g., schizophrenia) will not be addressed. In addition, bipolar disorders are not reviewed, as they are the focus of a separate chapter.

The chapter begins with a discussion of the prevalence, temporal order, and impact of each comorbid combination. The temporal precedence of comorbidity, or the degree to which depression consistently precedes or follows the other disorder, offers important clues into both the etiology and treatment of each condition. As will be seen, depression tends to develop after the other disorder rather than precede it (Hettema, Prescott, & Kendler, 2003). The chapter then reviews a sample of potential models accounting for comorbidity, illustrating the variety of possibilities with the combination of depression and substance use disorders.

The majority of depressed adolescents entering treatment have more than one condition (e.g., Biederman, Faraone, Mick, & Lelon, 1995). Thus, a major focus of the chapter is on the impact of comorbidity on treatment with depressed adolescents. The co-occurrence of disorders complicates the conceptualization and provision of treatment and is generally associated with greater treatment utilization, but possibly poorer engagement, lower recovery, and poorer maintenance of gains. Little is known regarding effective treatment delivery for comorbid conditions, however, because individuals with comorbidity have often been excluded from clinical trials. Whether treating one disorder significantly addresses the comorbid condition is considered, as are the small number of interventions specifically developed for the treatment of comorbid depressive conditions. The chapter concludes with implications for clinical practice, including assessment, treatment and prevention, and future research directions.

DATA SETS

My goal is to fairly represent the available research literature, but the review is not intended to be exhaustive. Given that my colleagues and I at the Oregon Research Institute have been actively interested in the occurrence and impact of comorbidity on adolescent depression for almost 20 years, many of the illustrations will be from data sets collected by our research group. The five most pertinent data sets are described next.

The Oregon Adolescent Depression Project (OADP)

The OADP is one of the largest longitudinal samples of diagnostically interviewed adolescents currently available, and began as a two-panel, randomly selected sample of high school adolescents (14–18 years) assessed between 1987 and 1990 (Lewinsohn, Hops, Roberts, Seeley, & Andrews, 1993). A total of 1,709 adolescents completed the initial (T1) interview and questionnaires, with an overall participation rate of 61%. Half of the T1 sample (53%) was female, with an average age of 16.6 years (*SD*=1.2). A total of 9% were non-White or Hispanic, and 53% were living with two biological parents. Approximately 1 year later, 1,507 participants (88%) returned for a readministration of the questionnaire and interview assessments. As participants reached their twenty-fourth birthday, a third wave of questionnaires and interviews (T3) was obtained from all participants with a history of psychopathology at T2 and a randomly selected subset of participants with no history of mental disorder (Lewinsohn, Rohde, Seeley, Klein, & Gotlib, 2003). Diagnostic data on the first-degree relatives of OADP probands were collected as part of a separate study (Klein, Lewinsohn, Seeley, & Rohde, 2001).

The Adolescent Coping With Depression Course (CWD-A)

The CWD-A (Clarke, Lewinsohn, & Hops, 1990), a group cognitive-behavioral treatment (CBT) for adolescent depression, was originally evaluated in two randomized controlled trials (RCTs). In the first (Lewinsohn, Clarke, Hops, & Andrews, 1990), 59 adolescents meeting DSM-III criteria for MDD or intermittent depression were randomly assigned to (a) an adolescent group only, (b) the adolescent group with a separate group for parents, or (c) wait-list. Participants and their parents were assessed to 24 months post-treatment. All significant improvement was accounted for by the two active treatment conditions compared to wait-list (Beck Depression Invention [BDI]; Beck, Ward, Mendelson, Mock, & Erbaugh, 1961; effect size d=1.18). Contrary to our expectation, differences between adolescent only and adolescent+parent conditions were minimal. Forty-six percent of treated adolescents no longer met diagnostic criteria for depression by the end of treatment (compared with 5% in the wait-list), and 83% had recovered by 6 months post-treatment.

The second clinical trial replicated the initial design, but involved 96 adolescents meeting DSM-III-R criteria for MDD or dysthymia (Clarke, Rohde, Lewinsohn, Hops, & Seeley, 1999). As in the first trial, recovery rates at post in the two active treatments were superior to wait-list (BDI $d=0.39$), with nonsignificant differences between the two active treatments. Sixty-seven percent of treated adolescents no longer met criteria at post-treatment versus 48% in the wait-list. By 12 months post-treatment, 81% had recovered (98% by 24 months).

Making a Plan for Success (MAPS)

The next RCT (Rohde, Clarke, Mace, Jorgensen, & Seeley, 2004a) evaluated the effectiveness of the CWD-A for depressed adolescents with comorbid conduct disorder (CD; 72% of whom also had a current substance use disorder at intake). Between 1998 and 2001, 93 adolescents (ages 13–17) meeting criteria for MDD/CD were recruited from a county department of juvenile justice, and randomly assigned to the CWD-A or a life skills/tutoring (LS) control group (a total of 182 youth were treated but not all met all inclusion/exclusion criteria). Participants were assessed to 12-month follow-up. To my knowledge, the MAPS project was the first reasonably powered RCT of a psychosocial intervention with comorbid depressed adolescents.

Treatment for Adolescents with Depression Study (TADS)

Dr. Anne Simons of the University of Oregon and I have been serving as codirectors of a treatment site in the NIMH-funded TADS project, and this chapter includes data on the presence and impact of comorbidity in this important study. TADS compared individual CBT, fluoxetine, combination CBT/fluoxetine, and a pill placebo with clinical management in adolescents, ages 12–17, with MDD (TADS Team, 2004). Using the Children's Depression Rating Scale-Revised (CDRS-R; Poznanski & Mokros, 1995) as the primary outcome, results from the acute (12-week) phase (TADS Team, 2004) indicated a significant advantage for combination treatment compared to pill placebo ($p=0.001$), which was not present for fluoxetine ($p=0.10$) or CBT ($p=0.40$) monotherapies. Combined treatment was also superior to fluoxetine ($p=0.02$) and CBT ($p=0.01$), while fluoxetine was superior to CBT ($p=0.01$). Using a dichotomous measure of recovery (Clinical Global Impression Improvement score), rates of response were 71% combination treatment, 61% fluoxetine, 43% CBT, and 35% pill placebo. Data regarding improvement during the entire 36-week course of treatment have recently been published (TADS Team, 2007) and indicate that treatments converge by their conclusion. Although the inclusion criteria for TADS required a primary diagnosis of MDD and excluded adolescents with a current severe CD or substance abuse/dependence diagnosis, almost half of the participants (48%) had at least one current comorbid diagnosis (TADS Team, 2005).

EPIDEMIOLOGY OF COMORBIDITIES

MDD and Dysthymia

The first examined comorbidity is the other unipolar affective disorder recognized by the DSM, namely dysthymia. For MDD and dysthymia to be concurrent, the acute episode MDD needs to be superimposed on a pre-existing chronic dysthymic episode, a condition that has been termed "double depression" (Keller &

Shapiro, 1982). The extent and nature of MDD/dysthymia comorbidity seems to have been examined in greatest detail in Lewinsohn, Rohde, Seeley, and Hops (1991), who described the prevalence and impact of MDD/dysthymia in the large community OADP sample at T1 (n=1,710) and in a large sample of community-residing adults (n=2,060). MDD was by far the more frequent form of depression. Among the depressed adolescents, 84% experienced only MDD (which we termed "pure MDD"), 9% experienced only dysthymia, and 7% experienced both MDD and dysthymia; comparable rates for adults were 79%, 11%, and 10%, respectively. Consistent with this distribution, in the TADS project, which required that all adolescents have current MDD, 10.5% also had concurrent dysthymia. Dysthymia in the Lewinsohn et al. study was highly comorbid with MDD, with concurrent comorbidity rates of Odds Ratio (*OR*)=20.2 for adolescents (compared to 4.4 for adults) and lifetime comorbidity rates of *OR*=3.4 for adolescents (1.6 for adults). Although comorbid, it is important to note that 93% of the adolescents with MDD had not experienced dysthymia and 58% of the adolescents with dysthymia had not had MDD. Gender differences in the distributions were nonsignificant.

Other studies have reported a significant degree of association between MDD and dysthymia in adolescents. In a community sample of 150 adolescents (Kashani et al., 1987), 12 participants had current dysthymia. Of these, 7 (58%) had a current diagnosis of MDD. Kovacs et al. (1984) reported that 70% of child/adolescents patients with a history of dysthymia developed MDD within 24 months of recovery from the index episode, compared to approximately 30% of those with no history of dysthymia.

Temporal Order

Among adolescents with both MDD and dysthymia, the dysthymia was more likely to precede than to follow MDD, with 91% experiencing their chronic disorder first, compared to 64% of adults with comorbid MDD/dysthymia (Lewinsohn et al., 1991). Because the diagnosis of dysthymia requires a duration of 1 year for young persons, rather than the 2-week duration required for MDD, there was the potential danger that the temporal pattern represented an artifact of the diagnostic system. However, the mean difference in onset age between MDD and dysthymia in the adolescents was substantially larger than 1 year (mean onset of MDD was 14.3 years of age versus mean onset of 11.1 years for dysthymia), which suggests that the distribution is not purely an artifact of the diagnostic system.

Impact

One difference between the adolescent and adult samples in the Lewinsohn et al. study was whether or not the depressed person was likely to receive mental health treatment. Among the depressed adolescents, differences in treatment utilization between the three depressed groups were nonsignificant, but a trend was present for the pure MDD group to be least likely to receive treatment (23% vs. 28% given pure dysthymia and 30% given comorbid MDD/dysthymia). Conversely, among adults, differences in treatment utilization were significant, with the pure dysthymia group being the least likely to receive treatment (27% versus 47% given pure MDD and 49% given comorbid MDD/dysthymia). These findings suggest that depression treatment utilization may be driven by chronicity in adolescents and by severity in adults.

MDD and Anxiety Disorders

The most common comorbidity with depression in adolescents appears to be anxiety (Essau, 2003; Karlsson et al., 2006), with 25–50% of depressed children and adolescents having a comorbid anxiety disorder and 10–15% of anxious youth having comorbid depression (Axelson & Birmaher, 2001). In a longitudinal community sample of 9- to 16-year-olds (Costello, Mustillo, Erkanli, Keeler, & Angold, 2003), depression and anxiety disorders had an *OR*=28.9 for girls and 27.9 for boys, controlling for other comorbidities. These were the highest associations with depression in that report. In a very large sample of British children, ages 5–15 years, Ford, Goodman, and Meltzer (2003) reported an adjusted OR between depression and anxiety of 17.0. The association between depression and anxiety disorders in the OADP, while significant, was lower in magnitude (*OR*=4.4; Lewinsohn et al., 1991), with no significant gender difference. In TADS, 27.4% of adolescent patients with MDD had a current anxiety disorder, with generalized anxiety disorder and social phobia being the two most common comorbid conditions (15.3% and 10.7%, respectively).

Reasons for the high degree of comorbidity between MDD and anxiety are unknown, although hypotheses include a common underlying construct of negative affect (i.e., a general tendency to experience distress and to worry), shared temperamental features (e.g., behavioral inhibition), and shared factors in neurotransmitter abnormalities and brain functioning responses (e.g., Angold & Costello, 1993; Axelson & Birmaher, 2001; Essau, 2003). Depression and anxiety disorders are known to cosegregate in families (e.g., Axelson & Birmaher, 2001; Williamson, Forbes, Dahl, & Ryan, 2005), and examination of the patterns of co-occurrence across family members can offer insight into the mechanisms for this phenomenon, as discussed in the section concerning models of comorbidity.

Temporal Order

Anxiety disorders generally have been found to precede rather than follow depression (e.g., Williamson et al., 2005). Among OADP adolescents with comorbid MDD/anxiety disorders, the anxiety disorders occurred first in 85% of the cases. In a large sample of German adolescents, 12–17 years of age, among participants who had comorbid depression and anxiety, 72% developed the anxiety disorder first (Essau, 2003). Regarding specific anxiety disorders, social anxiety increased the odds of future depressive disorder threefold in large sample of adolescents and young adults (ages 14–24) over a 3- to 4-year period (Stein et al., 2001). This temporal ordering of anxiety disorders preceding depression, however, has not been consistently noted (e.g., Breier, Charney, & Heninger, 1985), and Costello et al. (2003) found support for both depression predicting future anxiety and for anxiety to predict future depression in a large representative sample of 9- to 16-year-old youth. When analyses were conducted separately by gender, however, these associations were significant for only the female subset.

Impact

Comorbid MDD/social anxiety has been found to be associated with elevated rates of suicidal ideation and attempts (Stein et al., 2001). However, in Lewinsohn et al. (1995), we found that, compared to adolescents with pure

MDD, adolescents with comorbid MDD/anxiety disorder had higher rates of treatment utilization, but no other elevated rates of the negative consequences that were examined (i.e., poor global functioning, suicide attempts, poor physical health, academic problems, parental conflict).

MDD and Disruptive Behavior Disorders

Externalizing disorders were previously thought to "mask" adolescent depression (e.g., Glaser, 1967). Although this has been shown not to be the case, there is some truth to the fact that externalizing symptoms usually demand more attention from parents and teachers than internalizing symptoms, and thus, are more likely to result in treatment interventions. In their review, Nottelmann and Jensen (1995) found very high rates of comorbidity between the disruptive behavior disorders of CD, and oppositional defiant disorder (ODD), and depression in community samples, ranging from 42 to 82%. Fleming and Offord (1990) reviewed studies of child/adolescent depression and found that 17 to 79% of depressed youth had comorbid CD, 0–50% had comorbid ODD, and 0–57% had comorbid ADHD. In clinic samples, rates of concurrent CD in depressed adolescents range from 14 to 25% (Kovacs, Paulauskas, Gatsonis, & Richards, 1988; Marriage, Fine, Moretti, & Haley, 1986; Ryan et al., 1987); rates of lifetime comorbidity with CD are even higher (e.g., 36%; Kovacs et al., 1988). Similarly, rates of depression in samples of juvenile delinquents, the great majority of whom meet criteria for CD, are also elevated over base rates (e.g., Alessi, McManus, Grapentine, & Brickman, 1984; Chiles, Miller, & Cox, 1980). Several mechanisms for an association between adolescent depression and disruptive behavior disorders have been proposed, including possible shared environmental features (e.g., parental style and effectiveness) and a common genetic predisposition (e.g., McCracken, Cantwell, & Hanna, 1993).

In the OADP, the OR for lifetime comorbidity between depressive disorders and disruptive behavior disorders was 2.1 (Lewinsohn et al., 1991). Concurrent comorbidity had an $OR = 5.3$, but differed by gender. Currently depressed young men were significantly more likely than nondepressed young men to have current CD or ODD ($OR = 18.20$), whereas currently depressed young women were not ($OR = 0.99$). Ford et al. (2003) reported significant comorbidity between depression and CD (adjusted $OR = 15.4$), but noted that associations between depression and both ADHD and ODD became nonsignificant controlling for the presence of other disorders. The rates of disruptive behavior disorders in TADS were 23.5% (TADS Team, 2005), with 13.7% having current ADHD and 13.2% ODD. Severe CD was an exclusion criterion in TADS, and CD was diagnosed in only 0.5% of the patients at intake.

Costello et al. (2003) reported a different pattern of comorbidities for male and female adolescents. For female participants, ADHD was unrelated to depressive disorders, whereas CD and ODD were significantly comorbid in both unadjusted and adjusted analyses (which controlled for other comorbidities); adjusted $ORs = 10.6$ and 7.1, respectively. Among male participants, ADHD was significantly comorbid with depressive disorders in adjusted analyses ($OR = 3.4$), but CD and ODD were not.

Temporal Order

Depressive disorders and CD both accelerate in prevalence during adolescence (Cohen et al., 1993). It is unclear, however, whether depression tends to precede or follow CD. In our previous research (Rohde et al., 1991), depression typically followed rather than preceded the disruptive behavior disorder, occurring after the disruptive behavior disorder in 72% of the cases where it co-occurred. Other studies in which CD or conduct problems tended to precede depression include Biederman et al. (1995), Block and Gjerde (1990), and Riggs, Baker, Mikulich, Young, and Crowley (1995). However, other research (e.g., Drabick, Gadow, & Sprafkin, 2006; Geller, Chestnut, Miller, Price, & Yates, 1985) has found that the CD behaviors appeared at or following the onset of depression. More recent evidence exists for a bidirectional association between depression and externalizing problem behaviors in adolescents (Measelle, Stice, & Hogansen, 2006). Given the diagnostic requirement that it is evident prior to 7 years of age, ADHD almost always precedes MDD.

Impact

Capaldi (1991) found that sixth grade boys with both depression and conduct problems had the greatest functional impairments, exhibiting the adjustment problems associated with each disorder. The comorbid boys also had more problems with poor academics and substance use, more than boys with either pure conduct or pure depression problems. We also found that compared to adolescents with noncomorbid depression, young people with comorbid depression/disruptive behavior disorders were more likely to have academic problems (39% vs. 9%) (Lewinsohn et al., 1995). The comorbidity of CD and depression also has a significantly negative impact on both current and future psychosocial functioning (Ezpeleta, Domenech, & Angold, 2006; Fombonne et al., 2001; Marmorstein, & Iacono, 2001). Other research has found that comorbid conduct problems and depression in adolescents are associated with suicidal ideation (Capaldi, 1992), suicide attempts (Fombonne, Wostear, Cooper, Harrington, & Rutter, 2001; Miller, Chiles, & Barnes, 1982), and completed suicide (Shaffer, 1974). Patterson and Capaldi (1990) hypothesized that antisocial boys are vulnerable to developing depressed mood because their antisocial behaviors interfere with the development of prosocial skills in the academic and social areas, and Patterson and Stoolmiller (1991) found support for this dual failure model.

Whether CD impacts the course of depression is unclear. Comorbidity, in some studies, predicted a more chronic or recurrent course of depression (e.g., Keller, Beardslee, Lavori, Wunder, Drs, & Samuelson, 1988; Kovacs, Gatsonis, Paulauskas, & Richards, 1989). Conversely, other studies of youth at a variety of developmental periods found no indication that comorbid CD negatively impacted the course of depression (Campbell & Ewing, 1990; Harrington, Fudge, Rutter, Pickles, & Hill, 1991; Kovacs et al., 1988). It does not appear as though depression has a marked impact on the long-term course of CD (e.g., Chiles et al., 1980; Harrington et al., 1991), although comorbid depression has been found to be associated with an earlier onset of conduct symptoms (Riggs et al., 1995).

MDD and Substance Use Disorders

Depression, both at the level of diagnosis and the level of symptoms (subsyndromal depression), appears to have strong and consistent associations with substance use disorders (e.g., Brook, Whiteman, Finch, & Cohen, 1996; Helzer & Pryzbeck, 1988). Approximately 20–30% of community adolescents with depression have comorbid substance use disorder (Armstrong & Costello, 2002; Kandel et al., 1997; Kessler et al., 1996). Depression may have an even stronger association with substance use disorders in adolescents than adults (Clark, Kirisci, & Tarter, 1998; Kessler et al., 1994; Rohde et al., 1991). Concurrent and lifetime comorbidity rates of unipolar depression and substance use disorders were *OR*=8.0 and 4.4, respectively (Lewinsohn et al., 1991), with no significant gender differences. Costello et al. (2003) found that depressive disorders were significantly comorbid with substance use disorders among females (*OR*=2.9 in adjusted models), but not males (*OR*=0.2). Rates of comorbid depression/substance use disorder among clinical samples of adolescents may be even higher (e.g., Lewinsohn et al., 1995; Obando, Kliewer, Murrelle, & Svikis, 2004; Wise, Cuffe, & Fischer, 2001).

Temporal Order

The temporal precedence between depression and substance use disorders in adolescence is less predictable than either anxiety or disruptive behavior disorders. In the OADP sample, the substance use disorder preceded depression in 64% of the comorbid cases at T1 (Lewinsohn et al., 1991) and substance abuse predicted MDD at a future assessment (Rohde et al., 2001). On the other hand, depressive symptoms in a sample of female adolescents predicted increases in substance abuse symptoms (Measelle et al., 2006), and depression was a risk factor for future substance use disorders in male, but not female, adolescents (Sung, Erkanli, Angold, & Costello, 2004). Given the implications of temporal order on theories of etiology, more research on temporal ordering between these two conditions is provided in the next section, illustrating various models accounting for comorbid depression and substance use disorder.

Impact

Whereas both depression and substance use disorders each result in numerous negative consequences, their co-occurrence appears to be the single greatest risk factor for adolescent suicide attempt and completion (Aharonovich, Liu, Nunes, & Hasin, 2002; Vermeiren et al., 2003; Wagner, Cole, & Schwartzman, 1996). For example, suicide attempts occurred in 35% of OADP adolescents with comorbid MDD/substance use disorder compared to 19% in adolescents with pure MDD (Lewinsohn et al., 1995). Comorbid depression/substance use disorders are also associated with academic impairment (King et al., 1996; Lewinsohn et al., 1995; Marmorstein & Iacono, 2001; Wilens, Biederman, Abrantes, & Spencer, 1997); family dysfunction (Diamond et al., 2006; Rowe, Liddle, Greenbaum, & Henderson, 2004); increased functional impairment (Lewinsohn et al., 1995; Rowe, Liddle, & Dakof, 2001); and HIV risk (Dausey & Desai, 2003; Tubman, Wagner, & Langer, 2003).

MDD and Eating Disorders

The concurrent and lifetime ORs of unipolar depression and eating disorders in the OADP sample at T1 were 69.1 and 9.0, respectively (Lewinsohn et al., 1991). However, this association was significant only for female adolescents, as the rates of eating disorders were extremely low in the young men, regardless of whether or not they were depressed (lifetime prevalence of eating disorder was 0.12% in males at the first assessment, Lewinsohn et al., 1993). In a sample of 120 Canadian adolescents (93% female) with a variety of DSM-III-R eating disorders, 45% of the participants had a current MDD diagnosis (Geist, Davis, & Heinman, 1998). Among the subset of participants with the bingeing and purging symptoms associated with bulimia nervosa, 96% had MDD, or dysthymia, or ODD. Dansky et al. (1998) found that 36% of American women with binge eating disorder had a lifetime comorbid episode of MDD. An analysis of the OADP participants found that the association between dysthymia and bulimia was stronger than the association between MDD and bulimia (Perez, Joiner, & Lewinsohn, 2004). The rates of comorbid depressive disorders among patients being treated for eating disorders are substantially higher. For example, 94% of female inpatients treated for eating disorders had a comorbid mood disorder, which most commonly was MDD (Blinder, Cumella, & Sanathara, 2006), and 73% of young adolescents treated for anorexia had a depressive disorder during the course of their eating disorder (Lucka, 2006).

Temporal Order

Support for both directional hypotheses exist (Zaider, Johnson, & Cockell, 2002). Some researchers have hypothesized that depression predates the eating disorder, which actually represents a variant of mood disorder, whereas other research has suggests that the starvation or malnutrition from anorexia causes hormonal or neurotransmitter changes that lead to depression (O'Brien & Vincent, 2003). Eating disorder symptomatology have been found to predict future depression in adolescent females (Stice, Hayward, Cameron, Killen, & Taylor, 2000), and the presence of anorexia nervosa at age 16 increases the probability of depressive disorders in young adulthood (Ivarsson, Rastam, Wentz, Gillberg, & Gillberg, 2000). Conversely, negative affect in general, and depression in particular precede the onset of bulimic pathology (Measelle et al., 2006; Stice, Killen, Hayward, & Taylor, 1998), perhaps because the binge eating provides some comfort and distraction from negative emotions (McCarthy, 1990). The association between depression and future disordered eating may be stronger for female compared to male adolescents (McCabe & Vincent, 2003). Stice, Burton, and Shaw (2004) suggest that there may be reciprocal relations between eating disorder pathology and depression. It is possible that there is a feedback loop operating, wherein adolescents begin to binge and purge in an effort to regulate their negative affect, which results in even greater affective disturbances, and so on.

Impact

In a review of factors associated with negative outcomes among individuals with eating disorders, depression was the only factor associated with poorer outcomes for individuals with bulimia nervosa (Berkman, Lohr, & Bulik, 2007). Stice and Fairburn (2003) found that compared to nondepressed young women with bulimia, the depressive-dietary subtype reported greater social impairment and comorbidity. Anorexic adolescents who are depressed may have a greater likelihood of past child sexual abuse (Carter, Bewell, Blackmore, & Woodside, 2006), and while anorexia in general is associated with high rates of suicide, the risk is exacerbated by the presence of depression (Franko & Keel, 2006).

MODELS OF COMORBIDITY CAUSATION

Using Family Studies to Examine Models of Comorbidity

Although longitudinal epidemiologic studies of community samples probably provide the most accurate estimates of the prevalence of comorbidity, other designs, including family and twin studies, are better suited for testing models of etiology. Klein and Riso (1993) described six plausible explanations of the comorbidity between MDD and a comorbid disorder that can be explored using family studies. First, MDD and the comorbid disorder may share some or all of the same familial etiological factors. For example, Clark, Watson, and Mineka (1994) hypothesized that a temperament characterized by high negative affectivity predisposes individuals to both MDD and anxiety disorders. The second model is that the comorbid condition may have a causal influence on MDD, or vice versa. Third, the comorbid condition may be a third, independent disorder in its own right. Fourth, the comorbid condition may be a complex, or multiform, expression of one of the pure disorders, but differs from the other pure disorders. Fifth, the comorbid condition may be a heterogeneous mixture of expressions of pure MDD and expressions of the other pure disorder. Sixth, MDD and the comorbid disorder may be independently transmitted, and their co-occurrence may be due to assortative mating and/or nonfamilial etiological factors, such as childhood and adult adversity (Brown, Gleghorn, Schuckit, Myers, & Mott, 1996; Brown, Harris, & Eales, 1993).

We explored these six explanations for the comorbidity between MDD and anxiety disorders using a family study of the OADP sample and their first-degree relatives (Klein, Lewinsohn, Rohde, Seeley, & Shankman, 2003). Participants included 112 adolescents with a lifetime history of both MDD and one or more anxiety disorder, 290 adolescents with a history of MDD but no anxiety disorder, 43 adolescents with a history of one or more anxiety disorder but no MDD, 352 adolescents with no lifetime history of either MDD or anxiety, and the 2,608 first-degree relatives of these OADP participants. Compared with controls, MDD aggregated in the families of OADP participants with MDD, whether or not they had comorbid anxiety disorder. Similarly, anxiety disorders aggregated in the families of OADP participants with anxiety disorders, regardless of whether they had comorbid MDD. Comorbid MDD/anxiety disorders aggregated only in the families of OADP participants who had both MDD and anxiety disorder. These patterns were consistent with the independent transmission of MDD and anxiety disorders within families.

Models of Comorbidity Between Depression and Substance Use Disorders: An Illustration

The models and analyses proposed by Klein and Riso (1993) can be applied to any combination of two disorders. In addition, there are more specific models that address unique combinations of comorbid disorders, as illustrated next with the example of depression and substance use disorders. Although the significant comorbidity between depression and substance use disorders is well-documented, the causal nature of this association has been debated for some time (e.g., Kessler & Price, 1993; Merikangas, 1990). Four basic models could account for these associations.

Self-Medication Model

Many clinicians and patients believe that drug abuse is a maladaptive coping mechanism to mitigate depression (e.g., Khantzian, 1985). Consistent with this model, MDD has been found to predict substance use disorders in community adolescents (Costello, Erkanli, Federman, & Angold, 1999; Kuo, Gardner, Kendler, & Prescott, 2006; Rao, Daley, & Hammen, 2000; Whitmore et al., 1997). Also consistent with this model, CBT for depression improved substance abuse/dependence outcomes for depressed adults in addiction treatment (Brown, Evans, Miller, Burgess, & Mueller, 1997; Patten et al., 1998; Turner & Wehl, 1984), and antidepressants, compared to placebo, reduced depression and alcohol consumption in adults with MDD/alcoholism (Cornelius et al., 1997; McGrath et al., 1996). Others, however, have found that depression in community adolescents did not predict future substance use (e.g., Degenhardt, Hall, & Lynskey, 2003; Galaif, Sussman, Chou, & Wills, 2003; Hallfors, Waller, Bauer, Ford, & Halpern, 2006; Stice, Burton, & Shaw, 2004), and that the treatment of depression in adolescents did not reduce substance use disorders (e.g., Riggs, Mikulich, & Hall, 2001; Rohde et al., 2004a; Schmitz et al., 2001). In total, evidence for the model is mixed, and current support for the self-medication hypothesis alone, especially in adolescents, is not compelling.

Affective Consequences Model

According to this model, drug abuse creates or exacerbates depression. Prospective research has found that substance abuse predicts future depression (e.g., Brook, Brook, Zhang, Cohen, & Whiteman, 2002; Degenhardt et al., 2003; Hallfors et al., 2006; Rao et al., 2000; Rohde, Clarke, Lewinsohn, Seeley, & Kaufman, 2001; Swendsen & Merikangas, 2000). Among patients, substance use disorders precede depression in the majority of comorbid adults (e.g., Mirin & Weiss, 1991; Rounsaville, Weissman, Crits-Christoph, Wilber, & Kleber, 1982), and depression often remits in adults with substance abuse/dependence following detoxification (e.g., Brown & Schuckit, 1988; Brown et al., 1995). However, the likelihood of spontaneous depression remission following detoxification is less pronounced in adolescents with substance use disorders (e.g., Bukstein, Glancy, & Kaminer, 1992; Riggs et al., 1995; Subramaniam, Lewis, Stitzer, & Fishman, 2004). Moreover, the well-established fact that depression increases the risk of substance abuse/dependence relapse (Greenfield et al., 1998; McKay et al., 2002; Waldron, Turner, & Ozechowski, 2006) is inconsistent with a purely affective consequences model.

Independent Factors Model

This model posits that independent factors promote and maintain depression and substance use disorders. Thus, recovery in one condition would not automatically result in reductions in the other. Consistent with this model, in our research with depressed/conduct disordered adolescents, most of whom had one or more current substance use disorders, significant depression reductions occurred with no corresponding change in substance use disorder status (Rohde et al., 2004a). Also consistent with this model, CBT for women with comorbid PTSD/substance use disorder resulted in reduced alcohol use disorders, but no corresponding reductions in depression (Cohen & Hien, 2006). Overall, however, evidence fails to support the independent factors model. As noted previously, mixed findings for the impact of depression treatment on substance use disorders and higher relapse following drug/alcohol treatment for patients with comorbid substance use disorders and depression, while difficult to interpret, suggest that recovery in one condition is related in some way to recovery in the other. In addition, research has shown that the presence of comorbid depression reduces the effectiveness of substance use disorder treatment in adolescents and adults (e.g., Mueller, Lavori, Keller, & Swartz, 1994; Ritsher, McKellar, Finney, Otilingam, & Moos, 2002; Waldron et al., 2006).

Reciprocal Relations Model

The self-medication and affective consequences models are not mutually exclusive. In light of support for each model, a plausible perspective is that each disorder contributes to maintenance of the other. Given the magnitude of research supporting the self-medication and affective consequences models, empirical findings converge to provide the most support for a reciprocal relations perspective (although the evidence tends to favor the affective consequences model).

How one best addresses the reciprocal relations between depression and substance use disorders (and other comorbidities) remains an empirical question. Although, as noted earlier, epidemiologic and family/genetic studies have typically been proposed as methods for understanding the nature and mechanisms of comorbidity, RCTs are an underutilized but powerful tool for advancing theoretical conceptualizations (Glantz, 2002; Hinshaw, 2002). Unlike other designs, RCTs offer the possibility of experimentally controlling potentially relevant processes. This advantage is particularly relevant regarding the maintenance of comorbid conditions, in which the impact of each disorder on the other condition can be examined when treatments are provided in a sequenced approach. For example, one could first treat the depressive disorder and evaluate what impact depression treatment has on substance use, or conversely, first treat the substance use disorder and monitor potential reductions in depression. Prospective epidemiologic studies tend to reflect etiologic processes, whereas RCTs provide a method of testing models regarding maintenance processes. This is an important conceptual distinction because risk and maintenance processes could be quite different, and maintenance factors are actually more relevant for the development of effective treatment interventions. The various ways in which comorbidity can impact treatment is my next focus.

IMPACT OF COMORBIDITY ON TREATMENT

Comorbidity complicates the selection and delivery of treatment services (e.g., McKay, 2005; Star, Bober, & Gold, 2005), and interventions need to be tested to understand which treatments address which disorders in adolescents with comorbid conditions (Hibbs, 1995). Which disorder should be treated first? Should disorders be treated separately or simultaneously? Answers to basic service delivery questions such as these are currently unknown. Comorbidity can impact the treatment of depression in a number of ways, including increasing the likelihood of treatment utilization, increasing the severity of depression or functional impairment at intake, decreasing the depressed adolescent's engagement and retention in treatment, decreasing the effectiveness of the intervention in reducing depression, and reducing the adolescent's ability to maintain their gains. In addition, comorbid depression can decrease the effectiveness of treating the other conditions. It is also possible that an existing treatment designed for one disorder can successfully address both conditions. Lastly, new interventions explicitly developed for comorbid conditions may be needed, and a few such models have been proposed. Each of these potential scenarios is discussed next.

Comorbidity Increases Treatment Utilization

It has been repeatedly shown that individuals with two or more psychiatric conditions are over-represented in patient samples (e.g., Bukstein, Cornelius, Trunzo, Kelly, & Wood, 2005). To illustrate the magnitude of this effect, Lewinsohn et al. (1995) showed that the percent of OADP adolescents who had received treatment went from 4 to 25% to 50 to 66% among young people with 0, 1, 2, and 3, or more psychiatric disorders, respectively. Specifically regarding adolescent depression, 22% of adolescents with noncomorbid depression received treatment, compared to 49% of depressed adolescents with comorbid anxiety disorder, 61% of depressed adolescents with comorbid disruptive behavior disorder, and 65% of depressed adolescents with comorbid substance use disorder. This effect was not due to the other disorders necessarily resulting in greater treatment utilization, as treatment rates were 18% given pure anxiety disorder, 30% given pure disruptive behavior disorder, and 35% given pure substance use disorder adolescents. In Rohde et al. (1991), we noted that the pattern of treatment seeking among adults was noticeably different. Unlike adolescents, purely depressed adults were almost as likely as comorbid depressed adults to have sought treatment (35% vs. 39%, difference ns). Whereas we found no gender interactions in the impact of comorbidity on treatment seeking, Essau (2003) noted that comorbid anxiety disorders led to significantly greater increases in mental health utilization for depressed male compared to female adolescents.

Comorbid Adolescents are More Depressed and Impaired at Intake

Rohde et al. (2001) examined the impact of comorbidity on the CWD-A intervention with depressed adolescents. Our first hypothesis was that comorbidity would negatively affect the depressed adolescent by increasing the severity of his or her depression or functional impairment at the onset of treatment. BDI scores at intake were examined as a function of total lifetime comorbidity and specific comorbidity categories. Adolescents with any comorbidity had significantly higher BDI average intake scores compared with adolescents with no history of comorbidity. When BDI scores for the three constituent comorbidity diagnoses were compared, significant differences were found for the participants with anxiety disorders versus those with no anxiety (BDI Mean [*SD*]=29.8 [9.7] vs. 23.2 [10.0], $p<0.001$, Cohen's $d=0.66$). Differences as a function of comorbid substance use and disruptive behavior disorders were nonsignificant. In addition, global assessment of functioning (GAF) was significantly poorer in adolescents with any comorbidity (GAF Mean [*SD*]=54.4 [7.4] vs. 60.0 [7.4], $p<0.001$, Cohen's $d=0.76$).

Comorbidity Decreases Engagement and Retention

Different categories of comorbidity may have different effects on treatment. For example, in the treatment of adolescent substance abusers, the presence of comorbid mood disorders was associated with *higher* rates of treatment completion, whereas the presence of comorbid conduct disorders was associated with lower rates of treatment completion (Kaminer et al., 1992). Others have found that among adolescents with substance use disorder, comorbid depression predicts better treatment attendance (Pagnin, de Queiroz, & Saggese, 2005). In the area of depression, however, evidence suggests that comorbidity impairs engagement in depression treatment compared to adolescents with noncomorbid mood disorders. For example, Rowe, Sullivan, Mulder, and Joyce (1996) found that depressed patients with elevated CD symptoms were more likely to drop out of pharmacotherapy, although depression recovery rates did not differ as a function of past CD symptoms.

Another hypothesis in Rohde et al. (2001) was that depressed adolescents with comorbidity would show less participation in treatment, less consistent attendance, lower ratings on therapy homework completion, and lower levels of cohesiveness with the treatment group. Poor participation in treatment might act as a mediator for any negative treatment outcome effects associated with comorbidity. However, all correlations between the comorbidity categories (total, anxiety, disruptive behavior, substance use disorders) and the in-session process indicators (i.e., number of sessions attended, average homework completed, group cohesion scores at sessions 3, 8, and 16) were nonsignificant. Thus, within the limits of our experimental design, the presence of comorbidity was not a contraindication for use of our group CBT program.

Using data from the MAPS study, we identified the predictors of treatment engagement and retention among 182 multidisordered adolescents referred from juvenile corrections and randomly assigned to the CWD-A or life skills/tutoring. Engagement was defined as attending at least one session (yes/no) and retention was a continuous measure of number of sessions attended. Male drug abusers had a high likelihood of attending no sessions. Of the male participants who attended zero sessions, 47% had a drug use disorder versus 14% of males who attended one or more sessions; $OR=5.5$, 95% $CI=1.9–16.0$. Drug use disorder did not predict engagement for the female participants (drug use disorders were present in 25% of young women who attended zero sessions versus 36% who attended one or more sessions). Regarding retention, only one comorbidity measure predicted amount of attendance: adolescents with alcohol abuse/dependence attended fewer sessions ($M=8.9$; $SD=4.6$ sessions) than adolescents without alcohol abuse/dependence ($M=10.6$; $SD=4.8$ sessions), $t(153)=2.08$, $p=.039$. The other examined comorbid disorder categories (MDD, dysthymia, ADHD, CD, anxiety) did not predict either no-show or poor attendance. Although engagement and retention in treatment consist of much more than mere attendance, these findings suggest that substance use disorders appear to be the most salient factor lowering treatment engagement and retention for depressed adolescents. Future research should examine broader conceptualizations of engagement, including in-session participation, use of treatment techniques outside of session (i.e., homework completion), and the creation of a positive therapeutic alliance in the initial weeks of treatment.

Methods of Improving Engagement Given Comorbidity

Kennard, Ginsburg, Feeny, Sweeney, and Zagurski (2005) discussed the impact of comorbidity on successful implementation of the CBT intervention in TADS. In their review of various challenges to providing CBT to depressed adolescents, Kennard et al. (2005) noted that comorbid anxiety interferes with CBT depression treatment in various ways (e.g., increased difficulty completing social behavioral activation tasks), but that several strategies contained in depression CBT can address social anxiety, including relaxation skills, assertiveness, and social skills. In addition, in-session role-plays and social behavioral activation home practice can function as anxiety "exposure" work. Regarding CBT depression work when comorbid disruptive behavior disorders are present, they noted that it is often difficult to distinguish symptoms of depression from those of ODD and ADHD (e.g., negativity, irritability, poor concentration). Suggestions for addressing disruptive behavior disorders in a CBT intervention targeting adolescent depression included: educating the adolescent and family on the overlap of symptoms; greater care in development of the therapeutic alliance; family modules to help parents develop realistic expectations, positively reinforce desired behaviors, and improve contingency management skills; and possibly greater emphasis on behaviorally focused strategies.

Comorbidity Decreases Treatment Effectiveness in Reducing Depression

Several studies have found that depressed adolescents with comorbid conditions experience less and slower depression recovery, both by the end of acute treatment and during post-treatment follow-up (e.g., Brent et al., 1998; Emslie et al., 1997; Lewinsohn et al., 1995). Previous research has repeatedly found that comorbid anxiety disorders have a deleterious impact of depression response. In a discriminant function analysis with post-treatment recovery as per diagnosis as the dependent variable in the first evaluation of the CWD-A, Clarke et al. (1992) found that lower recovery rates at post-treatment were associated with higher initial state anxiety. Using data from the acute phase of treatment in TADS, Curry et al. (2006) examined whether comorbidities at intake (i.e., dysthymia, anxiety disorders, disruptive behavior disorders, total number of comorbid diagnoses) were either general predictors or treatment moderators of response (defined as reductions in depression levels) to acute treatment. Two comorbidity measures were general predictors of poorer response across treatment: adolescents with comorbid anxiety and those with more than one concurrent comorbid diagnoses benefited less from all acute interventions compared to adolescents with no anxiety disorder or those with no or only one comorbid condition. No comorbidity category moderated treatment response (i.e., identified adolescents who were more likely to benefit from one treatment compared to another). Examining the impact of comorbid anxiety on response to interpersonal psychotherapy for adolescents (IPT-A), Young, Mufson, and Davies (2006) found that comorbid anxiety disorders were associated with both more severe depression at intake and poorer depression outcomes post-treatment. However, reductions in depression in both the IPT-A and control treatment conditions were associated with improvements in anxiety disorder.

In our examination of the impact of comorbidity on the CWD-A (Rohde et al., 2001), one of the four comorbidity categories significantly predicted longer time to depression recovery: participants with lifetime substance use disorder had slower time to depression recovery during the 24-month follow-up period. The median recovery time from intake for participants with lifetime substance use disorders was 72.2 weeks compared with a median time of

10.0 weeks for participants with no lifetime history of substance use disorder. One positive aspect concerning recovery was that depressed adolescents with comorbid substance abuse/dependence (and other psychopathologies) eventually achieved comparable rates of improvement; recovery just took longer.

Few studies have evaluated the treatment of youth with comorbid depression and CD. Small medication trials indicate that antidepressant medications can be efficacious for adolescents with comorbidity (Puig-Antich, 1982; Riggs, Mikulich, Coffman, & Crowley, 1997), although adolescents with MDD/CD may be less responsive to medication than depressed adolescents with other comorbidities (Hughes et al., 1990). To address this gap in the research literature, we conducted an RCT evaluating the effectiveness of the CWD-A for depressed adolescents with comorbid CD (72% of whom also had current substance use disorder). Rohde et al. (2004) described our main findings in the MAPS study. A total of 93 adolescents (ages 13–17) meeting criteria for MDD/CD were recruited from a county juvenile justice department and randomly assigned to either the CWD-A or a life skills/tutoring (LS) control group. Participants were assessed out to 1-year post-treatment. MDD recovery post-treatment was greater in CWD-A (39%) compared to LS (19%) conditions; $OR=2.66$. In addition, participants receiving the group CBT intervention reported greater reductions in Beck Depression Inventory-II (BDI-II, Beck, Steer, & Brown, 1996; $d=0.48$, $p=0.033$) and Hamilton Depression Rating Scale (HDRS, Hamilton, 1960; $d=0.44$, $p=0.039$) scores, and improved social functioning ($d=0.52$, $p=0.019$) post-treatment. This study was the first RCT of a psychosocial intervention with depressed/CD adolescents. While the CWD-A course appeared to be an effective acute treatment for depression among adolescents with comorbid CD, the magnitude of the recovery in this study was somewhat lower than the diagnostic recovery rates in previous research with samples that excluded adolescent with current comorbidities (e.g., 39% in MAPS versus 46% in the first CWD-A trial and 67% in the second CWD-A trial). Perhaps the most important finding of the MAPS projects was that an empirically supported treatment for depression, previously evaluated in "ivory tower" settings, appears to be reasonably effective for real-world populations (i.e., depressed adolescents with comorbidities) compared with an alternative treatment (as opposed to wait-list control) and in the context of treatment as usual services. However, the findings also emphasized the need to improve term outcomes for comorbid adolescents.

We subsequently examined the factors that predicted time to MDD recovery (Rohde, Seeley, Kaufman, Clarke, & Stice, 2006). Although a number of variables were identified that predicted longer time to MDD recovery for both CBT and control group participants (e.g., early MDD onset, negative cognitions, low family cohesion, poor therapeutic alliance), none of the examined comorbid disorder categories (i.e., ADHD, substance use disorders, anxiety disorders) were related to MDD recovery time, either as a general predictor or a moderator of treatment condition.

Comorbidity Increases the Risk of Depression Recurrence

Compared to adolescents with a single psychiatric disorder, individuals with comorbid conditions may be at increased risk for depression recurrence after recovery (e.g., Emslie et al., 1997). It has also been found that compared to pure MDD, adolescents with double depression are at higher risk factor for depression recurrence following treatment (Birmaher, Arbelaez, & Brent, 2002). Rohde et al. (2001) examined the degree to which lifetime comorbidity at intake predicted recurrence following depression recovery from the CWD-A. Among the adolescents who recovered within 6 months of treatment, patients with a lifetime history of any comorbidity were not statistically more likely to experience recurrence. It should be noted, however, that the percent of comorbid patients who experienced recurrence was double the rate for noncomorbid patients (25% vs. 12%), and this difference would have been significant, given a larger sample. Among the specific comorbidity categories, participants with disruptive behavior disorders were more likely to relapse within the 24-month follow-up period: 36% of participants with disruptive behavior disorder experienced depression recurrence compared with 13% for participants with no such comorbidity history. While these findings need to be independently replicated, given the often chronic nature of attention-deficit and disruptive behavior disorders, these conditions might function as triggering factors in depression recurrence.

Impact of Depression on Treatment of Other Conditions

If treating one disorder reduces the other, this response could be due to several explanations. First, the skills (or medication) provided in treating the first disorder were applicable to the second. Second, the second disorder was secondary to the first (e.g., the depression was triggered by the stress associated with the other psychiatric disorder). Third, the "improvement" in the comorbid condition could be an artifact of diagnostic symptom overlap (i.e., not a true change). Fourth, the two conditions were not actually separate syndromes, but reflect a third diagnosis (e.g., mixed anxiety-depression), which was positively impacted by the treatment.

Regarding anxiety disorders, surprisingly few studies appear to have examined the impact of comorbid depressive disorders on the efficacy of anxiety disorder interventions with adolescents. In a pilot evaluation of a group CBT intervention for adolescents with social phobia (Baer & Garland, 2005), significant reductions were found in both interviewer- and self-reported anxiety symptoms for CBT patients compared to wait-list controls, but neither group showed any reductions in depressive symptoms. In adults, CBT treatment for panic disorder had a marginal impact on reducing depression (Tsao, Lewin, & Craske, 1998). Also in adults, depression was associated with poorer response or more impaired functioning post-treatment for social anxiety disorder patients (Erwin, Heimberg, Juster, & Mindlin, 2002) and those with obsessive-compulsive disorder (Abramowitz & Foa, 2000).

The occurrence of depression has been found to negatively impact the treatment response for conduct disorder. Gold and colleagues (Atwood, Gold, & Taylor, 1989; Gold, Mattlin, & Osgood, 1989) evaluated a typology proposed by Gold and Mann (1984) in which 306 incarcerated delinquent boys were classified as "buoyant" or "beset," based on self-report questionnaires of anxiety and depression at intake. In general, beset delinquents, who had problems with both depression and CD, had a more negative adjustment to the group treatment structure (e.g., greater frequency of misbehavior, greater tolerance for delinquency, greater opposition to staff).

A pattern is emerging in which depression may not negatively impact the adolescent's ability to engage and initially benefit from drug/alcohol treatment, but it does predict much greater risk of substance abuse relapse after treatment (e.g., McCarthy, Tomlinson, Anderson, Marlatt, & Brown, 2005; Rowe et al., 2004; Waldron et al., 2006; White et al., 2004). Other research, however, found that adolescent patients who maintained long-term abstinence were twice as likely to have been depressed at intake (Deskovitz, Key, Hill, & Franklin, 2004), which the authors interpreted as an indication of "hitting bottom." The impact of depression on substance use disorder treatment may be moderated by gender (Becker & Grilo, 2006), with depressed mood predicting better outcomes for younger female adolescents (Tapert et al., 2003). Substance use disorders also include nicotine dependence, and the presence of depression greatly impedes the ability of adult smokers to quit (e.g., Glassman et al., 1990; Rohde, Kahler, Lewinsohn, & Brown, 2004b). Several models have been proposed to account for the association between negative affect and smoking (Kassel, Stroud, & Paronis, 2003), including the nicotine withdrawal escape model (e.g., Parrott, 1999), in which smokers achieve a reduction in negative affect through relief of their nicotine withdrawal symptoms.

Waldron and colleagues have conducted several clinical trials examining a variety of family, individual, and group-based substance use disorder treatments with adolescents (e.g., Waldron & Kaminer, 2004; Waldron, Slesnick, Brody, Turner, & Peterson, 2001). As part of that research, Dr. Waldron examined whether drug/alcohol treatments would be effective with adolescents who displayed moderately elevated depressive symptoms at intake (Holly Barrett Waldron, personal communication, June, 2007). As found by others, youth with higher pre-treatment BDI scores (M=18.5 for females, 9.1 for males) had higher treatment engagement rates. However, controlling for pretreatment substance use and depression, a greater number of depressed adolescents had poorer outcomes in both the family therapy and nonfamily treatment conditions. The best longer-term outcomes were achieved by nondepressed substance abusing adolescents who received family therapy. Waldron et al. (2006) found that youth treated for problematic marijuana use by a family-based intervention clustered into two primary patterns: responders (64%) and relapsers (36%), with high depression scores at intake being a significant baseline predictors of being a relapser. These findings provide evidence suggesting that substance use disorder treatment alone may be insufficient for adolescents with comorbid depression, and that a combination of treatments could be more efficacious.

Regarding the impact of depression on treatment of eating disorders, comorbidity complicates the case conceptualization and subsequent decisions regarding the optimum treatment (O'Brien & Vincent, 2003). Stice and Fairburn (2003) found that compared to nondepressed young women with bulimia nervosa, those with a dietary-depressive subtype had greater treatment seeking but poorer treatment response, as indicated by bulimic symptom persistence over a 5-year follow-up. Among child and adolescent patients treated for anorexia nervosa and followed for 3 years, comorbid depression at intake was significantly predictive of eating disorder relapse (Waller et al., 2003).

An Intervention for One Disorder Treats Both Conditions

This section addresses the possibility that a depression-focused intervention will have the secondary benefit of significantly improving conditions, or conversely, that an intervention targeted at another condition will have the beneficial side effect of also reducing depression. In their recent meta-analysis of psychotherapy for depression in children and adolescents, Weisz, McCarty, and Valeri (2006) found that anxiety symptoms and disorders were also reduced (which was not the case for externalizing disorders). In that review, the effect size (ES) for anxiety (0.39) was only marginally lower than the ES for depression (0.57), whereas the ES for externalizing disorders (0.05) was significantly lower (and not significantly different from zero or no effects).

The impact of an intervention includes its ability to reduce future onset of disorders. A pilot evaluation with female adolescents of a CBT group intervention for social phobia (Hayward et al., 2000) found suggestive evidence that future rates of MDD among the subset of participants with a previous history of depression were lower for CBT participants compared to no-treatment controls (rates of MDD in the 1-year follow-up were 17% in the CBT group participants compared to 64% in controls), suggesting that an intervention targeting an anxiety disorder had the beneficial side effect of reducing future depression in an at-risk subset.

Although it has not been the focus of this review, prevention research aimed at one condition may also have the added benefit of reducing or preventing a second condition. Gillham et al. (2006) conducted a pilot study evaluating the impact of a school-based CBT depression prevention intervention, the Penn Resiliency Program for Children and Adolescents (PRP-CA), on depression and anxiety symptoms in 41 middle school students. The intervention was found to significantly reduce symptoms of both depression and anxiety during the 1-year follow-up.

Prior to the MAPS projects, previous studies evaluating treatment efficacy in cases with comorbid depression and CD had been extremely limited. Puig-Antich (1982) treated 43 prepubertal boys with MDD using imipramine. Of the 13 depressed boys with comorbid CD who showed a full response to antidepressant medication, 11 also no longer met criteria for CD. Friedman and Glickman (1987) examined the outcome of day treatment for 130 court-referred substance-abusing delinquent male adolescents as a function of psychiatric symptomatology at intake. Contrary to expectation, there was a tendency for boys who reported more psychiatric symptoms to improve more, rather than less, with treatment. The authors interpreted these findings as suggesting that delinquent male adolescents who were more willing to reveal their negative thoughts and feelings might be more trusting and motivated for counseling.

It is reasonable to assume that CBT interventions aimed at depression might positively impact externalizing problem behaviors. In CBT treatment of delinquency and aggression, adolescents are taught to self-monitor and observe the situations in which they become angry, recognize how they react and the consequences of their behavior, learn "self-talk" to diffuse anger, and learn problem-solving techniques (Lochman, White, & Wayland, 1991). These interventions parallel skills that are taught in the CWD-A course for adolescent depression. Morris (1993) evaluated a 12-week rational emotive therapy intervention with 12 adolescents diagnosed with CD. Participants changed significantly on all dependent variables (Irrational Beliefs Test, BDI, State-Trait Anger Expression Inventory). However, a second group, consisting of adolescents with ADHD, showed no significant change as a result of the intervention.

In the MAPS study, we found no evidence that the significantly greater reductions in depression during CBT treatment, compared to treatment as usual, were associated with greater reductions in CD symptoms. This negative finding suggests that acute reductions in depression symptomatology do not affect the course of CD. However, it is important to note that adolescents in both conditions had significant improvements in externalizing problem behaviors, and that adolescents in both conditions were allowed to receive the usual services provided to delinquent adolescents in the juvenile justice system, which often include treatments targeting delinquency and related externalizing problems.

Burton, Stice, Bearman, and Rohde (2007) conducted an RCT to test whether a CBT intervention designed to decrease depressive symptoms produced subsequent decreases in bulimic or substance use symptoms. A total of 145 female adolescents with elevated depressive symptoms were randomly assigned to a four-session depression intervention or a measurement-only condition, and assessed through 6-month follow-up. Relative to control participants, intervention participants showed significantly greater decreases in depressive symptoms and bulimic symptoms, but not substance use, with change in depressive symptoms mediating the effect for bulimic symptoms. These results provided experimental support for the theory that affect disturbances contribute to bulimic pathology, but did not support the affect regulation theory of substance use.

Pharmacotherapy interventions, especially the use of selective serotonin reuptake inhibitors (SSRIs), may be the most common intervention that treats two (or more) conditions. In addition to being a primary treatment for adolescent depression, SSRIs may be effective for anxiety disorder (Axelson & Birmaher, 2001; Labellarte, Walkup, & Riddle, 1998) and bulimia (Bellini & Merli, 2004). Imipramine plus CBT was superior to placebo/CBT for adolescents with comorbid anxiety/MDD in improving school attendance and depression (Bernstein et al., 2000). Small, uncontrolled trials evaluating SSRIs in depressed/substance use disordered adolescents (Cornelius et al., 2001; Cornelius et al., 2005; Deas, Randall, Roberts, & Anton, 2000; Riggs et al., 1997) generally report reductions in depression and substance use, although an open-label study of fluoxetine with 10 adolescents with comorbid MDD/substance use disorder (Cornelius et al., 2004; Cornelius et al., 2005) found that all patients had discontinued their medication by the second month of follow-up and 80% experienced MDD recurrence during 5-year follow-up. In a small uncontrolled trial with 14 adolescents with comorbid substance use disorders, ADHD, and mood disorder (Solhkhah et al., 2005), bupropion sustained release, an antidepressant medication that acts most directly on reducing the reuptake of dopamine, was associated with clinically significant reductions in drug use, ADHD symptoms, and depression. Riggs (2006) recently presented preliminary findings from the first large placebo-controlled RCT evaluating an SSRI (fluoxetine) in adolescents with comorbid substance use disorder/depression, finding significant reductions in depression at 13 and 17 weeks, but no medication effects for reduced drug use. For the adolescents with reduced depression (regardless of treatment), drug use was significantly reduced.

New Interventions Targeting Both Disorders

The last category of treatment reviews a small number of interventions specifically designed to address comorbid conditions. Actually, this section consists primarily of guiding principles and recommendations for the treatment of adolescents with comorbid disorders rather than manualized, theory-based, empirically evaluated interventions for treatments of two disorders.

In the area of comorbid depression/anxiety, many years ago, Kendall, Kortlander, Chansky, and Brady (1992) proposed a cognitive-behavioral synthesis for developing treatments for youth with comorbid depression and anxiety disorders. They noted that the first step is to recognize the heterogeneity of symptom presentation, even for adolescents with the same comorbid diagnostic labels. They recommended that treatment shift from interventions aimed at diagnostic categories to a focus on specific symptom patterns. Eight general treatment strategies were noted (e.g., education regarding affective states and labels, exposure and behavioral activation, cognitive work focused on the common distorted processes, problem solving, social skills training). Parental involvement was encouraged, although the authors also noted that parents of depressed adolescents may be more critical and less encouraging, and also are more likely to be struggling themselves with problems of depression and anxiety. Lastly, Kendall and colleagues suggest that when the anxiety disorder is more circumscribed, such as a phobic disorder, it might be most effective to initially focus treatment on interventions aimed at improving the adolescent's depression. Conversely, when the anxiety disorder is more pervasive and results in greater functional impairments, problems associated with both conditions will need to be addressed from the onset. To my knowledge, no manualized treatments have been developed to guide clinicians in the treatment of depressed adolescents with a variety of comorbid anxiety conditions.

A few multimodal, individualized, and long-term treatment models for comorbid depression and CD have been proposed (Rapp & Wodarski, 1997; Reinecke, 1995; Tolan & Loeber, 1993), but none have been evaluated in well-controlled trials. Rapp and Wodarski proposed a five-pronged treatment model utilizing: (1) individual CBT targeting problem solving, social skills, and cognitive distortions; (2) family interventions, including parent management training to enhance parental communication and supervision skills; (3) group interventions to take advantage of the important need for peer acceptance and support; (4) school programs to prevent academic failure and peer rejection; and (5) community resources, such as recreation and sports programs. Reinecke (1995) reviewed similarities and differences between the cognitive presentation and treatment of depression and conduct disorders, and suggested treatment focus on: (1) specific beliefs, expectations, and attributions; (2) social skills and problem-solving abilities; (3) affect regulation capability; and (4) the social environment of the adolescent. Given that interventions for comorbid adolescents have not been empirically evaluated, Reinecke suggested using a problem-solving framework to develop an individualized, integrated treatment plan.

The research base for comorbid depression/substance use disorders in adolescents is extremely limited, although clinically based guidelines have been proposed (Clark & Neighbors, 1996; Zeitlin, 1999). The most clear-cut guidelines (Riggs & Davies, 2002) recommend starting with motivational interviewing and an empirically supported substance use disorder treatment. Once substance use has dropped sufficiently, SSRIs should begin (or CBT or interpersonal psychotherapy, if SSRIs are unacceptable). Therapists should augment care with family therapy or 12-step groups, and treatment should be intensified if no change occurs by 2 months.

Regarding psychosocial treatments with adolescents with comorbid depression/substance use disorder, the literature appears to consist of a dual-focused treatment plan (adolescent group and family program; Lysaught & Wodarski, 1996), and two pilot studies of group psychotherapy (Pressman, Brook, Maidman, & Orlowski, 2001) or integrated group CBT plus family therapy (Curry, Wells, Lochman, Craighead, & Nagy, 2003). Curry and Wells published a single subject case study (Curry, Wells, Lochman, Craighead, & Nagy, 2001) and pilot study with 13 adolescents (Curry et al., 2003) of a treatment program named Family and Coping Skills (FACS) therapy, which was based on cognitive-behavioral family theory and research. Deficiencies in social cognitive processes identified in substance-abusing and depressed adolescents and their families (e.g., impulsivity, poor problem solving, affect dysregulation; poor parental monitoring and excessive criticism) are the targets of treatment in FACS. Treatment lasted approximately 3 months and consisted of assessment and feedback; twice-weekly 90-minute adolescent CBT group sessions (based on the CWD-A); weekly CBT-based family therapy sessions; random urine drug screens (results shared with parents and group); and monthly parent psychoeducation sessions. The CBT group consisted of 22 sessions, covering topics aimed at both depression and substance use disorder (e.g., increasing pleasant activities, learning to relax, responding assertively, recognizing and modifying automatic thoughts). Improved monitoring of the adolescent and use of appropriate consequences are provided to all families, with optional work on improved communication and problem solving, enhanced attachment, increased family pleasant activities, and recognition and modification of negative family beliefs. Retention and attendance rates in the pilot study were very good and FACS participants had significant reductions in depressive symptoms and marijuana use. Results of this open pilot study suggest that an outpatient CBT intervention is feasible and is associated with short-term improvement in target symptoms for depressed, substance-abusing adolescents. To date, this approach has not been further evaluated.

In the area of comorbid depression and eating disorders, Charpentier, Marttunen, Fadjukov, and Huttenen (2003) conducted an open trial pilot study evaluating a group CBT for reducing bulimic symptoms and comorbid depression in 28 female adolescents with eating disorders. The intervention was associated with reductions in both eating disorder symptoms and depressive symptoms that were maintained up to the 3-month follow-up.

CLINICAL IMPLICATIONS AND FUTURE DIRECTIONS

It is well-recognized that psychiatric comorbidity has a number of important implications (e.g., Achenbach, 1995; Hammen & Compas, 1994). Hopefully, the present review illustrates the complexity and importance of this issue in the area of adolescent depression. To conclude, here are some implications and suggestions for assessment, treatment, prevention, and etiologic research.

Implications for Assessment

The reality of comorbidity complicates assessment procedures and suggests that diagnostic conceptualizations of child and adolescent psychiatric disorders may be too simplistic to capture the complexity of psychopathology in youth. Given epidemiologic base rates, the possibility of comorbidity in depressed adolescents needs to be incorporated into assessment procedures, both at the onset of treatment and periodically throughout care. Given the presence of comorbidity, the adolescent needs more frequent monitoring for suicidality and impaired psychosocial functioning. While most adolescents are physically healthy, comorbidity includes physical conditions, and the depressed adolescent should be assessed for aspects of basic health, including nutrition, physical activity, medical illnesses, and sexuality. It is surprising how many depressed adolescents are not assessed for comorbid problem behaviors, including self-injurious behaviors (e.g., cutting, burning, other destruction of body tissue), eating pathology, and high-risk sexual activity. These are often present and if untreated, potentially contribute to the maintenance of depression or result in their own long-lasting consequences.

Implications for Treatment

The numerous ways in which comorbidity impacts the design, implementation, and success of depression treatment has been a major focus of this chapter. Given the frequency of comorbidity, clinicians have long treated comorbid depressed adolescents, relying on clinical judgment rather than decisions that are empirically derived. Psychotherapies need to be tested to understand which interventions are efficacious for which disorders in comorbid adolescents. In addition, knowledge concerning the temporal order of onset can guide treatment planning. If one psychiatric disorder is a trigger or a strong contributing factor for the subsequent disorder, it seems reasonable to primarily direct the therapeutic intervention at resolving the initial disorder rather than at addressing the secondary disorder. A second treatment approach is to rank problems by level of associated distress or impairment, and focus treatment on the problem behaviors that are most demanding of attention.

In the MAPS study, we attempted to treat MDD in a comorbid sample. Our intervention did not directly address CD (or other comorbid disorders), and we can offer no evidence that treatment interventions aimed at depression affect comorbid conditions. The MAPS results imply that interventions need to focus directly on the various presenting problems.

How can treatment outcomes be improved for depressed adolescents with comorbid conditions? In MAPS, although almost two-thirds of the participants in both treatment conditions recovered from the index MDD episode by 12 months post-treatment, the majority of patients in both conditions were still depressed at the end of acute care. The multidisordered youth in that study, on average, attended half of the treatment sessions and recovery rates might have been higher given better attendance (e.g., the more purely depressed adolescents in our previous efficacy studies attended on average 14 of 16 sessions). Additional methods of improving recovery rates would be to extend the duration of treatment or to incorporate families, peer groups, or the school system into treatment, as previously described.

On an encouraging note, we found no evidence of iatrogenic effects of group interventions for depressed youth with multiple disorders. Our clinical impression is that one strength of the CWD-A is its group format. Tempering our enthusiasm for a group modality was concern about creating a new deviant peer group, which might not adversely affect depression, but could increase rates of delinquency (Dishion & Andrews, 1995). We believe that this concern is more relevant to prevention interventions than to treatment interventions, where a deviant peer group has often already been established.

Implications for Prevention

Even more than treatment, prevention is a particularly understudied yet potentially powerful area of comorbidity research. To guide the development of effective prevention interventions, information regarding the temporal order of disorder onset is essential. Adolescents with one disorder may be considered a high-risk group for onset of the other disorder and therefore strong candidates for prevention work. Given that depression more often follows rather than precedes a mental disorder, depression prevention work should be an additional treatment goal for many adolescents with nondepression difficulties. In addition, if we knew any common factors that predisposed an adolescent to both comorbid conditions, treating that common factor could potentially reduce the incidence of both disorders. For instance, Reinecke (1995) discussed the possibility of emotional reactivity and affective dysregulation as common processes in comorbid depression/conduct disorder. If deficits in these processes were either found to precede the onset of full-blown diagnostic onset, interventions aimed at effective strategies for regulating mood might serve as a preventive intervention for both conditions.

Implications for Theory

Knowledge regarding the extent to which depression is comorbid with specific psychiatric disorders has important implications for theory. To the extent that a comorbid disorder consistently precedes or follows another disorder, the comorbid disorder may constitute an etiological trigger, a prodromal manifestation, or a residual stage for the other disorder. The degree to which one disorder precedes another may also have implications for nosologic categorizations. In addition, much of what we thought we knew about adolescent depression may actually refer to the effects of the other (comorbid) disorder or to the unique impact of having a combination of disorders rather than depression per se. Although it complicates and expands assessment demands, comorbidity should be assessed in all depression research wherever possible, as comorbidity is generally not controlled for or acknowledged in research studies. Stepping back, one can ask why is the rate of comorbidity in depressed adolescents so high?

The fact that comorbidity with adolescent depression exists is well established. The field is now ready for rigorously designed RCTs both to more effectively engage and treat the comorbidly depressed adolescent, and to better understand the processes by which comorbidity occurs and is maintained. Although the many potential permutations of comorbidity makes research in this area daunting, I believe this body of knowledge is approaching the point at which a paradigm shift can occur that synthesizes and advances our understanding of these phenomena and how best to treat the depressed multidisordered young person.

REFERENCES

Abramowitz, J. S., & Foa, E. B. (2000). Does major depressive disorder influence outcome of exposure and response prevention for OCD? *Behavior Therapy, 31*, 795–800.

Achenbach, T. M. (1995). Diagnosis, assessment, and comorbidity in psychosocial treatment research. *Journal of Abnormal Child Psychology, 23*, 45–65.

Aharonovich, E., Liu, X., Nunes, E., & Hasin, D. S. (2002). Suicide attempts in substance abusers: Effects of major depression in relation to substance use disorders. *American Journal of Psychiatry, 159*, 1600–1602.

Alessi, N. E., McManus, M., Grapentine, W. L., & Brickman, A. (1984). The characterization of depressive disorders in serious juvenile offenders. *Journal of Affective Disorder, 6*, 9–17.

Angold, A., & Costello, E. J. (1993). Depressive comorbidity in children and adolescents: Empirical, theoretical, and methodological issues. *American Journal of Psychiatry, 150*, 1779–1791.

Armstrong, T. D., & Costello, E. J. (2002). Community studies on adolescent substance use, abuse, or dependence and psychiatric comorbidity. *Journal of Consulting and Clinical Psychology, 70*, 1224–1239.

Atwood, R., Gold, M., & Taylor, R. (1989). Two types of delinquents and their institutional adjustment. *Journal of Consulting and Clinical Psychology, 57*, 68–75.

Axelson, D. A., & Birmaher, B. (2001). Relations between anxiety and depressive disorders in childhood and adolescent. *Depression and Anxiety, 14*, 67–78.

Baer, S., & Garland, E. J. (2005). Pilot study of community-based cognitive behavioral group therapy for adolescents with social phobia. *Journal of the American Academy of Child & Adolescent Psychiatry, 44*, 258–264.

Beck, A. T., Steer, R. A., & Brown, G. K. (1996). *Manual for Beck Depression Inventory-II.* San Antonio, TX: Psychological Corporation.

Beck, A. T., Ward, C. H., Mendelson, M., Mock, J., & Erbaugh, L. (1961). An inventory for measuring depression. *Archives of General Psychiatry, 4*, 561–571.

Becker, D. F., & Grilo, C. M. (2006). Prediction of drug and alcohol abuse in hospitalized adolescents: Comparisons by gender and substance type. *Behaviour Research and Therapy, 44*, 1431–1440.

Bellini, M., & Merli, M. (2004). Current drug treatment of patients with bulimia nervosa and binge-eating disorder: Selective serotonin reuptake inhibitors versus mood stabilizers. *International Journal of Psychiatry in Clinical Practice, 8*, 235–243.

Berkman, N. D., Lohr, K. N., & Bulik, C. M. (2007). Outcomes of eating disorders: A systematic review of the literature. *International Journal of Eating Disorders, 40*, 293–309.

Bernstein, G. A., Borchardt, C. M., Perwien, A. R., Crosby, R. D., Kushner, M. G., Turas, P. D., et al. (2000). Imipramine plus cognitive-behavioral therapy in the treatment of school refusal. *Journal of the American Academy of Child & Adolescent Psychiatry, 39*, 276–283.

Biederman, J., Faraone, S., Mick, E., & Lelon, E. (1995). Psychiatric comorbidity among referred juveniles with major depression: Fact or artifact? *Journal of the American Academy of Child & Adolescent Psychiatry, 34*, 579–590.

Birmaher, B., Arbelaez, C., & Brent, D. (2002). Course and outcome of child and adolescent major depressive disorder. *Child and Adolescent Psychiatric Clinics of North America, 11*, 619–638.

Blinder, B. J., Cumella, E. J., & Sanathara, V. A. (2006). Psychiatric comorbidities of female inpatients with eating disorders. *Psychosomatic Medicine, 68*, 454–462.

Block, J., & Gjerde, P. R. (1990). Depressive symptoms in late adolescence: A longitudinal perspective on personality antecedents. In J. Rolf, A. S. Masten, D. Cicchettie, K. H. Nuechterlein & S. Weintraub (Eds.), *Risk and protective factors in the development of psychopathology* (pp. 334–360). New York: Cambridge University Press.
Breier, A., Charney, D. S., & Heninger, G. R. (1985). The diagnostic validity of anxiety disorders and their relationship to depressive illness. *American Journal of Psychiatry, 142*, 787–797.
Brent, D. A., Kolko, D. J., Birmaher, B., Baugher, M., Bridge, J., Roth, C., et al. (1998). Predictors of treatment efficacy in a clinical trial of three psychosocial treatments for adolescent depression. *Journal of the American Academy of Child & Adolescent Psychiatry, 37*, 906–914.
Brook, D. W., Brook, J. S., Zhang, C., Cohen, P., & Whiteman, M. (2002). Drug use and the risk of major depressive disorder, alcohol dependence, and substance use disorders. *Archives of General Psychiatry, 59*, 1039–1044.
Brook, J. S., Whiteman, M., Finch, S., & Cohen, P. (1996). Young adult drug use and delinquency: Childhood antecedents and adolescent mediators. *Journal of the American Academy of Child & Adolescent Psychiatry, 35*, 1584–1592.
Brown, G. W., Harris, T. O., & Eales, M. J. (1993). Aetiology of anxiety and depressive disorders in an inner-city population: II. Comorbidity and adversity. *Psychological Medicine, 23*, 155–165.
Brown, R. A., Evans, M., Miller, I. W., Burgess, E. S., & Mueller, T. I. (1997). Cognitive-behavioral treatment for depression in alcoholism. *Journal of Consulting and Clinical Psychology, 65*, 715–726.
Brown, S. A., Gleghorn, A., Schuckit, M. A., Myers, M. A., & Mott, M. A. (1996). Conduct disorder among adolescent alcohol and drug abusers. *Journal of Studies on Alcohol, 57*, 314–324.
Brown, S. A., Inaba, R. K., Gillin, J. C., Schuckit, M. A., Stewart, M. A., & Irwin, M. R. (1995). Alcoholism and affective disorder: Clinical course of depressive symptoms. *American Journal of Psychiatry, 152*, 45–52.
Brown, S. A., & Schuckit, M. A. (1988). Changes in depression among abstinent alcoholics. *Journal of Studies on Alcohol, 49*, 412–417.
Bukstein, O. G., Cornelius, J., Trunzo, A. C., Kelly, T. M., & Wood, D. S. (2005). Clinical predictors of treatment in a population of adolescents with alcohol use disorders. *Addictive Behaviors, 30*, 1663–1673.
Bukstein, O. G., Glancy, L. J., & Kaminer, Y. (1992). Patterns of affective comorbidity in a clinical population of dually diagnosed adolescent substance abusers. *Journal of the American Academy of Child & Adolescent Psychiatry, 31*, 1041–1045.
Burton, E., Stice, E., Bearman, S. K., & Rohde, P. (2007). Experimental test of the affect-regulation model of bulimic symptoms and substance use: A randomized trial. *International Journal of Eating Disorders, 40*, 27–36.
Campbell, S. B., & Ewing, L. J. (1990). Follow up of hard to manage preschoolers: Adjustment at age 9 and predictors of continuing symptoms. *Journal of Child Psychology and Allied Professions, 31*, 871–889.
Capaldi, D. M. (1991). Co-occurrence of conduct problems and depressive symptoms in early adolescent boys: I. Familial factors and general adjustment at Grade 6. *Development and Psychopathology, 3*, 277–300.

Capaldi, D. M. (1992). Co-occurrence of conduct problems and depressive symptoms in early adolescent boys: II. A 2-year follow-up at Grade 8. *Development and Psychopathology, 4*, 125–144.

Carter, J. C., Bewell, C., Blackmore, E., & Woodside, D. B. (2006). The impact of childhood sexual abuse in anorexia nervosa. *Child Abuse and Neglect, 30*, 257–269.

Charpentier, P., Marttunen, M., Fadjukov, S., & Huttenen, A. (2003). CBT for adolescent eating disorder patients: Literature review and a report of an open trial of group CBT for adolescent outpatients with eating disorders. *Psychiatria Fennica, 34*, 80–98.

Chiles, J. A., Miller, M. L., & Cox, G. B. (1980). Depression in an adolescent delinquent population. *Archives of General Psychiatry, 37*, 1179–1184.

Clark, D. B., Kirisci, L., & Tarter, R. E. (1998). Adolescent versus adult onset and the development of substance use disorders in males. *Drug and Alcohol Dependence, 49*, 115–121.

Clark, D. B., & Neighbors, B. (1996). Adolescent substance abuse and internalizing disorders. *Child & Adolescent Psychiatric Clinics of North America, 5*, 45–71.

Clark, L. A., Watson, D., & Mineka, S. (1994). Temperament, personality, and the mood and anxiety disorders. *Journal of Abnormal Psychology, 103*, 103–116.

Clarke, G. N., Hops, H., Lewinsohn, P. M., Andrews, J. A., Seeley, J. R., & Williams, J. A. (1992). Cognitive-behavioral group treatment of adolescent depression: Prediction of outcome. *Behavior Therapy, 23*, 341–354.

Clarke, G. N., Lewinsohn, P. M., & Hops, H. (1990). *Instructor's manual for the Adolescent Coping with Depression Course.* Retrieved April 26, 2008, from http://www.kpchr.org/acwd/acwd.html.

Clarke, G. N., Rohde, P., Lewinsohn, P. M., Hops, H., & Seeley, J. R. (1999). Cognitive-behavioral treatment of adolescent depression: Efficacy of acute group treatment and booster sessions. *Journal of the American Academy of Child & Adolescent Psychiatry, 38*, 272–279.

Cohen, L. R., & Hien, D. A. (2006). Treatment outcomes for women with substance abuse and PTSD who have experienced complex trauma. *Psychiatric Services, 57*, 100–106.

Cohen, P., Cohen, J., Kasen, S., Velez, C. N., Hartmark, C., Johnson, J., et al. (1993). An epidemiological study of disorders in late childhood and adolescence: I. Age- and gender-specific prevalence. *Journal of Child Psychology and Psychiatry, 34*, 851–867.

Cornelius, J. R., Bukstein, O. G., Birmaher, B., Salloum, I. M., Lynch, K., Pollock, N. K., et al. (2001). Fluoxetine in adolescents with major depression and an alcohol use disorder: An open label trial. *Addictive Behaviors, 26*, 735–739.

Cornelius, J. R., Bukstein, O. G., Salloum, I. M., Kelly, T. M., Wood, D. S., & Clark, D. B., et al. (2004). Fluoxetine in depressed AUD adolescents: A 1-year follow-up evaluation. *Journal of Child and Adolescent Psychopharmacology, 14*, 33–38.

Cornelius, J. R., Clark, D. B., Bukstein, O. G., Birmaher, B., Salloum, I. M., & Brown, S. A., et al. (2005). Acute phase and five-year follow-up study of fluoxetine in adolescents with major depression and a comorbid substance use disorder: A review. *Addictive Behaviors, 30*, 1824–1833.

Cornelius, J. R., Salloum, I. M., Ehler, J. G., Jarret, P. J., Cornelius, M. D., Perel, J. M., et al. (1997). Fluoxetine in depressed alcoholics. *Archives of General Psychiatry, 54*, 700–705.

Costello, E. J., Erkanli, A., Federman, E., & Angold, A. (1999). Development of psychiatric comorbidity with substance abuse in adolescents: Effects of timing and sex. *Journal of Clinical Child Psychology, 28*, 298–311.

Costello, E. J., Mustillo, S., Erkanli, A., Keeler, G., & Angold, A. (2003). Prevalence and development of psychiatric disorders in childhood and adolescence. *Archives of General Psychiatry, 60*, 837–844.

Curry, J., Rohde, P., Simons, A., Silva, S., Vitiello, B., Kratochvil, C., et al. (2006). Predictors and moderators of acute outcome in the Treatment for Adolescents with Depression Study (TADS). *Journal of the American Academy of Child & Adolescent Psychiatry, 45*, 1427–1439.

Curry, J. F., Wells, K. C., Lochman, J. E., Craighead, W. E., & Nagy, P. D. (2001). Group and family cognitive behavior therapy for adolescent depression and substance abuse: A case study. *Cognitive and Behavioral Practice, 8*, 367–376.

Curry, J. F., Wells, K. C., Lochman, J. E., Craighead, W. E., & Nagy, P. D. (2003). Cognitive behavioral intervention for depressed, substance abusing adolescents: Development and pilot testing. *Journal of the American Academy of Child & Adolescent Psychiatry, 42*, 656–665.

Dansky, B. S., Brewerton, T. D., Kilpatrick, D. G., O'Neil, P. M., Resnick, H. S., Best, C. L., et al. (1998). The nature and prevalence of binge eating disorder in a national sample of women. In T. A. Widiger, A. J. Frances, H. A. Pincus, R. Ross, M. B. First, W. F. Davis, et al. (Eds.), *DSM-IV sourcebook* (pp. 515–531). Washington, DC: American Psychiatric Association Press.

Dausey, D. J., & Desai, R. A. (2003). Psychiatric comorbidity and the prevalence of HIV infection in a sample of patients in treatment for substance abuse. *Journal of Nervous and Mental Disease, 191*, 10–17.

Deas, D., Randall, C. L., Roberts, J. S., & Anton, R. F. (2000). A double-blind, placebo-controlled trial of sertraline in depressed adolescent alcoholics: A pilot study. *Human Psychopharmacology: Clinical and Experimental, 15*, 461–469.

Degenhardt, L., Hall, W., & Lynskey, M. (2003). Exploring the association between cannabis use and depression. *Addiction, 98*, 1493–1504.

Deskovitz, M., Key, D. E., Hill, E. M., & Franklin, J. T. (2004). Long-term family-oriented treatment for adolescents with substance-related disorders: An outcome study. *Child and Adolescent Social Work Journal, 21*, 265–284.

Diamond, G., Panichelli-Mindel, S. M., Shera, D., Dennis, M., Tims, F., & Ungemack, J. (2006). Psychiatric syndromes in adolescents with marijuana abuse and dependency in outpatient treatment. *Journal of Child and Adolescent Substance Abuse, 15*, 37–54.

Dishion, T. J., & Andrews, D. W. (1995). Preventing escalation in problem behaviors with high-risk young adolescents: Immediate and 1-year outcomes. *Journal of Consulting and Clinical Psychology, 63*, 538–548.

Drabick, D. A. G., Gadow, K. D., & Sprafkin, J. (2006). Co-occurrence of conduct disorder and depression in a clinic-based sample of boys with ADHD. *Journal of Child Psychology and Psychiatry, 47*, 766–774.

Emslie, G. J., Rush, A., Weinberg, W., Gullion, D., Rintelmann, J., & Hughes C. (1997). Recurrence of major depressive disorder in hospitalized children and adolescents. *Journal of the American Academy of Child & Adolescent Psychiatry, 36*, 785–792.

Erwin, B. A., Heimberg, R. G., Juster, H., & Mindlin, M. (2002). Comorbid anxiety and mood disorders among persons with social anxiety disorder. *Behaviour Research and Therapy, 40*, 19–35.

Essau, C. A. (2003). Comorbidity of anxiety disorders in adolescents. *Depression and Anxiety, 18*, 1–6.

Ezpeleta, L., Domenech, J. M., & Angold, A. (2006). A comparison of pure and comorbid CD/ODD and depression. *Journal of Child Psychology and Psychiatry, 47*, 704–712.

Fleming, J. E., & Offord, D. R. (1990). Epidemiology of childhood depressive disorders: A critical review. *Journal of the American Academy of Child & Adolescent Psychiatry, 29*, 571–580.

Fombonne, E., Wostear, G., Cooper, V., Harrington, R., & Rutter, M. (2001). The Maudsley long-term follow-up of child and adolescent depression: 2. Suicidality, criminality and social dysfunction in adulthood. *British Journal of Psychiatry, 179*, 218–223.

Ford, T., Goodman, R., & Meltzer, H. (2003). The British Child and Adolescent Mental Health Survey 1999: The prevalence of DSM-IV disorders. *Journal of the American Academy of Child & Adolescent Psychiatry, 42*, 1203–1211.

Franko, D. L., & Keel, P. K. (2006). Suicidality in eating disorders: Occurrence, correlates, and clinical implications. *Clinical Psychology Review, 26*, 769–782.

Friedman, A. S., & Glickman, N. W. (1987). Effects of psychiatric symptomatology on treatment outcome for adolescent male drug abusers. *Journal of Nervous and Mental Disease, 175*, 425–430.

Galaif, E. R., Sussman, S., Chou, C. P., & Wills, T. A. (2003). Longitudinal relations among depression, stress, and coping in high risk youth. *Journal of Youth and Adolescence, 32*, 243–258.

Geist, R., Davis, D., & Heinman, M. (1998). Binge/purge symptoms and comorbidity in adolescents with eating disorders. *Canadian Journal of Psychiatry, 43*, 507–512.

Geller, B., Chestnut, E. C., Miller, M. D., Price, D. T., & Yates, E. (1985). Preliminary data on DSM-III associated features of major depressive disorder in child and adolescents. *American Journal of Psychiatry, 142*, 643–644.

Gillham, J. E., Reivich, K. J., Freres, D. R., Lascher, M., Litzinger, S., Shatte, A., et al. (2006). School-based prevention of depression and anxiety symptoms in early adolescence: A pilot of a present intervention component. *School Psychology Quarterly, 21*, 323–348.

Glantz, M. D. (2002). Introduction to the special issue on the impact of childhood psychopathology interventions on subsequent substance abuse: Pieces of the puzzle. *Journal of Consulting and Clinical Psychology, 70*, 1203–1206.

Glaser, K. (1967). Masked depression in children and adolescents. *American Journal of Psychotherapy, 19*, 565–574.

Glassman, A. H., Helzer, J. E., Covey, L. S., Cottler, L. B., Stetner, F., Tipp, J. E., et al. (1990). Smoking, smoking cessation, and major depression. *Journal of the American Medical Association, 264*, 1546–1549.

Gold, M., & Mann, D. W. (1984). *Expelled to a friendlier place.* Ann Arbor, MI: University of Michigan Press.
Gold, M., Mattlin, J., & Osgood, D. W. (1989). Background characteristics and responses to treatment of two types of institutionalized delinquent boys. *Criminal Justice and Behavior, 16,* 5–33.
Greenfield, S. F., Weiss, R. D., Muenz, L. R., Vagge, L. M., Kelly, J. F., Bello, L. R., et al. (1998). The effect of depression on return to drinking: A prospective study. *Archives of General Psychiatry, 55,* 259–265.
Hallfors, D. D., Waller, M. W., Bauer, D., Ford, C. A., & Halpern, C. T. (2006). Which comes first in adolescent—sex and drugs or depression? *American Journal of Preventive Medicine, 29,* 163–170.
Hamilton, M. (1960). A rating scale for depression. *Journal of Neurology, Neurosurgery, and Psychiatry, 12,* 56–62.
Hammen, C., & Compas, B. E. (1994). Unmasking unmasked depression in children and adolescents: The problem or comorbidity. *Clinical Psychology Review, 14,* 585–603.
Harrington, R., Fudge, H., Rutter, M., Pickles, A., & Hill, J. (1991). Adult outcomes of childhood and adolescent depression: II. Links with antisocial disorders. *Journal of the American Academy of Child & Adolescent Psychiatry, 30,* 434–439.
Hayward, C., Varady, S., Albano, A. M., Thienemann, M., Henderson, L., & Schatzberg, A. F. (2000). Cognitive-behavioral group therapy for social phobia in female adolescents: Results of a pilot study. *Journal of the American Academy of Child & Adolescent Psychiatric, 39,* 721–726.
Helzer, J. E., & Pryzbeck, T. R. (1988). The co-occurrence of alcoholism with other psychiatric disorders in the general population and its impact on treatment. *Journal of Studies on Alcohol, 49,* 219–224.
Hettema, J. M., Prescott, C. A., & Kendler, K. S. (2003). The effects of anxiety, substance use and conduct disorders on risk of major depressive disorder. *Psychological Medicine, 33,* 1423–1432.
Hibbs, E. D. (1995). Child and adolescent disorders: Issues for psychosocial treatment research. *Journal of Abnormal Child Psychology, 23,* 1–10.
Hinshaw, S. P. (2002). Prevention/intervention trials and developmental theory: Commentary on the fast track special section (Commentary). *Journal of Abnormal Child Psychology, 3,* 53–59.
Hughes, C. W., Preskorn, S. H., Weller, E., Weller, R., Hassanein, R., & Tucker, S. (1990). The effect of concomitant disorders in childhood depression on predicting treatment response. *Psychopharmacology Bulletin, 26,* 235–238.
Ivarsson, T., Rastam, M., Wentz, E., Gillberg, I. C., & Gillberg, C. (2000). Depressive disorders in teenage-onset anorexia nervosa: A controlled longitudinal, partly community-based study. *Comprehensive Psychiatry, 41,* 398–403.
Kaminer, Y., Tarter, R. E., Bukstein, O. G., & Kabene, M. (1992). Adolescent substance abuse treatment: Staff, treatment completers', and noncompleters' perceptions of the value of treatment variables. *American Journal on Addictions, 1,* 115–120.
Kandel, D. B., Johnson, J. G., Bird, H. R., Canino, G., Goodman, S. H., Lahey, B. B., et al. (1997). Psychiatric disorders associated with substance use among children and adolescents: Finding from the methods for the epidemiology of child and adolescent mental disorders (MECA) study. *Journal of Abnormal Child Psychology, 25,* 121–132.

Karlsson, L., Pelkonen, J., Ruuttu, T., Kiviruusu, O., Heila, H., Holi, M., et al. (2006). Current comorbidity among consecutive adolescent psychiatric outpatients with DSM-IV mood disorders. *European Child and Adolescent Psychiatry, 15*, 220–231.

Kashani, J. H., Carlson, G. A., Beck, N. C., Hoeper, E. W., Corcoran, C. M., McAllister, J., et al. (1987). Depression, depressive symptoms, and depressed mood among a community sample of adolescents. *American Journal of Psychiatry, 144*, 931–934.

Kassel, J. D., Stroud, L. R., & Paronis, C. A. (2003). Smoking, stress, and negative affect: Correlation, causation, and context across stages of smoking. *Psychological Bulletin, 129*, 270–304.

Keller, M. B., Beardslee, W., Lavori, P. W., Wunder, J., Drs, D. L., & Samuelson, H. (1988). Course of major depression in non-referred adolescents: A retrospective study. *Journal of Affective Disorders, 15*, 235–243.

Keller, M. B., & Shapiro, R. W. (1982). "Double depression:" Superimposition of acute depressive episodes on chronic depressive disorders. *American Journal of Psychiatry, 139*, 438–442.

Kendall, P. C., Kortlander, E., Chansky, T. E., & Brady, E. U. (1992). Comorbidity of anxiety and depression in youth: Treatment implications. *Journal of Consulting and Clinical Psychology, 60*, 869–880.

Kennard, B. D., Ginsburg, G. S., Feeny, N. C., Sweeney, M., & Zagurski, R. (2005). Implementation challenges to TADS cognitive-behavioral therapy. *Cognitive and Behavioral Practice, 12*, 230–239.

Kessler, R. C., McGonagle, K. A., Zhao, S., Nelson, C. B., Hughes, M., Eshleman, S., et al. (1994). Lifetime and 12-month prevalence of DSM-III-R psychiatric disorders in the US: Results from the National Comorbidity Survey. *Archives of General Psychiatry, 51*, 8–19.

Kessler, R. C., Nelson, E. C., McGonagle, K. A., Edlund, M. J., Frank, R. G., & Leaf, P. J. (1996). The epidemiology of co-occurring addictive and mental disorders: Implications for prevention and service utilization. *American Journal of Orthopsychiatry, 66*, 17–31.

Kessler, R. C., & Price, R. H. (1993). Primary prevention of secondary disorders: A proposal and agenda. *American Journal of Community Psychology, 21*, 607–633.

Khantzian, E. J. (1985). The self-medication hypothesis of addictive disorders: Focus on heroin and cocaine dependence. *American Journal of Psychiatry, 142*, 1259–1264.

King, C. A., Ghaziuddin, N., McGovern, L., Brand, E., Hill, E., & Naylor, M. (1996). Predictors of comorbid alcohol and substance abuse in depressed adolescents. *Journal of the American Academy of Child & Adolescent Psychiatry, 35*, 743–751.

Klein, D. N., Lewinsohn, P. M., Rohde, P., Seeley, J. R., & Shankman, S. A. (2003). Family study of comorbidity between major depressive disorder and anxiety disorders. *Psychological Medicine, 33*, 703–714.

Klein, D. N., Lewinsohn, P. M., Seeley, J. R., & Rohde, P. (2001). A family study of major depressive disorder in a community sample of adolescents. *Archives of General Psychiatry, 58*, 13–20.

Klein, D. N., & Riso, L. P. (1993). Psychiatric disorders: Problems of boundaries and comorbidity. In C. G. Costello (Ed.), *Basic issues in psychopathology* (pp. 19–66). New York: Guilford Press.

Kovacs, M., Feinberg, T. L., Crouse-Novak, M., Paulauskas, S. L., Pollack, M., & Finkelstein, R. (1984). Depressive disorders in childhood: II. A longitudinal study of the risk for a subsequent major depression. *Archives of General Psychiatry, 41*, 643–649.

Kovacs, M., Gatsonis, C., Paulauskas, S. L., & Richards, C. (1989). Depressive disorders in childhood: IV. A longitudinal study of comorbidity with and risk for anxiety disorders. *Archives of General Psychiatry, 46*, 776–782.

Kovacs, M., Paulauskas, S., Gatsonis, C., & Richards, C. (1988). Depressive disorders in childhood: III. A longitudinal study of comorbidity with and risk for conduct disorders. *Journal of Affective Disorders, 15*, 205–217.

Kuo, P. H., Gardner, C. O., Jr., Kendler, K. S., & Prescott, C. A. (2006). The temporal relationship of the onsets of alcohol dependence and major depression: Using a genetically informative study design. *Psychological Medicine, 36*, 1153–1162.

Labellarte, M. J., Walkup, J. T., & Riddle, M. A. (1998). The new antidepressants: Selective serotonin reuptake inhibitors. *Pediatric Clinics of North America, 45*, 1137–1154.

Lewinsohn, P. M., Clarke, G. N., Hops, H., & Andrews, J. (1990). Cognitive-behavioral group treatment of depression in adolescents. *Behavior Therapy, 21*, 385–401.

Lewinsohn, P. M., Hops, H., Roberts, R. E., Seeley, J. R., & Andrews, J. A. (1993). Adolescent psychopathology: I. Prevalence and incidence of depression and other DSM-III-R disorders in high school students. *Journal of Abnormal Psychology, 102*, 133–144.

Lewinsohn, P. M., Rohde, P., & Seeley, J. R. (1995). Adolescent psychopathology: III. The clinical consequences of comorbidity. *Journal of the American Academy of Child & Adolescent Psychiatry, 34*, 510–519.

Lewinsohn, P. M., Rohde, P., Seeley, J. R., & Hops, H. (1991). Comorbidity of unipolar depression: I. Major depression with dysthymia. *Journal of Abnormal Psychology, 100*, 205–213.

Lewinsohn, P. M., Rohde, P., Seeley, J. R., Klein, D. N., & Gotlib, I. H. (2003). Psychosocial functioning of young adults who have experienced and recovered from major depressive disorder during adolescence. *Journal of Abnormal Psychology, 112*, 353–363.

Lochman, J. E., White, K. J., & Wayland, K. K. (1991). Cognitive-behavioral assessment and treatment with aggressive children. In P. C. Kendall (Ed.), *Child and adolescent therapy: Cognitive-behavioral procedures* (pp. 25–26). New York: Guilford Press.

Lucka, I. (2006). Depressive disorders in patients suffering from anorexia nervosa. *Archives of Psychiatry and Psychotherapy, 8*, 55–61.

Lysaught, E., & Wodarski, J. L. (1996). Model: A dual focused intervention for depression and addiction. *Journal of Child & Adolescent Substance Abuse, 5*, 55–72.

Marmorstein, N. R., & Iacono, W. G. (2001). An investigation of female adolescent twins with both major depression and conduct disorder. *Journal of the American Academy of Child & Adolescent Psychiatry, 40*, 299–306.

Marriage, K., Fine, S., Moretti, M., & Haley, G. (1986). Relationship between depression and conduct disorder in children and adolescents. *Journal of the American Academy of Child Psychiatry, 25*, 687–691.

McCabe, M. P., & Vincent, M. A. (2003). The role of biodevelopmental and psychological factors in disordered eating among adolescent males and females. *European Eating Disorders Review, 11*, 315–328.

McCarthy, D. M., Tomlinson, K. L., Anderson, K. G., Marlatt, G. A., & Brown, S. A. (2005). Relapse in alcohol and drug-disordered adolescents with comorbid psychopathology: Changes in psychiatric symptoms. *Psychology of Addictive Behaviors, 19*, 28–34.

McCarthy, M. (1990). The thin ideal, depression, and eating disorders in women. *Behavioral Research and Therapy, 28*, 205–218.

McCracken, J. T., Cantwell, D. P., & Hanna, G. L. (1993). Conduct disorder and depression. In H. S. Koplewicz & E. Klass (Eds.), *Depression in children and adolescents* (pp. 121–132). Philadelphia, PA: Harwood Academic.

McGrath, P. J., Nunes, E. V., Steward, J. W., Goldman, D., Algosti, V., Ocepek-Welikson, K., et al. (1996). Imipramine treatment of alcoholics with primary depression. *Archives of General Psychiatry, 53*, 232–240.

McKay, J. R. (2005). Co-occurring substance dependence and depression: Practical implications and next questions. *Addiction, 100*, 1755–1757.

McKay, J. R., Pettinati, H. M., Morrison, R., Feeley, M., Mulvaney, F. D., & Gallop. R. (2002). Relation of depression diagnoses to 2-year outcomes in cocaine-dependent patients in a randomized continuing care study. *Psychology of Addictive Behaviors, 16*, 225–235.

Measelle, J. R., Stice, E., & Hogansen, J. M. (2006). Developmental trajectories of co-occurring depressive, eating, antisocial, and substance abuse problems in female adolescents. *Journal of Abnormal Psychology, 115*, 524–538.

Merikangas, K. R. (1990). Comorbidity for anxiety and depression: Review of family and genetic studies. In J. D. Maser & C. R. Cloninger (Eds.), *Comorbidity of mood and anxiety disorders* (pp. 331–348). Washington, DC: American Psychiatric Press.

Miller, M. L., Chiles, J. A., & Barnes, V. E. (1982). Suicide attempters within a delinquent population. *Journal of Consulting and Clinical Psychology, 50*, 491–498.

Mirin, S. M., & Weiss, R. D. (1991). Substance abuse and mental illness. In R. J. Frances & S. I. Miller (Eds.), *Clinical textbook of addictive disorders* (pp. 271–298). New York: Guilford Press.

Morris, G. B. (1993). A rational-emotive treatment program with conduct disorder and attention-deficit hyperactivity disorder adolescents. *Journal of Rational Emotive and Cognitive Behavior Therapy, 11*, 123–134.

Mueller, T. I., Lavori, P. W., Keller, M. B., & Swartz, A. (1994). Prognostic effect of the variable course of alcoholism on the 10-year course of depression. *American Journal of Psychiatry, 151*, 701–706.

Nottelmann, E., & Jensen, P. (1995). Comorbidity of disorders in children and adolescents: Developmental perspectives. *Advances in clinical child psychology* (Vol. 17, pp. 109–155). New York: Plenum Press.

Nottelmann, E. D., & Jensen, P. S. (1999). Comorbidity of depressive disorders: Rates, temporal sequencing, course, and outcome. In E. A. Essau & F. Petermann (Eds.), *Depressive disorders in children and adolescents: Epidemiology, risk factors, and treatment* (pp. 137–191). Lanham, MD: Jason Aronson.

Obando, P., Kliewer, W., Murrelle, L., & Svikis, D. S. (2004). The comorbidity of substance abuse and depressive symptoms in Costa Rican adolescents. *Drug and Alcohol Dependence, 76*, 37–44.

O'Brien, K. M., & Vincent, N. K. (2003). Psychiatric comorbidity in anorexia and bulimia nervosa: Nature, prevalence and causal relationships. *Clinical Psychology Review, 23*, 57–74.

Pagnin, D., de Queiroz, V., & Saggese, E. G. (2005). Prediction of attrition from day treatment of adolescents with substance-related disorders. *Addictive Behaviors, 30*, 1065–1069.

Parrott, A. C. (1999). Does cigarette smoking cause stress? *American Psychologist, 54*, 817–820.

Patten, C. A., Martin, J. E., Myers, M. G., Mark, G., Calfas, K. J., & Williams, C. D. (1998). Effectiveness of cognitive-behavioral therapy for smokers with histories of alcohol dependence and depression. *Journal of Studies on Alcohol, 59*, 327–335.

Patterson, G., & Stoolmiller, M. (1991). Replication of a dual failure model for boys' depressed mood. *Journal of Consulting and Clinical Psychology, 59*, 491–498.

Patterson, G. R., & Capaldi, D. M. (1990). A mediational model for boys' depressed mood. In J. Rolf, A. S. Masten, D. Cicchettie, K. H. Nuechterlein, & S. Weintraub (Eds.), *Risk and protective factors in the development of psychopathology* (pp. 141–163). New York: Cambridge University Press.

Perez, M., Joiner, T. E., Jr., & Lewinsohn, P. M. (2004). Is major depressive disorder or dysthymia more strongly associated with bulimia nervosa? *International Journal of Eating Disorders, 36*, 55–61.

Poznanski, E., & Mokros, H. (1995). *Children's Depression Rating Scale-Revised (CDRS-R)*. Los Angeles, CA: WPS.

Pressman, M., Brook, D. W., Maidman, P., & Orlowski, B. (2001). Clinical improvement in adolescents comorbid for substance abuse and psychiatric diagnoses through multiple group psychotherapy. *Group, 25*, 321–332.

Puig-Antich, J. (1982). Major depression and conduct disorder in prepuberty. *Journal of the American Academy of Child Psychiatry, 21*, 118–128.

Rao, U., Daley, S. E., & Hammen, C. (2000). Relationship between depression and substance use disorders in adolescent women during the transition to adulthood. *Journal of the American Academy of Child & Adolescent Psychiatry, 39*, 215–222.

Rapp, L. A., & Wodarski, J. S. (1997). The comorbidity of conduct disorder and depression in adolescents: A comprehensive interpersonal treatment technology. *Family Therapy, 2*, 81–100.

Reinecke, M. A. (1995). Comorbidity of conduct disorder and depression among adolescents: Implications for assessment and treatment. *Cognitive and Behavioral Practice, 2*, 299–326.

Riggs, P. D. (2006). *Interventions for adolescent substance abusers with comorbid conduct disorder: Why can't we get it right.* Symposium presentation at JMATE, Baltimore, MD.

Riggs, P. D., Baker, S., Mikulich, S. K., Young, S. E., & Crowley, T. J. (1995). Depression in substance-dependent delinquents. *Journal of the American Academy of Child & Adolescent Psychiatry, 34*, 764–771.

Riggs, P. D., & Davies, R. D. (2002). A clinical approach to integrating treatment for adolescent depression and substance abuse. *Journal of the American Academy of Child & Adolescent Psychiatry, 41*, 1253–1255.

Riggs, P. D., Mikulich, S. K., Coffman, L. M., & Crowley, T. J. (1997). Fluoxetine in drug-dependent delinquents with major depression: An open trial. *Journal of Child and Adolescent Psychopharmacology, 7*, 87–95.

Riggs, P. D., Mikulich, S. K., & Hall, S. (2001). Effects of pemoline on ADHD, antisocial behaviors, and substance use in adolescents with conduct disorders and substance use disorder. In *Proceedings of the College on Problems of Drug Dependence, Sixty-Third Annual Scientific Meetings*, Scottsdale, AZ, June.

Ritsher, J. B., McKellar, J. D., Finney, J. M., Otilingam, P. G., & Moos, R. H. (2002). Psychiatric comorbidity, continuing care and mutual help as predictors of five-year remission from substance use disorders. *Journal of Studies on Alcohol, 63*, 709–715.

Rohde, P., Clarke, G. N., Lewinsohn, P. M., Seeley, J. R., & Kaufman, N. K. (2001). Impact of comorbidity on a cognitive-behavioral group treatment for adolescent depression. *Journal of the American Academy of Child & Adolescent Psychiatry, 40*, 795–802.

Rohde, P., Clarke, G. N., Mace, D. E., Jorgensen, J. S., & Seeley, J. R. (2004a). An efficacy/effectiveness study of cognitive-behavioral treatment for adolescents with comorbid major depression and conduct disorder. *Journal of the American Academy of Child & Adolescent Psychiatry, 43*, 660–668.

Rohde, P., Kahler, C. W., Lewinsohn, P. M., & Brown, R. A. (2004b). Psychiatric disorders, familial factors, and cigarette smoking: III. Associations with cessation by young adulthood among daily smokers. *Nicotine & Tobacco Research, 6*, 509–522.

Rohde, P., Lewinsohn, P. M., & Seeley, J. R. (1991). Comorbidity of unipolar depression: II. Comorbidity with other mental disorders in adolescents and adults. *Journal of Abnormal Psychology, 54*, 653–660.

Rohde, P., Seeley, J. R., Kaufman, N. K., Clarke, G. N., & Stice, E. (2006). Predicting time to recovery among depressed adolescents treated in two group interventions. *Journal of Consulting and Clinical Psychology, 74*, 80–88.

Rounsaville, B. J., Weissman, M. M., Crits-Christoph, K., Wilber, C., & Kleber, H. (1982). Diagnosis and symptoms of depression in opiate addicts. *Archives of General Psychiatry, 39*, 151–156.

Rowe, C. L., Liddle, H. A., & Dakof, G. A. (2001). Classifying clinically referred adolescent substance abusers by level of externalizing and internalizing symptoms. *Journal of Child and Adolescent Substance Abuse, 11*, 41–66.

Rowe, C. L., Liddle, H. A., Greenbaum, P. E., & Henderson, C. E. (2004). Impact of psychiatric comorbidity on treatment of adolescent drug abusers. *Journal of Substance Abuse Treatment, 26*, 129–140.

Rowe, J. B., Sullivan, P. F., Mulder, R. T., & Joyce, P. R. (1996). The effect of a history of conduct disorder in adult major depression. *Journal of Affective Disorders, 37*, 51–63.

Ryan, N. D., Puig-Antich, J., Ambrosin, P., Rabinovich, H., Robinsohn, D., Nelson, B., et al. (1987). The clinical picture of major depression in children and adolescents. *Archives of General Psychiatry, 44*, 854–861.

Schmitz, J. M., Averill, P., Stotts, A. L., Moeller, F. G., Rhoades, H. M., & Grabowski, J. (2001). Fluoxetine treatment of cocaine-dependent patients with major depressive disorder. *Drug and Alcohol Dependence, 63*, 207–214.

Shaffer, D. (1974). Suicide in childhood and early adolescence. *Journal of Child Psychology and Psychiatry, 15*, 275–291.

Solhkhah, R., Wilens, T. E., Daly, J., Prince, J. B., Van Patten, S. L., & Biederman, J. (2005). Bupropion SR for the treatment of substance-abusing outpatients adolescents with attention-deficit/hyperactivity disorder and mood disorders. *Journal of the Child and Adolescent Psychopharmacology, 15*, 777–786.

Star, J. E., Bober, D., & Gold, M. S. (2005). Double trouble: Depression and alcohol abuse in the adolescent patient. *Psychiatric Annals, 35*, 496–502.

Stein, M. B., Fuetsch, M., Muller, N., Hofler, M., Lieb, R., & Wittchen, H. U. (2001). Social anxiety disorder and the risk of depression: A prospective community study of adolescents and young adults. *Archives of General Psychiatry, 58*, 251–256.

Stice, E., Burton, E. M., & Shaw, H. (2004). Prospective relations between bulimic pathology, depression, and substance abuse: Unpacking comorbidity in adolescent girls. *Journal of Consulting and Clinical Psychology, 72*, 62–71.

Stice, E., & Fairburn, C. G. (2003). Dietary and dietary-depressive subtypes of bulimia nervosa show differential symptom presentation, social impairment, comorbidity, and course of illness. *Journal of Consulting and Clinical Psychology, 71*, 1090–1094.

Stice, E., Hayward, C., Cameron, R. P., Killen, J. D., & Taylor, C. B. (2000). Body-image and eating disturbances predict onset of depression among female adolescents: A longitudinal study. *Journal of Abnormal Psychology, 109*, 438–444.

Stice, E., Killen, J. D., Hayward, C., & Taylor, C. B. (1998). Support for the continuity hypothesis of bulimic pathology. *Journal of Consulting and Clinical Psychology, 66*, 784–790.

Subramaniam, G. A., Lewis, L. L., Stitzer, J. L., & Fishman, M. J. (2004). Depressive symptoms in adolescents during residential treatment for substance use disorders. *American Journal on Addictions, 13*, 253–267.

Sung, M., Erkanli, A., Angold, A., & Costello, E. J. (2004). Effects of age at first substance use and psychiatric comorbidity on the development of substance use disorders. *Drug and Alcohol Dependence, 75*, 287–299.

Swendsen, J. D., & Merikangas, K. R. (2000). The comorbidity of depression and substance use disorders. *Clinical Psychology Review, 20*, 173–189.

Tapert, S. F., Colby, S. M., Barnett, N. P., Spirito, A., Rohsenow, D. J., Myers, M. G., et al. (2003). Depressed mood, gender, and problem drinking in youth. *Journal of Child and Adolescent Substance Abuse, 12*, 55–68.

Tolan, P. H., & Loeber, R. (1993). Antisocial behavior. In P. H. Tolan & B. Cohler (Eds.), *Handbook of clinical research and practice with adolescents* (pp. 307–331). New York: Wiley-Interscience.

Tsao, J. C. I., Lewin, M. R., & Craske, M. G. (1998). The effects of cognitive-behavior therapy for panic disorder on comorbid conditions. *Journal of Anxiety Disorder, 12*, 357–371.

Treatment for Adolescents with Depression Study Team. (2004). The Treatment for Adolescents with Depression Study (TADS): Short-term effectiveness and safety outcomes. *Journal of the American Medical Association, 292*, 807–820.

Treatment for Adolescents with Depression Study Team. (2005). The Treatment for Adolescents with Depression Study (TADS): Demographic and clinical characteristics. *Journal of the American Academy of Child & Adolescent Psychiatry, 44*, 28–40.

Treatment for Adolescents with Depression Study (TADS) Team. (2007). The Treatment for Adolescents with Depression Study (TADS): Long-term effectiveness and safety outcomes. *Archives of General Psychiatry, 64*(10), 1132–1144.

Tubman, J. G., Wagner, E. F., & Langer, L. M. (2003). Patterns of depressive symptoms, drinking motives, and sexual behavior among substance abusing adolescents: Implications for health risk. *Journal of Child and Adolescent Substance Abuse, 13*, 37–57.

Turner, R. W., & Wehl, C. K. (1984). Treatment of unipolar depression in problem drinkers. *Advances in Behaviour Research and Therapy, 6*, 115–125.

Vermeiren, R., Schwab-Stone, M., Ruchkin, V. V., King, R. A., Van Heeringen, C., & Deboutte, D. (2003). Suicidal behavior and violence in male adolescents: A school-based study. *Journal of the American Academy of Child & Adolescent Psychiatry, 42*, 41–48.

Wagner, B. M., Cole, R. E., & Schwartzman, P. (1996). Comorbidity of symptoms among junior and senior high school suicide attempters. *Suicide and Life Threatening Behavior, 26*, 300–307.

Waldron, H. B., & Kaminer, Y. (2004). On the learning curve: The emerging evidence supporting cognitive-behavioral therapies for adolescent substance abuse. *Addiction, 99*(Suppl. 2), 93–105.

Waldron, H. B., Slesnick, N., Brody, J. L., Turner, C. W., & Peterson, T. R. (2001). Treatment outcomes for adolescent substance abuse at 4- and 7-month assessments. *Journal of Consulting and Clinical Psychology, 69*, 802–813.

Waldron, H. B., Turner, C. W., & Ozechowski, T. (2006). Profiles of change in behavioral and family interventions for adolescent substance abuse and dependence. In H. Liddle & C. Rowe (Eds.), *Adolescent substance abuse: Research and clinical advances.* (pp. 357–374). Cambridge: Cambridge University Press.

Waller, D. A., Mugan, M. N., Morshed, T., Setnick, J., Cummings, M., & Hynan, L. S. (2003). Three-year follow-up study of children and adolescents with anorexia nervosa initially treated in a continuum of care program. *Eating Disorders: The Journal of Treatment and Prevention, 11*, 63–72.

Weisz, J. R., McCarty, C. A., & Valeri, S. M. (2006). Effectives of psychotherapy in children and adolescents: A meta-analysis. *Psychological Bulletin, 132*, 132–149.

White, A. M., Jordan, J. D., Schroeder, K. M., Acheson, S. K., Georgi, B. D., Sauls, G., et al. (2004). Predictors of relapse during treatment and treatment completion among marijuana-dependent adolescents in an intensive outpatient substance abuse program. *Substance Abuse, 25*, 53–59.

Whitmore, E. A., Mikulich, S. K., Thompson, L. L., Riggs, P. D., Aarons, G. A., & Crowley, T. J. (1997). Influences on adolescent substance dependence: Conduct disorder, depression, attention-deficit hyperactivity disorder, and gender. *Drug and Alcohol Dependence, 47*, 87–97.

Wilens, T., Biederman, J., Abrantes, A., & Spencer, T. (1997), Clinical characteristics of psychiatrically referred adolescent outpatients with substance use disorders. *Journal of the American Academy of Child & Adolescent Psychiatry 36*, 941–947.

Williamson, D. E., Forbes, E. E., Dahl, R. E., & Ryan, N. D. (2005). A genetic epidemiologic perspective on comorbidity of depression and anxiety. *Child and Adolescent Psychiatric Clinics of North America, 14*, 707–726.

Wise, B., Cuffe, S. P., & Fischer, T. (2001). Dual diagnosis and successful participation of adolescents in substance abuse treatment. *Journal of Substance Abuse Treatment, 21*, 161–165.

Young, J. F., Mufson, L., & Davies, M. (2006). Impact of comorbid anxiety in an effectiveness study of interpersonal psychotherapy for depressed adolescents. *Journal of the American Academy of Child & Adolescent Psychiatry, 45*, 904–912.

Zaider, T. I., Johnson, J. G., & Cockell, S. J. (2002). Psychiatric disorders associated with the onset and persistence of bulimia nervosa and binge eating disorder during adolescence. *Journal of Youth and Adolescence, 31*, 319–329.

Zeitlin, H. (1999). Psychiatric comorbidity with substance misuse in children and teenagers. *Drug and Alcohol Dependence, 55*, 225–234.

Chapter Seven

Bipolar Disorder in Childhood and Adolescence

DAWN O. TAYLOR AND DAVID J. MIKLOWITZ

CONTENTS

There has been a growing awareness that the onset of bipolar disorder (BD) is often in childhood or adolescence, even though the typical symptom picture of mood dysregulation in adolescence is in many ways dissimilar to the symptom picture in adults.

We begin the chapter with a description of the early-onset form of the disorder and a discussion of the controversies surrounding the diagnosis of BD in younger populations. We present epidemiological findings, and discuss what we know about gender and racial/ethnic differences. The phenomenology of adolescent BD and the range of functional impairments involved are addressed, with special attention to researchers' attempts to define the core features of pediatric BD. We cover the research on the course and prognosis of the disorder, comorbidity, genetics and neurobiology, and neuropsychological investigations. Finally, we present research on psychosocial treatments, pharmacological treatments, and efforts at prevention.

Current models of etiology view BD as a primarily genetic illness whose onset and course are influenced by environmental stressors. We examine what is known about the environmental and biological protective and risk factors whose complex interplay over different periods of development result in the expression of the disorder.

DIAGNOSIS

Quinn and Fristad (2004) (see also Kowatch et al., 2005) acknowledged the difficulty of diagnosing early-onset BD and offered a comprehensive assessment approach including: (1) a timeline of the child's development, from birth to present, showing all prior mood episodes; (2) a structured clinical interview, including comorbid conditions; (3) a family history genogram to ascertain familial loading; (4) depression and mania rating scales to assess symptom severity and track treatment outcome; (5) global rating scales using multiple informants; and (6) use of mood logs. It is not clear, however, how frequently clinicians actually follow these recommendations in diagnosing the disorder.

The *Diagnostic and Statistical Manual of Mental Disorders*, fourth edition (DSM; American Psychiatric Association, 2000) spells out the criteria for diagnosing BD. Separate criteria sets define what constitutes a manic episode, a hypomanic episode, and a major depressive episode. Different combinations of these episodes are required to diagnose bipolar I versus bipolar II.

Manic episodes involve the experience of elated, expansive, or irritable mood (or any combination of these) plus at least three (four if the mood is only irritable) of the following symptoms: inflated self-esteem (or grandiosity); decreased need for sleep (e.g., feels rested after only 3 hours of sleep); more talkative than usual or pressure to keep talking; flight of ideas or subjective experience that thoughts are racing; distractibility (i.e., attention too easily drawn to unimportant or irrelevant external stimuli); increase in goal-directed activity (e.g., uninhibited people seeking) or psychomotor agitation; or excessive involvement in pleasurable activities that have a high potential for painful consequences (e.g., unrestrained buying sprees, sexual indiscretions, or foolish business investments in adults). These symptoms must be present for at least 1 week (or any duration if interrupted by hospitalization). The episode must cause marked impairment in social or occupational functioning, or necessitate hospitalization, or involve psychotic features.

Hypomanic episodes are defined by the same symptom set, but the criteria specify that the episode must last a minimum of 4 days rather than 7. The episode must represent an unequivocal change in functioning that is uncharacteristic of the person when not symptomatic and must be noticeable to others, but it cannot cause severe impairment (otherwise it is classified as a manic episode).

Major depressive episodes require a distinct period of sadness or anhedonia lasting at least 2 weeks, accompanied by five of the following seven symptoms: appetite change or weight gain or loss, hypersomnia or insomnia, psychomotor agitation or retardation, fatigue or low energy, feelings of worthlessness or guilt, problems with concentration or indecisiveness, and suicidal ideation or attempt.

A mixed episode is said to occur when criteria sets are met for both a manic and a major depressive episode (except for duration) during at least a 1-week period. With all four types of episodes, criteria specify that the symptoms are not due to the direct physiological effects of a substance (e.g., a drug of abuse, a medication, or other somatic treatment), or a general medical condition (e.g., hyperthyroidism).

Bipolar I is diagnosed when there is a current or past manic or mixed episode. Bipolar I can be used when there is a current manic episode and no history of any major depressive episode. In contrast, bipolar II requires the presence or history of a hypomanic episode and at least one major depressive episode (with no history of manic or mixed episodes). Cyclothymia involves hypomanic and depressive symptoms over a period of at least 2 years with no symptom-free periods of 2 months or longer.

In spite of the precision with which the DSM lays out criteria for diagnosing BD, the clinical presentation of the disorder in children and adolescents is widely debated. Areas of controversy include whether the diagnosis of BD in youth should require clearly demarcated mood episodes and, if so, of what duration, and whether specific hallmark symptoms (euphoria and grandiosity) should be required. The National Institute of Mental Health Research roundtable on prepubertal bipolar disorder (2001) agreed that pediatric BD can be described with "broad" or "narrow" phenotypes. The "narrow" phenotype is characterized by recurrent periods of major depression and mania or hypomania fitting the classic definitions of BD I and II, respectively. The broad phenotype has been variously defined, but may involve chronic mood lability/instability rather than discrete mood episodes, and irritability with no euphoria or depression.

Even when children do have classic symptoms of mania or hypomania, the symptom presentation is colored by the developmental stage of the child. Moreover, a great proportion of children do not meet the duration criteria of 4 (hypomania) or 7 (mania) days, and so are diagnosed as BD not otherwise specified (NOS). Children with the "broad" phenotype constitute the majority of referrals to clinicians and are characterized by severe irritability, "affective storms," mood lability, severe temper outbursts, depression, anxiety, hyperactivity, poor concentration, and impulsivity, all with or without clear mood episodicity. It is unclear whether broad phenotypes among children are true precursors to full bipolar I disorder in adulthood, although Birmaher et al. (2006) found that 25% of BD NOS children develop bipolar I or II disorder within an average of 22 months after their initial assessment.

Leibenluft, Charney, Towbin, Bhangoo, and Pine (2003) went one step further when they suggested classifying pediatric BD into "narrow," "intermediate," and "broad" phenotypes. The narrow phenotype includes those who meet the full DSM-IV criteria for mania or hypomania, including the duration criteria, and have the hallmark symptoms of elevated mood or grandiosity. The intermediate phenotype includes two subcategories: those with the hallmark symptom of elation but not meeting the duration criterion (i.e., symptoms lasting less than 4 days), and those meeting the duration criterion but with the less specific symptom of irritable mania or hypomania. (In the latter subcategory, elation is absent but the irritability must be episodic or periodic rather than chronic.) The broad phenotype consists of nonepisodic symptoms of severe irritability and hyperarousal without elation or grandiosity.

Rich et al. (2007) suggested the term "severe mood dysregulation" for children in the broad phenotype category, and developed a set of inclusion and exclusion criteria to further define the group. These are children who exhibit nonepisodic irritability accompanied by hyperarousal and hyper-reactivity to negative emotional stimuli, without elation or grandiosity.

In summary, children and adolescents who are diagnosed as bipolar in the community often fail to meet strict DSM-IV criteria. Future diagnostic systems should attempt to capture the broader phenotypes that are being treated in clinicians' offices, as these children—although not classically bipolar—often suffer from highly debilitating symptoms (Birmaher et al., 2006).

EPIDEMIOLOGY

Epidemiological studies have been hampered by the lack of consensus about how to define early-onset BD. Prevalence estimates vary depending on whether the narrow or broad phenotype is applied. Surveys that use strict DSM criteria reveal that the point prevalence of BD among youth is 1% or less. Kessler and Walters (1998) found that only a fraction of 1% of children and adolescents met DSM-III-R criteria for bipolar I.

In the Oregon Adolescent Depression Project, Lewinsohn, Klein, and Seeley (1995) used DSM-III-R criteria to assess a cohort of 1,709 high school students. They reported the lifetime prevalence of bipolar I, II, and cyclothymia to be 0.99% in their sample. In addition to the adolescents that met strict criteria, they identified 97 "core positive" cases (5.7% of the sample) who experienced a distinct period of elevated, expansive, or irritable mood, with an average of 2.9 associated manic symptoms.

Subjects in both groups were much more likely to report elevated or expansive than irritable mood, and relatively few subjects reported periods of irritable but not elevated mood. The most common manic symptom in both groups was increase in goal-directed activity. Other frequent symptoms included increased speech, inflated self-esteem, decreased need for sleep, and distractibility. Almost all symptoms were more frequent among the bipolar than core positive subjects. The authors also looked at the dimensional structure of the secondary ("B") manic symptoms during the most recent episode across the two groups. Using principal components analysis, the first component accounted for 38.2% of the variance and had relatively high and unique loadings on the following symptoms: decreased need for sleep, flight of ideas, distractibility, and poor judgment. This component reflects behavioral disorganization and impaired functioning; it correlated with total impairment ratings (social, family, and school). The second component accounted for an additional 14.6% of the variance, and loaded on inflated self-esteem and increase in goal-directed activity. It appears to represent the grandiose-hyperactive part of the manic syndrome. (This dimension resembles the behavioral facilitation or behavioral engagement system that Depue and Iacono [1989] hypothesized to represent the core neurobehavioral disturbance in BD.) Lewinsohn's study is limited by the reliance on self-report by adolescents, which may underestimate the frequency or severity of manic symptoms (Youngstrom, Findling, & Calabrese, 2004).

Lewinsohn, Klein, and Seeley (2000) followed a subset of their sample of high school students into young adulthood (n=1,507; mean age at entry was 16.6 years). In addition, all available first-degree relatives were interviewed. Using the Kiddie-Schedule for Affective Disorders and Schizophrenia (K-SADS), they identified adolescents who met DSM-III-R criteria for BD (n=17; mostly bipolar II and cyclothymia), subsyndromal BD (SUB; n=48), major depression (MDD; n=275), disruptive behavior disorder (n=49), and no disorder (n=307).

The BD and SUB groups were contrasted with each other and with the other diagnostic groups with respect to psychopathology during young adulthood. The BD group differed significantly from the SUB group only on total incidence of BD. Compared to the group with no disorders, the BD and SUB groups both showed significant impairment in psychosocial functioning and had higher mental health treatment utilization at age 24. About 1% of the MDD group "switched" to BD in young adulthood (a much lower rate of switching than found in clinical samples), and none of the SUB adolescents escalated to BD.

Although this study does not allow us to examine the continuity of BD from early childhood through adulthood, it gives clues about the relationship between "soft" signs of BD in adolescence (SUB) and BD in early adulthood. Notably, evidence for the premise that SUB is a risk factor for future BD was supported by the significantly elevated rates of BD and MDD in the relatives of adolescents with SUB compared to the relatives of adolescents with no disorders. In addition, SUB was significantly elevated in the relatives of BD cases. The fact that SUB probands did not escalate to BD, however, suggests that soft signs of BD in adolescence may be a risk factor for future psychopathology, but not specifically BD. Alternatively, adolescent self-report is not the most reliable means of obtaining data on precursor states.

A more recent community epidemiologic survey of mental disorder in youth, the Great Smoky Mountains Study of Youth, focused on a sample of 4,500 respondents in the age range 9 to 13 (Costello et al., 1996). None met criteria for bipolar I, and 0.1% met criteria for bipolar II in the 3 months before the interview. In a small (n=150) community sample of adolescents, 11.8% had a history of episodes lasting 2 days or longer in which they had four or more manic symptoms, but did not meet criteria for bipolar I, II, or cyclothymia (Carlson & Kashani, 1988).

Because of the complications surrounding the identification of cases of BD in youth, a useful approach in establishing prevalence is to work backward from the more clear-cut diagnosis of adult mania. Surveys of adults find that between 20 and 40% of those with a lifetime history of mania report that their first manic episode occurred during childhood or adolescence (e.g., Joyce, 1984; Kessler, Rubinow, Holmes, Abelson, & Zhao, 1997; Lish, Dime-Meenan, Whybrow, Price, & Hirschfeld, 1994). Given adult lifetime prevalence rates of BD in the range of 1 to 2%, it would appear that less than 1% of children and adolescents have manic symptoms that develop into adult BD. However, the cumulative lifetime prevalences of BD have increased in recent cohorts. A trend toward earlier age of onset of broadly defined BD with successively later years of birth has been reported (Rice et al., 1987). This is consistent with Kessler, Avenevoli, and Ries Merikangas (2001), who report that the lifetime prevalence as of age 18 in the recent National Comorbidity Survey (NCS) cohorts is 2.2%, which is 60 times higher than the prevalence in the oldest age cohorts of the NCS.

AGE OF ONSET

Goodwin and Jamison (1990), in a review of studies prior to 1990, describe the peak age of onset of BD as between 15 and 19 years old. In Lewinsohn et al.'s (1995) epidemiological study, the mean age of onset of the first affective episode for the 18 adolescents who met criteria for BD was 11.75 (SD=2.96).

This was significantly younger than the mean age of onset for the depressed, but not bipolar, adolescents in the sample. In the NCS-R, the mean age at onset was 18 (Merikangas et al., 2007).

Variation in age of onset may reflect underlying genetic heterogeneity in BD, as it does in Alzheimer's disease and breast cancer. Several studies have suggested that there may be three overlapping distributions of age of onset in BD (Bellivier, Golmard, Henry, Leboyer, & Schurhoff, 2001; Bellivier et al., 2003; Lin et al., 2006). Most recently, Lin et al. (2006) assessed 211 BD probands and their families as part of the NIMH Genetics Initiative for Bipolar Disorder. Using admixture analysis, they found three separate groups with different ages of onset. They assigned subjects to groups using cutoff points of less than age 21 for the first group, between 21 and 28 for the middle group, and greater than 28 for the third group. Earliest-onset subjects had higher risks of substance abuse, rapid cycling, and suicide attempts. Bipolar family members from a family with an earlier-onset proband were more likely than others to have an early onset (odds ratio=4.53, 95% CI=3.09–6.64).

Thus, it appears that age of onset may reflect underlying genetic heterogeneity and may aggregate within families. Age of onset may eventually be used to identify more homogenous subgroups of BD patients.

GENDER AND RACE/ETHNICITY

Although there are some findings on gender and ethnic differences in adult BD, reports of differences of this type in bipolar adolescents are sparse. Gender differences in depression have been found. Prepubertal boys have a slightly higher rate of depressed mood than girls, but in early adolescence there is a dramatic increase in depression among girls but not boys (e.g., Hankin et al., 1998; Wichstrom, 1999). There are apparently no comparable gender differences in rates of mania. The COBY (Course and Outcome of Bipolar Youth) study, described in detail in a later section of this chapter, compared sex and race across the three diagnostic groups of bipolar I, bipolar II, and bipolar NOS patients (Axelson et al., 2006). Racial differences were not in evidence across the three groups, but the proportion of males to females tended to differ across groups, with the lowest proportion of males (40%) in the bipolar II group. This parallels the finding in adults that women are more likely to be diagnosed with bipolar II, presumably because they report more depressive episodes than men (e.g., Schneck et al., 2004). Lewinsohn et al. (1995) noted few gender differences in their epidemiological sample and concluded that the prevalence, age of onset, phenomenology, and course of BD in adolescent males and females in a community setting was similar.

Patel, DelBello, and Strakowski (2006) examined ethnic differences in the symptom profiles of adolescents with BD at their first psychiatric hospitalization. Compared with the White cohort, African-American youths were diagnosed more frequently as having psychotic features and had higher ratings for auditory hallucinations. It is worth remembering that racial and gender differences found in clinical samples can reflect many differences that are independent of differences in the etiology of the disorder, including differences in the willingness to undergo treatment, and, particularly for children and adolescents, differences in the reactions of others (e.g., parents or teachers) to the clinical symptoms (Hartung & Widiger, 1998).

PHENOMENOLOGY

Several research groups have used semistructured interviews to examine the cross-sectional presentation of BD in clinical samples of youth (Axelson et al., 2006; Biederman, Faraone, Chu, & Wozniak, 1999; Findling et al., 2001; Geller et al., 2000). Geller and Luby (1997), in their review of child and adolescent BD, provided a particularly helpful description of how symptoms like euphoria, grandiosity, and hypersexuality manifest differently across developmental stages (child, adolescent, adult). For example, a common presentation of grandiosity in bipolar children is to instruct their teachers about how the class should be taught or to insist that stealing may be wrong for other people but not for them. Common adolescent grandiose delusions are that they will achieve a prominent profession even though they are failing in school.

Kowatch et al. (2005) performed a meta-analysis of seven studies examining the phenomenology of mania among children and adolescents aged 5 to 18. The most common symptoms during manic episodes were increased energy, distractibility, and pressured speech. Approximately 80% of subjects showed irritability and grandiosity; 70% had the symptoms of elated mood, decreased need for sleep, or racing thoughts. Hypersexuality and psychosis were less common.

Core Features

There has been ongoing controversy about how best to characterize mania in early onset BD. The pre-eminent criterion for mania/hypomania (an elated, expansive, or irritable mood that clearly represents a change from the individual's typical mood) contains the seeds of the dilemma(s). The first issue revolves around the affective nature of the mood (i.e., is elation required or is irritability enough to serve as a cardinal symptom of BD?); the second around the requirement that the mood syndrome is episodic and not an enduring characteristic of the individual.

Geller et al. (2001) felt that a method for differentiating BD from attention deficit hyperactivity disorder (ADHD) was needed because symptoms such as hyperactivity and distractibility are criteria for both disorders. They established a BD phenotype characterized by mania or hypomania with elation and/or grandiosity as one criterion for use in their longitudinal observation of a sample of early onset (prepubertal and early adolescent) BD subjects. Other researchers (e.g., Biederman, 1998) believe that severe, episodic irritability in the absence of elated mood can serve as a defining criterion for diagnosis of BD in children and adolescents (in keeping with DSM-IV). It is interesting that irritability has emerged consistently as a prominent symptom in clinical samples, and elated mood less so (although this could be an artifact of various research groups' differing definitions of mania), whereas in the epidemiological sample previously described (Lewinsohn et al., 1995) subjects were more likely to endorse elevated than irritable mood. It may be that irritability is overrepresented in clinical samples, and is one of the reasons these children are brought in for treatment. It is also possible that studies that use multiple informants will find more irritability than studies that rely on self-report only.

The requirement that mood syndromes be episodic is a particularly thorny one, especially for irritability and for euphoria (perhaps less so for depression, which more frequently presents as a discrete and extended mood state, even in children and adolescents). DSM-IV calls for 4 days duration to establish a hypomanic episode and 7 days for mania. Carlson and Kelly (1998) noted that a substantial proportion of children and adolescents report manic-like symptoms that persist for only a few hours or days and do not meet criteria for BD. These youngsters often are quite impaired, but there is considerable uncertainty about what these symptoms mean diagnostically. With the sort of mood lability seen in children and adolescents, moods are sometimes changing hourly, or at least several times in a day. How many hours in a day must be mood-affected for the day to count toward the duration criteria? Must they be contiguous hours? And if an adolescent is irritable for 2 hours every morning, is that characteristic (because it happens every day) or uncharacteristic (because after the morning irritability, the child is able to maintain a more level mood)? The same issues arise for elevated, silly, or giddy moods.

Attempts have been made to address some of these ambiguities, with promising results. Axelson et al. (2006) developed minimum criteria for a bipolar NOS diagnosis that included these clarifications: mood and symptom duration of a minimum of 4 hours within a 24-hour period for a day to "count;" and a minimum of 4 days (not necessarily consecutive) meeting the mood, symptom, duration, and functional change criteria over the subject's lifetime. Leibenluft et al. (2003), in work described earlier, offer an elegant approach for reconciling the complexities involved in early onset symptom pictures that may or may not include euphoria and grandiosity, may or may not meet duration criteria, and may or may not even appear to be episodic.

Irritability as a criterion for BD must be distinguished from irritability as a normal developmental phenomenon and as a common nonspecific psychiatric symptom. Leibenluft, Cohen, Gorrindo, Brook, and Pine (2006) developed scales measuring episodic and chronic irritability, and administered DSM-based structured interviews to 776 youths at three time points. They demonstrate that a child's irritability is likely to remain consistent in terms of its longitudinal course (i.e., episodic versus chronic). Chronic irritability at time 1 (mean age 13.8) predicted ADHD at time 2 (mean age 16.2) and major depression at time 3 (mean age 22.1). Episodic irritability at time 1 predicted simple phobia and mania at time 2. Episodic and chronic irritability in adolescents appear to be stable, distinct concepts, suggesting that the work differentiating narrow phenotype BD from (nonepisodic) severe mood dysregulation is essential to furthering our understanding of BD in youth.

COURSE AND IMPACT ON FUNCTIONING

Numerous studies point to dysfunctions associated with early-onset BD, regardless of whether the narrow or broad phenotype is applied. Some of these negative outcomes include high rates of hospitalization, suicidal behavior, psychosis, reckless behavior, aggression, and substance abuse; psychiatric, medical, and educational service utilization; severe family conflicts; significant caregiver burden; and chronic psychosocial impairment (Biederman et al., 2004; Biederman et al., 2003; Brent et al., 1988; Chang & Ketter, 2001; Craney & Geller, 2003; Findling et al., 2001; Geller et al., 2000;

Geller, Tillman, Craney, & Bolhofner, 2004; Lewinsohn et al., 2000; McClellan, McCurry, Snell, & DuBose, 1999; Perlis et al., 2004; Strober et al., 1995; Wilens et al., 2004). Two recent studies of adults found that early age at onset was associated with a rapid cycling course in adulthood (Coryell et al., 2003; Schneck et al., 2004).

Long-term follow-up studies illustrate the low recovery rates and high relapse rates associated with the disorder. One of the earliest was a 5-year naturalistic prospective follow-up of 54 consecutive admissions of bipolar I adolescents (mean age at entry was 16.0 years) to a university inpatient service (Strober et al., 1995). These subjects received aggressive pharmacotherapy, as well as equally intensive psychoeducation, family therapy, and individual therapy. Only 2 of the 54 subjects (3.7%) failed to achieve criteria for recovery at any time through the 260 weeks. Time to recovery varied by index episode polarity, with subjects with a purely manic or mixed episode recovering in a median of 9 or 11 weeks, respectively, whereas those with pure depression evidenced a median time to recovery of 26 weeks. Forty-four percent of those who recovered from their index episode had one or more relapses over the 5-year period. Comparing the results of this study with the findings on BD in adults (e.g., the NIMH Collaborative Study; Keller et al., 1986), it would appear that juveniles have a slower return to euthymia, but a lower relative risk of relapse, and longer time in remission than adult BD patients.

The COBY study (Axelson et al., 2006) was designed to extend the database on the cross-sectional presentation and longitudinal course of pediatric BD. Phenomenology (and family history) was examined as a function of bipolar I, bipolar II, or bipolar NOS diagnosis. Most subjects (58.2%) met criteria for bipolar I, with a few (6.8%) diagnosed as bipolar II, and a substantial number (34.9%) diagnosed as bipolar NOS, typically because they did not meet the episode duration criteria. The similarities among the three groups were perhaps more striking than the differences. Subjects with bipolar I had more severe lifetime manic symptoms, greater functional impairment, and higher rates of hospitalization, psychosis, and suicide attempts than those diagnosed bipolar NOS. The two groups were not different in age of onset, duration of illness, lifetime comorbidity, suicidal ideation, major depression, family history, and types of manic symptoms. The results suggest that all three diagnoses belong on a single continuum, with elevated mood as a common feature of youth with bipolar spectrum disorder.

This sample of children and adolescents (n=263, mean age 13 years) was followed for 2 years (Birmaher et al., 2006). Approximately 70% of subjects recovered (defined as eight consecutive weeks with minimal to no symptoms) from their index episode and 50% of those had at least one recurrence. There were no differences in rates of recovery among the three diagnostic subgroups, although subjects with BD NOS took a significantly longer time to recover than the other two groups. During 60% of the weeks of follow-up, subjects had syndromal or subsyndromal symptoms, and 3% of the time, psychosis. Twenty percent of bipolar II subjects converted to bipolar I, and 25% of bipolar NOS converted to bipolar I or II.

A number of predictors of recovery emerged. Subjects with childhood onset were less likely than those with adolescent onset to recover. Children with lower socioeconomic status longer duration of BD symptoms, and a diagnosis of BD NOS were less likely to recover. Birmaher et al. (2006) provided an additional analysis in which they compared the bipolar I youth in their sample with bipolar I adults in a 20-year follow-up of subjects with baseline mood disorders (Judd et al., 2002). Youth spent significantly more time symptomatic and had more mixed/cycling episodes, mood symptom changes, and polarity switches than adults.

Geller et al. (2004) reported on a 4-year naturalistic prospective outcome study of 86 subjects with an index episode of mania (defined by elated mood and/or grandiosity as one inclusion criterion) and a baseline age of 10.8 years. Follow-up assessments occurred every 6 months. Age of onset of the intake episode of mania was 7.4 years and episode duration was 79.2 consecutive weeks. Time to recovery was 60.2 weeks and the time to relapse after recovery was 40.4 weeks. Any BD diagnosis occurred during a mean of 67.1% of total follow-up weeks; subjects spent 56.9% of total weeks with mania or hypomania, and 47.1% with depression. Two predictors of relapse emerged; baseline psychosis (associated with more time ill with mania or hypomania), and low maternal warmth, which predicted earlier relapse to mania or hypomania. In contrast, coming from an intact biological family predicted a shorter time to recovery.

In Judd et al.'s (2002) 20-year follow-up of adult subjects with baseline mood disorders, depressive episodes predominated, whereas the children in Geller's sample spent more weeks with mania/hypomania than with depression. Methodological differences between the two studies may account for this difference, but it is also possible that mania or hypomania predominates during the prepubertal and early adolescent age range, and depressive states may become more dominant with age (or that Judd et al. [2002] had more adult-onset patients).

Birmaher et al. (2006) and Geller et al. (2004) make a case for continuity between child- and adult-onset BD based on the similarity of mania symptom distribution between the two, the occurrence of both within the same families, the occurrence of maternal warmth and psychosis as predictors of outcome of both, and the fact that, across the life span and especially in youth, BD usually follows a changeable and sinuous course.

COMORBIDITY

Virtually every study of early-onset BD has commented on the extensive comorbidities. Angold, Costello, and Erkanli (1999) presented a meta-analysis of 21 community studies that used standardized psychiatric interviews with parents and children to generate diagnoses (DSM-III, III-R, or IV) and report rates of comorbidity between pairs of disorders. They concluded that comorbidity cannot be explained as artifact, and is indeed a real phenomenon. Nonspecific symptoms like irritability blur the boundaries between diagnoses, calling for more work detailing the qualitative and quantitative aspects of individual symptoms in relation to different diagnoses. Nonetheless, studies find that comorbidity between disorders remains, even after overlapping symptoms are removed from the criteria for the two diagnoses (Milberger, Biederman, Faraone, Murphy, & Tsuang, 1995; ADHD and depression or generalized anxiety disorder]; Biederman, Faraone, Mick & Lelon, 1995; depression and ADHD or oppositional defiant disorder]). Angold et al. (1999) point to the importance of studying the development of patterns of symptomatology over time so that the developmental continuity of a single disease process is not obscured by current diagnostic categories.

The co-occurrence of BD and ADHD has been extensively studied by Biederman and colleagues. Biederman et al. (1996) contrasted 140 ADHD children (eligible subjects were 6 to 17 years of age) with and without BD at baseline and at 4-year follow-up; 11% of ADHD children at baseline were diagnosed with BD, and an additional 12% met criteria for BD after 4 years, rates significantly higher than those of controls at each assessment. Faraone, Biederman, Mennin, Wozniak, and Spencer (1997) administered structured psychiatric interviews to the 822 first-degree relatives of the entire sample of 260 ADHD and control children. Comparing ADHD children with and without BD, they found that relatives of ADHD+BD children had a fivefold elevated risk for BD and an elevated risk for major depression with severe impairment. The authors concluded that comorbid ADHD+BD is familially distinct from other forms of ADHD, and may be related to what others have termed childhood-onset BD (characterized by irritability rather than euphoria, a chronic rather than episodic course, and involving severe mood dysregulation leading to marked impairment).

A review of 17 studies that examined the co-occurrence of pediatric BD and ADHD in children, adolescents and, retrospectively, in adults (Singh, DelBello, Kowatch, & Strakowski, 2006) led to similar conclusions: "...the literature most strongly suggests that ADHD symptoms represent a prodromal or early manifestation of pediatric-onset bipolar disorder in certain at-risk individuals" (p. 710). Thus, ADHD may be a developmentally specific phenotype of early-onset BD among children with a positive family history of BD. One prognostic question is whether these comorbid children grow up to become typical BD adults (i.e., those with pure mania) or atypical BD adults with dysphoric, or mixed mania, or rapid cycling.

The only prospective study of the rate, risk, and predictors of switching from ADHD to prepubertal and early adolescent bipolar I (Tillman & Geller, 2006) followed 81 ADHD subjects (mean age 9.7) and 94 healthy controls over 6 years. To be considered a "switcher," a child had to meet criteria for a manic or mixed episode (with elated mood and/or grandiosity) of at least 2 weeks duration and impaired functioning. The cumulative risk of switching from ADHD to bipolar I through the 6-year follow-up was 28.5%, compared to a 2% switching rate for healthy controls.

A smaller body of literature documents the elevated risk for conduct disorder (CD) among children with mania. Reported comorbidity rates range from 42% in a sample of hospitalized adolescents with mania (Kutcher, Marton, & Korenblum, 1989) to 69% in a clinical outpatient sample of children and adolescents (Kovacs & Pollock, 1995). In a review of the literature on the diagnostic dilemmas surrounding diagnosis of childhood mania, ADHD, and CD, Kim and Miklowitz (2002) concluded that reliable and accurate diagnoses can be made despite the symptom overlap among the three disorders. They concurred with Faraone et al. (1997) that children with BD and ADHD may have a distinct familial subtype of BD. However, they cite work by Carlson, Loney, Salisbury, and Volpe (1998) that complicates the diagnostic picture by raising an alternative view: that the manic syndrome, at least as characterized by emotional lability, may be a part of the psychopathology of other disorders, and indeed has been recognized in children with schizophrenia, autism, and pervasive developmental disorders. This view suggests that manic symptoms sometimes represent "noise" that indicates the general severity of psychopathology, not specifically BD.

In summary, we must push beyond reporting rates of comorbidities to understanding what these co-occurring disorders represent. In order to do that, we will need universally accepted definitions of what childhood mania is, what comprises an episode, and longitudinal research that tracks the appearance and remission of different syndromes over different stages of development.

GENETICS AND NEUROBIOLOGY

BD is one of the most heritable of psychiatric illnesses, second only to autism. Family studies have shown that the relative risk to first-degree relatives of an individual with BD is about 7 (Satcher, 1999). Some degree of cofamiliality between unipolar and BD is supported, suggesting partial overlap in the familial risk factors for the two disorders (Pennington, 2002). Similarly, in family studies of bipolar I, bipolar II, and cyclothymia, each disorder increases the risk in relatives for the other two disorders, but to a lesser extent than the risk found when both proband and relative have the same phenotype.

Lapalme, Hodgins, and LaRoche (1997) performed a meta-analysis of studies of the phenomenology of bipolar offspring. Seventeen studies were examined, 11 of which included a comparison group of offspring of parents with no mental disorder. Over half (52%) of the bipolar offspring met DSM-III or III-R criteria for a psychiatric disorder compared to 29% of the controls. Furthermore, 5.4% of the bipolar offspring were diagnosed with BD, compared to 0% of the control group.

Twin studies further demonstrate the heritability of BD. Across studies, the average monozygotic concordance for BD is about 60%, whereas the average dizygotic concordance is about 12% (Kelsoe, 1997). Although genetic transmission is clearly significant, the fact that monozygotic concordance is less than 1.0 means that there must also be environmental influences on the development of BD. The mode of genetic transmission appears to be complex and likely involves multiple interacting genes (Satcher, 1999). Linkage studies have produced many initial "hits," few of which have been replicated. Chromosomes 13 and 22 may be the most promising candidates for carrying genes that contribute to BD, although the variance contributed by each of these may be quite small. For a thorough review of the genetics of BD literature, see Smoller and Finn (2003).

To understand what is different about the brain in BD, we need to understand what is disrupted in both the depressed and manic mood states. Some researchers have remarked on the frequent presentation of bipolar depression as atypical depression, while unipolar depression is more often associated with insomnia, anorexia, and psychomotor agitation (Kelley, 1987; Thase, 2007). Earlier studies suggested that bipolar and unipolar depression may be biologically as well as phenomenologically distinct. The symptoms of bipolar depression have been compared to animal models of mesolimbic dopamine depletion (Depue & Iacono, 1989; Swerdlow & Koob, 1987). The brain's motivation system is organized in layers ranging from the brainstem through the limbic system to the cortical level. Depue and Iacono (1989) term this the "behavioral facilitation" system, whose function is to mobilize approach behaviors to seek rewards and to remove obstacles to rewards. They argue that most of the symptoms of mania can be viewed as exaggerated functioning of this system, whereas bipolar depression reflects reduced functioning. The behavioral facilitation system corresponds to the main projection sites of the mesolimbic and mesocortical dopamine pathways. Alterations in dopaminergic neurotransmission could either over- or underactivate this system, with opposite consequences for the level of goal-directed activity, and the manifestation of either mania or bipolar depression. This theory of BD is supported by studies of reward-seeking behaviors in animal models and by evidence of alterations in dopamine neurotransmission in BD.

The symptoms of unipolar depression have been linked to deficiencies in norepinephrine (Schildkraut, 1965) and serotonin (Nemeroff, 1998; Prange, Wilson, Lynn, Alltop, & Stikeleather, 1974). Animal studies have demonstrated that stress and loss can alter levels of norepinephrine and serotonin, as well as altering the function of the stress response system (Mineka, Gunnar, & Champoux, 1986; Sapolsky, 1996; Stone, 1975). Gold and Chrousos (1999) presented endocrinological data indicating that the hypersomnia, hyperphagia, lethargy, fatigue, and relative apathy of the atypical syndrome are associated with concomitant hypofunctioning of the stress response system, while melancholic features (sustained anxiety and dread for the future with physiological hyperarousal) involve sustained hyperactivity of the stress response system. These findings on the biological distinctions between unipolar (nonatypical or melancholic) and bipolar (atypical) depression suggest that unipolar depression results from chronic stress (including loss) and that the opposite of unipolar depression is relief from chronic stress and the return of a normal capacity for pleasure. The opposite of bipolar depression is mania, an excessive pursuit and capacity for pleasure.

More recent research suggests that the distinction is not so straightforward. The concept of atypical depression emerged in the 1950s to describe individuals with unusual depressive symptoms (hypersomnia and weight gain rather than insomnia and loss of appetite) who were shown to respond better to monoamine oxidase inhibitors than to tricyclic antidepressants. Recent authors, however, have challenged the validity of the subtype, noting that consistency across and within types of depression has been unimpressive and, in the post-MAOI era, no group of drugs has been clearly shown to have greater efficacy in atypical depression (Davidson, 2007). Furthermore, unipolar depression can present with atypical features. Tremblay et al. (2005) examined the symptoms of anhedonia and decreased motivation or drive (atypical depression) in major depression. Using fMRI to compare subjects with major depression and healthy controls before and after receiving dextroamphetamine to stimulate the brain reward system, they found that individuals with major depression had a hypersensitive response to the rewarding effects of the stimulant (i.e., more positive reinforcing effects from the drug). There were significant positive correlations between the degree of dextroamphetamine reward and the severity of anhedonia. It may be that the dopamine pathways comprising the brain reward system are implicated in a specific component of depression (anhedonia), which may be differently represented in atypical versus nonatypical depression. Mapping the correspondence between melancholic versus atypical, and unipolar versus bipolar depression remains to be done. Understanding the biology of these differing mood presentations may shed light on phenomena such as mixed states, which are so common in child and adolescent BD.

There are other neurotransmitter and neuroendocrine abnormalities in adult BD. Alterations in norepinephrine levels are correlated with mood cycles in BD and may play a causal role in the switch between cycles. There is evidence for low levels of gamma-aminobutyric acid (the main cortical inhibitory neurotransmitter) in BD. The unaffected relatives of BD patients demonstrated sensitivity to the deleterious effects of tryptophan depletion (which lowers serotonin levels), suggesting that vulnerability to reduced tryptophan may represent an endophenotype for BD (Quintin et al., 2001: Sobczak et al., 2002). More recently, research in this area has moved from a focus on neurotransmitters and cell surface receptors to intracellular signaling pathways, or second messenger systems (the chemical cascade that occurs in the postsynaptic neuron after a neurotransmitter binds with a receptor). There is a growing consensus that the ability of medications, such as lithium and valproic acid, to treat multiple aspects of an illness as complex as BD arises from their major effects on intracellular signaling pathways, rather than on any single neurotransmitter system per se. Promising reports demonstrating neurotrophic and neuroprotective effects of mood stabilizers have emerged (Drevets, 2000; Moore, Bebchuk, Wilds, Chen, & Manji, 2000; Sassi et al., 2002). (Findings on neurotransmitters and cellular signaling pathways in adults are reviewed in Howland and Thase [1999], Manji et al. [2003], and Miklowitz and Johnson [2006].)

Both structural and functional neuroimaging studies have produced useful clues to understanding the adult mood-disordered brain. The two main structural findings—white matter hyperintensities (WMH; focal areas of high intensity signal, possibly caused by abnormalities in myelin or microinfarcts) and cortical atrophy—both suggest a neurodegenerative process. These findings are not accounted for by medication, and are correlated with the severity and chronicity of the disorder, cortisol levels, and age, leading to the hypothesis that the physiological changes associated with mood episodes cause neurodegeneration. Functional neuroimaging differences in adult BD include: (1) decreased frontal brain metabolism during a depressive episode (greater than that found in unipolar depression), (2) overall increases in brain metabolism with the switch to mania or hypomania, and (3) possible laterality differences in the frontal lobe metabolism between unipolar and BD (left hemisphere decreases in unipolar and right hemisphere decreases in bipolar). These changes are probably more accurately conceptualized as state rather than trait markers (Pennington, 2002).

DelBello, Adler, and Strakowski. (2006) provide a comprehensive overview of neuroimaging studies performed on children and adolescents from 1966 to 2005. Structural MRI studies suggest that severe prefrontal WMH occur in bipolar youth, similar to adults. Diffusion tensor imaging, a magnetic resonance technique that measures aspects of water diffusion, is used to assess subtler abnormalities in white matter tracts, like axonal disorganization. One study (Adler et al., 2006) reported that unmedicated first-episode bipolar adolescents, similar to bipolar adults, evidenced axonal disorganization. Since these indications were present at illness onset, they potentially represent an early biomarker of BD.

In addition to white matter abnormalities, structural MRI studies suggest abnormalities in the anterior cingulate, ventral prefrontal cortex, superior temporal gyral, amygdala, hippocampus, and putamen in bipolar youth. Some of these findings are similar to those reported in adults with BD. However, smaller amygdala volumes have been reported in bipolar youth (e.g., Chang et al., 2005), whereas the amygdala tends to be enlarged in adults. This discrepancy may suggest age-specific structural MRI abnormalities.

Magnetic resonance spectroscopy; a noninvasive neuroimaging technique that provides in vivo measurement of the concentration of specific neurochemicals in localized brain regions studies have found neurochemical abnormalities in second messenger metabolism, neuronal integrity, and possibly neurotransmission in the ventral and anterior cingulate prefrontal cortices and basal ganglia in bipolar children. Specifically, elevated prefrontal myo-inositol (a neurochemical involved in a second messenger pathway) has been reported in bipolar youth, and may be an early, specific biomarker of BD in children and adolescents. Davanzo et al. (2003) were able to demonstrate a significant reduction in myo-inositol/creatine levels with acute lithium treatment in 11 manic children.

Studies of both adults and children with BD suggest involvement of two interconnected brain pathways: a ventral-limbic (amygdala) pathway thought to regulate mood, and a dorsal-subcortical pathway (including the thalamus and basal ganglia) that modulates cognitive processes. Several investigators have hypothesized that dysfunction within these pathways underlies the neurophysiology of BD (Chang et al., 2004; Strakowski, DelBello, and Adler, 2005). Perhaps decreased amygdala volumes in bipolar youth lead to increases in ventral prefrontal activation in an attempt to regulate mood. Dysfunction in the ventral-limbic pathways leads to mood dysregulation as well as to secondary abnormalities in the dorsal-subcortical pathway.

NEUROPSYCHOLOGY

Pediatric BD is associated with a number of neuropsychological deficits. Attempts have been made to clarify the nature of these deficits, and to determine whether deficits are specific to mood states or whether they remain after symptomatic recovery.

Central findings from several small studies suggest that pediatric BD involves impairment in attention (Dickstein et al., 2004; Doyle et al., 2005), set shifting (Dickstein et al., 2004; Meyer et al., 2004), visuospatial memory (Dickstein et al., 2004; Olvera, Semrud-Clikeman, Pliszka, & O'Donnell, 2004), processing speed and interference control (Doyle et al., 2005), verbal memory (Doyle et al., 2005; McClure et al., 2005; Meyer et al., 2004) and abstract problem solving or executive function (Doyle et al., 2005; Murphy et al., 1999). The Performance IQ scores of pediatric bipolar patients on the Wechsler Intelligence Scale for Children were reported to be similar to those seen in schizophrenia spectrum disorders, and lower than those in ADHD, CD, ODD, and unipolar depression (McCarthy et al., 2004; Meyer et al., 2004).

Pavuluri et al. (2006) administered tests to assess attention, memory, visuospatial perception, and motor skills to pediatric BD patients who were medicated and euthymic, pediatric BD patients who were unmedicated and symptomatic, and healthy controls. Contrary to expectations, children with pediatric BD, regardless of medication and illness status, showed impairments in the domains of attention, executive functioning, working memory, and verbal learning compared to healthy individuals. Subjects with BD and ADHD performed worse on tasks assessing attention and executive function than patients with BD alone. Thus, there appear to be similar neurocognitive deficits in unmedicated acutely ill subjects and subjects who are medicated and clinically stable. However, this study used two separate cross-sectional groups of medicated and unmedicated patients. A design based on longitudinal follow-up of untreated patients through controlled treatment would be informative.

Rich et al. (2007) had children with severe mood dysregulation (broad phenotype; $n=21$), narrow-phenotype BD ($n=35$), and healthy comparison subjects ($n=26$) complete an attentional task that manipulated emotional demands (subjects were given verbal feedback regarding their response accuracy versus subjects who won or lost money based on their performance) and induced frustration (on a portion of correct responses, subjects were informed that they were too slow and lost money). The researchers measured mood response, behavior, and brain activity in response to the task. Both patient groups reported more arousal than healthy subjects during frustration. When frustrated, narrow-phenotype children showed brain activity suggestive of impairment in executive attention. Regardless of emotional context, broad-phenotype subjects evidenced impairments in the initial stages of attention. The authors concluded that the pathophysiology of irritability may differ between severe mood dysregulation and narrow-phenotype BD.

TREATMENT

Treatment of adolescent BD is based on pharmacotherapy and, where possible, psychotherapy. Here, we briefly review what is known about pharmacologic and psychosocial treatments. For a more comprehensive review, see Kowatch et al. (2005; practice guidelines for child psychiatrists).

Pharmacotherapy

In 2003, a group of 20 clinicians and Child and Adolescent Bipolar Foundation members met to develop a set of guidelines for the diagnosis and pharmacological treatment of pediatric BD (Kowatch et al., 2005). The assessment section of the guidelines provides a very useful adjunct to the DSM-IV criteria, providing suggestions for establishing symptom thresholds (i.e., how frequent or severe does a symptom have to be to count as present?) in making a diagnosis of childhood-onset patients. The guidelines also provide medication treatment algorithms for pediatric bipolar I. For acute phase treatment of manic or mixed symptoms without psychosis, monotherapy with a mood stabilizer or atypical antipsychotic is the first step, with lithium or divalproex as the recommendation of the majority of the panel. A decision tree is provided to guide the clinician through succeeding stages of therapy, based on whether the patient responds to the initial treatment, partially responds, or shows no response. For children with acute manic or mixed symptoms with psychosis, the initial treatment should be a combination of a mood stabilizer and an atypical antipsychotic. Again, a decision tree provides guidance on how and when to augment with added medication(s).

There was insufficient evidence to develop a treatment algorithm for children with bipolar I who are acutely depressed, but based on data on adults, lithium was recommended as a treatment option. Also covered are pharmacological treatment of comorbid disorders, maintenance/continuation treatment, and common side effects.

Randomized trials of various pharmacological agents have been undertaken, although a thorough review is beyond the scope of this chapter. (See Pavuluri, Birmaher, and Naylor [2005] for a presentation of the published pharmacotherapy trials in pediatric BD.) In the pharmacotherapy of adolescent mania, the best evidence is for lithium, divalproex, and atypical antipsychotics. Quetiapine (an atypical antipsychotic) appears to be effective alone or in conjunction with divalproex (DelBello, Schwiers, Rosenberg, & Strakowski, 2002; DelBello et al., 2006). A 61% rate of response was observed in an open-label trial of olanzapine (an atypical antipsychotic) for manic youths (Frazier et al., 2001). In a small sample of adolescents with bipolar depression, 84% responded to 8 weeks of lamotrigine (a mood stabilizer/anticonvulsant) treatment, with decreases in depression, mania, and aggression (Chang, Saxena, & Howe, 2006).

Psychotherapy

Several psychosocial treatments for BD have been shown to be effective with adults. Effectiveness is generally measured as longer time to relapse, more time well, improved functioning, and/or fewer or less severe symptoms/episodes. Included are cognitive-behavioral therapy (CBT) (Lam, Hayward, Watkins, Wright, & Sham, 2005), interpersonal and social rhythm therapy (frank et al. [2005] an enhancement of interpersonal psychotherapy for depression [Weissman, Markowitz, & Klerman, 2000] modified for BD), family-focused therapy (FFT; Miklowitz, George, Richards, Simoneau, and Suddath [2003] an approach that involves the patient and his/her family, and consists of psychoeducation about BD and training in communication and problem-solving skills), and group psychoeducation. The application of these approaches to pediatric BD is just beginning to receive attention.

Miklowitz, Biuckians, and Richards (2006) found in a small-scale open trial that adolescents with bipolar episodes who received FFT (family sessions consisting of education about BD, practice using four communication skills, and implementing family problem solving) and pharmacotherapy, stabilized over 24 months in mania symptoms (Cohen's $d=1.19$), depressive symptoms ($d=0.87$) and Child Behavior Checklist Problem Behavior scores ($d=0.99$). This approach is now being examined in a three-site randomized trial. In an open trial of FFT in combination with individual CBT, adjunctive to optimized pharmacotherapy, West, Henry, and Pavuluri (2007) observed improvements in symptoms (mania, aggression, psychosis, depression) and global functioning among bipolar children aged 5–17. These improvements were observed immediately following the 12-session treatment, and at 1, 2, and 3 years. This child- and family-focused CBT integrates principles of FFT and CBT, and focuses on the specific problems of children and families coping with BD. It is based on a biological theory of excessive reactivity to stimuli in interaction with environmental stressors in eliciting symptomatic states.

Fristad, Gavazzi, and Mackinaw-Koons (2003) examined multifamily psychoeducation groups (MFPG) as adjunctive to pharmacotherapy. Parents and children were provided with specific educational content, coached to practice communication skills, given workbooks containing materials presented in the sessions, and asked to complete family projects during the week. Parents in the MFPGs reported a greater understanding of mood disorder, more positive family interactions, and increased use of appropriate psychosocial and medical services than waiting-list parents.

Feeny, Danielson, Schwartz, Youngstrom, and Findling (2006) developed a manualized, individually delivered cognitive-behavioral intervention for adolescents with BD, and tested it in an open trial, as an adjunct to pharmacotherapy. The treatment included skill-oriented training (problem solving, social skills, relaxation, and relapse prevention) to improve mood symptoms and functioning. Using existing data, baseline characteristics and outcome were compared to a matched group of eight adolescents with BD who did not receive any psychosocial intervention. They concluded that the treatment was associated with symptom improvement in adolescents with BD and warrants evaluation in randomized controlled trials.

Clearly, the development and validation of psychosocial treatments for pediatric BD is a priority. Given the disadvantages of polypharmacy for the younger age groups (e.g., significant weight gain, rash, possibly increased suicide risk with antidepressants), the importance of developing effective psychosocial interventions is critical. Although all the psychosocial treatments tested to date have been adjuncts to pharmacotherapy, effective psychosocial agents could hopefully reduce the number of medications needed to stabilize patients with young-onset BD.

PREVENTION

Researchers are now beginning to identify and study populations at high risk for developing BD, in particular offspring of parents with BD, as a means of identifying populations with whom preventative interventions would be cost-effective. Kindling theory (Post, 1992) postulates that mood disorders are created by an interplay between a susceptible genetic diathesis and environmental stressors, which over time lead to the crossing of a neurobiological threshold for a mood episode. With the onset of each successive episode of mania or depression, biological changes accrue, leading to more frequent and spontaneous episodes which may or may not be elicited by environmental stressors.

Chang, Steiner, and Ketter (2003b) reviewed the research on numerous characteristics of bipolar offspring. Offspring of BD parents had elevated scores on the clinical scales of the Child Behavior Checklist (Dienes, Chang, Blasey, Adleman, & Steiner, 2002); tended toward temperaments that resulted in suboptimal reactions to psychosocial stressors, as measured from infancy to adolescence (Chang, Blasey, Ketter, & Steiner, 2003a; Gaensbauer, Harmon, Cytryn, and McKnew, 1984; Zahn-Waxler, Cummings, McKnew, & Radke-Yarrow, 1984); and had poorer psychosocial functioning (Pellegrini et al., 1986).

Based on findings such as those reported above, bipolar offspring often appear to have subsyndromal and possibly prodromal forms of BD. Chang et al. (2003a) investigated pharmacological interventions in this high-risk population. They reported clinical improvement after a 12-week open trial of divalproex in 78% of a cohort of 23 bipolar offspring with mood or behavior disorders. However, no placebo comparison was provided.

Findling et al. (2007) examined divalproex as monotherapy for children at risk for BD (i.e., diagnosis of BD NOS or cyclothymia and a first-degree relative with BD) in comparison with placebo in a randomized trial. No differences were observed over 5 years to medication discontinuation due to new mood episodes. Mood and psychosocial functioning ratings did not differ over time between the two groups, although both improved with time.

This study suggests that early pharmacological intervention may have no advantages over placebo in preventing the first onset of BD, although the issue has not been adequately examined. Psychosocial prevention studies for at-risk youth will be an important direction for the next wave of research on early-onset BD.

CONCLUSIONS

The advances in our understanding of BD in adolescence are encouraging, yet challenges remain. We need to learn more about the youth who often receive a diagnosis of BD in the community, but who better fit the criteria for "severe emotion dysregulation." What is their long-term outcome? Do the narrow versus broad phenotype children fall along the same continuum, or will neuropsychological and brain imaging studies reveal discontinuities? We need to articulate the multiple developmental pathways by which children arrive at a BD diagnosis in adolescence. In particular, how informative is age of onset, particularly pre- versus postpuberty, in illuminating course, prognosis, and treatment responsiveness? Is it possible to intervene with children at risk for developing BD, and forestall or eliminate the emergence of the disorder?

Further controlled studies of adjunctive psychotherapy approaches to adolescent BD are needed. It will be particularly important to examine which approaches work for which subgroups of this population, taking into account broad versus narrow phenotype and comorbid conditions. Early intervention may be a key to altering the deleterious course and functional impairments of BD over the lifespan.

REFERENCES

Adler, C. M., Adams, J., DelBello, M. P., Holland, S. K., Schmithorst, V., Levine, A., et al. (2006). Evidence of white matter pathology in bipolar disorder adolescents experiencing their first episode of mania: A diffusion tensor imaging study. *American Journal of Psychiatry, 163*(2), 322–324.

American Psychiatric Association (2000). *Diagnostic and statistical manual of mental disorders, 4th Ed. (Text Revision) (DSM-IV-TR).* Washington, DC: American Psychiatric Press.

Angold, A., Costello, J., & Erkanli, A. (1999). Comorbidity. *Journal of Child Psychology and Psychiatry, 40*(1), 57–87.

Axelson, D., Birmaher, B., Strober, M., Gill, M. K., Valeri, S., Chiappetta, L., et al. (2006). Phenomenology of children and adolescents with bipolar spectrum disorders. *Archives of General Psychiatry, 63,* 1139–1148.

Bellivier, F., Golmard, J. L., Henry, C., Leboyer, M., & Schurhoff, F. (2001). Admixture analysis of age at onset in bipolar I affective disorder. *Archives of General Psychiatry, 58,* 510–512.

Bellivier, F., Golmard, J. L., Rietschel, M., Schulze, T. G., Malafosse, A., Preisig, M., et al. (2003). Age at onset in bipolar I affective disorder: Further evidence for three subgroups. *American Journal of Psychiatry, 160,* 999–1001.

Biederman, J. (1998). Resolved: Mania is mistaken for ADHD in prepubertal children. *Journal of the American Academy of Child & Adolescent Psychiatry, 37*, 1096–1098.

Biederman, J., Faraone, S. V., Chu, M. P., & Wozniak, J. (1999). Further evidence of a bidirectional overlap between juvenile mania and conduct disorder in children. *Journal of the American Academy of Child & Adolescent Psychiatry, 38*, 468–476.

Biederman, J., Faraone, S. V., Mick, E., & Lelon, E. (1995). Psychiatric comorbidity among referred juveniles with major depression: Fact or artefact? *Journal of the American Academy of Child & Adolescent Psychiatry, 34*, 579–590.

Biederman, J., Faraone, S., Mick, E., Wozniak, J., Chen, L., Ouellette, C., et al. (1996). Attention-deficit hyperactivity disorder and juvenile mania: An overlooked comorbidity? *Journal of the American Academy of Child & Adolescent Psychiatry, 35*(8), 997–1008.

Biederman, J., Faraone, S. V., Wozniak, J., Mick, E., Kwon, A., & Aleardi, M., et al. (2004). Further evidence of unique developmental phenotypic correlates of pediatric bipolar disorder: Findings from a large sample of clinically referred preadolescent children assessed over the last 7 years. *Journal of Affective Disorders, 82S*, S45–S58.

Biederman, J., Mick, E., Faraone, S. V., Spencer, T., Wilens, T. E., & Wozniak, J. (2003). Current concepts in the validity, diagnosis and treatment of paediatric bipolar disorder. *International Journal of Neuropsychopharmacology, 6*, 293–300.

Birmaher, B., Axelson, D., Strober, M., Gill, M. K., Valeri, S., Chiappetta, L., et al. (2006). Clinical course of children and adolescents with bipolar spectrum disorders. *Archives of General Psychiatry, 63*(2), 175–183.

Brent, D. A., Perper, J. A., Goldstein, C. E., Kolko, D. J., Allan, M. J., Allman, C. J., et al. (1988). Risk factors for adolescent suicide: A comparison of adolescent suicide victims with suicidal inpatients. *Archives of General Psychiatry, 45*, 581–588.

Carlson, G. A., & Kashani, J. H. (1988). Manic symptoms in a nonreferred adolescent population. *Journal of Affective Disorders, 15*, 219–226.

Carlson, G. A., & Kelly, K. L. (1998). Manic symptoms in psychiatrically hospitalized children—what do they mean? *Journal of Affective Disorders, 51*, 123–135.

Carlson, G. A., Loney, J., Salisbury, H., & Volpe, R. (1998). Young referred boys with DICA-P manic symptoms vs. two comparison groups. *Journal of Affective Disorders, 121*, 113–121.

Chang, K., Adleman, N. E., Dienes, K., Simeonova, D. J., Menon, V., & Reiss, A. (2004). Anomalous prefrontal-subcortical activation in familial pediatric bipolar disorder: A functional magnetic resonance imaging investigation. *Archives of General Psychiatry, 61*(8), 781–792.

Chang, K., Karchemskiy, A., Barnea-Goraly, N., Garrett, A., Simeonova, D. I., & Reiss, A., et al. (2005). Reduced amygdalar gray matter volume in familial pediatric bipolar disorder. *Journal of the American Academy of Child & Adolescent Psychiatry, 44*, 565–573.

Chang, K., Saxena, K., & Howe, M. (2006). An open-label study of lamotrigine adjunct or monotherapy for the treatment of adolescents with bipolar depression. *Journal of the American Academy of Child & Adolescent Psychiatry, 45*(3), 298–304.

Chang, K., Steiner, H., & Ketter, T. (2003b). Studies of offspring of parents with bipolar disorder. *American Journal of Medical Genetics, 123C*, 26–35.

Chang, K. D., Blasey, C., Ketter, T. A., & Steiner, H. (2003a). Temperament characteristics of child and adolescent bipolar offspring. *Journal of Affective Disorders, 77*, 11–19.

Chang, K. D., & Ketter, T. A. (2001). Special issues in the treatment of pediatric bipolar disorder. *Expert Opinion on Pharmacotherapy, 2*, 613–622.

Coryell, W., Solomon, D., Turvey, C., Keller, M., Leon, A. C., Endicott, J., et al. (2003). The long-term course of rapid-cycling bipolar disorder. *Archives of General Psychiatry, 60*, 914–920.

Costello, E. J., Angold, A., Burns, B. J., Erkanli, A., Stangl, D., & Tweed, D., et al. (1996), The Great Smoky Mountains Study of youth: Functional impairment and severe emotional disturbance. *Archives of General Psychiatry 53*, 1137–1143.

Craney, J. L., & Geller, B. (2003). A prepubertal and early adolescent bipolar disorder-I phenotype: Review of phenomenology and longitudinal course. *Bipolar Disorders, 5*, 243–256.

Davanzo, P., Yue, K., Thomas, M. A., Belin, T., Mintz, J., Venkatraman, T. N., et al. (2003). Proton magnetic resonance spectroscopy of bipolar disorder versus intermittent explosive disorder in children and adolescents. *American Journal of Psychiatry, 160*(8), 1442–1452.

Davidson, J. R. (2007). A history of the concept of atypical depression. *Journal of Clinical Psychiatry, 68*(Suppl 3), 10–15.

DelBello, M. P., Adler, C. M., & Strakowski, S. M. (2006). The neuropsychology of childhood and adolescent bipolar disorder. *CNS Spectrums, 11*, 1–14.

DelBello, M. P., Kowatch, R. A., Adler, C. M., Stanford, K. E., Welge, J. A., Barzman, D. H., et al. (2006). A double-blind randomized pilot study comparing quetiapine and divalproex for adolescent mania. *Journal of the American Academy of Child & Adolescent Psychiatry, 45*(3), 305–313.

DelBello, M. P., Schwiers, M. L., Rosenberg, H. L., & Strakowski, S. M. (2002). A double-blind, randomized, placebo-controlled study of quetiapine as adjunctive treatment for adolescent mania. *Journal of the American Academy of Child & Adolescent Psychiatry, 41*(10), 1216–1223.

Depue, R. Q., & Iacono, W. G. (1989). Neurobehavioral aspects of affective disorders. *Annual Review of Psychology, 40*, 457–492.

Dickstein, D. P., Treland, J. E., Snow, J., McClure, E. B., Mehta, M. S., Towbin, K. E., et al. (2004). Neuropsychological performance in pediatric bipolar disorder. *Biological Psychiatry, 55*, 32–39.

Dienes, K. A., Chang, K. D., Blasey, C. M., Adleman, N. E., & Steiner, H. (2002). Characterization of children of bipolar parents by parent report CBCL. *Journal of Psychiatric Research, 36*, 337–345.

Doyle, A. E., Wilens, T. E., Kwan, A., Seidman, L. J., Faraone, S. V., Fried, R., et al. (2005). Neuropsychological functioning in youth with bipolar disorder. *Biological Psychiatry, 58*, 540–548.

Drevets, W. C. (2000). Neuroimaging studies of mood disorders. *Biological Psychiatry, 48*, 813–829.

Faraone, S. V., Biederman, J., Mennin, D., Wozniak, J., & Spencer, T. (1997). Attention-deficit hyperactivity disorder with bipolar disorder: A familial subtype? *Journal of the American Academy of Child & Adolescent Psychiatry, 36*(10), 1378–1390.

Feeny, N. C., Danielson, C. K., Schwartz, L., Youngstrom, E. A., & Findling, R. L. (2006). Cognitive-behavioral therapy for bipolar disorders in adolescents: A pilot study. *Bipolar Disorders, 8*(5 Pt 1), 508–515.

Findling, R. L., Frazier, T. W., Youngstrom, E. A., McNamara, N. K., Stansbrey, R. J., Gracious, B. L., et al. (2007). Double-blind, placebo-controlled trial of divalproex monotherapy in the treatment of symptomatic youth at high risk for developing bipolar disorder. *Journal of Clinical Psychiatry, 68*(5), 781–788.

Findling, R. L., Gracious, B. L., McNamara, N. K., Youngstrom, E. A., Demeter, C. A., Branicky, L. A., et al. (2001). Rapid, continuous cycling and psychiatric co-morbidity in pediatric bipolar I disorder. *Bipolar Disorders, 3*, 202–210.

Frank, E., Kupfer, D. J., Thase, M. E., Mallinger, A. G., Swartz, H. A., Fagiolini, A. M., et al. (2005). Two-year outcomes for interpersonal and social rhythm therapy in individuals with bipolar I disorder. *Archives of General Psychiatry, 62*(9), 996–1004.

Frazier, J. A., Biederman, J., Tohen, M., Feldman, P. D., Jacobs, T. G., Toma, V., et al. (2001). A prospective open-label treatment trial of olanzapine monotherapy in children and adolescents with bipolar disorder. *Journal of Child and Adolescent Psychopharmacology, 11*(3), 239–250.

Fristad, M. A., Gavazzi, S. M., & Mackinaw-Koons, B. (2003). Family psychoeducation: An adjunctive intervention for children with bipolar disorder. *Biological Psychiatry, 53*(11), 1000–1008.

Gaensbauer, T. J., Harmon, R. J., Cytryn, L., & McKnew, D. H. (1984). Social and affective development in infants with a manic-depressive parent. *American Journal of Psychiatry, 141*, 223–229.

Geller, B., Craney, J. L., Bolhofner, K., DelBello, M. P., Williams, M., & Zimerman, B. (2001). One-year recovery and relapse rates of children with a prepubertal and early adolescent bipolar disorder phenotype. *American Journal of Psychiatry, 158*(2), 303–305.

Geller, B., & Luby, J. (1997). Child and adolescent bipolar disorder: A review of the past 10 years. *Journal of the American Academy of Child & Adolescent Psychiatry, 36*(9), 1168–1176.

Geller, B., Tillman, R., Craney, J. L., & Bolhofner, K. (2004). Four-year prospective outcome and natural history of mania in children with a prepubertal and early adolescent bipolar disorder phenotype. *Archives of General Psychiatry, 61*, 459–467.

Geller, B., Zimerman, B., Williams, M., Bolhofner, K., Craney, J. L., Delbello M. P., et al. (2000). Diagnostic characteristics of 93 cases of a prepubertal and early adolescent bipolar disorder phenotype by gender, puberty and comorbid attention deficit hyperactivity disorder. *Journal of Child and Adolescent Psychopharmacology, 10*, 157–164.

Gold, P. W., & Chrousos, G. P. (1999). The endocrinology of melancholic and atypical depression: Relation to neurocircuitry and somatic consequences. *Procedures of the Association of American Physicians, 111*(1), 22–34.

Goodwin, F. K., & Jamison, K. R. (1990). *Manic-depressive illness*. New York: Oxford University Press.

Hankin, B. L., Abramson, L. Y., Moffitt, T. E., Silva, P. A., McGee, R., & Angell, K. E., et al. (1998). Development of depression from preadolescence to young adulthood: Emerging gender differences in a 10-year longitudinal study. *Journal of Abnormal Psychology, 107*, 128–140.

Hartung, C. M., & Widiger, T. A. (1998). Gender differences in the diagnosis of mental disorders: Conclusions and controversies of the DSM-IV. *Psychological Bulletin, 123*, 260–278.

Howland, R. H., & Thase, M. E. (1999). Affective disorders: Biological aspects. In T. Millon, P. H. Blaney, & R. D. Davis (Eds.), *Oxford textbook of psychopathology* (pp. 166–212). New York: Oxford University Press.

Joyce, B. R. (1984). Age of onset in bipolar affective disorder and misdiagnosis as schizophrenia. *Psychological Medicine, 14*, 145–149.

Judd, L. L., Akiskal, H. S., Schettler, P. J., Endicott, J., Maser, J., Solomon, D. A., et al. (2002). The long-term natural history of the weekly symptomatic status of bipolar I disorder. *Archives of General Psychiatry, 59*(6), 530–537.

Keller, M., Lavori, P., Coryell, W., Andreasen, J., Endicott, J., Clayton, P. J., et al. (1986). Differential outcome of episodes of illness in bipolar patients: Pure manic, mixed/cycling, and pure depressive. *Journal of the American Medical Association, 255*, 3138–3142.

Kelley, A. E. (1987). Dopamine and mental illness: Phenomenological and anatomical considerations. Open peer commentary to: N. R. Swerdlow & G. F. Koob (1987). *Behavioral and Brain Science, 10*, 197–245.

Kelsoe, J. R. (1997). The genetics of bipolar disorder. *Psychiatric Annals, 27*, 557–566.

Kessler, R. C., Avenevoli, S., & Ries Merikangas, K. (2001). Mood disorders in children and adolescents: An epidemiologic perspective. *Biological Psychiatry, 49*, 1002–1014.

Kessler, R. C., Rubinow, D. R., Holmes, C., Abelson, J. M., & Zhao, S. (1997). The epidemiology of DSM-III-R bipolar I disorder in a general population survey. *Psychological Medicine, 27*, 1079–1089.

Kessler, R. C., & Walters, E. E. (1998). Epidemiology of DSM-III-R major depression and minor depression among adolescents and young adults in the National Comorbidity Survey. *Depression and Anxiety, 7*, 3–14.

Kim, E. Y., & Miklowitz, D. J. (2002). Childhood mania, attention deficit hyperactivity disorder and conduct disorder: A critical review of diagnostic dilemmas. *Bipolar Disorders, 4*, 215–225.

Kovacs, M., & Pollock, M. (1995). Bipolar disorder and comorbid conduct disorder in childhood and adolescence. *Journal of the American Academy of Child & Adolescent Psychiatry, 34*, 715–723.

Kowatch, R. A., Fristad, M., Birmaher, B., Wagner, K. D., Findling, R. L., Hellander, M., et al. (2005). Treatment guidelines for children and adolescents with bipolar disorder. *Journal of the American Academy of Child & Adolescent Psychiatry, 44*(3), 213–235.

Kutcher, S., Marton, P., & Korenblum, M. (1989). Relationship between psychiatric illness and conduct disorder in adolescents. *Canadian Journal of Psychiatry, 34*, 526–529.

Lam, D. H., Hayward, P., Watkins, E. R., Wright, K., & Sham, P. (2005). Relapse prevention in patients with bipolar disorder: Cognitive therapy outcome after 2 years. *American Journal of Psychiatry, 162*, 324–329.

Lapalme, M., Hodgins, S., & LaRoche, C. (1997). Children of parents with bipolar disorder: A meta-analysis of risk for mental disorders. *Canadian Journal of Psychiatry, 42*(6), 623–631.

Leibenluft, E., Charney, D. S., Towbin, K. E., Bhangoo, R. K., & Pine, D. S. (2003). Defining clinical phenotypes of juvenile mania. *American Journal of Psychiatry, 160*(3), 430–437.

Leibenluft, E., Cohen, P., Gorrindo, T., Brook, J. S., & Pine, D. S. (2006). Chronic versus episodic irritability in youth: A community-based, longitudinal study of clinical and diagnostic associations. *Journal of Child and Adolescent Psychopharmacology, 16*(4), 456–466.

Lewinsohn, P. M., Klein, D. N., & Seeley, J. R. (1995). Bipolar disorders in a community sample of older adolescents: Prevalence, phenomenology, comorbidity, and course. *Journal of the American Academy of Child & Adolescent Psychiatry, 34*, 454–463.

Lewinsohn, P. M., Klein, D. N., & Seeley, J. (2000). Bipolar disorder during adolescence and young adulthood in a community sample. *Bipolar Disorders, 2*, 281–293.

Lin, P., McInnis, M. G., Potash, J. B., Willour, V., McKinnon, D. F., DePaulo, J. R., et al. (2006). Clinical correlates and familial aggregation of age at onset in bipolar disorder. *American Journal of Psychiatry, 163*, 240–246.

Lish, J. D., Dime-Meenan, S., Whybrow, P. C., Price, R. A., & Hirschfeld, R. M. (1994). The National Depressive and Manic Depressive Association (DMDA) survey of bipolar members. *Journal of Affective Disorders, 31*, 281–294.

Manji, H. K., Quiroz, J. A., Payne, J. L., Singh, J., Lopes, B. P., Viegas, J. S., et al. (2003). The underlying neurobiology of bipolar disorder. *World Psychiatry, 2*(3), 136–146.

McCarthy, J., Arreses, D., McGlashan, A., Rappaport, B., Kraseki, K., Conway, F., et al. (2004). Sustained attention and visual processing speed in children and adolescents with bipolar disorder and other psychiatric disorders. *Psychological Reports, 95*, 39–47.

McClellan, J., McCurry, C., Snell, J., & DuBose, A. (1999). Early-onset psychotic disorders: Course and outcome over a 2-year period. *Journal of the American Academy of Child & Adolescent Psychiatry, 38*, 1380–1388.

McClure, E. B., Treland, J. E., Snow, J., Dickstein, D. P., Towbin, K. E., Charney, D. S., et al. (2005). Memory and learning in pediatric bipolar disorder. *Journal of the American Academy of Child & Adolescent Psychiatry, 44*, 461–469.

Merikangas, K. R., Akiskal, H. S., Angst, J., Greenberg, P. E., Hirschfeld, R. M., Petukhova, M., et al. (2007). Lifetime and 12-month prevalence of bipolar spectrum disorder in the National Comorbidity Survey replication. *Archives of General Psychiatry, 64*(5), 543–552.

Meyer, S. E., Carlson, G. A., Wiggs, E. A., Martinez, P. E., Ronsaville, D. S., Klimes-Dougan, B., et al. (2004). A prospective study of the association among impaired executive functioning, childhood attentional problems, and the development of bipolar disorder. *Developmental Psychopathology, 16*, 461–476.

Miklowitz, D. J., Biuckians, A., & Richards, J. A. (2006). Early-onset bipolar disorder: A family treatment perspective. *Developmental Psychopathology, 18*(4), 1247–1265.

Miklowitz, D. J., George, E. L., Richards, J. A., Simoneau, T. L., & Suddath, R. L. (2003). A randomized study of family-focused psychoeducation and pharmacotherapy in the outpatient management of bipolar disorder. *Archives of General Psychiatry, 60*, 904–912.

Miklowitz, D. J., & Johnson, S. L. (2006). The psychopathology and treatment of bipolar disorder. *Annual Review of Clinical Psychology, 2*, 199–235.

Milberger, S., Biederman, J., Faraone, S. V., Murphy, J., & Tsuang, M. T. (1995). Attention deficit hyperactivity disorder and comorbid disorders: Issues of overlapping symptoms. *American Journal of Psychiatry, 152*, 1793–1800.

Mineka, S., Gunnar, M., & Champoux, M. (1986). Control and early socioemotional development: Infant rhesus monkeys reared in controllable versus uncontrollable environments. *Child Development, 57*, 1241–1256.

Moore, G. J., Bebchuk, J. M., Wilds, I. B., Chen, G., & Manji, H. K. (2000). Lithium-induced increase in human brain grey matter. *Lancet, 356*(9237), 1241–1242.

Murphy, F. C., Sahakina, B. J., Rubinsztein, J. S., Michael, A., Rogers, R. D., Robbins, T. W., et al. (1999). Emotional bias and inhibitory control processes in mania and depression. *Psychological Medicine, 29*, 1307–1321.

National Institute of Mental Health research roundtable on prepubertal bipolar disorder. (2001). *Journal of the American Academy of Child & Adolescent Psychiatry, 40*, 871–878.

Nemeroff, C. B. (1998). The neurobiology of depression. *Scientific American, 278*, 42–49.

Olvera, F. L., Semrud-Clikeman, M., Pliszka, S. R., & O'Donnell, L. (2004). Neuropsychological deficits in adolescents with conduct disorder and comorbid bipolar disorder: A pilot study. *Bipolar Disorders, 6*, 1–11.

Patel, N. C., DelBello, M. P., & Strakowski, S. M. (2006). Ethnic differences in symptom presentation of youths with bipolar disorder. *Bipolar Disorders, 8*, 95–99.

Pavuluri, M. N., Birmaher, B., & Naylor, M. W. (2005). Pediatric bipolar disorder: A review of the past 10 years. *Journal of the American Academy of Child & Adolescent Psychiatry, 44*(9), 846–871.

Pavuluri, M. N., Schenkel, L. S., Aryal, S., Harral, E., Hill, S. K., Herbener, E. S., et al. (2006). Neurocognitive function in unmedicated manic and medicated euthymic pediatric bipolar patients. *American Journal of Psychiatry, 163*, 286–293.

Pellegrini, D., Kosisky, S., Nackman, D., Cytryn, L., McKnew, D. H., Gershon, E., et al. (1986). Personal and social resources in children of patients with bipolar affective disorder and children of normal control subjects. *American Journal of Psychiatry, 143*, 856–861.

Pennington, B. F. (2002). *The development of psychopathology: Nature and nurture* (pp. 153–159). New York: Guilford Press.

Perlis, R. H., Miyahara, S., Marangell, L. B., Wisniewski, S. R., Ostacher, M., DelBello, M. P., et al. (2004). Long-term implications of early onset in bipolar disorder: Data from the first 1000 participants in the systematic treatment enhancement program for bipolar disorder (STEP-BD). *Biological Psychiatry, 55*, 875–881.

Post, R. M. (1992). Transduction of psychosocial stress into the neurobiology of recurrent affective disorder. *American Journal of Psychiatry 149*(8), 999–1010.

Prange, A., Wilson, I., Lynn, C., Alltop, L., & Stikeleather, R. (1974). L-tryptophan in mania: Contribution to a permissive hypothesis of affective disorders. *Archives of General Psychiatry, 30*, 56–62.

Quinn, C. A., & Fristad, M. A. (2004). Defining and identifying early onset bipolar spectrum disorder. *Current Psychiatry Reports, 6,* 101–107.
Quintin, P., Benkelfat, C., Launay, J. M., Arnulf, I., Pointereau-Bellenger, A., Barbault, S., et al. (2001). Clinical and neurochemical effect of acute tryptophan depletion in unaffected relatives of patients with bipolar affective disorder. *Biological Psychiatry, 50*(3), 184–190.
Rice, J., Reich, T., Andreasen, N. C., Endicott, J., Van Eerdewegh, M., Fishman, R., et al. (1987). The familial transmission of bipolar illness. *Archives of General Psychiatry, 44,* 441–447.
Rich, B. A., Schmajuk, M., Perez-Edgar, K. E., Fox, N. A., Pine, D. S., & Leibenluft, E. (2007). Different psychophysiological and behavioral responses elicited by frustration in pediatric bipolar disorder and severe mood dysregulation. *American Journal of Psychiatry, 164*(2), 309–317.
Sapolsky, R. M. (1996). *Why zebras don't get ulcers: A guide to stress, stress related diseases and coping.* New York: Freeman.
Sassi, R. B., Nicoletti, M., Brambilla, P., Mallinnger, A. G., Frank, E., Kupfer, D. J., et al. (2002). Increased gray matter volume in lithium-treated bipolar disorder patients. *Neuroscience Letters, 329*(2), 243–245.
Satcher, D. (1999). *Mental health: A report of the surgeon general.* Retrieved September 26, 2007 from http:www.surgeongeneral.gov/library/mental health/home.html.
Schildkraut, J. (1965). The catecholamine hypothesis of affective disorders: A review of supporting evidence. *American Journal of Psychiatry, 122,* 509–522.
Schneck, C. D., Miklowitz, D. J., Calabrese, J. R., Allen, M. H., Thomas, M. R., Wisniewski, S. R., et al. (2004). Phenomenology of rapid cycling bipolar disorder: Data from the first 500 participants in the Systematic Treatment Enhancement Program for Bipolar Disorder. *American Journal of Psychiatry, 161,* 1902–1908.
Singh, M. K., DelBello, M. P., Kowatch, R. A., & Strakowski, S. M. (2006). Co-occurrence of bipolar and attention-deficit hyperactivity disorders in children. *Bipolar Disorders, 8,* 710–720.
Smoller, J. W., & Finn, C. T. (2003). Family, twin, and adoption studies of bipolar disorder. *American Journal of Medical Genetics, Part C: Seminars in Medical Genetics, 123*(1), 48–58.
Sobczak, S., Riedel, W. J., Booij, I., Aan Het Rot, M., Deutz, N. E., & Honig, A. (2002). Cognition following acute tryptophan depletion: Difference between first-degree relatives of bipolar disorder patients and matched healthy control volunteers. *Psychological Medicine, 32*(3), 503–515.
Stone, E. A. (1975). Stress and catecholamines. In: A. J. Fredhoff (Ed.), *Catecholamines and behavior* (pp. 31–72). New York: Plenum Press.
Strakowski, S. M., DelBello, M. P., & Adler, C. M. (2005). The functional neuroanatomy of bipolar disorder: A review of neuroimaging findings. *Molecular Psychiatry, 10,* 106–116.
Strober, M., Schmidt-Lackner, S., Freeman, R., Bower, S., Lampert, C., & DeAntonio, M. (1995). Recovery and relapse in adolescents with bipolar affective illness: A five-year naturalistic, prospective follow-up. *Journal of the American Academy of Child & Adolescent Psychiatry, 34,* 724–731.

Swerdlow, N. R., & Koob, G. F. (1987). Dopamine, schizophrenia, mania, and depression: Toward a unified hypothesis of cortico-strito-pallido-thalamic function. *Behavioral and Brain Science, 10*, 197–245.

Thase, M. E. (2007). Recognition and diagnosis of atypical depression. *Journal of Clinical Psychiatry, 68*(Suppl 8), 11–16.

Tillman, R., & Geller, B. (2006). Controlled study of switching from attention-deficit/hyperactivity disorder to a prepubertal and early adolescent bipolar I disorder phenotype during 6-year prospective follow-up: Rate, risk, and predictors. *Development and Psychopathology, 18*, 1037–1053.

Tremblay, L. K., Naranjo, C. A., Graham, S. J., Herrmann, N., Mayberg, H. S., Hevenor, S., et al. (2005). Functional neuroanatomical substrates of altered reward processing in major depressive disorder revealed by a dopaminergic probe. *Archives of General Psychiatry, 62*, 1228–1236.

Weissman, M. M., Markowitz, J. C., & Klerman, G. L. (2000). *Comprehensive guide to interpersonal psychotherapy.* New York: Basic Books.

West, A. E., Henry, D. B., & Pavuluri, M. N. (2007). Maintenance model of integrated psychosocial treatment in pediatric bipolar disorder: A pilot feasibility study. *Journal of the American Academy of Child & Adolescent Psychiatry, 46*(2), 205–212.

Wichstrom, L. (1999). The emergence of gender difference in depressed mood during adolescence: The role of intensified gender socialization. *Developmental Psychology, 35*, 232–245.

Wilens, T. E., Biederman, J., Kwon, A., Ditterline, J., Forkner, P., Moore, H., et al. (2004). Risk of substance use disorders in adolescents with bipolar disorder. *Journal of the American Academy of Child & Adolescent Psychiatry, 43*, 1380–1386.

Youngstrom, E. A., Findling, R. L., & Calabrese, J. R. (2004). Effects of adolescent manic symptoms on agreement between youth, parent, and teacher ratings of behavior problems. *Journal of Affective Disorders, 82*(Suppl 1), S5–S16.

Zahn-Waxler, C., Cummings, E. M., McKnew, D. H., & Radke-Yarrow, M. (1984). Altruism, aggression, and social interactions in young children with a manic-depressive parent. *Child Development, 55*, 112–122.

Chapter Eight

Suicide and Nonsuicidal Self-Injurious Behaviors Among Youth: Risk and Protective Factors[1]

COLLEEN M. JACOBSON AND MADELYN GOULD

CONTENTS

Suicidal and nonsuicidal self-injurious behaviors among youth are multifaceted events, emerging from biological, cultural, sociological, psychological, and interpersonal factors. An understanding of how these factors, including depression, contribute to self-injurious behaviors among youth is critically needed given the magnitude of these behaviors. Seventeen hundred 15- to 19-year-olds, killed themselves in 2004, more than died from cancer, heart disease, birth defects, chronic respiratory disease, HIV, stroke, and diabetes combined (CDC, 2005). An additional 1.5 million high school students attempted suicide (Eaton et al., 2006), and up to 2.1 million high school students engaged in nonsuicidal self-injury (NSSI; Muehlenkamp & Gutierrez, 2007) in the past year. The goal of this chapter is to provide a review of the risk and protective factors for youth suicide and NSSI. In addition, treatment implications of the research findings discussed will be highlighted.

While reading this review, it is important to remain cognizant of the many challenges inherent in conducting sound research on self-injurious behaviors among youth. First, the classification of self-injurious behaviors is not a straightforward task. The field of suicidology has been plagued by inconsistent terminology across and even within research groups for many years (Silverman, 2006). The confusion in the field of suicidology regarding classification of self-injurious behaviors is quite likely linked to the ambivalent state commonly present among a person engaging in self-injury (Wagner, Wong, & Jobes, 2002). While a purely suicidal or nonsuicidal motive is occasionally present, a mixed motive is more common. Therefore, researchers are perpetually struggling to accurately classify self-injurious behaviors within their studies. (The classification struggle is discussed further in the next section of the chapter.) In addition, the manner in which data is collected (self-report or clinician interview) can affect the accuracy with which a self-injurious act is classified. Self-report techniques may encourage disclosure, but also leave the participant with the burden of appropriately categorizing his or her own behavior. Conversely, in-person interviews may yield more clinically accurate classification, but result in the reporting of fewer behaviors.

A substantial body of empirical research, albeit some of it with methodologic limitations, has addressed the rates, risk factors, and correlates of completed suicide, suicidal ideation and behaviors, and NSSI among adolescents, and will be summarized below. We performed searches using Psychinfo and Medline in addition to perusing the reference lists of relevant papers to gather the information for this chapter. Manuscripts that were in press or in preparation were not included in this review.

The information presented is separated into several sections. First, we will briefly summarize the definitions of self-injurious behaviors used throughout the research literature to be reviewed. Second, we will review the rates and patterns of completed suicide, followed by attempted suicide, and suicidal ideation. Third, we will review the rates of patterns of NSSI. Finally, we will summarize the research addressing the risk factors and correlates of suicidal and nonsuicidal behaviors. These sections are organized by risk factor/correlate with the data on both suicidal and nonsuicidal behaviors reviewed within each section.

DEFINITIONS OF SUICIDAL AND NONSUICIDAL SELF-INJURIOUS BEHAVIORS IN ADOLESCENTS

An explanation of the differential definitions of suicidal and nonsuicidal self-injurious behaviors is necessary before presenting their distinct rates, patterns, and risks. The adoption of reliable and clinically valid definitions for self-injurious behaviors is crucial in order to collect accurate rates of the behaviors, to conduct empirically sound research, and to provide appropriate clinical care (De Leo, Burgis, Bertolote, Kerkhof, & Bille-Brahe, 2006).

Fatal Suicidal Behavior

Most definitions of completed suicide mandate that the act was fatal, intentional, there was a desire to die, and it was carried out by the deceased himself or herself (Silverman, 2006; Silverman, Berman, Sanddal, O'Carroll, & Joiner, 2007). For example, suicide was defined by the WHO Working Group in 1986, as "an act with a fatal outcome which the deceased, knowing or expecting a fatal outcome, had initiated and carried out with the purpose of provoking the changes he desired" (World Health Organization, 1986). Note that this definition assumes that the person intended to die as a result of the act. The 1986 definition was updated in 1998 to read "The act of killing oneself deliberately, initiated and performed by the person concerned in the full knowledge or expectation of its fatal outcome," thus assuming full intention of death. More recently, De Leo and colleagues (2006) suggested that the definition of suicide be altered slightly to reflect the fact that many people who commit suicide may have been ambivalent about wanting to die. Their suggested definition reads, "Suicide is an act with a fatal outcome, which the deceased, knowing or expecting a *potentially* fatal outcome, has initiated and carried out with the purpose of bringing about wanted changes" (p. 2006). Because it is impossible to know what a person truly intended by a suicidal act once she/he is deceased, De Leo and colleagues proposed definition is likely the most accurate option of the three. Note that numerous definitions of suicide have been proposed in the literature; see De Leo et al. (2006) and Silverman (2006) for an overview of commonly cited definitions.

Nonfatal Self-Injurious Behavior

Unfortunately, many past research studies have failed to examine underlying motivations of nonfatal self-injurious behaviors, and thus did not separate NSSI from self-injury accompanied by suicidal intent. As such, there have been many terms used for self-injurious behavior not resulting in death: attempted suicide, parasuicide, deliberate self-harm, nonfatal suicidal behavior (Hjelmeland et al., 2002). Recent research studies have increasingly explored the motives underlying engagement in nonfatal self-injurious acts (e.g., Boergers, Spirito, & Donaldson, 1998; Hawton, Cole, O'Grady, & Osborn, 1982). For example, studies have been conducted in which a participant is given the choice of several different intentions, ranging from temporary escape from an impossible situation to wanting to die (Boergers et al., 1998; Hawton et al., 1982; Hjelmeland et al., 2002). This research has highlighted the wide range of intentions that drive self-injurious behaviors. Factor analyses indicate that three distinct dimensions of the intentions exist: wanting to die; temporary escape; and care seeking (Hjelmeland et al., 2002). Further, in one study, the factor associated with wanting to die was positively correlated with scores on a suicide intention scale, while the factors associated with care seeking and temporary escape were negatively correlated with suicidal intent (Hjelmeland et al., 2002). Thus, this research supports the validity of recent research that separates acts of self-harm based upon the absence or presence of accompanied suicidal intent, as has been the tradition in classifying completed suicide (Muehlenkamp, 2005; Nock & Kessler, 2006; Suyemoto, 1998).

We agree with the importance of the distinction between suicidal behaviors and NSSI, for both clinical and research-related reasons. In accordance, when we refer to a suicide attempt, we are indicating a nonfatal act that is carried out with at least some intent to die as a result of the act. Note that in this definition, a suicide attempt needs to be accompanied by only at least some intent to die. This "nonzero rule" was proposed by O'Carroll and colleagues (1996) and has since been adopted by many researchers in the field (e.g., Muehlenkamp & Gutierrez, 2007; Nock & Kessler, 2006; Posner, Oquendo, Stanley, Davies, & Gould, 2007). A self-injurious act that is not accompanied by any amount of intent to die will be referred to as NSSI and is not considered a suicide attempt. Note that all articles included in the NSSI sections of this chapter clarified that the behaviors in question were nonsuicidal in nature.

A common definition of NSSI is the purposeful destruction of one's own body tissue without the conscious intent to die (Favazza, 1998). Common methods of NSSI include cutting, burning, and hitting oneself (Muehlenkamp & Gutierrez, 2004, 2007; Ross & Heath, 2002; Zoroglu et al., 2003). Other commonly reported methods include pinching oneself, picking at a wound, and scratching oneself. Behaviors such as ingesting a toxic substance and engaging in risk-taking behaviors, including unsafe sex and risky driving, are not typically considered NSSI. Other terms used to refer to nonsuicidal self-injurious behaviors include self-mutilation and deliberate self-harm. However, it should be noted that self-mutilation and deliberate self-harm are not always distinguished from acts of self-injury that *are* accompanied by a wish to die. We prefer the term nonsuicidal self-injury, as the term itself clarifies that the behavior is nonsuicidal in nature. Note that NSSI can be engaged in for any number of reasons other than to kill oneself. As Walsh (2005) articulates, "the intent of the self-injuring person is to not to terminate consciousness (as in suicide) but to modify it" (p. 7). Common reasons for engaging in NSSI endorsed by adolescents include to make oneself feel better, to reduce negative feelings such as anxiety and depression, to increase feelings when none exist, to punish oneself, and to bring attention to oneself (Kumar, Pepe, & Steer, 2004; Nixon, Cloutier, & Aggarwai, 2002; Nock & Prinstein, 2004; Ross & Heath, 2003).

One other term that will be referred to in this chapter is suicidal ideation. Suicidal ideation refers to having thoughts about one's own death or of killing oneself that may or may not involve a plan as to how one may execute the suicidal act. Suicidal ideation includes several components, such as frequency, intensity, and duration of thoughts. Whether these thoughts lead to an attempt is influenced by a number of factors, including the individual's fearlessness about carrying out the behavior and his/her perceived deterrents (Beck, Kovacs, & Weissman, 1979). Empirical research indicates that having a desire for death and frequent ideation is correlated with elevated levels of depression and hopelessness, while a developed suicide plan in combination with perceived competence and intense ideation is linked to having made a suicide attempt (as opposed to only engaging in ideation) (Joiner, Rudd, & Rajab, 1997). The current chapter will include research addressing predictors of global suicidal ideation, as very little research has addressed the incidence and predictors of specific facets of suicidal ideation among youth. Readers interested in learning more about the components of suicidal ideation are directed to Beck and colleagues (1979), Joiner and colleagues (1997), and Steer, Rissmiller, Ranieri, and Beck (1993).

RATES AND PATTERNS OF COMPLETED SUICIDE

Suicide is the third leading cause of death among adolescents and young adults (15- to 24-year-olds) in the United States, behind only accidents and homicide. A total of 32,439 Americans died by suicide in 2004; 4,316 were those between the ages of 15 and 24 (CDC, 2005). The rate of death by suicide among 15- to 19-year-olds was 8.2 per 100,000; while it was 12.5 in 100,000 among 20- to 24-year-olds. Suicide among young children (10- to 14-year-olds) is much less common with a rate of 1.3 per 100,000 in 2004 (CDC, 2005). It is hypothesized by Shaffer and colleagues (1996) that the marked increase in the suicide rate at age 14 is linked to the onset of depression and exposure to substance use. The most commonly used method of suicide is firearms, accounting for 49% of suicides by the 15- to 24-year-old age group in 2004.

The suicide rate has not remained steady over time. Overall, the youth suicide rate has more than doubled since the 1950s, with the rate for white males tripling between 1964 and 1988 with a peak of 20 per 100,000 in 1988 (Gould, Greenberg, Velting, & Shaffer, 2003). However, the rate has fallen steadily over the past several years, declining by 28.5% since 1994 (CDC, 2005). The reasons for the initial increase are speculated to be linked to the increase in substance use among teenagers during those years, and increased accessibility to firearms (Gould et al., 2003). However, neither of these theories have direct empirical evidence. The marked decrease in youth suicide rates since the mid-1990s coincided with an increase in the use of antidepressants to treat adolescent depression (Olfson, Marcus, Weissman, & Jensen, 2002). A tandem increase in use of mental health services was not seen during that time, suggesting that the medications, specifically the SSRIs, are uniquely linked to the decrease in suicide (Gould et al., 2003).

Unfortunately, the youth suicide rate in 2004 was higher than the preceding year for the first time in 10 years. Specifically, the rate rose by 8.2% for males between 15 and 19 years of age and by nearly 25% for females between 15 and 19 years of age (CDC, 2005). It has been conjectured that this rise in the suicide rate is linked to the mandated "Black Box" warning on the use of antidepressants among youth issued by the FDA in 2004. Specifically, the Black Box warning was issued due to concern that antidepressant medication may increase suicidal ideation and suicidal behaviors among depressed youth. Recent research has indicated a decrease in the prescription rates of antidepressants for depressed youth following the FDA warning (Libby et al., 2007; Nemeroff et al., 2007). Youth suicide experts are concerned that the Black Box warning and subsequent failure to use antidepressants to treat depressed, suicidal adolescents, may to lead further increases in the suicide rate among adolescents in the coming years (Posner et al., 2007).

Completed suicide is much more common among adolescent males than females. In 2004, the rate among females aged 15 to 19 years was 3.5 per 100,000; for males it was 12.6 per 100,000. Similarly, the rate for females aged 20 to 24 was 3.6 per 100,000, and for males it was 20.8 per 100,000. Suicide rates also vary according to ethnicity. The highest rate of suicide in 2002 was among Native American youth (14.3/100,000), followed by white youth (8.2 in 100,000), Hispanic youth (5.7 in 100,000), African-American (4.0 in 100,000), and Asian Americans (3.9 in 100,000) (Anderson & Smith, 2005). The elevated rates of suicide among Native Americans may be linked to low social integration (resulting in limited access to mental health care), access to firearms, and alcohol and drug use (Borowsky, Resnick, Ireland, & Blum, 1999; Middlebrook, LeMaster, Beals, Novins, & Manson, 2001). The historic gap between the rates of suicide among white youth and African-American youth has been associated with the fact that African-Americans typically report greater levels of religiosity than white individuals, and African-Americans may tend to engage in "outwardly" rather than "inwardly" directed aggression (Gibbs, 1997; Shaffer, Gould, & Hicks, 1994). However, the gap between European and African-American youth suicide rates has decreased due to a large increase in the rate of suicide among African-American male youth from 1988 to 1994 (Gould et al., 2003). There are likely multiple reasons for the brief increase in suicide rates among African-American teens, with one potential reason being the difficulty this group has with accessing adequate psychiatric care (Gould et al., 2003).

RATES AND PATTERNS OF SUICIDAL IDEATION AND ATTEMPTED SUICIDE

Although the overall rate of completed suicide is relatively low, the rates of attempted suicide among youth are quite staggering. The Youth Risk Behavior Survey (YRBS) provides yearly prevalence rates for suicide attempts and suicidal ideation among a nationally representative group of high school students. The most recent statistics published from the YRBS (data collection from 10/2004 to 1/2006; Eaton et al., 2006) indicate that 16.9% of high school students seriously considered attempting suicide, 13.0% of students had made a suicide plan, and 8.4% had actually made a suicide attempt within the 12 months preceding the survey. Similar to rates of completed suicide, suicide attempts are quite rare among prepubertal children, and the rates increase throughout adolescence (Gould et al., 2003). For attempted suicide, the rates peak between 16 and 18 years of age and then markedly decline, especially among females (Lewinsohn, Rohde, Seeley, & Baldwin, 2001).

Unlike completed suicide, female adolescents are consistently more likely than male adolescents to consider or attempt suicide. In 2005, females were significantly more likely than males to have considered suicide (21.8% vs. 12.0%), made a suicide plan (16.2% vs. 9.9%), and attempted suicide (10.8% vs. 6.0%; Eaton et al., 2006). Females exceed males in rates of suicidal ideation, suicide plans, and attempted suicide across white, African-American, and Hispanic ethnicities. Hispanic females reported the highest rates of each type of behavior (ideation 24.2%, plan 18.5%, and attempt 14.9%), followed by white females (ideation 21.5%, plan 15.4%, and attempt 9.3%), and African-American females (ideation 17.1%, plan 13.5%, and attempt 9.8%); with the exception that African-American females reported an essentially equivalent rate of attempts as white females. Among the males, white males reported the highest level of ideation (12.4%), while Hispanic males reported the highest level of plans (10.7%) and attempts (7.8%). Higher attempt rates in females may be linked to the fact that females typically attempt suicide by overdose, whereas males are more likely to use firearms, the obviously more lethal choice.

Reasons for the elevated rates of suicidal ideation and attempts among Hispanic females remain unknown. It has been hypothesized that the combination of the cultural tradition of familism (centrality of the family in an individual's life) and authoritarian parenting style, paired with an emotionally vulnerable teenager who falls into conflict with her caregiver (mainly mother) over issues of individuality (often related to romantic relationships), may leave Hispanic females at increased risk for suicide (Zayas, Fortuna, Lester, & Cabassa, 2005). Empirical research has documented that a typical Hispanic female who attempts suicide is 15 to 16 years of age, highly acculturated to American values, and has immigrant parents who are low in acculturation (Ng, 1996; Razin et al., 1991). Zayas and colleagues (2005) hypothesized that a gap in acculturation between parent and adolescent paired with an inflexible parenting style may be highly problematic. In summary, the elevated rate of suicide attempts among Hispanic females in the United States is alarming, and further research is needed to find the causes of and the cure for this problem.

The rate of suicidal ideation across gender and ethnicity has dropped from 29.0% in 1991 to 21.8% in 2005, with a low of 16.9% in 2003. The suicide attempt rate across gender and ethnicity during this same period has remained relatively stable, ranging from a low of 7.3% in 1991 to a high of 8.7% in 1995. The rate of medically serious suicide attempts (i.e., an attempt that required medical attention) went from a low of 1.7% in 1991, to a high of 2.9% in 2003, falling to 2.3% in 2005 (CDC, 2007).

All data reported above comes from the YRBS, an anonymous, self-report survey. Attempt and ideation rates are typically lower when gathered via different means, such as one-on-one in-person interviews. For example, lifetime attempt rates from the Great Smoky Mountain Study (GSMS), a large-scale epidemiological study that involves in-person interviews conducted in western North Carolina, was 3.9% (4.6% for girls and 3.3% for boys; Foley, Goldston, Costello, & Angold, 2006). The 3-month prevalence rate of suicidal ideation was 0.69%, 0.3% for suicide plans, and 0.25% for attempts. Similar to the YBRS, girls were significantly more likely to endorse suicidal ideation, plans, and attempts. There were no differences in ideation, plans, or attempts based on ethnicity. The difference in rates of suicidality between the YRBS and the GSMS is unclear, and highlights the importance of understanding the methodology used in a study when interpreting the results. It is possible that the rates reported on the YRBS are inflated because there is no corroboration process included in the self-report survey. However, it is also possible that the rates reported in the YRBS are more accurate compared to the rates of suicidal behaviors reported in studies that utilize in-person interviews, as teens may be hesitant to report suicidal behaviors in person.

RATES AND PATTERNS OF NSSI

Unlike the data on suicide-related behaviors, data regarding the prevalence and patterns of NSSI are limited. No large scale, nationally representative, epidemiological study assessing the prevalence of NSSI in adolescents has been conducted. However, we can combine results from various smaller-scale, school-based studies to estimate prevalence rates. Among these studies, lifetime prevalence of NSSI among high school students ranges from 13.0 to 23.2% (Muehlenkamp & Gutierrez, 2004, 2007; Ross & Heath, 2002; Zoroglu et al., 2003), with the 12-month prevalence ranging from 2.5 to 12.5% (Garrison et al., 1993; Muehlenkamp & Gutierrez, 2007). The large difference in the 12-month prevalence rate reported in the Garrison et al. study and the Muehlenkamp and Gutierrez study is likely due to the fact that the participants in the latter study were older than those in the former study. In addition, the difference may be due to cohort effects, as the studies were conducted more than 10 years apart. Due to the limited amount of epidemiological research using nonreferred samples, little is known about the patterns of NSSI over time, although clinical lore suggests that it is increasing. Indirect evidence of increasing rates of NSSI is also evident in a study which found that the rates of self-cutting (for unknown intent) increased over threefold from 1990 to 2000 among adolescents in the United States presenting to the hospital following self-injury (Olfson, Gameroff, Marcus, Greenberg, & Shaffer, 2005).

The gender distribution of NSSI remains unclear. Although many assume the rates of NSSI are higher among females, only two (Muehlenkamp & Gutierrez, 2007; Ross & Health, 2002) of the five community-based studies of NSSI (Garrison et al., 1993; Muehlenkamp & Gutierrez, 2004; Zoroglu et al., 2003) identified significantly higher rates of NSSI among girls than boys. The common belief that girls engage in NSSI more frequently is likely linked to the fact that girls are more likely to seek treatment, and therefore be identified, and that NSSI has typically been associated with borderline personality disorder (BPD), a disorder more common in women than men (APA, 2000).

Data regarding the ethnic distribution of NSSI among youth is also unclear. Of the five community-based studies, two (Muehlenkamp and Gutierrez, 2004, 2007) identified significantly higher rates of NSSI among white youth than those of other ethnicities. None of the other three studies (Garrison et al., 1993; Ross & Heath, 2002; Zoroglu et al., 2003) reported on the significance of the ethnic breakdown of NSSI.

The age of onset of NSSI is between 12 and 14 years (Kumar et al., 2004, Muehlenkamp & Guterrez, 2004, 2007; Nixon et al., 2002; Nock & Prinstein, 2004; Ross & Heath, 2002). Because longitudinal research among adolescents is yet to exist, little is known about the course of NSSI, although it is common belief that NSSI peaks in midadolescence and decreases into adulthood. Further research is needed to determine the risk factors for engaging in single incident NSSI versus chronic NSSI.

RISK FACTORS AND CORRELATES OF SUICIDAL BEHAVIOR AND NSSI

Personal Characteristics

Psychopathology

A psychiatric disorder is a contributing factor to each type of self-injurious behavior. Psychological autopsy studies, in which a suicide victim's family and peers are interviewed extensively, indicate that up to 90% of adolescent suicide victims have at least one major psychiatric disorder (Beautrais, 2001; Brent, Baugher, Bridge, Chen, & Chiappetta, 1999; Moskos, Loson, Halbern, Keller, & Gray, 2005; Shaffer et al., 1996). Depressive disorders are the most commonly associated with suicide, increasing the odds of suicide by 11 to 27 times (Brent et al., 1988; Groholt, Ekeberg, Wichstrom, & Haldorsen, 1998; Shaffer et al., 1996; Shafii, Steltz-Lenarsky, Derrick, Beckner, & Whittinghill, 1988). Female youth who commit suicide are more likely than male youth to have an affective disorder (Brent et al., 1988; Shaffer et al., 1996).

Substance abuse is also elevated among youth suicide victims, especially older male victims (Marttunen, Aro, Henriksson, & Lohnqvist, 1991; Moskos et al., 2005; Shaffer et al., 1996), with the combination of depression and substance use being common as well (Brent et al., 1993; Shaffer et al., 1996). In addition, conduct disorder is present in approximately one-third of male youth suicide victims (Brent et al., 1993; Shaffer et al., 1996). Finally, rates of schizophrenia and bipolar disorder have not consistently been found to be elevated in youth suicides. Several studies have reported increased rates of both (up to 10%; Brent et al., 1988; Brent, 1993; Moskos et al., 2005), while other studies have not identified elevated rates (Apter et al., 1993; Brent et al., 1993; Marttunen et al., 1991; Shaffer et al., 1994, 1996). Consistent with completed suicide, research consistently finds an association between depressive disorders and youth suicide attempters (e.g., Beautrais, Joyce, & Mulder, 1996; Foley et al., 2006; Gould et al., 1998). A recent publication from the GSMS indicated that the risk of suicide attempt was greatest among adolescents with comorbid depression and anxiety, specifically generalized anxiety disorder (GAD). The odds ratio of attempting suicide among adolescents with depression and GAD compared to those without these disorders was 468.5 (Foley et al., 2006). In addition, depression plus a disruptive disorder also resulted in an extremely elevated risk for suicide attempts. This study failed to find a univariate relationship between substance use disorder and suicidality; however, the combination of depression and substance use was associated with increased risk. Additionally, anxiety was not independently associated with increased risk of suicide attempt in the GSMS study (Foley et al., 2006), however, panic attacks were independently associated with suicidal behaviors in other investigations (Gould, Fisher, Parides, Flory, & Shaffer, 1996; Pilowsky, Wu, & Anthony, 1999). Finally, recent research highlights the importance of overall symptom severity, rather than specific diagnoses (with the exception of depression plus GAD), in predicting suicidal behaviors in adolescents (Foley et al., 2006).

Research regarding NSSI in adolescents is relatively nascent; only one community-based study (i.e., Garrison et al., 1993) has examined the association between NSSI and psychiatric disorders. This study indicated that those with major depressive disorder were 8.3 times more likely to engage in NSSI, those with a specific phobia were 8.5 times more likely to engage in NSSI, and those with obsessive compulsive disorder (OCD) were 5.3 times more likely to engage in NSSI than those who did not have the respective diagnoses. All other research addressing the psychiatric profiles of adolescents who self-injure has been conducted among clinical settings, thus limiting the validity of the findings. Despite their shortcomings, these studies also identified elevated rates of depression, ranging from 41.6% to 58%, among adolescent self-injurers (Kumar et al., 2004; Nock, Joiner, Gordon, Lloyd-Richardson, & Prinstein, 2006). Elevated rates of externalizing disorders and substance use disorders (each around 60%) were also identified (Nock et al., 2006). Finally, preliminary research suggests that symptoms of BPD are common among youth engaging in NSSI (Nock et al., 2006).

Prior Attempts

A history of a prior suicide attempt is a strong risk factor for completing suicide as well as reattempting suicide. With regard to completed suicide, a history of a previous attempt increases the odds of suicide by 30 times among boys and 3 times among girls (Shaffer et al., 1996). Up to one-third of adolescent suicide victims have attempted suicide in the past (Groholt, Ekeberg, Wichstrom, & Haldorsen, 1997). Similarly, a prior suicide attempt leaves adolescents at an increased risk for attempting suicide in the future (Lewinsohn, Rhode, & Seeley, 1994; McKeown et al., 1998; Reinherz et al., 1995; Wichstrom, 2000).

As indicated above, those who have attempted suicide are at an increased risk of engaging in NSSI and vice versa; however, the temporal link between these two behaviors, i.e., which comes first, is yet unknown.

Cognitive and Personality Factors

Several cognitive and personality factors have received substantial attention regarding their relation to suicidality and NSSI among adolescents. Hopelessness has been linked to greater levels of suicidality in adolescents (Howard-Pitney, LaFromboise, Basil, September, & Johnson, 1992; Marcenko, Fishman, & Friedman, 1999; Overholser, Adams, Lehnert, & Brinkman, 1995; Rubenstein, Heeren, Housman, Rubin, & Stechler, 1989; Russell & Joyner, 2001; Shaffer et al., 1996). However, when other covariates, such as depression, are controlled for, the relationship between hopelessness and suicidality is greatly reduced (Cole, 1989; Howard-Pitney et al., 1992; Lewinsohn et al., 1994; Reifman & Windle, 1995; Rotheram-Borus & Trautman, 1988). At this time, no published research has investigated the relationship between hopelessness and NSSI among adolescents.

Poor interpersonal problem-solving ability is another cognitive factor that seems to be associated with suicidality (Asarnow, Carlson, & Guthrie, 1987; Rotheram-Borus, Trautman, Dopkins, & Shrout, 1990), even after controlling for factors such as depression (Rotheram-Borus et al., 1990). The fact that problem-solving abilities are linked to suicidality has great treatment implications. Indeed, psychosocial interventions for suicidal adults have received some empirical support (Evans et al., 1999; Linehan et al., 2006; Townsend et al., 2001; Tryer et al., 2003). Unfortunately, no published research addresses the relationship between basic problem-solving capacities and NSSI among adolescents, although this is likely an area that is currently of interest to investigators.

Impulsivity and aggression have also been linked to greater risk of suicidal behaviors and NSSI among adolescents (Apter, Plutchik, & van Praag, 1993; McKeown et al., 1998; Sourander, Helstela, Haavisto, & Bergroth, 2001). In addition, many adolescents describe their acts of NSSI as impulsive (Nock & Prinstein, 2005). It is possible that increasing one's general problem-solving ability, including ability to weigh options before acting, may act to decrease impulsivity and, therefore, impulsive acts.

A concept that has received recent attention regarding both suicidality and engagement in NSSI is emotional restrictedness, or alexithymia. Among clinical samples of adolescents, higher levels of alexithymia have been identified among people who engage in NSSI compared to those who do not (Kisiel & Lyons, 1999). Conversely, a recent study by Nock and colleagues (2008) found higher levels of emotional reactivity to be associated with engagement in NSSI. These two seemingly contradictory findings can be reconciled: people who engage in NSSI may experience emotions more intensely, but in light of their inability to *express* their emotions, they may be vulnerable to engaging in self-injury to relieve their unexpressed affect. Relatedly, one recent study found a greater tendency to suppress unwanted thoughts among people who engage in NSSI, with thought suppression acting as a mediator between emotional reactivity and NSSI (Najmi, Wegner, & Nock, 2007).

Finally, greater levels of hostility (Ross & Health, 2003; Zoroglu et al., 2003) and dissociation (Kiesel & Lyons, 1999) have been linked to NSSI among adolescents.

Sexual Orientation

Although the majority of youth who endorse same-sex sexual orientation do not report suicidality (Russell & Joyner, 2001), research indicates that rates of suicide attempts are two to six times greater among homosexual and bisexual teens than their heterosexual peers (Blake et al., 2001; Faulkner & Cranston, 1998; Garofalo et al., 1998; Remafedi, French, Story, Resnick, & Blum, 1998; Russell & Joyner, 2001). Further, in one large, epidemiological study, the association between sexuality and suicidality remained (although weakened) after accounting for depression, alcohol abuse, family history of attempts, and victimization (Russell & Joyner, 2001). These findings highlight the importance of addressing the issue of sexuality and comfort with one's own sexual preference among our depressed adolescent patients. To our knowledge, researchers are yet to address any link between NSSI and sexuality in adolescents.

Biological Factors

Although research is yet to identify specific genes or biological anomalies that are specifically linked to suicidal or nonsuicidal behavior in adolescents, research has yielded insight into abnormalities among impulsive and suicidal adults, regardless of diagnosis. Specifically, altered serotonergic function has been associated with suicidality and impulsivity (see Oquendo & Mann, 2000). Recent research indicates that people who engage in suicidal behaviors have less overall density of serotonin 1A receptors and serotonin transporter receptors in the prefrontal cortex (Arango et al., 2001). Mann, Waternaux, Haas, and Malone (1999) hypothesized that the anomalous serotonergic function is linked to a biological trait, which is manifest as impulsivity and/or aggression, which leaves people at increased risk for suicide in the face of external stress, thus supporting the diathesis-stress model of suicide.

There is a substantial amount of research that has attempted to identify genes or groups of genes that are specifically linked to suicide. One gene that received earlier attention was tryptophan hydroxylase (TPH); a poloymorphism on this gene was linked to suicide attempts in several studies (Mann & Stoff, 1997; Neilsen et al., 1994, ; Nielson et al., 1998). However, recent studies have resulted in inconsistent findings regarding TPH, and the one large study to address a link between TPH and suicide in adolescents failed to identify an association (Bennet et al., 2000). Finally, polymorphisms in the serotonin transporter (SERT) gene and the serotonin A receptor gene have been identified among suicide completers and attempters (Arango et al., 2001; Courtet et al., 2001; Du, Faludi, Palkovits, Bakish, & Hrdina, 2001; Neumeister et al., 2002).

Although no published research has specifically addressed a possible genetic component to NSSI, research has indicated that BPD, a diagnosis often characterized by engagement in NSSI, is moderately heritable (see Siever, Torgersen, Gunderson, Livesley, & Kendler, 2002). Therefore, it is likely that engagement in NSSI may have a genetic component, however further research focusing more specifically on the behavior of NSSI rather than a BPD diagnosis is needed.

Family Characteristics

Family History of Suicidal Behavior

A very strong risk factor for suicide (Agerbo, Nordentoft, & Mortensen, 2002; Brent, Bridge, Johnson, & Connolly, 1996; Brent et al., 1988; Brent et al., 1994; Gould et al., 1996; Shaffer, 1974; Shafii, Carrigan, Whittinghill, & Derrick, 1985) and suicide attempts (Bridge, Brent, Johnson, & Connolly, 1997; Glowinski et al., 2001; Johnson, Brent, Bridge, & Connolly, 1998) is a family history of suicidal behavior. This relationship remains after controlling for parental psychiatric history (Agerbo et al., 2002). A twin study of adolescents found that after controlling for psychiatric risk factors, the twin/co-twin odds ratio for making a suicide attempt was 5.6 for monozygotic twins and 4.0 for dizygotic twins, thus supporting some degree of heritability for suicide attempts (Glowinski et al., 2001). In addition, a large meta-analysis of twin data of people of all ages estimated the heritability for completed suicide to be 43% (McGuffin, Marusic, & Farmer, 2001). Based upon this large body of literature, it is extremely important to inquire about completed and attempted suicide in a patient's family when conducting a suicide assessment.

Parental Psychopathology, Divorce, and Parent–Child Relationships

The impact of parental psychopathology on suicidality among adolescents is unclear. Several research studies have identified a univariate relationship between parental psychopathology, mainly depression and substance abuse, and completed suicide (Brent et al., 1988; Brent et al., 1994; Gould et al., 1996) and attempted suicide and suicidal ideation (e.g., Fergusson & Lynskey, 1995; Joffe, Offord, & Boyle, 1998; Kashani, Goddard, & Reid, 1989). However, whether this relationship remains once the psychopathology of the suicide victim is taken into account is questionable, with one study finding that it does (Brent et al., 1994) and one study finding that it does not (Gould et al., 1996). No research has addressed the link between NSSI and parental psychopathology.

Similar to the issue of parental psychopathology, it appears that the univariate relationship between parental divorce and adolescent suicide and suicidality may be accounted for by other factors, such as parental psychopathology (Brent et al., 1994; Gould et al., 1996) and other psychosocial variables (Beautraiset al., 1996; Fergusson, Woodward, & Horwood, 2000; Groholt, Ekeberg, Wichstrom, & Haldorsen, 2000). Again, research is yet to address the relationship between divorce and engagement in NSSI.

Finally, the quality of parent–child relationships is important with respect to the child's overall functioning, and may be linked to suicide risk. Several studies have identified a link between poor parent–child relationships and suicide and suicide attempts (Beautrais et al., 1996; Brent et al., 1994; Brent et al., 1999; Fergusson & Lynskey, 1995; Fergusson et al., 2000; Gould et al., 1996; Lewinsohn, Rhode, & Seeley, 1993; Lewinsohn et al., 1994; Tousignant, Bastien, & Hamel, 1993). However, like the effects of divorce and perhaps parental psychopathology, the effect of relationship quality on suicidality weakens once the child's psychopathology is considered (Brent et al., 1994; Fergusson et al., 2000; Lewinsohn et al., 1993; McKeown et al., 1998). It is important to note that the frequency and satisfaction of parent–child communications was uniquely associated with suicidality even after adjusting for child pathology in one study (Gould et al., 1996). Research has not specifically addressed the effect of parent–child relationships on likelihood to engage in NSSI. However, it is quite likely that the two are related and research is needed in this area.

Social Stressors

Stressful Life Events

Stressful life events, including interpersonal loss and legal or disciplinary problems, have been found to be linked to completed suicide among several independent research studies (Beautrais, 2001; Brent et al., 1993; Gould et al., 1996; Marttunen, Aro, & Lohnqvist, 1993; Rich, Fowler, Fogarty, & Young, 1988; Runeson, 1990). This finding remains after controlling for psychopathology (Brent et al., 1993; Gould et al., 1996). It is likely that the combination of underlying psychopathology paired with an acute stressor typically leads to suicide.

Stressful life events, such as loss and disciplinary problems, are also linked to attempted suicide (Beautrais, Joyce, & Mulder, 1997; Fergusson et al., 2000; Lewinsohn, Rhode, & Seeley, 1996) and NSSI (Garrison et al., 1993). With respect to specific types of stressors, parental conflict is more commonly associated with suicide in younger adolescents, while romantic relationship difficulties are more strongly associated with suicide in older adolescents (Brent et al., 1999; Groholt et al., 1998). With respect to diagnosis, interpersonal loss is more commonly a precipitant among adolescents with substance disorders (Brent et al., 1993; Gould et al., 1996; Marttunen, Aro, Henrikkson, & Longqvist, 1994; Rich et al., 1988), while disciplinary crises are more commonly associated with suicide among adolescents with disruptive disorders (Brent et al., 1993; Gould et al., 1996) or substance disorders (Brent et al., 1993).

With regard to NSSI, minimal empirical research has addressed its link with stressful life events. One study found negative life events to be significantly associated with NSSI in a multivariate model, controlling for depression and suicidal ideation in addition to other covariates (Garrison et al., 1993). Additionally, an earlier study found that interpersonal loss, specifically in the form of the anticipation of an upcoming loss, was associated with increased engagement in NSSI among a clinical sample of adolescents (Rosen, Walsh, & Rode, 1990).

Bullying

Bullying is a specific stressful life event that has been the focus of recent research. A good deal of research has indicated that bullying behavior among adolescents is linked to suicidality (e.g., Brunstein-Klomek, Marrocco, Kleinman, Schonfeld, & Gould, 2007; Kaltiala-Heino, Rimpela, Marttunen, Rimpela, & Rantanen, 1999; Rigby & Slee, 1999; van der Wal, de Wit, & Hirasing, 2003). Specifically, a recent large epidemiological study indicated that being bullied and being a bully were both associated with a higher risk for suicidal ideation and suicide attempts, especially for girls (Brunstein-Klomek et al., 2007). Further, youth who are both victims and perpetrators of bullying behaviors seem to be at greater risk for both suicidal ideation and attempts (Brunstein-Klomek et al., 2007). For girls, being both a victim and a bully increased the odds of engaging in ideation or attempts by 10 to 12 times compared to those who were not involved in any bullying behavior. We are unaware of research addressing bullying behavior and NSSI.

Physical Abuse

Both psychological autopsy studies (Brent et al., 1999; Brent et al., 1994) and prospective longitudinal community studies (Brown, Cohen, Johnson, & Smailes, 1999; Johnson et al., 2002; Silverman, Reinherz, & Giaconia, 1996) have identified a link between physical abuse and suicide among adolescents. Physical abuse is also associated with an increased likelihood of making a suicide attempt, even after controlling for demographic characteristics, psychiatric symptoms, and parental psychopathology (Johnson et al., 2002). Johnson and colleagues (2002) found that interpersonal problems during middle adolescence mediated the relationship between childhood abuse and later suicide attempts, leaving the authors to conclude that abuse may lead to poor interpersonal effectiveness skills, thus leaving children isolated and at risk for suicidal behaviors. Early identification of and intervention, in the form of problem-solving skills, with children who have been abused may prevent later suicide attempts.

The relationship between physical abuse and NSSI is equivocal. Only one (Zoroglu et al., 2003) of three studies (Kiesel & Lyons, 1999; Lipschitz et al., 1999) to investigate this relationship among adolescents found a unique association between physical abuse and NSSI. In the other two studies, the effect of sexual abuse was much more strongly associated with NSSI than physical abuse, as is discussed in the next section.

Sexual Abuse

Contrary to physical abuse, a history of sexual abuse is a clear risk factor for engagement in NSSI (Kiesel & Lyons, 1999; Lipschitz et al., 1999; Zoroglu et al., 2003). Each of these studies among clinical samples of adolescents found sexual abuse to be predictive of NSSI in multivariate models. Interestingly, two of these studies (Kiesel & Lyons, 1999; Zoroglu et al., 2003) found that dissociation mediated the relationship between sexual abuse and NSSI, suggesting that sexual abuse leads some children to dissociate (in order to avoid the horrific experience) which then leads to engagement in NSSI. Indeed, one reason for engaging in NSSI cited by adolescents is to stop dissociation (Nock & Prinstein, 2004).

Childhood sexual abuse has also been found to be predictive of suicide attempts in longitudinal community studies (Fergusson, Horwood, & Lynskey, 1996; Silverman et al., 1996). Although the relationship between sexual abuse and suicide attempts weakened when covariates, such as parental substance abuse, were accounted for, it remained significant (Fergusson et al., 1996).

Environmental and Contextual Factors

Socioeconomic Status

Research addressing the effect of socioeconomic status on suicide and suicidal behaviors is somewhat mixed. Among studies of completed suicide victims, little or no effect of economic disadvantage on risk of suicide has been found (Agerbo et al., 2002; Brent et al., 1988; Gould et al., 1996). One interesting finding regarding African-Americans is that the African-American suicide victims had higher socioeconomic status than their general population peers (Gould et al., 1996). Conversely, studies of suicide attempters consistently find significantly higher rates of poverty among suicide attempters than their nonattempting peers (Beautrais et al., 1996; Fergusson et al., 2000; Foley et al., 2006; Wunderlich, Bronisch, & Wittchen, 1998). We are unaware of any empirical research addressing socioeconomic status and NSSI.

School Drop-Out and Homelessness

Not going to school and dropping out of high school or college have been associated with both attempted (Beautrais et al., 1996; Wunderlich et al., 1998) and completed suicide (Gould et al., 1996). Although no research has specifically addressed school attendance and incidence of NSSI, one study of a large group of homeless adolescents (n=428), many of whom were likely not attending school, identified extremely high rates of NSSI among the participants: overall prevalence of NSSI was 69%, prevalence of cutting was 45% (Tyler, Whitbeck, Hoyt, & Johnson, 2003).

Contagion

A common concern among parents, teachers, and clinicians is the occurrence of suicide contagion, referring to the phenomenon by which vulnerable adolescents may imitate suicidal behaviors performed by others. Research addressing "suicide contagion" has, unfortunately, confirmed this concern. Several studies have identified suicide clustering, in which suicides occur with greater temporal and spatial proximity than would be expected by past statistics (Brent et al., 1989; Gould, Wallenstein, & Kleinman, 1990a; Gould, Petrie, Kleinman, & Wallenstein, 1994; Gould, Wallenstein, Kleinman, O'Carroll, & Mercy, 1990b). This phenomenon seems to occur primarily among adolescents (Gould et al.,

1990a; Gould et al., 1990b). In addition, research supports clustering of suicide attempts (Gould et al., 1990a; Gould et al., 1990b). The observation of suicidal behaviors need not be first-hand to trigger a copy-cat act. Certain aspects of media coverage of suicide victims, including amount, duration, and prominence, is linked to increased rates of suicide in the United States and around the world (Etzersdorfe, Sonneck, & Nagel-Kuess, 1992; Fekete & Macsai, 1990; Hassan, 1995; Ishii, 1991; Jonas, 1992; Stack, 1996), and this effect is greatest for teenagers (Gould, 2001; Schmidtke & Schaller, 2000; Stack, 2000).

Although only minimal empirical research exists to document the phenomenon of contagion of nonsuicidal self-injurious behaviors (Rosen & Walsh, 1989), reports from schools suggest that NSSI is highly contagious. The concern is so great that specific protocols to address the spread of NSSI in schools have been developed (i.e., Walsh, 2005). The widespread use of the Internet among teenagers may also be cause for concern regarding the contagion of suicidal and nonsuicidal behaviors. One example of this is that preliminary research suggests there is an increasing number of self-injury message boards available on-line (Whitlock, Powers, & Echenrode, 2006).

Evidence of suicide clusters and contagion among teenagers should not deter parents, school personnel, or clinicians from asking about a youth's suicidality out of a fear of "putting ideas in his/her head." Evidence from a randomized controlled trial to evaluate the iatrogenic risk associated with assessing for suicide indicates that assessing suicidality in youth does not increase the rates of suicidal ideation or distress (Gould et al., 2005). The results of Gould et al.'s (2005) study have important clinical implications because a useful means of identifying teens at risk for suicide is to inquire about it in school and clinical settings.

PROTECTIVE FACTORS

Research addressing buffers to suicidal behaviors among adolescents is scarce compared to that addressing the risk factors for these behaviors. Nonetheless, three factors have been identified as potentially protective against suicidality in teens. Unfortunately, research addressing the protective factors for NSSI is nonexistent at this time.

Family cohesiveness, as indicated by the level of mutual involvement, shared interests, and emotional support, is linked to lower levels of suicidal behaviors among younger (McKeown et al., 1998) and older (Rubenstein, Halton, Kasten, Rubin, & Stechler, 1998; Rubenstein et al., 1989; Zhang & Jin, 1996) adolescents. Specifically, rates of suicidality were 3.5 to 5.5 lower among adolescents describing their families as high in cohesiveness compared to those who did not, even after taking depression and life stress levels into account (Rubenstein et al., 1998; Rubenstein et al., 1989). Consistent with these findings, interventions for suicidal youth (such as "Dialectical Behavior Therapy with Suicidal Adolescents" by Miller, Rathus, & Linehan, 2007) stress the importance of family involvement in the treatment of suicidal teens. Researchers interested in NSSI have yet to address the impact of family cohesiveness on the incidence of NSSI.

Religiosity is another protective factor that has received attention. Recent research among adolescents (Hilton, Fellingham, & Lyon, 2002; Siegrist, 1996; Zhang & Jin, 1996) confirmed the research conducted among adults (e.g.,

Hovey, 1999; Lester, 1992; Neeleman & Lewis, 1999; Stack, 1998) that higher levels of religiosity are linked to lower levels of suicidality. Reasons for the relationship between religiosity and suicide are less clear and may include the support provided by one's religious community, the stance of the religious institution toward suicide, and/or the sense of hope provided by the tenants of religion. The strength of the relationship between religiosity and suicidality in adolescents is yet unclear, as the existing studies failed to control for potentially confounding variables. Again, we are unaware of any empirical research that has addressed the relationship between religiosity and engagement in NSSI. The implications for clinicians of the role of religiosity in protecting against suicide are complex, as the extent to which a therapist should discuss religious issues with his/her patients is somewhat controversial (Lomax, Karff, & McKenny, 2002).

Finally, a fair amount of research has addressed the cognitive phenomenon of reasons for living and its relation to suicidality. Linehan and colleagues (1983) created the Reasons for Living Inventory, which assesses the extent to which a variety of factors may stop someone from attempting suicide. A significant negative association between the number of reasons for living endorsed and degree of suicidality among clinical and nonclinical samples of adults and college students has consistently been found (e.g., Connell & Meyer, 1991; Osman et al., 1993; Range & Penton, 1994). Further, growing evidence suggests that reasons for living are also an important protective factor among adolescents (Cole, 1989; Gutierrez, Osman, Kopper, & Barrios, 2000; Pinto, Whisman, & Conwell, 1998). One study found that three components of the Reasons for Living Inventory, i.e., survival and coping beliefs, moral objections, and fear of suicide, were significantly associated with lower levels of suicidal ideation, even after controlling for depression and hopelessness (Pinto et al., 1998). However, responsibility to family, and fear of failure, and social disapproval did not add unique variance to the model predicting suicidal ideation after adjusting for depression and hopelessness. Based on the apparent importance of having reasons for living, assessments of suicidal individuals should include an assessment of a person's perceived reasons to live, and treatments addressing suicidal teens should include a focus on increasing reasons to live.

Reasons for living has not been examined in relation to NSSI. Because people engage in NSSI for reasons other than to end their lives, the importance of identifying a link between NSSI and reasons for living is questionable.

CONCLUSIONS

There are several conclusions that can be drawn from this review. First and foremost, research indicates that the presence of psychopathology is an important risk factor for completed suicide, attempted suicide, and NSSI. Specifically, a diagnosis of depression is linked to each of these behaviors. Therefore, it is crucial that adolescent depression is taken seriously and treated aggressively in order to prevent subsequent suicide and/or self-injury. In addition, the research by Foley et al. (2006) highlights the danger of depression comorbid with generalized anxiety disorder for suicidal behaviors. Another perilous combination increasing the risk of suicidal behavior, particularly for males, is depression and substance abuse. Rates of depression and substance use, in addition to behavior disorders, are also elevated among adolescents engaging in NSSI. However, research assessing comorbid diagnoses of adolescents engaging in NSSI is limited by virtue of its use of clinical samples rather than nonreferred samples. Large-scale epidemiological studies of NSSI addressing co-occurring diagnoses are needed. Nonetheless, any adolescent who is identified as having made a suicide attempt or engaged in NSSI should be further evaluated for the possibility of the presence of an underlying and treatable mental disorder.

Engaging in self-injurious behavior leaves one at increased risk for engaging in future self-injurious behaviors. Although research has not yet indicated whether NSSI typically precedes suicidal behaviors or vice versa, it is known that the two types of behaviors tend to co-occur, and, as such, research indicates that adolescents who attempt suicide are at an increased risk for engaging in NSSI and vice versa (Garrison et al., 1993; Lipschitz et al., 1999; Muehlenkamp & Gutierrez, 2007). Some theories suggest that NSSI may serve as "practice" for ultimate suicide attempts and completed suicide (e.g., Joiner, 2005). This highlights the importance of carefully monitoring adolescents who report any engagement in self-injurious behaviors for future such behaviors. Because these types of behaviors may follow transient, yet stressful situations, and are often engaged in impulsively, an adolescent once again finding himself or herself in a similar crisis situation is likely to resort to self-injury to solve the problem.

Extensive research on suicidal behaviors has identified other important risk factors, including cognitive and personality-related characteristics, biologic vulnerabilities, family characteristics, adverse life circumstances, and socioenvironmental and contextual factors. Unfortunately, there still remain major gaps in our knowledge due to limited research about the risks of nonsuicidal self-injurious behavior.

Finally, a relatively small body of research has addressed protective factors for adolescent suicide, and virtually no research has addressed protective factors for NSSI. With regard to suicidality, evidence supports the potential importance of religiosity, family cohesiveness, and reasons for living in buffering against suicidality among teens. However, because the research in this area is somewhat limited, the effects of mediating and moderating variables that may account for a relationship with suicidality are yet unclear.

In summary, the goal of this chapter was to provide an overview of the rates, risk factors, and protective factors for suicidal and nonsuicidal self-injurious behaviors in adolescents. While self-injurious behaviors are prevalent in this age group, it is encouraging to note that research in this field is active. With regard to suicide and suicide attempts, the research addressing the risk factors for these behaviors among adolescents has yielded empirically based prevention and treatment efforts. Because the growth of empirical research addressing NSSI is more recent, efforts need to continue to focus on identifying risk factors for NSSI through epidemiological studies, in addition to beginning to explore potential effective treatments.

NOTE

1. Portions of this chapter were adapted from: M. S. Gould, T. Greenberg, D. M. Velting, & D. Shaffer. (2003). Youth suicide risk and preventive interventions: A review of the past 10 years. *Journal of the American Academy of Child & Adolescent Psychiatry, 42*(4), 386–405.

REFERENCES

Agerbo, E., Nordentoft, M., & Mortensen, P. B. (2002). Familial, psychiatric, and socioeconomic risk factors for suicide in young people: Nested case-control study. *British Medical Journal, 325*, 74.

American Psychiatric Association. (2000). *Diagnostic and statistical manual for mental disorders* (4th ed.) Text Revision. Washington, DC: American Psychiatric Association.

Anderson, R. N., & Smith, B. L. (2005). Deaths: Leading causes for 2002. *National Vital Statistics Reports, 53*(17), 1–89.

Apter, A., Bleich, A., King, R., Kron, S., Fluch, A., Kotler, M., et al. (1993). Death without warning? A clinical postmortem study of suicide in 43 Israeli adolescent males. *Archives of General Psychiatry, 50*, 138–142.

Apter, A., Plutchik, R., & van Praag, H. M. (1993). Anxiety, impulsivity and depressed mood in relation to suicidal and violent behavior. *Acta Psychiatrica Scandanavia, 87*, 1–5.

Arango, V., Underwood, M. D., Boldrini, M., Tamir, H., Kassir, S. A., Hsiung, S., et al. (2001). Serotonin 1A receptors, serotonin transporter binding and serotonin transporter mRNA expression in the brainstem of depressed suicide victims. *Neuropsychopharmacology, 25*, 892–903.

Asarnow, J., Carlson, G., & Guthrie, D. (1987). Coping strategies, self-perceptions, hopelessness, and perceived family environments in depressed and suicidal children. *Journal of Consulting and Clinical Psychology, 55*, 361–366.

Beautrais, A. L. (2001). Child and young adolescent suicide in New Zealand. *Australian and New Zealand Journal of Psychiatry, 35*, 647–653.

Beautrais, A. L., Joyce, P. R., & Mulder, R. T. (1996). Risk factors for serious suicide attempts among youths aged 13 through 24 years. *Journal of the American Academy of Child & Adolescent Psychiatry, 35*, 1174–1182.

Beautrais, A. L., Joyce, P. R., & Mulder, R. T. (1997). Precipitating factors and life events in serious suicide attempts among youths aged 13 through 24 years. *Journal of the American Academy of Child & Adolescent Psychiatry, 36*, 1543–1551.

Beck, A. T., Kovacs, M., & Weissman, M. (1979). Assessment of suicidal intention: The scale for suicide ideation. *Journal of Consulting and Clinical Psychology, 47*, 343–352.

Bennett, P. J., McMahon, W. M., Watabe, J., Achilles, J., Bacon, M., Coon, H., et al. (2000). Tryptophan hydroxylase polymorphisms in suicide victims. *Psychiatric Genetics, 10*, 13–17.

Blake, S. M., Ledsky, R., Lehman, T., Goodenow, C., Sawyer, R., & Hack, T. (2001). Preventing sexual risk behaviors among gay, lesbian, and bisexual adolescents: The benefits of gay-sensitive HIV instruction in schools. *American Journal of Public Health, 91*, 940–946.

Boergers, J., Spirito, A., & Donaldson, D. (1998). Reasons for adolescent suicide attempts: Associations with psychological functioning. *Journal of the American Academy of Child & Adolescent Psychiatry, 37*(12), 1287–1293.

Borowsky, I. W., Resnick, M. D., Ireland, M., & Blum, R. W. (1999). Suicide attempts among American Indian and Alaska Native youth: Risk and protective factors. *Archives of Pediatric and Adolescent Medicine, 153*, 573–580.

Brent, D. A., Baugher, M., Bridge, J., Chen, T., & Chiappetta, L. (1999). Age- and sex-related risk factors for adolescent suicide. *Journal of the American Academy of Child & Adolescent Psychiatry, 38*, 1497–1505.

Brent, D. A., Bridge, J., Johnson, B. A., & Connolly, J. (1996). Suicidal behavior runs in families: A controlled family study of adolescent suicide victims. *Archives of General Psychiatry, 53*, 1145–1152.

Brent, D. A., Kerr, M. M., Goldstein, C., Bozigar, J., Wartella, M. E., & Allan, M. J. (1989). An outbreak of suicide and suicidal behavior in high school. *Journal of the American Academy of Child & Adolescent Psychiatry, 28*, 918–924.

Brent, D. A., Perper, J. A., Goldstein, C. E., Kilko, D. J., Allan, M. J., Allman, C. J., et al. (1988). Risk factors for adolescent suicide: A comparison of adolescent suicide victims with suicidal inpatients. *Archives of General Psychiatry, 45*, 581–588.

Brent, D. A., Perper, J. A., Moritz, G., Allman, C. J., Friend, A., Roth, C., et al. (1993). Psychiatric risk factors for adolescent suicide: A case-control study. *Journal of the American Academy of Child & Adolescent Psychiatry, 32*, 521–529.

Brent, D. A., Perper, J. A., Moritz, G., Baugher, M., Roth, C., Balach, L., et al. (1993). Stressful life events, psychopathology and adolescent suicide: A case control study. *Suicide and Life Threatening Behavior, 23*, 179–187.

Brent, D. A., Perper, J. A., Moritz, G., Liotus, L., Schweers, J., Balach, L., et al. (1994). Familial risk factors for adolescent suicide: A case-control study. *Acta Psychiatrica Scandinavia, 89*, 52–58.

Bridge, J. A., Brent, D., Johnson, B. A., & Connolly, J. (1997). Familial aggregation of psychiatric disorders in a community sample of adolescents. *Journal of the American Academy of Child & Adolescent Psychiatry, 36*, 628–636.

Brown, J., Cohen, P., Johnson, J. G., & Smailes, E. M. (1999). Childhood abuse and neglect: Specificity of effects on adolescent and young adult depression and suicidality. *Journal of the American Academy of Child & Adolescent Psychiatry, 38*, 1490–1496.

Brunstein-Klomek, A., Marrocco, F., Kleinman, M., Schonfeld, I., & Gould, M. (2007). Bullying, depression, and suicidal ideation in adolescents. *Journal of the American Academy of Child & Adolescent Psychiatry, 46*, 40–49.

Centers for Disease Control and Prevention, National Center for Injury Prevention and Control. (2005). *Web-based injury statistics query and reporting system (WISQARS)*. Retrieved February 1, 2007, from http://www.cdc.gov/ncipc/wisqars.

Center for Disease Control and Prevention, National Center for Chronic Disease Prevention and Health Promotion. (2007). *National youth risk behavior survey (YRBS)*. Retrieved February 1, 2007 from http://www.cdc.gov/HealthyYouth/yrbs/pdf/yrbs07_us_suicide_related_behaviours_trend.pdf.

Cole, D. A. (1989). Psychopathology of adolescent suicide: Hopelessness, coping beliefs, and depression. *Journal of Abnormal Psychology, 98*, 248–255.

Cole, D. A. (1989). Validation of the reasons for living inventory in general and delinquent adolescent samples. *Journal of Abnormal Child Psychology, 17*, 13–27.

Connell, D. K., & Meyer, R. G. (1991). The reasons for living inventory and college population: Adolescent suicidal behaviors, beliefs, and coping skills. *Journal of Clinical Psychology, 47*, 485–489.

Courtet, P., Baud, P., Abbar, M., Boulenger, J. P., Castelnau, D., Mouthon, D., et al. (2001). Association between violent suicidal behavior and the low activity allele of the serotonin transporter gene. *Molecular Psychiatry, 6*, 338–341.

De Leo, D., Burgis, S., Bertolote, J. M., Kerkhof, A. J., & Bille-Brahe, U. (2006). Definitions of suicidal behavior: Lessons learned from the WHO/EURO Multicentre Study. *Crisis, 27*, 4–15.

Du, L., Faludi, G., Palkovits, M., Bakish, D., & Hrdina, P. D. (2001). Serotonergic genes and suicidality. *Crisis, 22*, 54–60.

Eaton, D. K., Kann, L., Kinchen, S., Ross, J., Hawkins, J., & Harris, W. (2006). Youth risk behavior survey surveillance-United States, 2005. *Morbidity and Mortality Weekly Report, 55*, 1–112.

Etzersdorfer, E., Sonneck, G., & Nagel-Kuess, S. (1992). Newspaper reports and suicide. *New England Journal of Medicine, 327*, 502–503.

Evans, K., Tryer, P., Catalan, J., Schmidt, U., Davidson, K., Dent, J., et al. (1999). Manual-assisted cogntive-behaviour therapy (MACT): A randomized controlled trial of a brief intervention with bibliotherapy in the treatment of recurrent deliberate self-harm. *Psychological Medicine, 29*, 19–25.

Faulkner, A. H., & Cranston, K. (1998). Correlates of same-sex behavior in a random sample of Massachusetts high school students. *American Journal of Public Health, 88*, 262–266.

Favazza, A. (1998). The coming of age of self-mutilation. *The Journal of Nervous and Mental Disease, 186*(5), 259–268.

Fekete, S., & Macsai, E. (1990). Hungarian suicide models, past and present. In G. Ferrari (Ed.), *Suicidal behavior and risk factors*, (pp. 149–156). Bologna: Monduzzi Editore.

Fergusson, D. M., Horwood, L. J., & Lynskey, M. T. (1996). Childhood sexual abuse and psychiatric disorder in young adulthood: II. Psychiatric outcomes of childhood sexual abuse. *Journal of the American Academy of Child & Adolescent Psychiatry, 35*, 1365–1374.

Fergusson, D. M., & Lynskey, M. (1995). Childhood circumstances, adolescent adjustment, and suicide attempts in a New Zealand birth cohort. *Journal of the American Academy of Child & Adolescent Psychiatry, 34*, 612–622.

Fergusson, D. M., Woodward, L. J., & Horwood, L. J. (2000). Risk factors and life processes associated with the onset of suicidal behaviour during adolescence and early adulthood. *Psychological Medicine, 30*, 23–39.

Foley, D. L., Goldston, D. B., Costello, E., & Angold, A. (2006). Proximal psychiatric risk factors for suicidality in youth: The Great Smoky Mountains Study. *Archives of General Psychiatry, 63*, 1017–1024.

Garofalo, R., Wolf, R., Cameron, M. S., Kessel, S., Palfrey, J., & DuRant, R. H., et al. (1998). The association between health risk behaviors and sexual orientation among a school-based sample of adolescents. *Pediatrics, 101*, 895–902.

Garrison, C. A., Cheryl, L. A., McKeown, R. E., Cuffe, S. P., Jackson, K. L., & Waller, J. L., et al. (1993). Nonsuicidal physically self-damaging acts in adolescents. *Journal of Child and Family Studies, 2*, 339–352.

Gibbs, J. T. (1997). African-American suicide: A cultural paradox. *Suicide and Life Threatening Behavior, 27*, 68–79.

Glowinski, A. L., Bucholz, K. K., Nelson, E. C., Fu, Q., Madden, P. A., Reich, W., et al. (2001). Suicide attempts in an adolescent female twin sample. *Journal of the American Academy of Child & Adolescent Psychiatry, 40*, 1300–1307.

Gould, M. S. (2001). Suicide and the media. In H. Hendin & J. J. Mann (Eds.), *Suicide prevention: Clinical and scientific aspects. Annals of the New York Academy of Sciences* (Vol. 932, pp. 200–224). New York: New York Academy of Sciences.

Gould, M. S., Fisher, P., Parides, M., Flory, M., & Shaffer, D. (1996). Psychosocial risk factors of child and adolescent completed suicide. *Archives of General Psychiatry, 53*, 1155–1162.

Gould, M., Greenberg, T., Velting, D. M., & Shaffer, D. (2003). Youth suicide risk and preventive interventions: A review of the past 10 years. *Journal of the American Academy of Child & Adolescent Psychiatry, 42*, 386–405.

Gould, M. S., King, R., Greenwald, S., Fisher, P., Schwab-Stone, M., Kramer, R., et al. (1998). Psychopathology associated with suicidal ideation and attempts among children and adolescents. *Journal of the American Academy of Child & Adolescent Psychiatry, 37*, 915–923.

Gould, M., Marrocco, F., Kleinman, M., Thomas, J. G., Mostkoff, K., Cote, J., et al. (2005). Evaluating iatrogenic risk of youth suicide screening programs: A randomized controlled trial. *Journal of the American Medical Association, 293*, 1635–1643.

Gould, M. S., Petrie, K., Kleinman, M., & Wallenstein, S. (1994). Clustering of attempted suicide: New Zealand National Data. *International Journal of Epidemiology, 23*, 1185–1189.

Gould, M. S., Wallenstein, S., & Kleinman, M. (1990a). Time-space clustering of teenage suicide. *American Journal of Epidemiology, 131*, 71–78.

Gould, M. S., Wallenstein, S., Kleinman, M., O'Carroll, P., & Mercy, J. (1990b). Suicide clusters: An examination of age-specific effects. *American Journal of Public Health, 80*, 211–212.

Groholt, B., Ekeberg, O., Wichstrom, L., & Haldorsen, T. (1997). Youth suicide in Norway, 1990–1992: A comparison between children and adolescents completing suicide and age- and gender-matched controls. *Suicide and Life Threatening Behavior, 2*, 250–263.

Groholt, B., Ekeberg, O., Wichstrom, L., & Haldorsen, T. (1998). Suicide among children and younger and older adolescents in Norway: A comparative study. *Journal of the American Academy of Child & Adolescent Psychiatry, 37*, 473–481.

Groholt, B., Ekeberg, O., Wichstrom, L., & Haldorsen, T. (2000). Young suicide attempters: A comparison between a clinical and an epidemiological sample. *Journal of the American Academy of Child & Adolescent Psychiatry, 39*, 868–875.

Gutierrez, P. M., Osman, A., Kopper, B. A., & Barrios, F. X. (2000). Why young people do not kill themselves: The Reasons for Living Inventory for Adolescents. *Journal of Clinical Child Psychology, 29*, 177–187.

Hassan, R. (1995). Effects of newspaper stories on the incidence of suicide in Australia: A research note. *Australian and New Zealand Journal of Psychiatry, 29*, 480–483.

Hawton, K., Cole, D., O'Grady, J., & Osborn, M. (1982). Motivational aspects of deliberate self-poisoning in adolescents. *British Journal of Psychiatry, 141*, 286–291.

Hilton, S. C., Fellingham, G. W., & Lyon, J. L. (2002). Suicide rates and religious commitment in young adult males in Utah. *American Journal of Epidemiology, 155*, 413–419.

Hjelmeland, H., Hawton, K., Nordvik, H., Bille-Brahe, U., DeLeo, D., Fekete, S., et al. (2002). Why people engage in parasuicide: A cross-cultural study of intentions. *Suicide and Life-Threatening Behaviors, 32*(4), 380–393.

Howard-Pitney, B., LaFromboise, T. D., Basil, M., September, B., & Johnson, M. (1992). Psychological and social indicators of suicide ideation and suicide attempts in Zuni adolescents. *Journal of Consulting and Clinical Psychology, 60*, 473–476.

Hovey, J. D. (1999). Religion and suicidal ideation in a sample of Latin American immigrants. *Psychological Reports, 85*, 171–177.

Ishii, K. (1991). Measuring mutual causation: Effect of suicide news on suicides in Japan. *Social Science Research, 20*, 188–195.

Joffe, R. T., Offord, D. R., & Boyle, M. H. (1988). Ontario Child Health Study: Suicidal behavior in youth aged 12–16 years. *American Journal of Psychiatry, 145*, 1420–1423.

Johnson, B. A., Brent, D. A., Bridge, J., & Connolly, J. (1998). The familial aggregation of adolescent suicide attempts. *Acta Psychiatrica of Scandanavia, 97*, 18–24.

Johnson, J. G., Cohen, P., Gould, M. S., Kasen, S., Brown, J., & Brook, J. S., et al. (2002). Childhood adversities, interpersonal difficulties, and risk for suicide attempts during late adolescence and early adulthood. *Journal of the American Academy of Child & Adolescent Psychiatry, 59*, 741–749.

Joiner, T. E. (2006). *Why people die by suicide*. Cambridge, MA: Harvard University Press.

Joiner, T. E., Rudd, M. D., & Rajab, M. H. (1997). The Modified Scale for Suicidal Ideation: Factors of suicidality and their relation to clinical and diagnostic variables. *Journal of Abnormal Psychology, 106*(2), 260–265.

Jonas, K. (1992). Modelling and suicide: A test of the Werther effect. *British Journal of Social Psychology, 3*, 295–306.

Kaltiala-Heino, R., Rimpela, M., Marttunen, M., Rimpela, A., & Rantanen, P. (1999). Bullying, depression, and suicidal ideation in Finnish adolescents: School survey. *British Medical Journal, 319*, 348–351.

Kashani, J. H., Goddard, P., & Reid, J. C. (1989). Correlates of suicidal ideation in a community sample of children and adolescents. *Journal of the American Academy of Child & Adolescent Psychiatry, 28*, 912–917.

Kisiel, C. L., & Lyons, J. S. (2001). Dissociation as a mediator of psychopathology among sexually abused children and adolescents. *American Journal of Psychiatry, 158*, 1034–1039.

Kumar, G., Pepe, D., & Steer, R. A. (2004). Adolescent psychiatric inpatients' self-reported reasons for cutting themselves. *The Journal of Nervous and Mental Disease, 192*(12), 830–836.

Lester, D. (1992). Religiosity, suicide and homicide: A cross-national examination. *Psychological Reports, 71*, 1282.

Lewinsohn, P. M., Rohde, P., & Seeley, J. R. (1993). Psychosocial characteristics of adolescents with a history of suicide attempt. *Journal of the American Academy of Child & Adolescent Psychiatry, 32*, 60–68.

Lewinsohn, P. M., Rohde, P., & Seeley, J. R. (1994). Psychosocial risk factors for future adolescent suicide attempts. *Journal of Consulting and Clinical Psychology, 62*, 297–305.

Lewinsohn, P. M., Rohde, P., & Seeley, J. R. (1996). Adolescent suicidal ideation and attempts: Prevalence, risk factors, and clinical implications. *Clinical Psychology-Science and Practice, 3*, 25–36.

Lewinsohn, P. M., Rohde, P., Seeley, J. R., & Baldwin, C. L. (2001). Gender differences in suicide attempts from adolescence to young adulthood. *Journal of the American Academy of Child & Adolescent Psychiatry, 40*, 427–434.

Libby, A. M., Brent, D. A., Morrato, E. H., Orton, H. D., Allen, R., & Valuck, R. J. (2007). Decline in treatment of pediatric depression after FDA advisory on risk of suicidality with SSRIs. *American Journal of Psychiatry, 164*, 884–891.

Linehan, M. M., Comtois, K., Murray, A. M., Brown, M. Z., Gallop, R. J., Heard, H. L., et al. (2006). Two-year randomized controlled trial and follow-up of dialectical behavior therapy versus therapy by experts for suicidal behaviors and borderline personality disorder. *Archives of General Psychiatry, 63*, 757–766.

Linehan, M. M., Goodstein, J. L., Nielson, S. L., & Chiles, J. A. (1983). Reasons for staying alive when you are thinking about killing yourself: The Reasons for Living Inventory. *Journal of Consulting and Clinical Psychology, 51*, 276–286.

Lipschitz, D. S., Winegar, R. K., Nicolaou, A. L., Hartnick, E., Wolfson, M., & Southwick, S. (1999). Perceived abuse and neglect as risk factors for suicidal behaviors in adolescent inpatients. *The Journal of Nervous and Mental Disease, 187*, 32–39.

Lomax, J. W., Karff, S., & McKenny, G. P. (2002). Ethical considerations in the integration of religion and psychotherapy: Three perspectives. *Psychiatric Clinics of North America, 25*(3), 547–559.

Mann, J. J., & Stoff, D. M. (1997). A synthesis of current findings regarding neurobiological correlates and treatment of suicidal behavior. *Annals of the New York Academy of Science, 836*, 352–363.

Mann, J. J., Waternaux, C., Haas, G. L., & Malone, K. M. (1999). Toward a clinical model of suicidal behavior in psychiatric patients. *American Journal of Psychiatry, 156*(2), 181–189.

Marcenko, M. O., Fishman, G., & Friedman, J. (1999). Reexamining adolescent suicidal ideation: A developmental perspective applied to a diverse population. *Journal of Youth and Adolescence, 28*, 121–138.

Marttunen, M. J., Aro, H. M., Henriksson, M. M., & Lonnqvist, J. K. (1991). Mental disorders in adolescent suicide. *Archives of General Psychiatry, 48*, 834–839.

Marttunen, M. J., Aro, H. M., Henrikksson, M. M., & Lonnqvist, J. K. (1994). Psychosocial stressors more common in adolescent suicides with alcohol abuse compared with depressive adolescent suicides. *Journal of the American Academy of Child & Adolescent Psychiatry, 33*, 490–497.

Marttunen, M. J., Aro, H. M., & Lonnqvist, J. K. (1993). Precipitant stressors in adolescent suicide. *Journal of the American Academy of Child & Adolescent Psychiatry, 32*, 1178–1183.

McGuffin, P., Marusic, A., & Farmer, A. (2001). What can psychiatric genetics offer suicidology? *Crisis, 22*(2), 61–65.

McKeown, R. E., Garrison, C. Z., Cuffe, S. P., Waller, J. L., Jackson, K. L., & Addy, C. L., et al. (1998). Incidence and predictors of suicidal behaviors in a longitudinal sample of young adolescents. *Journal of the American Academy of Child & Adolescent Psychiatry, 37*, 612–619.

Middlebrook, D. L., LeMaster, P. L., Beals, J., Novins, D. K., & Manson, S. M. (2001). Suicide prevention in American Indian and Alaska Native communities: A critical review of programs. *Suicide and Life Threatening Behavior, 31*(Suppl), 132–149.

Miller, A. L., Rathus, J. H., & Linehan, M. M. (2007). *Dialectical Behavior Therapy with suicidal adolescents.* New York: Guilford Press.

Moskos, M., Loson, L., Halbern, S., Keller, T., & Gray, D. (2005). Utah Youth Suicide Study: Psychological autopsy. *Suicide and Life Threatening Behavior, 35*, 536–546.

Muehlenkamp, J. J. (2005). Self-injurious behavior as a separate clinical syndrome. *American Journal of Orthopsychiatry, 75*(2), 324–333.

Muehlenkamp, J. J., & Gutierrez, P. M. (2004). An investigation of differences between self-injurious behavior and suicide attempts in a sample of adolescents. *Suicide and Life Threatening Behavior, 34*, 12–23.

Muehlenkamp, J. J., & Gutierrez, P. M. (2007). Risk for suicide attempts among adolescents who engage in non-suicidal self-injury. *Archives of Suicide Research, 11*, 69–82.

Najmi, S., Wegner, D. M., & Nock, M. (2007). Thought suppression and self-injurious thoughts and behaviors. *Behavior Research and Therapy, 45*, 1957–1965.

Neeleman, J., & Lewis, G. (1999). Suicide, religion, and socioeconomic conditions. An ecological study in 26 countries, 1990. *Journal of Epidemiology and Community Health, 53*, 204–210.

Nemeroff, C. B., Kalali, A., Keller, M. B., Charney, D. S., Lendarts, S. E., Cascade, E. F., et al. (2007). Impact of publicity concerning pediatric suicidality data on physician practice patterns in the United States. *Archives of General Psychiatry, 64*, 466–472.

Neumeister, A., Konstantinidis, A., Stastny, J., Schwarz, M. J., Vitouch, O., Willeit, M., et al. (2002). Association between serotonin transporter gene promoter polymorphism (5HTTLPR) and behavioral responses to tryptophan depletion in healthy women with and without family history of depression. *Archives of General Psychiatry, 59*, 613–620.

Ng, B. (1996). Characteristics of 61 Mexican Americans who attempted suicide. *Hispanic Journal of Behavioral Studies, 8*, 3–12.

Nielsen, D. A., Goldman, D., Virkkunen, M., Tokola, R., Rawlings, R., & Linnoila, M. (1994). Suicidality and 5-hydroxyindoleacetic acid concentration associated with a tryptophan hydroxylase polymorphism. *Archives of General Psychiatry, 51*(1), 34–38.

Nielsen, D. A., Virkkunen, M., Lappalainen, J., Eggert, M., Brown, G. L., Long, J. C., et al. (1998). A tryptophan hydroxylase gene marker for suicidality and alcoholism. *Archives of General Psychiatry, 55*(7), 593–602.

Nixon, M. K., Cloutier, P. F., & Aggarwai, S. (2002). Affect regulation and addictive aspects of repetitive self-injury in hospitalized adolescents. *Journal of the American Academy of Child & Adolescent Psychiatry, 41*(11), 1333–1341.

Nock, M., & Kessler, R. C. (2006). Prevalence of and risk factors for suicide attempts versus suicide gestures: Analysis of the National Comorbidity Study. *Journal of Abnormal Psychology, 115*, 616–623.

Nock, M., Joiner, T. E., Gordon, K. H., Lloyd-Richardson, E., & Prinstein, M. J. (2006). Non-suicidal self-injury among adolescents: Diagnostic correlates and relation to suicide attempts. *Psychiatry Research, 144*, 65–72.

Nock, M. K., & Prinstein, M. J. (2004). A functional approach to the assessment of self-mutilative behavior. *Journal of Consulting and Clinical Psychology, 72*(5), 885–890.

Nock, M. K., & Prinstein, M. J. (2005). Contextual features and behavioral functions of self-mutilation among adolescents. *Journal of Abnormal Psychology, 114*(1), 140–146.

Nock, M. K., Wedig, M. M., & Holmberg, E. B. (2008). The Emotion Reactivity Scale: Development, evaluation, and relation to self-injurious thoughts and behaviors. *Psychological Assessment, 39*, 107–116.

O'Carroll, P. W., Berman, A. L., Marris, R. W., Moscicki, E. K., Tanney, B. L., & Silverman, M. M. (1996). Beyond the Tower of Babel: A nomenclature for suicidology. *Suicide and Life Threatening Behavior, 26*, 237–252.

Olfson, M., Gameroff, M. J., Marcus, S. C., Greenberg, T., & Shaffer, D. (2005). National trends in hospitalization of youth with intentional self-inflicted injuries. *American Journal of Psychiatry, 162*, 1328–1333.

Olfson, M., Marcus, S. C., Weissman, M. M., & Jensen, P. S. (2002). National trends in the use of psychotropic medications by children. *Journal of the American Academy of Child & Adolescent Psychiatry, 41*, 514–521.

Oquendo, M. A., & Mann, J. J. (2000). The biology of impulsivity and suicidality. *Psychiatric Clinics of North America, 23*(1), 11–25.

Osman, A., Gifford, J., Jones, T., Lickiss, L., Osman, J., & Wenzel, R. (1993). Psychometric evaluation of the reasons for Living Inventory. *Psychological Assessment, 5*, 154–158.

Overholser, J. C., Adams, D. M., Lehnert, K. L., & Brinkman, D. C. (1995). Self-esteem deficits and suicidal tendencies among adolescents. *Journal of the American Academy of Child & Adolescent Psychiatry, 34*, 919–928.

Pilowsky, D. J., Wu, L., & Anthony, J. C. (1999). Panic attacks and suicide attempts in mid-adolescence. *American Journal of Psychiatry, 156*, 1545–1549.

Pinto, A., Whisman, M. A., & Conwell, Y. (1998). Reasons for living in a clinical sample of adolescents. *Journal of Adolescence, 21*, 397–405.

Posner, K., Oquendo, M. A., Stanley, B., Davies, M., & Gould, M. (2007). Columbia Classification Algorithm of Suicide Assessment (C-CASA): Classification of suicidal events in the FDA pediatric suicide risk analysis of antidepressants. *American Journal of Psychiatry, 164*, 1035–1043.

Range, L. M., & Penton, S. R. (1994). Hope, hopelessness, and suicidality in college students. *Psychological Reports, 75*, 456–458.

Razin, A. M., O'Dowd, M. A., Nathan, A., Rodriguez, I., Goldfield, A., Martin, C., et al. (1991). Suicidal behavior among inner-city Hispanic adolescent females. *General Hospital Psychiatry, 13*, 45–58.

Reifman, A., & Windle, M. (1995). Adolescent suicidal behaviors as a function of depression, hopelessness, alcohol use, and social support: A longitudinal investigation. *American Journal of Community Psychology, 23*, 329–354.

Reinherz, H. A., Giaconia, R. M., Silverman, A. B., Friedman, A., Pakiz, B., Frost, A. K., et al. (1995). Early psychosocial risks for adolescent suicidal ideation and attempts. *Journal of the American Academy of Child & Adolescent Psychiatry, 34*, 599–611.

Remafedi, G., French, S., Story, M., Resnick, M. D., & Blum, R. (1998). The relationship between suicide risk and sexual orientation: Results of a population-based study. *American Journal of Public Health, 88*, 57–60.

Rich, C. L., Fowler, R. C., Fogarty, L. A., & Young, D. (1988). San Diego Suicide Study: III. Relationships between diagnoses and stressors. *Archives of General Psychiatry, 45*, 589–592.

Rigby, K., & Slee, P. (1999). Suicidal ideation among adolescent school children, involvement in bully-victim problems, and perceived social support. *Suicide and Life Threatening Behaviors, 29*, 119–130.

Rosen, P., & Walsh, B. W. (1989). Patterns of contagion in self-mutilation epidemics. *American Journal of Psychiatry, 146*, 656–658.

Rosen, P., Walsh, B. W., & Rode, S. A. (1990). Interpersonal loss and self-mutilation. *Suicide and Life Threatening Behavior, 20*, 177–184.

Ross, S., & Heath, N. (2002). A study of the frequency of self-mutilation in a community sample of adolescents. *Journal of Youth and Adolescence, 31*(1), 67–77.

Ross, S., & Heath, N. (2003). Two models of adolescent self-mutilation. *Suicide and Life Threatening Behavior, 33*(3), 277–287.

Rotheram-Borus, M. J., & Trautman, P. D. (1988). Hopelessness, depression and suicidal intent among adolescent suicide attempters. *Journal of the American Academy of Child & Adolescent Psychiatry, 27*, 700–704.

Rotheram-Borus, M. J., Trautman, P. D., Dopkins, S. C., & Shrout, P. E. (1990). Cognitive style and pleasant activities among female adolescent suicide attempters. *Journal of Consulting and Clinical Psychology, 58*, 554–561.

Rubenstein, J. L., Halton, A., Kasten, L., Rubin, C., & Stechler, G. (1998). Suicidal behavior in adolescents: Stress and protection in different family contexts. *American Journal of Orthopsychiatry, 68*, 274–284.

Rubenstein, J. L., Heeren, T., Housman, D., Rubin, C., & Stechler, G. (1989). Suicidal behavior in "normal" adolescents: Risk and protective factors. *American Journal of Orthopsychiatry, 59*, 59–71.

Runeson, B. (1990). Psychoactive substance use disorder in youth suicide. *Alcohol Alcohol, 25*, 561–568.

Russell, S. T., & Joyner, K. (2001). Adolescent sexual orientation and suicide risk: Evidence from a national study. *American Journal of Public Health, 91*, 1276–1281.

Schmidtke, A., & Schaller, S. (2000). The role of mass media in suicide prevention. In K. Hawton & van K. Heeringen (Eds.), *The International Handbook of Suicide and Attempted Suicide* (pp. 675–698). New York: John Wiley & Sons.

Shaffer, D. (1974). Suicide in childhood and early adolescence. *Journal of Child Psychology and Psychiatry, 15*, 275–291.

Shaffer, D., Gould, M. S., Fisher, P., Trautman, P., Moreau, D., Kleinman, M., et al. (1996). Psychiatric diagnosis in child and adolescent suicide. *Archives of General Psychiatry, 53*, 339–348.

Shaffer, D., Gould, M., & Hicks, R. (1994). Worsening suicide rate in Black teenagers. *American Journal of Psychiatry, 151*, 1810–1812.

Shafii, M., Carrigan, S., Whittinghill, J. R., & Derrick, A. (1985). Psychological autopsy of completed suicide in children and adolescents. *American Journal of Psychiatry, 142*, 1061–1064.

Shafii, M., Steltz-Lenarsky, J., Derrick, A. M., Beckner, C., & Whittinghill, J. R. (1988). Comorbidity of mental disorders in the post-mortem diagnosis of completed suicide in children and adolescents. *Journal of Affective Disorders, 15*, 227–233.

Siegrist, M. (1996). Church attendance, denomination, and suicide ideology. *Journal of Social Psychology, 136*, 559–566.

Siever, L. J., Torgersen, S., Gunderson, J. G., Livesly, W. J., & Kendler, K. S. (2002). The borderline diagnosis III: Identifying endophenotypes for genetic studies. *Biological Psychiatry, 51*, 964–968.

Silverman, A. B., Reinherz, H. Z., & Giaconia, R. M. (1996). The long-term sequelae of child and adolescent abuse: A longitudinal community study. *Child Abuse and Neglect, 20*, 709–723.

Silverman, M. M. (2006). The language of suicidology. *Suicide and Life Threatening Behavior, 36*(5), 519–532.

Silverman, M. M., Berman, A. L., Sanddal, N. D., O'Carroll, P. W., & Joiner, T. E. (2007). Rebuilding the Tower of Babel: A revised nomenclature for the study of suicide and suicidal behaviors Part 1: Background, Rationale, & Methodology. *Suicide and Life Threatening Behavior, 37*(3), 264–277.

Sourander, A., Helstela, L., Haavisto, A., & Bergroth, L. (2001). Suicidal thoughts and attempts among adolescents: A longitudinal 8-year follow-up study. *Journal of Affective Disorders, 63*, 59–66.

Stack, S. (1996). The effect of the media on suicide: Evidence from Japan, 1955–1985. *Suicide and Life Threatening Behavior, 26*, 132–142.

Stack, S. (1998). Heavy metal, religiosity, and suicide acceptability. *Suicide and Life Threatening Behavior, 28*, 388–394.

Stack, S. (2000). Media impacts on suicide: A quantitative review of 293 findings. *Social Science Quarterly, 81*, 956–971.

Steer, R. A., Rissmiller, D. J., Ranieri, W. F., & Beck, A. T. (1993). Dimensions of suicidal ideation in psychiatric inpatients. *Behavioural Research and Therapy, 31*, 229–236.

Suyemoto, K. L. (1998). The functions of self-mutilation. *Clinical Psychology Review, 18*(5), 531–554.

Tousignant, M., Bastien, M. F., & Hamel, S. (1993). Suicidal attempts and ideations among adolescents and young adults: The contribution of the father's and mother's care and of parental separation. *Social Psychiatry and Psychiatric Epidemiology, 28*, 256–261.

Townsend, E., Hawton, K., Altman, D. G., Arensman, E., Gunnell, P., Hazell, P., et al. (2001). The efficacy of problem-solving treatments after deliberate self-harm: Meta-analysis of randomized controlled trials with respect to depression, hopelessness, and improvement in problems. *Psychological Medicine, 31*, 979–988.

Tryer, P., Thompson, S., Schmidt, U., Jones, V., Knapp, M., Davidson, K., et al. (2003). Randomized controlled trial of brief cognitive behavior therapy versus treatment as usual in recurrent deliberate self-harm: The POMPACT study. *Psychological Medicine, 33*, 969–976.

Tyler, K. A., Whitbeck, L. B., Hoyt, D. R., & Johnson, K. D. (2003). Self-mutilation and homeless youth: The role of family abuse, street experiences, and mental disorders. *Journal of Research on Adolescence, 13*(4), 457–474.

Van der Wal, M. F., de Wit, C. A., & Hirasing, R. A. (2003). Psychosocial health among young victims and offenders of direct and indirect bullying. *Pediatrics, 111*, 1312–1317.

Walsh, B. W. (2005). *Treating self-injury: A practical guide.* New York: Guilford Press.

Wagner, B. M., Wong, S. A., & Jobes, D. A. (2002). Mental health professionals' determinations of adolescent suicide attempts. *Suicide and Life Threatening Behavior, 32*, 284–300.

Whitlock, J., Powers, J. L., & Eckenrode, J. (2006). The virtual cutting edge: The internet and adolescent self-injury. *Developmental Psychology, 42*, 407–417.

Wichstrom, L. (2000). Predictors of adolescent suicide attempts: A nationally representative longitudinal study of Norwegian adolescents. *Journal of the American Academy of Child & Adolescent Psychiatry, 39*, 603–610.

World Health Organization. (1986). *Summary report, working group in preventative practices in suicide and attempted suicide.* Copenhagen: WHO Regional Office for Europe.

World Health Organization. (1998). *Primary prevention of mental, neurological and psychosocial disorders. Suicide.* Geneva: WHO.

Wunderlich, U., Bronisch, T., & Wittchen, H. U. (1998). Comorbidity patterns in adolescents and young adults with suicide attempts. *European Archives of Psychiatry and Clinical Neuroscience, 248*, 87–95.

Zayas, L. H., Fortuna, L. R., Lester, R. J., & Cabassa, L. J. (2005). Why do so many Latina teens attempt suicide? A conceptual model for research. *American Journal of Orthopsychiatry, 75*(2), 275–287.

Zhang, J., & Jin, S. (1996). Determinants of suicide ideation: A comparison of Chinese and American college students. *Adolescence, 31*, 451–467.

Zoroglu, S. S., Tuzun, U., Sar, V., Tutkin, H., & Savas, H. A. (2003). Suicide attempt and self-mutilation among Turkish high school students in relation with abuse, neglect, and dissociation. *Psychiatry and Clinical Neurosciences, 57*, 119–126.

Section III

BIOLOGICAL FACTORS

Chapter Nine

Early Onset Depression: Meanings, Mechanisms, and Processes[1]

IAN M. GOODYER

CONTENTS

The characteristics and severity of a depressive episode may depend on the extent of the involvement of both atypical early neurogenesis and acquired neuroendangerment in etiology. Future research studies must use genetically and physiologically sensitive designs to examine the nature of emotion regulation and cognitive processing in the onset, outcome, and treatment response of depressive disorders in young people.

Depressive syndromes in children and adolescents constitute a serious group of mental disorders with considerable risk for recurrence and subsequent psychosocial impairment with, in some cases, continuity into adult life (Dunn & Goodyer, 2006; Fombonne, Wostear, Cooper, Harrington, & Rutter, 2001; Pine, Cohen, Cohen, & Brook, 1999). The American Psychiatric Association Diagnostic and Statistical Manual (DSM) clinical criteria (American Psychiatric Association, 1994) successfully identifies the same clinical syndromes in school-age children, adolescents, and adults. In the prepubertal child, however, there has been emerging evidence that these criteria are insufficient to detect more developmentally sensitive forms of mood disorder (Egger & Angold, 2006). This paper considers possible processes and mechanisms involved in the onset of DSM-IV unipolar major depression from the perspective of recent advances in three neuroactive chemical components, serotonin, brain-derived neurotrophic factor, and cortisol. These will be considered in relation to genetic susceptibility, the current cognitive vulnerability map, and the role of social experience in the emergence of mood dysregulation and disorder during adolescence.

SEROTONIN AND AFFECTIVE DISORDERS

Chemical Emotion

The serotonin (5HT) system is large and complex in the mammalian brain and extremely old (>3,000,000 years), being found in many nonmammalian species including mollusks. The evolutionary significance remains unclear, but conservation and increased complexity of the system in humans is apparent with over 16 types and subtypes of receptor (Naughton, Mulrooney, & Leonard, 2000). The cell bodies are almost all located in the raphe nuclei in the brain stem, but the axons of these neurons innervate virtually the entire brain. 5HT is known to be involved in moderating a wide variety of physiological and behavioral processes, including mood, appetite, sleep, activity, and sexual behavior, all of which can be altered for the worse in depression. Because the 5HT system is modulatory in the brain, it is difficult to determine exact mechanisms and precise correlates with behavior. Thus, despite the fact that abnormal serotonergic (5HT) neurotransmission, and specifically depletion in the synaptic cleft, has been implicated as an etiological component of depressive disorder for over four decades, the precise mechanisms remain unknown. What is generally accepted is that unipolar depression is associated with diminished serotonergic function in the brain via a series of complex neurochemical events that lead to distortions and deficits in emotion and cognitive processing (Jans, Riedel, Markus, & Blokland, 2007). That is serotonergic depletion of itself does not "cause" depression, but alters the general sensitivity of the brain to make psychiatric disorders in general significantly more likely in the presence of other causative factors. Therefore, specific "depressogenic factors" are those that act in concert with serotonin sensitivity to induce mood disorder.

One key regulator is the serotonin transporter that is encoded by a single gene (SLC64A), which removes serotonin released into the synaptic cleft. The transcriptional activity of the human variation of this gene is modulated by several factors, including a repetitive sequence in a polymorphic region (5HTTLPR) composed of a short and a long version which results in differential 5HT expression (Canli & Lesch, 2007). Individuals may therefore be heterozygote (l/s) and homozygous (s/s) for the short form. This polymorphic variation was proposed as a possible genetic site for determining variation in risk for subsequent affective disorder (Collier et al., 1996). More recently, a single nucleotide polymorphism (SNP) has been located in the long version, one form of which has been shown to be low expressing, therefore functionally making the long form operate like a short form allele, resulting in a low clearance of serotonin from the synaptic cleft, in effect functioning like an s allelic form (Zalsman et al., 2006). Thus, the 5HTTLPR gene is triallelic with homozygotes for the long forms being of two types, La/La and La/Lg. The allelic variations denote an index of the time taken to clear serotonin from the synaptic cleft: La/La being the fastest followed by La/Lg and La/s, and the slowest being Lg/s and s/s carriers. It is important to note that recent cross-sectional imaging studies in adults have demonstrated no functional differences in the brain as a consequence of allelic variation in 5HTTLPR per se (Bhagwagar et al., 2006; Drevets et al., 2007; Parsey et al., 2006). This emphasizes the fact that allelic variations in the promoter are probably indexing and influencing downstream effects in some other component of this complex serotonergic modulatory system within the brain, and that these may well be set developmentally much earlier than would be detectable in the mature adult brain system.

Recent neuroscientific studies have examined the structure and function of neural systems in individuals grouped by their 5HTTLPR characteristics into those homozygous for the long form (l/l) and those with one or more copies of the short form (s/l+s/s). Hariri and colleagues (Hariri et al., 2002), using fMRI, were the first to report increased sensitivity in the amygdala to emotional stimuli in well adults with at least one copy of the 5HTTLPR 's' allele. 'S' carriers also have higher basal activity in emotionally sensitive areas of the brain (Canli et al., 2005; Canliet al., 2006), and are more likely to show increased difficulties over a range of behaviors and cognitions, including memory and attentional processes, alcohol and substance misuse, higher levels of worry and anxiety, and personality traits such as higher neuroticism and lower sociability (Canli et al., 2005; Jacobs et al., 2006; Kent et al., 2002; O'Hara et al., 2007; Roiser, Muller, Clark, & Sahakian, 2007; Sen, Burmeister, & Ghosh, 2004; Stein, Schork, & Gelernter, 2008). A recent PET study in adults reported in vivo data highlighting the central importance of the serotonergic system in general in the responsiveness of the human amygdala during emotional processing (Rhodes et al., 2007). Neuroimaging methods have also been used in younger populations to examine the relationships between depression and the amygdala, although participants have yet to be grouped by 5HTTLPR. For example, Roberson-Nay and colleagues (Roberson-Nay et al., 2006) recently demonstrated heightened amygdala activation in adolescent MDD during successful versus unsuccessful encoding of evocative faces. The level of activation in this and other studies mentioned above may depend not only on genetic variation, but the degree of emotional intensity within the stimulus (how fearful and arousing does a stimulus need to be to activate neuroaffective systems adaptively and maladaptively?); the competence of other psychological systems (e.g., individual differences in attentional processing may influence the processing of external stimuli in general); the emotional valence of the stimulus (activation in the amygdale and related structures may vary with the valence of the stimulus: negative emotions in a face or a picture could evoke stronger and/or preferential activation compared to positive or emotionally neutral in such stimuli); the maturity of the prefrontal systems in the brain involved in organization appraisal and response to stimuli.

The above findings also suggest that the appraisal and response to social experiences is likely to vary between individuals because of brain-mind-based differences. A recent study using fMRI and emotion psychology showed that typing 5HTTLPR allele reveals that those with an 's' brain (s/l or s/s) may indeed be tonically set at a higher level at rest than those homozygous for the 'l' (Canli & Lesch, 2007): This is potentially an example of a trait-organized function arising early in neural development. This would be obscured in fMRI experiments that rely on subtraction methodology to examine the state organized difference between groups in activation before and after an emotion stimulus. Canli and Lesch (2007) suggest that the origins of a higher resting level of blood flow in the amygdale in 's' carriers may arise as a function of a gene by environment interaction between 's' and early childhood adversities of some as yet unspecified type. Much further work is required to characterize if there is an early setting of brain readiness via gene by environment connections of one form or another (i.e., gene–environment correlations or interactions).

Overall there is clear-cut evidence that implicates serotonin in modulating emotion processing within the amygdala, the tonic level of which may, in part, be indexed by the 5HTTLPR genotype, but the resultant functions of which arise from more downstream elements of the serotonin system. Thus, it is not depletion of serotonin that may be the key, but its bioavailability and effects on the tissues. Higher levels of serotonin in the cleft in 's' carriers suggest less is taken up at postsynaptic sites with a resultant lower bioavailability or receptor sensitivity is lower. There may be further downstream differences and abnormalities at the level of the postsynaptic receptor sites with differential consequences on tissue sensitivity. It should be noted that in human studies, methodological variations in phenotype collection, variations in sample size, and heterogeneity in clinical assessment may inflate positive findings in any such studies (Munafo, Clark, Roberts, & Johnstone, 2006).

5HTTLPR, Life Events and Clinical Depression

Using a prospective strategy in the Dunedin birth cohort, Caspi and colleagues (Caspi et al., 2003) showed that by the third decade of life the liability for cumulative adverse life events to increase depressive episodes are significantly amplified in 's' carriers. This key finding demonstrated that in young adults the depressogenic risk that accrued from exposure to the cumulative effects of major negative life events over the prior 5 years (late teens to early twenties) in a dose-response manner was dependent on gene status: 's/s' individuals being the most sensitive, 's/l' in the middle, and 'l/l' the least. Note that there is no clear-cut association between being an 's' carrier and exposure to a single negative event, rather it is the cumulative effects over time together with the proposed genetic sensitivity to these events that is important.

There have now been a number of attempted replications and extensions of this key gene by environment interaction finding. Kaufman and colleagues (Kaufman et al., 2004) reported on a sample of 140 maltreated children: low social supports interacted with the 's' allele of 5HTTPLR resulting in increased depressive symptoms. In contrast, Surtees (Surtees et al., 2006) found a main effect of childhood adversities for major depression in a very large sample (>4,000), but neither a main effect nor an interaction with 5HTTPLR. Wilhelm et al. (Wilhelm, Mitchell, Niven, Finch, & Wedgwood, 2006) described a moderating effect of the 's' allele and cumulative events accruing over many years on subsequent depressive episodes, but Eley et al. (2004) reported similar findings using a range of ongoing social difficulties and briefer events in females only. Two studies have measured undesirable life events in the 6 or 12 months prior to the onset of a depressive episode. One provides a clear-cut 5HTTLPR by major event interaction (Cervilla et al., 2007), but the other an interaction only with rather more numerous minor events (Kendler, Kuhn, Vittum, Prescott, & Riley, 2005). Overall, the most consistent interaction between 5HTTLPR, social adversities, and subsequent depression seem to be with some form of cumulative index of stressful experience over months or years rather than days or weeks. Is this, therefore, a serotonergic gene effect reflecting the presence of early-formed distal vulnerabilities rather than a gene effect of current cognitive processing on acute events? As yet there have been no studies that have measured the environmental phenotype with sufficient precision to partition genetic effects by social adversities at differing points over the first two decades of life.

In addition, all the aforementioned studies tested 5HTTLPR moderation of the "depressogenic" effects of different forms of adverse experiences. Yet, the neurobiology of serotonin indicates no such specific psychological function is likely to be found: rather it moderates and tunes the brain to "events" both physiological and social, and hence has widespread and broader functions in contributing to social cognitive processing. A different but related notion, therefore, is to test a more general genetically sensitive hypothesis that variations in 5HTTLPR influence the generation *and* appraisal of the social environment. There is support for this proposition from behavioral genetic studies of life events research. Thus, Kendler and colleagues have recently shown in a meta-analysis that there are genetic influences on both the reporting and the experience of life events (Kendler & Baker, 2007). We do not yet know specifically whether the 's' allele of the 5HTTLPR genotype moderates the generation of highly proximal life events (PLEs) in the presence of more long-standing psychosocial adversities. Kendler suggests this may arise via genetic influences on sensitivity to the environment (Kendler et al., 2005), a conclusion which is markedly similar to the neuroscientific conclusions of Canli and Lesch (2007) that 5HTTLPR indexes a neurochemical process that is important for the formation of social cognitive processing. A recent prospective study of adolescents at high risk for depression provides some preliminary support for this notion of cognitive sensitivity, as the reporting and appraisal of recent life event was significantly amplified in 's' carriers with higher levels if prior adversities in their lives (Goodyer et al., 2007).

Overall, the likeliest primary psychological function of serotonin is to tune neural systems to adapt to environmental events, doing so through social cognitive systems of which a cognitive vulnerability system for depression would be one "pathological" example. Serotonin exerts effects on the amygdala and associated ventral prefrontal cortex, areas key to the emotion recognition and response process to experiences within and without the person. The evidence is preliminary but suggests that the tonic setting of the amygdala occurs as a result of a serotonin by environment interaction perhaps early in life, and that allelic variations in 5HTTLPR index group differences in sensitivity to the effects of these early experiences. These processes in the young child may result in individual differences in sensitivity to the subsequent social environment. Serotonin is not, however, the only chemical system to be implicated in abnormal mood states. Recent interest has grown in the role of a fundamental system of trophic agents involved in stimulating brain growth (neurogenesis) as potentially 'casual' agents in psychiatric disorders and depression in particular. Within this chemical family, brain-derived neurotrophic factor (BDNF) has been proposed as a key component in the onset of depressive disorders.

TROPHIC THEORY OF DEPRESSION

An existing body of knowledge from animal studies has shown that stress (generally meaning immediate depriving demands within an animal's environment, such as food restriction, foot shock, social isolation, or social defeat) is associated with many alterations in the brain including a decrease in key trophic elements involved in neuronal growth, development, and adaptive response to threat. The neurotrophic hypothesis of depression is based largely on these neuroscientific observations and, in particular, that decreases in BDNF levels are correlated with stress-induced depressive behaviors and that antidepressants enhance the expression of BDNF (Duman & Monteggia, 2006; Shirayama, Chen, Nakagawa, Russell, & Duman, 2002). The trophic hypothesis suggests an alternative to the serotonin and related monoamine theories in postulating that mood disorders arise from dysregulation of neuronal architecture and function via adverse effects on the trophic system in the brain responsible for normal neuronal growth. BDNF is known to have an important regulatory role in synaptic plasticity, and lowering BDNF levels can result in loss of this process with resultant neuronal atrophy.

Because trophic factors have a complex and varied biology in the regulation of synaptic growth, their specific associations with behavior in general and depressogenic processes in particular are difficult to disentangle and characterize (Martinowich, Manji, & Lu, 2007). Recent research has shown that of particular importance is to distinguish between pro-BDNF, a precursor form associated with long-term depression (LTD), and mature BDNF (mBDNF), which facilitates long-term potentiation (LTP) (Lu, Pang, & Woo, 2005; Pang et al., 2004; Woo et al., 2005). In neuroscience, LTP is the long-lasting enhancement in communication between two neurons that results from stimulating them simultaneously. Since neurons communicate via chemical synapses, and because memories are believed to be stored within these synapses, LTP and its opposing process, LTD, are widely considered the major cellular mechanisms that underlie learning and memory.

These two forms imply opposing cellular functions and may explain why BDNF may have opposing effects within the adult brain: an LTD effect on the stress system, which includes the hippocampus and hypothalamic-pituitary-adrenal (HPA) axis system, and an LTP effect on the brain reward system incorporating the nucleus accumbens and the ventral tegmental area. Acute stress can induce LTD in the hippocampus (and result in impairments in learning and memory), but it is not clear if this would be a cause or a consequence of depressive-like behaviors. This may depend on the form of BDNF. Thus, increases in mBDNF improve whereas stress impairs LTP in the hippocampus: an effect that in rodents can be reversed by antidepressants. Increased LTD may also have a role in depressive-like behaviors in rodents and can occur in the hippocampus under stressful conditions, but not otherwise. Again in rodents this can be reversed by antidepressants. Recent work suggests that increases in pro-BDNF within the hippocampus of juvenile rodents may facilitate LTD and therefore depressive-like behaviors as well as reduction of HPA control (Rosch, Schweigreiter, Bonhoeffer, Yves-Alain, & Korte, 2005; Woo et al., 2005); it remains to be shown if blocking pro-BDNF signaling pathways under stressful conditions prevents LTD and subsequent atrophy in the hippocampus. As yet, little is known about the effects of BDNF signaling on the reward system in humans, and this needs much further work as impairments in this system may well be associated with loss of pleasure or anhedonia and decreases in motivation leading to inattention and social withdrawal. Rodent evidence to date suggests important effects of BDNF on the reward system mediating long-term neural and behavioral plasticity in response to aversive social experiences (Krishnan et al., 2007).

Whether in animals these key BDNF-mediated effects are a cause or a consequence of stress-related and/or reward-related depressive-like behaviors remains to be firmly established, but evidence is growing for a key role for BDNF as part of a cascade of cellular events moderating the dopamine-mediated reward system in the brain (Berton et al., 2006; Nestler & Carlezon, 2006). Furthermore, such effects may be moderated by the genetic nature of the BDNF and epigenetic influences on behavioral adaptation to social experiences (Krishnan et al., 2007; McClung & Nestler, 2008). This animal evidence is sufficient for future human studies to consider that a number of key aspects of depressive disorders, including anhedonia, reduced motivation, and low energy may be mediated by impairments in mesolimbic areas of the brain that implicate BDNF as a moderator of individual differences in brain reward systems in humans (Monteggia et al., 2007; Nestler & Carlezon, 2006). From the genetic perspective, human studies have utilized the discovery of SNPs in BDNF gene that may contribute to dysfunction in the brain and subsequent mood disorders. A SNP was identified in the region encoding BDNF's pro-domain, leading to a valine at the amino acid 66 being substituted with a methionine (Val66-Met). A recent review of association studies between BDNF and depression in adults was not supportive of direct effects of this SNP with mood disorders (Groves, 2007). Interestingly, however, there is evidence for a significant association between the Val66Met allelic variations in BDNF gene in adults with a history of childhood depression compared to those without (Strauss et al., 2004; Strauss et al., 2005). In addition, nonclinical adolescent carriers with the Val66Val66 genotype and their mothers with the Val66Met genotype have been reported as having more depressive symptoms with the association mediated by higher levels of ruminative response style, one of the key cognitive vulnerability processes for clinical depression (Hilt, Sander, Nolen-Hoeksema, & Simen, 2007).

A further theoretical consideration is that there may be more indirect effects than is apparent from association studies: in other words gene x environment relationships rather than gene x clinical phenotype associations. There are, as yet, few such studies in the literature, but recently a gene to gene interaction with 5HTTLPR in predicting depression in maltreated children has been proposed with individuals with the Val66Met allele and being a 5HTTLPR 's' carrier showing higher depressive symptoms following maltreatment (Kaufman et al., 2006). These associations appeared to be particularly true for those heterozygous for the 's' allele suggesting an adverse genetic uplift for depressive symptoms of some type being obtained from the Val66Met and 's' genetic combination. The findings require replication, but lead to at least three possibilities: (i) direct trophic effects on serotonin systems in early brain development, (ii) serotonin influences on BDNF expression is differentially greater in those with a Val allele, and (iii) the impact of an adverse maltreatment environment may lower BDNF in those carrying the Val allele with consequential greater effects on those with an 's' allele in 5HTTLPR.

Interactions between BDNF and serotonin certainly occur biologically (Martinowich & Lu, 2008). For example, growth and survival of serotonin-rich neurons are promoted and facilitated by BDNF (Angelucci, Brene, & Mathé, 2005; Martinowich & Lu, 2008). This emphasizes that a common feature of the two systems is their ability to regulate the development and synaptic plasticity of neural circuits involved in emotion and cognition (Castren, Voikar, & Rantamäki, 2007). Thus, we now have modulatory models for both BDNF and serotonin in the brain operating not as genes for disease (always an unlikely proposition), but as susceptibility markers for physiological and psychological processing that arise via gene–environment relationships of different forms and perhaps most apparently in the first two decades of life.

Finally, two imaging studies on hippocampal volume and BDNF in humans to date suggest that it is the Met allele that is associated with reduced volume in the hippocampus and less gray matter density in the prefrontal cortex within normal adult volunteers and depressed patients (Frodl et al., 2007; Pezawas et al., 2004). Further genomic imaging studies at different ages and in well adults with a history of child onset depression are required to determine if there are functional as well as structural differences in emotion and cognition circuits that vary with the BDNF genotype. Currently, there are rather tantalizing suggestions of stress sensitive trophic effects on the development and integrity of the neural circuits that subserve emotion and cognition. These effects may be via two different trophic pathways, an early effect more apparent in childhood and adolescents and indexed by the presence of a Val allele in the gene; and later adult effect indexed by the Met allele within the same gene. The consequences may be deficits and or impairments in the hippocampal/HPA axis stress system across the lifespan and the brain reward system nucleus accumbens and the ventral tegmental area, in the maturing brain perhaps postadolescence. Much further work is now required to determine the reliability and validity of these complex but potentially important findings on the role of trophic agents in psychopathology and depression in particular.

In addition to the aforementioned BDNF–serotonin relationships, there is the intriguing biological association between BDNF and the HPA axis. Cortisol hypersecretion is one of the most robust pathophysiological markers for depression in adolescents and adults, but seemingly less so in prepubertal children. Would these findings be made more specific by a greater understanding of the associations between BDNF and cortisol?

CORTISOL AND DEPRESSION

Corticosteroids: An Essential but Temporally Complex Neuroendocrine Signal

Corticosteroids are among the most labile of all the hormonal systems (Herbert et al., 2006). Thus, the brain may be exposed to levels that vary greatly across time and between individuals. Values in the saliva of humans, a good indicator of "free" plasma levels and hence those in the tissues including the brain, vary by as much as eightfold during the day (Netherton, Goodyer, Tamplin, & Herbert, 2004). This diurnal rhythm tracks, but is not driven by, the daily cycle of activity and rest. Rather, the pacemaker driving the glucocorticoid cycle is an important signal connecting the central hypothalamic clock mechanism in the suprachiasmatic nucleus, synchronized by daylight, with peripheral "clocks" as target. This prepares the body for demands and opportunities offered by the solar cycle and can be termed "predictive" homeostasis. Absolute levels are determined by genotype, experience, age, and physiological state, but there is always a cyclical signal except under pathological conditions.

Corticosteroids also track more episodic events. This can be termed "reactive" homeostasis. Perturbations in the internal environments that challenge homeostasis, such as lack of food, water, salt, or excessive temperatures, all elicit increased corticosteroid secretion as part of the response to such demands or "stressors." External events, particularly those that threaten the individuals steady state (stress), also result in exaggerated glucocorticoid levels, and these may persist in situations of chronically threatening social adversities (Dallman et al., 2004). Added to these "group" effects are those related to individual differences in basal levels or the response to stressors. In both humans and rats (Grota, Bienen, & Felten, 1997; Stohr et al., 1998), there are marked individual and genotypic differences dependent upon both genetic processes and the occurrence of adverse events during fetal or neonatal life (Weaver et al., 2001, 2004). The exposure of the brain to corticosteroids in both the short and longer term rests on all the factors controlling their diurnal, episodic, or lifetime levels in the blood, and the way these are transmitted to the cells of the brain. As for changes in basal glucocorticoid levels, reactive homeostasis is governed by genetic, ontogenetic, and experiential factors.

The loss of the diurnal rhythm is among one of the most robust observations in patients with unipolar depression regardless of age. This loss reflects a deficit in the negative feedback system which has its control center in the hippocampus: circulating cortisol reaches receptors in this brain area which signal back through the HPA axis thereby controlling the release of cortisol from the adrenals. Loss of feedback sensitivity means that higher levels reaching the hippocampus do not shut down the system and excess cortisol is produced as a result, which is measurable in the saliva, blood, and urine. Salivary levels measure the "free" fraction which enters the brain and is an efficient marker of levels in the cerebral spinal fluid (CSF) (Guazzo, Kirkpatrick, Goodyer, Shiers, & Herbert, 1996). Adolescents both at risk for and those with depression have been shown to have altered HPA axis activity. At risk populations show higher morning cortisol levels than expected, which may reflect a higher tonic setting at the level of the brain for the production of circulating cortisol acting as a risk for the onset of disorder (Goodyer, Herbert, Tamplin, & Altham, 2000; Halligan, Herbert, Goodyer, & Murray, 2006; Harris, Borsanyi, Messari, Stanford, & Brown, 2000; Mannie, Harmer, & Cowen, 2007).

Early Life Experience Regulates Corticosteroids During Adulthood

One way in which early experience can modulate the HPA system is through the processes collectively referred to as epigenesis. This complex set of molecular and cellular events arise via environmental effects on the functions of genes involved in HPA axis regulation. The result is to alter the control mechanisms in the brain and change the tonic setting of the axis such that output levels of cortisol from the adrenals and associated behaviors show individual differences. Epigenesis occurs via one of two chemical processes: modulation of hippocampal glucocorticoid receptors by methylation of DNA and/or acetylation of DNA-associated histones (Waggoner, 2007). In general, DNA methylation silences genes, whereas histone-acetylation facilitates activation of transcription. These epigenetic mechanisms provide an added layer of transcriptional control of gene expression beyond those associated with variation in the sequence of the DNA. Variation in epigenetic regulation helps explain genetic diversity, but significant changes in epigenetic regulation can produce disease or vulnerabilities for disease. Epigenetic processing in man has yet to be directly described, but in rats lower levels of maternal care is associated with increased methylation of the consensus sequence for a neurotrophic growth factor, NGFI-A (a transcription factor) on the exon 1_7 promoter of glucocorticoid receptor (GR) gene, and this results in persistently decreased GR expression in the brain (Weaver et al, 2004; Weaveret al., 2001). There is a growing body of evidence that epigenesis is a key process in the formation of neuronal vulnerabilities for psychopathology including depression (Renthal et al., 2007; Tsankova, Renthal, Kumar, & Nestler, 2007).

Similar "programming" of the HPA axis in the young can follow adversity experienced during pregnancy (Holmes et al., 2006; Seckl & Meaney, 2004). This shows that maternal stress can also be transmitted to the young in a way that has long-lasting effects on neural systems that subserve emotion and cognition (Bhatnagar, Lee, & Vining, 2005; Dean, Yu, Lingas, & Matthews, 2001; Morley-Fletcher et al., 2003; Oitzl, Workel, Fluttert, Frösch, & de Kloet, 2000). Offspring whose mothers were stressed may themselves show increased levels of anxiety during adulthood as well as infancy. Anxiety is an essential ingredient of an adaptive response to a threatening situation, however excess or inappropriate anxiety may lead to a highly maladaptive state. The sensitive period for the programming actions of adversity thus begins in utero, and extends well into the neonatal period and perhaps beyond, at least in humans (Cushing & Kramer, 2005). Unfortunately, comparable data for humans is still not available, but there is growing evidence from prospective (human) studies for effects of maternal psychopathology and HPA function on infant HPA axis, behavior, and fetal functions (Azar, Paquette, Zoccolillo, Baltzer, & Tremblay, 2007; Davis et al., 2007; Halligan et al., 2006). The fetal environment can be altered if stress in the mother changes her hormonal profile, and in humans as well as rodents there is a strong correlation between maternal and fetal cortisol levels (Talge, Neal, & Glover, 2007). This putatively epigenetic developmental programming of the HPA axis may be one mechanism that accounts for individual differences in morning waking cortisol. Higher tonic setting of the HPA axis, and a relative increase in risk for psychopathology and neurodevelopmental difficulties in general may be a consequence of *atypical early neurogenesis*. Furthermore, neurogenesis occurs within the brain over time, and is likely to influence a wide and significant range of developmental trajectories beyond the early years, such as the continuing development of the prefrontal cortex into the third decade of life (Gottlieb, 2007; Karmiloff-Smith, 2007). Maturational stages, such as adrenarche, puberty, and the menopause, may all index epigenetic mechanisms that alter the sensitivity of the brain to a wide range of subsequent events including nutrition, exercise, and social experiences. The processes of growth and ageing may be in large part dependent on differential rates of epigenetic programming throughout the lifespan, and changes in a system such as the HPA axis may in part alter with time because of such epigenetic effects on the mechanism controlling cortisol output and rhythm and the response to this steroid at the level of the tissues.

Corticosteroid Acquired Neuroendangerment

The hippocampus seems particularly susceptible to the controlling or even damaging effects of corticosteroids (Sapolsky, 2000). This action, termed "neuroendangerment," implies that whilst higher corticosteroid levels may not in themselves damage cells, their vulnerability to other, adventitious, agents (e.g., anoxia or neurotoxins) may be accentuated. Excess glucocorticoid for a prolonged period of time (probably upwards of 3 hours) also induces atrophy of the apical dendrites of the pyramidal cells, thus potentially impeding their access to incoming information (McKittrick et al., 2000). This effect may arise quite independently of the tonic setting of the HPA axis and also influence the sensitivity of serotonin system via alterations to the binding of the of the serotonin transporter. This nondevelopmental mechanism may not only occur across the lifespan, but clearly indexes important interactions between the HPA axis and the serotonin system.

Whilst the immediate response to a threat is one of appraisal that facilitates coping strategies, it is equally important to form, encode, and consolidate memories about the nature and context of the experience itself. This enables individuals to reduce the chances of future exposure through avoidance strategies or enhances new coping strategies to be available for the next threatening experience. Indeed, memory formation for threatening events may occur most effectively in the context of high negative emotion (e.g., fear, sadness, disgust). Increases in systemic glucocorticoids at the point of exposure enhance such learning, but animal studies have shown that this encoding of experience in memory is prevented by lesions of the basolateral amygdala implying not some type of serotonin-cortisol effect in encoding emotionally valent, but also depend on interactions with noradrenalin within the same brain area (Roozendaal, Okuda, De Quervain, & McGaugh, 2006a; Roozendaal, Okuda, Van der Zee, & McGaugh, 2006b) . Such critical interactions between glucocorticoids and arousal-activated noradrenergic mechanisms within the basolateral amygdala may explain why glucocorticoids selectively enhance memory for emotionally arousing, and not emotionally neutral information (Buchanan, al'Absi, & Lovallo, 1999; Buchanan & Lovallo, 2001). In this context, it seems clear that glucocorticoids have an important and positive role to play in encoding and recalling memories of threat and aiding the development of coping strategies for adverse experience. Clearly this requires interactions with both serotonin and noradrenalin in the amygdala. Perhaps there is a similar interaction in the hippocampus that involves cortisol and mBDNF in particular to effect recall and use of consolidated information. This remains to be determined.

Current evidence suggests considerable interplay over time between cortisol and cognitive functions with both bottom-up (glucocorticoids on cognitive function), and top-down (cognitive processing on glucocorticoid secretion) effects in the human population (Lupien et al., 2005; Lupien, Maheu, Tu, Fiocco, & Schramek, 2007). This cortisol-cognitive interplay has implications for psychiatric disorders. For example, adult patients with severe unipolar depression show altered sensitivity of declarative memory as a function of glucocorticoids implicating dysfunctions in the hippocampus and anterior cingulate in mood disorders (Bremner et al., 2004a; Bremner, Vythilingam, Vermetten, Vaccarino, & Charney, 2004b). In adolescents, persistent depression (>18 months) is associated with antecedent cortisol hypersecretion and an increase in subsequent life events that involve danger to the self implicating steroid-related cognitive deficits in maintaining disorder (Goodyer, Herbert, & Tamplin, 2003; Goodyer, Park, & Herbert, 2001). Overall, individuals may, at any point in the lifespan and without necessarily having experiences consistent with the emergence of atypical early neurogenesis, undergo *acquired neuroendangerment* increasing their overall risk for depressive disorders.

Cortisol, Serotonin and BDNF

The notion of acquired neuroendangerment may represent a second process involving cortisol, serotonin, and BDNF that may lead to impairments in the neural systems, and the hippocampus in particular that subserve emotion and cognition thereby increasing the liability for depressive disorders. For example, at the neurocellular level serotonin may regulate the sensitivity of the progenitor cells in the dentate gyrus to glucocorticoid (Huang & Herbert, 2005). The rodent (but not yet human) data implicates both neurotrophic and serotonin systems in atypical epigenetic programming processes of the HPA axis that, as noted, appear to exert tonic effects on the amygdala and ventral prefrontal systems in particular.

Overall, the HPA axis may be implicated in two quite different ways in the onset and maintenance of unipolar major depression in young people. First, developmental vulnerabilities may arise via gene—environment mediated interactions giving rise to atypical early epigenesis that result in higher circulating levels of cortisol and different feedback sensitivities at the brain regions responsible for emotion processing. The amygdala and associated ventral prefrontal areas in particular are central, and variations in this neural system give rise to individual differences in emotion recognition and response to stimuli. These early developmental processes may be relatively stable leading to individual differences in predictive homeostasis. This may be indexed by individual differences in circulating morning basal cortisol levels. Such individuals are at risk for subsequent episodes of unipolar major depression. These developmental vulnerabilities will also set the tonic controls for emotion processing of the environment and result in differential levels of sensitivity to appraising and responding to subsequent social experience. In theory, one should see increased dysphoria and worry in difficult social circumstances as a consequence of atypical early epigenetic programming.

Second, episodic events may impact on the stress and reward systems in the brain, thereby lowering BDNF in cognitively important brain regions, altering the hippocampal control of the HPA and resulting in cortisol hypersecretion independently of any effects from atypical early neurogenesis (reactive homeostasis). Serotonin may moderate the effects of this process due to the role the system plays on BDNF function. If cortisol hypersecretion persists then individual differences in reactive homeostasis may occur, further exposing the hippocampus and perhaps the nucleus accumbens and ventral tegmentum to acquired neuroendangerment. In theory this would result in cognitive effects involving the hippocampus and associated memory functions, and the nucleus accumbens and ventral tegmental area (VTA) where activation to pleasure and controls on motivation are found. Down regulation of these areas would therefore most likely be involved in the development of negative cognitions toward the self, anhedonia, poor attention, and social withdrawal via loss of motivation.

CONCLUSIONS

Three neuroactive agents are purported to be involved in the etiology of depressive disorders, serotonin, BDNF, and cortisol. A literature review considers their contributions to the emergence of unipolar depressions both independently and collectively within two theoretical frameworks, termed atypical early epigenesis, representing an adverse developmental trajectory resulting in the formation of a vulnerable neuronal architecture increasing the likelihood of poor mood regulation when faced with environmental demands, and acquired neuroendangerment indicating the formation of a pathological brain process leading to synaptic plasticity and neuronal atrophy with resultant motivational, cognitive, and behavioral deficits at any point in development. There is evidence for both an atypical early neurogenesis and an acquired neuroendangerment framework for the evolving formation of neuropsychological vulnerabilities for subsequent clinical depressive episodes. Serotonin, BDNF, and cortisol act in concert rather than independently in both frameworks, but their relative effects on each other, related key neurochemistry notably dopamine and noradrenalin, and the neural systems that subserve emotion and cognition may differ according to underlying genetic characteristics and quality of the social experiences over time.

The psychological characteristics and severity of a depressive episode and perhaps thereby treatment response may depend on the extent of the involvement of both atypical early neurogenesis and acquired neuroendangerment in the etiology of affective disorders and whether the former predisposes individuals to the latter. Future research studies must use genetically and physiologically sensitive designs to examine the nature of emotion regulation and cognitive processing in the onset, outcome, and treatment response of depressive disorders in young people.

NOTE

1. The author is supported by program and project grants from the Wellcome Trust and a program grant from the MRC. The chapter is based in part on the Emmanuel Miller Lecture delivered to the Association of Child and Adolescent Mental Health (UK) in February 2007.

REFERENCES

American Psychiatric Association. (1994). *Diagnostic and statistical manual for mental and behavioural disorders*. Washington, DC: American Psychiatric Association.

Angelucci, F., Brene, S., & Mathé, A. A. (2005). BDNF in schizophrenia, depression and corresponding animal models. *Molecular Psychiatry, 10*(4), 345–352.

Azar, R., Paquette, D., Zoccolillo, M., Baltzer, F., & Tremblay, R. (2007). The association of major depression, conduct disorder, and maternal overcontrol with a failure to show a cortisol buffered response in 4-month-old infants of teenage mothers. *Biological Psychiatry, 62*(6), 573–579.

Berton, O., McClung, C. A., DiLeone, R. J., Krishnan, V., Renthal, W., & Russo, S. J. (2006). Essential role of BDNF in the mesolimbic dopamine pathway in social defeat stress. *Science, 311*(5762), 864–868.

Bhagwagar, Z., Hinz, R., Taylor, M., Fancy, S., Cowen, P., & Grasby, P. (2006). Increased 5-HT(2A) receptor binding in euthymic, medication-free patients recovered from depression: A positron emission study with [(11)C]MDL 100,907. *American Journal of Psychiatry, 163*(9), 1580–1587.

Bhatnagar, S., Lee, T. M., & Vining, C. (2005). Prenatal stress differentially affects habituation of corticosterone responses to repeated stress in adult male and female rats. *Hormones and Behavior, 47*(4), 430–438.

Bremner, J. D., Vythilingam, M., Vermetten, E., Anderson, G., Newcomer, J. W., & Charney, D. S. (2004a). Effects of glucocorticoids on declarative memory function in major depression. *Biological Psychiatry, 55*(8), 811–815.

Bremner, J. D., Vythilingam, M., Vermetten, E., Vaccarino, V., & Charney, D. S. (2004b). Deficits in hippocampal and anterior cingulate functioning during verbal declarative memory encoding in midlife major depression. *American Journal of Psychiatry, 161*(4), 637–645.

Buchanan, T. W., al'Absi, M., & Lovallo, W. R. (1999). Cortisol fluctuates with increases and decreases in negative affect. *Psychoneuroendocrinology, 24*(2), 227–241.

Buchanan, T. W., & Lovallo, W. R. (2001). Enhanced memory for emotional material following stress-level cortisol treatment in humans. *Psychoneuroendocrinology, 26*(3), 307–317.

Canli, T., & Lesch, K. P. (2007). Long story short: The serotonin transporter in emotion regulation and social cognition. *Nature Neuroscience, 10*(9), 1103–1109.

Canli, T., Omura, K., Haas, B. W., Fallgatter, A., Constable, R. T., & Lesch, K. P. (2005). Beyond affect: A role for genetic variation of the serotonin transporter in neural activation during a cognitive attention task. *Proceedings of the National Academy of Sciences of the United States of America, 102*(34), 12224–12229.

Canli, T., Qiu, M., Omura, K., Congdon, E., Haas, B. W., Amin, Z., et al. (2006). Neural correlates of epigenesis. *Proceedings of the National Academy of Sciences of the United States of America, 103*(43), 16033–16038.

Caspi, A., Sugden, K., Moffitt, T. E., Taylor, A., Craig, I. W., Harrington, H., et al. (2003). Influence of life stress on depression: Moderation by a polymorphism in the 5-HTT gene. *Science, 301*(5631), 386–389.

Castren, E., Voikar, V., & Rantamäki, T. (2007). Role of neurotrophic factors in depression. *Current Opinion in Pharmacology, 7*(1), 18–21.

Cervilla, J. A., Molina, E., Rivera, M., Torres-Gonzalez, F., Bellon, J. A., Moreno, B., et al. (2007). The risk for depression conferred by stressful life events is modified by variation at the serotonin transporter 5HTTLPR genotype: Evidence from the Spanish PREDICT-Gene cohort. *Molecular Psychiatry, 12*(8), 748–755.

Collier, D. A., Stober, G., Li, T., Heils, A., Catalano, M., Di Bella, D., et al. (1996). A novel functional polymorphism within the promoter of the serotonin transporter gene: Possible role in susceptibility to affective disorders. *Molecular Psychiatry, 1*(6), 453–460.

Cushing, B. S., & Kramer, K. M. (2005). Mechanisms underlying epigenetic effects of early social experience: The role of neuropeptides and steroids. *Neuroscience and Biobehavioral Reviews, 29*, 1089–1105.

Dallman, M. F., Akana, S. F., Strack, A. M., Scribner, K. S., Pecoraro, N., La Fleur, S. E., et al. (2004). Chronic stress-induced effects of corticosterone on brain: Direct and indirect. *Annals of the New York Academy of Sciences, 1018*(1), 141–150.

Davis, E. P., Glynn, L. M., Schetter, C. D., Hobel, C., Chicz-Demet, A., & Sandman, C. A. (2007). Prenatal exposure to maternal depression and cortisol influences infant temperament. *Journal of the American Academy of Child & Adolescent Psychiatry, 46*(6), 737–746.

Dean, F., Yu, C., Lingas, R. I., & Matthews, S. G. (2001). Prenatal glucocorticoid modifies hypothalamo-pituitary-adrenal regulation in prepubertal guinea pigs. *Neuroendocrinology, 73*(3), 194–202.

Drevets, W., Thase, M., Moses-Kolko, E., Price, J., Frank, E., Kupfer, D., et al. (2007). Serotonin-1A receptor imaging in recurrent depression: Replication and literature review. *Nuclear Medicine and Biology, 34*(7), 865–877.

Duman, R. S., & Monteggia, L. M. (2006). A neurotrophic model for stress-related mood disorders. *Biological Psychiatry, 59*(12), 1116–1127.

Dunn, V., & Goodyer, I. M. (2006). Longitudinal investigation into childhood- and adolescence-onset depression: Psychiatric outcome in early adulthood. *British Journal of Psychiatry, 188*, 216–222.

Egger, H. L., & Angold, A. (2006). Common emotional and behavioral disorders in preschool children: Presentation, nosology, and epidemiology. *Journal of Child Psychology and Psychiatry, and Allied Disciplines, 47*(3–4), 313–337.

Eley, T. C., Sugden, K., Corsico, A., Gregory, A. M., Sham, P., McGuffin, P., et al. (2004). Gene-environment interaction analysis of serotonin system markers with adolescent depression. *Molecular Psychiatry, 9*(10), 908–915.

Fombonne, E., Wostear, G., Cooper, V., Harrington, R., & Rutter, M. (2001). The Maudsley long-term follow-up of child and adolescent depression. 1. Psychiatric outcomes in adulthood. *British Journal of Psychiatry, 179*, 210–217.

Frodl, T., Schule, C., Schmitt, G., Born, C., Baghai, T., Zill, P., et al. (2007). Association of the brain-derived neurotrophic factor Val66Met polymorphism with reduced hippocampal volumes in major depression. *Archives of General Psychiatry, 64*(4), 410–416.

Goodyer, I., Bacon, A., Ban, M., Croudace, T., & Herbert, J. (2008). The 's' allele of the serotonin transporter (5HTTLPR) accentuates the association between morning cortisol and the onset of an episode of clinical depression in adolescents.. *British Journal of Psychiatry,* submitted.

Goodyer, I. M., Herbert, J., & Tamplin, A. (2003). Psychoendocrine antecedents of persistent first-episode major depression in adolescents: A community-based longitudinal enquiry. *Psychological Medicine, 33*(4), 601–610.

Goodyer, I. M., Herbert, J., Tamplin, A., & Altham, P. M. (2000). Recent life events, cortisol, dehydroepiandrosterone and the onset of major depression in high-risk adolescents. *British Journal of Psychiatry, 177*, 499–504.

Goodyer, I. M., Park, R. J., & Herbert, J. (2001). Psychosocial and endocrine features of chronic first-episode major depression in 8–16 year olds. *Biological Psychiatry, 50*(5), 351–357.

Gottlieb, G. (2007). Probabilistic epigenesis. *Developmental Science, 10*(1), 1–11.

Grota, L. J., Bienen, T., & Felten, D. L. (1997). Corticosterone responses of adult Lewis and Fischer rats. *Journal of Neuroimmunology, 74*(1–2), 95–101.

Groves, J. O. (2007). Is it time to reassess the BDNF hypothesis of depression? *Molecular Psychiatry, 12*(12), 1079–1088.

Guazzo, E. P., Kirkpatrick, P. J., Goodyer, I. M., Shiers, H. M., & Herbert, J. (1996). Cortisol, dehydroepandrosterone (DHEA), and DHEA sulfate in the cerebrospinal fluid of man: Relation to blood levels and the effects of age. *Journal of Clinical Endocrinology and Metabolism, 81*, 3951–3960.

Halligan, S. L., Herbert, J., Goodyer, I., & Murray, L. (2006). Disturbances in morning cortisol secretion in association with maternal postnatal depression predict subsequent depressive symptomatology in adolescents. *Biological Psychiatry, 62*, 40–46.

Hariri, A. R., Mattay, V. S., Tessitore, A., Kolachana, B., Fera, F., Goldman, D., et al. (2002). Serotonin transporter genetic variation and the response of the human amygdala. *Science, 297*(5580): 400–403.

Harris, T. O., Borsanyi, S., Messari, S., Stanford, K., & Brown, G. W. (2000). Morning cortisol as a risk factor for subsequent major depressive disorder in adult women. *British Journal of Psychiatry, 177*, 505–510.

Herbert, J., Goodyer, I. M., Grossman, A. B., Hastings, M. H., de Kloet, E. R., Lightman, S. L., et al. (2006). Do corticosteroids damage the brain? *Journal of Neuroendocrinology, 18*(6), 393–411.

Hilt, L. M., Sander, L. C., Nolen-Hoeksema, S., & Simen, A. A. (2007). The BDNF Val66Met polymorphism predicts rumination and depression differently in young adolescent girls and their mothers. *Neuroscience Letters, 429*(1), 12–16.

Holmes, M. C., Abrahamsen, C. T., French, K. L., Paterson, J. M., Mullins, J. J., & Seckl, J. R. (2006). The mother or the fetus? 11beta-hydroxysteroid dehydrogenase type 2 null mice provide evidence for direct fetal programming of behavior by endogenous glucocorticoids. *Journal of Neuroscience, 26*(14), 3840–3844.

Huang, G. J., & Herbert, J. (2005). Serotonin modulates the suppressive effects of corticosterone on proliferating progenitor cells in the dentate gyrus of the hippocampus in the adult rat. *Neuropsychopharmacology, 30*(2), 231–241.

Jacobs, N., Kenis, G., Peeters, F., Derom, C., Vlietinck, R., & van Os, J. (2006). Stress-related negative affectivity and genetically altered serotonin transporter function: Evidence of synergism in shaping risk of depression. *Archives of General Psychiatry, 63*(9), 989–996.

Jans, L. A., Riedel, W. J., Markus, C. R., & Blokland, A. (2007). Serotonergic vulnerability and depression: Assumptions, experimental evidence and implications. *Molecular Psychiatry, 12*(6), 522–543.

Karmiloff-Smith, A. (2007). Atypical epigenesis. *Developmental Science, 10*(1), 84–88.
Kaufman, J., Yang, B. Z., Douglas-Palumberi, H., Grasso, D., Lipschitz, D., Houshyar, S., et al. (2006). Brain-derived neurotrophic factor-5-HTTLPR gene interactions and environmental modifiers of depression in children. *Biological Psychiatry, 59*(8), 673–680.
Kaufman, J., Yang, B. Z., Douglas-Palumberi, H., Houshyar, S., Lipschitz, D., Krystal, J. H., et al. (2004). Social supports and serotonin transporter gene moderate depression in maltreated children. *Proceedings of the National Academy of Sciences of the United States of America, 101*(49), 17316–17321.
Kendler, K. S., & Baker, J. H. (2007). Genetic influences on measures of the environment: A systematic review. *Psychological Medicine, 37*(5), 615–626.
Kendler, K. S., Kuhn, J. W., Vittum, J., Prescott, C. A., & Riley, B. (2005). The interaction of stressful life events and a serotonin transporter polymorphism in the prediction of episodes of major depression: A replication. *Archives of General Psychiatry, 62*(5), 529–535.
Kent, L., Doerry, U., Hardy, E., Parmar, R., Gingell, K., Hawi, Z., et al. (2002). Evidence that variation at the serotonin transporter gene influences susceptibility to attention deficit hyperactivity disorder (ADHD): Analysis and pooled analysis. *Molecular Psychiatry, 7*(8), 908–912.
Krishnan, V., Han, M. H., Graham, D. L., Berton, O., Renthal, W., Russo, S. J., et al. (2007). Molecular adaptations underlying susceptibility and resistance to social defeat in brain reward regions. *Cell, 131*(2), 391–404.
Lu, B., Pang, P. T., & Woo, N. H. (2005). The yin and yang of neurotrophin action. *Nature Reviews. Neuroscience, 6*(8), 603–614.
Lupien, S. J., Fiocco, A., Wan, N., Maheu, F., Lord, C., Schramek, T., et al. (2005). Stress hormones and human memory function across the lifespan. *Psychoneuroendocrinology, 30*(3), 225–242.
Lupien, S. J. J., Maheu, F., Tu, M., Fiocco, A., & Schramek, T. E. E. (2007). The effects of stress and stress hormones on human cognition: Implications for the field of brain and cognition. *Brain and Cognition, 65*(3), 209–237.
Mannie, Z. N., Harmer, C. J., & Cowen, P. J. (2007). Increased waking salivary cortisol levels in young people at familial risk of depression. *American Journal of Psychiatry, 164*(4), 617–621.
Martinowich, K., & Lu, B. (2008). Interaction between BDNF and serotonin: Role in mood disorders. *Neuropsychopharmacology, 33*(1): 73–83.
Martinowich, K., Manji, H., & Lu, B. (2007). New insights into BDNF function in depression and anxiety. *Nature Neuroscience, 10*(9), 1089–1093.
McClung, C. A., and Nestler, E. J. (2008). Neuroplasticity mediated by altered gene expression. *Neuropsychopharmacology, 33*(1), 3–17.
McKittrick, C. R., Magarinos, A. M., Blanchard, C., Blanchard, R. J., McEwen, B. S., & Sakai, R. R. (2000). Chronic social stress reduces dendritic arbors in CA3 of hippocampus and decreases binding to serotonin transporter sites. *Synapse, 36*(2), 85–94.
Monteggia, L. M., Luikart, B., Barrot, M., Theobold, D., Malkovska, I., Nef, S., et al. (2007). Brain-derived neurotrophic factor conditional knockouts show gender differences in depression-related behaviors. *Biological Psychiatry, 61*(2), 187–197.

Morley-Fletcher, S., Darnaudery, M., Koehl, M., Casolini, P., Van Reeth, O., & Maccari, S. (2003). Prenatal stress in rats predicts immobility behavior in the forced swim test. Effects of a chronic treatment with tianeptine. *Brain Research, 989*(2), 246–251.

Munafo, M. R., Clark, T. G., Roberts, K. H., & Johnstone, E. C. (2006). Neuroticism mediates the association of the serotonin transporter gene with lifetime major depression. *Neuropsychobiology, 53*(1), 1–8.

Naughton, M., Mulrooney, J. B., & Leonard, B. E. (2000). A review of the role of serotonin receptors in psychiatric disorders. *Human Psychopharmacology, 15*(6), 397–415.

Nestler, E. J., & Carlezon, W. A., Jr. (2006). The mesolimbic dopamine reward circuit in depression. *Biological Psychiatry, 59*(12), 1151–1159.

Netherton, C., Goodyer, I., Tamplin, A., & Herbert, J. (2004). Salivary cortisol and dehydroepiandrosterone in relation to puberty and gender. *Psychoneuroendocrinology, 29*(2), 125–140.

O'Hara, R., Schroder, C. M., Mahadevan, R., Schatzberg, A. F., Lindley, S., Fox, S., et al. (2007). Serotonin transporter polymorphism, memory and hippocampal volume in the elderly: Association and interaction with cortisol. *Molecular Psychiatry, 12*(6), 544–555.

Oitzl, M. S., Workel, J. O., Fluttert, M., Frösch, F., & de Kloet, E. R. (2000). Maternal deprivation affects behaviour from youth to senescence: Amplification of individual differences in spatial learning and memory in senescent Brown Norway rats. *European Journal of Neuroscience, 12*(10), 3771–3780.

Pang, P. T., Teng, H. K., Zaitsev, E., Woo, N. T., Sakata, K., Zhen, S., et al. (2004). Cleavage of proBDNF by tPA/plasmin is essential for long-term hippocampal plasticity. *Science, 306*(5695), 487–491.

Parsey, R. V., Hastings, R. S., Oquendo, M. A., Hu, X., Goldman, D., Yung-yu Huang, M. S., et al. (2006). Effect of a triallelic functional polymorphism of the serotonin-transporter-linked promoter region on expression of serotonin transporter in the human brain. *American Journal of Psychiatry, 163*(1), 48–51.

Pezawas, L., Verchinski, B. A., Mattay, V. S., Callicott, J. H., Kolachana, B. S., Straub, R. E., et al. (2004). The brain-derived neurotrophic factor val66met polymorphism and variation in human cortical morphology. *Journal of Neuroscience, 24*(45), 10099–10102.

Pine, D. S., Cohen, E., Cohen, P., & Brook, J. (1999). Adolescent depressive symptoms as predictors of adult depression: Moodiness or mood disorder? *American Journal of Psychiatry, 156*(1), 133–135.

Renthal, W., Maze, I., Krishnan, V., Covington, III, H. E., Xiao, G., Kumar, A., et al. (2007). Histone deacetylase 5 epigenetically controls behavioral adaptations to chronic emotional stimuli. *Neuron, 56*(3), 517–529.

Rhodes, R. A., Murthy, N. V., Dresner, M. A., Selvaraj, S., Stavrakakis, N., Babar, S., et al. (2007). Human 5-HT transporter availability predicts amygdala reactivity in vivo. *Journal of Neuroscience, 27*(34), 9233–9237.

Roberson-Nay, R., McClure, E. B., Monk, C. S., Nelson, E. E., Guyer, A. E., Fromm, S. J., et al. (2006). Increased amygdala activity during successful memory encoding in adolescent major depressive disorder: An FMRI study. *Biological Psychiatry, 60*(9), 966–973.

Roiser, J. P., Muller, U., Clark, L., & Sahakian, B. J. (2007). The effects of acute tryptophan depletion and serotonin transporter polymorphism on emotional processing in memory and attention. *International Journal of Neuropsychopharmacology, 10*(4), 449–461.

Roozendaal, B., Okuda, S., De Quervain, D. J.-F., & McGaugh, J. L. (2006a). Glucocorticoids interact with emotion-induced noradrenergic activation in influencing different memory functions. *Neuroscience, 138*(3), 901–910.

Roozendaal, B., Okuda, S., Van der Zee, E. A., & McGaugh, J. L. (2006b). Glucocorticoid enhancement of memory requires arousal-induced noradrenergic activation in the basolateral amygdala. *Proceedings of the National Academy of Sciences of the United States of America, 103*(17), 6741–6746.

Rosch, H., Schweigreiter, R., Bonhoeffer, T., Yves-Alain, B., & Korte, M. (2005). The neurotrophin receptor p75NTR modulates long-term depression and regulates the expression of AMPA receptor subunits in the hippocampus. *Proceedings of the National Academy of Sciences of the United States of America, 102*(20), 7362–7367.

Sapolsky, R. M. (2000). Glucocorticoids and hippocampal atrophy in neuropsychiatric disorders. *Archives of General Psychiatry, 57*(10), 925–935.

Seckl, J. R., & Meaney, M. J. (2004). Glucocorticoid programming. *Annals of the New York Academy of Sciences, 1032*, 63–84.

Sen, S., Burmeister, M., & Ghosh, D. (2004). Meta-analysis of the association between a serotonin transporter promoter polymorphism (5-HTTLPR) and anxiety-related personality traits. *American Journal of Medical Genetics. Part B, Neuropsychiatric Genetics, 127*(1), 85–89.

Shirayama, Y., Chen, A. C., Nakagawa, S., Russell, D. S., & Duman, R. S. (2002). Brain-derived neurotrophic factor produces antidepressant effects in behavioral models of depression. *Journal of Neuroscience, 22*(8), 3251–3261.

Stein, M. B., Schork, N. J., & Gelernter, J. (2008). Gene-by-environment (serotonin transporter and childhood maltreatment) interaction for anxiety sensitivity, an intermediate phenotype for anxiety disorders. *Neuropsychopharmacology, 33*, 312–319.

Stohr, T., Wermeling, D. S., Szuran, T., Pliska, V., Domeney, A., Welzl, H., et al. (1998). Differential effects of prenatal stress in two inbred strains of rats. *Pharmacology, Biochemistry, and Behavior, 59*(4), 799–805.

Strauss, J., Barr, C. L., George, C. J., Devlin, B., Vetró, Á., Kiss, E., et al. (2005). Brain-derived neurotrophic factor variants are associated with childhood-onset mood disorder: Confirmation in a Hungarian sample. *Molecular Psychiatry, 10*(9), 861–867.

Strauss, J., Barr, C. L., George, C. J., King, N., Shaikh, S., Devlin, B., et al. (2004). Association study of brain-derived neurotrophic factor in adults with a history of childhood onset mood disorder. *American Journal of Medical Genetics. Part B, Neuropsychiatric Genetics, 131*(1), 16–19.

Surtees, P. G., Wainwright, N. W., Willis-Owen, S. A., Luben, R., Day, N. E., & Flint, J. (2006). Social adversity, the serotonin transporter (5-HTTLPR) polymorphism and major depressive disorder. *Biological Psychiatry, 59*(3), 224–229.

Talge, N. M., Neal, C., & Glover, V. (2007). Antenatal maternal stress and long-term effects on child neurodevelopment: How and why? *Journal of Child Psychology and Psychiatry, and Allied Disciplines, 48*(3–4), 245–261.

Tsankova, N., Renthal, W., Kumar, A., & Nestler, E. J. (2007). Epigenetic regulation in psychiatric disorders. *Nature Reviews Neuroscience, 8*(5), 355–367.

Waggoner, D. (2007). Mechanisms of disease: Epigenesis. *Seminars in Pediatric Neurology, 14*(1), 7–14.

Weaver, I. C., Cervoni, N., Champagne, F. A., D'Alessio, A. C., Sharma, S., Seckl, J. R., et al. (2004). Epigenetic programming by maternal behavior. *Nature Neuroscience, 7*(8), 847–854.

Weaver, I. C., La Plante, P., Weaver, S., Parent, A., Sharma, S., Diorio, J., et al. (2001). Early environmental regulation of hippocampal glucocorticoid receptor gene expression: Characterization of intracellular mediators and potential genomic target sites. *Molecular and Cellular Endocrinology, 185*(1–2), 205–218.

Wilhelm, K., Mitchell, P. B., Niven, H., Finch, A., & Wedgwood, L. (2006). Life events, first depression onset and the serotonin transporter gene. *British Journal of Psychiatry, 188*, 210–215.

Woo, N. H., Teng, H. K., Siao, C.-J., Chiaruttini, C., Pang, P. T., Milner, T. A., et al. (2005). Activation of p75NTR by proBDNF facilitates hippocampal long-term depression. *Nature Neuroscience, 8*(8), 1069–1077.

Zalsman, G., Huang, Y. Y., Oquendo, M. A., Burke, A. K., Hu, X.-Z., Brent, D. A., et al. (2006). Association of a triallelic serotonin transporter gene promoter region (5-HTTLPR) polymorphism with stressful life events and severity of depression. *American Journal of Psychiatry, 163*(9), 1588–1593.

Chapter Ten

The Genetics of Adolescent Depression

JENNIFER Y. F. LAU AND THALIA C. ELEY

CONTENTS

Genetics has become a strong contender in explaining individual differences on many aspects of human behavior, including indices of emotional well-being. This "genetic revolution" has unleashed a steady accumulation of studies aimed at disentangling the role of nature from nurture on internalizing phenotypes, such as depressive symptoms and disorders. As with most research in psychopathology, this emphasis began almost exclusively with examination of adult conditions, before shifting to conditions emerging earlier on in development. Recognition that developmental manifestations of depression are at least as important as adult conditions is driven by epidemiological findings of elevated prevalence of depressive disorders in this age range, and by increasing evidence that adult disorders have their roots in risk processes manifesting during critical periods in development. Nevertheless, extrapolating findings from adult studies to adolescent depression may be unsatisfactory, given unique biological and social changes characterizing adolescence. Among these are pubertal changes in the levels of circulating hormones; maturation of brain circuitry including those underlying affective and cognitive patterns of behavior; and the increasing salience of the peer group with corresponding decreases in the influence of family factors. Studying adolescent-onset depression thus provides a *tabula rasa* or blank slate to draw independent conclusions of the heritability of early onset conditions. While initial genetic studies focused on confirming the role of genetic influences on adolescent depression, a more recent trend has combined genetics with accounts of emotional problems that are rooted in psychology and neuroscience. This integrative approach promises greater understanding of intermediate pathways by which genetic risks impinge on behavior.

The current chapter reviews behavioral genetic studies of depressive disorders and related symptoms in adolescence. The first section presents a brief outline of the principles of behavioral genetic methodology utilized to explore the contributions of genes and the environment on behavioral phenotypes. Second, we describe how these methods have been applied to developmental research on depressive outcomes. Quantitative genetic studies generally support a heritable basis for adolescent depression in addition to substantial environmental contributions, but data also implicate complex trends in the size and nature of these effects relative to age and development, sex and the severity of the condition. We discuss these trends, contextualizing studies of adolescence within a wider literature of developmental changes in childhood and adolescence, a major theme of this section. The third section focuses on identifying specific genes that have been implicated in depressive disorders by molecular studies. As comparatively fewer studies are published with respect to adolescent depression, mainly adult studies are reviewed. In the final two sections, some of the more novel questions dominating the agenda of recent quantitative and molecular research are discussed. Rather than simply identifying the *level* of genetic and environmental influence, recent studies pose questions of *how* genetic and environmental risks are expressed through intermediate pathways to affect the phenotype, drawing on findings from psychology and neuroscience. Two main approaches are discussed. The first addresses the interplay between genetic and environmental factors on these phenotypes, whereas the second aims to identify specific risk markers, also termed endophenotypes, which potentially mediate risk effects associated with the distal genotype on the behavioral signs and symptoms of the phenotype.

TYPES OF GENETIC DESIGN

Behavioral genetic designs delineate the causes of behavioral variation between individual members as a function of genetic and environmental risk factors (for an introduction to behavioral genetics, the reader is referred to Plomin, DeFries, McClearn, & McGuffin, 2001). The direction of causation between genes and behavior is assumed to be one-way, such that naturally occurring variation in the sequencing of DNA molecules that characterize an individual's genotype affects behavior. Behaviors, in turn, cannot alter genetic variation except in unusual circumstances, such as exposure to high levels of ionizing radiation that may lead to genetic mutation. As genetic influences do not account for all variation on a phenotype, the remainder is assigned to shared and nonshared environmental factors (and measurement error). The first refers to aspects of the environment that make family members resemble one another, whereas the second are factors that make family members dissimilar. Shared environmental influences could include parental educational levels, socioeconomic status (SES), and parental psychopathology, which may contribute to similarity in the risk for depression on children growing up in the same family environment. Nonshared environmental influences may comprise family factors too, such as differential treatment by parents of siblings, and also extrafamilial sources, such as friendships. Partitioning individual variation on behavioral phenotypes into these contributions comprises one core component of behavioral genetic research. To this end, well-established quantitative designs, such as family, twin, and adoption studies, capitalize on the different genetic relationships between family members to infer genetic and environmental effects on phenotypes such as depression.

Whilst quantitative designs can demonstrate the heritability of depression, these are inferred and thus considered "unmeasured" with no assumptions made on the identity of specific genes. In contrast, *molecular* genetic approaches yield direct evidence for the role of genes by examining the effects of DNA polymorphisms, stretches of DNA containing variation in the sequencing of base-pair molecules on the observable behaviors of the phenotype (for more details on molecular genetic methods, the reader is referred to Eley & Craig, 2005; Eley & Rijsdijk, 2005). Depression, like other complex phenotypes, shows a mode of transmission implying the contribution of multiple genes of small effect size. These are known as quantitative trait loci (QTLs) and refer specifically to genes involved in determining individual differences of continuously measured traits, of which the extreme ends may comprise disordered individuals. As dimensional phenotypes differ from classic Mendelian traits (typically under the influence of a single gene), classical designs used for single-gene disorders may not be appropriate for complex phenotypes. Rather, designs with greater statistical power to detect their effects are needed. Linkage and association designs are two common strategies used to identify specific genes. Both methods make use of genetic markers, which are stretches of DNA that vary between members of a population. Linkage studies examine different genetic markers and levels of a phenotypic trait or disorder within families, and association studies examine gene-trait associations within populations. Often, association studies target certain genetic polymorphisms that have known functional effects within a neurobiological system that has been implicated in the pathogenesis of a disorder. Such an approach is known as a candidate gene approach. For depression, these have included extensive study of the serotonin system.

QUANTITATIVE GENETIC STUDIES OF DEPRESSION IN YOUNG PEOPLE

Family and twin studies converge broadly on the conclusion that early-onset depression symptoms are both familial and heritable with large contributions from environmental factors (for a review, see Rice, Harold, & Thapar, 2002a). Elevated rates of major depression in first-degree relatives of child probands (Birmaher, Ryan, Williamson, Brent, & Kaufman, 1996) and among the offspring of depressed parents (Weissman, Warner, Wichramaratne, Moreau, & Olfson, 1997) relative to family members of healthy and psychiatric controls have been reported in family studies. Similarly, twin studies document moderate genetic influences, weaker shared environmental effects, and large nonshared environmental contributions. Adoption studies, on the other hand, have reported negligible genetic and shared environmental effects (Eley, Deater-Deckard, Fombonne, Fulker, & Plomin, 1998; van den Oord, Boomsma, & Verhulst, 1994). Few convincing explanations for these conflictual findings exist, but one area of certainty is that patterns of genetic and environmental influences on vulnerability to depression are far from straightforward, with complex effects of age and development, sex and symptom severity on genetic and environmental parameters.

Age and Developmental Trends

As twin births are less common than singleton births, the recruitment of twins is as much driven by logistics as theoretical considerations. Thus, unlike non-genetic studies, it often becomes difficult to "pick and choose" subjects from a distinct subset of the population to test specific relationships. Rather than using rigorous experimental manipulations, twin studies examine age-related and developmental trends of genetic effects, by relying on cross-sectional comparisons of the magnitude of genetic and environmental indices in different age groups within one study or across the wider literature. The age range of each age group is typically wider than what is ideally required to detect more subtle developmental trends; such cross-sectional studies generally have shown larger genetic and smaller shared environmental effects in adolescents than in children (Eley & Stevenson, 1999; Hewitt, Silberg, Neale, Eaves, & Erickson, 1992; Rice et al., 2002; Scourfield et al., 2003; Silberg et al., 1999; Silberg, Rutter, & Eaves, 2001a; Thapar & McGuffin, 1994).

Whilst these results have important implications for the well-documented increases in rates of depression during adolescence, these conclusions are premature for at least three reasons. First, it is unclear whether age-related changes occur in both males and females. Two studies have reported larger genetic effects in adolescent females (Hewitt et al., 1992; Silberg et al., 1999; Silberg et al., 2001b), but another found increases in adolescent males only (Eley & Stevenson, 1999). Yet another showed greater genetic effects among both males and females in adolescence (Scourfield et al., 2003). These discrepant findings emphasize the importance of considering age-related changes in the context of sex effects. Second, it has been hard to reconcile findings of decreasing genetic effects over time during adolescence (O'Connor, McGuire, Reiss, Hetherington, & Plomin, 1998a; O'Connor, Neiderhiser, Reiss, Hetherington, & Plomin, 1998b) and the opposite trend during childhood: substantial genetic influences in early childhood (54–76% at 3 years) compared to middle childhood (34–48% between 7 and 12 years) (Boomsma, van Beijsterveldt, & Hudziak, 2005; van der Valk, van den Oord, Verhulst, & Boomsma, 2003). Thus, changes in heritability and shared environment across development appear to be nonlinear, possibly reflecting a u-shaped curve. Finally, different results may characterize severe populations, such that genetic influences are smaller and shared environmental factors larger in adolescent high-scorers (e.g., Deater-Deckard, Reiss, Hetherington, & Plomin, 1997; Eley, 1997; Gjone, Stevenson, Sundet, & Eilertsen, 1996; Rice et al., 2002). Far from providing simple answers, these discrepant findings point to further research.

A parallel line of enquiry to examining cross-sectional comparisons of age groups has studied continuity and change in genetic and environmental influences. While "continuity" in genetic and environmental influences is inferred by the presence of "stable" factors that persist across different ages (within individuals), "changes" in these etiological influences is reflected through age-specific factors that emerge during particular developmental periods. Two of these studies have demonstrated that whereas genetic factors persisted over a period of 3 years, "new" environmental effects emerged across time (O'Connor et al., 1998b; Silberg et al., 1999). A further three studies have reported results deviating from this pattern. Using a sample that spanned childhood as well as adolescence (5–14 years), Scourfield and colleagues (2003) showed the emergence of "new" genetic influences over a 3-year period with shared and some nonshared environmental influences remaining stable. In a second study of childhood only, "new" genetic factors also emerged at ages 3 and 7 with some persistence of genetic influence across time (van der Valk et al., 2003). Finally, our own work has explored genetic and environmental continuity and change at three time-points in adolescence and young adulthood where the average ages of the sample were: 14 years 5 months, 15 years, and 17 years and 8 months (Lau & Eley, 2008). Results showed a rather consistent profile of genetic effects across time (45%, 40%, and 45% at each time-point, respectively), decreasing shared environmental effects (19%, 9%, and 0%), but increasing nonshared environmental effects (36%, 51%, and 55%). Decomposing these influences into the effect of stable and new factors, genes contributed primarily towards the continuity of symptoms across time, although new genetic factors were evident at the second time-point, which corresponds roughly to midadolescence. "New" nonshared environmental effects emerged at each time-point and, overall, these factors contributed to change rather than stability of symptoms.

The reasons these differences between these studies exist is not immediately obvious. They may be due to design-related artifacts, such as the measure used to assess depression, the informant or rater, sex composition of the sample, or length of follow-up. A more intriguing alternative is that there are genuine differences between the distinct developmental transition periods assessed in each study (early childhood to middle childhood, middle childhood to adolescence, within adolescence, and adolescence to young adulthood), which are driven by developmentally sensitive etiological influences. The possibility that new genes and new environmental influences come "online" at different stages to account for developmental changes will require further investigation.

Sex Effects

As with age, sex-related differences in the size of genetic and environmental influences on depressive symptoms between males and females are indicated in some studies, though the direction of these differences has been difficult to decipher. Four studies show greater genetic effects among adolescent females (Boomsma et al., 2000; Jacobson & Rowe, 1999; Scourfield et al., 2003; Silberg et al., 1999) whilst two others report larger estimates in adolescent males (Eley & Stevenson, 1999; Rice et al., 2002). In children, there is some consensus that females show larger genetic effects (Eley & Stevenson, 1999; Happonen et al., 2002; Scourfield et al., 2003; van der Valk et al., 2003), although this has not always been replicated (Hewitt et al., 1992; van der Valk et al., 2003). Yet still other studies have found no sex differences in either age group (Bartels et al., 2003; Bartels et al., 2004; Gjone & Stevenson, 1997; Lau, Eley & Rijsdijk, 2006; Thapar & McGuffin, 1994). Together these studies provide only modest evidence of sex differences in the heritability of depression, with some suggestion that these variations may be relatively subtle, for example, emerging only at particular ages. Another possibility is that sex differences do not lie in the magnitude of genetic influences on depressive symptoms, but rather in the expression of the genetic vulnerability (e.g., Hankin & Abramson, 2001).

Extreme Scoring Individuals

At least six papers have reported genetic and environmental influences on various definitions of "extreme" depression: five of these have assessed high scores on questionnaire measures of depression (Deater-Deckard et al., 1997; Eley, 1997; Gjone et al., 1996; Rende, Plomin, Reiss, & Hetherington, 1993; Rice et al., 2002), and one has analyzed diagnostic data (Glowinski, Madden, Bucholz, Lynskey, & Heath, 2003). Compared with individuals scoring in the normal range, results of the former analyses are reasonably consistent in suggesting that there are nonsignificant trends for genetic effects to be lower and shared environmental factors to be greater among individuals reporting high scores on questionnaire measures (Deater-Deckard et al., 1997; Eley, 1997; Rende et al., 1993; Rice et al., 2002). Unexpectedly, this pattern does not extend to results from diagnostic data, which demonstrated comparable heritability and shared environmental effects to normal-ranged individuals. Given that this latter study constitutes only one of its kind, further replications will be needed before these results are interpreted to imply differences between data from questionnaires and from clinical interviews.

The papers analyzing extreme scores on questionnaire measures also hint at age-related trends, such that genetic influences are sizably larger and shared environmental effects smaller in high-scoring children, whilst nonsignificant decreases in genetic effects and increases in shared environmental effects characterize older high-scoring individuals (Gjone et al., 1996; Rice, Harold, & Thapar, 2003). Together, these results suggest that etiological influences in the development of "severe" depression are somewhat different between childhood and adolescence. These two studies also reported no significant sex differences in group heritability and shared environmental effects. Thus, at present until further study, etiological mechanisms operating at the extremes may be similar for girls and boys.

Summary

Exploration of more intricate trends in genetic and environmental effects on depressive symptoms, such as the effects of age and development, sex and the severity of symptoms has been made possible by the increased efforts to recruit large, epidemiological samples of child and adolescent twins and siblings over the last two decades. These findings have not always been definitive, nevertheless they provide a potential platform for explaining certain epidemiological findings in the presentation of depression. Most notably, changes in the size of genetic and environmental factors or in the emergence of "new" influences may provide possible accounts of observed age- and sex-related trends on prevalence rates during midpuberty. In addition, establishing the level of genetic and environmental effects in high scoring individuals (those presumably at increased risk for disorder) with those falling in the normal range can offer insight into whether the former set of individuals represent an etiological disjunction. This can, in turn, contribute towards resolving the conflicting categorical and dimensional conceptualizations of depression.

MOLECULAR GENETIC STUDIES OF DEPRESSION

The results from genome-wide scans of adult unipolar depression have only recently been published (for a more detailed review the reader is referred to Levinson, 2005), implicating broad regions within chromosomes 1, 2, 3, 4, 5, 6, 7, 8, 10, 11, 12, 15, and 18 as containing putative susceptibility genes. The areas identified are still too broad to pinpoint exact locations despite some overlap between studies (chromosomes 1, 4, 6, 7, 8, 11, and 12). Whereas conclusions from linkage studies have not been too fruitful, association studies guided by a priori knowledge that a particular genetic system is involved in the pathogenesis of depression have been more rewarding. The serotonergic (5HT) neurotransmitter system is by far the most popular neurobiological system targeted in locating candidate genes, a choice fuelled largely by prevailing physiological theories that the activity of monoaminergic neurotransmitters is somewhat compromised in individuals with depression (for a review on the neurobiology of depression, see Hirschfeld, 2000). Molecular genetic studies have concentrated on a number of genes known to code for different steps of this transmission, given that little is known about which regulatory processes involved in the chemical transmission of serotonin is responsible for the deficiency in levels (Manji, Drevets, & Charney, 2001). These have included genetic variants located within the serotonin transporter gene, serotonin receptor genes, and genes that code the monoamine oxidase type A (MAOA) and tryptophan hydroxylase (TPH1) enzymes. Both positive and negative results, replications and nonreplications, have been reported (for more details on individual studies, the reader is referred to Huezo-Diaz et al., 2005; Levinson, 2005). Thus far, there are good theoretically driven reasons for examining genetic variants involved in the release and regulation of serotonin, but the field is still in its infancy, and studies of children and adolescents have been rare.

Expansions into other candidate gene systems have included other members of the monoamine family, such as the noradrenergic and dopaminergic pathways, which may be involved in the brain reward systems; the hypothalamic-pituitary-adrenal axis, which is responsible for activating hormonal responses towards acute and chronic stressors (Villafuerte et al., 2002); and different neurotrophic factors, such as brain-derived neurotropic factor, which are implicated by more recent theories of the effects of neuroprotection and cellular resilience on the development of depression (Manji et al., 2001). Conclusions on their application within molecular genetic designs are far from definitive despite this relatively rich database of information on the functional significance of particular genes.

Identifying QTLs has proven challenging across almost all complex traits, and reports of high false positive rates and poor replicability across studies tend to characterize the field in general. The main reason is that complex phenotypes such as depression are multifactorial. This implies that not only are their multiple genes of small effect size accounting for the phenotype, but there are also important contributions by the social environment across time. Three different issues that contribute towards the issue of replication of linkage and association studies arise as a result of this complexity. First, because QTLs are probabilistic rather than deterministic, affected sibling pairs may not all share all chromosomal segments containing these. Or they may share many segments by chance. Second, there may be heterogeneity in the etiology of a phenotype. As phenotypes are defined essentially at the behavioral level (rather than by etiology), the same repertoire of symptoms may represent different genetic underpinnings or the sole effects of environmental adversity (phenocopies), which could lead to no differences observed in the comparison between groups. Finally, as there may be interplay between genetic and environmental influences (gene–environment interaction), there may be individuals who carry the susceptibility gene but who do not manifest the phenotype as they have not encountered the appropriate environmental event (reduced penetrance). Similarly, there may be interactions among different genetic loci (epistasis), which cannot be easily captured by studying genes independently.

Summary

The development of more sophisticated techniques to obtain and analyze DNA in recent years has made the collection of genotype information a very real possibility for many researchers. Although there are issues of high false positive rates and poor replicability across studies, somewhat dampening the excitement surrounding molecular genetics, gradual inclusion of genotype data in large, longitudinal samples promises to revolutionize the field of psychiatric genetics. Nowhere more exciting is the introduction of these applications within pediatric samples, which already possesses high-quality psychosocial and phenotypic data at their disposal. This first wave of studies can further engage questions on the role of development, providing a lens to view the dynamic expression of genetic and environmental factors across time.

GENE–ENVIRONMENT INTERPLAY AND DEPRESSIVE CONDITIONS

The importance of genetic influences on environmental risk exposure (gene–environment correlation) and genetic influences on the susceptibility to environmental risks (gene–environment interaction) in relation to depressive phenotypes has been confirmed by a growing body of literature. Examining these processes of interplay reflects one approach to understanding risk mechanisms leading to emotional outcomes. Each is discussed.

Gene–Environment Correlations

Gene–environment correlations imply the presence of genetic influences on exposure to an environmental condition. These may be manifested in three contexts (Scarr & McCartney, 1983). *Passive* gene–environment correlation (rG-E) comes about due to the sharing in biological families of both genes and environment. Thus, it occurs when the effects of parental genotype are related to the family environments their children are exposed to. For example, offspring of depressed mothers are likely to receive both a genetic predisposition for this condition and the environmental effects of a depressogenic parenting style, which may characterize the interpersonal styles of these mothers.

Evocative rG-E refers to the genetic propensity of some individuals to elicit or evoke certain reactions from others. Intermediate factors, such as temperament or cognitive style factors may mediate these effects. Thus, infants who cry easily or show irritability may be more likely to elicit negative reactions from caregivers, which may then impact on parenting style. Finally, *active* rG-E occurs when individuals select, create, and modify their environmental experiences based on particular genetically mediated dispositions. Behaviorally inhibited or shy individuals may be less likely to seek out friends instead choosing to engage in solitary play, thus ultimately influencing socioemotional development.

Mostly relying on findings from quantitative genetic designs, long-standing support for genetic influences on many aspects of the environment has been documented (Plomin & Bergeman, 1991). These studies have shown first that many "social" risks such as stressful life events aggregate in families (e.g., Rijsdijk et al., 2001), but more impressively, genetic influences have been found on an astonishing array of family environment variables, including family connectedness (Jacobson & Rowe, 1999), parent–child interaction as assessed by questionnaire (Plomin, Reiss, Hetherington, & Howe, 1994), observation (O'Connor, Hetherington, Reiss, & Plomin, 1995) or both (Pike, McGuire, Hetherington, Reiss, & Plomin, 1996), sibling interactions assessed by questionnaire alone (Plomin et al., 1994) or combined with observation (Pike et al., 1996), parental divorce (O'Connor, Caspi, DeFries, & Plomin, 2000), and life events (Silberg et al., 1999; Thapar, Harold, & McGuffin, 1998; Thapar & McGuffin, 1996). Collectively these findings suggest that the origins of the family environment are more complex than previously thought. Yet, what is most pertinent to studying risk mechanisms on depression is not that genes influence environments per se, but that genetic vulnerability involved in the phenotype is expressed through exposure towards high-risk environments. In other words, genes involved in the development of symptoms should overlap to some extent with those influencing aspects of the individual's environment. This has also been widely reported in many adolescent studies, including ours. We examined genetic and environmental influences on maternal punitive discipline and negative life events in our adolescent sample described previously (Lau & Eley, 2006). Moderate genetic effects emerged on both measures (at 31%), implicating the presence of gene–environment correlation. Next, we explored shared genetic influences between each social risk measure and depressive symptoms. Consistent with other examples in the literature (e.g., Eaves, Silberg, & Erkanli, 2003; Pike et al., 1996; Rice et al., 2003; Silberg et al., 1999; Thapar et al., 1998), there was significant overlap in genetic influences between symptoms and each social risk. Together, these results suggest that genetic liability on the phenotype may be expressed partly through creation of certain environmental risks.

Despite widespread evidence for gene–environment correlations, it has been challenging to analytically distinguish between the different types. The various psychosocial paths through which genetic effects may be expressed across development have been usefully speculated upon through this taxonomy. For example, it has been suggested that passive and evocative forms may be more salient in childhood, whilst active processes become increasingly important in adolescence when individuals play a more dynamic role in shaping their own experiences. Indeed, one study which has explored developmental differences, compared the relative contribution of genetic and environmental factors to the relationship between negative life events and depression in two age groups: 8–11 and 12–17 years (Rice et al., 2003). Genes played a larger role in this association among older adolescents compared to the child group, lending support to the notion that active gene–environment correlation, which presumably underlies the genetic effects on negative life events, is of stronger importance to symptoms in the older age group. The emergence of active processes could also reflect the new genetic influences that emerge in this age range (Lau & Eley, 2008; Scourfield et al., 2003).

Gene–Environment Interactions

Gene–environment interactions arise when environmental risk effects change as a function of genetic risk, or when genetic risks are expressed only in the presence of an environmental stressor. In terms of risk mechanisms, interactions may refer to genetic influences on reactivity towards the environment or when a stressor elicits (latent) genetic susceptibilities. In spite of difficulties demonstrating gene–environment interactions in depressive conditions, this has not prevented an accumulation of quantitative and molecular studies dedicated towards finding these effects.

One possibility for exploring interactions is through family designs. An earlier study of our adolescent sample exemplifies this approach, by examining the main and interactive effects of a composite index of parental familial vulnerability to anxiety, depression, and neuroticism and other social aspects of the family environment on self-reported depressive symptoms in the adolescent offspring (Eley et al., 2004a). The composite index of vulnerability maximizes familial liability to emotional conditions and is likely to reflect the effects of shared genes among family members (Sham et al., 2000). Of the environmental variables, only educational level, assessed on an eight-point scale ranging from no qualifications to postgraduate degree was a significant predictor of severe adolescent depressive symptoms independent of age, sex, parental familial vulnerability score, and parental BMI. Offspring of parents with no educational qualifications were more than twice as likely to score in the severe depressive symptoms group. Interestingly, a significant interaction also emerged between the continuous measure of genetic liability (labeled low, intermediate, and high G scores, Figure 10.1) and parental educational level on adolescent symptoms (see Figure 10.1). Adolescents who displayed high levels of familial risk for depression and whose parents had no educational qualifications had the highest symptom scores. This implies that adolescents in families with high rates of depression are particularly at risk for depression themselves if their parents lack qualifications. Coping strategies and ability to seek help may mediate this effect as these may all be improved in families where educational qualifications have been obtained.

Despite their provocativeness, these findings are also limited by a failure to discount the alternative suggestion that the familial composite reflects shared environmental influences rather than shared genes among family members. The twin design is again required to disentangle these sources. A study of adolescent females (Silberg, Rutter, Neale, & Eaves, 2001b) showed that negative life events (an environmental risk) exacerbated genetic effects on self-reported depressive (and anxiety) symptoms. Second, individuals at genetic risk for depression (and anxiety), indexed by the presence of parental

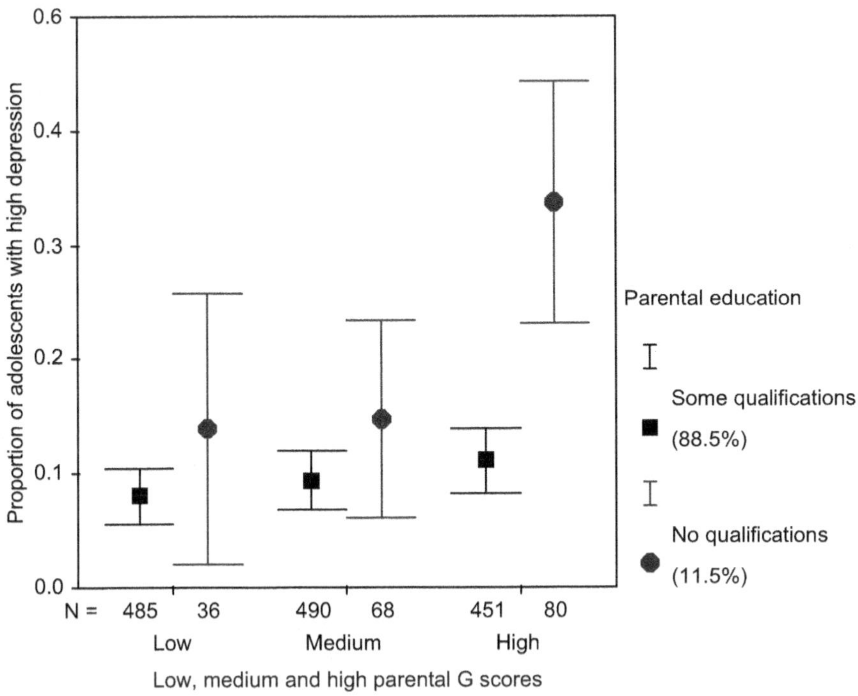

Figure 10.1 Parental educational influences on genetic risk to severe depression.

emotional disorders, were more likely to exhibit depressive symptoms following recent negative life events. Thus, the first test represents differences in genetic effects across levels of environmental risk, whereas the second showed genetic influences on reactivity towards environmental risk.

In studies of interactions, it is important to consider whether confounding effects are due to gene–environment correlation. Often, genetic risks for depression that increase social adversity may be misinterpreted as interactions. In fact the validity of interactions is premised on an assumption that there is no association between an individual's genetic makeup and their experience of particular environments. This can therefore be violated when gene–environment correlations are present, as these occur by definition when individuals with a certain genotype are more likely to be exposed to particular environmental events. What this amounts to is that when testing for interactions, it must be very clear that the environmental variable examined is not influenced by genes that are also associated with behavioral outcomes. Should this be the case, this may signify a gene–environment correlation on the phenotype rather than an interaction. Yet, as gene–environment correlations and interactions are likely to coexist, a more sophisticated approach is needed to simultaneously assess but differentiate these effects (Purcell, 2002).

To this end, we explored whether genetic effects on depressive outcomes varied as a function of maternal punitive discipline and negative life events (GxE) after controlling for genetic effects found on these variables. Both social risk measures reflected the joint presence of gene–environment correlation and interaction. Thus, genetic influences on adolescent depression were not only shared with those on punitive parenting or life events (gene–environment correlation), but they were also moderated by the presence of these risks (gene–environment interaction) such that genetic variance increased substantially with higher levels of each environmental risk. On the basis of these results, adolescents with higher genetic liability are more likely to be exposed to the double disadvantage of environmental risk (gene–environment correlation). Furthermore, under these high levels of adversity, genetic risks for depression have greater opportunity to be expressed (gene–environment interaction).

Using measures of the environment and candidate genes in molecular studies may represent a more precise method of assessing gene–environment interactions. A ground-breaking study first showed an interaction between a functional polymorphism in the serotonin (5-HT) transporter promoter region and the effect of life events, in relation to depression symptoms in adults (Caspi et al., 2003). The 5-HT transporter gene is involved in regulatory processes during stress (Hariri et al., 2002), making it an excellent candidate for interaction with environmental stress. The polymorphism exists in two forms, a "long" and a "short" form. The short allele is less efficient than the longer allele, thus leading to differences in available serotonin in the brain (Lesch et al., 1996). Analyses revealed that the effects of stressful life events were significantly stronger among individuals carrying one or two copies of the short form of the allele "s", as shown by an increase in symptom frequencies and severity. This allele also moderated the longitudinal prediction from childhood maltreatment to adult depression. We subsequently replicated this finding in adolescent females, with an interaction between the same serotonin transporter regulatory region and a family-based measure of environmental risk (including social adversity, family life events, and parental employment level) (Eley et al., 2004b). The effects of family-based environmental risk were significantly stronger among female adolescents who possessed at least one short allele (see Figure 10.2). Together, these findings suggest that this allelic variant augments effects of stress on emotional symptoms.

Convergence of both quantitative and molecular support has allowed the study of gene–environment interactions to become a topical area of research. However, these concepts are not entirely unfamiliar among psychologists,

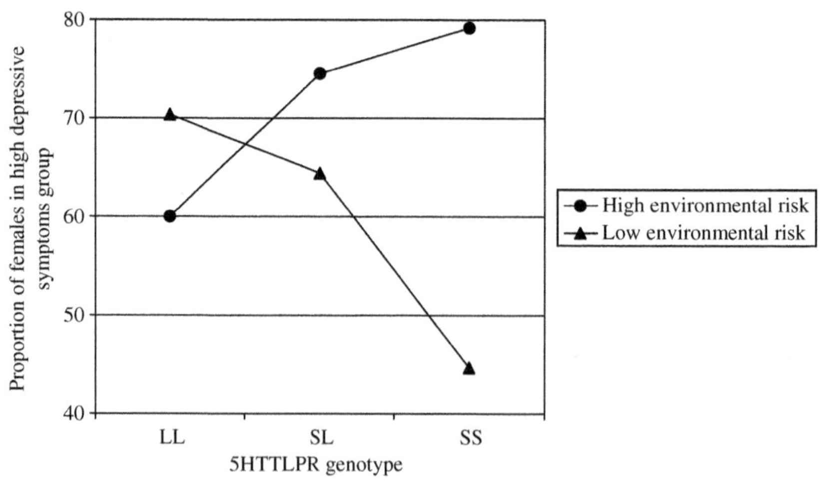

Figure 10.2 Impact of environmental risks on depressive symptom group by genotype in adolescent females.

who have long used diathesis-stress theories to define the mechanisms by which latent predispositions are elicited by the occurrence of environmental stressors. By suggesting that genetic effects act on core processes associated with stress reactivity, findings of gene–environment interaction may be viewed as an extension of these ideas. This possibility is touched upon in greater detail next.

INTERMEDIATE PHENOTYPES AS MEDIATORS OF GENETIC AND ENVIRONMENTAL RISK

The search for intermediate phenotypes that reflect or even mediate the risks associated with these influences is another approach to understanding genetic and environmental risk mechanisms on depression. Endophenotypes are risk markers or vulnerability traits that are more proximal to, and thus more directly influenced by the genes relevant to a behavioral disorder than are its signs and symptoms (Gottesman & Gould, 2003). As endophenotypes were assumed to share one or more of the same genes that confer vulnerability to the disorder of interest and to reflect more simplistic genetic phenomena, it follows that their use may result in greater statistical power for detection of susceptibility genes. A more subtle function of endophenotypes, however, lies in illuminating elusive pathways by which genes for behaviors are expressed. More specifically they provide a means for identifying traits "upstream" to the products of gene expression, but "downstream" from the clinical phenotype (Gottesman & Gould, 2003). As such, they can be identified at differing levels of analysis including neurophysiological, biochemical, endocrinological, neuroanatomical, cognitive, and neuropsychological measures. Several criteria have been proposed to help locate putative endophenotypes (e.g., Gottesman & Gould, 2003; Skuse, 2001; Waldman, 2005). First, the marker should co-occur with the disorder and its symptoms in the general population (as well as in clinical groups). Second, the marker should be relatively state-independent rather than an epiphenomenon of the illness and measured with good reliability. Ideally it should also possess temporal stability and be a developmental precursor to symptoms. The third and fourth criteria are that endophenotypes should show evidence of heritability and familial (genetic) overlap with the disorder of interest, respectively.

There are two possible approaches to identifying endophenotypes. Bottom-up accounts adopt a neuroscience explanation, beginning at the level of genes, to gene expression, to protein function, to neurotransmitters, neural circuitry, and behavior. In comparison, top-down accounts work in the opposite direction, working backwards from an individual's behaviors, reported cognitions, psychological mechanisms, brain function, and genes. Any of these intermediate levels could reflect plausible candidate markers. Despite extensive reviews of putative adult psychopathological and biological endophenotypes for affective disorders (Hasler, Drevets, Manji, & Charney, 2004), identifying endophenotypes of adolescent depression has been somewhat lacking, falling behind that of other juvenile phenotypes, such as ADHD, which have been the topic of various comprehensive reviews (Doyle et al., 2005a; Doyle et al., 2005b; Waldman, 2005). Given the relevance of gene–environment interactions on depression in younger samples, aspects of stress reactivity comprise particularly promising candidates. In our group, we have taken a top-down approach to the identification of these markers, with a particular interest in cognitive biases traditionally implicated in the development of these emotional behaviors. As some of these cognitive biases are considered to influence an individual's response towards external, particularly negative events, we speculated that they may reflect genetic risk markers that were expressed through increased stress reactivity, thus accounting for gene–environment interactions. Given that these cognitive factors were identified through many existing and well-articulated cognitive models of depression, their association with depression was already established. Thus, the next steps we took in evaluating their potential as genetic markers were to explore their genetic and environmental structure and the nature of their links with depressive conditions.

One of our first studies addressed these questions in relation to adolescent attributional style (Lau et al., 2006). According to the learned helplessness model (Abramson, Seligman, & Teasdale, 1978), later reformulated as the hopelessness theory (Alloy, Abramson, Metalsky, & Hartlage, 1988) attributional style is a risk factor for depression. Individuals who attribute negative events to internal (directed to the self), stable (likely to persist across time), and global (likely to affect many aspects of life) causes are thought to have increased risks for experiencing depression. These individuals may also possess an opposite pattern of attributions for positive events, such that these are interpreted using external, unstable, and specific reasons. This differential style of responding to environmental events is thought to be fully expressed in the presence of life events, as a diathesis to stress. Given robust evidence in favor of this (e.g., Hankin, Abramson, & Siler, 2001), we set out to unravel its genetic and environmental etiology. Analyses of self-reported data on adolescent attributional style revealed that like depressive symptoms this cognitive factor was primarily influenced by genes (35%) and nonshared environmental effects (60%) (Lau et al., 2006). Moreover, common genetic and nonshared environmental influences between attributional style and concurrent depressive symptoms, which contributed towards their phenotypic relationship, were found. Thus, negative attributions are more than just a learned trait, but are also heritable. More provocatively, these results are consistent with the interpretation that attributional style reflects some genetic liability on depression.

CONCLUDING REMARKS

Depression represents a common psychiatric problem reported in adolescence, a time in which prevalence rates soar against a backdrop of turbulent biological, psychological, and social changes. Given that such conditions are often associated with psychosocial impairment (Lewinsohn, Solomon, Seeley, & Zeiss, 2000) and with continuity into adulthood (Pine, Cohen, Cohen, & Brook, 1999), identifying risk factors poses a priority for mental health researchers. Behavioral genetics offers a unique approach by providing an integrative framework in which to study not only the effects of nature, but also of nurture. With the exception of some discrepancies in the results of particular study designs, the application of behavioral genetic methodology to the study of adolescent depressive symptoms and disorders has highlighted the importance of studying both these sources. Pairing more sophisticated conceptual questions with newer analytical tools has moved the field beyond examining the *extent* of genetic and environmental influences, to asking questions about first, the *nature* of these effects, and second, *how* these may be expressed.

The first set of questions is important because they may provide an explanatory framework for contextualizing results from the epidemiology of adolescent depression. Thus, findings of how genetic and environmental influences vary across age and development and sex may have important implications for understanding age- and sex-related trends in prevalence. Meanwhile, comparing genetic and environmental etiology of individuals reporting higher levels of symptoms with individuals falling in the normal range can offer insight into whether the former set of individuals represent an etiological disjunction, thus challenging (or validating) the proposed continuum between symptoms and disorders. The second set of questions, focusing on the interplay between genetic and environmental influences on the development of symptoms and possible intermediate factors and processes by which genetic and environmental risks take effect on behavioral outcomes is also relevant for the elucidation of risk mechanisms. A successful search for endophenotypes has necessitated the integration of different levels of explanation that stem from other disciplinary approaches, such as neuroscience and psychology within genetic studies. Moreover, such integrative studies should be considered in the context of developmental change, that is, the differences in the interplay between factors across different stages of development. This is where the collaboration between neuroscientists, psychologists, and behavioral geneticists will prove to be the most fruitful, with the opportunity to piece together what at first seem to be rather discrepant parts of a puzzle, to building an overall picture of the development of depression. At present, integrative studies have either selected top-down (behavior-cognitions-brains-genes) or bottom-up (genes-protein-function-behavior) approaches, but eventually studies need to attempt the more ambitious task of considering these approaches in parallel.

REFERENCES

Abramson, L. Y., Seligman, M. E. P., & Teasdale, J. D. (1978). Learned helplessness in humans: Critique and reformulation. *Journal of Abnormal Psychology, 87,* 49–74.

Alloy, L. B., Abramson, L. Y., Metalsky, G. I., & Hartlage, S. (1988). The hopelessness theory of depression: Attributional aspects. *British Journal of Clinical Psychology, 27,* 5–21.

Bartels, M., Boomsma, D. I., Hudziak, J. J., Rietveld, M. J., Van Beijsterveldt, T. C., & van den Oord, E. J. (2004). Disentangling genetic, environmental, and rater effects on internalizing and externalizing problem behavior in 10-year-old twins. *Twin Research, 7,* 162–175.

Bartels, M., Hudziak, J. J., Boomsma, D. I., Rietveld, M. J., Van Beijsterveldt, T. C., & van den Oord, E. J. (2003). A study of parent ratings of internalizing and externalizing problem behavior in 12-year-old twins. *Journal of the American Academy of Child & Adolescent Psychiatry, 42,* 1351–1359.

Birmaher, B., Ryan, N. D., Williamson, D. E., Brent, D. A., & Kaufman, J. (1996). Childhood and adolescent depression: A review of the past 10 years. Part II. *Journal of the American Academy of Child & Adolescent Psychiatry, 35,* 1575–1583.

Boomsma, D. I., Beem, A. L., van den Berg., M., Dolan, C. V., Koopmans, J. R., Vink, J. M., et al. (2000). Netherlands twin family study of anxious depression (NETSAD). *Twin Research, 3*, 323–334.

Boomsma, D. I., van Beijsterveldt, C. E. M., & Hudziak, J. J. (2005). Genetic and environmental influences on anxious/depression during childhood: A study from the Netherlands Twin Register. *Genes, Brain and Behavior, 4*(8), 466–481.

Caspi, A., Sugden, K., Moffitt, T. E., Taylor, A., Craig, I. W., Harrington, H., et al. (2003). Influence of life stress on depression: Moderation by a polymorphism in the 5-HTT gene. *Science, 301*, 386–389.

Deater-Deckard, K., Reiss, D., Hetherington, E. M., & Plomin, R. (1997). Dimensions and disorders of adolescent adjustment: A quantitative genetic analysis of unselected samples and selected extremes. *Journal of Child Psychology and Psychiatry, 38*, 515–525.

Doyle, A. E., Faraone, S. V., Seidman, L. J., Willcutt, E. G., Nigg, J. T., Waldman, I. D., et al. (2005a). Are endophenotypes based on measures of executive functions useful for molecular genetic studies of ADHD? *Journal of Child Psychology and Psychiatry, 46*, 774–803.

Doyle, A. E., Willcutt, E. G., Seidman, L. J., Biederman, J., Chouinard, V. A., Silva, J., et al. (2005b). Attention-deficit/hyperactivity disorder endophenotypes. *Biological Psychiatry, 57*, 1324–1335.

Eaves, L., Silberg, J., & Erkanli, A. (2003). Resolving multiple epigenetic pathways to adolescent depression. *Journal of Child Psychology and Psychiatry, 44*, 1006–1014.

Eley, T. C. (1997). Depressive symptoms in children and adolescents: Etiological links between normality and abnormality: A research note. *Journal of Child Psychology and Psychiatry, 38*, 861–866.

Eley, T. C., & Craig, I. W. (2005). Introductory guide to the language of molecular genetics. *Journal of Child Psychology and Psychiatry, 46*, 1039–1041.

Eley, T. C., Deater-Deckard, K., Fombonne, E., Fulker, D. W., & Plomin, R. (1998). An adoption study of depressive symptoms in middle childhood. *Journal of Child Psychology and Psychiatry, 39*, 337–345.

Eley, T. C., Liang, H., Plomin, R., Sham, P., Sterne, A., Williamson, R., et al. (2004a). Parental familial vulnerability, family environment, and their interactions as predictors of depressive symptoms in adolescents. *Journal of the American Academy of Child & Adolescent Psychiatry, 43*, 298–306.

Eley, T. C., & Rijsdijk, F. (2005). Introductory guide to the statistics of molecular genetics. *Journal of Child Psychology and Psychiatry, 46*, 1042–1044.

Eley, T. C., & Stevenson, J. (1999). Exploring the covariation between anxiety and depression symptoms: A genetic analysis of the effects of age and sex. *Journal of Child Psychology and Psychiatry, 40*, 1273–1284.

Eley, T. C., Sugden, K., Gregory, A. M., Sterne, A., Plomin, R., & Craig, I. W. (2004b). Gene–environment interaction analysis of serotonin system markers with adolescent depression. *Molecular Psychiatry 9*(10), 908–915.

Gjone, H., & Stevenson, J. (1997). The association between internalizing and externalizing behaviour in childhood and early adolescence: Genetic or environmental common influences. *Journal of Abnormal Child Psychology, 54*, 277–286.

Gjone, H., Stevenson, J., Sundet, J. M., & Eilertsen, D. E. (1996). Changes in heritability across increasing levels of behaviour problems in young twins. *Behavior Genetics, 26*, 419–426.

Glowinski, A. L., Madden, P. A., Bucholz, K. K., Lynskey, M. T., & Heath, A. C. (2003). Genetic epidemiology of self-reported lifetime DSM-IV major depressive disorder in a population-based twin sample of female adolescents. *Journal of Child Psychology and Psychiatry, 44*, 988–996.

Gottesman, I. I., & Gould, T. D. (2003). The endophenotype concept in psychiatry: Etymology and strategic intentions. *American Journal of Psychiatry, 160*, 636–645.

Hankin, B. L., & Abramson, L. Y. (2001). Development of gender differences in depression: An elaborated cognitive vulnerability-transactional stress theory. *Psychological Bulletin, 127*, 773–796.

Hankin, B. L., Abramson, L. Y., & Siler, M. (2001). A prospective test of the hopelessness theory of depression in adolescence. *Cognitive Therapy and Research, 25*, 607–632.

Happonen, M., Pulkkinen, L., Kaprio, J., Van der Meere, M. J., Viken, R. J., & Rose, R. J. (2002). The heritability of depressive symptoms: Multiple informants and multiple measures. *Journal of Child Psychology and Psychiatry, 43*, 471–479.

Hariri, A. R., Mattay, V. S., Tessitore, A., Kolachana, B., Fera, F., Goldman, D., et al. (2002). Serotonin transporter genetic variation and the response of the human amygdala. *Science, 297*, 400–403.

Hasler, G., Drevets, W. C, Manji, H. K., & Charney, D. S. (2004). Discovering endophenotypes for major depression. *Neuropsychopharmacology, 29*, 1765–1781.

Hewitt, J. K., Silberg, J. L., Neale, M. C., Eaves, L. J., & Erickson, M. (1992). The analysis of parental ratings of children's behavior using LISREL. *Behavior Genetics, 22*, 293–317.

Hirschfeld, R. M. (2000). History and evolution of the monoamine hypothesis of depression. *Journal of Clinical Psychiatry, 61*(Suppl. 6), 4–6.

Huezo-Diaz, P., Tandon, K., & Aitchison, K. J. (2005). The genetics of depression and related traits. *Current Psychiatry Reports, 7*, 117–124.

Jacobson, K. C., & Rowe, D. C. (1999). Genetic and environmental influences on the relationships between family connectedness, school connectedness, and adolescent depressed mood: Sex differences. *Developmental Psychology, 35*, 926–939.

Lau, J. Y. F., & Eley, T. C. (2006). Changes in genetic and environmental influences on depressive symptoms across adolescence and young adulthood. *British Journal of Psychiatry, 189*, 422—427.

Lau, J. Y. F., & Eley, T. C. (2008). Disentangling gene environment correlations and interactions in adolescent depression. *Journal of Child Psychology and Psychiatry, 42*, 142–150.

Lau, J. Y. F., Eley, T. C., & Rijsdijk, F. (2006). I think, therefore I am: A twin study of attributional style in adolescents. *Journal of Child Psychology and Psychiatry, 47*, 696–703.

Lesch, K. P., Bengel, D., Heils, A., Zhang Sabol, S., Greenburg, B. D., Petri, S., et al. (1996). Association of anxiety-related traits with a polymorphism in the serotonin transporter gene regulatory region. *Science, 274*, 1527–1531.

Levinson, D. F. (2005). The genetics of depression: A review. *Biological Psychiatry, 60*, 84–92.

Lewinsohn, P. M., Solomon, A., Seeley, J. R., & Zeiss, A. (2000). Clinical implications of "subthreshold" depressive symptoms. *Journal of Abnormal Psychology, 109*, 345–351.

Manji, H. K., Drevets, W. C., & Charney, D. S. (2001). The cellular neurobiology of depression. *Nature Medicine, 7*, 541–547.

O'Connor, T. G., Caspi, A., DeFries, J. C., & Plomin, R. (2000). Are associations between parental divorce in children's adjustment genetically mediated? An adoption study. *Developmental Psychology, 36*, 429–437.

O'Connor, T. G., Hetherington, E. M., Reiss, D., & Plomin, R. (1995). A twin-sibling study of observed parent-adolescent interactions. *Child Development, 66*, 812–829.

O'Connor, T. G., McGuire, S., Reiss, D., Hetherington, E. M., & Plomin, R. (1998a). Co-occurrence of depressive symptoms and antisocial behavior in adolescence: A common genetic liability. *Journal of Abnormal Psychology, 107*, 27–37.

O'Connor, T. G., Neiderhiser, J. M., Reiss, D., Hetherington, E. M., & Plomin, R. (1998b). Genetic contributions to continuity, change, and co-occurrence of antisocial and depressive symptoms in Adolescence. *Journal of Child Psychology and Psychiatry, 39*, 323–336.

Pike, A., McGuire, S., Hetherington, E. M., Reiss, D., & Plomin, R. (1996). Family environment and adolescent depressive symptoms and antisocial behavior: A multivariate genetic analysis. *Developmental Psychology, 32*, 590–603.

Pine, D. S., Cohen, E., Cohen, P., & Brook, J. (1999). Adolescent depressive symptoms as predictors of adult depression: Moodiness or mood disorder? *American Journal of Psychiatry, 156*, 133–135.

Plomin, R., & Bergeman, C. S. (1991). The nature of nurture: Genetic influences on "environmental" measures. *Behavioral and Brain Sciences, 14*, 373–427.

Plomin, R., DeFries, J. C., McClearn, G. E., & McGuffin, P. (2001). *Behavioral genetics* (4th ed.). New York: Worth.

Plomin, R., Reiss, D., Hetherington, E. M., & Howe, G. W. (1994). Nature and nurture: Genetic contributions to measures of the family environment. *Developmental Psychology, 30*, 32–43.

Purcell, S. (2002). Variance components models for gene–environment interaction in twin analysis. *Twin Research, 5*, 554–571.

Rende, R. D., Plomin, R., Reiss, D., & Hetherington, E. M. (1993). Genetic and environmental influences on depressive symptomatology in adolescence: Individual differences and extreme scores. *Journal of Child Psychology and Psychiatry, 34*, 1387–1398.

Rice, F., Harold, G., & Thaper, A. (2002a). The genetic aetiology of childhood depression: A review. *Journal of Child Psychology and Psychiatry, 43*, 65–80.

Rice, F., Harold, G. T., & Thapar, A. (2002b). Assessing the effects of age, sex and shared environment on the genetic aetiology of depression in childhood and adolescence. *Journal of Child Psychology and Psychiatry, 43*, 1039–1051.

Rice, F., Harold, G. T., & Thapar, A. (2003). Negative life events as an account of age-related differences in the genetic aetiology of depression in childhood and adolescence. *Journal of Child Psychology and Psychiatry, 44*, 977–987.

Rijsdijk, F. V., Sham, P. C., Sterne, A., Purcell, S., McGuffin, P., Farmer, A., et al. (2001). Life events and depression in a community sample of siblings. *Psychological Medicine, 31*, 401–410.

Scarr, S., & McCartney, K. (1983). How people make their own environments: A theory of genotype–environmental effects. *Child Development, 54*, 424–435.

Scourfield, J., Rice, F., Thapar, A., Harold, G. T., Martin, N., & McGuffin, P. (2003). Depressive symptoms in children and adolescents: Changing aetiological influences with development. *Journal of Child Psychology and Psychiatry, 44*, 968–976.

Sham, P. C., Sterne, A., Purcell, S., Cherny, S. S., Webster, M., Rijsdijk, F. V., et al. (2000). GENESiS: Creating a composite index of the vulnerability to anxiety and depression in a community-based sample of siblings. *Twin Research, 3*, 316–322.

Silberg, J., Pickles, A., Rutter, M., Hewitt, J., Simonoff, E., Maes, H., et al. (1999). The influence of genetic factors and life stress on depression among adolescent girls. *Archives of General Psychiatry, 56*, 225–232.

Silberg, J. L., Rutter, M., & Eaves, L. (2001a). Genetic and environmental influences on the temporal association between earlier anxiety and later depression in girls. *Biological Psychiatry, 49*, 1040–1049.

Silberg, J., Rutter, M., Neale, M., & Eaves, L. (2001b). Genetic moderation of environmental risk for depression and anxiety in adolescent girls. *British Journal of Psychiatry, 179*, 116–121.

Skuse, D. S. (2001). Endophenotypes and child psychiatry. *British Journal of Psychiatry, 178*, 395–396.

Thapar, A., Harold, G., & McGuffin, P. (1998). Life events and depressive symptoms in childhood–shared genes or shared adversity? A research note. *Journal of Child Psychology and Psychiatry, 39*, 1153–1158.

Thapar, A., & McGuffin, P. (1994). A twin study of depressive symptoms in childhood. *British Journal of Psychiatry, 165*, 259–265.

Thapar, A., & McGuffin, P. (1996). Genetic influences on life events in childhood. *Psychological Medicine, 26*, 813–820.

van den Oord, E. J., Boomsma, D. I., & Verhulst, F. C. (1994). A study of problem behaviors in 10- to 15-year-old biologically related and unrelated international adoptees. *Behavior Genetics, 24*, 193–205.

van der Valk, J. C., van den Oord, E. J., Verhulst, F. C., & Boomsma, D. I. (2003). Genetic and environmental contributions to stability and change in children's internalizing and externalizing problems. *Journal of the American Academy of Child & Adolescent Psychiatry, 42*, 1212–1220.

Villafuerte, S. M., Del-Favero, J., Adolfsson, R., Souery, D., Massat, I., Mendlewicz, J., et al. (2002). Gene-based SNP genetic association study of the corticotropin-releasing hormone receptor-2 (CRHR2) in major depression. *American Journal of Medical Genetics, 114*, 222–226.

Waldman, I. D. (2005). Statistical approaches to complex phenotypes: Evaluating neuropsychological endophenotypes for attention-deficit/hyperactivity disorder. *Biological Psychiatry, 57*, 1347–1356.

Weissman, M. M., Warner, V., Wickramaratne, P., Moreau, D., & Olfson, M. (1997). Offspring of depressed parents: 10 years later. *Archives of General Psychiatry, 54*, 932–940.

Chapter Eleven

Sleep and its Relationship to Adolescent Depression[1]

AMY R. WOLFSON AND ROSEANNE ARMITAGE

CONTENTS

There is a close association between sleep and depression throughout the life cycle, but the developmental changes in sleep and circadian rhythms that occur during adolescence may confer additional risk. Sleep disorders such as insomnia, sleep apnea, and delayed sleep phase syndrome (DSPS) often create a situation where the adolescent is not able to get an adequate amount of sleep on a regular basis. In turn, lack of sleep and irregular sleep patterns may contribute to excessive daytime sleepiness, irritability, and anhedonia for the adolescent. This may exacerbate daytime functioning difficulties, such as decreased academic performance, tardiness and absenteeism, and accidents (e.g., drowsy driving, etc.). This vicious cycle may lead to or explain adolescent depression. This chapter will discuss the relationship between sleep and depression in adolescents in more detail, highlighting how developmental changes in sleep may contribute to depression, the subjective and laboratory-based sleep characteristics of depression, and the relationship between depression and sleep disorders. Which sleep measures best predict relapse and recurrence and the clinical significance of these findings will also be discussed.

CHANGES IN SLEEP, CIRCADIAN RHYTHMS, AND BEHAVIOR

Behavioral scientists have argued that many health-compromising behaviors begin during adolescence, such as alcohol abuse, smoking, illicit drug use, unsafe sex, and other risk-taking behaviors (Donovan & Jessor, 1985; Duncan, Duncan, & Hops, 1998). Many of these behaviors are tied to peer culture, other societal influences, and sleep disturbances. Sleep problems in early childhood are associated with an elevated risk of developing symptoms of major depressive disorder (MDD) in later childhood and in early adulthood. There are a number of studies that indicate that parental reports of persistent sleep problems in early childhood predicted behavioral and emotional problems in midadolescence (Gregory & O'Connor, 2002). Further, irregular sleep habits and high motor activity during sleep have been associated with adolescent onset of depressive and anxiety symptoms (Ong, Wickramaratne, & Tang, 2006). Previous studies have already shown a higher incidence of sleep problems in those with anxiety and depression (Aronen, Paavonen, Fjalberg, Soininen, & Torronen, 2000; Johnson, Chilcoat, & Breslau, 2000). For example, a recent study of 300 8-year-old twins indicated significantly higher depression scores associated with bedtime resistance, delay of sleep onset, sleep anxiety, and parasomnias (Gregory et al., 2005). Similarly, children with sleep problems had higher scores on several dimensions of the Child Behavior Checklist, including anxiety/depression (Shang, Gau, & Soong, 2006).

Certain health compromising behaviors are connected to adolescents' self-presentation, such as their efforts to come across as sophisticated, cool, or tough in school or other social situations (Leary, Tchividjian, & Kraxberger, 1994). Moreover, adolescents find many such behaviors pleasurable or rewarding. Such habits as expressing a devaluing attitude toward sleep, staying up late, and sleeping until late in the morning have been linked to adolescent culture; however, adolescents' sleep patterns are also influenced by neurobiological development and environmental constraints.

Over the last two decades, researchers have established an increasingly more nuanced understanding of adolescents' sleep demands, patterns, and underlying bioregulatory processes (Carskadon & Acebo, 2002; Carskadon, Acebo, & Jenni, 2004). Data from longitudinal and cross-sectional assessments indicate that the "need" to sleep does not change from ages 10 to 17; if anything, older adolescents may require more sleep and fall asleep later in the evening (Carskadon, 1982; Carskadon & Acebo, 2002; Carskadon, Harvey, Duke, Anders, & Dement, 1980). Specifically, sleep need across chronological age, sex, and Tanner stage, is estimated at about 9 hours (Carskadon, 1982; Carskadon et al., 1980). In a study at a summer sleep camp at Stanford University during the 1970s, boys and girls who enrolled at 10 to 12 years of age were monitored yearly for 5 to 6 years. While researchers hypothesized that older children would need less sleep during the 10-hour nocturnal window they were given (i.e., 10 pm to 8 am), Carskadon and colleagues found that regardless of age, the children all slept about 9.2 of the 10 hours. In other words, as they progressed through adolescence, participants continued to get the same amount of sleep, but they no longer woke spontaneously before the end of the sleep window at 8 am (Carskadon et al., 1980). In addition, when the Multiple Sleep Latency Test (MSLT)—given at designated periods throughout the day to determine the speed of falling asleep, to measure sleepiness—was given to the adolescents, they showed greater alertness at 8 pm than earlier in the day, and even greater alertness at 10 pm.

In contrast, adolescents' *real world* sleep patterns show that many adolescents from a range of countries report sleeping from 1 to 2 (or more) hours less than 9 hours per night, particularly on school nights (Carskadon & Acebo, 2002; Wolfson & Carskadon, 1998). For example, the median school-night total sleep time reported by a large sample of high school students (aged 14 to 18 years) was 7.5 hours (Wolfson & Carskadon, 1998), and 70% of students in another large self-report survey reported less than 8.5 hours on school nights (Gibson et al., 2006). The recent National Sleep Foundation (2006) (NSF) sleep in America poll indicated that high school seniors report an average of 6.9 hours of sleep on school nights. By age 12 or 13, most adolescents report that they obtain significantly less sleep and have more irregular school-night versus weekend-night schedules in comparison to younger school-age children (Fredrikson, Rhodes, Reddy, & Way, 2004; Iglowstein, Jenni, Molinari, & Largo, 2003; Strauch & Meier, 1988; Thorleifsdottir, Bjornsson, Benediktsdottir, Gislason, & Kristbjarnarson, 2002; Wolfson, Acebo, Fallone, & Carskadon, 2003a; Wolfson et al., 2003b; Wolfson, Spaulding, Dandrow, & Baroni, 2007). School-night sleep length declines markedly over the adolescent years, whereas weekend and summer sleep schedules change less. Over this developmental phase, adolescents also report significantly delayed bedtimes and rise times, particularly on weekends (Carskadon & Acebo, 2002; Carskadon, Vieira, & Acebo, 1993; Carskadon, Wolfson, Acebo, Tzischinsky, & Seifer, 1998).

Another general trend is that the timing of sleep gets later as children enter and pass through adolescence, staying up later at night and sleeping in later in the morning. This delay of the sleep period is most obvious on weekend and vacation nights, whereas the timing of sleep is largely determined on school days by school start time schedules (Carskadon et al., 1998; Epstein, Chillag, & Lavie, 1998; Szymczak, Jasinska, Pawlak, & Swierzykowska, 1993). In one study attempting to investigate the association of sleep patterns and school start time, Carskadon and colleagues evaluated the impact of a 65-minute advance (earlier) of school start time for approximately 40 students across the transition from grade 9 (8:25 am start time) to grade 10 (7:20 am start time) (Carskadon et al., 1998). Objectively documented sleep records demonstrated that only 62% of the students in ninth grade, and fewer than half the students in tenth grade obtained an average of 7 hours or more of sleep on school nights. As expected, students woke significantly earlier on school days in tenth grade than in ninth grade. In tenth grade, students also displayed atypical sleep patterns on a laboratory nap test of sleepiness (MSLT). They fell asleep faster in tenth than in ninth grade (particularly an assessment at 8:30 am), and 48% of tenth grade participants' experienced at least one rapid eye movement (REM) sleep episode on the MSLT. This unusual pattern is disturbing because it mimics the clinical findings of patients with a major sleep disorder—narcolepsy (Guilleminault & Pelayo, 1998). These findings have been attributed to a combination of too little sleep occurring at a time mismatched to internal circadian rhythms (Carskadon et al., 1998).

Furthermore, two reviews by Carskadon and colleagues have shown that several distinct changes in the circadian process influence this sleep phase delay. Specifically, delay of intrinsic circadian phase, lengthening of the intrinsic period of the circadian clock, heightened sensitivity to evening light, or decreased sensitivity to morning light may contribute to the pubertal phase delay (Carskadon & Acebo, 2002; Carskadon et al., 2004). Likewise, a number of recent studies on sleep homeostasis (i.e., regulatory or balancing system enabling organisms to compensate for the loss of or surplus of sleep) in adolescents demonstrated that the rise rate of sleep need during the day is slower in mature adolescents in comparison to early pubertal adolescents, contributing to the delay in the timing of sleep over the course of puberty (Jenni, Achermann, & Carskadon, 2005; Jenni & Carskadon, 2004). This means that mature adolescents may be less sensitive to extended wakefulness and live with less sleep pressure at bedtime than younger, less mature adolescents. For example, Taylor and colleagues found that after being awake for 14.5, 16.5, and 18.5 hours, sleep tendency assessed by the time to fall asleep was significantly lower in postpubertal than prepubertal adolescents (Taylor, Jenni, Acebo, & Carskadon, 2005). These developmental changes in sleep homeostasis and circadian timing may decrease adolescents' sensitivity to sleep loss and increase tolerance for sleep pressure, making it easier to function in our adult 24/7 culture. Simultaneously, the adolescent delay in sleep onset (i.e., later bedtimes) may make it easier to participate in evening activities, yet increase the adolescents' vulnerability to sleep-wake disorders, such as DSPS and other physical and emotional consequences.

INADEQUATE, IRREGULAR SLEEP PATTERNS AND DEPRESSED MOOD

Adolescents' delayed sleep schedules and sleep needs mismatched with societal demands can negatively impact cognitive and emotional functioning. Teens from a variety of countries and cultural backgrounds report that they do not get enough sleep and feel poorly during the day (e.g., Gibson et al., 2006; Ledoux, Choquet, & Manfredi, 1994; Morrison, McGee, & Stanton, 1992; National Sleep Foundation, 2006; Wolfson, 2002; Wolfson & Carskadon, 1998; Yang, Kim, Patel, & Lee, 2005). According to one survey study of 3,000 adolescents, about half of the adolescents reported feeling tired or dragged out nearly every day (Wolfson, 2002). In this same study, approximately 30% stated that they rarely had a good night's sleep in the last two weeks, admitted that they fall asleep and/or struggle to stay awake in class, and said that they use 2 to 4 substances (e.g., caffeine, alcohol, cigarettes) at least once a day. Similarly, the NSF poll of about 1,600 adolescents and parents reported that only 20% of adolescents obtain the recommended 9 hours of sleep they need, and nearly one-half sleep less than 8 hours on school nights. The poll also indicated that at least once a week, 28% of high school students fall asleep in class and 14% are tardy or absent because they oversleep. More than one-third of the adolescents said that they felt cranky or irritable during the day and/or had trouble getting along with family members at least once a week (National Sleep Foundation, 2006). Insufficient sleep is unmistakably associated with irritability and depressed mood in adolescents (e.g., Wolfson & Carskadon, 1998). Similarly, affect regulation that requires the integration of high cognitive and emotional processing is particularly sensitive to inadequate or insufficient sleep, and may represent one of the most significant consequences of poor sleep patterns (Dahl, 1999).

Research has investigated the complex relationship between adolescents' sleep patterns and behavioral and emotional well-being. Studies have suggested cross-sectional associations between sleep problems, depressed mood, and other behavioral difficulties in teenagers (Kirmil-Gray, Eagleston, Gibson, & Thoresen, 1984; Morrison et al., 1992; Roberts, Lewinsohn, & Seeley,

1995; Saarenpaa-Heikkila, Laippala, & Koivikko, 2001; Wolfson & Carskadon, 1998). For example, in their retrospective survey of high school students, Wolfson and Carskadon (1998) found that high school age adolescents with more adequate sleep habits (defined as longer total sleep times and more regular sleep schedules across the week) reported lower levels of depressed mood, fewer complaints of daytime sleepiness, and fewer problematic sleep behaviors in comparison to students with inadequate sleep habits. Adolescents who reported more irregular sleep schedules had more behavior problems and increased substance abuse (e.g., cigarettes, marijuana, etc.; Wolfson, 2002). In another approach, studies categorized middle school age or young adolescents as sleepy or as poor sleepers. Using this design, studies found that the poor sleepers had more problematic coping behaviors (e.g., more difficulty recognizing, appraising, and adapting to stressful situations), displayed more behavior problems at home and in school, and/or reported higher levels or anxious and/or depressed mood (Fallone, Owens, & Deane, 2002; Morrison et al., 1992; Sadeh, Gruber, & Raviv, 2002; Wolfson et al., 1995).

More recently, researchers have utilized prospective methodologies such as sleep diaries and actigraphy to examine adolescents' sleep time, activities, and psychological well-being (e.g., Aronen et al., 2000; Hardway & Fuligni, 2006). Using diaries in a sample of 14- to 15-year-olds, Hardway and Fuligni found that adolescents who spent less time sleeping each night tended to report more negative and less positive daily moods. In particular, adolescents with more inconsistent nightly sleep reported more depressed mood, anxiety, and fatigue (Hardway & Fuligni, 2006). Likewise, using actigraphic estimates of sleep in a younger adolescent sample, Aronen and colleagues found that inadequate sleep was significantly associated with both externalizing and internalizing symptoms; particularly teacher-reported symptoms (Aronen et al., 2000).

Other research groups are attempting to look at specific depression symptoms, coping strategies, related risk factors, and sleep. Specifically, Carney, Edinger, Meyer, Lindman, and Istre (2006) investigated rumination and sleep disturbances in a sample of college students (Carney et al., 2006). Self-defined poor sleepers on the Pittsburgh Sleep Quality Index were more likely than good sleepers to ruminate (as measured on the Response Styles Questionnaire; Nolen-Hoeksema, 1991) in response to depressed mood and the ruminative content was symptom focused (e.g., dysphoria, concentration difficulties, and fatigue). Patten and colleagues evaluated the impact of depressive symptoms and cigarette smoking on adolescents' sleep problems (Patten, Choi, Gillin, & Pierce, 2000). In a sample of close to 8,000 12- to 18-year-olds, depressive symptoms and cigarette smoking predicted the development and maintenance of sleep problems over a 4-year period.

Taken together, studies strongly suggest that middle school through college-age adolescents with inadequate sleep, irregular school night to weekend sleep/wake schedules, and/or sleep disturbances struggle and cope less effectively with emotional/behavior difficulties. Yet, the direction, possible longitudinal nature, and the quality of the relationship between sleep quantity and schedules and emotional well-being is unclear. The quantity, quality, and timing of sleep seems to impact both internalizing emotional difficulties (e.g., such as depression) and externalizing difficulties (e.g., attention, conduct problems). It is essential to highlight the overlap between sleep regulation and behavioral/emotional problems in children and adolescents; there is clearly a two-way interaction between these two systems. Studies have shown that sleep loss may limit the ability to control mood and behavior; therefore insufficient sleep may contribute to the development or exacerbation of behavioral and emotional problems (Dahl, 1999). Adolescents who have trouble adapting to new school schedules and other changes (e.g., increased activities during the day, increased academic demands) may develop problematic sleeping behaviors leading to chronic sleepiness (Carskadon et al., 1998). Likewise, the development, regulation, and timing of sleep can be altered by behavioral/emotional disorders (Dahl et al., 1996). In general, however, sleep disturbances are more severe in those who meet diagnostic criteria for MDD.

SUBJECTIVE SLEEP DISTURBANCES IN DEPRESSION

Subjective sleep disturbances are a frequent complaint associated with MDD in adults as well as adolescents, and have been a consistent part of the Diagnostic and Statistical Manual of Mental Disorders (DSM)-based diagnostic criteria (DSM IV-TR, 2000). Up to 90% of depressed adults and adolescents have sleep complaints (Birmaher & Heydl, 2001; Ohayon, Caulet, & Lemoine, 1998; Reynolds & Kupfer, 1987; Tsuno, Besset, & Ritchie, 2005). Most often these include insomnia, hypersomnia, sleep continuity problems, daytime sleepiness, and circadian difficulties. Subjective sleep complaints are included in most depression symptom severity scales (Ivanenko, Crabtree, & Gozal, 2005), but are usually confined to insomnia items (Armitage, 2000). Thus, it is important to bear in mind how sleep disturbance was assessed when considering the findings. Although the majority of adolescents report insomnia during an episode of depression, 10–30% report hypersomnia (Ivanenko et al., 2005). Liu and colleagues specifically examined subjective sleep disturbances among 553 depressed children and adolescents using the Interview Schedule for Children and Adolescents, Diagnostic Version (Liu et al., 2007). This interview includes questions on insomnia and hypersomnia that were supplemented with questions about difficulty falling asleep, sleep quality, awakenings during the night, and the duration and prevalence of these sleep problems. Overall, 73% of the children had sleep disturbances including 54% with insomnia alone, 9% with hypersomnia, and 10% with both. Those who reported combined hypersomnia and insomnia showed the most severe depression, whereas those with no sleep disturbance showed the lowest symptom severity. In addition, the combined sleep disturbance group was also more likely to have recurrent depression and a longer duration of illness. As a group, those with sleep disturbances were more likely to report depressed mood, fatigue, anhedonia, sadness, guilt, weight loss, and diurnal variation than those children without sleep disturbances. Sleep disturbed children had a higher prevalence of anxiety disorders, but not other comorbid illnesses compared to those without sleep disturbance. Those who reported hypersomnia plus insomnia showed more symptoms of anhedonia, psychomotor retardation, weight loss, and fatigue than insomnia or hypersomnia alone. Those children who reported hypersomnia alone were more likely to have weight gain, psychomotor retardation, and fatigue than the insomnia alone group. These findings confirm the high prevalence of subjective sleep disturbance in early-onset depression and begin to identify different symptom profiles associated with the kind of sleep disturbance (Liu et al., 2007).

Bertocci and colleagues compared subjective sleep assessments in depressed children and adolescents to age-matched healthy controls and found significantly worse sleep quality, more difficulty waking in the morning, and twice as much time spent awake at night in the depressed children (Bertocci et al., 2005). The procedures for this study differed from other subjective sleep assessments in that subjective sleep data were collected after overnight sleep studies. In addition, study participants maintained a regularized sleep/wake schedule before participating in the overnight studies. Thus, subjective sleep disturbance is found in depressed adolescents even under more rigorous control of sleep/wake habits and sleep assessments.

Several other studies further underscore the clinical importance of sleep disturbances in adolescent depression. Greater suicidal ideation has been reported among those adolescents with most disturbed sleep (Liu & Buysse, 2005). More specifically, insomnia is more prevalent in adolescents with greater suicidal ideation (Barbe et al., 2005) and often accompanied by more nightmares (Choquet, Menke, & Ledoux, 1989). These findings were replicated in several different countries (cf. Liu & Buysse, 2005). As discussed below, laboratory-assessed sleep disturbances also relate to increased suicidal ideation.

SLEEP POLYSOMNOGRAPHY IN ADOLESCENT MDD

In addition to assessment of self-reported sleep, studies in depressed adolescent patients also include measurement of brain electroencephalography (EEG), eye movements, and motor activity to visually identify the timing and amount of REM and non-REM (NREM) sleep stages, identified below as sleep macroarchitecture. REM sleep is associated with relatively low-amplitude, mixed-frequency EEG activity and is not generally associated with feeling rested. In fact, brain metabolic output is often higher in REM sleep than in wakefulness. NREM sleep is comprised of Stage 1 (very light, nonrestorative sleep, most often present transition from wakefulness to sleep); Stage 2 sleep (associated with a move toward higher amplitude EEG activity and deeper sleep); and Stages 3 and 4 sleep (collectively identified as deep or slow-wave sleep because of the prevalence of high amplitude delta activity). Descriptions of standard sleep macroarchitecture can be found in the majority of sleep disorders textbooks (e.g., Carney, Berry, & Geyer, 2004; Kryger, Roth, & Dement, 2005; Mindell & Owens, 2003; Sheldon & Kryger, 2005).

There are also a growing number of studies of computerized algorithms for describing the EEG frequency structure within and across sleep stages, collectively referred to as sleep microarchitecture. Delta activity (0.5 up to 4 Hz) is most often quantified independent of sleep stage, and its time course across the night and response to sleep deprivation is presumed to model homeostasis in the brain, i.e., the recovery function of sleep. Beta EEG activity (16–32 Hz) is fast-frequency, low-amplitude activity that is present in abundance in wakefulness, in REM, and around the sleep onset interval (Armitage, Hoffmann, & Rush, 1999). There are numerous reports of sleep macro- and microarchitecture in adults with MDD. The majority of studies indicate that prolonged sleep onset, early occurrence of REM sleep, and reductions in deep, slow-wave NREM sleep characterize sleep macroarchitecture in MDD adults. Moreover, increased fast-frequency beta EEG activity and blunted slow-frequency delta activity are often reported as sleep microarchitectural findings in depressed adults (Armitage, 1995; Armitage, Hoffmann, Fitch, Trivedi, & Rush, 2000b; Armitage et al., 1992; Reynolds & Kupfer, 1987; Riemann, Kammerer, Low, & Schmidt, 1995). In addition, sleep EEG rhythms are poorly synchronized between the left and right hemisphere and within each hemisphere, reflected in significantly lower temporal coherence. Poorly synchronized sleep EEG rhythms produce chaotic and disorganized sleep states with little regularity across the night, and likely to impair the recovery function of sleep (Armitage et al., 1999). We review the findings on sleep macro- and microarchitecture in early-onset MDD below.

Sleep Macroarchitecture (Polysomnographic Data)

For the most part, earlier studies reported short REM latency (REML) in depressed adolescents compared to healthy controls (Dahl et al., 1990; Emslie, Rush, Weinberg, Rintelmann, & Roffwarg, 1994; Kutcher, Williamson, Marton, & Szalai, 1992; Lahmeyer, Poznanski, & Bellur, 1983; Riemann et al., 1995), particularly those with psychotic features of depression (Naylor, Shain, & Shipley, 1990; also see Ivanenko et al., 2005 for a review). Other studies have failed to confirm short REML as a characteristic of adolescent MDD (Appelboom-Fondu, Kerkhofs, & Mendlewicz, 1988; Dahl et al., 1991). However, four of the five studies that did report short REML in adolescents with MDD included only inpatients. Thus, the regularity of sleep schedules or severity of illness, or both may impact on REML and other sleep parameters. Research from Dahl and colleagues suggests that prolonged sleep latency may more reliably differentiate adolescents with MDD from healthy controls (Dahl, 1996, 1999; Dahl et al., 1996). In a meta-analysis, prolonged sleep latency was the only macro-architectural measure to differentiate between depressed and healthy control participants (Birmaher & Heydl, 2001). In fact, recent, more controlled studies have not shown robust differences in sleep macroarchitecture between depressed adolescents and healthy controls (Armitage, Emslie, Hoffmann, Rintelmann, & Rush, 2001; Armitage et al., 2000a). The study by Bertocci and colleagues (2005) described above, also included polysomnographic measures of sleep latency, minutes awake, and bed and rise times. Although no sleep architectural data were shown, the authors reported that only minutes of awake differentiated depressed from control groups. Restricting analysis to only those with the most disturbed subjective sleep resulted in no group differences (Bertocci et al., 2005).

There are a number of factors, however, that may contribute to the discrepancies between sleep findings in adult and early-onset depression. There are substantially fewer published studies in early-onset MDD and sample sizes are usually modest. In addition, many studies include both children and adolescents and are not able to take age and gender into consideration in statistical analyses due to limited sample size. One notable exception identified the most disturbed sleep architecture in adolescent males with MDD, characterized by the highest amount of light nonrestorative Stage 1 sleep, shortest REML, and the least amount of slow-wave sleep (Robert et al., 2006). The age-related differences in sleep architecture were also largest among the MDD boys, with minimal differences in sleep macroarchitecture between 8- and 12-year-old girls and those 13 to 18 years old. The results were very similar, with most disturbed sleep among pubertal boys, when Tanner maturation score was used to evaluate developmental changes instead of chronological age (Robert et al., 2006).

Moreover, challenge studies that either look at the sleep EEG response to a pharmacological agent, hormone, or sleep deprivation elicit larger and more reliable differences between depressed adolescents and healthy controls (cf., Dahl et al., 1994). Studies in adults support this position and have suggested that examining response to sleep challenge may provide the clearest description of sleep and brain regulatory abnormalities in depression rather than just monitoring static, baseline sleep characteristics (Armitage, 2007; Armitage & Hoffmann, 2001).

In summary, the majority of studies indicate that some sleep macroarchitectural measures differentiate depressed adolescents from controls, but that they are more likely to be found in adolescents, not younger children. Further, as shown in the meta-analysis of data on depressed adults (Benca, Obermeyer, Thisted, & Gillin, 1992), no single sleep macroarchitectural variable may discriminate young patients from controls across all studies. [See also limitations of studies below for further discussion.] Macroarchitectural measures, nevertheless, have shown some promise in predicting longitudinal course of depression. Rao and colleagues have shown that adolescent control participants who later went on to develop depression demonstrated greater sleep abnormality at baseline (Rao et al., 1996). Moreover, shorter REML and higher REM density in adolescents with MDD predicted a worse clinical outcome in young adulthood (Rao et al., 1996). In a prospective, naturalistic, follow-up study of children and adolescents with MDD, a greater probability of symptom recurrence was found in those with lower sleep efficiency (i.e., more nocturnal wake time) and longer sleep latency. Poor sleep efficiency was also associated with increased suicidality in those with recurrent symptoms (Emslie et al., 2001). Other studies have also indicated that some sleep macroarchitectural abnormalities are evident in those who have a family history of depression (Giles, Kupfer, Rush, & Roffwarg, 1998; Giles et al., 1989; Modell, Ising, Holsboers, & Lauer, 2005), or those who later develop depression (Goetz, Wolk, Coplan, Ryan, & Weissman, 2001). Sleep microarchitectural measures may show more specificity in identifying sleep abnormalities in depressed adolescents (Armitage, 1995; Farina et al., 2003).

Sleep Microarchitecture (Computer Analysis of Sleep EEG Frequencies)

Several studies have shown that the synchronization of sleep EEG frequencies and temporal coherence may be reduced in early-onset depression, particularly among adolescents 13–16 years of age (Armitage et al., 2000a, 2001). Depressed adolescent girls also showed poorly synchronized sleep EEG rhythms, particularly in fast-frequency beta activity. Elevated beta activity during sleep is most often associated with hyperarousal. Adolescent depressed girls also showed significantly lower delta activity in NREM sleep. Interestingly, the finding of lower delta activity in girls was contrary to the sex difference reported in depressed adults, where it is men with MDD who are most likely to show reduced delta activity (Armitage et al., 2000b; Armitage, Hoffmann, Fitch, Trivedi, & Rush, 2000c). Bertocci and colleagues (2005) also included some preliminary analyses of sleep microarchitecture in a subset of young participants, with no reported significant difference, although only limited data were shown. Once again, however, the sample sizes in the adolescent depression studies were much smaller than those in adults, and statistical power was limited.

A more recent study of children and adolescents confirmed that temporal coherence was significantly lower in adolescents with depression compared to healthy controls, but was lowest in depressed adolescent girls (Armitage, Hoffmann, Emslie, Rintelman, & Robert, 2006). This was in distinct contrast to the findings in sleep macroarchitecture, where depressed adolescent boys were most likely to show sleep disturbance (Robert et al., 2006). Interestingly, even young prepubertal depressed girls showed lower temporal coherence than their control group, whereas depressed prepubertal boys did not (Armitage et al., 2006). These findings indicate that at least some microarchitectural features of depression distinguish early-onset depressed females. It remains to be established if delta activity or associated sleep recovery functions are impaired in early-onset depression. A preliminary analysis of delta activity in this same sample has shown that delta activity in the first NREM period of the night is only lower in depressed adolescent boys, not girls (Hoffmann, Emslie, & Armitage, 2006), as found in depressed adults (Armitage et al., 2000c; Armitage et al., 2000b). The accumulation of delta in the first NREM period of the night and its subsequent time course are presumed to index sleep homeostasis and the recovery functions of sleep thus low delta could be interpreted as impaired homeostasis in depressed adolescent males. However, a sleep challenge study or sleep deprivation is required to confirm this suggestion, although such data are already available in depressed adults (Armitage, 2007).

Considering both sleep macro- and microarchitecture, the established findings support a different developmental time course in depressed boys and girls, and generally confirm the view that the pathophysiology of depression differs in adult men and women (Armitage, 2007). If impaired homeostasis is also confirmed in adolescent males, then clinical relevance of these sleep microarchitectural abnormalities may also be sex-dependent.

Two studies have identified lower temporal coherence in the unaffected first degree relatives of depressed patients (Fulton, Armitage, & Rush, 2000; Morehouse, Kusumakar, Kutcher, LeBlanc, & Armitage, 2002). Further, Morehouse and colleagues studied sleep EEG coherence in a group of 41 adolescent girls with depressed mothers and a group of age-matched controls with maternal history, and then prospectively followed the sample for 2 to 3 years (Morehouse et al., 2002). The high-risk girls had significantly lower temporal coherence than controls. Most importantly, those girls with the lowest temporal coherence were 10 times more likely to develop depressive symptoms 2 years later (Morehouse et al., 2002).

It is generally accepted that females are at higher lifetime risk for depression compared to males, from puberty until menopause (cf. Armitage, 2007; Armitage & Hoffman, 2001). There is also clear evidence that familial transmission of depression is sex-related, with a twofold higher rate of maternal transmission (Currier, Mann, Oquendo, Galfalvy, & Mann, 2006). The sex difference in temporal coherence and potentially in sleep homeostasis may be endophenotypes (intermediaries between genes and the final expression of depression) for further understanding sex differences in early-onset depression.

SLEEP DISORDERS AND DEPRESSED MOOD

Child and adolescent sleep disorders are common, affecting approximately 25% to 40% of children and adolescents (Meltzer & Mindell, 2006). Although there are several different sleep disorders that negatively impact adolescents, each sleep problem can have significant consequences for daytime functioning, such as depressed affect. Likewise, high rates of sleep problems exist among adolescents with neurodevelopmental, medical, and psychiatric problems. Reciprocal relationships occur between sleep disorders and psychiatric disorders such as depression. As discussed throughout this chapter, an adolescent diagnosed with depression often has coexisting sleep difficulties and, on the other hand, disrupted and inadequate sleep is often highly associated with affective, behavioral, and cognitive dysfunction. Studies in adult populations have shown that narcolepsy, insomnia, sleep apnea (sleep-disordered breathing; SDB), restless legs syndrome (RLS), periodic limb movement disorder (PLMD), and circadian disorders all show strong evidence for an association with depressed mood and/or mood disorders (Haba-Rubio, 2005; Vandeputte & de Weerd, 2003). For example, in a survey of nearly 1,000 individuals (ages 14–84) diagnosed with a sleep disorder (insomnia, RLS, PLMD, sleep apnea), more than 50% reported depression symptoms, and moderate to severe depression was found in close to 4% of the sample (Vandeputte & de Weerd, 2003). Less is known regarding adolescents; however in the section that follows, sleep disorders and depression and/or depressed mood in adolescents are briefly discussed.

A small number of studies have investigated the prevalence of insomnia in adolescents. Ohayon and colleagues estimate the prevalence of DSM-IV diagnosed insomnia to be 4% and the incidence of DSPS at 1% for 15- to 18-year-olds; however, approximately 18–25% reported insomnia symptoms in the past 30 days (Ohayon & Roberts, 2001; Roberts, Roberts, & Chen, 2002). DSPS (see reviews: Garcia, Rosen, & Mahowald, 2001; Wyatt, 2004) is manifested by sleep onset times that are delayed several hours relative to conventional bedtimes (3:00 am rather than 11:00 pm). Conversely, the normal time to wake up drifts to correspondingly later in the morning (11:00 am rather than 7:00 am). Both DSPS and insomnia are associated with daytime sleepiness, behavioral, and mood difficulties for adolescents. In particular, insomnia symptoms, such as nonrestorative sleep, difficulty initiating sleep, and daytime sleepiness, are associated with self-esteem difficulties, interpersonal relationship problems, symptoms of depression, and somatic complaints (Roberts, Lee, Hernandez, & Solari, 2004; Roberts et al., 2002). Likewise, adolescents with insomnia and/or hypersomnia are more likely to be depressed and to have comorbid anxiety disorders than depressed children and adolescents without sleep disturbances (Liu et al., 2007).

There seems to be a strong relationship between depression, altered circadian activity rhythms, and DSPS, in particular (Teicher et al., 1993). One study of adolescents with DSPS found that 36% had features of depression. Similarly, in a study of first-year college students (older adolescents) the researchers concluded that the sleep/wake patterns associated with DSPS and chronic insufficient sleep tend to result in lowered academic performance, depressed mood, and other daytime difficulties (Okawa, Uchiyama, Ozaki, Shibui, & Ichikawa, 1998). The relationship between DSPS and mood difficulties is poorly understood in that the inadequate sleep associated with DSPS may give rise to depression, or there may be a primary mood disorder that evokes the symptoms of DSPS (Okawa et al., 1998).

SDB or sleep apnea, RLS, PLMD, and narcolepsy (i.e., neurological syndrome characterized by daytime sleepiness, cataplexy, sleep paralysis, and hypnagogic hallucinations) can be associated with symptoms of depression in adults as well as adolescents (Baran & Richert, 2003; Deldin, Phillips, & Thomas, 2005; Picchietti & Winkelman, 2005; Sevim et al., 2004). Many symptoms of depression (e.g., sleep problems, sleepiness, concentration difficulties, irritability, and social withdrawal) overlap with symptoms of SDB, so it may be that neither causes the other but they are confused diagnostically. Studies have also suggested that the relationship between depression and SDB may be mediated by an additional factor such as obesity (Aloia et al., 2005; Crabtree, Varni, & Gozal, 2004). Aloia and colleagues found that depressive symptoms that are largely connected with the somatic aspects of depression (e.g., loss of energy) were more strongly associated with apnea severity, whereas cognitive depressive symptoms (e.g., negative thoughts) were more highly correlated with obesity (Aloia et al., 2005). Similarly, in a study of school-age children and young adolescents, children with probable SDB, regardless of the severity of apnea or the presence of obesity, had more impairments in quality of life and depressive symptoms than children without symptoms snoring (Crabtree et al., 2004). Since obesity and SDB are no longer considered only adult illnesses, these complex relationships need to be more closely examined in adolescents and young adults.

Failure to recognize narcolepsy, which often begins in childhood or adolescence, may lead to misdiagnosing a child as lazy, and an adolescent as depressed (Guilleminault & Pelayo, 2000). Additionally, adolescents with narcolepsy may have a coexisting diagnosis of depression or present with depressive symptoms, such as excessive sleepiness, difficulties with social functioning, and/or emotional lability. In a large study of 500 individuals diagnosed with narcolepsy, just over 50% had some degree of depression (Daniels, King, Smith, & Shneerson, 2001). Finally, some researchers have suggested that depression may be a symptom of narcolepsy (Adrien, 2002; Haba-Rubio, 2005), as reduced REM latency is seen in depression as well as narcolepsy (as discussed earlier). However, just because two disorders share a common endpoint sleep EEG characteristic, this does not mean that the same mechanisms or substrates underlie both diseases. Undoubtedly, there is symptom overlap among disorders associated with sleep disturbances. The sleep disturbances in MDDs, nevertheless, are pervasive.

INTERVENTIONS

Historically, it was believed that if the symptoms of depression were treated adequately, the sleep disturbances would also remit (Armitage, 2000). Available antidepressant agents at that time, however, were not particularly disturbing to sleep, as are many newer antidepressants. By contrast, newer antidepressants, such as serotonin reuptake inhibitors, have been associated with significant insomnia and increased sleep disruption (Rush et al., 1998; Trivedi et al., 1999; Vogel et al., 1998). Although there is some adaptation to the increased insomnia and sleep-disturbing effects over time, sleep macroarchitecture remains disturbed after several months of treatment, at least in adults with MDD (Hoffmann, Armitage, Trivedi, & Rush, 1999).

The majority of the studies of the effects of antidepressant drugs on sleep, however, have been conducted exclusively in adult patients. Thus, it is not known whether similar effects are observed in early-onset MDD. One small study does indicate that fluoxetine (Prozac™) also lightens sleep and increases wakefulness during the night in adolescents with MDD (Armitage, Emslie, & Rintelmann, 1997). In addition, the outcome of the Treatment of Adolescents with Depression (TADS) study does indicate that sleep disturbance is the most common residual symptom in adolescents, even after effective treatment (Kennard et al., 2006). Given the risk of relapse and recurrence with persistent sleep problems, it may be wise to consider adjunctive interventions for improving sleep.

Management of sleep complaints and problems, including regularizing the sleep-wake schedule as well as cognitive-behavioral approaches for insomnia, reportedly have a positive impact on depressive symptoms for many adolescents (Dahl, 1996, 1999; Manber, Bootzin, Acebo, & Carskadon, 1996). In a recent consensus conference on pharmacological management of insomnia in children and adolescents, Mindell and colleagues concluded that there is a need for pharmacological management of insomnia and related behavioral sleep problems in children and adolescents (Mindell et al., 2006). They also argued, however, that the field needs more appropriate, well-researched medication guidelines and methodologically sound, large-scale clinical trials (Mindell et al., 2006).

Currently, there is a tremendous need for treatment outcome studies focused on evaluating strategies for treating behavioral sleep problems in older school age, preadolescents, and adolescents with and without coexisting MDD or depression symptoms. Adult studies point out that cognitive-behavioral treatment (CBT) for insomnia has three courses of action—behavioral, cognitive, and educational. Over the last two decades, numerous studies have demonstrated that CBT is effective for 70 to 80% of adults, including young adults (Jacobs, Pace-Schott, Stickgold, & Otto, 2004; Morin, 2004) equivalent to the rates of response to pharmacotherapy. CBT is most effective with reducing sleep onset latency symptoms and increasing sleep efficiency. Again, unfortunately, few studies have evaluated the efficacy of CBT approaches for adolescents, particularly adolescents diagnosed with MDD.

The handful of studies that have looked at treatment efficacy for adolescent insomnia had small sample sizes and/or relied on a single-case design (Mindell, 2003). In particular, two case studies successfully utilized relaxation training and reduction of parental attention (Anderson, 1979; Weil & Goldfried, 1973), and another study treated three adolescents with a combination of relaxation training and biofeedback (Barowsky, Moskowitz, & Zweig, 1990).

Cognitive-behavioral strategies generally include sleep hygiene and, as Mindell points out, treatment plans for adolescents should include education about the specific components (Mindell, 2003). In particular, sleep hygiene includes the following: comfortable, dark, and quiet sleep environment; consistent bedtime and waking routines including weekends; avoiding excessive hunger or large amounts food close to bedtime; passing up naps in the late afternoon and early evening; steering clear of stimulating activities 1 hour before bedtime such as television watching, telephone conversations, computer activities, or exercising; and eliminating caffeine 4–6 hours before bedtime (Mindell, 2003).

Relaxation therapy (e.g., relaxation training, progressive muscle relaxation, meditation, etc.) helps the adolescent slow her/his racing thoughts and relaxes muscles so that she/he experiences a more restful, calm sleep. Stimulus control techniques consist of a set of procedures designed to curtail sleep-incompatible behaviors and regulate the sleep-wake schedule. Stimulus control therapy is meant to help the adolescent recondition herself/himself to associate bed and bedtime with sleep as opposed to other activities (e.g., studying, talking on the phone, using a laptop computer in bed). Also, adolescents learn to maximize cues that are associated with feeling sleepy and falling asleep, and to decrease the cues associated with staying awake.

Sleep restriction is another highly recommended behavioral treatment for insomnia (Spielman, Saskin, & Thorpy, 1987). This approach involves limiting the amount of time spent in bed, since some adolescents with insomnia tend to spend too much time in bed unsuccessfully trying to sleep. The allowed time in bed is increased or decreased by 15 to 20 minutes (or kept stable) for a given week depending on whether the adolescent's sleep efficiency that week increases, decreases, or stays the same. Many adolescents have numerous misconceptions or beliefs about sleep that actually interfere with their ability to fall asleep or to maintain sleep. Cognitive therapy helps the adolescent learn to get rid of her/his false beliefs and assumptions (e.g., misconceptions about causes of insomnia, faulty ideas about sleep promotion habits, etc.) and to replace them with appropriate and more helpful interpretations. Additional large-scale studies on the efficacy of these approaches for treating insomnia and related difficulties in adolescents would further advance the field. Similarly, treatment of sleep problems in adolescents with depression, substance abuse problems, and other behavioral and emotional difficulties requires careful assessment.

Bootzin and Stevens (2005) developed a behaviorally oriented group treatment (e.g., stimulus control, sleep hygiene education, cognitive therapy, and stress reduction) for sleep disturbances in adolescents being treated for substance abuse. Preliminary findings indicate that the adolescents in the program reported less insomnia-like symptoms and less daytime sleepiness, associated with reduced substance abuse problems (Bootzin & Stevens, 2005). Furthermore, Wolfson and colleagues are currently evaluating the efficacy of a prevention-oriented intervention designed to teach young adolescents sleep hygiene practices and, in so doing, prevent daytime behavioral difficulties, such as depressed mood. Pilot results suggested that the intervention was successful at improving students' sleep habits and their sense of self-efficacy (Vo, LeChasseur, Wolfson, & Marco, 2003).

In addition to insomnia type difficulties, DSPS, or delayed sleep phase, is especially troublesome for adolescents and, as discussed earlier, may coexist with depression. Adolescents with DSPS often present challenges if they are not motivated to change their sleep/wake patterns. Generally, intervention for DSPS or circadian rhythm disorders involves phototherapy (light) and/or chronotherapy along with collaboration with the school. Light therapy involves increasing morning light (e.g., using a light box at 10,000 lux or natural sunlight) and decreasing evening light (e.g., avoiding exposure to bright lights close to bedtime; Garcia et al., 2001). Chronotherapy, through progressive phase delay, regulates the timing of wakefulness and sleep to decrease excessive daytime sleepiness. Utilizing progressive phase delay, the adolescent delays bedtime and wake time 2 to 3 hours each day until a target sleep onset and wake time is obtained (Garcia et al., 2001). Furthermore, standard high school early start times are incompatible with most adolescents' sleep/wake patterns. Adolescents struggling with DSPS find early school start times impossible to manage.

Finally, there is also evidence that young depressed girls and adolescents of both sexes with MDD show weak circadian rest activity cycles and reduced daytime light exposure (Armitage et al., 2004). Adolescents with depression may benefit substantially from chronobiological interventions.

CONCLUSIONS

Inadequate sleep and irregular sleep schedules, common to adolescence, are frequently associated with depressed mood. Likewise, a number of sleep disorders seen in adolescents present with depression symptoms or may coexist with major depression. More importantly, MDDs are associated with significant sleep disturbance. Sleep disturbance also appears to be a risk factor for the initial development of depression and for risk of relapse and recurrence after a first onset. In addition, sleep problems are the most prevalent residual symptom of depression in adolescents. For the most part, subjective sleep disturbances are more prevalent than polysomnographic sleep measures. Newer procedures for quantifying sleep microarchitecture may prove to be a more sensitive metric in differentiating depressed adolescents from healthy controls.

Risk for the development of MDD is clearly higher in adolescence than in childhood, and there are developmental and environmental changes that impact sleep and sleep habits that may further contribute to this increased risk for depression. Early detection and intervention are important to reducing the economic and personal costs of depression, and there is good consensus that improving sleep is a key component of this goal (Bootzin & Stevens, 2005; Brunello et al., 2000; Manber et al., 1996). Understanding how developmental changes in sleep and circadian rhythms may exacerbate risk for depression will undoubtedly inform and improve intervention strategies. Educators, school psychologists, and health care professionals working with these adolescents need to advocate, collaborate, and develop education and treatment plans that alter the school environment in addition to recommending the treatment approaches discussed in this chapter.

NOTE

1. The authors would like to thank Kirstin Brown and Michaela Sparling for their dedicated research and editorial work on this chapter.

REFERENCES

Adrien, J. (2002). Neurobiological bases for the relation between sleep and depression. *Sleep Medicine Reviews, 6*, 341–351.

Aloia, M. S., Arnedt, J. T., Smith, L., Skrekas, J., Stanchina, M., & Millman, R. P. (2005). Examining the construct of depression in obstructive sleep apnea syndrome. *Sleep Medicine, 6*(2), 115–121.

Anderson, D. R. (1979). Treatment of insomnia in a 13-year-old boy by relaxation training and reduction of parental attention. *Journal of Behavior Therapy and Experimental Psychiatry, 10*, 263–265.

Appelboom-Fondu, J., Kerkhofs, M., & Mendlewicz, J. (1988). Depression in adolescents and young adults: Polysomnographic and neuroendocrine aspects. *Journal of Affective Disorders, 14*, 35–40.

Armitage, R. (1995). Microarchitectural findings in sleep EEG in depression: Diagnostic implications. *Biological Psychiatry, 37*, 72–84.

Armitage, R. (2000). The effects of antidepressants on sleep in patients with depression. *Canadian Journal of Psychiatry, 45*, 803–809.

Armitage, R. (2007). Sleep and circadian rhythms in mood disorders. *Acta Psychiatrica Scandinavica. Supplementum, 115*, 104–115.

Armitage, R., Emslie, G. J., Hoffmann, R. F., Rintelmann, J., & Rush, A. J. (2001). Delta sleep EEG in depressed adolescent females and healthy controls. *Journal of Affective Disorders, 63*, 139–148.

Armitage, R., Emslie, G. J., Hoffmann, R. F., Weinberg, W. A., Kowatch, R. A., Rintelmann, J., et al. (2000a). Ultradian rhythms and temporal coherence in sleep EEG in depressed children and adolescents. *Biological Psychiatry, 47*, 338–350.

Armitage, R., Emslie, G., & Rintelmann, J. (1997). The effect of fluoxetine on sleep EEG in childhood depression: A preliminary report. *Neuropsychopharmacology, 17*(4), 241–245.

Armitage, R., & Hoffmann, R. F. (2001). Sleep EEG, depression and gender. *Sleep Medicine Review, 5*, 237–246.

Armitage, R., Hoffmann, R., Emslie, G., Rintelman, J., Moore, J., & Lewis, K. (2004). Rest-activity cycles in childhood and adolescent depression. *Journal of the American Academy of Child & Adolescent Psychiatry, 43*(6), 761–769.

Armitage, R., Hoffmann, R., Emslie, G., Rintelman, J., & Robert, J. (2006). Sleep microarchitecture in childhood and adolescent depression: Temporal coherence. *Clinical EEG and Neuroscience, 37*(1), 1–9.

Armitage, R., Hoffmann, R., Fitch, T., Trivedi, M., & Rush, A. J. (2000b). Temporal characteristics of delta activity during NREM sleep in depressed outpatients and healthy adults: Group and sex effects. *Sleep, 23*(5), 607–617.

Armitage, R., Hoffmann, R. F., & Rush, A. J. (1999). Biological rhythm disturbance in depression: Temporal coherence of ultradian sleep EEG rhythms. *Psychological Medicine, 29*, 1435–1448.

Armitage, R., Hoffmann, R., Trivedi, M., & Rush, A. J. (2000c). Slow-wave activity in NREM sleep: Sex and age effects in depressed outpatients and healthy controls. *Psychiatry Research, 95*, 201–213.

Armitage, R., Roffwarg, H. P., Rush, A. J., Calhoun, J. S., Purdy, D. G., & Giles, D. E. (1992). Digital period analysis of sleep EEG in depression. *Biological Psychiatry, 31*, 52–68.

Aronen, E. T., Paavonen, E. J., Fjalberg, M., Soininen, M., & Torronen, J. (2000). Sleep and psychiatric symptoms in school-age children. *Journal of the American Academy of Child & Adolescent Psychiatry, 39*(4), 502–508.

Baran, A. S., & Richert, A. C. (2003). Obstructive sleep apnea and depression. *CNS Spectrum, 8*(2), 128–134.

Barbe, R. P., Williamson, D. E., Bridge, J. A., Birmaher, B., Dahl, R. E., Axelson, D. A., et al. (2005). Clinical differences between suicidal and nonsuicidal depressed children and adolescents. *Journal of Clinical Psychiatry, 66*(4), 492–498.

Barowsky, E. I., Moskowitz, J., & Zweig, J. B. (1990). Biofeedback for disorders of initiating and maintaining sleep. *Annals of the New York Academy of Science, 602*, 97–103.

Benca, R. M., Obermeyer, W. H., Thisted, R. A., & Gillin, J. C. (1992). Sleep and psychiatric disorders. A meta-analysis. *Archives of General Psychiatry, 49*, 651–668.

Bertocci, M. A., Dahl, R. E., Williamson, D. E., Josif, A. M., Birmaher, B., Axelson, D., et al. (2005). Subjective sleep complaints in pediatric depression: A controlled study and comparison with EEG measures of sleep and waking. *Journal of the American Academy of Child & Adolescent Psychiatry, 44*, 1158–1168.

Birmaher, B., & Heydl, P. (2001). Biological studies in depressed children and adolescents. *International Journal of Neuropsychopharmacology, 4*, 149–157.

Bootzin, R. R., & Stevens, S. J. (2005). Adolescents, substance abuse, and the treatment of insomnia and daytime sleepiness. *Clinical Psychology Review, 25*(5), 629–644.

Brunello, N., Armitage, R., Feinberg, I., Holsboer-Trachsler, E., Leger, D., Linkowski, P., et al. (2000). Depression and sleep disorders: Clinical relevance, economic burden and pharmacological treatment. *Neuropsychobiology, 42*(3), 107–119.

Carney, C. E., Edinger, J. D., Meyer, B., Lindman, L., & Istre, T. (2006). Symptom-focused rumination and sleep disturbance. *Behavioral Sleep Medicine, 4*(4), 228–241.

Carney, P. R., Berry, R. B., & Geyer, J. D. (2004). *Clinical sleep disorders*. Philadelphia, PA: Lippincott Williams & Wilkins.

Carskadon, M. A. (1982). The second decade. In C. Guilleminault (Ed.), *Sleeping and waking disorders: Indications and techniques*. Menlo Park, CA: Addison-Wesley.

Carskadon, M. A., & Acebo, C. (2002). Regulation of sleepiness in adolescents: Update, insights, and speculation. *Sleep, 25*(6), 606–614.

Carskadon, M. A., Acebo, C., & Jenni, O. G. (2004). Regulation of adolescent sleep: Implications for behavior. In R. Dahl (Ed.), *Annals of the New York Academy of Sciences, adolescent brain development: Vulnerabilities and opportunities* (Vol. 1021, pp. 276–291). New York: New York Academy of Sciences.

Carskadon, M. A., Harvey, K., Duke, P., Anders, T. F., & Dement, W. C. (1980). Pubertal changes in daytime sleepiness. *Sleep, 2*, 453–460.

Carskadon, M. A., Vieira, C., & Acebo, C. (1993). Association between puberty and delayed phase preference. *Sleep, 16*(3), 258–262.

Carskadon, M., Wolfson, A., Acebo, C., Tzischinsky, O., & Seifer, R. (1998). Adolescent sleep patterns, circadian timing, and sleepiness at a transition to early school days. *Sleep, 21*(8), 871–881.

Choquet, M., Menke, H., & Ledoux, S. (1989). Self-reported alcohol consumption among adolescents and the signification of early onset. A longitudinal approach. *Social Psychiatry Psychiatric Epidemiology, 24*(2), 102–112.

Crabtree, V. M., Varni, J. W., & Gozal, D. (2004). Health-related quality of life and depressive symptoms in children with suspected sleep-disordered breathing. *Sleep: Journal of Sleep and Sleep Disorders Research, 27*(6), 1131–1138.

Currier, D., Mann, M. J., Oquendo, M. A., Galfalvy, H., & Mann, J. J. (2006). Sex differences in the familial transmission of mood disorders. *Journal of Affective Disorders, 95*(1–3), 51–60.

Dahl, R. E. (1996). The regulation of sleep and arousal: Development and psychopathology. *Development and Psychopathology, 8*, 3–27.

Dahl, R. E. (1999). The consequences of insufficient sleep for adolescents: Links between sleep and emotional regulation. *Phi Delta Kappa, 80*(5), 354–359.

Dahl, R. E., Puig-Antich, J,, Ryan, N. D., Nelson, B., Dachille, S., Cunningham, S.L., et al. (1990). EEG sleep in adolescents with major depression: The role of suicidality and inpatient status. *Journal of Affective Disorders, 19*, 63–75.

Dahl, R. E., Ryan, N. D., Birmaher, B., al-Shabbout, M., Williamson, D. E., Neidig, M., et al. (1991). Electroencephalographic sleep measures in prepubertal depression. *Psychiatry Review, 38*, 201–214.

Dahl, R. E., Ryan, N. D., Matty, M. K., Birmaher, B., al-Shabbout, M., Williamson, D. E., et al. (1996). Sleep onset abnormalities in depressed adolescents. *Biological Psychiatry, 39*(6), 400–410.

Dahl, R. E., Ryan, N. E., Perel, J., Birmaher, B., al-Shabbout, M., Nelson, B., et al. (1994). Cholinergic REM induction test with arecoline in depressed children. *Psychiatry Research, 51*, 269–282.

Daniels, E., King, M. A., Smith, I. E., & Shneerson, J. M. (2001). Health-related quality of life in narcolepsy. *Journal of Sleep Research, 10*(1), 75–81.

Deldin, P. J., Phillips, L. K., & Thomas, R. J. (2005). A preliminary study of sleep-disordered breathing in major depressive disorder. *Sleep Medicine, 7*(2), 131–139.

Donovan, J. E., & Jessor, R. (1985). Structure of problem behavior in adolescence and young adulthood. *Journal of Consulting and Clinical Psychology, 53*, 890–904.

DSM IV-TR. (2000). *Diagnostic and statistical manual of mental disorders DSM-IV-TR* (4th ed.). Arlington, VA: American Psychiatric Association.

Duncan, S., Duncan, T. E., & Hops, H. (1998). Progressions of alcohol, cigarette, and marijuana use in adolescence. *Journal of Behavioral Medicine, 21*, 375–388.

Emslie, G. J., Armitage, R., Weinberg, W. A., Rush, A. J., Mayes, T. L., & Hoffman, R. F. (2001). Sleep polysomnography as a predictor of recurrence in children and adolescents with major depressive disorder. *International Journal of Neuropsychopharmacology, 4*, 159–168.

Emslie, G. J., Rush, A. J., Weinberg, W. A., Rintelmann, J. W., & Roffwarg, H. P. (1994). Sleep EEG features of adolescents with major depression. *Biological Psychiatry, 36*, 573–581.

Epstein, R., Chillag, N., & Lavie, P. (1998). Starting times of school: Effects of daytime functioning of fifth-grade children in Israel. *Sleep, 21*, 250–256.

Fallone, G., Owens, J. A., & Deane, J. (2002). Sleepiness in children and adolescents: Clinical implications. *Sleep Medicine Reviews, 6*, 287–306.

Farina, B., Marca, G. D., Grochocinski, V. J., Mazza, M., Buysse, D. J., Di Giannantonio, M., et al. (2003). Microstructure of sleep in depressed patients according to the cyclic alternating pattern. *Journal of Affective Disorders, 77*, 227–235.

Fredrikson, K., Rhodes, J., Reddy, R., & Way, N. (2004). Sleepless in Chicago: Tracking the effects of adolescent sleep loss during the middle school years. *Child Development, 75*(1), 84–95.

Fulton, M. K., Armitage, R., & Rush, A. J. (2000). Sleep electroencephalographic coherence abnormalities in individuals at high risk for depression: A pilot study. *Biological Psychiatry, 47*, 618–625.

Garcia, J., Rosen, G., & Mahowald, M. (2001). Circadian rhythms and circadian rhythm disorders in children and adolescents. *Seminars Pediatric Neurology, 8*, 229–240.

Gibson, E. S., Powles, A. C. P., Thabane, L., O'Brien, S., Molnar, D. S., Trajanovic, N., et al. (2006). "Sleepiness" is serious in adolescence: Two surveys of 3235 Canadian students. *BMC Public Health, 6*, 116.

Giles, D. E., Kupfer, D. J., Rush, A. J., & Roffwarg, H. P. (1998). Controlled comparison of electrophysiological sleep in families of probands with unipolar depression. *American Journal of Psychiatry, 155*(2), 192–199.

Giles, D. E., Kupfer, D. J., Rush, A. J., Roffwarg, H. P., Biggs, M. M., & Etzel, B. A. (1989). Polysomnographic parameters in first-degree relatives of unipolar probands. *Psychiatry Research, 27*, 127–136.

Goetz, R. R., Wolk, S. I., Coplan, J. D., Ryan, N. D., & Weissman, M. M. (2001). Premorbid polysomnographic signs in depressed adolescents: A reanalysis of EEG sleep after longitudinal follow-up in adulthood. *Biological Psychiatry, 49*, 930–942.

Gregory, A. M., Caspi, A., Eley, T. C., Moffitt, T. E., O'Connor, T. G., & Poulton, R. (2005). Prospective longitudinal associations between persistent sleep problems in childhood and anxiety and depression disorders in adulthood. *Journal of the American Academy of Child & Adolescent Psychiatry, 33*, 157–163.

Gregory, A. M., & O'Connor, T. G. (2002). Sleep problems in childhood: A longitudinal study of developmental change and association with behavioral problems. *Journal of the American Academy of Child & Adolescent Psychiatry, 41*(8), 964–971.

Guilleminault, C., & Pelayo, R. (2000). Narcolepsy in children: A practical guide to its diagnosis, treatment and follow-up. *Paediatric Drugs, 2*(1), 1–9.

Haba-Rubio, J. (2005). Psychiatric aspects of organic sleep disorders. *Dialogues Clinical Neuroscience, 7*(4), 335–346.

Hardway, C., & Fuligni, A. J. (2006). Dimensions of family connectedness among adolescents with Mexican, Chinese, and European backgrounds. *Developmental Psychology, 43*(6), 1246–1258.

Hoffmann, R. F., Armitage, R., Trivedi, M. H., & Rush, A. J. (1999). The effects of fluoxetine on quantitative sleep EEG in depressed outpatients. *Sleep and Hypnosis, 1*(4), 217–224.

Hoffmann, R. F., Emslie, G., & Armitage, R. (2006). The time course of slow-wave activity in depressed and healthy children and adolescents. *Sleep, 29*, A327.

Iglowstein, I., Jenni, O. G., Molinari, L., & Largo, R. H. (2003). Sleep duration from infancy to adolescence: Reference values and generational trends. *Pediatrics, 111*, 302–307.

Ivanenko, A., Crabtree, V. M., & Gozal, D. (2005). Sleep and depression in children and adolescents. *Sleep Medicine Review, 9*, 115–129.

Jacobs, G. D., Pace-Schott, E. F., Stickgold, R., & Otto, M. W. (2004). Cognitive behavior therapy and pharmacotherapy for insomnia: A randomized controlled trial and direct comparison. *Archives of Internal Medicine, 164*(17), 1888–1896.

Jenni, O. G., Achermann, P., & Carskadon, M. (2005). Homeostatic sleep regulation in adolescents. *Sleep, 28*(11), 1446–1454.

Jenni, O. G., & Carskadon, M. (2004). Spectral analysis of the sleep electroencephalogram during adolescence. *Sleep, 27*(4), 774–783.

Johnson, E. O., Chilcoat, H. D., & Breslau, N. (2000). Trouble sleeping and anxiety/depression in childhood. *Psychiatry Research, 94*(2), 93–102.

Kennard, B., Silva, S., Vitiello, B., Curry, J., Kratochvil, C., Simons, A., et al. (2006). Remission and residual symptoms after short-term treatment in the treatment of adolescents with depression study (TADS). *Journal of the American Academy of Child & Adolescent Psychiatry, 45*(12), 1404–1411.

Kirmil-Gray, K., Eagleston, J. R., Gibson, E., & Thoresen, C. E. (1984). Sleep disturbance in adolescents: Sleep quality, sleep habits, beliefs about sleep, and daytime functioning. *Journal of Youth and Adolescence, 13*(5), 375–384.

Kryger, M., Roth, T., & Dement, W. (Eds.). (2005). *Principles and practice of sleep medicine* (4th ed.). Philadelphia, PA: W.B. Saunders.

Kutcher, S., Williamson, P., Marton, P., & Szalai, J. (1992). REM latency in endogenously depressed adolescents. *British Journal of Psychiatry, 16*, 399–402.

Lahmeyer, H. W., Poznanski, E. O., & Bellur, S. N. (1983). EEG sleep in depressed adolescents. *American Journal of Psychiatry, 140*(9), 1150–1153.

Leary, M. R., Tchividjian, L. R., & Kraxberger, B. E. (1994). Self-presentation can be hazardous to your health: Impression management and health risk. *Health Psychology, 13*, 461–470.

Ledoux, S., Choquet, M., & Manfredi, R. (1994). Self-reported use of drugs for sleep or distress among French adolescents. *Journal of Adolescent Health, 15*(6), 495–502.

Liu, X., & Buysse, D. J. (2005). Sleep and youth suicidal behavior: A neglected field. *Current Opinion in Psychiatry, 19*, 288–293.

Liu, X., Buysse, D. J., Gentzler, A. L., Kiss, E., Mayer, L., Kapornai, K., et al. (2007). Insomnia and hypersomnia associated with depressive phenomenology and comorbidity in childhood depression. *Sleep, 30*(1), 83–90.

Manber, R., Bootzin, R. R., Acebo, C., & Carskadon, M. A. (1996). The effects of regularizing sleep-wake schedules on daytime sleepiness. *Sleep, 19*(5), 432–441.

Meltzer, L., & Mindell, J. (2006). Sleep and sleep disorders in children and adolescents. *Psychiatric Clinics North America, 29*(4), 1059–1076.

Mindell, J. A. (2003). Insomnia in children and adolescents. In M. P. Szuba, J. D. Kloss & D. F. Dinges (Eds.), *Insomnia principles and management* (pp. 125–135). New York: Cambridge University Press.

Mindell, J. A., Emslie, G., Blumer, J., Genel, M., Glaze, D., Ivanenko, A., et al. (2006). Pharmacologic management of insomnia in children and adolescents: Consensus statement. *Pediatrics, 117*(6), e1223–1232.

Mindell, J. A., & Owens, J. A. (2003). *A clinical guide to pediatric sleep: Diagnosis and management of sleep problems.* Philadelphia, PA: Lippincott Williams & Wilkins.

Modell, S., Ising, M., Holsboers, F., & Lauer, C. J. (2005). The Munich vulnerability study on affective disorders: Premorbid polysomnographic profile of affected high-risk probands. *Biological Psychiatry, 58*, 694–699.

Morehouse, R. L., Kusumakar, V., Kutcher, S. P., LeBlanc, J., & Armitage, R. (2002). Temporal coherence in ultradian sleep EEG rhythms in a never-depressed, high-risk cohort of female adolescents. *Biological Psychiatry, 51*, 446–456.

Morin, C. M. (2004). Cognitive-behavioral approaches to the treatment of insomnia. *Journal of Clinical Psychiatry, 65*(16), 33–40.

Morrison, D. N., McGee, R., & Stanton, W. R. (1992). Sleep problems in adolescence. *Journal of the American Academy of Child & Adolescent Psychiatry, 31*(1), 94–99.

National Sleep Foundation. (2006). *Sleep in America poll.* Washington, DC: National Sleep Foundation.

Naylor, M. W., Shain, B. N., & Shipley J. E. (1990). REM latency in psychiatrically depressed adolescents. *Biological Psychiatry, 28*, 161–164.

Nolen-Hoeksema, S. (1991). Responses to depression and their effects on the duration of depressive episodes. *Journal of Abnormal Psychology, 100*, 569–582.

Ohayon, M. M., Caulet, M., & Lemoine, P. (1998). Comorbidity of mental and insomnia disorders in the general population. *Comprehensive Psychiatry, 39*(4), 185–197.

Ohayon, M. M., & Roberts, R. E. (2001). Comparability of sleep disorders diagnoses using DSM-IV and ICSD classifications with adolescents. *Sleep, 24*(8), 920–925.

Okawa, M., Uchiyama, M., Ozaki, S., Shibui, K., & Ichikawa, H. (1998). Circadian rhythm sleep disorders in adolescents: Clinical trials of combined treatments based on chronobiology. *Psychiatry Clinical Neuroscience, 52*(5), 483–490.

Ong, S. H., Wickramaratne, P., & Tang, M. (2006). Early childhood sleep and eating problems as predictors of adolescent and adult mood and anxiety disorders. *Journal of Affective Disorders, 96*(1–2), 1–8.

Patten, C. A., Choi, W. S., Gillin, J. C., & Pierce, J. P. (2000). Depressive symptoms and cigarette smoking predict development and persistence of sleep problems in U.S. adolescents. *Pediatrics, 106*(2), 1–17.

Picchietti, D., & Winkelman, J. W. (2005). Restless legs syndrome, periodic limb movements in sleep, and depression. *Sleep, 28*(7), 891–898.

Rao, U., Dahl, R. E., Ryan, N. D., Birmaher, B., Williamson, D. E., Giles, D. E., et al. (1996). The relationship between longitudinal clinical course and sleep and cortisol changes in adolescent depression. *Biological Psychiatry, 40*, 474–484.

Reynolds, C. F., III, & Kupfer, D. J. (1987). Sleep research in affective illness: State of the art circa. *Sleep, 10*(3), 199–215.

Riemann, D., Kammerer, J., Low, H., & Schmidt, M. H. (1995). Sleep in adolescents with primary major depression and schizophrenia: A pilot study. *Journal of Child Psychology and Psychiatry, 36*, 313–326.

Robert, J., Hoffmann, R., Emslie, G., Rintelmann, J., Moore, J., & Armitage, R. (2006). Sleep macroarchitecture in childhood and adolescent depression. *Sleep, 29*(3), 342–349.

Roberts, R., Roberts, C., & Chen, I. G. (2002). Impact of insomnia on future functioning of adolescents. *Journal of Psychosomatic Research, 53*, 561–569.

Roberts, R. E., Lee, E. S., Hernandez, M., & Solari, A. C. (2004). Symptoms of insomnia among adolescents in the Lower Rio Grand Valley of Texas. *Sleep, 27*(4), 751–759.

Roberts, R. E., Lewinsohn, P. M., & Seeley, J. R. (1995). Symptoms of SSM-III-R major depression in adolescence: Evidence from an epidemiological survey. *Journal of the American Academy of Child & Adolescent Psychiatry, 34*(12), 1608–1617.

Rush, A. J., Armitage, R., Gillin, J. C., Yonkers, K. A., Winokur, A., Moldofsky, H., et al. (1998). Comparative effects of nefazodone and fluoxetine on sleep in outpatients with major depressive disorder. *Biological Psychiatry, 44*(2), 3–14.

Saarenpaa-Heikkila, O., Laippala, P., & Koivikko, M. (2001). Subjective daytime sleepiness and its predictors in Finnish adolescents in an interview study. *Acta Paediatrics, 90*(5), 552–557.

Sadeh, A., Gruber, R., & Raviv, A. (2002). Sleep, neurobehavioral functioning, and behavior problems in school-age children. *Child Development, 73*(2), 405–417.

Sevim, S., Dogu, O., Kaleagasi, H., Aral, M., Metin, O., & Camdeviren, H. (2004). Correlation of anxiety and depression symptoms in patients with restless legs syndrome: A population based survey. *Journal of Neurology, Neurosurgery & Psychiatry, 75*(2), 226–230.

Shang, C. Y., Gau, S. S.-F., & Soong, W. T. (2006). Association between childhood sleep problems and perinatal factors, parental mental distress and behavioral problems. *Sleep Research, 15*, 63–73.

Sheldon, S., & Kryger, M. (Eds.). (2005). *Principles and practice of pediatric sleep medicine*. Philadelphia, PA: W.B. Saunders.

Spielman, A. J., Saskin, P., & Thorpy, M. J. (1987). Treatment of chronic insomnia by restriction of time in bed. *Sleep, 10*(1), 45–56.

Strauch, I., & Meier, B. (1988). Sleep need in adolescents: A longitudinal approach. *Sleep, 11*(4), 378–386.

Szymczak, J. T., Jasinska, M., Pawlak, E., & Swierzykowska, M. (1993). Annual and weekly changes in the sleep-wake rhythm of school children. *Sleep, 16*, 433–435.

Taylor, D., Jenni, O., Acebo, C., & Carskadon, M. (2005). Sleep tendency during extended wakefulness: Insights into adolescent sleep regulation and behavior. *Journal of Sleep Research, 14*(3), 239–244.

Teicher, M. H., Glod, C. A., Harper, D., Magnus, E., Brasher, C., Wren, F., et al. (1993). Locomotor activity in depressed children and adolescents: I. Circadian dysregulation. *Journal of the American Academy of Child & Adolescent Psychiatry, 32*, 760–769.

Thorleifsdottir, B., Bjornsson, J. K., Benediktsdottir, B., Gislason, T. H., & Kristbjarnarson, H. (2002). Sleep and sleep habits from childhood to young adulthood over a 10-year period. *Journal of Psychosomatic Research, 53*, 529–537.

Trivedi, M. H., Rush, A. J., Armitage, R., Gullion, C. M., Grannemann, B. D., Orsulak, P. J., et al. (1999). Effects of fluoxetine on the polysomnogram in outpatients with major depression. *Neuropsychopharmacology, 20*(5), 447–459.

Tsuno, N., Besset, A., & Ritchie, K. (2005). Sleep and depression. *Journal of Clinical Psychiatry, 66*, 1254–1269.

Vandeputte, M., & de Weerd, A. (2003). Sleep disorders and depressive feelings: A global survey with the Beck Depression Scale. *Sleep Medicine, 4*(4), 343–345.

Vo, O. T., LeChasseur, K., Wolfson, A., & Marco, C. (2003). Sleepy pre-teens: Second pilot of sleep-smart program in 7th graders. *Sleep, 26*(Abstract Suppl), 1036.

Vogel, G. W., Kaplita, S. B., Fleming, J. B., Montplaisir, J., Erman, M. K., Albala, B. J., et al. (1998). Comparative effects of nefazodone and fluoxetine on sleep in outpatients with major depressive disorder. *Biological Psychiatry, 44*(1), 3–14.

Weil, G., & Goldfried, M. R. (1973). Treatment of insomnia in an eleven-year-old child through self-relaxation. *Behavior Therapy, 4*, 282–294.

Wolfson, A. (2002). Bridging the gap between research and practice: What will adolescents' sleep/wake patterns look like in the 21st Century? In M. A. Carskadon (Ed.), *Adolescent sleep patterns: Biological, social, and psychological influences.* New York: Cambridge University Press.

Wolfson, A. R., Acebo, C., Fallone, G., & Carskadon, M. A. (2003a). Actigraphically-estimated sleep patterns of middle school students. *Sleep (Abstract Supplement), 26*, G0313.

Wolfson, A. R., & Carskadon, M. A. (1998). Sleep schedules and daytime functioning in adolescents. *Child Development, 69*, 875–887.

Wolfson, A. R., Carskadon, M. A., Acebo, C., Seifer, R., Fallone, G., Labyak, S. E., et al. (2003b). Evidence for the validity of a sleep habits survey for adolescents. *Sleep, 26*(2), 213–216.

Wolfson, A. R., Spaulding, N., Dandrow, C., & Baroni, E. (2007). Middle school start times: The importance of a good night's sleep for young adolescents. *Behavioral Sleep Medicine, 5*(3), 194–209.

Wolfson, A., Tzischinsky, O., Brown, C., Darley, C., Acebo, C., & Carskadon, M. A. (1995). Sleep, behavior, and stress at the transition to senior high school. *Sleep Research, 24*, 115.

Wyatt, J. K. (2004). Delayed sleep phase syndrome: Pathophysiology and treatment options. *Sleep, 27*(6), 1195–1203.

Yang, C.-K., Kim, J. K., Patel, S. R., & Lee, J.-H. (2005). Age-related changes in sleep/wake patterns among Korean teenagers. *Pediatrics, 115*(1), 250–256.

Section IV

PSYCHOSOCIAL FACTORS

Chapter Twelve

Stress Exposure and Stress Generation in Adolescent Depression

CONSTANCE HAMMEN

CONTENTS

The current volume's focus on depression in adolescence is an acknowledgment of the distinctiveness of this age group in terms of epidemiological, etiological, course, and treatment considerations. The high rates of onset of depressive disorder and the emergence of dramatic gender differences in adolescence raise intriguing questions about the developmental psychopathology of depression, and foretell crucial clinical concerns about the impact and course of depressive disorders with adolescent onset. Indeed, it could be claimed that studies of adolescent depression are central to understanding unipolar depression in its most frequent and typical forms. One reason is that adolescence is one of the most common periods of onset of depression in recent birth cohorts, with high rates of recurrence even in community samples (e.g., Andrade et al., 2003; Kessler et al., 2003;

Lewinsohn, Rohde, Klein, & Seeley, 1999). A second is that compared to adolescent depression, those with childhood onset and later adult onset are likely different disorders with unique etiological and course features (e.g., Blazer, 2003; Weissman et al., 1999).

The purpose of the current chapter is to examine the role of stress in adolescent depression as a *predictor* of onset of depressive disorders and symptoms, as well as stress as a *consequence* of depression and characteristics of the depressed person and his or her environment (and such stress in turn may precipitate further depression). The research on stressful life events and their impact in adolescence is voluminous, spanning investigations of discrete stressors, such as a traumatic event or natural disaster, teen pregnancy, parental divorce, sexual assault, community violence, poverty, as well as studies of recent cumulative negative events. The current chapter will focus only on the latter—cumulative negative events—to limit the coverage and because such research forms the basis of most contemporary models and empirical tests of etiological mechanisms of depression and of explanations of gender differences. Also, excellent recent reviews of the wider range of stressors, both discrete and aggregated, in both child and adolescent samples covering psychopathology broadly, are available and generally draw similar conclusions about the stress-symptom relationship (e.g., Grant et al., 2003; Grant et al., 2006).

Most models of the origins of adolescent depression are either implicitly or explicitly diathesis-stress models, in which stressors play a necessary role, moderated or mediated by biological, socioemotional, and cognitive variables. Therefore, many of the chapters in Sections III and IV of this book will also present theory and research involving stressors. Consequently, the current chapter attempts to avoid duplication, and will present selective coverage of diathesis-stress models predicting depression.

Finally, the chapter attempts to emphasize issues that move beyond the basic observation that stress triggers depression. Thus, it notes certain methodological issues and addresses the measurement of stress, discusses whether adolescence is truly associated with increasing exposure to stress, reviews research on changing sensitivity to stressors, and explores evidence and mechanisms of stress generation. There is also discussion of gender differences in several topics: exposure to stressors, depressive reactions, specific sensitivity to interpersonal events, and the generation of stress.

METHODOLOGICAL CONSIDERATIONS

Stressor Assessment

Although research may examine depression in relation to a single specific stressor or situation (e.g., teen pregnancy, witnessing violence), considerable research examines occurrence of varied and multiple episodic (acute) stressful life events. While studies of adult depression have increasingly adopted interview methods of assessing stressors, with exceptions, most research on adolescent depression has used self-report checklists. Each of these approaches has advantages and limitations, which are elaborated below. Relatively few methods of evaluating ongoing, chronic stress have been developed, and pertinent issues are discussed.

Self-Report Checklists

A number of different checklists of negative life events have been reported. A review of methods for assessing life events in relation to youth psychopathology reported at least 11 such lists (Grant, Compas, Thurm, McMahon, & Gipson, 2004). Some of the more commonly used include the Adolescent Perceived Events Scale (APES; Compas, Davis, Forsythe, & Wagner, 1987) which covers both negative and positive experiences rated by the youth on valence (+3 extremely good to −3 extremely bad); the Life Events Questionnaire (LEQ; Coddington, 1972) originally developed for children but adapted for adolescents; and the Junior High Life Experiences Study (JHLES; Swearingen & Cohen, 1985), also covering positive and negative events. It is common for these instruments to be adapted by adding content relevant to the participant group, shortened to include only negative events, or only major events. A number of research groups have developed their own checklists, often borrowing items from these or similar instruments or generating items relevant to specific samples (e.g., Adolescent Stress Questionnaire; Byrne, Byrne, & Reinhart, 1995; Byrne & Mazanov, 2002; the Adolescent Life Change Event Scale; Waaktaar, Borge, Fundingsrud, Christie, & Torgersen, 2004; Yeaworth, York, Hussey, Ingle, & Goodwin, 1980). Scoring is variable across instruments, sometimes based on simple counts of event occurrence in the previous specified time frame, or sums of valence scores rated by youth for subjective impact. Recent research has established relatively sound psychometric properties of life event checklists, including test-retest reliability and concurrent validity (Grant et al., 2004). Some checklists target daily hassles, minor and daily events often highly subjective in nature—for example "schoolwork too hard" or "not enough fun things to do" (e.g., Everyday Life Events Scale [ELESC], Jose, Cafasso, and D'Anna [1994]; school-related [academic and peer] hassles questionnaire; Robinson, Garber, and Hilsman [1995]).

The advantages of checklists are evident. They are associated with low cost due to ease of administration and scoring. They are flexible and can be adapted for coverage of specific populations, and may be easily used in screening situations to detect potential needs for intervention. Disadvantages include reliance on idiosyncratic interpretation of the meaning of an item (e.g., "health problem of family member," "problems with classmates") as well as individual decisions about whether an event's occurrence rises to the threshold level for reporting ("brother or sister leaving home" [for how long?]), failure to include occurrence of personally significant events if rare or not represented on the questionnaire, and lack of dates of events' occurrence. Caution is also warranted about the content investigators choose to include on checklists. For example, Meadows, Brown, and Elder (2006), in the national Add Health study found that males scored higher on the stress index than females at all three waves of data, but they attributed the differences to the fact that the 12-item checklist contained more items likely to be experienced by males rather than representative of all stressors (e.g., expulsion from school, victim of violence, first involvement with law enforcement).

Conceptual criticisms may also be raised when events' scoring is based on subjective appraisal of negativity, as such research (appraisals of stress predicting depression) may involve tautology due to the effects of emotional state on perceptions.

Notably, checklists provide no information about the context in which stressful life events occur, or how multiple events may be related to each other—all of which may affect the significance, duration, and consequences of the events. The use of different checklists, administered to adolescents of different ages, also makes it difficult to compare across samples, or to draw conclusions about normative aspects of stress experiences among adolescents (e.g., Grant et al., 2004). Lack of standard widely used measures also limits understanding of stress-depression mechanisms, the clarity of which requires greater precision in measurement of objective aspects of stress exposure.

Interview Methods of Stressor Assessment

Several research groups have reported on stress-depression relationships based on methods of contextual threat assessment for adolescents, adapted from methods originally applied to adults (e.g., Brown & Harris, 1978). In this approach the interviewer elicits information from the participant (or in the case of children and younger adolescents, from both a parent and the child) concerning not only event occurrence, but also the date of occurrence and facts of the circumstances in which the event occurred. Contextual details include information about the event's features, but also about whether it was expected, what the consequences were, resources available, whether the person had prior experience with similar events, and the like. The idea is to obtain as much information as needed to distinguish how the same event might have different meaning and impact from one person to another depending on circumstances—for example, death of a grandmother might have largely different significance if she was the primary caretaker of a child or a geographically distant and rarely seen relative. In some life event assessment methods, the interviewer later presents to a rating team a narrative of the factual information blinded as to the person's actual reaction to the event. The rating team is also blind as to the participant's psychiatric status or history, and rates the severity of the event, according to the principle of scoring "objective impact" as how a typical person would experience the same event under the same circumstances. Raters may be guided by a written dictionary of scoring for similar items accumulated across usage of the procedure in comparable populations. Typically, raters also make judgments, from the contextual information, about the extent to which the event's occurrence is at least in part dependent upon or independent of the characteristics or behaviors of the person ("fateful").

Most of the existing stressor interviews for adolescents are based to some extent on the Life Events and Difficulties Schedule (LEDS; Brown & Harris, 1978). For example, the Pittsburgh group adapted the LEDS for American adolescents (Duggal et al., 2000; Williamson et al., 1998), and Garber, Keiley, and Martin (2002) used the Life Events Interview for Adolescents (LEIA) adapted from the LEDS and from the UCLA Life Stress Interview. The UCLA Life Stress Interview (Hammen, Adrian, Gordon, Jaenicke, & Hiroto, 1987) was based on the contextual threat approach, but is briefer and less time-intensive than the LEDS, and includes assessment of both chronic role-related stress (e.g., academic, romantic, friendship, family, and other domains) as well as episodic life events. The UCLA Life Stress Interview was initially developed for adults but has been adapted for use with children and adolescents (e.g., Adrian & Hammen, 1993; Hammen & Brennan, 2001; Hammen, Rudolph, Weisz, Rao, & Burge, 1999; Rudolph & Hammen, 1999). Rudolph and colleagues have further adapted the UCLA interview for younger adolescents (e.g., Rudolph & Flynn, 2007). Other context-based interview assessments include the Psychosocial Assessment of Childhood Experiences (PACE; Sandberg, McGuinness, Hillary, & Rutter, 1998; Sandberg, Rutter, Giles, & Owen, 1993) and methods developed by Goodyer and colleagues (e.g., Goodyer & Altham, 1991). Research has generally supported the reliability and validity of interview measures of stressors (reviewed in Grant et al., 2004).

Disadvantages of the contextual threat-based interview assessments include their expense: they are time-consuming to administer, require interview experience and training, and the scoring procedures may be labor-intensive especially if independent raters are used to evaluate magnitude of "objective" threat. The focus on objective severity of the event's impact has also been criticized for its neglect of "subjective" appraisal which, it is argued, reflects the individual's actual perception and experience of the event (e.g., Lazarus & Folkman, 1984). Moreover, it has been noted that "context" information that is elicited and folded into the threat ratings may itself consist of risk factors that account for some of the association between the purported event and depression—such as whether the event was expected or the availability of resources (Kessler, 1997; Mazure, 1998). Nevertheless, interview-based approaches and contextual threat scoring are commonly recommended because of the superior quality of information obtained, the precision in evaluation of timing of event occurrence in relation to symptom changes, and the potentially more complete coverage of stressors. Several studies have generally indicated that questionnaires may pick up items too minor to be rated as events in the interview, or that the instruments may each pick up something not noted by the other, but the two methods appear to be similarly predictive of depression (Lewinsohn, Rohde, & Gau, 2003; Zimmerman, Pfohl, & Stangl, 1986). In a small study comparing administration of the LEDS interview and the Life Events Checklist (Johnson & McCutcheon, 1980) in a clinical sample of youth with recent major depression and a non-ill comparison, Duggal et al. (2000) found that only about one-third of events considered by the interview to be severe and likely to have provoked the depression were identified on the checklist. The interview thus yielded a more complete record of the occurrence of events. The authors suggested that the interview not only assists in the recall of events, but also does not rely on the participant's own judgment and interpretation of whether the event was stressful. Furthermore, the interview is more suited to identify low base rate, but potentially highly personally relevant events that would not likely be included on checklists. It might also be noted that the contextual method of eliciting and scoring stressor information is suited to taking developmental considerations into account, an issue that sometimes makes checklists additionally problematic when administered to youth varying in ages between early and later adolescence within a study.

General Criticisms of Stressor Assessment Methods

As Grant and colleagues noted in their review (2004), only a small proportion of studies of adolescent stress-symptom associations used one of the few well-validated checklist or interview methods, and no single measure was used in more than 3% of the 500 studies they reviewed. The lack of standard instruments in wide use limits the comparability of findings across different populations, and impedes understanding of distributions of both normative and atypical levels and types of stress experienced by youth of different ages and environmental circumstances. It also means that most studies may be based on relatively less psychometrically developed measures. Grant et al. (2004) have called for the standardization of measures and development of taxonomies of stressor occurrence as important research targets.

Another important gap in stress assessment is the limited focus on conceptualization and measurement of chronic or ongoing stress. Episodic stressors—life events—typically have acute onsets and resolve within days or a few weeks. However, important information about enduring threats to youth may be ignored, and full account of stress-depression relationships is incomplete without factoring in the role of chronic stressful conditions, including, for example, medical and financial conditions, parental or parent–child discord, or chronic lack of stable friendships. Individual studies may focus on a particular ongoing stressor, such as parental conflict or divorce, or exposure to violence or poverty, but investigations typically do not sample across multiple domains. Most checklist methods do not capture such ongoing conditions as such, and while interview assessments may label "ongoing conditions," the latter may differ in how such events are defined or even fold information about enduring negative conditions into the background "context" of rating an episodic event so that its specific impact may be lost. More complete understanding of the extent to which environmental threats and challenges contribute to depression may be compromised by failure to assess chronic conditions systematically. One approach has been developed by Hammen and colleagues for adults and youth (e.g., Hammen et al., 1987) aimed at rating level of ongoing stressful circumstances in each of several role domains. For instance, for adolescents the domains include close friendships, peer/social life, romantic relationships, relationships with parents, academic performance, and finances. Chronic stress has been shown to predict depression in adolescents (e.g., Eberhart, Shih, Hammen, & Brennan, 2006), but further study is needed to understand its mechanisms and how it affects the timing of onset and recurrence of depression in youth.

Additional Methodological Notes

The vast majority of studies on the stress-depression relationship have employed questionnaire measures of depressive symptoms, with relatively few—as will be noted—including interview assessments of clinically significant depression. The question of whether symptom-based research can be generalized to more severe depression is an old and familiar issue, with acknowledgment that mild, subclinical symptoms, especially if stable, may be associated with impairment and predictive of future diagnoses of depression (Fergusson, Horwood, Ridder, & Beautrais, 2005; Lewinsohn, Solomon, Seeley, & Zeiss, 2000; Oldehinkel, Wittchen, & Schuster, 1999). While research based on subclinical samples is informative, it is nevertheless important for more studies of stress and depression processes to include clinically significant depression samples, especially in community populations that have broader generalizability than treatment populations. Also, it is a truism to say that longitudinal designs are needed to test contemporary versions of etiological models that attempt to clarify mechanisms of the stress-depression association. Longitudinal designs are needed not only to clarify the temporal, and possibly causal, sequence among variables, but also to assess changes in relationships among variables over time. Such designs are challenging, requiring considerable complexity and cost to evaluate transactional, multivariable models.

STRESS EXPOSURE AND DEPRESSIVE REACTIONS TO STRESS

In this section, several issues are explored: stress exposure (the amount of stress experienced by youth) and gender differences in stress exposure; stress reactivity and sensitivity to stress and gender differences in these topics. Later sections cover stress generation, and models of the moderators/mediators of the effects of stress. For some of these topics there is scant empirical research, while for others the amount of research is enormous, requiring selectivity. Unless noted otherwise, the studies cited generally employ checklists and subjective measures of stress.

Adolescence and Exposure to Stress

Two well-known demographic correlates of depression in adolescence are noteworthy: first onsets of depression commonly occur in adolescence, and the gender difference with female preponderance emerges. Do these patterns relate to stress exposure in adolescence? Is there greater stress exposure as youth progress from childhood to adolescence, and are girls and boys equally at risk for experiencing stressors?

It has often been noted that adolescence is a period of turmoil, marked by normative but challenging transitions affecting academic, peer, romantic, and parental domains, as several chapters in this volume describe. Arnett (1999) noted evidence for three aspects of adolescent "storm and stress," particularly among Westernized cultures: conflict with parents, mood disruptions, and increased risk behavior. McClure and Pine (2007) note that as well as the extensive biological changes that accompany emergence into adolescence, there are significant challenging social changes as well. They summarize that as youth become more autonomous, they change in the amount of support they seek from peers and parents; with increasing sexual maturation they seek romantic relationships, and attach greater salience to social stimuli and importance to social-evaluative concerns. At the same time they may have greater responsibility for performing tasks, chores, and work roles—as well as face greater academic and achievement challenges, including scholastic, recreational, or other competitive activity, which may have implications for later occupational roles.

It seems reasonable that as youth experience greater autonomy, they are also more exposed to stressors including a wider array of events to which they may contribute—in contrast to childhood experiences where most events occur beyond their personal control. Developmental changes also affect cognitions and the role they play in both the response to stressors and the occurrence of stressors. Alloy and Abramson (2007), elaborating on a cognitive vulnerability-transactional stress model of Hankin and Abramson (2001), note developmental changes, both neurological and psychosocial, occurring in the acquisition and function of negative cognitions emerging in adolescence. They predict that such vulnerability cognitions themselves may contribute to the occurrence of person-dependent negative events that trigger depression (e.g., Safford, Alloy, Abramson, & Crossfield, 2007).

In light of these speculations and observations, is there actual evidence of increases in adolescence of stressors predicting depression? Studies of changes in stress exposure are relatively infrequent, but a few longitudinal studies, as well as cross-sectional comparisons of different age groups, offer suggestive evidence that stress is indeed more common in adolescence than childhood. A classic cross-sectional study of fifth to ninth graders by Larson and Ham (1993) indicated that older students indeed experienced more negative life events than younger students, as reported by both the youth and their parents. The older youth reported higher rates in all domains, family, friends, school, and "other," and parents also reported more in all domains except family life. Older girls were especially likely to report more friend events, while boys reported more school events. Rudolph and Hammen (1999), in a cross-sectional study of clinic-referred youth, also showed higher rates of interview-assessed life event stress for older youth, with patterns varying by content and gender. Adolescent girls had more dependent interpersonal stress than preadolescent girls, but boys of the two age groups did not differ; adolescent boys showed higher levels of noninterpersonal stress (such as school events) than preadolescent boys, but girls did not differ. A large community sample of youth between 11 and 19 also found cross-sectional age-group differences in which older children reported more everyday hassles (Jose & Ratcliffe, 2004); both boys and girls showed higher rates with age, with girls' rates peaking in the age 14 group, and boys' rates increasing steadily by age. In a longitudinal study of youth from grades 6 to 10, Garber et al. (2002) found increases in the number of interview-assessed stressors over time. In contrast, Hankin, Mermelstein, and Roesch (2007) found general decreases in daily diary-reported events over three assessments in a 1-year period for eighth and tenth graders. However, complex patterns depending on grade cohort and time were reported; for instance, tenth graders reported more peer stressors than did eighth graders, and overall dependent stressors increased over time for tenth graders but decreased for eighth graders. Thus, changes may be related to content as well as to age group, and may depend in part on methodology—for example, daily hassles compared to life event checklists or interviews covering more major events over longer periods. Overall, the data generally support the idea that exposure to stressful events does increase in adolescence.

Gender Differences in Stress Exposure

In addition to age- or cohort-related gender differences noted above, several studies have examined overall gender differences in stress exposure, testing the hypothesis that girls experience more stress than boys. Ge, Lorenz, Conger, Elder, and Simons (1994) found that adolescent girls reported significantly more stressful life events than boys did in the Iowa Youth and Families Project. Overall, female higher frequencies were reported by Jose and Ratcliffe (2004) for everyday stressors/hassles on 26 of 50 items with only five reported more often by males.

Research has generally suggested domain-specific gender differences, and that interpersonal events are especially likely to be reported frequently by adolescent girls. In a clinical sample, Rudolph and Hammen (1999) found higher rates of interview-based interpersonal stress among girls, but boys had higher rates of noninterpersonal events, largely related to academic issues.

Shih, Eberhart, Hammen, and Brennan (2006) found that adolescent females reported significantly more total and interpersonal interview-assessed stress events in the past year than did males, using contextual interview assessments. Girls also reported more chronic interpersonal stress, whereas boys reported more chronic school-related stress. Reporting on everyday stressors, Hankin et al. (2007) found higher rates of stressors overall, and in interpersonal domains (peer, family, and romantic) among girls; boys reported more athletic stressors and a trend toward higher rates of achievement events. A review of peer relationship studies of children and adolescents by Rose and Rudolph (2006) found that girls—especially adolescents—generally reported greater exposure to peer stressors of most kinds than did boys.

Overall, therefore, girls appear to be exposed to greater levels of stressors, particularly in the interpersonal arena, whereas boys may experience more stressors in achievement-related domains, such as school and athletics. It could be considered that gender differences may simply be an artifact of girls' greater willingness to acknowledge and report negative events or provide greater details. Arguing against such an interpretation, Hankin et al. (2007) observed that their daily diary study found that boys and girls reported similar overall numbers of events in similar details. The differences in stress exposure, rather, are more likely to do with gender-related differentiation of domain-specific pursuits and values that intensify in adolescence and provide the context in which males and females are exposed to, generate, and perceive stressful experiences. Notably, as discussed more fully in a later section, females are especially likely to develop relational orientations that emphasize the maintenance of relationships and concerns with social approval (Cyranowski, Frank, Young, & Shear, 2000; Rose & Rudolph, 2006; Rudolph, 2002).

Finally, it should be noted that research has also found that females, especially adolescents, are more likely to experience exposure to traumatic events, such as sexual assault and victimization, death of a family member, and death of a friend—events all known to be predictive of depression (Fergusson, Swain-Campbell, & Horwood, 2002; Rheingold et al., 2004). Similarly, in a slightly older sample (average age 19–21) of 1,800 people, six of the nine recent (1-year) severe events that were assessed via checklist, with interviewed-assisted dating, occurred significantly more often to women than men, and several lifetime traumas occurred more often to women, such as sexual molestation, rape, physical or emotional abuse by a parent, and physical abuse by a spouse or partner. All of these items were predictive of depressive or anxiety disorders, although when exposure to violence events were included, men's total lifetime stress scores were higher than women's (Turner & Lloyd, 2004).

Depression Reactivity and Sensitivity to Stress

Research on adults provides extensive documentation of the extent to which depression is a reaction to stressful life events (e.g., reviewed in Hammen, 2006; Mazure, 1998). Most depressive episodes in both clinical and community samples are preceded by stressful events, but most negative life events do not trigger major depressive episodes. In this section, we discuss research on the link between stress and depression in adolescents, including gender differences in the extent to which males and females may differ in their reactivity (development of depression) following stressors. There is a large and convincing literature linking stress and depression, therefore, only selected material is reviewed to highlight general themes, and particular methods, designs, and samples.

A recent review by Grant et al. (2004) evaluated over 500 studies on stress and psychopathology in children and adolescents of which approximately 60 tested for associations between stress (including individual adversities like divorce, as well as studies with cumulative stressors) and symptoms in prospective studies, and many of these included internalizing symptoms. The authors concluded that the vast majority supported the predicted impact of recent stressors on subsequent symptoms. Most of the recent longitudinal research on the association between stress and depression has focused largely on depressive symptoms rather than disorders. Cole, Nolen-Hoeksema, Girgus, and Paul (2006) studied 708 young adolescents over six follow-ups approximately 6 months apart, and found that self-reported life events significantly predicted depressive symptoms; reciprocal effects were also observed, and stress-generation patterns are noted in a later section. Similarly, Kim, Conger, Elder, and Lorenz (2003) tested bidirectional effects in a 6-year study of youth internalizing and externalizing symptoms, and indicated that stressful life experiences predicted internalizing symptoms at each point from eighth through twelfth grade. Carter, Garber, Ciesla, and Cole (2006) studied peer and academic hassles as predictors of internalizing and externalizing symptoms over 4 years in a sample of youth at risk due to maternal depression. Higher stress levels predicted higher youth-reported internalizing symptoms a year later.

Comparatively few studies have assessed the role of stressful life events prior to onset of clinically diagnosed major depression in either treatment or community samples. However, the few available studies have reported significant associations, in cross-sectional and longitudinal designs, as indicated by several examples that used interview methods of stressor assessment. Goodyer (1995) reviewed several of his and colleagues' studies of clinically ascertained and community samples of depressed youth in which various psychosocial predictors, including stressful life events, were associated with onset compared with controls. Goodyer, Herbert, Tamplin, and Altham (2000) selected youth at suspected high risk due to various recent and life adversities; those who developed depressive episodes in the subsequent year were more likely to have experienced a significant interviewer-assessed loss or disappointment in the month before onset compared with those who did not develop depression. Williamson et al. (1998) reported on adolescents recruited from outpatient treatment, and found that 62% with a major depressive episode had experienced at least one severe event assessed via interview in the past year compared to only 27% among normal controls. Hammen, Shih, and Brennan (2004) found that interview-assessed chronic and episodic stress were proximal predictors of depression measured as a latent variable based in part on clinical diagnoses, in a mediational model of intergenerational transmission of depression. Several additional studies of major depression in youth used checklist assessments of life events. For instance, Lewinsohn, Joiner, and Rohde (2001) found that high levels of self-reported stress in combination with high levels of dysfunctional attitudes predicted major depression onset over a 1-year period. From the same sample, Monroe, Rohde, Seeley, and Lewinsohn (1999) had reported that recent romantic break-ups were particularly associated with first onset of major depression over a 1-year period. Burton, Stice, and Seeley (2004) examined stress-buffering effects, and found a main effect of life events predicting onset of clinically significant depression in young adolescent girls, but no evidence of stress buffering due to parent or peer support. Overall, there is little debate that depression is typically associated with prior occurrence of stressors.

Gender Differences in Depressive Reactions to Stress

In recent years, increasing numbers of researchers have attempted to shed light on the upsurge of depression in girls, compared to boys, that occurs in adolescence. In addition to the question of whether girls are exposed to more stress than boys are, several studies have addressed the issue of whether girls are more likely to become depressed—or more depressed—in response to stressors compared to boys. The overall review of stress-symptom studies in adolescents and children by Grant et al. (2006) generally supports the finding of higher levels of internalizing symptoms for girls in response to individual and cumulative stressors, although the results are qualified by type of stress and type of symptoms. Several recent studies specifically about depression and cumulative stressors are discussed below.

Most of the studies have been based on community samples, but in one study of clinic-referred children and adolescents, Rudolph and Hammen (1999) found stronger correlations between depressive symptoms and interview-assessed stressors in girls than boys. Among nonclinical studies, several published in the past few years are notable for longitudinal designs and/or relatively large samples, and aimed to specifically address the emergence of high rates of depression among adolescent females. Ge, Conger, and Elder (2001) in a study unique for its focus only on independent, or fateful, events in order to eliminate possibly confounding effects of the person on stress, observed complex gender–stress–pubertal status interactions. It appeared that early-maturing girls were especially likely to show depressive reactions to stressors, particularly in early adolescence. Little and Garber (2004) studied adolescents during the transition from eighth to ninth grade to address the personality-event congruence hypothesis in males and females, speculating that the genders would differ in their achievement and social orientations. Specifically they examined depression symptoms associated with achievement and interpersonal hassles in relation to achievement and interpersonal (dependency) orientations. They found that girls with high interpersonal orientation were more depressed than boys with high interpersonal orientation if they experienced high levels of peer stressors. Girls also showed higher levels of depressive symptoms in relation to academic hassles compared to boys, regardless of level of achievement orientation. Rudolph (2002) studied a large sample of fifth through eighth graders, focusing particularly on peer-related stressors and symptoms assessed via checklist. She found that both peer group and friendship stressors were significantly more associated with emotional distress among girls than boys. Gender differences were most pronounced at high levels of exposure to social stressors. Jose and Ratcliffe (2004) also found that gender moderated the association between stressor frequency and depressive symptoms, with girls showing higher depression than boys especially at high levels of stress.

Data from the National Longitudinal Study of Adolescent Health (Add Health) included assessments at baseline and for a subsample, two additional times over 7 years. Investigators Meadows et al. (2006) evaluated gender differences in depression symptoms in relation to stressful life events measured by a checklist. They found that stressors were significant predictors of symptoms at all time points for females, but for only one wave for males; overall, stressful life events were more associated with females' than males' depressive symptom patterns. Two additional studies specifically tested differential reactivity to stressors in males and females. Shih et al. (2006) found that at high levels of total interviewer-assessed life event stress in the past year, girls were more likely to be depressed (have a diagnosis of subclinical or full major depressive episode or dysthymia) than boys.

Hankin et al. (2007) also examined gender differences in stress reactivity, using daily diary measures of stressors for 1-week periods over three waves. They found that girls had significantly more depression than boys in response to stressful events.

Overall, therefore, the results are remarkably consistent, indicating that under conditions of exposure to high levels of stress, girls are significantly more likely to display depressive symptoms than boys are. It is noteworthy that many of the studies of gender differences in stress reactivity observed that girls were more reactive than boys to stress domains involving interpersonal relationships (although not limited to differences in reactivity in such domains). For instance, Shih et al. (2006) found girls were more reactive than boys to interpersonal life events, and Hankin et al. (2007) found borderline significant effects for girls' greater reactivity to interpersonal events and peer stressors. Rudolph and Hammen (1999) found that adolescent girls' depression was more associated with interpersonal and social conflict events compared to boys' depression. These findings are consistent with models of gender differences in relational orientation, in which girls are hypothesized to place higher value on social connections and evaluation by others (e.g., Cyranowski et al., 2000; Rudolph, 2002), such that their sense of self-regard and competence may be depleted in the face of interpersonal difficulties. Such a view of girls' social sensitivity and vulnerability to depression is supported not only by research on stressful life events, but also on studies of quality of peer or romantic relationships. For example, several studies have shown that indicators of high valuation of relationships, such as reassurance seeking, peer importance, and interpersonal sensitivity, may moderate the association between peer or romantic relationship quality and depressive symptoms in girls (e.g., Prinstein & Aikins, 2004; Prinstein, Borelli, Cheah, Simon, & Aikins, 2005; Rizzo, Daley, & Gunderson, 2006).

Stress Sensitization and Related Concepts

It has long been hypothesized that the nature of the stress-depression relationship changes over time within individuals, due to neurobiological effects of depression on stress-reactivity or due to cognitive and psychosocial factors that alter individuals' sensitivity to stressors (Post, 1992; Segal, Williams, Teasdale, & Gemar, 1996). A full review of this "kindling" model is beyond the scope of the current chapter, but Monroe and Harkness (2005) present a cogent conceptual and empirical discussion of the complex issues of this approach. One implication is that the association between stress and depression may be stronger for first onset versus later episodes of depression. Limited research on adolescents has tested this hypothesis, with mixed findings. As noted above, Monroe et al. (1999) found that romantic break-ups predicted first onset but not recurrence of depression. Lewinsohn, Allen, Seeley, and Gotlib (1999) also reported more generally from the same study that major life stress measured by checklist was a stronger predictor of first than recurrent major depressive episodes. However, Daley, Hammen, and Rao (2000), who employed interview measures of stress, found that episodic life events predicted both first onset and recurrences among young women followed from high school senior year for 5 years, but chronic stress was a stronger predictor of first onset than recurrence.

A variant of the kindling model suggests that individuals who have experienced prior stressful events and circumstances, especially those early in life, may be more vulnerable to development of depression when even low levels of stressors occur. Hammen, Henry, and Daley (2000) tested and found support for the hypothesis that young women who had experienced higher levels of childhood adversities would experience a major depressive episode following lower levels of interviewer-rated stress compared with women who did not have early adverse experiences. Similarly, Rudolph and Flynn (2007) found that pubertal girls with high levels of childhood adversity experienced significant depression at low, moderate, and high levels of stress, compared to those with low childhood adversity who experienced depression only at high stress exposure. Espejo et al. (2007) found that young adolescents who experienced adversity in their first 5 years, and who had prior diagnoses of anxiety disorders, had higher depression symptoms following both high and low levels of interviewer-rated negative life events; those who had only one of the risk factors—adversity or anxiety disorders—had depressive symptoms only if they had high levels of stress.

Harkness, Bruce, and Lumley (2006) reported evidence of stress sensitization in adolescents based on their reports of childhood adversity (parental antipathy, indifference, or physical or sexual abuse). Interestingly, evidence of lower levels of interviewer-assessed stress prior to onset of a depressive episode was observed only for independent (fateful) events and for first onsets. The authors noted that the absence of effects for dependent events (such as interpersonal stressors) might have been due to the confounding of "independence" and severity, in that independent events were rated as more severe compared to dependent stressors.

Although research on the topic of sensitization or kindling is limited in adolescent populations, the topic is an important reminder of the likely dynamic relationship between stress and depression. Monroe and Harkness (2005) observe that interventions early in the unfolding of the course of depression may have more success and enduring impact than later in the course because of the increasing sensitivity to, or even autonomy from stress, conferred by successive episodes. Thus, further research on the kindling hypothesis in adolescents is needed, and the identification of adolescents at risk for, or early in the course of depression, is a high priority as youth face increased challenges from stressful events during adolescence. Kindling research will also benefit from truly prospective research that can limit confounding of mood state on reporting of events, and which can examine within-person changes in the stress-depression association over time. Also, research on the role of early adversities on stress reactions requires further use of contemporaneous and objective measures of events in early childhood, reducing effects of depressive experiences on retrospective recall (e.g., see Espejo et al., 2007).

STRESS GENERATION AND DEPRESSION

Definitions and Empirical Evidence

In recent years the focus on the association between stress and depression has shifted from exclusive emphasis on the effects of stress on subsequent depression to include a bidirectional influence. The transaction between the person and the environment reflects the importance of viewing the person as an active agent who "selects" contexts and contributes to the circumstances of his or her life situations, rather than as a passive recipient of contextual influences (e.g., Buss, 1987). "Stress generation" is a term used by Hammen (1991) initially to describe the tendency of women with histories of unipolar depression to experience high levels of stressful life events judged to be at least partly dependent on their own characteristics, behaviors, or personal circumstances. An implication of increased stressor occurrence is the likelihood of risk for depression chronicity or recurrence. Thus, stress generation may have important implications for the course of depression, and for treatment and prevention.

Subsequent studies have replicated the stress generation finding in adults (see reviews in Hammen, 2006; Hammen & Shih, in press)—although not all studies have distinguished between the occurrence of all life events compared to events limited to those whose occurrence was judged to be dependent on the person. Dependent events commonly include stressors with interpersonal content, suggesting that stress generation often may reflect mechanisms relevant to the characteristics of depression-vulnerable individuals, such as beliefs, expectations, and actions related to relationships with others. The phenomenon of stress generation is consistent with, but not limited to, an interpersonal perspective on depression vulnerability and recurrence.

As with adults, stress generation has been observed to occur among adolescents with histories of major depression, including community samples of late adolescent women (Daley et al., 1997), adolescent males and females (Hammen & Brennan, 2001; Patton, Coffey, Posterino, Carlin, & Bowes, 2003), offspring of depressed mothers (Adrian & Hammen, 1993; Hammen et al., 2004), and clinical samples of children and adolescents (Rudolph & Hammen, 1999; Rudolph et al., 2000; Williamson, Birmaher, Anderson, Al-Shabbout, & Ryan, 1995). Most of these studies found that elevated rates of stressors among those with depression histories did not occur for independent (fateful) events, and were specific to person-dependent events. Except for Patton et al. (2003), the studies employed interviewer-assessed stress measures.

Studies have also shown stress generation patterns in youth with elevated depressive symptoms, and in more general measures of life events not restricted to those dependent on the person. For instance, Cole et al. (2006) found that scores from the Children Depression Inventory predicted checklist-based stressful life events prospectively in two longitudinal studies of school samples, one child and one adolescent. They also found the effect to be stronger for a latent trait (rather than state) factor of depression. Kim et al. (2003) found evidence of a stress generation effect in adolescents followed up multiple times between seventh and twelfth grades; indeed, as with many studies, they found evidence of reciprocal relations between stress and symptoms. Joiner, Wingate, Gencoz, and Gencoz (2005a) found that self-reported depressive symptoms predicted self-reported stressors, both those judged to be independent of the person and those contingent on the person, in college students 5 weeks later. Garber et al. (2002) did not find that symptoms predicted later stress when life events were assessed via interview of adolescents, but they did find a stress generation pattern when mother-reported symptoms were used to predict peer and academic "hassles" (Carter et al., 2006). Waaktaar et al. (2004) also found significant effects of depressive symptoms predicting stressful life events in a 1-year period in a Norwegian high school sample.

Correlates and Predictors of Stress Generation

The tendency of depressed individuals to experience elevated rates of stressful life events and circumstances to which they have contributed is not limited to the effects of depressive symptoms as such, although of course the irritability, pessimism, low energy, lack of enjoyment, and other features of the disorder doubtless affect the individual's transactions with the world. Stress generation effects have been observed to occur when individuals are not in depressive episodes, and when effects of depressive symptoms are statistically controlled. It is likely that stressors occur due to the person's environmental circumstances and to personal characteristics and behaviors, including both biologically-based and acquired characteristics. Research on adults has indicated that to a moderate extent, genetic factors play a role in stress generation presumably through heritable traits and dispositions that affect selection into environments as well as reactions to them (e.g., Kendler, Neale, Kessler, Heath, & Eaves, 1993; McGuffin, Katz, & Bebbington, 1988; Plomin, Lichtenstein, Pedersen, McClearn, & Nesselroade, 1990). Developmental psychopathologists have also emphasized the contribution of persons to stressful environments (e.g., Rutter et al., 1997; see also Champion, Goodall, & Rutter, 1995).

Among the variables that have been studied in relation to stress generation and depression, most have focused on personality characteristics that contribute to the quality of interpersonal relationships. Among adult samples, neuroticism, a trait reflecting high levels of emotionality and reactivity to situations, has been linked with life event occurrence (e.g., Fergusson & Horwood, 1987; Kendler, Gardner, & Prescott, 2003; Poulton & Andrews, 1992). Less research on personality factors has emerged from adolescent samples (see Hammen & Shih [in press] for further discussion of adult samples). However, several studies of late adolescents or college students have focused on sociotropy and autonomy personality styles. For instance, Daley et al. (1997) found that traits of autonomy (such as preference for independence and solitude, individual achievement) predicted occurrence of interpersonal conflict events over a longitudinal period among young women with histories of depression (see also Priel & Shahar, 2000). Shih (2006) found that sociotropy predicted increases in interpersonal but not achievement stress over weeks among women, but not men. Hankin, Kassel and Abela (2005) explored the role of attachment style (self-reported attachment cognitions) in college students. They found that insecure attachment (anxious and avoidant) predicted increased interpersonal but not achievement stressors, and mediated the path between attachment and later symptoms.

Dysfunctional cognitions have been speculated to play a role in stressor occurrence, perhaps associated with exhibiting attitudes and behaviors that elicit negative reactions from others, leading to interpersonal discord. For example, Joiner and colleagues (2005a) found that roommate rejection of the participant (a negative event rated by the roommate) was predicted by participant hopelessness cognitions. Joiner, Wingate, and Otamendi (2005b) further elaborated a hopelessness-interpersonal perspective on depression in college students, showing that the link between hopelessness and depression is partially mediated by the occurrence of interpersonal stressors. Safford et al. (2007) also demonstrated that negative cognitive style (a composite based on depressogenic attributions and dysfunctional attitudes) in college students was predictive of the occurrence of dependent minor and major life events but not independent events, as assessed with a checklist supplemented by interview. However, they did not find a stress generation effect associated with history of past depression; the authors speculated that their study did not include currently depressed or recently remitted people with depression, and that the stress-generating effect of depression may dissipate with extended periods since the person was depressed (in their study, an average of 28 months). Safford et al. (2007) interpret their findings to support the idea that it is not depression as such, but rather underlying cognitive style, that contributes to the occurrence of dependent and interpersonal stressors. Caldwell, Rudolph, Troop-Gordon, and Kim (2004) reported that negative self-views in adolescents predicted social disengagement that predicted peer stress.

Several of the original stress generation studies of youth were based on female samples (e.g., Daley et al., 1997), and did not examine gender effects in mixed samples (e.g., Carter et al., 2006; Joiner et al., 2005). However, several studies suggest that when gender differences are examined, girls are more likely to show stress generation effects (e.g., increased rates of dependent and interpersonal events) than boys (Hammen & Brennan, 2001; Rudolph & Hammen, 1999; Safford et al., 2007; Shih, 2006; Waaktaar et al., 2004).

Not all stress generation studies have distinguished between diagnostic groups. For instance, Sandberg et al. (1998) found that adolescents in treatment for a variety of internalizing and externalizing disorders were highly likely to experience dependent life events in the prior year compared to medical and normal control youth. It is likely that psychopathology in general is associated with impaired problem solving, or dysfunctional attitudes, or adverse environmental conditions that might contribute to higher levels of stress. Thus, for example, youth with disruptive behavior disorders or substance abuse disorder would be likely to experience stressors as consequences of their maladjustment. Thus, Carter et al. (2006) found that both mother-reported internalizing and externalizing symptoms were associated with later increases in peer and academic hassles. Rudolph et al. (2000) found that youth with externalizing disorders showed increased rates of dependent events, although girls had high rates of interpersonal events and boys had high rates of noninterpersonal (such as academic) events.

Less clear is whether there is something unique and specific about depression-related stressors, and whether those with histories of depression differ from those with other internalizing disorders. Only a handful of studies has explored whether depression or vulnerability to depression uniquely contributes to stressor occurrence, particularly interpersonal events, compared to those with anxiety. Joiner et al. (2005) found that anxiety symptoms did not predict stressors in a college sample, after controlling for depressive symptoms. Uhrlass and Gibb (2007) similarly found that anxiety symptoms did not predict increases in daily hassles over a 7-week period among college students, while depressive symptoms did. Finally, one study examined the stress generation issue among those with diagnoses of anxiety disorders: Connolly (2007) found that 15-year-olds with a history of a "pure" depressive disorder, compared with youth who had a "pure" anxiety disorder, reported significantly more interviewer-assessed dependent and interpersonal stressors in the past year. Although the analyses were retrospective, they suggest that characteristics of youth with depression are sufficiently distinct from those youth with anxiety disorders that the latter experience fewer stressors to which they have contributed. It might be speculated that anxious youth are more avoidant of conflict and are more risk averse in their environments in ways that may protect them from interpersonal losses and disruptions, compared to depressed youth.

Overall, the emerging stress-generation studies of adolescents point to the usefulness of studying what factors contribute to event occurrence, hence depression. The stress generation perspective has influenced some of the current models of depression, so that they include bidirectional, transactional effects of the person and environment, as noted in the next section. However, it is apparent that more research is needed to clarify the processes that lead to high levels of stressors that are due in part to the person's behaviors and environment.

MODELS OF THE STRESS-DEPRESSION RELATIONSHIP

As the current review and the more general stress-symptom relationship reviews of Grant et al. (2004) and Grant et al. (2006) indicate, the predictive effect of stressors on depression is empirically well-supported, and research attention should focus now on the moderators and mediators of the association in adolescent samples. Their broad review of stress-symptom studies in children and adolescents (Grant et al., 2006) noted that much of the research on moderators is inconclusive, and limited by lack of conceptually-driven models (with the exception of cognitive-vulnerability stress models). In contrast to moderation studies, Grant et al. (2006) note increasing sophistication in the development and testing of models of mediators that affect the relations between stressors and symptoms, and their review presents a comprehensive analysis of specific types of mediators associated with particular stressors and outcomes, in children and adolescents.

Most models of the causes of depression are diathesis-stress models, on the assumption that vulnerabilities for depression need to be triggered by stressors in order for depression to occur. Consequently, most of the chapters in Sections III and IV of this volume address such models in the context of their particular biological or psychosocial focus on vulnerabilities, and readers are referred to these chapters for more detailed coverage. In this section several recent examples of stress-depression models as applied to adolescents are noted, including those that focus on predictors of stress (stress generation) and those that focus on predictors of responses to stress. These models are discussed without extensive elaboration, in an attempt to acknowledge the kinds of questions, designs, and emerging findings that reflect the current state of the field.

There are several commonalities among current diathesis-stress models. First, most emphasize complex transactions among the person and environment, and among multiple variables. These features reflect the recognition that full understanding of depression requires inclusion of biological, cognitive, and social—as well as environmental—variables. The models also reflect acceptance of the role of the person in shaping his /her social world, and of the effects of biological and socioemotional development and the consequences of learning, and their progressive influences and changes over time. Additionally, most of the models selected for brief discussion aim to address the fundamental demographic realities of depression—the preponderance of females and the emergence of high rates of depression among adolescent girls.

Two of the models of the stress and depression link focus extensively on interpersonal factors as significant risk factors for depression. They particularly emphasize contributions to stress generation, with interpersonal stressors as the proximal predictors of depression. Hammen et al. (2004) used structural equation modeling to test predictors of youth depression from an intergenerational and interpersonal perspective, hypothesizing that maternal depression contributes to family and parent–child discord, which contributes to adolescents' interpersonal difficulties, which in turn predict the occurrence of interpersonal stressors. In a sample of over 800 15-year-olds and their mothers, Hammen et al. (2004) showed that the association between maternal (and grandmother) and youth depression is mediated by maternal family discord predicting poor parent–child relations, with both of these variables predicting youth interpersonal stressors and social competence, which were proximal predictors of youth depression.

Rudolph, Flynn, and Abaied (in press) presented a model with similar features but with greater elaboration of the specific characteristics of youth social functioning. They hypothesized that early family disruption (predicted by attachment insecurity and parental depression) would contribute to various youth social and behavioral deficits, which in turn predict relationship disturbances including stress and conflict in relationships, leading to depression. Rudolph et al. (in press) hypothesize that the stress and depression link is moderated by gender, personality and social-cognitive variables, and developmental transitions. The authors argue that normative social changes associated with transition to adolescence exacerbate interpersonal vulnerability (as an example, increased emphasis on peer relationships and social standing intersect with a youth's ineffective social problem solving to create interpersonal rejection or relationship conflict). A number of aspects of the model have been supported empirically, including their own and others' work (reviewed in Rudolph et al., in press), although a full test of the model has yet to be conducted. The Rudolph model implicitly predicts the emergence of gender differences in its emphasis on girls' typically greater endorsement of social connectedness and self-worth based on others' regard, and its interaction with girls' higher levels of exposure to social stressors (Rudolph, 2002).

Several models focus on the mechanisms by which stressors lead to depression. As an example of a stress-depression perspective in which biopsychosocial variables are emphasized, Ge and colleagues (2001) tested a model of the development of gender differences that includes attention to pubertal status and timing. They proposed that stressful life events would interact with pubertal status to predict depressive reactions. Specifically, early-maturing girls, especially those with earlier higher levels of depressive symptoms (pre-existing vulnerability), were hypothesized to become more depressed when encountering stressful life events. Using the youth sample from the 6-year Iowa Youth and Families study initially assessed in the seventh grade, and employing repeated self-rated measures of pubertal status, they found support for their hypotheses. Early-maturing girls with higher early symptoms manifested higher levels of symptoms in response to stressful events. They concluded that girls with early menarche had particular difficulty with adaptation in the face of life stress, and assert that their findings support the general interactive model of Nolen-Hoeksema and Girgus (1994), which proposes that girls' combination of pre-existing vulnerabilities plus new social and biological transitions predicts the emergence of gender differences in adolescence. Ge and colleagues (2001) acknowledge the limitations in their measures of symptoms and pubertal status, and urge further studies that include longitudinal hormonal assessments in studies of stress-depression linkages in adolescent samples.

Several models emphasize cognitive vulnerability variables as moderators of the stress-depression link. The "generic" cognitive vulnerability model predicts that depressogenic cognitions, such as dysfunctional attitudes or negative attributional style, moderate the association between stressful life events and depression. As reviewed in Grant et al. (2006), there is considerable support for this approach in adolescents. Hankin and Abramson (2001) presented an elaborated cognitive vulnerability-transactional stress theory that has components that specifically predict gender differences in depression. Among the changes in a basic cognitive model are the emphasis on negative affect as the initial response to negative life events, and elaborations and revisions concerning cognitive vulnerability. These include incorporation of ruminative response style as one form of maladaptive cognition in response to initial negative affect, and emphasis on specific domains of cognitive vulnerability, such as those that might be especially salient to female adolescents (e.g., body image dissatisfaction). The model also includes a transactional emphasis, noting the effect of depression and other vulnerabilities on the occurrence of stressful life events to which the person has contributed. Hankin and Abramson (2001) also acknowledge the importance of interpersonal characteristics and behaviors that may contribute to stress generation. Finally, the model incorporates pre-existing biological, personality, and environmental adversity factors that may have direct effects on cognitive vulnerability and life event occurrence. Their presentation of the model includes an extensive review of gender differences in the variables and mechanisms of the model, and emphasizes the various points at which such differences contribute to the ultimately higher rates of depression in girls compared to boys. On the basis of their daily diary study of stressors, conducted 3 times for 1 week each over 12 months, Hankin et al. (2007) provide support for key aspects of gender differences: girls' greater overall exposure to stressors, with greater levels of interpersonal events' mediating the association between gender and depressive symptoms, thus supporting a stress-generation approach as well as stress exposure. Interestingly, they did not show that girls display more depressive symptoms in reaction to stressors except in certain domains, including achievement and independent stressors, and girls did not show reactivity specifically with depression, as girls and boys displayed similar patterns of alcohol use in response to stressors.

Recently, Alloy and Abramson (2007) presented a similar but elaborated version of the Hankin and Abramson model, which they term the biocognitive vulnerability transactional stress model of gender differences in depression. There are five core elements of the model: negative life events, cognitive vulnerability, rumination, cognitive vulnerability × stress interactions, and hopelessness. They note that several of its key elements (cognitive vulnerability, stress interaction, rumination, and hopelessness) become operative in adolescence due to changes in hormones, brain, and cognitive development that enable the cognitive vulnerability processes that are necessary to the model. In addition to these five key elements, they emphasize the importance of biological factors, such as genetic vulnerability that may contribute to negative cognitive style as well as to depressive reactivity to stress, and maturational changes, such as developments in the prefrontal cortex that also affect information-processing and attributions about causality and implications for the self. An important element of the model is its emphasis on the factors and processes that contribute to the surge in depression and gender differences during adolescence. These include girls' greater exposure to stress, the consolidation of negative cognitive style, and rumination. Alloy and Abramson (2007) also note the role of familial factors such as modeling, reinforcement, and maladaptive parenting in the development of cognitive vulnerability. The authors review studies from their own and others' research programs that support various elements of the model, but the overall model has not been tested.

The essential element of the Hankin, Abramson, and Alloy models involves cognitive vulnerability and its interaction with stressors. A review of this research by Lakdawalla, Hankin, and Mermelstein (2007) focuses on such studies in child and adolescent samples, and presents analyses of findings for three cognitive perspectives: Beck's theory (dysfunctional attitudes), the hopelessness model (attribution style), and response styles (rumination). They generally conclude that the evidence supports each of these models, but more strongly for adolescents than children, and extensively review the measurement, design, statistical, and conceptual shortcomings of the research in this field. It is apparent that cognitive models of adolescent depression have empirical support, but there are many significant gaps to address.

CONCLUSIONS AND FUTURE DIRECTIONS

Studies of the predictors and mechanisms of adolescent depression provide critical contributions to the understanding of the most common forms of unipolar depression. Moreover, such contributions have the added benefit of helping to identify youth at greatest risk, and to help shape interventions to be delivered at a point of potentially great impact. One of several features that make adolescence unique is stress exposure. Increased stress exposure appears to be a considerable and fairly universal challenge, especially to girls, as they enter adolescence. Higher rates of stressors in adolescence occur as a function of increasing autonomy, changing sex-role related values and activities, and biological and cognitive developments that alter the youths' transactions with the world.

Increased levels of stressors and challenging circumstances may be difficult for all youth, but especially for those whose vulnerabilities mean that they are insufficiently able to cope with typical stressors, or whose stress burdens are exceptional. Further research on factors that contribute to the burden of stress, including those factors that are due to the person's own characteristics, behaviors, and circumstances, is needed. It is likely that such research needs to include heritable and dispositional characteristics, acquired cognitions about the self and others, and also a focus on how individuals select environments including friends and intimate partners. Just the act of forming a romantic relationship during adolescence, for example, may have powerful implications for stress and depression (e.g., Joyner & Udry, 2000). Models of the role of emotion regulation are also relevant to the understanding of the development of depression in youth in relation to stress (e.g., Garber, Braafladt, & Zeman, 1991; Silk, Shaw, Skuban, Oland, & Kovacs, 2006), although few studies have examined adolescents' emotion regulation specifically in the context of personally stressful life events. Such models have indicated that chronic stressors (such as negative family environment, parental marital discord, parental psychological disorders) likely contribute to dysfunctional emotion regulation, which of course may have a negative effect on social functioning and further stress occurrence (e.g., Cicchetti & Toth, 2005; Morris, Silk, Steinberg, Myers, & Robinson, 2007). Details and further developments are reported in Chapter 16 in this volume, and research that integrates this approach with other models and stress assessment will be an important direction to pursue.

Improvements can be made in the methods and conceptualization of stress assessment, especially those that enhance greater comparability and communicability across studies, and which illuminate more fully the contexts of episodic and chronic stress in the lives of adolescents. Furthermore, the field particularly needs further research that clarifies the nature of the vulnerabilities that moderate or mediate the effects of stress, and the mechanisms by which depressive reactions to stressors occur. Several integrative models of vulnerability and stress-reaction have been developed, and will inspire increasingly comprehensive tests of complex transactions. Other chapters in this volume will provide detail on particular biological and social-cognitive vulnerabilities and mechanisms.

As is true of all perspectives on depression, an interesting and important question is what is specific about depression? It is apparent (e.g., Grant et al., 2004; McMahon, Grant, Compas, Thurm, & Ey, 2003) that stressors may trigger or exacerbate a wide array of symptoms of psychopathology, but less is known about what specifically triggers depression rather than another disorder. This question is being pursued in part in research that addresses gender differences, with the suggestion that neurobiological and social-cognitive vulnerabilities in girls intersect with stressors that are experienced as depletion of self-worth, the latter often involving conflict or loss in the interpersonal domain. Thus, further research will clarify specific vulnerabilities, specific depression-reaction mechanisms, and specific stressors that trigger the vulnerabilities and reactions. The issue of comorbidity has not been discussed in the current chapter, but it clearly complicates the issue of specificity and presents challenges to conceptualization and methodology.

Another issue to pursue concerns the extent to which the impact of stressors on depressive reactions may alter over the course of depression, or as a function of accumulated or specific types of stress. Attention to the kindling/sensitization hypothesis and its apparent emerging empirical support suggests both methodological and theoretical issues to resolve. Methodologically, the issue reminds us to distinguish between those with first or recurrent episodes, and perhaps to factor distal stress exposure as well as recent exposure into analyses, among other challenges. Theoretically, of course, the sensitization issue requires conceptualization of the mechanisms that account for differing effects of stress on depression over time.

REFERENCES

Adrian, C., & Hammen, C. (1993). Stress exposure and stress generation in children of depressed mothers. *Journal of Consulting and Clinical Psychology, 61*, 354–359.

Alloy, L. B., & Abramson, L. Y. (2007). The adolescent surge in depression and emergence of gender differences: A biocognitive vulnerability-stress model. In D. Romer & E. F. Walker (Eds.), *Adolescent psychopathology and the developing brain* (pp. 284–312). New York: Oxford University Press.

Andrade, L., Caraveo-Anduaga, J. J., Berglund, P., Bijl, R. V., De Graaf, R., Vollebergh, W., et al. (2003). The epidemiology of major depressive episodes: Results from the International Consortium of Psychiatric Epidemiology (ICPE) Surveys. *International Journal of Methods in Psychiatric Research, 12*, 3–21.

Arnett, J. J. (1999). Adolescent storm and stress, reconsidered. *American Psychologist, 54*, 317–326.

Blazer, D. G. (2003). Depression in late life: Review and commentary. *Journal of Gerontology, 58A*, 249–265.

Brown, G. W., & Harris, T. (1978). *Social origins of depression.* London: Free Press.

Burton, E., Stice, E., & Seeley, J. R. (2004). A prospective test of the stress-buffering model of depression in adolescent girls: No support once again. *Journal of Consulting and Clinical Psychology, 72*, 689–697.

Buss, D. M. (1987). Selection, evocation, and manipulation. *Journal of Personality and Social Psychology, 53*, 1214–1221.

Byrne, D. G., Byrne, A. E., & Reinhart, M. I. (1995). Personality, stress and the decision to commence cigarette smoking in adolescence. *Journal of Psychosomatic Research, 39*, 53–62.

Byrne, D. G., & Mazanov, J. (2002). Sources of stress in Australian adolescents: Factor structure and stability over time. *Stress and Health: Journal of the International Society for the Investigation of Stress, 18*, 185–192.

Caldwell, M. S., Rudolph, K. D., Troop-Gordon, W., & Kim, D.-Y. (2004). Reciprocal influences among relational self-views, social disengagement, and peer stress during early adolescence. *Child Development, 75*, 1140–1154.

Carter, J. S., Garber, J., Ciesla, J. A., & Cole, D. A. (2006). Modeling relations between hassles and internalizing and externalizing symptoms in adolescents: A four-year prospective study. *Journal of Abnormal Psychology, 115*, 428–442.

Champion, L. A., Goodall, G., & Rutter, M. (1995). Behavior problems in childhood and stressors in early adult life: I. A 20 year follow-up of London school children. *Psychological Medicine, 25*, 231–246.

Cicchetti, D., & Toth, S. (2005). Child maltreatment. *Annual Review of Clinical Psychology, 1*, 409–438.
Coddington, R. D. (1972). The significance of life events as etiologic factors in the diseases of children: II. A study of a normal population. *Journal of Psychosomatic Research, 16*, 205–213.
Cole, D. A., Nolen-Hoeksema, S., Girgus, J., & Paul, G. (2006). Stress exposure and stress generation in child and adolescent depression: A latent trait-state-error approach to longitudinal analyses. *Journal of Abnormal Psychology, 115*, 40–51.
Compas, B. E., Davis, G. E., Forsythe, C. J., & Wagner, B. M. (1987). Assessment of major and daily stressful events during adolescence: The Adolescent Perceived Events Scale. *Journal of Consulting and Clinical Psychology, 55*, 534–541.
Connolly, N. (2007). *Comorbidity of depression and anxiety disorders in adolescence: Differential predictors and longitudinal trends.* Unpublished dissertation, University of California, Los Angeles.
Cyranowski, J. M., Frank, E., Young, E., & Shear, K. (2000). Adolescent onset of the gender difference in lifetime rates of major depression. *Archives of General Psychiatry, 57*, 21–27.
Daley, S. E., Hammen, C., Burge, D., Davila, J., Paley, B., Lindberg, N., et al. (1997). Predictors of the generation of episodic stress: A longitudinal study of late adolescent women. *Journal of Abnormal Psychology, 106*, 251–259.
Daley, S. E., Hammen, C., & Rao, U. (2000). Predictors of first onset and recurrence of major depression in young women during the 5 years following high school graduation. *Journal of Abnormal Psychology, 109*, 525–533.
Duggal, S., Malkoff-Schwartz, S., Birmaher, B., Anderson, B. P., Matty, M. K., & Houck, P. R. (2000). Assessment of life stress in adolescents: Self-report versus interview methods. *Journal of the American Academy of Child & Adolescent Psychiatry, 39*, 445–451.
Eberhart, N. K., Shih, J. H., Hammen, C. L., & Brennan, P. A. (2006). Understanding the sex difference in vulnerability to adolescent depression: An examination of child and parent characteristics. *Journal of Abnormal Child Psychology, 34*, 495–508.
Espejo, E., Hammen, C., Connolly, N., Brennan, P., Najman, J., & Bor, W. (2007). Stress sensitization and adolescent depressive severity as a function of childhood adversity: A link to anxiety disorders. *Journal of Abnormal Child Psychology, 35*, 287–299.
Fergusson, D. M., & Horwood, L. J. (1987). Vulnerability to life events exposure. *Psychological Medicine, 17*, 739–749.
Fergusson, D. M., Horwood, L. J., Ridder, E. M., & Beautrais, A. L. (2005). Subthreshold depression in adolescence and mental health outcomes in adulthood. *Archives of General Psychiatry, 62*, 66–72.
Fergusson, D. M., Swain-Campbell, N. R., & Horwood, L. J. (2002). Does sexual violence contribute to elevated rates of anxiety and depression in females? *Psychological Medicine, 32*, 991–996.
Garber, J., Braafladt, N., & Zeman, J. (1991). The regulation of sad affect: An information-processing perspective. In J. Garber & K. Dodge (Eds.), *The development of emotion regulation and dysregulation* (pp. 208–240). New York: Cambridge University Press.

Garber, J., Keiley, M. K., & Martin, N. C. (2002). Developmental trajectories of adolescents' depressive symptoms: Predictors of change. *Journal of Consulting and Clinical Psychology, 70*, 79–95.

Ge, X., Conger, R. D., & Elder, G. H. J. (2001). Pubertal transition, stressful life events, and the emergence of gender differences in adolescent depressive symptoms. *Developmental Psychology, 37*, 404–417.

Ge, X., Lorenz, F. O., Conger, R. D., Elder, G. H., & Simons, R. L. (1994). Trajectories of stressful life events and depressive symptoms during adolescence. *Developmental Psychology, 30*, 467–483.

Goodyer, I. M. (1995). Life events and difficulties: Their nature and effects. In I. M. Goodyer (Ed.), *The depressed child and adolescent* (pp. 171–193). New York: Cambridge University Press.

Goodyer, I. M., & Altham, P. M. E. (1991). Lifetime exit events and recent social and family adversities in anxious and depressed school-age children and adolescents: I. *Journal of Affective Disorders, 21*, 219–228.

Goodyer, I. M., Herbert, J., Tamplin, A., & Altham, P. M. E. (2000). Recent life events, cortisol, dehydroepiandrosterone and the onset of major depression in high-risk adolescents. *British Journal of Psychiatry, 177*, 499–504.

Grant, K. E., Compas, B. E., Stuhlmacher, A. F., Thurm, A. E., McHahon, S. D., & Halpert, J. A. (2003). Stressors and child and adolescent psychopathology: Moving from markers to mechanisms of risk. *Psychological Bulletin, 129*, 447–466.

Grant, K. E., Compas, B. E., Thurm, A. E., McMahon, S. D., & Gipson, P. Y. (2004). Stressors and child and adolescent psychopathology: Measurement issues and prospective effects. *Journal of Clinical Child and Adolescent Psychology, 33*, 412–425.

Grant, K. E., Compas, B. E., Thurm, A. E., McHahon, S. D., Gipson, P. Y., Campbell, A. J., et al. (2006). Stressors and child and adolescent psychopathology: Evidence of moderating and mediating effects. *Clinical Psychology Review, 26*, 257–283.

Hammen, C. (1991). The generation of stress in the course of unipolar depression. *Journal of Abnormal Psychology, 100*, 555–561.

Hammen, C. (2006). Stress generation in depression: Reflections on origins, research, and future directions. *Journal of Clinical Psychology, 62*, 1065–1082.

Hammen, C., Adrian, C., Gordon, D., Jaenicke, C., & Hiroto, D. (1987). Children of depressed mothers: Maternal strain and symptom predictors of dysfunction. *Journal of Abnormal Psychology, 96*, 190–198.

Hammen, C., & Brennan, P. A. (2001). Depressed adolescents of depressed and nondepressed mothers: Tests of an interpersonal impairment hypothesis. *Journal of Consulting and Clinical Psychology, 69*, 284–294.

Hammen, C., Henry, R., & Daley, S. (2000). Depression and sensitization to stressors among young women as a function of childhood adversity. *Journal of Consulting & Clinical Psychology, 68*, 782–787.

Hammen, C., Rudolph, K., Weisz, J., Rao, U., & Burge, D. (1999). The context of depression in clinic-referred youth: Neglected areas in treatment. *Journal of the American Academy of Child & Adolescent Psychiatry, 38*, 64–71.

Hammen, C., & Shih, J. (in press). Stress generation and depression. In K. Dobson & D. Dozois (Eds.), *Risk factors in depression*. Oxford: Elsevier Ltd.

Hammen, C., Shih, J. H., & Brennan, P. A. (2004). Intergenerational transmission of depression: Test of an interpersonal stress model in a community sample. *Journal of Consulting and Clinical Psychology, 72*, 511–522.

Hankin, B. L., & Abramson, L. Y. (2001). Development of gender differences in depression: An elaborated cognitive vulnerability-transactional stress theory. *Psychological Bulletin, 127,* 773–796.

Hankin, B. L., Kassel, J. D., & Abela, J. R. Z. (2005). Adult attachment dimensions and specificity of emotional distress symptoms: Prospective investigations of cognitive risk and interpersonal stress generation as mediating mechanisms. *Personality and Social Psychology Bulletin, 31*, 136–151.

Hankin, B. L., Mermelstein, R., & Roesch, L. (2007). Sex differences in adolescent depression: Stress exposure and reactivity models. *Child Development, 78*, 279–295.

Harkness, K. L., Bruce, A. E., & Lumley, M. N. (2006). The role of childhood abuse and neglect in the sensitization to stressful life events in adolescent depression. *Journal of Abnormal Psychology, 115*, 730–741.

Johnson, J. H., & McCutcheon, S. (1980). Assessing life events in older children and adolescents. Preliminary findings with the Life Events Checklist. In G. Sarason & C. D. Speilberger (Eds.), *Stress and anxiety*. Washington, DC: Hemisphere.

Joiner, T. E. J., Wingate, L. R., Gencoz, T., & Gencoz, F. (2005a). Stress generation in depression: Three studies on its resilience, possible mechanism, and symptom specificity. *Journal of Social and Clinical Psychology, 24*, 236–253.

Joiner, T. E. J., Wingate, L., & Otamendi, A. (2005b). An interpersonal addendum to the hopelessness theory of depression: Hopelessness as a stress and depression generator. *Journal of Social and Clinical Psychology, 24*, 649–664.

Jose, P. E., Cafasso, L. L., & D'Anna, C. A. (1994). Ethnic group differences in children's coping strategies. *Sociological Studies of Children, 6*, 25–53.

Jose, P. E., & Ratcliffe, V. (2004). Stressor frequency and perceived intensity as predictors of internalizing symptoms: Gender and age differences in adolescence. *New Zealand Journal of Psychology, 33*, 145–154.

Joyner, K., & Udry, J. R. (2000). You don't bring me anything but down: Adolescent romance and depression. *Journal of Health and Social Behavior, 41*, 369–391.

Kendler, K. S., Gardner, C. O., & Prescott, C. A. (2003). Personality and the experience of environmental adversity. *Psychological Medicine, 33*, 1193–1202.

Kendler, K. S., Neale, M. C., Kessler, R., Heath, A. C., & Eaves, L. J. (1993). A twin study of recent life events and difficulties. *Archives of General Psychiatry, 50*, 789–796.

Kessler, R. C. (1997). The effects of stressful life events on depression. *Annual Review of Psychology, 48,* 191–214.

Kessler, R. C., Berglund, P., Demler, O., Jin, R., Koretz, D., Merikangas, K. R., et al. (2003). The epidemiology of major depressive disorder. *Journal of the American Medical Association, 289*, 3095–3105.

Kim, K. J., Conger, R. D., Elder, G. H. J., & Lorenz, F. O. (2003). Reciprocal influences between stressful life events and adolescent internalizing and externalizing problems. *Child Development, 74*, 127–143.

Lakdawalla, Z., Hankin, B. L., & Mermelstein, R. (2007). Cognitive theories of depression in children and adolescents: A conceptual and quantitative review. *Clinical Child and Family Psychology Review, 10*, 1–24.

Larson, R., & Ham, M. (1993). Stress and "storm and stress" in early adolescence: The relationship of negative events with dysphoric affect. *Developmental Psychology, 29*, 130–140.

Lazarus, R., & Folkman, S. (1984). *Stress, appraisal, and coping*. New York: Springer.

Lewinsohn, P. M., Allen, N. B., Seeley, J. R., & Gotlib, I. H. (1999). First onset versus recurrence of depression: Differential processes of psychosocial risk. *Journal of Abnormal Psychology, 108*, 483–489.

Lewinsohn, P. M., Joiner, T. E. J., & Rohde, P. (2001). Evaluation of cognitive diathesis-stress models in predicting major depressive disorder in adolescents. *Journal of Abnormal Psychology, 110*, 203–215.

Lewinsohn, P. M., Rohde, P., & Gau, J. M. (2003). Comparability of self-report checklist and interview data in the assessment of stressful life events in young adults. *Psychological Report, 93*, 459–471.

Lewinsohn, P. M., Rohde, P., Klein, D. M., & Seeley, J. R. (1999). Natural course of adolescent major depressive disorder: I. Continuity into young adulthood. *Journal of the American Academy of Child & Adolescent Psychiatry, 38*, 56–63.

Lewinsohn, P. M., Solomon, A., Seeley, J. R., & Zeiss, A. (2000). Clinical implications of "subthreshold" depressive symptoms. *Journal of Abnormal Psychology, 109*, 345–351.

Little, S. A., & Garber, J. (2004). Interpersonal and achievement orientations and specific stressors predict depressive and aggressive symptoms. *Journal of Adolescent Research, 19*, 63–84.

Mazure, C. M. (1998). Life stressors as risk factors in depression. *Clinical Psychology: Science and Practice, 5*, 291–313.

McClure, E. B., & Pine, D. S. (2007). Social stress, affect, and neural function in adolescence. In D. Romer & E. F. Walker (Eds.), *Adolescent psychopathology and the developing brain* (pp. 219–244). New York: Oxford University Press.

McGuffin, P., Katz, R., & Bebbington, P. E. (1988). The Camberwell Collaborative Depression Study: III. Depression and adversity in the relatives of depressed probands. *British Journal of Psychiatry, 152*, 775–782.

McMahon, S. D., Grant, K. E., Compas, B. E., Thurm, A. E., & Ey, S. (2003). Stress and psychopathology in children and adolescents: Is there evidence of specificity? *Journal of Child Psychology and Psychiatry, 44*, 107–133.

Meadows, S. O., Brown, J. S., & Elder, G. H. J. (2006). Depressive symptoms, stress, and support: Gendered trajectories from adolescence to young adulthood. *Journal of Youth and Adolescence, 35*, 93–103.

Monroe, S., Rohde, P., Seeley, J. R., & Lewinsohn, P. M. (1999). Life events and depression in adolescence: Relationship loss as a prospective risk factor for first onset of major depressive disorder. *Journal of Abnormal Psychology, 108*, 606–614.

Monroe, S. M., & Harkness, K. L. (2005). Life stress, the "kindling" hypothesis, and the recurrence of depression: Considerations from a life stress perspective. *Psychological Review, 112*, 417–445.

Morris, A., Silk, J., Steinberg, L., Myers, S., & Robinson, L. (2007). The role of the family context in the development of emotion regulation. *Social Development, 16*, 361–388.

Nolen-Hoeksema, S. N., & Girgus, J. S. (1994). The emergence of gender differences in depression during adolescence. *Psychological Bulletin, 115*, 424–443.

Oldehinkel, A. J., Wittchen, H.-U., & Schuster, P. (1999). Prevalence, 20-month incidence and outcome of unipolar depressive disorders in a community sample of adolescents. *Psychological Medicine, 29*, 655–668.

Patton, G. C., Coffey, C., Posterino, M., Carlin, J. B., & Bowes, G. (2003). Life events and early onset depression: Cause or consequence. *Psychological Medicine, 33*, 1203–1210.

Plomin, R., Lichtenstein, P., Pedersen, N. L., McClearn, G. E., & Nesselroade, J. R. (1990). Genetic influence on life events during the last half of the life span. *Psychology and Aging, 5*, 25–30.

Post, R. M. (1992). Transduction of psychosocial stress into the neurobiology of recurrent affective disorder. *American Journal of Psychiatry, 149*, 999–1010.

Poulton, R. G., & Andrews, G. (1992). Personality as a cause of adverse life events. *Acta Psychiatrica Scandinavica, 85*, 35–38.

Priel, B., & Shahar, G. (2000). Dependency, self-criticism, social context and distress: Comparing moderating and mediating models. *Personality and Individual Differences, 28*, 515–525.

Prinstein, M. J., & Aikins, J. W. (2004). Cognitive moderators of the longitudinal association between peer rejection and adolescent depressive symptoms. *Journal of Abnormal Child Psychology, 32*, 147–158.

Prinstein, M. J., Borelli, J. L., Cheah, C. S. L., Simon, V. A., & Aikins, J. W. (2005). Adolescent girls' interpersonal vulnerability to depressive symptoms: A longitudinal examination of reassurance-seeking and peer relationships. *Journal of Abnormal Psychology, 114*, 676–688.

Rheingold, A. A., Smith, D. W., Ruggiero, K. J., Saunders, B. E., Kilpatrick, D. G., & Resnick, H. S. (2004). Loss, trauma exposure, and mental health in a representative sample of 12–17-year-old youth: Data from the National Survey of Adolescents. *Journal of Loss & Trauma. Special Issue: Risk and Resiliency Following Trauma and Traumatic Loss, 9*, 1–19.

Rizzo, C. J., Daley, S. E., & Gunderson, B. H. (2006). Interpersonal sensitivity, romantic stress and the prediction of depression: A study of inner-city, minority adolescent girls. *Journal of Youth and Adolescence, 35*, 469–478.

Robinson, N. S., Garber, J., & Hilsman, R. (1995). Cognitions and stress: Direct and moderating effects on depressive versus externalizing symptoms during the junior high school transition. *Journal of Abnormal Psychology, 104*, 453–463.

Rose, A. M., & Rudolph, K. D. (2006). A review of sex differences in peer relationship processes: Potential trade-offs for the emotional and behavioral development of girls and boys. *Psychological Bulletin, 132*, 98–131.

Rudolph, K. D. (2002). Gender differences in emotional responses to interpersonal stress during adolescence. *Journal of Adolescent Health, 30*, 3–13.

Rudolph, K. D., & Flynn, M. (2007). Childhood adversity and youth depression: Influence of gender and pubertal status. *Development and Psychopathology, 19*, 497–521.

Rudolph, K. D., & Hammen, C. (1999). Age and gender as determinants of stress exposure, generation, and reactions in youngsters: A transactional perspective. *Child Development, 70*, 660–677.

Rudolph, K. D., Hammen, C., Burge, D., Lindberg, N., Herzberg, D., & Daley, S. E. (2000). Toward an interpersonal life-stress model of depression: The developmental context of stress generation. *Development and Psychopathology, 12*, 215–234.

Rutter, M., Dunn, J., Plomin, R., Simonoff, E., Pickles, A., Maughan, B., et al. (1997). Integrating nature and nurture: Implications of person–environment correlations and interactions for developmental psychopathology. *Development and Psychopathology, 9*, 335–364.

Safford, S. M., Alloy, L. B., Abramson, L. Y., & Crossfield, A. G. (2007). Negative cognitive style as a predictor of negative life events in depression-prone individuals: A test of the stress generation hypothesis. *Journal of Affective Disorders, 99*, 147–154.

Sandberg, S., McGuinness, D., Hillary, C., & Rutter, M. (1998). Independence of childhood life events and chronic adversities: A comparison of two patient groups and controls. *Journal of the American Academy of Child & Adolescent Psychiatry, 37*, 728–735.

Sandberg, S., Rutter, M., Giles, S., & Owen, A. (1993). Assessment of psychosocial experiences in childhood: Methodological issues and some illustrative findings. *Journal of Child Psychology and Psychiatry, 34*, 879–897.

Segal, Z. V., Williams, J. M., Teasdale, J. D., & Gemar, M. (1996). A cognitive science perspective on kindling and episode sensitization in recurrent affective disorder. *Psychological Medicine, 26*, 371–380.

Shih, J. H. (2006). Sex differences in stress generation: An examination of sociotropy/autonomy, stress, and depressive symptoms. *Personality and Social Psychology Bulletin, 32*(4), 434–446.

Shih, J. H., Eberhart, N. K., Hammen, C. L., & Brennan, P. A. (2006). Differential exposure and reactivity to interpersonal stress predict sex differences in adolescent depression. *Journal of Clinical Child and Adolescent Psychology, 35*, 103–115.

Silk, J., Shaw, S., Skuban, E., Oland, A., & Kovacs, M. (2006). Emotion regulation strategies in offspring of childhood-onset depressed mothers. *Journal of Child Psychology and Psychiatry, 47*, 69–78.

Swearingen, E. M., & Cohen, L. H. (1985). Measurement of adolescents' life events: The Junior High Life Experiences Survey. *American Journal of Community Psychology, 13*, 69–85.

Turner, R. J., & Lloyd, D. A. (2004). Stress burden and the lifetime incidence of psychiatric disorder in young adults. *Archives of General Psychiatry, 61*, 481–488.

Uhrlass, D., & Gibb, B. (2007). Childhood emotional maltreatment and the stress generation model of depression. *Journal of Social and Clinical Psychology, 26*, 119–130.

Waaktaar, T., Borge, A. I. H., Fundingsrud, H. P., Christie, H. J., & Torgersen, S. (2004). The role of stressful life events in the development of depressive symptoms in adolescence: A longitudinal community study. *Journal of Adolescence, 27*, 153–163.

Weissman, M. M., Wolk, S., Wickramaratne, P., Goldstein, R. B., Adams, P., Greenwald, S., et al. (1999). Children with prepubertal-onset major depressive disorder and anxiety grown up. *Archives of General Psychiatry, 56,* 794–801.

Williamson, D. E., Birmaher, B., Anderson, B., Al-Shabbout, M., & Ryan, N. (1995). Stressful life events in depressed adolescents: The role of dependent events during the depressive episode. *Journal of American Academy of Child & Adolescent Psychiatry, 34,* 591–598.

Williamson, D. E., Birmaher, B., Frank, E., Anderson, B., Matty, M. K., & Kupfer, D. J. (1998). Nature of life events and difficulties in depressed adolescents. *Journal of the American Academy of Child & Adolescent Psychiatry, 37,* 1049–1057.

Yeaworth, R. C., York, J., Hussey, M. A., Ingle, M. E., & Goodwin, T. (1980). The development of an adolescent life change event scale. *Adolescence, 15,* 91–97.

Zimmerman, M., Pfohl, B., & Stangl, D. (1986). Life events assessment of depressed patients: A comparison of self-report and interview formats. *Journal of Human Stress, 12,* 13–19.

Chapter Thirteen

Cognitive Vulnerability to Depression in Adolescents: A Developmental Psychopathology Perspective

JOHN R. Z. ABELA AND BENJAMIN L. HANKIN

CONTENTS

Research examining the epidemiology of depression suggests that adolescence may be a critical period for understanding the development of this disorder for two reasons. First, although during childhood, sex differences in depression are not reliably found, during the transition from early to middle adolescence (i.e., ages 12–15) sex differences emerge, with girls reporting higher levels of both depressive symptoms (Angold, Erkanli, Silberg, Eaves, & Costello, 2002; Twenge & Nolen-Hoeksema, 2002) and disorders (Costello, Mustillo, Erkanli, Keeler, & Angold, 2003; Hankin et al., 1998) than boys. Second, the majority of individuals who develop depression experience their first clinically significant episode during the transition from middle to late adolescence (i.e., ages 15–18). Within this brief window of time, there is a dramatic sixfold increase in the prevalence of depression (Hankin et al., 1998; Kessler, Avenei, & Merikangas, 2001). Prevalence rates remain at similarly high levels throughout adulthood, with adult depression typically being preceded by adolescent depression (Kim-Cohen, Caspi, & Moffitt, 2003). Such startling facts strongly argue for the need to identify vulnerability factors to depression in adolescence so that intervention efforts can be initiated prior to the surge in depression rates and before sensitization factors lead to recurrences (Monroe & Harkness, 2005).

The current chapter examines the etiology of depression in adolescence from both a cognitive diathesis-stress and a developmental psychopathology perspective. We begin by discussing the central tenets of cognitive theories of vulnerability to depression. We next conduct a comprehensive review of research, examining six of the predominant cognitive models of depression: (1) the hopelessness theory (Abramson, Metalsky, & Alloy, 1989; Abramson, Seligman, & Teasdale, 1978), (2) Beck's (1967) cognitive theory, (3) the response styles theory (Nolen-Hoeksema, 1991), (4) Cole's (1990, 1991a) competency-based model, (5) theories of personality predispositions to depression (Beck, 1983; Blatt & Zuroff, 1992), and (6) Weisz's (1986) contingency-competence-control model. In the remaining sections, we (1) discuss theoretical, methodological, and statistical issues that may enhance empirical tests of the cognitive theories; (2) explore developmental findings, including whether cognitive vulnerability theories can be applied to understand the "big facts" of depression, such as the emergence of the sex difference in depression during early adolescence or the surge in depression rates during middle to late adolescence; and (3) present a theoretical framework to guide future research examining cognitive vulnerability to depression in youth.

COGNITIVE THEORIES OF DEPRESSION

Cognitive theories of depression are concerned with the relationship between human mental activity and the experience of depressive symptoms and episodes (Ingram, Miranda, & Segal, 1998). Cognition is thought to encompass the mental processes of perceiving, recognizing, conceiving, judging, and reasoning. According to cognitive theorists, these cognitive variables have significant causal implications for the onset, maintenance, and remission of depression.

Cognitive theories of depression operationalize vulnerability as an internal and stable feature of an individual that predisposes him or her to develop depression following negative events (Ingram et al., 1998). It is important to note that the majority of cognitive models are diathesis-stress models in that they posit that depression is produced by the *interaction* between an individual's cognitive vulnerability and certain environmental conditions that serve to trigger this diathesis into operation (for main-effect models, see Nolen-Hoeksema, 1991; Weisz, 1986; Weisz & Stipek, 1982). Under ordinary conditions, persons possessing cognitive vulnerability to depression are hypothesized to be no more likely than other individuals to report depressive symptoms. Only when vulnerable individuals are confronted with certain stressors are differences in symptom levels hypothesized to emerge (Ingram & Luxton, 2005; Monroe & Simons, 1991). For individuals who possess cognitive vulnerability factors, the occurrence of negative events is hypothesized to trigger a pattern of negative, biased, self-referent information processing that initiates a downward spiral into depression. Nonvulnerable individuals are hypothesized to react with an appropriate level of distress and depressive affect to the event, but not to spiral into depression.

Cognitive theories of vulnerability to depression are titration models (Abramson, Alloy, & Metalksy, 1988; Alloy, Hartlage, & Abramson, 1988). In other words, such theories posit that cognitive vulnerability is best conceptualized along a continuum with some individuals exhibiting higher levels of cognitive vulnerability than others. Similarly, negative events are best conceptualized along a continuum with some negative events being more negative than others. According to such a perspective, the higher the level of cognitive vulnerability an individual possesses, the less stressful negative events must be to trigger the onset of depressive symptoms/episodes. Conversely, even youth possessing average or low levels of cognitive vulnerability may be at risk for developing depression following the occurrence of extreme stressors.

Although a multitude of vulnerability factors have been posited by cognitive theorists, we will focus our review on the following vulnerability factors as they have been studied most extensively across child, early adolescent, and adolescent populations: (1) depressogenic inferential styles about causes, consequences, and the self (Abramson et al., 1978, 1989); (2) dysfunctional attitudes (Beck, 1967, 1983); (3) the tendency to ruminate in response to depressed mood (Nolen-Hoeksema, 1991); (4) low levels of self-perceived competence (Cole, 1990, 1991a); (5) personality predispositions to depression (Beck, 1983; Blatt & Zuroff, 1992); and (6) low levels of perceived control and contingency (Weisz, Southam-Gerow, & McCarty, 2001). In addition, wherever possible, we will focus our review on prospective studies, as they provide the most powerful tests of cognitive vulnerability theories (see Lakdawalla, Hankin, & Mermelstein [2007] for a quantitative review of this field).

Hopelessness Theory

The hopelessness theory is a cognitive diathesis-stress theory that posits a series of contributory causes that interact with one another to culminate in a proximal, sufficient cause of a specific subtype of depression: hopelessness depression (Abramson et al., 1989). The hopelessness theory postulates three distinct depressogenic inferential styles that serve as distal contributory causes of hopelessness depression: (1) the tendency to attribute negative events to global and stable causes, (2) the tendency to perceive negative events as having many disastrous consequences, and (3) the tendency to view the self as flawed or deficient following negative events. Each depressogenic inferential style predisposes individuals to the development of hopelessness depression by increasing the likelihood that they will make depressogenic inferences following negative events. Making such inferences increases the likelihood that hopelessness will develop. Once hopelessness develops, hopelessness depression is inevitable, as the hopelessness theory views hopelessness as the proximal, sufficient cause of hopelessness depression.

Depressogenic Inferential Style About Causes

The majority of research testing the diathesis-stress component of the hopelessness theory in children and adolescents has examined whether youth who possess a depressogenic inferential style about causes (also known as a depressogenic attributional style) are more likely than other youth to experience increases in depressive symptoms following negative events. Several studies have provided full support for the attributional vulnerability hypothesis in youth. For example, a depressogenic attributional style has been found to be associated with increases in depressive symptoms following the occurrence of negative events in third- through fifth-grade schoolchildren (Panak & Garber, 1992), third- through sixth-grade children (Brozina & Abela, 2006), 9- to 12-year-olds referred to summer camp for academic, behavioral, or interpersonal problems (Dixon & Ahrens, 1992), 9- to 17-year-old psychiatric inpatients (Joiner, 2000), sixth- through tenth-grade schoolchildren (Hankin, in press), ninth graders (Abela, Parkinson, Stolow, & Starrs, in press), ninth- through twelfth-grade students (Hankin, Abramson, & Siler, 2001 Southall & Roberts, 2002), and 15- to 17-year-old adolescents (Prinstein & Aikens, 2004).

Several other studies using youth samples have provided only partial support for the hopelessness theory's attributional vulnerability hypothesis. For example, studies comparing children at different stages of development have found support for the attributional vulnerability hypothesis in seventh- or eighth-grade students, but not in third-grade students (Abela, 2001; Nolen-Hoeksema, Girgus, & Seligman, 1986, 1992), and in fifth- but not sixth-grade students (Gibb & Alloy, 2006). Other studies examining the buffering role of high levels of self-esteem/competence have found support for the diathesis-stress component of the hopelessness theory in 12-year-olds with low, but not high self-esteem (Robinson, Garber, & Hilsman, 1995); in children aged 5 to 7 years, but not aged 8 to 10 years with low self-esteem (Conley, Haines, Hilt, & Metalsky, 2001), and in fifth and sixth graders with low, but not high, self-perceived competence and control (Hilsman & Garber, 1995). Using samples of twelfth-grade students, one study found a depressogenic attributional style to predict immediate, but not enduring, depressive mood reactions to a negative event (Abela & Seligman, 2000), whereas a second study found a depressogenic attributional style to predict enduring, but not immediate, depressive mood reactions to a negative event (Abela, 2002).

Other studies using youth samples have found no support for the hopelessness theory's attributional vulnerability hypothesis. For example, using community samples ranging in age from 11 to 13 years (Abela & Sarin, 2002; Bennett & Bates, 1995; Spence, Sheffield, & Donovan, 2002), three studies reported that the interaction between a depressogenic attributional style and negative events failed to predict change in depressive symptoms over time. Similarly, using samples of 8- to 16-year-olds with either affectively ill, medically ill, or control parents (Hammen, Adrian, & Hiroto, 1988), and ninth- through twelfth-grade students (Lewinsohn, Joiner, & Rohde, 2001), two studies reported that the interaction between a depressogenic attributional style and negative events did not predict the onset of depressive disorders.

Depressogenic Inferential Style About Consequences

Fewer studies have examined whether a depressogenic inferential style about consequences serves as a vulnerability factor to depressive symptoms in youth. Providing full support for the hopelessness theory, a depressogenic inferential style about consequences has been found to be associated with increases in depressive symptoms following the occurrence of negative events in third- and seventh-grade children (Abela, 2001) and third- through sixth-grade children (Brozina & Abela, 2006). Providing only partial support, however, for the hopelessness theory, using samples of twelfth-grade students, one study found a depressogenic inferential style about consequences to predict immediate, but not enduring, depressive mood reactions to a negative event (Abela & Seligman, 2000), whereas a second study found a depressogenic inferential style about consequences to predict enduring, but not immediate, depressive mood reactions to a negative event (Abela, 2002). Last, providing no support for the hopelessness theory, using a sample of seventh-grade schoolchildren, one study failed to find an association between a depressogenic inferential style about consequences and change in depressive symptoms following negative events (Abela & Sarin, 2002).

Depressogenic Inferential Style About the Self

Similarly, fewer studies have examined whether a depressogenic inferential style about the self serves as a vulnerability factor to depressive symptoms in youth. Providing full support for the hopelessness theory, a depressogenic inferential style about the self has been found to interact with negative events to predict increases in depressive symptoms in third- through sixth-grade schoolchildren (Brozina & Abela, 2006). Providing only partial support, however, for the hopelessness theory, another study reported a depressogenic inferential style about the self to be associated with increases in depressive symptoms following negative events in third- and seventh-grade girls, but not boys (Abela, 2001). Also providing only partial support for the theory, one study of twelfth-grade students found a depressogenic inferential style about the self to predict immediate, but not enduring, depressive mood reactions to a negative event (Abela & Seligman, 2000), whereas a second study found a depressogenic inferential style about the self to predict enduring, but not immediate, depressive mood reactions to a negative event (Abela, 2002). Last, providing no support for the hopelessness theory, one study failed to find an association between a depressogenic inferential style about the self and change in depressive symptoms following negative events in a sample of seventh-grade schoolchildren (Abela & Sarin, 2002).

Beck's Cognitive Theory

Similar to the hopelessness theory, Beck's cognitive theory is a diathesis-stress theory that posits a series of contributory causes that interact with one another to culminate in depression (Beck, 1967, 1983). Central to Beck's theory is the construct of schemas. Beck defines schemas as stored bodies of knowledge (i.e., mental representations of the self and prior experience) that are relatively enduring characteristics of a person's cognitive organization. When an individual is confronted with a situation, the schema most relevant to the situation is activated. Schema activation subsequently influences how the person perceives, encodes, and retrieves information regarding the situation.

Beck (1967, 1983) proposes that certain individuals possess depressogenic schemas that confer vulnerability to depression. Beck hypothesizes that depressogenic schemas are typically organized as sets of dysfunctional attitudes, such as "I am nothing if a person I love doesn't like me" or "If I fail at my work than I am a failure as a person." Such schemas are activated following the occurrence of negative life events. Once activated, depressogenic schemas trigger a pattern of negatively biased, self-referent information processing characterized by negative errors in thinking (e.g., negatively skewed interpretations of negative life events, such as overgeneralization and catastrophizing). Negative errors in thinking increase the likelihood that an individual will develop the negative cognitive triad. Beck defines the negative cognitive triad as containing three distinct, depressogenic, cognitive patterns: negative views of the self (e.g., the belief that one is deficient, inadequate, or unworthy), the world (e.g., construing life experiences in terms of themes of defeat or disparagement), and the future (e.g., the expectation that one's difficulties will persist in the future and there is nothing one can do to change this). As Beck views the negative cognitive triad as a proximal, sufficient cause of depressive symptoms, once an individual develops the negative cognitive triad, he or she will develop depressive symptoms.

To our knowledge, only five prospective studies have examined the diathesis-stress component of Beck's (1967, 1983) cognitive theory in adolescent samples. Two studies have obtained results consistent with Beck's theory. More specifically, higher levels of dysfunctional attitudes have been found to be associated with greater increases in depressive symptoms following the occurrence of negative events in sixth through tenth graders (Hankin, 2007). Similarly, higher levels of dysfunctional attitudes have been found to be associated with a greater likelihood of developing a clinically significant depressive episode following the experience of a high level of stress in 12- to 14-year-olds. At the same time, three studies have obtained results that provide only partial support for Beck's theory. More specifically, higher levels of dysfunctional attitudes have been found to interact with negative events to predict the onset of major depressive episodes in ninth- through twelfth-grade students—but only when dysfunctional attitudes exceed a certain threshold (Lewinsohn et al., 2001). In addition, among twelfth graders, dysfunctional attitudes have been found to interact with a negative university admissions outcome to predict increases in depressed mood the day that students received their admissions decision, but not 4 days later (Abela & D'Alessandro, 2002). Last, higher levels of dysfunctional attitudes have been found to be associated with greater increases in depressive symptoms following negative events in seventh graders possessing high, but not low, levels of social support and self-esteem (Abela & Sullivan, 2003).

Only two prospective studies have tested the vulnerability hypothesis of Beck's (1967, 1983) cognitive theory in child samples. Both of these studies have provided partial support for Beck's theory. More specifically, higher levels of dysfunctional attitudes have been found to be associated with increases in depressive symptoms following the occurrence of negative events in children (ages 6–14) of affectively ill parents possessing low, but not high, levels of self-esteem (Abela & Skitch, 2007). In addition, among third- through eighth-grade schoolchildren, higher levels of dysfunctional attitudes have been found to be associated with greater increases in depressive symptoms 4 days following, but not immediately after, receipt of a negative report card (D'Alessandro & Burton, 2006).

Response Styles Theory

The response styles theory posits that that the way in which individuals respond to their symptoms of depression determines both the severity and duration of such symptoms (Nolen-Hoeksema, 1991). Two such responses are proposed: rumination and distraction. Nolen-Hoeksema argues that individuals who engage in ruminative responses to depressed mood are likely to experience increased severity and duration of symptoms, whereas those who engage in distracting responses are likely to experience relief. The response styles theory was originally proposed to explain the finding that prevalence rates of depression are higher among women than men. Nolen-Hoeksema (1991) proposed that this difference could be accounted for, at least in part, by the differential response styles of the sexes. More specifically, she hypothesizes that women are more likely to ruminate in response to depressed mood, whereas men are more likely to distract.

To our knowledge, nine prospective studies have examined the vulnerability hypothesis of the response styles theory in youth. Results from these studies have been consistently supportive of the hypothesis that rumination is associated with greater severity of depressive symptoms over time. More specifically, in samples of third- and seventh-grade students (Abela, Brozina, & Haigh, 2002), sixth- through eighth-grade students (Burwell & Shirk, 2007; Hilt, McLaughlin, & Nolen-Hoeksema, 2007), sixth- through tenth-grade students (Hankin, in press-b), ninth-grade students (Abela, Parkinson, Stolow, & Starrs, 2007), ninth- through twelfth-grade students (Schwartz & Koenig, 1996), and 6- to 14-year-old children of affectively ill parents (Abela, Aydin, & Auerbach, 2007a), a ruminative response style has been found to be associated with increases in depressive symptoms over time. In addition, higher levels of rumination have been found to predict the onset of major depressive episodes in 12- to 14-year-old adolescents (Abela & Hankin, 2007), and in 11- to 15-year-old adolescent females (Nolen-Hoeksema, Stice, Wade, & Bohon, 2007). At the same time, results have been less supportive of the hypothesis that distractive responses are associated with decreases in depressive symptoms over time, with one study providing support for this hypothesis (Abela et al., 2007a), and two failing to obtain such support (Abela et al., 2002; Schwartz & Koenig, 1996).

COLE'S COMPETENCY-BASED MODEL OF DEPRESSION

Cole's (1991a) competency-based model of depression posits that the feedback a child receives about various areas of his/her life (e.g., academic, social, physical attractiveness, athletic ability, behavioral conduct, etc.) plays a critical role in the development of his/her sense of self-competence. In normal development, children are likely to receive and to focus on positive feedback from parents, teachers, and peers, and thus are likely to develop high levels of self-perceived competence. When normal development goes awry, however, and children receive and focus on negative feedback from such sources, they are likely to develop low levels of self-perceived competence. Low levels of self-perceived competence, in turn, are hypothesized to serve as a vulnerability and/or risk factor for the development of subsequent depression.

Cole's (1991a) competency-based model of depression has received a substantial degree of support in both child and early adolescent samples. Consistent with the model, evaluations of competence by parents, teachers, and/or peers have been found to predict change in children's self-perceived competencies over a 4-year follow-up interval in third graders (Cole, Jacquez, & Maschman, 2001), over a 30-week follow-up interval in fourth graders (Cole, 1991b), and over a 6-month follow-up interval in third and sixth graders (Cole, Martin, & Powers, 1997). At the same time, the relative predictive utility of parent versus peer versus teacher evaluations has been found to vary from one competency domain to another (Cole, 1991b), and as a function of sex (Cole et al., 1997). Also consistent with Cole's (1990, 1991a) competency-based model, lower levels of self-perceived competence have been found to be associated with increases in depressive symptoms over a 4-year follow-up interval in third graders (Cole et al., 2001), over a 2-year follow-up interval in sixth and seventh graders (Hoffman, Cole, Martin, Tram, & Seroczynski, 2000), and over a 6-month follow-up interval in both third (Cole et al., 1997; for exception see Cole, Martin, Powers, & Truglio, 1996) and sixth graders (Cole et al., 1997; Cole et al., 1996). Lower levels of self-perceived competence in the social (i.e., social competence, athletic competence, and physical appearance) but not academic (i.e., academic and behavioral competence) domains have also been found to be associated with increases in negative affect over a 2-year follow-up interval in seventh graders (Cole, Peeke, Dolezal, Murray, & Canzoniero, 1999b). Last, in line with Cole's mediational model, self-perceived competence has been found to mediate the association between evaluations of competence by parents, teachers, and/or peers and change in depressive symptoms over time in third and sixth graders (Cole et al., 1997).

Cole's (1991a) competency-based model has also been examined using children's *underestimations* of competence (i.e., discrepancy between child-report and other-report) as a vulnerability factor to depression rather than children's absolute levels of self-perceived competence. This approach to conceptualizing cognitive vulnerability, however, has resulted in inconsistent findings. More specifically, children's underestimations of their self-competence have been found to predict increases in depressive symptoms over a 1- to 3-year follow-up interval in both sixth and seventh graders (Hoffman et al., 2000), in seventh graders but not in either third through sixth graders or eighth graders (Cole, Martin, Peeke, Seroczynski, & Fier, 1999a; Cole, Martin, Peeke, Seroczynski, & Hoffman, 1998), and in some areas of competence (i.e., physical appearance and behavioral conduct), but not in others (i.e., academic, social, and athletic competence; Cole et al., 1998; Cole et al., 1999a).

Last, although several cross-sectional studies have examined whether self-perceived competence moderates the association between negative events and depressive symptoms (Cole & Turner, 1993), to date, only two prospective studies have done so. Consistent with a vulnerability-stress framework, in a prospective study of fifth and sixth graders, lower levels of academic competence were found to be associated with greater increases in depressive symptoms following the receipt of an unsatisfactory report card (Hilsman & Garber, 1995). At the same time, contrary to a diathesis-stress framework, in a 6-month prospective study of ninth graders, self-perceived competence was found to mediate, but not moderate, the association between negative events and the development of depressive symptoms (Tram & Cole, 2000).

Personality Predispositions to Depression

Researchers from diverse theoretical orientations have proposed that certain personality traits, also referred to as cognitive-affective styles, serve as vulnerability factors to depression (Beck, 1983; Blatt & Zuroff, 1992). Although differences exist in conceptualizations, each theory proposes a personality predisposition focused on interpersonal issues and another focused on achievement issues. These personality predispositions are labeled as dependency and self-criticism by psychodynamic theorists (Blatt & Zuroff, 1992), and as sociotropy and autonomy by cognitive theorists (Beck, 1983). Individuals high in dependency/sociotropy are concerned with interpersonal issues; they need the approval of others to maintain a sense of well-being. Dependent/sociotropic individuals are hypothesized to be at risk for developing depression when they perceive disruptions in their relationships with others, interpersonal loss, and/or social rejection. Individuals high in self-criticism/autonomy, on the other hand, are concerned with achievement issues; they need to meet their own and/or others' standards to maintain a sense of well-being. Self-critical/autonomous individuals are hypothesized to be at risk for developing depression when they perceive that they are not meeting such standards.

Support for the applicability of theories of personality predispositions to depression has been mixed. With respect to self-criticism/autonomy, consistent with such theories, higher levels of self-criticism have been found to be associated with increases in depressive symptoms following negative achievement, but not interpersonal, events among seventh graders (Abela, Sakellaropoulo, & Taxel, 2007e). At the same time, providing only partial support for such theories, higher levels of self-criticism have been found to be associated with greater increases in depressive symptoms in sixth- and seventh-grade girls but not boys (Shahar, Blatt, Zuroff, Kuperminc, & Leadbeater, 2004), following negative interpersonal, but not achievement, events (Shahar & Priel, 2003), following negative achievement, but not interpersonal, events among seventh-grade boys, but not girls, possessing low, but not high self-esteem (Abela & Taylor, 2003), and following both negative events in both the achievement and interpersonal domains among third graders possessing low, but not high levels of self-esteem (Abela & Taylor, 2003). Last, some prospective studies using samples of fifth- through eighth-grade students have failed to report an association between self-criticism/autonomy and change in depressive symptoms either as a main effect or in interaction with stressors (Little & Garber, 2000, 2004, 2005).

Results with respect to dependency/sociotropy have been equally mixed. Consistent with theories of personality predispositions to depression, among sixth graders, higher levels of sociotropy (e.g., neediness and connectedness) have been found to predict increases in depressive symptoms over time through the mediating role of dependent interpersonal negative events, but not dependent noninterpersonal negative events or independent negative events (Little & Garber, 2005). At the same time, providing only partial support for such theories, higher levels of sociotropy (e.g., neediness and connectedness) have been found to predict increases in depressive symptoms following negative peer, but not academic, events in eighth-grade girls but not boys (Little & Garber, 2004), and among fifth- through sixth-grade boys but not girls (connectedness only; Little & Garber, 2000). Also providing only partial support for such theories, higher levels of sociotropy (e.g., neediness and connectedness) have been found to be associated with increases in depressive symptoms over time among fifth and sixth graders (Little & Garber, 2000) and ninth graders (Shahar & Priel, 2003), irrespective of levels of negative events experienced. Last, some prospective studies of third- and seventh-grade students (Abela & Taylor, 2003), seventh-grade students (Abela et al., 2007e), and sixth- through seventh-grade students have failed to report an association between dependency and change in depressive symptoms either as a main effect or in interaction with stressors.

Weisz's Contingency-Competence-Control Model of Depression

Weisz and colleagues' (Weisz, 1986; Weisz & Stipek, 1983) two-dimensional model of control cognition posits that control-related beliefs play an important role in the development of youth depression. Within the context of this model, control, operationalized as the capacity to cause an intended outcome, is conceptualized as consisting of two factors: outcome contingency and personal competence. Outcome contingency refers to the degree to which the occurrence of a given outcome is dependent on the behavior of relevant individuals (i.e., children or adolescents of a similar age). Personal competence with respect to a given outcome refers to the individual's ability to produce the behavior upon which the outcome is contingent.

It is important to note that Weisz and colleagues' model maps onto earlier cognitive-behavioral models of depression. For example, similar to Weisz and colleagues' differentiation between outcome contingency and personal competence, Bandura (1986) distinguishes between outcome expectancies and self-efficacy expectancies. Outcome expectancies are operationalized as the probability that a given behavior will produce a desired outcome. In contrast, self-efficacy expectations are operationalized as the degree to which an individual believes he/she can successfully perform the behavior that produces the desired outcome. In addition, Weisz's constructs of personal competence and outcome contingency map onto Abramson and colleagues' (Abramson et al., 1978) constructs of personal helplessness and universal helplessness, respectively. More specifically, personal helplessness is operationalized as the belief that one's actions will not increase the likelihood of either the occurrence of positive outcomes or the nonoccurrence of negative outcomes while other individuals' actions will influence the likelihood of such outcomes.

In contrast, universal helplessness is operationalized as the belief that the occurrence of a positive outcome or the nonoccurrence of a negative outcome is not contingent upon the behavior of either the individual or relevant others.

A large body of research has accumulated demonstrating a cross-sectional association between lower levels of both perceived competence and/or perceived control and higher levels of depressive symptoms in community (Thurber & Weisz, 1997; Weisz, Sweeney, Proffitt, & Carr, 1993), clinic-referred (Han, Weisz, & Weiss, 2001; Magaro & Weisz, 2006; Weisz, Weiss, Wasserman, & Rintoul, 1987; Weisz et al., 2001), and inpatient (Weisz et al., 1989) samples of children and adolescents. Findings with respect to contingency-related beliefs, however, have been mixed, with some studies reporting an association between contingency-related beliefs and depressive symptoms (Weisz et al., 1989, Samples A and B; Weisz et al., 1993), some studies reporting an association between contingency-related beliefs in adolescents but not children (Weisz et al., 2001), and some studies failing to find such an association in either children or adolescents (Han et al., 2001; Weisz et al., 1989; Weisz et al., 1987, Samples C). To our knowledge, no prospective studies have examined whether control-related beliefs prospectively predict the development of depression in youth—particularly following the occurrence of negative events. Thus, it is unclear whether contingency-competency-control beliefs, as operationalized within the context of Weisz and colleagues' model, represent causes, correlates, or consequences of depression. At the same time, consistent with the hypothesis that control-related beliefs play a role in the development of depressive symptoms, interventions aimed at modifying such beliefs have been found to be effective in reducing depressive symptoms in youth (Weisz, Thurber, Sweeney, Proffitt, & LaGagnoux, 1997).

Empirical Status of Theories of Cognitive Vulnerability to Depression in Adolescents

There are several main points to emphasize based upon our brief review of the literature. First, it is clear that the majority of evidence supports the hypothesis that cognitive vulnerability factors interact with the occurrence of negative events to predict increases in depressive symptoms in children and adolescents—although the pattern of findings does not always conform exactly to what was originally proposed by the theories (e.g., reverse specificity for specific vulnerability hypothesis).

Second, the extant corpus of evidence supporting/contradicting theories of cognitive vulnerability to depression in child and adolescent samples parallels that found in adult samples (see Hankin & Abela [2005] for a review and elaboration on this point). On balance, there exist proportionally as many studies with adults as there are with both children and adolescents that support the cognitive theories of depression, as there are studies that do not.

Last, the various independent tests of cognitive diathesis-stress theories in child and adolescent samples yields what appears, at least on the surface, to be a picture of mixed support based on the use of traditional significance testing criteria (e.g., $p<0.05$; Cohen, 1994) as the foundation for determining whether a study supports or refutes cognitive theories. This "counting the significance stars" approach (Meehl, 1978), however, such as we have implicitly used in this chapter, may incorrectly lead one to conclude that there is evidence to refute cognitive theories (in adults as well as youth) when overall evidence supports them. Such an approach may also drive one to search for moderators to account for the "equivocal" evidence base when such a search is not needed. In contrast to counting how many studies have been supportive based on simple tests of significance, quantitative reviews, such as meta-analysis, can aggregate across the many individual studies, with varying samples sizes, methods, and designs, to provide a more accurate picture of the state of the field. We are aware of one such quantitative review (Lakdawala et al., 2007), and it provides relatively strong support for the hypothesis that cognitive vulnerability factors interact with negative events to predict increases in depressive symptoms in both children and adolescents.

There is still a need for research examining theories of cognitive vulnerability to depression in children and adolescents. In the remaining sections, we (1) discuss theoretical, methodological, and statistical issues that may enhance empirical tests of the cognitive theories; (2) explore developmental findings, including whether cognitive vulnerability theories can be applied to understand the "big facts" of depression, such as the emergence of the sex difference in depression during early adolescence or the surge in depression rates during middle to late adolescence; and (3) present a theoretical framework to guide future research examining cognitive vulnerability to depression in youth.

METHODOLOGICAL ISSUES

In recent years, there has been a surge in literature examining possible methodological reasons for inconsistencies in the findings of studies examining theories of cognitive vulnerability to depression in children, adolescents, and adults. We will briefly discuss some of these reasons as more methodologically rigorous research is likely to lead to greater consistency in findings in research examining cognitive vulnerability to depression at all stages of development. Topics covered include (1) the use of two time-point designs and nomothetic approaches to analysis versus the use of multiwave longitudinal designs and idiographic approaches to analysis, (2) operationalization of cognitive vulnerability (i.e., examining single vulnerabilities; examining multiple vulnerabilities using additive approach, multiplicative, or weakest link approaches), and (3) assessment of cognitive vulnerability factors (i.e., use of age-appropriate measures; psychometric properties of existing measures; use of priming procedures in the assessment of vulnerabilities; self-report measures versus information-processing techniques).

Approaches Towards Examining the Effect of Stress on Depressive Symptoms

In the typical study examining cognitive diathesis-stress theories of depression (e.g., Abela, 2001; Conley et al., 2001; Dixon & Ahrens, 1992; Gibb & Alloy, 2006; Hankin et al., 2001), cognitive vulnerability factors and depressive symptoms are assessed at Time 1. Depressive symptoms and negative events are assessed at Time 2. Analyses are then conducted examining whether each cognitive vulnerability factor interacts with negative events to predict increases in depressive symptoms. Implicit within such a design is the use of a nomothetic approach towards operationalizing high levels of stress. In other words, an individual is considered to be experiencing a high level of stress when his or her level of stress is higher than the sample's average level of stress. Although such an approach sounds plausible on the surface, it may lead to inaccurate predictions at the level of individual study participants. More specifically, a cognitively vulnerable individual can exhibit a sharp decrease in his/her level of stress between two consecutive time-points and yet still exhibit a level of stress that is higher than the sample's average level of stress. Similarly, a cognitively vulnerable individual can exhibit a sharp increase in his/her level of stress between any two consecutive time-points and yet still exhibit a level of stress that is lower than the sample average level of stress. Theories of cognitive vulnerability would predict that the individual whose stress level increased is more likely to show increases in depressive symptoms than the individual whose stress level decreased, given that cognitive theories posit that vulnerability factors interact with *increases* in levels of stress rather than *absolute* levels of stress to predict increases in depressive symptoms. Yet, a nomothetic approach towards operationalizing high levels of stress would make the exact opposite prediction.

The most powerful examination of the diathesis-stress component of theories of cognitive vulnerability to depression involves the use of a multiwave longitudinal design, in which negative events and depressive symptoms are assessed at multiple time points. The use of such a design allows researchers to operationalize high levels of stress from an idiographic perspective. From an idiographic perspective, an individual is considered to be experiencing a high level of stress when he or she is experiencing a level of stress that is higher than his or her own average level of stress. Thus, such an approach retains contextual information that may lead to more accurate predictions at the level of individual participants.

Essentially, when testing the cognitive diathesis-stress theories using a multiwave longitudinal design and an idiographic approach towards data analysis, researchers are examining whether the relationship between fluctuations in stress and fluctuations in depressive symptoms over time varies in children possessing varying levels of cognitive vulnerability. Thus, when using an idiographic approach towards analysis, the diathesis-stress component of cognitive theories would posit that stress and depressive symptoms will co-vary to a greater degree in children who possess cognitive vulnerability factors than in children who do not.

Although an idiographic approach to analysis is more consistent than a nomothetic approach with the diathesis-stress component of the cognitive theories, it is important to note that an idiographic approach does have limitations (and conversely that a nomothetic approach does have strengths). Most importantly, an idiographic approach treats any two given *increases in levels of stress* (i.e., the within-subject effect of stress) that are equal in magnitude (i.e., 0.5 sample mean within-subject *SD*) but that are occurring around different *absolute levels of stress* (i.e., the between-subject effect of stress) similarly when it is possible that the effect of such increases on depressive symptoms varies as a function of the absolute level of stress around which they are occurring (i.e., ±0.5 between-subject *SD*). In other words, it is possible that there exists a "threshold effect" in which increases in stress only trigger increases in depressive symptoms in cognitively vulnerable individuals if such increases pass a certain threshold. For example, an increase of 0.5 mean within-subject *SD* on a given measure of stress (1) may not be expected to predict increases in depressive symptoms in cognitively vulnerable individuals if it is bringing them from a low to an average level of stress in comparison to the sample's average levels of stress, yet (2) may be expected to predict increases in depressive symptoms in such individuals if it is bringing them from an average to a high level of stress in comparison to the sample's average levels of stress. The nomothetic approach that has been typically used to test the diathesis-stress component of the cognitive theories approximates a test of such a threshold model by examining whether cognitively vulnerable youth report increases in depressive symptoms when their level of stress is high in comparison to the sample's average level of stress. However, as stated earlier, such a nomothetic approach still contains missing information as it does not contain information as to whether participants' experienced a *within-subject* increase or decrease in their level of stress to arrive at this "final" level of stress.

In order to examine whether such a "threshold effect" exists, it is essential to examine the effect of stress on depressive symptoms using a cross-level approach (i.e., an approach that examines the interaction of the between- and within-subject effects of stress). Within such an approach, cognitively vulnerable youth are hypothesized to exhibit increases in depressive symptoms if (1) their level of stress is high in comparison to their own average level of stress, and (2) their level of stress is high in comparison to the sample's average level of stress. Such an approach may prove especially informative given that it contains important within-individual contextual information essential to providing an adequate test of the vulnerability hypothesis of the cognitive theories (i.e., idiographic approach) while simultaneously examining the impact of potentially important between-subject differences in stress levels (nomothetic approach).

Conceptualization of the Relation Among Multiple Vulnerabilities

Despite the etiology of depression being widely acknowledged as multifactorial in nature (e.g., Gotlib & Hammen, 2002; Hankin & Abela, 2005; Ingram & Price, 2001), relatively little research has considered possible relationships among the many risk, vulnerability, and protective factors proposed across the various cognitive and interpersonal theories of depression. It is unlikely that each cognitive and interpersonal theory of vulnerability is presenting an entirely distinct etiological pathway leading to the development of depression. Consequently, the richest examination of such theories will ultimately involve the integration of the various distinct risk, vulnerability, and protective factors proposed by empirically supported theories. Three models that have been proposed in an attempt to understand such inter-relationships are the multiplicative, additive, and weakest link models.

The Multiplicative Approach

Most research to date that has attempted to take an integrative approach has conceptualized the relation between the multiple vulnerability factors being examined (i.e., usually two) using a multiplicative approach. Such an approach posits that the vulnerability factors interact synergistically to potentiate the stress–depression relation, such as the greatest increases in depressive symptoms following increases in stress will be observed in individuals possessing both vulnerability factors. For example, within the context of cognitive theories, high levels of self-esteem buffers individuals who possess cognitive vulnerability factors against experiencing increases in depressive symptoms following negative events (Abela & Skitch, 2007; Abela & Taylor, 2003; Conley et al., 2001; Robinson et al., 1995; Southall & Roberts, 2002). Similarly, within the context of interpersonal theories, the association between negative attachment cognitions and depressive episodes has been found to be stronger among youth possessing high, as opposed to low, levels of excessive reassurance-seeking tendencies (Abela et al., 2005).

Although a multiplicative approach has proven useful in examining the integration of any given two models of cognitive and/or interpersonal vulnerability to depression, such an approach becomes more cumbersome, both theoretically and methodologically, when attempting to integrate a wider range of models. As the pool of cognitive and interpersonal vulnerability factors increases, the precision of the hypothesis becomes so exact that only those possessing the complete "depressogenic profile" are hypothesized to show increases in depressive symptoms following the occurrence of stressors.

The Additive Approach

A second approach towards conceptualizing the relation among multiple vulnerability factors is an additive approach. Such an approach assumes that an individual's degree of vulnerability to depression depends on the ultimate balance among his/her vulnerability, risk, and protective factors. Vulnerability factors exhibit a cumulative effect, with the presence of each additional vulnerability factor leading to a greater degree of vulnerability. Conversely, protective factors exhibit a cumulative effect with the presence of each additional protective factor leading to a lesser degree of vulnerability. This approach assumes that the factors work independently of one another. For example, the additive approach would predict that a person with a negative cognitive style, a high propensity to ruminate, and low self-esteem (three vulnerabilities) is more vulnerable to depression than a person with a negative cognitive style, a high propensity to ruminate, and average self-esteem (two vulnerabilities). Further, due to the counterbalancing effects of protective factors, such an approach would predict that a person with a negative cognitive style, an average propensity to engage in rumination, and average self-esteem (one vulnerability) is as vulnerable to depression as an individual with a negative cognitive style, a high propensity to ruminate, and high self-esteem (two vulnerabilities plus one protective factor).

Research examining the response styles theory has taken an additive approach by conceptualizing cognitive vulnerability to depression within the context of the response styles theory as the ratio between youths' scores on measures of rumination and distraction (Abela et al., 2007a). Youth with high ratio scores report a greater tendency to engaging in rumination, as opposed to distraction, following negative events. In support of such an approach, higher ratio scores were found to be associated with increases in depressive symptoms over time above and beyond the effects of both rumination and distraction.

Research examining the hopelessness theory of depression in adolescent and adult samples has also implicitly taken an additive approach to conceptualizing the relation among the three depressogenic inferential styles posited to serve as cognitive vulnerability factors by the theory as participants' cognitive vulnerability scores are set to equal the sum of their scores on measures assessing each of the three cognitive styles (Alloy et al., 2000;, Alloy et al., 2006; Hankin, Abramson, Miller, & Haeffel, 2004). Although several studies have demonstrated that such additive composite scores predict past and/or future depression—particularly following the occurrence of negative events, other studies have yielded less supportive findings (Abela, Aydin, & Auerbach, 2006; Abela & Sarin, 2002).

Finally, research examining Cole's (1990, 1991a) competency-based model of depression has taken an additive approach towards conceptualizing the relation among perceptions of competency in multiple life domains. More specifically, the model posits that receipt of negative feedback in multiple life domains has a cumulative effect on vulnerability to depression, such that low levels of self-perceived competence in two life domains results in a higher degree of vulnerability to depression than low levels of self-perceived competence in one life domain. At the same time, receipt of positive feedback in various life domains is hypothesized to counterbalance the receipt of negative feedback in other life domains. In other words, the likelihood of developing depression is lower in children with a high level of self-perceived competence in one or more life domains than in children who do not exhibit a high level of self-perceived competence in any life domains. Although Cole's model posits that both negative and positive feedback impact depression in youth, feedback about incompetence is hypothesized to be more strongly associated with depression. In other words, the difference in levels of depression in individuals exhibiting moderate versus high levels of self-perceived incompetence is hypothesized to be greater than the difference in levels of depression in individuals exhibiting moderate versus high levels of self-perceived competence. Last, although levels of self-perceived competence/incompetence in multiple life domains are hypothesized to impact youth depression, the relative importance of self-perceived competence and incompetence may vary from domain to domain.

The Weakest Link Approach

A third approach towards conceptualizing the relation among multiple vulnerability factors is a weakest link approach (Abela & Sarin, 2002). This approach posits that when multiple vulnerability factors predict depression through a similar mediating pathway (e.g., negative cognitive style, dysfunctional attitudes, and self-criticism/dependency each increase the likelihood an individual will engage in negative thinking following negative events and thus develop depression), then an individual's most depressogenic vulnerability is the best marker of his/her true propensity for developing depression. Thus, when considering similar vulnerabilities, this approach predicts an individual is as vulnerable to depression as his/her most depressogenic vulnerability makes him/her.

The weakest link approach was originally developed in the context of the hopelessness theory of depression. As the theory posits that depressogenic inferences about causes, consequences, and the self each predict depression through the mediating role of hopelessness, a youth's most depressogenic inferential style likely reflects the extent of their vulnerability to depression, as the inferences that are the product of such style likely reflect the greatest indicator of whether or not the child develops hopelessness.

In an initial test, Abela and Sarin (2002) reported that seventh graders' "weakest links" interacted with stressors to predict increases in depressive symptoms. In contrast, none of the individual cognitive vulnerability factors examined, nor their additive composite score, interacted with stressors to predict such increases. Similar findings have been reported in subsequent studies with children (Abela & McGirr, 2007; Abela, McGirr, & Skitch, 2007c; Abela & Payne, 2003; Abela, Skitch, Adams, & Hankin, 2006), adolescents (Abela & Hankin, 2007), and adults (Abela et al., 2006).

It is possible that a weakest link approach would prove beneficial in examining the relation among cognitive vulnerability factors on a broader level. In a preliminary study examining this possibility, Abela and Scheffler (2007) had children (ages 7–15) complete measures assessing depressive symptoms, four cognitive vulnerability factors (e.g., rumination, self-criticism, low self-esteem, and negative cognitive style), and four interpersonal vulnerability factors (e.g., low social support, negative attachment cognitions, dependency, and excessive reassurance seeking). Children were subsequently given handheld personal computers that were programmed to signal them to complete measures assessing depressive symptoms and negative events once a week, at a randomly selected time, for 6 weeks. With respect to cognitive vulnerability factors, a depressogenic weakest link was associated with increases in depressive symptoms following negative events. In contrast, additive composite scores were not associated with such increases. Interestingly, with respect to interpersonal vulnerability factors, both depressogenic weakest link and additive composite scores were associated with increases in depressive symptoms following negative events. Further, both scores exhibited unique effects. Such a pattern of findings suggests that the best approach to take when integrating multiple vulnerability factors may vary according to the type of vulnerability factor examined. In addition, such results indicate that it is possible that multiple types of integrative relationships are present for certain types of vulnerability factors.

Priming of Cognitive Vulnerability Factors

Several cognitive theorists have argued that cognitive vulnerability factors are typically latent and must be activated by negative mood states and/or the occurrence of stressors in order to be assessed accurately (Beck, 1967; Persons & Miranda, 1992; Riskind & Rholes, 1984; Teasdale, 1993). Therefore, studies that do not activate or prime cognitive vulnerability factors before assessing them are likely to inadequately assess the true propensity of participants' depressogenic thinking. A large body of research, using adult samples, has accumulated in recent years, providing support for this priming hypothesis (e.g., for review see Scher, Ingram, & Segal, 2005). Far fewer studies have examined the priming hypothesis in youth. Of those conducted, however, results have been consistently supportive.

In the first study, to our knowledge, to test the priming hypothesis in a youth sample (ages 8–12), Taylor and Ingram (1999) had children of currently and never depressed mothers complete a self-referent encoding task under one of two conditions: negative or neutral mood (induced by an autobiographical mood induction). In line with the priming hypothesis, high-risk children in the negative mood condition rated fewer positive words as self-descriptive than did both high-risk children in the neutral condition and low-risk children in either condition. Further, although high- and low-risk children did not differ in terms of recall of positive words, irrespective of mood condition, high-risk children in the negative mood condition recalled more negative words than did high-risk children in the neutral condition.

Providing equally strong support for the priming hypothesis, Timbremont and Braet (2004) had currently depressed, remitted depressed, and never depressed inpatient children complete a self-referent encoding task with intentional recall following viewing of a film centering around themes of social rejection. In terms of recall of negative and positive self-descriptive words, results were supportive of the priming hypothesis. More specifically, currently depressed children recalled more negative, and less positive, self-descriptive words than did never depressed children. In addition, although remitted and never depressed children were equally likely to recall negative self-descriptive words, remitted depressed children were less likely to recall positive self-descriptive words. Finally, although never depressed children recalled positive self-descriptive words more often than negative self-descriptive words, never and remitted depressed children did not differentially recall either group of words.

Last, some recent research has provided an indirect test of the priming hypothesis in a youth sample. Joorman, Talbot, and Gotlib (2007) compared daughters (ages 9–14) whose mothers had experienced recurrent major depressive episodes during their lifetime to daughters of never depressed mothers in terms of biased processing of emotional information. Following completion of a negative mood induction, daughters completed an emotional faces dot-probe task. Daughters at risk for depression selectively attended to negative facial expressions, whereas control daughters selectively attended to positive facial expressions.

To our knowledge, no past prospective studies examining theories of cognitive vulnerability to depression in youth have utilized priming procedures when assessing cognitive vulnerability factors. Thus, we cannot be certain that youths' true propensities for depressogenic thinking in such studies were accurately assessed. Future research is likely to benefit from incorporating priming techniques into their assessment procedures in order to increase the accuracy of their assessments of cognitive vulnerability factors.

DEVELOPMENTAL ISSUES

At what age do cognitive vulnerability factors emerge? Can cognitive vulnerability theories be applied to understand the "big facts" of depression, such as the dramatic rise in rates of depression starting in middle adolescence, the emergence of the sex difference in depression starting in early adolescence, and the strong continuity and recurrence of depression? These are the main questions that we will examine in this section.

The Emergence of Cognitive Vulnerability Factors

With respect to the question "At what age do cognitive vulnerability factors to depression emerge?" the following two main questions have been examined on both a theoretical and empirical level: (1) do cognitive vulnerability factors mediate the relationship between negative events and depression in younger children and moderate the association between negative events and depressive symptoms in older children? and (2) are there age-related changes in the latent organization of cognitive vulnerability factors such that they are more state-like in younger children and more trait-like in older children and adolescents?

There has been great debate in the literature on the developmental stage at which cognitive vulnerability factors emerge (Garber, 2000; Gibb & Coles, 2005; Hammen & Rudolph, 2003; Hankin & Abela, 2005). Several researchers have hypothesized that cognitive vulnerability factors do not begin to moderate the relationship between stress and depression until the transition from middle childhood to early adolescence—tying the emergence of such vulnerability factors to the influence of increasing levels of experience and cognitive-processing capacities. For example, from the perspective of Beck's (1967, 1983) cognitive theory, researchers have hypothesized that schemas do not become consolidated until adolescence or even early adulthood after repeated learning experiences have reinforced them (Hammen & Zupan, 1984; Young, 1999). From the perspective of the hopelessness theory (Abramson et al., 1989), researchers have hypothesized that a depressogenic attributional style only emerges as a vulnerability factor during the transition from childhood to adolescence when children acquire the ability to engage in abstract reasoning and formal operational thought (Nolen-Hoeksema et al., 1992; Turner & Cole, 1994).

In explaining mechanisms underlying such a developmental hypothesis, researchers have drawn from a wide variety of findings in the cognitive development literature—particularly those pertaining to middle childhood. For example, during middle childhood, children develop a more stable and less concrete sense of self (Rholes, Blackwell, Jordan, & Walters, 1980). Their self-views become increasingly differentiated (Abela & Véronneau-McArdle, 2002) as they shift their focus from concrete, behavioral characteristics in early childhood, to trait-like characteristics in middle childhood, to more abstract psychological constructs during adolescence (Harter, 1986, 1990). During this developmental period, children also become less here-and-now oriented (Shirk, 1988), and more likely to integrate past experience into working knowledge in a manner that informs interpretations and predictions (Rholes et al., 1980). Although very young children have a rudimentary understanding of causality (e.g., Oakes, 1994), it is not until middle childhood that children's use of stable personality traits to explain behavior increases dramatically (Corrigan, 1995). Last, it has been suggested that young children do not have the cognitive capacity to develop hopelessness because they have difficulty conceptualizing the sequencing of events as well as the length of time between events (Kaslow, Adamson, & Collins, 2000). Consequently, it is only in the transition from middle childhood to early adolescence when a future time orientation and the ability to assess probabilities emerge that hopelessness can develop (Kaslow et al., 2000).

The hypothesis that cognitive vulnerability emerges during the transition from middle childhood to early adolescence is largely based on early research examining the attributional vulnerability hypothesis of the hopelessness theory in youth. Results from three studies, in particular, provide the most compelling support for this hypothesis. In a 1-year longitudinal study of 8- to 11-year-old children, Nolen-Hoeksema and colleagues (1986) found that attributional style interacted with negative events to predict increases in depression in two out of four follow-up assessments. In a 5-year longitudinal study of third-grade schoolchildren, Nolen-Hoeksema and colleagues (1992) found that although early in childhood only the occurrence of negative events predicted increases in depression, later in childhood, the interaction between attributional style and negative events predicted increases in depression. Last, in a sample of fourth-, sixth-, and eighth-grade schoolchildren, Turner and Cole (1994) found that a depressogenic attributional style interacted with negative events to predict increases in depression in eighth-grade children, but not in fourth-or sixth-grade children.

When interpreting the results of these three studies, it is important to note that attributional style was assessed using the Children's Attributional Style Questionnaire (Seligman et al., 1984), a measure that is limited by its poor internal reliability (alphas range 0.4–0.6; Hankin & Abramson, 2002; Thompson, Kaslow, Weiss, & Nolen-Hoeksema, 1998). Subsequent research examining a wider range of cognitive vulnerability factors (e.g., depressogenic inferential styles about the self and consequences, a ruminative response style, dysfunctional attitudes, and self-criticism) and using improved measures of cognitive vulnerability, including more developmentally sensitive measures of attributional style (Conley et al., 2001), has yielded a pattern of findings that is contradictory to this developmental hypothesis. For example, five studies have provided support for theories of cognitive vulnerability to depression in third-grade schoolchildren (e.g., Abela, 2001; Abela et al., 2002; Abela, McGirr et al., 2007c; Abela & Payne, 2003; Abela & Taylor, 2003). Four studies using a sample of children between the ages of 6 and 14 have reported that the association between cognitive vulnerability factors and increases in depressive symptoms following negative events is not moderated by age (e.g., Abela et al., 2007a; Abela & McGirr, 2007; Abela & Skitch, 2007; Abela, Skitch et al., 2006). One study reported support for theories of cognitive vulnerability to depression in children aged 5 to 7 years, but not aged 8 to 10 years (Conley et al., 2001). Last, four studies have failed to provide support for theories of cognitive vulnerability to depression in either early adolescent (Abela & Sarin, 2002; Bennett & Bates, 1995; Spence et al., 2002) or middle adolescent (Lewinsohn et al., 2001) samples.

The Consolidation of Degree of Inter-Relatedness of Cognitive Vulnerability Factors

Although the pattern of results obtained in research examining theories of cognitive vulnerability to depression in youth suggests that such theories are applicable to children, early adolescents, and adolescents, it is likely that much change occurs with respect to cognitive vulnerability factors throughout childhood and adolescence. More specifically, it is possible that the accumulation of experience and increased cognitive processing abilities leads to (1) greater consolidation of specific cognitive vulnerability factors, and (2) greater inter-relatedness among different cognitive vulnerability factors.

The Consolidation of Cognitive Vulnerability Factors

To advance knowledge on how and when cognitive vulnerabilities emerge and stabilize, we have adapted and applied conceptual and empirical approaches from research on basic personality development (e.g., Caspi, Roberts, & Shiner, 2005; Fraley & Roberts, 2005), including examination of rank-order stability and mean-level changes in vulnerabilities over time. Different processes can explain how depression vulnerabilities maintain rank-order, or test-retest, stability over time. As seen in Figure 13.1, these include: (1) a trait-like model

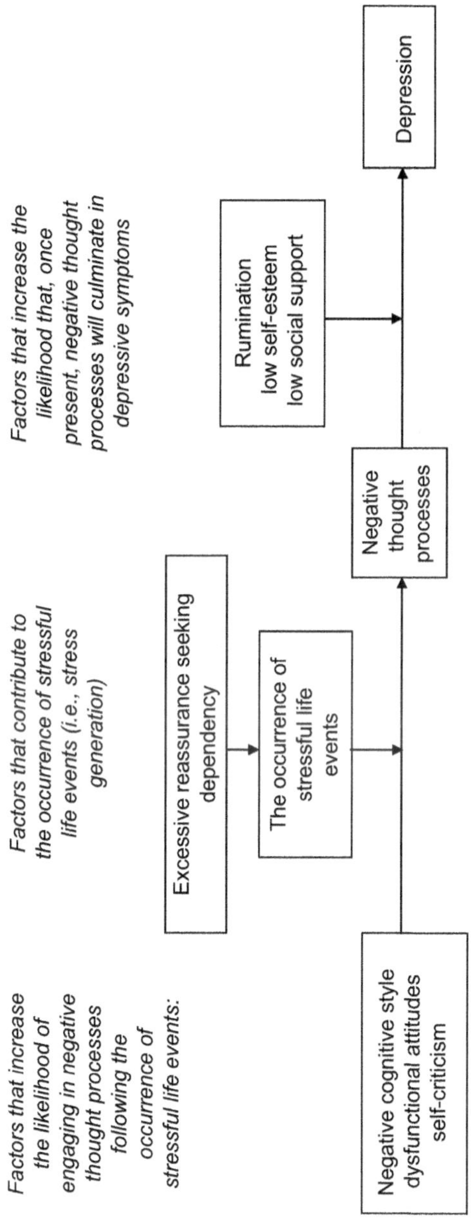

Figure 13.1 A cognitive-interpersonal integrative model of depression.

(top panel), (2) a contextual/autoregressive model (middle panel), and (3) a combined trait/contextual model (bottom panel). Trait models predict that the empirical test-retest correlations will be invariant (ignoring statistical fluctuations in measurement precision) as the length of test-retest interval increases because a stable psychological variable (i.e., a trait vulnerability) organizes the manifestation of depression vulnerability over time. In contrast, contextual models predict that the magnitude of the test-retest correlations for depression vulnerability will decrease monotonically as the size of the interval increases (i.e., an autoregressive simplex pattern; Kenny & Zautra, 2001) because there is no enduring trait vulnerability in the model contributing to stability over time.

To test these different organizing conceptual models rigorously, it is essential that multiple waves of data be used. The typical two time-point study (e.g., Burns & Seligman, 1989 in adults; Voelz, Walker, Petit, Joiner, & Wagner, 2003 in youth) most often used to demonstrate test-retest reliability is inadequate for formally examining the processes underlying the degree of test-retest reliability observed over those two time points, regardless of the length of time (Fraley & Roberts, 2005) because it is the pattern of test-retest correlations over time, not the strength of the test-retest correlation, that indicates whether the trait is organized best as a trait, contextual, or a combined manner. With multiwave data, structural equation modeling (SEM) can be used to examine the pattern of test-retest correlations over multiple follow-ups to determine whether a trait-like or autoregressive contextual model best explains the rank-order stability of data over time. Moreover, longitudinal analyses can evaluate whether mean levels of stability change significantly over time for the participants on average to investigate mean level stability.

Based on this personality framework, we (Hankin, Fraley, & Abela, 2005) recently provided the first examination of the *processes underlying stability of cognitive vulnerability*, in any age group, using data from a 35-day diary study with late adolescents (n=210). Participants completed daily ratings of the inferences they made for the most negative event experienced every day for a month, based on the hopelessness theory. We found rank-order stability: cognitive vulnerability (negative cognitive style) was moderately stable over time (average test-retest r=0.38, SD=0.08, range=0.56 to 0.15). Using SEM, the pattern of this test-retest stability was best explained by a trait-like model. The contextual/autoregressive model provided a poor fit to the test-retest data, and the combined trait and contextual model fit as well as the trait model alone. We also found mean level stability: cognitive vulnerability scores did not change on average over 35 days.

In addition, research with younger adolescents (grades 6–10; n=350; Hankin, in press-c) found that a negative cognitive style exhibited mean level stability, whereas rumination and dysfunctional attitudes showed some mean level change. Absolute magnitudes of test-retest reliabilities were strong for a negative cognitive style, and small to moderate for rumination and dysfunctional attitudes. SEM showed that enduring trait-like processes, but not contextual forces, contributed to the patterning of these test-retest reliabilities over time for a negative cognitive style, dysfunctional attitudes, and rumination. Finally, youths' grade was examined to evaluate whether grade, as a rough index of developmental level, influenced the fit of these models, given the developmental hypothesis that cognitive vulnerabilities likely emerge into a more stable, trait-like vulnerability as a function of increasing grade. Consistent with this hypothesis, the trait model and enduring processes fit for the older (ninth and tenth graders) youth well, and trait processes also fit for early adolescents (sixth to eighth graders) for a negative cognitive style. The trait model fit well for dysfunctional attitudes and rumination for middle adolescents, but neither trait nor contextual processes were significant for early adolescents. In sum, these results with early to middle and late adolescents (ages 12–16 and 18) provide initial evidence that cognitive vulnerabilities appear to have stabilized into a relatively stable, trait-like pattern, at least by sixth grade, although there likely is some continued change throughout early adolescence (sixth to eighth graders in this one study). It appears that cognitive vulnerabilities, especially a depressogenic inferential style, and dysfunctional attitudes and rumination to a lesser extent, have stabilized into coherent, fairly trait-like vulnerabilities to depression by middle adolescence and persist thereafter into adulthood.

The Inter-Relatedness of Cognitive Vulnerability Factors

The results from factor analytic studies suggest that cognitive vulnerability factors are more distinct in children than in adolescents and young adults (e.g., Adams, Abela, & Hankin, 2007; Hankin, Lakdawalla, Carter, Abela, & Adams, 2007; Joiner & Rudd, 1996). It appears that the various cognitive vulnerabilities may initially be relatively independent of one another, but then become more inter-related during the transition from childhood to adolescence. As multiple vulnerabilities coalesce into a consolidated *set* of moderately intercorrelated cognitive vulnerabilities, youths' degree of vulnerability to depression may heighten. Interestingly, this contamination process may occur around the same time that many researchers (Nolen-Hoeksema et al., 1992; Turner & Cole, 1994) have hypothesized that cognitive vulnerability to depression in youth first emerges.

Given that cognitive vulnerability factors become more inter-related with one another with age, different approaches towards conceptualizing the relationship between multiple cognitive vulnerability factors may be optimal for youth at different developmental stages. When youths' cognitive vulnerability factors are still relatively distinct, knowledge of any particular factor may convey minimal information about overall degree of vulnerability to depression, so a weakest link approach may be the most appropriate approach at this stage, as a child's most depressogenic vulnerability factor may likely be the best indicator of his/her propensity to engage in depressogenic thinking following stressors (Abela & Sarin, 2002). As cognitive vulnerability factors become more inter-related with one another over time, however, knowledge of a child's level with respect to any given vulnerability factor provides information about his/her levels with respect to other vulnerability factors. At this point in development, an additive approach may become more appropriate than a weakest link approach as the presence of multiple vulnerabilities may become an equally, if not more, important indicator of both the likelihood he/she engages in depressogenic thought processes as well as the degree of negativity and generality of such processes.

Developmental Changes in Levels of Cognitive Vulnerability and Stress

An alternative way in which theories of cognitive vulnerability could shed light on the pattern of depression rates observed in children, early adolescents, and adolescents is if *levels* of the vulnerability and risk factors featured in such theories vary as a function of development. In other words, although similar processes may be related to the onset of depression in both children and adolescents, differing levels of causal variables (e.g., vulnerability factors and stressors) may account for differing rates of depression in these age groups as well as differing rates between the sexes.

Age-Related Differences

The results from prospective studies examining levels of stressors experienced by youth at different developmental stages are consistent with this possibility. More specifically, both boys and girls begin to encounter more stressors starting around age 13 (Ge, Lorenz, Conger, Elder, & Simons, 1994; Rudolph & Hammen, 1999), and puberty, as a developmental transition, is associated with an increase in negative life events (Caspi & Moffitt, 1991; Graber, Brooks-Gunn, & Petersen, 1996). Thus, increasing levels of stress may explain, in part, the increase in overall depression rates for both boys and girls during the transitions from early to middle adolescence, and from middle to late adolescence.

Fewer studies have prospectively followed groups of youth over time, monitoring changes in levels of cognitive vulnerability. Thus, it is unclear whether cognitive vulnerability factors increase during the transition from childhood to adolescence. The results of two studies, however, provide support for this hypothesis. More specifically, Koestner, Zuroff, and Powers (1991) reported that levels of self-criticism increase during the transition from childhood to early adolescence. Similarly, Cole and colleagues (Cole et al., 2001) reported that perceived self-competence in the physical domain decreases during the transition from childhood to early adolescence. At the same time, other studies that have compared children and early adolescents in terms of levels of cognitive vulnerability factors, such as a negative cognitive style (Abela, 2001; Abela & Payne, 2003) and rumination (Abela et al., 2002; Abela, Vanderbilt, & Rochon, 2004), have failed to support this hypothesis, reporting either no age-related differences (Abela et al., 2002; Abela et al., 2004) or age-related differences in the direction of children reporting higher levels of such vulnerability factors than adolescents (Abela, 2001; Abela & Payne, 2003). A major barrier to interpreting age-related change, or lack of, in levels of vulnerability is that the degree to which current measures of cognitive vulnerability exhibit measurement invariance across age-groups is unknown. Consequently, the results reported in past studies should be interpreted with caution.

It is important to note that research examining age-related change in levels of cognitive vulnerability factors over time must not only consider the possibility that increases in levels of specific vulnerability factors contribute to increased depression rates, but also that *failure to show decreases* in levels of certain vulnerability factors may also contribute to increased depression rates. More specifically, several studies have reported a cross-sectional association between age and cognitive-interpersonal vulnerability factors such as dependency (Abela, Fishman, & Wagner, 2007b; Abela & Taylor, 2003) and reassurance seeking (e.g., Abela et al., 2005; Abela, Zuroff, Ho, Adams, & Hankin, 2006), with younger children reporting higher levels of such variables than older children. It is possible that elevated levels of such cognitive-interpersonal variables are both normative and adaptive in younger children, and consequently, elevated levels of such factors only begin to confer vulnerability to depression during the transition from childhood to early adolescence when they become developmentally atypical. It is likely that as normative base rates of variables such as dependency and reassurance seeking become increasingly lower, the interpersonal behaviors associated with them become more apt to be viewed as developmentally atypical, and consequently to elicit more negative responses from others (e.g., parents, peers, etc.). Providing indirect support for such a hypothesis, although elevated levels of dependency have been found to serve as a vulnerability factor to depressive symptoms in both adolescents and adults (see Zuroff, Santor, & Mongrain, 2004, dependency has not been found to confer vulnerability to depression in children (e.g., Abela et al., 2007e; Abela & Taylor, 2003). Further, although elevated levels of dependency have been found to be associated with impairment in social functioning in adolescents and adults (e.g., see Zuroff, Santor, & Mongrain, 2004), elevated levels of dependency have been found to be positively associated with social functioning in children (Fichman, Koestner, & Zuroff, 1996).

Sex Differences

The results from prospective studies examining sex differences in levels of stressors suggest that girls begin to encounter more stressors than boys starting around age 13 (Ge et al., 1994; Hankin, Mermelstein, & Roesch, 2007; Rudolph & Hammen, 1999) and that puberty, as a developmental transition, is associated with an increase in negative life events—particularly for girls (Graber, Brooks-Gunn, & Warren, 1995). Thus, the increasing levels of stressors observed in girls compared to boys during the transitions both from middle childhood to early adolescence and from early to middle adolescence may explain, in part, the emergence of sex differences in depression (e.g., girls become twice as likely as boys to experience depression; Hankin & Abramson, 2001).

Research examining sex differences in levels of cognitive vulnerability has reported mixed findings. More specifically, studies using child and early adolescent samples have failed to report sex differences in levels of cognitive vulnerability factors, such as depressogenic inferential styles about consequences and causes (Abela & McGirr, 2007), dysfunctional attitudes (e.g., Abela, 2001; Abela & Payne, 2003; Abela & Skitch, 2007), perceived competence in the academic domain (Bruce et al., 2006; Cole et al., 1998; Cole et al., 1999b), and rumination (Abela et al., 2007a; Abela et al., 2002; Abela et al., 2004; Broderick & Korteland, 2004; for exception see Ziegert & Kistner, 2002). At the same time, studies using child and early adolescent samples have reliably reported sex differences in cognitive vulnerability factors, such as depressogenic inferential style about the self (Abela, 2001; Abela & Payne, 2003), perceived competence in the interpersonal domain (Bruce et al., 2006; Cole et al., 1998; Cole et al., 1999b), and dependency (Abela et al., 2007e). With respect to adolescent samples, sex differences in levels of most cognitive vulnerability factors are reliably observed, with girls reporting higher levels of negative cognitive style (Abela et al., 2007; Hankin, in press; Hankin & Abramson, 2002; Hilt et al.,

2007; Mezulis, Abramson, Hyde, & Hankin, 2004; for exception see Hankin, et al., 2001) and rumination (Abela et al., 2007; Hankin, in press-b; Schwartz & Koenig, 1996) than boys, although boys may exhibit more dysfunctional attitudes than girls (Hankin, 2007; Haeffel et al., 2003). Finally, some research suggests that cognitive vulnerabilities may explain the sex difference in adolescent depression (Hankin, Wetter, & Cheely, 2008). In a cross-sectional study, Hankin and Abramson (2002) found that a negative cognitive style mediated the sex difference in depressive symptoms among high school students. Following this, Hankin (in press-d) used a multiwave prospective design with a sample of sixth to tenth graders and found that a negative cognitive style and stressors explained why girls exhibited increasing trajectories of depressive symptoms over time compared with boys.

Thus, regarding depressogenic inferential styles about causes and consequences, rumination, self-perceived competence in the academic domain, and self-criticism, results have provided support for the hypothesis that sex differences in cognitive vulnerability factors emerge in conjunction with sex differences in depression. At the same time, with respect to depressogenic inferential style about the self, results for self-perceived competence in the interpersonal domain, and dependency have provided support for the hypothesis that sex-differences in cognitive vulnerability factors pre-date the emergence of sex differences in depression.

A DEVELOPMENTAL PSYCHOPATHOLOGY MODEL OF VULNERABILITY TO DEPRESSION

Given the large number of vulnerability factors proposed by cognitive and interpersonal theories of depression (and consequently the large number of possible combinations among them), we use the following framework to guide us in our examination of cognitive vulnerability to depression in youth. In creating this framework, we were guided primarily by: (1) theory and research examining the causal mediation components of cognitive and interpersonal vulnerability theories, and (2) past research testing the diathesis-stress component of cognitive/interpersonal integrative models of depression (see Davilla, Ramsay, Stroud, & Steinberg, 2005; Hankin & Abela, 2005; Van Orden, Wingate, Gordon, & Joiner, 2005). This framework is meant to be viewed as a heuristic towards integrating theories rather than as a definitive statement of how the various vulnerabilities relate to each other—especially since we chose to group vulnerabilities into one of three mutually exclusive categories for the sake of simplicity and clarity.

As presented in Figure 13.1, within our integrative model, vulnerability factors are grouped into three categories: (1) factors that increase the likelihood of engaging in negative thought processes following the occurrence of negative events, (2) factors that contribute to the occurrence of stressful life events, and (3) factors that increase the likelihood that, once present, negative thought processes will culminate in depressive symptoms. As factors within the same category are hypothesized to be associated with depression through similar mediating pathways, in testing this integrative model, it will be important to examine whether a youth's degree of vulnerability *within each of the three categories* is best determined by his/her most depressogenic vulnerability factor within that category (weakest link approach) or whether the presence of multiple vulnerability factors within that category increases his/her degree of vulnerability in a cumulative fashion (additive approach). *Across categories*, we believe the model is best tested using a multiplicative approach, as categories are thought to encompass separate causal pathways that may interact synergistically to potentiate the stress–depression relationship.

Importantly, both cognitive and interpersonal vulnerability factors are included in our model, as we believe cognitive-interpersonal integrative models offer greater explanatory power than cognitive and interpersonal models alone. Within the framework of our model, we have chosen to focus on interpersonal vulnerability factors derived from two major categories of theories of interpersonal vulnerability: (1) theories that hypothesize an association between maladaptive interpersonal behaviors and depressive symptoms, and (2) theories that hypothesize an association between quality of interpersonal relationships and depressive symptoms (Rudolph, Flynn, & Abaied, 2008). Interpersonal theories of depression which fall within the first category posit that certain maladaptive interpersonal behaviors and/or styles render individuals vulnerable to depressive symptoms, either because they increase the likelihood of engaging in negative thought processes following negative interpersonal stressors, or because they play a role in stress generation processes. In this category, we include two constructs. First, *excessive reassurance seeking* (Joiner & Metalsky, 2001) is a relatively stable tendency to excessively and persistently seek assurances and comfort from others. Higher levels of reassurance seeking have been found to prospectively predict increases in depressive symptoms following negative events in youth (Abela, Morrison, & Starrs, 2007d; Abela, Zuroff, Ho, Adams, & Hankin, 2006) through the mediating role of stress-generation processes (Shih, Abela, & Starrs, 2007). Second, *dependency* is an exaggerated need for relatedness and a desire to be in direct, immediate contact with close others (e.g., parents, peers). Cross-sectional research shows that higher levels of dependency are associated with higher levels of depressive symptoms (Abela & Taylor, 2003; Fichman, Koestner, & Zuroff, 1994; Luthar & Blatt, 1993) and to predict increases in depressive symptoms following the occurrence of negative events (Abela et al., 2007e) through the mediating role of stress generation processes (Little & Garber, 2004). Interpersonal theories of depression that fall within the second category posit that interpersonal factors serve as buffers against depression following negative events (e.g., Brown & Harris, 1978). Such interpersonal factors are hypothesized to buffer against the deleterious effects of stress by enhancing one's coping abilities (Cohen & Wills, 1985). In this category, we include *social support*, which is a multidimensional concept defined as the availability of a network of people on whom a person can rely in times of need (Sarason, Pierce, & Bannerman, 1993). There are different types of social support (e.g., emotional, financial, informational), and a social support network might include family members, friends, romantic partners, and others. There is clear evidence of the buffering effects of social support across development (Garber & Little, 1999; Kashani, Carlson, & Beck, 1999). Adolescent depression is linked to low levels of support from families (e.g., Marcotte, Fortin, & Potvin, 2002; Sheeber, Hops, & Alpert, 1997) and friends (Klein, Lewinsohn, & Seeley, 1997).

It is important to note that both self-competence and perceived control were not included within this model. Our failure to include these two variables is the result of insufficient research to date examining whether these variables are best conceptualized as: (1) enduring cognitive vulnerabilities that interact with the occurrence of negative events to predict the development of depressive symptoms through the mediating role of negative thought processes; or (2) cognitive vulnerabilities that increase the likelihood that negative thoughts, once present, lead to the onset of more severe and long-lasting symptoms of depression. For example, with respect to Cole's (1991a) competency-based model of depression, only two studies have been conducted, to date, examining whether the occurrence of negative events moderates the association between perceived competence and change in depressive symptoms over time (Hilsman & Garber, 1995; Tram & Cole, 2000), and the results from these two studies were contradictory. Similarly, no prospective studies have examined whether control/contingency beliefs predict increases in depressive symptoms over time either as a main effect or in interaction with the occurrence of stressors. Thus, additional research examining the pathways through and conditions under which these cognitive vulnerability factors lead to depression is especially needed.

Last, it is important to note that the model presented above focuses on the more proximal causes of depression in youth. Such proximal causal pathways, however, are ultimately embedded within a broader framework delineating the more distal pathways through which cognitive and interpersonal vulnerability factors develop in the first place (e.g., Hankin & Abramson, 2001). To date, research has provided support for at least five of such pathways: (1) the experience of elevated levels of depressive symptoms (e.g., the scar hypothesis; Gibb et al., 2006; Nolen-Hoeksema et al., 1986, 1992); (2) repeated exposure to negative events occurring in multiple and likely interacting domains (i.e., family conflict, divorce, poverty; Garber & Flynn, 1998; Rudolph, Kurlakowsky, & Conley, 2001); (3) childhood emotional maltreatment (Gibb & Abela, in press; Gibb & Alloy, 2006; Gibb et al., 2006; Hankin, 2005); (4) maladaptive parenting practices including high levels of parental criticism, indifference, and control, and low levels of parental acceptance and care (Bruce et al., 2006; Jaenicke et al, 1987; Liu, 2003); and (5) modeling of feedback provided to the child by the parent (Alloy et al., 2001; Dweck, Davidson, Nelson, & Enna, 1978; Fincham & Cain, 1986; Garber & Flynn, 2001, Turk & Bry, 1992; for exception, see Gibb et al., 2006). Of utmost importance, such pathways are likely influenced by even more distal risk factors for depression, including the presence of parental psychopathology, genetic inheritance, sociocultural factors, and/or child temperament (Hankin & Abramson, 2001).

FUTURE DIRECTIONS

As this chapter illustrates, there now exists fairly convincing evidence demonstrating that various cognitive vulnerability factors interact with negative events to predict the development of depression in both children and adolescents. Although more research is needed in order to understand the parameters of this cognitive vulnerability-stress process in explaining the onset, maintenance, remission, and recurrence of depression in youth, it seems safe to conclude that cognitive factors, particularly in interaction with negative events, play an important etiological role in the development of youth depression. At the same time, much additional research is needed, aimed at developing a more comprehensive understanding of the role of cognitive factors in the development of depression in youth—particularly research addressing the following issues. First, as noted in this chapter, research investigating the developmental aspects of cognitive theories of vulnerability to depression is still in its infancy, and many questions crucial to understanding the development of depression from a developmental psychopathology perspective remain unanswered. Second, little research has integrated cognitive vulnerability factors with other theoretically interesting and empirically supported vulnerability factors, especially neural, genetic, social/interpersonal, and emotional influences (e.g., for notable exceptions see Abramson et al., 2002; Davidson, 2004; Gotlib, Joormann, Minor, & Cooney, 2006; Hankin & Abramson, 2001; Nelson, Leibenluft, McClure, & Pine, 2005). Third, the greater part of research conducted to date with youth examining cognitive theories of depression has assumed that negative events are independent of pre-existing diatheses as well as independent of baseline depression levels, rather than dependent upon characteristics and/or behaviors of youth themselves. Only recently have researchers begun to explore the association between youth and the negative events that occur in their environments from a transactional perspective (e.g., see Rudolph et al., 2000; Rudolph & Hammen, 1999; Shih et al., 2007). Finally, surprisingly little research has examined whether cognitive vulnerability factors, such as those discussed in the current chapter, either alone or in interaction with negative events, specifically predict the development of depressive symptoms as opposed to other forms of psychopathology (for exceptions, see Gladstone, Kaslow, Seeley, & Lewinsohn, 1997; Hankin, in press, 2007b; Lewinsohn, Zinbarg, Seeley, Lewinsohn, & Sack, 1997; Quiggle, Garber, Panak, & Dodge, 1992; Robinson et al., 1995; Weiss, Susser, & Catron, 1998). For example, in multiwave research in which depressive, anxious, and externalizing symptoms were assessed at each wave, baseline negative cognitive style interacted with within-youth stressors to predict depressive symptoms fluctuations over time specifically, whereas stressors predicted anxiety and externalizing symptoms (Hankin, in press). Likewise, baseline rumination predicted depressive symptoms, but not anxiety or externalizing problems, over time (Hankin, 2007). As literature examining these and other related questions accumulates, a stronger developmental psychopathology perspective on the etiology, maintenance, and recurrence of depression will emerge. Such an increased understanding will ultimately contribute to development of empirically supported treatment approaches for use with children and adolescents suffering from depression as well as the creation of effective depression prevention programs for those at risk.

REFERENCES

Abela, J. R. Z. (2001). The hopelessness theory of depression: A test of the diathesis-stress and causal mediation components in third and seventh grade children. *Journal of Abnormal Child Psychology, 29*, 241–254.

Abela, J. R. Z. (2002). Depressive mood reactions to failure in the achievement domain: A test of the integration of the hopelessness and self-esteem theories of depression. *Cognitive Therapy and Research, 26*, 531–552.

Abela, J. R. Z., Aydin, C., & Auerbach, R. P. (2006). Operationalizing the "vulnerability" and "stress" components of the hopelessness theory of depression: A multi-wave longitudinal study. *Behavior Research and Therapy, 44*, 1565–1583.

Abela, J. R. Z., Aydin, C., & Auerbach, R. P. (2007a). Responses to depression in children: Reconceptualizing the relation among response styles. *Journal of Abnormal Child Psychology, 35*, 913–927.

Abela, J. R. Z., Brozina, K., & Haigh, E. P. (2002). An examination of the response styles theory of depression in third and seventh grade children: A short-term longitudinal study. *Journal of Abnormal Child Psychology, 30*, 513–525.

Abela, J. R. Z., & D'Alessandro, D. U. (2002). Beck's cognitive theory of depression: A test of the diathesis-stress and causal mediation components. *British Journal of Clinical Psychology, 41*, 111–128.

Abela, J. R. Z., Fishman, M., & Wagner, C. (2007b). Personality predispositions to depression in children of affectively-ill parents. Manuscript submitted for publication.

Abela, J. R. Z., & Hankin, B. L. (2007). Rumination as a vulnerability factor to depression during the transition from early to middle adolescence: A multi-wave longitudinal study. Manuscript submitted for publication.

Abela, J. R. Z., Hankin, B. L., Haigh, E. A. P., Vinokuroff, T., Trayhern, L., & Adams, P. (2005). Interpersonal vulnerability to depression in high-risk children: The role of insecure attachment and reassurance seeking. *Journal of Clinical Child & Adolescent Psychology, 34*, 182–192.

Abela, J. R. Z., & McGirr, A. (2007). Operationalizing "cognitive vulnerability" and "stress" from the perspective of the hopelessness theory: A multi-wave longitudinal study of children of affectively-ill parents. *British Journal of Clinical Psychology, 46*, 377–395.

Abela, J. R. Z., McGirr, A., & Skitch, S. A. (2007c). Depressogenic inferential styles, negative events, and depressive symptoms in youth: An attempt to reconcile past inconsistent findings. *Behaviour Research and Therapy, 45*, 2397–2406.

Abela, J. R. Z., Morrison, E. J. P., & Starrs, C. (2007d). Excessive reassurance seeking, self-esteem, and depressive symptoms in children of affectively-ill parents: An experience sampling analysis. *Journal of Social and Clinical Psychology, 26*, 837–857.

Abela, J. R. Z., Parkinson, C., Stolow, D., & Starrs, C. (in press). A test of the integration of the hopelessness and response styles theories of depression in middle adolescence. *Journal of Clinical Child and Adolescent Psychology.*

Abela, J. R. Z., & Payne, A. V. L. (2003). A test of the integration of the hopelessness and self-esteem theories of depression in schoolchildren. *Cognitive Therapy & Research, 27*, 519–535.

Abela, J. R. Z., Sakellaropoulo, M., & Taxel, E. (2007e). Integrating two subtypes of depression: Psychodynamic theory and its relation to hopelessness depression in schoolchildren. *Journal of Early Adolescence, 27*, 363–385.

Abela, J. R. Z., & Sarin, S. (2002). Cognitive vulnerability to hopelessness depression: A chain is only as strong as its weakest link. *Cognitive Therapy and Research, 26*, 811–829.

Abela, J. R. Z., & Scheffler, P. (in press). Conceptualizing cognitive vulnerability to depression in youth: A comparison of the weakest link and additive approaches. *Journal of Cognitive Psychotherapy.*

Abela, J. R. Z., & Seligman, M. E. P. (2000). The hopelessness theory of depression: A test of the diathesis-stress component in the interpersonal and achievement domains. *Cognitive Therapy and Research, 24*, 361–378.

Abela, J. R. Z., & Skitch, S. A. (2007). Dysfunctional attitudes as a cognitive vulnerability factor for depression in children of affectively-ill parents: A multi-wave longitudinal study. *Behaviour Research and Therapy, 45*, 1127–1140.

Abela, J. R. Z., Skitch, S. A., Adams, P., & Hankin, B. L. (2006). The timing of parent and child depression: A hopelessness theory perspective. *Journal of Clinical Child and Adolescent Psychology, 35*, 253–263.

Abela, J. R. Z., & Sullivan, C. (2003). A test of Beck's cognitive diathesis-stress theory of depression in early adolescents. *Journal of Early Adolescence, 23*, 384–404.

Abela, J. R. Z., & Taylor, G. (2003). Specific vulnerability to depressive mood reactions in children: The moderating role of self-esteem. *Journal of Clinical Child and Adolescents Psychology, 32*, 408–418.

Abela, J. R. Z., Vanderbilt, E., & Rochon, A. (2004). A test of the integration of the response styles and social support theories of depression in third and seventh grade children. *Journal of Social and Clinical Psychology, 5*, 653–674.

Abela, J. R. Z., & Véronneau-McArdle, M. (2002). The relationship between self-complexity and depressive symptoms in third and seventh grade children: A short-term longitudinal study. *Journal of Abnormal Child Psychology, 30*, 155–166.

Abela, J. R. Z., Zuroff, D. C., Ho, R., Adams, P., & Hankin, B. L. (2006). Excessive reassurance seeking, hassles, and depressive symptoms in children of affectively-ill parents: A multi-wave longitudinal study. *Journal of Abnormal Child Psychology, 34*, 171–187.

Abramson, L. Y., Alloy, L. B., Hankin, B. L., Haeffel, J. G., MacCoon D. G., & Gibb, B. E. (2002). Cognitive vulnerability-stress models of depression in a self-regulatory and psychobiological context. In I. H. Gotlib & C. L. Hammen (Eds.), *Handbook of depression* (pp. 268–294). New York: Guilford Press.

Abramson, L. Y., Alloy, L. B., & Metalsky, G. I. (1988). The cognitive diathesis-stress theories of depression: Toward an adequate evaluation of the theories' validities. In L. B. Alloy (Ed.), *Cognitive processes in depression* (pp. 3–30). New York: Guilford Press.

Abramson, L. Y., Metalsky, G. I., & Alloy, L. B. (1989). Hopelessness depression: A theory-based subtype of depression. *Psychological Review, 96*, 358–372.

Abramson, L. Y., Seligman, M. E. P., & Teasdale, J. (1978). Learned helplessness in humans: Critique and reformulation. *Journal of Abnormal Psychology, 87*, 49–74.

Adams, P., Abela, J. R. Z., & Hankin, B. L. (2007). Factorial categorization of depression related constructs in children and early adolescents. *Journal of Cognitive Psychotherapy, 21*, 123–139.

Alloy, L. B., Abramson, L. Y., Hogan, M. E., Whitehouse, W. G., Rose, D. T., Robinson, M. S., et al. (2000). The Temple-Wisconsin Cognitive Vulnerability to Depression Project: Lifetime history of Axis-I psychopathology in individuals at high and low cognitive risk for depression. *Journal of Abnormal Psychology, 109*, 403–418.

Alloy, L. B., Abramson, L. Y., Tashman, N. A., Berrebbi, D. S., Hogan, M. E., Whitehouse, W. G., Crossfield, A. G., & Morocco, A. (2001). Developmental origins of cognitive vulnerability to depression: Parenting, cognitive, and inferential feedback styles of the parents of individuals at high and low cognitive risk for depression. *Cognitive Therapy and Research, 25*, 397–423.

Alloy, L. B., Abramson, L. Y., Whitehouse, W. G., Hogan, M. E., Panzarella, C., & Rose, D. T. (2006). Prospective incidence of first onsets and recurrences of depression in individuals at high and low cognitive risk for depression. *Journal of Abnormal Psychology, 115*, 145–156.

Alloy, L. B., Hartlage, S., & Abramson, L. Y. (1988). Testing the cognitive diathesis-stress theories of depression: Issues of research design, conceptualization, and assessment. In L. B. Alloy (Ed.), *Cognitive processes in depression* (pp. 31–73). New York: Guilford Press.

Angold, A., Erkanli, A., Silberg, J., Eaves, L., & Costello, E. J. (2002). Depression scale scores in 8–17-year-olds: Effects of age and gender. *Journal of Child Psychology & Psychiatry & Allied Disciplines, 43*, 1052–1063.

Bandura, A. (1986). *Social foundations of thought and action. A social-cognitive theory.* Englewood Cliffs, NJ: Prentice Hall.

Beck, A. T. (1967). *Depression: Clinical, experimental, and theoretical aspects.* New York: Harper & Row.

Beck, A. T. (1983). Cognitive therapy of depression: New perspectives. In P. J. Clayton & J. E. Barrett (Eds.), *Treatment of depression: Old controversies and new approaches.* New York: Raven Press.

Bennett, D. S., & Bates, J. E. (1995). Prospective models of depressive symptoms in early adolescence: Attributional style, stress, and support. *Journal of Early Adolescence, 15*, 299–315.

Blatt, S. J., & Zuroff, D. C. (1992). Interpersonal relatedness and self-definition: Two prototypes for depression. *Clinical Psychology Review, 12*, 527–562.

Broderick, P. C., & Korteland, C. (2004). A prospective study of rumination and depression in early adolescence. *Clinical Child Psychology and Psychiatry, 9*, 383–394.

Brown, G. W., & Harris, T. (1978). *Social origins of depression.* London: Tavistock.

Brozina, K., & Abela, J. R. Z. (2006). Symptoms of hopelessness depression and anxiety in children: Specificity of the hopelessness theory. *Journal of Clinical Child and Adolescent Psychology, 35*(4), 515–527.

Bruce, A. E., Cole, D. A., Dallaire, D. H., Jacquez, F. M., Pineda, A. Q., & LaGrange, B. (2006). Relation of parenting and negative life events to cognitive diatheses for depression in children. *Journal of Abnormal Child Psychology, 34*, 321–333.

Burns, M. O., & Seligman, M. E. P. (1989). Explanatory style across the life span: Evidence for stability over 52 years. *Journal of Personality and Social Psychology, 56*, 471–477.

Burwell, R. A., & Shirk, S. R. (2007). Subtypes of rumination in adolescence: Associations between brooding, reflection, depressive symptoms, and coping. *Journal of Clinical Child and Adolescent Psychology, 36*, 56–65.

Caspi, A., & Moffitt, T. E. (1991). Individual differences are accentuated during periods of social change: The sample case of girls at puberty. *Journal of Personality and Social Psychology, 61*, 157–168.

Caspi, A., Roberts, B. W., & Shiner, R. L. (2005). Personality development: Stability and change. *Annual Review of Psychology, 56*, 453–484.

Cohen, J. (1994). The earth is round ($p<0.05$). *American Psychologist, 49*, 997–1003.

Cohen, S., & Wills, T. A. (1985). Stress, social support, and the buffering hypothesis. *Psychological Bulletin, 98*, 310–357.

Cole, D. A. (1990). Relation of social and academic competence to depressive symptoms in childhood. *Journal of Abnormal Psychology, 99*, 422–429.

Cole, D. A. (1991a). Preliminary support for a competency-based model of depression in children. *Journal of Abnormal Psychology, 100*, 181–190.

Cole, D. A. (1991b). Change in self-perceived competence as a function of peer and teacher evaluation. *Developmental Psychology, 27*, 682–688.

Cole, D. A., Jacquez, F. M., & Maschman, T. L. (2001). Social origins of depressive cognitions: A longitudinal study of self-perceived competence in children. *Cognitive Therapy and Research, 25*, 377–395.

Cole, D. A., Martin, J. M., Peeke, L. A., Seroczynski, A. D., & Fier, J. (1999a). Children's over-and underestimation of academic competence: A longitudinal study of gender differences, depression, and anxiety. *Child Development, 70*, 459–473.

Cole, D. A., Martin, J. M., Peeke, L. G., Seroczynski, A. D., & Hoffman, K. (1998). Are cognitive errors of underestimation predictive or reflective of depression symptoms in children: A longitudinal study. *Journal of Abnormal Psychology, 107*, 481–496.

Cole, D. A., Martin, J. M., & Powers, B. (1997). A competency-based model of child depression: A longitudinal study of peer, parent, teacher, and self-evaluations. *Journal of Child Psychology and Psychiatry, 38*, 505–514.

Cole, D. A., Martin, J. M., Powers, B., & Truglio, R. (1996). Modeling causal relations between academic and social competence and depression: A multitrait-multimethod longitudinal study of children. *Journal of Abnormal Psychology, 105*, 258–270.

Cole, D. A., Maxwell, S. E., Martin, J. M., Peeke, L. G., Seroczynski, A. D., Tram, J. M., et al. (2001). The development of multiple domains of child and adolescent self-concept: A cohort sequential longitudinal design. *Child Development, 72*, 1723–1746.

Cole, D. A., Peeke, L., Dolezal, S., Murray, N., & Canzoniero, A. (1999b). A longitudinal study of negative affect and self-perceived competence in young adolescents. *Journal of Personality and Social Psychology, 77*, 851–862.

Cole, D. A., & Turner, J. E. (1993). Models of cognitive mediation and moderation in child depression. *Journal of Abnormal Psychology, 102*, 271–281.

Conley, C. S., Haines, B. A., Hilt, L. M., & Metalsky, G. I. (2001). The children's attributional style interview: Developmental tests of cognitive diathesis-stress theories of depression. *Journal of Abnormal Child Psychology, 29*, 445–463.

Corrigan, R. (1995). How infants and young children understand the causes of negative events. In N. Eiseberg (Ed.), *Social development* (pp. 1–26). Thousand Oaks, CA: Sage.

Costello, E. J., Mustillo, S., Erkanli, A., Keeler, G., & Angold, A. (2003). Prevalence and development of psychiatric disorders in childhood and adolescence. *Archives of General Psychiatry, 60*, 837–844.

D'Alessandro, D., & Burton, K. (2006). Development and validation of the Dysfunctional Attitudes Scale for Children: Test's of Beck's cognitive diathesis-stress theory of depression, of its causal mediation component, and of developmental effects. *Cognitive Therapy and Research, 30*, 335–353.

Davidson, R. (2004). Affective style: Causes and consequences. In J. T. Cacioppo & G. T. Berntson (Eds.), *Essays in social neuroscience* (pp. 77–91). Cambridge, MA: MIT Press.

Davilla, J., Ramsay, M., Stroud, C. B., & Steinberg, S. J. (2005). Attachment as vulnerability to the development of psychopathology. In B. L. Hankin & J. R. Z. Abela (Eds.), *Development of psychopathology: A vulnerability-stress perspective* (pp. 215–242). Thousand Oaks, CA: Sage.

Dixon, J. F., & Ahrens, A. H. (1992). Stress and attributional styles as predictors of self-reported depression in children. *Cognitive Therapy and Research, 16*, 623–634.

Dweck, C. S., Davidson, W., Nelson, S., & Enna, B. (1978). Sex differences in learned helplessness: II. The contingencies of evaluative feedback in the classroom and III. An experimental analysis. *Developmental Psychology, 14*, 268–276.

Fichman, L., Koestner, R., & Zuroff, D. C. (1994). Depressive styles in adolescence: Assessment, relation to social functioning, and developmental trends. *Journal of Youth and Adolescence, 23*(3), 315–330.

Fichman, L., Koestner, R., & Zuroff, D. C. (1996). Dependency, self-criticism, and perceptions of inferiority at summer camp: I'm even worse than you think. *Journal of Youth and Adolescence, 25*, 113–126.

Fincham, F. D., & Cain, K. M. (1986). Learned helplessness in humans: A developmental analysis. *Developmental Review, 6*, 301–333.

Fraley, C., & Roberts, B. W. (2005). Patterns of continuity: A dynamic model for conceptualizing the stability of individual differences in psychological constructs across the lifecourse. *Psychological Review, 112*, 60–74.

Garber, J. (2000). Development and depression. In A. J. Sameroff, M. Lewis & S. M. Miller (Eds.), *Handbook of developmental psychopathology* (pp. 467–490). New York: Kluwer.

Garber, J., & Flynn, C. (1998). Origins of the depressive cognitive style. In D. Routh & R. J. DeRebeis (Eds.), *The science of clinical psychology: Evidence of a century's progress* (pp. 53–93). Washington, DC: American Psychological Association.

Garber, J., & Flynn, C. (2001). Predictors of depressive cognitions in young adolescents. *Cognitive Therapy and Research, 25*, 353–376.

Garber, J., & Little, S. (1999). Predictors of competence among offspring of depressed mothers. *Journal of Adolescence Research, 14*, 44–71.

Ge, X., Lorenz, F. O., Conger, R. D., Elder, G. H., & Simons, R. L. (1994). Trajectories of stressful life events and depressive symptoms during adolescence. *Developmental Psychology, 30*, 467–483.

Gibb, B. E., & Abela, J. R. Z. (2008). Emotional abuse, verbal victimization, and the development of children's negative inferential styles and depressive symptoms. *Cognitive Therapy and Research, 32*, 161–176.

Gibb, B. E., & Alloy, L. B. (2006). A prospective test of the hopelessness theory of depression in children. *Journal of Clinical Child and Adolescent Psychology, 35*, 264–274.

Gibb, B. E., Alloy, L. B., Walshaw, P. D., Comer, J. S., Shen, G. H. C., & Villari, A. G. (2006). Predictors of attributional style change in children. *Journal of Abnormal Child Psychology, 34*, 425–439.

Gibb, B. E., & Coles, M. (2005). Cognitive vulnerability-stress models of psychopathology: A developmental perspective. In B. L. Hankin & J. R. Z. Abela (Eds.), *Development of psychopathology: A vulnerability-stress perspective* (pp. 104–135). Thousand Oaks, CA: Sage.

Gladstone, T. R. G., Kaslow, N. J., Seeley, J. R., & Lewinsohn, P. M. (1997). Sex differences, attributional style, and depressive symptoms among adolescents. *Journal of Abnormal Child Psychology, 25*, 297–305.

Gotlib, I. H., & Hammen, C. L. (Eds.). (2002). *Handbook of depression*. New York: Guilford Press.

Gotlib, I. H., Joormann, J., Minor, K. L., & Cooney, R. E. (2006). Cognitive and biological functioning in children at risk for depression. In T. Canli (Ed.), *Biology of personality and individual differences* (pp. 353–382). New York: Guilford Press.

Graber, J. A., Brooks-Gunn, J., & Petersen, A. C. (1996). *Transitions through adolescence: Interpersonal domains and context*. Hillsdale, NJ: Lawrence Erlbaum Associates.

Graber, J. A., Brooks-Gunn, J., & Warren, M. P. (1995). The antecedents of menarcheal age: Heredity, family environment, and stressful life events. *Child Development, 66*, 346–359.

Haeffel, G. J., Abramson, L. Y., Voelz, Z. R., Metalsky, G. I., Halberstadt, L., Dykman, B. M., et al. (2003). Cognitive vulnerability to depression and lifetime history of Axis I psychopathology: A comparison of negative cognitive styles (CSQ) and dysfunctional attitudes (DAS). *Journal of Cognitive Psychotherapy, 17*, 3–22.

Hammen, C., & Rudolph, K. D. (2003). Childhood mood disorders. In E. J. Mash & R. A. Barkley (Eds.), *Child psychopathology* (2nd ed., pp. 233–278). New York: Guilford Press.

Hammen, C., & Zupan, B. A. (1984). Self-schemas, depression, and the processing of personal information in children. *Journal of Experimental Child Psychology, 37*, 598–608.

Hammen, C. L., Adrian, C., & Hiroto, D. (1988). A longitudinal test of the attributional vulnerability model of depression in children at risk for depression. *British Journal of Clinical Psychology, 27*, 37–46.

Han, S. S., Weisz, J. R., & Weiss, B. (2001). Specificity of relations between children's control-related beliefs and internalizing and externalizing psychopathology. *Journal of Consulting and Clinical Psychology, 69*, 240–251.

Hankin, B. L. (2005). Childhood maltreatment and psychopathology: Prospective tests of attachment, cognitive vulnerability, and stress as mediating processes. *Cognitive Therapy*

Hankin, B. L. (in press). Cognitive vulnerability-stress model of depression in adolescence: Investigating symptom specificity in a multi-wave prospective study. *Journal of Abnormal Child Psychology. and Research, 29,* 645–671.

Hankin, B. L. (2007). Beck's cognitive theory of depression in adolescence: Prospective prediction of depressive symptoms and transactional influences in a multi-wave study. *International Journal of Cognitive Therapy.* Manuscript under review.

Hankin, B. L. (in press-b). Response styles theory and symptom specificity in adolescents: A multi-wave prospective study. *Journal of Clinical Child and Adolescent Psychology.*

Hankin, B. L. (in press-c). Stability of cognitive vulnerabilities to depression: A short-term prospective multi-wave study. *Journal of Abnormal Psychology.*

Hankin, B. L. (in press-d). Development of sex differences in depressive and co-occurring symptoms during adolescence: Descriptive trajectories and potential explanations in a multi-wave prospective study. *Journal of Clinical Child and Adolescent Psychology.*

Hankin, B. L., & Abela, J. R. Z. (2005). Depression from childhood through adolescence and adulthood: A developmental vulnerability-stress perspective. In B. L. Hankin & J. R. Z. Abela (Eds.), *Development of psychopathology: A vulnerability-stress perspective* (pp. 245–288). Thousand Oaks, CA: Sage.

Hankin, B. L., & Abramson, L. Y. (1999). Development of gender differences in depression: Description and possible explanations. *Annals of Medicine, 31,* 372–379.

Hankin, B. L., & Abramson, L. Y. (2001). Development of sex differences in depression: An elaborated cognitive vulnerability-transactional stress theory. *Psychological Bulletin, 127,* 773–796.

Hankin, B. L., & Abramson, L. Y. (2002). Measuring cognitive vulnerability to depression in adolescence: Reliability, validity, and gender differences. *Journal of Child and Adolescent Clinical Psychology, 31,* 491–504.

Hankin, B. L., Abramson, L. Y., Miller, N., & Haeffel, G. (2004). Cognitive vulnerability-stress theories of depression: Examining affective specificity in the prediction of depression versus anxiety in three prospective studies. *Cognitive Therapy and Research, 28,* 309–345.

Hankin, B. L., Abramson, L. Y., Moffitt, T. E., Silva, P. A., McGee, R., & Angell, K. A. (1998). Development of depression from preadolescence to young adulthood: Emerging gender differences in a 10 year longitudinal study. *Journal of Abnormal Psychology, 107,* 128–141.

Hankin, B. L., Abramson, L. Y., & Siler, M. (2001). A prospective test of the hopelessness theory of depression in adolescence. *Cognitive Therapy and Research, 25,* 607–632.

Hankin, B. L., Fraley, R. C., & Abela, J. R. Z. (2005). Daily depression and cognitions about stress: Evidence for a trait-like depressogenic cognitive style and the prediction of depressive symptoms trajectories in a prospective daily diary study. *Journal of Personality and Social Psychology, 88,* 673–685.

Hankin, B. L., Lakdawalla, Z., Carter, I., Abela, J. R. Z., & Adams, P. (2007). Are neuroticism, cognitive vulnerability and self-esteem overlapping or distinct risks for depression? Evidence from exploratory and confirmatory factor analyses. *Journal of Social and Clinical Psychology, 26*, 29–63.

Hankin, B. L., Mermelstein, R., & Roesch, L. (2007). Sex differences in adolescent depression: Stress exposure and reactivity. *Child Development, 78*, 279–295.

Hankin, B. L., Wetter, E., & Cheely, C. (2008). Sex differences in child and adolescent depression: A developmental psychopathological approach. In J. R. Z. Abela & B. L. Hankin (Eds.), *Handbook of depression in children and adolescents* (pp. 377–414). New York: Guilford Press.

Harter, S. (1986). Processes underlying the construction, maintenance, and enhancement of the self-concept in children. In J. Suis & A. Greenwald (Eds.), *Psychological perspectives on the self* (Vol. 3, pp. 137–181). Hillsdale, NJ: Lawrence Erlbaum Associates.

Harter, S. (1990). Causes, correlates, and the functional role of global self-worth: A life-span perspective. In R. J. Sternberg & J. Kolligan, Jr. (Eds.), *Competence considered* (pp. 67–97). New Haven, CT: Yale University Press.

Hilsman, R., & Garber, J. (1995). A test of the cognitive diathesis-stress model of depression in children: Academic stressors, attributional style, perceived competence, and control. *Journal of Personality and Social Psychology, 69*, 370–380.

Hilt, L. M., McLaughlin, K. A., & Nolen-Hoeksema, S. (2007). Gender and rumination in young adolescents: Predicting depressive symptoms and understanding the gender difference. Manuscript submitted for publication.

Hoffman, K. B., Cole, D. A., Martin, J. M., Tram, J., & Seroczynski, A. D. (2000). Are the discrepancies between self- and others' appraisals of competence predictive or reflective of depressive symptoms in children and adolescents: A longitudinal study, part II. *Journal of Abnormal Psychology, 109*, 651–662.

Ingram, R. E., & Luxton, D. D. (2005). Vulnerability-stress models. In B. L. Hankin & J. R. Z. Abela (Eds.), *Development of psychopathology: A vulnerability-stress perspective* (pp. 32–46). Thousand Oaks, CA: Sage.

Ingram, R. E., Miranda, J., & Segal, Z. V. (1998). *Cognitive vulnerability to depression*. New York: Guilford Press.

Ingram, R. E., & Price, J. M. (2001). *Vulnerability to psychopathology*. New York: Guilford Press.

Jaenicke, C., Hammen, C., Zupan, B., Hiroto, D., Gordon, D., Adrian, C., & Burge, D. (1987). Cognitive vulnerability in children at risk for depression. *Journal of Abnormal Child Psychology, 15*, 559–572.

Joiner, T. E., Jr. (2000). A test of the hopelessness theory of depression in youth psychiatric inpatients. *Journal of Clinical Child Psychology, 29*, 167–176.

Joiner, T. E., Jr., & Metalsky, G. I. (2001). Excessive reassurance seeking: Delineating a risk factor involved in the development of depressive symptoms. *Psychological Science, 12*, 371–378.

Joiner, T. E., Jr., & Rudd, M. D. (1996). Toward a categorization of depression-related psychological constructs. *Cognitive Therapy & Research, 20*, 51–68.

Joorman, J., Talbot, L., & Gotlib, I. H. (2007). Biased processing of emotional information in girls at risk for depression. *Journal of Abnormal Psychology, 116*, 135–143.

Kashani, J. H., Carlson, G. A., & Beck, N. C. (1999). Depression, depressive symptoms, and depressed mood among a community sample of adolescents. *American Journal of Psychiatry, 144*, 931–934.

Kaslow, N. J., Adamson, L. B., & Collins, M. H. (2000). A developmental psychopathology perspective on the cognitive components of child and adolescent depression. In A. J. Sameroff, M. Lewis & S. M. Miller (Eds.), *Handbook of developmental psychopathology* (pp. 491–510). New York: Kluwer.

Kenny, D. A., & Zautra, A. (2001). Trait-state models for longitudinal data. In L. M. Collins & A. G. Sayer (Eds.), *New methods for the analysis of change.* Washington, DC: American Psychological Association.

Kessler, R. C., Avenei, S., & Merikangas, K. R. (2001). Mood disorders in children and adolescents: An epidemiologic perspective. *Biological Psychiatry, 49*, 1002–1014.

Kim-Cohen, J., Caspi, A., & Moffitt, T. E. (2003). Prior juvenile diagnoses in adults with mental disorder: Developmental follow-back of a prospective-longitudinal cohort. *Archives of General Psychiatry, 60*, 709–717.

Klein, D. N., Lewinsohn, P. M., & Seeley, J. R. (1997). Psychosocial characteristics of adolescents with a past history of dysthymic disorder: Comparison with adolescents with past histories of major depressive and non-affective disorders, and never mentally ill controls. *Journal of Affective Disorders, 42*, 127–135.

Koestner, R., Zuroff, D. C., & Powers, T. A. (1991). Family origins of adolescent self-criticism and its continuity into adulthood. *Journal of Abnormal Psychology, 100*, 191–197.

Lakdawalla, Z., Hankin, B. L., & Mermelstein, R. (2007). Cognitive theories of depression in children and adolescents: A conceptual and quantitative review. *Clinical Child and Family Psychology Review, 10*(1), 1–24.

Lewinsohn, P. M., Joiner, T. E., & Rohde, P. (2001). Evaluation of cognitive diathesis-stress models in predicting major depressive disorder in adolescents. *Journal of Abnormal Psychology, 110*, 203–215.

Lewinsohn, P. M., Zinbarg, R., Seeley, J. R., Lewinsohn, M., & Sack, W. H. (1997). Lifetime comorbidity among anxiety disorders and between anxiety disorders and other mental disorders in adolescents. *Journal of Anxiety Disorders, 11*, 377–394.

Little, S. A., & Garber, J. (2000). Interpersonal and achievement orientations and specific stressors predicting depressive and aggressive symptoms in children. *Cognitive Therapy & Research, 24*, 651–670.

Little, S. A., & Garber, J. (2004). Interpersonal and achievement orientations and specific stressors predict depressive and aggressive symptoms. *Journal of Adolescent Research, 19*, 63–84.

Little, S. A., & Garber, J. (2005). The role of social stressors and interpersonal orientation in explaining the longitudinal relation between externalizing and depressive symptoms. *Journal of Abnormal Psychology, 114*, 432–443.

Liu, Y. (2003). The mediators between parenting and adolescent depressive symptoms: Dysfunctional attitudes and self-worth. *International Journal of Psychology, 38*, 91–100.

Luthar, S. S., & Blatt, S. J. (1993). Dependent and self-critical depressive experiences among inner-city adolescents. *Journal of Personality, 61*, 365–386.

Magaro, M. M., & Weisz, J. R. (2006). Perceived control mediates the relation between parental rejection and youth depression. *Journal of Abnormal Child Psychology, 34*, 867–876.

Marcotte, D., Fortin, L., & Potvin, P. (2002). Gender differences in depressive symptoms during adolescence: Role of gender-typed characteristics, self-esteem, body image, stressful life events, and pubertal status. *Journal of Emotional & Behavioral Disorders, 10*, 29–42.

Meehl, P. E. (1978). Theoretical risks and tabular asterisks: Sir Karl, Sir Ronald, and the slow progress of soft psychology. *Journal of Consulting and Clinical Psychology, 46*, 806–834.

Mezulis, A., Abramson, L. Y., Hyde, J. S., & Hankin, B. L. (2004). Is there a universal positivity bias in attributions? A meta-analytic review of individual, developmental, and cultural differences in the self-serving attributional bias. *Psychological Bulletin, 130*, 711–747.

Monroe, S. M., & Harkness, K. L. (2005). Life stress, the "kindling" hypothesis, and the recurrence of depression: Considerations from a life stress perspective. *Psychological Review, 112*, 417–445.

Monroe, S. M., & Simons, A. D. (1991). Diathesis-stress theories in the context of life stress research: Implications for the depressive disorders. *Psychological Bulletin, 110*, 406–425.

Nelson, E. E., Leibenluft, E., McClure, E., & Pine, D. S. (2005). The social reorientation of adolescence: A neuroscience perspective on the process and its relation to psychopathology. *Psychological Medicine, 35*, 163–174.

Nolen-Hoeksema, S. (1991). Responses to depression and their effects on the duration of depressive episodes. *Journal of Abnormal Psychology, 100*, 569–582.

Nolen-Hoeksema, S., Girgus, J. S., & Seligman, M. E. P. (1986). Learned helplessness in children: A longitudinal study of depression, achievement, and attributional style. *Journal of Personality and Social Psychology, 51*, 435–442.

Nolen-Hoeksema, S., Girgus, J. S., & Seligman, M. E. P. (1992). Predictors and consequences of childhood depressive symptoms: A five-year longitudinal study. *Journal of Abnormal Psychology, 101*, 405–422.

Nolen-Hoeksema, S., Stice, E., Wade, E., & Bohon, C. (2007). Reciprocal relations between rumination and bulimic, substance abuse, and depressive symptoms in female adolescents. *Journal of Abnormal Psychology, 116*, 198–207.

Oakes, L. M. (1994). Development of infants' use of continuity cues in their perceptions of causality. *Developmental Psychology, 30*, 869–879.

Panak, W. F., & Garber, J. (1992). Role of aggression, rejection, and attributions in the prediction of depression in children. *Development and Psychopathology, 4*, 145–165.

Persons, J. B., & Miranda, J. (1992). Cognitive theories of vulnerability to depression: Reconciling negative evidence. *Cognitive Therapy and Research, 16*, 485–502.

Prinstein, M. J., & Aikens, J. W. (2004). Cognitive moderators of the longitudinal association between peer rejection and adolescent depressive symptoms. *Journal of Abnormal Child Psychology, 32*, 147–158.

Quiggle, N. L., Garber, J., panak, W. F., & Dodge, K. A. (1992). Social information processing in aggressive and depressed children. *Child Development, 63*, 1305–1320.

Rholes, W. S., Blackwell, J., Jordan, C., & Walters, C. (1980). A developmental study of learned helplessness. *Developmental Psychology, 16*, 616–624.

Riskind, J. H., & Rholes, W. S. (1984). Cognitive accessibility and the capacity of cognitions to predict future depression: A theoretical note. *Cognitive Therapy and Research, 8*, 1–12.

Robinson, N. S., Garber, J., & Hilsman, R. (1995). Cognitions and stress: Direct and moderating effects on depressive versus externalizing symptoms during the junior high school transition. *Journal of Abnormal Psychology, 104*, 453–463.

Rudolph, K. D., Flynn, M., & Abaied, J. L. (2008). A developmental perspective on interpersonal theories of youth depression. In J. R. Z. Abela & B. L. Hankin (Eds.), *Handbook of depression in children and adolescents* (pp. 79–102). New York: Guilford Press.

Rudolph, K. D., & Hammen, C. (1999). Age and gender as determinants of stress exposure, generation, and reactions in youngsters: A transactional perspective. *Child Development, 70*, 660–677.

Rudolph, K.D., Hammen, C., Burge, D., Lindberg, N., Herzberg, D., & Daley, S.E. (2000). Toward an interpersonal life-stress model of depression: The developmental context of stress generation. *Development and Psychopathology, 12*, 215–234.

Rudolph, K. D., Kurlakowsky, K. D., & Conley, C. S. (2001). Developmental and social-contextual origins of depressive control-related beliefs and behavior. *Cognitive Therapy and Research, 25*, 447–475.

Sarason, B. R., Pierce, G. R., & Bannerman, A. (1993). Investigating the antecedents of perceived social support: Parents' views of and behavior toward their children. *Journal of Personality & Social Psychology, 65*, 1071–1085.

Scher, C. D., Ingram, R. E., & Segal, Z. V. (2005). Cognitive reactivity and vulnerability: Empirical evaluation of construct activation and cognitive diatheses in unipolar depression. *Clinical Psychology Review, 25*, 487–510.

Schwartz, J. A. J., & Koenig, L. J. (1996). Response styles and negative affect among adolescents. *Cognitive Therapy and Research, 20*, 13–36.

Seligman, M. E. P., Peterson, C., Kaslow, N. J., Tenenbaum, R. L., Alloy, L. B., & Abramson, L. Y. (1984). Attributional style and depressive symptoms among children. *Journal of Abnormal Psychology, 93*, 235–241.

Shahar, G., Blatt, S. J., Zuroff, D. C., Kuperminc, G., & Leadbeater, B. J. (2004). Reciprocal relations between depressive symptoms and self-criticism (but not dependency) among early adolescent girls (but not boys). *Cognitive Therapy and Research, 28*, 85–103.

Shahar, G., & Priel, B. (2003). Active vulnerability, adolescent distress, and the mediating/suppressing role of life events. *Personality and Individual Differences, 35*, 199–218.

Sheeber, L., Hops, H., & Alpert, A. (1997). Family support and conflict: Prospective relations to adolescent depression. *Journal of Abnormal Child Psychology, 25*, 333–344.

Shih, J., Abela, J. R. Z., & Starrs, C. (2007). Cognitive and interpersonal predictors of stress generation in children. Manuscript submitted for publication.

Shirk, S. R. (1988). Causal reasoning and children's comprehension of therapeutic interpretations. In S. R. Shirk (Ed.), *Cognitive development and child psychotherapy* (pp. 53–89). New York: Plenum Press.

Southall, D., & Roberts, J. E. (2002). Attributional style and self-esteem in vulnerability to adolescent depressive symptoms following life stress: A 14-week prospective study. *Cognitive Therapy and Research, 26*, 563–579.

Spence, S. H., Sheffield, J., & Donovan, C. (2002). Problem-solving orientation and attributional style: Moderators of the impact of negative life events on the development of depressives in adolescence? *Journal of Clinical Child Psychology, 31*, 219–229.

Taylor, L., & Ingram, R. E. (1999). Cognitive reactivity and depressotypic information processing in children of depressed mothers. *Journal of Abnormal Psychology, 108*, 202–210.

Teasdale, J. D. (1983). Negative thinking in depression: Cause, effect, or reciprocal relationship? *Advances in Behavior Research and Therapy, 5*, 3–25.

Thompson, M., Kaslow, N. J., Weiss, B., & Nolen-Hoeksema, S. (1998). Children's Attributional Style Questionnaire—Revised: Psychometric examination. *Psychological Assessment, 10*, 166–170.

Thurber, C. A., & Weisz, J. R. (1997). "You can try or you can just give up": The impact of perceived control and coping style on childhood homesickness. *Developmental Psychology, 33*, 508–517.

Timbremont, B., & Braet, C. (2004). Cognitive vulnerability in remitted depressed children and adolescents. *Behaviour Research and Therapy, 42*, 423–437.

Tram, J. M., & Cole, D. A. (2000). Self-perceived competence and the relation between life events and depressive symptoms in adolescence: Mediator or moderator? *Journal of Abnormal Psychology, 109*, 753–760.

Turk, E., & Bry, B. (1992). Adolescents' and parents' explanatory styles and parents' causal explanations about their adolescents. *Cognitive Therapy and Research, 16*, 349–357.

Turner, J. E., & Cole, D. A. (1994). Developmental differences in cognitive diatheses for child depression. *Journal of Abnormal Child Psychology, 22*(1), 15–32.

Twenge, J. M., & Nolen-Hoeksema, S. (2002). Age, gender, race, socioeconomic status, and birth cohort difference on the children's depression inventory: A meta-analysis. *Journal of Abnormal Psychology, 111*, 578–588.

Van Orden, K., Wingate, L. R., Gordon, K. H., & Joiner, T. E., Jr. (2005). Interpersonal factors as vulnerability to psychopathology over the life course. In B. L. Hankin & J. R. Z. Abela (Eds.), *Development of psychopathology: A vulnerability-stress perspective* (pp. 136–160). Thousand Oaks, CA: Sage.

Voelz, Z. R., Walker, R. L., Petit, J. W., Joiner, T. E., Jr., & Wagner, K. D. (2003). Depressogenic attributional style: Evidence of trait-like nature in youth psychiatric inpatients. *Personality and Individual Differences, 37*, 1129–1140.

Weiss, B., Susser, K., & Catron, T. (1998). Common and specific features of childhood psychopathology. *Journal of Abnormal Psychology, 107*, 118–128.

Weisz, J. R. (1986). Understanding the developing understanding of control. In M. Perlmutter (Ed.), *Cognitive perspectives on children's social and behavioral development: The Minnesota Symposia on child psychology* (pp. 219–285). Hillsdale, NJ: Erlbaum.

Weisz, J. R., Stevens, J. S., Curry, J. F., Cohen, R., Craighead, W. E., Burlingame, W. V., et al. (1989). Control-related cognitions and depression among inpatient children and adolescents. *Journal of the American Academy of Child & Adolescent Psychiatry, 28*, 358–363.

Weisz, J. R., & Stipek, D. J. (1982). Competence, contingency, and the development of perceived control. *Human Development, 25*, 250–281.

Weisz, J. R., Southam-Gerow, M. A., & McCarty, C. A. (2001). Control-related beliefs and depressive symptoms in clinic-referred children and adolescents: Developmental differences and model specificity. *Journal of Abnormal Psychology, 100*, 97–109.

Weisz, J. R., Sweeney, L., Proffitt, V. D., & Carr, T. (1993). Control-related beliefs and self-reported symptoms in late childhood. *Journal of Abnormal Psychology, 102*, 411–418.

Weisz, J. R., Thurber, C. A., Sweeney, L., Proffitt, V. D., & LaGagnoux, G. L. (1997). Brief treatment of mild-to-moderate child depression using primary and secondary control enhancement training. *Journal of Counseling and Clinical Psychology, 65*, 703–707.

Weisz, J. R., Weiss, B., Wasserman, A. A., & Rintoul, B. (1987). Control-related beliefs and depression among clinic-referred children and adolescents. *Journal of Abnormal Psychology, 96*, 58–63.

Young, J. E. (1999). *Cognitive therapy for personality disorders: A schema-focused approach* (3rd ed.). Sarasota, FL: Professional Resource Press.

Ziegert, D., & Kistner, J. (2002). Response styles theory: Downward extension to children. *Journal of Clinical Child and Adolescent Psychology, 31*(3), 325–334.

Zuroff, D. C., Santor, D. A., & Mongrain, M. (2004). Dependency, self-criticism, and maladjustment. In J. S. Auerbach, K. J. Levy & C. E. Schaffer (Eds.), *Relatedness, self-definition and mental representation: Essays in honor of Sidney J. Blatt* (pp. 75–90). London: Brunner-Routledge.

Chapter Fourteen

The Interpersonal Context of Adolescent Depression

KAREN D. RUDOLPH

CONTENTS

Adolescence is a stage of life marked by striking transformations in youths' social worlds. As youth progress through adolescence, they must negotiate the shift from a primary reliance on the family as a context for socialization and support to a more delicate balance between autonomy versus connectedness within the family (Allen, Hauser, Bell, & O'Connor, 1994). Moreover, youth must traverse the increasingly intricate and emotionally demanding landscape of peer and romantic relationships (Furman & Wehner, 1997; Laursen, 1996). Successfully meeting their basic need for relatedness during this pivotal period thus requires that youth possess strong personal and interpersonal resources. These complex social tasks of adolescence provide a developmental context of risk for the emergence of depression, particularly in youth with pre-existing personal characteristics or environmental experiences that compromise their ability to navigate the interpersonal challenges of adolescence. This chapter explores the interpersonal context of adolescent depression, with a focus on characteristics of youth and their environments that amplify or attenuate risk in the face of the social reorganization characterizing the transition through adolescence.

INTERPERSONAL PERSPECTIVES ON ADOLESCENT DEPRESSION

Several contemporary theories consider the importance of understanding adolescent depression within an interpersonal context. Collectively, these theories focus on the joint contribution of adolescents and their social contexts to the onset and progression of depression. Some of these theories also address two salient developmental features of depression: the sharp rise in depression and the emergence of a sex difference in depression during adolescence. Given the robust nature of this emerging sex difference, which portends higher rates of depression in females than males throughout the life course, it is important to consider how an interpersonal perspective can help to explain this notable developmental feature of depression. Although prior theories touch on critical interpersonal aspects of depression, a comprehensive, developmentally informed, interpersonal model of adolescent depression has not yet been formulated. This section briefly reviews relevant theories, and describes some of their limitations. In the following section, a comprehensive model is proposed that addresses the constraints on prior theories for understanding the interpersonal context of adolescent depression.

Nolen-Hoeksema and Girgus (1994) introduced a pioneering framework for understanding the emerging sex difference in depression. According to their framework, girls carry greater vulnerability than boys prior to adolescence; this vulnerability interacts with girls' heightened exposure to challenges relative to boys during adolescence to predict a sharper surge in depression in girls than in boys. Although this framework focuses on a broad range of vulnerabilities and adolescent challenges, personal and contextual influences of an interpersonal nature (e.g., interpersonal orientation, exposure to social challenges such as sexual abuse) play a central role (see also, Nolen-Hoeksema, 2001).

Providing a broader perspective on the divergent trajectories of emotional and behavioral development in girls and boys, Rose and Rudolph (2006) emphasize how peer socialization processes influence the emergence of emotional difficulties in girls. According to a speculative model—grounded in a systematic developmental analysis of the emergence and progression of sex differences in relationship processes—social-cognitive and behavioral aspects of peer relationships interact and transact with stress and coping processes within relationships to contribute to heightened risk for emotional disorders in girls. This model highlights a paradox in the development of sex-linked interpersonal processes, namely that female-linked relationship qualities and experiences confer emotional costs but also some social benefits, a point that will be elaborated at the end of the chapter.

Another recent model (Hankin & Abramson, 2001) expands cognitive vulnerability-stress theories to explain the emergence of a sex difference in depression during adolescence. This model suggests that cognitive vulnerabilities interact with stressful life events and consequent negative affect to predict increases in depression. There is some mention of interpersonal processes (e.g., the generation of interpersonal stress; the role of early environmental adversity), but the model does not provide much elaboration on interpersonal vulnerability.

Other recent theories focus on more precise interpersonal processes through which sex-linked vulnerability to depression unfolds across the adolescent transition. Cyranowski, Frank, Young, and Shear (2000) highlight how girls' affiliative needs, driven by both social and hormonal forces, interact with social challenges during the transition to foster depression in at-risk females. Similarly, Rudolph (2002) suggests that girls' heightened exposure to, generation of, and reactivity to interpersonal stress contribute to the emergence and maintenance of a sex difference in depression during adolescence. Female-linked relational orientation styles (e.g., a heightened psychological and emotional investment in relationships) are presumed to account in part for the sex difference in stress reactivity and depression. These two models shed light on interpersonal vulnerability in adolescent girls, but are somewhat limited in scope and do not consider the full range of interpersonal vulnerabilities or adolescent challenges that contribute to the surge in depression and the emerging sex difference in depression during adolescence.

These models share some features with interpersonal theories of adult depression. According to these theories, depressed individuals act in ways that elicit negative responses (Coyne, 1976; Joiner, Coyne, & Blalock, 1999) and generate stress and conflict in their relationships (Hammen, 2006); these relationship disturbances serve to perpetuate depressive symptoms. In brief, depressed individuals seek encouragement and reassurance of their worth, but then are unable to accept offers of support. Failure to accept support fosters negative affect and rejection by their partners, thereby confirming depressed individuals' negative self-views and maintaining their depression (Coyne, 1976; Joiner et al., 1999).

These theories provide a useful foundation on which to build an interpersonal model of adolescent depression, but they are limited in several ways. Most importantly, prior theories typically lack a developmental perspective. This adevelopmental approach is reflected in three ways. First, most prior interpersonal theories are silent on the developmental origins of interpersonal vulnerability to depression. Second, prior theories do not adequately consider which interpersonal processes are particularly relevant during adolescence, or how normative physical-maturational, cognitive-developmental, and social-contextual changes interact with individual differences in traits and experiences to account for the emergence of depression and the sex difference in depression during adolescence. Third, most prior theories focus on how youth *react* to their social worlds, rather than how they *contribute* to and *select* their social worlds. Addressing these three considerations—that is, identifying the mechanisms through which some youth develop interpersonal vulnerability, understanding the normative developmental context of adolescence, and examining the dynamic, transactional association between youth and their contexts—is crucial for learning which youth will develop interpersonal vulnerability, why these youth are at heightened risk for the development of depression during adolescence, and how depressed youths' attributes and behaviors contribute to the continuity of disorder over time. Moreover, elucidating these three developmental issues can inform prevention and intervention programs designed to divert youth toward more adaptive developmental pathways.

In addition, due in part to a relatively narrow focus on specific interpersonal processes rather than a broader perspective on the inter-relations among different components of adolescents' social contexts, prior theories rarely consider potential trade-offs of youths' interpersonal characteristics and experiences for vulnerability versus resilience to depression. Considering such trade-offs provides a more complex perspective that might help developmental scientists learn how to shift the balance away from risk and toward resilience in youth (for a more comprehensive discussion, see Rose & Rudolph, 2006).

The present chapter aims to extend prior theory by presenting a developmentally informed model of adolescent depression, which considers how individual differences in a range of interpersonal processes develop over time and intersect with normative developmental transitions to influence the onset and progression of depression across adolescence. The chapter also touches on how interpersonal vulnerability is linked to other domains of risk (genetic, biological, cognitive, and contextual). Directions for future research are suggested to address gaps in our knowledge about the interpersonal context of adolescent depression.

A Developmentally Informed Model of the Interpersonal Context of Adolescent Depression

The proposed model emphasizes the interplay among (a) youth characteristics that heighten susceptibility to depression (maladaptive relationship appraisals and social-behavioral deficits), (b) social-contextual influences that increase risk for depression (relationship disturbances and interpersonal stressors), and (c) normative transitions that create an interpersonal context of risk for depression during adolescence. The model draws from dynamic perspectives on development (Lerner, 1985; Magnusson, 1988) and psychopathology (Cicchetti & Rogosch, 2002) that highlight how ongoing interactions and transactions among youth and their environments influence emerging developmental trajectories. Accordingly, the central premises consider how youth play an active role in constructing, shaping, interpreting, and selecting their social worlds.

OVERVIEW OF THE MODEL

According to the model (see Figure 14.1; for related models, see Rudolph, Flynn, & Abaied, 2008; Rudolph, Hammen, & Daley, 2006), exposure to early family

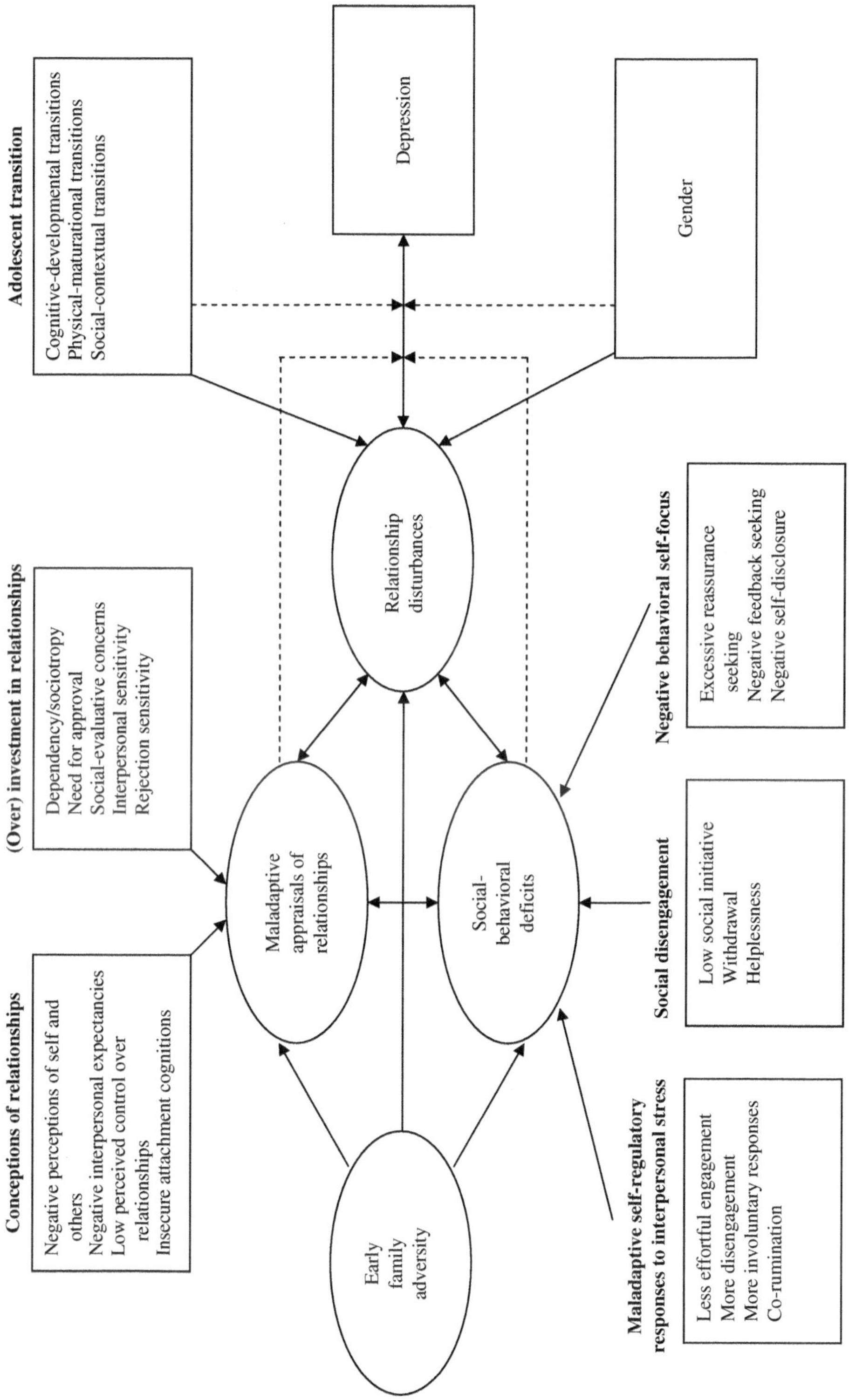

Figure 14.1 Theoretical model of the interpersonal context of adolescent depression.

adversity and parental depression fosters the development of maladaptive appraisals of relationships and social-behavioral deficits (Premise 7). Maladaptive relationship appraisals and social-behavioral deficits heighten vulnerability to depression (Premises 1 and 2), particularly in the face of relationship disturbances (Premise 3), and cause youth to generate stress in their relationships and to choose more stressful social contexts (Premise 4). The contributions of maladaptive relationship appraisals and social-behavioral deficits to depression are intensified during the passage through adolescence, especially in girls, due to the biological, psychological, and social changes occurring during this time (Premises 5 and 6). Finally, depression exacerbates maladaptive relationship appraisals, social-behavioral deficits, and relationship disturbances, accounting for the continuity of depression over time (Premise 8). This model emphasizes interpersonal processes that are hypothesized to be particularly relevant to girls' increasing risk for depression relative to boys over the course of adolescence.

ELABORATION OF THE MODEL

This section elaborates on the specific premises of the model and provides an analysis of the model components. A focus is placed on research with adolescents—for practical reasons, defined according to age and grade boundaries (11–18 years, fifth to twelfth grade). In some cases where research specific to adolescents is limited, studies that incorporate broader age ranges are included (and noted accordingly as "mixed-age" samples). A later section describes how indicators of development beyond chronological age (i.e., social-contextual changes, pubertal maturation, and cognitive-developmental advances) can and should be integrated into theory and research on the interpersonal context of adolescent depression.

Premise 1: Maladaptive Appraisals of Relationships Create a Vulnerability to Depression

The first premise is that maladaptive appraisals of relationships serve as a proximal contributor to depression. Several theoretical perspectives implicate maladaptive appraisals of relationships as a source of vulnerability. Attachment-based theories suggest that negative internal working models of relationships augment vulnerability to depression (Bowlby, 1980; Cummings & Cicchetti, 1990). Cognitive vulnerability-stress theories (Clark, Steer, Beck, & Ross, 1995) and psychodynamic theories (Blatt & Homann, 1992) suggest that individuals with a predisposition to base their self-worth on success in relationships (e.g., traits of sociotropy, dependency) are vulnerable to depression, particularly when confronted with interpersonal stress or failure. More broadly, the proposed model holds that appraisals involving heightened attention to, concern about, investment in, and negative conceptions of relationships constitute a form of interpersonal vulnerability to depression.

Youth who view themselves as incapable and unworthy of participating in rewarding relationships and who view others as unsupportive and untrustworthy (negative conceptions of self and others), who expect that interpersonal encounters will be aversive (pessimistic interpersonal expectancies), and who feel that they are unable to create positive interpersonal outcomes (low perceived control in relationships) might experience feelings of hopelessness about their social worlds. Negative conceptions and expectancies about the self and relationships might be generalized to future social encounters, resulting in maladaptive biases in the encoding, interpretation, and retrieval of interpersonal information (Baldwin, 1992; Main, Kaplan, & Cassidy, 1985; Rudolph, Hammen, & Burge, 1995). Feelings of hopelessness and a heightened focus on aversive aspects of interpersonal situations might set the stage for depression.

Likewise, youth who invest considerable time and emotional energy into worrying about their relationships and gaining approval from others, and who show heightened interpersonal sensitivity (i.e., excessive awareness of, and reactivity to, the behaviors and feelings of others; Boyce & Parker, 1989) or rejection sensitivity (i.e., tendency to anxiously expect, readily perceive, and over-react to rejection; Downey & Feldman, 1996) might be vulnerable to depression for a number of reasons (Rizzo, Daley, & Gunderson, 2006; Rudolph, Caldwell, & Conley, 2005; Rudolph & Conley, 2005). Such youth might show an excessive focus on trying to please others at the expense of their own needs (Fritz & Helgeson, 1998). Perceived failure to meet their personal standards for interpersonal success or to elicit adequate approval from others might lead these youth to experience self-disappointment and shame. Moreover, youth whose self-worth is contingent on social approval might experience more frequent or extreme fluctuations in their sense of self (Harter, Stocker, & Robinson, 1996). Finally, youth who possess a high need for approval and relatedness yet worry excessively about evaluation and potential rejection might attend disproportionately to negative compared to positive social cues. This constellation of inattention to one's own needs (Fritz & Helgeson, 1998), feelings of shame (Tangney, Burggraf, & Wagner, 1995), greater fluctuations in one's sense of self (Crocker & Wolfe, 2001), and heightened attention and sensitivity to negative social cues (Downey & Feldman, 1996), constitutes a strong vulnerability to depression.

Research supports the role of maladaptive relationship appraisals in adolescent depression. Youth who possess negative conceptions of the self in relationships (e.g., views of the self as unable to develop successful relationships, unworthy of positive regard, and ineffective at achieving desired interpersonal outcomes), negative conceptions of others (e.g., views of peers as untrustworthy and hostile), and insecure attachment cognitions experience more depressive symptoms concurrently and over time (Abela et al., 2005, in a mixed-age sample; Hammen et al., 1995; Rudolph & Clark, 2001; Rudolph, Kurlakowsky, & Conley, 2001). Research also links depressive symptoms to biased processing of interpersonal information (Shirk, Van Horn, & Leber, 1997, in a mixed-age sample). Moreover, depressed youth overestimate the stressfulness of challenging interpersonal events and their contribution to these events (Krackow & Rudolph, 2008, in a mixed-age sample), and underestimate their social competence relative to objective indicators (Cole, Martin, Peeke, Seroczynski, & Hoffman, 1998, in a mixed-age sample; Pomerantz & Rudolph, 2003, in a mixed-age sample; Rudolph & Clark, 2001). Heightened investment in, and concern about, relationships also are linked to emotional distress, including depression. For instance, youth who demonstrate dependency in relationships (Leadbeater, Kuperminc, Blatt, & Herzog, 1999), social-evaluative concerns (Rudolph & Conley, 2005), a strong need for approval (Rudolph et al., 2005, in a mixed-age sample), an interpersonal caring orientation (Gore,

Aseltine, & Colton, 1993), and interpersonal sensitivity (Rizzo et al., 2006) are more prone to depression concurrently and over time.

Research thus supports the idea that maladaptive relationship appraisals are linked to depression. However, only a few studies include prospective designs; more research needs to substantiate the idea that these appraisals contribute to subsequent depression. Moreover, little is known about the processes through which appraisals heighten vulnerability. A few possibilities are proposed earlier in this section; future research would benefit from a more direct examination of these and other explanatory processes. Finally, the proposed model highlights a range of relationship appraisals that confer vulnerability to depression, but it is unclear whether these appraisals reflect distinct constructs with independent contributions or whether a single relational orientation style underlies these constructs. Thus, research needs to be directed toward understanding the linkages among these appraisals.

Premise 2: Social-Behavioral Deficits Create a Vulnerability to Depression

According to the second premise, social-behavioral deficits heighten vulnerability to depression. Although research links a range of social-behavioral deficits to youth depression (for a review, see Rudolph et al., 2008), the present model focuses on a more narrow group of deficits that are viewed as particularly relevant to negotiating the transition through adolescence, including: (a) poor self-regulation in response to social challenges, (b) social disengagement, and (c) engagement in negative behavioral self-focus.

Poor Self-Regulation

One key aspect of social competence involves how youth regulate their emotions and behavior in response to challenge. Contemporary frameworks of self-regulation distinguish between effortful versus involuntary responses to stress (Compas, Connor-Smith, Saltzman, Thomsen, & Wadsworth, 2001; Rudolph, Dennig, & Weisz, 1995). Youth who act in purposeful, goal-directed ways and who effectively manage their emotions are more likely to deal successfully with social challenges and are less likely to become overwhelmed by their emotions than youth who react in an involuntary manner. Youth with the latter self-regulatory profile might become entrapped in a process of negative cognitive self-focus, in which they perseverate on their problems and negative emotions (i.e., rumination; Nolen-Hoeksema, 2000) or, alternatively, might act in an avoidant manner that prevents successful resolution of social difficulties. The failure to regulate negative cognitions and emotional arousal or to resolve social difficulties can foster a diminished sense of self-worth and self-efficacy, a sense of shame, and heightened negative emotions, which contribute to depression.

Consistent with these ideas, depressed youth show maladaptive self-regulation within their relationships. According to both youth and their parents, when faced with challenges in their relationships, depressed youth engage in fewer effortful engagement (e.g., problem solving, support seeking) and more involuntary responses to stress (e.g., rumination, emotional arousal) (Connor-Smith, Compas, Wadsworth, Thomsen, & Saltzman, 2000, using a measure of anxiety/depressive symptoms; Flynn & Rudolph, 2007, in a mixed-age sample; Jaser et al., 2005; Langrock, Compas, Keller, Merchant,

& Copeland, 2002, in a mixed-age sample) than nondepressed youth. Internalizing symptoms also are associated with co-rumination, or the extensive discussion of personal problems in the context of a dyadic relationship (Rose, 2002). Although much of this research relies on concurrent data, some research suggests that maladaptive responses to stress (Tolan, Gorman-Smith, Henry, Chung, & Hunt, 2002, using a measure of internalizing symptoms; Wadsworth & Berger, 2006, using a measure of anxiety/depressive symptoms) and co-rumination (Rose, Carlson, & Waller, 2007) predict heightened depression over time.

Observations also reveal poor self-regulation within relationships. During challenging peer interactions, depressed youth are less effective at negotiating conflict and show heightened emotion dysregulation compared to nondepressed youth (Rudolph, Hammen, & Burge, 1994, in a mixed-age sample). Similarly, during challenging mother–child interactions, depressed youth show less problem solving and faciliative behavior (e.g., positive affect, affirmation) than nondepressed youth, although they do not exhibit more aversive behavior (Sheeber & Sorensen, 1998). Unfortunately, little is known about whether observed emotion and behavior regulation within relationships contributes to future depression, although one study using multi-informant report, including observations, revealed that less supportive and more conflictual parent–child relationships predicted depression over time (Sheeber, Hops, Alpert, Davis, & Andrews, 1997).

Social Disengagement

A tendency to disengage from relationships might also create a vulnerability to depression. Youth who are less actively involved in positive relationships and who show low social initiative will lack the opportunity for rewarding interactions and social support, and might feel isolated, lonely, and alienated (Joiner, 2002). Social disengagement might have particularly adverse effects during the adolescent transition when normative social-contextual changes promote heightened social relatedness in youth, particularly within the peer group (Laursen, 1996).

Research supports the role of social disengagement in depression. According to teachers, depressed adolescents engage in less positive approach behavior and more social withdrawal than nondepressed adolescents (Rudolph & Clark, 2001). Teacher reports also link helpless social behavior, as reflected in a lack of social initiative and persistence, with adolescent depressive symptoms (Nolen-Hoeksema, Girgus, & Seligman, 1992). During observations of family interactions, depressed youth demonstrate more solitary behavior and fewer positive reactions to others (Messer & Gross, 1995, in a mixed-age sample). Although little longitudinal research examines whether social disengagement predicts subsequent depression in adolescents, research with younger youth (Boivin, Hymel, & Bukowski, 1995, in a mixed-age sample) supports this prospective association (cf. Nolen-Hoeksema et al., 1992), suggesting that this type of research would be worthwhile to pursuing with adolescents.

Negative Behavioral Self-Focus

The model also proposes that a tendency to engage in negative behavioral self-focus contributes to depression. Negative behavioral self-focus can be reflected in several types of behavior. As discussed earlier, an interpersonal theory of adult depression (Coyne, 1976; Joiner et al., 1999) suggests that depression-prone individuals engage in excessive attempts to seek reassurance from close relationship partners, contributing to a cycle of interpersonal rejection and depression. These attempts might be enacted in the form of negative statements about the self, accompanied by efforts to elicit a counter-argument by partners. Alternatively, researchers have suggested that depression-prone individuals engage in negative feedback seeking, or active efforts to solicit feedback that verifies their negative self-concept (Borelli & Prinstein, 2006). Receiving this negative feedback confirms their low sense of self-worth, thereby heightening depression. Finally, negative behavioral self-focus might take the form of excessive or one-sided negative self-disclosures in the context of relationships (e.g., comments about one's negative characteristics or experiences). This type of negative behavioral self-focus might contribute to depression both by drawing youths' attention to their perceived deficiencies and problems as well as by compromising the quality of their relationships. Negative behavioral self-focus might be particularly relevant to understanding depression during adolescence due to the heightened self-focus that accompanies this stage (Buss, 1980; Garber, Weiss, & Shanley, 1993).

In support of this perspective, excessive reassurance seeking (Prinstein, Borelli, Cheah, Simon, & Aikins, 2005) and negative feedback seeking (Borelli & Prinstein, 2006) predict heightened adolescent depression concurrently and over time. Research has not examined the role of negative self-disclosure in adolescent depression. However, research shows that depressed college students make more negative statements, including self-focused comments (e.g., negative self-disclosures) and other-focused comments (e.g., criticisms, disagreements), during conversation with friends compared to nondepressed individuals (Segrin & Flora, 1998). During interactions with their mothers, depressed youth engage in more "depressive" behaviors marked by negative affect and self-derogatory comments compared to nondepressed youth (Sheeber & Sorensen, 1998).

Overall, research suggests that social-behavioral deficits play a role in adolescent depression, with more limited evidence indicating that these deficits predict future depression. However, more work is needed to elaborate on the specific nature of these deficits and to better understand why and how particular deficits heighten vulnerability. Much of the research to date examines deficits at a fairly broad level (e.g., global responses to interpersonal challenges, social withdrawal), with far less investigation into the specific interpersonal behaviors that occur during moment-to-moment interactions. Although research on excessive reassurance seeking and negative feedback seeking takes a first step toward addressing this gap, this research does not specify precisely how these behaviors are enacted within relationships, how the partners of depressed youth perceive and react to these behaviors, or how these behaviors foster the dissolution of relationships. Additional work is also needed to differentiate the influence of social-behavioral deficits across varying interpersonal contexts, such as the broader peer group versus dyadic interactions and intimate relationships.

Premise 3: Maladaptive Appraisals and Social-Behavioral Deficits Interact with Relationship Disturbances to Heighten Risk for Depression

Consistent with vulnerability-stress models of psychopathology, the third premise holds that maladaptive appraisals of relationships and social-behavioral deficits are particularly likely to foster depression when youth encounter challenges in their relationships. In particular, youth with these vulnerabilities are more likely to interpret and react to interpersonal difficulties in ways that create a risk for depression than youth without these vulnerabilities.

Youth who have pessimistic views of their social worth or efficacy and whose self-worth is contingent on social approval are likely to draw negative self-inferences following interpersonal stress or failure. These youth might blame themselves for their difficulties and focus on their inability to change their situation, thus experiencing a sense of shame and hopelessness. Heightened interpersonal sensitivity might activate cognitive distortions, such as catastrophization when faced with interpersonal challenges (e.g., "If I have an argument with my friend, our friendship is over"), or might undermine youths' perceived ability to cope with interpersonal problems (Rizzo et al., 2006). Similarly, rejection-sensitive youth presumably interpret perceived rejection as reflecting an inability to achieve a highly valued goal (i.e., interpersonal acceptance; Downey & Feldman, 1996). Youth with maladaptive self-regulatory styles will be particularly likely to experience emotional arousal when faced with interpersonal challenges. Finally, interpersonal stress is likely to exacerbate pre-existing tendencies to engage in excessive reassurance seeking or negative self-disclosures within relationships. In contrast, youth with maladaptive appraisals and social-behavioral deficits might be less likely to develop depression in the context of more supportive, less stressful relationships. Thus, maladaptive relationship appraisals and social-behavioral deficits likely interact with relationship disturbances to predict depression.

Substantial evidence confirms that adolescent depression occurs in the context of disturbances within peer, romantic, and family relationships. This research is briefly summarized, followed by a review of research investigating whether youth with maladaptive appraisals of relationships and social-behavioral deficits are particularly vulnerable to depression when faced with these disturbances.

According to multiple perspectives, depressive symptoms in adolescents are associated with less popularity and more rejection and isolation in the peer group (Nolan, Flynn, & Garber, 2003; Rudolph & Clark, 2001). Depressed youth also elicit negative responses from unfamiliar peers. During dyadic interactions, observers report that the partners of depressed youth respond more negatively than the partners of nondepressed youth (Baker, Milich, & Manolis, 1996; Rudolph et al., 1994, in a mixed-age sample); these negative reactions are apparent in partner ratings following dyadic interactions (Baker et al., 1996; Connolly, Geller, Marton, & Kutcher, 1992).

Depressed adolescents also report difficulties in their close relationships, such as poorer friendship quality (e.g., less intimacy and poor conflict resolution; more conflict and perceived criticism) and more friendship stress (e.g., arguments, break-ups) (Borelli & Prinstein, 2006; La Greca & Harrison, 2005; Prinstein et al., 2005; Rudolph, 2002). However, friend reports do not corroborate these views, revealing either no differences (Brendgen, Vitaro, Turgeon, & Poulin, 2002) or differences that favor depressed adolescents (Daley & Hammen, 2002). Explanations for this discrepancy have not yet been investigated. It might be that self-reports of poor friendship quality reflect a negative bias on the part of depressed youth, consistent with evidence that depressed adolescents have more negative views of their peer relationships than warranted (Rudolph & Clark, 2001). Alternatively, the friends of depressed youth might initially offer extra support, but become frustrated if these efforts are not perceived as genuine or helpful and, subsequently, withdraw from the friendship. Both depressed adolescents and their romantic partners report more negative relationship qualities (e.g., conflict, criticism, and exclusion) and less provision of emotional support from the partners compared to nondepressed adolescents and their partners (Daley & Hammen, 2002; La Greca & Harrison, 2005).

Reports by youth and their parents also link family disturbances with adolescent depression. These disturbances are reflected in more hostile and less intimate, satisfying, and warm parent–child relationships (Herman-Stahl & Petersen, 1999; Puig-Antich et al., 1993), as well as parenting styles characterized by less acceptance, and more psychological control (Garber, Robinson, & Valentiner, 1997) and criticism (Frye & Garber, 2005). Compared to nondepressed youth, depressed youth characterize their families as less cohesive and adaptable, less open to emotional expressiveness, and more rejecting and conflictual (Hops, Lewinsohn, Andrews, & Roberts, 1990; Sheeber & Sorensen, 1998).

Confirming the reports of adolescents and their parents, observations reveal that the mothers of depressed youth show more dominance and anger (Kobak, Sudler, & Gamble, 1991) and less faciliative behavior (Sheeber & Sorensen, 1998) during parent–child interactions than the mothers of nondepressed youth. Observations of family-wide interactions reveal that mothers of depressed youth direct more aversive attention toward their children than do the mothers of nondepressed youth (Dadds, Sanders, Morrison, & Rebgetz, 1992, in a mixed-age sample), but observations do not always confirm self-reports of overt hostility (Sheeber & Sorensen, 1998).

Taking a global perspective, considerable research examines youths' exposure to stressful interpersonal life events and circumstances. Using differing methodologies, including extensive semistructured interviews and daily diaries, evidence links exposure to everyday hassles, ongoing strain, and severe events within relationships to depression in adolescents (Daley & Hammen, 2002; Hankin, Mermelstein, & Roesch, 2007; Krackow & Rudolph, 2008 in a mixed-age sample; Wagner & Compas, 1990).

Once again, much of this research involves concurrent designs that provide only a first step toward supporting the idea that relationship disturbances contribute to future depression. However, a growing body of evidence reveals that disturbances across peer (Conley & Rudolph, in press, in a mixed-age sample; Hankin et al., 2007; Nolan et al., 2003), romantic (Hankin et al., 2007; Monroe, Rohde, Seeley, & Lewinsohn, 1999), and family (Davies & Windle, 1997; Hankin et al., 2007; Lewinsohn et al., 1994; Sheeber et al., 1997; Stice, Ragan, & Randall, 2004) relationships predict future depression in youth.

Building on the idea that relationship disturbances contribute to depression, Premise 3 specifies that some youth will be more vulnerable to these disturbances than will others. Although significant evidence establishes support for vulnerability-stress models of adolescent depression, most theory and research in this vein focus on general cognitive vulnerability-stress interactions (for a review, see Hankin & Abela, 2005). In contrast, the proposed model is more specific in the hypothesis that two forms of interpersonal vulnerability (maladaptive relationship appraisals and social-behavioral deficits) heighten reactivity to relationship disturbances.

Some research supports an interpersonal vulnerability-stress model of depression. Several forms of maladaptive relationship appraisals interact with relationship disturbances to predict depression. For example, one study revealed that late-adolescent girls with insecure attachment cognitions experience more depression than those with secure attachment cognitions when faced with interpersonal stress (Hammen et al., 1995). Mixed support has emerged for the joint contribution of sociotropy/dependency and interpersonal stress to depression, with some research supporting an interactive effect (Abela, McIntyre-Smith, & Dechef, 2003; Fichman, Koestner, & Zuroff, 1997, in a mixed-age sample), and other research failing to find support (Abela & Taylor, 2003). Several studies reveal that a heightened investment in relationships interacts with relationship stress to predict depression. In one study, youth with an elevated need for approval were more likely to experience depression when exposed to high than low levels of peer victimization (Rudolph et al., 2005, in a mixed-age sample). In another study, a high investment in peer acceptance interacted with peer rejection to predict subsequent depression in girls (Prinstein & Aikins, 2004). Finally, interpersonal sensitivity amplified depressive responses to romantic relationship stress in adolescent girls (Rizzo et al., 2006), and rejection sensitivity predicted heightened emotional distress in youth who were exposed to an experimentally manipulated peer rejection (Downey, Lebolt, Rincon, & Freitas, 1998).

Some research also supports the idea that social-behavioral deficits interact with relationships disturbances to predict depression. In a study of early adolescents, youth with a tendency toward social disengagement showed stable high or increasing trajectories of depression over time in the context of high peer exclusion, but stable low or decreasing trajectories of depression over time in the context of low peer exclusion (Gazelle & Rudolph, 2004). In a sample of college students, shyness predicted increases in depressive symptoms in the absence, but not in the presence, of social support (Joiner, 1997; cf. Brozina & Abela, 2006, for a nonsignificant interaction of behavioral inhibition and daily hassles in a mixed-age sample). In a mixed-age sample, excessive reassurance seeking interacted with daily hassles (not specifically of an interpersonal nature) to predict depressive symptoms over time in older but not in younger youth (Abela, Zuroff, Ho, Adams, & Hankin, 2006).

Overall, this research suggests the promise of an interpersonal vulnerability-stress model of adolescent depression, wherein pre-existing interpersonal vulnerability is activated in the context of relationship disturbances. This work provides a promising step toward understanding why some youth are more susceptible than others to depression when they encounter relationship disturbances. However, longitudinal research needs to confirm the interactive effect of prior vulnerability and recent stress on subsequent depression. Moreover, future research needs to identify the processes through which maladaptive relationship appraisals and social-behavioral deficits confer vulnerability to depression in the face of interpersonal stress. Some possibilities were suggested earlier, but empirical investigations of these processes are needed.

Premise 4: Maladaptive Relationship Appraisals and Social-Behavioral Deficits Foster Relationship Disturbances

According to Premise 4, maladaptive relationship appraisals and social-behavioral deficits not only *amplify* depressive responses to relationship disturbances, but also cause adolescents to *create* stress in their social worlds. As such, certain youth shape their environments in ways that compromise their relationships and heighten risk for depression. These influences are proposed to be particularly salient during the transition to adolescence in light of the social reorganization that occurs during this period (see Premise 5).

Maladaptive relationship appraisals are likely to foster social-behavioral deficits and consequent relationship disturbances. Youth with negative conceptions of self and others, a diminished sense of control over relationships, elevated dependency and need for approval, and heightened interpersonal sensitivity might disengage from relationships in response to their hopelessness about affecting change or in an effort to avoid disapproval. This disengagement might foster social isolation and relationship disturbances. Indeed, youth with negative self-appraisals within peer relationships show heightened social disengagement over time, which predicts increases in peer-related stress (Caldwell, Rudolph, Troop-Gordon, & Kim, 2004).

Alternatively, youth with maladaptive relationship appraisals might engage in behaviors that elicit overt rejection and conflict. For example, youth with negative self-appraisals or a heightened need for approval might engage in excessive reassurance seeking in an effort to relieve their self-doubt, or excessive negative self-disclosures to their relationship partners. Although "co-rumination" between friends might benefit youths' relationships to the extent that it is mutual and collaborative (Rose, 2002), a one-sided behavioral focus on one's self-doubt and difficulties might undermine close relationships. Consistent with these pathways, heightened sociotropy (Shih, 2006, in female college students) and reassurance seeking (Potthoff, Holahan, & Joiner, 1995, in college students) predict the subsequent generation of stress in relationships, and youth characterized by heightened rejection sensitivity experience more peer victimization and conflicts over time (Downey et al., 1998). Youth who demonstrate involuntary and dysregulated responses to interpersonal problems are also likely to be at higher risk for social difficulties, such as rejection and conflict, than those who engage in planful, goal-directed responses.

Beyond creating disturbances in existing relationships, social-behavioral deficits might cause youth to enter into maladaptive relationships, due either to purposeful self-selection or to exclusion from adaptive relationships. For example, youth with poor self-regulatory skills might affiliate with deviant peers because they view these peers as similar or because they fail to integrate into the mainstream peer group. Moreover, a tendency toward negative feedback seeking might lead youth to affiliate with peers who provide negative evaluations that verify their poor self-concept (Borelli & Prinstein, 2006). Consequently, youth with these types of social-behavioral deficits might participate in stressful friendships and romantic relationships.

Thus, according to the proposed model, maladaptive relationship appraisals and social-behavioral deficits not only have adverse intrapersonal consequences (e.g., a sense of shame or hopelessness) that create a vulnerability to depression, but also heighten risk through a process of stress generation, relationship disruption, and relationship selection. These interpersonal difficulties then exacerbate youths' maladaptive self-appraisals and social-behavioral deficits, creating a self-perpetuating cycle of dysfunction (Caldwell et al., 2004). Although research supports the Premise 4 idea that youth with maladaptive appraisals and social-behavioral deficits select and construct adverse interpersonal environments, little is known about the particular processes through which these vulnerabilities operate. Moreover, few studies examine reciprocal linkages among maladaptive appraisals, social-behavioral deficits, and relationship disturbances. Future research needs to identify the specific behaviors (e.g., lack of persistence, disengagement, excessive reassurance seeking, negative self-disclosure) through which depression-prone youth shape specific aspects of their environments (e.g., social isolation, rejection, conflict).

Premises 5 and 6: Interpersonal Vulnerability to Depression is Intensified During the Transition Through Adolescence; Girls are More Vulnerable to These Transition Effects Than are Boys

As noted earlier, a developmentally informed interpersonal model of adolescent depression should address two robust developmental phenomena: the sharp rise in depression and the emergence of a sex difference in depression during adolescence (Hankin & Abramson, 2001; Nolen-Hoeksema & Girgus, 1994; Rudolph et al., 2006). Accordingly, a major focus of the proposed model is to elucidate the developmental context of interpersonal vulnerability to depression, emphasizing how the transitions of adolescence amplify risk in vulnerable youth. This perspective is consistent with models of development and psychopathology that view developmental transitions as potential periods of risk that accentuate pre-existing individual differences in vulnerability (Caspi & Moffitt, 1991; Nolen-Hoeksema & Girgus, 1994). In particular, the proposed model considers social-contextual, physical-maturational, and cognitive-developmental changes that help explain increasing risk for depression among vulnerable youth during the adolescent transition. Moreover, the model postulates that sex differences in interpersonal vulnerability, social risk, and normative developmental challenges collectively contribute to the emerging sex difference in depression during this period.

Social-Contextual Transitions that Create and Interact with Interpersonal Vulnerability

Adolescence is marked by social-contextual transitions that result from broader changes in social settings (e.g., school transitions) and more proximal changes in social roles, relationships, and expectations (e.g., onset of dating, shifting parental expectations). It is proposed that these disruptions in youths' social worlds heighten risk for depression, particularly in vulnerable youth. This risk is intensified in adolescent girls relative to boys due to girls' greater exposure and reactivity to social challenges during this time (Hankin & Abramson, 2001; Nolen-Hoeksema, 2001; Nolen-Hoeksema & Girgus, 1994; Rudolph, 2002; Rudolph et al., 2006).

A critical task of adolescence is the development of an independent social network outside of the family, one that provides not only socialization opportunities, but also intimacy and support (Brown, Dolcini, & Leventhal, 1997; Furman & Buhrmester, 1992). Paradoxically, at the same time that youth negotiate this shift, they often face disruptions in their peer groups due to school transitions (Simmons, Burgeson, Carlton-Ford, & Blyth, 1987). Other hallmarks of the adolescent transition include increasing immersion in platonic heterosexual relationships and romantic involvement. Negotiating these novel relationships can present challenges as adolescents need to learn new skills to cope with the frequent instability of early romantic relationships (Compian & Hayward, 2003; Furman & Wehner, 1997; Leaper & Anderson, 1997).

Adolescence is also characterized by significant changes in the family context, including increases in parent–child conflict and decreases in emotional closeness (for reviews, see Laursen, 1996; Paikoff & Brooks-Gunn, 1991). These changes might result in part from discrepant parent and youth expectations about the responsibilities and privileges that should be accorded to adolescents. Youth also need to strike a balance between autonomy and connectedness within the family (Allen et al., 1994). Related to this challenge, adolescent peer group norms might begin to conflict with family norms and values, potentially fueling greater strain within the family. Dealing with this reorganization and renegotiation of family relationships likely presents challenges to the developing adolescent that might heighten risk for depression.

In addition to heightened stress stemming from normative changes in relationships and social expectations, adolescents might create more interpersonal stress than preadolescents. Adolescents might succumb to peer pressure or the temptation to seek out new experiences, causing them to engage in risky behaviors (e.g., early sexual behavior, substance use; Donovan, Jessor, & Costa, 1988; Prinstein & La Greca, 2004). In fact, research shows that levels of many risk-taking behaviors rise during adolescence (Centers for Disease Control and Prevention, 2006). Such behaviors might increase adolescents' exposure to stress in their relationships (e.g., unwanted pregnancies, conflicts with authority figures). Furthermore, adolescents generally exert greater control over certain aspects of their lives than do preadolescents (e.g., selecting friends and dating partners). The growing ability to actively shape their environments (Scarr & McCartney, 1983) enables adolescents to engage in stress-inducing behaviors and to enter into stressful social situations and relationships.

Indeed, research indicates that the adolescent transition is accompanied by intensified social challenges. Moreover, consistent with Premise 6, there are sex-differentiated effects. Girls' exposure to interpersonal stress, particularly self-generated stress, increases significantly from preadolescence to adolescence, whereas boys' exposure remains consistent (Rudolph & Hammen, 1999) and significantly lower than that of girls (Davies & Windle, 1997; Gore et al., 1993; Hankin et al., 2007; Shih, Eberhart, Hammen, & Brennan, 2006). When specific aspects of relationships are distinguished, this heightened stress emerges particularly in the context of dyadic friendships (e.g., problems with friends, end of friendships), youths' vicarious experience of the stress of others in their social networks (for a review, see Rose & Rudolph, 2006), and exposure to sexual abuse (Hayward & Sanborn, 2002; Nolen-Hoeksema & Girgus, 1994).

As discussed earlier, greater exposure to relationship disturbances predicts depression, but little research directly examines whether heightened interpersonal stress in girls relative to boys accounts for the emerging sex difference in adolescent depression. However, limited data show that sex-linked exposure to stress within one's friendships (Rudolph, 2002), stressors experienced by friends (Gore et al., 1993), and overall interpersonal stressors (Hankin et al., 2007; Shih et al., 2006), mediate the sex difference in adolescent depression. This pattern of elevated and increasing interpersonal stress in girls relative to boys across adolescence likely helps to explain the intensification of the sex difference in depression.

Although most youth face social challenges during adolescence, Premise 5 further implicates individual differences in depressive responses to these demands that are contingent upon youths' interpersonal vulnerability. Specifically, these social-contextual changes are likely to amplify risk in youth with compromised personal resources (i.e., maladaptive appraisals of relationships and social-behavioral deficits) and pre-existing relationship disturbances.

A positive and secure sense of self and others in the context of relationships, and a sense of control over one's success in relationships are likely to facilitate youths' ability to navigate the unfamiliar territory of adolescent relationships. In contrast, youth who have pessimistic beliefs about their own social worth and competence, and who view others as hostile or unsupportive are likely to encounter difficulties negotiating changes in existing relationships and forging new relationships. Moreover, youth who show an excessive reliance on others for approval or who worry extensively about evaluation or abandonment in relationships are more likely to become depressed in the face of the relationship disruptions that often accompany the transition.

Youth who enter the transition with social-behavioral deficits are also likely to be more reactive to normative interpersonal changes, and to actively create difficulties in their relationships. For instance, responding to social challenge with involuntary and dysregulated responses (e.g., rumination, avoidance) rather than with effortful, planful responses (e.g., problem solving, emotional expression) will likely confer vulnerability to depression when youth are confronted with transition-related social challenges, particularly given that youth receive less external support for coping compared to earlier stages of life. Moreover, youth with this self-regulatory profile might act in ways that undermine their relationships, as they are less likely to engage in effective strategies for resolving interpersonal dilemmas that arise during the transition. Lack of social initiative and a tendency toward social disengagement are also likely to be exacerbated during the adolescent transition, as youth might decide that it is easier to withdraw from relationships than to face the new social demands. Similarly, a predisposition to engage in negative behavioral self-focus is likely to be activated by the ambiguity that often characterizes adolescent relationships. For example, reassurance-seeking or negative feedback-seeking behaviors might be intensified as youth attempt to confirm the security of their existing relationships or to develop new relationships in the context of adolescent social transitions. Finally, youth with social-behavioral deficits might become excluded from the mainstream peer group and gravitate toward norm-breaking peers during adolescence, thereby enhancing their likelihood of participating in stressful social contexts. Together, these interpersonal processes likely heighten adolescents' risk for the development of depression during this period.

Youth who enter the transition period with pre-existing disturbances in their relationships will also likely find it more difficult to adapt to the changing social demands of adolescence. For instance, youth who receive little support from their family and friends or who already have conflictual relationships might become overwhelmed when faced with the social challenges of adolescence, resulting in increasing levels of depression.

A final component of Premises 5 and 6 suggests that girls are more likely than boys to show depressive responses to the adolescent transition because girls possess higher levels, than boys, of several interpersonal vulnerabilities. Compared to boys, girls show a heightened investment in the quality of their close relationships; the sex difference in some aspects of this investment seems to be present during preadolescence, whereas the sex difference in other aspects of this investment seems to intensify during adolescence (for a review, see Rose & Rudolph, 2006). This investment is reflected, in part, in the form of maladaptive relationship appraisals, such as those discussed earlier. However, it is also reflected in other types of appraisals (e.g., empathy, interpersonal caring orientation, connection-oriented goals) that might be adaptive in some circumstances, but could heighten depression when girls face disruption in their social networks (Rudolph, 2002). That is, if girls value intimacy and harmony in their relationships more so than boys, normative transition-related changes in peer groups or parent–child relationships might present a greater threat to girls' than to boys' well-being. Moreover, some types of relationship appraisals, such as interpersonal caring orientations (Gore et al., 1993) and a need for approval (Rudolph et al., 2005) are linked more strongly to depression in girls than in boys.

Girls also show more particular social-behavioral deficits than boys. Specifically, girls are more likely than boys to engage in certain types of maladaptive responses to interpersonal difficulties (i.e., rumination and co-rumination), and this sex difference becomes more pronounced during adolescence (for a review, see Rose & Rudolph, 2006). Although girls demonstrate more self-disclosure within close friendships than do boys (for a review, see Rose & Rudolph, 2006), it is unknown whether they engage in more excessive or one-sided negative self-disclosure. Thus far, research does not demonstrate sex differences in negative feedback seeking (Borelli & Prinstein, 2006) or excessive reassurance seeking (Abela et al., 2006, in a mixed-age sample) in youth.

Consistent with the idea that girls show greater vulnerability to relationship disturbances than boys, girls perceive interpersonal problems as more stressful than boys (Wagner & Compas, 1990), and show heightened depression in the face of relationship disturbances, both concurrently and over time (Goodyer & Altham, 1991; Hankin et al., 2007; Rudolph, 2002; Rudolph & Hammen, 1999, in a mixed-age sample; Rudolph et al., 2000; Shih et al., 2006). Moreover, romantic relationship involvement predicts larger increases in depression in adolescent girls than boys (Joyner & Udry, 2000). However, research has not yet established whether particular types of interpersonal vulnerability account for this sex difference in stress reactivity.

To summarize, several lines of research support the proposed influence of social-contextual transitions on risk for depression. First, research documents that the changes occurring within relationships during this period are reflected in heightened exposure to stress. Second, evidence is consistent with the idea that sex differences in exposure and reactivity to relationship disturbances contribute to the emerging sex difference in depression during adolescence. Research is needed to test the proposal that the social-contextual transitions of adolescence amplify risk specifically, or more prominently, in youth with pre-existing interpersonal vulnerabilities, and that these vulnerabilities explain girls' heightened interpersonal stress reactivity relative to boys during adolescence.

Physical-Maturational Transitions that Create and Interact with Interpersonal Vulnerability

Interpersonal vulnerability to depression is also probably amplified by youths' progression through puberty. Puberty represents a complex and pivotal developmental transition, marked by hormonal and somatic changes, as well as psychological and social reorganization (for a review, see DeRose, Wright, & Brooks-Gunn, 2006). Although negotiating this transition presents a challenge to many youth, it is especially likely to intensify risk in those with preexisting interpersonal vulnerabilities. Specifically, it is proposed that youth with maladaptive relationship appraisals, social-behavioral deficits, and relationship disturbances will be most adversely affected by the progression through puberty. This intensification effect is expected to be more salient in girls than in boys.

A growing body of evidence suggests that pubertal development contributes to depression and helps to account for the emerging sex difference in depression (Angold, Costello, & Worthman, 1998; Ge, Conger, & Elder, 2001; Hayward, Gotlib, Schraedley, & Litt, 1999), although some recent research also implicates pubertal maturation as a contributor to depression in boys (for a review, see Huddleston & Ge, 2003). The present chapter proposes several interpersonal processes that explain how the pubertal transition heightens risk for depression. Consistent with the interpersonal focus of the model, this chapter highlights the intersection between puberty and youths' social worlds. Specifically, puberty is viewed as a process that unfolds within an interpersonal context, with accompanying implications for social interactions and relationships (DeRose et al., 2006; Graber, 2003). However, these interpersonal processes are likely linked to the biological changes of puberty (e.g., changes in sex hormones drive attitudes and behaviors associated with dating and opposite-sex relationships; Compian & Hayward, 2003), and thus must be considered part of a more complex package of influences.

First, the somatic changes of puberty (e.g., growth of secondary sexual characteristics, changes in body mass and weight distribution) might have adverse effects on youths' self-appraisals in the context of relationships. Moreover, these negative psychological effects might be more salient in girls than in boys. Many of the puberty-induced somatic changes are viewed as socially undesirable in girls (e.g., increased weight and body fat), but socially desirable in boys (e.g., increased height, muscle mass, and athleticism; for reviews, see Alsaker, 1995; Petersen, Silbereisen, & Sorensen, 1996; Stice, 2003). The undesirable nature of these changes in girls might undermine their sense of worth and competence in relationships, and might heighten their sensitivity to social evaluation and their need for approval from others. These effects might be exacerbated in early-maturing girls, who not only experience these changes prior to their peers, but also show lasting differences in their body size and shape (Simmons, Blyth, & McKinney, 1983).

Several studies confirm that more advanced pubertal status and early maturation are linked to negative self-appraisals in the form of body image and weight concerns in girls (Simmons et al., 1983; Tobin-Richards, Boxer, & Petersen, 1983), although the evidence is mixed regarding whether these concerns are translated into lower global self-worth (Simmons et al., 1983; Wichstrom, 1999). Indeed, pubertal development is associated with some types of positive self-appraisals in girls in the context of relationships (e.g., perceptions of the self as more popular with boys; Simmons et al., 1983). However, it is possible that, despite these positive self-appraisals, girls demonstrate increases in their concerns about evaluation and approval, which might still confer vulnerability to depression. Moreover, the proposed model suggests that the adverse effects of puberty intensify pre-existing interpersonal vulnerability. Thus, girls who enter the pubertal transition with maladaptive appraisals might show declines in their sense of self-worth and competence in relationships, whereas those with adaptive appraisals might show few ill effects.

Second, the passage through puberty might create or exacerbate social-behavioral deficits. For example, early-maturing girls might feel insecure or alienated from their peer group due to their differing physical and social status, causing them to engage in more reassurance seeking or to disengage from their relationships. Alternatively, early-maturing girls might engage in more negative self-disclosures in their relationships due to their concerns about their differing status, or might participate in co-ruminative discussions with similarly developed peers in an effort to seek understanding and support. Research has not examined whether pubertal development contributes to the emergence or exacerbation of depression-linked social-behavioral deficits or sex differences therein. Future research in this area could help to elucidate some of the specific interpersonal behaviors through which puberty heightens vulnerability to depression, as well as to examine whether puberty amplifies depression in youth with pre-existing social-behavioral deficits.

Third, puberty has direct implications for youths' peer, romantic, and family relationships that might heighten risk for depression. Pubertal development is accompanied by somatic changes that convey meaning to youth and their social networks about social roles, expectations, and status (DeRose et al., 2006; Graber, 2003). Although both parents and youth likely view emerging physical changes as signs of maturity, their perspective on the meaning of this maturity might differ. Parents might develop higher expectations of youth while also fearing the potential risks associated with increasing maturity. Youth might view these changes as signals that they are ready to assume more independence and autonomy from their families. Discrepancies in these perspectives might create tension within the family. Indeed, increased conflict and decreased closeness in parent–adolescent relationships are intensified with more advanced pubertal status and, in particular, early maturation (Crockett & Petersen, 1987; Hill, 1988; Steinberg, 1987; for reviews, see Alsaker, 1995; Paikoff & Brooks-Gunn, 1991; Susman & Rogol, 2004).

The pubertal transition also heightens social challenges in the peer context. As discussed earlier, many of the somatic changes of puberty are viewed as undesirable for girls but desirable for boys within the peer group. Indeed, despite the fact that girls' breast development is associated with some positive features of peer relationships (e.g., greater perceived social support; Brooks-Gunn & Warren, 1988; greater perceived attractiveness; Tobin-Richards et al., 1983), breast development is also the target of teasing (Brooks-Gunn, 1984). More generally, early-maturing youth more often are targets of sexual harassment and social victimization than their on-time and late-maturing peers (Craig, Pepler, Connolly, & Henderson, 2001). Thus, the transition through puberty, particularly when it is encountered early relative to one's peers, might contribute to disturbances in girls' relationships. Early-developing youth, both girls and boys, are also more likely to enter into risky peer contexts that contribute to greater social challenges. Specifically, early-developing youth are more likely than on-time and late-developing youth to befriend older peers (Magnusson, 1988; Weichold, Silbereisen, & Schmitt-Rodermund, 2003), to participate earlier in romantic relationships (Silbereisen & Kracke, 1997), and to associate with peers who engage in norm-breaking behavior (Magnusson, Stattin, & Allen, 1986). Participation in these risky social contexts might heighten the likelihood that early-maturing youth generate stress in their relationships (Rudolph, in press).

Research thus supports the idea that the pubertal transition contributes to relationship disturbances and social challenges, particularly in early-maturing youth and in girls. Little research directly examines whether sex differences in puberty-linked relationship disturbances contribute to the emerging sex difference in adolescent depression. However, a recent study indicates that exposure to heightened peer stress partially mediates the association between early pubertal timing and depression in girls, but not in boys (Conley & Rudolph, 2008). These findings are consistent with the proposal that adolescent girls' heightened risk for depression is due, in part, to the social implications of their transition through puberty.

Premises 5 and 6 also consider the interactive contribution of pre-existing relationship disturbances and the pubertal transition to the emerging sex difference in depression. Youth who enter this transition with compromised social networks face the synergistic effects of challenges in multiple life domains (Magnusson, 1988; Simmons, Blyth, Van Cleave, & Bush, 1979). Only a few studies examine the joint contribution of puberty and social context to adolescent depression. Some research suggests that puberty interacts with the normative social-developmental challenges of adolescence to heighten risk for depression in girls. For example, engagement in platonic (Ge, Conger, & Elder, 1996) and romantic (Hayward & Sanborn, 2002; Natsuaki, Biehl, & Ge, in press) heterosexual relationships amplifies risk for depression and associated psychological distress in girls with more advanced pubertal status and in girls with off-time pubertal development, particularly early-developing girls. In another study, the adverse effects of pubertal timing on depression were exacerbated in the context of high-stress peer relationships, but tempered in the context of low-stress peer relationships (Conley & Rudolph, in press). Interestingly, data from this study suggested that *early* actual and perceived pubertal timing in girls, and *late* actual and perceived timing in boys heightened risk for depression at elevated levels of peer stress.

In sum, preliminary research supports the premise that puberty both *contributes to* and *interacts with* interpersonal vulnerability to heighten depression over the adolescent transition. Moreover, some evidence suggests that this intensification process is more salient in girls than in boys. More work is needed to elucidate the precise interpersonal pathways through which puberty exerts its effects (DeRose et al., 2006). For instance, relatively little is known about the influence of pubertal changes on youths' appraisals of relationships or specific social-behavioral deficits associated with depression. In addition, research has only begun to explore how puberty interacts with youths' pre-existing interpersonal vulnerabilities or social contexts to predict depression. Because puberty does not have universal adverse effects, it will be essential to determine the conditions under which this transition contributes to depression.

Cognitive-Developmental Transitions that Create and Interact with Interpersonal Vulnerability

Youth also experience significant cognitive maturation over the adolescent transition that might provide a developmental context for the emergence or exacerbation of interpersonal vulnerability to depression. Many of these cognitive advances can be adaptive, as they enable the maturing adolescent to reason more effectively, and to engage in more complex problem solving, decision making, and perspective taking (Keating, 2004). At the same time, these advances might have some paradoxical adverse interpersonal consequences, especially for youth with a pre-existing tendency toward maladaptive appraisals of relationships, social-behavioral deficits, and relationship disturbances.

Over the course of adolescence, several cognitive transformations occur that might exacerbate maladaptive relationship appraisals and social-behavioral deficits. During this time, youth develop a more integrated, complex, and abstract knowledge system regarding the self and relationships (Damon & Hart, 1982; Harter, 1988; Selman, 1980). Moreover, adolescents begin to evaluate the self and others according to stable psychological attributes and competencies rather than concrete and unstable actions, allowing youth to engage in social comparison processes based on enduring traits (Higgins, 1991; Ruble & Rholes, 1981). Advances in cognitive abilities are also reflected in an increasing capacity to generalize across situations and time, resulting in less context-specific and more generalized self-appraisals (Higgins, 1991).

These cognitive-developmental changes might confer interpersonal advantages for youth with primarily positive appraisals of the self and relationships. However, in youth with negative appraisals, these changes might instead drive an intensification of concerns about one's worth, the judgments of others, and one's ability to engage in effective control over the social world. Specifically, with advances in the tendency to evaluate the self according to dispositional attributes and to generalize across situations and time, negative beliefs about one's worth, competence, and control in relationships, and about the social orientation of others might become more consolidated and resistant to change. Moreover, with advances in social comparison and perspective taking, vulnerable youth might become especially likely to worry about social evaluation and to base their self-worth on approval by others. Accompanying these changes, vulnerable youth also might show increases in certain social-behavioral deficits that heighten risk for depression. For example, these youth might engage in excessive reassurance seeking to elicit positive judgments from others, or in excessive negative self-disclosure to gain others' perspectives on their problems. These cognitive-developmental changes might be especially likely to undermine appraisals and behavior in adolescent girls due to socialization forces that guide them to be more invested in the quality of their relationships and the evaluations of others (Hill & Lynch, 1983; Rose & Rudolph, 2006).

Cognitive maturation also might directly influence the quality of youths' relationships. Paikoff and Brooks-Gunn (1991) summarize how cognitive transformations during adolescence might undermine parent–child relationships. In brief, they suggest that changes in expectations, attributional processes, perspective taking, complexity of social understanding, and self-definition set the stage for emerging conflict and tension in parent–adolescent relationships. Consistent with these ideas, more advanced cognitive processing is linked to certain disturbances in parent–adolescent relationships (for a review, see Paikoff & Brook-Gunn, 1991). However, the disruptive effect of these changes might depend, in part, on the quality of the relationship prior to adolescence. That is, families with supportive parent–child relationships might more effectively navigate the changes that accompany advances in adolescents' cognitive capacities, whereas those with conflictual or distant relationships might more readily succumb to the challenges that accompany these cognitive transitions. Similar adverse changes might occur in peer relationships as youth begin to question the perspectives of their peers.

Thus, although many of the cognitive-developmental advances that characterize the adolescent transition carry benefits for growth and development, these same changes might trigger or exacerbate interpersonal vulnerability in a subset of youth with pre-existing maladaptive relationship appraisals, social-behavioral deficits, and relationship disturbances. However, relatively little research establishes a direct connection between cognitive-developmental maturation and changes in interpersonal vulnerability, and virtually no research examines possible interactive effects. Because it is essential to place the emergence of psychopathology during adolescence into the context of normative adolescent cognitive development, it would be beneficial to examine empirically whether and how cognitive-developmental transitions create or interact with interpersonal vulnerability to depression.

Premise 7: Early Family Adversity Contributes to Interpersonal Vulnerability to Depression

According to the proposed model, interpersonal vulnerability develops in the context of early family adversity, including parental depression and other severe family disruptions (e.g., insecure parent–child attachment, child maltreatment, maladaptive parent socialization). This perspective is consistent with other theories regarding the intergenerational transmission of vulnerability to depression, and with significant evidence that parental (particularly maternal) depression (for reviews, see Goodman & Gotlib, 1999; Hammen, 1991) and early adversity (for reviews, see Goodman, 2002; Harkness & Lumley, in press) are associated with youth depression. More specifically, the model implicates maladaptive relationship appraisals, social-behavioral deficits, and relationship disturbances as explanatory processes that link early adversity to depression. Thus, this model expands prior interpersonal theories of depression by elaborating on the developmental origins of interpersonal vulnerability. Because of the large scope of research examining the role of early adversity in youth depression, some representative examples are presented to illustrate possible interpersonal mechanisms through which risk is transmitted.

Early Adversity and Maladaptive Appraisals of Relationships

It is proposed that early family adversity fosters the internalization of negative conceptions of self and others within relationships and, more speculatively, an excessive focus on gaining positive evaluation and approval. A common dimension that is believed to underlie the impact of various forms of adversity (e.g., maternal depression, insecure attachment, maltreatment, parental loss) on appraisals of relationships is exposure to a punitive and/or unpredictable family environment.

According to attachment theory, for example, early parent–child interactions characterized by a lack of caregiver sensitivity and responsiveness are encoded in memory in the form of internal working models of the self as unworthy of love, and others as unresponsive and untrustworthy; these internal working models are believed to cause biased processing of social information (Ainsworth, Blehar, Waters, & Wall, 1978; Bowlby, 1969, 1982; Main et al., 1985). Other forms of early family adversity, such as maternal depression and child maltreatment, might contribute to negative conceptions of self and others by fostering insecure attachment, or through alternate pathways, such as maladaptive parent socialization. For example, depressed mothers demonstrate more hostility and criticism (Lovejoy, Graczyk, O'Hare, & Neuman, 2000), and less contingent parenting (Cox, Puckering, Pound, & Mills, 1987). Similar styles characterize parenting in the context of maltreatment (Cicchetti & Howes, 1991). Exposure to critical and unpredictable parenting might convey the message that youth are not competent and that their environment is not responsive, thereby undermining their sense of control within relationships. Similarly, experience of severe disruptions within family relationships (e.g., parental death or divorce) might cause youth to feel that interpersonal events and relationships are uncontrollable. Indeed, youth exposed to family adversity in the form of insecure attachment, maternal depression, and maltreatment demonstrate less adaptive conceptions of the self and others, and biased processing of social information in early and middle childhood (Lynch & Cicchetti, 1998; Murray, Woolgar, Cooper, & Hipwell, 2001; Toth, Cicchetti, Macfie, & Emde, 1997). Moreover, adolescents with insecure attachment styles report more negative appraisals of their social competence (Cooper, Shaver, & Collins, 1998). Research also supports the idea that parent socialization styles characterized by intrusiveness, hostility, and noncontingency compromise youths' sense of control (Grolnick & Ryan, 1989). Exposure to moderate or severe parent separation or loss (e.g., death, divorce, parental abandonment) is also associated with lower perceptions of control within parent–child relationships (Rudolph et al., 2001).

It is further proposed that early family adversity fosters heightened sensitivity to evaluation in relationships. Youth exposed to unpredictable or overly punitive family environments might be especially attuned to cues regarding social evaluation, and especially sensitive to feedback regarding a lack of approval. Little research examines the developmental origins of social-evaluative concerns and a heightened need for approval, although it has been suggested that adolescents exposed to early maltreatment develop heightened rejection sensitivity (Downey, Khouri, & Feldman, 1997). Because it is possible, however, that some types of early family adversity foster a devaluation of relationships and a disinvestment in relationships as a source of self-worth, future work needs to examine how adversity is linked to these types of appraisals.

Early Adversity and Social-Behavioral Deficits

Early family adversity is also presumed to drive the emergence of social-behavioral deficits associated with youth depression. Youth who are exposed to serious family adversity are more likely to feel overwhelmed when faced with challenge, and thus might demonstrate involuntary rather than planful responses to stress. More specifically, for instance, according to attachment theory, parent–child attachment and resulting internal working models form the cornerstone for subsequent responses to stress (Bowlby, 1969, 1982; Cassidy, 1994). Youth with a history of insecure attachment might therefore have greater difficulty effectively regulating their emotions and behavior in response to social challenges. Likewise, exposure to maternal depression might lead to maladaptive responses to social challenge through either modeling of ineffective maternal coping or through explicit socialization practices. As discussed earlier, exposure to significant family disruption or loss also might engender a sense of a lack of control, which results in less active, planful responses to stress, lower social initiative, and a tendency to disengage from stressful social situations. Finally, early family adversity might foster an interpersonal style characterized by negative behavioral self-focus. For example, youth exposed to overly critical parenting might make excessive negative self-statements aimed at either seeking reassurance of their worth or eliciting negative feedback that is consistent with their self-view.

Research supports the idea that early family adversity constitutes a risk factor for the emergence of social-behavioral deficits linked to depression, although much of this research focuses on early to middle childhood rather than adolescence. For example, insecure attachment is linked to less effective emotion regulation during infancy and toddlerhood (Diener, Mangelsdorf, McHale, & Frosch, 2002; Kochanska, 2001), but these findings are not specific to responses to social challenges. During adolescence, insecurely attached youth engage in less support seeking (Shirk, Gudmundsen, & Burwell, 2005) and more maladaptive avoidant responses to stress (Howard & Medway, 2004); again, these findings are not specific to social challenge, but are consistent with a tendency toward social disengagement. During adolescence, insecurely attached youth seek less positive feedback than securely attached youth (Cassidy, Ziv, Mehta, & Feeney, 2003). Research also shows that early adolescents exposed to a moderate or severe disruption in parent–child relationships demonstrate more helplessness when faced with social challenges than those exposed to no disruption or to a mild disruption (Rudolph et al., 2001). Finally, maternal depression is linked to less active socialization of responses to stress in youth (Abaied & Rudolph, 2007, in a mixed-age sample).

Early Adversity and Relationship Disturbances

Premise 7 further holds that early family adversity is reflected in, and contributes to, disturbances in adolescent relationships. Many forms of early adversity are likely to be expressed in the form of ongoing family stressors (e.g., low parental support, heightened parent–child conflict). Moreover, it is proposed that a history of adversity increases youths' tendency to *create* disturbances in their relationships as a result of their social-behavioral deficits. Finally, early adversity might enhance youths' *reactivity* to relationship disturbances. A history of adversity might lower the threshold for depressive responses to interpersonal stress, such that youth show heightened depression even in the presence of mild stress. Alternatively, a history of adversity might amplify stress reactivity at high levels of interpersonal stress, such that recent stress is more strongly associated with depression in youth exposed to high than low levels of adversity (Rudolph & Flynn, 2007).

Consistent with this premise, research links family adversity to relationship disturbances. Examining the interpersonal processes underlying the intergenerational transmission of depression, Hammen, Shih, and Brennan (2004) found that heightened interpersonal stress experienced by depressed mothers undermined parenting quality; maladaptive parenting predicted disturbances in adolescents' peer relationships and the generation of interpersonal stress. Research also links insecure attachment (Troy & Sroufe, 1987; Youngblade & Belsky, 1992) and child maltreatment (Shields, Cicchetti, & Ryan, 1994) to relationship disturbances during early and middle childhood, such as peer rejection, exposure to peer victimization, and lower quality friendships.

Moreover, research supports the idea that youth exposed to early family adversity show heightened reactivity (i.e., depressive responses) to recent stressors (Hammen, Henry, & Daley, 2000; Harkness, Bruce, & Lumley, 2006), particularly those involving relationships (Rudolph & Flynn, 2007). This heightened reactivity differs as a function of sex and pubertal status (Rudolph & Flynn, 2007), demonstrating the importance of considering the developmental and sex-linked nature of interpersonal vulnerability.

Summary

Overall, research supports the idea that early family adversity contributes to the emergence of maladaptive relationship appraisals, social-behavioral deficits, and relationship disturbances that increase vulnerability to depression. This contribution likely occurs through multiple pathways, including internalization of negative conceptions of the self and relationships, modeling and socialization of maladaptive interpersonal styles, transmission of relationship disturbances, and both biological and psychological sensitization to interpersonal stress. Future research needs to elucidate how specific types of early adversity foster specific types of interpersonal vulnerability.

Premise 8: Depression has Negative Interpersonal Consequences

The final premise holds that depression undermines youths' appraisals of relationships, amplifies social-behavioral deficits, and causes youth to generate disturbances in their relationships. Although pioneering interpersonal models of adult depression (Coyne, 1976; Joiner et al., 1999), and developmental psychopathology models of depression (Cicchetti & Toth, 1998; Hammen, 1992; Rudolph et al., 2006) emphasize transactional processes, most theory and research on the interpersonal context of adolescent depression focuses on interpersonal dysfunction as an antecedent of depression. However, it is equally important to consider how depression contributes to future interpersonal dysfunction. Given the rapid growth and change characterizing the transition through adolescence, depression might have particularly detrimental interpersonal effects during this stage by hampering the natural maturation of abilities and the successful negotiation of new challenges. Thus, adolescent depression not only might have proximal adverse effects on interpersonal functioning during acute episodes, but also might exert long-term effects resulting from interference with normative developmental trajectories.

With regard to appraisals, depressive symptoms might cause youth to develop more negative conceptions of self and others for several reasons. Negative mood states induce heightened attention to, and memory for, negative information, thereby increasing the likelihood that youth will begin to view themselves and others in a negative light (Pomerantz & Rudolph, 2003). Moreover, rumination that is associated with depression promotes a focus on negative aspects of the self (Lyubomirsky, Caldwell, & Nolen-Hoeksema, 1998). Depressive symptoms, such as self-doubt and a poor self-concept, might cause youth to question their worth in relationships, and to therefore place greater reliance on evaluation and approval by others. Because conceptions of self and others likely begin to stabilize and generalize during adolescence, negative conceptions developed at this time might continue beyond the acute episode. Indeed, research shows that depressive symptoms predict subsequent declines in youths' views of self and relationships (Cole, Peeke, Dolezal, Murray,

& Canzoniero, 1999, in a mixed-age sample; Pomerantz & Rudolph, 2003, in a mixed-age sample), although there is no evidence to evaluate whether these declines are particularly salient or long-lasting during adolescence.

Specific symptoms and associated characteristics of depressed youth also might create or exacerbate social-behavioral deficits. In the short term, symptoms such as fatigue, anhedonia, and hopelessness might impair youths' efforts to cope actively with social challenges, and might cause youth to disengage from their relationships. Symptoms such as low self-worth might result in excessive reassurance seeking or a tendency to engage in excessive negative self-disclosures within relationships. Moreover, difficulties with emotion regulation might cause depressed youth to respond to social challenges in a dysregulated, rather than a planful, manner. In the long term, depressive symptoms might leave an interpersonal "scar" (Nolen-Hoeksema et al., 1992; Rohde, Lewinsohn, & Seeley, 1990) by interfering with the development of adaptive social skills. Research generally supports the idea that depressive symptoms create proximal deficits in social behavior (for a review, see Rudolph et al., 2008). Far less research examines long-term interpersonal consequences, but a growing body of evidence shows that depressive symptoms predict increases in social-behavioral deficits, such as social helplessness and negative feedback seeking, over short periods of time (for a review, see Rudolph et al., 2008).

Finally, depression might contribute to disturbances in youths' relationships either due to the immediate effects of depressive symptoms (e.g., irritability leading to interpersonal conflict) or due to the concomitant social-behavioral deficits (e.g., excessive reassurance seeking or social disengagement leading to social isolation or dissolution of relationships). In support of this idea, adolescent depression predicts subsequent disturbances in peer and romantic relationships (e.g., friendship instability, poor friendship quality, and peer rejection) and the generation of interpersonal stress (for a review, see Rudolph et al., 2008).

The adverse interpersonal consequences of depression might help to explain the continuity of depression over time. That is, depressive symptoms and associated impairment intensify pre-existing interpersonal vulnerabilities, thereby perpetuating or exacerbating depression. This transactional process sets the stage for chronic or recurrent depression, accounting for the continuity of depression through adolescence and adulthood. Moreover, this process might contribute to the growing sex difference in depression. Specifically, given the complex and emotionally challenging nature of adolescent girls' relationships, depression and associated behaviors might be more likely to disrupt adolescent girls' than boys' relationships (Prinstein et al., 2005; Rudolph, Ladd, & Dinella, 2007), thereby fueling the cycle of interpersonal dysfunction and depression in girls. Indeed, research shows that transactions between depression and interpersonal stress contribute to the continuity of depression over time in adolescent girls, but not boys (Rudolph, Flynn, Abaied, Groot, & Thompson, in press). Given the implications of this self-perpetuating cycle for youths' long-term development, additional prospective studies are needed to investigate the possible effects of depression on interpersonal adjustment.

SUMMARY AND FUTURE DIRECTIONS

To summarize the proposed interpersonal model of adolescent depression (see Figure 14.1), early family adversity (e.g., parental depression, insecure attachment, maltreatment) contributes to the emergence of maladaptive appraisals of relationships and social-behavioral deficits. These interpersonal vulnerabilities potentiate depressive responses to future interpersonal challenges, as well as cause youth to generate disturbances in their relationships and to select into more stressful social contexts. Notably, this model considers how the transition through adolescence—marked by normative social-contextual, physical-maturational, and cognitive-developmental changes—serves as a sensitive period for the activation of interpersonal vulnerability to depression. Girls are particularly vulnerable to this intensification process because they possess heightened interpersonal vulnerability and are exposed to more social challenges during this transition. Finally, depression exacerbates preexisting interpersonal vulnerabilities and relationship disturbances, and interferes with the development of new interpersonal competencies, thereby fueling an ongoing cycle of disturbance that accounts, in part, for the continuity of depression through adolescence and into adulthood.

Empirical data support many components of this model, although prospective longitudinal research needs to distinguish the interpersonal antecedents versus consequences of youth depression. Moreover, explicit examination of the proposed effects of the adolescent transition would be helpful for clarifying the precise processes through which developmental changes influence interpersonal vulnerability to depression and the emergence of a sex difference in depression during this stage. In addition to closer empirical scrutiny of this model, advances in theory and research on the interpersonal context of adolescent depression require linking interpersonal theories with other prominent theories to provide a more comprehensive perspective on the emergence and progression of depression over time.

Perhaps one of the most pressing needs is to integrate interpersonal theories with genetic and biological theories of depression. From the perspective of interpersonal theories, this integration could elucidate possible genetic and/or biological pathways that underlie the intergenerational transmission of interpersonal vulnerability. Conversely, from the perspective of genetic and biological theories, this integration could elucidate how genetic and biological influences are translated into psychosocial dysfunction. For example, the family might contribute to interpersonal vulnerability not only through exposure to early adversity and maladaptive socialization processes, but also through transmission of a genetic liability (e.g., a temperamental predisposition to heightened interpersonal stress generation or stress reactivity). Indeed, some research documents a genetic liability to stress exposure (Silberg et al., 1999) and stress reactivity (Eley et al., 2004), particularly in adolescent girls. Moreover, exposure to early family adversity might trigger biological sensitization to stress (Post, 1992), which is expressed in the form of maladaptive self-regulation in response to subsequent relationship disturbances. Linking interpersonal and biological perspectives on adolescent depression would also help to clarify how biological, psychological, and social changes associated with puberty independently or jointly contribute to risk for depression.

Theory and research would also benefit from considering the interpersonal context of *resilience* to depression, particularly with regard to how the interpersonal characteristics and experiences of girls might buffer them from depression. In recent years, growing attention has focused on how girls' orientation toward relationships and interpersonal experiences intensify their risk for depression during the adolescent transition, as reflected in the proposed model. Yet, adolescent girls' heightened investment in relationships also has adaptive counterparts (e.g., connection-oriented goals, valuing of intimacy and friendship, empathy) that can serve a protective function by helping girls to develop positive appraisals about relationships and interpersonal competencies, and to establish supportive and rewarding social bonds (for a comprehensive review of the socioemotional trade-offs of sex-linked relationship processes, see Rose & Rudolph, 2006). Thus, it is critical to supplement interpersonal theories of depression that highlight the "dark side" of girls' relationships with perspectives that consider how to build on the strengths of these relationships as a protective mechanism against depression.

Recent research supports the potential promise of this complementary perspective. In one study, low stress, supportive peer relationships buffered girls against the depression-inducing effects of early maturation (Conley & Rudolph, in press). Another study revealed that adolescent girls' positive social self-perceptions buffered them from depression (Eberhart, Shih, Hammen, & Brennan, 2006). In some cases, therefore, characteristics of girls' relationships might provide resilience against the interpersonal challenges of the adolescent transition. A key mission for future research is to identify how to reap the benefits of girls' investment in relationships without encumbering the emotional drawbacks. Moreover, despite adolescent girls' elevated risk for depression relative to boys, it should not be forgotten that some adolescent boys do suffer from depression. Research is needed to determine whether similar interpersonal vulnerabilities and social challenges account for depression in adolescent boys as in girls, or whether boys follow alternate pathways to depression.

Finally, the proposed model focuses on the role of the adolescent transition as a developmental context of risk for interpersonal vulnerability to depression. However, transitions represent turning points at which youth either can progress along maladaptive developmental trajectories or can move toward more adaptive pathways (Schulenberg, Maggs, & Hurrelmann, 1997). For example, reorganization of peer groups might provide youth with the opportunity to redirect patterns that are ingrained in context of former relationships. Similarly, romantic relationships might provide novel contexts for the development of intimacy that youth were previously unable to attain. Considering the prospects, rather than just the pitfalls, presented by the adolescent transition would contribute significantly not only to theory aimed at understanding the onset and progression of adolescent depression, but also to interventions aimed at preventing depression during this critical developmental stage.

REFERENCES

Abaied, J., & Rudolph, K. D. (2007). *Maternal socialization of coping during early adolescence.* Manuscript submitted for publication.

Abela, J. R. Z., Hankin, B. L., Haigh, E. A. P., Adams, P., Vinokuroff, T., & Trayhern, L. (2005). Interpersonal vulnerability to depression in high-risk children: The role of insecure attachment and reassurance seeking. *Journal of Clinical Child and Adolescent Psychology, 34*, 182–192.

Abela, J. R. Z., McIntyre-Smith, A., & Dechef, M. L. E. (2003). Personality predispositions to depression: A test of the specific vulnerability and symptom specificity hypotheses. *Journal of Social and Clinical Psychology, 22*, 493–514.

Abela, J. R. Z., & Taylor, G. (2003). Specific vulnerability to depressive mood reactions in schoolchildren: The moderating role of self-esteem. *Journal of Clinical Child and Adolescent Psychology, 32*, 408–418.

Abela, J. R. Z., Zuroff, D. C., Ho, M. R., Adams, P., & Hankin, B. L. (2006). Excessive reassurance seeking, hassles, and depressive symptoms in children of affectively ill parents: A multiwave longitudinal study. *Journal of Abnormal Child Psychology, 34*, 171–187.

Ainsworth, M. D., Blehar, M., Waters, E., & Wall, S. (1978). *Patterns of attachment: A psychological study of the strange situation.* Hillsdale, NJ: Lawrence Erlbaum.

Allen, J. P., Hauser, S. T., Bell, K. L., & O'Connor, T. G. (1994). Longitudinal assessment of autonomy and relatedness in adolescent-family interactions as predictors of adolescent ego development and self-esteem. *Child Development, 65*, 179–194.

Alsaker, F. D. (1995). Timing of puberty and reactions to pubertal changes. In M. Rutter (Ed.), *Psychosocial disturbances in young people: Challenges for prevention* (pp. 37–82). Cambridge: Cambridge University Press.

Angold, A., Costello, E. J., & Worthman, C. M. (1998). Puberty and depression: The roles of age, pubertal status and pubertal timing. *Psychological Medicine, 28*, 51–61.

Baker, M., Milich, R., & Manolis, M. (1996). Peer interactions of dysphoric adolescents. *Journal of Abnormal Child Psychology, 24*, 241–255.

Baldwin, M. W. (1992). Relational schemas and the processing of social information. *Psychological Bulletin, 112*, 461–484.

Blatt, S. J., & Homann, E. (1992). Parent–child interaction in the etiology of dependent and self-critical depression. *Clinical Psychology Review, 12*, 47–91.

Boivin, M., Hymel, S., & Bukowski, W. M. (1995). The roles of social withdrawal, peer rejection, and victimization by peers in predicting loneliness and depressed mood in childhood. *Development and Psychopathology, 7*, 765–785.

Borelli, J. L., & Prinstein, M. J. (2006). Reciprocal, longitudinal associations between adolescents' negative feedback-seeking, depressive symptoms, and friendship perceptions. *Journal of Abnormal Child Psychology, 34*, 159–169.

Bowlby, J. (1969, 1982). *Attachment and loss: Vol. I. Attachment.* New York: Basic Books.

Bowlby, J. (1980). *Attachment and loss: Vol. 3. Loss: Sadness and depression.* New York: Basic Books.

Boyce, P., & Parker, G. (1989). Development of a scale to measure interpersonal sensitivity. *Australian and New Zealand Journal of Psychiatry, 23*, 341–351.

Brendgen, M., Vitaro, F., Turgeon, L., & Poulin, F. (2002). Assessing aggressive and depressed children's social relations with classmates and friends: A matter of perspective. *Journal of Abnormal Child Psychology, 30*, 609–624.

Brooks-Gunn, J. (1984). The psychological significance of different pubertal events to young girls. *Journal of Early Adolescence, 4*, 315–327.

Brooks-Gunn, J., & Warren, M. P. (1988). The psychological significance of secondary sexual characteristics in nine- to eleven-year-old girls. *Child Development, 59*, 1061–1069.

Brown, B. B., Dolcini, M. N., & Leventhal, A. (1997). Transformations in peer relationships at adolescence: Implications for health-related behavior. In J. Schulenberg, J. L. Maggs & K. Hurrelmann (Eds.), *Health risks and developmental transitions during adolescence* (pp. 161–189). New York: Cambridge University Press.

Brozina, K., & Abela, J. R. Z. (2006). Behavioural inhibition, anxious symptoms, and depressive symptoms: A short-term prospective examination of a diathesis-stress model. *Behaviour Research and Therapy, 44*, 1337–1346.

Buss, A. (1980). *Self-consciousness and social anxiety.* San Francisco, CA: W.H. Freeman.

Caldwell, M. S., Rudolph, K. D., Troop-Gordon, W., & Kim, D. (2004). Reciprocal influences among relational self-views, social disengagement, and peer stress during early adolescence. *Child Development, 75*, 1140–1154.

Caspi, A., & Moffitt, T. E. (1991). Individual differences are accentuated during periods of social change: The sample case of girls at puberty. *Journal of Personality and Social Psychology, 61*, 157–168.

Cassidy, J. (1994). Emotion regulation: Influences of attachment relationships. *Monographs of the Society for Research in Child Development, 59*, 228–283.

Cassidy, J., Ziv, Y., Mehta, T. G., & Feeney, B. C. (2003). Feedback seeking in children and adolescents: Associations with self-perceptions, attachment representations, and depression. *Child Development, 74*, 612–628.

Centers for Disease Control and Prevention. (2006). Youth risk behavior surveillance–United States, 2005. *Morbidity and Mortality Weekly Report, 55*, 1–108.

Cicchetti, D., & Howes, P. W. (1991). Developmental psychopathology in the context of the family: Illustrations from the study of child maltreatment. *Canadian Journal of Behavioural Science, 23*, 257–281.

Cicchetti, D., & Rogosch, F. A. (2002). A developmental psychopathology perspective on adolescence. *Journal of Consulting and Clinical Psychology, 70*, 6–20.

Cicchetti, D., & Toth, S. L. (1998). The development of depression in children and adolescents. *American Psychologist, 53*, 221–241.

Clark, D. A., Steer, R. A., Beck, A. T., & Ross, L. (1995). Psychometric characteristics of revised sociotropy and autonomy scales in college students. *Behavior Research and Therapy, 33*, 325–334.

Cole, D. A., Martin, J. M., Peeke, L. G., Seroczynski, A. D., & Hoffman, K. (1998). Are cognitive errors of underestimation predictive or reflective of depressive symptoms in children: A longitudinal study. *Journal of Abnormal Psychology, 107*, 481–496.

Cole, D. A., Peeke, L., Dolezal, S., Murray, N., & Canzoniero, A. (1999). A longitudinal study of negative affect and self-perceived competence in young adolescents. *Journal of Personality and Social Psychology, 77*, 851–862.

Compas, B. E., Connor-Smith, J. K., Saltzman, H., Thomsen, A. H., & Wadsworth, M. E. (2001). Coping with stress during childhood and adolescence: Progress, problems, and potential in theory and research. *Psychological Bulletin, 12*, 87–127.

Compian, L., & Hayward, C. (2003). Gender differences in opposite sex relationships: Interactions with puberty. In C. Hayward (Ed.), *Gender differences at puberty* (pp. 77–92). New York: Cambridge University Press.

Conley, C. S., & Rudolph, K. D. (in press). The emerging sex difference in adolescent depression: Interacting contributions of puberty and peer stress. *Development and Psychopathology.*

Conley, C. S., & Rudolph, K. D. (2008). The role of peer stress in mediating links between pubertal development and depression in adolescence. Manuscript in preparation.

Connolly, J., Geller, S., Marton, P., & Kutcher, S. (1992). Peer responses to social interaction with depressed adolescents. *Journal of Clinical Child Psychology, 21*, 365–370.

Connor-Smith, J. K., Compas, B. E., Wadsworth, M. E., Thomsen, A. H., & Saltzman, H. (2000). Responses to stress in adolescence: Measurement of coping and involuntary stress responses. *Journal of Consulting and Clinical Psychology, 68*, 976–992.

Cooper, M. L., Shaver, P. R., & Collins, N. L. (1998). Attachment styles, emotion regulation, and adjustment in adolescence. *Journal of Personality and Social Psychology, 74*, 1380–1397.

Cox, A. D., Puckering, C., Pound, A., & Mills, M. (1987). The impact of maternal depression in young children. *Journal of Child Psychology and Psychiatry, 28*, 917–928.

Coyne, J. C. (1976). Depression and the response of others. *Journal of Abnormal Psychology, 85*, 186–193.

Craig, W. M., Pepler, D., Connolly, J., & Henderson, K. (2001). Developmental context of peer harassment in early adolescence: The role of puberty and the peer group. In J. Juvonen & S. Graham (Eds.), *Peer harassment in school: The plight of the vulnerable and victimized* (pp. 242–261). New York: Guilford Press.

Crocker, J., & Wolfe, C. T. (2001). Contingencies of self-worth. *Psychological Review, 108*, 593–623.

Crockett, L. J., & Petersen, A. C. (1987). Pubertal status and psychosocial development: Findings from the early adolescence study. In R. M. Lerner & T. T. Foch (Eds.), *Biological-psychosocial interactions in early adolescence* (pp. 173–188). Hillsdale, NJ: Erlbaum.

Cummings, E. M., & Cicchetti, D. (1990). Towards a transactional model of relations between attachment and depression. In M. Greenberg, D. Cicchetti & M. Cummings (Eds.), *Attachment in the preschool years* (pp. 339–372). Chicago, IL: University of Chicago Press.

Cyranowski, J. M., Frank, E., Young, E., & Shear, K. (2000). Adolescent onset of the gender difference in lifetime rates of depression. *Archives of General Psychiatry, 57*, 21–27.

Dadds, M. R., Sanders, M. R., Morrison, M., & Rebgetz, M. (1992). Childhood depression and conduct disorder: II. An analysis of family interaction patterns in the home. *Journal of Abnormal Psychology, 101*, 505–513.

Daley, S. E., & Hammen, C. (2002). Depressive symptoms and close relationships during the transition to adulthood: Perspectives from dysphoric women, their best friends, and their romantic partners. *Journal of Consulting and Clinical Psychology, 70*, 129–141.

Damon, W., & Hart, D. (1982). The development of self-understanding from infancy through adolescence. *Child Development, 53*, 841–864.

Davies, P. T., & Windle, M. (1997). Gender-specific pathways between maternal depressive symptoms, family discord, and adolescent adjustment. *Developmental Psychology, 33*, 657–668.

DeRose, L. M., Wright, A. J., & Brooks-Gunn, J. (2006). Does puberty account for the gender differential in depression? In C. L. M. Keyes & S. H. Goodman (Eds.), *Women and depression: A handbook for the social, behavioral, and biomedical sciences* (pp. 89–128). New York: Cambridge University Press.

Diener, M. L., Mangelsdorf, S. C., McHale, J. L., & Frosch, C. A. (2002). Infants' behavioral strategies for emotion regulation with fathers and mothers: Associations with emotional expressions and attachment quality. *Infancy, 3*, 153–174.

Donovan, J. E., Jessor, R., & Costa, F. M. (1988). Syndrome of problem behavior in adolescence: A replication. *Journal of Consulting and Clinical Psychology, 56*, 762–765.

Downey, G., & Feldman, S. I. (1996). Implications of rejection sensitivity for intimate relationships. *Journal of Personality and Social Psychology, 70*, 1327–1343.

Downey, G., Khouri, H., & Feldman, S. (1997). Early interpersonal trauma and adult adjustment: The mediational role of rejection sensitivity. In D. Cicchetti & S. Toth (Eds.), *Rochester Symposium on Developmental Psychopathology: Vol. 8. The effects of trauma on the developmental process* (pp. 85–114). Rochester, NY: University of Rochester Press.

Downey, G., Lebolt, A., Rincon, C., & Freitas, A. L. (1998). Rejection sensitivity and children's interpersonal difficulties. *Child Development, 69*, 1072–1089.

Eberhart, N. K., Shih, J. H., Hammen, C. L., & Brennan, P. A. (2006). Understanding the sex difference in vulnerability to adolescent depression: An examination of child and parent characteristics. *Journal of Abnormal Psychology, 34*, 495–508.

Eley, T. C., Sugden, K., Corsico, A., Gregory, A. M., Sham, P., McGuffin, P., et al. (2004). Gene-environment interaction analysis of serotonin system markers with adolescent depression. *Molecular Psychiatry, 9*, 908–918.

Fichman, L., Koestner, R., & Zuroff, D. C. (1997). Dependency and distress at summer camp. *Journal of Youth and Adolescence, 26*, 217–232.

Flynn, M., & Rudolph, K. D. (2007). Perceptual asymmetry and youths' responses to stress: Understanding vulnerability to depression. *Cognition and Emotion, 21*, 773–788.

Fritz, H. L., & Helgeson, V. S. (1998). Distinctions of unmitigated communion from communion: Self-neglect and over involvement with others. *Journal of Personality and Social Psychology, 75*, 121–140.

Frye, A. A., & Garber, J. (2005). The relations among maternal depression, maternal criticism, and adolescents' externalizing and internalizing symptoms. *Journal of Abnormal Child Psychology, 33*, 1–11.

Furman, W., & Buhrmester, D. (1992). Age and sex differences in perceptions of networks of personal relationships. *Child Development, 63*, 103–115.
Furman, W., & Wehner, E. A. (1997). Adolescent romantic relationships: A developmental perspective. In S. Shulman & W. A. Collins (Eds.), *New directions for child development: Adolescent romantic relationships* (pp. 21–36). San Francisco, CA: Jossey-Bass.
Garber, J., Robinson, N. S., & Valentiner, D. (1997). The relation between parenting and adolescent depression: Self-worth as a mediator. *Journal of Adolescent Research, 12*, 12–33.
Garber, J., Weiss, B., & Shanley, N. (1993). Cognitions, depressive symptoms, and development in adolescents. *Journal of Abnormal Psychology, 102*, 47–57.
Gazelle, H., & Rudolph, K. D. (2004). Moving toward and away from the world: Social approach and avoidance trajectories in anxious solitary youth. *Child Development, 75*, 829–849.
Ge, X., Conger, R. D., & Elder, G. H., Jr. (1996). Coming of age too early: Pubertal influences on girls' vulnerability to psychological distress. *Child Development, 67*, 3386–3400.
Ge, X., Conger, R. D., & Elder, G. H., Jr. (2001). Pubertal transition, stressful life events, and the emergence of gender differences in adolescent depressive symptoms. *Developmental Psychology, 37*, 404–417.
Goodman, S. H. (2002). Depression and early adverse experiences. In I. H. Gotlib & C. Hammen (Eds.), *Handbook of depression* (pp. 245–267). New York, NY: Guilford Press.
Goodman, S. H., & Gotlib, I. H. (1999). Risk for psychopathology in the children of depressed mothers: A developmental model for understanding mechanisms of transmission. *Psychological Review, 106*, 458–490.
Goodyer, I. M., & Altham, P. M. E. (1991). Lifetime exit events in anxiety and depression in school age children: I. *Journal of Affective Disorders, 21*, 219–228.
Gore, S., Aseltine, R. H., & Colton, M. E. (1993). Gender, social-relational involvement, and depression. *Journal of Research on Adolescence, 3*, 101–125.
Graber, J. A. (2003). Puberty in context. In C. Hayward (Ed.), *Gender differences at puberty* (pp. 307–325). New York: Cambridge University Press.
Grolnick, W. S., & Ryan, R. M. (1989). Parent styles associated with children's self-regulation and competence in school. *Journal of Educational Psychology, 81*, 143–154.
Hammen, C. (1991). The generation of stress in the course of unipolar depression. *Journal of Abnormal Psychology, 100*, 555–561.
Hammen, C. (1992). Cognitive, life stress, and interpersonal approaches to a developmental psychopathology model of depression. *Development and Psychopathology, 4*, 191–208.
Hammen, C. (2006). Stress generation in depression: Reflections on origins, research, and future directions. *Journal of Clinical Psychology, 62*, 1065–1082.
Hammen, C., Burge, D., Daley, S. E., Davila, J., Paley, B., & Rudolph, K. D. (1995). Interpersonal attachment cognitions and prediction of symptomatic responses to interpersonal stress. *Journal of Abnormal Psychology, 104*, 436–443.

Hammen, C., Henry, R., & Daley, S. E. (2000). Depression and sensitization to stressors among young women as a function of childhood adversity. *Journal of Consulting and Clinical Psychology, 68*, 782–787.

Hammen, C., Shih, J. H., & Brennan, P. A. (2004). Intergenerational transmission of depression: Test of an interpersonal stress model in a community sample. *Journal of Consulting and Clinical Psychology, 72*, 511–522.

Hankin, B. L., & Abela, J. R. Z. (2005). *Development of psychopathology: A vulnerability-stress perspective*. London: Sage.

Hankin, B. L., & Abramson, L. Y. (2001). Development of gender differences in depression: An elaborated cognitive vulnerability-transactional stress theory. *Psychological Bulletin, 127*, 773–796.

Hankin, B. L., Mermelstein, R., & Roesch, L. (2007). Sex differences in adolescent depression: Stress exposure and reactivity models in interpersonal and achievement contextual domains. *Child Development, 78*, 279–295.

Harkness, K. L., Bruce, A. E., & Lumley, M. N. (2006). The role of childhood abuse and neglect in the sensitization to stressful life events in adolescent depression. *Journal of Abnormal Psychology, 115*, 730–741.

Harkness, K. L., & Lumley, M. N. (2008). Child abuse and neglect and the development of depression in children and adolescents. In J. R. Z. Abela & B. L. Hankin (Eds.), *Handbook of depression in children and adolescents* (pp. 466–488). New York: Guilford Press

Harter, S. (1988). Developmental and dynamic changes in the nature of the self-concept: Implications for child psychotherapy. In S. R. Shirk (Ed.), *Cognitive development and child psychotherapy* (pp. 119–160). New York: Plenum Press.

Harter, S., Stocker, C., & Robinson, N. S. (1996). The perceived directionality of the link between approval and self-worth: The liabilities of a looking glass self-orientation among young adolescents. *Journal of Research on Adolescence, 6*, 285–308.

Hayward, C., Gotlib, I. J., Schraedley, P. K., & Litt, I. F. (1999). Ethnic differences in the association between pubertal status and symptoms of depression in adolescent girls. *Journal of Adolescent Health, 25*, 143–149.

Hayward, C., & Sanborn, K. (2002). Puberty and the emergence of gender differences in psychopathology. *Journal of Adolescent Health, 30*, 49–58.

Herman-Stahl, M., & Petersen, A. C. (1999). Depressive symptoms during adolescence: Direct and stress-buffering effects of coping, control beliefs, and family relationships. *Journal of Applied Developmental Psychology, 20*, 45–62.

Higgins, E. T. (1991). Development of self-regulatory and self-evaluative processes: Costs, benefits, and tradeoffs. In M. R. Gunnar & L. A. Sroufe (Eds.), *Self processes and development: The Minnesota Symposia on Child Development* (Vol. 23, pp. 125–166). Hillsdale, NJ: Lawrence Erlbaum.

Hill, J. P. (1988). Adapting to menarche: Familial control and conflict. In M. Gunnar & W. A. Collins (Eds.), *Minnesota symposia on child development* (Vol. 21, pp. 43–77). Hillsdale, NJ: Lawrence Erlbaum.

Hill, J. P., & Lynch, M. E. (1983). The intensification of gender-related role expectations during early adolescence. In J. Brooks-Gunn & A. C. Petersen (Eds.), *Girls at puberty* (pp. 201–228). New York: Plenum Press.

Hops, H., Lewinsohn, P. M., Andrews, J. A., & Roberts, R. E. (1990). Psychosocial correlates of depressive symptomatology among high school students. *Journal of Clinical Child Psychology, 3*, 211–220.

Howard, M. S., & Medway, F. J. (2004). Adolescents' attachment and coping with stress. *Psychology in the Schools, 41*, 391–402.

Huddleston, J., & Ge, X. (2003). Boys at puberty: Psychosocial implications. In C. Hayward (Ed.), *Gender differences at puberty* (pp. 113–134). New York: Cambridge University Press.

Jaser, S. S., Langrock, A. M., Keller, G., Merchant, M. J., Benson, M. A., Reeslund, K., et al. (2005). Coping with the stress of parental depression II: Adolescent and parent reports of coping and adjustment. *Journal of Clinical Child and Adolescent Psychology, 34*, 193–205.

Joiner, T. E., Jr. (1997). Shyness and low social support as interactive diatheses, with loneliness as mediator: Testing an interpersonal-personality view of vulnerability to depressive symptoms. *Journal of Abnormal Psychology, 106*, 386–394.

Joiner, T. E. (2002). Depression in its interpersonal context. In I. H. Gotlib & C. L. Hammen (Eds.), *Handbook of depression* (pp. 295–313). New York: Guilford.

Joiner, T. E., Coyne, J. C., & Blalock, J. (1999). On the interpersonal nature of depression: Overview and synthesis. In T. E. Joiner & J. C. Coyne (Eds.), *The interactional nature of depression* (pp. 3–19). Washington, DC: American Psychological Association.

Joyner, K., & Udry, J. R. (2000). You don't bring me anything but down: Adolescent romance and depression. *Journal of Health and Social Behavior, 41*, 369–391.

Keating, D. P. (2004). Cognitive and brain development. In R. M. Lerner & L. Steinberg (Eds.), *Handbook of adolescent psychology* (pp. 45–84). Hoboken, NJ: John Wiley & Sons.

Kobak, R. R., Sudler, N., & Gamble, W. (1991). Attachment and depressive symptoms during adolescence: A developmental pathways analysis. *Development and Psychopathology, 3*, 461–474.

Kochanska, G. (2001). Emotional development in children with different attachment histories: The first three years. *Child Development, 72*, 474–490.

Krackow, E., & Rudolph, K. D. (2008). Life stress and the accuracy of cognitive appraisals in depressed youth. *Journal of Clinical Child and Adolescent Psychology, 37*, 376–385.

La Greca, A. M., & Harrison, H. M. (2005) Adolescent peer relations, friendships, and romantic relationships: Do they predict social anxiety and depression? *Journal of Clinical Child and Adolescent Psychology, 34*, 49–61.

Langrock, A. M., Compas, B. E., Keller, G., Merchant, M. J., & Copeland, M. E. (2002). Coping with the stress of parental depression: Parents' reports of children's coping, emotional, and behavioral problems. *Journal of Clinical Child and Adolescent Psychology, 31*, 312–324.

Laursen, B. (1996). Closeness and conflict in adolescent peer relationships: Interdependence with friends and romantic partners. In W. M. Bukowski & A. F. Newcomb (Eds.), *The company they keep: Friendship in childhood and adolescence. Cambridge studies in social and emotional development* (pp. 186–210). New York: Cambridge University Press.

Leadbeater, B. J., Kuperminc, G. P., Blatt, S. J., & Herzog, C. (1999). A multivariate model of gender differences in adolescents' internalizing and externalizing problems. *Developmental Psychology, 35*, 1268–1282.

Leaper, C., & Anderson, K. J. (1997). Gender development and heterosexual romantic relationships during adolescence. In S. Shulman & W. A. Collins (Eds.), *Romantic relationships in adolescence: Developmental perspectives. New directions for child development, 78* (pp. 85–103). San Francisco, CA: Jossey-Bass.

Lerner, R. M. (1985). Adolescent maturational changes and psychosocial development: A dynamic interactional perspective. *Journal of Youth and Adolescence, 14*, 355–372.

Lewinsohn, P. M., Roberts, R. E., Seeley, J. R., Rohde, P., Gotlib, I. H., & Hops, H. (1994). Adolescent psychopathology: II. Psychosocial risk factors for depression. *Journal of Abnormal Psychology, 103*, 302–315.

Lovejoy, C. M., Graczyk, P. A., O'Hare, E., & Neuman, G. (2000). Maternal depression and parenting behavior: A meta-analytic review. *Clinical Psychology Review, 20*, 561–592.

Lynch, M., & Cicchetti, D. (1998). Trauma, mental representation, and the organization of memory for mother-referent material. *Development and Psychopathology, 10*, 739–759.

Lyubomirsky, S., Caldwell, N. D., & Nolen-Hoeksema, S. (1998). Effects of ruminative and distracting responses to depressed mood on retrieval of autobiographical memories. *Journal of Personality and Social Psychology, 75*, 166–177.

Magnusson, D. (1988). *Individual development from an interactional perspective: A longitudinal study*. Hillsdale, NJ: Lawrence Erlbaum.

Magnusson, D., Stattin, H., & Allen, V. L. (1986). Differential maturation among girls and its relation to social adjustment: A longitudinal perspective. In P. B. Baltes, D. L. Featherman & R. M. Lerner (Eds.), *Life-span development and behavior* (Vol. 7, pp. 135–172). Hillsdale, NJ: Lawrence Erlbaum.

Main, M., Kaplan, N., & Cassidy, J. (1985). Security in infancy, childhood, and adulthood: A move to the level of representation. In I. Bretherton & E. Waters (Eds.), Growing points in attachment theory and research. *Monographs of the Society for Research in Child Development, 50*, 66–104.

Messer, S. C., & Gross, A. M. (1995). Childhood depression and family interaction: A naturalistic observation study. *Journal of Clinical Child Psychology, 24*, 77–88.

Monroe, S. M., Rohde, P., Seeley, J. R., & Lewinsohn, P. M. (1999). Life events and depression in adolescence: Relationship loss as a prospective risk factor for first onset of major depressive disorder. *Journal of Abnormal Psychology, 108*, 606–614.

Murray, L., Woolgar, M., Cooper, P., & Hipwell, A. (2001). Cognitive vulnerability to depression in 5-year-old children of depressed mothers. *Journal of Child Psychology and Psychiatry, 42*, 891–899.

Natsuaki, M. N., Biehl, M. C., & Ge, X. (in press). Trajectories of depressed mood from early adolescence to young adulthood: The effects of pubertal timing and adolescent dating. *Journal of Early Adolescence.*

Nolan, S. A., Flynn, C., & Garber, J. (2003). Prospective relations between rejection and depression in young adolescents. *Journal of Personality and Social Psychology, 85*, 745–755.

Nolen-Hoeksema, S. (2000). The role of rumination in depressive disorders and mixed anxiety/depressive symptoms. *Journal of Abnormal Psychology, 109*, 504–511.

Nolen-Hoeksema, S. (2001). Gender differences in depression. *Current Directions in Psychological Science, 10*, 173–176.

Nolen-Hoeksema, S., & Girgus, J. S. (1994). The emergence of gender differences in depression in adolescence. *Psychological Bulletin, 115*, 424–443.

Nolen-Hoeksema, S., Girgus, J. S., & Seligman, M. E. (1992). Predictors and consequences of childhood depressive symptoms: A 5-year longitudinal study. *Journal of Abnormal Psychology, 101*, 405–422.

Paikoff, R. L., & Brooks-Gunn, J. (1991). Do parent–child relationships change during puberty? *Psychological Bulletin, 110*, 47–66.

Petersen, A. C., Silbereisen, R. K., & Sorensen, S. (1996). Adolescent development: A global perspective. In K. Hurrelmann & S. F. Hamilton (Eds.), *Social problems and social contexts in adolescence: Perspectives across boundaries* (pp. 3–37). Hawthorne, NY: de Gruyter.

Pomerantz, E. M., & Rudolph, K. D. (2003). What ensues from emotional distress? Implications for competence estimation. *Child Development, 74*, 329–345.

Post, R. M. (1992). Transduction of psychosocial stress into the neurobiology of recurrent affective disorder. *American Journal of Psychiatry, 149*, 999–1010.

Potthoff, J. G., Holahan, C. J., & Joiner, T. E. (1995). Reassurance seeking, stress generation, and depressive symptoms: An integrative model. *Journal of Personality and Social Psychology, 68*, 664–670.

Prinstein, M. J., & Aikins, J. W. (2004). Cognitive moderators of the longitudinal association between peer rejection and adolescent depressive symptoms. *Journal of Abnormal Child Psychology, 32*, 147–158.

Prinstein, M. J., Borelli, J. L., Cheah, C. S. L., Simon, V. A., & Aikins, J. W. (2005). Adolescent girls' interpersonal vulnerability to depressive symptoms: A longitudinal examination of reassurance-seeking and peer relationships. *Journal of Abnormal Psychology, 114*, 676–688.

Prinstein, M. J., & La Greca, A. M. (2004). Childhood peer rejection and aggression as predictors of externalizing and health risk behaviors: A six-year longitudinal study. *Journal of Consulting and Clinical Psychology, 72*, 103–112.

Puig-Antich, J., Kaufman, J., Ryan, N. D., Williamson, D. E., Dahl, R. E., Lukens, E., et al. (1993). The psychosocial functioning and family environment of depressed adolescents. *Journal of the American Academy of Child & Adolescent Psychiatry, 32*, 244–253.

Rohde, P., Lewinsohn, P. M., & Seeley, J. R. (1990). Are people changed by the experience of having an episode of depression? A further test of the scar hypothesis. *Journal of Abnormal Psychology, 99*(3), 264–271.

Rizzo, C. J., Daley, S. E., & Gunderson, B. H. (2006). Interpersonal sensitivity, romantic stress, and the prediction of depression: A study of inner-city, minority adolescent girls. *Journal of Youth and Adolescence, 35*, 444–453.

Rose, A. J. (2002). Co-rumination in the friendships of girls and boys. *Child Development, 73*, 1830–1843.

Rose, A. J., Carlson, W., & Waller, E. M. (2007). Prospective associations of co-rumination with friendship and emotional adjustment: Considering the socioemotional trade-offs of co-rumination. *Developmental Psychology, 43*, 1019–1031.

Rose, A. J., & Rudolph, K. D. (2006). A review of sex differences in peer relationship processes: Potential trade-offs for the emotional and behavioral development of girls and boys. *Psychological Bulletin, 132*, 98–131.
Ruble, D. N., & Rholes, W. S. (1981). The development of children's perceptions and attributions about their social world. In J. D. Harvey, W. Ickes, & R. F. Kidd (Eds.), *New directions in attribution research* (Vol. 3, pp. 3–36). Hillsdale, NJ: Lawrence Erlbaum.
Rudolph, K. D. (2002). Gender differences in emotional responses to interpersonal stress during adolescence. *Journal of Adolescent Health, 30*, 3–13.
Rudolph, K. D. (in press). Developmental influences on interpersonal stress generation in depressed youth. *Journal of Abnormal Psychology.*
Rudolph, K. D., Caldwell, M. S., & Conley, C. S. (2005). Need for approval and children's well-being. *Child Development, 76*, 309–323.
Rudolph, K. D., & Clark, A. G. (2001). Conceptions of relationships in children with depressive and aggressive symptoms: Social-cognitive distortion or reality? *Journal of Abnormal Child Psychology, 29*, 41–56.
Rudolph, K. D., & Conley, C. S. (2005). The socioeconomic costs and benefits of social-evaluative concerns: Do girls care too much? *Journal of Personality, 73*, 115–137.
Rudolph, K. D., Dennig, M. D., & Weisz, J. R. (1995). Determinants and consequences of children's coping in the medical setting: Conceptualization, review, and critique. *Psychological Bulletin, 11*, 328–357.
Rudolph, K. D., & Flynn, M. (2007). Childhood adversity and youth depression: The role of gender and pubertal status. *Development and Psychopathology, 19*, 497–521.
Rudolph, K. D., Flynn, M., & Abaied, J. L. (2008). A developmental perspective on interpersonal theories of youth depression. In J. R. Z. Abela & B. L. Hankin (Eds.), *Handbook of depression in children and adolescents* (pp. 79–102). New York: Guilford.
Rudolph, K. D., Flynn, M., Abaied, J. L., Groot, A., & Thompson, R. (in press). Why is past depression the best predictor of future depression? Stress generation as a mechanism of depression continuity in girls. *Journal of Clinical Child and Adolescent Psychology.*
Rudolph, K. D., & Hammen, C. (1999). Age and gender determinants of stress exposure, generation, and reactions in youngsters: A transactional perspective. *Child Development, 70*, 660–677.
Rudolph, K. D., Hammen, C., & Burge, D. (1994). Interpersonal functioning and depressive symptoms in childhood: Addressing the issues of specificity and comorbidity. *Journal of Abnormal Child Psychology, 22*, 355–371.
Rudolph, K. D., Hammen, C., & Burge, D. (1995). Cognitive representations of self, family, and peers in school-age children: Links with social competence and sociometric status. *Child Development, 66*, 1385–1402.
Rudolph, K. D., Hammen, C., Burge, D., Lindberg, N., Herzberg, D., & Daley, S. (2000). Toward an interpersonal life-stress model of depression: The developmental context of stress generation. *Development and Psychopathology, 12*, 215–234.
Rudolph, K. D., Hammen, C., & Daley, S. E. (2006). Mood disorders. In D. A. Wolfe & E. J. Mash (Eds.), *Behavioral and emotional disorders in adolescents: Nature, assessment, and treatment* (pp. 300–342). New York: Guilford Press.

Rudolph, K. D., Kurlakowsky, K. D., & Conley, C. S. (2001). Developmental and social-contextual origins of depressive control-related beliefs and behavior. *Cognitive Therapy and Research, 25*, 447–475.

Rudolph, K. D., Ladd, G., & Dinella, L. (2007). Gender differences in the interpersonal consequences of early-onset depressive symptoms. *Merrill-Palmer Quarterly, 53*(3), 461–488.

Scarr, S., & McCartney, K. (1983). How people make their own environments: A theory of genotype environment effects. *Child Development, 54*, 424–435.

Schulenberg, J., Maggs, J. L., & Hurrelmann, K. (1997). Negotiating developmental transitions during adolescence and young adulthood: Health risks and opportunities. In J. Schulenberg, J. L. Maggs & K. Hurrelmann (Eds.), *Health risks and developmental transitions during adolescence* (pp. 1–19). New York: Cambridge University Press.

Segrin, C., & Flora, J. (1998). Depression and verbal behavior in conversations with friends and strangers. *Journal of Language and Social Psychology, 17*, 492–503.

Selman, R. L. (1980). *The growth of interpersonal understanding: Developmental and clinical analyses.* San Diego, CA: Academic Press.

Sheeber, L., Hops, H., Alpert, A., Davis, B., & Andrews, J. A. (1997). Family support and conflict: Prospective relations to adolescent depression. *Journal of Abnormal Child Psychology, 25*, 333–344.

Sheeber, L., & Sorensen, E. (1998). Family relationships of depressed adolescents: A multimethod assessment. *Journal of Clinical Child Psychology, 27*, 268–277.

Shields, A., Cicchetti, D., & Ryan, R. M. (1994). The development of emotional and behavioral self-regulation and social competence among maltreated school-age children. *Development and Psychopathology, 6*, 57–75.

Shih, J. H. (2006). Sex differences in stress generation: An examination of sociotropy/autonomy, stress, and depressive symptoms. *Personality and Social Psychology Bulletin, 32*, 434–446.

Shih, J. H., Eberhart, N. K., Hammen, C. L., & Brennan, P. A. (2006). Differential exposure and reactivity to interpersonal stress predict sex differences in adolescent depression. *Journal of Clinical Child and Adolescent Psychology, 35*, 103–115.

Shirk, S. R., Gudmundsen, G. R., & Burwell, R. A. (2005). Links among attachment-related cognitions and adolescent depressive symptoms. *Journal of Clinical Child and Adolescent Psychology, 34*, 172–181.

Shirk, S. R., Van Horn, M., & Leber, D. (1997). Dysphoria and children's processing of supportive interactions. *Journal of Abnormal Child Psychology, 25*, 239–249.

Silbereisen, R. K., & Kracke, B. (1997). Self-reported maturational timing and adaptation in adolescence. In J. Schulenberg, J. L. Maggs, & K. Hurrelman (Eds.), *Health risks and developmental transitions during adolescence* (pp. 85–109). New York: Cambridge University Press.

Silberg, J. L., Pickles, A., Rutter, M., Hewitt, J., Simonoff, E., Maes, H., et al. (1999). The influence of genetic factors and life stress on depression among adolescent girls. *Archives of General Psychiatry, 56*, 225–232.

Simmons, R. G., Blyth, D. A., & McKinney, K. L. (1983). The social and psychological effects of puberty on white females. In J. Brooks-Gunn & A. C. Petersen (Eds.), *Girls at puberty: Biological and psychosocial perspectives* (pp. 229–272). New York: Plenum Press.

Simmons, R. G., Blyth, D. A., Van Cleave, E. F., & Bush, D. M. (1979). Entry into early adolescence: The impact of school structure, puberty, and early dating on self-esteem. *American Sociological Review, 44*, 948–967.

Simmons, R. G., Burgeson, R., Carlton-Ford, S., & Blyth, D. A. (1987). The impact of cumulative change in early adolescence. *Child Development, 58*, 1220–1234.

Steinberg, L. D. (1987). Impact of puberty on family relations: Effects of pubertal status and pubertal timing. *Developmental Psychology, 23*, 451–460.

Stice, E. (2003). Puberty and body image. In C. Hayward (Ed.), *Gender differences at puberty* (pp. 61–76). New York: Cambridge University Press.

Stice, E., Ragan, J., & Randall, P. (2004). Prospective relations between social support and depression: Differential direction of effects for parent and peer support? *Journal of Abnormal Psychology, 113*, 155–159.

Susman, E. J., & Rogol, A. (2004). Puberty and psychological development. In R. M. Lerner & L. Steinberg (Eds.), *Handbook of adolescent psychology* (2nd ed., pp. 15–44). Hoboken, NJ: Wiley.

Tangney, J. P., Burggraf, S. A., & Wagner, P. E. (1995). Shame-proneness, guilt-proneness, and psychological symptoms. In J. P. Tangey & K. W. Fisher (Eds.), *Self-conscious emotions: The psychology of shame, guilt, embarrassment, and pride* (pp. 343–367). New York: Guilford Press.

Tobin-Richards, M. H., Boxer, A. M., & Petersen, A. C. (1983). The psychological significance of pubertal change: Sex differences in perceptions of self during early adolescence. In J. Brooks-Gunn & A. C. Petersen (Eds.), *Girls at puberty: Biological and psychosocial perspectives* (pp. 127–154). New York: Plenum Press.

Tolan, P. H., Gorman-Smith, D., Henry, D., Chung, K., & Hunt, M. (2002). The relation of patterns of coping of inner-city youth to psychopathology symptoms. *Journal of Research on Adolescence, 12*, 423–449.

Toth, S. L., Cicchetti, D., Macfie, J., & Emde, R. N. (1997). Representations of self and other in the narratives of neglected, physically abused, and sexually abused preschoolers. *Development and Psychopathology, 9*, 781–796.

Troy, M., & Sroufe, L. A. (1987). Victimization among preschoolers: Role of attachment history. *American Academy of Child and Adolescent Psychiatry, 26*, 166–172.

Wadsworth, M. E., & Berger, L. E. (2006). Adolescents coping with poverty-related family stress: Prospective predictors of coping and psychological symptoms. *Journal of Youth and Adolescence, 35*, 57–70.

Wagner, B. M., & Compas, B. E. (1990). Gender, instrumentality, and expressivity: Moderators of the relation between stress and psychological symptoms during adolescence. *American Journal of Community Psychology, 18*, 383–406.

Weichold, K., Silbereisen, R. K., & Schmitt-Rodermund, E. (2003). Short-term and long-term consequences of early versus late physical maturation in adolescents. In C. Hayward (Ed.), *Gender differences at puberty* (pp. 241–276). New York: Cambridge University Press.

Wichstrom, L. (1999). The emergence of gender difference in depressed mood during adolescence: The role of intensified gender socialization. *Developmental Psychology, 35*, 232–245.

Youngblade, L. M., & Belsky, J. (1992). Parent–child antecedents of 5-year-olds' close friendships: A longitudinal analysis. *Developmental Psychology, 28*, 700–713.

Chapter Fifteen

Coping and Emotion Regulation: Implications for Understanding Depression During Adolescence[1]

BRUCE E. COMPAS, SARAH S. JASER, AND MOLLY A. BENSON

CONTENTS

Adolescence is a critical period for the development of the capacity to regulate emotions and cope with stress. It is during this period that increased autonomy emerges in the ability to regulate one's behavior, emotion, cognition, physiology, and one's relationship with the social environment. Growth in the capacity for emotion regulation and coping is driven by important biological changes, including significant developments in brain structure and function, as well as changes in social contexts and social relationships. However, these major advances in the capacity for coping and emotion regulation also make adolescence a time of increased vulnerability in the development of regulatory processes. Regulatory skills, including the ability to cope with stress, are still being actively shaped and acquired during a time of heightened stress and challenge, increasing the risk that the development of these processes will be disrupted or delayed.

It is noteworthy that depression also increases significantly in its incidence and prevalence during adolescence, as depression can be conceptualized as a problem of impaired or disrupted emotion regulation. The emergence of depression during adolescence is due in part to the interplay of significant psychosocial stress with the simultaneous emergence of the ability for coping and emotion regulation in the face of stress. If coping skills are impaired or fail to develop in some adolescents, these individuals are most vulnerable to the effects of stress, particularly in terms of risk for depression.

In this chapter we examine the central role of coping with stress, and related processes of emotion regulation, in the development of and recovery from depression during adolescence. We first discuss depression as a disorder of dysregulation in major psychological and biological systems. We then describe theory and research related to the role of coping and emotion regulation in depression as it emerges during adolescence. As part of this discussion, we address conceptual and methodological issues in the integration of the somewhat disparate lines of work on coping and emotion regulation, with a goal of contributing to greater synthesis of these two important constructs. Third, we review studies of coping and emotion regulation as they relate to depression in adolescence, with a special emphasis on offspring of depressed parents as a high-risk group for understanding these processes. Finally, we consider future directions for research in this burgeoning area of investigation, including issues in measurement, research integrating behavioral and biological aspects of coping and emotion regulation, and careful examination of the role of coping and emotion regulation as components of interventions for the prevention and treatment of depression during adolescence.

DEPRESSION AND DYSREGULATION

Depression involves the dysregulation of several important biological and psychological systems. Major depressive disorder (MDD) is striking in that its central characteristics include dysregulation of processes that reflect *either* excessive *or* insufficient levels of certain responses. For example, disruptions in sleep and appetite are seen in either hypo- or hypersomnia and hypo- or hyperphagia, respectively. Depression is not simply a matter of over regulation/over control, but rather of failed regulatory processes that manifest in either over or under control, over or under regulation. Thus, depression reflects disrupted and unregulated psychological and biological systems, processes that are accentuated under stress. These processes are perhaps best captured by the concept of allostatic load that reflects the degree of chronic demands on psychological and biological systems due to repeated or prolonged stress (McEwen, 2004).

At the biological level, depression is associated with disruptions in the activation and recovery of the hypothalamic-pituitary-adrenal (HPA) axis in response to stress, typically measured in alterations in the production of cortisol (e.g., Bale, 2005). Considerable research has shown that the HPA axis is hyper-reactive to stress among depressed individuals, as measured by excessively high circulating levels of cortisol (e.g., Steimer, Python, Schulz,

& Aubry, 2007). Further, the HPA axis may be slow to return to baseline or a homeostatic level in depressed individuals. However, there is also evidence of hypocortisolism in individuals with depression, particularly in the presence of comorbid post-traumatic stress disorder, indicating that this system is not simply dysregulated in one direction (Luecken, Dausch, Gulla, Hong, & Compas, 2003).

The dysregulation of both positive and negative emotions is also a central feature of depression. Anhedonia, or the inability to experience positive affect, is a hallmark symptom of MDD. The ability to mobilize and experience positive emotions is important in enhancing and repairing one's mood, increasing appetitive motivation, and increasing approach and active behavior (e.g., Joorman & Gotlib, 2007; Shaw et al., 2006). Generating and maintaining positive affect, particularly in the face of significant stress, may be an important process in decreasing the risk for the development of sad and dysphoric mood. Conversely, the dysregulation of negative emotions, especially sadness and irritability, is also a hallmark feature of depression. Taken together, these patterns suggest that depression is characterized by the inability to activate one emotional state (positive affect) accompanied by the inability to dampen, modulate, or palliate another emotional state (sadness).

Psychosocial stress plays a central role in triggering the dysregulation of the psychological and biological processes central to depression. Stressful life events, recurring minor stressors, and chronic adversity are all associated with psychological symptoms and disorders, including depressive symptoms and disorders, in children and adolescents (for reviews of stress in young people see Grant, Compas, Stuhlmacher, Thurm, & McMahon, 2003; Grant, Compas, Thurm, McMahon, & Gipson, 2004; Grant et al. 2006; McMahon et al., 2003). For example, in a sample of young adolescents, Carter, Garber, Ciesla, and Cole (2006) found that daily stressors predicted internalizing symptoms, including symptoms of depression, over a period of 1 year even after controlling for initial symptoms. Similarly, Cole, Nolen-Hoeksema, Girgus, and Paul (2006) showed that stressors predicted subsequent depressive symptoms, controlling for the stability of these symptoms, in children and adolescents. Consistent with a model emphasizing the importance of dysregulation in depression, Cole et al. also found that depressive symptoms predicted increases in stress over time, suggesting that depressive symptoms are associated with disruptions in the external environment (i.e., depressive symptoms contribute to stressful events) as well as dysregulation of internal processes.

The dysregulation of these multiple systems in depression suggests that a central feature of this disorder is the failure to develop and/or failure to activate processes of self-regulation in response to stress. Therefore, it is important to consider the regulation of emotion, behavior, cognition, and physiology in relation to depression. Further, it is essential to consider these regulatory processes as they occur, or breakdown, in response to stress. The concept of coping is central to understanding emotion regulation and other regulatory processes that are activated in response to stress.

COPING AND EMOTION REGULATION

Before further examining the role of coping and emotion regulation in depression during adolescence, it is important to consider the nature of each of these constructs and their inter-relations. Research on coping and emotion regulation has grown somewhat independently. Each has been the subject of extensive reviews (e.g., Compas, Connor-Smith, Saltzman, Thomsen, & Wadsworth, 2001; Davidson, Jackson, & Kalin, 2000; Skinner, Edge, Altman, & Sherwood, 2003), and each has been the subject of handbooks providing comprehensive references to relevant theory and research (e.g., Gross, 2007; Wolchick & Sandler, 1997; Zeidner & Endler, 1996). Thus, coping and emotion regulation have been represented by separate and extensive research enterprises. However, there is now considerable recognition of the close links between them. At a broad level, emotion regulation refers to changes associated with activated emotions, including changes in an emotion or in other psychological processes related to an emotion (Cole, Martin, & Dennis, 2004). Coping is at once both *broader* and *more specific* than emotion regulation (Compas et al., 2001; Skinner & Zimmer-Gembeck, 2007). Specifically, coping refers to the regulation of emotions *and* other important psychological and biological processes; as such, emotion regulation can be seen as a subset of coping. On the other hand, coping refers to emotion regulation under a *specific* set of circumstances, that is, in response to stress. Since emotion regulation is an ongoing process that occurs under both stressful and nonstressful circumstances, coping is a special case of emotion regulation under stress (e.g., Eisenberg et al., 2001).

Regulatory processes, especially in response to stress, include both automatic and controlled processes (Compas et al., 2001). Automatic (or involuntary) processes occur either within or outside of conscious awareness but are not under conscious control, whereas controlled (or voluntary) responses to stress and regulatory processes are within conscious awareness and are experienced as under personal control. Dual process theories that encompass automatic and controlled processes are pervasive in psychological science (Feldman Barrett, Tugade, & Engle, 2004). Dual process models have been applied to social cognition (e.g., Lieberman, 2007), mental control (e.g., Wenzlaff & Wegner, 2000), emotions and emotional disorders (Mathews & MacLeod, 2005), and self-regulation (e.g., Bargh & Ferguson, 2000). Empirical support for the distinction between controlled or volitional responses and automatic or involuntary responses is extensive. For example, attention to and responses to threatening cues in the environment, which are experienced as stressful and therefore may initiate coping behavior, are processed on both an automatic, uncontrolled level as well as on a controlled, strategic level (see Mathews & MacLeod, 2005, for a review of research with adults). Research has recently begun to examine these two levels of attentional processing and biases in children and adolescents (e.g., Boyer et al., 2006). Automatic and controlled processes are critical to coping and emotion regulation. However, as outlined below, emotion regulation includes both of these processes (Gross & Thompson, 2007), whereas coping exclusively refers to controlled, effortful responses to stress (Compas et al., 2001).

Emotion Regulation

Much of the seminal work on emotion regulation has been conducted from a developmental perspective, driven by an interest in understanding how the capacity for self-regulation emerges with development. A widely accepted definition of emotion regulation has been offered by Thompson (1994): "The extrinsic and intrinsic processes responsible for monitoring, evaluating, and modifying emotional reactions, especially their intensive and temporal feature, to accomplish one's goals" (pp. 27–28). This definition includes the child and her/his social context as part of the regulatory process, both of which are of central importance in the development of emotion regulation. Young children rely on parents and other adult caregivers to soothe and manage negative emotions, but during adolescence emotion regulation may become more internal and autonomous. Thompson also points to the multiple facets of emotion regulation that range from recognizing and understanding one's emotions, to taking steps to try to alter or modify their intensity and duration. Cole et al. (2004) further distinguish between two types of regulation—emotion as *regulating* and emotion as *regulated*. In the former, changes are observed in other domains (e.g., behavior or cognition) as a result of an emotion, whereas the latter refers to changes in the valence, intensity, or time course of an emotion that may occur within an individual or between individuals.

The complexity of emotion regulation is further reflected in the distinction between automatic and controlled regulatory processes. Temperamental differences in emotionality have been identified in early childhood and reflect automatic patterns of emotional arousal in response to novelty, discomfort, or threat (Rothbart & Bates, 1998). Evidence for automatic emotion regulation processes that may be rooted in temperament have also been identified in adults (e.g., Haas, Omura, Constable, & Canli, 2007). In contrast to emotionality, effortful control is a dimension of temperament that involves self-regulation, including the ability to purposefully focus or shift attention as needed to regulate emotional responses to the environment (e.g., Eisenberg et al., 2001; Rothbart & Bates, 1998).

The underlying neurobiology of emotion regulation is also becoming clearer from recent research. Neuroimaging studies have provided some evidence regarding brain regions that are involved in automatic emotion regulation (i.e., those activated by implicit tasks; Haas et al., 2007), and those that are involved in controlled, purposeful efforts to regulate emotional arousal, such as cognitive reframing or reappraising a situation (e.g., Oschner, Bunge, Gorss, & Gabrieli, 2002). For example, the dorsolateral prefrontal cortex and the anterior cingulate cortex have been shown to activate in response to tasks that require higher order cognitive processes, including working memory, decision making, and inhibitory control (Davidson, 2003). Further, the relative activation of the left and right prefrontal cortical regions is implicated in emotion regulation (e.g., Davidson, 2003), as is the regulation of emotional arousal by the vagas nerve as reflected in respiratory sinus arrhythmia (e.g., Porges, 2007). We return to the neurobiology of coping and emotion regulation later in our discussion of future directions for research in this area.

A contemporary synthesis of views on emotion regulation is offered by Gross and Thompson (2007), who define emotion regulation as "a heterogeneous set of processes by which emotions are themselves regulated" (p. 7). Emotion regulation includes both automatic and controlled processes which are characterized as intrinsic (actions by the individual to regulate one's own emotions) and extrinsic (actions by others to regulate an individual's emotions). Gross and Thompson take an inclusive perspective, including actions taken to either increase or decrease positive or negative emotions in their definition of emotion regulation. They further note that the distinction between conscious and nonconscious and automatic and controlled processes is not static, as emotion regulation acts that are initially conscious and purposeful may become automatized over time, and initially automatic responses may be brought under conscious control (see Compas et al., 2001, for a similar view of coping and stress reactivity). Finally, Gross and Thompson do not identify maladaptive versus maladaptive emotion regulation on an a priori basis; efficacy depends on features of the individual and the context.

Definitions of emotion regulation have also been generated specifically with regard to the development of depression during childhood and adolescence. For example, Forbes and Dahl (in press) define the construct as "the internal and external processes involved in the initiation, maintenance, or modification of the quality, intensity, or chronometry of affective responses" (p. 831). Shaw et al. (2006), also studying depression in children/adolescents, defined emotion regulation as a "biologically based reaction that co-ordinates biologically and psychologically adaptive responding to stimuli" (p. 491). Kovacs et al. (2006) note that the ability to focus attention away from the source of distress or the associated feelings represents a primary goal of emotion regulation, which starts in early childhood. In addition, they posit that most emotion regulation responses to distress are the products of learning, shaped by social contexts, particularly the family. Finally, adaptive emotion regulation responses are those that down-regulate the emotion, while maladaptive emotion regulation responses exacerbate or prolong the emotion (Kovacs et al.).

Coping

Similar to the challenges in understanding emotion regulation, theory and research on coping with stress has been characterized by problems in conceptualization and measurement. In a seminal review of coping research and theory, Skinner et al. (2003) delineated multiple levels of analysis of coping processes, including specific categories of coping responses (e.g., distraction, emotional expression), broader families of coping (e.g., problem solving, accommodation), and even broader adaptive processes (e.g., co-ordinating actions and contingencies in the environment). The complexity of and, perhaps, problems in the field are reflected by more than 400 specific categories of coping responses identified in the literature by Skinner et al. (2003).

Progress has been made toward consensus on understanding the varied aspects of coping during childhood and adolescence (e.g., Compas et al., 2001; Skinner et al., 2003; Skinner & Zimmer-Gembeck, 2007). Skinner et al. (2003) point to the contribution of top-down, theory-driven research that have used confirmatory factor analysis to test models of coping as an important alternative to early work that relied on bottom-up methods using exploratory factor analysis to examine rather disparate sets of coping responses. Top-down methods are reflected in the work of Walker, Smith, Garber, and Van-Slyke (1997), as well as our own research on coping as part of a dual process model of responses to stress (e.g., Compas et al., 2006; Connor-Smith, Compas, Wasworth, Thomsen, Saltzman, 2000).

Dual Process Model of Coping and Responses to Stress

We view coping as one aspect of a broader set of processes that are enacted in response to stress. We define coping as "conscious volitional efforts to regulate emotion, cognition, behavior, physiology, and the environment in response to stressful events or circumstances" (Compas et al., 2001, p. 89). Similarly,

Skinner and Zimmer-Gembeck (2007) define coping as "action regulation under stress" (p. 122), and Eisenberg, Fabes, and Guthrie (1997) identify coping as "involving regulatory processes in a subset of contexts—those involving stress" (p. 42). Regulation under stress involves a broad array of responses, including efforts to (a) initiate; (b) terminate or delay; (c) modify or change the form or content; (d) modulate the amount or intensity of a thought, emotion, behavior, or physiological reaction; or (e) redirect thought or behavior toward a new target (Compas et al., 2001). These regulatory processes both draw on and are constrained by the biological, cognitive, social, and emotional development of the individual. An individual's developmental level both contributes to the resources that are available for coping, and limits the types of coping responses the individual can enact.

The broad array of controlled and automatic responses to stress is further distinguished along a dimension of engagement versus disengagement (Connor-Smith et al., 2000). Engagement responses involve orienting or directing responses toward the source of stress or one's emotional responses to a stressor, whereas disengagement responses orient away from the stressor or one's reaction to it. Automatic engagement responses include emotional and physiological arousal, intrusive cognitions, and impulsive action. Disengagement responses that occur automatically in response to stress include escape behavior, emotional numbing, and cognitive interference. In contrast to automatic responses to stress, three types of controlled (coping) responses have been identified. Controlled disengagement responses represent disengagement coping, which includes avoidance, denial, and wishful thinking. Drawing on developmental models of perceived control and the importance of these perceptions in responses to stress, controlled engagement responses are differentiated as primary control coping and secondary control coping (Compas et al., 2001). Primary control coping is characterized by responses aimed at resolving the source of stress or direct attempts to change one's emotional responses to a stressor, including problem solving, controlled (regulated) expression of emotions, and emotion modulation. Primary control coping is hypothesized to be best suited to stressors that are experienced as under personal control. Secondary control coping involves efforts to adapt to a stressor and is, therefore, best suited to stress that is experienced as beyond personal control. Examples of secondary control coping responses include acceptance, distraction, cognitive restructuring, and optimistic thinking. Related to the pursuit of the underlying neurobiology of coping and emotion regulation, recent research has identified brain structures, functions, and physiology associated with perceptions of control (Declerck, Boone, & de Brabander, 2006), suggesting that it may be possible to map the neuroanatomy of a control-based model of coping.

The dual process model of coping and stress reactivity has been tested using adolescent self-reports and parents' reports about adolescents on the Responses to Stress Questionnaire (Connor-Smith et al., 2000). This model has been supported using confirmatory factor analyses in diverse samples of adolescents and adults coping with a wide range of different types of stress, including Euro-American adolescents coping with social/interpersonal stress (Connor-Smith et al., 2000), Navajo adolescents coping with social/interpersonal stress (Wadsworth, Reickmann, Benson, & Compas, 2004), and children and adolescents coping with recurrent pain (Compas et al., 2006). Findings from these studies suggest that this model is robust and replicable across a wide range of different types of stress, different age groups, and diverse cultural and ethnic groups. Further, this model has been supported in latent variable analyses combining parent and adolescent reports of adolescents' coping, indicating that it is not limited to self-report measures (Compas et al., 2006).

This model has emphasized active forms of engagement coping as reflected in efforts to regulate the source of stress and one's emotions in primary control coping and one's cognitions and attention in secondary control coping. However, passive forms of engagement coping as represented by ruminative coping (e.g., focusing on one's negative emotions, searching for a cause of one's problems) are also important (Nolen-Hoeksema, 2004), especially in regard to depression. Rumination includes self-reflection (e.g., "analyzing recent events and try to understand why I am upset;" "writing down what I am thinking and analyzing it"), and brooding (e.g., "thinking about how alone I feel;" "thinking about how upset I feel"). In examining the role of coping in relation to depression, it will be valuable to integrate models of coping in children and adolescents that include both active and passive coping responses.

Integrating Coping and Emotion Regulation

A number of clear links can be seen between recent conceptualizations of coping and emotion regulation. Both refer to processes of the regulation of emotions and physiological responses to stress (Skinner & Zimmer-Gembeck, 2007). Coping includes strategies that are intended to manage and modulate negative emotions in response to stress. This type of coping was originally included in the diffuse category of emotion-focused coping, which has proven problematic as it has typically encompassed a very broad and heterogeneous set of coping strategies. More recent conceptualizations of emotional approach coping (Stanton, Kirk, Cameron, & Danoff-Burg, 2000) and the inclusion of emotional expression and emotional modulation have provided a more precise picture of the types of coping strategies that reflect successful regulation of negative emotions under stress.

Several response types are common to coping and emotion regulation. For example, cognitive reappraisal and distraction, both types of secondary control coping, have been studied extensively as examples of emotion regulation (e.g., Oschner et al., 2002). Cognitive reappraisal appears to be an adaptive form of secondary control or emotional approach coping, and an effective way of regulating one's emotions when faced with an uncontrollable source of stress, or an emotionally arousing situation or stimulus that cannot be changed (e.g., Compas et al., 2006). Distraction, or shifting one's attention to an alternative stimulus, has also been studied as a form of coping and emotion regulation that appears to be adaptive when faced with situations that demand adaptation rather than direct action.

Executive Function as a Unifying Construct

Coping and the controlled, intentional, aspects of emotion regulation can be further linked as examples of the broad category of executive function (Compas, 2006). Executive functions include a broad array of cognitive processes, including planning, cognitive flexibility, abstract thinking, rule acquisition, initiating appropriate actions and inhibiting inappropriate actions, and selecting relevant sensory information. Executive function processes operate on a continuous basis, as they are central in information processing in daily life.

However, these processes and skills also provide the foundation for effective coping and emotion regulation. As such, coping is the process of bringing executive functions online during times of stress. For example, Copeland and Compas (2007) found that coping mediated the relation between measures of executive function (performance on tasks requiring inhibitory control) and externalizing problems in adolescents. Specifically, performance on laboratory tasks measuring inhibitory control was related to greater use of primary and secondary control coping, which accounted for the relationship between inhibitory control and externalizing problems (Copeland & Compas, 2007). Further, the link between executive function and emotion regulation is explicit in many conceptual models, as emotion regulation is often included as one form of executive function (Compas, 2006).

Establishing the link of executive function with coping and emotion regulation points to common brain structures and functions that are shared by these processes. Functional magnetic resonance imaging (fMRI) studies have located executive functions within the prefrontal cortex. For example, strategic control of attention, a process involved when distraction is used as a form of coping, is regulated by the lateral prefrontal, orbital, and parietal areas (Hampshire & Owen, 2005). Working memory, which is involved in coping strategies such as problem solving and cognitive reappraisal/cognitive restructuring, is regulated by the dorsolateral prefrontal cortex (Feldman Barrett et al., 2004). Thus, executive function may represent a critical link between coping and emotion regulation at a behavioral and a biological level.

RESEARCH ON COPING, EMOTION REGULATION, AND DEPRESSION DURING ADOLESCENCE

An accumulating body of evidence suggests that coping and emotion regulation play a central role in the development and course of depressive symptoms, and perhaps depressive disorders, in adolescence. Studies have been carried out with adolescents at varying levels of risk for depression, with an emphasis on children and adolescents of parents with current or past depressive symptoms and disorders.

Coping and Depression

Several studies have examined the relation between coping and depressive symptoms in community samples of adolescents exposed to varying levels of risk. For example, Nolen-Hoeksema, Stice, Wade, and Bohon (2007) found, in a longitudinal study, that rumination predicted onset of MDD in adolescent girls. Similarly, Grant et al. (2004) found that ruminative coping, a passive form of engagement coping, was associated with higher depressive symptoms in a sample of low-income, urban, African-American adolescents. Burwell and Shirk (2007) examined two subtypes of ruminative coping, brooding and reflection, as predictors of depressive symptoms in urban adolescents. They found that brooding, but not reflection, was predictive of increases in depressive symptoms. Papadakis, Prince, Jones, and Strauman (2006) report a similar relation between brooding as a ruminative coping strategy and depressive symptoms in a sample of middle to upper class adolescent girls.

In contrast to the adverse effects of rumination, there is evidence for the adaptive consequences of primary and secondary control coping. In a series of studies of rural low-income adolescents, Wadsworth and colleagues (Wadsworth & Berger, 2006; Wadsworth & Compas, 2002; Wadsworth, Raviv, Connor-Smith, & Compas, 2005) found that primary and secondary control coping with economic stress and strain were associated with lower symptoms of mixed anxiety/depression. Benson et al. (2007) found that secondary control coping strategies were related to lower internalizing symptoms, including depressive symptoms, across three samples of Bosnian adolescents coping with three types of postwar stressors, including reminders of trauma and loss. These studies suggest that ruminative coping is related to increased risk and secondary control coping is associated with reduced risk for depressive symptoms.

Adolescent offspring of depressed parents are perhaps at greatest risk for depression, and have been the focus of perhaps the most extensive research on the role of coping and depression in adolescence. Children of depressed parents are at increased risk for developing internalizing and externalizing symptoms and psychopathology, especially depression (e.g., Beardslee, Versage, & Gladstone, 1998; Weissman, Warner, Wickramaratne, Moreau, & Olfson, 1997). One of the hypothesized mechanisms of risk for the transmission of depression from depressed parents to their children is exposure to a stressful environment that is a consequence of the parent's depression. For example, Hammen, Brennan, and Shih (2004) found that adolescent children of mothers with current or past MDD or dysthymia experienced significantly greater levels of conflict and stress in their family than children of never-depressed mothers, and that these children were more reactive to stress. Parental depression is associated with at least three types of family stress: stress that results from parental withdrawal and unavailability to the child, parental irritability and intrusiveness with the child, and interparental conflict (Jaser et al., 2005; Langrock, Compas, Keller, Merchant, & Copeland, 2002). All three of these sources of stress can be conceptualized as beyond the child's control, therefore secondary control coping responses may be most adaptive in the face of these stressors.

Our research group has studied coping and stress responses in three samples of adolescent offspring of depressed parents. First, we examined these processes in a sample of adolescents whose mother or father had a history of depression, and who had experienced at least one episode of depression in the adolescent's lifetime (Jaser et al., 2007; Jaser et al., 2005; Langrock et al., 2002). We found that adolescents' use of secondary control coping (i.e., positive thinking, distraction, acceptance, and cognitive restructuring) was related to lower symptoms of mixed anxiety/depression, both within and across adolescents' and parents' reports of adolescents' coping and symptoms. Further, higher levels of involuntary engagement stress reactivity (emotional and physiological arousal, intrusive thoughts) were related to higher symptoms of anxiety/depression. A troubling pattern was identified in these adolescents—as levels of stress (parental withdrawal and parental intrusiveness) increased, adolescents used less secondary control coping and reported higher levels of stress reactivity (Jaser et al., 2005; Langrock et al., 2002). That is, as stress increases and adaptive coping becomes more important, adolescents' use less secondary control coping and experience higher levels of reactivity. This is consistent with the notion that stress contributes to dysregulation (heightened stress reactivity) and interferes with controlled self-regulation and coping, both of which lead to increased risk for depressive symptoms.

Second, we have examined coping and stress responses in adolescents whose mothers had a history of depression compared with a demographically matched sample of adolescents whose mothers did not have a history of depression (Jaser et al., in press). As expected, adolescents of mothers with a history of depression were higher in depressive symptoms and externalizing problems than adolescents whose mothers did not have a history of depression. Further, adolescent children of mothers with a history of depression reported higher levels of stress reactivity (e.g., emotional and physiological arousal, intrusive thoughts) than children of mothers with no history of depression. Mothers' reports of their current depressive symptoms and observations of maternal sadness during parent–child interactions in the laboratory were both related to higher levels of adolescents' depressive symptoms and externalizing problems, higher stress reactivity, and lower levels of secondary control coping. Finally, adolescents' use of secondary control coping and stress reactivity accounted for the relation between maternal history of depression and adolescents depressive symptoms. These findings replicate those found by Jaser et al. (2005) and Langrock et al. (2002), but extend the previous studies by using direct observations to assess parental depressive symptoms and parent–child interactions.

Third, we have examined stress and coping in adolescent offspring of mothers and fathers with a history of depression (Fear et al., 2008). In this sample, our focus was on adolescents' coping with interparental conflict, and a very similar pattern of findings emerged. Once again we found support for secondary control coping as a predictor of lower internalizing and externalizing symptoms, after accounting for method variance in adolescent and parent reports of coping and symptoms. Further, secondary control coping partially or fully accounted for the association between interparental conflict and adolescent symptoms (Fear et al.).

Emotion Regulation and Depression

Studies of emotion regulation and depression suggest that disruption of emotion regulation is related to lower positive and higher negative emotion in depressed youth. In one study of adolescents' ratings of their emotional responses to daily life events, participants who reported low regulation of negative affect experienced higher levels of depressive symptoms than those reporting higher regulation (Silk, Steinberg, & Morris, 2003). A study of children and adolescents with affective disorders found that youth with MDD or comorbid anxiety/depression exhibited significantly longer response times to negative emotional background information presented during a working memory task, compared to neutral backgrounds (Ladouceur et al., 2005). Children and adolescents in a low-risk control group in the same sample had longer response times to positive distracting background information presented during the task (Ladouceur et al., 2005).

In a study of a community sample of adolescents, Garnefski and Kraaij (2006) used the Cognitive Emotion Regulation Questionnaire (CERQ; Garnefski, Boon, & Kraaij, 2003; Garnefski, Rieffe, Jellesma, Terwogt, & Kraaji, 2007), consisting of nine subscales: self-blame, other-blame, rumination, catastrophizing, putting into perspective, positive refocusing, positive reappraisal, acceptance, and refocus on planning. These scales share item content with several scales from the Responses to Stress Questionnaire (Connor-Smith et al., 2000) that has been used in studies of coping, stress reactivity, and depression. For example, rumination on the CERQ is similar to involuntary engagement on the Responses to Stress Questionnaire, whereas the CERQ scales putting into perspective, positive refocusing, positive reappraisal, and acceptance are similar to secondary control coping. Garnefski and Kraaij (2006) and Garnefski et al. (2007) found that adolescents' reports of rumination, catastrophizing, and self-blame were related to greater symptoms of depression, and the use of positive reappraisal and positive refocusing was related to fewer symptoms of depression. The overlap in the items on these measures of coping and emotion regulation highlight the substantial overlap in these two constructs.

Researchers have also begun to examine emotion regulation in children of depressed parents; however, studies with this population have not yet examined emotion regulation in adolescents. The most extensive work has been conducted by Kovacs and colleagues, and has used direct observation methods to assess young children's (age 3- to 7-years-old) emotion regulation in response to laboratory stress tasks, and examined the relation between children's emotion regulation and their depressive symptoms (Forbes, Fox, Cohn, Galles, & Kovacs, 2006a; Forbes et al. 2006b; Silk, Shaw, Forbes, Lane, & Kovacs, 2006a; Silk, Shaw, Skuban, Oland, & Kovacs, 2006b). Because of the relevance of understanding emotion regulation and depression in young people, these studies will be reviewed here. These studies are noteworthy for several reasons, including inclusion of a particularly high-risk sample, children whose mothers had themselves first experienced depression during childhood, and the use of direct observations and physiological measures of emotion regulation.

Silk and colleagues (2006a) observed children's responses to a delay of gratification task as an example of an emotionally arousing (frustration) context for children and their mothers. Silk et al. found that children of mothers with childhood-onset depression were more likely to focus on a delay object (a response that is similar to rumination in that it is a form of passive engagement with the source of stress or source of emotional arousal) than children of mothers without a history of depression. Further, the use of positive reward anticipation (displays of joy and information gathering, a component of problem solving, a form of primary control engagement coping) was related to fewer internalizing symptoms in children of mothers with childhood-onset depression and current depressive symptoms, but not for children of mothers without a history of depression (Silk et al., 2006b).

The measurement of emotion regulation in the context of responses to emotionally arousing tasks in the laboratory highlights some of the challenges in conceptualizing and measuring emotion regulation. In one study, the codes used by Silk et al. (2006a) for emotion regulation included children's expressions of joy, anger, and sadness, along with behaviors of active distraction, focus on delay object, passive waiting, information gathering, and physical comfort seeking. Three factors emerged from a factor analysis of these codes—negative focus on delay (displays of sadness and anger and focus on delay object), behavioral distraction (active distraction and the converse of passive waiting), and positive reward anticipation (displays of joy and information gathering). Thus, codes for emotion regulation included observed levels of positive and negative emotion. However, in another study using the same population and task, Silk et al. (2006b) utilized only observed behaviors for coding emotion regulation strategies, including active distraction, focusing on the delay object, passive waiting, and information gathering. Similarly, Forbes et al. (2006a) coded for five affective behaviors (anger, sadness, worry, disgust, and smiling), and three self-regulatory behaviors (active, passive, and disruptive). Composite variables were created for approach (smiling and active self-regulation) and withdrawal (sadness, worry, disgust, and passive self-regulation) (Forbes et al.). The inclusion versus exclusion of emotions as part of the measurement of emotion regulation reflects the dichotomy highlighted by Cole et al. (2004) between "emotion as regulating" (emotions lead to changes in other aspects of behavior and cognition) and "emotion as regulated" (emotions are changed as a consequence of other processes).

Zeeman and colleagues have identified both adaptive and maladaptive aspects of emotion regulation that are related to internalizing symptoms, including depression in children and adolescents (Garber, Braafladt, & Zeeman, 1991). For example, Zeeman, Shipman, and Suveg (2002) found that higher levels of internalizing symptoms were associated with the inability to identify emotional states, the inhibition of anger, and the dysregulation of anger and sadness. They have further identified association between similar deficits in emotion regulation skills and symptoms of depression in children and adolescents with anxiety disorders (Suveg & Zeeman, 2004), and eating disorders (Sim & Zeeman, 2004). This work suggests that deficits in emotion regulation skills may be a common risk factor associated with a wide range of internalizing symptoms and disorders (Zeeman, Cassano, Perry-Parrish, & Stegall, 2006).

SUMMARY AND FUTURE DIRECTIONS

The closely related processes of coping and emotion regulation are central in understanding the effects of stress, and in the relation between stress and depressive symptoms, during adolescence. We now summarize what research has shown thus far, and suggest several important directions for future research.

Summary of Current Research

Although research on coping, emotion regulation, and depression in adolescence is in its early stages, several consistent findings have emerged. Secondary control engagement coping strategies and the closely related emotion regulation strategy of distraction are associated with lower symptoms of depression. Secondary control coping includes distracting or shifting attention to positive stimuli to manage negative emotions that arise in response to stress. However, secondary control coping also includes acceptance of a negative situation (e.g., "I just have to take things as they are, to go with the flow"), and cognitive restructuring or reappraising a situation. This includes emphasizing the positive aspects of a stressful situation, and maintaining an optimistic but realistic outlook under stress. These forms of coping and emotion regulation are well suited for managing sources of stress that are uncontrollable or perceived as beyond personal control.

In contrast, passive forms of engagement, including rumination and focusing on stimuli that are triggers for negative emotions are related to higher depressive symptoms. Rumination that involves brooding about one's negative emotions and searching for causes of one's negative emotions appears to be a particularly problematic form of coping. Ruminative coping appears to be closely related to automatic negative thoughts (e.g., intrusive thoughts about a stressor). This form of passive engagement coping may be problematic in part because it triggers automatic negative thoughts and sustains the arousal of negative emotions. These findings are reflected in research on both coping and emotion regulation and in the use of questionnaires and behavioral observations, and they set the stage for the next steps in this important area of research.

Future Directions

Measurement of Coping and Emotion Regulation

One important next step in research on coping and emotion regulation in relation to depression in adolescence will involve improving and refining measures. We believe an important step in this direction will be to declare a moratorium on the development of new questionnaires to assess either of these constructs. Efforts should be devoted instead to carefully documenting the overlap in the content of current measures of coping and emotion regulation. As noted above, many measures of these constructs include scales with common names (e.g., acceptance), and many share very similar items. A core set of items could be identified that captures the important aspects of coping and emotion regulation in their relationship to depression.

In addition to refining the content of questionnaire measures, future research would benefit from the use of multiple methods and multiple sources to assess both constructs. For example, relevant methods include adolescents' self-reports, parents' reports, observations of behavior, and performance on laboratory tasks. The use of multiple methods in combination has been rare, however. The use of multiple methods and data analytic strategies that combine these varied types of data (e.g., latent variable modeling) will increase the methodological rigor of coping and emotion regulation research, and help to control for problems of shared method variance in the assessment of both of these constructs and depression.

Linking Behavior with Brain Structure and Function

One of the most promising areas for research integrating coping and emotion regulation involves the identification of brain structures and functions associated with specific aspects of the coping process (Lewis & Stieben, 2004). Current research points to frontal and prefrontal regions in the brain as playing the central role in coping and emotion regulation, and more detailed specification of brain function and structure has several implications for understanding these processes. It appears that adaptive forms of emotion regulation and coping, including cognitive reappraisal and other forms of secondary control coping, are part of the broader set of processes included in executive functions. Because executive functions also include problem solving and other forms of primary control coping, it appears that emotion regulation and secondary control coping may be closely linked to other regulatory mechanisms. An important task for future research is to chart the course of the development of these executive functions, and how they are brought online in response to stress and the arousal of negative emotions.

Intervention Research

Enhancement of coping and emotion regulation skills plays an implicit role in many psychological interventions with adolescents, and an increasingly explicit role in several recent treatment and preventive interventions. One of the most researched evidence-based treatments for adolescent depression, cognitive-behavioral therapy, focuses on the development of cognitive and behavioral coping skills that are hypothesized to improve adolescents' ability to cope with stressors and decrease their focus on negative emotion, while increasing their attention to positive activities and emotion. Common elements of these interventions include emotion regulation strategies, such as emotion identification, self-monitoring, relaxation, pleasant activity scheduling, and specific coping skills including cognitive restructuring and problem solving. One recently developed cognitive-behavioral intervention, Primary and Secondary Control Enhancement Training (Weisz, Thurber, Sweeney, Profit, & LeGagnoux, 1997), specifically targets coping and regulation skills linked to the concepts of primary and secondary control.

Based on the research of emotion regulation in children of depressed parents, Kovacs and colleagues (2006) developed contextual emotion regulation therapy (CERT) to treat children with MDD. This treatment is based on the idea that problems in the adaptive self-regulation of distress and dysphoria compromise a child's ability to cope, increasing the likelihood for clinical depression in children. CERT is individually tailored to account for individual and developmental differences in emotion regulation; the child's inclination toward one domain of emotion regulation responses (biological, behavioral, cognitive, or social/interpersonal) is used to remediate deficits. In addition, children and their parents receive "coping skills training," which consists of reviewing emotion-naming, causes for emotions, and identifying adaptive responses (Kovacs et al., 2006).

We have developed a family-based intervention for children of parents who suffer from depression (Compas, Forehand, & Keller, in press). One arm of the intervention is designed to teach secondary control coping skills to children and adolescents to build more efficacious ways to manage the chronic stress associated with parental depression. Children and adolescents are taught to accept their parents' depression without blaming themselves or taking on responsibility for the problem. Cognitive reappraisal is another component of the intervention, with the intent of helping children and adolescents to reframe their parents' depression in a less pessimistic or hopeless manner. Finally, the use of pleasant activities as a way to distract themselves from the stress associated with their parents' depression is also emphasized. Data from a pilot trial indicate that children and adolescents can improve their use of these secondary control coping skills, and that the intervention is associated with reductions in internalizing symptoms. An ongoing study is testing the efficacy of the intervention in a randomized controlled trial.

CONCLUSION

The constructs of coping and emotion regulation are central to understanding the nature and development of depression during adolescence. Deficits in coping and emotion regulation skills and the use of maladaptive strategies to regulate emotions (e.g., rumination) are important sources of risk in the development of depression during adolescence. The field will benefit from greater integration of these two rich but relatively independent lines of research with regard to both basic underlying processes and the development of interventions for the prevention and treatment of depression in adolescence.

NOTE

1. Preparation of this chapter was supported by grant R01 MH069928 from the National Institute of Mental Health.

REFERENCES

Bale, T. L. (2005). Sensitivity to stress: Dysregulation of CRF pathways and disease development. *Hormones and Behavior, 48*, 1–10.

Bargh, J. A., & Ferguson, M. J. (2000). Beyond behaviorism: On the automaticity of higher mental processes. *Psychological Bulletin, 126*, 925–945.

Beardslee, W. R., Versage, E. M., & Gladstone, T. (1998). Children of affectively ill parents: A review of the past 10 years. *Journal of the American Academy of Child & Adolescent Psychiatry, 37*, 1134–1141.

Benson, M. A., Compas, B. E., Layne, C. M., Pasalic, H., Katalinksi, R., Saltzman, W., et al. (2007). Measurement of coping and stress responses in the aftermath of war: A study of Bosnian adolescents. Manuscript submitted for publication.

Boyer, M. C., Compas, B. E., Stanger, C., Colletti, R. B., Konik, B. S., Morrow, S. B., et al. (2006). Attentional biases to pain and social threat in children with recurrent abdominal pain. *Journal of Pediatric Psychology, 31*, 209–220.

Burwell, R. A., & Shirk, S. R. (2007). Subtypes of rumination in adolescence: Associations between brooding, reflection, depressive symptoms, and coping. *Journal of Clinical Child and Adolescent Psychology, 36*, 56–65.

Carter, J. S., Garber, J., Ciesla, J. A., & Cole, D. A. (2006). Modeling relations between hassles and internalizing and externalizing symptoms in adolescence: A four-year prospective study. *Journal of Abnormal Psychology, 116*, 428–442.

Cole, D. A., Nolen-Hoeksema, S., Girgus, J., & Paul, G. (2006). Stress exposure and stress generation in child and adolescent depression: A latent trait-state-error approach to longitudinal analyses. *Journal of Abnormal Psychology, 115*, 40–51.

Cole, P. M., Martin, S. E., & Dennis, T. A. (2004). Emotion regulation as a specific construct: Methodological challenges and directions for child development research. *Child Development, 75*, 317–333.

Compas, B. E. (2006). Psychobiological processes of stress and coping: Implications for resilience in childhood and adolescence. *Annals of the New York Academy of Sciences, 1094*, 226–234.

Compas, B. E., Boyer, M. C., Stanger, C., Colletti, R. B., Thomsen, A. H., Dufton, L. M., et al. (2006). Latent variable analysis of coping, anxiety/depression, and somatic symptoms in adolescents with chronic pain. *Journal of Consulting and Clinical Psychology, 74*, 1132–1142.

Compas, B. E., Connor-Smith, J. K., Saltzman, H., Thomsen, A. H., & Wadsworth, M. E. (2001). Coping with stress during childhood and adolescence: Problems, progress, and potential in theory and research. *Psychological Bulletin, 127,* 87–127.

Compas, B. E., Forehand, R., & Keller, G. (in press). Preventive intervention in families of depressed parents: A family cognitive-behavioral intervention. In T. J. Strauman, P. R. Costanzo, J. Garber, & L. Y. Abramson (Eds.), *Preventing depression in adolescent girls: A multidisciplinary approach.* New York: Guilford Press.

Connor-Smith, J. K., Compas, B. E., Wadsworth, M. E., Thomsen, A. H., & Saltzman, H. (2000). Responses to stress in adolescence: Measurement of coping and involuntary stress responses. *Journal of Consulting and Clinical Psychology, 68,* 976–992.

Copeland, W. E., & Compas, B. E. (2007). Neuropsychological correlates of coping: The role of executive inhibition. Manuscript submitted for publication.

Davidson, R. J. (2003). Affective neuroscience and psychophysiology: Toward a synthesis. *Psychophysiology, 40,* 655–665.

Davidson, R. J., Jackson, D. C., & Kalin, N. H. (2000). Emotion, plasticity, context, and regulation: Perspectives from affective neuroscience. *Psychological Bulletin, 126,* 890–909.

Declerck, C. H., Boone, C., & de Brabander, B. (2006). On feeling in control: A biological theory for individual differences in control perception. *Brain and Cognition, 62*(2), 143–176.

Eisenberg, N., Cumberland, A., Spinrad, T. L., Fabes, R. A., Shepard, S. A., Reiser, M., et al. (2001). The relations of regulation and emotionality to children's externalizing and internalizing problem behavior. *Child Development, 72,* 1112–1134.

Eisenberg, N., Fabes, R. A., & Guthrie, I. K. (1997). Coping with stress: The roles of regulation and development. In S. A. Wolchik, & I. N. Sandler (Eds.), *Handbook of children's coping: Linking theory and intervention* (pp. 41–70). New York: Plenum Press.

Fear, J., Forehand, R., Colletti, C., Roberts, L., Champion, J., Reeslund, K., et al. (2008). Parental depression and interparental conflict: Adolescents' self-blame and coping responses. Manuscript submitted for publication.

Feldman Barrett, L., Tugade, M. M., & Engle, R. W. (2004). Individual differences in working memory capacity and dual process theories of the mind. *Psychological Bulletin, 130,* 553–573.

Forbes, E. E., Fox, N. A., Cohn, J. F., Galles, S. F., & Kovacs, M. (2006a). Children's affect regulation during a disappointment: Psychophysiological responses and relation to parent history of depression. *Biological Psychology, 71,* 264–277.

Forbes, E. E., & Dahl, R. E. (in press). Alterations of positive affect in childhood and adolescent depression. *Development and Psychopathology.*

Forbes, E. E., Shaw, D. S., Fox, N. A., Cohn, J. F., Silk, J. S., & Kovacs, M. (2006b). Maternal depression, child frontal asymmetry, and child affective behavior as factors in child behavior problems. *Journal of Child Psychology and Psychiatry, 47,* 79–87.

Garber, J., Braafladt, N., & Zeeman, J. (1991). The regulation of sad affect: An information-processing perspective. In K. A. Dodge & J. Garber (Eds.), *The development of emotion regulation and dysregulation* (pp. 208–240). New York: Cambridge University Press.

Garnefski, N., Boon, S., & Kraaij, V. (2003) Relationships between cognitive strategies of adolescents and depressive symptomatology across different types of life events. *Journal of Youth & Adolescence, 32,* 401–408.

Garnefski, N., & Kraaij, V. (2006). Relationships between cognitive emotion regulation strategies and depressive symptoms: A comparative study of five specific samples. *Personality and Individual Differences, 40,* 1659–1669.

Garnefski, N., Rieffe, C., Jellesma, F., Terwogt, M. M., & Kraaji, V. (2007). Cognitive emotion regulation strategies and emotional problems in 9-11-year-old children. *European Child and Adolescent Psychiatry, 16,* 1–9.

Grant, K. E., Compas, B. E., Stuhlmacher, A. F., Thurm, A. E., & McMahon, S. D. (2003). Stress and child/adolescent psychopathology: Moving from markers to mechanisms of risk. *Psychological Bulletin, 129,* 447–466.

Grant, K. E., Compas, B. E., Thurm, A. E., McMahon, S. D., & Gipson, P. Y. (2004). Stressors and child/adolescent psychopathology: Measurement issues and prospective effects. *Journal of Clinical Child and Adolescent Psychology, 33,* 412–425.

Grant, K. E., Compas, B. E., Thurm, A. E., McMahon, S. D., Gipson, P. Y., Campbell, A. J., et al. (2006). Stressors and child and adolescent psychopathology: Evidence of moderating and mediating effects. *Clinical Psychology Review, 26,* 257–283.

Gross, J. J., & Thompson, R. A. (2007). Emotion regulation: Conceptual foundations. In J. J. Gross (Ed.), *Handbook of emotion regulation* (pp. 3–24). New York: Guilford Press.

Gross, J. J. (2007). (Ed.), *Handbook of emotion regulation.* New York: Guilford Press.

Haas, B. W., Omura, K., Constable, R. T., & Canli, T. (2007). Is automatic emotion regulation associated with agreeableness? *Psychological Science, 18,* 130–132.

Hammen, C., Brennan, P. A., & Shih, J. H. (2004). Family discord and stress predictors of depression and other disorders in adolescent children of depressed and nondepressed women. *Journal of the American Academy of Child & Adolescent Psychiatry, 43,* 994–1002.

Hampshire, A., & Owen, A. M. (2005). Fractionating attentional control using event-related fMRI. *Cerebral Cortex, 16,* 1679–1689.

Jaser, S. S., Champion, J. E., Reeslund, K., Keller, G., Merchant, M. J., Benson, M., et al. (2007). Cross-situational coping with peer and family stressors in adolescent offspring of depressed parents. *Journal of Adolescence, 30*(6), 917–932.

Jaser, S. S., Fear, J. M., Reeslund, K. L., Champion, J. E., Reising, M. M., & Compas, B. E. (in press). Maternal sadness and adolescents' responses to stress in offspring of mothers with and without a history of depression. *Journal of Clinical Child and Adolescent Psychology.*

Jaser, S. S., Langrock, A. M., Keller, G., Merchant, M. J., Benson, M., Reeslund, K., et al. (2005). Coping with the stress of parental depression II: Adolescent and parent reports of coping and adjustment. *Journal of Clinical Child and Adolescent Psychology, 34,* 193–205.

Joorman, J., & Gotlib, I. H. (2007). Selective attention to emotional faces following recovery from depression. *Journal of Abnormal Psychology, 116*, 80–85.

Kovacs, M., Sherrill, J., George, C., Pollock, M., Tumuluru, R., & Ho, V. (2006). Contextual emotion-regulation therapy: Description and pilot testing of a new intervention. *Journal of the American Academy of Child and Adolescent Psychiatry, 45*, 892–903.

Ladouceur, C. D., Dahl, R. D., Williamson, D. E., Birmaher, B., Ryan, N. D., & Casey, B. J. (2005). Altered emotional processing in pediatric anxiety, depression, and comorbid anxiety-depression. *Journal of Abnormal Child Psychology, 33*, 165–177.

Langrock, A. M., Compas, B. E., Keller, G., Merchant, M. J., & Copeland, M. E. (2002). Coping with the stress of parental depression: Parents' reports of children's coping, emotional, and behavioral problems. *Journal of Clinical Child and Adolescent Psychology, 31*, 312–324.

Lieberman, M. D. (2007). Social cognitive neuroscience: A review of core processes. *Annual Review of Psychology, 58*, 259–289.

Luecken, L. J., Dausch, B., Gulla, V., Hong, R., & Compas, B. E. (2003). Alterations in morning cortisol associated with PTSD in women with breast cancer. *Journal of Psychosomatic Research, 55*, 1–3.

Lewis, M. D., & Stieben, J. (2004). Emotion regulation in the brain: Conceptual issues and directions for developmental research. *Child Development, 75*, 371–376.

Mathews, A., & MacLeod, C. (2005). Cognitive vulnerability to emotional disorders. *Annual Review of Clinical Psychology, 1*, 167–195.

McEwen, B. S. (2004). Protection and damage from acute and chronic stress. *Annals of the New York Academy of Sciences, 1032*, 1–7.

McMahon, S. D., Grant, K. E., Compas, B. E., Thurm, A. E., & Ey, S. (2003). Stress and psychopathology in children and adolescents: Is there evidence of specificity? *Journal of Child Psychology and Psychiatry, 44*, 1–27.

Nolen-Hoeksema, S. (2004). The response styles theory. In C. Papageorgiou & A. Wells (Eds.), *Depressive rumination: Nature, theory, and treatment of negative thinking in depression* (pp. 107–123). New York: Wiley.

Nolen-Hoeksema, S., Stice, E., Wade, E., & Bohon, C. (2007). Reciprocal relations between rumination and bulimic, substance abuse, and depressive symptoms in female adolescents. *Journal of Abnormal Psychology, 116*, 198–207.

Oschner, K. N., Bunge, S. A., Gorss, J. J., & Gabrieli, J. D. E. (2002). Rethinking feelings: An fMRI study of cognitive regulation of emotion. *Journal of Cognitive Neuroscience, 14*, 1215–1229.

Papadakis, A. A., Prince, R. P., Jones, N. P., & Strauman, T. J. (2006). Self-regulation, rumination, and vulnerability to depression in adolescent girls. *Development and Psychopathology, 18*, 815–829.

Porges, S. W. (2007). A phylogenetic journey through the vague and ambiguous Xth cranial nerve: A commentary on contemporary heart rate variability research. *Biological Psychology, 74*, 301–307.

Rothbart, M. K., & Bates, J. E. (1998). Temperament. In W. Damon & N. Eisenberg (Eds.), *Handbook of child psychology* (Vol. 3, pp. 105–176). New York: Wiley.

Shaw, D. S., Schonberg, M., Sherrill, J., Huffman, D., Lukon, J., Obrosky, D., et al. (2006). Responsivity to offspring's expression of emotion among childhood-onset depressed mothers. *Journal of Clinical Child and Adolescent Psychology, 35*, 490–503.

Silk, J. S., Shaw, D. S., Forbes, E. E., Lane, T. L., & Kovacs, M. (2006a). Maternal depression and child internalizing: The moderating role of child emotion regulation. *Journal of Clinical Child and Adolescent Psychology, 35*, 116–126.

Silk, J. S., Shaw, D. S., Skuban, E. M., Oland, A. A., & Kovacs, M. (2006b). Emotion regulation strategies in offspring of childhood-onset depressed mothers. *Journal of Child Psychology and Psychiatry, 47*, 69–78.

Silk, J. S., Steinberg, L., & Morris, A. S. (2003). Adolescents' emotion regulation in daily life: Links to depressive symptoms and problem behavior. *Child Development, 74*, 1869–1880.

Sim, L., & Zeeman, J. (2004). Emotion awareness and identification skills in adolescent girls with bulimia nervosa. *Journal of Clinical Child and Adolescent Psychology, 33*, 760–771.

Skinner, E. A., Edge, K., Altman, J., & Sherwood, H. (2003). Searching for the structure of coping: A review and critique of category systems for classifying ways of coping. *Psychological Bulletin, 129*, 216–269.

Skinner, E. A., & Zimmer-Gembeck, M. J. (2007). The development of coping. *Annual Review of Psychology, 58*, 119–144.

Stanton, A. L., Kirk, S. B., Cameron, C. L., & Danoff-Burg, S. (2000). Coping through emotional approach: Scale construction and validation. *Journal of Personality and Social Psychology, 78*, 1150–1169.

Steimer, T., Python, A., Schulz, P. E., & Aubry, A. (2007). Plasma corticosterone, dexamethasone (DEX) suppression and DEX/CRH tests in a rat model of genetic vulnerability to depression. *Psychoneuroimmunology, 32*(5), 575–579.

Suveg, C., & Zeeman, J. (2004). Emotion regulation in children with anxiety disorders. *Journal of Clinical Child and Adolescent Psychology, 33*, 750–759.

Thompson, R. A. (1994). Emotion regulation: A theme in search of definition. *Monographs of the Society for Research in Child Development, 59*, 25–52.

Wadsworth, M. E., & Berger, L. E. (2006). Adolescents coping with poverty-related family stress: Prospective predictors of coping and psychological symptoms. *Journal of Youth and Adolescence, 35*, 57–70.

Wadsworth, M. E., & Compas, B. E. (2002). Coping with family conflict and economic strain: The adolescent perspective. *Journal of Research on Adolescence, 12*, 243–274.

Wadsworth, M. E., Raviv, T., Compas, B. E., & Connor-Smith, J. K. (2005). Parent and adolescent responses to poverty-related stress: Tests of mediated and moderated coping models. *Journal of Child and Family Studies, 14*, 283–298.

Wadsworth, M. E., Reickmann, T., Benson, M., & Compas, B. E. (2004). Coping and responses to stress in Navajo adolescents: Psychometric properties of the Responses to Stress Questionnaire. *Journal of Community Psychology, 32*, 391–411.

Walker, L. S., Smith, C. A., Garber, J., & Van-Slyke, D. A. (1997). Development and validation of the pain response inventory for children. *Psychological Assessment, 9*, 392–405.

Weissman, M. M., Warner, V., Wickramaratne, P., Moreau, D., & Olfson, M. (1997). Offspring of depressed parents. 10 years later. *Archives of General Psychiatry, 54*(10), 932–940.

Weisz, J. R., Thurber, C. A., Sweeney, L., Profit, V. D., & LeGagnoux, G. L. (1997). Brief treatment of mild-to-moderate child depression using primary and secondary control enhancement training. *Journal of Consulting and Clinical Psychology, 65*, 703–707.

Wenzlaff, R. M., & Wegner, D. M. (2000). Thought suppression. *Annual Review of Psychology, 51*, 59–91.

Wolchick, S. A., & Sandler, I. N. (1997). *Handbook of children's coping: Linking theory and intervention.* New York: Plenum Press.

Zeeman, J., Cassano, M., Perry-Parrish, C., & Stegall, S. (2006). Emotion regulation in children and adolescents. *Journal of Developmental and Behavioral Pediatrics, 27*, 155–168.

Zeeman, J., Shipman, K., & Suveg, C. (2002). Anger and sadness regulation: Predictions to internalizing and externalizing symptoms in children. *Journal of Clinical Child and Adolescent Psychology, 31*, 393–398.

Zeidner, M., & Endler, N. S. (Eds.). (1996). *Handbook of coping: Theory, research, and applications.* Oxford: John Wiley & Sons.

Chapter Sixteen

Parental Depression: Impact on Offspring and Mechanisms Underlying Transmission of Risk

JUTTA JOORMANN, FANNY EUGÈNE, AND IAN H. GOTLIB

CONTENTS

Depression is a debilitating disorder with high personal and economic costs. It is estimated that 24% of women and 15% of men will experience clinically significant depression (Kessler et al., 2003). Approximately 80% of these individuals will experience more than one major depressive episode over the course of their lives (Belsher & Costello, 1988; Boland & Keller, 2002). The high prevalence and high recurrence rate of depressive episodes is particularly disconcerting when we take into account that depression not only affects the depressed person, but also has a great impact on the person's social environment, specifically on family members. In fact, it is now accepted that depression is a familial disorder with a significantly increased risk of depression onset in offspring of depressed parents (Goodman, Adamson, Riniti, & Cole, 1994; Weissman et al., 2005). Still, we have little understanding of the impact of parental depression on their offspring, and even less understanding of the mechanisms that underlie the elevated risk of offspring to develop psychiatric disorders themselves.

Parental depression has also been found to be associated with an earlier onset and more severe course of depression in the offspring (Lieb, Isensee, Hofler, Pfister, & Wittchen, 2002). Because first episodes of depression are occurring at increasingly younger ages (Kessler et al., 2003), and because early-onset depression has been found to predict both poorer course and more adverse outcomes (e.g., Lewinsohn, Rohde, Seeley, Klein, & Gotlib, 2000; Rao, Hammen, & Daley, 1999), researchers have underscored the importance of assessing the functioning of youth in helping to understand risk for this disorder. Indeed, research conducted during the past several decades has documented that depressive disorders affect children and adolescents, that most youngsters who suffer from major depression are at high risk for recurrent episodes as they grow into adulthood, and conversely, that up to 45% of young adults with mood disorders had been depressed during their preteen or early teenage years (e.g., Birmaher et al., 1996; Kessler, Avenevoli, & Merikangas, 2001). Indeed, most depressive disorders in young adulthood are preceded by depression during adolescence (Pine, Cohen, Gurley, Brook, & Ma, 1998). Further, in a national sample of respondents, about 15% of 15- to 16-year-olds had already had episodes of major depression (Kessler & Walters, 1998).Understanding the factors that lead to depressive episodes in children and adolescents may therefore provide help to prevent adult depression. Examining the functioning of offspring of depressed parents and the impact of parents' depression on their offspring may thus provide valuable information for the prevention of depression onset and for the development of effective early interventions.

Numerous studies report adverse effects of parents' depression on their children. In fact, negative effects of parental depression have been found in children ranging in age from infancy through adolescence (e.g., Rahman, Lovel, Bunn, Iqbal, & Harrington, 2004; Whiffen & Gotlib, 1989). Having parents who suffer from depression is associated with a three to fivefold increase in the risk to the offspring for developing a depressive episode during early adolescence (Beardslee, Versage, & Gladstone, 1998; Williamson, Birmaher, Axelson, Ryan, & Dahl, 2004). Importantly, parental depression has also been found to be associated with an increased risk in the offspring for substance abuse, anxiety disorders, and externalizing disorders, such as oppositional defiant disorder or conduct disorder (for reviews, see Cummings & Davies, 1994; Gotlib & Goodman, 1999; Hammen, 1991). In a 5-year follow-up, Biederman et al. (2006) reported that offspring of parents with a major depressive disorder (MDD) were more likely not only to develop MDD, but also to present with multiple anxiety disorders, specific phobias, and disruptive behavior disorders. In a large, longitudinal study, the risk for developing anxiety disorders, major depression, social impairment, and substance dependence was approximately three times as high in the offspring of depressed parents as in the offspring of nondepressed parents (Weissman et al., 2006). The authors followed offspring of depressed and nondepressed parents for about 20 years, to age 35, and reported higher rates of medical problems and mortality in the offspring of depressed parents as they reached middle age. The highest incidence of depression in this sample was between ages 16 and 20, mostly in females. Interestingly, the earlier onset of depression in the offspring of depressed parents was not offset by later onset of depressive episodes in the low-risk group.

Because depression is twice as common in women as in men (Eaton et al., 1997; Kessler, McGonagle, Nelson, & Hughes, 1994), most of the literature on parental depression has focused on the risks associated with maternal depression. Nevertheless, of the few studies that have looked specifically at the impact of having a depressed father, most have found that paternal depression is also associated with emotional problems in the offspring (see Klein, Lewinsohn, Rohde, Seeley, & Olino, 2005; Phares, Duhig, & Watkins, 2002). For example, in a recent meta-analysis, Kane and Garber (2004) reported that paternal depression was significantly related to offspring internalizing and externalizing disorders (see also Connell & Goodman, 2002). Lewinsohn, Olino, and Klein (2005) demonstrated that while maternal depression was associated with offspring experiencing more minor stressors, for example, fights with parents and siblings, and greater levels of physical symptoms, paternal depression was associated with experiencing more major stressors, for example, difficulties at school, trouble with the law, having lower perceived social competence, and being more likely to attempt suicide during adolescence.

Importantly, children with two depressed parents are at significantly greater risk for disorder than children with one depressed parent (Weissman et al., 1984). Similarly, paternal depression was found to exacerbate the effect of maternal depression during infancy, but only in families in which fathers spent significant amounts of time caring for the children (Mezulis, Hyde, & Clark, 2004). From a more positive perspective, however, the presence of a healthy father in the home was associated with lower rates of disorder among school-aged children of depressed mothers (Conrad & Hammen, 1993). Even more troubling are recent findings indicating that psychopathology in children of depressed parents is moderated by grandparental depression status (Weissman et al., 2005). The authors reported that at age 12, almost 60% of all the grandchildren with two generations of MDD exhibited psychiatric disorders, particularly anxiety disorders. Interestingly, in families with depressed parents, but without depressed grandparents, parent diagnosis did not affect the rate of psychiatric disorders in the grandchildren, but did affect overall psychosocial functioning. These studies demonstrate that although maternal depression has been the focus of the majority of studies, the impact of paternal depression on offspring and the role that other caregivers and family members play in altering the risk of emotional disorders in these children clearly warrants more attention.

Given the findings reviewed above, it is critical that we identify the mechanisms that place offspring of depressed parents at elevated risk for depression. Although investigators have provided important data regarding the magnitude of this risk, we know little about the specific factors that are implicated in the development of depression in these offspring or about the mechanisms involved in the intergenerational transmission of risk. Certainly, there is a genetic component that contributes to these children's risk (see Chapter 10 in this volume). Indeed, heritability of depression has been estimated at approximately 37% (Sullivan, Neale, & Kendler, 2000). It is almost certain, therefore, that the effects of parental depression on offspring are transmitted through multiple mechanisms, including heritability, innate dysfunctional regulatory mechanisms that affect stress reactivity and emotion regulation abilities, exposure to negative maternal cognitions, behaviors, affect, and the stressful context of the children's lives (Goodman & Gotlib, 1999). Understanding the operation of these factors is crucial if we are to develop effective programs to prevent the onset of this debilitating disorder.

Goodman and Gotlib (1999) emphasized the importance of adopting a developmental perspective when examining the intergenerational transmission of depression; consequently, we begin this chapter by examining the impact of parental depression at different stages of the child's development. Although the focus of this handbook is on depression in adolescence, studies suggest that parental depression affects the development of biological reactivity to stress and emotion regulation skills early in life, thereby setting the stage for increased risk of depression throughout adolescence and early adulthood (Goodman & Gotlib, 1999). As we will discuss later in this chapter, parent's regulation of their children's emotions may be needed most at early stages of development. Children may find it particularly difficult to recover from the negative effects of early exposure to parental depression not only because dysfunctional emotion regulation strategies, behavioral patterns, and cognitive schemas are established, but also because children have acquired a peer status that is difficult to alter. Recent studies have found that the adverse impact of maternal postnatal depression on risk for emotional disorders in adolescence is associated with the chronicity and severity of the mother's depression (Halligan, Murray, Martins, & Cooper, 2007a; Hammen & Brennan, 2003).

Thus, our main focus in this chapter is on the identification of underlying mechanisms of risk, and we believe that it is essential to examine the impact of parental psychopathology at different stages of development in order to gain a better understanding of these mechanisms. Therefore, in the second part of this chapter, we examine family environment, cognitive vulnerability to depression, and biological determinants of stress reactivity and emotion regulation in offspring of depressed parents. Finally, we discuss treatment implications and outline future directions for this important line of research.

THE IMPACT OF PARENTAL DEPRESSION ON OFFSPRING

It is important to recognize that the impact of a parent's depression on the offspring is a function of the offspring's age and, more importantly, of his or her biological and psychosocial development. As Goodman and Gotlib (1999) noted, a developmental perspective is often lacking in studies of offspring of depressed parents. Moreover, the observation that parental depression increases the offspring's risk not only for depression, but also for other forms of psychopathology, implies that parental depression affects the development of general risk factors that are associated with a range of emotional disorders. We should not expect, therefore, that parents and their offspring will exhibit substantial overlap in their specific symptoms of depression. Individual differences in responding to stressful life events and, specifically, in recovery from stressful experiences and negative affect, are important concepts in understanding risk for psychopathology.

Indeed, in recent years, depression has been conceptualized as a disorder of emotion dysregulation and stress reactivity. Theorists have suggested that it is not so much an abnormal initial response to a stressor, such as a stressful life event, which characterizes individuals who are vulnerable to depression, but rather an inability to regulate the duration and intensity of the ensuing negative affect (e.g., Teasdale, 1988). The construct of emotion regulation, which evolved from the broader concept of coping with stress, involves the utilization of behavioral and cognitive strategies in an effort to modulate affect intensity and duration (Thompson, 1994). Although the assessment of emotion regulation is not an easy endeavor, given its importance for well-being, this construct has been the focus of increasing attention in the developmental literature (Cole, Martin, & Dennis, 2004). Indeed, children's development of emotion regulation is considered to be one of the cornerstones of socialization (Eisenberg, 2000). Researchers have identified a developmental sequence, progressing from a basic limited self-regulatory capacity for managing emotion, through toddlers engaging in mutually regulatory interactions with their mothers, culminating in the development of a wider array of self-regulatory strategies in adolescents. Importantly, the developmental literature continues to document the long-term negative consequences related to difficulties in these stages.

The unfolding of emotion regulation responses also depends on the maturation of brain regions that support the development of sensory, motor, perceptual, cognitive, linguistic, and social skills. Overall, such skills are at rudimentary levels during infancy, show very rapid development during early and middle childhood, and more gradual increments after late childhood (Anderson, Anderson, Northam, Jacobs, & Catroppa, 2001; Klenberg, Korkman, & Lahti-Nuuttila, 2001; Korkman, Kemp, & Kirk, 2001). But even across childhood, age-specific trajectories of different skills vary and probably affect the rate of acquisition and extent of sophistication of some emotion regulation responses. And notable gains in some cognitive skills (e.g., working memory) appear only around late adolescence (Swanson, 1999). In this context, it is important to note that brain regions associated with primary functions, such as motor and sensory systems, mature first, followed by temporal and parietal association cortices that underlie basic language skills and spatial attention. Prefrontal cortex (PFC) and lateral temporal cortices are among the last areas to mature (Casey, Tottenham, Listen, & Durston, 2005). Several regions of the PFC, including the orbitofrontal cortex (OFC), the medial prefrontal cortex (MPFC), and the anterior cingulate cortex (ACC), play a critical role in the cognitive regulation of emotion, including refocusing of attention, distraction, and reappraisal. Consequently, it has been proposed that the development of emotion regulation depends critically on the development of the PFC (Stuss, 1992). Individual differences in the development of emotion regulation skills are therefore likely to be closely related to individual differences in the development of brain structure and function.

Importantly, the development of emotion regulation is achieved through interactions among the maturing infant, caregivers, and other individuals, or factors in the environment. While interaction with the primary caregivers and their modeling of responses to negative affect might play a crucial role in early childhood and infancy, social skills, cognitive abilities, self-regulation of negative affect, and peer relations likely become more important in later development. In the next section, we describe research examining the functioning of children of depressed parents at different stages of development. We focus in particular on the development of emotion regulation and stress reactivity in childhood and adolescence, and on the role of the caregivers in affecting this development.

Impact of Parental Depression in Infants and Preschool-Aged Children

A number of theorists contend that the impact of parental depression, and particularly maternal depression, should be most pronounced during the early years of the child's life (for a discussion of this point, see Goodman and Gotlib [1999]). Mothers are likely to be the primary caregivers of young children. Similarly, school-aged children will have more contact with others, and may, therefore, benefit from supportive peer and other adult relationships. In addition, because early mother–infant relationships form a foundation for children's self-perceptions and social relations, maternal depression also likely interferes with younger children's mastery of developmentally salient tasks. Emotion regulation in infancy, for example, is largely dependent on caregiver–child relations. Given that the young child lacks cognitive skills necessary for self-regulation, and only possesses very rudimentary skills for self-soothing, parents play a primary role in the regulation of negative affect during this developmental period.

Indeed, the results of a growing number of investigations indicate that parental, and particularly, maternal, depression is associated with problematic functioning in infants and toddlers. It is important to point out, though, that the majority of studies in this area rely on parent report. Given the well-replicated finding that depression is characterized by biased processing of negative material and by reporting biases, depressed parent's reports of problematic child behavior may, in part, reflect these biases (Brewin, Andrews, & Gotlib, 1993; Goodman & Gotlib, 1999). Keeping this caveat in mind, numerous studies have reported that infants of women with elevated depression scores were rated as more drowsy or fussy, and as less relaxed or content than infants of nondepressed women; other studies similarly found maternal reports of infant crying and unsoothability to be correlated with depressive symptomatology (Field et al., 2007; Weinberg, Olson, Beeghly, & Tronick, 2006). Indeed, changes in infant's play behavior, sleep pattern, affect, activity level, and physiological changes (i.e., cortisol, vagal tone, and heart rate) have been observed for the duration of their mother's depression (Field, 1995).

Whiffen and Gotlib (1989) assessed the effects of a diagnosable episode of depression during the postpartum on infants' cognitive and socioemotional development. At 9–10 weeks postpartum, the depressed mothers reported more difficulties with infant care and perceived their infants as more bothersome than did the nondepressed mothers. Observers rated the infants of the depressed mothers as more tense and less happy. Perhaps most importantly, the infants of the depressed mothers obtained lower scores on the Bayley Scales of Infant Development, particularly on the Mental or Cognitive Development subscale. This effect was independent of maternal level of education. Moreover, at 3 years of age, children of the depressed mothers obtained significantly lower scores on the verbal, perceptual performance, general cognitive, and memory subscales, and a marginally lower score on the quantitative subscale, than children of the control mothers. In addition, the previously depressed mothers also rated their children on the Child Behavior Checklist (CBCL) as more aggressive and destructive.

Similar results were reported by Carro, Grant, Gotlib, and Compas (1993), who found that fathers' depressive symptoms at 1 month postpartum predicted children's internalizing and externalizing problem behaviors at 2–3 years of age, and the interaction of the fathers' and mothers' depressive symptoms predicted childrens' subsequent internalizing problems. In a community sample, preschool children's social competence and behavior problems, as reported by their day care providers, were related to early maternal depression

(Gross, Conrad, Fogg, Willis, & Garvey, 1995). Other studies have found difficulties in social behavior in infants and toddlers. Withdrawn infant behavior towards the clinician was related to the mother's report of whether she had felt depressed since birth (Matthey, Guedeney, Starakis, & Barnett, 2005). In a similar study, toddlers of depressed mothers exhibited fewer social skills and more defiance when interacting with their mothers than did toddlers of nondepressed mothers (Dietz, Jennings, & Abrew, 2005).

One of the important indicators of infant adjustment is attachment behavior, which is assumed both to reflect the quality of the mother–child relationship (see Ainsworth, Blehar, Waters, & Wall, 1978) and to provide an important link to the child's later interpersonal and emotion regulation competence. Indeed, 2- to 3-year-old children of unipolar and bipolar depressed mothers were found to be characterized by higher rates of insecure attachment than control children (Carter, Garrity Rokous, Chazan Cohen, Little, & Briggs Gowan, 2001; Righetti Veltema, Bousquet, & Manzano, 2003). In a recent meta-analysis of attachment studies, infants of depressed mothers were less likely to be securely attached (Martins & Gaffan, 2000). Because secure attachment is important for exploratory behavior, it is not surprising that infant negative behavioral responses to novelty were found to be related to levels of maternal depression and anxiety (Davis et al., 2004).

Investigators examining the interactions of depressed mothers and their children report that these children are more "maladaptively empathic." Thus, their own activity was disrupted when other people experienced distress, and they were more likely to suppress the expression of affect. Given these findings, investigators have hypothesized that children of depressed mothers are overly sensitive to their mothers' negative affect, while being unable to seek or accept comfort for their own emotional distress (e.g., Zahn-Wexler, Cummings, Iannotti, & Radke-Yarrow, 1984). Furthermore, infant–mother dyads in which the mother suffered from postpartum depression were characterized by little verbal interaction and playing behavior (Righetti Veltema et al., 2003). Depressed mothers also demonstrated less repair of interrupted interactions than nondepressed mothers, and their toddlers were less likely to maintain interactions (Jameson, Gelfand, Kulcsar, & Teti, 1997).

It is clear from these studies that infants and toddlers of depressed mothers exhibit a range of behavioral, emotional, and cognitive difficulties. Moreover, several longitudinal studies indicate that these difficulties are quite stable. Behavioral and social difficulties in a 5-year follow-up assessment were related to postnatal depression in their mothers (Hipwell, Murray, Ducournau, & Stein, 2005; Murray, Sinclair, Cooper, Ducournau, & Turner, 1999). Negative effects of postnatal maternal depression were even found in a 13-year follow-up assessment (Halligan et al., 2007a; Murray, Halligan, Adams, Patterson, & Goodyer, 2006). Given the high rate of recurrence of depressive episodes, mothers with postpartum depression are also likely to experience further episodes during their children's lifetime. It is unclear whether maternal depression during infancy has particularly pernicious effects on the children's development or if the stability of the children's problems is the result of the repeated exposure to maternal depression. Halligan et al. (2007a) assessed depressive symptoms in adolescents who had or had not been exposed to maternal postnatal depression, and found that maternal postnatal depression was associated with increased risk for depression in adolescent offspring only if the mother had suffered additional depressive episodes during the child's life. This result suggests that chronicity of maternal depression is more important than the timing of the episode. They also found, however, that maternal postnatal depression was associated with increased risk for anxiety disorders in offspring even if there had been no additional depressive episode during the child's life. Similarly, other studies suggest that despite the importance of chronicity, even relatively short exposure to severe maternal depression can have a deleterious impact on a child's emotional functioning. Indeed, in a related study, severity of maternal depression was a better predictor of adolescent offspring's risk for depression than chronicity (Hammen & Brennan, 2003).

We also do not know whether the children's difficulties are due to transient problematic behaviors that are a consequence of experiencing a depressive episode, or to more stable underlying personality characteristics of women who are prone to experiencing episodes of depression (see Barnett and Gotlib [1988] and Gotlib and Hammen [1992] for reviews of this literature). Finally, we do not know whether children's behavioral problems are a consequence of their parent's depression or, alternatively, a reflection of an underlying vulnerability in the children to experience emotional disorders that is expressed in early behavioral problems or temperament. For example, a recent study in preschool children reported that low positive emotionality (a propensity to experience positive mood states, high sociability, and high environmental engagement), but not high negative emotionality (a propensity to experience negative mood states similar to the concept of neuroticism) or behavioral inhibition (characterized by wariness, fear, and low exploration in novel situations) was related to maternal mood disorder (Durbin, Klein, Hayden, Buckley, & Moerk, 2005). These authors propose that low positive emotionality in children represents a temperamental risk factor for depression. Importantly, maternal depression during pregnancy was related to negative affect and behavioral inhibition in the children, which predicted affective disorders (Huot, Brennan, Stowe, Plotsky, & Walker, 2004). Thus, offspring of depressed parents might early on exhibit temperamental risk factors that influence parent–child interactions and cause some of the difficulties that we reviewed above. Other child characteristics might also be important moderators of risk. Horowitz and Garber (2003), for example, found that IQ moderated the relation between chronicity of maternal depression and depressive disorders in adolescents. Interestingly, for children of mothers with no or less chronic depression, higher IQ was associated with lower likelihood of depression. In contrast, for children of mothers with a history of more chronic depression, higher levels of IQ were significantly associated with a greater likelihood of depression. In a related study, higher levels of verbal ability were related to less reporting of depressive symptoms and internalizing problems (Malcarne, Hamilton, Ingram, & Taylor, 2000). It will be important for future research to address these issues more explicitly.

Impact of Parental Depression in School-Age Children and/or Adolescents

Social relationships and self-regulation skills become more important for emotion regulation and stress reactivity as children start attending school. Although one might expect that parental depression in this phase of development has a weaker impact on children, findings in the literature suggest that this is not the case. The continued adverse impact of parental depression might be due to the lasting effects of earlier exposure to subclinical or clinical depression in the parents, or to the effects of repeated exposure to parental depression. It may also indicate that parental support continues to play an important role in development despite the reduced time that primary caregivers spend with their children.

In several early investigations, researchers interviewed depressed mothers about the functioning of their school-age children. In general, these studies show that, compared to never-depressed parents, both currently and formerly depressed parents describe their children as having a greater number of physical and psychological problems (Billings & Moos, 1983). It is important to bear in mind, though, that these data are based on parental reports rather than on direct observations of the children and, therefore, may be biased (e.g., Brewin et al., 1993; Webster Stratton & Hammond, 1988).

A number of investigators have examined more directly the psychosocial functioning of older children of depressed mothers, and reported that children of depressed parents demonstrate poorer functioning than do children of nondepressed parents (Goodman et al., 1994; Orvaschel, Walsh, & Ye, 1988). Lee and Gotlib (1989), for example, examined the psychological adjustment of four groups of school-age children: children of depressed psychiatric patient mothers, children of nondepressed psychiatric patient mothers; children of nondepressed medical patient mothers, and children of community mothers. Children of depressed mothers had more severe psychiatric symptoms on the Child Assessment Schedule (CAS) and poorer overall adjustment on the Global Assessment Scale for Children than did the children of nondepressed mothers. The children of depressed mothers were also rated by their mothers as having a greater number of both internalizing and externalizing problems compared with the children of the nondepressed control mothers; indeed, two-thirds of the children of the depressed mothers were placed in the clinical range on the CBCL (greater than the 90th percentile), an incidence three times greater than that observed in the nondepressed controls. Interestingly, the children of depressed mothers typically did not differ from the children of nondepressed psychiatric patient mothers, suggesting that the effects of maternal depression on child dysfunction may be nonspecific.

In a 10-month follow-up assessment of these children, Lee and Gotlib (1991a) reported that despite a significant reduction in the mothers' depressive symptoms, the formerly depressed women continued to describe their children as having a higher number of internalizing and externalizing problems than the nondepressed controls. Moreover, interviewer ratings on the CAS indicated that children of both the depressed and the nondepressed psychiatric patient mothers were rated as having a greater number of mood symptoms and somatic complaints than children of the community mothers. Thus, children of both depressed and nondepressed mothers demonstrated problematic adjustment, even when their mothers were no longer overtly symptomatic, indicating that there may be a substantial lag between alleviation of maternal symptomatology and improvement in child functioning. Finally, in a recent study examining 7- to 17-year-old children of depressed treatment-seeking mothers, about a third of the children had a current psychiatric disorder, and nearly half had a lifetime history of psychopathology, including disruptive behavior and anxiety disorders (Pilowsky et al., 2006a).

Impact of Parental Depression in Adolescence

Adolescence, and in particular, puberty, is a time of elevated risk for the development of depression in girls (Birmaher et al., 1996; Hayward, Gotlib, Schraedley, & Litt, 1999; Kessleret al. 1994); indeed, pubert status has been found to be a better predictor of depression in girls than age (Angold, Costello, & Worthman, 1998). In a study that compared the functioning of adolescent children of unipolar depressed parents, arthritic parents, and community control parents, the investigators found that although the children of depressed parents reported more symptoms than offspring in the community group, there were no significant differences between the children of the depressed and the arthritic patients (Hirsch, Moos, & Reischl, 1985).

Other studies have assessed the adjustment of adolescent offspring of depressed and nondepressed parents (Beardslee, Schultz, & Selman, 1987). These investigators assessed parental and adolescent reports on the Diagnostic Interview for Children and Adolescents and reported that 38% of the adolescents in the high-risk group received a diagnosis of past or current affective disorder, whereas only 2% of the adolescents in the low-risk group received such diagnoses. Similarly, 7- to 19-year-old children of depressed parents were found to demonstrate cognitive impairment in the form of subtest variability on the WISC-R (Hirsch et al., 1985). Recent studies have examined offspring of depressed parents in adolescents and early adulthood and reported that maternal depression was associated with higher levels of physical symptoms during adolescence, higher levels of minor stressors, and higher risk of using mental health services during adulthood (Lewinsohn et al., 2005). Paternal depression was associated with more major stressors, higher likelihood of attempted suicide during adolescence, and lower perceived social competence during adolescence and young adulthood. Halligan et al. (2007a) reported that maternal postnatal depression was associated with higher rates of affective disorders in adolescent offspring, but only if there were later episodes of maternal depression; higher rates of anxiety disorders were independent of the occurrence of subsequent maternal depression. Finally, a recent longitudinal study reported that parental depression was associated with depression recurrence, chronicity, and severity, and with elevated rates of anxiety disorders as formerly depressed adolescence entered adulthood (Rohde, Lewinsohn, Klein, & Seeley, 2005).

This brief overview of the literature clearly demonstrates that parental depression has important and lasting effects on children's development and psychosocial adjustment. We now turn to a closer investigation of mechanisms that may underlie these negative effects and place offspring at increased risk for psychopathology. As we outlined at the beginning of the chapter, risk for depression is associated with a multitude of environmental and innate factors that influence the development of stress reactivity and the ability to regulate emotions. Indeed, contemporary models of adult depression are explicitly diathesis-stress formulations, positing that events perceived as stressful will interact with an "endogenous" vulnerability that contributes to the onset of the disorder (cf. Monroe & Simons, 1991). A sizeable body of research has documented a strong and consistent association between stress and depression in adults (see Gotlib & Hammen, 2002). Similarly, longitudinal studies with adolescents have found life stress to predict the onset of MDD (Goodyer, Herbert, Tamplin, & Altham, 2000; Lewinsohn, Rohde, Klein, & Seeley, 1999); research has also demonstrated that responsive caretakers and social support may buffer the risk for the onset of depression (Werner & Smith, 2001). In this context, recent research examining the development of negative outcomes in depression has focused on the link between individual predispositions and stressful experiences by assessing the constructs of stress reactivity and emotion regulation. We first focus on environmental factors and then present recent research that suggests that offspring of depressed parents are characterized by cognitive biases and neuroendocrine and neurobiological abnormalities that affect response to stressors and the ability to regulate emotional states.

MECHANISMS OF RISK

Family Environments of Children of Depressed Parents

Children of depressed parents are likely to be exposed to stressful family environments. In a recent review, Burke (2003) found that families of depressed women were characterized by elevated levels of conflict and marital discord. Interestingly, these authors reported that a significant percentage of men reported developing depression when their partners became depressed. This finding is particularly noteworthy because, as we noted earlier, children with two depressed parents are at greater risk of negative outcome than children with only one depressed parent. In a related study, parental depression was also associated with poor marital adjustment, parent–child discord, low family cohesion, affectionless control, and parental divorce (Pilowsky, Wickramarante, Nomura, & Weissman, 2006b). These authors also reported that family discord factors were associated with increased risk for depression and substance abuse in the offspring in a 20-year follow-up. More generally, parenting and family environments have been found to be more negative in families of depressed mothers. Interestingly, Hammen and colleagues have found that chronic familial stress and negative parenting behavior, such as high expressed emotion and high criticism, mediate the relation between parent and offspring depression (e.g., Hammen, Brennan, & Shih, 2004a; Hammen, Shih, & Brennan, 2004b; Nelson, Hammen, Brennan, & Ullman, 2003). In a large community sample, for example, Hammen et al. (2004a) reported significant interactions between maternal depression and family discord/stress variables. Hammen et al. (2004b) also demonstrated that maternal depression (and depression in the maternal grandmother) contributed to chronic interpersonal stress in the mothers, affecting the quality of parenting and youth's social competence. In turn, poor social functioning and interpersonal life events caused at least in part by the youths themselves were proximal predictors of current depression. The association between maternal and child depression was mediated by the family and interpersonal stress effects. High expressed emotion in the parents also proved to be an intervening variable between maternal depression and child functioning in this sample (Nelson et al., 2003). Finally, Nomura, Wickramaratne, Warner, Mufson, and Weissman (2002) reported in their longitudinal study that parental depression was the most important predictor of offspring MDD and anxiety disorders, whereas family discord was the most important predictor of substance abuse. These findings strongly suggest that children who grow up in a household with one or two depressed parents are exposed to higher levels of conflicts and more interpersonal stressors than control children, and that these stressors affect the development of social competence in the youth, thereby increasing their risk for the onset of emotional disorders.

Several researchers have directly examined the behaviors of depressed parents with their children. Compared with nondepressed psychiatric and nonpsychiatric controls, depressed mothers have been observed in direct interactions with their children to be less positive, and more negative and retaliatory with their children, and to engage in more angry and intrusive, hostile and conflictual behavior (Goodman et al., 1994; Hammen, 1991), to display more sad and irritable affect (Cohn, Campbell, Matias, & Hopkins, 1990; Hops et al., 1987), and to either be ineffective in resolving conflicts or to alternate between harsh, punitive discipline and undercontrol (e.g., Dumas, Gibson, & Albin, 1989). In a recent meta-analysis of behavioral studies, Lovejoy, Graczyk, O'Hare, and Neuman (2000) reported a strong association between negative maternal behavior and depression, and weaker associations between depression and disengagement from the child. Current depression in the mother had the largest effects. Importantly, low levels of parental control, high levels of maternal warmth, and low levels of maternal overinvolvement interacted with maternal depression to predict resilient outcomes in youth (Brennan, Le Brocque, & Hammen, 2003).

We outlined in the beginning of the chapter that the parent's support of the development of emotion regulation skills in their offspring very much depends on the child's age and, more importantly, the child's biological and psychosocial maturation. In the early stages of this development, parents need to foster an attachment relationship and facilitate the development of emotional self-regulation. Insensitive or unresponsive parenting has been found to be among the strongest predictors of insecure attachment and, further, may be related to problems in infants' development of innate regulatory mechanisms (e.g., Field, 1992). Relative to their nondepressed counterparts, depressed mothers have been observed to provide lower amounts and lower quality stimulation for their infants (Livingood, Daen, & Smith, 1983), to use less reciprocal vocalization and affectionate contact with their infants, and to be slower in responding, and less contingently responsive to their infants (Field, 1984; Field, Healy, Goldstein, & Guthertz, 1990).

For toddlers and preschool-aged children, parents must support their children in developing an accurate understanding of social and emotional situations (Cicchetti & Schneider-Rosen, 1986). This includes providing their child with emotional language acquisition and socialization (Gottman, Katz, & Hooven, 1996), guiding the behaviors of their toddlers in social referencing situations, and facilitating relationships with their peers (cf. Campos & Steinberg, 1981; Walden & Ogan, 1988). These aspects of emotion regulation development are important so that children develop effective autonomous functioning, manage emotionally arousing situations, and develop their ability to organize and co-ordinate environmental resources (Cicchetti & Schneider-Rosen, 1986).

It is important to note, therefore, that depressed mothers compared to control mothers have been found to spend less time mutually engaged with their children in a shared activity (Goldsmith & Rogoff, 1997). They also tend to exhibit less encouragement to sustain attention, but instead initiate and terminate their children's attention to objects more frequently (Breznitz & Friedman, 1988).

In school-aged children and adolescents, parents need to provide general social support or stress buffering (Lee & Gotlib, 1991b). They need to support children in coping with new stressors, help their children to maintain their focus on the cognitive-intellectual and social environment, and monitor their children's behavior and provide consistent reinforcement of desired, rather than of undesired behavior (Hops et al., 1987; Hops, Sherman, & Biglan, 1990). Thus, studies have reported that depressed mothers suppress their dysphoric affect in response to their children's aggressive affect, thereby reinforcing the children's misbehavior (e.g., Hops et al., 1987). Moreover, a number of investigators have found that depressed mothers, compared with their nondepressed counterparts, have more negative appraisals of, and lower tolerance for their children's behaviors. Both of these variables, in turn, have been found to be associated with more punitive parenting, and might further be expected to be associated with higher thresholds for rewarding desired behavior (e.g., Forehand, Lautenschlager, Faust, & Graziano, 1986; Schaughency & Lahey, 1985). Furthermore, in their confluence model, Dishion, Patterson, and Griesler (1994) describe poor parental discipline and poor monitoring of peer relations by the parents as two important factors that increase the risk of antisocial behavior in adolescents. More specifically, lack of reinforcement of desired behaviors and parent–child interactions that reinforce aggressive and coercive behavior, combined with decreased monitoring by the parents, increases the likelihood of affiliation with deviant peers, which may be related to the increased risk of externalizing disorders in these children.

Cognitive Vulnerability in Offspring of Depressed Parents

One of the major approaches over the past two decades to understanding the etiology of MDD, the functioning of depressed individuals, and vulnerability to this disorder are cognitive models of depression. In general, these models emphasize the importance of cognitive constructs, like schemas, in placing individuals at elevated risk for experiencing episodes of depression, and in hindering the recovery process (Beck, 1967, 1976; Bower, 1981; Teasdale, 1988). Thus, cognitive theories posit that vulnerable and depressed individuals selectively attend to negative stimuli, filter out positive stimuli, and perceive negative or neutral information as being more negative than is actually the case. These processing biases will have an adverse effect on emotion regulation and stress reactivity by maintaining negative affective states and hindering recovery from stressful events. As in other diathesis-stress models, negative schemas, developed through adverse early experiences, are posited to be latent until they are activated when individuals experience a stressful life event. In early interactions with their primary caregivers, therefore, children can develop dysfunctional schemas, such as the idea that they are worthless if they are not liked by everyone. These schemas do not necessarily lead to negative automatic thoughts or distortions, but they are easily activated by stressful events, negative mood states, or situations that resemble the situation under which the schemas were acquired, for example, the establishing of close peer relationships. Depressive affect innervates the negative schemas and reinforces their activity. Early life experiences and interactions with primary caregivers likely play an important role in the formation of functional and dysfunctional cognitive schemas, and might thereby increase depressive vulnerability.

As in the adult literature, studies relying on self-report measures indicate that depressed children endorse more cognitive errors and more negative attributions than nondepressed children (e.g., Tems, Stewart, Skinner, & Hughes, 1993). Jaenicke et al. (1987) examined attributional styles in 8- to 16-year-old children of mothers diagnosed with MDD, bipolar disorder (BD), or a physical medical illness, and of healthy mothers. Consistent with the hopelessness theory of depression, children of mothers with MDD or BD had significantly more depressotypic attributional styles than children of medically ill or healthy mothers. An important limitation to this study, however, is that many of the children had diagnosable past episodes of depression. Because this was not controlled for in the analyses, the negative attributional style of high-risk children in this study could represent a consequence of, rather than a vulnerability to, depression. In addition, Hammen (1991) later reported that many of these children of BP and MDD mothers had high levels of depressive symptoms at the time of the study. Differences between high- and low-risk children could thus have reflected the presence of current depression in children of BD and MDD mothers. In a more recent study however, Garber and Robinson (1997) found that, even after controlling for children's current depressive symptomatology, children of unipolar depressed mothers had more negative attributional styles than children of never-depressed mothers.

Because attributional style is usually assessed through self-report questionnaires, it has been difficult to study in very young children. Children under 8 years of age have been found to provide unreliable answers to self-report questionnaire items, which are often inconsistent with their actual behavior (Vitaro & Pelletier, 1991). To avoid this problem, investigators exposed 5-year-old children whose mothers had been depressed at least once since their birth to a situation of mild stress (the threat of losing in a children's card game). Compared to children whose mothers had never been depressed, children of depressed mothers were more likely to express hopelessness and pessimism when losing a card deal (Murray, Woolgar, Cooper, & Hipwell, 2001). Given the association between depressotypic attributions and hopelessness, this suggests that children who have been exposed to maternal depression could show a cognitive vulnerability to depression as early as the age of five.

More recently, self-report measures of cognitive functioning in depression have been largely replaced by more sophisticated methodologies, many derived from research in experimental cognitive psychology (Gotlib & MacLeod, 1997). Using experimental tasks, researchers have found evidence of biases in both attention and memory in depressed adults (see Mathews & MacLeod, 2005, for a recent review), and similar results are beginning to be found in samples of depressed children (e.g., Bishop, Dalgleish, & Yule, 2004; Neshat-Doost, Taghavi, Moradi, Yule, & Dalgleish, 1998; Timbremont & Braet, 2004). Very few studies, however, have examined cognitive biases in offspring of depressed parents. Jaenicke et al. (1987) found high-risk children of unipolar depressed mothers to endorse or recall fewer positive self-descriptive adjectives than children of control mothers. Other researchers used a recall paradigm following a negative mood induction in children between the ages of 8 and 12, whose mothers met diagnostic criteria for major depression or dysthymia at the time of the study (Taylor & Ingram, 1999). These children recalled significantly more negative than neutral words. This recall bias was not found in children whose mothers had never been depressed. It is important to note, however, that children's prior history of depression was not assessed in this study. More recently, Joormann, Talbot, and Gotlib (2007) investigated whether never-disordered daughters whose mothers have experienced recurrent episodes of depression during their daughters' lifetime were characterized by biased processing of emotional information. Following a negative mood induction, participants completed an emotional faces dot-probe task. Daughters of depressed, but not of never-disordered, mothers selectively attended to negative facial expressions; in contrast, only control daughters selectively attended to positive facial expressions.

Taken together, the results of these studies indicate that depressed children and adults are characterized by biases in attention to, and memory for, negative emotional material. There is also growing evidence of the operation of negative cognitive schemas in offspring of depressed parents, particularly as these children experience negative mood states, a finding that supports the formulation that the biases that are apparent in depressed adults have their origins in childhood. It is critical to note, however, that there is little direct evidence that negative cognitive schemas play a causal role in the onset of diagnosable depressive episodes, either in children or in adults. Longitudinal studies are needed to investigate whether these cognitive factors predict the first onset of depressive episodes in children at risk for depression.

Biological Risk Factors

As Goodman and Gotlib (1999) describe in detail, two primary mechanisms that underlie the elevated depression risk in offspring are 1) heritability and 2) exposure to a depressed mother who models negative behaviors and cognitions and exposes the offspring to high levels of stress. Although the reported degree of heritability for MDD varies across studies, it is almost certain that what is inherited is not unipolar depression itself, but rather traits and characteristics that confer an increased vulnerability to depression, such as heightened stress reactivity and problematic self-regulatory processes (e.g., Plomin, Reiss, Hetherington, & Howe, 1994). Indeed, behavior genetics studies have demonstrated that several correlates of (and potential risk factors for) depression in children are highly heritable, including temperament, shyness, low self-esteem, and expression of negative emotions (cf. Loehlin, 1992). In fact, Goldsmith, Buss, and Lemery (1997) presented intriguing data indicating that identical twins were more similar than fraternal twins on parental reports of emotion regulation. Importantly, there is now evidence that the quality of parent–child interactions can affect the maturational trajectory of corticolimbic neurocircuits and neuroregulatory mechanisms in the offspring that influence the development of effective emotion regulation skills (Dawson, 1994; Kaufman, Plotsky, Nemeroff, & Charney, 2000). Indeed, a number of recent studies have documented the adverse effects of stress exposure on human physiology, brain structure, and function (Bremner et al., 2000). Moreover, individual differences in the development of emotion regulation skills are likely to be closely related to individual differences in brain structure and function.

Stress Reactivity in Children of Depressed Parents

Investigators have begun to focus on the neuroendocrine and neural bases of emotion regulation and coping as an alternative to self-report methodologies, a shift that has helped to elucidate the biological foundations of emotion dysregulation and risk for depression. In particular, a focus on cortisol as a reflection of the stress response system has allowed investigators to examine immediate response to stress, as well as longer-term physiological and emotional arousal (e.g., Gunnar, Marvinney, Isensee, & Fisch, 1989). The hypothalamic-pituitary-adrenocortical (HPA) system and the resultant production of cortisol are conceptualized as the psychophysiological substrates of the regulation and coping systems. Cortisol is released spontaneously throughout the day (basal cortisol), and is also released in response to stressors (cortisol reactivity), and researchers have examined reactivity of the HPA axis and basal cortisol levels in relation to depression. The reactivity of the HPA system represents the core of human stress response, secreting cortisol when under stress as a means of mobilizing resources necessary for sustaining the physical and psychological activity needed for action (Stansbury & Gunnar, 1994). Indeed, investigators have argued that levels of cortisol produced under stress reflect individuals' ability to regulate and cope (Gunnar, Connors, & Isensee, 1989). Even basal HPA functioning is of interest to researchers examining emotion regulation because basal cortisol, that is, naturally occurring cortisol levels at a given point during the day, varies across the day, promotes various adaptive functions, and may reflect individuals' baseline physiological and emotional arousal. Given that the functioning of the HPA system is so integrally related to the human stress response, it is not surprising that atypical patterns of both basal HPA functioning and HPA reactivity have recently been documented in depression (Gunnar & Cheatham, 2003). More specifically, cortisol secretion following an acute stressor has been found to be elevated in depressed patients (Parker, Schatzberg, & Lyons, 2003), reflecting the difficulties of depressed adults in regulating negative emotion.

Moreover, both in animal studies and in studies with humans, early exposure to stressful life circumstances, separation from caregivers, and differences in caregiving behavior have been found to be associated with variations in cortisol levels. Rhesus monkeys that were separated from their mothers and reared with peers, for example, exhibit increases in cortisol responses to a variety of stressful situations through adolescence (Fahlke et al., 2000; Suomi, 1999). Gunnar, Morison, Chisholm, and Schuder (2001) found that Romanian orphans raised under suboptimal conditions for several months early in life had elevated levels of cortisol, even after adoption. In a similar vein, caregiving behavior has been shown to buffer neuroendocrine responses to stress in infants separated from their mothers for short periods of time (Gunnar, Larson, Hertsgaard, & Harris, 1992), and secure attachment has been found to buffer cortisol response to injections (Gunnar et al., 1992).

Research examining the neuroendocrine functioning of depressed children and adolescents is limited and results have been mixed. Several investigators have found children's internalizing problems, including symptoms of mood disorders, to be associated with low basal cortisol (e.g., Granger et al., 1998). Goodyer, Herbert, Moor, and Altham (1991), however, found that elevated baseline cortisol secretion occurred in many, but not in all, child and adolescent participants with major depression; moreover, these investigators also found that baseline HPA dysregulation was associated with more severe depressive symptomatology. A longitudinal study reported that elevations in evening cortisol levels among depressed children predicted a recurrent course of the disorder at a 7-year follow-up assessment (Rao et al., 1996). Similarly, Mathew et al. (2003) found that elevations of daytime cortisol in depressed adolescents predicted subsequent suicide attempts over a 10-year follow-up period. Finally, in a 3-year longitudinal study, Goodyer and colleagues (2000) demonstrated that peak levels of morning cortisol and late-afternoon levels of dehydroepiandrosterone (DHEA; another hormone that indexes HPA activity) among adolescents predicted the subsequent onset of MDD. In fact, DHEA hypersecretion was found in this sample to precede the onset of the depressive episode. In contrast, other longitudinal studies have found that *low* basal cortisol levels in children were associated with increased externalizing problems, such as aggression and impulsivity, at a 5-year follow-up assessment when children reached adolescence (cf. Klimes-Dougan, Hastings, Granger, Usher, & Zahn-Wexler, 2001; Shoal, Giancola, & Kirillova, 2003).

Even fewer studies have examined cortisol reactivity in depressed children. In a recent study, Luby et al. (2003) found depressed preschoolers exhibited HPA axis reactivity in response to a discrete stressor. Coplan et al. (2002) reported elevated baseline cortisol levels among children diagnosed with depression and/or anxiety during anticipation of a laboratory stressor (i.e., inhaling CO_2), suggesting that HPA-axis dysfunction in this population might emerge in the face of a stressor. In addition, in a longitudinal study, Shoal et al. (2003) found that cortisol response to stressors was associated with internalizing problems and anxiety at a 6-month follow-up. Thus, although depression-associated HPA-axis dysfunction has not been found consistently in children and adolescents in cross-sectional investigations, there is evidence that basal levels of diurnal cortisol secretion predict recurrence of depression and suicide attempts.

Only recently, researchers have examined whether HPA dysregulation represents a biological marker of risk for depression in youth. Goodman and Gotlib (1999) postulated that one of the consequences of maternal depression is the chronic activation of the HPA axis in the child as a result of repeated exposure to stress of living with a depressed parent. Walker, Walder, and Reynolds (2001) proposed that an increase in basal cortisol levels with puberty is related to the increased incidence of emotional disorders after this developmental period. This suggests that dysregulated HPA functioning is a mechanism that might underlie the risk for MDD in children of depressed mothers. Consistent with this formulation, Halligan, Herbert, Goodyer, and Murray (2004) reported that having a depressed mother was associated with higher and more variable morning cortisol in adolescents, an index of baseline HPA functioning and emotional arousal. Interestingly, elevated morning cortisol secretion at 13 years of age was found to predict higher levels of depressive symptoms when these adolescents were 16, suggesting that baseline HPA functioning mediates the association of maternal depression and adolescent offspring's depressive symptomatology (Halligan, Herbert, Goodyer, & Murray, 2007b). In a similar study, Essex, Klein, Cho, and Kalin (2002) found that preschool-age children of depressed mothers exhibited elevated cortisol levels that were associated prospectively with higher levels of psychological symptoms in first grade. Although few studies have examined cortisol reactivity, abnormal HPA reactivity in response to a laboratory stressor has been observed in samples of children whose mothers were depressed, but who themselves were not depressed (Ashman, Dawson, Panagiotides, Yamada, & Wilkinson, 2002).

In sum, offspring of depressed parents have been found to be characterized by elevated and/or more variable levels of cortisol secretion than their low-risk counterparts. It appears, therefore, that dysregulated HPA axis functioning, both basal and in response to a stressor, may serve as a risk factor for the development of an episode of major depression in children of depressed parents. Indeed, these data are consistent with Goodman and Gotlib's (1999) formulation that a critical consequence for children of depressed mothers is chronic activation of the HPA axis as a result of the stress of living with a depressed parent, reflecting an impaired ability to cope effectively with stress and regulate negative affect. It is important to note here that chronic activation of the HPA axis, resulting in high levels of cortisol, can disrupt functioning in regions of the brain that are responsible for the regulation of emotion (e.g., the PFC, the ACC, and the amygdala), which may represent a mechanism through which HPA axis activation is related to a child's ability to cope with stress.

Neurobiological Functioning

Investigators have recently begun to delineate neural aspects of emotion regulation (e.g., Ochsner, Bunge, Gross, & Gabrieli, 2002). In particular, medial and dorsolateral prefrontal brain areas have been found to modulate emotion-processing areas, such as the amygdala and the OFC (Elliott, Rubinsztein, Sahakian, & Dolan, 2002; Siegle, Steinhauer, Thase, Stenger, & Carter, 2002). Importantly, these brain areas have also been implicated in depression (e.g., Mayberg, 2007; Siegle et al., 2002). In contrast to the growing literature in adults, neuroimaging studies of depressed children are rare, and imaging studies of children at risk for depression are virtually nonexistent. MacMillan et al. (2003) reported marginally significant elevations in amygdala volume among depressed adolescents. Thomas et al. (2001) examined patterns of neural activation in depressed and anxious children, relative to healthy controls, as they viewed fearful and neutral faces. Thomas et al. found that whereas the anxious children exhibited an exaggerated amygdala response to the fearful faces, the five depressed girls in this study demonstrated a blunted amygdala response to the fearful faces. This blunted neural response is intriguing because it mirrors findings of blunted psychophysiological reactivity to emotional stimuli among depressed adults (e.g., Rottenberg, Gross, Wilhelm, Najmi, & Gotlib, 2002). Roberson Nay et al. (2006), in contrast, reported increased activation in the amygdala in depressed compared to control children during encoding of emotional faces.

Researchers have now begun to investigate the possible mediating role of neurobiological functioning in the intergenerational transmission of depression. Monk et al. (2008), for example, used fMRI to investigate neural correlates of the processing of emotional stimuli in offspring of depressed parents. These investigators reported that, compared to children of nondepressed parents, children of depressed parents exhibited greater activation in amygdala and nucleus accumbens activation to fearful faces and less activation in the nucleus accumbens to happy faces. In addition, studies measuring baseline EEG activity in adolescent offspring of depressed mothers found that, compared to adolescents of never-depressed mothers, they showed a pattern of relative left frontal hypoactivity on alpha-band measures (Tomarken, Dichter, Garber, & Simien, 2004). In addition to these differences in baseline EEG activity, other investigators have reported that having a depressed parent is associated with difference in electrophysiological activation during a cognitive task (Perez-Edgar, Fox, Cohn, & Kovacs, 2006). These authors recorded event-related potentials (ERPs) in children of depressed and never-depressed parents while they performed a Posner selective attention task. They found that when task performance was associated with a potential stressor (having to give an embarrassing speech), at-risk children had slower reaction times and larger P3 and slow wave amplitudes in frontal regions than children of never-depressed mothers. The authors interpreted this finding as reflecting a deficit in selective attention in children of depressed parents that leads them to recruit more processing resources in anterior regions in order to perform as well as other children. Importantly, Pérez-Edgar et al. (2006) did not find any behavioral or neural difference between the two groups of children when no stressor was present, which is consistent with a diathesis-stress model of depression vulnerability. In a related study, relative greater left frontal activity in response to receiving a disappointing toy in children at risk for depression was associated with concurrent internalizing and externalizing problems (Forbes et al., 2006). The high-risk children also showed poor heart period recovery after disappointment.

Importantly, the neurobiological literature suggests that the development of emotion regulation abilities occurs in concert with more fine-tuned functioning of frontal areas. The studies also suggest that emotion regulation and maturation of PFC functioning are intimately related to the development of cognitive abilities over the life span, and specifically to the development of cognitive control. This suggests that a closer investigation of individual differences in the ability to over-ride prepotent responses and inhibit the processing of irrelevant but distracting material would increase our understanding of neural processes underlying the ability to regulate negative affect in response to stressful events and, therefore, might have important implications for research on typical and atypical development. We clearly need more studies investigating the neurobiology of emotion regulation in the offspring of depressed parents to evaluate these propositions.

CONCLUSIONS AND FUTURE DIRECTIONS

Our review of the literature demonstrates that parental depression has a negative impact on the development of offspring. We also emphasized, however, that a multitude of factors are involved in the onset of depression and in the transmission of risk from parents to children and adolescents. Future studies need to take this complexity into account by further investigating characteristics of offspring, the depressed mother, the family, or other aspects of the environment that affect the nature of the association between maternal depression and negative outcome in the offspring. An increasing number of studies have demonstrated, for example, that the presence of psychiatrically well husbands of depressed mothers is associated with lower rates of disorder among school-aged children (Conrad & Hammen, 1993; Hops et al., 1987). Other studies show that characteristics of the offspring, such as temperament, gender, and intelligence play an important role in risk for depression (e.g., Burt et al., 2005; Horowitz & Garber, 2003). Although intriguing for their potential to function as protective factors, offspring variables, such as low intelligence, may also represent early manifestations of psychopathology. Clearly, future research is needed to investigate factors that increase or decrease the risk for offspring of depressed parents.

Increasingly, studies have identified mechanisms of risks and have proposed mechanisms of transmission. In our view, the most important direction now for future research to take is for investigators to address implications for interventions; very few studies have examined effective ways to intervene and prevent the onset of psychopathology in offspring of depressed parents, and most of these studies have found small to moderate effect sizes (for a recent meta-analysis, see Horowitz & Garber, 2006). Two main ways to conceptualize interventions seem obvious to us: interventions can focus on reducing the parent's psychopathology and/or on increasing the offspring's coping skills. Researchers have reported that offsprings' functioning improves when family adversities, not specifically parental depression, decrease (e.g., Cicchetti & Schneider-Rosen, 1986). On the other hand, Timko, Cronkite, Berg, and Moos (2002) found that 10 years after a parent's depressive episode, children of stably remitted parents experienced more psychological distress than offspring of never-depressed parents. In fact, they experienced as much psychological distress as offspring of nonremitted or partially remitted parents. In a noteworthy study, Weissman et al. (2006) reported that remission of maternal depression after 3 months of treatment with antidepressants was associated with decreases in rates of diagnosis in the children. In fact, 33% of children who had a diagnosis at baseline and whose mothers remitted in response to the treatment recovered from their diagnosis compared to 12% of children whose mothers did not remit. Importantly, all children whose mothers remitted and who did not have a diagnosis at baseline remained diagnosis-free, whereas 17% of children whose mothers remained depressed acquired a diagnosis. These findings suggest that successful treatment of the parent's depression can not only help their offspring recover, but perhaps more importantly, can prevent the onset of disorder. Treatment can also target mother–child interactions and parenting. Verduyn, Barrowclough, Roberts, Tarrier, and Harrington (2003), for example, conducted a randomized controlled trial and investigated the effectiveness of a CBT group for depression combined with parenting skills enhancement. These authors reported that after 6- and 12-month follow-ups, participants in this group exhibited lower levels of maternal depression and fewer child problems.

Results of recent studies suggest that the way in which offspring cope with their parent's depression and, more generally, individual differences in emotion regulation in high-risk offspring, can affect resilience. Secondary control coping strategies, like positive thinking, acceptance, and distraction have been found to mediate the relation between adolescent's reports of parental stress and depressed parent's report of their adolescent's anxiety/depression symptoms (Jaser et al., 2005). In a similar sample, the use of secondary coping strategies in response to family stress and the use of primary control coping, such as problem solving and emotional expression, in response to stress with peers was found to be related to lower self-reported anxiety and stress (e.g., Langrock, Compas, Keller, Merchant, & Copeland, 2002). Importantly, the use of involuntary engagement responses, like rumination or intrusive thoughts, was associated with increased symptoms (Langrock et al., 2002). Finally, Silk, Shaw, Forbes, Lane, and Kovacs (2006) reported that positive reward anticipation in a delayed reward task, compared to distraction or negative focus on the delay, moderated the effects of maternal depression on children's internalizing problems, particularly if mothers had current depressive symptoms. These examples of studies investigating coping skills and individual differences in emotion regulation abilities suggest that treatment programs that focus on improving these skills in children at high risk for depression might provide important ways to prevent the onset of disorder in these children.

REFERENCES

Ainsworth, M. S., Blehar, M. C., Waters, E., & Wall, S. (1978). *Patterns of attachment: A psychological study of the strange situation*. Oxford: Lawrence Erlbaum.

Anderson, V. A., Anderson, P., Northam, E., Jacobs, R., & Catroppa, C. (2001). Development of executive functions through late childhood and adolescence in an Australian sample. *Developmental Neuropsychology, 20*, 385–406.

Angold, A., Costello, E. J., & Worthman, C. M. (1998). Puberty and depression: The roles of age, pubertal status and pubertal timing. *Psychological Medicine, 28*, 51–61.

Ashman, S. B., Dawson, G., Panagiotides, H., Yamada, E., & Wilkinson, C. W. (2002). Stress hormone levels of children of depressed mothers. *Development & Psychopathology, 14*, 333–349.

Barnett, P. A., & Gotlib, I. H. (1988). Psychosocial functioning and depression: Distinguishing among antecedents, concomitants, and consequences. *Psychological Bulletin, 104*, 97–126.

Beardslee, W., Versage, E., & Gladstone, T. (1998). Children of affectively ill parents: A review of the past 10 years. *Journal of the American Academy of Child & Adolescent Psychiatry, 37*, 1134–1141.

Beardslee, W. R., Schultz, L. H., & Selman, R. L. (1987). Level of social-cognitive development, adaptive functioning, and DSM-III diagnoses in adolescent offspring of parents with affective disorders: Implications for the development of the capacity for mutuality. *Developmental Psychology, 23*, 807–815.

Beck, A. T. (1967). *Depression: Clinical, experimental, and theoretical aspects*. New York: Harper & Row.

Beck, A. T. (1976). *Cognitive therapy and the emotional disorders*. New York: New American Library.

Belsher, G., & Costello, C. G. (1988). Relapse after recovery from unipolar depression: A critical review. *Psychological Bulletin, 104*, 84–96.

Biederman, J., Petty, C., Hirashfeld Becker, D. R., Henin, A., Faraone, S. V., Dang, D., et al. (2006). A controlled longitudinal 5-year follow-up study of children at high and low risk for panic disorder and major depression. *Psychological Medicine, 36*, 1141–1152.

Billings, A. G., & Moos, R. (1983). Comparison of children of depressed and nondepressed parents: A social environmental perspective. *Journal of Abnormal Child Psychology, 11*, 483–486.

Birmaher, B., Ryan, N. D., Williamson, D. E., Brent, D. A., Kaufman, J., Dahl R. E., et al. (1996). Childhood and adolescent depression: A review of the past 10 years. *Journal of the American Academy of Child and Adolescent Psychiatry, 35*, 1427–1439.

Bishop, S. J., Dalgleish, T., & Yule, W. (2004). Memory for emotional stories in high and low depressed children. *Memory, 12*, 214–230.

Boland, R. J., & Keller, M. B. (2002). Course and outcome of depression. In I. H. Gotlib & C. L. Hammen (Eds.), *Handbook of depression* (pp. 43–60). New York: Guilford Press.

Bower, G. H. (1981). Mood and memory. *American Psychologist, 36*, 129–148.

Bremner, J. D., Innis, R. B., Southwick, S. M., Staib, L., Zoghbi, S., & Charney, D. S. (2000). Decreased benzodiazepine receptor binding in prefrontal cortex in combat-related posttraumatic stress disorder. *American Journal of Psychiatry, 157*, 1120–1126.

Brennan, P. A., Le Brocque, R., & Hammen, C. (2003). Maternal depression, parent–child relationships, and resilient outcomes in adolescence. *Journal of the American Academy of Child and Adolescent Psychiatry, 42*, 1469–1477.

Brewin, C. R., Andrews, B., & Gotlib, I. H. (1993). Psychopathology and early experience: A reappraisal of retrospective reports. *Psychological Bulletin, 113*, 82–98.

Breznitz, Z., & Friedman, S. L. (1988). Toddlers' concentration: Does maternal depression make a difference? *Journal of Child Psychology and Psychiatry, 29*, 267–279.

Burke, L. (2003). The impact of maternal depression on familial relationships. *International Review of Psychiatry, 15*, 243–255.

Burt, K. B., Van Dulmen, M. H. M., Carlivati, J., Egeland, B., Sroufe, L. A., Forman, D. R., et al. (2005). Mediating links between maternal depression and offspring psychopathology: The importance of independent data. *Journal of Child Psychology and Psychiatry, 46*, 490–499.

Campos, J. J., & Steinberg, C. R. (1981). Perception, appraisal and emotion: The onset of social referencing. In M. E. Lamb & L. R. Sherrod (Eds.), *Infant social cognition: Empirical and theoretical considerations* (pp. 273–314). Hillsdale, NJ: Lawrence Erlbaum Associates.

Carro, M. G., Grant, K. E., Gotlib, I. H., & Compas, B. E. (1993). Postpartum depression and child development: An investigation of mothers and fathers as sources of risk and resilience. *Development and Psychopathology, 5*, 567–579.

Carter, A. S., Garrity Rokous, F. E., Chazan Cohen, R., Little, C., & Briggs Gowan, M. J. (2001). Maternal depression and comorbidity: Predicting early parenting, attachment security, and toddler social-emotional problems and competencies. *Journal of the American Academy of Child & Adolescent Psychiatry, 40*, 18–26.

Casey, B. J., Tottenham, N., Listen, C., & Durston, S. (2005). Imaging the developing brain: What have we learned about cognitive development? *Trends in Cognitive Sciences, 9*, 104–110.

Cicchetti, D., & Schneider-Rosen, K. (1986). An organizational approach to childhood depression. In M. Rutter, C. E. Izard & P. B. Read (Eds.), *Depression in young people: Developmental and clinical perspectives* (pp. 71–134). New York: Guilford Press.

Cohn, J. F., Campbell, S. B., Matias, R., & Hopkins, J. (1990). Face-to-face interactions of postpartum depressed and nondepressed mother-infant pairs at 2 months. *Developmental Psychology, 26*, 15–23.

Cole, P. M., Martin, S. E., & Dennis, T. A. (2004). Emotion regulation as a scientific construct: Methodological challenges and directions for child development research. *Child Development, 75*, 317–333.

Connell, A. M., & Goodman, S. H. (2002). The association between psychopathology in fathers versus mothers and children's internalizing and externalizing behavior problems: A meta-analysis. *Psychological Bulletin, 128*, 746–773.

Conrad, M., & Hammen, C. (1993). Protective and resource factors in high- and low-risk children: A comparison of children with unipolar, bipolar, medically ill, and normal mothers. *Development and Psychopathology, 5*, 593–607.

Coplan, J. D., Moreau, D., Chaput, F., Martinez, J. M., Hoven, C. W., Mandell, D. J., et al. (2002). Salivary cortisol concentrations before and after carbon-dioxide inhalations in children. *Biological Psychiatry, 51*, 326–333.

Cummings, E. M., & Davies, P. T. (1994). Maternal depression and child development. *Journal of Child Psychology & Psychiatry & Allied Disciplines, 35*, 73–112.

Davis, E. P., Snidman, N., Wadhwa, P. D., Glynn, L. M., Schetter, C. D., & Sandman, C. A. (2004). Prenatal maternal anxiety and depression predict negative behavioral reactivity in infancy. *Infancy, 6*, 319–331.

Dawson, G. (1994). Development of emotional expression and emotion regulation in infancy: Contributions of the frontal lobe. In G. Dawson & K. W. Fischer (Eds.), *Human behavior and the developing brain* (pp. 346–379). New York: Guilford Press.

Dietz, L. J., Jennings, K. D., & Abrew, A. J. (2005). Social skill in self-assertive strategies of toddlers with depressed and nondepressed mothers. *Journal of Genetic Psychology, 166*, 94–116.

Dishion, T. J., Patterson, G. R., & Griesler, P. C. (1994). Peer adaptations in the development of antisocial behavior: A confluence model. In L. R. Huesmann (Ed.), *Aggressive behavior: Current perspectives* (xix ed., pp. 61–95). New York: Plenum Press.

Dumas, J. E., Gibson, J. A., & Albin, J. B. (1989). Behavioral correlates of maternal depressive symptomatology in conduct-disorder children. *Journal of Consulting and Clinical Psychology, 57*, 516–521.

Durbin, C. E., Klein, D. N., Hayden, E. P., Buckley, M. E., & Moerk, K. C. (2005). Temperamental emotionality in preschoolers and parental mood disorders. *Journal of Abnormal Psychology, 114*, 28–37.

Eaton, W. W., Anthony, J. C., Gallo, J., Cai, G., Tien, A., Romanoski, A., et al. (1997). Natural history of diagnostic interview Schedule/DSM-IV major depression: The Baltimore epidemiologic catchment area follow-up. *Archives of General Psychiatry, 54*, 993–999.

Eisenberg, N. (2000). Emotion, regulation, and moral development. *Annual Review of Psychology, 51*, 665–697.

Elliott, R., Rubinsztein, J. S., Sahakian, B. J., & Dolan, R. J. (2002). The neural basis of mood-congruent processing biases in depression. *Archives of General Psychiatry, 59*, 597–604.

Essex, M. J., Klein, M. H., Cho, E., & Kalin, N. H. (2002). Maternal stress beginning in infancy may sensitize children to later stress exposure: Effects on cortisol and behavior. *Biological Psychiatry, 52*, 776–784.

Fahlke, C., Lorenz, J. G., Long, J., Champoux, M., Suomi, S. J., & Higley, J. D. (2000). Rearing experiences and stress-induced plasma cortisol as early risk factors for excessive alcohol consumption in nonhuman primates. *Alcoholism: Clinical and Experimental Research, 24*, 644–650.

Field, T. (1984). Early interactions between infants and their postpartum depressed mothers. *Infant Behavior and Development, 7*, 517–522.

Field, T. (1992). Infants of depressed mothers. *Development and Psychopathology, 4*, 9–66.

Field, T. (1995). Infants of depressed mothers. *Infant Behavior and Development, 18*, 1–13.

Field, T., Healy, B., Goldstein, S., & Guthertz, M. (1990). Behavior state matching and synchrony in mother-infant interactions of nondepressed versus depressed dyads. *Developmental Psychology, 26*, 7–14.

Field, T., Hernandez Reif, M., Diego, M., Feijo, L., Vera, Y., Gil, K., et al. (2007). Still-face and separation effects on depressed mother-infant interactions. *Infant Mental Health Journal, 28*, 314–323.

Forbes, E. E., May, J. C., Siegle, G. J., Ladouceur, C. D., Ryan, N. D., Carter, C. S., et al. (2006). Reward-related decision-making in pediatric major depressive disorder: An fMRI study. *Journal of Child Psychology and Psychiatry, 47*, 1031–1040.

Forehand, R., Lautenschlager, G. J., Faust, J., & Graziano, W. G. (1986). Parent perceptions and parent-child interactions in clinic-referred children: A preliminary investigation of the effects of maternal depressive moods. *Behavior Research and Therapy, 24*, 73–75.

Garber, J., & Robinson, N. S. (1997). Cognitive vulnerability in children at risk for depression. *Cognition & Emotion, 11*, 619–635.

Goldsmith, D. F., & Rogoff, B. (1997). Mothers' and toddlers' coordinated joint focus of attention: Variations with maternal dysphoric symptoms. *Developmental Psychology, 33*, 113–119.

Goldsmith, H. H., Buss, K. A., & Lemery, K. S. (1997). Toddler and childhood temperament: Expanded content, stronger genetic evidence, new evidence for the importance of environment. *Developmental Psychology, 33*, 891–905.

Goodman, S. H., Adamson, L. B., Riniti, J., & Cole, S. (1994). Mothers' expressed attitudes: Associations with maternal depression and children's self-esteem and psychopathology. *Journal of the American Academy of Child and Adolescent Psychiatry, 33*, 1265–1274.

Goodman, S. H., & Gotlib, I. H. (1999). Risk for psychopathology in the children of depressed mothers: A developmental model for understanding mechanisms of transmission. *Psychological Review, 106*, 458–490.

Goodyer, I., Herbert, J., Moor, S., & Altham, P. (1991). Cortisol hypersecretion in depressed school-aged children and adolescents. *Psychiatry Research, 37*, 237–244.

Goodyer, I. M., Herbert, J., Tamplin, A., & Altham, P. M. E. (2000). Recent life events, cortisol, dehydroepiandrosterone and the onset of major depression in high-risk adolescents. *British Journal of Psychiatry, 177*, 499–504.

Gotlib, I. H., & Goodman, S. H. (1999). Children of parents with depression. In W. K. Silverman & T. H. Ollendick (Eds.), *Developmental issues in the clinical treatment of children* (pp. 415–432). Needham Heights, MA: Allyn & Bacon.

Gotlib, I. H., & Goodman, S. H. (Eds.). (2002). *Children of depressed parents: Mechanisms of risk and implications for treatment* (viii ed.). Washington, DC: American Psychological Association.

Gotlib, I. H., & Hammen, C. L. (1992). *Psychological aspects of depression: Toward a cognitive-interpersonal integration.* Oxford: John Wiley & Sons.

Gotlib, I. H., & Hammen, C. L. (2002). *Handbook of depression.* New York: Guilford Press.

Gotlib, I. H., & MacLeod, C. (1997). Information processing in anxiety and depression: A cognitive developmental perspective. In J. Burack & J. Enns (Eds.), *Attention, development, and psychopathology* (pp. 350–378). New York: Guilford Press.

Gottman, J. M., Katz, L. F., & Hooven, C. (1996). Parental meta-emotion philosophy and the emotional life of families: Theoretical models and preliminary data. *Journal of Family Psychology, 10*, 243–268.

Granger, D. A., Serbin, L. A., Schwartzman, A., Lehoux, P., Cooperman, J., & Ikeda, S. (1998). Children's salivary cortisol, internalising behaviour problems, and family environment: Results from the concordia longitudinal risk project. *International Journal of Behavioral Development, 22*, 707–728.

Gross, D., Conrad, B., Fogg, L., Willis, L., & Garvey, C. (1995). A longitudinal study of maternal depression and preschool children's mental health. *Nursing Research, 44*, 96–101.

Gunnar, M. R., Connors, J., & Isensee, J. (1989). Lack of stability in neonatal adrenocortical reactivity because of rapid habituation of the adrenocortical response. *Developmental Psychobiology, 22*, 221–233.

Gunnar, M. R., Larson, M. C., Hertsgaard, L., & Harris, M. L. (1992). The stressfulness of separation among nine-month-old infants: Effects of social context variables and infant temperament. *Child Development, 63*, 290–303.

Gunnar, M. R., Morison, S. J., Chisholm, K., & Schuder, M. (2001). Salivary cortisol levels in children adopted from Romanian orphanages. *Development and Psychopathology, 13*, 611–628.

Gunnar, M., Marvinney, D., Isensee, J., & Fisch, R. O. (1989). Coping with uncertainty: New models of the relations between hormonal, behavioral, and cognitive processes. In D. S. Palermo (Ed.), *Coping with uncertainty: Behavioral and developmental perspectives* (pp. 101–129). Hillsdale, NJ: Lawrence Erlbaum Associates.

Gunnar, M. R., & Cheatham, C. L. (2003). Brain and behavior interfaces: Stress and the developing brain. *Infant Mental Health Journal, 24*, 195–211.

Hales, R. E., & Yudofsky, S. C. (Eds.). (2004). *Essentials of neuropsychiatry and clinical neurosciences* (xiv ed.). Washington, DC: American Psychiatric Publishing.

Halligan, S. L., Herbert, J., Goodyer, I. M., & Murray, L. (2004). Exposure to postnatal depression predicts elevated cortisol in adolescent offspring. *Biological Psychiatry, 55*, 376–381.

Halligan, S. L., Murray, L., Martins, C., & Cooper, P. J. (2007a). Maternal depression and psychiatric outcomes in adolescent offspring: A 13-year longitudinal study. *Journal of Affective Disorders, 9*, 145–154.

Halligan, S. L., Herbert, J., Goodyer, I., & Murray, L. (2007b). Disturbances in morning cortisol secretion in association with maternal postnatal depression predict subsequent depressive symptomatology in adolescents. *Biological Psychiatry, 62*, 40–46.

Hammen, C. (1991). *Depression runs in families: The social context of risk and resilience in children of depressed mothers.* New York: Springer-Verlag.

Hammen, C., & Brennan, P. A. (2003). Severity, chronicity, and timing of maternal depression and risk for adolescent offspring diagnoses in a community sample. *Archives of General Psychiatry, 60*, 253–258.

Hammen, C., Brennan, P. A., & Shih, J. H. (2004a). Family discord and stress predictors of depression and other disorders in adolescent children of depressed and nondepressed women. *Journal of the American Academy of Child & Adolescent Psychiatry, 43*, 994–1002.

Hammen, C., Shih, J. H., & Brennan, P. A. (2004b). Intergenerational transmission of depression: Test of an interpersonal stress model in a community sample. *Journal of Consulting and Clinical Psychology, 72*, 511–522.

Hayward, C., Gotlib, I. H., Schraedley, P. K., & Litt, I. F. (1999). Ethnic differences in the association between pubertal status and symptoms of depression in adolescent girls. *Journal of Adolescent Health, 25*, 143–149.

Hipwell, A. E., Murray, L., Ducournau, P., & Stein, A. (2005). The effects of maternal depression and parental conflict on children's peer play. *Child: Care, Health and Development, 31*, 11–23.

Hirsch, B. J., Moos, R. H., & Reischl, T. M. (1985). Psychosocial adjustment of adolescent children of a depressed, arthritic, or normal parent. *Journal of Abnormal Psychology, 94*, 154–164.

Hops, H., Biglan, A., Sherman, L., Arthur, J., Friedman, L., & Osteen, V. (1987). Home observations of family interactions of depressed women. *Journal of Consulting and Clinical Psychology, 55*, 341–346.

Hops, H., Sherman, L., & Biglan, A. (1990). Maternal depression, marital discord, and children's behavior: A developmental perspective. In G. R. Patterson (Ed.), *Depression and aggression in family interactions* (pp. 185–208). New York: Lawrence Erlbaum Associates.

Horowitz, J. L., & Garber, J. (2003). Relation of intelligence and religiosity to depressive disorders in offspring of depressed and nondepressed mothers. *Journal of the American Academy of Child & Adolescent Psychiatry, 42*, 578–586.

Horowitz, J. L., & Garber, J. (2006). The prevention of depressive symptoms in children and adolescents: A meta-analytic review. *Journal of Consulting and Clinical Psychology, 74*, 401–415.

Huot, R. L., Brennan, P. A., Stowe, Z. N., Plotsky, P. M., & Walker, E. F. (2004). Negative affect in offspring of depressed mothers is predicted by infant cortisol levels at 6 months and maternal depression during pregnancy, but not postpartum. In B. McEwen & R. Yehuda (Eds.), *Biobehavioral stress response: Protective and damaging effects* (xvi ed., pp. 234–236). New York: New York Academy of Sciences.

Jaenicke, C., Hammen, C., Zupan, B., Hiroto, D., Gordon, D., Adrian, C., et al. (1987). Cognitive vulnerability in children at risk for depression. *Journal of Abnormal Child Psychology, 15*, 559–572.

Jameson, P. B., Gelfand, D. M., Kulcsar, E., & Teti, D. M. (1997). Mother–toddler interaction patterns associated with maternal depression. *Development and Psychopathology, 9*, 537–550.

Jaser, S. S., Langrock, A. M., Keller, G., Merchant, M. J., Benson, M. A., Reeslund, K., et al. (2005). Coping with the stress of parental depression II: Adolescent and parent reports of coping and adjustment. *Journal of Clinical Child and Adolescent Psychology, 34*, 193–205.

Joormann, J., Talbot, L., & Gotlib, I. H. (2007). Biased processing of emotional information in girls at risk for depression. *Journal of Abnormal Psychology, 116*, 135–143.

Kane, P., & Garber, J. (2004). The relations among depression in fathers, children's psychopathology, and father-child conflict: A meta-analysis. *Clinical Psychology Review, 24*, 339–360.

Kaufman, J., Plotsky, P. M., Nemeroff, C. B., & Charney, D. S. (2000). Effects of early adverse experiences on brain structure and function: Clinical implications. *Biological Psychiatry, 48*, 778–790.

Kessler, R. C., Avenevoli, S., & Merikangas, K. R. (2001). Mood disorders in children and adolescents: An epidemiologic perspective. Biological Psychiatry, 49, 1002–1014.

Kessler, R. C., Berglund, P., Demler, O., Jin, R., Koretz, D., Merikangas, K. R., et al. (2003). The epidemiology of major depressive disorder: Results from the National Comorbidity Survey Replication (NCS-R). *Journal of the American Medical Association, 289*, 3095–3105.

Kessler, R. C., McGonagle, K. A., Nelson, C. B., & Hughes, M. (1994). Sex and depression in the national comorbidity survey: II. cohort effects. *Journal of Affective Disorders, 30*, 15–26.

Kessler, R. C., & Walters, E. E. (1998). Epidemiology of DSM-III-R major depression and minor depression among adolescents and young adults in the national comorbidity survey. *Depress Anxiety, 7*, 3–14.

Klein, D. N., Lewinsohn, P. M., Rohde, P., Seeley, J. R., & Olino, T. M. (2005). Psychopathology in the adolescent and young adult offspring of a community sample of mothers and fathers with major depression. *Psychological Medicine, 35*, 353–365.

Klimes-Dougan, B., Hastings, P. D., Granger, D. A., Usher, B. A., & Zahn-Waxler, C. (2001). Adrenocortical activity in at-risk and normally developing adolescents: Individual differences in salivary cortisol basal levels, diurnal variation, and responses to social challenges. *Development & Psychopathology Stress and Development: Biological and Psychological Consequences, 13*, 695–719.

Korkman, M., Kemp, S. L., & Kirk, U. (2001). Effects of age on neurocognitive measures of children ages 5 to 12: A cross-sectional study on 800 children from the United States. *Developmental Neuropsychology, 20*, 331–354.

Langrock, A. M., Compas, B. E., Keller, G., Merchant, M. J., & Copeland, M. E. (2002). Coping with the stress of parental depression: Parents' reports of children's coping, emotional, and behavioral problems. *Journal of Clinical Child and Adolescent Psychology, 31*, 312–324.

Lee, C. M., & Gotlib, I. H. (1989). Clinical status and emotional adjustment of children of depressed mothers. *American Journal of Psychiatry, 146*, 478–483.

Lee, C. M., & Gotlib, I. H. (1991a). Adjustment of children of depressed mothers: A ten-month follow-up. *Journal of Abnormal Psychology, 100*, 473–477.

Lee, C. M., & Gotlib, I. H. (1991b). Family disruption, parental availability, and child adjustment: An integrative review. In R. J. Prinz (Ed.), *Advances in the behavioral assessment of children and families* (Vol. 5, pp. 166–199). London: Jessica Kingsley.

Lewinsohn, P. M., Olino, T. M., & Klein, D. N. (2005). Psychosocial impairment in offspring of depressed parents. *Psychological Medicine, 35*, 1493–1503.

Lewinsohn, P. M., Rohde, P., Klein, D. N., & Seeley, J. R. (1999). Natural course of adolescent major depressive disorder: I. Continuity into young adulthood. *Journal of the American Academy of Child & Adolescent Psychiatry, 38*, 56–63.

Lewinsohn, P. M., Rohde, P., Seeley, J. R., Klein, D. N., & Gotlib, I. H. (2000). Natural course of adolescent major depressive disorder in a community sample: Predictors of recurrence in young adults. *American Journal of Psychiatry, 157*, 1584–1591.

Lieb, R., Isensee, B., Hofler, M., Pfister, H., & Wittchen, U. H. (2002). Parental major depression and the risk of depression and other mental disorders in offspring: A prospective-longitudinal community study. *Archives of General Psychiatry, 59*, 365–374.

Livingood, A. B., Daen, P., & Smith, B. D. (1983). The depressed mother as a source of stimulation for her infant. *Journal of Clinical Psychology, 39*, 369–375.

Loehlin, J. C. (1992). *Genes and environment in personality development.* Thousand Oaks, CA: Sage Publications.

Lovejoy, M. C., Graczyk, P. A., O'Hare, E., & Neuman, G. (2000). Maternal depression and parenting behavior: A meta-analytic review. *Clinical Psychology Review, 20*, 561–592.

Luby, J. L., Heffelfinger, A., Mrakotsky, C., Brown, K., Hessler, M., & Spitznagel, E. (2003). Alteration in stress cortisol reactivity in depressed preschoolers relative to psychiatric and no-disorder comparison groups. *Archives of General Psychiatry, 60*, 1248–1255.

MacMillan, S., Szeszko, P. R., Moore, G. J., Madden, R., Lorch, E., Ivey, J., et al. (2003). Increased amygdala: Hippocampal volume ratios associated with severity of anxiety in pediatric major depression. *Journal of Child and Adolescent Psychopharmacology, 13*, 65–73.

Malcarne, V. L., Hamilton, N. A., Ingram, R. E., & Taylor, L. (2000). Correlates of distress in children at risk for affective disorder: Exploring predictors in the offspring of depressed and nondepressed mothers. *Journal of Affective Disorders, 59*, 243–251.

Martins, C., & Gaffan, E. A. (2000). Effects of early maternal depression on patterns of infant-mother attachment: A meta-analytic investigation. *Journal of Child Psychology and Psychiatry, 41*, 737–746.

Mathew, S. J., Coplan, J. D., Goetz, R. R., Feder, A., Greenwald, S., Dahl, R. E., et al. (2003). Differentiating depressed adolescent 24h cortisol secretion in light of their adult clinical outcome. *Neuropsychopharmacology, 28*, 1336–1343.

Mathews, A., & MacLeod, C. (2005). Cognitive vulnerability to emotional disorders. *Annual Review of Clinical Psychology, 1*, 167–195.

Matthey, S., Guedeney, A., Starakis, N., & Barnett, B. (2005). Assessing the social behavior of infants: Use of the ADBB scale and relationship to mother's mood. *Infant Mental Health Journal, 26*, 442–458.

Mayberg, H. S. (2007). Defining the neural circuitry of depression: Toward a new nosology with therapeutic implications. *Biological Psychiatry, 61*, 729–730.

Mezulis, A. H., Hyde, J. S., & Clark, R. (2004). Father involvement moderates the effect of maternal depression during a child's infancy on child behavior problems in kindergarten. *Journal of Family Psychology, 18*, 575–588.

Monk, C. S., Klein, R. G., Telzer, E. H., Schroth, B. A., Mannuzza, S., Moulton, J. L., et al. (2008). Amygdala and nucleus accumbens activation to emotional facial expressions in children and adolescents at risk for major depression. *American Journal of Psychiatry, 165*, 90–98.

Monroe, S. M., & Simons, A. D. (1991). Diathesis-stress theories in the context of life-stress research: Implications for depressive disorders. *Psychological Bulletin, 110*, 406–425.

Murray, L., Halligan, S. L., Adams, G., Patterson, P., & Goodyer, I. M. (2006). Socioemotional development in adolescents at risk for depression: The role of maternal depression and attachment style. *Development and Psychopathology, 18*, 489–516.

Murray, L., Sinclair, D., Cooper, P., Ducournau, P., & Turner, P. (1999). The socioemotional development of 5-year-old children of postnatally depressed mothers. *Journal of Child Psychology and Psychiatry, 40*, 1259–1271.

Murray, L., Woolgar, M., Cooper, P., & Hipwell, A. (2001). Cognitive vulnerability to depression in 5-year-old children of depressed mothers. *Journal of Child Psychology and Psychiatry, 42*, 891–899.

Nelson, D. R., Hammen, C., Brennan, P. A., & Ullman, J. B. (2003). The impact of maternal depression on adolescent adjustment: The role of expressed emotion. *Journal of Consulting and Clinical Psychology, 71*, 935–944.

Neshat-Doost, H. T., Taghavi, M. R., Moradi, A. R., Yule, W., & Dalgleish, T. (1998). Memory for emotional trait adjectives in clinically depressed youth. *Journal of Abnormal Psychology, 107*, 642–650.

Nomura, Y., Wickramaratne, P. J., Warner, V., Mufson, L., & Weissman, M. M. (2002). Family discord, parental depression and psychopathology in offspring: Ten-year follow-up. *Journal of the American Academy of Child & Adolescent Psychiatry, 41*, 402–409.

Ochsner, K. N., Bunge, S. A., Gross, J. J., & Gabrieli, J. D. E. (2002). Rethinking feelings: An fMRI study of the cognitive regulation of emotion. *Journal of Cognitive Neuroscience*, 14, 1215–1229.

Orvaschel, H., Walsh Allis, G., & Ye, W. (1988). Psychopathology in children of parents with recurrent depression. *Journal of Abnormal Child Psychology, 16*, 17–28.

Parker, K. J., Schatzberg, A. F., & Lyons, D. M. (2003). Neuroendocrine aspects of hypercortisolism in major depression. *Hormones & Behavior, 43*, 60–66.

Perez Edgar, K., Fox, N. A., Cohn, J. F., & Kovacs, M. (2006). Behavioral and electrophysiological markers of selective attention in children of parents with a history of depression. *Biological Psychiatry, 60*, 1131–1138.

Phares, V., Duhig, A. M., & Watkins, M. M. (2002). Family context: Fathers and other supports. In S. H. Goodman & I. H. Gotlib (Eds.), *Children of depressed parents: Mechanisms of risk and implications for treatment* (pp. 203–226). Washington, DC: American Psychological Association.

Pilowsky, D. J., Wickramaratne, P. J., Rush, A. J., Hughes, C. W., Garber, J., Malloy, E., et al. (2006a). Children of currently depressed mothers: A STAR*D ancillary study. *Journal of Clinical Psychiatry, 67*, 126–136.

Pilowsky, D. J., Wickramarante, P. J., Nomura, Y., & Weissman, M. M. (2006b). Family discord, parental depression, and psychopathology in offspring: 20-year follow-up. *Journal of the American Academy of Child & Adolescent Psychiatry, 45*, 452–460.

Pine, D., Cohen, P., Gurley, D., Brook, J., & Ma, Y. (1998). The risk for early-adulthood anxiety and depressive disorders in adolescents with anxiety and depressive disorders. *Archives of General Psychiatry, 55*, 56–64.

Plomin, R., Reiss, D., Hetherington, E. M., & Howe, G. W. (1994). Nature and nurture: Genetic contributions to measures of the family environment. *Developmental Psychology, 30*, 32–43.

Rahman, A., Lovel, H., Bunn, J., Iqbal, Z., & Harrington, R. (2004). Mohers' mental health and infant growth: A case-control study from Rawalpindi, Pakistan. *Child: Care, Health & Development, 30*, 21–27.

Rao, U., Dahl, R. E., Ryan, N. D., Birmaher, B., Williamson, D. E., Giles, D. E., et al. (1996). The relationship between longitudinal clinical course and sleep and cortisol changes in adolescent depression. *Biological Psychiatry, 40*, 474–484.

Rao, U., Hammen, C., & Daley, S. E. (1999). Continuity of depression during the transition to adulthood: A 5-year longitudinal study of young women. *Journal of the American Academy of Child & Adolescent Psychiatry, 38*, 908–915.

Righetti Veltema, M., Bousquet, A., & Manzano, J. (2003). Impact of postpartum depressive symptoms on mother and her 18-month-old infant. *European Child and Adolescent Psychiatry, 12*, 75–83.

Roberson Nay, R., McClure, E. B., Monk, C. S., Nelson, E. E., Guyer, A. E., Fromm, S. J., et al. (2006). Increased amygdala activity during successful memory encoding in adolescent major depressive disorder: An fMRI study. *Biological Psychiatry, 60*, 966–973.

Rohde, P., Lewinsohn, P. M., Klein, D. N., & Seeley, J. R. (2005). Association of parental depression with psychiatric course from adolescence to young adulthood among formerly depressed individuals. *Journal of Abnormal Psychology, 114*, 409–420.

Rottenberg, J., Gross, J. J., Wilhelm, F. H., Najmi, S., & Gotlib, I. H. (2002). Crying threshold and intensity in Major Depressive Disorder. *Journal of Abnormal Psychology, 111*, 302–312.

Schaughency, E. A., & Lahey, B. B. (1985). Mothers and fathers perceptions of child deviance: Roles of child behavior, parental depression, and marital satisfaction. *Journal of Consulting and Clinical Psychology, 53*, 718–723.

Schneiderman, N., Field, T. M., & McCabe, P. M. (Eds.). (1992). *Stress and coping in infancy and childhood* (xv ed.). Hillsdale, NJ: Lawrence Erlbaum Associates.

Shoal, G. D., Giancola, P. R., & Kirillova, G. P. (2003). Salivary cortisol, personality, and aggressive behavior in adolescent boys: A 5-year longitudinal study. *Journal of the American Academy of Child & Adolescent Psychiatry, 42*, 1101–1107.

Siegle, G. J., Steinhauer, S. R., Thase, M. E., Stenger, V. A., & Carter, C. S. (2002). Can't shake that feeling: Event-related fMRI assessment of sustained amygdala activity in response to emotional information in depressed individuals. *Biological Psychiatry, 51*, 693–707.

Silk, J. S., Shaw, D. S., Forbes, E. E., Lane, T. L., & Kovacs, M. (2006). Maternal depression and child internalizing: The moderating role of child emotion regulation. *Journal of Clinical Child and Adolescent Psychology, 35,* 116–126.

Stansbury, K., & Gunnar, M. R. (1994). Adrenocortical activity and emotion regulation. *Monographs of the Society for Research in Child Development, 59,* 108–134, 250–283.

Sullivan, P. F., Neale, M. C., & Kendler, K. S. (2000). Genetic epidemiology of major depression: Review and meta-analysis. *American Journal of Psychiatry, 157,* 1552–1562.

Suomi, S. J. (1999). Attachment in rhesus monkeys. In J. Cassidy & P. R. Shaver (Eds.), *Handbook of attachment: Theory, research, and clinical applications* (pp. 181–197). New York: Guilford Press.

Stuss, D. T. (1992). Biological and psychological development of executive functions. *Brain and Cognition, 20,* 8–23.

Swanson, H. L. (1999). What develops in working memory? A life span perspective. *Developmental Psychology, 35,* 986–1000.

Taylor, L., & Ingram, R. E. (1999). Cognitive reactivity and depressotypic information processing in children of depressed mothers. *Journal of Abnormal Psychology, 108,* 202–208.

Teasdale, J. D. (1988). Cognitive vulnerability to persistent depression. *Cognition and Emotion, 2,* 247–274.

Tems, C. L., Stewart, S. M., Skinner, J. R., & Hughes, C. W. (1993). Cognitive distortions in depressed children and adolescents: Are they state dependent or traitlike? *Journal of Clinical Child Psychology, 22,* 316–326.

Thomas, K. M., Drevets, W. C., Dahl, R. E., Ryan, N. D., Birmaher, B., Eccard, C. H., et al. (2001). Amygdala response to fearful faces in anxious and depressed children. *Archives of General Psychiatry, 58,* 1057–1063.

Thompson, R. A. (1994). Emotion regulation: A theme in search of definition. *Monographs of the Society for Research in Child Development, 59,* 25–52, 250–283.

Timbremont, B., & Braet, C. (2004). Cognitive vulnerability in remitted depressed children and adolescents. *Behaviour Research & Therapy, 42,* 423–437.

Timko, C., Cronkite, R. C., Berg, E. A., & Moos, R. H. (2002). Children of parents with unipolar depression: A comparison of stably remitted, partially remitted, and nonremitted parents and nondepressed controls. *Child Psychiatry and Human Development, 32,* 165–185.

Tomarken, A. J., Dichter, G. S., Garber, J., & Simien, C. (2004). Resting frontal brain activity: Linkages to maternal depression and socio-economic status among adolescents. *Biological Psychology, 67,* 77–102.

Verduyn, C., Barrowclough, C., Roberts, J., Tarrier, N., & Harrington, R. (2003). Maternal depression and child behaviour problems: Randomised placebo-controlled trial of a cognitive-behavioural group intervention. *British Journal of Psychiatry, 183,* 342–348.

Vitaro, F., & Pelletier, D. (1991). Assessment of children's social problem-solving skills in hypothetical and actual conflict situations. *Journal of Abnormal Child Psychology, 19,* 505–518.

Walden, T. A., & Ogan, T. A. (1988). The development of social referencing. *Child Development, 59,* 1230–1240.

Walker, E. F., Walder, D. J., & Reynolds, F. (2001). Developmental changes in cortisol secretion in normal and at-risk youth. *Development and Psychopathology, 13*, 721–732.

Webster Stratton, C., & Hammond, M. (1988). Maternal depression and its relationship to life stress, perceptions of child behavior problems, parenting behaviors, and child conduct problems. *Journal of Abnormal Child Psychology, 16*, 299–315.

Weinberg, M. K., Olson, K. L., Beeghly, M., & Tronick, E. Z. (2006). Making up is hard to do, especially for mothers with high levels of depressive symptoms and their infant sons. *Journal of Child Psychology and Psychiatry, 47*, 670–683.

Weissman, M. M., Prusoff, B. A., Gammon, G. D., Merikangas, K. R., Leckman, J. F., & Kidd, K. K. (1984). Psychopathology in the children (ages 6–18) of depressed and normal parents. *Journal of the American Academy of Child Psychiatry, 23*, 78–84.

Weissman, M. M., Wickramaratne, P., Nomura, Y., Warner, V., Pilowsky, D., & Verdeli, H. (2006). Offspring of depressed parents: 20 years later. *American Journal of Psychiatry, 163*, 1001–1008.

Weissman, M. M., Wickramaratne, P., Nomura, Y., Warner, V., Verdeli, H., Pilowsky, D. J., et al. (2005). Families at high and low risk for depression: A 3-generation study. *Archives of General Psychiatry, 62*, 29–36.

Werner, E. E., & Smith, R. S. (2001). *Journeys from childhood to midlife: Risk, resilience, and recovery*. Ithaca, NY: Cornell University Press.

Whiffen, V. E., & Gotlib, I. H. (1989). Infants of postpartum depressed mothers: Temperament and cognitive status. *Journal of Abnormal Psychology, 98*, 274–279.

Williamson, D., Birmaher, B., Axelson, D., Ryan, N., & Dahl, R. (2004). First episode of depression in children at low and high familial risk for depression. *Journal of the American Academy of Child Psychiatry, 43*, 291–297.

Zahn-Waxler, C., Cummings, E. M., Iannotti, R. J., & Radke-Yarrow, M. (1984). Young children of depressed parents: A population at risk for affective problems. In D. Cicchetti & K. Schneider-Rosen (Eds.), *Childhood depression. New directions for child development* (pp. 81–105). San Francisco, CA: Jossey-Bass.

Section V

TREATMENT OF ADOLESCENT DEPRESSION

Chapter Seventeen

Cognitive Behavioral Therapy for Youth Depression: The ACTION Treatment Program

KEVIN D. STARK, LAUREN S. KRUMHOLZ, KRISTEN P. RIDLEY, AND AMY HAMILTON

CONTENTS

OVERVIEW

As noted in Weersing and Gonzalez'schapter (see Chapter 21), cognitive-behavioral therapy (CBT) is one of the preferred and most empirically tested psychosocial interventions for depressive disorders among youth. CBT for depressed youth represents a downward extension of the adult models for treating depression (e.g., Beck, Rush, Shaw, & Emery, 1979). In general, there are few differences in the content of the treatment programs for youth relative to adults. The differences are in the way that the interventions are delivered to children and adolescents. The core treatment components, including affective education, coping skills, problem solving, and cognitive restructuring are the same, however, they are taught to youngsters using a more interactive and experiential approach. Adults can learn and will commonly apply the skills following a didactic presentation. Children, in contrast, need an engaging didactic presentation, then they need to actually enact the skill and experience the benefits of it on mood in order to learn it and try to independently use it. For example, the girls in our latest treatment study taught us how to best help them learn to use cognitive restructuring strategies. They benefit from externalizing the negative cognitions to an external source (the Muck Monster), and then they can learn to talk back to the negative thoughts that are directed at them from the Muck Monster. Girls also need repeated practice before they understand how to use the skill, and are likely to independently use it outside of the meetings. There are a number of other important differences between standard CBT for depression in adults and youth. Therapeutic homework is a central part of CBT for the treatment of depression. Adults seem to have a higher rate than children and adolescents of completing therapeutic homework. Another difference between adult and child clients may be that adult clients enter therapy of their own volition because they are experiencing pain, or recognize that they are having some problems. Thus, they are motivated to use therapy. Children, in contrast, are often brought to treatment by their parents and don't think that they need it so they are not as motivated to engage in therapy. Adults have an intuitive idea about what therapy is going to entail or they learn about it through the media. Children have no idea what to expect during therapy, and they don't know how to maximize the benefits of treatment. We have found that it is important to teach children and adolescents "good client" behaviors so that they can maximize their experiences. Another difference between the existing studies with children and adults is that the child treatments are commonly delivered using a group format, whereas the adult treatments are commonly delivered using an individual format. In a few studies, parents are involved in the child treatments, but parents commonly are included in their child's treatment in clinical practice.

The authors of this chapter have completed a 5-year study evaluating the efficacy of a gender- and age-specific CBT intervention for depressed 9- to 14-year-old girls. While we are in the process of analyzing the data, we can address the clinical significance of the treatment. Approximately 84% of the girls who completed the CBT, and 80% of the girls who completed CBT plus parent training no longer received a diagnosis of a depressive disorder following treatment, in contrast to 47% of the girls who participated in a minimal contact control condition. Thus, the CBT with and without parent training produced a nearly two to one improvement rate. By design, the activities, coping skills, and illustrations in the ACTION program's treatment manuals are specific to girls in this age group. Although the activities and workbooks for the ACTION program would need to be modified for boys and for older youth, the core therapeutic components and the sequence in which they are implemented are appropriate for females and males as well as for youth 9 years and older. The intervention requires modifications to address the individual needs of girls with various additional comorbid conditions, and it would have to be one component of a multimodal treatment for girls with comorbid obsessive compulsive disorder post-traumatic stress syndrome conduct disorder, attention-deficit hyperactivity disorder, and substance abuse disorders. Since the ACTION program is effective in treating depression in pre- and early-adolescent girls and prototypic of CBT interventions, the focus of this chapter will be on the ACTION program (i.e., the girl treatment and parent training components), and clinical insights gained over the past 5 years during its implementation. Ideally, during the ACTION program, girls learn coping strategies, problem solving, and cognitive restructuring skills at the same time that their environments are being changed through parent training and consultation. In addition, parents and teachers work with the therapist to encourage the girls to apply the therapeutic skills to their everyday lives.

OVERVIEW OF CHILD TREATMENT

ACTION is a group treatment that follows a structured therapist's manual (Stark, Simpson, Schnoebelen, Glenn, & Hargrave, 2007) and workbook (Stark, Schnoebelen, Simpson, Hargrave, & Glenn, 2007). Each of the 20 group and two individual meetings (see Table 17.1 for a session-by-session outline) lasts approximately 60 minutes, and is conducted twice a week for 11 weeks. The treatment materials can be adapted for use with individual clients. However,

Table 17.1 Session-by-Session Outline of Primary Child Treatment Components

1. Introductions and discussion of pragmatics
2. Affective education and introduction to coping
3. Affective education, coping skills, and introduction to Catch the Positive Diaries
Individual meeting: review therapeutic concepts and establish treatment goals
4. Extend group cohesion, review participant goals, application of coping skills
5. Extend coping skills, introduction to problem solving
6. Cognition and emotion, introduction to cognitive restructuring
7. Apply problem solving
8. Apply problem solving
9. Apply problem solving
Individual meeting: review therapeutic concepts, identify common negative thoughts, individualize Catch the Positive Diaries, and introduce cognitive restructuring
10. Prepare for cognitive restructuring and introduction to cognitive restructuring
11. Cognitive restructuring
12. Cognitive restructuring and self-maps
13. Cognitive restructuring and self-maps
14. Cognitive restructuring and self-maps
15. Cognitive restructuring and self-maps
16. Cognitive restructuring and self-maps
17. Cognitive restructuring and self-maps
18. Cognitive restructuring and self-maps
19. Cognitive restructuring and self-maps
20. Bring it all together and termination activity

it is important to note that results of a qualitative study (Molnar, 2007) indicate that some of the program's effectiveness is attributable to the group format. The participants noted the importance of forming relationships with girls who are also depressed, and that the other group members were helpful in the process of acquiring and applying the skills. More specifically, sharing of emotional experiences by one group member appears to be the trigger for the other girls starting to share their personal experiences. This enables the therapist to begin to help the girls apply the therapeutic skills to their problems and experiences.

The ACTION treatment program is designed to be fun and engaging while teaching youngsters a variety of skills that are applied to their depressive symptoms, interpersonal difficulties, and other stressors. It is important that the meetings are enjoyable to increase participant's engagement, and to facilitate better recall of learned skills and in-session experiences. In addition, any experience that even temporarily improves the mood of depressed youth is useful, in that it may lead to improvements in brain functioning. These mood-enhancing experiences also lead to some cognitive restructuring in and of themselves as they counter the belief that "I always feel depressed" and "I never feel good." The skills are taught to the girls through didactic presentations and activities, are rehearsed during in-session activities where the participants experience the benefits of the treatment procedures, and are applied and practiced through therapeutic homework.

To make the intervention developmentally appropriate, whenever the girls are taught a therapeutic concept or skill, they should experience the benefits of it in session. Experiencing these benefits in session combats their helpless and pessimistic thoughts (e.g., "Nothing can help me"), increases treatment credibility (e.g., "This stuff really helps"), and provides them with a sense of personal efficacy (e.g., "I can make myself feel better"). Application of the therapeutic skills outside of meetings is critical for successful treatment as the participants have to practice using the strategies to provide themselves with relief from depressive symptoms, and they have to reduce stress and eliminate stressful situations. Thus, skill application is monitored and recorded through completion of therapeutic homework, which is encouraged through an in-session reward system.

The treatment program is based on a self-regulation model in which girls use skills to achieve and to maintain a pleasant mood, or they use a change in mood or negative thoughts as a sign to engage in coping, problem solving and/or cognitive restructuring. As discussed in more detail below, the girls are taught to use the "3Bs" (brain, body, and behavior) to identify their emotional experiences. Activities completed within the meetings and as homework help the girls to become more aware of their personal experiences and the links between their thoughts, behaviors, and emotions. By paying attention to the thoughts in their heads, the reactions of their bodies, and their own behavior, the girls become better aware of their emotions. Over the course of therapy, they additionally become more aware of changes in their emotions, and more skilled at using the changes as cues to engage in coping, problem solving, or cognitive restructuring.

Depressed youth often experience undesirable situations that are not within their control and thus cannot be changed by them. In such situations, the girls can take action to improve their mood and other depressive symptoms through coping skills that are taught and applied during the first nine meetings. Participants experience the benefits of using coping skills within session, and they are encouraged to use these skills outside of meetings through self-monitoring and recording their use.

Some undesirable situations that occur within the lives of depressed youth are within their control and can be changed or managed. The girls are taught a five-step problem-solving procedure to change undesirable situations, and thus to reduce distress and the accompanying emotional upset. Successful use of problem solving provides the participants with learning experiences that teach them that they are efficacious and can impact their lives in a positive way. Once again countering a belief of helplessness and providing evidence for a new belief of personal efficacy. By the middle of treatment, the youngsters typically are proficient at using coping and problem-solving skills which leads to an improvement in mood, and this enables them to focus on identifying and changing negative thoughts.

Depressed youth are taught to recognize and then evaluate negative thoughts using a number of cognitive restructuring strategies. It is assumed that the negative thoughts are a reflection of a negatively distorted style of thinking that arises from one or more of the following core beliefs: (1) I am unlovable; (2) I am worthless; and (3) I am helpless. A variety of within-session activities and therapeutic homework exercises are used to teach youngsters to be "Thought Judges" who evaluate the validity of their negative thoughts using two questions: (1) What is another way of looking at it? (2) What is the evidence? The therapist also provides the girls with discovery learning experiences that help them come to new more adaptive conclusions, and thus new more adaptive beliefs.

The core beliefs of depressed youth are still developing as a result of their negative life experiences. Thus, some of their negative thoughts are going to be valid representations of reality. When their negative thoughts are realistic and reflect situations that can be changed, the youngster is encouraged to use problem solving to develop and follow a plan that produces improvement in the situation. If the situation is real but cannot be changed, then a coping strategy is used to manage her reaction to the situation.

The core therapeutic components of the ACTION program are affective education, goal setting, coping skills training, self-monitoring through use of the Catch the Positive Diary (CPD), training and application of problem solving, cognitive restructuring strategies, and expanding the girl's beliefs about the self through self-map activities. Affective education is used to teach girls about the model of depression and how to treat it. Thus, the link between thoughts, feelings, and behaviors is established during the first few meetings. Affective education is also used to teach the girls to recognize and to identify the variety and magnitude of their emotional experiences. Initially, treatment efforts are focused on pleasant emotions and positive experiences as a means of creating an improvement in mood. Goal setting is used as a procedure for collaboratively devising the direction of treatment, and for motivating the girl to work toward the change that she desires. Coping skills are taught to the girls as a means of improving their mood at any time, and as a strategy to use when they begin to experience negative emotions. The girls are taught to use emotion-focused coping when their mood is adversely affected by an event that they cannot change. The purpose of self-monitoring using the CPD is to change the girls' attention from processing predominantly negative to positive events, and to help them attend to information that would discredit negative beliefs and provide evidence for more positive and realistic beliefs. Monitoring positive desirable events also serves as a tool for increasing the girls' engagement in such events. Problem solving is taught to the girls as a strategy that they can use to change stressful situations that are within their control or influence. Effective use of problem solving helps to not only reduce stress and improve the girl's life circumstances, but also to restructure the helplessness belief. Cognitive restructuring strategies are a central part of the ACTION treatment program. From the start of treatment, therapists are trying to help the girls understand the link between their thoughts, emotions, and behaviors, and to understand that their thoughts may not be valid. A good deal of time and therapeutic effort is spent helping the girls understand this point, which is a necessary precursor to effectively using cognitive restructuring strategies. A developmentally appropriate strategy for restructuring the beliefs of children is the Muck Monster procedure, in which negative thoughts are attributed to this common enemy that is external to the girls. This appears to depersonalize the procedure to some extent. Using this strategy, the girls learn how to question their negative thoughts and beliefs, and how to develop more positive and realistic beliefs. The self-mapping activity is the final treatment strategy used in the program because it requires the girls to be open to seeing their positive qualities; cognitive restructuring strategies are used to help meet this objective.

The ACTION program is designed to change the family environment through a hybrid program of parent training and cognitive-behavioral family therapy. Parent training is designed to teach parents to use positive reinforcement as the primary means of managing behavior, and to decrease use of punitive and coercive behavior management procedures. Parents are taught empathic listening as well as other communication skills. Family problem solving and conflict resolution skills are taught as a means of reducing stress due to conflict within the family. Another important aspect of the parent-training component is to help parents understand how they can support their daughters in the application of the ACTION skills in the home environment. Finally, parents are encouraged to apply the skills that their daughters are learning to their own lives.

A more complete description of each treatment component appears in the following sections. A session-by-session treatment outline appears in Table 17.1. In general, the first nine sessions primarily emphasize affective education and teaching coping and problem-solving skills. Sessions 10 through 19 focus on learning and applying cognitive restructuring, improving the girls' core beliefs about the self, and continued application of coping and problem-solving strategies.

CASE CONCEPTUALIZATION

While the ACTION treatment program is manualized, it cannot be effectively applied in a cookbook fashion. To be effective, the therapist must be able to develop a conceptualization of the girl's depressive disorder, and then use this conceptualization to individualize the treatment program for each girl. The manual is the guide to the therapeutic procedures and the order in which they are used, and the conceptualization provides the targets and the probable content to which the therapeutic procedures will be applied. The conceptualization is like a road map that directs the therapist and client to where they need to go to effectively manage depressive symptoms, and to change the core beliefs that underlie the depressive disorder. In addition, the therapist must have an understanding of the objectives of each session of the manual so that he/she can artfully and flexibly apply the core therapeutic skills to the experiences that each girl brings to meetings. Every meeting is guided by an integration of the case conceptualization, the session objectives, and the issues the girls bring to the meeting.

Case conceptualization is an ongoing hypothesis generating and testing process, which begins during the initial assessment prior to treatment, and is revised as necessary throughout treatment. The therapist tries to evaluate the validity of the conceptualization for each girl during meetings and modifies the conceptualization as new information is revealed. This process is intimately tied to theory. Theory provides the model of disturbances that may be causing the girl's depression.

Based on cognitive theory of depression (Beck et al., 1979), it is hypothesized that maladaptive core beliefs underlie the negatively distorted thinking that is evident in depression and appears to cause depressive symptoms. The three primary core beliefs that underlie depression are (1) I am helpless, (2) I am worthless, and/or (3) I am unlovable. The therapist uses assessment data, historical information, the automatic thoughts that are verbalized during treatment, and patterns in the girl's behavior to develop and test hypotheses about core beliefs. To determine which core belief(s) are operating for each girl, the therapist listens to the girl's self-references and the meanings that she draws from daily experiences. The beliefs are reflected in the themes and consistencies found in each girl's thoughts. The meanings of events can be deduced from the discussions and by asking, "What does it mean about you if…?" and by following this answer with additional similar questions until the most basic meaning is uncovered. J. Beck (1995) refers to this procedure as the "downward arrow" technique. In addition, the meaning of events can be revealed by asking questions, such as "What would it mean to you if…?" When the therapist believes that he/she has identified a core belief, he/she asks the girl whether it fits or rings true. In other words, the therapist discloses his/her hypothesis about the existence of a core belief and asks the girl to consider whether the hypothesis is accurate or not. Once the core beliefs have been successfully identified, the therapist continually and very actively looks for ways to change them as well as the environmental events that maintain them.

The next step in the case conceptualization process is identification of the environmental events that have maintained, or are maintaining the beliefs. To accomplish this, the therapist remains cognizant of the girl's core beliefs while assessing the girl's interactions with her caregivers and significant others and looks for patterns that could provide learning experiences that would lead to the development and maintenance of the core beliefs. Similarly, the girl's relationships with, and patterns of interacting with peers are assessed to determine whether they could be contributing to the development and maintenance of the core beliefs. Moreover, other achievement-related experiences provide the girl with additional learning experiences that shape core beliefs. Children and adolescents are active information processors who are constantly deriving meaning from events in their lives. They are continuously trying to understand what an event means about the self, the world, and the future. For example, a girl's father has been absent from her life and her mother is abusing substances. Consequently, the mother does not nurture her daughter as she is seeking the next high or intoxicated experience. At times, the daughter may be left without adequate care, and at other times, the parent may be irritable and emotionally attack the girl. The daughter then asks herself why her mother does not pay more attention to her, and why her mother does not seem to love her. Over time with repeated experiences such as these, the girl draws the conclusion that she is unlovable and this becomes internalized and structuralized. Once this belief is internalized, the girl begins to interact with others in a fashion that is consistent with this belief, leading to additional experiences that support it, and she interprets ambiguous events as further evidence that she is unlovable.

The case conceptualization guides the therapist's decision making during meetings. For example, if a girl holds the core belief that she is unlovable, the therapist should look for opportunities within the girl's life experiences that provide her with evidence that she is loved and lovable. The therapist should also try to change environmental events that support the belief that she is unlovable, and attempt to provide the girl with new learning experiences that support the belief that she is loved and lovable.

In addition to conceptualizing the nature of the girl's cognitive disturbances, the therapist assesses the girl's coping and problem-solving skills. During all encounters with the parents, and especially during conjoint parent–daughter meetings, the therapist observes the interactions between the parents and him/herself and between the parents and their daughter. The purpose of attending to these interactions is to evaluate the parents' behavior management, communication, and conflict resolution skills, as well as the degree of warmth and supportiveness in the parent–daughter relationship. These characteristics of the parents' interactions are important, for they may lead to the development of a negative affective tone in the home. Negative affect is both a stressor and it affects the daughter's mood. In addition, the therapist assesses the parents' emotion regulation and problem-solving skills, as parents often serve as models for their children. The presence of parental psychopathology is formally assessed during completion of pretreatment measures and, since many parents do not accurately report this information, ongoing assessment is completed during interactions with the parents.

IMPLEMENTATION

Duration and Spacing of Meetings

To date, researchers have not reached a consensus regarding the minimum number of meetings needed to produce an effective outcome nor the number of meetings required for the maximum positive impact. It is possible that the number of sessions required is idiosyncratic to each client. Currently, our treatment groups complete 20 meetings plus two individual meetings over 11 weeks. A session-by-session list of the therapeutic components and objectives appear in Table 17.1 and Table 17.2. Additional individual meetings are

Table 17.2 Objectives by Meeting

Meeting No.	Objectives
1	Discuss parameters of meetings, introduce counselors and participants, establish rationale for treatment, discuss confidentiality, establish group rules, build group cohesion, establish within group incentive system
2	Introduce participants to chat time and agenda setting, establish pragmatics of completing homework, introduce mood meter and Take ACTION List, complete within-session coping activity
3	Discuss importance of thinking about meetings and doing practice, introduce clients to various therapeutic components including: focusing on the positive, Catch the Positive Diaries, affective education, and coping strategies
Individual meeting 1	Review therapeutic concepts, development of treatment goals
4	Extend group cohesion, review participant goals and strategies, discuss application of coping strategies, complete coping skills activity within session
5	Experience impact of coping skills activity within session, introduction, extension and application of problem solving, introduction to brainstorming step of problem solving
6	Demonstrate the role of cognition in emotion and behavior, introduce connection of thoughts to feelings, enactment of coping skills activity within session
7	Apply problem solving to real-life situations, practice brainstorming activity, experience coping skills activity within session
8	Apply problem solving to teasing, experience coping skills activity within session
9	Apply problem solving to interpersonal problems, experience coping skills activity within session
Individual meeting 2	Review therapeutic concepts, identify common negative thoughts, individualize Catch the Positive Diaries, introduce cognitive restructuring
10	Prepare for cognitive restructuring, experience coping skills activity within session, practice cognitive restructuring
11	Introduce how perceptions are constructed, illustrate how depression distorts thinking, provide rationale for changing negative thoughts
12	Practice identifying negative thoughts of group members, introduce client strengths through a self-map, practice cognitive restructuring
13	Practice identifying negative thoughts, continue identifying strengths for the self-maps, practice cognitive restructuring with questions using alternative interpretations
14	Continue identifying negative thoughts, adding strengths to the self-maps, and practicing cognitive restructuring
15	Continue identifying negative thoughts and adding strengths to the self-maps, introduce examining evidence as a tool for cognitive restructuring
16	Continue identifying negative thoughts and adding strengths to the self-maps, practice cognitive restructuring, prepare for termination
17	Continue adding strengths to the self-maps, integrate and apply cognitive restructuring, continue preparing for termination
18	Continue adding strengths to the self-maps, integrate and apply all of the learned skills, continue preparing for termination
19	Draw conclusions from self-maps, empowerment activity for clients to continue using skills on their own, prepare for group termination
20	Say goodbye to the group, say goodbye to negative thoughts and feelings, terminate

conducted during this period on an as-needed basis. The duration of each meeting has been prescribed by the time permitted by each school principal, and has typically ranged from 45 to 75 minutes. However, in the ideal situation, it may be wise to base the duration of the meetings on developmental level with longer meetings scheduled for older youth and less time for younger girls. We prefer 1-hour meetings with groups of 9- and 10-year-olds, and 75-minute meetings with girls 11 and older. Experience suggests that children and younger adolescents benefit from meeting twice per week rather than once per week. There are numerous advantages to twice-weekly meetings (see Stark, Hargrave, Schnoebelen, Simpson, & Molnar, 2005).

Structure and Format of Meetings

CBT sessions for depression are structured and each meeting follows a sequence of events (Beck, 1995). We have modified this sequence to be developmentally appropriate. The structuring of meetings results in an efficient use of time, and forces the therapist to develop a plan for each meeting and to use time wisely. The skilled therapist should be flexible in the ordering of and amount of time devoted to each segment of the session. This flexibility should be based on the nature of the material the girls bring to the sessions. For example, a participant may be describing her experience with a homework assignment. Additional time may then be invested in this discussion if it has important implications for skill acquisition, changing a maladaptive behavior pattern, eliminating a problem, or changing a belief. Similarly, the order of the segments can be altered if needed to improve the flow of the discussion or of a learning experience.

The ACTION treatment program, as described in the manuals, is a small group intervention (two to five girls). Interventions for girls with depression that utilize a small group format have several advantages over individual treatment. A small group format often allows for some degree of normalization for girls suffering from depression because the girls have the opportunity to listen to other group members who are struggling with similar problems. This tends to validate each member's feelings, and helps them feel less isolated and alone. In addition, sharing similar problems and experiences is a useful way for girls to practice problem-solving skills, as the group members can help one another generate possible solutions. Some group members are also able to suggest what worked and did not work for them in comparable situations.

Girls and adolescents suffering from depression occasionally have significant social difficulties and few friends. Using a small group format often facilitates friendships among the group members, which allows them to build their social skills and develop more confidence. Group members are encouraged to build off of the other members' strengths. For example, if one of the girls in the group makes friends easily and another girl does not have any friends, the sociable girl can model "chit chat" conversation and provide feedback for the more socially isolated girl. Additionally, group formats allow for modeling of sharing feelings by the more social or outgoing group members, which typically increases the likelihood that the other members will feel safe to share their feelings. Group members are able to provide support for each other not only within sessions, but outside of sessions, and following termination of the intervention. Some therapists find that their group members are eager to offer support and encouragement to one another and tend to be proud of themselves when they are able to help.

Another benefit to a small group approach is that it can provide unique insight into the daily behavior of the group members at school. Group members who attend the same school are able to provide direct examples of when they observe each other using the skills that they learn in session. In addition, they can usually offer evidence against the other group members' negative thoughts. Most therapists find that hearing compliments and evidence against negative thoughts from a peer is often more meaningful and effective to the group members than hearing these from a therapist. In addition, group members have the opportunity to test out their negative thoughts about how others view them by asking for the opinions of their fellow group members. For instance, there is nothing more powerful for a girl who believes that nobody likes her than to hear the rest of the group saying, "What do you mean? We all love hanging out with you. You're funny, nice, and a great friend." The group format also allows for role-playing activities. Oftentimes, members in a group are able to accurately role-play different social situations.

A small group approach to intervention for depression is therapeutic to the extent that group cohesion is achieved. For example, for group members who have been rejected interpersonally, being part of a cohesive group is a powerful intervention in itself and creates a different experience for them. Although the amount of time it takes to achieve group cohesion varies by the group and its members, therapists typically find that achieving cohesion within a group does not occur until the fourth or fifth session. Cohesion may be more easily achieved within groups of younger girls. To facilitate group cohesion, the therapist emphasizes the importance of each member to the group, and uses skill-building activities in session that foster relationships between group members. Therapists find that group cohesion typically occurs following the sharing of personal goals. Another technique to enhance cohesion is for the therapist to have the members compliment one another during session to practice "catching the positive." Furthermore, reinforcing prosocial or "good friend" behaviors between group members and using language that reflects a team approach serves to build group cohesion.

Despite the numerous advantages to using a group format in depression interventions, this format may actually hinder the progress and therapeutic effects of the intervention in some cases. Difficulties achieving group cohesion can impede the treatment process and may arise when group members overtly dislike each other, are in different grades, have dissimilar interests, are overly critical of other members, or display features of an emerging personality disorder. Under these circumstances, the therapist should try to incorporate many group-building activities, which provide additional opportunities for group members to positively interact with one another. Therapists may also find it beneficial to try to elicit similarities between group members, help them see positives in one another, and emphasize that they do not have to be best friends but could be more like teammates. In some situations, the therapist may find it effective to talk about issues openly, either by giving feedback to the individual girl or in the group by emphasizing positive interactions and the importance of taking turns. Individuals who show signs that indicate the presence of an emerging personality disorder are perhaps the most difficult to include in group interventions due to their manipulative behavior.

In most cases, these girls will significantly interfere with the progress of the other group members in the intervention; therefore, these girls should usually be removed from the group and offered individual treatment.

CORE THERAPEUTIC COMPONENTS

Affective Education

Affective education is the component of treatment in which participants learn about depression. They are taught the CBT model of depression including its causes, and how this model applies to them. They are provided with the rationale for treatment, and they learn how they are going to manage their depression. The affective education component helps participants become more self-aware, particularly of therapeutically relevant experiences, such as their depressive thoughts, unpleasant emotions, and other depressive symptoms. Participants are then taught to use these experiences as cues to engage in cognitive strategies, problem solving, and/or coping skills to manage their unpleasant emotions. Affective education is threaded throughout the program and is especially evident during the first few meetings.

Due to developmental limitations, children are taught a simplified model of depression in which sadness is caused by negative thoughts, undesirable outcomes, and a deficit in skills to overcome and manage these undesirable outcomes. If depression results from these experiences, then it makes sense that the following treatment strategies would alleviate depression: (1) if you feel bad because of negative thoughts, then change those thoughts; (2) if the undesirable outcomes/situations cannot be changed, use coping strategies to help yourself feel better; and (3) if the undesirable situation can be changed, use problem solving to improve it. In order to use these three broad strategies, the youngsters have to recognize their unpleasant emotions, the presence of a problem, and their accompanying negative thoughts. Girls aged 9- to 14-years-old are taught to identify their emotions by acting like "emotion detectives" who investigate their own experience of the 3 Bs: **B**ody (how their body is reacting), **B**rain (what they are thinking), and **B**ehavior (how they are behaving). This process increases the girls' awareness of their emotional experiences. During the meetings, when a girl states that she is feeling a particular emotion, the therapist asks her to describe what is happening in her body, what she is thinking, and how she is behaving. Simultaneously, the therapist may use a simple cookie cutout drawing of a girl to illustrate what is happening in her body, brain, and behavior. As treatment progresses and the girls become more proficient at this process, they complete the drawings themselves. The girls also complete therapeutic homework assignments in which they identify their emotional experiences and independently assess their experience of the 3 Bs. When working with adolescents, we refer to the 3 Bs, but we do not use the cookie-cutter drawings, and we expect the girls to be able to describe their emotional experiences in greater detail. Similarly, the therapist wouldn't use the term emotion detective as a means of capturing the process in a memorable fashion.

To help the girls recognize that a problem exists, they are taught to look for the signs that they are experiencing a problem. Possible signs include a shift to unpleasant affect, the occurrence or potential occurrence of an undesirable outcome, and feeling anxious or worried. An interpersonal conflict, a failure experience, and a loss, all represent problems to be solved.

A number of strategies and activities are used to help the girls learn about the distorted nature of depressive cognition. In addition, they learn how to become aware of negative thoughts. The methods for accomplishing this are described in the section on cognitive restructuring. This appears to be an important but often overlooked part of the cognitive restructuring process.

Goal Setting

CBT is a collaborative approach to therapy in which the client is fully informed of the treatment objectives, and the methods that are going to be employed to achieve these objectives. Central to this collaborative process is helping the participant identify her goals for therapy (e.g., J. Beck, 1995). In the case of treating children, this may also involve helping the parents identify their goals for their child's treatment and their goals for changing their family interaction, parenting practices, and sometimes themselves.

In the ACTION program, the therapist begins the goal-setting process by reviewing the pretreatment assessment information. This information is used to complete an initial case conceptualization that is translated into treatment goals, which are positively worded statements about desired outcomes. Between the third and fourth group meetings, the therapist merges the goals that he/she has generated during the case conceptualization with the girl's goals and concerns, to develop a set of three or four collaboratively generated goals. We limit the number of goals that are set with each girl because of hopelessness and helplessness that is often experienced by depressed youth. They would likely consider more than three or four goals an overwhelming and impossible task to achieve. In addition, they would see the list of goals and think, "Wow, I must really be a mess if I have all of these things wrong with me." Thus, while the therapist identifies many goals for the participant, he/she only discusses a limited number of them at any given time. As goals are achieved, additional goals are collaboratively established. In addition to setting goals with the girl, the therapist describes how each of the three core treatment procedures (coping skills, problem solving, and cognitive restructuring) will be used to help her achieve each of these goals. Before the end of the goals meeting, the therapist asks the girl if she would be willing to share her goals with the group. During the fourth group meeting, with each girl's permission, they share goals with each other and brainstorm how they can help each other reach their goals. The strategies for helping each other are recorded on girls' goals sheets so that they can refer to them as needed. At the beginning of every subsequent meeting, there is a "goals check-in" time to report progress toward goal attainment and to celebrate progress.

Coping Skills Training

A central objective of CBT for depression is to behaviorally activate the depressed youngsters. In the ACTION program, coping skills (Beck & Emery, 1985) are used to achieve this therapeutic objective. Emotion-focused coping is taught both as a general strategy for enhancing mood, and more specifically for when the participant is experiencing an undesirable or stressful situation that she cannot change (e.g., Weiten & Lloyd, 2006). Coping skills are described and practiced during meetings two through nine, although the therapists can use a coping skills activity at any time during treatment when a girl is experiencing an unpleasant or flat mood. For example, during one of the meetings, a girl described her thoughts and feelings about her father once again forgetting her birthday. The fact that he did not call or come over to get her for his standard visitation triggered her "I am unlovable" belief, which resulted in her feeling extreme sadness and some anger. The girl described how the situation with her father made her feel irritable and act "snappy" with her mother. Her mother then "snapped" back that she was "tired of these pity parties," and when the girl slammed her door and said "I hate you," the mother grounded her daughter. The sum of these events activated the "I am worthless" belief and some self-destructive ideation. The therapist made an initial attempt to restructure these beliefs, but the girl appeared to be stuck in her negative affect and unable to think more objectively. Therefore, the therapist decided to use a fun team-based coping activity to enhance mood and the girl's sense of connection with others. By using a coping skills activity in session, the therapist models for the girl how to spontaneously use these strategies to cope and enhance mood. When the girl's mood improved, the therapist went back to the cognitive restructuring and then processed with the group how the combination of coping and "thought detective questions" helped the girl feel better. Coping skills training is emphasized at the beginning of treatment because these skills help the girls experience an immediate improvement in mood. This improvement in mood eases the girls' ability to learn and benefit from problem solving and cognitive restructuring, which are taught later.

As part of the development of the ACTION treatment, a pilot study was completed to identify naturally occurring coping strategies used by 9- to 14-year-old children to manage sadness and anger/irritability. Teachers selected resilient 9- to 14-year-old students, who were then placed into same gender and age focus groups. Five broad categories of coping skills emerged from these focus groups: (1) do something fun and distracting; (2) do something soothing and relaxing; (3) seek social support; (4) do something that expends lots of energy; and (5) change your thinking. The girls experience the benefits of examples of coping skills from each of the five broad categories within the treatment sessions. The therapist chooses the coping skills to be taught and applied during each meeting based on what he/she believes is most needed by the group. For example, the group may be exhibiting flat affect. The therapist would do something fun and energizing as a means of enlivening the group.

Solely discussing coping skills and how they work is not adequate as it becomes nothing more than an intellectual exercise for children. Children, and to a lesser extent adolescents, have to experience the benefits of coping skills before they will try to use them. When a coping strategy is taught, the therapist asks the girls to rate their mood at that moment and then to participate in an activity in which they use one of the coping skills. For example, the girls may play with hula hoops for 5 minutes along with the therapist (fun and distracting), or they may play freeze tag (exerting energy), wiggle their toes in sand while imaging a relaxing beach scene (soothing and relaxing), they may talk with one another about a stressor (talk to someone), or they may be asked to talk back to their negative thoughts (change your thinking). After completing the activity, they re-rate their moods. Inevitably, their moods dramatically improve. The therapist processes the experience with them. After the coping strategies are taught, the girls are asked to generate a list of examples of activities they can do for each of the five categories of coping strategies.

In addition to teaching coping strategies, the therapist helps the girls identify situations where it is most advantageous to use specific coping skills. For example, doing something fun and distracting can help lift mood and reduce anger or anxiety. Soothing and relaxing coping skills are emphasized as methods for reducing anger, irritability, and anxiety in general, and for creating a calm, pleasant, emotional state. Expending energy is useful for generating more energy, reducing stress, elevating mood, and fostering better sleep hygiene. Talking to someone can be used as a way to calm down, distract oneself from something that is upsetting, gain another's perspective, and feel more connected. Early in treatment, participants are taught to change their thinking by using simple coping statements as a means of managing mood. These statements are designed to help the girls, at least temporarily, combat depressive thinking. Coping statements are used by participants prior to and during the time they are acquiring more complex cognitive restructuring strategies, and are not to be confused with the more elegant cognitive restructuring procedures described later in the chapter.

While youngsters can learn and benefit from using coping skills, therapeutic improvement is dependent on applying the skills outside of meetings. To facilitate application of coping strategies, therapeutic homework is assigned. This homework progresses from identifying changes in emotion and the accompanying thoughts, to identifying the context of emotional change and the coping skill used to improve mood. In general, participants enjoy using coping strategies and have a relatively easy time learning coping skills and applying them to their depressive symptoms.

The coping skills training procedure is similar for adolescent girls. The difference is that the actual skills used would be developmentally specific. For example, a 15-year-old girl might choose to listen to music on her iPod while an 8-year-old might choose to watch a specific video to relax, or she might choose a different type of music. Adolescents also need fewer within-session experiences with the coping skill before they trust that it will work and start to use it outside of the meetings.

CPD: A Tool to Promote Activation and Coping

As the name suggests, the Catch the Positive Diary (Lewinsohn & Graf, 1973) is designed to help the girls catch (attend to) positive events by helping them self-monitor and record the occurrence of a variety of therapeutically important positive events. When treating depressed youth, the CPD is used to (1) behaviorally activate the girls through engagement in fun activities; (2) redirect the girls' attention from negative to positive events; (3) increase the girls' completion of therapeutically relevant activities; and (4) help the girls find evidence that supports new, more adaptive beliefs, and counters negative beliefs.

The CPD consists of three parts: (1) a list of events to be self-monitored; (2) a set of rows that extends from the list of positive events, and a series of columns that designates the days of the week, forming a grid of cells; and (3) a place for rating the girl's mood each day of the week. Since the list of events to be monitored increases and changes over the course of treatment, the list is placed on a separate form that can be replaced and/or additional copies can be added as the list grows. Using blank lists rather than preconstructed lists allows each girl to create an individualized set of positive events that specifically addresses her case conceptualization.

Self-monitoring of enjoyable activities leads to an increase in the frequency of engagement in these activities. Engagement in fun and distracting activities as a means of enhancing mood and coping with stress is the first coping strategy taught, so enjoyable activities are the first events on the list. To further increase engagement in these activities, the therapist educates the girls about the mood enhancing quality of engaging in recreational activities, and gives the girls therapeutic homework to participate in as many of the activities on their list as they can each day. To further motivate the girls, the therapist graphs each girl's mood and the number of recreational activities completed each day. The graph visually illustrates that mood improves as girls participate in more "fun" activities. An overarching goal of the treatment program and of the CPD is to improve mood by increasing the frequency and types of coping skills used by the girls. As noted earlier, this produces behavioral activation that is one of the overarching goals of treatment. As the other categories of coping skills are taught to the girls and the benefits are experienced in session, the girls' favorite examples of these coping skills are added to the list. Thus, the list expands from fun activities to include soothing and relaxing activities, activities that vigorously expend energy, social activities, and coping thoughts.

Because depressed youth generally fail to notice commonly occurring positive events, and thus mood enhancing events, participants may be asked to include these events on the list, to redirect their attention towards positive occurrences and restructure the belief that "nothing good ever happens to me." For example, the girls may be instructed to add to their lists receiving a compliment, getting a good grade, playing an instrument, doing a nice job on an art project, hearing something funny, laughing with friends, acting silly, hearing a song that you like, and dancing.

Based on each girl's case conceptualization and the negative thoughts that she verbalizes during meetings, the girls are instructed to add specific events to their list that will lead to changes in core beliefs. Thus, self-monitoring of these events restructures core beliefs and the negative thoughts that arise from them. For example, a girl may hold the distorted belief that she is unlovable. If the therapist has proof that she is loved, he/she could help the girl construct a list of critical events that are evidence that she is loved. Examples might include: My mom said she loves me; my dad hugged me; my parents take care of me; and my brother plays with me. As the events occur, the girls check them off in their diaries and the outcome of the assignment is processed during the next meeting. When such tasks are given to the girls, it is useful to complete the list early in the meeting so that they can practice monitoring the occurrence of the target events during the meeting with the assistance of the therapist. The CPD is a flexible tool that can be used for various therapeutic purposes. Since it is individualized, it can be used with youth of all ages.

Problem-Solving Training

As the girls acquire a better understanding of their emotions, accurately identify them, recognize their impact on behavior and thinking, and understand that they can take action to moderate the intensity and impact of their emotions, the girls are taught that some of the undesirable situations that lead to unpleasant emotions can be changed. Problem solving is the strategy used to develop a plan for changing undesirable situations. The five-step problem-solving sequence is formally introduced during the fifth meeting. During this meeting, the group also creates a comprehensive list of problems that girls their age typically face. Then the group goes through the list and determines whether or not each problem can be changed. If the girls decide they cannot change a problem, the therapist inquires about which coping skill they would use to moderate the impact of the problem. Learning to identify whether or not a problem can be changed by the girls is an important and somewhat difficult concept for the girls to grasp. Adolescents tend to have a better grasp of this concept. Thus, typically the older the client the greater their understanding of the concept of controllability and the less time has to be spent directly trying to help them to learn how to gauge the amount of control they have over a situation. Through interviews of past participants in the treatment, we have learned that some of the girls who did not improve from treatment stopped believing in the efficacy of the ACTION treatment because they were attempting to apply problem solving to situations that were not within their control (e.g., parental divorce). Their therapists were unaware of this at the time, so they could not intervene to help the participant use her coping skills and possibly cognitive restructuring strategies to deal with such situations. Children can learn to distinguish situations they can impact from ones they cannot by asking themselves: Can I control the outcome of this situation? Can I independently prevent the situation from occurring? Who is in control of the situation? The girls have to learn how to think through situations and determine whether or not the situations are out of their control. Depressed youth may err in either direction. They can hold a helplessness belief, which leads them to believe they cannot control or positively impact any negative situations. In this instance, the therapist has to help the girls begin to believe that they can affect negative situations that occur in their lives. In contrast, some girls fail to see the limits of their own abilities, perhaps as a result of a developmental limitation. In this situation, the therapist has to aid the girls in recognizing that some situations are simply out of their control.

The problem-solving procedure used in the ACTION treatment is a modified version of the one described by Kendall (e.g., Kendall & Braswell, 1993). Participants are taught to break problem solving down into five steps through education, modeling, coaching, rehearsal, and feedback. To simplify the process and to help the girls remember the steps, the therapist refers to the steps as the "5Ps." The steps include: (1) problem definition (**P**roblem), (2) goal definition (**P**urpose), (3) solution generation (**P**lans), (4) consequential thinking (**P**redict and pick), and (5) self-evaluation (**P**at on the back). The steps are defined in a developmentally sensitive manner and activities are used to illustrate the meaning and purpose of each step. When working with adolescents, we let them know that they can help themselves to remember the five steps involved in problem solving by thinking of the process as involving the 5 Ps. Adolescents also seem to have a better grasp of the second step—goal definition. They understand what a goal is and have had some experience with setting personal goals, so it requires less explanation and they are more capable of independently setting their goals for a particular problem. In general, the adolescents grasp the problem-solving procedure more quickly than children, so they require fewer training sessions before they can independently employ problem solving.

The first step in the process is problem identification and definition. This may be the most difficult step for depressed youth to learn, as they often view a problem as a personal threat. To a depressed girl, existence of a problem means that there is something wrong with herself, or the problem represents an impending loss. In addition, depressed youngsters with a helpless core belief feel overwhelmed by problems, think that they cannot solve them, and believe that if they did solve an existing problem, it would be replaced by another problem. Thus, their sense of hopelessness has to be combated through concrete evidence from their life experiences demonstrating that they can overcome problems. The therapist tries to help the girls develop an attitude that problems are a normal part of life and they represent challenges that can be eliminated or managed. They simply represent frustrations that need to be attacked and solved.

It is difficult for children to recognize that a problem exists and to identify it early in treatment. At the beginning of treatment, 9- to 14-year-old girls note that they feel bad and often do not know why. As they progress through treatment, the therapist helps them to identify the problems (as well as the negative thoughts) that lead to the upset. As a result of participating in this process, the girls learn how to independently identify their problems. They essentially learn to ask themselves: What is bothering me? What caused me to feel upset? The first problem solving related therapeutic homework assignment that the girls complete is to identify problems and the clues that they used to identify them. This independent practice appears to be helpful. The therapist processes the girls' reports, which further sensitizes them to the clues that a problem exists.

The second step of problem solving is goal definition. The key to helping depressed youth identify their goals for problem solving is helping them choose constructive goals and avoid destructive ones. Their tendency is to choose ineffective or self-defeating goals. They can get caught up in self-destructive patterns of behavior that lead to punishment, rejection, and loss in general. Thus, it is important for the therapist to help the girls choose effective goals that will lead to desirable outcomes. Cognitive restructuring may have to be used during this step, as the girls' helplessness belief could prevent them from believing that there is any chance that the desirable goals will come true, so they do not bother to set them. Another example of how a dysfunctional belief may impact the girl's goal setting is the case where a depressed girl may expect rejection from peers so she sets as her goal rejecting peers before they can reject her and this perpetuates the destructive cycle. The therapist would have to work with this girl to test the belief that others may like her and set goals that would create a new learning history that supports this alternative positive belief.

The third step of problem solving is solution generation. Generating alternative solutions is difficult for depressed youngsters, especially those with a helpless core belief, since they typically believe that nothing will work or help them. Therefore, once again, it may be necessary to uncover maladaptive thoughts and to use cognitive restructuring strategies during this step. Youngsters often learn how to brainstorm during science and other classes at school. Thus, many participants have had some experience with this process. An important aspect to the brainstorming process is teaching girls to suspend judgment and to simply generate as many possible solutions to a problem as they can without evaluating the solutions. During this process it is helpful for the therapist to model the process by providing the girls with ridiculous plans that clearly will not work, so that they can laugh with the therapist and see that they can generate any plan, even ones that will not work. Some depressed youngsters also appear to lack knowledge of potential solutions to the problems they face. They need suggestions from the therapist, other helpful adults, and the group members. As a practical rule, we try to help the girls to generate at least five solutions for each problem.

The fourth step in the problem-solving process is consequential thinking, which involves thinking ahead to the potential outcome for each generated plan and then choosing a plan. During this step, it is necessary for the therapist to combat pessimism, as it is easier for the girls to generate reasons for why a plan would not work rather than why it would work. Even when girls cannot identify specific reasons for why they believe a plan will not work, they base their predictions of the plan failing on how they are feeling (emotional reasoning). Thus, the therapist has to be prepared to help the girls see possible positive outcomes and to combat the girls' sense of helplessness. When a girl is stuck in the helplessness, it is useful to stop the discussion and enact a coping strategy to elevate mood, which seems to free up their thinking and allow them to see positive alternatives. It is also useful to discuss the fact that the girl is stuck and explain the negative effects of being stuck on the girl's ability to solve the problem and on the girl's mood.

The final step of self-evaluation involves assessing the outcome of the implementation of a plan and then reinforcing oneself or re-evaluating the problem and trying another plan. When the girls first start using problem solving, the therapist should process the outcome with the girls, as depressed youngsters are likely to minimize their successes and magnify the significance of their failed attempts, while attributing failures to themselves. There are numerous times when depressed youth do not recognize a success or a partial success. If the outcome is not blatantly positive, they may not recognize the success. Therefore, it is important to walk the client through the attempt at problem solving and the outcome in detail. To help combat the disappointment of a failed plan, the girls are taught to use coping statements as well as other coping skills to manage the upset. Furthermore, the therapist aids the girls in seeing that the initial failure to achieve their goal is not a waste of time or effort, as it provides them with additional information that is useful for crafting a new, more effective plan. Thus, a failure experience is reframed as an opportunity to acquire new information that they did not have, so they can develop more effective plans.

After the girls are educated about the purpose of each problem-solving step and how to apply them, they are provided with practice applying the steps through games and/or hypothetical situations. Because games and hypothetical situations are less emotionally charged than real-life problems, the girls and therapist are able to focus on the problem-solving process rather than on the meaning and affect attached to the situation. By applying the steps during these games and hypothetical situations, the therapist can help the girls better understand each step of the process and how important it is to implement the steps in the proper sequence. This practice with problem solving also gives the therapist a window into how the girls are likely to react to successful and unsuccessful attempts to solve problems. The girls verbalize their negative thoughts during failure experiences, which provides the therapist with an opportunity to help the girls cope with failure or to restructure the girls' distorted thoughts (e.g., I can't do anything right! Nothing ever goes right for me!).

Once the girls have learned the problem-solving steps and begin applying their problem-solving skills to real-life problems that are within their control, the therapist and other group members work together to generate plans that have a high probability of successfully fixing the problem. Then, the girls must try the plans. They are more likely to try plans if they believe that the plans will work, and if they believe that they possess the ability to successfully implement them. Thus, it is important to discuss both of these issues with the girls as plans are developed and the girls are assigned homework to implement the plans. It may be useful to ask the girls if they foresee anything that would get in the way of trying the plans. A problem-solving homework form can be completed during the meeting as the therapist and other group members help each other work through the steps and develop plans. They can then refer to this form as they attempt to implement the plans. It is helpful to begin applying problem solving to simpler problems with solutions that are more likely to be successful. Thus, the girls develop a learning history of success with problem solving, which increases the likelihood that they will use problem solving in the future.

Problem solving can be derailed by negative thinking. Two strategies that are useful in helping the girls overcome negative thinking are cognitive restructuring and coping skills. Cognitive restructuring strategies should be used to get the girls over the cognitive roadblocks that prevent them from using problem solving outside of the meetings. It often takes the girls a number of weeks to build enough of a new learning history to begin to believe that they can use problem solving to produce significant changes in their lives. Another useful strategy is to teach the girls to combine coping skills with problem solving. They are taught to use the coping skills to elevate their mood or to overcome their pessimism, and then they engage in problem solving when they have more emotional distance and can think more realistically about the problem.

Cognitive Restructuring

Establishing the Rationale for Cognitive Restructuring

In order to effectively restructure a youngster's distorted thoughts and beliefs, it is necessary to first establish a relationship between negative thoughts, unpleasant mood, and other depressive symptoms. This can be accomplished through various methods. Since cognitive restructuring is specifically taught to the girls during the latter sessions, it is possible to establish this relationship during the earlier meetings. From the first meeting forward in treatment, the therapist watches for opportunities to educate the girls about the relationship between their negative thoughts and unpleasant mood as well as other depressive symptoms. Whenever a group member states how she feels, the therapist links the feelings to her thoughts. For example, (Girl) "I felt horrible last night." (Therapist) "What were you thinking when you felt horrible?" (Girl) "That my only friend had dumped me." (Therapist) "Oh I see. If you think that your only friend no longer likes you, you feel horrible. How would you have felt if you had thought that she was upset but that she would be over it tomorrow?" This procedure of using the girl's own experiences to illustrate the link between thoughts and feelings is the most desirable way to build her understanding of this relationship. It is necessary to repeatedly do this throughout treatment. The therapist's modeling of the process helps the girls begin to try to independently make the link between their thoughts and mood.

A number of within-session activities are used to supplement the linking of the girls' own thoughts and emotions. Early in treatment when the relationship between thoughts and feelings is still being established, the therapist writes thoughts on cutouts of thought bubbles and the names of various emotions on heart-shaped cutouts. These cutouts are placed inside a paper bag. The girls take turns pulling a cutout from the bag. If a thought bubble is chosen, then the girl is instructed to state the emotion that goes with it. If an emotion cutout is chosen, then the girl is instructed to state a thought that is likely to cause that emotion. The other group members can help as needed or offer additional examples. The therapist can choose to complete more processing, such as: "When was the last time that you felt that way? What was happening? What were you thinking?" The therapist should try to make the thought and emotion cutouts real for the girls by using thoughts that the girls have verbalized during meetings, and by using examples of the girls' emotional experiences as reported in previous meetings. With adolescents, the therapist will spend more time processing the girls' emotional experiences and be more likely to ask the girls to elaborate on their thoughts and to try to recall them in the exact words that they first appeared.

Many of these activities are designed to be experiential in nature. In other words, they are designed to teach the girls through their own within-session experiences. In addition, they are used to extend the girls' understanding of the nature of cognition and its relationship to emotional adjustment. The girls should understand that they construct their thoughts, that their thoughts may not be true, and that they can change them. During one activity used to accomplish this, the therapist shows the girls a cartoon of a situation commonly experienced by girls their age that is open to multiple interpretations. The girls are instructed to each write a short story about what is happening in the cartoon. Typically, they all create different stories. The girls share their stories and then the therapist processes this with them, by asking questions such as: "How could all of you be looking at the same picture but see it in a different way?" "What does this tell us about the way we think?" "Which story is correct?" "What does that tell us about the way we think?" "Debbie, can you see the same thing that Lisa saw? Shaniqua, can you see it the way that Melissa did?" "So, you can change the way that you think about things?" "Who can tell us about a time when she thought something and it turned out that you saw it in the wrong way—you misunderstood it?" "When you are depressed, what do you think happens to your thinking?" "Are your thoughts more positive or more negative?" "Did you know that often times when you are depressed your thoughts aren't true? They lie to you and make you see things in a negative way that is not true."

To illustrate the negative bias in depressive thinking and to help the girls experience this phenomenon in session, the participants complete a task in which they are given a large bead to put into their shoe between the sole and the bottom of their foot. Then they are given a hard piece of fruity candy to suck on. The girls are instructed to walk around and notice the discomfort of the bead. Then they are asked to concentrate on the fruity, sweet flavor of the candy. (Therapist) "What happens when you concentrate on the candy?" (Girl) "The bad feeling goes away." (Therapist) "What happens when you concentrate on the bead?" (Girl) "You forget about the candy and get annoyed at the bead." (Therapist) "So two things are happening at the same time and you can notice one or the other depending on which one you attend to?" "When someone is feeling depressed, which one do you think that person attends to?" (Girl) "The bead." (Therapist) "What happens to the good things like the candy that are occurring at the same time?" (Girl) "They are ignored." (Therapist) "Right. When someone is feeling depressed, she is likely to only notice the unpleasant, negative, or unwanted things that are going on and then she misses the good things that are happening. So, if you only noticed the negative things that are going on, how would you feel?" (Girl) "Really down." (Therapist) "Right. What would happen if you also noticed the good things that were happening?" (Girl) "You would feel good." (Therapist) "Right, and how would you feel if you noticed both things?" (Girl) "Okay." (Therapist) "Yes. So, if you want to feel better, should you pay more attention to the beads in your life or the sweet things?" "Were you able to do this just a minute ago when you were walking around?" (Girl) "Yes." (Therapist) "Ah ha, so that is what we are going to work on. Noticing the sweet and good things."

When establishing the rationale for cognitive restructuring with the girls, another important concept to teach them is that often their thoughts are not true. "Just because you think it, it doesn't mean that it is true" (J. Beck, 2005). This is a surprising revelation for 9- to 14-year-old girls. They are under the assumption that if they think something, then it has to be true. The activities used within the group and examples from the girls' lives are used to illustrate this point. Another important message to relay to the girls is that we are continually confronted with multiple ways of thinking about situations, and that we are making choices about what we want to think and believe. In many situations, we can choose what we want to believe because there is no clear-cut, definitive way of thinking that is correct. The participants should be taught that sometimes we have to look at the practical outcome of believing a negative thought and then weigh the advantages of choosing to believe a viable and possibly true, alternative thought. Once again, real-life situations are used to make this point.

By the time the girls are beginning to focus on their own negative thoughts, and are learning how to evaluate and restructure them so that they are more realistic, they understand that their thoughts affect their emotions, that their thoughts are constructed, that they may not be true, and that it is desirable to think more positively and realistically because it will help them feel better.

Identifying Negative Thoughts

In order to independently restructure negative thoughts and the beliefs that underlie them, the girls must become aware of their own thoughts. The extent to which the girls need direct training in the metacognitive process of recognizing their own thoughts is a function of developmental level. Adolescents can do this much more easily than younger girls. Regardless of age, it is easier to recognize when someone else expresses negative thoughts; therefore, therapists begin by asking the girls to identify others' negative thoughts as a bridge to recognizing and identifying their own negative thoughts. To accomplish this, the therapist and girls discuss how to recognize negative thoughts and then they make a game of catching each other's negative thoughts. The girls are instructed to call out "negative thought" whenever someone expresses one through their in-group statements. The therapist purposely makes many negative statements to give the girls practice at doing this and to normalize being the recipient of the negative thought comment. Subsequently, the girls are asked to catch and record their own negative thoughts on homework forms that they bring to the group. The process of identifying negative thoughts is a metacognitive act. The girls learn to listen to their thoughts and to look for clues that their thoughts possess negative content. The experience with identifying the negative thoughts of other group members facilitates the process of learning how to identify one's own negative thoughts.

Cognitive Restructuring Strategies

A primary objective of the ACTION treatment for depressed youth is to change negatively distorted thinking to more positive and realistic thinking. More specifically, the objective is to identify the negative core beliefs that underlie the girl's depressive disorder, and help her evaluate these core beliefs while providing learning experiences that help her build new, positive, and realistic core beliefs. Thus, if a girl believes she is helpless, the therapist collaboratively devises learning experiences that demonstrate to her that she is efficacious. If she believes that she is unlovable, then the therapist helps her develop the core belief that she is lovable. Similarly, if a girl believes that she is worthless, then the therapist helps her develop the belief that she has value/worth. To accomplish any of these objectives, the therapist must first identify the core beliefs that underlie the youngster's depressive thoughts and then develop a plan for providing the girl with corrective learning experiences. The most important thoughts to focus on are those that reflect and support negative core beliefs. Corrective learning experiences can be completed through verbal discussions, or by using a more powerful strategy of giving the girl a behavioral experiment that allows her to have a new experience that contradicts the negative belief while supporting a new, more realistic, and positive belief.

Negative thoughts are restructured by the therapist throughout treatment as they are identified. The girls are introduced to the cognitive restructuring procedure during meeting six, so they can better understand what the therapist is helping them do during the early meetings. During the first nine meetings, the therapist identifies negative thoughts and asks the questions that lead to cognitive restructuring. Consequently, the girls are not required to do much self-reflection outside of the meetings. Cognitive restructuring becomes the focus of treatment later (meetings 10–20) because it requires the youngsters to focus on negative thoughts that can heighten depressive symptoms. By providing the girls with coping and problem-solving skills earlier in treatment, they can manage the upset that comes with increased self-focus. In addition, these skills produce symptom relief including an improvement in mood that appears to loosen negative thinking. This improvement in mood also appears to help the girls create emotional distance from their depressive thoughts and beliefs, which seems to open them to restructuring. The cognitive restructuring completed by the therapist helps start the shift in thinking and serves as a model for how to restructure negative thoughts and beliefs.

Once a negative thought has been identified, the 9- to 14-year-old girl asks one of the two thought detective questions to evaluate the thought's validity and to develop adaptive thoughts to replace the negative thoughts. The two thought detective questions are: (1) What's another way to think about it? and (2) What's the evidence (Beck et al., 1979)? The girls learn the question that is best suited for different negative thoughts. "What's another way to think about it" is the easiest cognitive restructuring question for girls to learn. They use this question to generate alternative, plausible, and positive thoughts. So, this is a good question to use when the girls draw a negative conclusion from a situation that has many other viable conclusions. "What's the evidence" is used when the objective facts do not support the girl's negative thought.

For adolescents, therapists teach them two additional questions (Beck et al., 1979) that they can use including "What would I tell my best friend?" and "What is the worst that could happen, the best that could happen, and what is most realistic to expect?" "What would I tell my best friend?" is used when the girl is setting unrealistically stringent or perfectionistic standards for herself. "What is the worst…" is used when the youngster is experiencing catastrophic thinking. If the therapist finds that he/she is using "What would I tell my best friend" frequently, then she states in an empathic way "Wouldn't it be nice if you could be your own best friend?" For some girls this is a powerful concept that they can build upon.

The standard cognitive restructuring procedure is difficult to teach children to use because of the developmental difference between children and adults. One powerful tool to enhance the accessibility of cognitive restructuring to youth is an activity that the girls refer to as "Talking back to the Muck Monster." When the participants are having difficulty changing or letting go of negative thinking, therpists refer to this as being "stuck in the negative muck." The girls understand and enjoy this metaphor. When they are stuck in the negative muck, it is the Muck Monster that is filling them with negative thoughts and holding them back from extricating themselves from the muck. The girls consistently report having an image of their Muck Monster. They are eager to describe their Muck Monster and they are asked to draw it in preparation for the activity.

Establishing the Muck Monster as the source of the girls' depressive thoughts is useful in a number of ways. It depersonalizes the negative thinking; thus, the Muck Monster is the source of negative thoughts rather than the girl. Attributing the negative thoughts to the Muck Monster also creates emotional distance between the girl and her depressive thinking, which seems to make it slightly easier to let go of or actively work to counter the negative thoughts. The Muck Monster also becomes a common opponent to defeat. Talking back to the Muck Monster is completed as many times as is needed to help the girls learn how to restructure their negative thoughts between the tenth meeting and termination. Therapists don't use the term Muck Monster with adolescents, rather, they ask them to either give the source of their depression a name or just refer to it as "that is your depression talking to you." "What are you going to say to your depression to argue against the negative thoughts—the lies it is telling you?"

Preparation for cognitive restructuring begins prior to treatment during the assessment process and continues throughout treatment. The therapist maintains a list of each girl's negative thoughts. The list includes thoughts that were endorsed on the pretreatment assessment measures, verbalized during treatment meetings, and recorded on homework forms. This list represents the content of each girl's Muck Monster. During an individual meeting that occurs between meetings 10 and 11, the therapist discusses each girl's list with her to confirm that the content of the list "rings true," and to heighten her awareness of these thoughts and beliefs as well as their impact on emotions, behavior, and interpersonal relationships. The beliefs are written inside the girls' drawings of their Muck Monsters, and the thoughts that stem from the beliefs are written in thought bubbles around the Muck Monster.

As mentioned previously, to help the girls learn to independently apply cognitive restructuring, they are asked to talk back to the Muck Monster using the two thought detective questions. For this activity, an extra chair is brought to the group meetings. The chair is for the Muck Monster. The therapist moves to the empty chair and holds the girl's picture of the Muck Monster while he/she states one of the girl's negative thoughts. The girl forcefully uses the two thought detective questions to guide her talking back to the Muck Monster. Group members help her do this by providing additional evidence or alternative interpretations. The girls may be encouraged to forcefully talk back to the Muck Monster by yelling at it. Other group members assist and cheer the girl on as she evaluates negative thoughts and then replaces them with more realistic positive thoughts. Sometimes it is beneficial to have the girl play the role of the Muck Monster and have her hold the drawing of the Muck Monster while verbalizing her own negative thoughts. The therapist then forcefully talks back to the Muck Monster using the two thought detective questions. The girls enjoy this activity and it helps them learn how to use cognitive restructuring. To provide the girls with additional help applying cognitive restructuring outside of the meetings, the workbook has forms that guide the process of catching, evaluating, and replacing negative thoughts. A parallel procedure is used with adolescents, but the terms thought detective questions and Muck Monster are not used. Developmentally appropriate terms that the girls use to refer to the cognitive restructuring questions and the source of their depressive thinking are used instead.

Restructuring of negative thoughts is also completed indirectly through guided learning experiences incorporated into treatment. These learning experiences are chosen based on the case conceptualization initially developed before treatment meetings begin, and is further refined over the ensuing meetings. At the same time that the therapist is refining the case conceptualizations, he/she is watching for opportunities to use the girl's own experiences to help her process evidence that contradicts her negative beliefs and supports new, more adaptive beliefs. For example, a girl whose underlying core belief is "I am unlovable" which results in the intermediate belief "No one likes me" states that the following events happened between meetings: She talked with a friend on the Internet. She had a friend sleepover during the weekend. She was invited to a birthday party. She and her mom baked Christmas cookies together. Her mom tucks her into bed and says prayers with her every night. Through Socratic questioning, each of these events can be used as evidence that she is liked by her friends and loved by significant others. The therapist also gives the girl specific homework assignments that provide her with learning experiences that contradict existing negative beliefs and build new, more adaptive beliefs.

Building a Positive Sense of Self

The primary objective of cognitive restructuring is to help girls build positive core beliefs about the self. During the last eight meetings, additional activities are used to help build these positive core beliefs. The cognitive restructuring treatment component appears last because all of the previously learned skills are used during the process of working towards self-improvement and recognizing positive aspects of the self. Depressed youth evaluate their performances, possessions, and personal qualities more negatively than nondepressed youth, and their self-evaluations tend to be negatively distorted (Kendall, Stark, & Adam, 1990). In other words, they tend to be unrealistically and unreasonably negative in their self-evaluations. Youngsters can be taught to evaluate themselves more reasonably and positively when it is realistic to do so. During cognitive restructuring, participants learn to recognize their positive attributes, outcomes, and possessions.

One of the tools used to help children and adolescents develop more positive beliefs about themselves is the "self-map". Each circle within the figure represents an area of the girl's life and an aspect of self-definition. Overall, the self-map helps the girls broaden their self-definition and recognize more personal strengths than they previously acknowledged. Girls are asked to fill in each bubble with relevant strengths. In addition, parents and teachers are interviewed by the therapist to identify their perceptions of the girl's strengths in each of the domains. This information is provided to the girls by the therapist. We have found that this information can be powerful, as the girls enjoy receiving compliments from their parents and teachers. The girls are often quite surprised that these adults think very positively about them. In addition to the adult input, group members provide each other with positive feedback for each circle. Once again, receiving this information from peers appears to be poignant and believable to the girls. This procedure seems to work well with both girls and adolescents without modification.

The CPD is used as the girls are asked to self-monitor evidence that supports the positive self-description outlined on the self-map. For example, a girl may base much of her self-worth on her musical talent. She would be instructed to self-monitor her successes during class, individual instruction, practice, and concerts. In addition, emphasis would be placed on her effort toward becoming a better musician rather than on comparing herself to others. Furthermore, the personal pleasure she derives from playing her instrument would be emphasized.

In some instances, the girls' negative self-evaluations are accurate and they can benefit from self-improvement. In such instances, the goal of treatment is to help the girls translate personal standards into realistic goals, and then to develop and carry out plans for attaining their goals. Following the translation process, they prioritize the areas in which they are working towards self-improvement. Initially, a plan is formulated for producing improvement in an area where success is probable. The long-term goal is broken down into subgoals, and problem solving is used to develop plans that will lead to subgoal and eventually goal attainment. Prior to enacting plans, the girls identify possible impediments to carrying out the plans. Once again, problem solving is used to develop contingency plans for overcoming the impediments. Once the plans, including contingency plans, have been developed, the girls self-monitor their progress toward change. Alterations to plans are made along the way.

OVERVIEW OF PARENT TRAINING

The parent component of the ACTION treatment program (Stark, Simpson, Yancy, & Molnar, 2007a, 2007b) is a hybrid of traditional parent training and cognitive-behavioral family therapy. It is designed to support the child treatment component by teaching parents how to help their daughters use therapeutic skills and how to reinforce their daughter's efforts to use therapeutic skills. Another objective is to teach parents how to apply the ACTION skills to themselves. In addition, the girls and their parents learn a number of skills designed to remediate possible disturbances in family functioning and in the family environment. This parent-training component was specifically designed for families that have a daughter who is between the ages of 9 and 14. The efficacy of the intervention and appropriateness with families that have an adolescent girl is questionable, as other investigators have found inclusion of a parent component in the treatment of depressed adolescents to be aversive for the adolescent who is trying to individuate from parents (Brent, Holder, & Kolko, 1997). So, much more clinical judgment would have to go into deciding how to include parents in the treatment of a depressed adolescent. It is believed that the core components and objectives for the parent training remain relevant to a family with a depressed adolescent, especially the meetings on empathic listening, communication training, and conflict resolution.

Parent training meetings are completed in groups at the daughter's school after school hours. Meetings are conducted by the girl's therapist and last approximately 90 minutes. There are eight group parent meetings and two individual family meetings completed over the 11 weeks that their daughters are participating in treatment. The individual family meetings occur between the third and fourth group meetings and again between the seventh and eighth group meetings. The daughters also participate in half of the parent meetings and both individual family meetings. The meetings are structured similarly to the girls meetings. However, there is an addition, prior to reviewing the main points from the previous parent meeting, the girls provide the parents with a description of the skills they have learned.

Parent Training Skills

Parents are provided with information about depression in girls and young teens, our model of depression, and how to successfully treat depression. To create a more positive environment, parents are taught to manage their daughter's behavior through the use of reinforcement for desirable behavior. At the same time, they are instructed to decrease their use of punitive and coercive strategies. Teaching parents this approach to managing their daughter's behavior creates a home environment that has a positive affective valence and sends the girls an encouraging message about themselves ("I am a good person") and about their parents ("They pay attention to me"). During the first two meetings, parents learn how to effectively use positive reinforcement, and are taught the impact of positive reinforcement on their daughter's behavior. The parents are asked to apply reinforcement during the meetings when their daughters are present. By observing the parents use of reinforcement, the therapist can praise the parents and provide them with corrective feedback. In addition, the therapist can help the parents recognize when opportunities to use reinforcement present themselves. When a parent seems resistant to using reinforcement, the therapist can restructure the parental beliefs that inhibit the use of reinforcement. Parents are instructed to monitor their use of reinforcement at home through completion of forms in the parents' workbook.

Positive reinforcement is only effective if the rewards delivered by the parents are truly desirable to their daughters. Oftentimes, parents are unaware of what the most meaningful rewards to their daughters are. During the second meeting, the girls work with their parents to develop a reward menu and to identify areas in which they seek more parental encouragement. During this meeting, parents also experience the power of doing fun things with their daughters as they play a game together. Parents are encouraged to help their daughters participate in additional fun activities as a coping strategy and to engage in more recreational activities as a family. Results of our research clearly indicate that families with depressed daughters partake in fewer social and recreational activities than families with nondepressed daughters. Low levels of social and recreational activities are one of the strongest family environment predictors of depression in 9- to 14-year-old girls (Greenberg, Sander, & Stark, 2008).

During the third meeting, the parents are taught the deleterious effects of excessive use of punishment. They are asked to identify the forms of punishment they use. Parents are then encouraged to decrease the use of punishment and to replace punishment with positive reinforcement. This can be difficult for families caught in a coercive pattern and for depressed parents who tend to see their daughters as exhibiting more misbehavior than is actually present. Depressed parents are more likely to punish their daughters than nondepressed parents. Thus, it may be necessary to treat the parents' depression in order to reduce their use of punishment and increase their use of reinforcement.

During the same week that participants set their goals for treatment and work with the therapist to identify plans for obtaining their goals, the therapist conducts individual family meetings and collaborates with the parents to identify the parents' goals for their daughter and their family. In addition, with the girl's permission, the therapist and daughter describe the girl's goals for treatment and the intervention plans for achieving these goals to the parents. Parents are encouraged to support these goals through actions that help their daughter.

Parents are taught numerous communication skills. Initially, they are taught empathic listening. This skill is important because it communicates to the daughters that they are being listened to and understood, which leads to a sense of being loved and worthy. In addition, it is a cornerstone of healthy communication. The girls are taught to ask their parents if it is a good time to talk when they are feeling upset or experiencing a problem. Likewise, the parents are taught to initiate a conversation with their daughter when they sense she is upset. Once the conversation is initiated, the parent clears his or her mind of distractions and then listens to the daughter without providing her with any quick comforts or solutions. The parent should be trying to uncover the emotion or message underlying the daughter's statements. This is challenging for parents, as they have a hard time just listening and an even harder time identifying the underlying emotions or broader meaning. Extensive role-playing and coaching are typically necessary for the parents to be able to listen empathically. In some cases, the most that can be accomplished is teaching the parent to become an active listener. Parents are taught the following additional communication skills: (1) keep it brief, (2) don't blame,

(3) be specific, (4) make feeling statements, and (5) give options if possible. These skills are modeled by the therapists, role-played by the therapists and parents, and practiced during sessions by the parents and their daughters. The communication training begins with discussions about easy topics, and then progresses to more emotionally laden topics.

Parents are taught the same five-step problem-solving procedure that the girls learn. Parents are instructed to view misbehavior and problems faced by the family as problems-to-be-solved. The girls teach their parents the steps and then play a game with their parents to demonstrate the meaning of each step as well as how to apply each step to the simple situation of the game. Once the parents have been exposed to the steps and understand the process, the therapist breaks the parents and daughters into family units and provides the families with a hypothetical family problem to be solved.

Elevated levels of conflict are commonly reported in families with depressed girls (Stark, Humphrey, Crook, & Lewis, 1990) and are related to the duration of time taken for the natural remission of a depressive episode. Therefore, parents are taught conflict resolution skills. More specifically, they learn how to structure and use family meetings as a tool for reducing conflict. The first step in the family meeting is to say something positive about each family member. Then, the person who calls the meeting sets the agenda. The person who calls the meeting, next states the issue and gives examples of the personal impact of the point of conflict. This person then initiates a discussion about alternative behaviors that would solve the problem, and the family discusses potential outcomes for each alternative. Finally, a plan is chosen and initiated. The families role-play the meeting process with coaching from the therapists. Emphasis is placed on identifying the conflict early before the upset is exacerbated and cannot be constructively managed. Over the course of the next few meetings, the therapist works with the parents to eliminate barriers to resolving conflict (e.g., parent beliefs).

Parents can play a significant role in helping their daughters catch, evaluate, and restructure negative thoughts and beliefs. During the second individual family meeting and during the seventh and eighth group parent meetings, the parents learn about the impact of negative thinking on their daughters' emotional well-being. Parents are taught to consider the messages they inadvertently relay to their daughters through their actions and verbal exchanges. During the individual family meeting and while the families are divided into their family constellations within the larger group meeting, the girls describe the effects that their specific negative thoughts have on their emotions. Then the parents help their daughters talk back to the negative thoughts. Parents are encouraged to identify their own negative thoughts and to restructure them using the same procedures as their daughters.

CLINICAL INSIGHTS FROM IMPLEMENTATION OF THE ACTION PROGRAM

Individualizing a Group Intervention

Although the ACTION treatment is a manualized group intervention, therapists individualize the intervention for each participant. The ability of the therapists to individually tailor the intervention for each girl plays a significant role in the overall success of the treatment. By individualizing the intervention, the therapist makes the treatment applicable to each girl's particular experience with depression. This increases the probability that the girls will use the intervention strategies and consider them effective. Given the importance of individualizing treatment, some methods to accomplish this will be discussed. Therapists should focus on meeting the main objectives of each meeting, while also individually applying the activities within each session to address the case conceptualizations for the group members. The case conceptualizations, which are created based on the assessment prior to the initiation of treatment, are critical to individualizing treatment. These conceptualizations are continually revised as the therapist learns more about each girl during meetings and through consultation with parents, teachers, and counselors. By remaining aware of the conceptualizations during the sessions, therapists help the girls recognize the unique ways they experience emotions and the coping strategies that are most effective for them; they collaborate with the girls to design problem-solving plans that address their unique challenges; and they individualize cognitive restructuring activities for each girl's specific negative thoughts. Remaining aware of each girl's case conceptualization allows therapists to collect evidence from the girl as well as from teachers and parents, which is contradictory to the girl's negative thoughts and dysfunctional beliefs. For example, if a girl believes that she is a terrible student, the therapist can gather information from teachers about assignments, tests, or report cards, in which the girl performed well. Therapists are able to begin restructuring core beliefs and negative thoughts early in treatment and consistently throughout treatment by presenting the contradictory evidence collected from the girls' life experiences. For example, a girl's case conceptualization indicated that she often had the thought that her mother hated her. Using this information, the therapist paid close attention to when the girl talked about her mother and highlighted times that the girl mentioned an interaction with her mother, in which the mother displayed care or concern for the girl. The therapist could then use this evidence to help the girl see the discrepancy between her belief that her mother hated her and her mother's caring behaviors.

Another method for individualizing treatment involves the therapist utilizing case conceptualizations to create CPDs. These diaries have specific prompts for the girls to use to catch positive experiences they notice throughout the day. For example, if a girl believes that she is helpless, then her diary may have a prompt asking her to write down whenever she uses ACTION skills to help herself feel better. A girl with the belief that she is unlovable may be asked to note each time someone acts in a caring way to her, such as when her parents hug her, her friends compliment her, or her teachers assist her in class.

Treatment is also individualized by asking each girl to work collaboratively with the therapist and other group members to develop personalized treatment goals. The therapist and other group members additionally help each girl create plans for accomplishing her goals. The girls' progress towards these goals is discussed at every other meeting, and the girls receive stickers when they make progress on an individual goal. The therapist often creates opportunities for the girls to work on their goals during the group meetings. For instance, if a girl has the goal to be more open about her feelings with others, the therapist could encourage her to work on this goal by expressing her feelings during the sessions.

The structure of the meetings also fosters individualization of treatment, as the girls are encouraged to add their specific concerns and the situations they want to discuss to the agenda at the beginning of each meeting. This allows the therapist to individually adapt activities to the situations that are of greatest concern to each girl. For example, if the therapist was planning to work on problem solving, he/she could use a situation a girl mentioned to illustrate how to use problem solving.

Another way to individualize treatment is to have participants use coping strategies that the therapist knows are most useful to the girls based on the symptoms they are presently experiencing. This first requires that therapists have participants determine which coping strategies are most effective for them overall and in certain situations. Then, based on the youngsters' current symptoms, the therapist can ask the group members to employ the coping strategy that they find most helpful for their specific emotional state. For example, when group members appeared anxious one day because they were worried about statewide testing, the therapist asked each of them to select the coping strategy that is most effective for them at reducing anxiety and then practice the coping strategy during the group meeting. Similarly, when a therapist was working with girls who were struggling with insomnia, the therapist and group members discussed a variety of coping strategies that could help the girls fall asleep more quickly, such as listening to relaxing music, progressive muscle relaxation, and journaling, and then the therapist instructed the girls to identify and employ the strategy that is most effective for each of them.

Overcoming Obstacles to Treatment

We encountered various obstacles during the implementation of the ACTION program, which are useful to be aware of when treating depression in youth. These obstacles as well as suggestions for overcoming them will be discussed. The obstacles involve factors related to the parents, to meeting in schools, and to the match between therapist and clients.

The obstacles associated with working with parents include dealing with the parents' psychopathology and maintaining parents' participation in treatment. A parent's psychopathology can interfere with his or her ability to acknowledge improvement in their daughter, to contribute to the girl's treatment in a constructive fashion, and to use strategies to help maintain the child's improvement. To overcome this obstacle, the therapist should facilitate a referral for the parent to engage in his or her own treatment. Although finding treatment for a parent can be time consuming, it represents time well spent, as it is beneficial to the well-being of the girl. When the therapist is unsuccessful at having a parent begin therapy, the therapist should provide the youngster with examples of how people in one's life, including parents, can prevent them from improving and then see if this discussion rings true. If so, the therapist can use problem solving and coping skills to develop strategies for managing these negative influences. For example, if a girl lives with a father who is overly punitive due to his own psychological concerns, the therapist may help the girl develop plans that would enable her to spend more time outside of the home doing extracurricular activities that are valued by the father and enjoyed by the girl. Extracurricular activities would improve the girl's mood because they are enjoyable and would minimize the time that she spends with the father who is likely to punish her unnecessarily. Role-playing may also be used to provide the girls with practice dealing with the negative influences in their lives.

Another potential obstacle involving parents is keeping parents engaged in their daughter's treatment. There are numerous reasons why parents may be unable or unwilling to attend meetings and return phone calls. In most cases, the therapist should be flexible by trying to accommodate the parents' schedules. Prior to meeting, the therapist should call the parents to remind them of the meeting. An alternative solution to this obstacle that can be used in conjunction with the aforementioned solutions is to take a preventative stance from the onset of therapy by collaboratively setting up a weekly phone check-in time with parents. The phone check-in is additionally useful to therapists for assessing home improvement and the parents' ongoing concerns for their daughter. If parents are not participating in treatment because they speak a language other than English, the therapist should work with another therapist who can act as a translator.

Because ACTION was implemented in a school setting, numerous obstacles related to meeting at school arose. These obstacles include schedule conflicts, student absences, and teacher reluctance to allow students to miss class. The key ingredients for addressing these obstacles are the use of flexibility and creativity. When there are schedule conflicts or students are absent, the therapist needs to be prepared to reschedule the meeting and/or individualize and reorganize a particular session from the manual. The therapist must also be willing to collaborate with teachers, who are concerned with students missing their class, and work around teachers' schedules, which will occasionally involve compromise.

Obstacles when treating childhood depression may also occur based on the lack of match between a therapist and a client's gender, culture, religion, or race. In these situations, the therapist should work to build a strong therapeutic alliance with the girl and the parents, while remaining sensitive to these differences. The therapist should be open to learning about and discussing these differences with the girl and the parents.

SUMMARY

CBT is one of the most widely used and empirically validated psychosocial treatment approaches for depressive disorders among youth. The authors of this chapter have completed a 5-year study assessing the efficacy of a CBT intervention for 9- to 14-year-old girls, known as the ACTION treatment program. Following treatment, girls who participated in CBT and CBT plus parent training were twice as likely as girls in the minimal contact control condition to no longer qualify for a diagnosis of a depressive disorder.

While the ACTION program is a manualized group treatment program for depressed preadolescent girls, the program with some modifications to the content of session activities can be used with boys as well as older youth. Although the intervention is delivered using a group format, therapists individualize the intervention through the development of a case conceptualization for each participant. The conceptualization is initially developed prior to treatment through an integration of the pretreatment assessment materials and evolves as it is informed by new information that becomes evident during treatment meetings. The case conceptualization provides the therapist with a scheme for identifying experiences in the girl's life that provide contradictory evidence for existing depressive beliefs and help build more realistic and positive beliefs. Learning experiences for each girl that tear down negative beliefs and build new, more adaptive core beliefs are designed and implemented based on the case conceptualization.

Researchers have not yet reached a consensus on the minimum number of sessions required for the maximum positive impact of CBT on depressive symptoms; in fact, the number of sessions required may be idiosyncratic to each client. The ACTION program involves 20 group meetings and two individual sessions. The duration of CBT meetings should depend on the developmental level of the child. We prefer 1-hour meetings for 9- and 10-year-old girls and 75 minute meetings for girls aged 11 years and older. Our experience suggests that girls and younger adolescents benefit from meeting twice per week rather than once per week.

The format and structure of sessions are important elements of CBT interventions for depressed youth. The ACTION program uses a small group format (two to five girls). A small group format has numerous advantages over an individual format, including normalization for girls suffering from depression, opportunities to practice CBT skills as a group, and the potential facilitation of friendships and improvement in social skills. When employing a small group format, building cohesion among group members, which strongly affects girls' progress during treatment, is a critical task for therapists. CBT sessions should be structured and involve a sequence of events (J. Beck, 1995). The structuring of sessions results in an efficient use of time and necessitates that therapists develop a plan for each session. The plan should be flexible depending on the material brought to the session by clients. The sequence of the ACTION sessions is developmentally appropriate for the participating girls.

The core therapeutic components of child treatment in the ACTION program are affective education, goal setting, coping skills training, problem-solving training, and cognitive restructuring. Affective education is the part of treatment in which girls learn about depression, including a simplified CBT model of depression. The goal-setting phase of therapy is a collaborative approach that entails the girl and the therapist working together to establish treatment objectives and discuss methods for achieving those objectives. The purpose of the coping skills training is for girls to become behaviorally activated and learn how to enhance their mood when they are faced with a difficult situation they cannot change. A beneficial tool for promoting behavioral activation and coping, which is individualized and useful for youth of all ages, is the CPD (Lewinsohn & Graf, 1973). During problem-solving training, girls learn a five-step strategy for altering undesirable situations. Cognitive restructuring involves teaching girls to identify their negative distorted thinking, and modify it to make it more positive and realistic. The overarching goal of cognitive restructuring is to promote the development of positive core beliefs about the self. To effectively facilitate the acquisition and application of coping skills, problem solving, and cognitive restructuring strategies for youth, it is recommended that a therapist use experiential, interactive, and engaging didactic presentations of CBT material, and provide opportunities for clients to practice and experience the benefits of these techniques.

Clinical judgment should be used when determining how to include parents in the treatment of their child's depression. The parent-training component of the ACTION program is a hybrid of traditional parent training and cognitive-behavioral family therapy. Parents learn to help their daughters use therapeutic skills (i.e., problem solving and cognitive restructuring), reinforce their daughters' use of therapeutic skills, and apply these skills to themselves. Parents are also taught additional skills, such as reinforcement of desirable behavior, empathic listening, and conflict resolution, to assuage disturbances in family functioning and in the family environment.

Our experiences implementing the ACTION program have highlighted the paramount importance of individualizing treatment within a group therapy format. Individualizing treatment enhances the applicability of a treatment program to each girl's experience with depression and increases the likelihood that the girl will use the therapeutic skills beyond the treatment program. In addition, obstacles such as the presence of parental psychopathology or cultural differences between the therapist and the clients, may arise while treating childhood depression and should be dealt with using creativity, openness, and flexibility.

REFERENCES

Beck, A. T., & Emery, G. (1985). *Anxiety disorders and phobias.* New York: Guilford Press.

Beck, A. T., Rush, J., Shaw, B. F., & Emery, G. (1979). *Cognitive therapy of depression.* New York: Basic Books.

Beck, J. (1995). *Cognitive therapy: Basics & beyond.* New York: Guilford Press.

Beck, J. (2005). *Cognitive therapy for challenging problems: What to do when the basics don't work.* New York: Guilford Press.

Brent, D. A., Holder, D., & Kolko, D. (1997). A clinical psychotherapy trial for adolescent depression comparing cognitive, family, and supportive therapy. *Archives of General Psychiatry, 54*, 877–885.

Greenberg, M., Sander, J. B., & Stark, K. D. (2008). Family predictors of depression in early adolescent girls. Manuscript submitted for publication.

Kendall, P. C., & Braswell, L. (1993). *Cognitive-behavioral therapy for impulsive girls* (2nd ed.). New York: Guilford Press.

Kendall, P. C., Stark, K. D., & Adam, T. (1990). Cognitive deficit or cognitive distortion in girlhood depression. *Journal of Abnormal Girl Psychology, 18*, 255–270.

Lewinsohn, P. M., & Graf, M. (1973). Pleasant activities and depression. *Journal of Consulting and Clinical Psychology, 41*, 261–268.

Molnar, J. (2007). *Variables that predict treatment outcome in girls who have completed the ACTION treatment program for depression: A qualitative investigation.* Unpublished dissertation, University of Texas, Austin.

Stark, K. D., Hargrave, J. L., Schnoebelen, S., Simpson, J. P., & Molnar, J. (2005). Treatment of child hood depression. In P. C. Kendall (Ed.), *Child and adolescent therapy: Cognitive behavioral procedures* (3rd ed.). New York: Guilford Press.

Stark, K. D., Humphrey, L. L., Crook, K., & Lewis, K. (1990). Perceived family environments of depressed and anxious girls: Girl's and maternal figure's perspectives. *Journal of Abnormal Girl Psychology, 18*, 527–547.

Stark, K. D., Schnoebelen, S., Simpson, J., Hargrave, J., & Glenn, R. (2007). *Treating depressed girls: Therapist manual for "ACTION"*. Ardmore, PA: Workbook.

Stark, K. D., Simpson, J., Schnoebelen, S., Glenn, R., & Hargrave, J. (2007). *ACTION workbook.* Ardmore, PA: Workbook.

Stark, K. D., Simpson, J., Yancy, M., & Molnar, J. (2007a). *Parent's workbook for ACTION.* Ardmore, PA: Workbook.

Stark, K. D., Yancy, M., Simpson, J., & Molnar, J. (2007b). *Treating depressed girls: Therapist manual for parent component of "ACTION"*. Ardmore, PA: Workbook.

Weiten, W., & Lloyd, M. A. (2006). *Psychology applied to modern life* (8th ed.). Belmont, CA: Thomson Wadsworth.

Chapter Eighteen

Interpersonal Psychotherapy for Depressed Adolescents

MEREDITH L. GUNLICKS AND LAURA MUFSON

CONTENTS

Interpersonal psychotherapy for depressed adolescents (IPT-A; Mufson, Dorta, Moreau, & Weissman, 2004) is a time-limited psychotherapeutic intervention adapted from interpersonal psychotherapy for adults (IPT; Klerman, Weissman, Rounsaville, & Chevron, 1984; Weissman, Markowitz, & Klerman, 2000). There is a large body of research demonstrating the efficacy of IPT for depressed adults (Weissman et al., 2000). IPT is based on the principle that, regardless of the underlying cause of the depression, the disorder occurs within an interpersonal context. It assumes that depression can negatively impact interpersonal relationships, and problematic relationships and social interactions can have negative effects on mood. The goal of IPT is to decrease depressive symptoms by focusing on current interpersonal difficulties and helping the individual improve his or her relationships and interpersonal interactions.

RATIONALE FOR INTERPERSONAL PSYCHOTHERAPY

The theoretical basis for IPT stems from the work of Adolf Meyer, Harry Stack Sullivan, and other interpersonal theorists who have stated that interpersonal interactions form the basis of personality and functioning. Meyer (1957) viewed psychopathology as an expression of the patient's attempts to adapt to his or her environment. He further posited that the manner in which the patient attempts to negotiate his or her environment is determined by prior experiences, particularly early experiences in the family and the patient's social and cultural context. Sullivan (1953) also emphasized the need for a person's actions to be understood from their historical and present interpersonal context. He believed that a significant component of psychiatric illness develops out of and is perpetuated by problems in interpersonal interactions. Therefore, appropriate treatment would focus on identifying and understanding interpersonal problems, and learning more adaptive interpersonal behaviors. Consistent with this, IPT focuses on helping the patient increase awareness of his or her current communication patterns and understand how changing his or her communication style can elicit different responses from others. The patient can then observe that by altering communication patterns, the nature of the patient's relationships are altered, and this, in turn, can lead to changes in the patient's mood.

IPT also has roots in attachment theory. Bowlby (1978) argued that people have a tendency and need to develop strong bonds to significant others. When these bonds are disrupted in some way, the individual experiences emotional distress, including symptoms of depression. IPT recognizes and addresses the role of attachment in depression. It targets interpersonal conflicts, transitions, and grief in relationships that may affect the patient's attachment experiences and contribute to the development of depression.

Developmental psychopathology theories of depression are also relevant for IPT. They propose that depression arises when an individual is unable to achieve essential developmental tasks (Cicchetti & Toth, 1995). The achievement of normal developmental tasks, such as the development of a healthy sense of self, the capacity to effectively regulate emotions, and the ability to develop close relationships while still maintaining a degree of autonomy emerges within the context of adaptive relationships. Relationship problems and interpersonal stress can interfere with these normal processes by leading to the internalization of maladaptive beliefs about the self and relationships, acquisition of ineffective strategies for coping with interpersonal problems, and a sense of helplessness and hopelessness about one's ability to successfully negotiate interpersonal situations. IPT provides patients with the interpersonal tools that they need to successfully develop meaningful relationships and manage interpersonal stressors, which may facilitate mastery of developmental tasks and lead to reductions in depressive symptoms.

There is strong empirical support for an interpersonal perspective on depression (Hammen, 1999; Rudolph et al., 2000; Sheeber, Hops, & Davis, 2001). Interpersonal stressors have been found to be more strongly linked to adolescent depression than noninterpersonal stressors (Blechman, McEnroe, Carella, & Audette, 1986; Rudolph et al., 2000), and this is particularly the case for girls (Hankin, Mermelstein, & Roesch, 2007). Depression has also been found to precipitate interpersonal stress (Hammen, 1991; Rudolph et al., 2000). For adolescents specifically, problems in relationships with family members and peers, or a loss or lack of relationships seem to be most relevant for depression. Conflictual and unsupportive relationships with parents have been found to be associated with both depressive disorders and subdiagnostic symptoms of depression in adolescents (Sheeber, Davis, Leve, Hops, & Tildesley, 2007). Depressed adolescents have also been found to display more negative affect during interactions with their parents than healthy adolescents (Sanders, Dadds, Johnston, & Cash, 1992; Sheeber, Allen, Davis, & Sorensen, 2000). This may interfere with their ability to communicate or problem solve effectively, leading to continued interpersonal difficulties and ongoing risk for depression (Gotlib & Hammen, 1992).

Depression is also related to problems in peer relationships. Peer rejection, experience of teasing/bullying, unsupportive friendships, and poor communication patterns with peers are all associated with depression in adolescents (Allen et al., 2006; Galambos, Leadbeater, & Barker, 2004; Klomek, Marrocco, Kleinman, Schonfeld, & Gould, 2007; Nolan, Flynn, & Garber, 2003). Social withdrawal and a lack of peer relations are also predictors and consequences of depression (Allen et al., 2006; Joiner, 2000). IPT-A addresses these kinds of impairments in family and peer relationships and provides adolescents with skills that will be helpful in both current and future interpersonal contexts.

ADAPTATION OF IPT FOR USE WITH DEPRESSED ADOLESCENTS

IPT was originally designed as an intervention for nonpsychotic depressed adults treated as outpatients (Klerman et al., 1984; Weissman et al., 2000). The rationale for the adaptation of IPT for adolescents is based on the observation that there are similarities between adolescent and adult depressive symptoms (Ryan et al., 1987), and that adolescent depression is associated with difficulties in interpersonal relationships and impaired social functioning. While the adult model is delivered in a 16–20 week model, IPT-A has been delivered as a 12–16 week model, the latter time frame allowing for some flexibility of session frequency after session 8. Both IPT and the adaptation for adolescents (IPT-A) have the same goals to reduce depressive symptoms by improving interpersonal relationships and social functioning. Many of the relationship problems targeted in IPT-A are similar to IPT, such as conflicts with family members, difficulties with changes that occur in life, loneliness and social isolation, as well as the experience of death of a loved one. IPT-A has been adapted to also address interpersonal issues that are more relevant to adolescence, including parental separation or divorce, negotiation of peer relationships and peer pressure, and the development of romantic relationships. IPT-A can address problems in any significant relationship; however, it often focuses on improving relationships within the family, as these relationships are most frequently related to adolescents' depression. Family relations are particularly relevant for adolescents, as one of the primary developmental tasks for adolescents is to learn to individuate from parents, that is, to learn to negotiate greater autonomy from parents while still maintaining a degree of closeness and intimacy (Steinberg, 1990). Communication and interpersonal problem-solving skills learned during IPT-A can facilitate successful individuation, and thereby promote healthy development. Relationships with parents also act as models for other intimate relationships. The skills adolescents learn within the context of improving their relationships with their family members can generalize to other nonfamilial relationships. In this way, IPT-A addresses current interpersonal problems that are associated with adolescents' depressive symptoms, and also provides skills that will be helpful to adolescents in future relationships.

Because of the frequent focus on relationships within the family, one of the adaptations of IPT-A is the addition of an optional parent component. IPT-A is conceptualized as an individual treatment that highly recommends, but does not require parental participation. Because of the dynamic nature of communication, intervening only in the adolescent's communication patterns can positively influence the manner in which parents' communicate with their adolescents, as well. However, having parents participate in treatment, when possible, is advisable and helpful for promoting the adolescent's well-being and successful treatment. Parental participation is flexible and can range from no attendance to attendance at several sessions. No attendance is strongly discouraged, but is sometimes necessary, depending on the family's circumstances. It is desirable to have parents at least attend one session in the initial phase of treatment in order to be educated about depression and the IPT-A treatment, and at least one session in the termination phase in order to learn about the adolescent's warning signs of depression and strategies for managing potential recurrence. Therapists are encouraged to have this level of parental involvement at a minimum. Parental participation can also be helpful in the middle phase of treatment, as this provides adolescents with opportunities to practice the interpersonal skills they have learned in treatment with their parents and with the therapist present to help facilitate the interaction.

The techniques used to work towards improving adolescents' relationship functioning and decreasing depressive symptoms have also been modified so that they are more developmentally appropriate. Whereas adults may be asked how they are feeling in an open-ended way, in IPT-A, adolescents are asked to rate their mood on a weekly basis using a 1–10 scale. This method is more concrete and makes it easier for adolescents to monitor their mood. To help the adolescents identify the important people in their life, the therapist utilizes a "closeness circle," described later in this chapter, to help the adolescent begin to visualize the differences in their feelings and experiences of different people in their lives. The treatment also includes work on more basic social skills, perspective-taking skills to counteract adolescents' tendencies towards black-and-white thinking about solutions to problems, and strategies for specifically handling parent–adolescent tensions. Finally, tactics have been developed for other issues that may arise over the course of treatment, including school refusal, physical or sexual abuse, involvement of child protective agencies, and suicidality.

DETERMINING SUITABILITY OF IPT-A

Prior to initiating IPT-A, a complete diagnostic evaluation should be conducted with the adolescent to assess current symptoms and diagnoses, as well as psychiatric, family, developmental, medical, social, and academic history. IPT-A is designed to treat adolescents, ages 12–18 years, with nonpsychotic, unipolar depression. It is frequently the case that depressed adolescents will also present with comorbid psychiatric diagnoses. Depressed adolescents with comorbid anxiety disorders, attention deficit disorder, and oppositional defiant disorder have been successfully treated with IPT-A, though IPT-A is most effective when the depression diagnosis is the primary diagnosis and the comorbid diagnoses are limited. IPT-A is not recommended for adolescents with mental retardation active suicidal or homicidal behaviors, psychotic behavior, or bipolar disorder. It is also not indicated for adolescents who are actively abusing substances. For these adolescents, it may be more beneficial to treat the substance abuse prior to addressing the depression.

Among adolescents with nonpsychotic, unipolar depression, it is our experience that adolescents are more likely to benefit from psychotherapy of any kind if they are open to the idea of developing a one-to-one relationship with a therapist, are willing to attend therapy sessions, and are motivated to discuss feelings and problems. Adolescents whose families are supportive and encouraging of therapy attendance are also likely to benefit more from treatment, though families are not required to actively participate in IPT-A. Since part of the treatment includes regularly reviewing the adolescent's depressive symptoms and linking these symptoms to interpersonal events, IPT-A will be most effective for depressed adolescents who are able to acknowledge that they are depressed and agree with the therapist that they are experiencing at least one difficulty of an interpersonal nature.

COURSE OF TREATMENT

IPT-A is a time-limited treatment that is designed to be delivered once a week for 12 weeks, though the treatment schedule can be more flexible if necessary. In a study recently completed in school-based clinics, adolescents received IPT-A for eight consecutive weeks, and the remaining four sessions were scheduled over an additional 8-week time period depending on the adolescent's need and school schedule (Mufson et al., 2004). Additionally, if a crisis occurs or supplementary sessions are needed for other reasons, the treatment can be extended for a longer period of time, or there is the flexibility to temporarily meet more than once a week to address the crisis for a brief period of time. It is important though to maintain treatment as time-limited while being flexible about whether it is 12 or 16 weeks.

IPT-A is divided into three treatment phases: the initial phase, the middle phase, and the termination phase. Throughout the treatment, the sessions begin with the therapist assessing the adolescent's depressive symptoms and asking the adolescent to rate his or her mood using a 10-point scale. Any changes in depressive symptoms that occurred over the course of the week are noted and linked to interpersonal events that happened during the week. Following the review of symptoms, the therapist and adolescent focus on tasks that are specific to the phase of treatment that they are in at the time.

INITIAL PHASE

The initial phase of treatment generally consists of the first four sessions. As noted earlier, we recommend that the parent(s) participate in at least one session during the initial phase of treatment, typically the first session. The goals of the initial phase of treatment are to (1) confirm the depression diagnosis and suitability of IPT-A, (2) provide psychoeducation about depression and assign adolescent the "limited sick role," (3) explain the theory and goals of IPT-A, (4) conduct the interpersonal inventory to obtain a sense of the adolescent's social functioning and interpersonal relationships, (5) identify the interpersonal problem area(s), and (6) make the treatment contract (Mufson et al., 2004). Goals 1–3 can generally be achieved during the first session, leaving the remainder of the initial phase sessions to complete the interpersonal inventory, identify the interpersonal problem area(s), and develop the treatment plan.

Confirm the Depression Diagnosis and Suitability of IPT-A

Prior to entering IPT-A, the adolescent should have already undergone a complete psychiatric evaluation; however, it is important to confirm the depression diagnosis in the first session. Using a clinical interview, the therapist should assess current and past depressive symptoms, as well as symptoms of other disorders that might make IPT-A an unsuitable treatment. The therapist should also confirm that the adolescent is willing to acknowledge experiencing symptoms of depression, and is willing to discuss the interconnections between his or her depression and relationships.

Provide Psychoeducation about Depression

Once the depression diagnosis is confirmed, the therapist should educate the adolescent and his or her family about depression. This involves describing the symptoms and behaviors associated with depression. For example, many adolescents and parents do not realize that irritability is a symptom of depression. They also may not realize that a decline in academic performance may be a function of reduced concentration, anhedonia, fatigue, and other symptoms of depression, rather than an indication that the adolescent is being oppositional or lazy. It is also helpful to describe depression as a medical illness that can be treated. This can decrease the stigma that can be associated with depression, it takes the blame off the adolescent for causing the depression, and it provides an optimistic prognosis for the depression improving with treatment.

Another component of the psychoeducation involves assigning the adolescent the limited sick role. This involves explaining that like someone with a medical illness, adolescents who have symptoms of depression may not be able to do as many things or do things as well as they did before the depression developed. For example, adolescents may have more difficulty with school work, they may not help out as much around the house, and they may withdraw socially. While adolescents may have more difficulty doing these things, it is important for the adolescent to do as much as possible. The goal of the limited sick role is for the adolescent to try to do as many of his or her usual activities as possible, with the acknowledgement and acceptance that he or she might not do these things as well as before the depression developed. It is important for the family to understand the limited sick role, so that they can be more supportive of the adolescent's efforts in these activities, and less critical of the performance or outcomes.

Explain the Theory and Goals of IPT-A

It is important to explain the theory and structure of IPT-A to the adolescent and family so that they know what to expect during the course of treatment, and why the treatment focuses on relationships rather than other aspects of the adolescent's life. This involves educating the family about the interpersonal context of depression. Specifically, regardless of what initially caused the depression, depression affects people's relationships, and relationships affect people's mood. Thus, the focus of treatment will be on improving the adolescent's relationships by teaching communication and interpersonal problem-solving skills, which can then lead to improvements in the adolescent's mood.

Conduct the Interpersonal Inventory

The goal of the interpersonal inventory is to identify the interpersonal issues that are most closely related to the onset or persistence of the adolescent's depression and are most affected by the adolescent's depression. The first step of the interpersonal inventory is for the adolescent to identify the significant relationships in his or her life. This is done by completing a closeness circle. A closeness circle is a series of concentric circles that resembles a bull's-eye. The adolescent writes his or her name in the innermost circle and puts the names of the people in his or her life in the other circles depending on the closeness of their relationship. People that the adolescent feels the closest to, even if the relationship is not always positive, are put in the circle closest to the adolescent, people that the adolescent feels less close to are put in the next circle, and people the adolescent feels the least close to are put in the largest circle that is farthest away from the adolescent. Once the closeness circle has been completed, the therapist inquires about the adolescent's relationships in more depth, making sure to discuss the relationships that the adolescent feels are most related to his or her mood in either positive or negative ways. For each relationship, the therapist will want to make sure to inquire about the frequency and content of their interactions, terms and expectations for the relationship, positive and negative aspects of the relationship, how the relationship has changed since the adolescent became depressed, and changes the adolescent would like to make in the relationship.

Identify the Interpersonal Problem Area(s)

Based on the interpersonal inventory, the therapist helps the adolescent understand the relationship between interpersonal events and his or her depressive symptoms. The therapist identifies common themes or problems in the adolescent's relationships, and together with the adolescent, identifies one of four interpersonal problems areas that will be the focus of treatment. The four problem areas that form the basis for treatment are grief due to death, interpersonal role disputes, interpersonal role transitions, and interpersonal deficits. Generally, only one interpersonal problem area is identified, but it is also possible to identify two problem areas. When this happens, the therapist and adolescent will need to discuss how to address both problem areas over the course of treatment.

Grief Due to Death

Grief is selected as the problem area when an adolescent experiences the death of a loved one, and the loss is associated with prolonged grief, significant depressive symptoms, and impairment in functioning. Grief over losses that are not due to death, such as parents' divorce or the end of a romantic relationship, is conceptualized within the problem area of interpersonal role transitions, which is described later in the chapter. IPT-A may be particularly helpful for bereaved adolescents who had a conflictual relationship with the deceased or experienced a significant disruption in their support network as a result of the death, as these have been identified as risk factors for more complicated bereavement (Clark, Pynoos, & Goebel, 1994). The goal of IPT-A for adolescents with this problem area is to facilitate the delayed normal mourning process, and to develop or improve other relationships that can provide the support, nurturance, companionship, or guidance that has been lost. For adolescents, IPT-A also has been shown to be effective in helping adolescents with a depression that has occurred during the normal bereavement period.

Interpersonal Role Disputes

An interpersonal role dispute occurs when an individual and at least one significant other have nonreciprocal expectations about the terms and/or guidelines for behavior within the relationship (Klerman et al., 1984; Weissman et al., 2000). Some examples of common role disputes that adolescents experience include disagreements with parents about levels of freedom and independence, arguments with parents about selection of peer group with whom they are associating, and disagreements with a romantic partner about amount of time spent with friends. Several empirical studies have documented the link between adolescent depression and conflict with family members and peers (Lewinsohn et al., 1994; Sheeber et al., 2007; Vernberg, 1990). However, it is important to note that while adolescents frequently experience conflicts within their relationships, conflicts are not always associated with depression. Interpersonal role dispute is selected as the problem area if the adolescent's depressive episode coincides with a relationship conflict. Conflicts that are chronic may leave the adolescent feeling helpless to resolve the dispute, and can lead to the development of depression. Conversely, adolescents who are experiencing depression are often more irritable or display other symptoms that make it difficult for them to negotiate interpersonal conflicts successfully (Sanders et al., 1992; Sheeber et al., 2000). In these cases, the conflict may exacerbate the adolescent's depression. The goal of treatment is to help the adolescent develop skills to resolve the dispute, if possible. If resolution is not possible, the goal is to help the adolescent develop strategies for coping with the relationship.

Interpersonal Role Transitions

A role transition involves adjustment to a life change that requires an alteration of behavior from an old role to a new role (Klerman et al., 1984; Weissman et al., 2000). Role transitions mark the turning points between major stages of life. They may be biologically determined (transitioning from childhood to puberty) or a result of social and cultural practices (transitioning from high school to college). In addition to these more normative transitions, adolescents may also experience unexpected events that require them to relinquish an old social role and take on a new one, such as a sudden illness of a loved one, changes in family structure due to parents' separation or divorce, or the ending of a romantic relationship or significant friendship. These types of transitions have all been found to predict the development of adolescent depression (Grant & Compas, 1995; Monroe, Rohde, Seeley, & Lewinsohn, 1999; Strohschein, 2005). Both positive and negative life changes can lead to depression because they involve a loss of familiarity and comfort with the current stage or role. An adolescent may develop symptoms of depression in response to a role transition if the role is placed upon him or her unexpectedly, the role is undesired, the adolescent is not psychologically or emotionally prepared for the new role, or the old role is missed. Depression may also exacerbate the adolescent's ability to successfully negotiate the transition. For these adolescents, the goal of IPT-A is to help the adolescent mourn the old role and develop the skills they need to manage their new role more successfully.

Interpersonal Deficits

Interpersonal deficits refer to deficiencies in social and communication skills that impair the adolescent's ability to develop positive relationships (Klerman et al., 1984; Weissman et al., 2000). Deficits may include difficulty initiating or maintaining relationships, expressing one's feelings verbally, or eliciting information from others to establish communication. This problem area is typically selected when the interpersonal inventory indicates a history of social withdrawal and minimal social relationships. Both of these have been found to be associated with adolescent depression (Allen et al., 2006; Joiner, 2000). Adolescents who have difficulty developing positive relationships may become depressed because they experience prolonged loneliness and low self-esteem. Depression may also cause social withdrawal, resulting in a developmental lag in interpersonal skills that perpetuates the depression (Joiner, 2000). The goal of treatment for these adolescents is to help them develop the interpersonal skills needed to have more satisfying relationships and reduce social isolation. Due to the time-limited nature of IPT-A, it is best suited for adolescents whose interpersonal deficits are less pervasive or are a consequence of their depression or a specific stressor. Adolescents with more severe or pervasive social skills deficits may need more intensive treatment.

Make the Treatment Contract

Once the problem area(s) have been identified, the adolescent and therapist make a verbal treatment contract. This contract specifies the adolescent's and therapist's roles in treatment, the interpersonal problem area(s) that will be the focus of treatment, and the practical details of the treatment. This involves discussing the number of treatment sessions remaining, and the importance of the adolescent coming to treatment on time and calling to cancel, if necessary. The therapist explains to the adolescent that in order for the treatment to be most helpful, the adolescent will need to bring in information about relationships and interpersonal interactions each week for the therapist and adolescent to work on. In addition, the adolescent is informed that his or her parent(s) may be invited to attend a treatment session to work on the identified problem area(s).

MIDDLE PHASE

The middle phase of treatment consists of sessions five through nine. It is during this phase of treatment that the therapist and adolescent begin to work directly on the identified interpersonal problem area(s). This is accomplished by further clarification of the problem area, identifying effective strategies for managing the problem, and practicing and implementing the strategies. Some of the therapeutic techniques utilized during this phase of treatment are specific to the identified problem area(s); however, there are also several techniques that are used across problem areas. When using the techniques to help adolescents improve their communication and relationship functioning, it is best to start with a topic that is manageable and has a high likelihood of success. This generates hope in the adolescents that the strategies they learn can help facilitate change in their relationships and improve their mood.

General Techniques

Encouragement of Affect and Linkage with Interpersonal Events

Encouragement of affect refers to techniques used to help the adolescent become aware, acknowledge, and accept painful emotions about events and relationships, and understand their impact on relationships (Klerman et al., 1984; Weissman et al., 2000). It is our experience that adolescents tend to present in one of two ways. Some adolescents experience their emotions intensely and can readily express them, but have little understanding of how the events in their lives are related to their affective states. Other adolescents can easily describe events in their lives, but relay these events without any mention of affect. For both types of adolescents, it is important to help them link any interpersonal events with their mood. This may involve reviewing the week in great detail to unearth an event or relationship that may have led to a change in mood. If the adolescent describes a difficult interaction with a significant other without awareness of the feelings associated with the interaction, it may involve asking the adolescent how the event made the adolescent feel and how it affected his or her depressive symptoms. This educates the adolescent about the link between interpersonal events and mood, and helps the adolescent become more comfortable and skilled in identifying, understanding, and communicating his or her feelings.

Communication Analysis

The purpose of communication analysis is to explore the adolescent's patterns of interacting with others in order to identify ways in which the adolescent's communication is ineffective and the skills the adolescent needs to master to have better communication. Communication analysis involves asking the adolescent to describe, in detail, an interpersonal event that happened during the week. Together, the therapist and adolescent analyze the communication to help the adolescent recognize the impact of his or her words on others, the feelings he or she conveyed verbally and nonverbally, the feelings that arose during the interactions, and changes in the communication that could have altered the outcome of the interaction and the adolescent's associated feelings. This is accomplished by asking questions such as: How did the discussion start? When and where did it take place? What exactly did the adolescent say? What did the other person say back? Then what happened? How did that make the adolescent feel? How does the adolescent think it made the other person feel? Is that the outcome the adolescent wanted (Mufson et al., 2004)?

Once the therapist has a clear understanding of the interaction, the therapist and adolescent discuss how altering the communication at various points might have led to a different outcome and different emotional experience. This includes discussion of things the adolescent could have said or done differently. It is helpful to first ask the adolescent to attempt to generate some ideas about how he or she could have behaved differently, though the therapist will most likely need to also use directive techniques to build the adolescent's interpersonal skills and competence. Some common communication techniques to be taught and modeled include (1) communicating feelings and opinions directly ("I statements"), (2) putting yourself in the other person's shoes to see their perspective, (3) selecting an optimal time to initiate a conversation with someone (e.g., not asking mom for a raise in allowance when she is paying the bills), (4) being specific when talking about a problem and focusing on the present problem at hand (avoid "you always" or "you never"), and (5) generating some solutions to the problem prior to the conversation and being willing to compromise.

Decision Analysis

Once the adolescent and therapist have used communication analysis to identify communication problems and alternative communication strategies that may lead to more desirable outcomes, it is useful to conduct a decision analysis to determine the best course of action. This is similar to problem-solving techniques that are used in other treatments, but is focused more specifically on addressing interpersonal problems. Decision analysis involves selecting an interpersonal situation that is causing the adolescent problems, determining the goal, generating a list of alternative strategies (some of these may come out of the communication analysis), evaluating the pros and cons of each potential solution or strategy, and selecting a strategy to try. Once a strategy has been attempted, the outcome should be evaluated and the need for selecting a second option determined.

Role-Playing

Role-playing should be used following both communication analysis and decision analysis. It is a way for adolescents to practice the communication and interpersonal problem-solving skills that they have learned in order to feel more comfortable using them in real life. To be most useful, the therapist and adolescent should not simply talk about what it would be like to have the conversation using the new strategies, but they should actually act it out. Adolescents are often self-conscious about this at first. It is helpful for the therapist to be comfortable doing role-play him or herself and to have a sense of humor about it. The therapist may also choose to talk through the scenario before doing the role-play so the adolescent feels more prepared. The adolescent should be instructed that he or she will have the opportunity to play both roles to better understand the other person's perspective, and to help the therapist understand the adolescent's experience of the other person. It is also helpful to try the role-play more than once, with different outcomes to the interactions, both positive and negative, so that the adolescent can become more skilled in handling different kinds of situations that might develop.

Problem Area Specific Techniques

Grief Due to Death

The treatment goal for adolescents with the identified problem area of grief is to facilitate the delayed normal grieving process. This involves reviewing in detail the adolescent's relationship with the deceased, including both positive and negative aspects of the relationship, conflicts in the relationship, and special qualities of the relationship. As part of the exploration of the adolescent's relationship with the deceased, the therapist should also gently encourage expression of affect about the relationship and its loss. Treatment also involves helping the adolescent to connect symptoms of depression and current behaviors to feelings surrounding the death. As the treatment progresses, the therapist helps the adolescent develop skills for communicating about the loss and associated feelings, and applying those skills to other significant relationships in the adolescent's life. The idea is to help the adolescent develop new relationships or further develop existing relationships to replace the support that was lost with the death of the loved one.

Interpersonal Role Disputes

For adolescents experiencing an interpersonal role dispute, the dispute may be in one of three stages: renegotiation, impasse, and dissolution (Klerman et al., 1984; Weissman et al., 2000). An adolescent and significant other are in the renegotiation stage if they are still communicating with one another and are attempting to resolve the conflict. In the impasse stage, the adolescent and significant other are no longer attempting to discuss the conflict and social distancing (or "the silent treatment") commonly occurs. In the dissolution stage, the adolescent and significant other have already decided that the dispute cannot be resolved and they have chosen to end the relationship. For adolescents whose disputes are in the renegotiation or impasse stages, the goal of treatment is to help the adolescent define and resolve the dispute. This involves working with the adolescent and the other person, if possible, to identify and explore the dispute, identify existing patterns of communication, and use communication analysis and decision analysis to teach new communication skills and generate solutions to the dispute. If complete resolution of the problem does not appear to be possible, the therapist works with the adolescent to develop strategies for coping with the relationship that cannot be changed. This may include developing other relationships that can provide a means of support. It can be helpful to point out to the adolescent that while a relationship may not be able to be changed completely, simply decreasing the frequency or intensity of conflict can lead to improved mood. If the dispute is in the dissolution stage, treatment focuses on mourning the loss of the relationship. This involves exploring the dispute and lost relationship, developing an understanding of what occurred, and helping the adolescent to feel comfortable and competent to establish new relationships.

Interpersonal Role Transitions

Treatment for adolescents experiencing an interpersonal role transition involves identifying and defining the role transition, helping the adolescent relinquish the old role and accept the new one, and helping the adolescent develop a sense of mastery and competence in the new role. Specifically, the therapist should provide the adolescent and parents, when possible, with information about the impact of transitions and the association between the transition and the adolescent's depressive symptoms. This is followed by discussions with the adolescent about what the transition means to the adolescent, feelings and expectations about the old and new roles, and gains and losses associated with the transition. The therapist also helps the adolescent to learn new communication and interpersonal problem-solving skills needed to manage the new role and develop relationships that can provide ongoing support around the transition.

Interpersonal Deficits

Treatment of this problem area begins with a thorough review of current relationships to identify and label repetitive interpersonal problems, and connect feelings and depression symptoms to problems in relationships. If the adolescent does not have many current significant relationships, the therapist can review past relationships to look for patterns of difficulty as well as strengths upon which to build. The therapist can also use his or her own relationship with the adolescent to explore the adolescent's interpersonal deficits. The therapist then teaches the adolescent new skills for building and maintaining relationships and uses role-play to help the adolescent practice the new skills. Skills taught might include initiating and sustaining a conversation, asking a peer to join in an activity, or sharing feelings with someone. The therapist then helps the adolescent to identify existing relationships that he or she would like to build upon and/or new people with whom the adolescent would like to form relationships. The adolescent is encouraged to try the new strategies with these individuals outside of the therapy session. It is important with these adolescents to focus on strengths as much as on deficits. The therapist should highlight skills the adolescent has used in other relationships or in the therapy session to help the adolescent build a sense of confidence and competence and to reinforce positive communication patterns.

TERMINATION PHASE

The termination phase of IPT-A typically consists of the last three or four sessions, and is similar to termination phases of other treatments. There are several goals for this treatment phase. First, it is important to review the course of the adolescent's depressive symptoms and how these symptoms have changed, also noting the warning symptoms of depression that are particular to that adolescent so he or she will be aware if the depression recurs. A second objective of the termination phase is to review the changes that have occurred in the adolescent's communication style and relationship functioning, link these changes to the improvement in the adolescent's mood, and highlight the skills and strategies the adolescent developed that were particularly useful. It is also helpful to discuss potential future situations that the adolescent anticipates having difficulty with, and reviewing strategies that the adolescent can use to negotiate those situations. As part of termination, it is also important to discuss the feelings the adolescent has about ending the treatment and the relationship with the therapist. Finally, it is important to discuss the possibility of recurrence of depression and strategies for managing such a recurrence. It is useful for parents to attend a session during the termination phase in order to review progress made, plans for managing future interpersonal difficulties, warning signs for recurrence of depression, and strategies for managing the depression should it recur.

EMPIRICAL SUPPORT FOR IPT-A

The American Psychological Association Division 12 has developed criteria for evaluating the extent to which a psychotherapy has received sufficient empirical evidence for treatment efficacy to warrant its dissemination (Chambless et al., 1998; Chambless et al., 1996). Based on their criteria, psychotherapies are categorized as "experimental," "probably efficacious," or "well-established." IPT-A meets the criteria for a "well-established" psychotherapy for depression in youth.

IPT-A DELIVERED AS INDIVIDUAL PSYCHOTHERAPY

There have been a number of clinical trials supporting the efficacy and effectiveness of IPT-A: an open clinical trial (Mufson et al., 1994), two efficacy studies (Mufson, Weissman, Moreau, & Garfinkel, 1999; Rossello & Bernal, 1999), and an effectiveness study (Mufson et al., 2004). The samples for three of the studies were predominately female, Hispanic, and of low socioeconomic status (Mufson et al., 2004; Mufson et al., 1994; Mufson et al., 1999). A fourth study involved male and female Hispanic adolescents living in Puerto Rico (Rossello & Bernal, 1999). The open clinical trial was conducted to refine the treatment manual and test the feasibility and acceptability of the treatment. Fourteen adolescents who met criteria for a nonbipolar depressive disorder were treated with IPT-A in a hospital outpatient clinic (Mufson et al., 1994). Adolescents demonstrated a significant decrease in depressive symptoms, psychological distress, and physical distress, and an improvement in functioning over the course of treatment. In addition, none of the adolescents qualified for a depression diagnosis at the end of treatment, as determined using a semistructured diagnostic interview. The majority of the adolescents continued to report fewer depressive symptoms and maintained their gains in functioning 1 year following the completion of treatment (Mufson & Fairbanks, 1996).

Following the open clinical trial, the efficacy of IPT-A was evaluated in a randomized, controlled clinical trial. Forty-eight adolescents with major depressive disorder were randomized to receive weekly IPT-A or biweekly clinical monitoring (Mufson et al., 1999). Significantly more IPT-A patients completed treatment than did control patients, suggesting that adolescents were more engaged by the IPT-A treatment. Adolescents who received IPT-A reported significantly fewer symptoms of depression post-treatment and had significantly greater recovery rates than adolescents in the control condition. Adolescents in the IPT-A condition also demonstrated greater improvements in social functioning and problem-solving skills.

To assess the effectiveness of IPT-A, a randomized clinical trial of IPT-A versus treatment as usual (TAU) was conducted in school-based mental health clinics. Sixty-three adolescents who met criteria for a nonbipolar depressive disorder were randomized to receive IPT-A or TAU from school-based health clinic clinicians (Mufson et al., 2004). Post-treatment, adolescents who were treated with IPT-A demonstrated fewer depressive symptoms, better social functioning, and better global functioning compared to adolescents who received TAU.

Another research group has also tested the efficacy of IPT for adolescents using their own adaptation. Rossello and Bernal (1999) conducted a randomized clinical trial of IPT, cognitive-behavioral therapy (CBT), and wait-list control with depressed adolescents in Puerto Rico. They found that both IPT and CBT resulted in a significantly greater reduction in depressive symptoms than the wait-list condition. In addition, adolescents who received IPT demonstrated greater improvements in self-esteem and social functioning than adolescents in the wait-list condition.

IPT-A DELIVERED AS GROUP PSYCHOTHERAPY

IPT-A also has been adapted to be delivered in a group format (IPT-AG; Mufson, Gallagher, Dorta, & Young, 2004). The idea to adapt IPT-A as a group treatment developed out of observations that adolescents sometimes struggled to practice new communication and problem-solving skills in between individual therapy sessions, and adolescents' questions about whether other adolescents had similar problems with their relationships. Group therapy provides a context for adolescents to see that they are not alone and to practice new interpersonal techniques. An additional benefit is the potential cost-effectiveness of treating adolescents in a group format.

IPT-AG has the same primary goals of the individual treatment with two additional goals: (1) to increase adolescents' experience with positive social interaction and reduce social isolation, and (2) to increase the positive resolution of interpersonal difficulties in a supportive group setting. The treatment consists of a combination of individual and group therapy sessions delivered over the course of 14 weeks. Two individual pregroup sessions are conducted with each adolescent and his or her parent(s) to obtain information about the adolescent's particular depressive symptoms and significant relationships, and to identify the interpersonal problem area(s). Middle and termination phase work is conducted in the group setting. Group exercises are used to encourage adolescents to coach each other to use better communication and problem-solving skills. In addition, they report to each other on their experiences trying the new techniques at home, such that they can learn from each other's successes and mistakes. Parents are also invited to participate in a family session midtreatment and post-treatment. The midtreatment session provides the adolescent with an opportunity to practice the new communication skills he or she has been learning in the group. The post-treatment session is an opportunity to review with parents the progress the adolescent has made and strategies for managing potential recurrence of depression. A pilot study was conducted comparing the group to the individual model of IPT-A: 10 adolescents were treated in two groups and eight adolescents were treated individually. Results suggested that the group treatment was as effective as the individual treatment in reducing depression symptoms and improving functioning (Mufson, 2004).

A clinical trial of IPT-AG has also been conducted in rural Uganda (Bolton et al., 2007). In this study, a large sample of adolescents was screened using locally developed measures of depression and functioning. Adolescents were randomized to IPT-AG, a version of creative play, or a wait-list condition. Adolescents who received IPT-AG demonstrated a significant improvement in depressive symptoms compared to adolescents in the other two treatment conditions, and this was particularly true for girls. There were no treatment group effects for level of functioning.

In order to provide a model of treatment for less severely symptomatic adolescents, a modified version of IPT-AG, entitled interpersonal psychotherapy-adolescent skills training (IPT-AST) has been developed as a prevention intervention for adolescents with elevated symptoms of depression (Young, Mufson, & Davies, 2006). IPT-AST follows the format of IPT-AG, but focuses more on psychoeducation and skill building that can be applied to multiple relationships, rather than a particular problem area. An efficacy study was recently conducted with adolescents who had elevated symptoms of depression, but did not meet criteria for a current major depressive episode (Young et al., 2006). Forty-one adolescents were randomized to receive IPT-AST or school counseling as delivered by guidance counselors and social workers. Adolescents who received IPT-AST had significantly fewer depressive symptoms and depressive diagnoses and had better overall functioning post-treatment than adolescents who received school counseling. These gains were maintained at 3- and 6-month follow-ups.

FUTURE DIRECTIONS

Based on the empirical support for IPT-A, other applications and adaptations of IPT-A are being developed and clinical trials are underway. Currently, IPT-A is being adapted and tested for use with depressed adolescents who are engaging in nonsuicidal self-injury, depressed pregnant teenagers (Miller, 2004), prepubertal youth with symptoms of depression and anxiety, bipolar adolescents, and offspring of bipolar parents. A combined treatment of IPT-A and medication is also being tested for adolescents with treatment-resistant depression.

IPT-A is now established as a viable treatment for adolescent depression. In addition, there is evidence that IPT-A can be successfully implemented and disseminated to community treatment settings and community clinicians can be trained in IPT-A with relative ease (Mufson, 2006). Given the high rates of adolescent depression, its association with concurrent and future impairments in functioning, and its result in significant health care expenditures, greater dissemination of treatments such as IPT-A will be critical for decreasing this significant public health problem.

REFERENCES

Allen, J. P., Insabella, G., Porter, M. R., Smith, F. D., Land, D., & Phillips, N. (2006). A social-interactional model of the development of depressive symptoms in adolescence. *Journal of Consulting and Clinical Psychology, 74*, 55–65.

Blechman, E. A., McEnroe, M. J., Carella, E. T., & Audette, D. P. (1986). Childhood competence and depression. *Journal of Abnormal Psychology, 95*, 223–227.

Bolton, P., Bass, J., Betancourt, T., Speelman, L., Neugebauer, R., Onyango, G., et al. (2007). A randomized controlled trial of interventions for psychosocial problems among war-affected adolescents in Northern Uganda. *Journal of the American Medical Association, 298(5)*, 519–527.

Bowlby, J. (1978). Attachment theory and its therapeutic implications. *Adolescent Psychiatry, 6*, 5–33.

Chambless, D. L., Baker, M. J., Baucom, D. H., Beutler, L. E., Calhoun, K. S., Crits-Christoph, P., et al. (1998). Update on empirically validated therapies, II. *Clinical Psychologist, 51*, 3–16.

Chambless, D. L., Sanderson, W. C., Shoham, V., Bennett Johnson, S., Pope, K. S., Crits-Christoph, P., et al. (1996). An update on empirically validated therapies. *Clinical Psychologist, 49*, 5–18.

Cicchetti, D., & Toth, S. L. (1995). Developmental psychopathology and disorders of affect. In D. Cicchetti & D. J. Cohen (Eds.), *Developmental psychopathology: Risk, disorder, and adaptation* (Vol. 2, pp. 369–420). New York: Wiley.

Clark, D., Pynoos, R., & Goebel, A. (1994). Mechanisms and processes of adolescent bereavement. In R. Haggerty (Ed.), *Stress, risk, and resilience in children and adolescents: Processes, mechanisms, and interventions* (pp. 100–145). Cambridge, UK: Cambridge University Press.

Galambos, N. L., Leadbeater, B. J., & Barker, E. T. (2004). Gender differences in and risk factors for depression in adolescence: A 4-year longitudinal study. *International Journal of Behavior Development, 28*, 16–25.

Gotlib, I. H., & Hammen, C. L. (1992). *Psychological aspects of depression: Toward a cognitive-interpersonal integration*. Chichester, UK: Wiley.

Grant, K. E., & Compas, B. E. (1995). Stress and anxious-depressed symptoms among adolescents: Searching for mechanisms of risk. *Journal of Consulting and Clinical Psychology, 63*, 1015–1021.

Hammen, C. (1991). The generation of stress in the course of unipolar depression. *Journal of Abnormal Psychology, 100*, 555–561.

Hammen, C. (1999). The emergence of an interpersonal approach to depression. In T. Joiner & J. C. Coyne (Eds.), *The interactional nature of depression: Advances in interpersonal approaches* (pp. 21–35). Washington, DC: American Psychological Association.

Hankin, B. L., Mermelstein, R., & Roesch, L. (2007). Sex differences in adolescent depression: Stress exposure and reactivity models. *Child Development, 78*, 279–295.

Joiner, T. E. (2000). Depression's vicious scree: Self-propagating and erosive processes in depression chronicity. *Clinical Psychology: Science and Practice, 7*, 203–218.

Klerman, G. L., Weissman, M. M., Rounsaville, B. J., & Chevron, E. S. (1984). *Interpersonal psychotherapy of depression*. New York: Basic Books.

Klomek, A. B., Marrocco, F., Kleinman, M., Schonfeld, I. S., & Gould, M. S. (2007). Bullying, depression, and suicidality in adolescents. *Journal of the American Academy of Child & Adolescent Psychiatry, 46*, 40–49.

Lewinsohn, P. M., Roberts, R. E., Seeley, J. R., Rohde, P., Gotlib, I. H., & Hops, H. (1994). Adolescent psychopathology II: Psychosocial risk factors for depression. *Journal of Abnormal Psychology, 103*, 302–315.

Meyer, A. (1957). *Psychobiology: A science of man*. Springfield, IL: Thomas.

Miller, L. (2004). A spiritual formulation of interpersonal psychotherapy for depression in pregnant girls. In P. S. Richards & A. E. Bergin (Eds.), *Casebook for a spiritual strategy in counseling and psychotherapy* (pp. 75–86). Washington, DC: American Psychological Association.

Monroe, S. M., Rohde, P., Seeley, J. R., & Lewinsohn, P. M. (1999). Life events and depression in adolescence: Relationship loss as a prospective risk factor for first onset of major depressive disorder. *Journal of Abnormal Psychology, 108*, 606–614.

Mufson, L. (2004). *Interpersonal psychotherapy for depressed adolescents group adaptation (IPT-AG): Preliminary efficacy.* Paper presented at the American Academy of Child and Adolescent Psychiatry annual meeting, Washington, DC.

Mufson, L. (2006). *IPT-A: The challenges of effectiveness studies and therapist training in the community.* Paper presented at the International Society for Interpersonal Psychotherapy biennial meeting, Toronto, Canada.

Mufson, L., Dorta, K. P., Moreau, D., & Weissman, M. M. (2004). *Interpersonal psychotherapy for depressed adolescents* (2nd ed.). New York: Guilford Press.

Mufson, L., Dorta, K. P., Wickramaratne, P., Nomura, Y., Olfson, M., & Weissman, M. M. (2004). A randomized effectiveness trial of interpersonal psychotherapy for depressed adolescents. *Archives of General Psychiatry, 61*, 577–584.

Mufson, L., & Fairbanks, M. D. (1996). Interpersonal psychotherapy for depressed adolescents: A one-year naturalistic follow-up study. *Journal of the American Academy of Child & Adolescent Psychiatry, 35*, 1145–1155.

Mufson, L., Gallagher, T., Dorta, K. P., & Young, J. F. (2004). A group adaptation of interpersonal psychotherapy for depressed adolescents. *American Journal of Psychotherapy, 58*, 220–237.

Mufson, L., Moreau, D., Weissman, M. M., Wickramaratne, P., Martin, J., & Samoilov, A. (1994). Modification of interpersonal psychotherapy with depressed adolescents (IPT-A): Phase I and II studies. *Journal of the American Academy of Child & Adolescent Psychiatry, 33*, 695–705.

Mufson, L., Weissman, M. M., Moreau, D., & Garfinkel, R. (1999). Efficacy of interpersonal psychotherapy for depressed adolescents. *Archives of General Psychiatry, 56*, 573–579.

Nolan, S. A., Flynn, C., & Garber, J. (2003). Prospective relations between rejection and depression in young adolescents. *Journal of Personality and Social Psychology, 85*, 745–755.

Rossello, J., & Bernal, G. (1999). The efficacy of cognitive-behavioral and interpersonal treatments for depression in Puerto Rican adolescents. *Journal of Consulting and Clinical Psychology, 67*, 734–745.

Rudolph, K. D., Hammen, C., Burge, D., Lindberg, N., Herzberg, D., & Daley, S. E. (2000). Toward an interpersonal life-stress model of depression: The developmental context of stress generation. *Development and Psychopathology, 12*, 215–234.

Ryan, N. D., Puig-Antich, J., Ambrosini, P., Rabinovich, H., Robinson, D., Nelson, B., et al. (1987). The clinical picture of major depression in children and adolescents. *Archives of General Psychiatry, 44*, 854–886.

Sanders, M. R., Dadds, M. R., Johnston, B. M., & Cash, R. (1992). Childhood depression and conduct disorder: I. Behavioral, affective and cognitive aspects of family problem-solving interactions. *Journal of Abnormal Psychology, 101*, 495–504.

Sheeber, L., Allen, N., Davis, B., & Sorensen, E. (2000). Regulation of negative affect during mother-child problem-solving interactions: Adolescent depressive status and family processes. *Journal of Abnormal Child Psychology, 28*, 467–479.

Sheeber, L., Hops, H., & Davis, B. (2001). Family processes in adolescent depression. *Clinical Child and Family Psychology Review, 4*, 19–35.

Sheeber, L. B., Davis, B., Leve, C., Hops, H., & Tildesley, E. (2007). Adolescents' relationships with their mothers and fathers: Associations with depressive disorder and subdiagnostic symptomatology. *Journal of Abnormal Psychology, 116*, 144–154.

Steinberg, L. (1990). Autonomy, conflict, and harmony in the family relationship. In S. Feldman & G. Elliot (Eds.), *At the threshold: The developing adolescent* (pp. 255–276). Cambridge, MA: Harvard University Press.

Strohschein, L. (2005). Parental divorce and child mental health trajectories. *Journal of Marriage and Family, 67*, 1286–1300.

Sullivan, H. S. (1953). *The interpersonal theory of psychiatry.* New York: Norton.

Vernberg, E. M. (1990). Psychological adjustment and experiences with peers during early adolescence: Reciprocal, incidental, or unidirectional relationships? *Journal of Abnormal Child Psychology, 18*, 187–198.

Weissman, M. M., Markowitz, J. C., & Klerman, G. L. (2000). *Comprehensive guide to interpersonal psychotherapy.* New York: Basic Books.

Young, J. F., Mufson, L., & Davies, M. (2006). Efficacy of interpersonal psychotherapy-adolescent skills training: An indicated preventive intervention for depression. *Journal of Child Psychology and Psychiatry, 47*, 1254–1262.

Chapter Nineteen

Family-Based Treatment for Adolescent Depression

NADINE J. KASLOW, MICHELLE ROBBINS BROTH, NATALIE COWLES ARNETTE, AND MARIETTA H. COLLINS

CONTENTS

Depression in adolescents is common, recurrent and often chronic; associated with psychosocial functional impairment, morbidity, and mortality typically associated with suicide; and co-occurs with other disorders (Ryan, 2005). Growing attention has been paid to evidence-based psychosocial interventions (David-Ferdon & Kaslow, 2008; Weisz, McCarty, & Valeri, 2006) for depressed adolescents. Most psychosocial interventions have focused on the individual and typically include cognitive behavior therapy (CBT) or interpersonal therapy (IPT) (David-Ferdon & Kaslow, 2008). Psychosocial interventions have produced moderate, clinically meaningful treatment gains (David-Ferdon & Kaslow, 2008; Michael & Crowley, 2002; Sander & McCarty, 2005; Weisz et al., 2006). Several prevention programs also show promise (Horowitz & Garber, 2006; Sutton, 2007). There are also pharmacological interventions for depressed youth, and a number of studies have supported the efficacy of specific serotonin reuptake inhibitors (SSRIs) (Cheung, Emslie, & Mayes, 2005, 2006; Emslie & Mayes, 2001; Mann et al., 2006; Olfson, Marcus, & Shaffer, 2006; Varley, 2006; Wagner & Ambrosini, 2001). Only recently have family interventions appeared in the literature (Asarnow, Tompson, & Berk, 2005; Cottrell, 2003; Sander & McCarty, 2005). The aforementioned interventions may occur independently or in conjunction, either sequentially or concurrently.

Depressive disorders in youth reflect an interaction of genetic and environmental factors (Caspi et al., 2003; Kaufman et al., 2006; Kaufman et al., 2004; Rende, Slomkowski, Lloyd-Richardson, Stroud, & Niaura, 2006; Rice, Harold, & Thapar, 2002a, 2002b, 2003; Silberg, Rutter, & Eaves, 2001). Not only does depression run in families from a genetic perspective, but also family dynamics and adverse family environments may be associated with the development and maintenance of depressive symptoms and disorders in adolescents (Duggal, Carlson, Sroufe, & Egeland, 2001; Pineda, Cole, & Bruce, 2007) in different racial-ethnic groups (Sagrestano, Paikoff, Holmbeck, & Fendrich, 2003). Moreover, a teenager's depression impacts significantly on the family system and is associated with significant family burden (Angold et al., 1998). Conversely, protective factors within the family system can reduce a child's risk for depression and can be associated with a more positive course and prognosis for a depressed adolescent (Avison & McAlpine, 1992; Brennan, Le Brocque, & Hammen, 2003; Dallaire et al., 2006; Hoeltje, Zubrick, Silburn, & Garton, 1996; Richmond, Stocker, & Rienks, 2005). To that end, parents and siblings have been found to influence adolescent attitudes about depression and choices about accessing treatment (Wisdom & Agnor, 2007). Thus, family-based interventions that attend to the individual characteristics of all family members and the larger family and social context may be ideally suited for depressed youth and their families (Asarnow et al., 2005; Avenevoli & Merikangas, 2006; Cottrell, 2003; Sander & McCarty, 2005).

This chapter examines family risk factors for adolescent depression, family patterns associated with depression in teenagers, and family protective factors. A perspective on a relational diagnosis of depressive disorders in young people is presented. Focus is then given to the indications and contraindications for family-based interventions. This section is followed by a discussion of evidence-based research on interventions for depressed youth with varying degrees of parental and family involvement. Guiding principles for effective family interventions for depressed adolescents are proffered, and directions for future research are given.

FAMILY RISK FACTORS AND CORRELATES

The family serves as a child's primary social contact and plays a central role in the development and maintenance of depression in adolescents (Asarnow et al., 2005; Herring & Kaslow, 2002; Kaslow, Jones, & Palin, 2005; Kaslow, Mintzer, Meadows, & Grabill, 2000; Sexson, Glanville, & Kaslow, 2001). Family risk factors and correlates may be precursors, negative sequelae, or contributors to the maintenance of depression in adolescents. It is imperative that families are not blamed for their youth's depression, but rather a systemic perspective should be incorporated that appreciates the relative role of the youth, the family, and the biopsychosocial make-up of each family member, as well as the sociocultural context within which the youth's depression is embedded.

Genetic Risk Factors and Correlates

A family history of mood disorders confers significant genetic risk (Rice et al., 2002a, 2002b). Children with a family history of depression are at increased risk for major depressive disorder (MDD) and dysthymic disorder (DD) (Goodman & Gotlib, 1999, 2002; Hammen, 1991; Klein, Lewinsohn, Seeley, & Rohde, 2001; Rice et al., 2002b; Weissman, Warner, Wickramaratne, Moreau, & Olfson, 1997; Weissman et al., 2005). The first-degree relatives of youth with MDD or DD have an increase in depression (Klein et al., 2001; Klein, Shankman, Lewinsohn, Rohde, & Seeley, 2004; Rice et al., 2002b) and substance use disorders (Klein et al., 2001). Adoption (Rice et al., 2002b) and twin studies (Hudziak, Rudiger, Neale, Heath, & Todd, 2000; Marmorstein & Iacono, 2001) provide further genetic support.

Environmental Risk Factors and Correlates

Genetic factors do not explain all of the variance in youth depression (Eley, Deater-Deckard, Fombonne, Fulker, & Plomin, 1998; Fendrich, Warner, & Weissman, 1990; Jacobson & Rowe, 1999) and twin, family, and adoption studies suggest that the development of depression in youth reflects an interaction of genetic, demographic, and environmental factors (Caspi et al., 2003; Kaufman et al., 2006; Kaufman et al., 2004; Pike, McGuire, Hetherington, Reiss, & Plomin, 1996; Rice et al., 2002a; Scourfield et al., 2003; Silberg et al., 1999; Silberg et al., 2001). Several environmental (i.e., non-genetic) family risk factors are associated with an increased vulnerability to depression in adolescents, including prenatal factors (e.g., delivery complications, low birth weight), family structure variables (e.g., single-parent families, divorced families, teen mothers), and acute and chronic negative family life events and stressors (e.g., loss, childhood maltreatment—physical and sexual abuse, neglect, exposure to interpersonal violence, poverty, racial discrimination) (Cuffe, McKeown, Addy, & Garrison, 2005; Danielson, De Arellano, Kilpatrick, Saunders, & Resnick, 2005; Duggal et al., 2001; Durbin, Klein, & Schwartz, 2000; Flament, Cohen, Choquet, Jeammet, & Ledoux, 2001; Ge, Natsuaki, & Conger, 2006; Gilman, Kawachi, Fitzmaurice, & Buka, 2002; Goodman, Slap, & Huang, 2003; Grych, Fincham, Jouriles, & McDonald, 2000; Harkness, Bruce, & Lumley, 2006; Kaslow et al., 2003; Kaufman & Charney, 2001; Kilpatrick et al., 2003; Pilowsky, Wickramaratne, Nomura, & Weissman, 2006; Sagrestano et al., 2003; Turner, Finkelhor, & Ormrod, 2006). Further, the parenting practices that often characterize depressed mothers and fathers, as well as the family discord and conflict commonly found in homes in which there is parental depression, negatively impact children's adjustment (Goodman & Gotlib, 2002; Kane & Garber, 2004; Pilowsky et al., 2006; Radke-Yarrow, Martinez, Mayfield, & Ronsaville, 1998). The negative effects of the combination of parental depression and maladaptive family factors on the youth's psychological adjustment persist as they enter young adulthood (Nomura, Wickramaratne, Warner, Mufson, & Weissman, 2002).

A number of family relational patterns are linked to the development and/or maintenance of depression in youth and include insecure parent–child attachment, low levels of family cohesion and support, low levels of parental warmth, problematic family boundaries (e.g., enmeshment, disengagement), parental rejection, low levels of parental involvement, inappropriate levels of family control, high levels of conflict and hostility, poor conflict resolution skills, harsh and inconsistent discipline, difficulties with affect regulation, high levels of expressed emotion (i.e., hostility, overinvolvement, critical comments) and guilt-inducing statements, parental and sibling negativity, depressotypic cognitions (including negative views of the self, world, and future) and attributional styles, low marital satisfaction in parents, and a poorness of fit between child temperament and family interactional style (Asarnow, Tompson, Woo, & Cantwell, 2001; Bohnert, Martin, & Garber, 2007; Drabick, Beauchaine, Gadow, Carlson, & Bromet, 2006; Duggal et al., 2001; Focht-Birkerts & Beardslee, 2000; Formoso, Gonzales, & Aiken, 2000; Graham & Easterbrooks, 2000; Hammen, Brennan, & Shih, 2004; Herring & Kaslow, 2002; Jacobvitz, Hazen, Curran, & Hitchens, 2004; Jewell & Stark, 2003; Kane & Garber, 2004; Kim et al., 2003; Patton, Coffey, Posterino, Carlin, & Wolfe, 2001; Pilowsky et al., 2006; Pineda et al., 2007; Reinherz, Paradis, Gioconia, Stashwick, & Fitzmaurice, 2003; Sagrestano et al., 2003; Sexson et al., 2001; Sheeber, Hops, & Davis, 2001; Shirk, Gudmundsen, & Burwell, 2005; Simons et al., 2002; Stein et al., 2000; Zahn-Waxler, Klimes-Dougan, & Slattery, 2000). These family relational patterns are observed across ethnic and cultural groups (Chen, Rubin, & Li, 1995; Simons et al., 2002), although the patterns may show variability by ethnic group (Gutman & Eccles, 2007; Herman, Ostrander, & Tucker, 2007). Of note, changes in family functioning are linked with changes for depression in youth (Sagrestano et al., 2003). In addition, family functioning mediates the link between interparental conflict and depressed mood in youth (Unger, Brown, Tressell, & McLeod, 2000). Despite the proliferation of evidence supporting a link between family functioning and the development and/or maintenance of depression in youth, not all investigations support such an association (Tamplin & Goodyer, 2001).

Cumulative Risk Factor Model

Myriad family factors have emerged in cumulative risk factor models of depression. For example, the combination of attachment security, maternal depressive symptoms, and economic risk accounted for 47% of the variance in school-aged children's depression scores in one study (Graham & Easterbrooks, 2000), while another investigation found that depressive symptoms in children were accounted for by the cumulative effects of maternal depressive symptoms, early care lacking in emotional supportiveness, abuse, and family stressors (Duggal et al., 2001). Among ethnic-minority children from high-risk urban communities, the combination of economic destitution, exposure to traumatic life events, parenting styles, individual coping styles, and cognitive development have been associated with increased risk for the development of depression (Barreto & McManus, 1997). For African American inner-city youth, the following combinations of factors predicted depressive symptoms: (1) child maltreatment, lower levels of maternal education, higher levels of maternal depression, maternal intimate partner violence experiences, and life stress (Johnson & Kliewer, 1999); and (2) uninvolved parenting, racial discrimination, and criminal victimization (Simons et al., 2002).

Intergenerational Transmission of Risk Factors, Correlates, and Depression

There are countless mechanisms by which the intergenerational transmission of depression may occur, such as genetic predisposition, emotional unavailability of depressed caregivers, exposure to adverse family environments, family interactions that perpetuate and reinforce the adolescent's depression, and problematic family dynamics associated with affect regulation and cognitive processing (Goodman & Gotlib, 1999; Sheeber et al., 2001). There may be a "family heritage," consisting of the intergenerational transmission of depression through family interactions, family coping with negative events, and daily family functioning that significantly accounts for the manifestation of depression in young people (Wisdom & Agnor, 2007).

PROTECTIVE FACTORS

From a developmental psychopathology framework, understanding depression in youth requires an emphasis on protective factors and resilience (Goldstein & Brooks, 2005; Luthar, Cicchetti, & Becker, 2000). This section combines the research on children at risk for depression and those who already are depressed. In general, the greater the number of protective factors, regardless of the presence of risk factors, the lower the child's risk for depressive symptoms or disorders (Resnick et al., 1997).

Many protective factors within youth serve as buffers with regard to preventing depression or helping the depression to be associated with more positive outcomes. One significant protective factor against the development of depression is a secure attachment bond to parents and other family members (Formoso et al., 2000; Graham & Easterbrooks, 2000; Leech, Larkby, Day, & Day, 2006; Muris, Meesters, van Melick, & Zwambag, 2001; O'Connor & Paley, 2006; Samaan, 2000). A positive relationship with a nondepressed parent can serve as a protective factor against insecure attachment (Herring & Kaslow, 2002). Protective factors related to family dynamics include having a close relationship with one's parents while demonstrating the capacity to think and act separately from one's parents (Beardslee & Podorefsky, 1988; Beardslee, Versage, & Gladstone, 1998; Gutman & Sameroff, 2004). Additional family factors that serve a buffering function include supportive positive parenting; high levels of parental care; warm attitudes toward children; high levels of family support and cohesion; low parental psychological control; low maternal overinvolvement; low levels of parental indifference; appropriate levels of parental monitoring; positive messages to children; strong sibling bonds; and skilled communication among family members (Brennan et al., 2003; Dallaire et al., 2006; Formoso et al., 2000; Klein & Forehand, 2000; Liu, 2003; Richmond et al., 2005; Sugawara et al., 2002). Some variability in these findings exists based upon both the gender of the parent and the child (Liu, 2003; Sugawara et al., 2002), although these findings appear true cross-culturally (Liu, 2003). Further, remission of maternal depression is associated with improved child adjustment (Weissman et al., 2006).

RELATIONAL DISORDERS

Increasing attention has been paid to relational disorders, disorders that reflect that the bond among family members is disordered (Beach, Wamboldt, Kaslow, Heyman, First, & Underwood, 2006a; Beach, Wamboldt, Kaslow, Heyman, & Reiss, 2006b; First et al., 2002; Kaslow, 1996), despite the fact that, historically, psychiatric diagnoses have focused on the individual rather than on the individual in context. Characteristics of relational disorders include: having distinctive features for classification; causing severe emotional, social, and occupational impairment; maintaining a recognizable clinical course; comprising recognizable patterns of comorbidity; upholding patterns of family aggregation; reflecting biological, psychological, and social etiological contributions; responding to specific treatments; and having the capacity to be prevented (First et al., 2002). A number of suggestions have been made regarding ways in which relational considerations can be included in the DSM-V (Beach et al., 2006a; Beach et al., 2006b).

Kaslow and colleagues presented criteria for a relational diagnosis of depression in youth (Kaslow, Deering, & Ash, 1996; Kaslow et al., 2005). According to these criteria, the individual must: (1) be younger than 18 years of age; (2) meet criteria for the fourth edition of the Diagnostic and Statistical Manual of Mental Disorders (DSM-IV) (American Psychiatric Association [APA], 1994) for at least one of these disorders: MDD, DD, adjustment disorder with depressed mood/other adjustment subcategory that includes depression, reactive attachment, depressive personality, minor depression, recurrent brief depression, and mixed anxiety-depression; (3) reside in a family in which at least one of the following relational patterns is present: attachment problems, low cohesion and low support, inappropriate levels of family control, high levels of family conflict and ineffective conflict resolution, family violence, affect regulation difficulties, transmission of depressive cognitions, and impaired communication patterns; and (4) demonstrate a relationship pattern with peers, teachers, or other significant adults that continues over time and is characterized by social isolation, rejection, or criticism of the youth, and which is associated with low social self-esteem and/or difficulties in interpersonal problem solving.

FAMILY-BASED INTERVENTIONS

Indications and Contraindications

As discussed above, several family patterns associated with adolescent depression render a family-based intervention desirable and perhaps optimal. When adolescent depression occurs in the context of attachment problems, low family cohesion or support, impaired family communications (e.g., parent–youth, parent–parent), inappropriate levels of family control, high levels of family conflict and ineffective conflict resolution, or cross-generational affect regulation difficulties and depressotypic cognitions, then family-based treatments may be the most efficient means of targeting the teenager's depression by addressing the contextual factors that maintain it. In cases where the adolescent's depression occurs in the context of lower cognitive functioning, family involvement may be essential to reduce symptoms and enhance functioning in the teenager. Further, family interventions are likely to be particularly helpful for depressed youth with depressed parents (Cottrell, 2003). Finally, they may be more helpful for younger than older adolescents (Brent et al., 1998).

In contrast, family-based treatment for adolescent depression is contraindicated in several situations. First, family treatments should not be used when safety cannot be assured. High levels of family violence must be addressed primary to the family's involvement in the adolescent's treatment for depression. In such cases, reducing the violence becomes the target of treatment, and the adolescent's depression should be treated in a corollary fashion. Second, when a family member's psychopathology or substance abuse negates their appropriate participation in family treatment, an alternative therapy should be used to treat the adolescent's depression.

Finally, there are instances in which family interventions should co-occur with other modalities. Depressed youth may benefit simultaneously or sequentially from other psychosocial interventions and/or pharmacological treatments, in addition to family interventions. Moreover, when parents or caregivers are themselves depressed, such depression may need to be a specific target of intervention in addition to that of the adolescent.

Evidence-Based Interventions

Family interventions can be divided into two categories: those that target all children and children at-risk for depression (primary and secondary preventive interventions), and those that target children already depressed (tertiary preventive interventions). Further, evidence-based family interventions vary in the degree to which they involve parents. Specifically, there are interventions that focus on parent–child relational issues in working alone with adolescents (and not their parents) or that include parents as partners in the treatment. Other intervention programs consist of separate meetings for parents and youth. Finally, some interventions include the entire family. The different types of family-based interventions are discussed in turn. Details about many of these interventions can be found in other chapters in this book.

Family Interventions: Universal Prevention

The only family intervention associated with a universal prevention program involved a school-based prevention program that added a parent component. The Resourceful Adolescent Program (RAP) is a cognitive-behavioral universal depression prevention protocol (Merry, McDowell, Wild, Bir, & Cunliffe, 2004; Shochet et al., 2001; Shochet & Ham, 2004). One study compared RAP for adolescents only (RAP-A), RAP for adolescents plus parent involvement (RAP-F), and a control group (Shochet et al., 2001). The three-session parent group complemented the 11-session strengths-based, skill building, and problem-solving approach used in the adolescent RAP intervention by providing strategies to enhance parental effectiveness, promote parents' efforts to build their children's self-esteem, and improve parent–child communication and conflict management. At post-intervention and 10-month follow-up, adolescents in either active intervention (RAP-A, RAP-F) had lower levels of depressive symptoms and hopelessness than their peers in the control group, but there were no differences between the two active interventions. Although this study provides evidence for the efficacy of RAP, it does not show added value for the parent component, which may be attributable, in part, to low levels of parental participation and the brevity of the parent component.

Family Interventions for At-Risk Youth

Significant strides have taken place with regard to developing and testing interventions to prevent depressive symptoms and disorders in children and adolescents (Barrett & Turner, 2004; Beardslee & Gladstone, 2001; Sutton, 2007). Selective and indicated prevention programs are more effective than universal programs, and effect sizes for the aforementioned programs tend to be small to moderate (Horowitz & Garber, 2006). Since most preventive intervention programs focus on preadolescent youth, we include literature pertaining to prevention work with elementary and middle-school aged children and their families, as well as those for depressed teens.

Children of Depressed Parents

One group of at-risk youth for whom prevention efforts are most relevant to this chapter is children of depressed parents. This section describes family-oriented interventions for children of depressed parents. Beardslee and colleagues, guided by a developmental perspective, have conducted a programmatic line of research targeting the family of a depressed parent as a unit. Their program focuses on families with 8- to 15-year-old children. The program, designed to reduce risk factors and enhance protective factors for the children by bringing about parental change, has been found to be safe, feasible, and helpful to families with parental affective disorder (Beardslee et al., 1992). In an outpatient clinic setting, Beardslee and colleagues conducted a random assignment study in which they compared clinician-based versus lecture-based cognitive psychoeducational prevention programs for addressing family members' behaviors and attitudes toward depression (Beardslee et al., 1993). Approximately 18 weeks postintervention, an assessment revealed that families assigned to both conditions were satisfied, found the intervention they received to be advantageous, and had decreases in their level of upset regarding issues of concern. However, compared to those in the lecture-based group, those in the clinician-based group were more satisfied, noted more positive changes with regard to their behaviors and attitudes concerning the parental mood disorder, and reported receiving more assistance with their primary concern. According to parent report, these results were sustained over 3 years (Beardslee, Wright, Rothberg, Salt, & Versage, 1996). Findings at 1 and a half years after completion of the intervention revealed that, in comparison to peers whose families were assigned randomly to the lecture-only condition, youth in the clinician-based group reported greater understanding about their parents' mood disorder and had better adaptive functioning (Beardslee et al., 1997). Parents in this condition reported better communication with their children, enhanced comprehension of their children's experience, and greater responsiveness to their children's affect; they also indicated that their children had gained a greater understanding of their mood disorder (Beardslee et al., 1997; Focht-Birkerts & Beardslee, 2000). Such changes are associated with improvements in parents' ability to manage children at risk for depression and in at-risk children's use of adaptive coping strategies, thus reducing children's risk for depression (Beardslee et al., 1993).

Subsequently, Beardslee and colleagues developed the Family Depression Program, a videotape-based program geared toward families with at least one depressed parent and a child aged 7–12 (Butler, Budman, & Beardslee, 2000). The program, designed to enhance resiliency and reduce the risk of depression in children, consists of one videotape for parents and one for children and a parent manual providing guidance on using the tapes and obtaining mental health services for the children. The parent videotape, a documentary-type film entitled "Depression: Helping Families Cope," realistically portrays families and outlines the effects of depression on families. Emphasis is placed upon the effects depression within the family can have on children. The child tape recounts the experiences of a child whose family appears in the parent tape. In the child tape, the young adolescent learns about parental depression and the utility of treatment, ways to gain support from other family members in the face of parental depression, and the importance of continuing with age-appropriate peer and educational activities. The parent manual provides education on recognizing depression in young people, promoting resiliency in children, and obtaining resources for depressed youth or those unable to cope effectively. In a study in which families were assigned randomly to the Family Depression Program or a wait-list control group, results demonstrated the safety of the family prevention program and a high degree of satisfaction with the program itself. Participation in the intervention correlated with reductions in parental fears about the effects of depression on their children, greater degree of reported communication among family members regarding the caregiver's mood disorder, and an increase in support and understanding among the adults in the family.

Beardslee and coworkers (Beardslee, Gladstone, Wright, & Cooper, 2003) conducted a large scale efficacy trial of two manual-based psychoeducational interventions targeting the relatively well-adjusted children of parents with mood disorders. One intervention was facilitated by a clinician and conducted with each family as a single entity (in individual sessions and family meetings), while the other was conducted in lecture format to groups of parents. In both interventions, education was provided to parents regarding the causes and symptoms of depression in both adults and children, and the impact of parental mood disorders on the family as a whole, with an emphasis on alleviating parental guilt and stressing the potential for resiliency among the children of depressed adults. Parents in both conditions reported improvements in child-related behaviors and attitudes; this change was more striking in the parents receiving the clinician-facilitated intervention than in those participating in the lecture-only format. Further, youth in both conditions experienced a reduction of internalizing symptoms and manifested a better understanding of their parents' mood disorders after the intervention. Moreover, the growth in children's understanding of parental depression was correlated with parental report of improvement in the child's behavior postintervention. There is a need to assess the generalizability of these findings to diverse samples (Beardslee et al., 2003).

Summary

Taken together, family-oriented interventions for children of depressed parents that are facilitated by clinicians are safe, feasible, and helpful to families. Positive outcomes reported for youth include greater understanding of parental mood disorder, better adaptive functioning, and greater reduction in internalizing symptoms. With regard to outcomes for parents, participation in clinician-led interventions results in better ability of parents to manage their at-risk children's behavior, better communication with children, enhanced comprehension of their children's experience, and greater responsiveness to their children's affect.

Interventions for Depressed Youth that Address Family Concerns or Include Parents Flexibly as Partners

Interpersonal Therapy for Depressed Adolescents (IPT-A) (Mufson et al., 2004; Mufson, Weissman, Moreau, & Garfinkel, 1999; Rossello & Bernal, 1999), a probably efficacious intervention for depressed teens (David-Ferdon & Kaslow, 2008), can be conducted in an individual or group format in community or school setting. IPT-A focuses on interpersonal issues relating to the parent–child relationship and changes in the parent–adolescent relationship due to shifts in closeness and authority. Although not a family intervention per se, in some studies of IPT-A, parents were engaged in the assessments, interviewed before and after the therapy, and allowed to address issues related to the treatment, without the adolescents' confidentiality being violated (Rossello & Bernal, 1999). In a more recent study, parents were included as partners in therapy in the beginning, middle, and end phases of the intervention program to facilitate treatment goal attainment (Mufson et al., 2004). At the initial visit, they received information about depression model; were invited to provide information about the background of the problem; and were asked to commit their support to their child's participation in the program. On an as needed basis, parents were encouraged to participate in the midphases of the intervention to support the young person's new found efforts to communicate and problem-solve in interpersonal situations, and facilitate a change in the quality and style of the family interactions. At the final session, they were involved to address the adolescent's current symptoms and perspectives on the intervention, and to work with the team on developing a plan for additional mental health services for the youth. In this protocol, parental involvement was limited and focused on the youth. Further, no assessment was made of the added value of parent involvement.

Another well-researched, adolescent-focused intervention program that includes parents flexibly is the Treatment for Adolescents with Depression Study (The Treatment for Adolescents with Depression Study Team, 2003, 2005; Treatment for Adolescents with Depression Study (TADS) Team, 2004). At a minimum, parents receive education about depression, learn the rationale for the intervention, and are engaged in joint goal setting. Families could be flexibly engaged in the CBT intervention, particularly during sessions focused on parent–adolescent concerns. Unfortunately, no information has been reported to date on the degree and nature of family involvement, nor has this variable been examined regarding its influence on treatment outcome.

Summary

The two intervention programs that have involved parents flexibly as partners in their adolescent's treatment for depression—IPT-A and TADS—did not evaluate the added value of the parents' involvement as it relates to treatment outcome. Thus, the potential benefit of incorporating parents or families into these treatments for adolescent depression remains an empirical question.

Interventions for Depressed Youth with a Parent Component

Interventions that have been tested with and without a parent component or have compared a program with a parent component to a control group are described in this section, along with relevant outcome data. Details on these interventions can be found in other chapters in this book.

Penn Resiliency Program (PRP)

PRP (Cardemil, Reivich, Beevers, Seligman, & James, 2007; Cardemil, Reivich, & Seligman, 2002; Gillham, Hamilton, Freres, Patton, & Gallop, 2006; Gillham & Reivich, 1999; Gillham, Reivich, Jaycox, & Seligman, 1995; Gillham et al., 2006; Gillham et al., 2007; Jaycox, Reivich, Gillham, & Seligman, 1994; Pattison & Lynd-Stevenson, 2001; Roberts, Kane, Thomson, Bishop, & Hart, 2003; Yu & Seligman, 2002), a CBT approach, has been deemed a probably efficacious intervention for depressed youth (David-Ferdon & Kaslow, 2008). Recently, PRP was enhanced by adding a parent component, which involved a manualized group intervention designed to support parents' resiliency by educating them about the comparable skills taught to their children in the children's program, and by training them to model these skills in their parenting and to support their use with their children (Gillham et al., 2006). Students and their parents were assigned randomly to either the enhanced PRP or a control group (usual care). Results revealed that students in the enhanced PRP that included the parent component had more significant decreases in symptoms of depression and anxiety during the 1-year follow-up period than their counterparts in the control condition. These findings suggest that the PRP with a parent component is potentially efficacious. However, until the program is compared to the PRP without a parent component, the added value of the parent group remains an empirical question.

Self-Control Therapy (SCT)

SCT (Stark, Reynolds, & Kaslow, 1987; Stark, Rouse, & Livingston, 1991), also a CBT intervention, has been classified as a probably efficacious intervention for depressed youth (David-Ferdon & Kaslow, 2008). In one test of SCT for youth with depressive symptoms, youth were assigned to a control condition or SCT, and both groups had monthly family meetings. Family meetings for the SCT encouraged parents to assist their children in applying their new skills and to increase the frequency of positive family activities. Monthly family sessions for the traditional counseling condition addressed improving communication and increasing pleasant family events. The extent to which targeted family work added to the more positive outcome for the SCT youth at postintervention and follow-up with regard to greater reductions in depressive symptoms and cognitions relative to youth in the control group is unclear.

Adolescent Coping with Depression Program (CWD-A)

A number of investigations have tested the CWD-A program (Clarke et al., 1995; Clarke et al., 2001; Clarke et al., 2002; Clarke, Rohde, Lewinsohn, Hops, & Seeley, 1999; Kaufman, Rohde, Seeley, Clarke, & Stice, 2005; Lewinsohn, Clarke, Hops, & Andrews, 1990; Lewinsohn, Clarke, Rohde, Hops, & Seeley, 1996; Rohde, Clarke, Mace, Jorgensen, & Seeley, 2004), which has been classified as probably efficacious (David-Ferdon & Kaslow, 2008). In some tests of the CWD-A program, parents were included as agents of change to promote parental acceptance and reinforcement of the anticipated improvements in their adolescent's functioning. In one study (Lewinsohn et al., 1990), depressed adolescent students were randomized to CWD-A adolescent group only, CWD-A adolescent group-plus-parent, or a wait-list control. In the parent groups, parents were informed about the general topics being addressed in the CWD-A program, the skills being taught, and the rationale for their use. Relative to youth in the control condition, youth in the CWD-A adolescent group with and without a parent component manifested more significant reductions in depression according to self and clinician, but not parent, ratings. In both CWD-A groups, there was a noteworthy reduction in the number of teenagers meeting diagnostic criteria for depression at post-treatment relative to the control group. Positive gains were maintained at the 2-year follow-up for the CWD-A adolescent group only and the CWD-A adolescent group-plus-parent; no data were available for the wait-list control group. One relevant factor associated with recovery was parent involvement in treatment (Clarke et al., 1992). These data suggest that the CWD-A adolescent group-plus-parent component is effective, and mixed support for the contention that it may be associated with greater treatment gains than the CWD-A adolescent group alone. They indicate that family involvement is linked with better rates of recovery.

A replication study (Clarke et al., 1999; Lewinsohn et al., 1996), which included skills training throughout the protocol and added booster sessions, offered additional support for the CWD-A program for depressed adolescents in the community. Youth were randomized to (1) intervention condition—CWD-A, CWD-A-plus-parent, or a wait-list control; and (2) follow-up conditions—booster sessions-plus-assessment or assessment-only. At postintervention, adolescents in the CWD-A and CWD-A-plus-parent groups had higher depression recovery rates and greater improvements in self-reported depressive symptoms than adolescents in the wait-list control. Parent and interviewer data regarding the youth's symptoms were less compelling. Thus, the parent component had no apparent effect on outcomes, a finding potentially attributable to the lack of emphasis on the development of the parent component; the inconsistent attendance of parents, particularly fathers; and lack of evidence for a change in family conflict levels as a result of the intervention (Clarke et al., 1999).

In a third hybrid efficacy-effectiveness examination of CWD-A, youth from the Department of Corrections, who met criteria for both MDD and conduct disorder, were assigned randomly to CWD-A-plus-parent or a life skills/tutoring control group (Rohde et al., 2004). Postintervention, but not follow-up data, demonstrated that adolescents in the CWD-A-plus-parent condition had better rates of recovery from depression than youth in the control group, particularly according to teen reports. While this study suggests some value to the CWD-A-plus-parent program, it was not compared to another active intervention and gains were not sustained over time.

ACTION Program

The ACTION Treatment Program is designed for depressed girls, and the intervention is offered alone and in combination with a parent-training component (Stark et al., 2007; Stark et al., 2006a; Stark, Herren, & Fisher, in press; Stark et al., 2006b). The parenting training program aims to strengthen the family environment and support the child treatment component by educating parents about depression and its treatment and effective behavior management strategies. It also teaches parents the skills their child is learning (e.g., communication, problem solving, conflict management, cognitive restructuring), how to support their depressed child's efforts to learn and apply the therapeutic skills, techniques for enhancing their behavior management and communication and reducing conflict, and strategies for assisting their child in reducing his or her negative cognitions. Parents are to collaborate with their child in identifying goals for the family and devising a treatment plan to achieve those goals. Parents receive their own workbook. The protocol also involves a teacher consultation. Preliminary findings support the efficacy of the ACTION program, as it is associated with over a 70% recovery rate when the intervention is offered alone or in combination with the parent component. Youth whose parents participated in the parent-training component had a more positive outcome than those whose parents were not assigned to receive that intervention.

Summary

Interventions for depressed youth with a parent component have produced overall positive results for the inclusion of parents. However, some studies were problematic methodologically, and failed to produce replicated results. The ACTION Program offered the most promising preliminary findings.

Interventions for the Parents of Depressed Youth

Family Psychoeducation

Fristad and colleagues (Fristad, Arnett, & Gavazzi, 1998) examined the impact of a 90-minute psychoeducational workshop that addressed the symptom presentation, etiology, course, prognosis, and treatment of childhood depression as well as family factors (e.g., expressed emotion) that impact the outcome (Fristad et al., 1998). The workshop, provided to parents of mood-disordered adolescent inpatients, resulted in decreased levels of expressed emotion and increased understanding of mood disorders in the caregivers, most notably in fathers, both immediately upon completion and at 4-month follow-up.

Depression Experience Journal (EJ)

A recent investigation examined the feasibility and safety of the Depression Experience Journal (EJ), a computer-based psychoeducational intervention for families of psychiatrically hospitalized depressed youth (Demaso, Marcus, Kinnamon, & Gonzalez-Heydrich, 2006). The EJ is guided by a narrative approach focused on mutual self-disclosure of personal stories about childhood depression. The EJ is a web-based forum of parents', siblings, patients', and hospital staff's descriptions of pediatric depression. For the study protocol, parents of hospitalized youth completed a semistructured interview on a laptop computer regarding their experiences with the child's depression, history of other mental health problems, reasons for admission, and treatment history. Then, they were invited to explore the EJ web-based forum for 30 minutes. Two to four weeks later via telephone, they completed a second 30-minute semistructured interview that elicited quantitative and qualitative information regarding satisfaction with the EJ's presentation and experience, concerns or areas for improvement, impressions of the EJ's impact on their lives and their coping, and attitudinal change. Results revealed that parents experienced generally high satisfaction and a low sense of concern for harmfulness with the EJ experience. Suggestions included adding material for a younger audience (e.g., siblings) and adding information about depression beyond the hospitalization experience.

Summary

Interventions for the parents of depressed youth have included in-person workshops and computer-based psychoeducational programs. These interventions are considered safe and have resulted in an increased understanding of mood disorder symptoms and decreased levels of expressed emotion within families.

Interventions for Depressed Youth with a Family Component

Family Psychoeducation

Fristad and colleagues have developed and examined the impact of a multiple-family psychoeducation program for families of children with mood disorders (Fristad, Gavazzi, Centolella, & Soldano, 1996; Fristad, Gavazzi, & Soldano, 1998; Fristad, Goldberg-Arnold, & Gavazzi, 2003; Goldberg-Arnold, Fristad, & Gavazzi, 1999). This intervention program was designed to lower the levels of expressed emotion found in families of depressed youth by means of education and support. It is intended to serve as an adjunct to the ongoing medication management and individual/family therapy a depressed child receives. The six-session, multiple-family psychoeducation program is structured so that at each session families experience segments together as a family and segments separately for parents and children. The goals for the parent groups are to provide social support, information, and skill building. The parent sessions provide the caregivers with a better understanding of mood disorder symptoms and more knowledge about the cause, course, prognosis, and treatment of mood disorders; they are designed to reduce the caregiver's sense of guilt and blame for their child's illness, to enhance the family's coping techniques, to reduce expressed emotion in the family system, and to increase their awareness of available resources. Family projects and role-playing are used to concretize the didactic material provided during each session. The developmentally informed youth sessions focus on building cohesion, teaching about symptoms and their management and how to complete a cost-benefit analysis of treatment, and providing an opportunity to overcome the social impairment associated with their disorder. The adolescent groups also focus on peer issues specific to teenagers, including substance use, preventing self-harm, identity development, and academic achievement. The overarching goals for the youth groups are to decrease social isolation and enhance social acceptance, increase knowledge about mood disorders, and provide an opportunity to bolster their social skills. Role-playing and team-building exercises are major strategies used.

One open trial offered preliminary efficacy data for this multifamily psychoeducation group intervention (Fristad et al., 1998). Findings indicated high levels of family satisfaction with the intervention program. Parents who attended the program believed that there was an overall improvement in the quality of the family climate following the intervention, which was sustained over 4 months. Fathers had more positive feedback and response than mothers. Six-month follow-up data indicated that most parents evidenced a positive attitudinal shift toward their adolescent with a mood disorder; they reported more positive thinking about their child and his/her mood disorder, the family situation, and the educational and mental health care systems (Goldberg-Arnold et al., 1999). Since the families participated in multiple interventions simultaneously, it is difficult to determine the extent to which the improvements are attributable to the multifamily psychoeducation group. Further, the generalizability of the findings is unclear given that the ethnic status of the samples in these studies is unknown, and the sample sizes are relatively small and predominantly middle- and upper-class (Fristad et al., 1998).

In a randomized controlled trial, children with mood disorders and their families were assigned randomly to immediate multifamily psychoeducation groups-plus-treatment-as-usual or a 6-month wait-list control condition-plus-treatment-as-usual (Fristad et al., 2003). At 6-month follow-up, there were between-group differences in the predicted direction. Compared to families in the control group, families in the immediate multifamily psychoeducation group reported greater gains in parental knowledge regarding childhood mood disorder symptoms, more marked increase in positive family interactions in terms of positive emotional expression according to parental report, more positive perceptions of parental and peer support from the children, and greater use of appropriate services by the families. Expected decreases in negative family interactions were not associated with participation in the immediate multifamily psychoeducation group. Data from this psychoeducational program yields some promising findings in terms of family knowledge and interactions, but there is no information about the impact of this program on youths' depression.

Other investigations have examined a different psychoeducational model for depressed adolescents (Sanford et al., 2006). These authors conducted a randomized, controlled trial comparing standard group and individual therapy (usual treatment) to therapy enhanced with family psychoeducation (usual treatment plus family psychoeducation; FPE). The FPE program consisted of twelve 90-minute in-home sessions with all consenting family members residing with the identified patient. Sessions were held within the first 6 months following enrollment in the study, with one booster session at 3-month follow-up. Session goals were to: (1) increase the family's knowledge about adolescent depression and their understanding of the impact of depression on the family; (2) strengthen the family's communication by reducing hostile or isolating interactions and to foster supportive interactions; and (3) enhance coping, problem solving, and crisis management skills. At 3-month follow-up, FPE families reported high rates of satisfaction with treatment and improvement in adolescent–parent relationships, as well as a decline in depressive symptoms. This preliminary research suggests that FPE shows promise as a component of treatment for depression in adolescents as well as younger children.

Stress-Busters

One treatment development study focused on the acceptability and efficacy of a combined cognitive-behavioral family education intervention, Stress-Busters, for children with depressive symptoms (Asarnow, Scott, & Mintz, 2002). This 10-session school-based intervention included: (1) the provision of cognitive-behavioral strategies (e.g., problem identification, problem solving, social skills, goal setting, relaxation training, affect regulation, pleasant activity scheduling, link between thoughts and feelings, cognitive restructuring, development of personal stress reduction plan) to ameliorate depression and comorbid symptoms and disorders in the youth, and to enhance their capacity to cope with life stress; (2) the development and showing of a videotape by the children for the parents in the family session regarding the skills the youngster learned in the cognitive-behavioral sessions; and (3) a one-session family education component to enhance generalizability and encourage a more supportive family environment. The family education session introduced parents to the intervention goal and the skills learned, emphasized the key role parents play in assisting their children to effectively use these skills, aided youth in feeling positive about their accomplishments in the intervention, empowered the children to experience a sense of mastery in displaying their skills by consulting their parents, and promoted effective parent–child interactions to support the child's progress. At postintervention, compared to youth in the control group, those in the Stress-Busters program had fewer depressive symptoms, negative cognitions, and maladaptive coping responses. There was also a high level of satisfaction with the program. Although promising, this combined intervention has not been evaluated in comparison to the Stress-Busters program without the addition of a family component, nor has it been examined with clinically depressed youth.

Summary

Interventions for depressed adolescents that incorporate a family component yielded encouraging outcomes. These family psychoeducation programs generally have resulted in high levels of family satisfaction; greater improvements in the family climate; more positive emotional expression; and increases in parents' positive attitudes toward their adolescents and their mood disorder, their family, and the mental health care and educational systems. Children also report more positive perceptions of support from parents and peers as a result of these family psychoeducation programs. However, the effect of these programs on youth's depressive symptoms is mixed.

Family Interventions for Depressed Youth

Systemic Behavioral Family Therapy (SBFT)

One study compared the efficacy of family, CBT, and supportive psychosocial treatments for adolescents with MDD (Brent et al., 1997). Parents of youth assigned to both the CBT and family interventions received education about depression, however only the family protocol entailed full parental involvement with parents as partners of change. The family intervention was SBFT, and it combined interventions from functional family therapy and problem-solving therapy. In the early phase of this 12- to 16-session program, the therapist identifies the family's concerns and offers a series of reframing statements to enhance treatment engagement and highlight maladaptive family interaction patterns. The latter phase of the treatment focuses on improving communication and problem-solving skills and changing dysfunctional family interactions.

Both the CBT and the SBFT yielded small effect sizes (ES=0.36 and 0.18, respectively), however, the CBT showed a more rapid treatment response and greater reductions in depressive symptoms. No differences between the groups were found with regard to measures of suicidality or functional impairment (Stein et al., 2001). After acute treatment, the cognitive-behavioral intervention was the most effective in reducing cognitive distortions, and at 2-year follow-up, it was equally effective as the supportive treatment in relieving symptoms of anxiety (Kolko, Brent, Baugher, Bridge, & Birmaher, 2000). However, at 2-year follow-up, SBFT had a more positive impact than CBT on decreasing family conflict and parent–child relationship problems, but was equivalent to supportive therapy (Kolko et al., 2000). Outcomes were not mediated by cognitive distortions or family functioning. However, the CBT appeared less effective in the presence of maternal depression (Brent et al., 1998). Although these findings did not provide strong support for SBFT as a treatment for youth depression, at least relative to CBT, they do suggest that family interventions may have a lasting influence on family relationships, particularly for children compared to adolescents (Brent et al., 1998). Unfortunately, however, the family intervention was found to be the least credible of the three treatments by parents (Stein et al., 2001), raising questions about buy-in.

Behavioral and Strategic Youth-Focused Family Interventions

One study compared the effects of strategic and behavioral family therapies for depressive symptoms in youth, although the children did not meet diagnostic criteria for depression (Steinberg, Sayger, & Szykula, 1997). The child-focused behavioral family therapy was brief and lasted 8–12 weeks, and it focused on setting up for success, modeling, behavioral contracts, home token-economy, incentive programs, social reinforcement, communication skills, and self-monitoring to increase prosocial behaviors. In this program, families define specific problems that require remediation, identify contexts that trigger problem behaviors, and discuss prior strategies at problem management and resolution. The intervention was a nonmanualized educational approach to teaching parenting skills and behavioral self-control to the children. The child-focused strategic family therapy used strategic interviewing techniques to identify problem behavior sequences and problem resolution strategies, offered reframes and suggestions of untried solutions, and incorporated paradoxical interventions, benevolent doubt, and metaphorical storytelling. At follow-up, both family interventions were equally effective in reducing parent-reported behavior problems and depressive symptoms in children. These results support the potential value of both family protocols, but do not indicate a relative advantage to either treatment.

Attachment-Based Family Therapy (ABFT)

ABFT involves a family systems-oriented approach offered with the parent–adolescent subsystem (Diamond, Reis, Diamond, Siqueland, & Isaacs, 2002; Diamond & Siqueland, 1995; Diamond, Siqueland, & Diamond, 2003). A semistructured manualized treatment specifically tailored to the needs of depressed adolescents and their families. Based on attachment theory (Bowlby, 1969), this treatment model seeks to repair ruptures in the attachment relationship and build trust between adolescents and their parents. For parents, this process involves a focus on criticism, disengagement, personal stressors, and parenting skills. For adolescents, affect regulation, self-concept, motivation, and disengagement are the primary foci. The model uses five primary treatment tasks: relational reframing (shifting the focus from fixing the adolescent to modifying the family context by reducing blame and criticism), alliance building with both parent and adolescent, reattachment (i.e., rebuilding an emotional family attachment bond), and promoting competency. Particular attention is paid to bolstering the therapist–parent alliance within the context of family therapy for depressed adolescents (Diamond, Diamond, & Liddle, 2000).

Thus far, the empirical study of this model has generated promising results. In a clinical trial comparing ABFT to a minimal contact control, Diamond and colleagues found that members of the ABFT group were less likely to meet criteria for MDD after completion of the 12-week program, a finding maintained at 6-month follow up (Diamond et al., 2002). ABFT was more successful in reducing symptoms of depression and anxiety, hopelessness, and suicidal ideation, and was linked to greater improvements in mother–adolescent attachments as measured by the Inventory of Parent and Peer Attachment (Armsden & Greenberg, 1987). A medium effect size of .72 has been reported for ABFT.

In addition to ABFT in general, empirical attention (Moran, Diamond, & Diamond, 2005) has been paid to the value of the relational reframing intervention with families of depressed adolescents. Relational reframes early in treatment result in parents increasingly constructing problems from an interpersonal, rather than intrapersonal, frame. Further, in sessions in which there was a positive therapist–family alliance, parents' constructions of difficulties in interpersonal terms led to therapists' increased use of relational reframes. These findings suggest that relational reframing is a potentially powerful treatment technique for enhancing relational attachment in families with a depressed youth.

Summary

In studies of family interventions for depressed youth, CBT was more effective than SBFT after acute treatment. The reverse was true at follow-up. Of concern, SBFT was less credible than other interventions. When behavioral and strategic youth-focused family interventions were compared, both were equally effective. Empirical studies of ABFT have offered promising preliminary results. Thus, it appears that family interventions may be effective for depressed youth, but premature to conclude this definitively. Further, no one form of family treatment has been demonstrated to be superior to any other form of family treatment.

GUIDING PRINCIPLES FOR EFFECTIVE FAMILY INTERVENTIONS

We offer the following principles as guides for effective family-based interventions with depressed youth. These suggestions are based on the aforementioned review of the myriad family-oriented interventions for depressed youth, and as a result have an empirical basis. Attention is paid to both assessment and intervention phases of treatment, and to developmental, gender, and cultural considerations.

Distinct developmental challenges occur in the transitional stage of adolescence, and parents are key in enhancing adolescents' progress through this stage by fostering autonomy and providing connection, guidance, and protection (Asarnow et al., 2005). Parents must still take care of their adolescents and help them take care of themselves. This inevitable tension may be complicated by social-contextual factors, including families with single parents or dual-working parents who must focus on a multitude of demands and have less time to interact with their children. As such, assessments should be ecologically-based, as well as developmentally-informed. Assessments should not only focus on the depressed child, but also on family structure and functioning as related to the family's attributions regarding the child's depression and behavior, handling of negative events and conflict, boundaries, family closeness and support, parental control, communication patterns, subsystem relationships, and strengths and competencies of each member and the system as a whole (Kaslow et al., 2000). A thorough assessment is needed across domains to identify intervention targets to optimize symptom reduction and family functioning. The assessment should focus on situations in which family-based interventions are indicated and contraindicated and treatment plans generated accordingly.

In making treatment decisions, child and family needs and preferences must also be considered, and the child and family must be engaged actively (www.nice.org.uk). Given that depression runs in families, biopsychosocial interventions for other family members need to be considered (www.nice.org.uk). A treatment plan must be developed collaboratively with the depressed youth and his/her family (Kaslow et al., 2000), focusing on the needs of depressed youth, individual family members, and the family system. Sometimes it is necessary to conduct family interventions concurrent with or sequential to interventions with individual family members or family subsystems (Racusin & Kaslow, 1994). With regard to individual or subsystem sessions, confidentiality must be addressed, which is especially important given the developmental tasks of adolescence (Asarnow et al., 2005). Fathers—who have historically been neglected in the literature—and mothers, as well as other significant adults in the household, should be included in both assessment and intervention phases (Sander & McCarty, 2005). Like assessments, interventions must be guided by a developmental psychopathology perspective (Hammen, Rudolph, Weisz, Rao, & Burge, 1999; Zahn-Waxler et al., 2000) and attend to areas of competence and strength as well as dysfunction.

Interventions should include a psychoeducational component, not only about the disorder and maladaptive family factors, but also about the treatment recommendations and plan. It is important to convey evidence-based information to the family in a culturally informed fashion (www.nice.org.uk). Interventions that incorporate structural, cognitive-behavioral, and attachment-based components may be valuable (Cottrell, 2003; Cottrell & Boston, 2002; Diamond et al., 2002; Diamond & Siqueland, 1995; Diamond et al., 2003; Herring & Kaslow, 2002; Sander & McCarty, 2005). They must target family relational patterns salient to the development and maintenance of depressive disorders in youth (Kaslow et al., 1996; Kaslow et al., 2005). Such interventions should decrease family stress levels, enhance social support within the family system, bolster attachment quality, facilitate effective parent–child communication, increase family-based problem solving, and disrupt negative parent–child interactions (Carr, 2000; Diamond & Siqueland, 1995; Diamond et al., 2002; Diamond et al., 2003; Herring & Kaslow, 2002; Kaslow et al., 2005; Sexson et al., 2001). Parents need to become cognizant of the depressogenic communications that they have with their children and alter these dialogues to help bolster their children's views of themselves, the world, and the future.

Effective family intervention programs will also be most beneficial if they are designed to be developmentally appropriate and gender-sensitive (Chaplin et al., 2006; Horowitz & Garber, 2006; Stark et al., 2007; Stark et al., 2006a; Stark et al., in press; Stark et al., 2006b). Given that family factors may be important differentially in depressed female and male adolescents, gender considerations should guide family-based interventions. Some studies found stronger effects of family variables for females than males. For example, among suicidal adolescents recently hospitalized, family support is negatively correlated with females', but not males', sense of hopelessness, depressive symptoms, and suicidal ideation (Kerr, Preuss, & King, 2006). Similarly, parent relationships and physical attractiveness have a stronger effect on adolescent depression for females, while sense of academic competence has a stronger effect on adolescent depression for males (Makri-Botsari, 2005). Nonetheless, family factors may be relevant for adolescent males, but follow a different pattern than for females. One longitudinal study of adolescent males into adulthood found that parents' marital transitions were the most significant predictor of depressive symptoms in early adolescence; furthermore, the relationship between mothers' and sons' depressive symptoms was moderated by fathers' depressive symptoms (Kim, Capaldi, & Stoolmiller, 2003).

It behooves therapists devising and conducting family interventions to take into account sociocultural variables, such as ethnicity/race and social class. Although depressive symptoms and disorders are evident in adolescents in all cultures, there are differential prevalence rates (Kistner, David, & White, 2003; Leech et al., 2006; Sen, 2004; Twenge & Nolen-Hoeksema, 2002; Wight, Aneshensel, Botticello, & Sepulveda, 2005) and variations in symptom presentation (Das, Olfson, McCurtis, & Weissman, 2006) across ethnic groups. These cross-cultural differences reflect other risk factors (e.g., family structure, household income), barriers to detection and treatment, rates of service utilization, and cultural norms regarding emotional displays and coping patterns (Das et al., 2006; Gee, 2004; Sen, 2004; Wight et al., 2005; Wu et al., 2001), but may be less apparent when social class is taken into account (Doi, Roberts, Takeuchi, & Suzuki, 2001). Family interventions also require attention to cultural variables related to protective factors. For example, family support was found to be a critical protective factor against emotional difficulties in Filipino adolescents who immigrated to Hawaii with their families (Guerrero, Hishinuma, Andrade, Nishimura, & Cunanan, 2006). In a parallel fashion, having grandparents in the household of African American families was associated with fewer depressive symptoms among adolescents (Hamilton, 2005). Understanding such cultural factors is key to providing services that will engage the family in treatment and that will meet the family's needs effectively.

Further support for the contention that family assessments and interventions should be culturally competent comes from the burgeoning evidence for the value of culture-specific interventions for depressed youth and their families (Breland-Noble, Bell, & Nicolas, 2006; Griffith, Zucker, Bliss, Foster, & Kaslow, 2001; McClure, Connell, Zucker, Griffith, & Kaslow, 2005), the likelihood that such approaches facilitate treatment engagement (Breland-Noble et al., 2006), the fact that some interventions may be more effective for youth from some ethnic groups than for others (Cardemil et al., 2002, 2007), and the possibility of differential treatment effects across cultures (Pattison & Lynd-Stevenson, 2001; Roberts et al., 2003; Yu & Seligman, 2002). While cross-cultural considerations should be paramount, there is evidence of the cultural transportability of evidence-based protocols for depressed youth (Rossello & Bernal, 1999).

FUTURE DIRECTIONS FOR RESEARCH

In addition to the aforementioned guiding principles for the conduct of family-focused interventions for depressed youth, the following are suggestions for future research on family-based interventions. Assessment protocols for pre- and postintervention and follow-up should be multitrait, multimethod, and multi-informant. Although more time-consuming and potentially burdensome and threatening to family adherence (Asarnow et al., 2005), such an approach is essential to gathering a full picture of the functioning of the youth, family members, and family unit. A relational diagnostic perspective should guide these assessments (Kaslow et al., 2005), which requires gathering data about and from multiple individuals within the family system and using observational methodologies that examine family interactional styles. Assessments should enable researchers to ascertain if interventions were effective with regard to symptom reduction and the child's functional status, as well as changes in the family environment and the development of greater resilience in each family member.

Samples need to be diverse and this diversity needs to be described. This is important because much of the research has been conducted with primarily Caucasian samples (Shaffer, Forehand, Kotchick, & The Family Health Project Research Group, 2002). This homogeneity limits the generalizability of the findings to ethnically diverse populations, and fails to account for possible cultural variables that may be present when working with diverse populations (Hocking & Lochman, 2005). The limited research suggests possible racial and ethnic differences in the development and expression of depressive symptoms (Cardemil et al., 2002; Sagrestano et al., 2003; Shaffer et al., 2002), a finding that may be attributable, in part, to social class (Cardemil et al., 2002; Shaffer et al., 2002).

With regard to theoretical perspective, assessments and interventions for depressed youth and their families and for at-risk youth and their families should: be integrative (McClure et al., 2005); incorporate developmental psychopathology (Hammen et al., 1999; Zahn-Waxler et al., 2000) and family systems (Cottrell & Boston, 2002; Kaslow, Kaslow, & Farber, 1999) perspectives; include strategies from other evidence-based psychosocial models, such as CBT and IPT (Reinecke & Simons, 2005; Stark et al., 2007; Stark et al., 2006a; Stark et al., in press-b); and promote resilience (Luthar & Cicchetti, 2000; Luthar et al., 2000). Optimally, these family interventions will be designed and implemented in a culturally competent fashion (Griffith et al., 2001; Lopez, Edwards, Pedrotti, Ito, & Rasmussen, 2002; McClure et al., 2005), with attention to youth and families of diverse cultures (Das et al., 2006; Munoz, Penilla, & Urizar, 2002). Doing so will enhance treatment engagement (Breland-Noble et al., 2006). Culturally informed issues should be examined empirically so that, as more evidence is gathered, treatments may be matched to the family's needs.

Family-based interventions should target modifying the family relational patterns described above, with ongoing and thorough assessment of these patterns. These interventions should be designed to decrease family stress, enhance the availability of social support within the family system, bolster attachment relationships, facilitate clear parent–child communication and reduce depressotypic messages, promote systematic family-based problem solving, resolve family conflict, disrupt negative parent–child interactions, enhance positive reinforcement, and offer skill building in the areas of family interactional styles, role management, positive parenting behaviors, and parental monitoring and supervision of children (Brent, Kolko, Birmaher, Baugher, & Bridge, 1999; Carr, 2000; Diamond & Siqueland, 1995; Hammen et al., 1999; Herring & Kaslow, 2002; Ingram, 2003; Lewinsohn et al., 1990; Lewinsohn et al., 1996; Reinecke & Simons, 2005; Sagrestano et al., 2003; Sander & McCarty, 2005; Sexson et al., 2001; Stark, Swearer, Kurowski, Sommer, & Bowen, 1996). While studies document the importance of these areas for family and youth functioning, increased empirical emphasis on these targeted areas for intervention is warranted. More investigations need to examine how best to alter these family factors and dynamics that permeate the context of adolescent depression.

Hybrid efficacy-effectiveness designs will be valuable (Rohde et al., 2004). Designs should compare family interventions that include all family members versus separate youth and parent conditions, particularly given the relative dearth of interventions tested to date that actually involve all family members (Sanford et al., 2006). Family interventions may be tested both concurrent with and sequential to interventions with the depressed youth themselves, as well as singularly versus in combined form (Racusin & Kaslow, 1994). There should be studies that ascertain which family factors are associated with more positive treatment outcomes, so that studies matching families to treatment modality can be conducted. It is essential that we examine the relative efficacy of family interventions for depressed youth with other forms of psychotherapy and with psychopharmacological interventions, building upon the exiting research base (Birmaher et al., 2000; Brent et al., 1997; Brent et al., 1999; Brent et al., 1998; Kolko et al., 2000; Rossello & Bernal, 1999). It behooves researchers to study longer-term interventions and the value of booster sessions, as mood disorders persist and recur. When multiple family members are depressed, it will be essential to test the efficacy of targeting each person's depression (American Academy of Child and Adolescent Psychiatry, 1998).

In terms of data analyses, it may be useful to assess the relative efficacy of various family intervention approaches, taking into account family structure and family relational processes. Research should test mediators and moderators of outcome (Sander & McCarty, 2005), taking into account genetic and environmental risk and protective factors (Beardslee & Gladstone, 2001; Focht-Birkerts & Beardslee, 2000). Although not all studies have found family variables to mediate or moderate treatment outcome of adolescents (Kolko et al., 2000), most investigations have shown family factors to be influential in predicting recovery and recurrence (Birmaher et al., 2000; Rohde, Seeley, Kaufman, Clarke, & Stice, 2006), including parental involvement (Clarke, DeBar, & Lewinsohn, 2003), parental depression (Weersing & Brent, 2003), and family factors. The efficacy of the family programs needs to be considered over longer follow-up time intervals, particularly given that at long-term follow-up, participation in family interventions is associated more strongly with reductions in family conflict and with improvements in parent–child relationships than involvement in CBT (Kolko et al., 2000). With that in mind, attention should be given to evaluating the efficacy of different treatment modalities and programs in conjunction with various outcomes, ranging from the individual's depressive symptoms to the family's interactional quality, with various foci on emotional, interpersonal, behavioral, and cognitive factors.

Attention should also be paid to developing family-oriented preventive intervention programs for adolescents at risk for depression (e.g., youth of depressed parents) (Beardslee, 2002; Goodman & Gotlib, 2002). This work could build on existing research with youth of depressed parents (Clarke et al., 2001; Clarke et al., 2002), family interventions for youth of depressed parents (Beardslee et al., 2003; Beardslee et al., 1992; Beardslee et al., 1993; Beardslee et al., 1997a; Beardslee et al., 1996; Beardslee et al., 1997b), and interventions for depressed mothers and their young children (Cicchetti, Rogosch, & Toth, 2000; Field, Grizzle, Scafidi, & Schanberg, 1996; Sanders & McFarland, 2000; van Doesum, Hosman, & Riksen-Walraven, 2005).

Much of the existing literature on family-based treatments has provided limited support for the additional benefit of involving parents beyond interventions with the youth themselves (Clarke et al., 1999; Lewinsohn et al., 1996; Sanford et al., 2006). Nonetheless, few studies actually evaluated a standard family therapy component with all family members present. In contrast, intervention studies involving family members typically included an adjunct parent component, frequently involving adult sessions separate from those of the depressed youth (Asarnow et al., 2002; Clarke et al., 2005; Clarke et al., 2001; Clarke et al., 2002; Clarke et al., 1999; Diamond et al., 2002; Muratori, Picchi, Bruni, Patarnello, & Romagnoli, 2003; Nelson, Barnard, & Cain, 2003; Pfeffer, Jiang, Kakuma, Hwang, & Metsch, 2002; Rohde et al., 2004; Sanford et al., 2006). One study including all family members involved a family psychoeducation enhancement component that did not reduce adolescent depressive symptoms beyond the control condition, but did improve the adolescent's social functioning and the adolescent–parent relationship (Sanford et al., 2006). Such findings highlight the need for future investigations to examine various forms of family therapy for depressed youth, and to involve the entire family constellation, including siblings and significant individuals from multiple generations, rather than only one parent (Cottrell, 2003; Kaslow et al., 2000). Such results also emphasize the importance of family/contextual variables as treatment targets. Developing and evaluating interventions that prevent future episodes by addressing the family context is essential. Attention should be given to the increased involvement of key individuals, such as parents, to support the development of more adaptive skills and foster generalization beyond the therapy environment (Asarnow et al., 2002; Nelson et al., 2003). When family-based interventions have evaluated aspects of the family as targets of treatment, such interventions enhance family members' knowledge about depression, increase utilization of appropriate services, and improve family interactions and adolescents' social functioning (Fristad et al., 1998a; Fristad et al., 1998b; Fristad et al., 2003).

Two additional areas of concern are the long-term follow-up of family-based treatment interventions (Asarnow et al., 2005; Sander & McCarty, 2005), especially in comparison with other forms of treatment, and the transition of beneficial family-focused interventions for depressed youth from research laboratories to clinical settings (Asarnow et al., 2005). Family-based treatment for depressed youth in practice settings may present different challenges than those found in research settings, particularly with regard to third party reimbursement. Future research, then, must focus on the generalizability of findings beyond laboratory settings in order for family-based treatments for depressed youth to reach their full potential.

CONCLUDING COMMENTS

To date, there is a dearth of well-conducted research examining family interventions for depressed youth, despite the well-documented links between depression and family factors (Cottrell, 2003; Sander & McCarty, 2005). A recent review found that only 32% of intervention studies included parents in any capacity (Sander & McCarty, 2005). Most investigations have focused on separate parent groups, with little attention paid to family interventions involving the entire family system (Sherrill & Kovacs, 2002). In general, treatments that involve youth alone versus treatments that incorporate parents or the family systems as agents or facilitators of change are relatively comparable in terms of their effectiveness (Sander & McCarty, 2005). Given the limited study thus far, it is premature to conclude that family therapy is ineffective or to assert that family therapy has the requisite evidence base to support it as the treatment of choice for youth depression (Asarnow et al., 2005; Cottrell & Boston, 2002; Harrington, Whittaker, & Shoebridge, 1998). In fact, a recent meta-analysis (Sander & McCarty, 2005) found that for five treatment outcome studies that included a parent component or were family-based, the mean weighted effect size was .40, which was comparable to the 0.45 found for treatment outcome studies with adolescents only. In addition, when parents are partners in treatment, there is a small positive benefit, with a mean effect size of 0.25 (Sander & McCarty, 2005). Nonetheless, how well youth with depression respond to treatment is influenced by family factors (Asarnow, Goldstein, Thompson, & Guthrie, 1993; Birmaher et al., 2000). Thus, for practical and clinical reasons, it is wise to engage parents directly in the care of the depressed youth (Sherrill & Kovacs, 2002). In addition, since depression in a family member impacts all others in the family and since family dynamics influence the course and outcome of a youth's depression, families are likely to be critical change agents.

REFERENCES

American Academy of Child and Adolescent Psychiatry. (1998). Practice parameters for the assessment and treatment of children and adolescents with depressive disorders. *Journal of the American Academy of Child and Adolescent Psychiatry, 37* (supplement), 63S–83S.

Angold, A., Messer, S. C., Stangl, D., Farmer, E. M., Costello, E. J., & Burns, B. J. (1998). Perceived parental burden and service use for child and adolescent psychiatric disorders. *American Journal of Public Health, 88*, 75–80.

Armsden, G. C., & Greenberg, M. T. (1987). The Inventory of Parent and Peer Attachment: Individual differences and their relationship to psychological well-being. *Journal of Youth and Adolescence, 16*, 427–454.

Asarnow, J. R., Goldstein, M. J., Thompson, M., & Guthrie, D. (1993). One-year outcomes of depressive disorders in child psychiatric in-patients: Evaluation of the prognostic power of a brief measure of expressed emotion. *Journal of Child Psychology and Psychiatry, 34*, 129–137.

Asarnow, J. R., Scott, C. V., & Mintz, J. (2002). A combined cognitive-behavioral family education intervention for depression in children: A treatment development study. *Cognitive Therapy and Research, 26*, 221–229.

Asarnow, J. R., Tompson, M. C., & Berk, M. S. (2005). Adolescent depression: Family-focused treatment strategies. In W. M. Pinsof & J. L. Lebow (Eds.), *Family psychology: The art of the science* (pp. 425–450). Oxford: Oxford University Press.

Asarnow, J. R., Tompson, M., Woo, S., & Cantwell, D. P. (2001). Is expressed emotion a specific risk factor for depression or a nonspecific correlate of psychopathology. *Journal of Abnormal Child Psychology, 29*, 573–583.

Avenevoli, S., & Merikangas, K. R. (2006). Implications of high-risk family studies for prevention of depression. *American Journal of Preventive Medicine, 31*, S126–S135.

Avison, W. R., & McAlpine, D. D. (1992). Gender differences in symptoms of depression among adolescents. *Journal of Health and Social Behavior, 33*, 77–96.

Barreto, S., & McManus, M. (1997). Casting the net for "depression" among ethnic minority children for the high risk urban communities. *Clinical Psychology Review, 17*, 823–845.

Barrett, P. M., & Turner, C. M. (2004). Prevention of childhood anxiety and depression. In P. M. Barrett & T. H. Ollendick (Eds.), *Handbook of interventions that work with children and adolescents: Prevention and treatment* (pp. 429–474). New York: John Wiley and Sons.

Beach, S. R. H., Wamboldt, M. Z., Kaslow, N. J., Heyman, R. E., First, M. B., Underwood, L. G., et al. (Eds.). (2006a). *Relational processes and DSM-V: Neuroscience, assessment, prevention, and treatment.* Washington, DC: American Psychiatric Association.

Beach, S. R. H., Wamboldt, M. Z., Kaslow, N. J., Heyman, R. E., & Reiss, D. (2006b). Describing relationship problems in DSM-V: Toward better guidance for research and clinical practice. *Journal of Family Psychology, 20*, 359–368.

Beardslee, W. R. (2002). *Out of the darkened room when a parent is depressed: Protecting the children and strengthening the family.* New York: Little, Brown, and Company.

Beardslee, W. R., & Gladstone, T. R. (2001). Prevention of childhood depression: Recent findings and future prospects. *Biological Psychiatry, 49*, 1101–1110.

Beardslee, W. R., Gladstone, T. R. G., Wright, E. J., & Cooper, A. B. (2003). A family-based approach to the prevention of depressive symptoms in children at risk: Evidence of parental and child change. *Pediatrics, 112*, 119–131.

Beardslee, W. R., Hoke, L., Wheelock, I., Rothberg, P. C., van de Velde, P., & Swatling, S. (1992). Initial findings on preventive intervention for families with parental affective disorders. *American Journal of Psychiatry, 149*, 1335–1340.

Beardslee, W. R., & Podorefsky, M. A. (1988). Resilient adolescents whose parents have serious affective and other psychiatric disorders: Importance of self-understanding and relationships. *American Journal of Psychiatry, 145*, 63–69.

Beardslee, W. R., Salt, P., Porterfield, K., Rothberg, P., Van de Velde, P., Swatling, S., et al. (1993). Comparison of preventive interventions for families with parental affective disorder. *Journal of the American Academy of Child & Adolescent Psychiatry, 32*, 254–263.

Beardslee, W. R., Salt, P., Versage, E. M., Gladstone, T. R. G., Wright, E. J., & Rothberg, P. C. (1997a). Sustained change in parents receiving preventive interventions for families with depression. *American Journal of Psychiatry, 154*, 510–515.

Beardslee, W. R., Versage, E. M., & Gladstone, T. R. G. (1998). Children of affectively ill parents: A review of the past 10 years. *Journal of the American Academy of Child & Adolescent Psychiatry, 37*, 1134–1141.

Beardslee, W. R., Wright, E., Rothberg, P. C., Salt, P., & Versage, E. (1996). Response of families to two preventive intervention strategies: Long-term differences in behavior and attitude change. *Journal of the American Academy of Child & Adolescent Psychiatry, 35*, 774–782.

Beardslee, W. R., Wright, E. J., Salt, P., Drezner, K., Gladstone, T. R., Versage, E. M., et al. (1997b). Examination of children's responses to two preventive intervention strategies over time. *Journal of the American Academy of Child & Adolescent Psychiatry, 36*, 196–204.

Birmaher, B., Brent, D. A., Kolko, D., Baugher, M., Bridge, J., Holder, D., et al. (2000). Clinical outcome after short-term psychotherapy for adolescents with major depressive disorder. *Archives of General Psychiatry, 57*, 29–36.

Bohnert, A. M., Martin, N. C., & Garber, J. (2007). Predicting adolescents' organized activity involvement: The role of maternal depression history, family relationship quality, and adolescent cognitions. *Journal of Research on Adolescence, 17*, 221–244.

Bowlby, J. (1969). *Attachment and loss: Attachment* (Vol. I). London: Hogarth Press.

Breland-Noble, A. M., Bell, C. C., & Nicolas, G. (2006). Family first: The development of an evidence-based family intervention for increasing participation in psychiatric clinical care and research in depressed African American adolescents. *Family Process, 45*, 153–169.

Brennan, P. A., Le Brocque, R., & Hammen, C. L. (2003). Maternal depression, parent-child relationships, and resilient outcomes in adolescence. *Journal of the American Academy of Child and Adolescent Psychiatry, 42*, 1469–1477.

Brent, D. A., Holder, D., Kolko, D., Birmaher, B., Baugher, M., Roth, C., et al. (1997). A clinical psychotherapy trial for adolescent depression comparing cognitive, family, and supportive therapy. *Archives of General Psychiatry, 54*, 877–885.

Brent, D. A., Kolko, D., Birmaher, B., Baugher, M., & Bridge, J. (1999). A clinical trial for adolescent depression: Predictors of additional treatment in the acute and follow-up phases of the trial. *Journal of the American Academy of Child & Adolescent Psychiatry, 38*, 263–269.

Brent, D. A., Kolko, D. J., Birmaher, B., Baugher, M., Bridge, J., Roth, C., et al. (1998). Predictors of treatment efficacy in a clinical trial of three psychosocial treatments for adolescent depression. *Journal of the American Academy of Child & Adolescent Psychiatry, 37*, 906–914.

Butler, S. F., Budman, S. H., & Beardslee, W. R. (2000). Risk reduction in children from families with parental depression: A videotape psychoeducation program. *National Academies of Practice Forum, 2*, 267–276.

Cardemil, E. V., Reivich, K. J., Beevers, C. G., Seligman, M. E. P., & James, J. (2007). The prevention of depressive symptoms in low-income, minority children: Two-year follow-up. *Behaviour Research and Therapy, 45*, 313–327.

Cardemil, E. V., Reivich, K. J., & Seligman, M. E. P. (2002). The prevention of depressive symptoms in low-income minority middle school students. *Prevention and Treatment, 5*, 32–37.

Carr, A. (2000). Evidence-based practice in family therapy and systemic consultation: I. Child-focused problems. *Journal of Family Therapy, 22*, 29–60.

Caspi, A., Sugden, K., Moffitt, T. E., Taylor, A., Craig, I. W., Harrington, H., et al. (2003). Influence of life stress on depression: Moderation by a polymorphism in the 5-HTT gene. *Science, 301*, 386–389.

Chaplin, T. M., Gillham, J. E., Reivich, K., Elkon, A. G. L., Samuels, B., Freres, D. R., et al. (2006). Depression prevention for early adolescent girls: A pilot study of all girls versus co-ed groups. *Journal of Early Adolescence, 26*, 110–126.

Chen, X., Rubin, K. H., & Li, B.-S. (1995). Depressed mood in Chinese children: Relations with schools performance and family environment. *Journal of Consulting and Clinical Psychology, 63*, 938–947.

Cheung, A. H., Emslie, G. J., & Mayes, T. L. (2005). Review of the efficacy and safety of antidepressants in youth depression. *Journal of Child Psychology and Psychiatry, 46*, 735–754.

Cheung, A. H., Emslie, G. J., & Mayes, T. L. (2006). The use of antidepressants to treat depression in children and adolescents. *Canadian Medical Association Journal, 174*, 193–200.

Cicchetti, D., Rogosch, F. A., & Toth, S. L. (2000). The efficacy of toddler-parent psychotherapy for fostering cognitive development in offspring of depressed mothers. *Journal of Abnormal Child Psychology, 28*, 135–148.

Clarke, G. N., Debar, L., Lynch, F., Powell, J., Gale, J., O'Connor, E., et al. (2005). A randomized effectiveness trial of brief cognitive-behavioral therapy for depressed adolescents receiving antidepressant medication. *Journal of the American Academy of Child & Adolescent Psychiatry, 44*, 888–898.

Clarke, G. N., DeBar, L. L., & Lewinsohn, P. M. (2003). Cognitive-behavioral group treatment for adolescent depression. In A. E. Kazdin & J. R. Weisz (Eds.), *Evidence-based psychotherapies for children and adolescents* (pp. 120–147). New York: Guilford Press.

Clarke, G. N., Hawkins, W., Murphy, M., Sheeber, L., Lewinsohn, P. M., & Seeley, J. (1995). Targeted prevention of unipolar depressive disorder in an at risk sample of high school adolescents: A randomized trial of a group cognitive intervention. *American Academy of Child and Adolescent Psychiatry, 34*, 312–321.

Clarke, G. N., Hops, H., Lewinsohn, P. M., Andrews, J., Seeley, J. R., & Williams, J. (1992). Cognitive-behavioral group treatment of adolescent depression: Prediction of outcome. *Behavior Therapy, 23*, 341–352.

Clarke, G. N., Hornbrook, M., Lynch, F., Polen, M., Gale, J., Beardslee, W. R., et al. (2001). A randomized trial of a group cognitive intervention for preventing depression in adolescent offspring of depressed parents. *Archives of General Psychiatry, 58*, 1127–1134.

Clarke, G. N., Hornbrook, M., Lynch, F., Polen, M., Gale, J., O'Connor, E., et al. (2002). Group cognitive-behavioral treatment for depressed adolescent offspring of depressed parents in a health maintenance organization. *Journal of the American Academy of Child & Adolescent Psychiatry, 41*, 305–313.

Clarke, G. N., Rohde, P., Lewinsohn, P. M., Hops, H., & Seeley, J. (1999). Cognitive-behavioral treatment of adolescent depression: Efficacy of acute group treatment and booster sessions. *Journal of the American Academy of Child & Adolescent Psychiatry, 38*, 272–279.

Cottrell, D. (2003). Outcome studies of family therapy in child and adolescent depression. *Journal of Family Therapy, 25*, 406–416.

Cottrell, D., & Boston, P. (2002). Practitioner review: The effectiveness of systemic family therapy for children and adolescents. *Journal of Child Psychology and Psychiatry, 43*, 573–586.

Cuffe, S. P., McKeown, R. E., Addy, C. L., & Garrison, C. Z. (2005). Family and psychosocial risk factors in a longitudinal epidemiological study of adolescents. *Journal of the American Academy of Child & Adolescent Psychiatry, 44*, 121–129.

Dallaire, D. H., Pineda, A. Q., Cole, D. A., Ciesla, J. A., Jacquez, F. M., LaGrange, B., et al. (2006). Relation of positive and negative parenting to children's depressive symptoms. *Journal of Clinical Child and Adolescent Psychology, 35*, 313–322.

Danielson, C. K., De Arellano, M. A., Kilpatrick, D. G., Saunders, B. E., & Resnick, H. S. (2005). Child maltreatment in depressed adolescents: Differences in symptomatology based on history of abuse. *Child Maltreatment, 10*, 37–48.

Das, A. K., Olfson, M., McCurtis, H. L., & Weissman, M. M. (2006). Depression in African Americans: Breaking barriers to detection and treatment. *Journal of Family Practice, 55*, 30–39.

David-Ferdon, C., & Kaslow, N. J. (2008). Evidence-based psychosocial interventions for child and adolescent depression. *Journal of Clinical Child and Adolescent Psychology, 37(1)*, 62–104.

Demaso, D. R., Marcus, N. E., Kinnamon, C., & Gonzalez-Heydrich, J. (2006). Depression Experience Journal: A computer-based intervention for families facing childhood depression. *Journal of the American Academy of Child and Adolescent Psychiatry, 45*, 158–165.

Diamond, G. M., Diamond, G. S., & Liddle, H. A. (2000). The therapist-parent alliance in family-based therapy for adolescents. *Journal of Clinical Psychology, 56*, 1037–1050.

Diamond, G. S., Reis, B. F., Diamond, G. M., Siqueland, L., & Isaacs, L. (2002). Attachment-based family therapy for depressed adolescents: A treatment development study. *Journal of the American Academy of Child & Adolescent Psychiatry, 41*, 1190–1196.

Diamond, G. S., & Siqueland, L. (1995). Family therapy for the treatment of depressed adolescents. *Psychotherapy: Theory, Research, Practice, Training, 32*, 77–90.

Diamond, G. S., Siqueland, L., & Diamond, G. M. (2003). Attachment-based family therapy for depressed adolescents: Programmatic treatment development. *Clinical Child and Family Psychology Review, 6*, 107–127.

Doi, Y., Roberts, R. E., Takeuchi, K., & Suzuki, S. (2001). Multiethnic comparison of adolescent major depression based on the DSM-IV criteria in a U.S.-Japan study. *Journal of the American Academy of Child and Adolescent Psychiatry, 40*, 1308–1315.

Drabick, D. A. G., Beauchaine, T. P., Gadow, K. D., Carlson, G. A., & Bromet, E. J. (2006). Risk factors for conduct problems and depressive symptoms in a cohort of Ukrainian children. *Journal of Clinical Child and Adolescent Psychology, 35*, 244–252.

Duggal, S., Carlson, E. A., Sroufe, L. A., & Egeland, B. (2001). Depressive symptomatology in childhood and adolescence. *Development and Psychopathology, 13*, 143–164.

Durbin, C. E., Klein, D. N., & Schwartz, J. E. (2000). Predicting the 2 1/2 year outcome of dysthymic disorder: The roles of childhood adversity and family history of psychopathology. *Journal of Consulting and Clinical Psychology, 68*, 57–63.

Eley, T. C., Deater-Deckard, K., Fombonne, E., Fulker, D. W., & Plomin, R. (1998). An adoption study of depressive symptoms in middle chidhood. *Journal of Clinical Psychology and Psychiatry, 39*, 337–345.

Emslie, G. J., & Mayes, T. L. (2001). Mood disorders in children and adolescents: Psychopharmacological treatment. *Biological Psychiatry, 49*, 1082–1090.

Fendrich, M., Warner, V., & Weissman, M. M. (1990). Family risk factors, parental depression, and psychopathology in offspring. *Developmental Psychology, 26*, 40–50.

Field, T., Grizzle, N., Scafidi, F., & Schanberg, S. (1996). Massage and relaxation therapies' effects on depressed adolescent mothers. *Adolescence, 31*, 904–911.

First, M. B., Bell, C. C., Cuthbert, B., Krystal, J. H., Malison, R., Offord, D. R., et al. (2002). Personality disorders and relational disorders: A research agenda for addressing crucial gaps in DSM. In D. J. Kupfer, M. B. First & D. A. Regier (Eds.), *A research agenda for DSM-V* (pp. 123–200). Washington, DC: American Psychiatric Publishing.

Flament, M. F., Cohen, D., Choquet, M., Jeammet, P., & Ledoux, S. (2001). Phenomenology, psychosocial correlates, and treatment seeking in major depression and dysthymia of adolescence. *Journal of the American Academy of Child & Adolescent Psychiatry, 40*, 1070–1078.

Focht-Birkerts, L., & Beardslee, W. R. (2000). A child's experience of parental depression: Encouraging relational resilience in families with affective illness. *Family Process, 39*, 417–434.

Formoso, D., Gonzales, N. A., & Aiken, L. S. (2000). Family conflict and children's internalizing and externalizing behavior: Protective factors. *American Journal of Community Psychology, 28*, 175–199.

Fristad, M. A., Arnett, M. M., & Gavazzi, S. M. (1998a). The impact of psychoeducational workshops on families of mood-disordered children. *Family Therapy, 25*, 151–159.

Fristad, M. A., Gavazzi, S. M., Centolella, D. M., & Soldano, K. W. (1996). Psychoeducation: A promising intervention strategy for families of children and adolescents with mood disorders. *Contemporary Family Therapy, 18*, 371–383.

Fristad, M. A., Gavazzi, S. M., & Soldano, K. W. (1998b). Multi-family psychoeducation groups for childhood mood disorders: A program description and preliminary efficacy data. *Contemporary Family Therapy, 20*, 385–402.

Fristad, M. A., Goldberg-Arnold, J. S., & Gavazzi, S. M. (2003). Multi-family psychoeducation groups in the treatment of children with mood disorders. *Journal of Marital and Family Therapy, 29*, 491–504.

Ge, X., Natsuaki, M. N., & Conger, R. D. (2006). Trajectories of depressive symptoms and stressful life events among male and female adolescents in divorced and nondivorced families. *Development and Psychopathology, 18*, 253–273.

Gee, C. B. (2004). Assessment of anxiety and depression in Asian American youth. *Journal of Clinical Child and Adolescent Psychology, 33*, 269–271.

Gillham, J. E., Hamilton, J., Freres, D. R., Patton, K., & Gallop, R. (2006). Preventing depression among early adolescents in the primary care setting: A randomized controlled study of the Penn Resiliency Program. *Journal of Abnormal Child Psychology, 34*, 203–219.

Gillham, J. E., Reivich, K., Freres, D. R., Lascher, M., Litzinger, S., Shatte, A. J., et al. (2006). School-based prevention of depression and anxiety symptoms in early adolescence: A pilot of a parent intervention component. *School Psychology Quarterly, 21*, 323–348.

Gillham, J. E., Reivich, K., Jaycox, L., & Seligman, M. E. P. (1995). Prevention of depressive symptoms in school children: Two year follow-up. *Psychological Science, 6*, 343–351.

Gillham, J. E., & Reivich, K. J. (1999). Prevention of depressive symptoms in school children: A research update. *Psychological Science, 10*, 461–462.

Gillham, J. E., Reivich, K. J., Freres, D. R., Chaplin, T. M., Shatte, A. J., Samuels, B., et al. (2007). School-based prevention of depressive symptoms: A randomized controlled study of the effectiveness and specificity of the Penn Resiliency Program. *Journal of Consulting and Clinical Psychology, 75*, 9–19.

Gilman, S. E., Kawachi, I., Fitzmaurice, G. M., & Buka, S. L. (2002). Socioeconomic status in childhood and the lifetime risk of major depression. *International Journal of Epidemiology, 31*, 359–367.

Goldberg-Arnold, J. S., Fristad, M. A., & Gavazzi, S. M. (1999). Family psychoeducation: Giving caregivers what they want and need. *Family Relations, 48*, 1–7.

Goldstein, S., & Brooks, R. B. (Eds.). (2005). *Handbook of resilience in children.* New York: Kluwer Academic/Plenum Press.

Goodman, E., Slap, G. B., & Huang, B. (2003). The public health impact of socioeconomic status on adolescent depression and obesity. *American Journal of Public Health, 93*, 1844–1850.

Goodman, S. H., & Gotlib, I. H. (1999). Risk for psychopathology in the children of depressed mothers: A developmental model for understanding mechanisms of transmission. *Psychological Review, 106*, 458–490.

Goodman, S. H., & Gotlib, I. H. (Eds.). (2002). *Children of depressed parents: Mechanisms of risk and implications for treatment.* Washington, DC: American Psychological Association.

Graham, C. A., & Easterbrooks, M. A. (2000). School-aged children's vulnerability to depressive symptomatology: The role of attachment security, maternal depressive symptomatology, and economic risk. *Development and Psychopathology, 12*, 201–213.

Griffith, J., Zucker, M., Bliss, M., Foster, J., & Kaslow, N. J. (2001). Family interventions for depressed African American adolescent females. *Innovations in Clinical Practice, 19*, 159–173.

Grych, J. H., Fincham, F. D., Jouriles, E. N., & McDonald, R. (2000). Interparental conflict and child adjustment: Testing the mediational role of appraisals in the cognitive-contextual framework. *Child Development, 71*, 1648–1661.

Guerrero, A. P. S., Hishinuma, E. S., Andrade, N. N., Nishimura, S. T., & Cunanan, V. L. (2006). Correlations among socioeconomic and family factors and academic, behavioral, and emotional difficulties in Filipino adolescents in Hawai'i. *International Journal of Social Psychiatry, 52*, 343–359.

Gutman, L. M., & Eccles, J. S. (2007). Stage-environment fit during adolescence: Trajectories of family relations and adolescent outcomes. *Developmental Psychology, 43*, 522–537.

Gutman, L. M., & Sameroff, A. J. (2004). Continuities in depression from adolescence to young adulthood: Contrasting ecological influences. *Development and Psychopathology, 16*, 967–984.

Hamilton, H. A. (2005). Extended families and adolescent well-being. *Journal of Adolescent Health, 36*, 260–266.

Hammen, C. L. (1991). *Depression runs in families: The social context of risk and resilience in children of depressed mothers.* New York: Springer-Verlag.

Hammen, C. L., Brennan, P. A., & Shih, J. H. (2004). Family discord and stress predictors of depression and other disorders in adolescent children of depressed and nondepressed women. *Journal of the American Academy of Child & Adolescent Psychiatry, 43*, 994–1002.

Hammen, C. L., Rudolph, K. D., Weisz, J., Rao, U., & Burge, D. (1999). The context of depression in clinic-referred youth: Neglected areas in treatment. *Journal of the American Academy of Child & Adolescent Psychiatry, 38*, 64–71.

Harkness, K. L., Bruce, A. E., & Lumley, M. N. (2006). The role of childhood abuse and neglect in the sensitization to stressful life events in adolescent depression. *Journal of Abnormal Psychology, 115*, 730–741.

Harrington, R., Whittaker, J., & Shoebridge, P. (1998). Psychological treatment of depression in children and adolescents: A review of treatment research. *British Journal of Psychiatry, 173*, 291–298.

Herman, K. C., Ostrander, R., & Tucker, C. M. (2007). Do family environments and negative cognitions of adolescents with depressive symptoms vary by ethnic group. *Journal of Family Psychology, 21*, 325–330.

Herring, M., & Kaslow, N. J. (2002). Depression and attachment in families: A child-focused perspective. *Family Process, 41*, 494–518.

Hocking, M. C., & Lochman, J. E. (2005). Applying the transactional stress and coping model to sickle cell disorder in insulin-dependent diabetes mellitus-Identifying psychosocial variables related to adjustment and intervention. *Clinical Child and Family Psychology Review, 8*, 221–246.

Hoeltje, C. O., Zubrick, S. R., Silburn, S. R., & Garton, A. F. (1996). Generalized self-efficacy: Family and adjustment correlates. *Journal of Clinical Child Psychology, 25*, 446–453.

Horowitz, J. L., & Garber, J. (2006). The prevention of depressive symptoms in children and adolescents: A meta-analytic review. *Journal of Consulting and Clinical Psychology, 74*, 401–415.

Hudziak, J. J., Rudiger, L. P., Neale, M. C., Heath, A. C., & Todd, R. D. (2000). A twin study of inattentive, aggressive, and anxious/depressed behaviors. *Journal of the American Academy of Child & Adolescent Psychiatry, 39*, 469–476.

Ingram, R. E. (2003). Origins of cognitive vulnerability to depression. *Cognitive Therapy and Research, 27*, 77–88.

Jacobson, K. C., & Rowe, D. C. (1999). Genetic and environmental influences on the relationships between family connectedness, school connectedness, and adolescent depression mood: Sex differences. *Developmental Psychology, 35*, 926–939.

Jacobvitz, D., Hazen, N., Curran, M., & Hitchens, K. (2004). Observations of early triadic family interactions: Boundary disturbances in the family predict symptoms of depression, anxiety, and attention-deficit/hyperactivity disorder in middle childhood. *Development and Psychopathology, 16*, 577–592.

Jaycox, L., Reivich, K., Gillham, J. E., & Seligman, M. E. P. (1994). Prevention of depressive symptoms in school children. *Behavioral Research and Therapy, 32*, 801–816.

Jewell, J. D., & Stark, K. D. (2003). Comparing the family environments of adolescents with conduct disorder or depression. *Journal of Child and Family Studies, 12*, 77–89.

Johnson, P. D., & Kliewer, W. (1999). Family and contextual predictors of depressive symptoms in inner-city African American youth. *Journal of Child and Family Studies, 8*, 181–192.

Kane, P., & Garber, J. (2004). The relations among depression in fathers, children's psychopathology, and father-child conflict: A meta-analysis. *Clinical Psychology Review, 24*, 339–360.

Kaslow, F. W. (1996). *Handbook of relational diagnosis and dysfunctional family patterns*. New York: John Wiley and Sons.

Kaslow, N. J., Deering, C., & Ash, P. (1996). Relational diagnosis of child and adolescent depression. In F. W. Kaslow (Ed.), *Handbook of relational diagnosis and dysfunctional family patterns* (pp. 171–185). New York: John Wiley and Sons.

Kaslow, N. J., Heron, S., Roberts, D. K., Thompson, M., Guessous, O., & Jones, C. K. (2003). Family and community factors that predict internalizing and externalizing symptoms in low-income, African American children: A preliminary report. *New York Academy of Sciences, 1008*, 55–68.

Kaslow, N. J., Jones, C. A., & Palin, F. (2005). A relational perspective on depressed children: Family patterns and interventions. In W. M. Pinsof & J. L. Lebow (Eds.), *Family psychology: The art of the science* (pp. 397–424). Oxford: Oxford University Press.

Kaslow, N. J., Kaslow, F., & Farber, E. (1999). Theories and techniques of marital and family therapy. In M. B. Sussman, S. K. Steinmetz & G. W. Peterson (Eds.), *Handbook of marriage and the family* (pp. 767–792). New York: Plenum Press.

Kaslow, N. J., Mintzer, M., Meadows, L., & Grabill, C. (2000). A family perspective on assessing and treating childhood depression. In E. Bailey (Ed.), *Working with children: Using the family as a resource in children's therapy* (pp. 215–241). New York: W.W. Norton.

Kaufman, J., & Charney, D. (2001). Effects of early stress on brain structure and function: Implications for understanding the relationship between child maltreatment and depression. *Development and Psychopathology, 13*, 451–471.

Kaufman, J., Yang, B.-Y., Douglas-Palumberi, H., Grasso, D., Liptschitz, D., Houshyar, S., et al. (2006). Brain-derived neurotrophic factors-5-HTTLPR gene interactions and environmental modifiers of depression in children. *Biological Psychiatry, 59*, 673–680.

Kaufman, J., Yang, B., Douglas-Palumberi, H., Houshyar, S., Lipschitz, D., Krystal, J. H., et al. (2004). Social supports and serotonin transporter gene moderate depression in maltreated children. *PNAS, 101*, 17316–17321.

Kaufman, N. K., Rohde, P., Seeley, J. R., Clarke, G., & Stice, E. (2005). Potential mediators of cognitive-behavioral therapy for adolescents with comorbid major depression and conduct disorder. *Journal of Consulting and Clinical Psychology, 73*, 38–46.

Kerr, D. C., Preuss, L. J., & King, C. A. (2006). Suicidal adolescents' social support from family and peers: Gender-specific associations with psychopathology. *Journal of Abnormal Child Psychology, 34*, 103–114.

Kilpatrick, D. G., Ruggiero, K. J., Acierno, R., Saunders, B. E., Resnick, H. S., & Best, C. L. (2003). Violence and risk of PTSD, major depression, substance abuse/dependence, and comorbidity: Results from the National Survey of Adolescents. *Journal of Consulting and Clinical Psychology, 71*, 692–700.

Kim, H. K., Capaldi, D. M., & Stoolmiller, M. (2003). Depressive symptoms across adolescence and young adulthood in men: Predictions from parental and contextual risk factors. *Development and Psychopathology, 15*, 469–495.

Kim, I. J., Ge, X., Brody, G. H., Conger, R. D., Gibbons, F. X., & Simons, R. L. (2003). Parenting behaviors in the occurrence and co-occurrence of depressive symptoms and conduct problems among African American children. *Journal of Family Psychology, 17*, 571–583.

Kistner, J. A., David, C. F., & White, B. A. (2003). Ethnic and sex differences in children's depressive symptoms: Mediating effects of perceived and actual competence. *Journal of Clinical Child and Adolescent Psychology, 32*, 341–350.

Klein, D. N., Lewinsohn, P. M., Seeley, J., & Rohde, P. (2001). A family study of major depressive disorder in a community sample of adolescents. *Archives of General Psychiatry, 58*, 13–20.

Klein, D. N., Shankman, S. A., Lewinsohn, P. M., Rohde, P., & Seeley, J. R. (2004). Family study of chronic depression in a community sample of young adults. *American Journal of Psychiatry, 161*, 646–653.

Klein, K., & Forehand, R. (2000). Family processes as resources for African American children exposed to a constellation of sociodemographic risk factors. *Journal of Clinical Child Psychology, 29*, 53–65.

Kolko, D., Brent, D. A., Baugher, M., Bridge, J., & Birmaher, B. (2000). Cognitive and family therapies for adolescent depression: Treatment specificity, mediation, and moderation. *Journal of Consulting and Clinical Psychology, 68*, 603–614.

Leech, S. L., Larkby, C. A., Day, R., & Day, N. L. (2006). Predictors and correlates of high levels of depression and anxiety symptoms among children at age 10. *Journal of the American Academy of Child & Adolescent Psychiatry, 45*, 223–230.

Lewinsohn, P. M., Clarke, G., Hops, H., & Andrews, J. (1990). Cognitive-behavioral treatment for depressed adolescents. *Behavior Therapy, 21*, 385–401.

Lewinsohn, P. M., Clarke, G., Rohde, P., Hops, H., & Seeley, J. (1996). A course in coping: A cognitive-behavioral approach to the treatment of adolescent depression. In E. D. Hibbs & P. S. Jensen (Eds.), *Psychosocial treatments for child and adolescent disorders: Empirically based strategies for clinical practice* (pp. 109–135). Washington, DC: American Psychological Association.

Liu, Y.-L. (2003). Parent–child interaction and children's depression: The relationships between parent-child interaction and children's depressive symptoms in Taiwan. *Journal of Adolescence, 26*, 447–457.

Lopez, S. J., Edwards, L. M., Pedrotti, J. T., Ito, A., & Rasmussen, H. N. (2002). Culture counts: Examinations of recent applications of the Penn Resiliency Program or, toward a rubric for examining cultural appropriateness of prevention programming. *Prevention and Treatment, 5*, Article 12.

Luthar, S. S., & Cicchetti, D. (2000). The construct of resilience: Implications for interventions and social policies. *Development and Psychopathology, 12*, 857–885.

Luthar, S. S., Cicchetti, D., & Becker, B. (2000). The construct of resilience: A critical evaluation and guidelines for future work. *Child Development, 71*, 543–562.

Makri-Botsari, E. (2005). Risk/protective effects on adolescent depression: Role of individual, family, and peer factors. *Psychological Studies, 50*, 50–61.

Mann, J. J., Graham, E., Baldessarini, R. J., Beardslee, W. R., Fawcett, J. A., Goodwin, F. K., et al. (2006). ACNP Task Force Report on SSRIs and suicidal behavior in youth. *Neuropsychopharmacology, 31*, 473–492.

Marmorstein, N. R., & Iacono, W. G. (2001). An investigation of female adolescent twins with both major depression and conduct disorders. *Journal of the American Academy of Child & Adolescent Psychiatry, 40*, 299–306.

McClure, E. B., Connell, A., Zucker, M., Griffith, J. R., & Kaslow, N. J. (2005). The Adolescent Depression Empowerment Project (ADEPT): A culturally sensitive family treatment for depressed, African American girls. In E. D. Hibbs & P. S. Jensen (Eds.), *Psychosocial treatments for child and adolescent disorders: Empirically based strategies for clinical practice* (2nd ed., pp. 149–164). Washington, DC: American Psychological Association.

Merry, S., McDowell, H., Wild, C. J., Bir, J., & Cunliffe, R. (2004). A randomized placebo-controlled trial of a school-based depression prevention program. *Journal of the American Academy of Child & Adolescent Psychiatry, 43*, 538–547.

Michael, K. D., & Crowley, S. L. (2002). How effective are treatments for child and adolescent depression? A meta-analytic review. *Clinical Psychology Review, 22*, 247–269.

Moran, G., Diamond, G. M., & Diamond, G. S. (2005). The relational reframe and parents' problem constructions in attachment-based family therapy. *Psychotherapy Research, 15*, 226–235.

Mufson, L. H., Dorta, K. P., Wickramaratne, P., Nomura, Y., Olfson, M., & Weissman, M. M. (2004). A randomized effectiveness trial of interpersonal psychotherapy for depressed adolescents. *Archives of General Psychiatry, 61*, 577–584.

Mufson, L. H., Weissman, M. M., Moreau, D., & Garfinkel, R. (1999). Efficacy of interpersonal psychotherapy for depressed adolescents. *Archives of General Psychiatry, 56*, 573–579.

Munoz, R. F., Penilla, C., & Urizar, G. (2002). Expanding depression prevention research with children of diverse cultures. *Prevention and Treatment, 5.*

Muratori, F., Picchi, L., Bruni, G., Patarnello, M., & Romagnoli, G. (2003). A two-year follow-up of psychodynamic psychotherapy for internalizing disorders in children. *Journal of the American Academy of Child and Adolescent Psychiatry, 42*, 331–339.

Muris, P., Meesters, C., van Melick, M., & Zwambag, L. (2001). Self-reported attachment style, attachment quality, and symptoms of anxiety and depression in young adolescents. *Personality and Individual Differences, 30*, 809–818.

Nelson, E. L., Barnard, M., & Cain, S. (2003). Treating childhood depression over videoconferencing. *Telemedicine Journal and e-Health, 9*, 49–55.

Nomura, Y., Wickramaratne, P. J., Warner, V., Mufson, L. H., & Weissman, M. M. (2002). Family discord, parental depression, and psychopathology in offspring: Ten-year follow-up. *Journal of the American Academy of Child & Adolescent Psychiatry, 41*, 402–409.

O'Connor, M. J., & Paley, B. (2006). The relationship of prenatal alcohol exposure and the postnatal environment to child depressive symptoms. *Journal of Pediatric Psychology, 31*, 50–64.

Olfson, M., Marcus, S. C., & Shaffer, D. A. (2006). Antidepressant drug therapy and suicide in severely depressed children and adults: A case-control study. *Journal of the American Academy of Child & Adolescent Psychiatry, 63*, 865–872.

Pattison, C., & Lynd-Stevenson, R. M. (2001). The prevention of depressive symptoms in children: The immediate and long-term outcomes of a school-based program. *Behaviour Change, 18*, 92–102.

Patton, G. C., Coffey, C., Posterino, M., Carlin, J. B., & Wolfe, R. (2001). Parental "affectionless control" in adolescent depressive disorder. *Social Psychiatry and Psychiatric Epidemiology, 36*, 475–480.

Pfeffer, C., Jiang, H., Kakuma, T., Hwang, J., & Metsch, M. (2002). Group intervention for children bereaved by the suicide of a relative. *Journal of the American Academy of Child & Adolescent Psychiatry, 41*, 505–513.

Pike, A., McGuire, S., Hetherington, E. M., Reiss, D., & Plomin, R. (1996). Family environment and adolescent depressive symptoms and antisocial behavior: A multivariate genetic analysis. *Developmental Psychology, 32*, 590–603.

Pilowsky, D. J., Wickramaratne, P., Nomura, Y., & Weissman, M. M. (2006). Family discord, parental depression, and psychopathology and offspring: 20-year follow-up. *Journal of the American Academy of Child & Adolescent Psychiatry, 45*, 452–460.

Pineda, A. Q., Cole, D. A., & Bruce, A. E. (2007). Mother-adolescent interactions and adolescent depressive symptoms: A sequential analysis. *Journal of Social and Personal Relationships, 24*, 5–19.

Racusin, G. R., & Kaslow, N. J. (1994). Child and family therapy combined: Indications and implications. *American Journal of Family Therapy, 22*, 237–246.

Radke-Yarrow, M., Martinez, M., Mayfield, A., & Ronsaville, D. (Eds.). (1998). *Children of depressed mothers: From early childhood to maturity*. New York: Cambridge University Press.

Reinecke, M., & Simons, A. (2005). Vulnerability to depression among adolescents: Implications for cognitive-behavioral treatment. *Cognitive and Behavioral Practice, 12*, 166–176.

Reinherz, H. Z., Paradis, A. D., Gioconia, R. M., Stashwick, C. K., & Fitzmaurice, G. M. (2003). Childhood and adolescent predictors of major depression in the transition to adulthood. *American Journal of Psychiatry, 160*, 2141–2147.

Rende, R., Slomkowski, C., Lloyd-Richardson, E., Stroud, L., & Niaura, R. (2006). Estimating genetic and environmental influences on depressive symptoms in adolescents: Differing effects on higher and lower levels of symptoms. *Journal of Clinical Child and Adolescent Psychology, 35*, 237–243.

Resnick, M. D., Bearman, P. S., Blum, R. W., Bauman, K. E., Harris, K. M., Jones, J., et al. (1997). Protecting adolescents from harm: Findings from the National Longitudinal Study of Adolescent Health. *Journal of the American Medical Association, 278*, 823–832.

Rice, F., Harold, G. T., & Thapar, A. (2002a). Assessing the effects of age, sex, and shared environment on the genetic aetiology of depression in childhood and adolescence. *Journal of Child Psychology and Psychiatry and Allied Disciplines, 43*, 1039–1051.

Rice, F., Harold, G. T., & Thapar, A. (2002b). The genetic aetiology of childhood depression: A review. *Journal of Child Psychology and Psychiatry, 43*, 65–79.

Rice, F., Harold, G. T., & Thapar, A. (2003). Negative life events as an account of age-related differences in the genetic aetiology of depression in childhood and adolescence. *Journal of Child Psychology and Psychiatry, 44*, 977–987.

Richmond, M. K., Stocker, C. M., & Rienks, S. L. (2005). Longitudinal associations between sibling relationship quality, parental differential treatment, and children's adjustment. *Journal of Family Psychology, 19*, 550–559.

Roberts, C., Kane, R., Thomson, H., Bishop, B., & Hart, B. (2003). The prevention of depressive symptoms in rural school children: A randomized controlled trial. *Journal of Consulting and Clinical Psychology, 71*, 622–628.

Rohde, P., Clarke, G., Mace, D. E., Jorgensen, J. S., & Seeley, J. R. (2004). An efficacy/effectiveness study of cognitive-behavioral treatment for adolescents with comorbid major depression and conduct disorder. *Journal of the American Academy of Child & Adolescent Psychiatry, 43*, 660–668.

Rohde, P., Seeley, J. R., Kaufman, N. K., Clarke, G. N., & Stice, E. (2006). Predicting time to recovery among depressed adolescents treated in two psychosocial group interventions. *Journal of Consulting and Clinical Psychology, 74*, 80–88.

Rossello, J., & Bernal, G. (1999). The efficacy of cognitive-behavioral and interpersonal treatments for depression in Puerto Rican adolescents. *Journal of Consulting and Clinical Psychology, 67*, 734–745.

Ryan, N. D. (2005). Treatment of depression in children and adolescents. *Lancet, 366*, 933–940.

Sagrestano, L., Paikoff, R. L., Holmbeck, G. N., & Fendrich, M. (2003). A longitudinal examination of familial risk factors for depression among inner-city African American adolescents. *Journal of Family Psychology, 17*, 108–120.

Samaan, R. A. (2000). The influences of race, ethnicity, and poverty on the mental health of children. *Journal of Health Care for the Poor and Underserved, 11*, 100–110.

Sander, J. B., & McCarty, C. A. (2005). Youth depression in the family context: Familial risk factors and models of treatment. *Clinical Child and Family Psychology Review, 8*, 203–219.

Sanders, M. R., & McFarland, M. (2000). Treatment of depressed mothers with disruptive children: A controlled evaluation of cognitive behavioral family intervention. *Behavior Therapy, 31*, 89–112.

Sanford, M., Boyle, M., McCleary, L., Miller, J. G., Steele, M., Duku, E., et al. (2006). A pilot study of adjunctive family psychoeducation in adolescent major depression: Feasibility and treatment effect. *Journal of the American Academy of Child and Adolescent Psychiatry, 45*, 386–395.

Scourfield, J., Rice, F., Thapar, A., Harold, G. T., Martin, N., & McGuffin, P. (2003). Depressive symptoms in children and adolescents: Changing etiological influences with development. *Journal of Child Psychology and Psychiatry, 44*, 968–976.

Sen, B. (2004). Adolescent propensity for depressed mood and help seeking: Race and gender differences. *Journal of Mental Health Policy and Economics, 7*, 133–145.

Sexson, S. B., Glanville, D. N., & Kaslow, N. J. (2001). Attachment and depression: Implications for family therapy. *Child and Adolescent Psychiatric Clinics of North America, 10*, 465–486.

Shaffer, A., Forehand, R., Kotchick, B. A., & The Family Health Project Research Group. (2002). A longitudinal examination of correlates of depressive symptoms among inner-city African American children and adolescents. *Journal of Child and Family Studies, 11*, 151–164.

Sheeber, L., Hops, H., & Davis, B. (2001). Family processes in adolescent depression. *Clinical Child and Family Psychology Review, 4*, 19–35.

Sherrill, J. T., & Kovacs, M. (2002). Treatment of mood disorders in children and adolescents: Nonsomatic treatment of depression. *Child and Adolescent Psychiatric Clinics of North America, 11*, 579–594.

Shirk, S. R., Gudmundsen, G. R., & Burwell, R. A. (2005). Links among attachment-related cognitions and adolescent depressive symptoms. *Journal of Clinical Child and Adolescent Psychology, 34*, 172–181.

Shochet, I. M., Dadds, M. R., Holland, D., Whitefield, K., Harnett, P. H., & Osgarby, S. M. (2001). The efficacy of a universal school-based program to prevent adolescent depression. *Journal of Clinical Child Psychology, 30*, 303–315.

Shochet, I. M., & Ham, D. (2004). Universal school-based approaches to preventing adolescent depression: Past findings and future directions of the Resourceful Adolescent Program. *International Journal of Mental Health Promotion, 6*, 17–25.

Silberg, J., Pickles, A., Rutter, M., Hewitt, J., Simonoff, E., Maes, H., et al. (1999). The influence of genetic factors and life stress on depression among adolescent girls. *Archives of General Psychiatry, 56*, 225–232.

Silberg, J. L., Rutter, M., & Eaves, L. J. (2001). Genetic and environmental influences on the temporal association between earlier anxiety and later depression in girls. *Biological Psychiatry, 49*, 1040–1049.

Simons, R. L., Murry, V., McLoyd, V., Lin, K., Cutrona, C. E., & Conger, R. D. (2002). Discrimination, crime, ethnic identity, and parenting as correlates of depressive symptoms among African American children: A multilevel analysis. *Development and Psychopathology, 14*, 371–393.

Stark, K. D., Hargrave, J., Hersh, B., Greenberg, M., Herren, J., & Fisher, M. (2007). Treatment of childhood depression: The ACTION treatment program. In J. R. Z. Abela & B. L. Hankin (Eds.), *Child and adolescent depression: Causes, treatment, and prevention*. New York: Guilford Press.

Stark, K. D., Hargrave, J., Sander, J., Schnoebelen, S., Simpson, J., & Molnar, J. (2006a). Treatment of childhood depression: The ACTION treatment program. In P. C. Kendall (Ed.), *Child and adolescent therapy: Cognitive-behavioral procedures* (3rd ed., pp. 169–216). New York: Guilford Press.

Stark, K. D., Herren, J., & Fisher, M. (in press). Treatment of childhood depression. In M. J. Mayer, R. V. Acker, J. Lochman & F. M. Gresham (Eds.), *Cognitive-behavioral interventions for students with emotional/behavioral disorders*. New York: Guilford Press.

Stark, K. D., Reynolds, W. M., & Kaslow, N. J. (1987). A comparison of the relative efficacy of self-control therapy and behavior problem-solving therapy for depression in children. *Journal of Abnormal Child Psychology, 15*, 91–113.

Stark, K. D., Rouse, L., & Livingston, R. (1991). Treatment of depression during childhood and adolescence: Cognitive behavioral procedures for the individual and family. In P. Kendall (Ed.), *Child and adolescent therapy* (pp. 165–206). New York: Guilford Press.

Stark, K. D., Sander, J., Hauser, M., Simpson, J., Schnoebelen, S., Glenn, R., et al. (2006b). Depressive disorders during childhood and adolescence. In E. J. Mash & R. A. Barkley (Eds.), *Treatment of childhood disorders* (3rd ed., pp. 336–407). New York: Guilford Press.

Stark, K. D., Swearer, S., Kurowski, C., Sommer, D., & Bowen, B. (1996). Targeting the child and the family: A holistic approach to treating child and adolescent depressive disorders. In E. D. Hibbs & P. S. Jensen (Eds.), *Psychosocial treatments for child and adolescent disorders: Empirically based strategies for clinical practice* (pp. 207–238). Washington, DC: American Psychological Association.

Stein, D., Brent, D. A., Bridge, J., Kolko, D., Birmaher, B., & Baugher, M. (2001). Predictors of parent-rated credibility in a clinical psychotherapy trial for adolescent depression. *Journal of Psychotherapy Practice and Research, 10*, 1–7.

Stein, D., Williamson, D. E., Birmaher, B., Brent, D. A., Kaufman, J., Dahl, R. E., et al. (2000). Parent-child bonding and family functioning in depressed children and children at high risk and low risk for future depression. *Journal of the American Academy of Child & Adolescent Psychiatry, 39*, 1387–1395.

Steinberg, E. B., Sayger, T. V., & Szykula, S. A. (1997). The effects of strategic and behavioral family therapies on child behavior and depression. *Contemporary Family Therapy, 19*, 537–551.

Sugawara, M., Akiko, Y., Noriko, T., Tomoe, K., Haya, S., Kensuke, S., et al. (2002). Marital relations and depression in school-age children: Links with family functioning and parental attitudes toward child rearing. *Japanese Journal of Educational Psychology, 50*, 129–140.

Sutton, J. M. (2007). Prevention of depression in youth: A qualitative review and future suggestions. *Clinical Psychology Review, 27*, 552–571.

Tamplin, A., & Goodyer, I. M. (2001). Family functioning in adolescents at high and low risk for major depressive disorder. *European Child and Adolescent Psychiatry, 10*, 170–179.

The Treatment for Adolescents with Depression Study Team. (2003). Treatment for Adolescents with Depression Study (TADS): Rationale, design, and methods. *Journal of the American Academy of Child & Adolescent Psychiatry, 42*, 531–542.

The Treatment for Adolescents with Depression Study Team. (2005). The Treatment for Adolescents with Depression Study (TADS): Demographic and clinical characteristics. *Journal of the American Academy of Child & Adolescent Psychiatry, 44*, 28–40.

Treatment for Adolescents with Depression Study (TADS) Team. (2004). Fluoxetine, cognitive-behavioral therapy, and their combination for adolescents with depression: Treatment for Adolescents with Depression Study (TADS) randomized controlled trial. *Journal of the American Medical Association, 292*, 807–820.

Turner, H. A., Finkelhor, D., & Ormrod, R. (2006). The effect of lifetime victimization on the mental health of children and adolescents. *Social Science and Medicine, 62*, 13–27.

Twenge, J. M., & Nolen-Hoeksema, S. (2002). Age, gender, race, socioeconomic status, and birth cohort differences on the Children's Depression Inventory: A meta-analysis. *Journal of Abnormal Psychology, 111*, 578–588.

Unger, D. G., Brown, M. B., Tressell, P. A., & McLeod, L. E. (2000). Interparental conflict and adolescent depressed mood: The role of family functioning. *Child Psychiatry and Human Development, 31*, 23–41.

van Doesum, K. T. M., Hosman, C. M. H., & Riksen-Walraven, J. M. (2005). A model-based intervention for depressed mothers and their infants. *Infant Mental Health Journal, 26*, 157–176.

Varley, C. K. (2006). Treating depression in children and adolescents: What options now? *CNS Drugs, 20*, 1–13.

Wagner, K. D., & Ambrosini, P. (2001). Childhood depression: Pharmacological therapy/treatment (Pharmacotherapy of childhood depression). *Journal of Clinical Child Psychology, 30*, 88–97.

Weersing, V. R., & Brent, D. A. (2003). Cognitive-behavioral therapy for adolescent depression: Comparative efficacy, mediation, moderation, and effectiveness. In A. E. Kazdin & J. R. Weisz (Eds.), *Evidence-based psychotherapies for children and adolescents* (pp. 135–147). New York: Guilford Press.

Weissman, M. M., Pilowsky, D. J., Wickramaratne, P. J., Talati, A., Wisniewski, S. R., Fava, M., et al. (2006). Remissions in maternal depression and child psychopathology: A STAR*D-child report. *Journal of the American Medical Association, 295*, 1389–1398.

Weissman, M. M., Warner, V., Wickramaratne, P., Moreau, D., & Olfson, M. (1997). Offspring of depressed parents: 10 years later. *Archives of General Psychiatry, 54*, 932–940.

Weissman, M. M., Wickramaratne, P., Nomura, Y., Warner, V., Verdeli, H., Pilowsky, D. J., et al. (2005). Families at high and low risk for depression: A 3-generation study. *Archives of General Psychiatry, 62*, 29–36.

Weisz, J. R., McCarty, C. A., & Valeri, S. M. (2006). Effects of psychotherapy for depression in children and adolescents: A meta-analysis. *Psychological Bulletin, 132*, 132–149.

Wight, R. G., Aneshensel, C. S., Botticello, A. L., & Sepulveda, J. E. (2005). A multilevel analysis of ethnic variation in depressive symptoms among adolescents in the United States. *Social Science and Medicine, 6*, 2073–2084.

Wisdom, J. P., & Agnor, C. (2007). Family heritage and depression guides: Family and peer views influence adolescent attitudes about depression. *Journal of Adolescence, 30*, 333–346.

Wu, P., Hoven, C. W., Cohen, P., Liu, X., Moore, R. E., Tiet, Q., et al. (2001). Factors associated with use of mental health services for depression by children and adolescents. *Psychiatric Services, 52*, 189–195.

Yu, D. L., & Seligman, M. E. P. (2002). Preventing depressive symptoms in Chinese children. *Prevention and Treatment, 5*, Article 9.

Zahn-Waxler, C., Klimes-Dougan, B., & Slattery, M. J. (2000). Internalizing problems of childhood and adolescence: Prospects, pitfalls, and progress in understanding the development of anxiety and depression. *Development and Psychopathology, 12*, 443–466.

Chapter Twenty

Pharmacotherapy for Adolescent Depression[1]

GIL ZALSMAN, GAL SHOVAL, AND LIAD ROTSTEIN

CONTENTS

Epidemiological studies estimate prevalence rates of major depression disorder (MDD) to be as high as 1–2.5% among prepubertal children (with no gender difference), while in adolescence, rates climb to 3–8% (with female predominance of 2:1) (Goodyer, 1999). The prevalence of this disorder in late adolescence is very close to that of adults (Lewinsohn, Rohde, & Seeley, 1998). Significant morbidity and mortality are likely. Adolescent-onset depression has a marked increased risk of recurring later in life relative to adult-onset depressive disorder, and the same is true for suicide (Weissman et al., 1999). Most depressive episodes in adolescents recur within 5 years of onset (Birmaher et al., 1996b), a rate that may surpass recurrence rates of adult-onset depression (Emslie, Mayes, & Ruberu, 2005). One study reported a 40% recurrence rate in adolescents within 1 year (Emslie et al., 1998).

Depression causes not only immense agony, but also a marked disturbance in functioning and a life-threatening complication: suicide. Depression in youth is one of the strongest predictors of suicidal thoughts and attempts. Psychological autopsies have revealed that approximately two-thirds of adolescents who complete suicide suffered from depression (Marttunen, Aro, Henriksson, & Lonnqvist, 1991). The controversy over the possible elevation of suicidality as a result of the use of antidepressant pharmacotherapy is dealt with later in this chapter.

Despite being a prevalent and recurrent disorder, pediatric depression currently remains widely underdiagnosed and undertreated. This may be due partly to the relatively nonspecific presentation of the disorder, and the relatively late recognition of the disorder in children and adolescents. Due to a long-time misconception that depression is extremely rare in the pediatric age group, there is a paucity of studies on pediatric depression in general, and a lack of large-scale controlled studies of different drug therapies for pediatric depression in particular.

The biological mechanisms behind depression in children and adolescents are not clear yet, but seem to be different from adult depression (Zalsman et al., 2006c). A few mechanisms have been suggested, such as disturbances in the hypothalamic-pituitary-adrenal (HPA) axis, dysregulation of growth hormone, and dysregulation of serotonin (Goodyer, 1999; Goodyer et al., 1996). It seems that the dysregulation of serotonin, but not epinephrine, is more important in the creation of pediatric depression (Goodyer, 1999; Goodyer, Herbert, Tamplin, & Altham, 2000).

The treatment for adolescent depression includes nonpharmacological treatments, which are covered in other chapters of this book, such as cognitive-behavioral therapy (CBT), interpersonal therapy for adolescent (IPT-A), and family-based therapy (FBT); and pharmacological therapies (AACAP, 1998; Birmaher & Brent, 2003; Birmaher, Ryan, Williamson, Brent, & Kaufman, 1996a; Birmaher et al., 1996b; Moreno, Roche, & Greenhill, 2006; Shaffer & Waslick, 2002; Zalsman, Brent, & Weersing, 2006a). The nonpharmacological therapies are discussed elsewhere in this book. In many cases, the combination of nonpharmacological and pharmacological modalities is warranted (Murray, de Vries, & Wong, 2004). For review, see AACAP practice parameters for adolescent depression (AACAP, 1998; AACAP Consensus Group, 2007—unpublished draft) and the Treatment of Adolescent Depression Study (TADS) study group report (2003). The main goals of pharmacotherapy for adolescent depression are to achieve remission, prevent suicidal behavior, and prevent relapse and recurrence of depressive episodes (Birmaher et al., 1996a; Birmaher et al., 1996b, Birmaher et al., 2003; Moreno et al., 2006; Shaffer & Waslick., 2002; Zalsman et al., 2006a).

This chapter encompasses the description of the treatment phases, description of various groups of antidepressants, other biological therapies, and the controversy over the danger of suicidality, concluding with treatment algorithm and recommendations.

PHASES OF TREATMENT AND RESPONSE

Treatment of adolescent depression can be divided into three clinical phases: (i) acute, (ii) continuation, and (iii) maintenance (Birmaher et al., 1996b; Birmaher et al., 2003). The acute phase takes 6–12 weeks, and its main goals are to achieve a treatment response characterized by rapid symptom reduction and return to more adaptive psychosocial functions. *Response* is defined as a significant reduction of symptoms and impairments for at least 2 weeks (Birmaher et al., 2003). In recent trials, this has taken considerably longer than 6–12 weeks, with only around 50–60% of patients showing one or no symptoms by 12 weeks. Remission is defined as the period following response where there are less than two symptoms of depression lasting for at least 8 weeks together with a return to psychosocial functions at home and at school. After a period of two consecutive months symptom-free, *recovery* is defined. It is likely that around no more than two-thirds of depressed adolescents attending mental health clinics will achieve full remission by 4 months following the inception of **any form of treatment**. *Relapse* is a return of a depressive episode during remission and *recurrence* is a relapse within the recovery period (Birmaher et al., 2003). A predictor of relapse is the persistence of residual symptoms during the remission phase (i.e., patients who in fact do no better than partial remission by 4 months after starting treatment). Of particular concern is the likelihood of around one-third of patients showing treatment resistance and remaining fully depressed at 4 to 6 months after the acute phase of treatment.

The continuation phase is the 6-month period from the time that the patient is in full remission and/or defined as recovered, and NOT from the time treatment was started. The maintenance phase is after 1 year in remission or recovery in which prevention of recurrence is the main goal of treatment. During each phase, the comorbidities, resistance, and complications have to be considered in the decision of which treatment program should be used. There is no clear-cut, evidence-based, protocol for the full management of depressive episodes from acute through to the maintenance phase. In routine outpatient practice, no depressed child or adolescent should be managed by medication alone. Active clinical care involves attention to current psychosocial difficulties, psychoeducation about the nature and characteristics of depression, acute family and peer group conflicts and, where appropriate, liaison with other agencies, such as social services.

Specific Antidepressants

Tricyclic Antidepressants (TCAs)

In the 1980s, TCAs were the first group of medications to be prescribed in children and adolescents with depression. This was done as an extrapolation of the proved efficacy of these drugs among the adult depressed population and with very little scientific basis. Despite the clear efficacy demonstrated in adults, later trials of TCAs among children as well as adolescents were mostly negative (Geller, Cooper, Graham, Marsteller, & Bryant, 1990; Geller, Cooper, McCombs, Graham, & Wells, 1989; Kashani, Shekim, & Reid, 1984; Kramer & Feiguine, 1981; Petti & Law, 1982). The fact that many studies grouped together prepubertal children and postpubertal adolescents may have served to confound the results (Cheung, Emslie, & Mayes, 2005). A meta-analysis of studies of TCAs showed better results among depressed adolescents than among depressed children (Hazell, O'Connell, Heathcote, & Henry, 2000). Another obstacle to proving a therapeutic effect was, and still is today, the high placebo effect reported in the young population (50–60% in some studies). Some authors still see TCAs, especially amitriptyline, as a good second line agent, especially in treatment-resistant depression (Barbui & Hotopf, 2001). However, two controlled double-blind studies failed to demonstrate any advantage over placebo in depressed and resistant patients (Birmaher et al., 1998; Kye et al., 1996). The same is true for the TCA desipramine (Klein et al., 1998; Kutcher et al., 1994).

Taking into account the unimpressive results of TCAs in young patients, together with the potential wide range of side effects caused by these drugs, such as vertigo, dry mouth, urinary retention, constipation, tachycardia, and orthostatic hypotension, the indication for the use of TCAs for pediatric depression remained very much in doubt (Goodyer, 1999; Kutcher et al., 1994; Kye et al., 1996). The risk of lethality due to overdose and several case reports of sudden death of children (with desipramine and imipramine) made the use of TCAs even more rare (Goodyer, 1994).

Selective Serotonin Reuptake Inhibitors (SSRIs)

The group of SSRI medications include: fluoxetine (Prozac), sertraline (Zoloft), paroxetine (Paxil), citalopram (Celexa), escitalopram (Lexapro), and fluvoxamine (Luvox). Fluoxetine is the only SSRI approved by the American Food and Drug Administration (FDA) for adolescent depression. The class of SSRIs was introduced in the late 1980s as antidepressant and anxiolytic agents with a relatively low profile of adverse effects. Despite their selective effect on serotonin, they were shown to be as effective in alleviating depression and anxiety in adults as the TCAs, with a significantly lower rate of side effects and markedly diminished cardiotoxicity, even in cases of overdose.

Similar to TCAs, SSRIs were prescribed for pediatric depression based on the positive results in the adult population, but it was not until 1997 that a study on fluoxetine reported efficacy in the treatment of depression in children and adolescents (Emslie et al., 1997). Subsequent studies showed no difference compared to placebo (Emslie et al., 2002; Simeon, Dinicola, Ferguson, & Copping, 1990). It was only in 2004 that the multisite large-scale NIMH-funded study, the TADS, showed effective results for fluoxetine (March et al., 2004). In this study (n = 439), fluoxetine alone had a response rate of 60.6% and was more effective than CBT alone (43.2%). A combination of both therapies was even more effective, with a response rate of 71%. Some clinicians found the response rate on CBT surprisingly low in the TADS study and suggested some explanation to this finding (AACAP Consensus Group, 2007—unpublished draft). It is of note that a recent study done in the UK (Goodyer et al., 2007) on a sample of 208 adolescents aged 11–17, with moderate to severe depression, found no evidence that the combination of CBT plus an SSRI is superior to SSRI with routine clinical care. It is also important to bear in mind that the placebo effect in the young population may be as high as 60%, warranting extra precaution when analyzing the medication efficacy study results in this age (AACAP Consensus Group, 2007; Birmaher et al., 1996b; Bridge et al., 2007; March et al., 2004).

Fluoxetine was shown in a series of double-blind, placebo-controlled trials of adolescent depression to be effective for all phases of treatment: acute, maintenance, and relapse prevention of MDD (Emslie et al., 2004; Emslie et al., 2002; Emslie et al., 1998). In adolescents suffering from depression, dosages higher than 20 mg and b.i.d. administration may be needed due to rapid metabolization of the active compound (Brent & Birmaher, 2002). Despite the FDA's 2004 black box warning of SSRI and the risk of suicidality (see later in this chapter), and the existence of other alternatives, fluoxetine is still the most widely used antidepressant for adolescent depression.

Across studies, fluoxetine has shown a larger difference between medication and placebo than other antidepressants. This may be due to actual differences in the effect of the fluoxetine, other related properties of this medication (e.g., long half-life may lessen the impact of poor adherence to treatment), or because the studies involving fluoxetine were better designed and conducted, or used on more severely depressed patients.

Randomized controlled trials have also been performed on sertraline, paroxetine, and citalopram producing conflicting results (Keller et al., 2001; Wagner et al., 2003; Wagner et al., 2004). For instance, efficacy was not clearly demonstrated for paroxetine compared with placebo in depressed adolescents (Keller et al., 2001). Other studies of this medication were only presented in scientific meetings and are yet to be published. Negative results were found for sertraline in two randomized, controlled, multisite trials. Their combined data was later analyzed and sertraline was found to be significant in alleviating depression (63% vs. 53%, $p = 0.05$) (Wagner et al., 2003). To date, only one study of citalopram has shown significant efficacy in the treatment of adolescent-onset depression (Wagner et al., 2004). Its L-isomer (one of the mirror 3-D structures of the molecule) escitalopram was found to be only equal to placebo for depression in this age group (Wagner, Jonas, Findling, Ventura, & Saikali, 2006).

SSRIs Side Effects

All the SSRIs share similar side-effect profiles, and tolerance over time is the rule in most cases. Most of the side effects are dose-dependent and mild.

The most common side effects are:

1. Gastrointestinal system: nausea, diarrhea, stomach discomfort, decreased appetite, and decreased or increased weight.
2. Nervous system: headaches, restlessness (akathysia-like), tremor, jitteriness, agitation and disinhibition, insomnia or hypersomnia, vivid dreams and nightmares.
3. Sexual dysfunction: delayed or painful ejaculation, anorgasmia.
4. Psychiatric: SSRI can trigger hypomania or mania especially in 10- to 14-year-olds (Martin et al., 2004; Shaffer et al., 2002). Other psychiatric adverse events were described in a systemic chart review of adolescents treated with SSRIs, and all were reversible (Wilens et al., 2003).

Rare side effects of SSRIs described in adolescents include allergic reactions, growth retardation (Weintrob, Cohen, Klipper-Aurbach, Zadik, & Dickerman, 2002), extrapyramidal syndrome (a Parkinson-like syndrome which is a common side effect of psychiatric medications), and nocturnal reversible enuresis and hyponatremia (low natrium level in the blood) (Cheung et al., 2005; Kandil, Aksu, & Ozyavuz, 2004; Ryan, 2005; Shaffer et al., 2002).

SSRIs and the Risk of Suicidal Behavior

Following the accumulation of reports that adolescent patients receiving SSRI treatment had expressed increased suicidal behavior, in December 2002, the British Drug Authority issued a warning to refrain from prescribing this group of medications to patients less than 18 years of age. A few months later, the FDA published its warning against the use of paroxetine in children and adolescents. Following strong public pressure, the FDA held a hearing on the subject. Despite the fact that there were only indications of an increase in suicide gestures or attempts, and not of completed suicide, in October 2004, the FDA issued a black box warning stating that antidepressant medications may increase the risk for suicide ideation and suicide behavior in children and adolescents with depression and other psychiatric disturbances. It was recommended that this risk be weighed against the clinical need to treat depression, which may lead to suicidality by itself. Published data suggest a favorable risk-benefit profile for some SSRIs; however, addition of unpublished data indicated that risks could outweigh benefits of these drugs, except fluoxetine, to treat depression in children and young people (Whittington et al., 2004).

Many researchers, as well as the American Academy of Child and Adolescent Psychiatry, objected to the FDA warning, claiming that it may lead to undertreatment of depressive disorders, which are already underdiagnosed and undertreated (Brent, 2004; Brent & Birmaher, 2004). One study by Olfson, Marcus, and Shaffer (2006) demonstrated a negative correlation between the number of SSRI prescriptions and rates of suicide in various counties in the United States of America (Olfson et al., 2006). An increase of 1% in SSRI prescriptions to adolescents was associated with a decrease of 0.23:100,000 in the rates of completed adolescent suicide.

A recent meta-analysis of randomized, controlled, trials of children aged 6- to 19 years (Bridge et al., 2007) has shown that the risk difference of suicidal ideation/attempt within the indication of MDD was 0.9% and was not significant (risk difference is defined as the absolute difference in the event rate of two comparison groups). The authors concluded that benefits of antidepressant appear to be much greater than the risks from suicidal ideation and attempts.

The authors of this chapter retain the conviction that according to up-to-date studies, SSRI class medications should play an important role in the treatment of depression. Nonetheless, they must be used with the necessary precautions: the patient follow-up should be more intensive than in the past, extra attention should be directed toward suicidal behavior of any kind, and dose titration should be gradual. In patients with many risk factors for suicide, the option of a day-care psychiatric unit or a closed unit may be considered, at least upon treatment initiation. Thus, SSRIs could serve not only to alleviate depression, but also prevent suicide among the young population, in which it is the second or third cause of death (Bridge et al., 2007; Olfson et al., 2006).

Although the SSRIs are the safest and the most effective and widely used antidepressants in pediatrics, other groups of antidepressants are used for specific indications or when depression is resistant.

Serotonin and Norepinephrine Reuptake Inhibitors (SNRIs)

The SNRI group includes venlafaxine and duloxetine. Both are potent inhibitors of serotonin and norepinephrine, and usually serve as second or third line in the decision tree of the psychiatrist. One study (Mandoki, Tapia, Tapia, Sumner, & Parker, 1997) evaluated the efficacy and side effect profile of venlafaxine in the treatment of depression in children and adolescents. In a double-blind, placebo-controlled, 6-week study, 33 subjects between the ages of 8 and 17 who met the criteria for MDD were treated with either venlafaxine and psychotherapy or placebo and psychotherapy (Mandoki et al., 1997). The results indicated a significant mean improvement over time, but it could not be attributed to venlafaxine drug therapy. Low dosage and short length of treatment may account for the lack of efficacy (Mandoki et al., 1997). Secondary analysis of other venlafaxine trials showed an age effect, with these medications being better than placebo for depressed adolescents, but not depressed children. However, children were treated with low venlafaxine dosages (for review, see Bridge et al., 2007).

Our group and others are currently studying the SNRI duloxetine in adolescent depression, but data are still lacking.

Monoamine Oxidase (MAOA) Inhibitors

MAOA inhibitors are a class of antidepressants that selectively and reversibly inhibit MAOA enzyme, resulting in elevating levels of biogenic amines and neurotransmitters in the brain. Because of a potential risk in drug–drug interaction and drug–food interaction, use of the MAOA inhibitors is very limited in adolescents (Birmaher et al., 1996a; Birmaher et al., 2003; Ryan, 2005). At least 2 weeks are needed before an SSRI or TCA can be given to a patient who was treated with MAOA inhibitors because of the possibility of drug–drug interactions. Tyramine-containing foods, such as red wine and some cheeses, are dangerous potential interactions. Hyperadrenergic crisis (life-threatening hypertension) and serotonin syndrome (hyperthermia, flushing and loss of consciousness) are the major complications. Some studies have shown some benefit in atypical depression, depression with comorbid attention deficit hyperactive disorder (ADHD), and comorbid Tourette syndrome, a tic disorder (Birmaher et al., 1996a; Birmaher et al., 2003; Ryan, 2005).

Other Antidepressants

Nefazodone is a direct antagonist of the serotonin 5HT2 receptor and has serotonin-reuptake blocking properties. One study of depressed adolescents failed to show an improvement in the Children's Depression Rating Scale-revised (CDRS-R) score. In another study of both children and adolescents, results were negative (Birmaher & Brent, 2003).

Mirtazapine blocks the pre- and postsynaptic alpha 2 receptor, as well as the serotonin reuptake 5HT2 and 5HT3. There are no data on the efficacy of mirtazapine in pediatric populations with MDD. Because of the sedative effect of mirtazapine, its use is limited to MDD patients with severe insomnia (Shaffer et al., 2002).

Bupropion is an aminoketone compound that structurally resembles amphetamine. The neurochemical actions responsible for its antidepressant activity are not fully known. We found no controlled data on its use in a pediatric population with MDD. Its use is limited to youth with both ADHD and MDD.

Omega 3 was recently suggested as an effective treatment for mild to moderate childhood depression (Nemets, Nemets, Apter, Bracha, & Belmaker, 2006) as well as St. John's Wart (Hypericum) (Shaffer & Waslick, 2002), but these findings need independent controlled replications.

Other Biological Therapies

Electro Convulsive Therapy (ECT)

Considered a well-accepted, effective, and safe procedure in adults, ECT is indicated for patients with either depressive or bipolar disorder who present with a catatonic state or psychotic features, are suicidal, or are refractory or unresponsive to pharmacotherapy (Stein, Weizman, & Bloch, 2006). While adverse events of ECT are usually minor and transient and no absolute contraindications exist, this treatment is less studied in the pediatric population, and therefore limited (Stein et al., 2006; Zalsman et al., 2006a). Currently, the rates of ECT-use in children and adolescents are significantly low relative to adults. It was shown that it is only rarely used as a first-line treatment in this population (Stein et al., 2006). Stigma and prejudice have raised public concern over the use of ECT in minors (Birmaher et al., 1996a; Stein et al., 2006). However, the literature lacks any data that could support the assumption that ECT may damage the developing brain.

There are currently no well-accepted guidelines for the application of ECT in the young population (Stein et al., 2006). There is a remarkable variability between different countries. Well-designed and large-scale studies are needed in order to create evidence-based guidelines for safe and effective treatment for depressed children and adolescents. Despite the poor quality and methodology of the studies in the area, two reviews of the literature have suggested that efficacy of ECT is high also in the pediatric population (AACAP, 1998; Stein et al., 2006), with better results in unipolar patients than in bipolar patients.

Transcranial Magnetic Stimulation (TMS)

TMS, also known as repetitive transcranial magnetic stimulation (rTMS), is being studied as a new alternative for the treatment of depression. TMS involves daily exposure of the patient's brain to electromagnetic field. The main advantage of TMS is that it is a noninvasive and nonradiating method.

A review of seven meta-analyses (including a Cochrane Review—the most extensive meta-analysis system in medicine) published so far concluded that the effect of TMS in the treatment of adult depression is at best moderate, evidently less effective than ECT (Loo & Mitchell, 2005). However, alternative methods of administering TMS are currently being studied, such as the use of TMS with different frequencies, placement of the magnetic coil on the brain, number of stimuli, and course length. Since TMS is to date more of a research tool than a clinical tool, very little data have been collected on its use and application in pediatric depression (Stein et al., 2006). One group in Tel Aviv University is currently studying the TMS effect on adolescent depression.

Sleep Deprivation

Primary sleep disorders may result in MDD and vice versa in both adults and children. Subjective sleep complaints are a very prominent component of early-onset depression, although subjective complaints and objective observations of sleep in a sleep laboratory are not closely correlated (Zalsman et al., 2006c).

Depressed patients take a longer time to fall asleep, have increased number of awakenings and decreased sleep efficiency, or time spent asleep divided by time spent in bed. They have less slow wave sleep (Stage 3 and 4 nonrapid eye movement [REM] sleep), and more REM sleep. Depressed patients also show more phasic eye movements during REM sleep (greater REM density) and a more rapid onset of REM sleep (shorter REM latency) (Zalsman et al., 2006c).

It has been shown that sleep deprivation, even of a few hours, may result in mood elation in adult patients with MDD (Sadeh, Gruber, & Raviv, 2003). We are currently assessing this strategy in an adolescent population (Sadeh & Zalsman—unpublished data).

Treatment Algorithm and Recommendations

Based on the Practice Parameters of the American Academy of Child and Adolescent Psychiatry from both 1998 (AACAP, 1998) and the unpublished parameters from 2007 (AACAP Consensus Group, 2007—unpublished draft), a few basic recommendations can be drawn. A suggested algorithm by the Texas Consensus Conference Panel on Medication Treatment of Childhood MDD (Hughes et al., 2007) is presented in Figure 20.1.

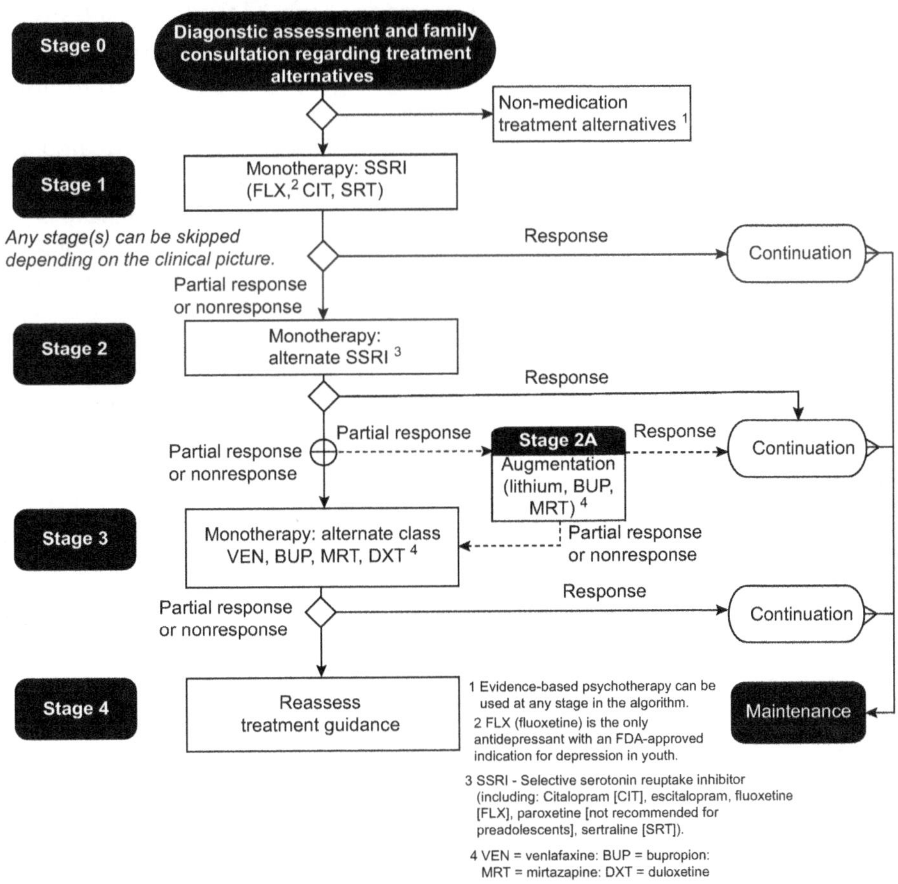

Figure 20.1 Medication algorithm for treating children and adolescents with MDD (Revised based on Hughes et al., 2007, with permission).

As noted earlier, several studies show small or no differences between the SSRIs and placebo, in part because the rates of placebo response are high. This is more obvious in depressed children than adolescents. Thus, it is possible that depressive symptoms in youth may be highly responsive to supportive management. It is also possible that studies showing no effects of SSRIs included subjects with mild depressions, or that other methodological issues are responsible for the lack of difference between medication and placebo, such as low medication dosages. In fact, the difference between the response to SSRIs and placebo was inversely related to the number of sites involved in the study (Bridge et al., 2007). TCAs are no more efficacious than placebo for the treatment of child and adolescent depression and should *not* be used as a first-line medication. Moreover, they are associated with more side effects than the SSRIs and can be fatal after an overdose.

After a thorough interview with the adolescent and both parents (if available), and after other diagnoses and medical conditions are ruled out, a diagnosis of MDD is made. Brief supportive and psychoeducation treatments may suffice a mild depression (AACAP Consensus Group, 2007—unpublished draft). For others, treatment should be 2 to 4 weeks of active routine clinical care. About 20% of depressive episodes may respond to such routine methods without recourse to more specialist psychotherapies (Goodyer et al., 2007). Evidence-based psychotherapy, such as CBT or IPT-A, by a trained clinician should be the second line of treatment in first episode noncomplicated cases. If there is no response after 3 months of psychological treatment, an antidepressant should be added to ongoing psychological therapies. In severe and complicated cases, most clinicians agree that medications are indicated as the first line (AACAP, 1998). When pharmacotherapy is needed, based on the data presented in this chapter, we recommend starting with a SSRI agent with the lowest dose available as a test dose for a few days to avoid side effects (side effects are dose dependent and tolerance is quick), and afterward, tapering up to a standard dose (fluoxetine 20 mg, citalopram 20 mg, sertralin 50 mg, escitalopram 10 mg, etc.). Based on the data available at the time this chapter was written, we suggest to start with fluoxetine, which seems to be the most studied, safe, and effective, and which has the best benefit to risk ratio of all SSRIs in the pediatric age (Whittington et al., 2004). On 2003, FDA approved fluoxetine as the first and only SSRI approved for depression in youth aged 7 to 17 years (www.fda.org). Response is expected in 4 to 8 weeks. If well tolerated and response is delayed, within a month the dose should be increased to 40 mg divided into two doses (Brent, 2004; Brent & Birmaher, 2006). Switching to another SSRI is the first step in case of treatment resistance. Citalopram or sertraline are the second choices (Hughes et al., 2007). Resistance should be declared only after twice a day of double standard dose for 6 weeks (AACAP, 1998; Shaffer et al., 2002; TADS, 2003). If monotherapy with a second SSRI fails, then augmentation and SNRI should be used (Hughes et al., 2007) (Fig. 20.1). According to the AACAP practice parameters, all patients need a continuation therapy for 6 to 12 months after the acute phase and some may need a maintenance therapy (AACAP, 1998; AACAP Consensus Group, 2007—unpublished draft).

The treatment for all patients should continue for at least 6 months after full remission. Patients should be assessed every other week, and subsequently once a month if no comorbidity or complications such as suicidal behavior occur (AACAP, 1998; AACAP Consensus Group, 2007; Birmaher et al., 2003; Brent et al., 2002; Shaffer et al., 2002).

Relapse and recurrence are very high in adolescent depression (40–60%), therefore maintenance therapy may be recommended to the patient on completion of the continuation phase (6–12 months of remission) (Birmaher et al., 1996a; Birmaher et al., 1996b; Brent et al., 2002; Shaffer et al., 2002). The clinician should consider who should get the maintenance treatment. Clear recommendations are currently missing, and the decision should take into account the number of previous episodes, suicidality, severity of the episode, comorbid mental disorders, and the will of the patient and his/her parents. The patient and the family should be informed by the physician of all the risks and benefits currently known for both maintenance and, alternatively, cessation of the drug. The discussion and decision should be recorded in the medical file.

Treatment for Specific Types of Depression

Psychotic Depression

Sometimes young patients with major depression also have psychotic symptoms, such as auditory hallucinations or delusions, usually with self-derogatory, paranoid, or depressive content. In these cases, antipsychotic medication should be added, but discontinued as the depression remits because of the risk for tardive dyskinesia in a long-term treatment with these agents (Birmaher et al., 2003; Shaffer et al., 2002; TADS, 2003). ECT is also an effective and safe treatment for psychotic depression (Stein et al., 2006).

Atypical Depression

In adults, MAO inhibitors seem to have some benefit for people with atypical depression, but this has not been studied in adolescents (Birmaher et al., 1996b).

Seasonal Depression

Light therapy has been studied in adults with seasonal depression and seems effective, but has the risk of inducing hypomania or mania. Data in adolescent are missing (Birmaher et al., 1996b).

Bipolar Depression

Patients with bipolar depression may need a mood stabilizer in addition to the antidepressant treatment. Psychotic features and family history of bipolar disorder in a depressed adolescent may indicate that the depressive episode is part of a future bipolar disorder.

Treatment of Resistant Depression

Approximately 20–30% of adolescents with MDD have partial or no response (Brent & Birmaher, 2006). The most accepted definition to nonresponse is less than 50% improvement from baseline CDRS-R (Brent & Birmaher, 2006). A common reason for nonresponsiveness is noncompliance (Birmaher et al., 1996a; Brent et al., 2006; Moreno et al., 2006; Zalsman et al., 2006a). Adolescents don't like to take medication, a fact that is true for other medical disorders in the pediatric age, such as diabetes mellitus. Another common reason is undertreatment: too low dosage or too brief trial of medication. Some adolescents are rapid metabolizers of SSRIs and may need double dosage (Brent et al., 2002).

In some cases, the depression has atypical features and needs second- or third-line (choice) medications (Klein et al., 1998).

Strategies in the case of resistant depression are similar to those of adults, although controlled studies in the pediatric age group on resistant depression are missing. The strategies used in adults include switching to another SSRI, augmentation with thyroxine or lithium, SNRI, other medication groups, ECT and even IV clomipramine (Birmaher et al., 2003). Stress reduction, decrease in family discord, a supportive environment, psychiatric treatment of other family members, and psychotherapy for Axis 2 disorders may lower the rate of nonresponse and recurrence. Psychoeducation of patient and family seems to turn many "nonresponders" into responders (Birmaher et al., 2003; Brent et al., 2002; Brent et al., 2006).

Treatment of Comorbidities

Comorbidity is very common in depressed adolescents, especially in clinical samples (Angold, Costello, & Erkanli, 1999). Comorbidity with depression may arise because of shared risk factors that are common to both conditions (Fergusson & Woodward, 2002). Anxiety is frequently a precursor of mood disorder and may also occur simultaneously with depression. Alcohol, drug, and tobacco abuse are associated with depression, and longitudinal studies suggest a bidirectional causality, with substance abuse both leading to and occurring as a consequence of depression (Rohde, Kahler, Lewinsohn, & Brown, 2004a, 2004b; Rohde, Lewinsohn, Brown, Gau, & Kahler, 2003). ADHD and depression are also often comorbid, and the two disorders may be cotransmitted in families (Biederman et al., 1992). Conduct disorder is frequently comorbid with depression, particularly in prepubertal samples (Harrington, Rutter, & Fombonne, 1996). Comorbidity may also arise because a condition is either a precursor to or a consequence of depression, as in the cases of anxiety and tobacco use, respectively. The treatment of comorbidities and related features must accompany the treatment of depression, otherwise the rate of response and recurrence are high (Birmaher et al., 2003; Brent et al., 2002; TADS, 2003). Each of the comorbidities should be treated specifically as recommended by the specific AACAP practice parameters. A specific algorithm for the treatment of childhood MDD with and without comorbidities, was recently suggested by the Texas Consensus Conference Panel on Medication Treatment of Childhood MDD (Hughes et al., 2007).

FUTURE DIRECTIONS

The development of antidepressants for adolescents was based on drugs developed for adults and extrapolated into the pediatric age group. We hope that in the future, with better understanding of the neurobiology of pediatric depression (Zalsman et al., 2006c), more specific agents may be developed and meet the specific developmental characteristics of MDD in the youth. Pharmacogenetic strategies may help in matching the right drug to each individual. Understanding the developing brain and the impact of pharmacotherapy on synaptic plasticity and pruning may be another field to be explored. Several studies suggested that neuropsychological traits and deficits may be used as markers or predictors to SSRI response and nonresponse. These traits include deficits in psychomotor speed (Taylor et al., 2006) and lower executive functions as measured by the Wisconsin Cards Sorting Test (WCST) (Dunkin et al., 2000). Our own data found a specific profile in young SSRI nonresponders of poorer global cognitive functioning and pronounced deficits in executive functions, language, and working memory (Gorlyn et al., unpublished data). We hope that these findings will be replicated with an adolescents population and serve as another tool in predicting response. Studies on gene X environment interaction (Caspi et al., 2003; Zalsman et al., 2006b) may shed a light on genetic effects under specific environmental conditions (e.g., maltreatment, negative life events) in the development of depression in the youth population and help in designing a gene-therapy strategy in the future.

NOTE

1. The authors wish to thank Dr Ian Goodyer from Cambridge University, UK, Dr Abraham Weizman and Dr Alan Apter from Tel Aviv University, Israel, Dr Boris Birmaher from Pittsburgh University, and Dr Andres Martin from Yale University, USA, for their remarks on this chapter and/or on the clinical recommendation section. We also wish to thank S. Zrachya and M. Gerchak for English editing of the text. We thank Dr Hughes and JAACAP for permission to use the algorithm in Figure 20.1.

REFERENCES

AACAP. (1998). Practice parameters for the assessment and treatment of children and adolescents with depressive disorders. *Journal of the American Academy of Child & Adolescent Psychiatry, 37*, 63S–83S.

AACAP Consensus Group. (2007). *Practice parameters for the assessment and treatment of children and adolescents with depressive disorder.* Unpublished draft.

Angold, A., Costello, E. J., & Erkanli, A. (1999). Comorbidity. *Journal of Child Psychology and Psychiatry, 40*, 57–87.

Barbui, C., & Hotopf, M. (2001). Amitriptyline v. the rest: Still the leading antidepressant after 40 years of randomised controlled trials. *British Journal of Psychiatry, 178*, 129–144.

Biederman, J., Faraone, S. V., Keenan, K., Benjamin, J., Krifcher, B., Moore, C., et al. (1992). Further evidence for family-genetic risk factors in attention deficit hyperactivity disorder: Patterns of comorbidity in probands and relatives in psychiatrically and pediatrically referred samples. *Archives of General Psychiatry, 49*, 728–738.

Birmaher, B., Axelson, D. A., Monk, K., Kalas, C., Clark, D. B., Ehmann, M., et al. (2003). Fluoxetine for the treatment of childhood anxiety disorders. *Journal of the American Academy of Child & Adolescent Psychiatry, 42*, 415–423.

Birmaher, B., & Brent, D. A. (2003). Depressive disorders. In A. Martin, L. Scahill, D. S. Charney & J. F. Leckman (Eds.), *Pediatric psychopharmacology* (1st ed., pp. 466–483). New York: Oxford University Press.

Birmaher, B., Ryan, N. D., Williamson, D. E., Brent, D. A., & Kaufman, J. (1996a). Childhood and adolescent depression: A review of the past 10 years. Part II. *Journal of the American Academy of Child & Adolescent Psychiatry, 35*, 1575–1583.

Birmaher, B., Ryan, N. D., Williamson, D. E., Brent, D. A., Kaufman, J., Dahl, R. E., et al. (1996b). Childhood and adolescent depression: A review of the past 10 years. Part I. *Journal of the American Academy of Child & Adolescent Psychiatry, 35*, 1427–1439.

Birmaher, B., Waterman, G. S., Ryan, N. D., Perel, J., McNabb, J., Balach, L., et al. (1998). Randomized, controlled trial of amitriptyline versus placebo for adolescents with "treatment-resistant" major depression. *Journal of the American Academy of Child & Adolescent Psychiatry, 37*, 527–535.

Brent, D. A. (2004). Antidepressants and pediatric depression—the risk of doing nothing. *New England Journal of Medicine, 351*, 1598–1601.

Brent, D. A., & Birmaher, B. (2002). Clinical practice. Adolescent depression. *New England Journal of Medicine, 347*, 667–671.

Brent, D. A., & Birmaher, B. (2004). British warnings on SSRIs questioned. *Journal of the American Academy of Child & Adolescent Psychiatry, 43*, 379–380.

Brent, D. A., & Birmaher, B. (2006). Treatment-resistant depression in adolescents: Recognition and management. *Child and Adolescent Psychiatric Clinics of North America, 15*, 1015–1034.

Bridge, J. A., Iyengar, S., Salary, C. B., Barbe, R. P., Birmaher, B., Pincus, H. A., et al. (2007). Clinical response and risk for reported suicidal ideation and suicide attempts in pediatric antidepressant treatment: A meta-analysis of randomized controlled trials. *Journal of the American Medical Association, 297*, 1683–1696.

Caspi, A., Sugden, K., Moffitt, T. E., Taylor, A., Craig, I. W., Harrington, H., et al. (2003). Influence of life stress on depression: Moderation by a polymorphism in the 5-HTT gene. *Science, 301*, 386–389.

Cheung, A. H., Emslie, G. J., & Mayes, T. L. (2005). Review of the efficacy and safety of antidepressants in youth depression. *Journal of Child Psychology and Psychiatry, 46*, 735–754.

Dunkin, J. J., Leuchter, A. F., Cook, I. A., Kasl-Godley, J. E., Abrams, M., & Rosenberg-Thompson, S. (2000). Executive dysfunction predicts nonresponse to fluoxetine in major depression. *Journal of Affective Disorders, 60*, 13–23.

Emslie, G. J., Heiligenstein, J. H., Hoog, S. L., Wagner, K. D., Findling, R. L., McCracken, J. T., et al. (2004). Fluoxetine treatment for prevention of relapse of depression in children and adolescents: A double-blind, placebo-controlled study. *Journal of the American Academy of Child & Adolescent Psychiatry, 43*, 1397–1405.

Emslie, G. J., Heiligenstein, J. H., Wagner, K. D., Hoog, S. L., Ernest, D. E., Brown, E., et al. (2002). Fluoxetine for acute treatment of depression in children and adolescents: A placebo-controlled, randomized clinical trial. *Journal of the American Academy of Child & Adolescent Psychiatry, 41*, 1205–1215.

Emslie, G. J., Mayes, T. L., & Ruberu, M. (2005). Continuation and maintenance therapy of early-onset major depressive disorder. *Paediatric Drugs, 7*, 203–217.

Emslie, G. J., Rush, A. J., Weinberg, W. A., Kowatch, R. A., Carmody, T., & Mayes, T. L. (1998). Fluoxetine in child and adolescent depression: Acute and maintenance treatment. *Depression and Anxiety, 7*, 32–39.

Emslie, G. J., Rush, A. J., Weinberg, W. A., Kowatch, R. A., Hughes, C. W., Carmody, T., et al. (1997). A double-blind, randomized, placebo-controlled trial of fluoxetine in children and adolescents with depression. *Archives of General Psychiatry, 54*, 1031–1037.

Fergusson, D. M., & Woodward, L. J. (2002). Mental health, educational, and social role outcomes of adolescents with depression. *Archives of General Psychiatry, 59*, 225–231.

Geller, B., Cooper, T. B., Graham, D. L., Marsteller, F. A., & Bryant, D. M. (1990). Double-blind placebo-controlled study of nortriptyline in depressed adolescents using a "fixed plasma level" design. *Psychopharmacology Bulletin, 26*, 85–90.

Geller, B., Cooper, T. B., McCombs, H. G., Graham, D., & Wells, J. (1989). Double-blind, placebo-controlled study of nortriptyline in depressed children using a "fixed plasma level" design. *Psychopharmacology Bulletin, 25*, 101–108.

Goodyer, I., Dubicka, B., Wilkinson, P., Kelvin, R., Roberts, C., Byford, S., et al. (2007). Selective serotonin reuptake inhibitors (SSRIs) and routine specialist care with and without cognitive behaviour therapy in adolescents with major depression: Randomised controlled trial. *British Medical Journal, 335*, 142–149.

Goodyer, I. M. (1999). *The depressed child and adolescent*. Cambridge: Cambridge University Press.

Goodyer, I. M., Herbert, J., Altham, P. M., Pearson, J., Secher, S. M., & Shiers, H. M. (1996). Adrenal secretion during major depression in 8- to 16-year-olds, I. Altered diurnal rhythms in salivary cortisol and dehydroepiandrosterone (DHEA) at presentation. *Psychological Medicine, 26*, 245–256.

Goodyer, I. M., Herbert, J., Tamplin, A., & Altham, P. M. (2000). First-episode major depression in adolescents. Affective, cognitive and endocrine characteristics of risk status and predictors of onset. *British Journal of Psychiatry, 176*, 142–149.

Harrington, R., Rutter, M., & Fombonne, E. (1996). Developmental pathways in depression: Multiple meanings, antecedents, and endpoints. *Development and Psychopathology, 8*, 601–616.

Hazell, P., O'Connell, D., Heathcote, D., & Henry, D. (2000). Tricyclic drugs for depression in children and adolescents. *Cochrane Database of Systematic Reviews*, CD002317.

Hughes, C. W., Emslie, G. J., Crismon, M. L., Posner, K., Birmaher, B., Ryan, N., et al. (2007). Texas Children's Medication Algorithm Project: Update from Texas Consensus Conference Panel on Medication Treatment of Childhood Major Depressive Disorder. *Journal of the American Academy of Child & Adolescent Psychiatry, 46*, 667–686.

Kandil, S. T., Aksu, H. B., & Ozyavuz, R. (2004). Reversible nocturnal enuresis in children receiving SSRI with or without risperidone: Presentation of five cases. *Israel Journal of Psychiatry and Related Sciences, 41*, 218–221.

Kashani, J. H., Shekim, W. O., & Reid, J. C. (1984). Amitriptyline in children with major depressive disorder: A double-blind crossover pilot study. *Journal of the American Academy of Child Psychiatry, 23*, 348–351.

Keller, M. B., Ryan, N. D., Strober, M., Klein, R. G., Kutcher, S. P., Birmaher, B., et al. (2001). Efficacy of paroxetine in the treatment of adolescent major depression: A randomized, controlled trial. *Journal of the American Academy of Child & Adolescent Psychiatry, 40*, 762–772.

Klein, R. G., Mannuzza, S., Koplewicz, H. S., Tancer, N. K., Shah, M., Liang, V., et al. (1998). Adolescent depression: Controlled desipramine treatment and atypical features. *Depression and Anxiety, 7,* 15–31.

Kramer, A. D., & Feiguine, R. J. (1981). Clinical effects of amitriptyline in adolescent depression. A pilot study. *Journal of the American Academy of Child Psychiatry, 20,* 636–644.

Kutcher, S., Boulos, C., Ward, B., Marton, P., Simeon, J., Ferguson, H. B., et al. (1994). Response to desipramine treatment in adolescent depression: A fixed-dose, placebo-controlled trial. *Journal of the American Academy of Child & Adolescent Psychiatry, 33,* 686–694.

Kye, C. H., Waterman, G. S., Ryan, N. D., Birmaher, B., Williamson, D. E., Iyengar, S., et al. (1996). A randomized, controlled trial of amitriptyline in the acute treatment of adolescent major depression. *Journal of the American Academy of Child & Adolescent Psychiatry, 35,* 1139–1144.

Lewinsohn, P. M., Rohde, P., & Seeley, J. R. (1998). Major depressive disorder in older adolescents: Prevalence, risk factors, and clinical implications. *Clinical Psychology Review, 18,* 765–794.

Loo, C. K., & Mitchell, P. B. (2005). A review of the efficacy of transcranial magnetic stimulation (TMS) treatment for depression, and current and future strategies to optimize efficacy. *Journal of Affective Disorders, 88,* 255–267.

Mandoki, M. W., Tapia, M. R., Tapia, M. A., Sumner, G. S., & Parker, J. L. (1997). Venlafaxine in the treatment of children and adolescents with major depression. *Psychopharmacology Bulletin, 33,* 149–154.

March, J., Silva, S., Petrycki, S., Curry, J., Wells, K., Fairbank, J., et al. (2004). Fluoxetine, cognitive-behavioral therapy, and their combination for adolescents with depression: Treatment for Adolescents with Depression Study (TADS) randomized controlled trial. *Journal of the American Medical Association, 292,* 807–820.

Martin, A., Young, C., Leckman, J. F., Mukonoweshuro, C., Rosenheck, R., & Leslie, D. (2004). Age effects on antidepressant-induced manic conversion. *Archives of Pediatrics & Adolescent Medicine, 158,* 773–780.

Marttunen, M. J., Aro, H. M., Henriksson, M. M., & Lonnqvist, J. K. (1991). Mental disorders in adolescent suicide. DSM-III-R axes I and II diagnoses in suicides among 13- to 19-year-olds in Finland. *Archives of General Psychiatry, 48,* 834–839.

Moreno, C., Roche, A. M., & Greenhill, L. L. (2006). Pharmacotherapy of child and adolescent depression. *Child and Adolescent Psychiatric Clinics of North America, 15,* 977–998.

Murray, M. L., de Vries, C. S., & Wong, I. C. (2004). A drug utilisation study of antidepressants in children and adolescents using the general practice research database. *Archives of Disease in Childhood, 89,* 1098–1102.

Nemets, H., Nemets, B., Apter, A., Bracha, Z., & Belmaker, R. H. (2006). Omega-3 treatment of childhood depression: A controlled, double-blind pilot study. *American Journal of Psychiatry, 163,* 1098–1100.

Olfson, M., Marcus, S. C., & Shaffer, D. (2006). Antidepressant drug therapy and suicide in severely depressed children and adults: A case-control study. *Archives of General Psychiatry, 63,* 865–872.

Petti, T. A., & Law, W., III. (1982). Imipramine treatment of depressed children: A double-blind pilot study. *Journal of Clinical Psychopharmacology, 2,* 107–110.

Rohde, P., Kahler, C. W., Lewinsohn, P. M., & Brown, R. A. (2004a). Psychiatric disorders, familial factors, and cigarette smoking: II. Associations with progression to daily smoking. *Nicotine and Tobacco Research, 6*, 119–132.

Rohde, P., Kahler, C. W., Lewinsohn, P. M., & Brown, R. A. (2004b). Psychiatric disorders, familial factors, and cigarette smoking: III. Associations with cessation by young adulthood among daily smokers. *Nicotine and Tobacco Research, 6*, 509–522.

Rohde, P., Lewinsohn, P. M., Brown, R. A., Gau, J. M., & Kahler, C. W. (2003). Psychiatric disorders, familial factors and cigarette smoking: I. Associations with smoking initiation. *Nicotine and Tobacco Research, 5*, 85–98.

Ryan, N. D. (2005). Treatment of depression in children and adolescents. *Lancet, 366*, 933–940.

Sadeh, A., Gruber, R., & Raviv, A. (2003). The effects of sleep restriction and extension on school-age children: What a difference an hour makes. *Child Development, 74*, 444–455.

Shaffer, D., & Waslick, B. (2002). *The many faces of depression in children and adolescents* (1st ed.). Washington, DC: American Psychiatric Association.

Simeon, J. G., Dinicola, V. F., Ferguson, H. B., & Copping, W. (1990). Adolescent depression: A placebo-controlled fluoxetine treatment study and follow-up. *Progress in Neuropsychopharmacology & Biological Psychiatry, 14*, 791–795.

Stein, D., Weizman, A., & Bloch, Y. (2006). Electroconvulsive therapy and transcranial magnetic stimulation: Can they be considered valid modalities in the treatment of pediatric mood disorders? *Child and Adolescent Psychiatric Clinics of North America, 15*, 1035–1056.

TADS. (2003). Treatment for Adolescents with Depression Study (TADS): Rationale, design, and methods. *Journal of the American Academy of Child & Adolescent Psychiatry, 42*, 531–542.

Taylor, B. P., Bruder, G. E., Stewart, J. W., McGrath, P. J., Halperin, J., Ehrlichman, H., et al. (2006). Psychomotor slowing as a predictor of fluoxetine nonresponse in depressed outpatients. *American Journal of Psychiatry, 163*, 73–78.

Wagner, K. D., Ambrosini, P., Rynn, M., Wohlberg, C., Yang, R., Greenbaum, M. S., et al. (2003). Efficacy of sertraline in the treatment of children and adolescents with major depressive disorder: Two randomized controlled trials. *Journal of the American Medical Association, 290*, 1033–1041.

Wagner, K. D., Jonas, J., Findling, R. L., Ventura, D., & Saikali, K. (2006). A double-blind, randomized, placebo-controlled trial of escitalopram in the treatment of pediatric depression. *Journal of the American Academy of Child & Adolescent Psychiatry, 45*, 280–288.

Wagner, K. D., Robb, A. S., Findling, R. L., Jin, J., Gutierrez, M. M., & Heydorn, W. E. (2004). A randomized, placebo-controlled trial of citalopram for the treatment of major depression in children and adolescents. *American Journal of Psychiatry, 161*, 1079–1083.

Weintrob, N., Cohen, D., Klipper-Aurbach, Y., Zadik, Z., & Dickerman, Z. (2002). Decreased growth during therapy with selective serotonin reuptake inhibitors. *Archives of Pediatrics & Adolescent Medicine, 156*, 696–701.

Weissman, M. M., Wolk, S., Goldstein, R. B., Moreau, D., Adams, P., Greenwald, S., et al. (1999). Depressed adolescents grown up. *Journal of the American Medical Association, 281*, 1707–1713.

Whittington, C. J., Kendall, T., Fonagy, P., Cottrell, D., Cotgrove, A., & Boddington, E. (2004). Selective serotonin reuptake inhibitors in childhood depression: Systematic review of published versus unpublished data. *Lancet, 363,* 1341–1345.

Wilens, T. E., Biederman, J., Kwon, A., Chase, R., Greenberg, L., Mick, E., et al. (2003). A systematic chart review of the nature of psychiatric adverse events in children and adolescents treated with selective serotonin reuptake inhibitors. *Journal of Child and Adolescent Psychopharmacology, 13,* 143–152.

Zalsman, G., Brent, D. A., & Weersing, V. R. (2006a). Depressive disorders in childhood and adolescence: An overview epidemiology, clinical manifestation and risk factors. *Child and Adolescent Psychiatric Clinics of North America, 15,* 827–841.

Zalsman, G., Huang, Y. Y., Oquendo, M. A., Burke, A. K., Hu, X. Z., Brent, D. A., et al. (2006b). Association of a triallelic serotonin transporter gene promoter region (5-HTTLPR) polymorphism with stressful life events and severity of depression. *American Journal of Psychiatry, 163,* 1588–1593.

Zalsman, G., Oquendo, M. A., Greenhill, L., Goldberg, P. H., Kamali, M., Martin, A., et al. (2006c). Neurobiology of depression in children and adolescents. *Child and Adolescent Psychiatric Clinics of North America, 15,* 843–868.

Chapter Twenty-One

Effectiveness of Interventions for Adolescent Depression: Reason for Hope or Cause for Concern?[1]

V. ROBIN WEERSING AND ARACELI GONZALEZ

CONTENTS

Thirty years ago, the existence of adolescent depression was still a subject of scientific debate. However, as the wide prevalence and substantial impact of depression in adolescence became well-established, efforts to develop effective interventions quickly followed. By the end of the 1980s, the first randomized controlled trial (RCT) had been published (Reynolds & Coats, 1986); the 1990s brought 10 RCTs, and in the next decade, 18 clinical trials targeting adolescent depression have already appeared in the literature. The path of these treatments from conception to testing is a familiar one to observers of the youth therapy literature. Successful adult interventions were "child-sized" for teens—dose adjusted, content simplified, structure increased. As a result, the three best-supported interventions for youths with depression map directly onto the list of empirically supported adult depression treatments—cognitive-behavioral therapy (CBT), interpersonal psychotherapy (IPT), and the use of selective serotonin reuptake inhibitors (SSRI), particularly fluoxetine. In contrast, research on "developmental" interventions, such as family-based or parenting-focused treatments has lagged far behind, as discussed by Garber, Webb, and Horowitz in this volume.

In this chapter, we review the available empirical evidence on the effectiveness of adolescent depression treatment, restricting our review to studies including youth aged 12 to 18, and focusing our review on the "big three" of CBT, SSRIs, and IPT. Across these models, we prioritize findings from RCTs appearing in peer-reviewed, English language journals. We structure our review to map onto the core questions of intervention research; namely:

1. Do interventions for adolescent depression produce positive effects? Are they efficacious in clinical trials and effective in clinical practice?
2. How do treatments for depression achieve their effects? What is the available evidence for treatment mediation and therapy mechanisms of action?
3. For whom do these interventions work? What are the predictors and moderators of treatment outcome?

We conclude with a summary of unanswered questions in treatment research for depression in adolescents and propose some fruitful areas for additional study.

EFFICACY AND EFFECTIVENESS OF MAJOR THERAPEUTIC APPROACHES

To date, there are 26[2] clinical trials for adolescent depression that focus on CBT, IPT, or SSRIs. Until very recently, the story told by these studies was a simple one. Without question, CBT was the best researched and most well-supported intervention for adolescent depression. In eight RCTs, CBT had outperformed control conditions ranging from wait lists to alternate treatments (e.g., family therapy; Brent et al., 1997), and the intervention was fast on the way to becoming the standard of care for health systems and professional practice organizations (e.g., National Health and Medical Research Council, 1997). The status of CBT was further enhanced by national and international regulatory concerns about possible increases in suicidality associated with the use of antidepressant medications in children and adolescents (National Institute for Health and Clinical Excellence, 2005; U.S. Food and Drug Administration [FDA], 2007), and, more recently, young adults (U.S. FDA, 2007).

This clear picture was blurred substantially in 1994 by the publication of the Treatment of Adolescents with Depression Study (TADS), the largest clinical trial ever conducted in depressed youths. TADS compared the effects of CBT, fluoxetine, CBT and fluoxetine in combination, and a placebo control condition, and came to the surprising conclusion that CBT did not appear to outperform the effects of the placebo control (TADS Team, 2004). On the heels of TADS, a new meta-analysis of the youth depression literature has suggested that previous reviews may have overestimated the size of CBT effects by a factor of 3 (Weisz, McCarty, & Valeri, 2006). Although CBT did demonstrate a significant effect in this meta-analysis, what were once considered the largest effects of psychotherapy in the youth treatment literature (e.g., Lewinsohn & Clarke, 1999; Reinecke, Ryan, & Dubois, 1998) are now proposed to be among the smallest. Furthermore, as data on the efficacy of CBT and safety of SSRIs have been in flux, a small but consistent body of evidence has developed supporting the use of IPT in adolescent depression. Although there are only three RCTs focusing on IPT, the intervention model has already begun to demonstrate efficacy compared to alternate treatments, effectiveness in practice, and independent replication (apart from the original development team).

Taken together, these findings raise considerable questions about what should be considered the best practice intervention model for adolescent depression. To aid in our review of this complicated literature, we summarize the empirical outcomes across all published CBT, IPT, and SSRI clinical trials in Table 21.1. We provide clinically significant response rates for treatment and control conditions, and also compute a metric well-known in evidence-based medicine, the number-needed-to-treat (NNT) ratio. The NNT provides useful shorthand for clinical decision making by estimating the number of treated cases, on average, needed to produce one clinical recovery (see Guyatt & Rennie, 2002, pp. 358–360, for discussion and definition of NNT). As such, low NNT numbers are considered good, with the rough rubric of a NNT of 10 or less being medically acceptable. As can be seen in the table, there is tremendous variability in depression treatment response and NNT, with ratios ranging from 1 to infinity (treatment worse than control).

To capture slope and dimensional outcomes of treatment, Figure 21.1 depicts change in youth-reported depression symptoms, from intake to post-treatment, for this same set of clinical trials. To facilitate comparison of results across different self-report scales, the figure displays depression symptoms in a standardized, *normative z score* format. Computing a normative z score is a simple procedure that uses data from the original measure development papers to standardize depression scores relative to a "normal" community sample of youth.[3] These calculations use the formula $z_{nt}(\bar{x}_t - \mu)/(\sigma)$, where $\bar{x}_t$ is the mean score on the depression measure in the group of interest (e.g., intake depression score for a CBT treatment group), μ is the normal population mean, and σ is the normal population standard deviation for the depression measure (Kendall & Grove, 1988). An intake z score of 2.0 indicates that the mean level of symptoms is two standard deviations above the community mean for depression, roughly the 98th percentile. By definition, a normative z score of 0 is equivalent to a "normal" level of depression (the community mean), and return of symptoms to this level is another index of clinically significant change (Weersing, 2005). As with Table 21.1, perhaps the most striking feature of the figure is the substantial variability in initial severity of symptoms and

Table 21.1 Response Rates and NNT Ratios for Treatments for Adolescent Depression

Experimental Treatment	Study	Total *n*	Control Group	Definition of Response	Response Rate		
					Experimental	Control	NNT
CBT	Ackerson et al. (1998)	22	WL	Normal HRSD and RCI	59	NA	NA
CBT	Brent et al. (1997)	107	NST	No mood diagnosis and normal BDI	60	39	5
CBT	Clarke et al. (1999)	124	WL	No mood diagnosis	65	48	6
CBT+P	Clarke et al. (1999)	124	WL	No mood diagnosis	69	48	5
CBT+TAU	Clarke et al. (2002)	88	TAU	No mood diagnosis	58	53	20
CBT	Kerfoot et al. (2004)	52	TAU	No mood symptoms or diagnosis	23	20	33
CBT	Lewinsohn et al. (1990)	69	WL	No mood diagnosis	43	5	3
CBT+P	Lewinsohn et al. (1990)	69	WL	No mood diagnosis	47	5	2
CBT	Melvin et al. (2006)	73	CBT+SERT	No mood diagnosis	86	50	3
CBT	Melvin et al. (2006)	73	SERT	No mood diagnosis	86	46	3
CBT	Reynolds and Coats (1986)	30	WL	Normal BDI	83	0	1
CBT	Roselló and Bernal (1999)	71	WL	Normal CDI	59	NA	NA
CBT	Rohde et al. (2004)	93	Life skills	No mood diagnosis	39	19	5
CBT	TADS (2004)	439	PLA	CGI-I ≥2	43	35	13
CBT	Vostanis et al. (1996)	63	NST	No mood diagnosis	86	75	9
CBT	Wood et al. (1996)	53	Relaxation	"Clinical remission"	54	21	3
IPT-A	Mufson et al. (1999)	48	WL	Normal HRSD	75	46	3
IPT-A	Mufson et al. (2004)	63	School TAU	Normal HRSD	50	34	6
IPT-A	Roselló and Bernal (1999)	71	WL	Normal CDI	82	NA	NA

Citalopram	Wagner et al. (2004)	174	PLA	Normal CDRS-R	36	24	8
Citalopram	von Knorring et al. (2006)	244	PLA	≥50% decrease in MADRS or no anhedonia/dysphoria	61	59	50
Escitalopram	Wagner et al. (2006)	268	PLA	≥50% decrease in MADRS	63	52	9
FLX	Emslie et al. (1997)	96	PLA	CGI-I ≤2	56	33	4
FLX	Emslie et al. (2002)	219	PLA	≥30% decrease in CDRS-R	65	54	9
FLX	Simeon et al. (1990)	40	PLA	CGI-I ≤2	NA	NA	NA
FLX	TADS (2004)	439	PLA	CGI-I ≤2	61	35	4
Paroxetine	Berard et al. (2006)	286	PLA	≥50% decrease in MADRS	61	58	33
Paroxetine	Emslie et al. (2006)	201	PLA	CGI-I ≤2	49	46	33
Paroxetine	Keller et al. (2001)	177	PLA	HAM-D ≤8 or ≥50% decrease	67	55	8
SERT	Wagner et al. (2003)	364	PLA	CGI-I ≤2	63	53	10
CBT+FLX	TADS (2004)	439	PLA	CGI-I ≤2	71	35	3
CBT+FLX	TADS (2004)	439	FLX	CGI-I ≤2	71	61	10
CBT+SSRI	Clarke et al. (2005)	152	TAU	No mood diagnosis	77	72	20
CBT+TAU	Asarnow et al. (2005)	418	TAU	Normal CES-D	69	58	9
CBT+SERT	Melvin et al. (2006)	73	SERT	No mood diagnosis	50	46	25

Note: CBT = cognitive behavior therapy; CBT + P = cognitive behavior therapy plus parent component; TAU = treatment as usual; IPT-A = interpersonal psychotherapy for adolescents; FLX = fluoxetine; SSRI = selective serotonin reuptake inhibitor; SERT = sertraline; WL=wait list; NST = nondirective supportive therapy; PLA = placebo; HRSD = Hamilton Rating Scale for Depression; RCI = reliable change index; BDI = Beck Depression Inventory; CDI = Children's Depression Inventory; CGI-I = Clinical Global Impressions-Improvement; CDRS-R = Children's Depression Rating Scale-Revised; MADRS = Montgomery-Asberg Depression Rating Scale; HAM-D = Hamilton Rating Scale for Depression; CES-D = Center for Epidemiologic Studies Depression Scale; NA = data not available.

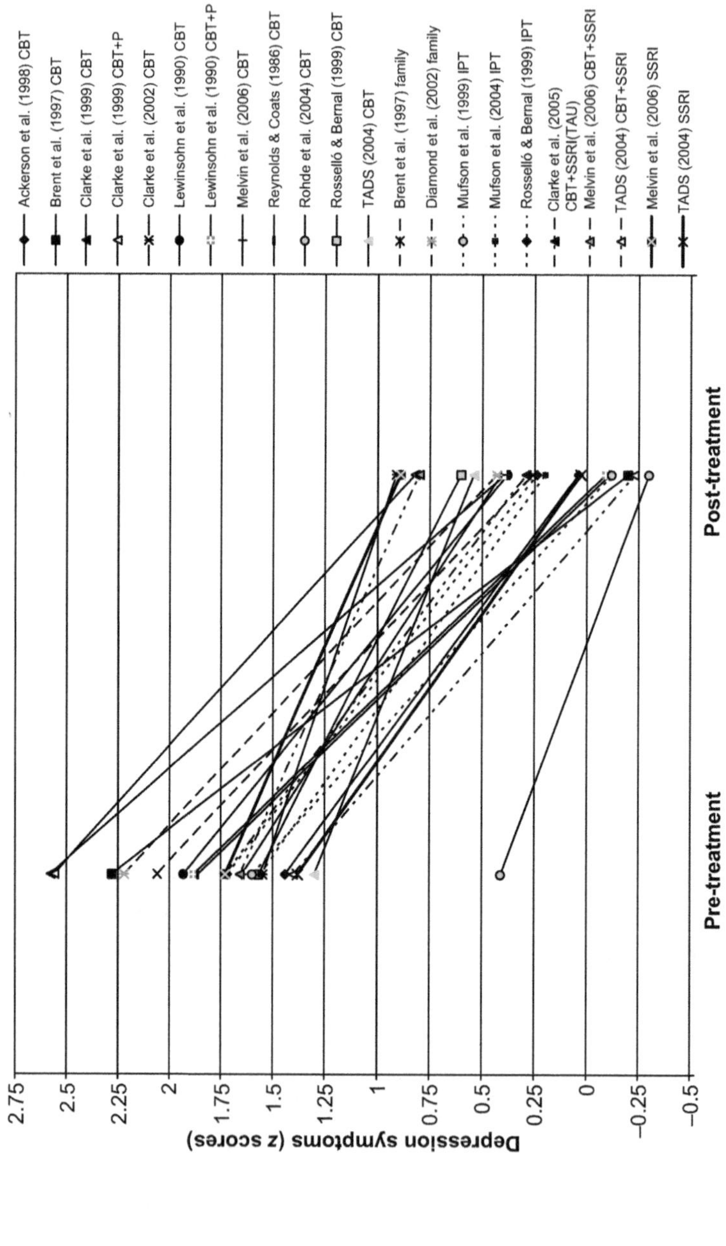

Figure 21.1 Shape of symptom change in treatment of adolescent depression.

post-treatment z scores, with a range of over a standard deviation at each time point. The symptom slope across investigations also varies notably, although all studies in the sample display a strong trend of reduction in symptoms over the course of time.

We next unpack these broad results by reviewing key findings within the treatment literature for each of the target intervention models. In this review, we begin with the foundational efficacy studies for each approach, and progress to studies with clinically complicated samples and investigations based in real-world practice settings (when available). We group these traditional "efficacy" and "effectiveness" studies together in an effort to highlight the development of specific intervention models and available data on the robustness of the treatment program.

Cognitive-Behavioral Therapy

As shown in Table 21.1, the majority of adolescent depression clinical trials are investigations of CBT. These studies differ in sample size, composition of control groups, inclusion and exclusion criteria, and specific CBT treatment programs. This last point—variability in CBT content—is perhaps the most meaningful. CBT is a family of interventions that draw on a range of cognitive and behavioral mood regulation techniques, and CBT manuals differ markedly in their inclusion of these specific elements and the dose (number of sessions) devoted to each core technique. In the development of the literature, three different "flavors" of CBT have been particularly important: (a) the Coping with Depression course (CWD-A; Lewinsohn, Clarke, Hops, & Andrews, 1990), (b) a brief CBT protocol developed in the United Kingdom (Wood, Harrington, & Moore, 1996), and (c) the Pittsburgh Cognitive Therapy program (Brent et al., 1997). These three programs serve as the source manuals for 12 of the 15 CBT clinical trials, and the two United States-based manuals (CWD-A and Pittsburgh) were combined and adapted to form the TADS CBT manual. We review the empirical findings associated with these three core manuals before turning to a discussion of TADS.

Coping With Depression (CWD-A)

More than half (8/15) of published CBT studies for adolescent depression have used CWD-A as the basis for their intervention programs. As with many CBT programs, CWD-A began as a skills group for depressed adults and was adapted to be more developmentally appropriate for adolescents (e.g., by including cartoon examples for cognitive restructuring). CWD-A is designed to be a comprehensive program including a wide range of CBT techniques, such as psychoeducation, pleasant activity scheduling, social skills training, problem-solving training, relaxation, and cognitive restructuring. The treatment is a didactic group therapy "course" with structured activities, a teen workbook, and standardized in-class exercises and homework assignments to practice skills (Clarke, DeBar, & Lewinsohn, 2003).

In an attempt to map onto the developmental needs of adolescents, a CWD-A parent curriculum was also created and tested in early clinical trials. The focus of this curriculum appears to be treatment support and teaching the general skills reviewed in youth sessions, rather than an attempt at family therapy or direct treatment of depression in parents who may also be suffering from a concurrent mood disorder. In the first randomized CWD-A investigation by Lewinsohn and colleagues (Lewinsohn et al., 1990), the CBT plus the enhanced parent program (CBT+P) was compared against teen-only CWD-A and a wait list. While the two CBT conditions outperformed the wait list, the extra parent sessions did not significantly improve treatment response. In an enhanced replication of the Lewinsohn study, Clarke, Rohde, Lewinsohn, Hops, and Seeley (1999) found very similar results. CWD-A with and without parent sessions reduced depression significantly more than wait list at post-intervention and follow-up (see Table 21.1), but addition of parent sessions did not improve the effects of teen-only group CBT. In this trial, booster sessions were provided after the termination of the acute treatment phase, although they were poorly attended by teens. These booster sessions did not reduce the rate of depression recurrence for those who had remitted by the end of treatment, but booster sessions did appear to assist teens that had not yet recovered from depression at the end of the acute treatment phase.

Given the general success of the program, CWD-A has been adapted for samples of clinically complicated depressed youth, including adolescents with comorbid major depression and conduct disorder (Rohde, Clarke, Mace, Jorgensen, & Seeley, 2004) and depressed adolescent offspring of parents who are themselves currently depressed (Clarke et al., 2002). In general, the intervention has been less efficacious in these extensions. In the comorbid sample, the NNT ratio in favor of CBT was very good (5), but the absolute response rate in the intervention group was substantially lower (39%) than in previous CWD-A studies in pure depression samples (43–69%). Furthermore, significant differences between treatment and control did not persist at 6- or 12-month follow-up. In a similar vein, CWD-A fared poorly in the depressed offspring sample. While the NNT ratio in the original trials were all less than 10, in the offspring sample, 20 youths would need to be treated with CBT in order to see one recovery more than in the control condition. Statistically, CWD-A did not separate from the control condition on any measure of depression outcome in the sample with depressed parents.

On the other end of the severity spectrum, CWD-A has been shortened for the purpose of treating mild to moderately depressed teens seen for services in primary care. In the larger of these two investigations, youths with high symptoms of depression were screened and randomized to either primary care treatment as usual (TAU) or a quality improvement arm that included access to CBT (short CWD-A) and/or medication management (Asarnow et al., 2005). Overall, youths randomized to the arm with access to CBT demonstrated better outcomes over time than TAU teens, and adolescents reported preferring (and used more) CBT services than other intervention options, such as medication. However, another primary care study did not demonstrate significant benefit for a CWD-A-based primary care manual (Clarke et al., 2005). In this study youths receiving SSRI treatment in pediatric primary care were randomized to continue with treatment as usual (TAU SSRI) or to receive cognitive-behavioral treatment (CWD-A) adjunctive to their TAU SSRI medication management. Depressed adolescents who received standard antidepressant medication management had outcomes equivalent to youths whose SSRI care was supplemented by participation in CWD-A . Of note, depressed teens in the CWD-A condition reduced their use of antidepressants by 20% over the course of this study, a result that complicates interpretation of the "no difference" outcome between the two arms.

Brief CBT

Three trials in the United Kingdom have examined the effects of a set of similar, very brief CBT protocols. Vostanis and colleagues (Vostanis, Feehan, & Grattan, 1998; Vostanis, Feehan, Grattan, & Bickerton, 1996a; Vostanis, Feehan, Grattan, & Bickerton, 1996b) compared three to five sessions of CBT to a supportive therapy control in a sample of depressed teen outpatients. There were no statistically significant differences between the treatment groups in depression response (86% vs. 75%) despite a NNT of 9 in favor of CBT. In contrast to the Vostanis results, Wood et al. (1996) found a similar brief CBT program to be superior to relaxation therapy for adolescent outpatients across multiple indices, with an impressive NNT of 3. Over follow-up, the two treatment groups in the Wood trial converged due to continued improvement in the relaxation group and relapse in the CBT group. The addition of CBT booster sessions after acute treatment appeared to result in a much lower relapse rate than acute treatment alone, compared to a historical control condition (20% vs. 50%; Kroll et al., 1996).

In the final brief CBT investigation, the Wood program was adapted for use in general outpatient clinical settings and taught to Masters-level therapists in the United Kingdom. This CBT effectiveness study suffered from many methodological limitations including difficulty recruiting social workers, difficulty recruiting depressed teens, and youth attrition from treatment. Under these conditions, the outcomes of CBT and usual case management services did not differ significantly (Kerfoot, Harrington, Harrington, Rogers, & Verduyn, 2004), and the CBT NNT ratio was very high (33). It is interesting to note that the therapists in this study reported high satisfaction with CBT training, despite difficulty recruiting therapists into the trial and poor outcomes for youths within the trial.

The Pittsburgh Cognitive Therapy Study

The final, seminal CBT program in the adolescent literature is the cognitive therapy program developed and tested by the Pittsburgh depression research group (Brent et al., 1997). The dose of CBT in the Pittsburgh manual was the same as CWD-A (16 sessions); however, the structure of the Pittsburgh program was significantly more flexible. The treatment was individual (versus group) therapy, driven by a classic Beckian cognitive case conceptualization with no pre-set exercises or homework assignments (see Brent et al., 1996, for case examples). Content of the intervention focused primarily on cognitive restructuring with use of behavioral activation and problem-solving skills as deemed clinically necessary (Weersing & Brent, 2003).

In the 1997 clinical trial of the protocol, adolescents with major depression were randomly assigned to CBT, family therapy, or a supportive therapy control. The majority of teens were recruited from clinical settings (including discharge from inpatient care), and the sample appears to have been significantly depressed with a high rate of current suicidal ideation and past attempt. At post-treatment, significantly more teens receiving CBT than supportive therapy no longer met diagnostic criteria for major depression (Brent et al., 1997), and full remission of depression was also more common in CBT (60%) than in either family (38%) or supportive (39%) therapy, translating to a very favorable NNT ratio of 5. By 2-year follow-up, depression remission and recovery rates between the three treatments were no longer significantly different

(Birmaher et al., 2000), although the descriptive data again favored CBT (94% in remission) over family (77%) and supportive (74%) therapy (Weersing & Brent, 2003), and the NNT ratio remained constant over time.

While there have been no formal replications of the Brent findings, the treatment program has served as the model for an outpatient depression clinical service in Pittsburgh for the last decade. Archival medical records data from this clinic revealed that youths treated with CBT had outcomes similar to teens enrolled in the clinical trial, when controlling for baseline differences in the two samples (Weersing, Iyengar, Kolko, Birmaher, & Brent, 2006). These data serve as a partial replication of effects, and also speak to the potential effectiveness of CBT in settings and samples of youth less rarefied than clinical trials (e.g., youths with severe comorbid diagnoses, such as substance abuse and eating disorders, youths referred from inpatient units post-suicide attempt).

TADS

As discussed in the introduction, the picture of CBT effects was redrawn in 2004 with the publication of the TADS trial (TADS, 2004). TADS was designed to be a well-powered test of the relative efficacy of 12 weeks of treatment with fluoxetine, CBT, and their combination in treating serious depression in adolescents. As with most randomized clinical trials, an independent evaluator blind to treatment conditions rated adolescent outcomes. While adolescents in the medication-only group were blind to whether they were receiving active fluoxetine or placebo control, those receiving combination treatment were aware that they were receiving both forms of active treatment.

The TADS CBT intervention manual was created by combining elements of CWD-A, aspects of the Pittsburgh cognitive therapy manual, and the investigators' expertise in CBT and family interventions for substance abuse (see Curry & Wells, 2005). The 15-session treatment was delivered in an individual format, although sessions were closely scripted with many required elements and specific homework exercises. Outside of a small number of required, core sessions (sessions 1–6), therapists and supervisors were allowed to select different treatment modules for the remaining nine sessions to map onto individual case presentations and comorbid conditions (e.g., communication training for family conflict). This approach was selected to mimic the structure and comprehensive nature of the group-based CDW-A protocol, while providing for some of the individualized case conceptualization elements of the Pittsburgh cognitive therapy model.

Overall, outcomes of TADS were not good news for CBT. Across multiple measures, CBT failed to outperform pill placebo, with an NNT of 13 on the main measure of clinically significant response. In contrast, conditions including medication—fluoxetine alone and combination treatment—showed very postive effects, with NNTs of 4 and 3, respectively, compared to placebo control. There was some evidence that participation in CBT in the combination cell may have had a weak beneficial effect in buffering youths against negative life stress and suicidal feelings compared to the fluoxetine alone condition. However, this finding may simply be due to the increased number of sessions in combination treatment, rather than reflecting a specific benefit associated with CBT.

Understanding the outcomes of the TADS investigation has been quite difficult, in part because the results appear anomalous with respect to both the CBT and the SSRI literature. The response rate for CBT reported in TADS (34%) is the lowest in the literature, save the methodologically suspect Kerfoot effectiveness study (23%). Conversely, the NNT for fluoxetine in TADS ties for highest in the antidepressant literature (see Table 21.1). It has been suggested that this pattern of findings may reflect greater depression severity in the TADS sample, and that many CBT investigations may have enrolled adolescents on the mild end of the depression spectrum (e.g., Ackerson, Scogin, McKendree-Smith, & Lyman, 1998). This argument may have some merit; however, at least one study speaks directly to this critique. The Pittsburgh cognitive therapy study sample appears to have been as severely depressed and impaired as TADS and likely more suicidal (Bridge & Brent, 2004), yet the Pittsburgh CBT response rate was 23% higher than the rate reported in TADS.

The other leading critique of the TADS results has focused on the content and quality of the CBT implementation. As discussed earlier, the TADS manual was based on two of the most well-supported manuals in the CBT literature. However, while the TADS therapy program was built on an empirically-informed base, the adapted protocol had never been tested prior to the trial, and, in essence, was a novel CBT therapy program. Commentators have questioned the investigators' success at merging the very structured, group-administered CWD-A program with the principle-driven, individual therapy manual of Pittsburgh (Hollon, Garber, & Shelton, 2005). The "flexible module" approach of TADS has also drawn comment (see Weersing & Brent, 2006). While the strategy of allowing therapists and supervisors to pick from a range of possible CBT technique modules is intuitively appealing, in application it may have led to many youths receiving a lower dose of "core" CBT techniques (e.g., cognitive restructuring) than in other protocols, with techniques less central to the CBT model of depression dominating treatment (e.g., rekindling parent-teen attachment).

At this time, additional analyses of long-term TADS effects and potential site differences in implementation of the manual modules are still ongoing. The field awaits the results of these important investigations. Regardless of the outcome of these studies, the data from TADS provide an important caveat to the efficacy of CBT and will likely inform the psychotherapy research agenda in adolescent depression for years to come.

Pharmacotherapy

The outcomes of the TADS study provided critical empirical support for the use of SSRIs in depressed adolescents at a time when the safety of antidepressants was under serious question. Historically, RCTs of antidepressants in children and adolescents reported mixed outcomes at best. Studies of tricyclic antidepressants found little to no effects of these agents in youth (for review, see Moreno, Roche, & Greenhill, 2006), and the first antidepressant trial with a positive outcome in adolescents did not appear until the late 1990s (Emslie et al., 1997). Following the publication of this first successful trial of fluoxetine, further positive data on the efficacy of fluoxetine emerged in the literature (Emslie et al., 2002), followed by clinical trials for paroxetine (Keller et al., 2001) and sertraline (Wagner et al., 2003), producing results that are more difficult to interpret (e.g., disagreement over definitions of clinical response and need to pool studies to increase power, respectively). This developing empirical base grew alongside a dramatic upsurge in off-label use of SSRIs in youth, with antidepressant prescription rates rising 200% from the late 1980s through the late 1990s (Olfson, Marcus, Weissman, & Jensen, 2002; Zito et al., 2002).

Suicidality in SSRI Treatment

Against this backdrop, there has been growing public, scientific, and regulatory scrutiny of the SSRI side-effect profile, particularly reports of increased suicidality in children and adolescents undergoing antidepressant treatment. These concerns were first acted on in the United Kingdom, with a review of evidence leading to a restriction in SSRI use for all agents except fluoxetine, and with the recommendation that nonpharmacological interventions be used as a first choice treatment for depression in youth (National Institute for Health and Clinical Excellence, 2005). The Food and Drug Administration (FDA) in the United States followed with public hearings and a commissioned meta-analysis of adverse events in antidepressant treatment across all youth diagnostic groups (i.e., including anxiety disorders) in all published and unpublished antidepressant data. Notably, there were no completed suicides in the published or unpublished SSRI data sets; however, the FDA meta-analysis did find a higher rate of spontaneously reported, "suicide-related" adverse events (4% vs. 2%; Hammad, Laughren, & Racoosin, 2006, such as increased suicidal ideation, self-injury, formation of a plan, or suicide attempt. As a result, these proceedings led to a black box warning label on antidepressants use in youth and, more recently, in young adults (U.S. FDA, 2007).

The FDA black box warning was implemented before the TADS data were published, and the addition of the TADS sample to the literature more than doubled the number of youths enrolled in clinical trials of fluoxetine (from 355 to 794). In addition, since the publication of TADS, two additional clinical trials of paroxetine (Berard, Fong, Carpenter, Thomason, & Wilkinson, 2006; Emslie et al., 2006), two trials of citalopram (von Knorring, Olsson, Thomsen, Lemming, & Hultén, 2006; Wagner et al., 2004), and one trial of escitalopram (Wagner, Jonas, Findling, Ventura, & Saikali, 2006) have been published. Results of these studies have continued to be mixed, with studies of fluoxetine generally reporting good separation of drug from placebo, but trials of other agents producing more inconclusive results, as mentioned previously.

Bridge and colleagues recently published a meta-analysis including all of these new clinical trials as well as unpublished industry data and found that antidepressants were generally efficacious for the treatment of depression and anxiety in children and adolescents (Bridge et al., 2007). Across all investigations, the average response rate for antidepressants was 60% compared to 49% for placebo, leading to an NNT of 9 (Bridge et al., 2007). Outcomes were better for anxiety than for depression and for adolescents than children. The authors also coded and calculated suicide-related adverse events rates in all extant data and found that 2.5% of youths in antidepressant treatment met criteria for increased suicidality versus 1.7% of youths in placebo conditions, with rates higher in depressed samples than anxious samples. This "suicide signal" was statistically significant, but, notably, the number needed to *harm* (NNH) based on these data is 125, and the ratio of youths helped by SSRIs (NNT = 9) compared to those who become suicidal (NNH = 125) is approximately 14:1 (Bridge et al., 2007).

Furthermore, the clinical significance of these "suicide-related" adverse events are unclear. Almost all were increased suicidal ideation, with very few attempts and no completions (see e.g., Hammad, Laughren, & Racoosin, 2006). Moreover, adolescent suicide rate has declined over the past decade, as the rates of SSRI use have been dramatically increasing in the population. Pharmacoepidemiological studies find a relationship between increased prescription and sales of SSRIs by county and a decline in completed suicides, which is particularly strong among youth (see e.g., Olfson, Gameroff, Marcus, & Waslick, 2003).

Fluoxetine

Taken together, these data on efficacy and safety suggest that fluoxetine is a well-supported treatment for adolescent depression with an acceptable risk-benefit profile. Data on other SSRIs are much weaker; consequently, fluoxetine is the only antidepressant to receive FDA and Medicine and Healthcare Products Regulatory Agency (MHRA) approval for the treatment of depression in children and adolescents. As summarized in Table 21.1, in three published studies of fluoxetine, a higher proportion of those treated with fluoxetine were "much or very much improved" compared to those treated with placebo, with a NNT ranging from 4 to 9 (Emslie et al., 2002; Emslie et al., 1997; March, 2004). One early study of fluoxetine did not show statically significant results, and this investigation did not provide sufficient data for the calculation of an NNT ratio (Simeon, Dinicola, Ferguson, & Copping, 1990).

Combination Treatments

As described in our discussion of the TADS CBT results, it has been suggested that the combination of CBT and fluoxetine may provide the greatest benefit to adolescents with moderate to severe depression. The combination cell had the highest rates of clinical response (71%) in the trial, and combination was superior to fluoxetine alone in producing depression remission (37% vs. 20%; Kennard et al., 2006). The TADS team has suggested that combination treatment may also help buffer adolescents against any possible increases in suicidality associated with SSRI use, although this effect in TADS may simply be due to the increased number of sessions in combination treatment, rather than resulting from specific elements of CBT.

Data from two additional clinical trials bear on the question of the acceptability and efficiency of combination treatment. As discussed in the review of CBT, the CDW-A program has been adapted by multiple investigative teams as a primary care treatment intervention. In the Clarke et al. (2005) trial, the addition of CDW-A to primary care-based prescription of SSRIs did not improve depression treatment response. Although the CDW-A program was specifically designed to support medication treatment, teens in the CBT arm significantly reduced their medication use over the course of the trial. The primary care quality improvement investigation by Asarnow and colleagues had a similar finding. In this trial, adolescents with likely diagnoses of major depression were randomly assigned to primary care TAU or a quality improvement intervention that included access to CBT, SSRIs, or a combination of both. In these circumstances, adolescents predominantly chose CBT as their main treatment option (Asarnow et al., 2005). These data are in accordance with community and provider surveys indicating a reluctance to employ antidepressant or combination care for youths, and a preference for psychosocial interventions as a front-line treatment for depression (e.g., Wisdom, Clarke, & Green, in press).

Interpersonal Psychotherapy

We next turn to a less-researched, but promising area of psychosocial intervention—interpersonal psychotherapy for depression. Thus far, there have been three randomized trials examining the efficacy (Mufson, Weissman, Moreau, & Garfinkel, 1999; Roselló & Bernal, 1999) or effectiveness (Mufson et al., 2004) of IPT for depressed adolescents. Two teams of investigators created developmentally appropriate treatment manuals adapted from an original IPT adult manual developed by Klerman, Weissman, Rounsaville, and Chevron (1984). To examine the efficacy of their intervention, Mufson and colleagues (1999) randomized clinic-referred depressed adolescents to 12 weeks of IPT or to clinical monitoring (once a month review of depression symptoms and functioning). As can be seen in Table 21.1, 75% of youth receiving IPT met clinician-rated recovery criteria compared to 46% of youth assigned to clinical monitoring, producing a very promising NNT of 3. Due in part to high attrition among youth receiving clinical monitoring (54%), follow-up data were not available. To address this issue, Mufson et al. conducted intent-to-treat analyses for the dimensional symptom measures. Even after carrying the last score forward, the data support the superiority of IPT to clinical monitoring in reducing symptoms of depression in adolescents.

Results of the Rosselló and Bernal (1999) trial provide independent replication of these positive IPT findings. The IPT treatment protocol developed by Rosselló and Bernal (1999) included relevant cultural and developmental adaptations for use with an adolescent population living in Puerto Rico. In this trial, the investigators randomized Puerto Rican teenagers with diagnosable depression to 12 weeks of IPT, CBT, or wait list control. At post-treatment, 82% of the youths receiving IPT for depression reported clinically significant change (moving them from the clinical to normative range on a youth self-report measure) compared with 59% of those youth receiving CBT. This difference was not statistically significant. Insufficient data were reported to calculate the NNT ratio, and this study had substantial attrition rates and rates of out-of-protocol use of other treatment services (e.g., 48% of those receiving IPT).

Having demonstrated the efficacy of IPT in controlled settings, Mufson et al. (2004) transported their treatment protocol to school-based mental health clinics to examine the effectiveness of the intervention. The treatment was delivered to depressed students by school counseling staff who were randomly assigned to receive IPT training or to continue TAU. At post-treatment, 50% of youth randomized to receive IPT compared to 34% receiving school TAU, met the recovery criterion (see Table 21.1). In addition, youth receiving IPT showed faster improvement of depression symptoms and greater improvement in overall functioning. Attrition rates in this study were low (11% of total sample) and IPT treatment gains were maintained at 1-month follow-up. Although the recovery rate in this trial is lower than those reported in the efficacy trials conducted by Mufson and colleagues (1999, 2004), these results are within the range of effects reported across the IPT and CBT literature (see Figure 21.1), and the NNT of 6 is still well above the guideline for acceptable treatments (see Table 21.1).

As a whole, data from these three trials strongly suggest that IPT may be an effective treatment for depressed adolescents, especially compared to no treatment, wait list, and school counseling. The effectiveness of IPT compared with active interventions, such as CBT or SSRI, remains uncertain, and data representing the maintenance of clinical gains at follow-up are almost nonexistent.

CORE PROCESSES AND MECHANISMS IN TREATMENT

In this section, we move from broad questions of efficacy and effectiveness to an examination of the processes underlying treatment effects. This section focuses on the two psychosocial interventions for depressed teens, CBT and IPT. As will be seen in our review, the psychotherapy process literature is quite sparse—across all investigations of CBT and IPT, only three CBT investigations formally test whether change in cognitive, behavioral, or interpersonal process variables accounts for differences in treatment outcome. However, while formal tests of mediation are rare, many of the CBT and IPT therapy studies contain findings relevant to the question of treatment mechanism. It is common for investigations of CBT to include cognitive change measures as outcomes, and all published studies of IPT assess change in social adaptation as a function of treatment. These outcome-focused investigations do not provide critical data on the timing of change in potential mediators; logically, for a mediator to produce an outcome, change in the mediator must happen first (see e.g., Kazdin & Nock, 2003; Weersing & Weisz, 2002). However, these RCTs can demonstrate whether there is specificity in processes—for example, that CBT has a larger impact on cognitive change than control conditions—and serve as a useful first step in understanding mechanisms of treatment action.

To aid in our summary of these effects, we reviewed each measure in every clinical trial for CBT or IPT and coded whether these measures assessed depression outcomes, cognitive processes (e.g., negative self-talk), behavioral skills (e.g., pleasant activity scheduling), or interpersonal functioning (e.g., quality of friendships). We then computed unadjusted effect sizes[4] for youth self-reported depression symptoms and for the three classes of process variables. Figure 21.2 displays the mean effect sizes by each domain for CBT and IPT. Note that these effect sizes are presented for illustrative rather than inferential purposes. Many of the effect size "means" are single effect sizes drawn from a single clinical trial, and some process areas have not been investigated at all (e.g., behavioral self-regulation in IPT). Effect size data are intended to provide a descriptive rubric for discussing the size and strength of relationships rather than simply relying on counts of statistically significant effects across studies, particularly given the dramatic differences in sample size and power across the body of psychotherapy clinical trials (total *n (STET)* ranging from 22 to 439, see Table 21.1).

Cognitive-Behavioral Therapy

Cognitive Processes

As can be seen in Figure 21.2, on average, CBT produced greater change on measures of depressogenic cognitions than did comparison conditions, with a cognitive process effect size nearly equal to the impact of CBT on depression symptoms (0.44 vs. 0.49). Following treatment, depressed youth reported a

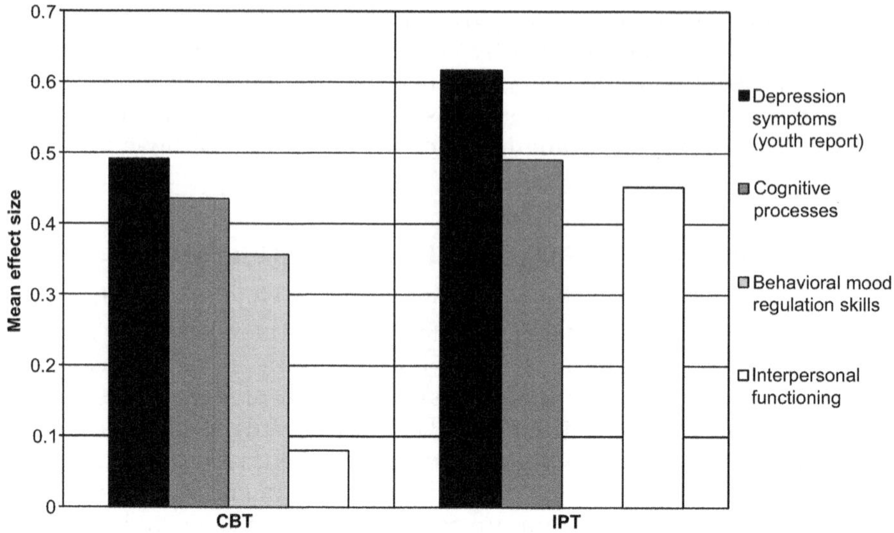

Figure 21.2 Effects of CBT and IPT on depression symptoms and potential mediating processes.

more positive view of themselves, had a less hopeless view of their futures, and formed more benign explanations for the negative events in their lives. Three investigations formally tested whether this change in cognitions mediated the impact of CBT on depression: (a) a reanalysis of the Brent et al. (1997) clinical trial of the Pittsburgh cognitive therapy model by Kolko, Brent, Baugher, Bridge, and Birmaher (2000); (b) the Ackerson et al. (1998) trial of cognitive bibliotherapy for teens with mild depression; and (c) a paper by Kaufman, Rohde, Seeley, Clarke, and Stice (2005) examining the process and outcome of CWD-A adapted for youths with depression and comorbid conduct problems (Rohde et al., 2004).

In the original Brent clinical trial (1997), CBT for depressed adolescents was compared to family and supportive therapy, and CBT was found to be more efficacious than these alternate treatments on multiple measures of depression, including indices of clinically significant change. Kolko et al. (2000) investigated the mediating role of several cognitive and family process variables in producing these treatment effects. Data were available on symptom and process change at midpoint of treatment as well as at outcome, aiding in the interpretation of any possible mediating effects. As hypothesized, CBT did have a significantly greater effect on cognitive distortions, but CBT was not superior to alternate interventions in changing the specific cognitions of hopelessness. In addition, Kolko and colleagues were not able to demonstrate that change in cognitive distortion mediated the effect of CBT on depression symptoms, although low power may have limited their ability to find significant effects (e.g., the subsample youth with complete data did not even show a significant effect of the intervention on depression symptoms).

Stronger support for the role of specific, cognitive change in CBT outcome comes from an investigation of a CBT bibliotherapy program for depressed teens. Ackerson et al. (1998) found that youths who were given a CBT self-help book demonstrated a reduction in depression symptoms 4 weeks later (youth self-report ES = 1.23). Teens also had a significant reduction in depressogenic thinking as assessed by the Dysfunctional Attitudes Scale (DAS ES = 2.13), but they did not show significant change in negative automatic thoughts, as assessed with the Automatic Thoughts Questionnaire (ATQ) despite a positive effect size in favor of CBT (ES = 0.69). Change in dysfunctional attitudes did mediate the effects of the intervention on youth-reported depression symptoms, but the conditions for mediation were not met for other measures of depression (i.e., interviewer ratings). Again, power may have been a limiting factor in this investigation, as cell sizes were below 15 and only the largest effects demonstrated statistical significance.

In the Kaufman reanalysis of the Rohde et al. (2004) trial, CBT was also found to significantly impact one cognitive process measure, and change in cognitions did statistically mediate program effects on depression symptoms (all constructs were measured post-treatment). However, effects were inconsistent across measures of cognition, and the specific pattern of findings was opposite to that of Ackerson—significant effects on the ATQ (ES = 0.19) and nonsignificant results for the DAS (ES = −0.10).

Behavioral Processes

Three studies assessed behavioral mechanisms of CBT effects. Lewinsohn et al. (1990) measured the frequency and enjoyment of pleasant activities before and after CBT. As targeted in the CDW-A intervention, CBT beneficially impacted pleasant activities, although insufficient data were provided in the published report to allow for effect size computation. Vostanis and colleagues reported similar, specific effects of CBT on the quality of spare time activities (ES = 0.38), and quality of spare time predicted level of depression over follow-up (Vostanis et al., 1998; Vostanis et al., 1996a, 1996b). Kaufman et al. (2005) created "face valid" subscales from the Pleasant Events Schedule to capture engagement in relaxing activities and other behavioral activation tasks. Participants in CBT did not improve more from pre- to post-treatment than youth in the control group, although post-treatment effect sizes favored CBT (effect sizes of 0.48 and 0.21).

Interpersonal Processes

Five CBT clinical trials examined the role of social skills and interpersonal adaptation in depression recovery. Evidence on the effects of CBT are mixed, with one study reporting improved social skills and functioning after CBT, but no differential effects on depression (Vostanis et al., 1996a), three investigations indicating that CBT did produce positive effects on depression, but did *not* outperform comparison conditions on social skills and peer adaptation (Kaufman et al., 2005; Rosselló & Bernal, 1999; Wood et al., 1996), and one trial suggesting that CBT was as effective as family therapy at improving family relationships (Kolko et al., 2000). As discussed previously, only the Kolko paper assessed the possible mediating role of interpersonal processes in CBT effects, and evidence for mediation was not found.

Interpersonal Psychotherapy

Cognitive Processes

Although IPT-A targets interpersonal processes over cognitive change, several studies did include measures of depressogenic cognitive style. These cognitive measures may be useful in examining the validity of mechanism findings. Logically, interpersonal therapies should not affect cognitive measures better than wait list conditions, and they should produce significantly inferior effects than CBT.

Although the effect size was small (0.15), Rosselló and Bernal (1999) found that IPT-A was significantly superior to wait list in improving youths' self-concepts and was equivalent in effect to CBT. Mufson and colleagues (1999) assessed change in specific social problem-solving skills—a cognitive process closely tied to tasks of IPT-A. Adolescents who participated in IPT-A showed significant improvements, relative to wait list, on several subscales of the social problem-solving measure. At post-treatment, teens were able to generate multiple solutions to problem situations, and engage in solution implementation and verification. Youth did not change significantly on their overall problem solving orientation (negative problem orientation, impulsivity/carelessness, or avoidance). Unfortunately, descriptive statistics were not provided on this measure, and effect sizes could not be computed.

Behavioral Processes

None of the investigations of IPT included measures of behavioral change processes, such as participation in pleasant and meaningful activities.

Interpersonal Processes

In contrast, all of the IPT RCTs included interpersonal process measures, and IPT did produce significant changes in youths' self-reported social functioning relative to wait list (Mufson et al., 1999), CBT (Rosselló & Bernal, 1999), and school counseling services (Mufson et al., 2004). As with cognitive change in CBT, the specific interpersonal domains that demonstrated statistically significant improvement varied across the three studies. However, across investigations, IPT appeared to show the most consistently positive effects on dating relationships, and the most variable effects on family functioning and relationships (ES ranging from −0.30 to 0.33). Mediation was not assessed in any of these investigations.

PREDICTORS AND MODERATORS OF OUTCOME

We turn next to an examination of predictors and moderators of treatment response. There has been only one investigation of treatment predictors in IPT-A (Young, Mufson, & Davies, 2006), and a follow-up to the TADS study (Curry et al., 2006) provides the only pharmacotherapy predictor data within a randomized design. As a result, our review is heavily focused on CBT trials, and the majority of these studies compare CBT to an inactive control condition, such as a wait list. The significant predictor variables uncovered in our review may, therefore, be predictors of response to CBT or could predict response to intervention for adolescent depression in general. Where there are data indicating differential response to one form of intervention—that is, evidence of treatment moderation—we highlight these findings. We cluster our discussion of predictors and moderators into three main categories of severity, comorbidity, and family context.

Severity of Depression

A range of severity indices has been related to poor outcomes of intervention for depression in adolescents. Greater severity of symptoms at intake (Birmaher et al., 2000; Brent et al., 1998; Clarke, Hops, Lewinsohn, & Andrews, 1992), greater chronicity and earlier age of first depression onset (Curry et al., 2006; Rohde et al., 2001), poor functioning at intake (Curry et al., 2006; Jayson, Wood, Kroll, Fraser, & Harrington, 1998; Rohde et al., 2006), less engagement in and enjoyment of pleasant activities (Clarke et al., 1992), and more severe cognitive distortions and feelings of hopelessness (Brent et al. 1998; Clarke et al., 1992; Curry et al., 2006; Rohde et al., 2006) have predicted poor response across CBT, SSRI, combination treatment, family therapy, and supportive therapy. Of these factors, hopelessness seems particularly problematic. In addition to its negative association with post-treatment response, hopelessness predicted early removal from the Brent clinical trial (Brent et al. 1998), and hopelessness appeared to mediate the moderating effects of suicidality in that same trial. In a reanalysis of the Brent data, Barbe and colleagues (2004a) found that CBT produced significantly better outcomes than supportive therapy for depressed adolescents with current or lifetime suicidality (87% vs. 36% recovery rates), and this outcome appears to be due to CBT protocol's superior effect on reducing hopelessness, compared to supportive treatment.

Comorbidity

As discussed by Rohde (this volume), the relationship between comorbidity and depression treatment response appears to be complex, and contradictory findings have been reported in the literature. In the treatment of depressed teens, comorbid anxiety has been found to predict poor outcomes to CBT, IPT, fluoxetine and combination treatment (e.g., Clarke et al., 1992; Curry et al., 2006; Young et al., 2006), positive outcome to CBT (e.g., Rohde, Clarke, Lewinsohn, Seeley, & Kaufman, 2001), and superior outcome to CBT versus alternate interventions (treatment moderation; Brent et al., 1998). Similarly, comorbid disruptive behavior problems have been unrelated to outcome in some samples (Clarke et al., 1992), and predictive of poor treatment response in other studies (Rohde et al., 2001; Rohde et al., 2006). The effects of major depression comorbid with dysthymia also have been unclear (cf. Brent et al., 1998; Clarke et al., 1992).

Family Environment and Parental Depression

Aspects of the family environment also appear to impact on depression treatment outcome. Across treatment types, parent-child conflict was associated with depression recurrence over follow-up in the Brent RCT sample (Birmaher et al., 2000). However, conflict was not a significant predictor or moderator in the TADS study (Curry et al., 2006), and cohesion was unrelated to outcome in the families of youths with comorbid depression and conduct disorder (Rohde et al., 2006). In contrast, higher family income (greater than $75,000 per year) moderated treatment effects such that youths from high income family did as well in CBT as in the combination treatment of CBT + fluoxetine (Curry et al., 2006).

Parental depression also predicted poor outcome in several CBT trials (Clarke et al., 1992; Jayson et al., 1998), although this effect was not found in the TADS investigation (Curry et al., 2006) or the Rohde et al. (2004) treatment trial with comorbid youths (Rohde et al., 2006). Presence of parental depression did eliminate the significant difference favoring CBT over family and supportive therapies in the Brent study (1998). In addition, familial depression may account for the poor outcome of the Clarke et al. (2002) investigation, in which the generally successful CDW-A program did not outperform a usual care control condition. The Clarke sample in this study was composed entirely of depressed youths who also had one or more parents with a history of affective illness.

CONCLUSIONS AND FUTURE DIRECTIONS

In sum, the adolescent depression treatment literature provides both reason for hope and cause for concern. The three leading interventions for depressed adolescents—CBT, SSRI, and IPT—have all demonstrated efficacy in replicated clinical trials, with response rates in some studies ranging as high as 90% (e.g., Lewinsohn et al., 1990). However, while there is evidence that these interventions *can* work well, there are also data to suggest that these treatments frequently do not work well and that they may perform poorly in the groups of adolescents most in need of intervention.

Response rates and NNT ratios range dramatically across the literature, as do definitions of what constitutes a good clinical response. When adopting the most stringent criteria for depression recovery, results of even the best clinical trials are sobering—for example, *response* to combination treatment in TADS was over 70% at post-treatment; but only 37% of youths met criteria for *remission* of depression symptoms (Kennard et al., 2006). Questions about the safety of antidepressant treatment raise additional concern. In a recent meta-analysis, the benefit to risk ratio for antidepressant medication in youth was estimated as 14:1 in favor of treatment (Bridge et al., 2007). However, this meta-analysis relied upon the weaker definition of "response" employed by clinical trials in weighing these risks, and the ratio of healing to harm would certainly shift should more stringent outcome criteria of remission or recovery be used in clinical trials. Furthermore, adolescents who suffer the most symptomatic and functional impairment may reap the least benefit of our treatment. Severity of depression, presence of comorbid psychiatric conditions, family adversity and conflict, and parental depression history have all been identified as predictors of poor treatment response.

As might be predicted from this list of negative treatment indicators, data on the effectiveness of these interventions in real-world clinical practice settings and samples is mixed. In our review, we identified five investigations that examined the effects of evidence-based treatment for adolescent depression delivered under conditions approximating active clinical service. Four of the five focused on disseminating CBT to health care systems, either testing the effects of CBT alone (Kerfoot et al., 2004) or CBT delivered with the option of adjunctive SSRI treatment (Asarnow et al., 2005; Clarke et al., 2005; Weersing et al., 2006). Two of these four studies did not find that the addition of CBT improved on the typical package of services available for depressed youths in their settings (Clarke et al., 2005; Kerfoot et al., 2004. Furthermore, data from the positive CBT effectiveness studies do not provide a ringing endorsement on the effectiveness of CBT in practice. In a quasi-experimental study, Weersing and colleagues (2006) found that CBT delivered as part of the regular services of an outpatient tertiary care clinic had outcomes very similar to clinical trials of CBT, adjusting for differences between samples enrolled in clinical trials versus clinical practice. In our view, these findings have two implications. First, these data do suggest that the clinical trial literature on the efficacy of CBT is relevant to practice. However, the second implication is that the samples enrolled in most efficacy studies may be easier to treat than the population of youths typically encountered in active practice. Again, these results are concordant with "efficacy" findings on poor treatment response for clinically complicated youths from adverse environments.

Taken together, these data on treatment response and effectiveness in practice suggest the need to develop strong, more robust interventions for depressed adolescents. This treatment development process is hampered, however, by a limited understanding of the mechanisms of action and core processes of currently available interventions. Cognitive change appears to be associated with response to CBT, but the data supporting this link are far from definitive. Patterns of results vary across measures and reverse across studies, and statistical mediation has only been demonstrated in two clinical trials—both of which measured cognitive change as a simple post-treatment outcome. Similarly, IPT seems to have significant impact on interpersonal functioning and social skills, but these potential treatment processes have yet to be probed in a single mediation study. Understanding the active ingredients of combination treatments suffers from a similar level of uncertainty. For example, it is an open question whether the "protective" effect of CBT on suicide-related adverse events associated with fluoxetine is a function of specific elements of CBT treatment, or epiphenomenal to the increased dose of intervention in the TADS combination condition. Without solid data to address these core questions of process, it is difficult to programmatically refine interventions into more efficient forms.

Future treatment development might also be enhanced by greater attention to development itself. The three best supported interventions for adolescent depression are direct translations from the adult depression treatment literature. Adolescents differ from adults in physical, cognitive, and emotional maturity, and with minor exceptions, they are still subject to the care and authority of parents (for discussion, see Weisz & Weersing, 1999). The families of depressed youth suffer from serious parental psychopathology, chaotic life circumstances, and harsh parenting practices (Hammen, Rudolph, Weisz, Rao, & Burge, 1999). Parental depression is the strongest single predictor of depression in adolescents (Beardslee, Versage, & Gladstone, 1998), and remission of maternal depression is correlated with reductions in children's symptoms and diagnoses (Weissman et al., 2006). The field seems ripe for the development and investigation of conjoint or sequenced treatment for depressed parents and teens, as well as other interventions that address the very stressful and negative life context of depressed adolescents.

Similar arguments may be used to support the need for additional work in early intervention and depression prevention (as discussed by McLaughlin, this volume). Given data that severity and chronicity are associated with poor response across depression treatments, it may be efficient to target public health efforts at adolescents earlier in the trajectory of disorder. Intervening with youths in the mild to moderate range of depression also may allow for the use of more acceptable interventions for youth and families. As discussed in our review of combination treatments, many teens and families are unwilling to initiate a course of antidepressant treatment, despite positive efficacy data, and report a preference for psychosocial interventions. Adolescent CBT trials have begun to target pediatric primary care as a potential site for such services (e.g., Asarnow et al., 2005), and the IPT group has conducted a successful effectiveness study based in school health clinics (Mufson et al., 2004). Investigations like these may serve the dual purpose of testing the impact of early intervention while also addressing key questions about the "robustness" of evidence-based treatments for adolescent depression in real-world service delivery systems.

NOTES

1. V. Robin Weersing and Araceli Gonzalez, Joint Doctoral Program in Clinical Psychology, San Diego State University and University of California at San Diego. This work was made possible by support from the William T. Grant Foundation to the first author. Many thanks to Elyse Homel and Patrick Walker for their assistance in manuscript preparation.
2. This number excludes studies that focus on children as well as adolescents, but do not report adolescent outcome data separately.
3. Study measures and normative data were as follows: Children's Depression Inventory ($\mu = 9.09$, $\sigma = 7.04$; Smucker, Craighead, Craighead, & Green, 1986); Beck Depression Inventory ($\mu = 7.17$, $\sigma = 7.50$; Roberts, Lewinsohn, & Seeley, 1991); Center for Epidemiologic Studies Depression Scale ($\mu = 16.98$, $\sigma = 10.65$; Roberts et al., 1991); Reynolds Adolescent Depression Scale ($\mu = 60.18$, $\sigma = 14.29$; Reynolds, 1986; Reynolds & Mazza, 1998). For the Mood and Feelings Questionnaire (MFQ-C; Kent, Vostanis, & Feehan, 1997), the only published psychometric data were collected in samples of child and adolescent outpatients. These outpatient samples are likely to have higher means on the MFQ-C than samples of nonclinic, community youth, leading to artificially low z scores compared to investigations that utilized a different dimensional symptom measure. Thus, we chose to exclude studies employing the MFQ-C (Vostanis et al., 1996b; Wood et al., 1996) from the figure.
4. Uncorrected Cohen's $d = (\bar{x}_c - \bar{x}_t) / S$, where $\bar{x}_c =$ mean of control group, $\bar{x}_t =$ mean of experimental group, and s_c= standard deviation of control group.

REFERENCES

Ackerson, J., Scogin, F., McKendree-Smith, N., & Lyman, R. D. (1998). Cognitive bibliotherapy for mild and moderate adolescent depressive symptomatology. *Journal of Consulting & Clinical Psychology, 66*, 685–690.

Asarnow, J. R., Jaycox, L. H., Duan, N., LaBorde, A. P., Rea, M. M., Murray, P., et al. (2005). Effectiveness of a quality improvement intervention for adolescent depression in primary care clinics: A randomized controlled trial. *Journal of the American Medical Association, 293*, 311–319.

Barbe, R. P., Bridge, J., Birhamer, B., Kolko, D., & Brent, D. A. (2004a). Suicidality and its relationship to treatment outcome in depressed adolescents. *Suicide & Life-Threatening Behavior, 34*, 44–55.

Barbe, R. P., Bridge, J. A., Birmaher, B., Kolko, D. J., & Brent, D. A. (2004b). Lifetime history of sexual abuse, clinical presentation, and outcome in a clinical trial for adolescent depression. *Journal of Clinical Psychiatry, 65*, 77–83.

Beardslee, W. R., Versage, E. M., & Gladstone, T. R. (1998). Children of affectively ill parents: A review of the past 10 years. *Journal of the American Academy of Child & Adolescent Psychiatry, 37*, 1134–1141.

Berard, R., Fong, R., Carpenter, D. J., Thomason, C., & Wilkinson, C. (2006). An international, multicenter, placebo-controlled trial of paroxetine in adolescents with major depressive disorder. *Journal of Child and Adolescent Psychopharmacology, 16*, 59–75.

Birmaher, B, Brent, D. A., Kolko, D., Baugher, M., Bridge, J., Holder, D., et al., (2000). Clinical outcome after short-term psychotherapy for adolescents with major depressive disorder. *Archives of General Psychiatry, 57(1)*, 29-36.

Brent, D. A., Holder, D., Kolko, D., Birmaher, B., Baugher, M., Roth, C., et al. (1997). A clinical psychotherapy trial for adolescent depression comparing cognitive, family, and supportive therapy. *Archives of General Psychiatry, 54*, 877–885.

Brent, D. A., Kolko, D. J., Birmaher, B., Baugher, M., Bridge, J., Roth, C., et al. (1998). Predictors of treatment efficacy in a clinical trial of three psychosocial treatments for adolescent depression. *Journal of the American Academy of Child & Adolescent Psychiatry, 37*, 906–914.

Brent, D. A., Roth, C. A., Holder, D., Kolko, D., Birmaher, B., Johnson, B., et al. (1996). Psychosocial interventions for treating adolescent suicidal depression: A comparison of three psychosocial interventions. In E. D. Hibbs & P. S. Jensen (Eds.) *Psychosocial treatments for child and adolescent disorders: Empirically based strategies for clinical practice* (pp. 187–206). Washington, DC, US: American Psychological Association.

Bridge, J. A., & Brent, D. A. (2004). Adolescents with depression [Letter to the editor]. *Journal of the American Medical Association, 292(21)*, 2578.

Bridge, J. A., Iyengar, S., Salary, C. B., Barbe, R. P., Birmaher, B., Pincus, H. A., et al. (2007). Clinical response and risk for reported suicidal ideation and suicide attempts in pediatric antidepressant treatment: A meta-analysis of randomized controlled trials. *Journal of the American Medical Association, 297*, 1683–1696.

Clarke, G., Debar, L., Lynch, F., Powell, J., Gale, J., O'Connor, E., et al. (2005). A randomized effectiveness trial of brief cognitive-behavioral therapy for depressed adolescents receiving antidepressant medication. *Journal of the American Academy of Child & Adolescent Psychiatry, 44*, 888–898.

Clarke, G., Hops, H., Lewinsohn, P. M., & Andrews, J. (1992). Cognitive-behavioral group treatment of adolescent depression: Prediction of outcome. *Behavior Therapy, 23*, 341–354.

Clarke, G. N., DeBar, L. L., & Lewinsohn, P. M. (Eds.) (2003). *Cognitive-behavioral group treatment for adolescent depression*. New York: Guilford Press.

Clarke, G. N., Hornbrook, M., Lynch, F., Polen, M., Gale, J., O'Connor, E., et al. (2002). Group cognitive-behavioral treatment for depressed adolescent offspring of depressed parents in a health maintenance organization. *Journal of the American Academy of Child & Adolescent Psychiatry, 41*, 305–313.

Clarke, G. N., Rohde, P., Lewinsohn, P. M., Hops, H., & Seeley, J. R. (1999). Cognitive-behavioral treatment of adolescent depression: Efficacy of acute group treatment and booster sessions. *Journal of the American Academy of Child & Adolescent Psychiatry, 38*, 272–279.

Curry, J., Rohde, P., Simons, A., Silva, S., Vitiello, B., Kratochvil, C., et al. (2006). Predictors and moderators of acute outcome in the treatment for adolescents with depression study (TADS). *Journal of the American Academy of Child & Adolescent Psychiatry, 45*, 1427–1439.

Curry, J. F., & Wells, K. C. (2005). Striving for effectiveness in the treatment of adolescent depression: Cognitive behavior therapy for multisite community intervention. *Cognitive and Behavioral Practice, 12*, 177–185.

Emslie, G., Wagner, K. D., Kutcher, S., Krulewicz, S., Fong, R., Carpenter, D. J., et al. (2006). Paroxetine treatment in children and adolescents with major depressive disorder: A randomized, multicenter, double-blind, placebo-controlled trial. *Journal of the American Academy of Child & Adolescent Psychiatry, 45*, 709–719.

Emslie, G. J., Heiligenstein, J. H., Wagner, K. D. M., Hoog, S. L., Ernest, D. E., Brown, E. P., et al. (2002). Fluoxetine for acute treatment of depression in children and adolescents: A placebo-controlled, randomized clinical trial. *Journal of the American Academy of Child & Adolescent Psychiatry, 41*, 1205–1215.

Emslie, G. J., Rush, J., Weinberg, W. A., Kowatch, R. A., Hughes, C. W., Carmody, T., et al. (1997). A double-blind, randomized, placebo-controlled trial of fluoxetine in children and adolescents with depression. *Archives of General Psychiatry, 54*, 1031–1037.

Guyatt, G., & Rennie, D. (2002). *Users' guide to the medical literature: A manual for evidence-based clinical practice*. Chicago, IL: AMA Press.

Hammen, C., Rudolph, K., Weisz, J., Rao, U., & Burge, D. (1999). The context of depression in clinic-referred youth: Neglected areas in treatment. *Journal of the American Academy of Child & Adolescent Psychiatry, 38*, 64–71.

Hammad, T. A., Laughren, T., & Racoosin, J. (2006). Suicidality in pediatric patients treated with antidepressant drugs. *Archives of General Psychiatry, 63*, 332–339.

Hollon, S. D., Garber, J., & Shelton, R. C. (2005). Treatment of depression in adolescents with cognitive behavior therapy and medications: A commentary on the TADS project. *Cognitive and Behavioral Practice, 12*, 149–155.

Jayson, D., Wood, A., Kroll, L., Fraser, J., & Harrington, R. (1998). Which depressed patients respond to cognitive-behavioral treatment? *Journal of the American Academy of Child & Adolescent Psychiatry, 37*, 35–39.

Kaufman, N. K., Rohde, P., Seeley, J. R., Clarke, G. N., & Stice, E. (2005). Potential mediators of cognitive-behavioral therapy for adolescents with comorbid major depression and conduct disorder. *Journal of Consulting and Clinical Psychology, 73*, 38–46.

Kazdin, A. E., & Nock, M. K. (2003). Delineating mechanisms of change in child and adolescent therapy: Methodological issues and research recommendations. *Journal of Child Psychology & Psychiatry & Allied Disciplines, 44*, 1116–1129.

Keller, M. B., Ryan, N. B., Strober, M., Klein, R. G., Kutcher, S. P., Birmaher, B., et al. (2001). Efficacy of paroxetine in the treatment of adolescent major depression: A randomized, controlled trial. *Journal of the American Academy of Child and Adolescent Psychiatry, 40(7)*, 762–772.

Kendall, P. K., & Grove, W. (1988). Normative comparisons in therapy outcome. *Behavioral Assessment, 10*, 147–158.

Kennard, B., Silva, S., Vitiello, B., Curry, J., Kratochvil, C., Simons, A., et al. (2006). Remission and residual symptoms after short-term treatment in the Treatment of Adolescents with Depression Study (TADS). *Journal of the American Academy of Child & Adolescent Psychiatry, 45*, 1404–1411.

Kent, L., Vostanis, P., & Feehan, C. (1997). Detection of major and minor depression in children and adolescents: Evaluation of the Mood and Feelings Questionnaire. *Journal of Child Psychology and Psychiatry, 38*, 565–573.

Kerfoot, M., Harrington, R., Harrington, V., Rogers, J., & Verduyn, C. (2004). A step too far? Randomized trial of cognitive-behaviour therapy delivered by social workers to depressed adolescents. *European Child and Adolescent Psychiatry, 13*, 92–99.

Klerman, G. K., Weissman, M. M., Rounsaville, B. J., & Chevron, E. S. (1984). *Interpersonal psychotherapy of depression: A brief, focused, specific strategy.* Northvale, NJ: Jason Aronson.

Kolko, D. J., Brent, D. A., Baugher, M., Bridge, J., & Birmaher, B. (2000). Cognitive and family therapies for adolescent depression: Treatment specificity, mediation, and moderation. *Journal of Consulting and Clinical Psychology, 68*, 603–614.

Kroll, L., Harrington, R., Jayson, D., Fraser, J., & Gowers, S. (1996). Pilot study of continuation cognitive-behavioral therapy for major depression in adolescent psychiatric patients. *Journal of the American Academy of Child & Adolescent Psychiatry, 35*, 1156–1161.

Lewinsohn, P. M., & Clarke, G. N. (1999). Psychosocial treatments for adolescent depression. *Clinical Psychology Review, 19*, 329–342.

Lewinsohn, P. M., Clarke, G. N., Hops, H., & Andrews, J. A. (1990). Cognitive-behavioral treatment for depressed adolescents. *Behavior Therapy, 21*, 385–401.

March, J. S. (2004). 'Fluoxetine, cognitive-behavioral therapy, and their combination for adolescents with depression: Treatment for Adolescents With Depression Study (TADS) randomized controlled trial': Reply. *Journal of the American Medical Association, 292*, 2578–2579.

Melvin, G. A., Tonge, B. J., King, N. J., Heyne, D., Gordon, M. S., & Klimkeit, E. (2006). A comparison of cognitive-behavioral therapy, sertraline, and their combination for adolescent depression. *Journal of the American Academy of Child & Adolescent Psychiatry, 45*, 1151–1161.

Moreno, C., Roche, A. M., & Greenhill, L. L. (2006). Pharmacotherapy of child and adolescent depression. *Child and Adolescent Psychiatric Clinics of North America, 15*, 977–998.

Mufson, L., Dorta, K. P., Wickramaratne, P., Nomura, Y., Olfson, M., & Myrna, M. W. (2004). A randomized effectiveness trial of interpersonal psychotherapy for depressed adolescents. *Archives of General Psychiatry, 61*, 577–584.

Mufson, L., Weissman, M. M., Moreau, D., & Garfinkel, R. (1999). Efficacy of interpersonal psychotherapy for depressed adolescents. *Archives of General Psychiatry, 56*, 573–579.

National Health and Medical Research Council. (1997). *Depression in young people: Clinical practice guidelines.* Canberra: Australian Government Publishing Service.

National Institute for Health and Clinical Excellence. (2005). *Depression in children and young people: NICE guideline*. Retrieved May 4, 2007, from http://www.nice.org.uk/pdf/word/CG028NICEguideline.doc.

Olfson, M., Gameroff, M. J., Marcus, S. C., & Waslick, B. D. (2003). Outpatient treatment of child and adolescent depression in the United States. *Archives of General Psychiatry, 60*, 1236–1242.

Olfson, M., Marcus, S. C., Weissman, M. M., & Jensen, P. S. (2002). National trends in the use of psychotropic medications by children. *Journal of the American Academy of Child & Adolescent Psychiatry, 41*, 514–521.

Reinecke, M. A., Ryan, N. E., & Dubois, D. L. (1998). Cognitive-behavioral therapy of depression and depressive symptoms during adolescence: A review and meta-analysis. *Journal for the American Academy of Child & Adolescent Psychiatry, 37*, 26–34.

Reynolds, W. (1986), *Reynolds Adolescent Depression Scale*. Odessa, FL: Psychological Assessment Resources.

Reynolds, W. M., & Coats, K. I. (1986). A comparison of cognitive-behavioral therapy and relaxation training for the treatment of depression in adolescents. *Journal of Consulting and Clinical Psychology, 54*, 653–660.

Reynolds, W. M., & Mazza, J. (1998). Reliability and validity of the Reynolds Adolescent Depression Scale with young adolescents. *Journal of School Psychology, 36*, 295–312.

Roberts, R. E., Lewinsohn, P. M., & Seeley, J. R. (1991). Screening for adolescent depression: A comparison of depression scales. *Journal of the American Academy of Child & Adolescent Psychiatry, 30*, 58–66.

Rohde, P., Clarke, G. N., Lewinsohn, P. M., Seeley, J. R., & Kaufman, N. K. (2001). Impact of comorbidity on a cognitive-behavioral group treatment for adolescent depression. *Journal of the American Academy of Child & Adolescent Psychiatry, 40*, 795–802.

Rohde, P., Clarke, G. N., Mace, D. E., Jorgensen, J. S., & Seeley, J. R. (2004). An efficacy/effectiveness study of cognitive-behavioral treatment for adolescents with comorbid major depression and conduct disorder. *Journal of the American Academy of Child & Adolescent Psychiatry, 43*, 660–668.

Rosselló, J., & Bernal, G. (1999). The efficacy of cognitive-behavioral and interpersonal treatments for depression in Puerto Rican adolescents. *Journal of Consulting and Clinical Psychology, 67*, 734–745.

Simeon, J. G., Dinicola, V. F., Ferguson, H., & Copping, W. (1990). Adolescent depression: A placebo-controlled fluoxetine treatment study and follow-up. *Progress in Neuro-Psychopharmacology and Biological Psychiatry, 14*, 791–795.

Smucker, M. R., Craighead, W. E., Craighead, L. W., & Green, B. J. (1986). Normative and reliability data for the Children's Depression Inventory. *Journal of Abnormal Child Psychology, 14*, 25–39.

TADS Team. (2004). Fluoxetine, cognitive-behavioral therapy, and their combination for adolescents with depression: Treatment for Adolescents with Depression Study (TADS) randomized controlled trial. *Journal of the American Medical Association, 292*, 807–820.

U.S. Food and Drug Administration. (2007). *Antidepressant use in children, adolescents, and adults*. Accessed May 5, 2007, from http://www.fda.gov/cder/drug/antidepressants/default.htm.

von Knorring, A., Olsson, G. I., Thomsen, P. H., Lemming, O. M., & Hultén, A. (2006). A randomized, double-blind, placebo-controlled study of citalopram in adolescents with major depressive disorder. *Journal of Clinical Psychopharmacology, 26*, 311–315.

Vostanis, P., Feehan, C., & Grattan, E. (1998). Two-year outcome of children treated for depression. *European Child and Adolescent Psychiatry, 7*, 12–18.

Vostanis, P., Feehan, C., Grattan, E., & Bickerton, W. L. (1996a). A randomised controlled out-patient trial of cognitive-behavioural treatment for children and adolescents with depression: 9-month follow-up. *Journal of Affective Disorders, 40*, 105–116.

Vostanis, P., Feehan, C., Grattan, E., & Bickerton, W. L. (1996b). Treatment for children and adolescents with depression: Lessons from a controlled trial. *Clinical Child Psychology and Psychiatry, 1*, 199–212.

Wagner, K. D., Ambrosini, P., Rynn, M., Wohlberg, C., Yang, R., Greenbaum, M. S., et al. (2003). Efficacy of sertraline in the treatment of children and adolescents with major depressive disorders. *Journal of the American Medical Association, 290*, 1033–1041.

Wagner, K. D., Jonas, J., Findling, R. L., Ventura, D., & Saikali, K. (2006). A double-blind, randomized, placebo-controlled trial of escitalopram in the treatment of pediatric depression. *Journal of the American Academy of Child & Adolescent Psychiatry, 45*, 280–288.

Wagner, K. D., Robb, A. S., Findling, R. L., Jin, J., Gutierrez, M. M., & Heydorn, W. E. (2004). A randomized, placebo-controlled trial of citalopram for the treatment of major depression in children and adolescents. *American Journal of Psychiatry, 161*, 1079–1083.

Weersing, V. R. (2005). Benchmarking the effectiveness of psychotherapy: Program evaluation as a component of evidence-based practice. *Journal of the American Academy of Child & Adolescent Psychiatry, 44*, 1058–1062.

Weersing, V. R., & Brent, D. A. (2003). Cognitive-behavioral therapy for adolescent depression: Comparative efficacy, mediation, moderation, and effectiveness. In A. E. Kazdin & J. R. Weisz (Eds.), *Evidence-based psychotherapies for children and adolescents* (pp. 135–147). New York: Guilford Press.

Weersing, V. R., & Brent, D. A. (2006). Cognitive behavioral therapy for depression in youth. *Child and Adolescent Psychiatric Clinics of North America, 15*, 939–957.

Weersing, V. R., Iyengar, S., Kolko, D. J., Birmaher, B., & Brent, D. A. (2006). Effectiveness of cognitive-behavioral therapy for adolescent depression: A benchmarking investigation. *Behavior Therapy, 37*, 36–48.

Weersing, V. R., & Weisz, J. R. (2002). Mechanisms of action in youth psychotherapy. *Journal of Child Psychology and Psychiatry, 43*, 3–29.

Weissman, M. M., Pilowsky, D. J., Wickramaratne, P. J., Talati, A., Wisniewski, S. R., Fava, M., et al. (2006). Remissions in maternal depression and child psychopathology: A STAR*D-Child report. *Journal of the American Medical Association, 295*, 1389–1398.

Weisz, J. R., McCarty, C. A., & Valeri, S. M. (2006). Effects of psychotherapy for depression in children and adolescents: A meta-analysis. *Psychological Bulletin, 132*, 132–149.

Weisz, J. R., & Weersing, V. R. (1999). Psychotherapy with children and adolescents: Efficacy, effectiveness, and developmental concerns. In D. Cicchetti & S. L. Toth (Eds.), *Rochester Symposium on Developmental Psychopathology: Vol. 9. Developmental approaches to prevention and intervention* (pp. 341–386). Rochester, NY: University of Rochester Press.

Wisdom, J. P., Clarke, G. N., & Green, C. A. (2006). What teens want: Barriers to seeking care for depression. *Administration and Policy in Mental Health and Mental Health Services Research, 33*(2), 133–145.

Wood, A., Harrington, R., & Moore, A. (1996). Controlled trial of a brief cognitive-behavioural intervention in adolescent patients with depressive disorders. *Journal of Child Psychology & Psychiatry and Allied Disciplines, 37*, 737–746.

Young, J. F., Mufson, L., & Davies, M. (2006). Impact of comorbid anxiety in an effectiveness study of interpersonal psychotherapy for depressed adolescents. *Journal of the American Academy of Child & Adolescent Psychiatry, 45*, 904–912.

Zito, J. M., Safer, D. J., dosReis, S., Gardner, J. F., Soeken, K., Boles, M., et al. (2002). Rising prevalence of antidepressants among US youths. *Pediatrics, 109*, 721–727.

Section VI

PREVENTION OF ADOLESCENT DEPRESSION

Chapter Twenty-Two

Prevention of Depression in Adolescents: A Review of Selective and Indicated Programs

JUDY GARBER, CHRISTIAN A. WEBB, AND JASON L. HOROWITZ

CONTENTS

ADOLESCENCE: A WINDOW OF OPPORTUNITY FOR PREVENTING DEPRESSION

Earlier chapters in this Handbook have described important issues concerning the epidemiology, comorbidities, biological, and psychosocial risk factors, and treatment of depression in adolescents. Clearly, depression is a serious public health problem for which efforts at prevention are needed. Point prevalence of adolescent depression is estimated to be between 3 and 8%, and approximately 18 to 20% of adolescents will have a depressive episode by age 18 (Costello, Mustillo, Erkanli, Keerler, & Angold, 2003; Merikangas & Knight Chapter 3 of this volume). Moreover, depression has a chronic, episodic course marked by considerable and persistent impairment (Lewinsohn, Rohde, Seeley, Klein, & Gotlib, 2003; Pickles et al., 2001) including dysfunctional interpersonal relationships, academic problems, cigarette smoking, substance use problems, high-risk sexual behavior, physical health problems, and increased risk of suicide (Birmaher et al., 1996; Brent et al., 1993; Le, Munoz, Ippen, & Stoddard, 2003; Rohde, Lewinsohn, & Seeley, 1994; Stolberg, Clark, & Bongar, 2002). These associated problems account for a substantial proportion of the health care costs incurred by this age group, and are a significant economic and social burden to society (World Health Organization, 2001).

The average depressive episode in youth lasts between 6 and 8 months (Kaminski & Garber, 2002; Kovacs, 1996; Lewinsohn, Clarke, Seeley, & Rohde, 1994). Longer depressive episodes are associated with worse functioning over time (Rao, Hammen, & Daley, 1999), and are more difficult to treat (Judd et al., 1998; Thase & Howland, 1994). Particularly relevant to prevention is the fact that depression is quite recurrent. An episode of depression during childhood or adolescence increases the risk of subsequent depressive episodes during adolescence (Emslie et al., 1997; McCauley et al., 1993) and adulthood (Lewinsohn, Rohde, Klein, & Seeley, 1999b; Rao et al., 1999; Weissman et al., 1999). Recurrence rates have ranged from 40 to 72% over 3 to 7 years (Emslie et al., 1997; Harrington, Fudge, Rutter, Pickle, & Hill, 1990; Kovacs et al., 1984; Lewinsohn et al., 1999b). Thus, the majority of individuals with early-onset depressions will experience another episode in their adult life (Kandel & Davies, 1986; Rao, Ryan, Birmaher, & Dahl, 1995), and most cases of recurrent adult depression have their initial onsets during adolescence (Kessler, Wai, Demler, & Walters, 2005; Pine, Cohen, Gurley, Brook, & Ma, 1998). Therefore, adolescence may be a particularly critical and opportune developmental window during which to intervene to prevent the onset and recurrence of depressive disorders and their associated impairment.

WHY FOCUS ON PREVENTION?

Although efficacious psychosocial and pharmacological treatments for adolescent depression exist (Vitiello, & Swedo, 2004; Weisz, McCarty, & Valari, 2006), such approaches only help about 65% of those treated (Brent et al., 1997; Emslie et al., 1998, 2002; Mufson, Weissman, Moreau, & Garfinkel, 1999; Treatment for Adolescents with Depression Study (TADS) Team, 2004, 2007; Wagner, Robb, Findling, Gutierrez, & Heydorn, 2004), and only about 25% of depressed adolescents ever receive treatment (Hirshfeld et al., 1997; Newman et al., 1996). Moreover, no matter how well treatments work once an episode occurs, they do not prevent the onset of new cases. Thus, despite the potential benefits of treatment to individuals, society ultimately will be better off if depression can be prevented in the first place (Heller, 1996).

In addition, factors such as chronicity, comorbidity, and parental depression can render efficacious treatments less likely to work well (Birmaher et al., 2000; Brent et al., 1998; Clarke et al., 1992; Emslie et al., 1998). Further, given concerns that certain classes of medications (e.g., serotonin reuptake inhibitors [SSRIs] other than fluoxetine) may increase risk for developing suicidal ideation or facilitate suicidal behaviors (Committee on Safety of Medicines, 2004), interventions that can prevent or reduce the need for such treatment are becoming even more imperative. Therefore, prevention of depression, particularly among high-risk youth, may be more cost-effective and safe as well as less distressing for individuals than waiting for the condition to appear, and then trying to treat a full depressive episode.

TYPES OF PREVENTION

In the past, types of prevention were described as primary, secondary, and tertiary (Caplan, 1964). Reducing the incidence of new cases of disorder in individuals who have not had the disorder was primary prevention; reducing the duration and severity of symptoms was secondary prevention (i.e., treatment); and reducing the recurrence of disorder and its associated impairment in those who have already had it was tertiary (maintenance). The Institute of Medicine (IOM; Mrazek & Haggerty, 1994) found this distinction too broad, and instead classified prevention programs into three categories (universal, selective, and indicated) based on the population groups to whom the interventions are directed. Although these categories do not exactly map on to primary, secondary, and tertiary prevention, the IOM classification has been increasingly used over the last decade.

Universal preventive intervention is administered to all members of a population, and does not select participants based on risk. Selective prevention is given to a subgroup of a population whose risk is deemed to be above average. Indicated preventive interventions are provided to individuals who have detectable, subclinical levels of signs or symptoms of the disorder, but who do not currently meet diagnostic criteria for disorder. The present review focuses on the latter two "targeted" preventions (i.e., selective and indicated), which are given to a subset of a population identified as being at greater risk of the disorder than the general population. (See Spence & Shortt [2007] and McLaughlin [this volume] for a discussion of universal depression prevention programs).

Some studies have included both selective (e.g., offspring of depressed parents, family conflict) and indicated (i.e., subsyndromal depressive symptoms) samples in order to identify a particularly high-risk group (e.g., Clarke et al., 2001; Garber et al., 2007; Jaycox, Reivich, Gillham, & Seligman, 1994; Yu & Seligman, 2002). Cuijpers (2003) has suggested that high-risk samples are likely to have greater statistical power to detect a prevention effect due to the increased probability of finding disorder in the no-intervention group. On the other hand, given the etiological complexity of mood disorders, no single risk factor is likely to identify all individuals who will develop the disorder, and not all individuals who develop the condition will have that particular risk factor. Therefore, it might make sense to recruit individuals who have multiple risk factors, although the cost of screening to find such a sample may be prohibitive, and the results might not generalize. For a more extensive discussion of the advantages and disadvantages of the different types of preventive interventions, see Offord, Kraemer, Kazdin, Jensen, and Harrington (1998).

Several qualitative (Garber & McCauley, 2002; Gillham, Shatté, & Freres, 2000; Merry & Spence, 2007; Munoz, Le, Clarke, & Jaycox, 2002; Sutton, 2007) and quantitative (Horowitz & Garber, 2006; Jané-llopis, Hosman, Jenkins, & Anderson, 2003; Merry, McDowell, Hetrick, Bir, & Muller, 2004) reviews of studies testing interventions to prevent depression in children and adolescence have been conducted recently. Whereas qualitative reviews generally summarize and synthesize findings across multiple studies, meta-analyses amalgamate effect sizes from different studies with various numbers of participants, and allow for the examination of other study characteristics that can influence effect sizes, such as the type of intervention, the age and sex of the participants, and the length of follow-up. This chapter provides a combined qualitative and quantitative review of selective and indicated programs aimed at preventing depression in children and adolescents at risk. In particular, we review prevention programs in relation to the risk factors they are designed to address. Next, we provide a meta-analysis, which updates our earlier quantitative review (Horowitz & Garber, 2006) by including follow-up information for several of the selective studies and reviewing an additional six indicated studies. Finally, we suggest several directions for future research.

WHO IS AT RISK FOR DEPRESSION?

According to Mrazek and Haggerty (1994), risk factors to be targeted for prevention are not necessarily causally related to the outcome and may include biological, psychological, and/or environmental variables. Potential risk factors for depression include gender (Hankin et al., 1998; Hilt & Nolen-Hoeksema, this volume), genes (Lau & Eley, this volume; Sullivan, Neale, & Kendler, 2000), parental depression (Goodman & Gotlib, 1999; Joorman, Eugene, & Gotlib, this volume), anxiety (Pine et al., 1998; Rohde, this volume), subsyndromal levels of depressive symptoms (Fergusson, Horwood, Ridder, & Beautrais, 2005; Judd et al., 1998), neurobiological dysregulation (Goodyer, this volume; Kaufman, Martin, King, & Charney, 2001), temperament/personality (Kendler, Gardner, & Prescott, 2002; Yap, Allen, & Sheeber, 2007), negative cognitions (Abela & Hankin, this volume), problems in self-regulation and coping (Compas, Jaser, & Benson, this volume), stressful life events (Hammen, this volume), and interpersonal difficulties (Rudolph, this volume). A review of depression prevention programs (see Table 22.1) reveals that some, but not all, of these variables have been used to select at-risk individuals for prevention trials.

Selective prevention programs have targeted family factors such as divorce (Gwynn & Brantley, 1987; Wolchik et al., 1993, 2002), parental death (Sandler et al., 1992, 2003), parental depression (Beardslee et al., 1997, 2007 Clarke et al., 2001), parental alcoholism (Clair & Genest, 1987; Roosa, Gensheimer, Short, Ayers, & Shell, 1989), and family conflict (Gillham, Reivich, Jaycox, & Seligman 1995; Jaycox et al., 1994; Yu & Seligman, 2002), environmental stressors such as poverty (Cardemil, Reivich, & Seligman, 2002) and school transitions (Quayle, Dzuirawiec, Roberts, Kane, & Ebsworthy, 2001), and individual characteristics such as a negative cognitive style (Seligman, Schulman, DeRubeis, & Hollon, 1999). Depression prevention programs that targeted participants based on particular risk factors are reviewed next.

Table 22.1 Description of studies of selective and indicated samples used in the meta-analysis

Study	Selective sample (risk)	*n* (% female)	Age (years)	Length of intervention (# of sessions)	Dep. measure	Postintervention effect size	Effect size follow-up closest to 6 months	Effect size last follow-up	Summary of intervention
Gwynn and Brantley (1987)	Divorced parents	60 (50%)	9–11	8 wkly group	CDI	1.37	–	–	Educational support group: divorce education, encourage emotional expression, problem-solving skills
Roosa et al. (1989)	Alcoholic parent	81 (50%)	9–13 *M*=10.3	8 wkly group	CDI	0.41	–	–	Education about alcoholism, improve self-esteem, emotion-focused coping strategies
Sandler et al. (1992)	Parent died <2 yrs ago	72 (49%)	7–17 *M*=12.4	9 family and 6 parent-only	CDI	0.24	–	–	**Family Bereavement Program:** grief workshop, target parent demoralization, parent warmth, stable positive events, stress management
Sandler et al. (2003)	Parent died 4–30 mo. ago	244 (49%)	8–16 *M*=11.4	8 child- and parent-only 2-hr+6 family sessions	CDI	0.06	0.11 (11 mo)	0.11 (11 mo)	**Family bereavement program:** grief workshops, coping, stress management, control-related beliefs, self-esteem, problem solving, discipline practices

(*Continued*)

Table 22.1 (Continued)

Study	Selective sample (risk)	*n* (% female)	Age (years)	Length of intervention (# of sessions)	Dep. measure	Postintervention effect size	Effect size follow-up closest to 6 months	Effect size last follow-up	Summary of intervention
Wolchik et al. (1993)	Divorced parents	94 (39%)	8–15 *M*=10.6	2 individual and 10 wkly group	CDI	–0.06	–	–	**New Beginnings:** mother program (MP): improve mother–child relationship, teach discipline skills, schedule positive activities, improve child's contact with father
Wolchik et al. (2002)	Divorced parents	218 (50%)	9–12 *M*=10.7	11 wkly 105-min	CDI	MP=0.01 MPCP=0.06	–0.07 (6 mo) 0.06 (6 mo)	–0.04 (6 mo) –0.04 (72 mo)	**New Beginnings:** MP; MP plus child program (MPCP): CP-recognition, labeling feelings, problem solving, relaxation, cognitive reframing, communication skills
Beardslee et al. (1997, 2003, 2007)	Parents with an affective disorder	52 (40%)	8–15 *M*=11.5	6–10 meetings with parents, child, or both	CDI	0.20	0.42 (18 mo.)	0.42 (18 mo.)	**Cognitive education program:** increase understanding within family, educate about mood disorders; control condition received two 1-hr lectures
Seligman et al. (1999)	Low ASQ scores	235 (52%)	College freshman	8 wkly 2-hr group and 6 individual next 2 yrs	BDI	0.32	0.12 (6 mo.)	0.25 (36 mo.)	**Cognitive-behavioral program:** cognitive restructuring, empirical hypothesis testing, behavioral activation, interpersonal skills training

Quayle et al. (2001)	School transition	47 (100%)	11–12	8 wkly 80-min	CDI	–0.62	0.62 (6 mo.)	0.62 (6 mo.)	**Penn Prevention Program (PPP)** adapted for Australian children
Cardemil et al. (2002, 2007)	Low income			12 wkly 90-min group	CDI				**Modified Penn Resiliency Program:** changed ethnicity of children in examples, focus on problems of low income families, single-parent homes, managing interpersonal conflict
Study 1	Latino;	53 (45%)	*M*=11.3			0.99	1.24 (6 mo.)	0.66 (24 mo.)	
Study 2	African-American	115 (55%)	*M*=10.9			0.16	0.31 (6 mo.)	–0.10 (24 mo.)	
Gillham and Reivich (1999), Gillham et al. (1995), Jaycox et al. (1994)	Depressive symptoms and/or family conflict	143 (46%)	10–13 *M*=11.4	12 wkly 90-min group	CDI	0.18	0.32 (6 mo.)	0.20 (36 mo.)	**Penn Prevention Program:** cognitive: link between thoughts and feelings; social problem solving, goal setting, perspective taking, decision making, generating action alternatives
Clarke et al. (1995)	Depressive symptoms	150 (70%)	*M*=15.3	15 45-min group 3 times a week	CES-D	0.31	–0.07 (6 mo.)	–0.01 (12 mo.)	**Cognitive-behavioral program:** identify and challenge negative thoughts, develop effective coping strategies
Reivich (1996), Shatté (1996)	Depressive symptoms	152 (47%)	12–14 *M*=12.7	12 wkly 2-hr group	CDI	0.12	0.40 (4 and 8 mo.)	0.22 (12 mo.)	**Penn Optimism Program:** same as PPP; Penn Enhancement Program: affect-focused, emotional expression
Lamb et al. (1998)	Depressive symptoms	41 (56%)	14–19 *M*=15.8	8 wkly	RADS	0.70	–	–	**Cognitive skills program:** coping, problem solving, communication skills

(Continued)

Table 22.1 (Continued)

Study	Selective sample (risk)	*n* (% female)	Age (years)	Length of intervention (# of sessions)	Dep. measure	Postintervention effect size	Effect size follow-up closest to 6 months	Effect size last follow-up	Summary of intervention
Forsyth (2001)	Depressive symptoms	59 (97%)	18–25 $M = 19.4$	4 group	BDI	1.51	1.95 (12 mo.)	1.95 (12 mo.)	**Interpersonal program:** role disputes, transitions, emotional expression
Clarke et al. (2001)	Depressed parents; depressive symptoms	94 (60%)	13–18 $M = 14.6$	15 1-hr group	CES-D	0.41	0.47 (12 mo.)	0.04 (24 mo.)	**Cognitive-behavioral program:** cognitive restructuring, target parent-related beliefs
Peden et al. (2001)	Depressive symptoms	92 (100%)	18–24 $M = 19.3$	6 wkly 1-hr	BDI and CES-D	0.73	0.82 (6 mo.)	0.31 (18 mo.)	**Cognitive-behavioral program:** reduce negative thinking, thought stopping, affirmations
Yu and Seligman (2002)	Depressive symptoms and/or family conflict	220 (45%)	8–15 $M = 11.8$	10 wkly 2-hr group	CDI	0.23	0.30 (3 mo.)	0.30 (3 mo.)	Modified **Penn Optimism Program:** adapted for use with Chinese children
Puskar et al. (2003)	Depressive symptoms	89 (82%)	14–18 $M = 16$	10 wkly 45-min group	RADS	0.55	0.60 (6 mo.)	0.31 (12 mo.)	**Teaching Kids to Cope:** cognitive restructuring, coping, affect regulation
Roberts et al. (2003, 2004)	Depressive symptoms	189 (50%)	11–13 $M = 11.9$	12 wkly 90-min group	CDI	0.05	0.07 (6 mo.)	0.15 (30 mo.)	**Penn Prevention Program:** cognitive and social problem solving
Gillham et al. (2006b)	Depressive symptoms.	271 (53%)	11–12	12 wkly 90-min group	CDI	–0.02	0.22 (6 mo.)	0.07 (24 mo.)	**Penn Resiliency Program:** same as Penn Prevention Program

Gillham et al. (2006a)	Depressive symptoms	44 (30%)	Sixth and seventh grade	Children: 8 90-min group parents: 6 90-min	CDI	0.08	0.59 (6 mo.)	0.38 (12 mo.)	Shorter **Penn Resiliency Program:** same components for children; parents were taught core skills their children were learning
Sheffield et al. (2006)	Depressive symptoms	521 (69%)	13–15 *M*=14.3	(a) 8 wkly 45-min group (Universal) (b) 8 wkly 90-min group (Indicated) (c) both	CDI	a=0.08 b=0.14 c=–0.02	a=–0.08 (3 mo.) b=–0.05 (3 mo.) c=–0.15 (12 mo.)	a=–0.02 (15 mo.) b=–0.09 (15 mo.) c=–0.15 (12 mo.)	**Cognitive-behavioral program:** cognitive restructuring, problem solving, interpersonal skills training, self-reward training
Young et al. (2006)	Depressive symptoms	41 (85%)	11–16 *M*=13.4	2 individual and 8 wkly 90-min group	CES-D	1.05	0.81 (6 mo.)	0.81 (6 mo.)	**Interpersonal Psychotherapy Adolescent Skills Training:** communication skills, link between feelings and interpersonal interactions, learn about depression and prevention
Stice et al. (2006)	Depressive symptoms	225 (70%)	15–22 *M*=18.4	4 wkly 1-hr	CES-D and BDI	CBT vs. WL=0.76 vs. SE=–0.37 vs. Bib=0.14 vs. EW=–0.13 vs. Jrn=0.29	0.13 (6 mo.) –0.34 –0.49 0.01 –0.06	0.13 (6 mo.) –0.34 –0.49 0.01 –0.06	**Brief CB program:** cognitive restructuring, behavioral activation, coping versus wait-list control, bibliotherapy, expressive writing, or journaling
Burton et al. (2007)	Depressive symptoms	145 (100%)	14–23 *M*=18.6	4 wkly 1-hr	CES-D and BDI	0.52	0.05 (6 mo.)	0.05 (6 mo.)	**Cognitive-behavioral program** based on Clarke et al. (1995): identify and challenge negative thoughts, behavioral activation, coping

Note: BDI=Beck Depression Inventory; CDI=Children's Depression Inventory; CES-D=Center for Epidemiological Studies-Depression scale; RADS=Reynolds Adolescent Depression Scale; ASQ=Attributional Style Questionnaire; CB=Cognitive-Behavioral; WL=Wait-list; SE=supportive-expressive group therapy; Bib=bibliotherapy; EW=Expressive writing; Jrn=Journaling; Dep.=Depression; mo.=months; wkly=weekly; min=minutes; hr=hour.

Family Risk Factors

Two prevention programs developed to work with children of divorced parents included measures of depressive symptoms. The preventive intervention created by Gwynn and Brantley (1987) functioned as an educational support program. Five groups of six children met for eight weekly sessions to learn how to talk about divorce with friends and teachers, express their feelings, solve problems related to their parents' divorce, and handle situations and feelings during visitation. They also discussed issues involving stepfamilies, and conflict with parents. Behavioral rehearsal and role-playing with puppets were used. Results showed that children in the intervention group had lower levels of depressive symptoms on the Children's Depression Inventory (CDI) at post-treatment than the children in the control group.

Wolchik et al. (1993) took a different approach to working with children of divorce. The "New Beginnings" program for parents who had been divorced targeted five hypothesized mediators of the relation between divorce and depression in children, including the quality of the custodial parent–child relationship, discipline strategies, contact with the noncustodial parent, anger management and listening skills, and enhancing social support from other adults. Wolchik et al. found significant differences between the intervention and control group on the quality of the parent–child relationship and the number of negative divorce-related events, but found no effect on children's depressive symptoms on the CDI compared to controls.

In a subsequent study, Wolchik et al. (2000, 2002) developed a dual-component prevention program for children of divorced parents that consisted of concurrent but separate interventions for mothers and children. The child component emphasized the recognition and labeling of feelings, divorce information, problem solving, cognitive reframing, communication skills, and relaxation. The dual-component program was compared to a mother-only intervention and a self-study condition in which mothers and children read age-appropriate self-help books about divorce. At postintervention, the mother-only program (MP) was better than the self-study condition on relationship quality, discipline, and child adjustment problems; program effects on externalizing problems were maintained at 6-month follow-up (Wolchik et al., 2000). At the 6-year follow-up, adolescents in the MP and the MP plus child program had lower rates of mental disorders and lower levels of externalizing problems and substance use (Wolchik et al., 2002); no significant differences were found on depression, however.

The New Beginnings program was not designed to explicitly prevent depression, and therefore might not have addressed depression relevant risk factors. Moreover, one of the exclusion criteria for entry into the study was a CDI score of 17 or greater. Thus, it is likely that the very children whose depression might have improved or worsened were excluded. Future studies should test the efficacy of this program with children who are experiencing the full range of depressive symptoms, given the known relation between divorce and depression in youth (e.g., Amato, 2001).

Another important risk factor for depression is death of a parent (e.g., Lutzke, Ayers, Sandler, & Barr, 1997; Tremblay & Israel, 1998). Sandler et al. (1992, 2003) created the Family Bereavement Program, which sought to bring together families with similar experiences. The first part involved a three-session grief workshop that focused on communication about feelings between the child and the surviving parent. The second part was a 12-session family adviser program that targeted (a) parental demoralization by giving emotional support, (b) parental warmth through teaching positive exchanges and communication skills, (c) stable positive events through planning regular times for the parent and child to have fun together, and (d) negative life events through emotion-focused and problem-focused coping.

Sandler et al. (2003) reported increased warmth in the parent–child relationship, fewer negative events, more positive events, and better family coping and cohesion for those in the treatment group compared to controls. At postintervention, no significant effect was found on depressive symptoms as measured with the CDI, but at the 11-month follow-up, the baseline X gender X program interaction was significant, indicating that among girls who had higher levels of depressive symptoms at baseline, those who were in the program had lower depression scores at follow-up compared to girls in the control group. Thus, the inclusion of children with high levels of depressive symptoms at baseline likely allowed them to show an effect of the program on depression. Sandler et al. speculated that the reduction in depressive symptoms in girls might have been partially due to the positive effects of the program on improving coping and reducing their negative thoughts about stressful events.

Parental psychopathology, particularly mood disorders, is probably one of the strongest predictors of depression in children and adolescents (e.g., Beardslee, Versage, & Gladstone, 1998; Goodman & Gotlib, 1999). Beardslee and colleagues (1997, 2003, 2007) have examined two preventive interventions for children ages 8 through 15, who had a parent with an affective disorder. The active intervention was a clinician-facilitated program that included 6 to 11 individual meetings with the children and parents, as well as a meeting with the entire family together. In addition, telephone contacts or refresher meetings were conducted at 6- to 9-month intervals. This clinician-facilitated intervention (a) presented psychoeducational material about mood disorders and about risks and resilience in children; (b) linked the psychoeducational material to family members' unique life experiences with the illness; (c) decreased feelings of guilt and blame in the children; and (d) helped children develop relationships both within and outside of the family to facilitate their independent functioning in school and in activities outside of the home. In contrast, the lecture "control" condition consisted of two 1-hour lectures with parents, delivered in a group format without children present. The psychoeducational material mirrored that presented in the clinician-facilitated condition and family discussion was encouraged, but there was no attempt to link the lecture material to family members' particular experiences with the parents' illness. Parents were encouraged to talk to their children about mood disorders, but they had to decide whether or not to initiate such conversations.

Results showed that children in the clinician-facilitated program reported greater understanding of parental affective disorder, more change in child-related behaviors, attitudes, and problem-solving strategies, and better adaptive functioning compared to those in the control condition. Internalizing scores decreased over time for children in both groups, but there were no significant differences between the two conditions on change in children's depressive symptoms at the 1-, 2-, and 4.5-year follow-up. Thus, the clinician-facilitated program showed some beneficial effects on children's development, although its effect on changes in depression in particular needs to be studied further. The absence of a no-intervention control group may have limited their ability to show a significant intervention effect.

Another possible reason for Beardslee and colleagues not finding an effect on depression may be that they excluded all children who had ever been diagnosed with a mood disorder. Given the high rate of recurrence of depression (e.g., Emslie et al., 1997; Weissman et al., 1999), it is possible that they eliminated the very youth who would have been most likely to show an intervention effect. That is, the rates of depression in children in the control condition probably would have been greater, thereby resulting in a significant group difference. We discuss further this issue of selecting on current or past depression later in this chapter (see also Clarke et al., 2001).

Parental alcohol problems have also been linked with psychopathology in offspring (e.g., Clair & Genest, 1987). Roosa et al. (1989) implemented an 8-week preventive intervention for children of alcoholics. Children met in groups to learn about alcohol and alcohol abuse, problem-solving techniques, situation-specific appraisal, and emotion-focused coping strategies, and to participate in exercises designed to improve self-esteem. Group leaders used a variety of techniques including didactic presentations, structured homework, role-playing, videotaped models, and behavioral rehearsal. Results showed that at post-treatment, children in the intervention group had marginally lower levels of depressive symptoms as reported on the CDI than those in the control group. The relatively small sample size ($n = 81$) might have reduced their power to find a significant effect.

Environmental Stressors

In addition to the family risk factors described above, other stressors that have been the target of prevention have included low income and school transitions. Low socioeconomic status (SES) has been found to correlate with a greater prevalence of depression (Blazer, Kessler, McGonagle, & Swartz, 1994). Cardemil and colleagues (Cardemil, Reivich, Beevers, Seligman, & James, 2007; Cardemil et al., 2002) conducted two studies of children at risk as a function of their being low income as well as being an ethnic minority—Latino or African-American. Cardemil and colleagues modified the Penn Resiliency Program (PRP) to match the ethnicity of the children in the clinical materials to that of the participants, focus on life problems specific to low-income families, address the issue of single-parent homes, and increase time spent on alternative ways of handling conflict. Children were taught social cognitive and problem-solving skills, such as generating and evaluating explanations for negative life events, and handling conflict with family members and peers. Cardemil and colleagues found lower levels of depressive symptoms on the CDI at post-treatment and at the 3- and 6-month, and 2-year follow-up evaluations for Latino children in the treatment group compared to controls. No significant differences were found on depression between the intervention and control group in the African-American sample.

Whether or not being an ethnic minority is a sufficient risk factor for depression in children and adolescents is not known. There is some evidence that certain ethnic minority youth (e.g., Latino) report higher levels of depressive symptoms than Caucasian adolescents (Twenge & Nolen-Hoeksema, 2002). If so, then prevention effects might be stronger for these groups because more of the youth in the no-intervention group would show an increase in depressive symptoms. Depression prevention programs generally have not been developed specifically for particular ethnic groups, and few studies have tested whether the effects of a preventive intervention differ as a function of ethnicity. The Penn Prevention Program (PPP) has been found to be efficacious with Chinese (Yu & Seligman, 2002) and Latino, but not African-American children (Cardemil et al., 2007; Cardemil et al., 2002). In addition, a depression prevention program based on interpersonal psychotherapy (IPT) has been found to be effective in a Latino sample of predominantly female adolescents (Young, Mufson, & Davies, 2006). It is far too early to conclude whether or not depression can be prevented in children and adolescents from different ethnic minority groups. Much more careful descriptive research needs to be done to address questions of prevalence, course, etiology, and treatment response in these samples, which then can be used to inform the development of ethnically sensitive depression prevention programs.

Another potential life stressor for adolescents is school transition (Roeser & Eccles, 1998; Rudolph, Lambert, Clark, & Kurlakowsky, 2001). Quayle et al. (2001) conducted a randomized, controlled trial with 47 girls making the transition from seventh grade to high school. This study might be considered a universal intervention because it was offered to all students in this small school. Nevertheless, because it focused particularly on girls making the school transition, we included it here among selective studies. Twenty-four students were assigned to the Optimism and Life Skills program, which was based on the PPP (Jaycox et al., 1994), and 23 students were in the control group.

Quayle et al. (2001) found significant group effects on depressive symptoms (CDI) at the 6-month follow-up, but not at post-test. The effect was due to both a decrease in depression scores in the prevention group and an increase in the control group. The authors suggested that the somewhat unusual finding of a significant effect at follow-up but not immediately postintervention might have been due to a latency effect, whereby some time needed to pass for the skills learned to be adopted and integrated into their lives. Interestingly, however, they found no significant effects on the measure of attributional style, although this could have been due, in part, to the small sample.

Negative Cognitions

There is now considerable evidence that in the context of stress, negative cognitions (e.g., attributional style, self-worth, hopelessness, and dysfunctional attitudes) are risk factors for depression (e.g., Abela & Hankin, this volume). Nevertheless, despite this theoretical and empirical link and the fact that the majority of preventive interventions in youth have focused on cognitive restructuring and problem solving, few depression prevention studies have selected participants based on negative cognitions, per se. Seligman et al. (1999) implemented a prevention program for college freshmen identified as being at risk for depression by scoring in the most pessimistic quartile on the Attributional Style Questionnaire (ASQ; Seligman, Abramson, Semmel, & von Baeyer, 1979). The intervention included eight weekly sessions in groups of 10, and six individual meetings over the following 3 years. Cognitive-Behavioral (CB) techniques were used, including identifying automatic negative thoughts and underlying beliefs, empirical hypothesis testing, cognitive restructuring, behavioral activation strategies, and interpersonal skills training. Seligman et al. found lower levels of depressive symptoms for participants in the intervention group compared to controls as reported on the BDI immediately post-treatment and at each 6-month follow-up over 3 years. Moreover, they reported that changes in attributional style, hopelessness, and dysfunctional attitudes from pre to postintervention mediated the effect of the intervention on depressive symptoms averaged across postintervention and follow-up.

Although not selecting on the basis of negative cognitions, several other studies (Cardemil et al., 2002; Gillham, Hamilton, Freres, Patton, & Gallop, 2006b; Horowitz, Garber, Ciesla, Young, & Mufson, 2007; Jaycox et al., 1994; Quayle et al., 2001; Yu & Seligman, 2002) have also examined whether negative cognitions changed as a function of having received a CB, depression prevention program. For example, Gillham et al. (2006b) reported that their prevention program improved explanatory style for positive events, and for girls, improved attributions for negative events as well. In addition, some studies (e.g., Jaycox et al., 1994; Yu & Seligman, 2002) have shown that changes in negative cognitions (e.g., attributional style, automatic negative thoughts) partially mediated the effect of prevention programs on subsequent depression. Moreover, this mediation effect has been found to be specific to the CB intervention compared to an interpersonal prevention program (Horowitz et al., 2007). Much more research is needed to identify the cognitive or other active components of successful prevention programs so that they can be targeted more efficiently in future intervention efforts.

Selective prevention programs have not yet been developed and tested specifically for individuals at risk based on genes, psychobiology, or temperament/personality, which presumably are more stable and less malleable. More information is needed regarding which genes and neurobiological markers to target before interventions can be designed specifically for individuals with such risk factors. Surprisingly, however, several other important variables that are known to predict depression have not yet been used to specifically target participants for selective programs to prevent depression. This includes many other types of stressors (e.g., peer victimization, romantic break-ups, academic failure), anxiety, and gender, although the latter two have been examined as possible moderators of the effect of some interventions on depression.

Anxiety

Two groups have tested whether anxiety moderated the effects of universal prevention programs on depression (Hains & Ellmann, 1994; Lowry-Webster, Barrett, & Dadds, 2001; Lowry-Webster, Barrett, & Lock, 2003). Hains and Ellmann found that their universal stress inoculation training program significantly lowered depressive symptoms for children with high, but not low, emotional arousal measured at baseline. Similarly, in their universal CB program, known as FRIENDS, Lowry-Webster and colleagues found a reduction in depressive symptoms for those children who were clinically anxious at pre-test. In both of these studies, however, the positive results for the subgroup with anxiety may have been due to their also having higher levels of depressive symptoms, rather than the intervention affecting anxiety symptoms per se.

Other studies (Gillham et al., 2006a; Roberts, Kane, Thomson, Bishop, & Hart, 2003; Seligman et al., 1999) have used versions of the PPP with youth reporting subclinical levels of depression, and have shown a reduction in symptoms of anxiety in the intervention group. In a sample of seventh grade students, Roberts et al. found that the children in the PPP group had lower levels of self-reported anxiety than the control group at postintervention and at the 6-month follow-up, although they did not differ significantly on depressive symptoms. Children's scores on the CDI in both the intervention and control groups decreased across time. In addition, baseline levels of anxiety did not moderate the relation between intervention and depression. Evidence of a preventive effect on depression will possibly become apparent as these children move further into adolescence when the rates of depression are known to increase, although at the 30-month follow-up, again no effect on depression was found (Roberts, Kane, Bishop, Matthews, & Thomson, 2004).

A recent pilot study investigating the effectiveness of the PRP for Children and Adolescents (PRP-CA) when combined with a parent intervention component (Gillham et al., 2006a) found that this integrated program significantly reduced symptoms of both anxiety and depression at the 6- and 12-month follow-up period, although not at the postintervention assessment. Across the follow-up period, fewer PRP participants reported high levels of symptoms compared to controls. Although the pattern of results was similar for depression and anxiety, only the intervention effect on anxiety symptoms was significant.

Thus, the PPP has been found to reduce anxiety symptoms, possibly even more than it reduces symptoms of depression. The extent to which the reduction in anxiety mediates the effects of the intervention on depression still needs to be explored. Moreover, although potentially promising, the strategy of preventing depression by explicitly reducing anxiety in youth has yet to be adequately tested in a way that disentangles the baseline levels of both anxiety and depression. Future studies should also determine the effect of the preventive intervention on both negative and positive affectivity (Watson & Clark, 1984).

Gender

The use of gender as a selection factor is even more complicated. Although much has been written about the increasing rate of depression in girls during adolescence (Cyranowski, Frank, Young, & Shear, 2000; Hankin & Abramson, 2001; Nolen-Hoeksema & Hilt, this volume), a better understanding of the reasons for this gender effect is needed to inform the development of gender appropriate depression prevention programs. Garber (2006) highlighted the distinction between gender differences in risk versus in response to preventive interventions. Although adolescent females are at greater risk for depression than males, this does not necessarily mean that there will be sex differences in response to preventive intervention programs. The effect of a preventive intervention may appear to be stronger for females than males because the rates of depression in the no-intervention control group will probably be greater for females than males. Thus, the higher rate of depression in females is relevant to prevention research, in that a significant group by gender interaction could be due to within-gender effects of the intervention and/or within-intervention effects for gender. That is, girls and boys may respond similarly to an intervention, but girls in the no-intervention control group may show an increase in depression. Alternatively, boys could do better than girls in the intervention, and there could be no difference in girls as a function of condition.

Among studies of prevention programs that have examined sex differences, some have found that girls responded better than boys (Gillham et al., 2006b; Petersen, Leffert, Graham, Alwin, & Ding, 1997; Schmiege, Khoo, Sandler, Ayers, & Wolchik, 2006; Seligman et al., 1999), others have found that boys did better than girls (Clarke, Hawkins, Murphy, & Sheeber, 1993; Ialongo et al., 1999; Kellam, Rebok, Mayer, Ialongo, & Kalodner, 1994), and still others have found no gender differences (Horowitz et al., 2007). It is noteworthy that universal programs have tended to show no sex differences or better effects for males than females, whereas targeted programs generally have found stronger effects for females (although see Petersen et al. [1997] for an exception).

Given that adolescent girls are at greater risk for depression compared to males, how might this affect prevention research? Should the nature of the intervention be different for girls and boys? There is some evidence that girls may respond better to a more interpersonally focused program. For example, the Penn Enhancement Program (PEP), which is a more social-emotional program, was found to be more effective for girls than boys, whereas the Penn Optimism Program (POP), which is a CB skills training program, was more effective for boys than girls (Reivich, 1996; Shatté, 1996). In a study testing an interpersonally oriented prevention program with a predominantly female sample, Forsyth (2001) found one of the highest effect sizes of any program tested to date. Without a male sample for comparison, however, it is not possible to know if this program would have worked as well for males. Nevertheless, the Forsyth study is consistent with the idea that an interpersonal approach may be effective for females. Horowitz et al. (2007) directly compared a CB versus a program based on IPT, and found that both programs were significantly more effective than a no-intervention control group in reducing depressive symptoms, but no significant effects were found for gender.

Given limited resources, should depression prevention programs target girls in particular, due to their greater risk? Boys also get depressed, however, and if depression serves as a precursor for other problems (e.g., substance use, suicide) (Angold, Costello, & Erkanli, 1999), then boys should be provided with depression prevention programs as well. Thus, although adolescent females are at greater risk for depression than their male peers, the evidence is inconclusive regarding gender differences in the efficacy of one type of program versus another. Few studies have separated boys from girls in their data analyses, thus making it impossible to examine differential effects of their programs by gender. Moreover, despite the various speculations about why females are at greater risk of depression (Nolen-Hoeksema & Hilt, this volume), depression prevention programs generally have not yet been designed to specifically target these hypothesized mechanisms. The translation of basic knowledge about the processes that account for gender differences in rates of depression to the actual content of prevention programs should be the focus of future research.

In summary, a variety of risk factors have been used in selective programs aimed at preventing depressive symptoms in adolescents. Five of the eleven studies of selective prevention programs found some effect on depressive symptoms after the intervention. Two of those studies (Gwynn & Brantley, 1987; Roosa et al., 1989), however, did not conduct follow-up analyses, thus making it impossible to assess the long term preventive effects of these programs. Of the studies that did conduct follow-up analyses, three (Cardemil et al., 2002,

2007; Quayle et al., 2001; Seligman et al., 1999) reported preventive effects on depressive symptoms at 6 months. Cardemil et al. (2007) found significant preventive effects for Latino youth at 2 years, and Seligman et al. continued to find preventive effects at each 6-month follow-up over 3 years.

Subsyndromal Depressive Symptoms

Indicated preventive interventions target individuals who are already showing subclinical signs or symptoms of the disorder that is the focus of the prevention effort. Subsyndromal levels of depressive symptoms have been found to significantly increase the risk of having a full major depressive episode (MDE) in children (e.g., Kovacs et al., 1984), adolescents (Fergusson et al., 2005; Pine, Cohen, Cohen, & Brook, 1999), and adults (e.g., Judd et al., 1998). For example, in a prospective study, Pine et al. (1999) showed that a difference of two standard deviations from the mean in depressive symptoms in adolescents predicted a two to threefold greater risk of an episode of major depression in adulthood; the symptoms of anhedonia and morbid ideation were particularly predictive of subsequent depressive episodes. Subsyndromal levels of depression can also negatively impact academic/occupational and interpersonal functioning (Lewinsohn et al., 2003; Lewinsohn, Solomon, Seeley, & Zeiss, 2000; Wells, Bushnell, Hornblow, & Joyce, 1989). Thus, targeting individuals with subsyndromal depression for preventive intervention may not only ameliorate existing levels of distress and dysfunction, but may also reduce risk of future MDEs and impairment.

Indicated interventions require an additional step to the recruitment process because all potential participants must be screened to determine if their level of symptoms qualifies them for the program. Although this increases the initial time and cost, it also maximizes the likelihood that those receiving the intervention are at a high level of need. Similar to selective interventions, indicated programs typically have been implemented in a small group format.

TYPES OF PREVENTION PROGRAMS

The majority of depression prevention programs administered to children and adolescents have been based on CB therapy (CBT) principles (Beck, Rush, Shaw, & Emery, 1979). CBT, which helps individuals identify, evaluate, and modify depressive cognitions, and develop coping and problem-solving skills, has been shown to significantly reduce depressive symptoms in both adults (Hollon, Thase, & Markowitz, 2002) and youth (Curry, 2001; Reinecke, Ryan, & DuBois, 1998). Meta-analyses evaluating the efficacy of CBT for adolescent depression have found that main effects obtained at post-treatment were quite large, –1.02 (Lewinsohn & Clarke, 1999) and 1.27 (Reinecke et al., 1998). The recently completed multisite Treatment for Adolescents with Depression Study (TADS) indicated that fluoxetine plus CBT outperformed medication alone, which in turn was superior to CBT alone and placebo, which were equally efficacious at the 12-week assessment (TADS, 2004), although by weeks 18 and 36, CBT alone caught up with medication alone as a monotherapy (TADS, 2007). Given the efficacy of CBT in the treatment of depression in both adults and adolescents, many prevention programs have made CB techniques primary features of their interventions. In fact, 16 of the 25 studies reviewed here focused primarily on CB techniques including cognitive restructuring, assertiveness training, and coping and problem-solving skills; an additional six programs emphasized coping and problem solving.

The Penn Prevention Programs

Perhaps the most widely tested and most successful preventive intervention in youth is the PPP developed by Jaycox et al. (1994). This 12-session program uses CB techniques to teach coping strategies, enhance a sense of mastery and competence, and combat deficits, such as lower academic achievement, poor peer relationships, low self-esteem, and behavior problems. The program has both a cognitive and a social problem-solving component. The cognitive component teaches participants the link between thoughts and feelings, how to evaluate the accuracy of their beliefs, and how to replace negative thoughts with more realistic, less pessimistic interpretations. The social problem-solving component teaches skills such as goal setting, perspective taking, information gathering, decision making, anticipating consequences, assertiveness, negotiation, self-instruction, and generating alternative actions. Participants are also taught a variety of coping strategies, such as distraction, relaxation, and distancing from stress.

Many studies of indicated (Gillham & Reivich, 1999; Gillham et al., 2006b; Gillham et al., 2006a; Gillham et al., 1995; Jaycox et al., 1994; Reivich, 1996; Roberts et al., 2004; Roberts et al., 2003; Shatté, 1996, Yu & Seligman, 2002) as well as selective (Cardemil et al., 2007; Cardemil et al., 2002; Quayle et al., 2001) samples have used some variation of the PPP. In the first study to test this program, the Penn group (Gillham et al., 1995; Jaycox et al., 1994) found significantly lower levels of depressive symptoms in children in the intervention group compared to controls at post-treatment and at each 6-month follow-up for 2 years. The effect faded after 2 years, however, and the difference between children in the PPP condition and controls was no longer significant at a 3-year follow-up (Gillham & Reivich, 1999). One limitation of the study by Jaycox et al. (1994) was that they did not use random assignment to condition; rather the intervention group was compared to children in a matched no-treatment control group. The prevention and control groups did not differ significantly on any of the initial measures of risk level, depressive symptoms, and explanatory style, or demographic characteristics (e.g., age, race, parents' marital status, fathers' education level), except control families had significantly higher incomes and mothers with higher education levels than prevention families. To statistically control for these differences, family income and mother's education level were entered as covariates in all analyses. Although the lack of randomization is a limitation (Merry & Spence, 2007), comparable effects have been replicated in other studies using the same or similar program.

Since its creation, the PPP has been studied with different populations and with some variations in the procedures, and has been referred to by various names, including the Penn Optimism Program (POP) and the Penn Resiliency Program (PRP). Reivich (1996) and Shatté (1996) evaluated two indicated preventive interventions in a sample of subclinically depressed young adolescents. In these studies, the POP was compared to the PEP, which was a more affect-focused and less cognitive-focused program. The PEP sessions were more experiential in nature, using simulation activities in place of didactic presentations. Each PEP session focused on a different risk factor for depression, including peer pressure, trust, study skills, setting and achieving goals, friendship, families, self-esteem, and body image. Results indicated lower levels of depressive symptoms in children in the POP condition at 4 months and 8 months compared to controls (Reivich, 1996; Shatté, 1996), and lower levels of depressive symptoms in children in the PEP condition at 8 months and 12 months compared to controls (Shatté, 1996). Thus, both types of programs appeared to have some benefits.

Yu and Seligman (2002) conducted a study in China with children who had subclinical levels of depressive symptoms. They modified the Penn program for Chinese children, but maintained all the central components of the POP program including both cognitive and social problem-solving training. Yu and Seligman found lower CDI scores for children in the POP group at both the postintervention assessment and the 3-month follow-up compared to children in the control group.

Another variation of the PRP has been to add a parent component, consisting of six 90-minute sessions, in which parents are taught the core skills that their children are learning in the child component. Gillham et al. (2006a) found that children in the combined child and parent intervention condition had lower levels of depressive symptoms on the CDI than children in the control condition at the 6- and 12-month follow-up, although not at the postintervention assessment. Moreover, because there was no condition that included the child component of the PRP without the parent component, it is not possible to discern the unique contribution of the parent component. Given the importance of parents in children's development and the association between poor parenting and depression in youth (e.g., Rapee, 1997; Sheeber, Hops, & Davis, 2001), further development and testing of prevention programs that actively include parents are needed.

As an attempt to examine the feasibility of dissemination of their depression prevention program, Gillham et al. (2006b) implemented the PRP delivered by therapists in a primary care setting. Participants were 271 children, aged 11 and 12 (53% female), who had elevated levels of depressive symptoms. Results indicated that for girls, but not boys, lower levels of depressive symptoms were found for those in the intervention group compared to those in the usual care control condition. For the full sample, PRP did not prevent depressive disorders, but among high symptom youth, PRP did significantly prevent a broader range of depression and anxiety disorders when combined.

Overall, the PPP has shown small to moderate effects that last as long as 2 years. As expected, the strongest findings for the Penn programs have been in studies conducted by the developers and research team. In two of these studies (Cardemil et al., 2002; Gillham et al., 1995), groups were led by the PRP developers, members of their research team, and/or psychology graduate students supervised by the research team. Cardemil and colleagues (Cardemil et al., 2002, Study 1) found large effects through their 6-month follow-up, and Gillham and colleagues (1995) found moderate to large effects at their 12- to 24-month evaluations. Smaller effects were found in a study in which PRP groups were led by school teachers trained by the research team (Yu & Seligman, 2002). Results of other studies by research groups in Australia, not directly affiliated with the Penn group, have found mixed results (Quayle et al., 2001; Roberts et al., 2004; Roberts et al., 2003). Thus, the PPPs have shown some promise, and their further study is warranted.

The Coping with Depression Course

A second CB program that has been relatively successful in preventing depression in indicated samples was developed by Clarke, Lewinsohn and colleagues (Clarke et al., 1995; Clarke et al., 2001), and recently has been more widely tested (Burton, Stice, Bearman, & Rohde, 2007; Garber et al., 2007; Stice, Burton, Bearman, & Rohde, 2006). Clark et al. (1995) used a CB program adapted from the Adolescent Coping with Depression Course (Clarke, Lewinsohn, & Hops, 1990). Students in ninth and tenth grade who had depressive symptoms, met in 45-minute sessions three times a week for 5 weeks. The intervention focused on identifying and challenging negative cognitions, and used group discussions and role-playing to help adolescents develop effective coping strategies. Clarke et al. (1995) found lower levels of depressive symptoms at post-treatment, but not at a 6- or 12-month follow-up.

In another study (Clark et al., 2001), the sample was comprised of adolescents who had current subclinical depressive symptoms and/or a prior depressive disorder, and had a parent with a history of depression. During the 15 one-hour sessions, youth were taught cognitive-restructuring skills for challenging their irrational, unrealistic, negative thoughts, with a particular focus on negative cognitions related to having a depressed parent. In addition, the program provided three parent informational meetings, discussing the specific content of the program sessions. A particular strength of these studies was their inclusion of psychiatric interviews, allowing for the assessment of clinically significant depressive episodes in addition to self-reported depressive symptoms. Clarke et al. (2001) found lower levels of depressive symptoms for the intervention group compared to the treatment as usual comparison group at post-treatment and at a 12-month follow-up. By the 24-month follow-up, however, differences between the groups were no longer significant. Clarke et al. also reported a significant effect for depressive diagnoses, such that participants in the intervention group had significantly fewer diagnoses at the 12-month follow-up compared to controls, and this effect persisted at a diminished level at the 18- and 24-month follow-up.

Recently, Garber and colleagues (2007) conducted a study that attempted to replicate and extend the findings of Clarke et al. (2001). High-risk youth were again selected on the basis of having a parent with a history of depression, and the teen having current subsyndromal depressive symptoms as measured on the CES-D, and/or having had a depressive disorder in the past. The prevention program consisted of eight weekly 90-minute group sessions plus six monthly continuation sessions. Survival analyses from baseline through the 8-month follow-up indicated that significantly more adolescents in the treatment-as-usual group had depressive episodes compared to those in the intervention group. This sample is continuing to be followed through 32 months from baseline.

Stice and colleagues (Burton et al., 2007; Stice et al., 2006) developed a brief, CB preventive intervention (the Blues Group), which drew upon the work of Clarke et al. (1995) and Clarke et al. (2001). This four session program minimized didactic presentations, actively engaged participants through in-session exercises, assigned homework to help participants learn to apply the skills to their daily life, and used motivational enhancement exercises to increase their willingness to use the skills, strategic self-presentation to facilitate internalization of key principles, behavioral techniques to reinforce use of the skills, and group activities to foster feelings of social support and group cohesion.

Stice et al. (2006) compared this brief group CB depression prevention program to a wait-list control condition, as well as to a supportive-expressive group, expressive writing, bibliotherapy, or journaling. The 225 adolescents (70% female; mean age = 18) with elevated depressive symptoms on the CES-D were randomized to CB, wait-list, or one of the four placebo or alternative interventions; they completed assessments at baseline, post, and 1- and 6-month follow-up. All five active interventions showed significantly greater reductions in depressive symptoms at postintervention than wait-list controls; effects for the CB program and bibliotherapy persisted into follow-up, and participants in the CB, supportive-expressive, and bibliotherapy conditions also showed significantly greater decreases in depressive symptoms than those in the expressive writing and journaling groups at follow-up. Stice et al. argued that there may be multiple ways to reduce depressive symptoms in high-risk adolescents, although the influence of other factors, such as expectancies, demand characteristics, and attention, also need to be considered.

Using the same brief CB intervention, Burton et al. (2007) conducted a randomized trial designed to decrease depressive symptoms, and thereby subsequently decrease bulimic and substance use symptoms. A sample of 145 female participants with elevated depressive symptoms was randomly assigned to their brief preventive intervention or to an assessment-only condition. Relative to the control group, intervention participants showed decreases in depressive symptoms through the 6-month follow-up, and also showed significantly greater reductions in bulimic symptoms. Particularly interesting was that changes in depressive symptoms partially mediated the effect of the intervention on bulimic symptoms. Thus, even brief CB programs can have at least a short-term prevention effect.

Interpersonal Therapy Approaches

Although the majority of depression prevention programs have made CB techniques central components of their interventions, a few depression prevention programs (Forsyth, 2001 Young et al., 2006) have been based on interpersonal theories of and therapies for depression, such as IPT (Weissman, Markowitz, & Klerman, 2000). IPT targets several different interpersonal problems hypothesized to be related to depression, including role transitions, grief, interpersonal deficits, and interpersonal disputes.

Studies of the efficacy of IPT for the treatment of depression in adults indicate that IPT tends to outperform minimal contact control, usual care, or placebo, but is not superior to tricyclic antidepressant medications, medications plus IPT, or cognitive therapy (DiMascio et al., 1979; Elkin et al., 1989; Frank et al., 1990; Schulberg et al., 1996). IPT has been adapted for adolescents (Mufson, Dorta, Moreau, & Weissman, 2004a) and addresses developmental issues assumed to be etiologically related to depression in youth, including separation from parents, authority and autonomy issues, development of dyadic interpersonal relationships, peer pressure, loss, and problems related to single-parent families. Results from two IPT-A depression treatment trials by Mufson and colleagues (Mufson et al., 2004b; Mufson, Weissman, Moreau & Garfinkel, 1999) indicated that IPT-A, compared to clinical monitoring and treatment as usual, was associated with significantly greater reductions on the Hamilton Depression Rating Scale (HAM-D), better overall social functioning, and improvement in both overall functioning and on clinician's ratings of global improvement.

Given the promising results emerging from efficacy studies of IPT for the treatment of depression in both adults and youth, Forsyth (2001) developed and evaluated a four-session, IPT-based, indicated depression prevention program for college students. Session 1 dealt with the relation between life events, role transitions, and interpersonal difficulties. Session 2 focused on the four main tasks of role transitions: giving up roles, expressing guilt, anger, and loss, acquiring new skills, and developing new attachments and support groups. The last two sessions dealt with the resolution of role disputes and working through role transitions. Results of this brief intervention conducted with a small sample of predominantly female, older adolescents indicated that those in the intervention group had significantly lower BDI scores compared to the control group at both post-treatment and the 3-month follow-up.

Young et al. (2006) developed and tested an IPT-adolescent skills training (IPT-AST) group prevention program based on IPT-A. The program consisted of two individual sessions and eight weekly 90-minute group sessions, targeting three types of interpersonal problems: interpersonal role disputes, role transitions, and interpersonal deficits. In the psychoeducation component, participants learned about prevention, depression, and the link between feelings and interpersonal interactions. The second component was aimed at developing interpersonal and communication skills. The results of their small prevention trial with an indicated and predominantly female, Latino sample also showed good effects. Thus, interpersonally oriented preventive interventions are showing some promise when conducted with females with subsyndromal levels of depressive symptoms compared to no intervention. IPT-A prevention approaches need to be tested further with larger samples of males and females at various ages across adolescence.

Several other targeted prevention programs have included an interpersonal component, although it was not necessarily the central focus of the intervention. For example, as described above, the PPPs consisted of both a cognitive and a social problem-solving component (Cardemil et al., 2007; Gillham et al., 2006b; Gillham et al., 2006a; Gillham et al., 1995; Jaycox et al., 1994; Quayle et al., 2001; Reivich, 1996; Roberts et al., 2003; Shatté, 1996; Yu & Seligman, 2002). In addition, various other prevention programs have included social skills training or a social problem-solving component (Eggert, Thompson, Herting, & Nicholas, 1995; Lamb, Puskar, Sereika, & Corcoran, 1998; Seligman et al., 1999; Sheffield et al., 2006). Because these interpersonal components were part of a broader program, however, it is not possible to determine from these studies the specific contribution of the interpersonal components of the interventions.

In summary, 13 of the 16 indicated prevention studies found some small to moderate positive effect on depressive symptoms either at the postintervention assessment and/or at follow-up. A summary of descriptive characteristics of all selective and indicated depression prevention studies can be found in Table 22.1. Next, we present the results of a meta-analysis of these depression prevention programs.

META-ANALYSIS OF SELECTIVE AND INDICATED DEPRESSION PREVENTION PROGRAMS

Similar to our early meta-analysis (Horowitz & Garber, 2006), we identified relevant studies through a computer search of the PsychInfo database using the keywords "depression" and "prevention." Each study was then inspected for selective and indicated depression prevention studies involving children and adolescents. To reduce publication bias, unpublished dissertations, obtained through interlibrary loan or directly from the author, were included. In addition, we examined references of all obtained studies to identify any additional relevant articles. Finally, a manual search was conducted of all journals within which an obtained study had been published, dating back to 1971 through December 2006, thereby updating Horowitz and Garber (2006), which only had studies through 2004. These journals included: *Archives of General Psychiatry*, the *Journal of the American Academy of Child & Adolescent Psychiatry*, *Prevention and Treatment*, *Psychological Science*, *Psychology in the Schools*, *School Psychology Quarterly*, the *International Journal of Mental Health Promotion*, the *American Journal of Community Psychology*, *Behavior Research and Therapy*, *Family Relations*, the *Journal of Abnormal Child Psychology*, the *Journal of Consulting and Clinical Psychology*, the *Journal of American College Health*, the *Journal of the American Medical Association*, and the *International Journal of Eating Disorders*.

To be included in the current meta-analysis, studies had to meet the following criteria: (a) one of the goals involved preventing depressive symptoms in children or adolescents, (b) the study had a selective and/or indicated sample, (c) participants were randomly assigned to condition, (d) the study compared an active intervention with a control condition, (e) the study included some or all participants under the age of 21, and (f) depressive symptoms were assessed using a generally accepted measure.

Effect sizes for each study were calculated by dividing the postintervention difference between the control group and intervention group depression scores by the standard deviation of the control group. Interventions may produce greater variability in the treatment group than in the control group. Therefore, following the suggestion of several meta-analysis experts (e.g., Weiss & Weisz, 1990; Weisz, Weiss, Han, Granger, & Morton, 1995), rather than using the pooled standard deviation, we calculated effect sizes with the standard deviation of the control group because it is presumed to be a more accurate estimate of the population variance. This calculation yields Cohen's *d* (Cohen, 1977), whereby an effect size of 0.2 is considered small, 0.5 is moderate, and 0.8 is large. In the few cases where means or standard deviations were not reported, we requested the data directly from the author(s). If the necessary data were not provided, we used the procedures suggested by Smith, Glass, and Miller (1980) to derive effect sizes using alternative statistical data (e.g., *t* or *F* values).

To preserve independence of effect size estimates, we used only one effect size from each subject sample in the analysis (Weiss & Weisz, 1990; Wilson, Lipsey, & Derzon, 2003). In addition, two studies (Reivich, 1996; Wolchik et al., 2002) included two variations of an intervention and a control group. Given that the two interventions did not differ on any of the characteristics assessed in the current meta-analysis, results for both intervention groups were pooled and compared to the one control group. In contrast, Sheffield and colleagues

(2006) compared an indicated, universal, and a combined universal plus indicated program to a control condition. Given that the purpose of the current chapter was to review targeted (i.e., selective or indicated) interventions, only the indicated condition was included and compared to the control group. Finally, one study (Stice et al., 2006) compared a CBT intervention to a wait-list control condition and four placebo or alternative interventions. Given the significant differences among the placebo and alternative conditions, and for the sake of consistency, in this meta-analysis we used the comparison of the CBT intervention group to the wait-list control condition.

All of the studies reviewed here included a self-report measure of depressive symptoms; far fewer included diagnostic interviews as well. Therefore, we computed effect sizes for all studies using data from the self-report measures. The most common self-report depression measure was the CDI (i.e., used in 17/27 studies). The self-report measures used in the effect size calculations for each study are presented in Table 22.1.

In every study reviewed here, depressive symptoms were assessed at baseline and immediately postintervention; several studies also conducted follow-up assessments ranging from as short as 1 month to as long as 6 years; the most common follow-up period was 6 months. In the current meta-analysis, we computed effect sizes for immediately postintervention, at the follow-up closest to 6 months (range = 3 to 18 months), and at the last conducted follow-up assessment.

Given that effect sizes from small samples are known to be biased estimates of population parameters, an adjustment for small sample bias was applied to each effect size (Hedges & Olkin, 1985). In addition, to give more weight to effect sizes from studies with larger samples and with smaller standard errors, each effect size was weighted by the inverse of its variance (Hedges & Olkin, 1985).

RESULTS

To test whether effect size values differed significantly from zero, we used SPSS macros created by Wilson (2005), which generate z tests. To examine whether the various effect sizes in the meta-analysis were estimating the same population mean, we conducted a homogeneity analysis based on Hedges and Olkin's (1985) Q statistic, which is designed to test whether the observed variability across effect sizes is greater than expected from subject-level sampling error. Potential moderators of effect size variability were examined using a meta-analytic analog to the analysis of variance (ANOVA) for categorical independent variables (e.g., type of intervention), and using a modified weighted regression for continuous variables (e.g., percent of females, mean age, number of sessions, length of follow-up; Lipsey & Wilson, 2001). All analyses were conducted using inverse-variance weighted, maximum likelihood, random effects models (Hunter & Schmidt, 2000; Lipsey & Wilson, 2001).

We identified 27 studies that met the inclusion criteria. Of these studies, 11 were selective and 16 were indicated. Table 22.1 presents effect size values and descriptive characteristics for each study. Positive effect sizes reflect lower levels of depressive symptoms in the intervention group relative to controls. Studies that had samples comprised primarily of college-age students (i.e., Burton et al., 2007; Forsyth, 2001; Peden, Rayens, Hall, & Beebe, 2001;

Seligman et al., 1999) were included because they are still considered to be "adolescents" (Steinberg & Lerner, 2004), and the transition to young adulthood is a time of heightened risk for depression (Rao et al., 1999; Reinherz, Giaconia, Hauf, Wasserman, & Silverman, 1999).

At postintervention, effect sizes ranged from –0.62 to 1.51. The weighted overall mean effect size was 0.33, which is considered small to moderate (Cohen, 1977). This effect was significantly different from 0 ($z=4.81$, $p<0.001$). At follow-up, effect sizes ranged from –0.07 to 1.95. The weighted overall mean effect size was 0.38, which was also significantly different from 0 ($z=4.52$, $p<0.001$).

Effect size distributions were significantly heterogeneous at both postintervention ($Q=86.41$, $p<0.0001$) and follow-up ($Q=72.61$, $p<0.0001$), indicating that the various effect sizes may not be estimating a common population mean and that their variability is greater than expected from sampling error alone. Potential moderators of this variability were then examined.

Type of Intervention

At postintervention, the weighted mean effect size for the selective studies was 0.26 ($z=2.20$, $p<0.05$), and for indicated prevention programs was 0.40 ($z=4.02$, $p<0.001$). This difference in effect sizes was not significant, $Q(1,25)=0.80$, $p=0.37$. At follow-up, the weighted mean effect size for selective studies was 0.34 ($z=2.26$, $p<0.05$), and indicated prevention programs was 0.36 ($z=3.49$, $p<0.001$). This difference in effect sizes was not significant, $Q(1,20)=0.02$, $p=0.89$.

Sex of Participants

Sex was operationalized as the percent of female participants in the sample. At postintervention, the effect of sex showed a nonsignificant trend ($z=1.87$, $p=0.06$, $B=0.31$), indicating that studies with a greater percent of female participants had slightly larger effect sizes. This effect was not significant at follow-up ($z=1.42$, $p=0.15$, $B=0.28$).

Age of Participants

There was a significant effect for age of participants at postintervention ($z=2.91$, $p<0.01$, $B=0.45$), such that larger effect sizes were found for studies of older participants. This effect was not significant at follow-up ($z=0.96$, $p=0.33$, $B=0.19$).

Length of Intervention and Length of Follow-Up

There was a significant effect for the number of sessions in the intervention on the effect size at postintervention ($z=-2.63$, $p<0.01$, $B=-0.42$). Specifically, studies with fewer sessions yielded larger effect sizes. At follow-up, this effect was no longer significant. ($z=-1.56$, $p=0.12$, $B=-0.30$). The number of months of the last conducted follow-up was not significantly related to the magnitude of the effect size at that follow-up ($z=-1.04$, $p=0.30$, $B=-.20$).

DISCUSSION

Consistent with other meta-analyses (Horowitz & Garber, 2006; Merry et al., 2004), we found that short-term effects (i.e., at postintervention) of depression prevention programs have been small but positive, whereas sustained effects over the course of follow-up have been less consistent. Moreover, the effect sizes for both selective and indicated programs were in the small to moderate range, and did not differ significantly from each other. Because we only focused on targeted programs, however, we could not replicate the fairly consistent finding that the effect sizes for selective and indicated programs tend to be larger than those of universal programs.

One difference between our meta-analyses and the one conducted by Merry et al. (2004) is in how gender was operationalized. For the moderation analyses by gender, Merry et al. included only the eight studies that had reported symptom results separately by gender, and they used pooled effect sizes for male versus female participants. They concluded that intervention was associated with significantly decreased symptoms at postintervention for boys, but not for girls, although in the six studies that used diagnostic outcomes, significant postintervention effects were found for girls, but not for boys. For either outcome, there were no significant gender differences during follow-up.

One limitation of analyzing only those studies that provide data for males and females separately is that the number of studies becomes very small (e.g., $n=8$). In contrast, because we operationalized sex as the percentage of females in each particular sample, all studies could be used. We found a somewhat larger effect on postintervention symptoms for samples with a higher percentage of females; this effect was not significant at follow-up, however. These differences across meta-analyses highlight the importance of researchers presenting the results of their intervention studies (i.e., means and standard deviations) broken down by sex.

The moderator analyses indicated that the effects at postintervention were stronger in studies with older teens and a higher percentage of females. This may be partly explained by the fact that the younger participants and boys in the no-intervention control group would be less likely than older girls to show increases in their levels of depressive symptoms at subsequent assessments. That is, epidemiological studies of community samples have shown that the rates of depression increase, particularly among females, around age 15 (Hankin et al., 1998). Thus, the prevention effect may be more apparent among older female samples because those in the control condition are likely to show increased depression. It is also possible that these depression prevention programs do not work as well with younger participants and males.

To examine whether the four studies of college-age participants were largely responsible for the findings with regard to age and gender, we reanalyzed the data with these samples removed. Results indeed showed that the age and gender effects were no longer significant. The extent to which the efficacy of depression prevention programs differs by age and gender among children and younger adolescents requires further study. In addition to needing large samples in order to show a prevention effect when using younger samples, the content of the interventions may need to be altered further to make them more developmentally appropriate, particularly programs that require metacognitive abilities and social perspective taking.

Prevention Versus Treatment

A "prevention" effect has been defined as one in which there is a diminished or no increase in symptoms or disorders in the intervention group relative to controls. In contrast, a "treatment" effect is one in which there is a greater reduction in symptoms or disorders in the intervention group relative to controls (Gillham et al., 2000; Horowitz & Garber, 2006). Among selective studies, Quayle et al. (2001) showed a prevention effect; that is, the control group had greater increases in depressive symptoms than the intervention group. Sandler et al. (2003) also found a prevention effect in girls' self-report of internalizing symptoms, although not for depressive symptoms, in particular. The other selective studies showed "treatment" effects; that is, depressive symptoms decreased in the intervention group compared to controls. Similarly, among indicated studies, most effects would be considered treatment. A few indicated studies, however, have shown prevention effects; that is, an increase in depressive symptoms (Gillham et al., 2006b; Jaycox et al., 1994; Reivich, 1996) or disorders (Clarke et al., 2001; Garber et al., 2007) in the control group, and either a decrease or no increase in depressive symptoms, or lower rates of depressive disorders, in the intervention group.

A related issue is whether the term "prevention" should be reserved for only the first onset of a disorder, or whether it can be extended to prevention of recurrence. According to Mrazek and Haggerty (1994), prevention refers to "interventions that occur before the initial onset of a disorder" (p. 23). Given that the processes underlying first versus subsequent depressive episodes may differ (e.g., Lewinsohn, Allen, Seeley, & Gotlib, 1999a; Monroe & Harkness, 2005), it is important to determine whether a particular intervention can prevent a first onset and/or a recurrence. Participants should be either screened-out based on history of depression or the analyses should be conducted in a way that separates first onsets from recurrences. In the studies by Clarke and colleagues (Clarke et al., 1995; Clarke et al., 2001; Garber et al., 2007), the samples contained a substantial number of participants with histories of depression; therefore, the analyses should examine whether the pattern of results differed for individuals with and without prior MDEs. Interventions that occur subsequent to a diagnosis of depression are considered by some to be treatment rather than prevention (Sutton, 2007). Although the prevention of relapse and recurrence of MDD is important, it is not "pure" or "primary" prevention because the first onset was not prevented. This distinction may simply be semantic, although both theory and empirical research suggest that the processes underlying first versus recurrent depressive episodes may differ, and therefore different types of interventions may be necessary to prevent them.

Following the recommendations of Mrazek and Haggerty (1994) regarding an intervention spectrum, we suggest that the broader construct of intervention be conceptualized along a continuum from "primary" prevention of the first onset of symptoms and disorder, to preventing onset in "selective" at risk samples, to "indicated" prevention aimed at keeping subsyndromal states from becoming a full disorder, to prevention of recurrence of new episodes among individuals who already have had an episode, to treatment of individuals experiencing a current depressive episode that includes a relapse prevention component and maintenance (see Figure 22.1). An important question is whether the essence of the interventions at these different points along the continuum can be the same, but in different doses, frequencies, and intensities, or rather are fundamentally different approaches to prevention and treatment needed?

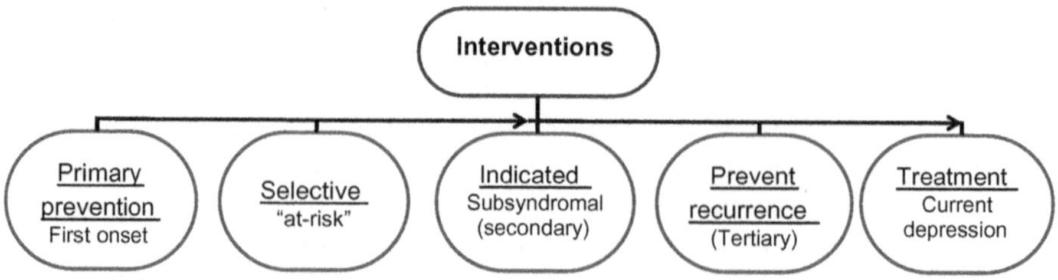

Figure 22.1 An intervention spectrum from prevention to treatment.

Thus far, there has been a tendency to start with existing treatments that have been efficacious in reducing symptoms in currently depressed adolescents (e.g., CBT, IPT) and then translating them into prevention programs. Although this is a logical approach, it may not be the most efficient or effective strategy. Basic cognitive processes, such as state-dependent learning and transfer of training, may influence whether knowledge learned during a non-depressed state will generalize to the more affectively charged depressive state. Moreover, adolescents' motivation to participate and learn depression prevention strategies when they are euthymic should be addressed early in the intervention. Anecdotally, our experience has been that no matter what the content of a prevention program is, any intervention with youth should be guided by a few basic principles: keep it simple, keep it interesting, and make it relevant. These are likely the "nonspecifics" that are necessary, although probably not sufficient.

CONCLUSIONS AND FUTURE DIRECTIONS

Although there have now been over 30 studies testing the efficacy of programs for preventing depression in at-risk youth, many important issues remain. If we were just beginning to construct a program for preventing depression in adolescents, where would we start? Should prevention programs be based on known risk and protective factors, successful psychosocial treatments, or other considerations? What relevant advances in genetics, neuroscience, epidemiology, psychosocial predictors, developmental psychopathology, and animal models can be used to inform the development of new approaches to prevention? and what basic research still needs to be conducted?

Epidemiologic and clinical research indicates that increased risk for depression is associated with being female, parental history of depression, subclinical depressive symptoms, anxiety, stressful life events, neurobiological dysregulation, neuroticism, negative cognitions, problems in self-regulation and coping, and interpersonal dysfunction (Garber, 2006). These vulnerabilities both increase individuals' chances of encountering stress and decrease their ability to deal with the stress once it occurs. Although several depression prevention programs have targeted one or more of these risk factors, a comprehensive program for preventing depression in adolescents that includes multiple intervention components, each of which addresses risk and protective factors across different domains and levels of analysis has not yet been developed or tested.

Have we been targeting the wrong things? Should we focus on the contexts (e.g., family, schools, peers, poverty) that burden the individual, rather than on the individual? Albee (2005) suggested that focusing on strengthening the individual's resistance to stressors ignores the need for the larger society to directly reduce or eliminate the stressors themselves. Thus, current prevention approaches that emphasize building individual skills and resiliency should be complemented by improvements in the quality of children's homes, schools, neighborhoods, and community environments.

Another basis for the development of prevention programs has been to take treatments that have been found to be effective in reducing depressive disorders and modify them into preventive interventions. Thus far, this has been the case for CB approaches in particular (e.g., Clarke et al, 1995; Clarke et al., 2001; Gillham & Reivich, 1999; Gillham et al., 1995), and for programs based on IPT for adolescents (e.g., Young et al., 2006). Such treatments have been somewhat successful in reducing current depression in teens, but can the same techniques be used to prevent depression? Are the processes that reduce depression in treatment, the same as those that produce the onset of depressive symptoms and disorder? Moreover, to what extent do the skills (e.g., cognitive, coping, communication) taught in these therapies transfer if learned during a nondepressed state? Are the persons targeted for depression prevention programs motivated to develop skills for changing depressive symptoms if they are not currently experiencing or have never had them? Finally, what developmental, cultural, and gender differences need to be considered when developing programs for preventing depression? How do we construct depression prevention programs that are appropriately sensitive to these differences?

Efficacy trials examine whether the intervention of interest "works" better than doing nothing. The definition of "working" involves how large was the effect size? How long did the effects persist? Were the effects of the intervention specific to the primary outcome (i.e., depression) or were other symptoms and disorders (e.g., anxiety, externalizing) affected as well? Did the study find a prevention versus a treatment effect?

The next important question is how does the preventive intervention work? What are the essential ingredients? This can be addressed by comparing the program to an active control or alternative intervention that is similar in most respects (e.g., number and length of sessions, therapist training) to the program of interest, except for the components that presumably are responsible for the preventive effect. To date, only a few studies of targeted samples have examined whether the preventive intervention outperformed an active credible control intervention (e.g., Stice et al., 2006). Dismantling studies can also be used whereby different components or combinations of components are compared to each other as well as to a no-intervention control. This approach has been used, for example, to examine the incremental contribution of adding a child or parent component (e.g., Wolchik et al., 2002).

Another way to examine *how* an intervention works is by testing whether the hypothesized processes actually *mediate* the relation between the intervention and the outcome. For example, do CB programs prevent depression by teaching youth how to change negative cognitions and/or problem-solve? Is IPT effective because it changes interpersonal relationships? Does the intervention produce change in the putative mediator, which in turn leads to change in depression? The study of the Family Bereavement Program (Sandler et al., 2003; Schmiege et al., 2006) provides a nice example of how to test mediation in the context of a prevention trial.

Equally important is to identify why a program did *not* work or did not work as well as expected. Possible reasons for weak findings could be that the intervention was not designed and/or implemented well. For example, the therapist might have delivered the program with inadequate fidelity and/or poor quality. Other possible reasons for a program not working may be due to a failure to identify the "right" parameters with regard to the number, length, and frequency of sessions, and over what period of time. Are booster/continuation sessions necessary? If so, how many and how often? How long should the intervention effect last? Is the preventive intervention best implemented individually, in groups, families, or groups of families? Should groups be same or mixed gender? What is the best age range of the participants in a group? How many participants should be in a group? How many group leaders are needed? Who should deliver the intervention—professional clinicians, teachers, graduate students, peers?

Another way to try to understand the processes underlying the effects of a preventive intervention is to identify for whom it does and does not work. Moderator variables affect the size and/or direction of the relation between the intervention and outcome (i.e., changes in depression), and are tested by analyzing the interaction between intervention condition (active versus control) and a presumed moderator (e.g., sex, age, initial levels of depressive symptoms) to predict the level of depressive symptoms at postintervention and follow-up evaluations. By identifying significant moderators, we can then focus our efforts on the participant and design features (e.g., older, female, single-gender groups, booster sessions) that are associated with the largest effects sizes. It is equally important, however, to identify for whom the intervention was least effective (e.g., younger, male), determine possible reasons for the small effects with such individuals, and then modify or supplement the intervention to address these limitations.

Replication studies conducted by independent investigators should also be conducted. Although the positive intervention effects for three programs have replicated across studies conducted by the same laboratory, including the PRP (Cardemil et al., 2007 Gillham et al., 2006a; Seligman et al., 1999), the Coping with Stress program (Clarke et al., 1995; Clarke et al., 2001), and the Blues Program (Burton et al., 2007 Stice et al., 2006) most have not been replicated by independent laboratories, with the exception of the PRP. Given that independent replication is a necessary step in establishing the efficacy of a program, (American Psychological Association Task Force on Psychological Intervention Guidelines, 1995), this is an important area for future study.

Given this long list of questions that remain, some have argued that the depression prevention field is still in the efficacy stage, and may not be ready for effectiveness trials and more widespread dissemination (e.g., Merry & Spence, 2007). It would be more efficient to conduct trials that could inform us about both efficacy and effectiveness simultaneously, but that would leave too many uncontrolled variables. Future studies of programs aimed at preventing depression in youth need to examine potential mediators and moderators, evaluate the fidelity and adherence of program implementation, assess participant attendance, compliance, and retention rates, and conduct longer follow-up periods. At this point, even the best studies have produced only small to moderate effect sizes, and the effects tend not to endure. Future studies of depression prevention programs for children and adolescents should test theoretically and empirically informed interventions, include no-intervention and active control groups, randomly assign participants to condition, use independent evaluators to do the evaluations, assess both symptom and diagnostic outcomes specific to depression as well as comorbid disorders and levels of functional impairment, conduct longer follow-up periods, and examine moderators and mediators of the effect of the intervention on depression. Determining how and for whom an intervention works will allow us to more efficiently and effectively disseminate it to those who need it most.

NOTE

1. Judy Garber was supported in part by grants (R01 MH57822; R01 MH64735) and an Independent Research Scientist Development Award (K02 MH66249) from the National Institute of Mental Health, and a grant from the William T. Grant Foundation (173096); Christian Webb was supported in part by a Social Sciences and Humanities Research Council of Canada (SSHRC) Doctoral Fellowship during completion of this work.

REFERENCES

Albee, G. W. (2005). Call to revolution in the prevention of emotional disorders. *Ethical Human Psychology and Psychiatry, 7*, 37–44.

Amato, P. R. (2001). Children of divorce in the 1990s: An update of the Amato and Keith (1991) meta-analysis. *Journal of Family Psychology, 15*, 355–370.

American Psychological Association Task Force on Psychological Intervention Guidelines. (1995). *Template for developing guidelines: Interventions for mental disorders and psychological aspects of physical disorders.* Washington, DC: APA.

Angold, A., Costello, E. J., & Erkanli, A. (1999). Comorbidity. *Journal of Child Psychology and Psychiatry, 40*, 57–87.

Beardslee, W., Gladstone, T., Wright, E., & Cooper, A. (2003). A family-based approach to the prevention of depressive symptoms in children at risk: Evidence of parental and child change. *Pediatrics, 112*, 119–131.

Beardslee, W. R., Versage, E. M., & Gladstone, T. R. G. (1998). Children of affectively ill parents: A review of the past 10 years. *Journal of the American Academy of Child & Adolescent Psychiatry, 37*, 1134–1141.

Beardslee, W., Wright, E., Gladstone, T., & Forbes, P. (2007). Long-term effects from randomized trial of two public health preventive interventions for parental depression. *Journal of Family Psychology, 21*, 703–713.

Beardslee, W. R., Wright, E. J., Salt, P., Drezner, K., Gladstone, T. R. G., Versage, E. M., et al. (1997). Examination of children's responses to two preventive intervention strategies over time. *Journal of the American Academy of Child and Adolescent Psychiatry, 36*, 196–204.

Beck, A. T., Rush, A. J., Shaw, B. F., & Emery, G. (1979). *Cognitive therapy of depression.* New York: Guilford Press.

Birmaher, B., Brent, D. A., Kolko, D., Baugher, M., Bridge, J., Iyengar, S., et al. (2000). Clinical outcome after short-term psychotherapy for adolescents with major depressive disorder. *Archives of General Psychiatry, 57*, 29–36.

Birmaher, B., Ryan, N., Williamson, D., Brent, D., Kaufman, J., Dahl, R., et al. (1996). Childhood and adolescent depression: A review of the past 10 years, Part I. *Journal of the American Academy of Child & Adolescent Psychiatry, 35*, 1427–1439.

Blazer, D. G., Kessler, R. C., McGonagle, K. A., & Swartz, M. S. (1994). The prevalence and distribution of major depression in a national community sample: The National Comorbidity Survey. *American Journal of Psychiatry, 151*, 979–986.

Brent, D. A., Holder, D., Kolko, D., Birmaher, B., Baugher, M., Roth, C., et al. (1997). A clinical psychotherapy trial for adolescent depression comparing cognitive, family, and supportive therapy. *Archives of General Psychiatry, 54*, 877–885.

Brent, D. A., Kolko, D. J., Birmaher, B., Baugher, M., Bridge, J., Roth, C., et al. (1998). Predictors of treatment efficacy in a clinical trial of three psychosocial treatments for adolescent depression. *Journal of the American Academy of Child & Adolescent Psychiatry, 37*, 906–914.

Brent, D. A., Perper, J. A., Moritz, G., Allman, C., Friend, A., Roth, C., et al. (1993). Psychiatric risk factors for adolescent suicide: A case-control study. *Journal of the American Academy of Child & Adolescent Psychiatry, 32*, 521–529.

Burton, E. M., Stice, E., Bearman, S. K., & Rohde, P. (2007). An experimental test of the affect-regulation theory of bulimic symptoms and substance use: A randomized trial. *International Journal of Eating Disorders, 40*, 27–36.

Caplan, G. (1964). *Principles of preventive psychiatry.* New York: Basic Books.

Cardemil, E. V., Reivich, K. J., Beevers, C. G., Seligman, M. E. P., & James, J. (2007). The prevention of depressive symptoms in low-income minority children: Two-year follow-up. *Behaviour Research and Therapy, 45*, 313–327.

Cardemil, E. V., Reivich, K. J., & Seligman, M. E. P. (2002). The prevention of depressive symptoms in low-income minority middle-school students. *Prevention & Treatment*, Article 8. Retrieved April 17, 2004 from http://journals.apa.org./prevention/volume5/pre0050008a.html.

Clair, D., & Genest, M. (1987). Variables associated with the adjustment of offspring of alcoholic fathers. *Journal of Studies on Alcohol, 47*, 180–182.

Clarke, G. N., Hawkins, W., Murphy, M., & Sheeber, L. B. (1993). School-based primary prevention of depressive symptomatology in adolescents: Findings from two studies. *Journal of Adolescent Research, 8*, 183–204.

Clarke, G. N., Hawkins, W., Murphy, M., Sheeber, L. B., Lewinsohn, P. M., & Seeley, J. R. (1995). Targeted prevention of unipolar depressive disorder in an at-risk sample of high school adolescents: A randomized trial of a group cognitive intervention. *Journal of the American Academy of Child & Adolescent Psychiatry, 34*, 312–321.

Clarke, G. N., Hops, H., Lewinsohn, P. M., Andrews, J., Seeley, J. R., & Williams, J. (1992). Cognitive behavioral group treatment of adolescent depression: Prediction of outcome. *Behavior Therapy, 23*, 341–354.

Clarke, G. N., Hornbrook, M., Lynch, F., Polen, M., Gale, J., Beardslee, W., et al. (2001). A randomized trial of a group cognitive intervention for preventing depression in adolescent offspring of depressed parents. *Archives of General Psychiatry, 58*, 1127–1134.

Clarke, G. N., Lewinsohn, P. M., & Hops, H. (1990). *Instructor's manual for the Adolescent Coping with Depression Course.* Eugene, OR: Castalia Press.

Cohen, J. (1977). *Statistical power analysis for the behavioral sciences* (rev. ed.). New York: Academic Press.

Committee on Safety of Medicines. (2004). *Use of selective serotonin reuptake inhibitors in children and adolescents with major depressive disorder.* Retrieved January 16, 2006, from http://www.antidepressantsfacts.com/2003–12-10-CSM-SSRIs-childrenUK_bestanden/csmhomemain.htm.

Costello, E. J., Mustillo, S., Erkanli, A., Keeler, G., & Angold, A. (2003). Prevalence and development of psychiatric disorders in childhood and adolescence. *Archives of General Psychiatry, 60*, 837–844.

Cuijpers, P. (2003). Examining the effects of prevention programs on the incidence of new cases of mental disorders: The lack of statistical power. *American Journal of Psychiatry, 160*, 1385–1391.

Curry, J. F. (2001). Specific psychotherapies for childhood and adolescent depression. *Biological Psychiatry, 49*, 1091–1100.

Cyranowski, J. M., Frank, E., Young, E., & Shear, K. (2000). Adolescent-onset of the gender difference in lifetime rates of major depression. *Archives of General Psychiatry, 57*, 21–27.

DiMascio, A., Weissman, M. M., Prusoff, B. A., Neu, C., Zwilling, M., & Klerman, G. L. (1979). Differential symptom reduction by drugs and psychotherapy in acute depression. *Archives of General Psychiatry, 36*, 1450–1456.

Eggert, L. L., Thompson, E. A., Herting, J. R., & Nicholas, L. J. (1995). Reducing suicide potential among high-risk youth: Tests of a school-based prevention program. *Suicide & Life-Threatening Behavior, 25*, 276–296.

Elkin, I., Shea, M. T., Watkins, J. T., Imber, S. D., Sotsky, S. M., Collins, J. F., et al. (1989). National Institute of Mental Health Treatment of Depression Collaborative Research Program: General effectiveness of treatments. *Archives of General Psychiatry, 46*, 971–982.

Emslie, G. J., Heiligenstein, J. H., Wagner, K. D., Hoog, S. L., Ernest, D. E., Brown, E., et al. (2002). Fluoxetine for acute treatment of depression in children and adolescents. *Journal of the American Academy of Child & Adolescent Psychiatry, 41*, 1205–1215.

Emslie, G. J., Rush, A. J., Weinberg, W. A., Gullion, C. M., Rintelmann, J., & Hughes, C. W. (1997). Recurrence of major depressive disorder in hospitalized children and adolescents. *Journal of the American Academy of Child & Adolescent Psychiatry, 36*, 785–792.

Emslie, G. J., Rush, A. J., Weinberg, W. A., Kowatch, R. A., Carmody, T., & Mayes, T. L. (1998). Fluoxetine in child and adolescent depression: Acute and maintenance treatment. *Depression and Anxiety, 7*, 32–39.

Fergusson, D. M., Horwood, L. J., Ridder, E. M., & Beautrais, A. L. (2005). Subthreshold depression in adolescence and mental health outcomes in adulthood. *Archives of General Psychiatry, 62*, 66–72.

Flay, B. R. (1986). Efficacy and effectiveness trials (and other phases of research) in the development of health promotion programs. *Preventive Medicine, 15*, 451–474.

Forsyth, K. M. (2001). The design and implementation of a depression prevention program (Doctoral dissertation, University of Rhode Island). *Dissertation Abstracts International, 61*(12), 6704B (UMI No. 9999536).

Frank, E., Kupfer, D. J., Perel, J. M., Cornes, C., Jarrett, D. B., Mallinger, A. G., et al. (1990). Three-year outcomes for maintenance therapies in recurrent depression. *Archives of General Psychiatry, 47,* 1093–1099.

Garber, J. (2006). Depression in children and adolescents: Linking risk research and prevention. *American Journal of Preventive Medicine, 31*(Suppl. 1), 104–125.

Garber, J., Brent, D., Clarke, G., Beardslee, W. R., Weersing, R. V., Gladstone, T., et al. (2007, September). *Prevention of depression in at-risk adolescents: Short-term outcome.* Invited paper presented at the Child and Adolescent Depression Consortium, Pittsburgh, PA.

Garber, J., & McCauley, E. (2002). Prevention of depression and suicide in children and adolescents. In M. Lewis (Ed.), *Child and adolescent psychiatry: A comprehensive text* (3rd ed., pp. 805–821). Baltimore, MD: Williams & Wilkins.

Gillham, J. E., Hamilton, J., Freres, D. R., Patton, K., & Gallop, R. (2006b). Preventing depression among early adolescents in the primary care setting: A randomized controlled study of the Penn Resiliency Program. *Journal of Abnormal Child Psychology, 34,* 203–219.

Gillham, J. E., & Reivich, K. J. (1999). Prevention of depressive symptoms in school children: A research update. *Psychological Science, 10,* 461–462.

Gillham, J. E., Reivich, K. J., Freres, D. R., Lascher, M., Litzinger, S., Shatté, A., et al. (2006a). School-based prevention of depression and anxiety symptoms in early adolescence: A pilot of a parent intervention component. *School Psychology Quarterly, 21,* 323–348.

Gillham, J. E., Reivich, K. J., Jaycox, L. H., & Seligman, M. P. E. (1995). Prevention of depressive symptoms in schoolchildren: Two-year follow-up. *Psychological Science, 6,* 343–351.

Gillham, J. E., Shatté, A. J., & Freres, D. R. (2000). Preventing depression: A review of cognitive-behavioral and family interventions. *Applied & Preventive Psychology, 9,* 63–88.

Goodman, S. H., & Gotlib, I. H. (1999). Risk for psychopathology in the children of depressed mothers: A developmental model for understanding mechanisms of transmission. *Psychological Review, 106,* 458–90.

Gwynn, C. A., & Brantley, H. T. (1987). Effects of a divorce group intervention for elementary school children. *Psychology in the Schools, 24,* 161–164.

Hains, A. A., & Ellman, S. W. (1994). Stress inoculation training as a preventive intervention for high school youths. *Journal of Cognitive Psychotherapy: An International Quarterly, 8,* 219–232.

Hankin, B. L., & Abramson, L. Y. (2001). Development of gender differences in depression: An elaborated cognitive vulnerability-transactional stress theory. *Psychological Bulletin, 127,* 773–796.

Hankin, B. L., Abramson, L. Y., Moffitt, T. E., Silva, P. A., McGee, R., & Angell, K. A. (1998). Development of depression from preadolescence to young adulthood: Emerging gender differences in a 10 year longitudinal study. *Journal of Abnormal Psychology, 107,* 128–141.

Harrington, R.C., Fudge, H., Rutter, M., Pickles, A., & Hill, J. (1990) Adult outcomes of childhood and adolescent depression. I. Psychiatric status. *Archives of General Psychiatry, 47,* 465–473.

Hedges, L. V., & Olkin, I. (1985). *Statistical methods for meta-analysis.* Orlando, FL: Academic Press.

Heller, K. (1996). Coming of age of prevention science: Comments on the 1994 National Institute of Mental Health–Institute of Medicine Prevention Reports. *American Psychologist, 51*, 1123–1127.

Hirshfeld, R., Keller, M., Panico, S., Arons, B., Barlow, D., Davidoff, F., et al. (1997). The National Depressive and Manic-Depressive Association consensus statement on the undertreatment of depression. *Journal of the American Medical Association, 277*, 333–340.

Hollon, S. D., Thase, M. E., & Markowitz, J. C. (2002). Treatment and prevention of depression. *Psychological Science in the Public Interest, 3*, 39–77.

Horowitz, J. L., & Garber, J. (2006). The prevention of depressive symptoms in children and adolescents: A meta-analytic review. *Journal of Consulting and Clinical Psychology, 74*, 401–415.

Horowitz, J. L., Garber, J., Ciesla, J. A., Young, J., & Mufson, L. (2007). Prevention of depressive symptoms in adolescents: A randomized trial of cognitive-behavioral and interpersonal prevention programs. *Journal of Consulting and Clinical Psychology, 75*, 693–706.

Hunter, J. E., & Schmidt, F. L. (2006). Fixed effects vs. random effects meta-analysis models: Implications for cumulative research knowledge. *International Journal of Selection and Assessment, 8*, 275–292.

Ialongo, N. S., Werthamer, L., Kellam, S. G., Brown, C. H., Wang, S., & Lin, Y. (1999). Proximal impact of two first-grade preventive interventions on the early risk behaviors for later substance abuse, depression, and antisocial behavior. *American Journal of Community Psychology, 27*, 599–641.

Jané-Llopis, E., Hosman, C., Jenkins, R., & Anderson, P. (2003). Predictors of efficacy in depression prevention programmes. *British Journal of Psychiatry, 183*, 384–97.

Jaycox, L. H., Reivich, K. J., Gillham, J., & Seligman, M. E. P. (1994). Prevention of depressive symptoms in school children. *Behavior Research and Therapy, 32*, 801–816.

Judd, L. L., Akiskal, H. S., Maser, J. D., Zeller, P. J., Endicott, J., Coryell, W., et al. (1998). A prospective 12-year study of subsyndromal and syndromal depressive symptoms in unipolar major depressive disorders. *Archives of General Psychiatry, 55*, 694–700.

Kaminski, K. M., & Garber, J. (2002). Depressive spectrum disorders in adolescents: Episode duration and predictors of time to recovery. *Journal of the American Academy of Child & Adolescent Psychiatry, 41*, 410–418.

Kandel, D. B., & Davies, M. (1986). Adult sequelae of adolescent depressive symptoms. *Archives of General Psychiatry, 43*, 255–262.

Kaufman, J., Martin, A., King, R. A., & Charney, D. (2001). Are child-, adolescent-, and adult-onset depression one and the same disorder? *Biological Psychiatry, 49*, 980–1001.

Kellam, S. G., Rebok, G. W., Mayer, L. S., Ialongo, N., & Kalodner, C. R. (1994). Depressive symptoms over first grade and their response to a developmental epidemiologically based preventive trial aimed at improving achievement. *Development and Psychopathology, 6*, 463–481.

Kendler, K. S., Gardner, C. O., & Prescott, C. A. (2002). Toward a comprehensive developmental model for major depression in women. *American Journal of Psychiatry, 159*, 1133–1145.

Kessler, R. C., Wai, T. C., Demler, O., & Walters, E. E. (2005). Prevalence, severity, and comorbidity of 12-month DSM-IV disorders in the National Comorbidity Survey Replication. *Archives of General Psychiatry, 62*, 617–627.

Kovacs, M. (1996). The course of childhood-onset depressive disorders. *Psychiatric Annals, 26*, 326–330.

Kovacs, M., Feinberg, T. L., Crouse-Novak, M., Paulauskas, S. L., Pollock, M., & Finkelstein, R. (1984). Depressive disorders in childhood. II. A longitudinal study of the risk for a subsequent major depression. *Archives of General Psychiatry, 41*, 653–649.

Lamb, J. M., Puskar, K. R., Sereika, M., & Corcoran, M. (1998). School-based intervention to promote coping in rural teens. *American Journal of Maternal and Child Nursing, 23*, 187–194.

Le, H., Munoz, R. F., Ippen, C. G., & Stoddard, J. L. (2003). Treatment is not enough: We must prevent major depression in women. *Prevention & Treatment, 6*(2). Retrieved March 10, 2005, from http://journals.apa.org/prevention/volume6/pre0060010a.html.

Lewinsohn, P. M., Allen, N. B., Seeley, J. R., & Gotlib, I. H. (1999a). First onset versus recurrence of depression: Differential processes of psychosocial risk. *Journal of Abnormal Psychology, 108*, 483–489.

Lewinsohn, P. M., & Clarke, G. N. (1999). Psychosocial treatments for adolescent depression. *Clinical Psychology Review, 19*, 329–342.

Lewinsohn, P. M., Clarke, G. N., Seeley, J. R., & Rohde, P. (1994). Major depression in community adolescents: Age at onset, episode duration, and time to recurrence. *Journal of the American Academy of Child & Adolescent Psychiatry, 33*, 809–818.

Lewinsohn, P. M., Rohde, P., Klein, D. N., & Seeley, J. R. (1999b). Natural course of adolescent major depressive disorder. I: Continuity into young adulthood. *Journal of the American Academy of Child & Adolescent Psychiatry, 38*, 56–63.

Lewinsohn, P. M., Rohde, P., Seeley, J. R., Klein, D. N., & Gotlib, I. H. (2003). Psychosocial characteristics of young adults who have experienced and recovered from major depressive disorder during adolescence. *Journal of Abnormal Psychology 112*, 353–363.

Lewinsohn, P. M., Solomon, A., Seeley, J. R., & Zeiss, A. (2000). Clinical implications of "subthreshold" depressive symptoms. *Journal of Abnormal Psychology, 109*, 345–351.

Lipsey, M. W., & Wilson, D. B. (2001). *Practical meta-analysis: Applied social research methods series* (Vol. 49). Thousand Oaks, CA: Sage.

Lowry-Webster, H. M., Barrett, P. M., & Dadds, M. R. (2001). A universal prevention trial of anxiety and depressive symptomatology in childhood: Preliminary data from an Australian study. *Behaviour Change, 18*, 36–50.

Lowry-Webster, H. M., Barrett, P. M., & Lock, S. (2003). A universal prevention trial of anxiety symptomatology during childhood: Results at 1-year follow-up. *Behaviour Change, 20*, 25–43.

Lutzke, J. R., Ayers, T. S., Sandler, I. N., & Barr, A. (1997). Risks and interventions for the parentally bereaved child. In S. A. Wolchik & I. N. Sandler (Eds.), *Handbook of children's coping with common life stressors: Linking theory, research and interventions* (pp. 215–243). New York: Plenum Press.

McCauley, E., Myers, K., Mitchell, J. Calderon, R., Scholredt, K., & Treder, R. (1993). Depression in young people: Initial presentation and clinical course. *Journal of the American Academy of Child & Adolescent Psychiatry, 32*, 714–722.

Merry, S., McDowell, H., Hetrick, S., Bir, J., & Muller, N. (2004). Psychological and/or educational interventions for the prevention of depression in children and adolescents. *The Cochrane Database of Systematic Reviews, 2*, CD003380.

Merry, S. N., & Spence, S. H. (2007). Attempting to prevent depression in youth: A systematic review of the evidence. *Early Intervention in Psychiatry, 1*, 128–137.

Monroe, S. M., & Harkness, K. L. (2005). Life stress, the "Kindling" hypothesis, and the recurrence of depression: Considerations from a life stress perspective. *Psychological Review, 112*, 417–445.

Mrazek, P. J., & Haggerty, R. J. (Eds.). (1994). *Reducing risks for mental disorders: Frontiers for preventive intervention research.* Washington, DC: National Academy Press.

Mufson, L., Dorta, K. P., Moreau, D., & Weissman, M. M. (2004a). *Interpersonal psychotherapy for depressed adolescents* (2nd ed.). New York: Guilford Press.

Mufson, L., Dorta, K. P., Wickramaratne, P., Nomura, Y., Olfson, M., & Weissman, M. M. (2004b). A randomized effectiveness trail of interpersonal psychotherapy for depressed adolescents. *Archives of General Psychiatry, 61*, 577–584.

Mufson, L., Weissman, M. M., Moreau, D., & Garfinkel, R. (1999). Efficacy of interpersonal psychotherapy for depressed adolescents. *Archives of General Psychiatry, 56*, 573–579.

Munoz, R. F., Le, H. N., Clarke, G. N., & Jaycox, L. H. (2002). Preventing the onset of major depression. In I. H. Gotlib & C. L. Hammen (Eds.), *Handbook of depression* (pp. 343–359). New York: Guilford Press.

Newman, D. L., Moffitt, T. E., Caspi, A., Magdol, L., Silva, P. A., & Stanton, W. R. (1996). Psychiatric disorder in a birth cohort of young adults: Prevalence, comorbidity, clinical significance, and new case incidence from ages 11 to 21. *Journal of Consulting and Clinical Psychology, 64*, 552–562.

Offord, D. R., Kraemer, H. C., Kazdin, A. E., Jensen, P. S., & Harrington, R. (1998). Lowering the burden of suffering from child psychiatric disorder: Trade-offs among clinical, targeted, and universal interventions. *Journal of the American Academy of Child & Adolescent Psychiatry, 37*, 686–694.

Peden, A. R., Rayens, M. K., Hall, L. A., & Beebe, L. H. (2001). Preventing depression in high-risk college women: A report of an 18-month follow-up. *Journal of American College Health, 49*, 299–306.

Petersen, A. C., Leffert, N., Graham, B., Alwin, J., & Ding, S. (1997). Promoting mental health during the transition into adolescence. In J. Schulenberg, J. L. Muggs & A. K. Hierrelmann (Eds.), *Health risks and developmental transitions during adolescence* (pp. 471–497). New York: Cambridge University Press.

Pickles, A., Rowe, R., Simonoff, E., Foley, D., Rutter, M., & Silberg, J. (2001). Child psychiatric symptoms and psychosocial impairment: Relationship and prognostic significance. *British Journal of Psychiatry, 179*, 230–235.

Pine, D. S., Cohen, E., Cohen, P., & Brook, J. (1999). Adolescent depressive symptoms as predictors of adult depression: Moodiness or mood disorder? *American Journal of Psychiatry, 156*, 133–135.

Pine, D. S., Cohen, E., Gurley, D., Brook, J., & Ma, Y. (1998). The risk for early-adulthood anxiety and depressive disorders in adolescents with anxiety and depressive disorders. *Archives of General Psychiatry, 55*, 56–64.

Puskar, K. R., Sereika, S. M., & Tusaie-Mumford, K. (2003). Effect of the Teaching Kids to Cope (TKC) Program on outcomes of depression and coping among rural adolescents. *Journal of Child and Adolescent Psychiatric Nursing, 16*, 71–80.

Quayle, D., Dzuirawiec, S., Roberts, C., Kane, R., & Ebsworthy, G. (2001). The effect of an optimism and life skills program on depressive symptoms in preadolescence. *Behaviour Change, 18*, 194–203.

Radloff, L. S. (1977). The CES-D Scale: A self-report depression scale for research in the general population. *Applied Psychological Measurement, 1*, 385–401.

Rao, U., Hammen, C., & Daley, S. E. (1999). Continuity of depression during the transition to adulthood: A 5-year longitudinal study of young women. *Journal of the American Academy of Child & Adolescent Psychiatry, 38*, 908–915.

Rao, U., Ryan, N. D., Birmaher, B., & Dahl, R. E. (1995). Unipolar depression in adolescents: Clinical outcome in adulthood. *Journal of the American Academy of Child & Adolescent Psychiatry, 34*, 566–578.

Rapee, R. M. (1997). Potential role of childrearing practices in the development of anxiety and depression. *Clinical Psychology Review, 17*, 47–67.

Reinecke, M. A., Ryan, N. E., & DuBois, D. L. (1998). Cognitive-behavioral therapy of depression and depressive symptoms during adolescence: A review and meta-analysis. *Journal of the American Academy of Child & Adolescent Psychiatry, 37*, 26–34.

Reinherz, H. Z., Giaconia, R. M., Hauf, A. M. C., Wasserman, M. S., & Silverman, A. B. (1999). Major depression in the transition to adulthood: Risks and impairments. *Journal of Abnormal Psychology, 108*, 500–510.

Reivich, K. (1996). The prevention of depressive symptoms in adolescents (Doctoral Dissertation, University of Pennsylvania). *Dissertation Abstracts International, 57*(4), 2881B. (UMI No. 9627995). Retrieved March 10, 2004.

Roberts, C., Kane, R., Bishop, B., Matthews, H., & Thomson, H. (2004). The prevention of depressive symptoms in rural school children: A follow-up study. *International Journal of Mental Health Promotions, 6*, 4–16.

Roberts, C., Kane, R., Thomson, H., Bishop, B., & Hart, B. (2003). The prevention of depressive symptoms in rural school children: A randomized controlled trial. *Journal of Consulting and Clinical Psychology, 71*, 622–628.

Roeser, R. W., & Eccles, J. S. (1998). Adolescents' perceptions of middle school: Relation to longitudinal changes in academic and psychological adjustment. *Journal of Research on Adolescence, 8*, 123–158.

Rohde, P., Lewinsohn, P. M., & Seeley, J. R. (1994). Are adolescents changed by an episode of major depression? *Journal of the American Academy of Child & Adolescent Psychiatry, 33*, 1289–1298.

Roosa, M. W., Gensheimer, L. K., Short, J. L., Ayers, T. S., & Shell, R. (1989). A preventive intervention for children in alcoholic families: Results of a pilot study. *Family Relations, 38*, 295–300.

Rudolph, K. D., Lambert, S. F., Clark, A. G., & Kurlakowsky, K. D. (2001). Negotiating the transition to middle school: The role of self-regulatory processes. *Child Development, 72*, 929–946.

Sandler, I. N., Ayers, T. S., Wolchik, S. A., Tien, J., Kwok, O., Haine, R. A., et al. (2003). The Family Bereavement Program: Efficacy evaluation of a theory-based prevention program for parentally bereaved children and adolescents. *Journal of Consulting and Clinical Psychology, 71*, 587–600.

Sandler, I. N., West, S. G., Baca, L., Pillow, D. R., Gersten, J. C., Rogosch, F., et al. (1992). Linking empirically based theory and evaluation: The family bereavement program. *American Journal of Community Psychology, 20*, 491–521.

Schmiege, S. J., Khoo, S. T., Sandler, I. N., Ayers, T. S., & Wolchik, S. A. (2006). Symptoms of internalizing and externalizing problems: Modeling recovery curves following death of a parent. *American Journal of Preventive Medicine, 31*(Suppl. 5), 152–160.

Schulberg, H. C., Block, M. R., Madonia, M. J., Scott, C. P., Rodriguez, E., & Imber, S. D. (1996). Treating major depression in primary care practice. Eight-month clinical outcomes. *Archives of General Psychiatry, 53*, 913–919.

Seligman, M. E. Abramson, L. P., Semmel, A., & von Baeyer, C. (1979), Depressive attributional style. *Journal of Abnormal Psychology, 88*, 242–247.

Seligman, M. E., Schulman, B. S., DeRubeis, R. J., & Hollon, S. D. (1999). The prevention of depression and anxiety. *Prevention & Treatment, 2*, Article 8. Retrieved June 9, 2000, from http://journals.apa.org/prevention/volume2/pre0020008a.html.

Shatté, A. J. (1996). Prevention of depressive symptoms in adolescents: Issues of dissemination and mechanisms of change (Doctoral Dissertation, University of Pennsylvania). (UMI No. 9713001)

Sheeber, L., Hops, H., & Davis, B. (2001). Family processes in adolescent depression. *Clinical Child and Family Psychology Review, 4*, 19–35.

Sheffield, J. K., Spence, S. H., Rapee, R. M., Kowalenko, N., Wignall, A., Davis, A., et al. (2006). Evaluation of universal, indicated, and combined cognitive-behavioral approaches to the prevention of depression among adolescents. *Journal of Consulting and Clinical Psychology, 74*, 66–79.

Smith, M. L., Glass, G. V., & Miller, T. I. (1980). *The benefits of psychotherapy.* Baltimore, MD: Johns Hopkins University Press.

Spence, S. H., & Shortt, A. L. (2007). Research review: Can we justify the widespread dissemination of universal, school-based interventions for the prevention of depression among children and adolescents? *Journal of Child Psychology and Psychiatry, 48*, 526–542.

Steinberg, L., & Lerner, R. M. (2004). The scientific study of adolescence: A brief history. *Journal of Early Adolescence, 24*, 45–54.

Stice, E., Burton, E., Bearman, S. K., & Rohde, P. (2006). Randomized trial of a brief depression prevention program: An elusive search for a psychosocial placebo control condition. *Behavior Research and Therapy, 45*, 863–876.

Stolberg, R. A., Clark, D. C., & Bongar, B. (2002). Epidemiology, assessment, and management of suicide in depressed patients. In I. H. Gotlib & C. L. Hammen (Eds.), *Handbook of depression* (pp. 581–601). New York: Guilford Press.

Sullivan, P. F., Neale, M. C., & Kendler, K. S. (2000). Genetic epidemiology of major depression: Review and meta-analysis. *American Journal of Psychiatry, 157*, 1552–1562.

Sutton, J. M. (2007). Prevention of depression in youth: A qualitative review and future suggestions. *Clinical Psychology Review, 27*, 552–571.

Thase, M. E., & Howland, R. H. (1994). Refractory depression: Relevance of psychosocial factors and therapies. *Psychiatric Annals, 24*, 232–240.

Treatment for Adolescents with Depression Study (TADS) Team. (2004). Fluoxetine, cognitive-behavioral therapy, and their combination for adolescents with depression: Treatment for Adolescents with Depression Study (TADS) randomized controlled trial. *Journal of the American Medical Association, 292*, 807–820.

Treatment for Adolescents with Depression Study (TADS) Team. (2007). The Treatment for Adolescents with Depression Study (TADS): Long term effectiveness and safety outcomes. *Archives of General Psychiatry, 64*, 1132–1144.

Tremblay, G. C., & Israel, A. C. (1998). Children's adjustment to parental death. *Clinical Psychology: Science and Practice, 5*, 424–438.

Twenge, J. M., & Nolen-Hoeksema, S. (2002). Age, gender, race, socioeconomic status, and birth cohort differences on the Children's Depression Inventory: A meta-analysis. *Journal of Abnormal Psychology, 111*, 578–588.

Vitiello, B., & Swedo, S. (2004). Antidepressant medications in children. *New England Journal of Medicine, 350*, 1489–1491.

Wagner, K. D., Robb, A. S., Findling, R. L., Gutierrez, M. M., & Heydorn, W. E. (2004). A randomized, placebo-controlled trial of citalopram for the treatment of major depression in children and adolescents. *American Journal of Psychiatry, 161*, 1079–1083.

Watson, D., & Clark, L. A. (1984). Negative affectivity: The disposition to experience aversive emotional states. *Psychological Bulletin, 96*, 465–490.

Weiss, B., & Weisz, J. R. (1990). The impact of methodological factors on child psychotherapy outcome research: A meta-analysis for researchers. *Journal of Abnormal Child Psychology, 18*, 639–670.

Weissman, M. M., Markowitz, J. C., & Klerman, G. L. (2000). *Comprehensive guide to interpersonal psychotherapy.* New York: Basic Books.

Weissman, M. M., Wolk, S., Goldstein, R., Moreau, D., Adams, P., Greenwald, S., et al. (1999). Depressed adolescents grown up. *Journal of the American Medical Association, 281*, 1707–1713.

Weisz, J. R., McCarty, C. A., & Valeri, S. M. (2006). Effects of psychotherapy in children and adolescents: A meta-analysis. *Psychological Bulletin, 132*, 132–149.

Weisz, J. R., Weiss, B., Han, S. S., Granger, D., & Morton, T. (1995). Effects of psychotherapy with children and adolescents revisited: A meta-analysis of treatment outcome studies. *Psychological Bulletin, 117*, 450–468.

Wells, J. E., Bushnell, J. A., Hornblow, A. R., & Joyce, P. R. (1989). Christchurch Psychiatric Epidemiology Study. I. Methodology and lifetime prevalence for specific psychiatric disorders. *Australian and New Zealand Journal of Psychiatry, 23*, 315–326.

Wilson, D. B. (2005). *SPSS macros.* Retrieved March 3, 2007, from http://mason.gmu.edu/~dwilsonb/ma.html.

Wilson, S. J., Lipsey, M. W., & Derzon, J. H. (2003). The effects of school-based intervention programs on aggressive behavior: A meta-analysis. *Journal of Consulting and Clinical Psychology, 71*, 136–139.

Wolchik, S. A., Sandler, I. N., Milsap, R. E., Plummer, B. A., Greene, S. M., Anderson, E. R., et al. (2002). Six-year follow-up of preventive interventions for children of divorce: A randomized controlled trial. *Journal of the American Medical Association, 288*, 1874–1881.

Wolchik, S. A., West, S. G., Sandler, I. N., Tein, J. Y., Coatsworth, D., Lengua, L., et al. (2000). An experimental evaluation of theory-based mother and mother-child programs for children of divorce. *Journal of Consulting & Clinical Psychology, 68*, 843–856.

Wolchik, S. A., West, S. G., Westover, S., Sandler, I. N., Martin, A., Lustig, J., et al. (1993). The children of divorce parenting intervention: Outcome evaluation of an empirically based program. *American Journal of Community Psychology, 21*, 293–331.

World Health Organization. (2001). *World Health Report 2001. Mental health: New understanding, new hope.* Retrieved June 4, 2006, from http://www.who. int/whr2001/2001/main/en/.

Yap, M. B. H., Allen, N. B., & Sheeber, L. (2007). Using an emotion regulation framework to understand the role of temperament and family processes in risk for adolescent depressive disorders. *Clinical Child and Family Psychology Review, 10*, 180–196.

Young, J. F., Mufson, L., & Davies, M. (2006). Efficacy of interpersonal psychotherapy-adolescent skills training: An indicated preventive intervention for depression. *Journal of Child Psychology and Psychiatry, 47*, 1254–1262.

Yu, D. L., & Seligman, M. E. P. (2002). Preventing depressive symptoms in Chinese children. *Prevention & Treatment, 5,* Article 9. Retrieved May 17, 2004, from http://journals.apa.org/prevention/volume5/pre0050009a.html.

Chapter Twenty-Three

Universal Prevention for Adolescent Depression

KATIE A. MCLAUGHLIN

CONTENTS

Major depression among adolescents represents a serious public health problem. The prevalence of major depression among adolescents has been steadily increasing over time (e.g., Kessler & Walters, 1998), and adolescent-onset depression is associated with myriad negative consequences for affected individuals in both adolescence and later in adulthood (e.g., Georgiades, Lewinsohn, Monroe, & Seeley, 2006; Lewinsohn, Soloman, Seeley, & Zeiss, 2000; Pine, Cohen, Cohen, & Brooke, 1999). To address this growing public health problem, a number of preventive interventions for adolescent depression have been developed and tested. These interventions vary markedly across a number of dimensions, including the targeted population, the individuals who are trained to administer the intervention, the site for recruitment of participants, the outcomes assessed, and the ultimate efficacy of the intervention being tested. This chapter focuses specifically on universal preventive interventions for adolescent depression. Universal prevention programs for adolescent depression represent interventions that target all eligible adolescents rather than those selected to be at high risk for depression based on current symptom levels or family history of depression. Indicated prevention programs are reviewed by Judy Garber in Chapter 22 of this volume. Definitions relevant to the distinctions between the major types of preventive interventions are first covered, followed by reviews of the need for prevention of adolescent depression and of the current literature on universal preventive interventions. Finally, challenges to universal prevention research, and directions for future research are provided.

PREVENTION DEFINITIONS

Prevention ultimately aims to prevent the occurrence of some event before it happens. Prevention, as it relates to mental health, is concerned with preventing the onset of psychopathological conditions before they emerge. In 1994, the Institute of Medicine (IOM) released definitions, guidelines, and recommendations for prevention research focused on mental disorders. The framework that was created to classify preventive interventions differs somewhat from the public health classification system for disease prevention. Within the public health nosology, three types of prevention are delineated: primary, secondary, and tertiary (Commission on Chronic Illness, 1957). Primary prevention involves efforts to reduce the incidence of a disease by decreasing the number of new cases. Secondary prevention aims to reduce the prevalence of a disease by decreasing the number of active cases in the population. Finally, tertiary prevention is concerned with reducing the amount of disability associated with a disease among already diagnosed cases. Within the IOM mental health framework, these definitions were modified somewhat to be more relevant to mental disorders, as opposed to medical diseases, and are referred to as universal, indicated, and selected prevention (IOM, 1994). *Universal* preventive interventions are those that are intended for all eligible individuals in the population, regardless of their risk status for a particular mental disorder. The benefits of universal preventive interventions should outweigh the risks for all individuals, and are particularly effective when the cost is low and efficacy is high across large segments of the population. *Indicated* prevention efforts target individuals who are already manifesting early signs or symptoms of a mental disorder, but who do not yet meet full diagnostic criteria. Indicated interventions may be warranted even if they involve higher costs and somewhat greater risk than universal interventions (IOM, 1994). *Selective* prevention targets individuals considered to be at high risk for developing a particular mental disorder based on the presence of an identified risk factor. The goal of all three types of preventive interventions is to reduce the incidence of new cases of a particular mental disorder (IOM, 1994).

NEED FOR PREVENTION OF ADOLESCENT DEPRESSION

Adolescent depression is common and is associated with a multitude of deleterious consequences. By the end of adolescence the prevalence of depression is approximately the same as in adult populations, with approximately 15–20% of adolescents experiencing a major depressive episode by age 18 (Hankin et al., 1998; Kessler & Walters, 1998; Lewinsohn, Hops, Roberts, Seeley, & Andrews, 1993). Depression in adolescents is associated with substantial functional impairment and an elevated risk for suicide attempts, with more than 20% of depressed adolescents reporting at least one lifetime suicide attempt (Kessler & Walters, 1998). Adolescents who have experienced a major depressive episode are at particularly high risk for experiencing recurrent problems with depression and for relapse in adulthood (Fombonne, Wostear, Cooper, Harrington, & Rutter, 2001; Lewinsohn, Rhode (STET—Rohde), Klein, & Seeley, 1999; Pine, Cohen, Gurley, Brook, & Ma, 1998). The vast majority of currently depressed adolescents have already experienced recurrent depressive episodes; the average number of episodes for a depressed adolescent is 5.4, and the average length of the longest episode is 32.5 weeks (Kessler & Walters, 1998). Adolescent depression is also associated with an increased risk for the development of substance use disorders and anxiety disorders in adulthood (Georgiades et al., 2006; Lewinsohn et al., 2000; Pine et al., 1998). Although not all adolescents with depressive symptoms develop anxiety and depression in adulthood, the majority of adults with these conditions experienced problems with depressive disorders in adolescence. As such, adolescent-onset depression represents a particularly insidious condition because of its strong association with chronic and recurrent emotional problems in adulthood.

Prevention of adolescent depression represents an important goal for a number of reasons. Depression in this age group is not only associated with a host of negative consequences for adolescents during a depressive episode, but also portends the development of serious problems later in life. In addition, many adolescents who develop major depression do not receive adequate treatment. Lewinsohn, Rohde, and Seeley (1998) reported that 40% of depressed adolescents have never received treatment of any kind, and a recent community study found that only 23% of depressed adolescents had utilized mental health services (Essau, 2005). The number of adolescents who receive *adequate* treatment for depression is undoubtedly lower. Only a minority of adults with major depression receives adequate treatment. A large study found that only 30% of individuals with major depression or an anxiety disorder receive appropriate care (Young, Klap, Sherbourne, & Wells, 2001), and in the National Comorbidity Survey-Replication, only 37.5% with major depressive disorder (MDD) received adequate treatment (Wang et al., 2005). It is likely that adequate treatment is obtained even less commonly among adolescents given lower rates of treatment seeking in this population (e.g., Essau, 2005), given that empirically supported treatments for adolescent depression have only recently been identified relative to treatments for adult depression, and given the widespread use of selective serotonin reuptake inhibitors for adolescent depression despite their serious adverse side effects and questionable risk-benefit profile (e.g., Jureidini et al., 2004). Research suggests that depressed adolescents treated in the community have worse outcomes than adolescents treated in efficacy trials, and that community treatment results in outcomes no better than found among control groups in efficacy trials (Weersing & Weisz, 2002). Treatment of adolescent depression has not been found to have a positive impact on relapse in young adulthood (Lewinsohn et al., 1998), suggesting that treatments for adolescent depression do not have a lasting impact, and may not prevent the onset of future depressive episodes.

The negative consequences of adolescent depression are clear, and the majority of depressed adolescents do not receive adequate treatment. For these reasons, adolescent depression represents an important target for prevention efforts. For a complete review of the epidemiology of adolescent depression, please see Merikangas & Knight, Chapter 23 of this volume.

BENEFITS OF UNIVERSAL PREVENTION FOR ADOLESCENT DEPRESSION

Universal prevention, by definition, involves delivering an intervention to a large number of individuals who are at varied levels of risk for developing a disorder; those at high risk are not targeted exclusively. This type of prevention is most useful for disorders in which a much larger proportion of the population is at-risk for developing the disorder than the proportion that already has the disorder (e.g., McKinlay & Marceau, 2000; Rose, 1992). Major depression among adolescents represents an excellent candidate for such interventions, as the prevalence of depression among adults is relatively high (approximately 16–17%; Kessler et al., 1994: Kessler et al., 2003), while the prevalence among young adolescents is substantially lower (2–3%; e.g., Costello, Mustillo, Erkanli, Keeler, & Angold, 2003). The risk for developing major depression increases substantially across adolescence, and by the end of this period the prevalence of depression is similar to the prevalence among adults (e.g., Hankin et al., 1998). As such, adolescence represents a particularly important period of risk for the development of depression. At the beginning of adolescence, a substantially higher proportion of adolescents are at-risk for developing major depression than those who already have the disorder, which makes adolescent depression an ideal candidate for universal prevention efforts.

Universal prevention has several benefits over indicated prevention that justify targeting larger unselected samples of individuals. The first advantage involves community implementation of interventions following research trials. Indicated prevention programs are typically delivered by mental health professionals or trained psychology graduate students (e.g., Clarke et al., 2001), because trained professionals may adhere more effectively to intervention manuals than other intervention deliverers. Unfortunately, using highly trained professionals reduces the likelihood that the intervention will actually be implemented in the community once the research trial is over (see Glasgow, Lichtenstein, & Marcus, 2003). This represents a serious problem with current prevention programs. A number of indicated interventions have been found to be effective in research trials (e.g., Clarke et al., 2001; Gillham, Reivich, Jaycox, & Seligman, 1995; Jaycox, Reivich, Gillham, & Seligman, 1994), but the methods used to test these interventions have rendered them unfeasible to sustain in community settings. In contrast, designing an intervention that is implemented by teachers or other individuals working with adolescents in the community, or that is bundled with delivery of other health services (e.g., Muñoz et al., 1995) and is readily transportable to other settings will greatly increase the chances that it will be sustained in the community if it is demonstrated to be effective. Given that the goal of prevention is to reduce the incidence of a disorder on a population level, interventions must be designed that are easily transportable to a variety of settings and that do not require substantial financial resources or highly trained professionals to implement.

Another advantage of universal prevention is that it targets a larger population of individuals at risk and, therefore, does not necessitate identification of those at highest risk for the development of depression. There are a number of difficulties associated with identifying high-risk adolescents to target with indicated preventive interventions. There have traditionally been two ways in which indicated and selective prevention research trials have identified high-risk participants: selecting adolescents with depressed parents (e.g., Clarke et al., 2001) and selecting adolescents with high scores on symptom measures of depression (e.g., Jaycox et al., 1994). Identification of adolescents with depressed parents represents a challenging endeavor for a number of reasons. Clarke and colleagues (2001) identified high-risk adolescents by searching a large health care provider database for parents who had been treated for affective disorders. Out of a large pool of eligible individuals, a relatively small number of adolescents with depressed parents were identified. This strategy would also be difficult to implement on a large scale due to issues related to access to medical records and confidentiality. Other methods for identifying adolescents with depressed parents, such as screening in primary care or other health care facilities, require a lot of effort spent identifying each high-risk adolescent and are thus not feasible to implement in the community. Identifying high-risk adolescents on the basis of depressive symptomatology is also problematic. Adolescents who are not symptomatic at the time of assessment will not be included in indicated interventions, although this group may ultimately contribute more cases of major depression than the group who are already symptomatic (see Rose, 1992). Another problem associated with screening for adolescents with high levels of depressive symptoms involves stigma. This problem is particularly concerning if high-risk students are singled out for interventions that take place at school.

Other problems with identifying high-risk participants for indicated prevention studies are also noteworthy. Currently, screening instruments are not yet reliable at identifying adolescents who are experiencing problems with depression. A recent study examined the ability of widely used self-report measures of anxiety and depression to identify young adolescents experiencing high levels of symptomatology (Dierker et al., 2001). When the results of the self-report measures were compared to the results of a structured diagnostic interview, none of the self-report measures demonstrated high accuracy in identifying children with internalizing disorders based on the interview. Because screening instruments are not highly accurate at identifying adolescents with high levels of subdiagnostic depressive symptoms versus adolescents with MDD, our ability to accurately identify adolescents who should be targeted by indicated prevention using screening instruments is thus also poor. As such, many adolescents who are experiencing significant depressive symptoms, or who may go on to develop major depression, but would not be included in indicated preventive interventions, will receive an adequate dose of intervention in universal prevention. At the same time, those adolescents at highest risk (i.e., those who would be targeted by indicated prevention studies) will still receive the full dose of the intervention.

Targeting a larger population of adolescents is warranted for other reasons as well. Evidence suggests that the presence of even mild symptoms of depression in adolescence is associated with impairment and risk for future psychopathology. A substantial proportion of adolescents experience depressive symptoms in the absence of a full-blown diagnosis (Angold, Costello, Farmer, Burns, & Erkanli, 1999; Kessler & Walters, 1998), and subthreshold depressive symptoms also portend serious consequences later in life. Subthreshold depressive symptoms in adolescence have been consistently associated with significant functional impairment, reduced quality of life, and increased utilization of health services (e.g., Angold et al., 1999; Gonzalez-Tejera et al., 2005; Lewinsohn et al. 2000). The presence of subthreshold symptoms among adolescents is associated with an increased risk for developing MDD in adulthood (Fergusson, Horwood, Ritter, & Beautrais, 2005; Pine et al. 1999) and for attempting suicide (Fergusson et al., 2005; Judd, Akiskal, & Paulus, 1997). One-third of individuals who experience a first-onset of major depression in adulthood, experienced at least one depressive symptom during adolescence compared to only 7% of adults with no history of depression (Wilcox & Anthony, 2003). Moreover, the presence of even one depressive symptom in adolescence is associated with greater risk for future psychopathology: sad mood has been demonstrated to predict the onset of MDD, and sleep disturbance had been found to predict the onset of substance abuse (Georgiades et al., 2006). Adolescent depressive symptoms are also associated with an increased risk for the development of substance use disorders (Georgiades et al., 2006; Lewinsohn et al., 2000) and for the onset of anxiety disorders in adulthood (Pine et al., 1998). Adolescents who experience only mild symptoms of depression or who experience one or two severe symptoms of depression may not be identified as candidates for indicated prevention efforts despite the significant impairment and future risk associated with this symptom profile. In contrast, this group would be included in universal prevention programs. As such, preventive interventions targeting depression among adolescents with mild to moderate but subthreshold symptoms have the potential to prevent some of the pernicious consequences associated with depressive symptoms among this age group.

A final advantage of universal prevention, particularly school-based universal prevention, involves the ability to deliver doses of the intervention over longer periods of time. Indicated prevention trials typically demonstrate a weakening of the preventive effects of the intervention over time (e.g., Clarke et al., 1995; Clarke et al., 2001). When the intervention is delivered after school or in special sessions outside of the typical school environment, the length of the intervention is somewhat limited and booster sessions can be difficult to implement. Interventions delivered in a classroom setting or via the Internet, on the other hand, can be implemented over longer periods of time. If weakening of preventive effects is observed, booster sessions can easily be delivered at a later point in time.

REVIEW OF UNIVERSAL PREVENTION STUDIES

This section will provide a review of the extant literature examining the efficacy of universal prevention interventions for adolescent depression. To be included in the review, studies had to meet several criteria. First, the target population for the intervention had to include all eligible adolescents in the sampling frame. Studies that selected participants based on symptom levels, family history, or other indications of future risk for depression (e.g., Beardslee et al., 1993) were excluded. Second, the study had to compare a preventive intervention for adolescent depression to some type of control condition. Open trials and pilot studies that did not include control groups were excluded. Finally, the intervention being evaluated had to target adolescent depression specifically. Studies that examined more general interventions focused, for example, on the prevention of negative responses to stress (e.g., Hains & Ellman, 1994) or on promotion of general well-being among adolescents were excluded. Finally, doctoral dissertations that were not published as scholarly articles or book chapters were also excluded.

The first empirical evaluations of universal prevention programs for adolescent depression involved examination of two brief interventions that were presented in videotape format to participants during health class (Clarke,

Hawkins, Murphy, & Sheeber, 1993). The first intervention was a three-session educational intervention that provided information on the symptoms, causes, and treatments of depression, and encouraged participants to seek treatment if they were feeling depressed. The educational intervention also included a component focused on increasing pleasurable activities to prevent depression, but no active skill training took place. Participants were 622 ninth and tenth graders from two high schools and one middle school, and randomization to experimental and control groups occurred at the classroom level. Self-reported depressive symptoms served as the primary outcome. Following the intervention, a reduction in depressive symptoms was reported by boys who had received the educational program relative to controls, but no difference in symptoms was found among girls. At 12-week follow-up, no differences in depressive symptoms were found between the intervention and control groups. The intervention had no effect on knowledge about depression or willingness to seek treatment (Clarke et al., 1993); as such, the lack of intervention efficacy at reducing depressive symptoms is unsurprising.

The second intervention examined by Clark and colleagues (1993) was a five-session behavioral skills training program focused on increasing participants' engagement in pleasurable activities. Information regarding the symptoms, causes, and treatments of depression was also presented. Three hundred and eighty students in the ninth and tenth grade from the same schools that received the first intervention participated. Randomization again occurred at the classroom level, and self-reported depressive symptoms served as the primary outcome. The skills training program had no effect on depressive symptoms immediately following intervention administration or at the 12-week follow-up. Similar to the first intervention, the skills training program had no effect on knowledge about depression or willingness to seek treatment. The lack of efficacy of the programs evaluated in these studies likely resulted from an inadequate dose of intervention being administered to participants given that both interventions were brief and circumscribed in nature. Studies that followed this initial evaluation have focused on interventions that are longer and more comprehensive with respect to the therapeutic techniques intended to prevent the onset of depression.

The Penn Resiliency Program (PRP) represents an intervention intended to prevent the onset of depression in children and adolescents that has been demonstrated to be effective in adolescents across a number of indicated prevention trials (e.g., Gillham et al., 1995; Jaycox et al., 1994; Seligman, Schulman, DeRubeis, & Holland, 1999). The PRP is a 12-session cognitive-behavioral intervention that involves both cognitive restructuring and social problem-solving components. Cardemil, Reivich, and Seligman (2002) examined the efficacy of the PRP in preventing the onset of depressive symptoms in a sample of low-income minority adolescents. This study utilized a sample of low-income adolescents given that low socioeconomic status (SES) is a documented risk factor for depression (e.g., Blazer, Kessler, McGonagle, & Swartz, 1994); however, students were not individually selected for the study based on high-risk status. Rather, the entire population of students in grades 5 and 6 at two low-income schools participated. Because adolescents were not individually selected to participate based on pre-existing depressive symptoms, maternal depression, or other important risk factors for major depression, this study qualifies as a universal prevention study. The intervention was administered during school hours in weekly 90-minute sessions by well-trained psychology graduate students. Self-reported depressive symptoms served as the primary outcome of the study. The results were presented separately for Latino and African-American participants given that the two participating schools differed markedly in their racial/ethnic composition. The PRP was found to be effective at reducing depressive symptoms among the Latino participants following the intervention, and these effects were maintained at 6-month follow-up (Cardemil et al., 2002). Importantly, these effects were found for participants both high and low in initial depressive symptomatology. The intervention was not found to be effective at reducing depressive symptoms among the African-American participants. This finding partially resulted from reductions in depressive symptoms among the control participants in that sample. The investigators speculated that differential treatment efficacy may have resulted from reductions over time in depressive symptoms among the entire African-American sample due to factors related to the school or other factors that differed systematically across the two study samples. These explanations were speculative, and to date no empirical evidence speaks to the issue of differential efficacy of universal programs for adolescent depression across racial/ethnic groups.

A more recent evaluation of the PRP examined the efficacy of the intervention when administered by school teachers and counselors to a large unselected sample of adolescents (Gillham et al., 2007). This study also included an attention control condition to provide a more methodologically sound evaluation of the efficacy of the PRP, and to examine the specificity of the intervention compared to other nonacademic school programming. Participants were recruited from three middle schools across a 3-year period, and were not selected based on elevated depressive symptoms at baseline. Six hundred and seventy-nine adolescents in sixth to eighth grade were randomly assigned to receive the PRP, a competing attention control intervention, the Penn Enhancement Program (PEP; Reivich, 1996), or were assigned to a control group. The PEP was a group intervention focused on discussion of stressors in adolescence including peer pressure, trust and betrayal, and body image, and a number of other developmentally relevant topics. Each intervention was delivered in twelve 90-minute sessions after school, and teachers, counselors, and graduate students not affiliated with the research program were trained to administer the intervention. In addition to an initial 30-hour training session, biweekly supervision was provided to all intervention administrators. All sessions were audiotaped, and four sessions from each administrator were coded for adherence. The primary outcome measure was self-reported symptoms of depression. In addition, participants reporting elevated depressive symptoms were asked to complete a semistructured interview designed to assess depressive symptoms in youth. Outcomes were assessed prior to the start of the intervention, 2 weeks following intervention completion, and every 6 months for a 3-year follow-up period.

The results indicated that the PRP did not reduce depressive symptoms over the course of the study compared to either of the control conditions (Gillham et al., 2007). The PRP was effective at preventing elevated levels of depressive symptoms (defined as depressive symptoms above a threshold established on the self-report measure) compared to the control condition, but was not more effective than the PEP attention control intervention. However, a school X intervention condition interaction was found such that the PRP was more effective at reducing depressive symptoms and preventing elevated depression than both control conditions in two of the schools, but was not effective in one of the schools. The impacts of the PRP on depressive symptoms in the two schools in which it had an effect were maintained through the follow-up period. Differences between the schools were not found that could explain the differential school effects. Overall, the PRP did not impact depressive symptoms to a greater extent than an attention control in the full sample. However, the PRP led to lasting reductions in depressive symptoms in two of the schools in which the study was conducted, suggesting that it may be effective when administered as a universal prevention intervention.

Quayle, Dziurawiec, Roberts, Kane, and Ebsworthy (2001) examined the efficacy of a modified version of the PRP in preventing depression among a small sample of preadolescent females in Australia. The original PRP was modified in format from twelve 90-minute sessions to eight 80-minute sessions. The materials were also modified to be relevant to Australian youth. Forty-seven participants from an all-female school were randomized to intervention and control groups. The intervention was administered in small groups of approximately 12 participants during school hours. Two facilitators administered the intervention to each group, and facilitators were postgraduate clinical psychology students. Facilitators received 30 hours of training in intervention administration and received weekly supervision. The primary outcome was self-reported symptoms of depression, and outcomes were assessed prior to the start of the intervention, postintervention, and at a 6-month follow-up. Attendance to the intervention sessions was poor, with participants attending an average of 3.4 sessions, and attrition at the 6-month follow-up was high. Only 33 participants completed the follow-up assessment. The results indicated no difference in depressive symptoms between the intervention and control group postintervention; however, at 6-month follow-up, participants in the intervention condition reported fewer depressive symptoms than participants in the control group. Results of this study should be interpreted with caution given the extremely small sample size, poor attendance to intervention sessions, and high attrition.

While the PRP represents a depression prevention program that was designed as an indicated intervention used with high-risk groups that was modified to be applicable as a universal preventive intervention, a number of interventions have been designed specifically as universal prevention programs. All of these interventions have been designed and evaluated outside of the United States. The Resourceful Adolescent Program (RAP) represents the first of these interventions, and was designed to be implemented in schools to an unselected population of students. The RAP is a cognitive-behavioral intervention that occurs during 11 sessions lasting 40–50 minutes. Problem solving, cognitive restructuring, and self-management techniques are included. This intervention was first evaluated in a small trial in Australia (Shochet et al., 2001). Two hundred and sixty students in the ninth grade of one Australian high school participated in the study. The intervention was designed to be administered to small groups, typically 8–10 students. As such, classrooms were divided into 2–3 groups, each with a different intervention facilitator, and all facilitators were trained psychologists. This study did not randomly assign participants to groups: all ninth graders during one school year served as the control group, and all ninth graders during the following school year served as the intervention group. Within the intervention group, half of participants were assigned to receive only the RAP and half were assigned to receive the RAP plus an additional three-session intervention for parents. The parental component included parenting, stress management, and familial conflict resolution components, as well as information on adolescent development and self-esteem. Self-report measures of depressive symptomatology were used as the primary outcomes for the study, and participants were followed for 10 months following completion of the intervention. Participants in both intervention conditions experienced a significantly greater reduction in depressive symptoms than participants in the control group, and the two intervention groups did not differ from one another. The reduction in depressive symptoms resulting from the intervention was maintained at 10-month follow-up.

An intervention that was recently evaluated in New Zealand, the RAP-Kiwi (Merry, McDowell, Wild, Bir, & Cunliffe, 2004b), was adapted from the RAP described above. The RAP-Kiwi is an 11-session intervention that includes both cognitive-behavioral and interpersonal components. The structure of the RAP was left unchanged, but some of the materials were modified to be relevant to adolescents in New Zealand as opposed to Australia. The RAP-Kiwi was evaluated in a trial that utilized an active placebo control group. The active placebo was focused on "having fun" (Merry et al., 2004b, p. 540) and contained no components thought to influence depressive symptoms. Participants were 392 students from two New Zealand schools: the participants were in the ninth grade class at one school and the tenth grade class at the other. The intervention was administered by teachers, who received two and a half days of training focused on implementation of the RAP-Kiwi. Self-report measures of depression served as the primary outcome. The results indicated that the intervention led to a greater decrease in depressive symptoms than the active placebo. At 18-month follow-up, the intervention group continued to experience lower levels of depressive symptoms than the control group, although the effect was small in magnitude.

Another universal preventive intervention, the Problem Solving for Life Program (PSLP), was developed in Australia (Spence, Sheffield, & Donovan, 2003), and evaluations of this intervention represent the largest investigations of universal prevention for adolescent depression to date. The PSLP is an eight-session cognitive-behavioral intervention that involves both cognitive restructuring and problem-solving skill training components. Each session takes approximately 45–50 minutes, and sessions are designed to be administered once a week. In the first evaluation of this intervention, 1,500 eighth grade students from 16 high schools in Australia participated, and randomization occurred at the school level. Teachers in the intervention condition received a 6-hour training session before implementing the intervention. Self-report measures of symptomatology were used as the primary outcome measures; however, a particular strength of this study involved the use of a structured diagnostic interview with all high-risk students (i.e., those scoring above a cutoff on symptom measures of depression). Participants were followed for 12 months following completion of the intervention. The results of this study indicated that the PSLP led to clinically significant reductions in depressive symptoms immediately following the intervention among high-risk adolescents, and a greater reduction in depressive symptoms among low-risk adolescents relative to participants in the control group (Spence et al., 2003). However, the effects of the intervention were not maintained at the 12-month follow-up. No significant differences in the incidence of depressive disorders were found between the intervention and control groups over the follow-up period.

The PSLP was recently evaluated in a much larger sample of Australian adolescents in a study that aimed to examine the efficacy of both universal and indicated prevention programs alone and in combination (Sheffield et al., 2006). Approximately 5,000 ninth grade students in 36 schools participated in the study. Schools were matched on location (urban-rural), SES, and type of school (state, parochial, etc.) and randomized within strata to one of four experimental conditions: universal, indicated, universal plus indicated, and no-intervention control. Participants scoring in the highest 20% on a measure of depressive symptoms at baseline were considered high risk, and participated in the indicated program in those conditions that included the indicated intervention. The indicated intervention contained cognitive restructuring, problem-solving skill training, interpersonal skill training, and self-reward components and was administered in eight sessions to small groups of 8–10 students. In the combined universal and indicated condition, the universal program was completed during the first school semester and the indicated intervention was completed during the second semester. Self-report symptom measures served as the primary outcomes, and structured diagnostic interviews were also administered to all high-risk adolescents.

No effect of either the universal or indicated intervention was found in this study: neither intervention resulted in decreases in depressive symptoms or in a reduced incidence of depressive disorders compared to the no-intervention control condition. Moreover, the combined universal and indicated program was no more effective than either intervention administered alone and was not demonstrated to be superior to the control condition. The results of this study are inconsistent with previous findings suggesting that the PSLP is an effective universal prevention program (Spence et al., 2003) and with evidence that clearly supports the efficacy of indicated cognitive-behavioral interventions in preventing adolescent depression among high-risk individuals (e.g., Clarke et al., 2001; Gillham et al., 1995; Jaycox et al., 1994; Seligman et al., 1999). A potential explanation for these inconsistent findings is that participants did not receive an adequate dose of the intervention and therefore did not acquire the necessary skills (e.g., problem solving) to impact upon depression risk. Analyses indicated that students in the intervention conditions did not develop better problem-solving skills, one of the mechanisms by which the intervention is designed to reduce depressive symptoms, while a previous test of the PSLP found significant improvements in problem-solving skills for those in the intervention (Spence et al., 2003). This lack of skill acquisition may have occurred due to lower adherence to the intervention by teachers in the larger study compared to the initial study completed on a smaller, and potentially more well-controlled scale.

The final universal prevention program that has been evaluated empirically, the LISA-T (Pössel, Horn, Groen, & Hautzinger, 2004a), was developed and tested in Germany. The LISA-T was designed using Dodge's (1993) social information processing model of social competence, and utilizes traditional cognitive-behavioral techniques for treating depression. The program aims to teach participants the relationships between thoughts, emotions, and behaviors, to identify and modify dysfunctional thoughts, to increase self-confidence, and to improve social competence. The LISA-T was examined in a study that randomized classrooms to intervention and control conditions in participating middle schools. Two hundred participants received the intervention and 174 served as the control group. The intervention was administered over 10 weekly sessions by trained psychologists or psychology graduate students. The intervention group classrooms were split by gender, and the LISA-T was administered separately to males and females. The primary outcome was self-reported depressive symptoms, and this was assessed prior to and immediately following intervention implementation, as well as at 3- and 6-month follow-up intervals. The results indicated that the intervention did not have an impact on the development of depressive symptoms for the entire sample, as there were no differences in symptoms for the intervention and control groups. However, participants who reported low levels of symptoms prior to the intervention did not report increases in symptoms over time in the intervention group, but did develop increased depressive symptoms in the control group. In addition, participants with subsyndromal depression reported a decrease in symptoms over time in the intervention group, and an increase in symptoms in the control group. As such, the LISA-T resulted in the prevention of the development of depressive symptoms, but only in participants who were experiencing minimal or subsyndromal depression at the beginning of the study. The intervention was not effective for those participants with clinically relevant depressive symptoms.

Summary of Universal Prevention Studies

To date, a number of universal preventive interventions for depression have been empirically evaluated. All interventions have been cognitive-behavioral in nature and have been administered in school settings. Some studies have utilized teachers as intervention administrators, while others have used trained study personnel, typically mental health professionals or psychology graduate students. The majority of studies have utilized self-reported depressive symptomatology as the universal outcome, although two recent studies have also included structured diagnostic interviews of high-risk adolescents to examine depressive disorders in addition to symptoms. The efficacy of the interventions that have been examined in reducing depressive symptoms and the incidence of depressive disorders has varied markedly across studies.

A recent meta-analysis examined the efficacy of universal prevention studies targeting adolescent depression and concluded that such programs are not effective at reducing depressive symptoms (Merry, McDowell, Hetrick, Bur, & Muller, 2004a). When examining the efficacy of these programs at preventing the onset of depressive disorders, the analyses also indicated that universal prevention programs were not effective at reducing the incidence of depression over the follow-up period following the intervention. However, these analyses did not include all of the universal prevention studies reviewed above due to a number of exclusion criteria and because several studies were published after the meta-analysis was conducted (e.g., Gillham et al., 2007; Merry et al., 2004b; Sheffield et al., 2006). Only the studies conducted by Cardemil and colleagues (2002), Spence and colleagues (2003), and Quayle and colleagues (2001) were included in the meta-analysis. As such, the efficacy of existing universal prevention programs as a whole remains somewhat unclear. However, several consistent patterns of findings across the universal prevention studies that have been conducted are worth noting.

Among the comprehensive interventions that have been evaluated (i.e., those that include an adequate number of sessions and that cover a range of material), all have demonstrated some measurable effect on depressive symptoms immediately following implementation of the intervention. The PRP, RAP and its variants, and the PSLS have each demonstrated efficacy in this regard. However, the beneficial effects of these interventions typically disappear, or are at least substantially reduced, over the follow-up period (e.g., Spence et al., 2003). As such, one conclusion from the universal prevention literature is that comprehensive prevention programs are at least moderately successful at reducing depressive symptomatology in the short term, but do not have lasting effects once the intervention has been completed. Given that the goal of universal prevention is to reduce the incidence of depressive disorders, efforts must be made to improve preventive interventions to create more lasting effects on depression incidence over time.

Another consistent finding across universal prevention studies is that adolescents at low risk for depression, typically based on low levels of depressive symptomatology at the start of the intervention, benefit equally from preventive interventions as adolescents initially at high risk for depression (e.g., Cardemil et al., 2002). This finding is important, given that an argument against universal prevention is that it is inefficient because interventions will not be relevant or helpful to those individuals at low risk for developing the disorder in question. Given that universal preventive interventions for adolescent depression appear to be effective at reducing depressive symptoms even among low-risk adolescents, the potential benefits of these interventions for all adolescents are clear.

Across universal prevention studies, programs that utilize teachers as intervention administrators tend to be less efficacious (e.g., Sheffield et al., 2006) than programs that utilize mental health professionals or psychology graduate students (e.g., Shochet et al., 2001). This is not surprising, given that mental health professionals and graduate students are specifically trained in psychopathology and mental health interventions. This training likely leads to better adherence to the intervention techniques, better ability to manage and respond effectively to individual participant's reactions to the program, and better flexibility in tailoring the intervention to be appropriate for different groups of participants. Unfortunately, using mental health professionals and graduate students to administer preventive interventions does not represent a sustainable approach to prevention. As such, prevention researchers should focus efforts on improving teacher training, creating intervention materials that are straightforward and easy to follow, and utilizing other techniques that allow uniformity of intervention administration and fidelity to intervention techniques (e.g., Internet-based approaches, see Future Directions section).

CHALLENGES TO UNIVERSAL PREVENTION OF ADOLESCENT DEPRESSION

A considerable amount of questions remain unanswered regarding the efficacy of universal preventive interventions for adolescent depression. However, this type of research faces a number of challenges that make it difficult to design and implement studies that are methodologically sound enough to make firm conclusions about the efficacy of universal prevention. The first challenge involves the need to utilize large enough sample sizes and to include long enough follow-up periods to be able to detect preventive effects if they do, in fact, exist. If a preventive intervention is effective, the incidence of MDD will be lower among individuals who received the intervention than among those who did not. However, 1-year incidence rates of MDD are low among adolescents, even though this developmental period is marked by the highest risk for depression among any age group (e.g., Blazer et al., 1994). As such, samples must be large enough to have an adequate number of cases develop over the study period. Following that logic, the follow-up period of the study must also be long enough to allow an adequate number of cases to emerge. Inclusion of large samples and utilization of long follow-up periods is difficult due to high cost. To date, most studies examining the efficacy of universal preventive interventions have been relatively small in scale when one considers the sample size and follow-up period necessary to detect differences in depression incidence between study groups. Follow-up periods typically last 6–12 months, and most studies have not included participant assessments after 1 year of follow-up.

The largest preventive intervention that has been conducted (Spence et al., 2003) utilized a large sample and an adequate follow-up time. However, this intervention failed to find preventive effects for an intervention that was demonstrated to be effective in prior evaluations. The inconsistency in these findings likely relates to poorer adherence to the preventive intervention in the larger study, and demonstrates another challenge associated with universal prevention research. Larger studies that utilize more intervention administrators and sites inevitably involve the sacrifice of some degree of investigator control over intervention implementation. It is undoubtedly easier to train and monitor a small number of intervention administrators located at one site as opposed to a large number spread across many intervention sites. Studies that include a larger number of participants must typically utilize more intervention administrators and more intervention sites. As such, studies that include adequate sample sizes inherently involve some loss of experimental control.

Given that the goal of prevention is to reduce the incidence of MDD, a preventive intervention can be considered effective only if it is associated with a reduction in the number of new cases of major depression among those who received the intervention compared to controls. As such, studies of universal preventive interventions must measure the incidence of major depression among study participants to truly demonstrate intervention efficacy. None of the studies that have been conducted to date have measured depression incidence, although several studies have measured depression incidence among a small group of study participants (e.g., Sheffield et al., 2006). Instead, symptoms of depression have been used as the primary outcome in virtually all universal prevention studies. Given the cost associated with conducting diagnostic interviews with large numbers of participants, it is understandable that depression incidence has not been measured in prevention studies. However, the consequence is that conclusions about the actual preventive effects of interventions cannot be made. Interventions that reduce symptom levels may not have an impact on depression incidence. Measurement of the incidence of major depression in intervention and control groups represents a challenge faced by prevention researchers to which there are no easy solutions.

Another series of obstacles to conducting universal prevention research involves the need to rely on schools to conduct studies. All universal prevention studies for adolescent depression to date have been conducted within schools, and working with schools creates a unique set of challenges for conducting intervention studies. The first involves the vast number of other demands placed on teachers and schools and the existence of important academic standards that teachers and schools must meet. Since the inception of the No Child Left Behind (NCLB) legislation, teachers in public schools have been expected to meet benchmarks for student test scores on achievement tests, particularly in reading and math. NCLB standards are of critical importance for school districts to meet given that federal funds are withdrawn from districts that cannot meet federal achievement score benchmarks, and teachers who do not meet standards for test scores are at risk of losing their jobs (U.S. Department of Education, 2006). Given the importance of meeting achievement standards, classroom time must be prioritized for the academic material that is covered on achievement tests. The demands placed on teachers to improve test scores and meet academic benchmarks likely results in less investment in using classroom time to focus on mental health issues, and a decreased willingness to complete lengthy intervention components that detract from academic teaching. Even teachers who believe in the importance of these interventions probably have difficulty allocating enough classroom time to the intervention to result in good adherence to the materials, given the extent of competing academic demands.

Gaining access to schools that are willing to participate in intervention studies represents another challenge for school-based universal prevention research. Given the NCLB legislation and increased focused on standardized testing in the United States, finding schools that are willing to dedicate classroom time to mental health intervention represents a daunting challenge. Schools may also be hesitant to participate without evidence that the intervention being examined has been previously demonstrated to be effective. Even if school administrators are invested in an intervention, school boards must often approve curriculum-changes, and in many places, mental health interventions may be viewed as controversial or not appropriate for use during class time. Once a school has been found that is interested in mental health interventions, a number of other obstacles remain to conducting a sound research study. Randomization at the classroom or teacher level, which is necessary to conduct experimental research studies in the absence of recruiting a large number of schools, is often not appealing to school officials. School administrators typically prefer administering interventions to entire schools given the logistical difficulties associated with training some teachers in a school but not others, and the importance of randomization at the classroom level can be difficult to convey. These challenges to gaining access to schools appear to be particularly difficult to overcome in the United States, perhaps partly due to NCLB legislation. With the exception of Cardemil and colleagues (2002) and Clarke and colleague (1993), all universal prevention studies to date have been conducted outside the United States. Efforts must be made to create incentives for schools to participate in universal prevention studies or to find alternative methods for administering preventive interventions (see Future Directions section).

Perhaps the largest obstacle for universal prevention researchers to overcome involves intervention integrity. Intervention integrity involves the extent to which an intervention is implemented as intended (see Perepletchikova & Kazdin, 2005). To date, all universal preventive intervention targeting adolescent depression have been school-based, and have utilized mental health professionals, psychology graduate students, or teachers as intervention administrators. The problem of sustainability associated with using mental health professionals or graduate students in this capacity has already been reviewed. Training teachers to administer universal prevention may represent a more sustainable approach to intervention delivery, but ensuring adherence to the intervention techniques can be difficult. A number of characteristics of teachers and the school environment render it challenging to achieve good adherence to intervention materials. First, teachers' lack of training in psychopathology and mental health intervention delivery means that extensive training is likely necessary to ensure teacher competence with intervention materials. For good adherence to the intervention to be achieved, teachers should understand not only the intervention materials, but also the underlying mechanisms of change (e.g., cognitive restructuring). If the rationale for using intervention techniques and mechanisms of action are not well-understood, teachers may have difficulty adapting intervention delivery to the needs of different classrooms while maintaining the core intervention techniques. Moreover, adequate teacher training is often difficult to achieve. Schools cannot provide unlimited time to train teachers. District in-service days, which are limited in number, typically must be used, and for contractual reasons school districts cannot require teachers to stay after school for training even if they are being paid overtime. As such, providing adequate training to ensure competence with intervention materials is difficult. Another challenge to intervention integrity involves teacher investment in the intervention. Teachers may be resistant to the idea of using classroom time to administer mental health interventions, or may not believe that such interventions are worthwhile or likely to be effective with their students. A number of other factors may also contribute to low teacher investment in the intervention, and it is likely that teachers who do not believe in the importance of the intervention will administer the intervention in a way that does not involve optimal adherence. The numerous competing demands on teacher time in the classroom that were previously mentioned also serve as a challenge to good adherence to interventions. Even teachers who are invested in the intervention may not be able to devote the necessary classroom time to achieve good adherence.

Given lack of adequate time for teacher training, the competing demands for covering academic material and the importance of meeting NCLB benchmarks, and the probable lack of investment in the intervention from at least some teachers, ensuring that a universal preventive intervention is administered in the way that it is intended represents an enormous challenge. Even when these obstacles can be overcome, sound assessment of integrity of the intervention is difficult in classroom settings. Unlike psychotherapy trials in which every session of therapy can be videotaped, reviewed, and coded for adherence, videotaping a number of teachers administering an intervention across numerous classrooms at variable times of the day or week is difficult. As such, intervention integrity in universal prevention trials is often unknown.

FUTURE DIRECTIONS FOR UNIVERSAL PREVENTION RESEARCH

In this section, suggestions for overcoming some of the challenges to universal prevention studies outlined in the previous section are made. Specific attention is paid to the use of innovative methods for recruiting participants and administering interventions with the goals of increasing access to preventive interventions, improving the efficacy of interventions and integrity to intervention techniques during administration, and increasing the sustainability of interventions following research trials.

One current challenge facing universal prevention researchers involves reliance on schools for recruitment of participants. Because schools provide access to large numbers of adolescents, and because youth are required to attend school and are thus a captive audience, using schools as sites for recruitment of participants and for intervention administration has been a logical choice. However, there are numerous problems to be faced when using schools as the sites for universal prevention studies, and the identification of sites other than schools to recruit participants for such studies represents an important area for future research. The number of demands placed on schools is myriad, particularly since the NCLB legislation was passed. Finding schools that are willing to commit classroom time to mental health interventions represents a challenging task, and many schools must often be approached before finding school administrators that are willing to even consider allocating time for mental health interventions. In addition, school boards often must approve the use of interventions. Given these challenges, identifying other opportunities for accessing large numbers of adolescents for participating in universal prevention studies is critical.

Primary care and family medicine clinics represent one alternative to using schools to recruit participants. These sites provide access to large numbers of adolescents, as do schools. Recruitment of participants through medical clinics would require cooperation from the clinic and the provision of study personnel at the clinic over a period of time to recruit participants. Although this method may appear to involve more work than recruiting a school to provide participants, it does not necessarily involve more effort. As stated previously, recruiting a school can require a large investment of time in order to gain support from school administrators at the district and building levels, the school board, and from teachers. Once a school has agreed to participate, individual consent from students and parents must also be obtained. This can be a lengthy and time-consuming process, particularly if institutional review boards require active consent from parents, and may involve multiple mailings and even direct calls to parents who do not return consent forms. As such, recruitment of adolescents through medical clinics would not necessarily involve greater expenditures of time and money for researchers. In fact, one of the first universal prevention studies targeting depression was conducted in primary care clinics (Muñoz et al., 1995). This study focused on adults rather than adolescents, but nevertheless demonstrates the feasibility of this approach to recruitment. In this study, approximately half of individuals who were approached by study personnel at the primary care clinic agreed to participate in screening for eligibility (Muñoz & Ying, 1993). Of 707 potential participants screened, 150 were eventually randomized to participate in the study (Muñoz & Ying, 1993). This study found positive effects of a group cognitive-behavioral intervention on the prevention of increases in depressive symptoms over time, and suggests that recruitment of participants through medical clinics represents a viable approach for future universal prevention studies. One indicated prevention study targeting adolescent depression successfully used a health maintenance organization to recruit adolescents of depressed mothers for a preventive intervention (Clarke et al., 2001), indicating that other methods of recruitment of adolescents in particular are feasible alternatives to school-based methods. Recruitment of adolescents through such sites would be beneficial for trials of Internet-delivered interventions or group interventions led by facilitators other than teachers, and would eliminate the need to collaborate with schools.

Another large challenge facing universal prevention research involves the reliance on teachers, trained mental-health professionals, or graduate students to administer interventions. Given the adherence issues associated with using teachers as intervention administrators, and the sustainability issues associated with using trained professionals, other approaches to delivering universal preventive interventions targeting adolescent depression should be explored. Internet-based interventions represent an approach that may hold great promise in this regard. Internet-based interventions are increasingly being used in public health and in clinical psychology to administer treatments to large numbers of people. Evidence suggests that Internet-based approaches to intervention delivery can be equally effective as those delivered by clinicians and can reach a substantial number of individuals at a low cost. For example, an Internet-based intervention for smoking cessation that utilized cognitive-behavioral mood management techniques was found to be effective at increasing quit rates, particularly among previously depressed participants (Muñoz et al., 2006). This study recruited a large sample size over a short period of time given the ability of the Internet to attract large numbers of people and given the convenience of completing an intervention from home or work.

Internet-based preventive interventions targeting adolescent depression may solve many of the problems that arise when teachers are responsible for administering interventions during class time. In Internet-based approaches, the intervention is delivered exactly as intended and uniformly across all participants, making adherence a nonissue. Teacher investment in the intervention is unnecessary, given that the intervention can be completely administered in the absence of teacher participation. Intervention materials can be completed at home or during breaks in the school day (e.g., study halls) rather than during class time that would otherwise be devoted to academic material. Moreover, the exact dosage of the intervention that is received by each participant (e.g., how many modules, lessons, or activities were completed) can be carefully monitored. Internet-based approaches also solve the problems of sustainability that are associated with using mental health professionals or graduate students to administer interventions. Internet-based preventive interventions thus represent a sustainable and cost-effective method for providing access to effective interventions to large segments of the population.

Future studies should aim to modify existing interventions that have been found to be effective, such as the PRP, so that they may be administered via the Internet. Partnering with schools would aid in the testing of such interventions. Schools have the authority to assign intervention materials as homework and allow access to large populations of adolescents. Administrators tend to be invested in reducing mental health problems in schools given their negative consequences for academic and social functioning, and would likely support mental-health interventions that do not require use of class time or teacher in-service time for training. The use of the Internet to deliver preventive interventions represents a strategy that, if effective, could be used to access large segments of the population and have substantial impacts upon public health. These approaches could solve many of the problems associated with using teachers to administer interventions, particularly problems of adherence, and the sustainability problems associated with using trained mental health professionals.

CONCLUSION

To date, a number of universal preventive interventions for adolescent depression have been developed and empirically evaluated. The results of these evaluations have been decidedly mixed; many of the interventions that have been examined have been found to be effective in some trials (e.g., Spence et al., 2003) but not in others (e.g., Sheffield et al., 2006). The inconsistent results that have been typical in this literature have likely resulted from a number of methodological and logistical challenges that face universal prevention researchers. These challenges range from the need to test interventions on large samples of adolescents and utilize lengthy follow-up periods, to a host of difficulties inherent in working with schools to conduct intervention research. Universal prevention researchers must develop innovative strategies for designing and testing preventive interventions and for overcoming the myriad challenges that are present in this type of research. Until then, the true benefits of universal preventive interventions will remain unclear. Ultimately, universal preventive interventions for adolescent depression may provide the best strategy for reducing the incidence of major depression at a population level if researchers are able to design effective interventions that are sustainable in communities. The public health impact of such interventions would be far-reaching, and universal prevention researchers are encouraged to continue developing strategies to test interventions for adolescent depression in spite of the numerous challenges that must be overcome.

REFERENCES

Angold, A., Costello, E. J., Farmer, E. M. Z., Burns, B. J., & Erkanli, A. (1999). Impaired but undiagnosed. *Journal of the American Academy of Child & Adolescent Psychiatry, 38*, 129–137.

Beardslee, W. R., Salt, P., Porterfield, K., Rothberg, P. C., van de Velde, P., Swatling, S., et al. (1993). Comparisons of preventive interventions for families with parental affective disorder. *Journal of the American Academy of Child & Adolescent Psychiatry, 32*, 254–263.

Blazer, D. G., Kessler, R. C., McGonagle, K. A., & Swartz, M. S. (1994). The prevalence and distribution of major depression in a national community sample: The National Comorbidity Survey. *American Journal of Psychiatry, 151*, 979–986.

Cardemil, E. V., Reivich, K. J., & Seligman, M. E. P. (2002). The prevention of depressive symptoms in low-income minority middle school students. *Prevention and Treatment, 5*, Article 8.

Clarke, G. N., Hawkins, W., Murphy, M., & Sheeber, L. B. (1993). School-based primary prevention of depressive symptomatology in adolescents: Findings from two studies. *Journal of Adolescent Research, 8*, 183–204.

Clarke, G. N., Hawkins, W., Murphy, M., Sheeber, L. B., Lewinsohn, P. M., & Seeley, J. R. (1995). Targeted prevention of unipolar depressive disorder in an at-risk sample of high school adolescents: A randomized trial of a group cognitive intervention. *Journal of the American Academy of Child & Adolescent Psychiatry, 34*, 312–321.

Clarke, G. N., Hornbrook, M., Lynch, F., Polen, M., Gale, J., Beardslee, W., et al. (2001). A randomized trial of a group cognitive intervention for preventing depression in adolescent offspring of depressed parents. *Archives of General Psychiatry, 58*, 1127–1134.

Commission on Chronic Illness. (1957). *Chronic illness in the United States* (Vol. 1). Cambridge, MA: Harvard University Press.

Costello, E. J., Mustillo, S., Erkanli, A., Keeler, G., & Angold, A. (2003). Prevalence and development of psychiatric disorders in childhood and adolescence. *Archives of General Psychiatry, 60*, 837–844.

Dierker, L. C., Albano, A. M., Clarke, G. N., Heimberg, R. G., Kendall, P. C., Merikangas, K. E., et al. (2001). Screening for anxiety and depression in early adolescence. *Journal of the American Academy of Child & Adolescent Psychiatry, 40*, 929–936.

Dodge, K. A. (1993). Social-cognitive mechanisms in the development of conduct disorder and depression. *Annual Review of Psychology, 44*, 559–584.

Essau, C. A. (2005). Frequency and patterns of mental health services utilization among adolescents with anxiety and depressive disorders. *Depression and Anxiety, 22*, 130–137.

Fergusson, D. M., Horwood, J., Ritter, E. M., & Beautrais, A. L. (2005). Subthreshold depressive symptoms in adolescence and mental health outcomes in adulthood. *Archives of General Psychiatry, 62*, 66–72.

Fombonne, E., Wostear, G., Cooper, V., Harrington, R., & Rutter, M. (2001). The Maudsley long-term follow-up of child and adolescent depression: 1. Psychiatric outcomes in adulthood. *British Journal of Psychiatry, 179*, 210–217.

Georgiades, K., Lewinsohn, P. M., Monroe, S. M., & Seeley, J. R. (2006). Major depressive disorder in adolescence: The role of subthreshold symptoms. *Journal of the American Academy of Child & Adolescent Psychiatry, 45*, 936–944.

Gillham, J. E., Reivich, K. J., Freres, D. M., Chaplin, T. M., Shatté, A. J., Samuels, B., et al. (2007). School-based prevention of depressive symptoms: A randomized controlled study of the effectiveness and specificity of the Penn Resiliency Program. *Journal of Consulting and Clinical Psychology, 75*, 9–19.

Gillham, J. E., Reivich, K. J., Jaycox, L. H., & Seligman, M. E. P. (1995). Prevention of depressive symptoms in schoolchildren: Two-year follow-up. *Psychological Science, 6*, 343–351.

Glasgow, R. E., Lichtenstein, E., & Marcus, A. C. (2003). Why don't we see more translation of health promotion research to practice? Rethinking the efficacy-to-effectiveness transition. *American Journal of Public Health, 93*, 1261–1267.

Gonzalez-Tejera, G., Canino, G., Ramirez, R., Chavez, L., Shrout, P., Bird, H., et al. (2005). Examining minor and major depression in adolescence. *Journal of Child Psychology and Psychiatry, 46*, 888–899.

Hains, A. A., & Ellman, S. W. (1994). Stress inoculation straining as a preventative intervention for high school youths. *Journal of Cognitive Psychotherapy: An International Quarterly, 8*, 219–232.

Hankin, B. L., Abramson, L. Y., Moffitt, T. E., Silva, P. A., McGee, R., & Angell, K. E. (1998). Development of depression from preadolescence to young adulthood: Emerging gender differences in a 10-year longitudinal study. *Journal of Abnormal Psychology, 107*, 128–140.

Institute of Medicine. (1994). *Reducing risks for mental disorders: Frontiers for preventive intervention research*. Washington, DC: National Academy Press.

Jaycox, L. H., Reivich, K. J., Gillham, J. E., & Seligman, M. E. P. (1994). Prevention of depressive symptoms in school children. *Behaviour Research & Therapy, 32*, 801–816.

Judd, L. L., Akiskal, H. S., & Paulus, M. P. (1997). The role and clinical significance of subsyndromal depressive symptoms (SSD) in unipolar major depressive disorder. *Journal of Affective Disorders, 45*, 5–18.

Jureidini, J. N., Doecke, C. J., Mansfield, P. R., Haby, M. M., Menkes, D. B., & Tonkin, A. L. (2004). Efficacy and safety of antidepressants for children and adolescents. *British Medical Journal, 328*, 879–883.

Kessler, R. C., Berglund, P., Demler, O, Jin, R., Koretz, D., Merikangas, K. R., et al. (2003). The epidemiology of major depressive disorder: Results from the National Comorbidity Survey Replication (NCS-R). *Journal of the American Medical Association, 289*, 3095–3105.

Kessler, R. C., McGonagle, K. A., Zhao, S., Nelson, C. B., Hughes, M., Eshleman, S., et al. (1994). Lifetime and 12-month prevalence of DSM-III-R psychiatric disorders in the National Comorbidity Survey. *Archives of General Psychiatry, 51*, 8–19.

Kessler, R. C., & Walters, E. E. (1998). Epidemiology of DSM-III-R major depression and minor depression among adolescents and young adults in the National Comorbidity Survey. *Depression & Anxiety, 7*, 3–14.

Lewinsohn, P. M., Hops, H., Roberts, R. E., Seeley, J. R., & Andrews, J. A. (1993). Adolescent psychopathology: I. Prevalence and incidence of depression and other DSM-III-R disorders in high school students. *Journal of Abnormal Psychology, 102*, 133–144.

Lewinsohn, P. M., Rohde, P., Klein, D. N., & Seeley, J. R. (1999). Natural course of adolescent major depressive disorder: I. Continuity into young adulthood. *Journal of the American Academy of Child & Adolescent Psychiatry, 38*, 56–63.

Lewinsohn, P. M., Rohde, P., & Seeley, J. R. (1998). Treatment of adolescent depression: Frequency of services and impact on functioning in young adulthood. *Depression and Anxiety, 7*, 47–52.

Lewinsohn, P. M., Soloman, A., Seeley, J. R., & Zeiss, A. (2000). Clinical implications of subthreshold depressive symptoms. *Journal of Abnormal Psychology, 109*, 345–351.

McKinlay, J., & Marceau, L. (2000). US public health and the 21st century: Diabetes mellitus. *The Lancet, 356*, 757–761.

Merry, S., McDowell, H., Hetrick, S., Bir, J., & Muller, N. (2004a). Psychological and/or educational interventions for the prevention of depression in children and adolescents. *Cochrane Database of Systematic Reviews, 2*, CD003380.

Merry, S., McDowell, H., Wild, C. J., Bir, J., & Cunliffe, R. (2004b). A randomized placebo controlled trial of a school-based depression prevention program. *Journal of the American Academy of Child & Adolescent Psychiatry, 43*, 538–547.

Muñoz, R. F., Lenert, L. L., Delucchi, K., Stoddard, J., Perez, J. E., Penilla, C., et al. (2006). Toward evidence-based Internet interventions: A Spanish/English website for international smoking cessation trials. *Nicotine and Tobacco Research, 8*, 77-87.

Muñoz, R. F., & Ying, Y.-W. (1993). *The prevention of depression: Research and practice.* Baltimore, MD: The Johns Hopkins University Press.

Muñoz, R. F., Ying, Y.-W., Bernal, G., Pérez-Stable, E. J., Sorensen, J. L., Hargreaves, W. A., et al. (1995). Prevention of depression with primary care patients: A randomized controlled trial. *American Journal of Community Psychology, 23*, 199–222.

Perepletchikova, F., & Kazdin, A. E. (2005). Treatment integrity and therapeutic change: Issues and research recommendations. *Clinical Psychology: Science and Practice, 12*, 365–383.

Pine, D. S., Cohen, E., Cohen, P., & Brooke, J. (1999). Adolescent depressive symptoms as predictors of adult mood disorders: Moodiness or mood disorder? *American Journal of Psychiatry, 156*, 133–135.

Pine, D. S., Cohen, P., Gurley, D., Brook, J., & Ma, Y. (1998). The risk for early adulthood anxiety and depressive disorders in adolescents with anxiety and depressive disorders. *Archives of General Psychiatry, 55*, 56–64.

Pössel, P., Horn, A. B., Groen, G., & Hautzinger, M. (2004a). School-based prevention of depressive symptoms in adolescents: A 6-month follow-up. *Journal of the American Academy of Child & Adolescent Psychiatry, 43*, 1003–1010.

Pössel, P., Horn, A. B., Seeman, S., & Hautzinger, M. (2004b). *Trainingsprogramm zur Prävention von Depressionen bei Jugendlichen. LARS&LISA: Lust an realistischer sicht & leichtigkeit im sozialen alltag.* Göttingen: Hogrefe.

Quayle, D., Dziurawiec, S., Roberts, C., Kane, R., & Ebsworthy, G. (2001). The effect of an optimism and lifeskills program on depressive symptoms in preadolescence. *Behaviour Change, 18*, 194–203.

Reivich, K. J. (1996). *The prevention of depressive symptoms in adolescents.* Unpublished doctoral dissertation, University of Pennsylvania, Philadelphia.

Rose, G. (1992). *The strategy of preventive medicine* (1st ed.). Oxford: Oxford University Press.

Seligman, M. E. P., Schulman, P., DeRubeis, R. J., & Holland, S. D. (1999). The prevention of depression and anxiety. *Prevention & Treatment, 2*, Article 8. Retrieved July 11, 2007, from http://www.journals.apa.org/prevention/volume2/pre0020008a.html.

Sheffield, J. K., Spence, S. H., Rapee, R. M., Kowalenko, N., Wignall, A., Davis, A., et al. (2006). Evaluation of primary, indicated, and combined cognitive-behavioral approaches to the prevention of depression among adolescents. *Journal of Consulting and Clinical Psychology, 74*, 66–79.

Shochet, I., Dadds, M. R., Holland, D., Whitefield, K., Harnett, P. H., & Osgarby, H. M. (2001). The efficacy of a universal school-based program to prevent adolescent depression. *Journal of Clinical Child Psychology, 30*, 303–315.

Spence, S. H., Sheffield, J. K., & Donovan, C. L. (2003). Preventing adolescent depression: Evaluation of the Problem Solving for Life Program. *Journal of Consulting and Clinical Psychology, 71*, 3–13.

U.S. Department of Education (2006). Schools not making adequate yearly progress. Retrieved July 11, 2007, from http://answers.ed.gov.

Wang, P. S., Lane, M., Olfson, M., Pincus, H. A., Wells, K. B., & Kessler, R. C. (2005). 12-month use of mental health services in the United States. *Archives of General Psychiatry, 62*, 629–640.

Weersing, V. R., & Weisz, J. R. (2002). Community clinic treatment of depressed youth: Benchmarking usual care against CBT trials. *Journal of Consulting and Clinical Psychology, 70*, 299–310.

Wilcox, H. C., & Anthony, J. C. (2003). Child and adolescent clinical features as forerunners of adult-onset major depressive disorder: Retrospective evidence from an epidemiologic study. *Journal of Affective Disorders, 82*, 9–20.

Young, A. S., Klap, R., Sherbourne, C. D., & Wells, K. B. (2001). The quality of care for depressive and anxiety disorders in the US. *Archives of General Psychiatry, 58*, 55–61.

Chapter Twenty-Four

Integration and Remaining Questions

SUSAN NOLEN-HOEKSEMA AND LORI M. HILT

As we come to the end of the process of editing this volume, we are struck both by how much we know, and how much we still do not know about adolescent depression. There has been a great deal of research on adolescent depression in the last decade or two, as evidenced by the citations in the chapters in this book. Thanks in part to many researchers having taken a developmental psychopathology approach (Cicchetti & Toth, this volume), we understand much more about the appropriate assessment and diagnosis of depression in adolescents (Essau & Ollendick, this volume). This has allowed for more valid and accurate epidemiological studies of adolescent depression and suicide, and conditions that tend to be comorbid with adolescent depression, across cultures, ethnicities, and socioeconomic status (see Allen & Astuto, this volume; Jacobson & Gould, this volume; Merikangas & Knight, this volume; Rohde, this volume). A developmental psychopathology approach has also informed recent studies of the emergence of gender differences in depression in adolescence (see Hilt & Nolen-Hoeksema, this volume), and the nature, course, and causes of bipolar disorder in adolescence (see Taylor & Miklowitz, this volume).

Research on the biological changes of adolescence has exploded in recent years, advancing our understanding of the role of genetic, neurobiological, hormonal, and sleep-related factors in adolescent depression (see Goodyer, this volume; Lau & Eley, this volume; Wolfson & Armitage, this volume). Similarly, our methods for studying psychosocial change in adolescence, and its impact on depression, have improved greatly, leading to a large research base (see Abela & Hankin, this volume; Compas, Jaser, & Benson, this volume; Hammen, this volume; Joormann, Eugène, & Gotlib, this volume; Rudolph, this volume). Finally, state-of-the-art methods for conducting randomized clinical trials have been used to assess a number of different intervention and prevention programs for adolescent depression in the last decade or so, to the point that meta-analyses of this research are possible (see Garber, Webb, & Horowitz, this volume; Gunlicks & Mufson, this volume; Kaslow, Broth, Cowles Arnette, & Collins, this volume; McLaughlin, this volume; Stark, Krumholz, Ridley, & Hamilton, this volume; Weersing & Gonzalez, this volume; Zalsman, Shoval, & Rotstein, this volume).

Still, there is so much we do not know. Each of the authors in this book could provide his or her own list of critical questions that should motivate future research. We will highlight three major questions, each of which cuts across many chapters in this book.

First, *how do we understand continuity in adolescent depression*? Developmental psychopathologists distinguish between homotypic continuity, the continuation of a process over time in a relatively unchanging form, and heterotypic continuity, the continuation of a process but in different forms over time (see Angold, Costello, & Erkanli, 1999). As several authors in this volume have pointed out, there is substantial homotypic continuity in adolescent depression (e.g., see Garber et al., this volume). Depression in adolescence tends to be chronic and characterized by frequent recurrences in adolescence and into adulthood. What accounts for the high degree of chronicity and recurrence in adolescent depression? It seems likely that an episode of depression during this crucial developmental time could have long-term effects on biological systems (e.g., the prefrontal cortex, the hypothalamic-pituitary-adrenal axis) and psychosocial systems (e.g., family relationships, peer relationships, self-competencies). Understanding the impact of depression in adolescence on the development of these systems will be critical to understanding the nature of this disorder and to developing treatment programs that mitigate its impact.

There may also be substantial heterotypic continuity in adolescent depression. Some have argued that the developmental precursor of adolescent depression is childhood anxiety (e.g., Kovacs, Gatsonis, Paulauskas, & Richards, 1989), and many depressed adolescents were anxious as children (Pine, Cohen, Gurley, Brook, & Ma, 1998). Childhood anxiety transforming into adolescent depression might be an instance of heterotypic continuity. If anxiety is the precursor for depression, what accounts for the transition from anxiety to depression? Perhaps cognitive development makes the hopeless cognitions characteristic of depression (see Abela & Hankin, this volume) possible in adolescence. Perhaps it takes the interaction of preadolescent biological or psychosocial vulnerabilities plus the biological or psychosocial changes of early adolescence to trigger episodes. If childhood anxiety is the developmental precursor to adolescent depression, we might expect the same factors that predict adolescent depression to predict childhood anxiety. Alternately, childhood anxiety may result in changes in the developing child that puts him or her at greater risk for later depression. As yet, however, these issues remain relatively unexplored.

Some depressed adolescents eventually are rediagnosed with bipolar disorder. We have learned a great deal in recent years about the nature and biological underpinnings of pediatric bipolar disorder (see Taylor & Miklowitz, this volume). Much more remains to be known about the overlap and distinctions between unipolar and bipolar syndromes in youth, and methods for accurately diagnosing bipolar disorder in youth, however.

Adolescent depression increases risk for the development of several other disorders, including substance use disorders, eating disorders, and anxiety disorders (see Rohde, this volume). This is an instance of what Angold et al. (1999) call heterotypic comorbidity—the comorbidity of different syndromes. Depressed adolescents who have comorbid conditions may be more likely to seek help, but are often more difficult to treat (Weersing & Gonzalez, this volume). Research on the mechanisms by which adolescent depression increases vulnerability for these other syndromes is needed to prevent their development and to improve treatments.

A second overarching question remaining to be answered is *how we understand the convergence of biological and psychosocial risk factors for adolescent depression*. We will propose one integrative model based on the research reviewed in this volume, but we recognize there are many ways biological and psychosocial risk factors could converge to create depression.

Genetic factors may set the stage for adolescent depression (see Lau & Eley, this volume). Genetic factors may contribute directly to the development of depression, but more likely they lead to the development of any or all of the neurobiological and psychosocial risk factors discussed in this volume. Thus, there may be genetic influences in the functioning of neurotransmitter and hormonal systems, sleep physiology, the tendency to experience stressful events, cognitive and interpersonal styles, and coping and emotion regulation styles. And of course, one way parental depression may contribute to depression in adolescents is through genetic transmission.

The psychosocial risk factors likely also influence each other. For example, early life stress, including having a depressed parent, may lead to depressogenic cognitive styles, deficits in interpersonal skills, or poor coping and emotion regulation skills (see Hammen, this volume; Joormann et al., this volume). On the other hand, youth with maladaptive cognitive styles and/or interpersonal skills are likely to create more stress in their lives, and poor coping or emotion regulation skills would exacerbate the effects of that stress on well-being (see Abela & Hankin, this volume; Compas et al., this volume; Rudolph, this volume).

The genetic, neurobiological, and psychosocial risk factors discussed in this volume may interact with changes in hormones and sleep physiology in early adolescence, and with increased social stress, to trigger first episodes of depression. Young adolescents with poor emotion-regulation skills may manage these early episodes badly, leading to more chronic and recurrent episodes.

Timing is likely to make an important difference in the impact of biological and psychosocial change. As Steinberg and colleagues (2006) describe, increases in circulating sex steroids and the development of mature secondary sex characteristics tend to precede the maturation of prefrontal areas of the brain, in some children by years. Hormonal change and the development of secondary sex characteristics could, in some children, create emotional arousal because it creates physiological arousal, and because peers and adults may begin reacting to the children as if they were adults (e.g., showing sexual interest in children with mature secondary sex characteristics). Prefrontal cortex development, which could facilitate cognitive control over emotion, often lags behind these other biological changes, however. Children who are confronted with major stressors during this lag time between pubertal changes and cortical development may have particular difficulty coping effectively, and as a result, be at increased risk for the development of depression. In addition, children who begin puberty early relative to their peers may have a large window of vulnerability. As summarized by Hilt and Nolen-Hoeksema (this volume), some studies suggest that girls who go through the peak pubertal changes (e.g., menarche, weight gain, development of secondary sex characteristics) several months or more before their female peer group are more likely than girls who mature around the same time as their peer group to show depression.

This integrative model raises the third set of critical questions that remain to be answered: *how do we improve treatment and prevention programs for adolescent depression*? As Weersing and Gonzalez (this volume, pp. 589–616) conclude, "the adolescent depression treatment literature provides both reason for hope and cause for concern." While depressed adolescents respond to several types of psychosocial and pharmacological interventions (see Sections V and VI), the remission rate for any treatment is relatively low, and relapse rates are high.

The fact that so many risk factors influence the development of depression suggests there are many targets for intervention and prevention programs, and this may be why many modes of intervention appear to be somewhat helpful. But our integrative model suggests there are many reciprocal effects of the risk factors for depression on each other, so that focusing interventions on any single system may not be effective because the processes in other systems may overwhelm the intervention effects. This may be, in part, why no intervention has a consistently excellent response or remission rate.

Multimodal interventions, targeting biological systems, psychological factors (e.g., cognitions, interpersonal skills, coping and emotion-regulation skills), and the adolescent's social context (family and peers), would seem most appropriate for depressed adolescents, given our integrative perspective. There is some evidence from recent therapy outcome studies that the combination of medication and psychotherapy, or the combination of individual psychotherapy and family-based intervention, are more effective than either alone (e.g., see Kaslow et al., this volume; Weersing & Gonzalez, this volume). We await further research on interventions with combined foci on multiple systems operating to increase adolescents' risk for depression.

Another implication for treatment and prevention of our integrative model is that we need to take developmental factors into consideration in the design and timing of programs. A young adolescent, whose prefrontal cortex is still developing, may benefit from skills training in cognitive control of emotion (e.g., reappraisal); yet, he or she may find learning these skills more difficult compared to an older adolescent. On the other hand, an older adolescent, whose prefrontal cortex is more developed, may have more rigid cognitive styles than a younger adolescent whose cognitions may be more malleable. This might suggest that interventions targeting multiple systems (e.g., behavioral interventions, pharmacological interventions) would be important to consider. Treatments that consider developmental factors would also utilize different interventions depending on the child's cognitive, social, and biological development.

The pace of developmental change in adolescents is potentially quite different for different systems. Physiological and cognitive change can happen quite rapidly—a 14-year-old can seem like an entirely different creature physiologically and psychologically than he or she was at age 13. But there is often much slower change in the adolescent's social context. Depressed adolescents may have a reputation among peers that is hard to change even after their depression has lifted, spontaneously or through treatment. Adolescents' family context is also difficult to change. Unlike adults, adolescents cannot easily change schools or divorce their family if they choose. Thus, some forms of intervention (e.g., cognitive-behavioral therapy and pharmacotherapy) may need to be adjusted frequently to adapt to an adolescent whose physiology and cognitive capacity are changing rapidly, and some (e.g., interpersonal therapy and family therapy) may need to take the slow pace of change in the adolescent's context into account and help the adolescent cope with this.

Of course, only a minority of depressed adolescents receive any treatment, a problem that has been exacerbated by recent worries about the safety of antidepressant medications (see Zalsman et al., this volume). Thus, prevention programs that forestall first onsets or recurrences of depression are sorely needed. As Garber et al. (this volume) and McLaughlin (this volume) note, some studies suggest prevention programs can be effective, but there is much room for improvement. Even with universal prevention programs, access is an issue. Innovative modes of delivery of preventive interventions, such as over the Internet, may improve access for adolescents who could benefit from these programs, at a low cost and a low level of intrusiveness (McLaughlin, this volume).

The chapters in this volume offer a wealth of information on adolescent depression, much of it quite new, that helps us understand the nature and impact of the disorder on adolescents' lives, the risk factors, and what treatments and prevention programs might be effective. These chapters also point to areas where more research is needed. If we can better understand, and thus better treat, depression in adolescents, it will have a huge positive impact across their lifespan.

REFERENCES

Angold, A., Costello, E. J., & Erkanli, A. (1999). Comorbidity. *Journal of Child Psychology and Psychiatry, 40*, 57–87.

Kovacs, M., Gatsonis, C., Paulauskas, S. L., & Richards, C. (1989). Depressive disorders in childhood: IV: A longitudinal study of comorbidity with and risk for anxiety disorders. *Archives of General Psychiatry, 46*, 776–782.

Pine, D. S., Cohen, P., Gurley, D., Brook, J., & Ma, Y. (1998). The risk for early adulthood anxiety and depressive disorders in adolescents with anxiety and depressive disorders. *Archives of General Psychiatry, 55*, 56–64.

Steinberg, L., Dahl, R., Keating, D., Kupfer, D. J., Masten, A. S., & Pine, D. (2006). The study of developmental psychopathology in adolescence: Integrating affective neuroscience with the study of context. In D. Cicchetti & D. Cohen (Eds.), *Developmental psychopathology, Vol. 2: Developmental neuroscience* (pp. 710–741). New York: Wiley.

Index

H

I